CLASSICAL AND MEDIEVAL LITERATURE CRITICISM

Guide to Gale Literary Criticism Series

For criticism on	Consult these Gale series
Authors now living or who died after December 31, 1959	*CONTEMPORARY LITERARY CRITICISM (CLC)*
Authors who died between 1900 and 1959	*TWENTIETH-CENTURY LITERARY CRITICISM (TCLC)*
Authors who died between 1800 and 1899	*NINETEENTH-CENTURY LITERATURE CRITICISM (NCLC)*
Authors who died between 1400 and 1799	*LITERATURE CRITICISM FROM 1400 TO 1800 (LC)* *SHAKESPEAREAN CRITICISM (SC)*
Authors who died before 1400	*CLASSICAL AND MEDIEVAL LITERATURE CRITICISM (CMLC)*
Black writers of the past two hundred years	*BLACK LITERATURE CRITICISM (BLC)*
Authors of books for children and young adults	*CHILDREN'S LITERATURE REVIEW (CLR)*
Dramatists	*DRAMA CRITICISM (DC)*
Hispanic writers of the late nineteenth and twentieth centuries	*HISPANIC LITERATURE CRITICISM (HLC)*
Native North American writers and orators of the eighteenth, nineteenth, and twentieth centuries	*NATIVE NORTH AMERICAN LITERATURE (NNAL)*
Poets	*POETRY CRITICISM (PC)*
Short story writers	*SHORT STORY CRITICISM (SSC)*
Major authors from the Renaissance to the present	*WORLD LITERATURE CRITICISM, 1500 TO THE PRESENT (WLC)*

ISSN 0896-0011

Volume 19

CLASSICAL AND MEDIEVAL LITERATURE CRITICISM

Excerpts from Criticism of the Works of World
Authors from Classical Antiquity through the
Fourteenth Century, from the First Appraisals
to Current Evaluations

**Jelena O. Krstović
Daniel G. Marowski**
Editors

GALE

DETROIT · NEW YORK · TORONTO · LONDON

STAFF

Daniel G. Marowski, *Editor*
Jelena Krstović, *Contributing Editor*
Susan Trosky, *Managing Editor*

Marlene S. Hurst, *Permissions Manager*
Margaret A. Chamberlain, Maria Franklin, Kimberly F. Smilay, *Permissions Specialists*
Diane Cooper,
Edna Hedblad, Michele Lonoconus, Maureen Puhl, Shalice Shah,
Permissions Associates
Sarah Chesney, Jeffrey Hermann, *Permissions Assistants*

Victoria B. Cariappa, *Research Manager*
Laura C. Bissey, Julia Daniel, Tamara C. Nott, Michele P. Pica, Tracie A. Richardson, Cheryl Warnock, *Research Associates*

Mary Beth Trimper, *Production Director*
Deborah Milliken, *Production Assistant*

Sherrell Hobbs, *Macintosh Artist*
Pamela A. Hayes, *Photography Coordinator*
Randy Bassett, *Image Database Supervisor*
Robert Duncan, *Imaging Specialist*

∞™
This book is printed on acid-free paper that meets the minimum requirements of American National Standard for Information Sciences—Permanence Paper for Printed Library Materials, ANSI Z39.48-1984.

Library of Congress Catalog Card Number 88-658021
ISBN 0-8103-9982-2
ISSN 0896-0011
Printed in the United States of America

10 9 8 7 6 5 4 3 2 1

Contents

Preface   vii

Acknowledgments   xi

Preface

Since its inception in 1988, *Classical and Medieval Literature Criticism* has been a valuable resource for students and librarians seeking critical commentary on the writers and works of these periods in world history. Major reviewing sources have assessed *CMLC* as "useful" and "extremely convenient," noting that it "adds to our understanding of the rich legacy left by the ancient period and the Middle Ages," and praising its "general excellence in the presentation of an inherently interesting subject." No other single reference source has surveyed the critical reaction to classical and medieval literature as thoroughly as *CMLC*.

Scope of the Series

CMLC is designed to serve as an introduction for students and advanced readers of the works and authors of antiquity through the fourteenth century. The great poets, prose writers, dramatists, and philosophers of this period form the basis of most humanities curricula, so that virtually every student will encounter many of these works during the course of a high school and college education. By organizing and reprinting an enormous amount of commentary written on classical and medieval authors and works, *CMLC* helps students develop valuable insight into literary history, promotes a better understanding of the texts, and sparks ideas for papers and assignments. Each entry in *CMLC* presents a comprehensive survey of an author's career, an individual work of literature, or a literary topic, and provides the user with a multiplicity of interpretations and assessments. Such variety allows students to pursue their own interests; furthermore, it fosters an awareness that literature is dynamic and responsive to many different opinions.

CMLC continues the survey of criticism of world literature begun by Gale's *Contemporary Literary Criticism (CLC)*, *Twentieth-Century Literary Criticism (TCLC)*, *Nineteenth-Century Literature Criticism (NCLC)*, *Literature Criticism from 1400 to 1800 (LC)*, and *Shakespearean Criticism (SC)*. For additional information about these and Gale's other criticism series, users should consult the Guide to Gale Literary Criticism Series preceding the title page in this volume.

Coverage

Each volume of *CMLC* is carefully compiled to present:

- criticism of authors and works which represent a variety of genres, time periods, and nationalities

- both major and lesser-known writers and works of the period (such as non-Western authors and literature, increasingly read by today's students)

- 4-6 authors or works per volume

- individual entries that survey the critical response to each author, work, or topic, including early criticism, later criticism (to represent any rise or decline in the author's reputation), and current retrospective analyses. The length of each author or work entry also indicates relative importance, reflecting the amount of critical attention the author, work, or topic has received from critics writing in English, and from foreign criticism in translation.

An author may appear more than once in the series if his or her writings have been the subject of a substantial amount of criticism; in these instances, specific works or groups of works by the author will be covered in separate entries. For example, Homer will be represented by three entries, one devoted to the *Iliad,* one to the *Odyssey,* and one to the Homeric Hymns.

Starting with Volume 10, *CMLC* will also occasionally include entries devoted to literary topics. For example, *CMLC*-10 focuses on Arthurian Legend and includes general criticism on that subject as well as individual entries on writers or works central to that topic—Chrétien de Troyes, Gottfried von Strassburg, Layamon, and the Alliterative *Morte Arthure.*

Organization of the Book

An author entry consists of the following elements: author heading, biographical and critical introduction, principal English translations or editions, excerpts of criticism (each preceded by a bibliographic citation and an annotation), and a bibliography of further reading.

■ The **Author Heading** consists of the author's most commonly used name, followed by birth and death dates. If the entry is devoted to a work, the heading will consist of the most common form of the title in English translation (if applicable), and the original date of composition. Located at the beginning of the introduction are any name or title variations.

■ A **Portrait** of the author is included when available. Many entries also feature illustrations of materials pertinent to the author or work, including manuscript pages, book illustrations, and representations of people, places, and events important to a study of the author or work.

■ The **Biographical and Critical Introduction** contains background information that concisely introduces the reader to the author, work, or topic.

■ The list of **Principal Works** and **English Translations** or **Editions** is chronological by date of first publication and is included as an aid to the student seeking translated versions or editions of these works for study. The list will focus primarily on twentieth-century translations, selecting those works most commonly considered the best by critics.

■ **Criticism** is arranged chronologically in each entry to provide a useful perspective on changes in critical evaluation over the years. All titles by the author featured in the critical entry are printed in boldface type to enable the user to ascertain without difficulty the works being discussed. Also for purposes of easier identification, the critic's name and the publication date of the essay are given at the beginning of each piece of criticism. Anonymous criticism is preceded by the title of the journal in which it appeared. Publication information (such as publisher names and book prices) and parenthetical numerical references (such as footnotes or page and line references to specific editions of works) have been deleted at the editors' discretion to provide smoother reading of the text. Many critical entries in *CMLC* also contain translations to aid the users.

■ A complete **Bibliographic Citation** provides original publication information for each piece of criticism.

■ Critical excerpts are also prefaced by **Annotations** providing the reader with information about both the critic and the criticism, the scope of the excerpt, the growth of critical controversy, or changes in critical trends regarding an author or work. In some cases, these notes include cross-references to excerpts by critics who discuss each other's commentary. Dates in parentheses within the annotation refer to a book publication date when they follow a book title, and to an essay date when they follow a critic's name.

- An annotated bibliography of **Further Reading** appears at the end of each entry and lists additional secondary sources on the author or work. In some cases it includes essays for which the editors could not obtain reprint rights. When applicable, the Further Reading is followed by references to additional entries on the author in other literary reference series published by Gale.

Topic Entries are subdivided into several thematic rubrics in which criticism appears in order of descending scope.

Cumulative Indexes

Each volume of *CMLC* includes a cumulative **author index** listing all authors who have appeared in Gale's Literary Criticism Series, along with cross references to such biographical series as *Contemporary Authors* and *Dictionary of Literary Biography*. For readers' convenience, a complete list of Gale titles included appears on the page prior to the author index. Useful for locating an author within the various series, this index is particularly valuable for those authors who are identified with a certain period but who, because of their death date, are placed in another, or for those authors whose careers span two periods. For example, Geoffrey Chaucer, who is usually considered a medieval author, is found in *Literature Criticism from 1400 to 1800* because he died after 1399.

Beginning with the tenth volume, *CMLC* includes a cumulative index listing all topic entries that have appeared in the Gale Literary Criticism Series *Classical and Medieval Literature Criticism, Contemporary Literary Criticism, Literature Criticism from 1400 to 1800, Nineteenth-Century Literature Criticism,* and *Twentieth-Century Literary Criticism.*

Beginning with the second volume, *CMLC* also includes a cumulative nationality index. Authors and/or works are grouped by nationality, and the volume in which criticism on them may be found is indicated.

Title Index

Each volume of *CMLC* also includes an index listing the titles of all literary works discussed in the series. Foreign language titles that have been translated are followed by the titles of the translations—for example, *Slovo o polku Igorove (The Song of Igor's Campaign)*. Page numbers following these translated titles refer to all pages on which any form of the title, either foreign language or translated, appears. Titles of novels, dramas, nonfiction books, and poetry, short story, or essay collections are printed in italics, while those of all individual poems, short stories, and essays are printed in roman type within quotation marks. In cases where the same title is used by different authors, the author's name or surname is given in parentheses after the title, e.g. *Collected Poems* (Horace) and *Collected Poems* (Sappho).

Critic Index

An index to critics, which cumulates with the second volume, is another useful feature of *CMLC*. Under each critic's name are listed the authors and/or works on whom the critic has written and the volume and page number where criticism may be found.

A Note to the Reader

When writing papers, students who quote directly from any volume in the Literary Criticism Series may use the following general forms to footnote reprinted criticism. The first example pertains to material drawn from a periodical, the second to material reprinted from books.

Rollo May, "The Therapist and the Journey into Hell," *Michigan Quarterly Review,* XXV, No. 4 (Fall 1986), 629-41; excerpted and reprinted in *Classical and Medieval Literature Criticism,* Vol. 3, ed. Jelena O. Krstović (Detroit: Gale Research, 1989), pp. 154-58.

Dana Ferrin Sutton, *Self and Society in Aristophanes* (University of Press of America, 1980); excerpted and reprinted in *Classical and Medieval Literature Criticism,* Vol. 4, ed. Jelena O. Krstović (Detroit: Gale Research, 1990), pp. 162-69.

Suggestions Are Welcome

Readers who wish to make suggestions for future volumes, or who have other comments regarding the series, are cordially invited to write or call the editors (1-800-347-GALE, Fax: (313) 961-6815).

Acknowledgments

Pearl, portrait. The British Library. Reproduced by permission.

Pearl, river of snakes. The British Library. Reproduced by permission.

Pearl, text. The British Library. Reproduced by permission.

Pearl, trees and flowers. The British Library. Reproduced by permission.

Confucius

551(?) B.C.-479 B.C.

(The name Confucius is a Latinized version of the transliteration K'ung-fu-tzu.) Chinese philosopher.

INTRODUCTION

A thinker of unmatched influence in Eastern civilization, Confucius was a teacher and minor government official whose philosophy has been preserved in the *Lun-yu* (*The Analects*), a collection of sayings attributed to him and his disciples. *The Analects* contains remarks on a wide variety of subjects, including government, personal conduct, warfare, and family, and has been subject to diverse, even diametrically conflicting interpretations. For over two thousand years, Confucianism has endured as the foundation of Chinese philosophy.

Biographical Information

It is generally believed that Confucius was born in the state of Lu during the Chou dynasty and was orphaned at an early age. Some of Confucius's ancestors had been aristocrats in the state of Sung, but the family had immigrated to Lu to escape political unrest and intrigue. As a descendent of ancient nobility, Confucius occupied a middle position in Chinese society—between the impoverished peasantry and the ruling aristocracy. By the age of fifteen he had decided to become a scholar and worked to educate himself in music, literature, and ancient history. He began teaching in his early twenties and also served for a time as manager of Lu's state granary and supervisor of public fields. He also studied ancient governments under a scholar known as the master of Tan. Making use of an informal, discursive teaching style, Confucius became extremely popular with his students, many of whom became important government officials. In 479 B.C. Confucius left Lu on a sometimes perilous fourteen-year journey during which he taught and spread his ideas on society and government throughout China. Confucius's son died the year he returned to Lu, and two years later his student Yan Hui died. Reportedly inconsolable over the death of his beloved student, Confucius died less than three years later.

Major Works

The objective of Confucianism, the body of thought and writings inspired by Confucius, is the elucidation and encouragement of three main principles: *Jen, Tao,* and *Li.* In his teachings, which have been recorded in

such works as *The Analects, Li Chi* (*Book of Rites*), and *I Ching* (*Book of Changes*), Confucius encouraged his students to think for themselves; he also endeavored to define concepts in an abstract manner so that they could be universalized and applied to all cultures. Confucius's principles therefore are never succinctly defined and have engendered a multitude of interpretations, resulting in diverse readings of his works. Although scholars acknowledge problems with *The Analects* as the direct transcription of Confucius's utterances, it is nonetheless regarded as the best possible summation of his philosophy. *The Analects* are composed of twenty books, each made up of aphorisms, questions, and notes attributed to Confucius and twenty of his disciples, most notably Master Tseng, who is credited with twelve sayings of his own; Jan Ch'iu, who went on to become a lieutenant in the powerful Chi Family; and Tzu-kung, who went on to become a prominent diplomat. Alternately translated as "humanity," "good," "love," and "reciprocity," *Jen,* according to Arthur Waley, is "a sublime moral attitude, transcendental perfection attained to by legendary heroes . . .

but not by any living or historical person." This opinion contradicts the belief, often espoused by earlier scholars, that all humans are endowed with *Jen.* Thomas Cleary argues that "humanity is to love people" and contends that "Confucius believed the moral foundation of social order must rest on the primary virtue of . . . humanity." *Tao,* translated as "way," had been used before Confucius to describe both positive and negative ways of doing things. Confucius's innovation, according to H.G. Creel, was to recast the word as "the way . . . that individuals, states, and the world should conduct themselves and be conducted." Taoism, the philosophical school based upon the *Tao te Ching* of Lao Tzu—who may have been a contemporary of Confucius—offers a similar interpretation of the term, albeit in a more mystical and personal context. Benjamin I. Schwartz defines *Li* as "all those 'objective' prescriptions of behavior, whether involving rite, ceremony, manners, or general deportment, that bind human beings and the spirits together in networks of interacting roles within the family, within human society, and with the numinous realm beyond." The discipline required of strict adherence to the ideals of duty and etiquette has inspired some political leaders to impose dictatorial rule on their subjects in the name of Confucius. Confucius's teachings, however, stress the opposite, as one of the philosopher's central tenets is that a state should be designed to serve the people. According to Thomas Cleary, Confucius "envisioned a social order guided by reasonable, humane, and just sensibilities, not by the passions of individuals arbitrarily empowered by hereditary status, and warned of the social consequences if men in positions of power considered personal profit and advantage over public humanity and justice. Confucius believed in the regeneration of public and private conscience through education and the influence of unifying cultural ideals."

Critical Reception

The first important thinker to expand upon Confucius's work was Meng-tzu, better known by his Latinized name, Mencius. Active during the fourth century B.C., Mencius, like Confucius, was a teacher and counselor. In the collection of his teachings, the *Mencius,* he furthered the concept of *Jen,* arguing that the potential for exemplifying such an honorable trait exists in every human being. In direct contrast, the teachings of Hsun-tzu, the prominent Confucian thinker of the third century B.C., stress the evil nature of humanity. For Hsun-tzu, *Li* functions to suppress selfish instincts. Subsequent philosophers of the ancient world incorporated mystical schemes, numerology, and aspects of Taoism into traditional Confucian thought. Although the resulting philosophy was in many ways a diluted and contradictory imitation of Confucianism, it was during this period that the movement gained wide

acceptance, becoming the official state religion of China in the second century B.C. and eventually spreading to other Asian nations. Wang Ch'ung, a logician of the first century A.D., is credited with eliminating the mystical and supernatural elements of Confucianism as superfluous. Most of the first millennium A.D. is regarded as a period of relative diminution for the influence of Confucianism in China, during which time Taoism and Buddhism flourished. Neo-Confucianism arose in the eleventh century largely owing to the scholarship of Chu Hsi, whose historical writings focused on what are now known as the Classical Confucian texts—thirteen works of ancient origin that deal with a wide range of topics pertaining to Confucianism. Chu Hsi also explored the metaphysical side of Confucianism, engineering a path to spiritual enlightenment that has been viewed as a response to the challenge posed by Buddhism. During the seventeenth century a second wave of Neo-Confucianism arose; comparable to the earlier efforts of Wang Ch'ung, it aimed at reestablishing the original intent of *The Analects,* necessitating the purgation of all extraneous commentary and speculation. The influx of Western culture into twentieth-century China considerably altered the society's political and philosophical traditions. Mao Tse-Tung neglected Confucius in favor of Marxist ideology when he organized the People's Republic of China in 1949, effectively removing the Confucian tradition from political discourse, although its principles survive in literature and philosophy. Ironically, the decline of Confucianism in China was accompanied by a recognition—evinced by the numerous English translation of *The Analects*—on the part of the Western world of the depth and sophistication of Confucianism. Many scholars have observed similarities between the teachings of Confucius and those of Socrates and Jesus and often debate whether Confucianism should be characterized as a religion or a secular philosophy of ethics. Commentaries on Confucius usually center on differing interpretations of such key terms as *Li* and *Jen* as well as themes of proper government and individual behavior. D. Howard Smith celebrated the profundity of Confucius as a thinker: "He was convinced that there was a divine order which worked for love and righteousness, and taught that in obedience to that divine order man will find his highest goal."

PRINCIPAL WORKS

Lun-yu [*The Analects*] (philosophy) c. 400 B.C.
*Shih Ching [*Book of Songs*] (poetry)
Ch'un Ch'iu [*Spring and Autumn*] (history)
†*Li Chi* [*Book of Rites*] (philosophy)

I Ching [*Book of Changes*] (philosophy)
Shu Ching [*Book of History*] (history)

*According to popular tradition, Confucius was the editor of this collection.

†The works known as the *Great Learning* and the *Doctrine of the Mean* are chapters from this book.

CRITICISM

James Legge (essay date 1893)

SOURCE: "Confucius and His Immediate Disciples," in *The Chinese Classics, Vol. I,* Oxford at the Clarendon Press, 1893, pp. 90-111.

[*In the following excerpt, Legge remarks on the veneration of Confucius and discusses the philosopher's views on government.*]

1. Confucius died . . . complaining that of all the princes of the kingdom there was not one who would adopt his principles and obey his lessons. He had hardly passed from the stage of life, when his merit began to be acknowledged. When the duke Âi heard of his death, he pronounced his eulogy in the words, 'Heaven has not left to me the aged man. There is none now to assist me on the throne. Woe is me! Alas! O venerable Nî!' Tsze-kung complained of the inconsistency of this lamentation from one who could not use the master when he was alive, but the prince was probably sincere in his grief. He caused a temple to be erected, and ordered that sacrifice should be offered to the sage, at the four seasons of the year.

The sovereigns of the tottering dynasty of Châu had not the intelligence, nor were they in a position, to do honour to the departed philosopher, but the facts detailed in the first chapter of these prolegomena, in connexion with the attempt of the founder of the Ch'in dynasty to destroy the literary monuments of antiquity, show how the authority of Confucius had come by that time to prevail through the nation. The founder of the Han dynasty, in passing through Lû, B.C. 195, visited his tomb and offered the three victims in sacrifice to him. Other sovereigns since then have often made pilgrimages to the spot. The most famous temple in the empire now rises near the place of the grave. The second and greatest of the rulers of the present dynasty, in the twenty-third year of his reign, the K'ang-hsî period, there set the example of kneeling thrice, and each time laying his forehead thrice in the dust, before the image of the sage.

In the year of our Lord 1, began the practice of conferring honorary designations on Confucius by imperial authority. The emperor P'ing then styled him— 'The duke Nî, all-complete and illustrious.' This was changed, in A.D. 492, to—'The venerable Nî, the accomplished Sage.' Other titles have supplanted this. Shun-chih, the first of the Man-châu dynasty, adopted, in his second year, A. D. 1645, the style,—'K'ung, the ancient Teacher, accomplished and illustrious, all-complete, the perfect Sage;' but twelve years later, a shorter title was introduced,—'K'ung, the ancient Teacher, the perfect Sage.' Since that year no further alteration has been made.

At first, the worship of Confucius was confined to the country of Lû, but in A.D. 57 it was enacted that sacrifices should be offered to him in the imperial college, and in all the colleges of the principal territorial divisions throughout the empire. In those sacrifices he was for some centuries associated with the duke of Châu, the legislator to whom Confucius made frequent reference, but in A.D. 609 separate temples were assigned to them, and in 628 our sage displaced the older worthy altogether. About the same time began the custom, which continues to the present day, of erecting temples to him,—separate structures, in connexion with all the colleges, or examination-halls, of the country.

The sage is not alone in those temples. In a hall behind the principal one occupied by himself are the tablets—in some cases, the images—of several of his ancestors, and other worthies; while associated with himself are his principal disciples, and many who in subsequent times have signalized themselves as expounders and exemplifiers of his doctrines. On the first day of every month, offerings of fruits and vegetables are set forth, and on the fifteenth there is a solemn burning of incense. But twice a year, in the middle months of spring and autumn, when the first *ting* day of the month comes round, the worship of Confucius is performed with peculiar solemnity. At the imperial college the emperor himself is required to attend in state, and is in fact the principal performer. After all the preliminary arrangements have been made, and the emperor has twice knelt and six times bowed his head to the earth, the presence of Confucius's spirit is invoked in the words, 'Great art thou, O perfect sage! Thy virtue is full; thy doctrine is complete. Among mortal men there has not been thine equal. All kings honour thee. Thy statutes and laws have come gloriously down. Thou art the pattern in this imperial school. Reverently have the sacrificial vessels been set out. Full of awe, we sound our drums and bells.'

The spirit is supposed now to be present, and the service proceeds through various offerings, when the first of which has been set forth, an officer reads the following, which is the prayer on the occasion:—'On this

. . . month of this . . . year, I, *A.B.,* the emperor, offer a sacrifice to the philosopher K'ung, the ancient Teacher, the perfect Sage, and say,—O Teacher, in virtue equal to Heaven and Earth, whose doctrines embrace the past time and the present, thou didst digest and transmit the six classics, and didst hand down lessons for all generations! Now in this second month of spring (or autumn), in reverent observance of the old statutes, with victims, silks, spirits, and fruits, I carefully offer sacrifice to thee. With thee are associated the philosopher Yen, Continuator of thee; the philosopher Tsăng, Exhibiter of thy fundamental principles; the philosopher Tsze-sze, Transmitter of thee; and the philosopher Măng, Second to thee. May'st thou enjoy the offerings!'

I need not go on to enlarge on the homage which the emperors of China render to Confucius. It could not be more complete. He was unreasonably neglected when alive. He is now unreasonably venerated when dead.

2. The rulers of China are not singular in this matter, but in entire sympathy with the mass of their people. It is the distinction of this empire that education has been highly prized in it from the earliest times. It was so before the era of Confucius, and we may be sure that the system met with his approbation. One of his remarkable sayings was,—'To lead an uninstructed people to war is to throw them away.' When he pronounced this judgment, he was not thinking of military training, but of education in the duties of life and citizenship. A people so taught, he thought, would be morally fitted to fight for their government. Mencius, when lecturing to the ruler of T'ăng on the proper way of governing a kingdom, told him that he must provide the means of education for all, the poor as well as the rich. 'Establish,' said he, '*hsiang, hsü, hsio,* and *hsiâo,*—all those educational institutions,—for the instruction of the people.'

At the present day, education is widely diffused throughout China. In few other countries is the schoolmaster more abroad, and in all schools it is Confucius who is taught. The plan of competitive examinations, and the selection for civil offices only from those who have been successful candidates,—good so far as the competition is concerned, but injurious from the restricted range of subjects with which an acquaintance is required,—have obtained for more than twelve centuries. The classical works are the text books. It is from them almost exclusively that the themes proposed to determine the knowledge and ability of the students are chosen. The whole of the magistracy of China is thus versed in all that is recorded of the sage, and in the ancient literature which he preserved. His thoughts are familiar to every man in authority, and his character is more or less reproduced in him.

The official civilians of China, numerous as they are, are but a fraction of its students, and the students, or those who make literature a profession, are again but a fraction of those who attend school for a shorter or longer period. Yet so far as the studies have gone, they have been occupied with the Confucian writings. In the schoolrooms there is a tablet or inscription on the wall, sacred to the sage, and every pupil is required, on coming to school on the morning of the first and fifteenth of every month, to bow before it, the first thing, as an act of reverence. Thus all in China who receive the slightest tincture of learning do so at the fountain of Confucius. They learn of him and do homage to him at once. I have repeatedly quoted the statement that during his life-time he had three thousand disciples. Hundreds of millions are his disciples now. It is hardly necessary to make any allowance in this statement for the followers of Tâoism and Buddhism, for, as Sir John Davis [*The Chinese*] has observed, 'whatever the other opinions or faith of a Chinese may be, he takes good care to treat Confucius with respect.' For two thousand years he has reigned supreme, the undisputed teacher of this most populous land.

3. This position and influence of Confucius are to be ascribed, I conceive, chiefly to two causes:—his being the preserver, namely of the monuments of antiquity, and the exemplifier and expounder of the maxims of the golden age of China; and the devotion to him of his immediate disciples and their early followers. The national and the personal are thus blended in him, each in its highest degree of excellence. He was a Chinese of the Chinese; he is also represented as, and all now believe him to have been, the *beau ideal* of humanity in its best and noblest estate.

4. It may be well to bring forward here Confucius's own estimate of himself and of his doctrines. It will serve to illustrate the statements just made. The following are some of his sayings:—'The sage and the man of perfect virtue;—how dare I rank myself with them? It may simply be said of me, that I strive to become such without satiety, and teach others without weariness.' 'In letters I am perhaps equal to other men; but the character of the superior man, carrying out in his conduct what he professes, is what I have not yet attained to.' 'The leaving virtue without proper cultivation; the not thoroughly discussing what is learned; not being able to move towards righteousness of which a knowledge is gained; and not being able to change what is not good;—these are the things which occasion me solicitude.' 'I am not one who was born in the possession of knowledge; I am one who is fond of antiquity and earnest in seeking it there.' 'A transmitter and not a maker, believing in and loving the ancients, I venture to compare myself with our old P'ăng.'

Confucius cannot be thought to speak of himself in these declarations more highly than he ought to do.

Rather we may recognise in them the expressions of a genuine humility. He was conscious that personally he came short in many things, but he toiled after the character, which he saw, or fancied that he saw, in the ancient sages whom he acknowledged; and the lessons of government and morals which he laboured to diffuse were those which had already been inculcated and exhibited by them. Emphatically he was 'a transmitter and not a maker.' It is not to be understood that he was not fully satisfied of the truth of the principles which he had learned. He held them with the full approval and consent of his own understanding. He believed that if they were acted on, they would remedy the evils of his time. There was nothing to prevent rulers like Yâo and Shun and the great Yü from again arising, and a condition of happy tranquillity being realised throughout the kingdom under their sway.

If in anything he thought himself 'superior and alone,' having attributes which others could not claim, it was in his possessing a divine commission as the conservator of ancient truth and rules. He does not speak very definitely on this point. It is noted that 'the appointments of Heaven was one of the subjects on which he rarely touched.' His most remarkable utterance was that which I have already given in the sketch of his Life:—'When he was put in fear in K'wang, he said, "After the death of king Wăn, was not the cause of truth lodged here in me? If Heaven had wished to let this cause of truth perish, then I, a future mortal, should not have got such a relation to that cause. While Heaven does not let the cause of truth perish, what can the people of K'wang do to me?"' Confucius, then, did feel that he was in the world for a special purpose. But it was not to announce any new truths, or to initiate any new economy. It was to prevent what had previously been known from being lost. He followed in the wake of Yâo and Shun, of T'ang, and king Wăn. Distant from the last by a long interval of time, he would have said that he was distant from him also by a great inferiority of character, but still he had learned the principles on which they all happily governed the country, and in their name he would lift up a standard against the prevailing lawlessness of his age.

5. The language employed with reference to Confucius by his disciples and their early followers presents a striking contrast with his own. I have already, in writing of the scope and value of 'The Doctrine of the Mean,' called attention to the extravagant eulogies of his grandson Tsze-sze. He only followed the example which had been set by those among whom the philosopher went in and out. We have the language of Yen Yüan, his favourite, which is comparatively moderate, and simply expresses the genuine admiration of a devoted pupil. Tsze-kung on several occasions spoke in a different style. Having heard that one of the chiefs of Lû had said that he himself—Tsze-kung—was superior to Confucius, he observed, 'Let me use the com-

parison of a house and its encompassing wall. My wall only reaches to the shoulders. One may peep over it, and see whatever is valuable in the apartments. The wall of my master is several fathoms high. If one do not find the door and enter by it, he cannot see the rich ancestral temple with its beauties, nor all the officers in their rich array. But I may assume that they are few who find the door. The remark of the chief was only what might have been expected.'

Another time, the same individual having spoken revilingly of Confucius, Tsze-kung said, 'It is of no use doing so. Chung-nî cannot be reviled. The talents and virtue of other men are hillocks and mounds which may be stepped over. Chung-nî is the sun or moon, which it is not possible to step over. Although a man may wish to cut himself off from the sage, what harm can he do to the sun and moon? He only shows that he does not know his own capacity.'

In conversation with a fellow-disciple, Tsze-kung took a still higher flight. Being charged by Tsze-ch'in with being too modest, for that Confucius was not really superior to him, he replied, 'For one word a man is often deemed to be wise, and for one word he is often deemed to be foolish. We ought to be careful indeed in what we say. Our master cannot be attained to, just in the same way as the heavens cannot be gone up to by the steps of a stair. Were our master in the position of the prince of a State, or the chief of a Family, we should find verified the description which has been given of a sage's rule:—He would plant the people, and forthwith they would be established; he would lead them on, and forthwith they would follow him; he would make them happy, and forthwith multitudes would resort to his dominions; he would stimulate them, and forthwith they would be harmonious. While he lived, he would be glorious. When he died, he would be bitterly lamented. How is it possible for him to be attained to?'

From these representations of Tsze-kung, it was not a difficult step for Tsze-sze to take in exalting Confucius not only to the level of the ancient sages, but as 'the equal of Heaven.' And Mencius took up the theme. Being questioned by Kung-sun Ch'âu, one of his disciples, about two acknowledged sages, Po-î and Î Yin, whether they were to be placed in the same rank with Confucius, he replied, 'No. Since there were living men until now, there never was another Confucius;' and then he proceeded to fortify his opinion by the concurring testimony of Tsâi Wo, Tsze-kung, and Yû Zo, who all had wisdom, he thought, sufficient to know their master. Tsâi Wo's opinion was, 'According to my view of our master, he is far superior to Yâo and Shun.' Tsze-kung said, 'By viewing the ceremonial ordinances of a prince, we know the character of his government. By hearing his music, we know the character of his virtue. From the distance of a hundred ages after, I can arrange, ac-

Confucius

cording to their merits, the kings of those hundred ages;—not one of them can escape me. From the birth of mankind till now, there has never been another like our master.' Yû Zo said, 'Is it only among men that it is so? There is the ch'î-lin among quadrupeds; the fung-hwang among birds; the T'âi mountain among mounds and ant-hills; and rivers and seas among rain-pools. Though different in degree, they are the same in kind. So the sages among mankind are also the same in kind. But they stand out from their fellows, and rise above the level; and from the birth of man-kind till now, there never has been one so complete as Confucius.' I will not indulge in farther illustra-tion. The judgment of the sage's disciples, of Tsze-sze, and of Mencius, has been unchallenged by the mass of the scholars of China. Doubtless it pleases them to bow down at the shrine of the Sage, for their profession of literature is thereby glorified. A reflec-tion of the honour done to him falls upon themselves. And the powers that be, and the multitudes of the people, fall in with the judgment. Confucius is thus, in the empire of China, the one man by whom all possible personal excellence was exemplified, and by

whom all possible lessons of social virtue and politi-cal wisdom are taught.

6. The reader will be prepared by the preceding account not to expect to find any light thrown by Confucius on the great problems of the human condition and destiny. He did not speculate on the creation of things or the end of them. He was not troubled to account for the origin of man, nor did he seek to know about his hereafter. He meddled neither with physics nor metaphysics. The tes-timony of the **Analects** about the subjects of his teach-ing is the following:—'His frequent themes of discourse were the Book of Poetry, the Book of History, and the maintenance of the rules of Propriety.' 'He taught let-ters, ethics, devotion of soul, and truthfulness.' 'Ex-traordinary things; feats of strength; states of disorder; and spiritual beings, he did not like to talk about.'

Confucius is not to be blamed for his silence on the subjects here indicated. His ignorance of them was to a great extent his misfortune. He had not learned them. No report of them had come to him by the ear; no vision of them by the eye. And to his practical mind the toiling of thought amid uncertainties seemed worse than useless.

The question has, indeed, been raised, whether he did not make changes in the ancient creed of China, but I cannot believe that he did so consciously and design-edly. Had his idiosyncrasy been different, we might have had expositions of the ancient views on some points, the effect of which would have been more beneficial than the indefiniteness in which they are now left, and it may be doubted so far, whether Confucius was not unfaithful to his guides. But that he suppressed or added, in order to bring in articles of belief originating with himself, is a thing not to be charged against him.

I will mention two important subjects in regard to which there is a conviction in my mind that he came short of the faith of the older sages. The first is the doctrine of God. This name is common in the **Shih-ching** and **Shû-ching**. *Tî* or *Shang-Tî* appears there as a personal being, ruling in heaven and on earth, the author of man's moral nature, the governor among the nations, by whom kings reign and princes decree justice, the rewarder of the good, and the punisher of the bad. Confucius preferred to speak of Heaven. Instances have already been given of this. Two others may be cited:— 'He who offends against Heaven has none to whom he can pray?' 'Alas!' said he, 'there is no one that knows me.' Tsze-kung said, 'What do you mean by thus say-ing that no one knows you?' He replied, 'I do not murmur against Heaven. I do not grumble against men. My studies lie low, and my penetration rises high. But there is Heaven;—THAT knows me!' Not once throughout the Analects does he use the personal name. I would say that he was unreligious rather than irreli-gious; yet by the coldness of his temperament and

6

intellect in this matter, his influence is unfavourable to the development of ardent religious feeling among the Chinese people generally; and he prepared the way for the speculations of the literati of mediæval and modern times, which have exposed them to the charge of atheism.

Secondly, along with the worship of God there existed in China, from the earliest historical times, the worship of other spiritual beings,—especially, and to every individual, the worship of departed ancestors. Confucius recognised this as an institution to be devoutly observed. 'He sacrificed to the dead as if they were present; he sacrificed to the spirits as if the spirits were present. He said, "I consider my not being present at the sacrifice as if I did not sacrifice."' The custom must have originated from a belief in the continued existence of the dead. We cannot suppose that they who instituted it thought that with the cessation of this life on earth there was a cessation also of all conscious being. But Confucius never spoke explicitly on this subject. He tried to evade it. 'Chî Lû asked about serving the spirits of the dead, and the master said, "While you are not able to serve men, how can you serve their spirits?" The disciple added, "I venture to ask about death," and he was answered, "While you do not know life, how can you know about death."' Still more striking is a conversation with another disciple, recorded in the 'Narratives of the School.' Tsze-kung asked him, saying, 'Do the dead have knowledge (of our services, that is), or are they without knowledge?' The master replied, 'If I were to say that the dead have such knowledge, I am afraid that filial sons and dutiful grandsons would injure their substance in paying the last offices to the departed; and if I were to say that the dead have not such knowledge, I am afraid lest unfilial sons should leave their parents unburied. You need not wish, Ts'ze, to know whether the dead have knowledge or not. There is no present urgency about the point. Hereafter you will know it for yourself.' Surely this was not the teaching proper to a sage. He said on one occasion that he had no concealments from his disciples. Why did he not candidly tell his real thoughts on so interesting a subject? I incline to think that he doubted more than he believed. If the case were not so, it would be difficult to account for the answer which he returned to a question as to what constituted wisdom:—'To give one's self earnestly,' said he, 'to the duties due to men, and, while respecting spiritual beings, to keep aloof from them, may be called wisdom.' At any rate, as by his frequent references to Heaven, instead of following the phraseology of the older sages, he gave occasion to many of his professed followers to identify God with a principle of reason and the course of nature; so, in the point now in hand, he has led them to deny, like the Sadducees of old, the existence of any spirit at all, and to tell us that their sacrifices to the dead are but an outward form, the mode of expression which the principle of filial piety requires them to adopt when its objects have departed this life.

It will not be supposed that I wish to advocate or to defend the practice of sacrificing to the dead. My object has been to point out how Confucius recognised it, without acknowledging the faith from which it must have originated, and how he enforced it as a matter of form or ceremony. It thus connects itself with the most serious charge that can be brought against him,—the charge of insincerity. Among the four things which it is said he taught, 'truthfulness' is specified, and many sayings might be quoted from him, in which 'sincerity' is celebrated as highly and demanded as stringently as ever it has been by any Christian moralist; yet he was not altogether the truthful and true man to whom we accord our highest approbation. There was the case of Măng Chih-fan, who boldly brought up the rear of the defeated troops of Lû, and attributed his occupying the place of honour to the backwardness of his horse. The action was gallant, but the apology for it was weak and unnecessary. And yet Confucius saw nothing in the whole but matter for praise. He could excuse himself from seeing an unwelcome visitor on the ground that he was sick, when there was nothing the matter with him. These were small matters, but what shall we say to . . . his deliberately breaking the oath which he had sworn, simply on the ground that it had been forced from him? I should be glad if I could find evidence on which to deny the truth of that occurrence. But it rests on the same authority as most other statements about him, and it is accepted as a fact by the people and scholars of China. It must have had, and it must still have, a very injurious influence upon them. Foreigners charge a habit of deceitfulness upon the nation and its government;—on the justice or injustice of this charge I say nothing. For every word of falsehood and every act of insincerity, the guilty party must bear his own burden, but we cannot but regret the example of Confucius in this particular. It is with the Chinese and their sage, as it was with the Jews of old and their teachers. He that leads them has caused them to err, and destroyed the way of their paths.

But was not insincerity a natural result of the un-religion of Confucius? There are certain virtues which demand a true piety in order to their flourishing in the heart of man. Natural affection, the feeling of loyalty, and enlightened policy, may do much to build up and preserve a family and a state, but it requires more to maintain the love of truth, and make a lie, spoken or acted, to be shrunk from with shame. It requires in fact the living recognition of a God of truth, and all the sanctions of revealed religion. Unfortunately the Chinese have not had these, and the example of him to whom they bow down as the best and wisest of men, does not set them against dissimulation.

7. I go on to a brief discussion of Confucius's views on government, or what we may call his principles of political science. It could not be in his long intercourse with his disciples but that he should enunciate many

maxims bearing on character and morals generally, but he never rested in the improvement of the individual. 'The kingdom, the world, brought to a state of happy tranquillity,' was the grand object which he delighted to think of; that it might be brought about as easily as 'one can look upon the palm of his hand,' was the dream which it pleased him to indulge. He held that there was in men an adaptation and readiness to be governed, which only needed to be taken advantage of in the proper way. There must be the right administrators, but given those, and 'the growth of government would be rapid, just as vegetation is rapid in the earth; yea, their government would display itself like an easily-growing rush.' The same sentiment was common from the lips of Mencius. Enforcing it one day, when conversing with one of the petty rulers of his time, he said in his peculiar style, 'Does your Majesty understand the way of the growing grain? During the seventh and eighth months, when drought prevails, the plants become dry. Then the clouds collect densely in the heavens; they send down torrents of rain, and the grain erects itself as if by a shoot. When it does so, who can keep it back?' Such, he contended, would be the response of the mass of the people to any true 'shepherd of men.' It may be deemed unnecessary that I should specify this point, for it is a truth applicable to the people of all nations. Speaking generally, government is by no device or cunning craftiness; human nature demands it. But in no other family of mankind is the characteristic so largely developed as in the Chinese. The love of order and quiet, and a willingness to submit to 'the powers that be,' eminently distinguish them. Foreign writers have often taken notice of this, and have attributed it to the influence of Confucius's doctrines as inculcating subordination; but it existed previous to his time. The character of the people moulded his system, more than it was moulded by it.

This readiness to be governed arose, according to Confucius, from 'the duties of universal obligation, or those between sovereign and minister, between father and son, between husband and wife, between elder brother and younger, and those belonging to the intercourse of friends.' Men as they are born into the world, and grow up in it, find themselves existing in those relations. They are the appointment of Heaven. And each relation has its reciprocal obligations, the recognition of which is proper to the Heaven-conferred nature. It only needs that the sacredness of the relations be maintained, and the duties belonging to them faithfully discharged, and the 'happy tranquillity' will prevail all under heaven. As to the institutions of government, the laws and arrangements by which, as through a thousand channels, it should go forth to carry plenty and prosperity through the length and breadth of the country, it did not belong to Confucius, 'the throneless king,' to set them forth minutely. And indeed they were existing in the records of 'the ancient

sovereigns.' Nothing new was needed. It was only requisite to pursue the old paths, and raise up the old standards. 'The government of Wăn and Wû,' he said, 'is displayed in the records,—the tablets of wood and bamboo. Let there be the men, and the government will flourish; but without the men, the government decays and ceases.' To the same effect was the reply which he gave to Yen Hûi when asked by him how the government of a State should be administered. It seems very wide of the mark, until we read it in the light of the sage's veneration for ancient ordinances, and his opinion of their sufficiency. 'Follow,' he said, 'the seasons of Hsiâ. Ride in the state-carriages of Yin. Wear the ceremonial cap of Châu. Let the music be the Shâo with its pantomimes. Banish the songs of Chăng, and keep far from specious talkers.'

Confucius's idea then of a happy, well-governed State did not go beyond the flourishing of the five relations of society which have been mentioned; and we have not any condensed exhibition from him of their nature, or of the duties belonging to the several parties in them. Of the two first he spoke frequently, but all that he has said on the others would go into small compass. Mencius has said that 'between father and son there should be affection; between sovereign and minister righteousness; between husband and wife attention to their separate functions; between old and young, a proper order; and between friends, fidelity.' Confucius, I apprehend, would hardly have accepted this account. It does not bring out sufficiently the authority which he claimed for the father and the sovereign, and the obedience which he exacted from the child and the minister. With regard to the relation of husband and wife, he was in no respect superior to the preceding sages who had enunciated their views of 'propriety' on the subject. We have a somewhat detailed exposition of his opinions in the 'Narratives of the School.'— 'Man,' said he, 'is the representative of Heaven, and is supreme over all things. Woman yields obedience to the instructions of man, and helps to carry out his principles. On this account she can determine nothing of herself, and is subject to the rule of the three obediences. When young, she must obey her father and elder brother; when married, she must obey her husband; when her husband is dead, she must obey her son. She may not think of marrying a second time. No instructions or orders must issue from the harem. Woman's business is simply the preparation and supplying of drink and food. Beyond the threshold of her apartments she should not be known for evil or for good. She may not cross the boundaries of the State to attend a funeral. She may take no step on her own motion, and may come to no conclusion on her own deliberation. There are five women who are not to be taken in marriage:—the daughter of a rebellious house; the daughter of a disorderly house; the daughter of a house which has produced criminals for more than one generation; the daughter of a leprous house; and the daughter who has lost her father and elder brother. A wife may be divorced for seven reasons, which, however, may be overruled by three considerations. The grounds for divorce are disobedience to her husband's parents; not giving birth to a son; dissolute conduct; jealousy—(of her husband's attentions, that is, to the other inmates of his harem); talkativeness; and thieving. The three considerations which may overrule these grounds are—first, if, while she was taken from a home, she has now no home to return to; second, if she have passed with her husband through the three years' mourning for his parents; third, if the husband have become rich from being poor. All these regulations were adopted by the sages in harmony with the natures of man and woman, and to give importance to the ordinance of marriage.'

With these ideas of the relations of society, Confucius dwelt much on the necessity of personal correctness of character on the part of those in authority, in order to secure the right fulfilment of the duties implied in them. This is one grand peculiarity of his teaching. I have adverted to it in the review of 'The Great Learning,' but it deserves some further exhibition, and there are three conversations with the chief Chî K'ang in which it is very expressly set forth. 'Chî K'ang asked about government, and Confucius replied, "To govern means to rectify. If you lead on the people with correctness, who will dare not to be correct?"' 'Chî K'ang, distressed about the number of thieves in the State, inquired of Confucius about how to do away with them. Confucius said, "If you, sir, were not covetous, though you should reward them to do it, they would not steal."' 'Chî K'ang asked about government, saying, "What do you say to killing the unprincipled for the good of the principled?" Confucius replied, "Sir, in carrying on your government, why should you use killing at all? Let your evinced desires be for what is good, and the people will be good. The relation between superiors and inferiors is like that between the wind and the grass. The grass must bend, when the wind blows across it."'

Example is not so powerful as Confucius in these and many other passages represented it, but its influence is very great. Its virtue is recognised in the family, and it is demanded in the church of Christ. 'A bishop'—and I quote the term with the simple meaning of overseer—'must be blameless.' It seems to me, however, that in the progress of society in the West we have come to think less of the power of example in many departments of state than we ought to do. It is thought of too little in the army and the navy. We laugh at the 'self-denying ordinance,' and the 'new model' of 1644, but there lay beneath them the principle which Confucius so broadly propounded,—the importance of personal virtue in all who are in authority. Now that Great Britain is the governing power over the masses of India, and that we are coming more and more into

contact with tens of thousands of the Chinese, this maxim of our sage is deserving of serious consideration from all who bear rule, and especially from those on whom devolves the conduct of affairs. His words on the susceptibility of the people to be acted on by those above them ought not to prove as water spilt on the ground.

But to return to Confucius.—As he thus lays it down that the mainspring of the well-being of society is the personal character of the ruler, we look anxiously for what directions he has given for the cultivation of that. But here he is very defective. 'Self-adjustment and purification,' he said, 'with careful regulation of his dress, and the not making a movement contrary to the rules of propriety;—this is the way for the ruler to cultivate his person.' This is laying too much stress on what is external; but even to attain to this is beyond unassisted human strength. Confucius, however, never recognised a disturbance of the moral elements in the constitution of man. The people would move, according to him, to the virtue of their ruler as the grass bends to the wind, and that virtue would come to the ruler at his call. Many were the lamentations which he uttered over the degeneracy of his times; frequent were the confessions which he made of his own shortcomings. It seems strange that it never came distinctly before him, that there is a power of evil in the prince and the peasant, which no efforts of their own and no instructions of sages are effectual to subdue.

The government which Confucius taught was a despotism, but of a modified character. He allowed no *jus divinum,'* independent of personal virtue and a benevolent rule. He has not explicitly stated, indeed, wherein lies the ground of the great relation of the governor and the governed, but his views on the subject were, we may assume, in accordance with the language of the **Shû-ching**:—'Heaven and Earth are the parents of all things, and of all things men are the most intelligent. The man among them most distinguished for intelligence becomes chief ruler, and ought to prove himself the parent of the people.' And again, 'Heaven, protecting the inferior people, has constituted for them rulers and teachers, who should be able to be assisting to God, extending favour and producing tranquillity throughout all parts of the kingdom.' The moment the ruler ceases to be a minister of God for good, and does not administer a government that is beneficial to the people, he forfeits the title by which he holds the throne, and perseverance in oppression will surely lead to his overthrow. Mencius inculcated this principle with a frequency and boldness which are remarkable. It was one of the things about which Confucius did not like to talk. Still he held it. It is conspicuous in the last chapter of 'The Great Learning.' Its tendency has been to check the violence of oppression, and maintain the self-respect of the people, all along the course of Chinese history.

I must bring these observations on Confucius's views of government to a close, and I do so with two remarks. First, they are adapted to a primitive, unsophisticated state of society. He is a good counsellor for the father of a family, the chief of a clan, and even the head of a small principality. But his views want the comprehension which would make them of much service in a great dominion. Within three centuries after his death, the government of China passed into a new phase. The founder of the Ch'in dynasty conceived the grand idea of abolishing all its feudal kingdoms, and centralizing their administration in himself. He effected the revolution, and succeeding dynasties adopted his system, and gradually moulded it into the forms and proportions which are now existing. There has been a tendency to advance, and Confucius has all along been trying to carry the nation back. Principles have been needed, and not 'proprieties.' The consequence is that China has increased beyond its ancient dimensions, while there has been no corresponding development of thought. Its body politic has the size of a giant, while it still retains the mind of a child. Its hoary age is in danger of becoming but senility.

Second, Confucius makes no provision for the intercourse of his country with other and independent nations. He knew indeed of none such. China was to him 'The Middle Kingdom,' 'The multitude of Great States,' 'All under heaven.' Beyond it were only rude and barbarous tribes. He does not speak of them bitterly, as many Chinese have done since his time. In one place he contrasts their condition favourably with the prevailing anarchy of the kingdom, saying 'The rude tribes of the east and north have their princes, and are not like the States of our great land which are without them.' Another time, disgusted with the want of appreciation which he experienced, he was expressing his intention to go and live among the nine wild tribes of the east. Some one said, 'They are rude. How can you do such a thing?' His reply was, 'If a superior man dwelt among them, what rudeness would there be?' But had he been a ruler-sage, he would not only have influenced them by his instructions, but brought them to acknowledge and submit to his sway, as the great Yü did. The only passage of Confucius's teachings from which any rule can be gathered for dealing with foreigners, is that in the 'Doctrine of the Mean,' where 'indulgent treatment of men from a distance' is laid down as one of the nine standard rules for the government of the country. But 'the men from a distance' are understood to be *pin* and *lü* simply,—'guests,' that is, or officers of one State seeking employment in another, or at the royal court; and 'visitors,' or travelling merchants. Of independent nations the ancient classics have not any knowledge, nor has Confucius. So long as merchants from Europe and other parts of the world could have been content to appear in China as suppliants, seeking the privilege of trade, so long the government would have ranked them with the barbarous

hordes of antiquity, and given them the benefit of the maxim about 'indulgent treatment,' according to its own understanding of it. But when their governments interfered, and claimed to treat with that of China on terms of equality, and that their subjects should be spoken to and of as being of the same clay with the Chinese themselves, an outrage was committed on tradition and prejudice, which it was necessary to resent with vehemence.

I do not charge the contemptuous arrogance of the Chinese government and people upon Confucius; what I deplore, is that he left no principles on record to check the development of such a spirit. His simple views of society and government were in a measure sufficient for the people while they dwelt apart from the rest of mankind. His practical lessons were better than if they had been left, which but for him they probably would have been, to fall a prey to the influences of Tâoism and Buddhism, but they could only subsist while they were left alone. Of the earth earthy, China was sure to go to pieces when it came into collision with a Christianly-civilized power. Its sage had left it no preservative or restorative elements against such a case.

It is a rude awakening from its complacency of centuries which China has now received. Its ancient landmarks are swept away. Opinions will differ as to the justice or injustice of the grounds on which it has been assailed, and I do not feel called to judge or to pronounce here concerning them. In the progress of events, it could hardly be but that the collision should come; and when it did come it could not be but that China should be broken and scattered. Disorganization will go on to destroy it more and more, and yet there is hope for the people, with their veneration for the relations of society, with their devotion to learning, and with their habits of industry and sobriety;—there is hope for them, if they will look away from all their ancient sages, and turn to Him, who sends them, along with the dissolution of their ancient state, the knowledge of Himself, the only living and true God, and of Jesus Christ whom He hath sent.

8. I have little more to add on the opinions of Confucius. Many of his sayings are pithy, and display much knowledge of character; but as they are contained in the body of the Work, I will not occupy the space here with a selection of those which have struck myself as most worthy of notice. The fourth Book of the **Analects**, which is on the subject of zăn, or perfect virtue, has several utterances which are remarkable.

Thornton [*History of China*] observes:—'It may excite surprise, and probably incredulity, to state that the golden rule of our Saviour, 'Do unto others as you would that they should do unto you,' which Mr. Locke designates as 'the most unshaken rule of morality, and foundation of all social virtue,' had been inculcated by Confucius, almost in the same words, four centuries before.' I have taken notice of this fact in reviewing both 'The Great Learning' and 'The Doctrine of the Mean.' I would be far from grudging a tribute of admiration to Confucius for it. The maxim occurs also twice in the **Analects**. In Book XV. xxiii, Tsze-kung asks if there be one word which may serve as a rule of practice for all one's life, and is answered, 'Is not reciprocity such a word? What you do not want done to yourself do not do to others.' The same disciple appears in Book V. xi, telling Confucius that he was practising the lesson. He says, 'What I do not wish men to do to me, I also wish not to do to men;' but the master tells him, 'Ts'ze, you have not attained to that.' It would appear from this reply, that he was aware of the difficulty of obeying the precept; and it is not found, in its condensed expression at least, in the older classics. The merit of it is Confucius's own.

When a comparison, however, is drawn between it and the rule laid down by Christ, it is proper to call attention to the positive form of the latter,—'All things whatsoever ye would that men should do unto you, do ye even so to them.' The lesson of the gospel commands men to do what they feel to be right and good. It requires them to commence a course of such conduct, without regard to the conduct of others to themselves. The lesson of Confucius only forbids men to do what they feel to be wrong and hurtful. So far as the point of priority is concerned, moreover, Christ adds, 'This is the law and the prophets.' The maxim was to be found substantially in the earlier revelations of God. Still it must be allowed that Confucius was well aware of the importance of taking the initiative in discharging all the relations of society. . . .

But the worth of the two maxims depends on the intention of the enunciators in regard to their application. Confucius, it seems to me, did not think of the reciprocity coming into action beyond the circle of his five relations of society. Possibly, he might have required its observance in dealings even with the rude tribes, which were the only specimens of mankind besides his own countrymen of which he knew anything, for on one occasion, when asked about perfect virtue, he replied, 'It is, in retirement, to be sedately grave; in the management of business, to be reverently attentive; in intercourse with others, to be strictly sincere. Though a man go among the rude uncultivated tribes, these qualities may not be neglected.' Still, Confucius delivered his rule to his countrymen only, and only for their guidance in their relations of which I have had so much occasion to speak. The rule of Christ is for man as man, having to do with other men, all with himself on the same platform, as the children and subjects of the one God and Father in heaven.

How far short Confucius came of the standard of Christian benevolence, may be seen from his remarks when asked what was to be thought of the principle that injury should be recompensed with kindness. He replied, 'With what then will you recompense kindness? Recompense injury with justice, and recompense kindness with kindness.' The same deliverance is given in one of the Books of the **Lî Chî**, where he adds that 'he who recompenses injury with kindness is a man who is careful of his person.' Chăng Hsüan, the commentator of the second century, says that such a course would be 'incorrect in point of propriety.' This 'propriety' was a great stumbling-block in the way of Confucius. His morality was the result of the balancings of his intellect, fettered by the decisions of men of old, and not the gushings of a loving heart, responsive to the promptings of Heaven, and in sympathy with erring and feeble humanity.

This subject leads me on to the last of the opinions of Confucius which I shall make the subject of remark in this place. A commentator observes, with reference to the inquiry about recompensing injury with kindness, that the questioner was asking only about trivial matters, which might be dealt with in the way he mentioned, while great offences, such as those against a sovereign or a father, could not be dealt with by such an inversion of the principles of justice. In the second Book of the **Lî Chî** there is the following passage:—'With the slayer of his father, a man may not live under the same heaven; against the slayer of his brother, a man must never have to go home to fetch a weapon; with the slayer of his friend, a man may not live in the same State.' The *lex talionis* is here laid down in its fullest extent. The Châu Lî tells us of a provision made against the evil consequences of the principle, by the appointment of a minister called 'The Reconciler.' The provision is very inferior to the cities of refuge which were set apart by Moses for the manslayer to flee to from the fury of the avenger. Such as it was, however, it existed, and it is remarkable that Confucius, when consulted on the subject, took no notice of it, but affirmed the duty of blood-revenge in the strongest and most unrestricted terms. His disciple Tsze-hsiâ asked him, 'What course is to be pursued in the case of the murder of a father or mother?' He replied, 'The son must sleep upon a matting of grass, with his shield for his pillow; he must decline to take office; he must not live under the same heaven with the slayer. When he meets him in the marketplace or the court, he must have his weapon ready to strike him.' 'And what is the course on the murder of a brother?' 'The surviving brother must not take office in the same State with the slayer; yet if he go on his prince's service to the State where the slayer is, though he meet him, he must not fight with him.' 'And what is the course on the murder of an uncle or a cousin?' 'In this case the nephew or cousin is not the principal. If the principal on whom the revenge devolves can take it, he has only to stand behind with his weapon in his hand, and support him.'

Sir John Davis has rightly called attention to this as one of the objectionable principles of Confucius. The bad effects of it are evident even in the present day. Revenge is sweet to the Chinese. I have spoken of their readiness to submit to government, and wish to live in peace, yet they do not like to resign even to government the 'inquisition for blood.' Where the ruling authority is feeble, as it is at present, individuals and clans take the law into their own hands, and whole districts are kept in a state of constant feud and warfare.

But I must now leave the sage. I hope I have not done him injustice; the more I have studied his character and opinions, the more highly have I come to regard him. He was a very great man, and his influence has been on the whole a great benefit to the Chinese, while his teachings suggest important lessons to ourselves who profess to belong to the school of Christ.

Ernst Faber (essay date 1896)

SOURCE: "A Missionary View of Confucianism," in *A Systematical Digest of the Doctrines of Confucius,* The General Evangelical Protestant Missionary Society of Germany, 1902, pp. 89-99.

[*In the excerpt below, Faber compares Confucianism and Christianity.*]

This subject is still but little known. As I have an exhaustive work in preparation I will take the liberty of stating here its programme:—

I. The Thirteen Sacred Books of Confucianism. The origin of every portion of them. A history of the text. Remnants of ancient texts; various readings, quotations, etc. History of the Confucian Canon.

II. The other Ancient Literature of China, *i.e.,* a description of all the original works still in existence and not included in the Confucian Sacred Books.

III. Outline of a History of the Pre-Confucian Period, from these sources (under II), compared with such accidental notices as the Confucian Classics (under I) may contain.

IV. The Life and Work of Confucius, with a sketch of the history of his time.

V. The Doctrinal Contents of the thirteen Classics.

VI. The Historical Development of Confucianism. Its divisions, causes of opposition, relation to Taoism and

Buddhism, etc. Its influence on the interpretation of the Classics.

VII. The Relation of the Classics;

(*a.*) to the Christian Religion,

(*b.*) to the Needs of Modern Life.

VIII. Characteristics of Modern Confucianism.

As for my present task I have only a few pages at my disposal I thought it best to confine myself strictly to

A MISSIONARY VIEW OF CONFUCIANISM.

In order to avoid misunderstanding the reader is reminded that Confucianism is not identical with Chinese life. There have always been other agencies at work for good and for evil in China. Though we do not confine Confucianism to the person of Confucius, nor to the teachings of the Classics, fairness requires us to regard as genuine only such later developments as can be shown to have their roots in the Classics. The Classics again have to be explained in the spirit of the whole contents of the Canon, and care must be taken not to force a meaning into single passages which may be contrary to that spirit. To the question: How far is Confucianism responsible for the present corrupt state of Chinese life? the correct answer seems to be, *so far as the principles which led to this corruption are sanctioned in the Classics.* The missionary view of Confucianism can treat of nothing but the relation between Confucianism and Christianity. When we speak of such a relation we mean that both systems have points of similarity and agreement. A clear statement of these and the cheerful acknowledgment of their harmonious teaching makes mutual understanding between adherents of the two systems possible and easy. There are also points of difference and antagonism, and a clear perception of these will guard against confusion and perversion of truth. There are other points which may exist in a rudimentary state in one system and be highly developed in the other, or may only occur in one and be absent in the other. This points to deficiencies in one system which may be supplemented from the other. Our subject divides itself accordingly into three parts:—1. Points of similarity which form a basis of agreement between Confucianism and Christianity. 2. Points of antagonism which form obstacles and must be removed. 3. Points of deficiency in Confucianism which are perfect in Christianity.

I. POINTS OF SIMILARITY.

1. *Divine Providence* over human affairs and visitation of human sin are acknowledged. Both Confucius and Mencius had a firm belief in their special mission. A plain and frequent teaching of the Classics, on the other

hand, is that calamities visit a country and ruin overcomes a dynasty through the displeasure of heaven. The metaphysical speculations of Chu Fu-tsze and his school (Sung) only differ in their explanation of it, not in the fact.

2. *An Invisible World* above and around this material life is firmly believed in. Man is considered to stand in connection with spirits, good and bad.

3. *Moral Law* is positively set forth as binding equally on man and spirits. The spirits appear as the executors of the moral law. This is, however, little understood by the Chinese people who attempt to bribe and cheat the spirits as well as their mandarins. Still the Moral Law is proclaimed in the Classics.

4. *Prayer* is offered in public calamities as well as for private needs, in the belief that it is heard and answered by the spiritual powers.

5. *Sacrifices* are regarded as necessary to come into closer contact with the spiritual world. Even its deeper meanings of self-sacrifice and of a *vicarious sacrifice* are touched upon, which are two important steps toward an understanding of the sacrificial death of Christ.

6. *Miracles* are believed in as the natural *efficacy of Spirits.* This is a fruitful source of superstition among the people. Western science, on the other hand, lays all stress on force inherent in matter and stimulates scepticism. We can point to the great power of the human intellect over the material forces. God's intellect is all comprehensive. God is working miracles, not by suspending the laws of nature, *nor by acting contrary to them,* but by *using them,* as their omnipotent Master, to serve *His will and purpose.* The Divine purpose distinguishes God's miracles from miraculous occurrences.

7. *Moral Duty* is taught, and its obligations in the five human relations—sovereign and minister, father and son, husband and wife, elder brother and younger, friend and friend. There are errors connected with the Confucian teaching of these duties pointed out below II, 8-13 and defects, illustrated III, 13. It remains, nevertheless, an excellent feature of Confucianism that moral duty is inculcated, and that the *social* obligations are made so prominent. We may say that it is the quintessence of Confucian education.

8. *Cultivation of the Personal Moral Character* is regarded as the basis for the successful carrying out of the social duties. That self-control should *not be abandoned in private when no moral being is near to observe it,* is repeatedly emphasized.

9. *Virtue* is valued above riches and honor. The strong tendency of the great mass of Chinese is certainly to money and pleasure, but it is to be *regretted* that foreign improvements are too often recommended on account of their *profit,* or because they would improve the material conditions of comfortable living. The Christian view is first of all the kingdom of God, then all other things as natural results. The dominion of virtue, though not identical with the kingdom of God, is a close approximation to it. It is a solemn lesson which we may learn from ancient and modern history, that *wealth has ruined more nations than poverty.*

10. *In case of failure* in political and social life the moral self-culture and the practice of humanity are to be attended to even more carefully than before, according to opportunities. This is *the great moral victory which Confucius gained,* and the same may be said of his distinguished followers, the greatest among whom are Mencius and Chu Fu-tsze. None of these pillars of Confucianism turned to money-making or sought vain glory in the service of the State by sacrificing their principles to gain access to official employment or by a promise to keep their conviction secret in their own bosoms. They gained greater ultimate success by their failure in life. The cross of Christ has a similar meaning, and we should not expect worldly triumph *as long as our Lord is despised* and even *blasphemed* among the higher classes of China.

11. *Sincerity and truth* are shown to be the only basis for self-culture and the reform of the world. This gives to self-culture a high moral tone. It is not only external culture, such as fine manners and good works, nor is it intellectual improvement but a normal state of the *intentions of* the mind, combined with undefiled feelings and emotions of the heart. We should not question whether any Chinaman ever reached this ideal, but ask those we have to deal with, Have *you* attained it? If not, what is the cause of your failure? Will you not seek and find it in Christ?

12. *The Golden Rule* is proclaimed as the principle of moral conduct among our fellow-men. This is egoism ennobled by altruism. The rule is given not only in a negative *but also in the positive form.* It can, however, be fully understood and carried out only by one born of God, whom the love of Christ constraineth. Still, that this rule entered a Chinese mind and found expression from the mouth of Confucius *raises Confucianism to a high standard of morality.* We may welcome it as a powerful assistance to bring about a conviction of sin among the Chinese; for who ever acted up to it?

13. Every ruler should carry out a *Benevolent Government* for the benefit of the people. He must not endure the suffering of the people. If the Chinese emperors and mandarins would really act up to what they pretend to be (viz., the fathers and mothers of the people) with the same care, affection and even self-sacrifice,

as good parents do for their children, China would be in a different condition. Still, we can avail ourselves of this high ideal and show *its fulfilment in Christ* who gave His life for the world.

II. POINTS OF ANTAGONISM.

1. *God,* though dimly known, is not the only object of religious worship. This cannot be regarded as only a deficiency, it is a fatal error. *Polytheism* is taught in the Classics. Idolatry is the natural consequence, and all the superstitions in connection with it among the people are its inevitable results.

2. The *Worship of Spiritual Beings* is not done in spirit and in truth, but by punctilious observance of prescribed ceremonies to the minutest detail. The offerings and sacrifices consist in materials procurable with money. Though the Classics also point to a deeper meaning, this superficial ritualism, with absence of elevating devotional feeling and renovating influence in heart and life, has grown from the seed sown by the Classics.

3. *The Worship of Ancestral Spirits,* tablets and graves, we have to regard as a sin, for it takes the place of the worship of God. It is an *error* so far as it rests on wrong notions in regard to the departed in the other world; their happiness being thought dependent on the sacrifices from their descendants and the fortune of the living as caused by the dead. It is an *evil,* because selfish considerations take the place of moral and religious motives. The superstitions of geomancy, spiritualism, exorcism and all kinds of deceit practised by Buddhist and Taoist priests, have their origin in it. Confucianism is responsible for all this religious corruption, for sacrificing to the dead is taught as the highest filial duty in the Classics, and Mencius sanctions polygamy on its account. The ritual duties for the dead in dressing the corpse, burial, mourning and periodical sacrifices, are so numerous, onerous and expensive that, if carried out conscientiously by everybody, very little of wealth and of energy could be left for anything else. Christianity acknowledges no other duty to the dead beyond a decent burial and tender memory, remembering and honoring all their good for our imitation. This is in accordance even with some Confucian teaching in the Classics.

4. *The Erection of Temples* to great warriors and to other men of eminence in which sacrifices are offered and incense is burned to their shades. They are invoked to be present at the service; prayers are offered, and help is asked and believed to have been received more or less frequently. This goes far beyond the honor due to benefactors of mankind. There are certainly over a hundred thousand such temples in China. They absorb a great proportion of the revenue without giving any return but the increase of superstition. Noble am-

bition could be inspired more effectively in the Christian way. Though the practice of building temples to heroes arose shortly after the classical period its roots can be found in the Classics. The spirits of departed benefactors were appointed by Imperial authority to certain offices in the invisible world. This is one of the Imperial prerogatives in Confucianism. We consider it, of course, either as a sacrilege or as nonsense. The myriads of War-god Temples, dedicated to Kwan-ti, an ancient warrior, may suffice as a striking example of the extent of this error.

5. *The Memorial Arches* erected to persons that committed *suicide,* especially to widows, are throwing a sad light on the morality of a community where such *crimes* are necessitated. Confucianism is responsible for it by the low place it allows to women, by the wrong feeling of honor it awakens in men and women and by the meagre religious consolation it can provide for the afflicted. Death is sought as the only escape from unbearable misery.

6. *Oracles,* by stalks and the tortoise-shell, are declared necessary for the right conduct of human affairs. They certainly point to the need of a revelation of the Divine Will. It is, however, sought in a mechanical way, and chance is taken instead. Astrology and magic, in all its modern forms, are the evil results, and a confusion between what is right and wrong is the moral consequence. The interpretation of the oracles is in the hands of shrewd persons who take advantage of it for their own benefit. The whole system of divination is a caricature of biblical *revelation* and its corresponding human side of *inspiration.* God reveals Himself, but the human mind must be prepared to receive it as an inspiration, *i.e.,* must come under the influence of God's spirit.

7. *Choosing Lucky Days* is a sacred duty demanded by the Classics and enforced by law. This duty involves much loss of valuable time to all Chinese. The yearly publication of the Imperial Almanac, the standard for this absurdity, demonstrates the fossilized state of the Chinese mind. European astronomy has been taught to the Chinese Imperial court for over three hundred years; many books have been published too, the influence of which is so imperceptible because only the Confucian Classics fill and shape the Chinese mind. Many other superstitions prevail for the same reason.

8. *Polygamy* is not only wrong; it has ever been a curse in Chinese history. Many intrigues, crimes and wars have been caused by it. Confucianism has not only no censure for it, not even for its detestable accumulation in the Imperial palace, that greatest slum of the world, but sanctions it in the Classics. Confucianism is, therefore, responsible for this great social and political evil. The misery of eunuchs, secondary wives, slave-girls, feet-binding, degradation of women

in general, are accompaniments which magnify this vice. Instead of extolling the Confucian moral teaching on the five human relations all Confucianists, together with their foreign admirers, ought to hide their faces in shame that the most important of the human relations is treated so viciously.

9. *Rebellion.* Confucius praising Yao and Shun as the highest pattern of moral accomplishment points principally to the fact that both rulers selected the worthiest of their subjects to become their co-regents and their successors. This high example has not found one follower among 244 emperors (according to Mayer's Reader's Manual) of China, from Confucius' death to the present day. This in spite of Confucianism as the state-religion of China. Confucius himself appears to have regarded with favor rebellious movements in the hope of bringing a sage to the throne. Mencius is certainly very outspoken in this respect. He justifies dethroning and even the murder of a bad ruler. No wonder then that rebellions have occurred, on a large scale, over fifty times in about 2,000 years, and local rebellions are almost yearly events. It is impossible to calculate how many hundred millions of human lives have been sacrificed during these rebellions. Confucianism is to blame for it. Neither Confucius himself, nor one of his followers, ever thought of establishing a constitutional barrier against tyranny and providing a magna charta for the security of life and property of the ministers and people of China. The hands of the executioner ended the noble lives of many of China's best men. It cannot be otherwise as long as the capricious will of a self-conceited ruler is supreme law. The remedy has been found in Western (Christian) countries in the separation of the *executive* from the *legislative* power. Law is no more the will of one man, but of the majority of the people, its formulation is done by an assembly of chosen men, etc. The people must also have a legal way to make their grievances known and find relief in a peaceful manner. Confucianism, however, regards the people as little children that must be fed, protected and taught their duties. They have only the right to obey under these circumstances and to rebel if the contrary should become intolerable.

10. Confucianism attaches too high *authority to the Emperor.* He is called the son of Heaven, the only supreme authority on earth. Every law and custom must emanate from him. The emperor of China cannot acknowledge another sovereign as his equal. In this respect he can be compared with the pope of Rome. The treaties with foreign powers have already upset this fundamental doctrine of Confucianism.

11. *Patria Potestas.* Corresponding to the extreme view of Imperial authority Confucianism has also fostered an extreme idea of paternal power. A father may kill his offspring, may sell even grown sons and daughters into slavery. Their property belongs to him under all circumstances, even their families are absolutely subject to him, as long as he, the father, lives.

12. *Blood Revenge.* It is a strict demand of Confucius in the Classics, that a son should lose no time in revenging the death of his father, or of a near relative. A younger brother has the same duty in regard to the death of an older, and a friend to a friend. This means that they have to take the law into their own hands. They will be guided by their feelings, and in many cases more serious wrong is done by their revenge than by the original act which may present mitigating circumstances, or be not murder at all, perhaps even justifiable under enlightened examination. If the accompanying circumstances are not taken into consideration by impartial judges, where and when can the shedding of blood be stopped? Logically only with the total extermination of one of the respective families. Even several families may share this fate, as friends have to take up the same cause. The *jus talionis* belongs to a primitive period of human society. Moses mitigated it and brought it under the control of impartial legal authority. Confucius not only sanctioned an ancient usage, but raised it to a moral duty, poisoning by it three of his five social relations. As the remaining two relations have been shown as vicious in part (see above Nos. 4 and 5) Confucianists have really no reason for their extravagant boasting.

13. The absolute *Subordination* of sons to their fathers and of younger brothers to their eldest brother during life-time, is also a source of many evils. It may work well enough in a primitive society and in wealthy families, but not in a dense population among poor people. In China the inevitable result has been much misery and contention in families; ruins everywhere testify to it. Progress is also made impossible, as there will always be some old people obstinately against any modern improvement. *Nepotism* also is made a moral obligation by the Classics.

14. *Official corruption* is to a great extent due to the custom of making presents to the superior in office. This bad usage is sanctioned in the classics and by Confucius himself carrying such presents with him on his journeys. Its worst abuse is the sale of offices and bribery. Present-giving and receiving should be confined to friendly intercourse, but official relations should be kept free from it under penalty of dismissal from office. See the Old Testament on this point.

15. *The Sacredness of a promise,* contract, oath, treaty, etc., is often violated when opportunity is favorable to a personal advantage. Though Christian nations commit also too many trespasses of this kind, the difference is, that the teaching and example of Christ and His apostles is against it, even against falsehood of any shape. But *Confucius himself broke a solemn oath and excused it.* The Chinese moral sentiment is, there-

fore, misguided, whereas the Christian feeling is up to the standard. Lying and deceitfulness are so highly developed in China, probably to a great extent, from this cause.

16. *Identity* of physical, moral and political law is presumed by Confucianism and finds its canonical expression especially in the **I-king** or **Book of Changes**. But the same idea runs through all the Classics and later doctrinal developments of Confucianism. The truth of this doctrine can only be sought in the person of one almighty God, but it is a serious error when applied to man, especially to sinful man. This is the deeper root of Confucian pride and of much nonsense in regard to natural events. It is also the source of Taoist magic, charms, etc., shared by modern Chinese Buddhism.

III. POINTS OF DEFICIENCY IN CONFUCIANISM WHICH ARE PERFECT IN CHRISTIANITY.

1. The God of Confucianism is the majestic *Ruler on High* inaccessible to the people. The emperor of China is the only person privileged to approach Him. God is not known in His nature of love as our *Heavenly Father*.

2. The Confucian *Divine Providence* appears in conflict with the Confucian notion of *Fate*. Providence presupposes a *personal* God, omnipresent, omniscient and omnipotent, a God who can feel compassion with living creatures, as in Christianity.

3. Confucianism acknowledges a *Revelation of God* in nature and in human history, but a revelation of God's nature, will and intentions (plan) for the salvation and education of the human race remains unknown. See II, 6.

4. There is no conviction of an unconditioned *Responsibility* to God, the majestic Ruler of the universe who will judge in righteousness. Therefore a deep sense of sin and sinfulness is absent.

5. The necessity of *an Atonement* is not conceived, because neither the holiness of God, nor the depth of human sin are taught in the Classics.

6. As the deepest cause of death and of all the evils in the world is not sought and found in sin, therefore the *need of a Saviour* is not felt; salvation is sought in external performances, in self-correction too, but not in the grace of God who sent the only true Saviour from Heaven to Earth to reunite man with God.

7. Confucianism has produced many theories on the *Nature of Man,* but none that man is the image of the personal God. Hence the perfect union of the divine and the human, as it has been realized in the person

of Christ, has never been anticipated by a Chinese mind.

8. As every man has to save himself there cannot be a *Universality of salvation* in Confucianism. Such can *only* be the case when salvation is God's work; God was in Christ and reconciled the world to Himself. The conditions of a participation cannot be in man's own judgment, but are laid down by God himself—faith in Christ. Through it every man can become a partaker of God's grace.

9. Confucianists remain, in spite of their best efforts, *estranged from God*. They may improve themselves and come into communion with the spirits of the departed (?), but NOT with the *Spirit of God,* for enlightenment in eternal truths, for strength to a holy living, for comfort in the struggles of life, for peace and hope in death.

10. Confucianism teaches the immortality of the soul, but in a disembodied state dependant for all its needs on the goodwill of living men. Resurrection in a spiritual body for eternal happiness in God's glory is unknown.

11. The highest ideal of Confucianism, its *summum bonum,* is political, the government and state of China. This has ever remained an utopian idea, a fiction like the republic of Plato. Christ shows us another ideal, the *Kingdom of God.* It begins in the heart of the believer which becomes regenerated. It then extends to the Church, *i.e.,* a brotherhood of men in Christian spirit, embraces all nations and finds its glorious perfection at the second coming of Christ in the resurrection of the dead, *i.e.,* the reunion of all generations of mankind and the new heaven and new earth, when God will be all in all.

12. Christianity can supplement striking deficiencies not only in religion proper but also in the morality of Confucianism. *Self-examination,* for example, one of the excellent fundamental principles of Confucianism, has a deeper meaning in Christianity. We attend to it before God, the most holy one, who is perfection in every sense, and who is our pattern, especially in His incarnate form of Christ. Every other merely human model has imperfections. Yao and Shun had theirs, and Confucius was conscious of his own. We certainly estimate Confucius higher for his expressions of humility than for the pompous eulogies from his haughty followers.

13. *Self-culture* also has a deeper sense in Christianity. It implies *purity* in every way. Sexual impurity is tolerated by Confucianism to a shocking extent. Confucius himself was pure, and the Classics are remarkable for the spirit of purity that permeates the whole of them. There is, however, nowhere an intimation given of the

importance of consistent purity of soul and body for the improvement of personal character as well as for society. Internal purity and external cleanliness are deficient qualities in Confucian morality. It has not even the same moral standard of purity for male and female persons. We have to confess that there is still much impurity exhibited in Christian lands, but it is of heathen origin, against the principles of Christianity, and true Christians feel ashamed of it.

14. *The Human Relations.* The grave errors of Confucianism in regard to the social relations have already been exposed (II, 8-13). But there are besides deficiencies apparent, for the five do not exhaust all human relations. One important relation has become prominent in all civilized countries in our times, that of the employer to the employed, or as it is sometimes put impersonally of "capital to labour." Christian brotherhood contains the solution of this problem (see Paul's letter to Philemon, etc.). There is another relation of the Wealthy to the Poor and Needy. Christ's answer to the question, "Who is my neighbour," is the best possible. There is a relation to Foreigners. In this we know it is our duty to bring the Gospel and all its blessings to all creatures. When compared with this UNIVERSAL SPIRIT of the Christian human relations Confucianism appears primitive and clannish.

15. Confucianism keeps certain days as festivals, but has no regular day of rest, no *Sabbath*-day. This deficiency leaves not only the working classes without a relief in their hardships, but allows the nobler aspirations of human nature to be submerged in the unbroken turmoil of daily life. The Christian Sabbath is no more the Jewish Sabbath of the law, but God's rest in the reborn heart of man as His temple, and man's rest from earthly toil and care, a foretaste of the eternal rest in God.

16. *The Fulness of Christian Life.* Christians become, through faith in Christ, children of God, members of the body of the glorified Christ, co-inheritors of the heavenly kingdom. Christ is born in the hearts of His believers. Our bodies are then temples of the triune God and become gradually instruments of His glory. Although on earth our treasure is kept in earthen vessels, though we still live by faith, not by sight, though it has not yet appeared what we shall be—still we have the assurance of it in the ever present communion with God in His grace. Confucianism has nothing of the kind. Its cold abstract morality and cool ceremonial religion cannot produce the warmth of feeling on which human life depends. There is nothing approaching to the Lord's prayer in Confucianism, nor to that concise expression of the fullness of Christian life in the apostolic blessing, "the grace of our Lord Jesus Christ, the love of God and the communion of the Holy Spirit be with you." Although theologians differ in their metaphysical explanations of this mystery, the trinity of

divine life animates every true Christian's heart. Its absence separates the non-Christian from the Christian. What Confucianism really needs is this Divine Life. May God's Spirit move the field of dry bones!

Arthur Waley (essay date 1938)

SOURCE: An introduction to and "Terms," in *The Analects of Confucius,* George Allen & Unwin Ltd, 1938, pp. 13-26, 27-50.

[*In the following excerpt, Waley comments on Confucius's life, his disciples, and the origins of the* Analects. *The critic also defines several key terms used in the* Analects.]

I

Thought grows out of environment. Ideally speaking the translator of such a book as the *Analects* ought to furnish a complete analysis of early Chinese society, of the processes which were at work within it and of the outside forces to which it reacted. Unfortunately our knowledge of the period is far too incomplete for any such synthesis to be possible. The literary documents are scanty and of uncertain date; scientific archaeology in China has suffered constant setbacks and is still in its infancy. All that I have attempted in the following pages is to arrange such information as is accessible under a series of disconnected headings, in a convenient order, but without pretence of unity or logical sequence.

CONFUCIUS

The Confucius of whom I shall speak here is the Confucius of the *Analects.* One could construct half a dozen other Confuciuses by tapping the legend at different stages of its evolution. We should see the Master becoming no longer a moral teacher but a 'wise man' according to the popular conception of wisdom that existed in non-Confucian circles in China and in our own Middle Ages, an answerer of grotesque conundrums, a prophet, a magician even. We should see the disappointed itinerant tutor of the *Analects* turning into a successful statesman and diplomatist, employed not only in his own country but in neighbouring States as well.[1]

But I shall act here on the principle recently advocated by that great scholar Ku Chieh-kang, the principle of 'one Confucius at a time.' Not that we can regard the Confucius of the *Analects* as wholly historical; still less, that we must dismiss as fiction all data about the Master that do not happen to occur in this book. But in the first place the biographical facts deducible from the *Analects* are those which are most relevant to an understanding of the book itself; and secondly, the picture of Confucius given in the *Analects,* besides being the earliest that we possess, differs from that of all other books in that it contains no elements that bear patently and obviously the stamp of folk-lore or hagiography. What then was Confucius? It appears from the *Analects* that he was a private person who trained the sons of gentlemen in the virtues proper to a member of the ruling classes. It is clear, however, that he was not content with this position and longed for a more public one, either in his own State or in some other, which would give him the opportunity to put into practice the Way which he regarded as that of the Former Kings, the Way of Goodness, long ago discarded by the rulers of the world in favour of a Way of violence and aggression. There is not the slightest indication that he ever obtained such a position. Twice, however, he speaks of himself as 'following after' the Great Officers of Court. Those who ranked next to the Great Officers (*Ta Fu*) were the Knights (*shih*), and if Confucius ranked immediately after the Great Officers (as he seems to suggest) he must at the time have been *Shih-shih,* [2] Leader of the Knights, which was not politically speaking a position of any importance. Discontented with the slow progress of his doctrines in the land of Lu, Confucius travelled from State to State,[3] seeking for a ruler who would give the Way its chance. The only disciples actually mentioned as accompanying him are Jan Ch'iu, Tzu-lu, and his favourite disciple Yen Hui. The States and towns which they visited (Ch'i, Wei, Ch'ên, Ts'ai and K'uang) all lay within the modern provinces of Shantung and Honan. The strangers evidently met with a hostile reception, and had occasionally to endure severe privation. Several of the disciples were in the service of Chi K'ang-tzu, the dictator of Lu; and it may have been owing to their good offices that Confucius was at last encouraged to return to his native State.

Concerning his private life, we learn from the *Analects* that he had been brought up in humble circumstances.[4] Of his marriage nothing is said; but two children are mentioned, a daughter[5] and a son whom the Master outlived.[6] An older brother is mentioned, but Confucius seems to have acted as head of the family, and this is explained by later tradition as due to the fact that the elder brother was a cripple.

Confucius speaks of himself in one place (II, 4) as being over seventy. As to the exact dates of his birth and death the *Analects* tell us nothing. It can be inferred, however, from references to contemporary persons and events, that the time of his main activity was the end of the sixth and the first twenty years or so of the fifth century.[7]

After his apotheosis in the Han dynasty Confucius was credited with the omniscience and moral infallibility of the Divine Sage. This view of him appears, indeed,

to have been current even during his lifetime; for we find him at pains to disclaim any such attributes.[8] Nor would he allow himself to be regarded as Good,[9] a disclaimer that is natural enough, seeing that he accords this title only to a few legendary heroes of the remote past. Even in the social virtues which formed the basis of his teaching he claimed no pre-eminence. There was not, he said, a hamlet of ten houses but could produce men as loyal and dependable as himself. He denied (though one disciple at least seems to have had the opposite impression) that he possessed any unusual stock of knowledge;[10] still less would he admit that such knowledge as he possessed was innate or inspired.[11] What he regarded as exceptional in himself was his love of 'learning,' that is to say, of self-improvement, and his unflagging patience in insisting upon the moral principles that had (in his view) guided the godlike rulers of the remote past. His task, then, like that of the English trainer of *chün-tzu* (gentlemen's sons) in the great Public Schools, was not so much to impart knowledge as to inculcate moral principles, form character, hand down unaltered and intact a great tradition of the past.[12] He speaks of himself as a veritable P'êng Tsu (i.e. Nestor) in his devoted reliance upon 'antiquity'; and if we want further to define what he meant by this reliance on the past, we find it, I think, in Mencius's saying: Follow the rules of the Former Kings, and it is impossible that you should go wrong.[13]

What then was this antiquity, who were the great figures of the past whom Confucius regarded as the sole source of wisdom?

THE ANCIENTS

Were we to take them in the order of their importance to him, I think we should have to begin with the founders and expanders of the Chou dynasty; for in his eyes the cultures of the two preceding dynasties found their climax and fulfilment in that of the early Chou sovereigns.[14] Above all, we should have to deal first with Tan, Duke of Chou, who had not only a particular importance in the Lu State, but also a peculiar significance for Confucius himself.[15] But it is more convenient to take them in their 'chronological' order, that is to say, in the order in which the mythology of Confucius's day arranged them. We must begin then with the *Shêng,* the Divine Sages.[16] These were mythological figures, historicized as rulers of human 'dynasties'; but still endowed with divine characteristics and powers. The *Analects* mention three of them, Yao, Shun and Yü the Great; but they occupy a very restricted place in the book.[17] Yao and Shun are twice[18] mentioned in the stock phrase (if a man were to do this), then 'even Yao and Shun could not criticize him'; meaning that such a man would himself be to all intents and purposes a *shêng.* Yao appears otherwise only in the eulogy of VIII, 19, where he is exalted as the equal of God.[19] The eulogy of Shun which follows tells us that with only five servants to help him he kept order 'everywhere under Heaven.' Elsewhere[20] he is said to have ruled by *wu-wei* (non-activity), through the mere fact of sitting in a majestic attitude 'with his face turned to the South.' We have here the conception, familiar to us in Africa and elsewhere, of the divine king whose magic power regulates everything in the land. It is one which is common to all early Chinese thought, particularly in the various branches of Quietism that developed in the fourth century B.C. The *shêng*, however, only 'rules by non-activity' in the sense that his divine essence (*ling*) assures the fecundity of his people and the fertility of the soil. We find Shun assisted in his task by 'five servants,'[21] who are clearly conceived of as performing the active functions of government.

Yao and Shun are not mentioned in the ***Book of Songs,*** and there is reason to suppose that their cult did not form part of the Chou tradition. The third Divine Sage, Yü the Great, generally[22] associated in Chinese legend with a Deluge Myth akin to that of the Near East, figures in the ***Analects*** not as the subduer of the Flood but as patron of agriculture. He drains and ditches the land[23] and tills the fields,[24] his name being coupled with that of the harvest-god Hou Chi. Yü the Great is 'historicized' as founder of the Hsia dynasty, whose 'times' (i.e. calendar of agricultural operations) Confucius recommends, in answer to a question about the ideal State.[25]

T'ang, the founder of the Shang-Yin dynasty which preceded the Chou, is only once mentioned. It was supposed in Confucius's day that the remnants of the Shang-Yin people had settled in Sung and that the Sung State perpetuated the traditions of the fallen dynasty. But Confucius himself doubted whether Yin culture could really be reconstructed by evidence supplied from Sung.[26]

THE DISCIPLES

Later tradition credits Confucius with seventy-two[27] disciples; but the compilers are hard put to it to bring the number up to anything like so imposing a total. In the ***Analects*** some twenty people figure, who might possibly be regarded as disciples, in so far as they are represented as addressing questions to Confucius. But far fewer appear as definite 'frequenters of his gate.' The most important of them, in the history of Confucianism, is Master Tsêng, who is credited in the ***Analects*** with twelve sayings of his own. The Master Tsêng of Book VIII is, however, a very different person from the Master Tsêng of Book I, the latter resembling far more closely the Tsêng of later tradition, and of the *Tsêng Tzu* fragments.[28] Humanly the most distinctive of the disciples are Yen Hui and Tzu-lu, who are perfect examples of the contrasted types of character that psychologists call introvert and extravert. Both

of them died before Confucius, and were thus unable to influence the subsequent development of the school. Tzu-lu played a considerable part in contemporary history and is mentioned in the chronicles from 498 down to the time of his death in 480. Two other disciples are well known to history, Jan Ch'iu appears as a lieutenant of the usurping Chi Family from 484 till 472; and Tzu-kung figures largely in inter-State diplomacy from 495 till 468.

The name of Master Yu, who figures so prominently in Book I, only to disappear almost completely in the remaining Books, happens by chance to occur in the *Tso Chuan* Chronicle under the year 487. But he was evidently not a person of high social status; for he served as a foot-soldier.

It is clear that after the Master's death, Tzu-hsia, like Master Tsêng, founded a school of his own; for his disciples are spoken of in Book XIX. To him, too, are attributed about a dozen sayings. Two other disciples, Tzu-chang and Tzu-yu, are also obviously regarded by the compliers of the ***Analects*** as being of special importance; for they, too, are credited with sayings of their own.

THE ANALECTS[29]

There is not much doubt that ***Lun Yü*** (***Analects,*** to use the English equivalent that Legge's translation has made so familiar) means 'Selected Sayings.' *Lun,* as a term connected with the editing of documents, occurs indeed in ***Analects,*** XIV, 9. The contents of the book itself make it clear that the compilation took place long after the Master's death. Several of the disciples already have schools of their own, and the death of Master Tsêng, which certainly happened well into the second half of the fifth century, is recorded in Book VIII. It is clear, too, that the different Books are of very different date and proceed from very different sources. I should hazard the guess that Books III-IX represent the oldest stratum. Books X and XX (first part) certainly have no intrinsic connexion with the rest. The former is a compilation of maxims from works on ritual; the latter consists of stray sentences from works of the ***Shu Ching*** type. Book XIX consists entirely of sayings by disciples. The contents of XVIII and of parts of XIV and XVII are not Confucian in their origin, but have filtered into the book from the outside world, and from a world hostile to Confucius. Book XVI is generally and rightly regarded as late. It contains nothing characteristic of the milieu that produced Books III-IX, and it would not be difficult to compile a much longer book of just the same character by stringing together precepts from works such as the *Tso Chuan* and *Kuo Yü.* Only in one passage of the ***Analects*** do we find any reference to ideas the development of which we should be inclined to place later than the ordinarily accepted[30] date of the book, namely the middle of the fourth century. I refer to the disquisition on 'correcting names' in XIII, 3. In *Mencius* (early third century B.C.) there is not a trace of the 'language crisis,'[31] and we have no reason to suppose that the whole sequence of ideas embodied in this passage could possibly be earlier in date than the end of the fourth century. That the writer of the passage realized its incompatibility with the doctrines of Confucius—the insistence on punishments is wholly un-Confucian—is naïvely betrayed in the introductory paragraphs. Tzu-lu is made to express the greatest astonishment that Confucius should regard the reform of language as the first duty of a ruler and tells him impatiently that his remark is quite beside the point.

We may, of course, be wrong in thinking that the whole complex of ideas connected with 'reforming language in order to adjust penalties' dates from as late as the end of the fourth century. There may be special reasons why we find no echo of such ideas in *Mencius.* Or again, the compilation of the *Analects* may be much later than we suppose; but this alternative involves linguistic difficulties. It may, on the other hand, be a better solution to regard this passage as an interpolation on the part of Hsün Tzu or his school, for whom the absence of any reference in the sayings of Confucius to what they themselves taught as a fundamental doctrine must certainly have been inconvenient.

It is curious that only one pre-Han text shows definite evidence of familiarity with the *Analects*. The ***Fang Chi*** (part of the ***Li Chi;*** supposed to be an extract from the ***Tzu Ssu Tzu***) quotes *Analects,* II, 11, and names the ***Lun Yü*** as its source. The ***Fang Chi*** also quotes books of the ***Shu Ching*** which were unknown in Han times, not being found either in the official collection or among the books rediscovered but uninterpreted. It is therefore certainly a pre-Han work. There are, apart from this, many cases in which pre-Han authors, such as Hsün Tzu, Lü Pu-wei, Han Fei Tzu, use maxims or anecdotes that are also used in the *Analects*. But there is nothing to show that the writer is quoting the book as we know it now. Mencius, it is clear, used a quite different collection of sayings, which contained, indeed, a certain number of those which occur in the *Analects,* often differently worded and allotted to quite different contexts; but he quotes at least three times as many sayings that do not occur in the *Analects* at all.

It would be rash, however, to conclude that the *Analects* were not known or did not exist in the days of Mencius and Hsün Tzu. We possess only a very small fragment of early Confucian literature. Could we read all the works that are listed in the *Han Shu* bibliography, we should very likely discover that some particular school of Confucianism based its teaching on the *Analects,* just as Mencius based his on another collection of sayings. The *Doctrine of the Mean* and the *Great Learning,* works of very uncertain date but certainly pre-

Han, both use sayings from the *Analects,* which may well be actual quotations.

The history of the text from *c.* 150 B.C.[32] till the time (second century A.D.) when at the hands of Chêng Hsüan the book received something like its present form I must leave to others to write. The task is one which involves great difficulties. The data are supplied not by scientific bibliographers but by careless repeaters of legend and anecdote. Some of the relevant texts (e.g. *Lun Hêng,* P'ien 81) are hopelessly corrupt; the real dates of supposedly early Han works which show knowledge of the *Analects* are impossible to ascertain. At every turn, in such studies, we are forced to rely, without any means of checking their statements, upon writers who clearly took no pains to control their facts.

This much, however, is certain: during the period 100 B.C. to A.D. 100 two versions were currently used, the Lu version (upon which our modern version is chiefly based) and the Ch'i version,[33] which had two extra chapters. Much later (second century A.D.?)[34] a third version came into general use. This was the Ku Wên (ancient script) text collated by Chêng Hsüan when he made his famous edition, of which fragments have been recovered from Tun-huang. We know[35] some twenty-seven instances in which the Ku version differed from the Lu, and in all but two of these instances the version we use to-day follows Ku not Lu. I state these facts merely that the reader may know roughly what is meant when in the course of this book I mention Ku and Lu readings. The real origin of the Ku version[36] remains very uncertain and a discussion of the question, bound up as it is with the history of the other Ku Wên texts, would lead us too far afield.

A last question remains to be answered. How far can we regard any of the sayings in the *Analects* as actual words of Confucius? In searching for such authentic sayings we must use certain precautions. Obviously, we shall not find them in Book X,[37] nor in Book XX.[38] Books XVI-XVII clearly do not emanate from a source at all near to the earliest Confucianism. Book XVIII is, indeed, full of anti-Confucian stories, of just the same sort that we find in Taoist works, naïvely accepted by the compilers; Book XIV has a considerable element of the same description (34, 41, 42). The story of the meeting with Yang Huo (XVII, 1) is of just the same kind. We shall have to remember that in ancient Chinese literature sayings are often attributed to a variety of people; (indifferently, for example, to Master Tsêng and Confucius, or to Confucius and Yen Tzu) and bear in mind that such sayings were probably more or less proverbial. We certainly must not forget that Confucius describes himself as a transmitter, not an originator, and that the presence of rhyme or archaic formulae, or of proverbial shape in the sayings often definitely stamps them as inherited from the past. Bearing all these facts in mind I think we are justified in suppos-

"Master Kung wept when the strange beast was captured and killed for he felt that this event presaged his death and the failure of his policies."

ing that the book does not contain many authentic sayings, and may possibly contain none at all. As I have already pointed out, I use the term 'Confucius' throughout this book in a conventional sense, simply meaning the particular early Confucians whose ideas are embodied in the sayings.

Supposing, however, someone should succeed in proving that some particular saying was really uttered by the Master, it would still remain to be proved that the context in which the remark occurred in the *Analects* was really the original one; and the context of a remark profoundly affects its meaning. In later literature, particularly the *Li Chi* (**Book of Rites**) and *Shih Chi* (**Historical Records**), we find a good many of Confucius's more cryptic remarks given contexts, put into settings of an explanatory description, and it has been suggested that in such cases we have the original form and intention of the sayings, which in the *Analects* have for some reason become divorced from their proper surroundings. That this should be so is against all the canons of textual history. Always, in similar cases, we find that the contexts have been invented as glosses upon the original *logia*. In the oldest strata of the Synoptic Gospels isolated sayings occur which in the more recent strata are furnished, often very arbitrarily, with an explanatory setting. It is a process that we can see at work over and over again in Buddhist hagiography. I have therefore seldom called attention

to these manipulations of the text by the later Confucian schools, and have been content to leave the isolated *logia* as I found them.

II

TERMS

JÊN

This word in the earliest Chinese means freemen, men of the tribe, as opposed to *min,* 'subjects,' 'the common people.' The same word, written with a slight modification, means 'good' in the most general sense of the word, that is to say, 'possessing the qualities of one's tribe.' For no more sweeping form of praise can be given by the men of a tribe than to say that someone is a 'true member' of that tribe. The same is true of modern nations; an Englishman can give no higher praise than to say that another is a true Englishman. In the ***Book of Songs*** the phrase 'handsome and good' (*jên*) occurs more than once as a description of a perfectly satisfactory lover. *Jên,* 'members of the tribe' show a forbearance towards one another that they do not show to aliens, and just as the Latin *gens,* 'clan,' gave rise to our own word 'gentle,' so *jên* in Chinese came to mean 'kind,' 'gentle,' 'humane.' Finally, when the old distinction between *jên* and *min,* freemen and subjects, was forgotten and *jên* became a general word for 'human being,' the adjective *jên* came to be understood in the sense 'human' as opposed to 'animal,' and to be applied to conduct worthy of a man, as distinct from the behaviour of mere beasts.

Of this last sense (human, not brutal) there is not a trace in the ***Analects***. Of the sense 'kind,' 'tenderhearted' there are only two examples,[39] out of some sixty instances in which the word occurs. Confucius's use of the term, a use peculiar to this one book, stands in close relation to the primitive meaning. *Jên*, in the ***Analects,*** means 'good' in an extremely wide and general sense. 'In its direction'[40] lie unselfishness and an ability to measure other people's feelings by one's own. The good man is 'in private life, courteous; in public life, diligent; in relationships, loyal.'[41] Goodness (on the part of a ruler) is complete submission to ritual.[42] The Good do not grieve[43] and will necessarily be brave.[44] At the same time, it cannot be said that *jên* in the ***Analects*** simply means 'good' in a wide and general sense. It is, on the contrary, the name of a quality so rare and peculiar that one 'cannot but be chary in speaking of it.'[45] It is a sublime moral attitude, a transcendental perfection attained to by legendary heroes such as Po I, but not by any living or historic person. This, however, is far from being understood by the disciples, who suggest as examples of goodness not only Tzu-wên (seventh century B.C.), Ch'ên Wêntzu (sixth century), Kuan Tzu (seventh century), but even contemporaries and associates such as Tzu-lu, Jan Ch'iu, Kung-hsi Hua, Jan Yung. All such claims the Master abruptly dismisses. Indeed so unwilling is he to accord the title *jên* that he will not even allow it to a hypothetical person who 'compassed the salvation of the whole State.'[46] Such a one would be a Divine Sage (*shêng*), a demi-god; whereas *jên* is the display of human qualities at their highest. It appears indeed that *jên* is a mystic entity not merely analogous to but in certain sayings practically identical with the Tao of the Quietists. Like Tao, it is contrasted with 'knowledge.' Knowledge is active and frets itself away; Goodness is passive and therefore eternal as the hills.[47] Confucius can point the way to Goodness, can tell 'the workman how to sharpen his tools,'[48] can speak even of things 'that are near to Goodness.' But it is only once, in a chapter bearing every sign of lateness,[49] that anything approaching a definition of Goodness is given.

In view of this repeated refusal to accept any but remote[50] mythological figures as examples of *jên*, to accept[51] or give a definition of Goodness, there is surely nothing surprising in the statement of Book IX (opening sentence) that 'the Master rarely discoursed upon Goodness.'[52]

It seems to me that 'good' is the only possible translation of the term *jên* as it occurs in the ***Analects***. No other word is sufficiently general to cover the whole range of meaning; indeed terms such as 'humane,' 'altruistic,' 'benevolent' are in almost every instance inappropriate, often ludicrously so. But there is another word, *shan,* which though it wholly lacks the mystical and transcendental implications of *jên,* cannot conveniently be translated by any other word but 'good.' For that reason I shall henceforward translate *jên,* by Good (Goodness, etc.) with a capital; and *shan* by good, with a small g.

TAO

Unlike, *jên, tao* has not in the ***Analects*** a technical or peculiar meaning, but is used there in just the same sense as in early Chinese works in general. *Tao* means literally a road, a path, a way. Hence, the way in which anything is done, the way in which, for example, a kingdom is ruled; a method, a principle, a doctrine. It usually has a good meaning. Thus 'when *tao* (the Way) prevails under Heaven' means when a good method of government prevails in the world; or rather 'when *the* good method prevails,' for Confucius 'believed in the ancients,' that is to say, he believed that the one infallible method of rule had been practised by certain rulers of old, and that statecraft consisted in rediscovering this method. But there seem to have been other 'Ways'; for Confucius[53] speaks of 'this Way' and 'my Way.' Moreover, in one passage[54] he is asked about *shan- jên chih Tao,* 'the Way of the good people,' and replies (according to my interpretation) disapprovingly that 'those who do not tread in the tracks (of the ancients)' cannot hope to 'enter into the sanctum.' 'Good people' is a term often applied in Chinese to those who share one's views. Thus Quietists called other Quietists 'good people.' The 'good people' here intended evidently sought guidance from some source other than the example of the ancients, and they may well have been Quietists.

But we are also told that Confucius did not discourse about the Will of Heaven[55] or about 'prodigies' and 'disorders' (of Nature).[56] We have only to read other early books to see that the world at large attached extreme importance to the Will of Heaven as manifested by portents such as rainbows, comets, eclipses; and to monstrosities such as two-headed calves and the like. It may be that the doctrine of those who sought guidance from such signs rather than from the records of the Former Kings came to be known as the 'Way of the good people.' In general, however, the word *Tao* in the ***Analects*** means one thing only, the Way of the ancients as it could be reconstructed from the stories told about the founders of the Chou dynasty and the demi-gods who had preceded them.

The aspect of Confucius's Way upon which Western writers have chiefly insisted is his attitude towards the supernatural. It has been rightly emphasized that he was concerned above all with the duties of man to man and that he 'did not talk about spirits.'[57] From a false interpretation of two passages (VI, 20 and XI, 11) the quite wrong inference has, however, been drawn that his attitude towards the spirit-world was, if not sceptical, at least agnostic. In the first passage a disciple asks about wisdom. The wisdom here meant is, of course, that of the ruler or member of the ruling classes, and the point at issue is one frequently debated in early Chinese literature: which should come first, the claims of the people or those of the spirit-world? In concrete terms, should the security of the whole State, which depends ultimately on the goodwill of the Spirits of grain, soil, rivers and hills, be first assured by lavish offerings and sacrifices, even if such a course involves such heavy taxation as to impose great hardship on the common people? Or should the claims of the people to what it is 'right and proper' (*i*) for them to have be satisfied before public expenditure is lavished upon the protecting spirits? The reply of Confucius is that the claims of the people should come first; but that the spirits must be accorded an attention sufficient to 'keep them at a distance,' that is to say, prevent them from manifesting their ill-will by attacking human beings; for just as we regard sickness as due to the onslaught of microbes, the Chinese regarded it as due to demoniacal 'possession.'

The same question concerning the priority in budget-making of human and ghostly claims is discussed in the second passage. Tzu-lu asks about 'the service of spirits,' meaning, as has generally been recognized, the outlay of public expenditure on sacrifice and other ceremonies of placation. The Master's reply is, 'How can there be any proper service of spirits until living men have been properly served?' Tzu-lu then 'asked about the dead.' A much debated question was whether the dead are conscious; and it was suggested that if they are not, it must clearly be useless to sacrifice at any rate to that portion of the spirit-world which consists of the spirits of the dead, as opposed to those of hills, streams, the soil, etc. Confucius does not wish to commit himself to any statement about, for example, the consciousness or unconsciousness of the dead, and adroitly turns the question by replying, 'Until a man knows about the living,[58] how can he know the dead?' All that is meant by the reply (which is a rhetorical one and must not be analysed too logically) is that for the *chün-tzu* questions about the existence led by the dead are of secondary importance as compared to those connected with the handling of living men.

There is not, as Western writers have often supposed, any allusion to an abstract metaphysical problem concerning the ultimate nature of Life. Nor are the two passages discussed above in any way isolated or exceptional. They are, on the contrary, characteristic of the general diversion of interest from the dead to the living, from the spirit-world to that of everyday life, which marks the break-up of the old Chou culture, founded upon divination and sacrifice.[59]

TÊ[60]

This word corresponds closely to the Latin *virtus*. It means, just as *virtus* often does, the specific quality or 'virtue' latent in anything. It never (except by some accident of context) has in early Chinese the meaning of virtue as opposed to vice, but rather the meaning of 'virtue' in such expressions as 'in virtue of' or 'the virtue of this drug.' In individuals it is a force or power closely akin to what we call character and frequently contrasted with *li*, 'physical force.' To translate it by 'virtue,' as has often been done, can only end by misleading the reader, who even if forewarned will be certain to interpret the word in its ordinary sense (virtue as opposed to vice) and not in the much rarer sense corresponding to the Latin *virtus*. For this reason I have generally rendered *tê* by the term 'moral force,' particularly where it is contrasted with *li*, 'physical force.' We cannot, however, speak of a horse's *tê* as its 'moral force.' Here 'character' is the only possible equivalent; and in the case of human beings the term 'prestige' often comes close to what is meant by *tê*.

SHIH

This word is often translated 'scholar'; but this is only a derived, metaphorical sense and the whole force of many passages in the *Analects* is lost if we do not understand that the term is a military one and means 'knight.' A *shih* was a person entitled to go to battle in a war-chariot, in contrast with the common soldiers who followed on foot. Confucius, by a metaphor similar to those embodied in the phraseology of the Salvation Army, calls the stout-hearted defenders of his Way 'Knights'; and hence in later Chinese the term came to be applied to upholders of Confucianism and finally to scholars and literary people in general. The burden of most of the references to *shih* in the *Analects* is that the Knight of the Way needs just the same qualities of endurance and resolution as the Soldier Knight. A saying such as 'A knight whose thoughts are set on home is not worthy of the name of knight'[61] refers in the first instance to real knights, and is only applied by metaphor to the spiritual warriors of Confucius's 'army.' If like Legge we translate 'the scholar who cherishes his love of comfort . . . ,' we lose the whole point. As we shall see later, Confucius was himself a knight in the literal sense, and it is probable, as we have seen, that in his later years he was senior knight, 'leader of the knights,' responsible for their discipline. . . .

Notes

[1] The legend of Confucius's worldly success, transferred to the West, has continued its growth on Euro-

pean soil. Meyer's *Konversationslexicon* (1896) goes so far as to say that he was 'received with the highest honours at every Court' in China.

[2] The original function of the *shih-shih* was to 'keep the Knights in order'; Cf. *Mencius* I, 2, VI, 2. In practice he acted under the orders of the Minister of Justice and functioned as a sort of police-magistrate. In the second stage of its development the Confucian legend represents the Master as achieving the position of Minister of Justice, an idea which may well have grown out of his having in fact been Leader of the Knights.

[3] This mobility was typical of Chinese society. Not only moralists, but warriors, craftsmen and even peasants moved from State to State, if they thought that by doing so they could improve their chances of success.

[4] IX, 6. But the saying from which we learn this was a disputed one, and an alternative version of it is given immediately afterwards, 'But Lao says the Master said . . .' etc. This alternative version refers to lack of official employment, but not to poverty.

[5] V, 1.

[6] XI, 7.

[7] I will not here enter into the difficult question of how the dates (551-479 B.C.) later accepted as official were first arrived at. Cf. Maspero, *La Chine Antique,* p. 455, and below, p. 78.

[8] VII, 33.

[9] *Ibid.*

[10] XV, 2.

[11] VII, 19.

[12] VII, 1.

[13] *Mencius,* IV, 1. I.

[14] III, 14.

[15] VII, 5.

[16] See *The Way and Its Power,* p. 91. Mencius and later writers use the term *shêng* in a much wider sense, applying it even to a comparatively recent person such as Liu-hsia Hui.

[17] I except Book XX, which has not necessarily anything to do with the beliefs of Confucius. Yü is legendary; but the Hsia dynasty is probably not wholly mythological.

[18] VI, 28; XIV, 45.

[19] *T'ien;* literally, 'Heaven'.

[20] XV, 4.

[21] VIII, 20. One of them was presumably Kao Yao, mentioned in XII, 22.

[22] But not in the *Songs,* where he generally appears as a Creator connected indeed with irrigation, only once as a flood-subduer.

[23] VIII, 21.

[24] XIV, 6.

[25] XV, 10.

[26] III, 9. Systematic excavation at An-yang, the site of one of the Yin capitals, has put us in possession of far more information about Yin culture than Confucius was able to obtain.

[27] Seventy-two is a sacred number, connected with the quintuple division of the year of 360 days. Cf. XI, 25.

[28] Collected by Yüan Yüan, *Huang Ch'ing Ching Chieh,* 803-806.

[29] This section might well be omitted by readers without special knowledge of Chinese literature.

[30] I mean accepted by scholars as the date of the material contained in the book. The date of its compilation may well be later.

[31] See *The Way and Its Power,* p. 59. *Mencius,* VI, 2. VI, is unintelligible, and has in any case never been interpreted as relevant.

[32] It is quoted by name in the *Han Shih Wai Chuan,* which presumably dates from the middle of the second century.

[33] Now lost, save for a few fragments.

[34] Legge's suggestion that Chang Yü (died 5 B.C.) used the Ku version is not borne out by the texts.

[35] Through the *Shih Wên* and the fragments from Tun-huang. The *Hsin-lun* of Huan T'an (*c.* A.D. 1) says that Ku had four hundred characters different from Lu.

[36] Alleged to have been found, (1) during the Emperor Ching's reign (156-141 B.C.); (2) at the beginning of the Han Emperor Wu's reign (140 B.C.); (3) at the end of his reign (87 B.C.); by (1) Prince Kung of Lu (in Lu from 154-127 B.C.; (2) the Emperor Wu himself; (1) during the demolition of Confucius's house; (2) before the demolition, which was at once suspended; (1) ac-

cording to some accounts without supernatural manifestations; (2) according to others, to the accompaniment of supernatural music.

The accounts also differ considerably as to what books were found and as to who hid them there.

[37] Which is simply a collection of traditional ritual maxims.

[38] Which, apart from the few sayings appended at the end, is a collection of sentences from texts of the *Shu Ching* type.

[39] XII, 22 and XVII, 21.

[40] VI, 28.

[41] XIII, 19.

[42] XII, 1.

[43] IX, 28.

[44] XIV, 5.

[45] XII, 3.

[46] VI, 28.

[47] VI, 21.

[48] XV, 9.

[49] XVII.

[50] Po I, Shu Ch'i, Pi Kan, Wei Tzu and Chi Tzu is the complete list. All of them belonged, according to legend, to the end of the Yin dynasty. The last three occur in Book XVIII, which emanated from non-Confucian circles.

[51] Cf. XIV, 2.

[52] A vast mass of discussion has centred round this passage. Cf. *Journal of the American Oriental Society,* December 1933 and March 1934.

[53] It would be pedantic always to say 'the early Confucians' or the compilers of the *Analects;* though that is, strictly speaking, what I mean when I say 'Confucius.'

[54] XI, 19.

[55] V, 12.

[56] VII, 20.

[57] VII, 20.

[58] Or 'knows about life.' . . .

[59] Cf. *The Way and Its Power,* pp. 24 seq.

[60] Cf. *The Book of Songs,* p. 346. . . .

[61] VIII, 4.

Lin Yutang (essay date 1942)

SOURCE: An introduction to *The Wisdom of China and India,* Random House, 1942, pp. 3-52.

[*In the following excerpt, Yutang outlines the basic tenets of Confucianism, which he describes as a system of ideas that sought a rationalized social and political order "by laying the basis for it in a moral order."*]

I. THE CHARACTER OF CONFUCIAN IDEAS

Can one be enthusiastic about Confucianism nowadays? I wonder. The answer seems to depend on whether one can be enthusiastic about sheer good sense, a thing which people usually cannot work up very much enthusiasm for. The more important question seems to be whether one can believe in Confucianism nowadays. This is especially important to the modern Chinese of today, a question that directly challenges their minds and cannot be brushed aside. For there is a centrality or, shall I say, universality, about the Confucian attitude and point of view, reflected in a joy in Confucian belief that I see even among maturing modern Chinese who have received a Western education. The centrality and basic appeal of its humanism have a strange strength of their own. During the political chaos and battle of ideas in the centuries immediately following Confucius, Confucianism won the victory over Taoism, Motianism, Naturalism, Legalism, Communism and a host of other philosophies. It maintained this supremacy over the Chinese people for the length of two thousand five hundred years, with the exception of a few periods, and it always came back to its own stronger than ever. Apart from Taoism which was in fashion in the third to sixth centuries A.D., its strongest rival was Buddhism, which attained a great vogue with the Sung scholars. But with all its fine metaphysics, Buddhism succeeded only in modifying the interpretation of the method of arriving at knowledge and the aim of this humanist culture. It shifted the emphasis to certain ideas originally in the Confucian classics and directed a fuller attention to them, but did not replace Confucianism itself. Perhaps it was merely the old prestige of Confucius, but there was a great pride among the Confucian scholars, a belief in their own correctness, which made these scholars renounce Buddhism and look askance at it with toleration or contempt, as the case may have been. The same common sense that crushed the mysticism of Chungtse also made them renounce the mysticism of Buddhism. Today Confucianism meets a still greater rival, not Christianity, but the entire system of Western thought and life and the coming of a new social order, brought about by the industrial age. As a political system aiming at the restoration of a feudal order, Confucianism will probably be put out of date by the developments of modern political science and economics. But as a system of humanist culture, as a fundamental viewpoint concerning the conduct of life and of society, I believe it will still hold its own. We have not yet progressed so far that, for instance, the doctrines of Karl Marx and Confucius no longer meet, or have no longer a common meeting point. Confucianism, as a live force in the Chinese people, is still going to shape our national conduct of affairs and modify Communism in China, if it is ever introduced. We will merely repeat the fight with Western Communism that Mencius fought with the early Chinese Communists and won. It is in this sense that a study of Confucianism and its fundamental beliefs will be of interest to people of the Western world, in helping them fundamentally to understand the Chinese *ethos* and Chinese *mores*.

To Western readers, Confucius is chiefly known as a wise man speaking in aphorisms or moral maxims, which hardly suffices to explain the depth of the influence of Confucianism. Without a deeper unity of belief or system of thought, no mere collection of aphorisms could dominate a nation's history as Confucianism has dominated China. The answer to the puzzle of Confucius' great prestige and influence has to be sought elsewhere. Without a fundamental system of beliefs which is accepted to be true, maxims and proverbs might easily grow stale and outworn. The *Analects,* the Confucian Bible, is such a collection of moral maxims, and it is chiefly through the *Analects* that Confucianism has been made known to the West. But the *Analects* after all is only a collection of the cream of Confucius' sayings, often torn apart from their contexts, which are found with a fuller elucidation in *The Book of Mencius, Liki* and other books. After all, Confucius did not talk the whole day in staccato sentences. It would be impossible, therefore, to arrive at a full appreciation of the influence and prestige of Confucius without an understanding of the system of Confucian ideas as a system.

To put it briefly, Confucianism stood for a rationalized social order through the ethical approach, based on personal cultivation. It aimed at political order by laying the basis for it in a moral order, and it sought political harmony by trying to achieve the moral harmony in man himself. Thus its most curious characteristic was the abolition of the distinction between politics and ethics. Its approach was definitely an ethical

approach, differing from the Legalists who tried to bring about a strong nation by a rigid enforcement of the law. It was also a positive point of view, with a keen sense of responsibility toward one's fellow men and the general social order, as distinguished from the negative cynicism of Taoism. Fundamentally, it was a humanist attitude, brushing aside all futile metaphysics and mysticism, interested chiefly in the essential human relationships, and not in the world of spirits or in immortality. The strongest doctrine of this particular type of humanism, which accounts for its great enduring influence, is the doctrine that "the measure of man is man," a doctrine which makes it possible for the common man to begin somewhere as a follower of Confucianism by merely following the highest instincts of his own human nature, and not by looking for perfection in a divine ideal.

To be more specific, Confucianism was definitely aiming at the restoration of a rationalized feudal order, with clear gradations of rank, at a time when the feudal system of the Chou Dynasty was breaking down. In order to understand this, one has to go back to a conception of the collapse of the feudal system in Confucius' days and the centuries immediately following. There were hundreds of duchies, baronies, and townships, which had emerged as independent states, with the stronger states growing in power and territory and constantly warring with one another. The power of the Emperor, still holding a theoretic sovereignty over the Chinese Empire, had dwindled to nothing; in fact to such an extent that neither Confucius in his time nor Mencius later, who went about to persuade different kings to put their doctrines into practice, did not even bother to go and see the Emperor. This was a contradiction of his own theory of a rationalized social order, upholding loyalty to the highest authority. The situation was so bad that there was no point in either one of them trying to see the weak Emperor at all. There was, therefore, an international anarchy, resembling conditions in modern Europe. Treaties were scrapped, and there were alliances and big and little ententes, which never lasted very long. Taxation was frightful, in order to keep up the growing armies, and the smaller states were constantly worried about invasions by the powerful neighboring states. Conferences were constantly held, now with the ruler of one leading state and now with that of another sitting as the chairman. Philosophers began to develop the distinction between "offensive" and "defensive" warfare and between "aggressors" and "victims." Curiously, there developed a kind of intellectual internationalism; scholars moved about and switched their allegiance from one state to another. The ancient rites and insignias of rank had fallen into a terrible confusion; there was great inequality of wealth; and this moral and political chaos set every keen mind thinking about the best way of bringing about peace and order. In this atmosphere, the greatest intellectual activity, coupled with the greatest freedom of thought, brought about the greatest richness and variety in Chinese philosophy. Some repudiated civilization entirely, as Laotse and Chuangtse did; some became budding Communists, believing that every man should work for his living with his hands; some taught the oneness of God, the love of God, and a humanitarian, unselfish and even ascetic personal life, to the extent of repudiating music itself, as Motse did; and there were Sophists, Stoics, Hedonists, Epicureans and downright Naturalists. Many people, like modern Europeans, began to suspect civilization itself, and harked back to the primitive life, as some modern thinkers are harking back to the African jungle or the Island of Bali. Some others, like Confucius, were like the modern Christians, who believe in the force of moral ideals, in education, in the arts, in continuity with the past, and in maintaining some sort of international decencies and a high moral standard in human relationships, which were all part of the Confucian faith.

The chapter "On the Conduct of the Confucianists" in *Liki* (*Juhsing,* Ch. XLI) distinguishes this school of scholars from the rest. The term *Ju* (Confucianism is known in China as "the religion of the *Ju*" since Confucius' time) was already current in Confucius' day, and the scholars styled as *Ju* were probably a special set of people, conservative in point of view, backed by historical scholarship, and wearing a special *Ju* cap and *Ju* gown as symbols of their belief in the past. The following are a few extracts showing the high moral idealism of this group of followers of Confucius:

> The Duke Ai of Lu asked Confucius, "Is the Master's dress that of the *Ju*?" Confucius replied, "I grew up in Lu and wore a gown with broad sleeves, and stayed later in Sung and therefore wore a cap of black cloth. I have heard it said that a gentleman is broad in his scholarship, but wears the gown of his own country. I do not know if this gown that I wear may be called a *Ju* gown." "What about the conduct of the *Ju*?" asked the Duke, and Confucius replied, "I shall not be able to finish it if I were to describe all the details, and if I did, I would have to stop over here and yet not be able to cover it all, even after you have changed the attendants several times." The Duke then asked Confucius to sit down on the mat, and Confucius sat in his company and said,

> "A *Ju* is like one who has jewels in his keeping waiting for sale; he cultivates his knowledge morning and night to prepare himself for requests for advice; he cherishes integrity and honesty of character against the time when he is appointed; he endeavors to order his personal conduct against the time when he shall be in office. Such is his independence!

> "A *Ju* is orderly in his dress and careful in his actions; his great refusals seem like lack of respect and his little refusals seem like false manners; when he appears on public occasions, he looks awe-inspiring, and on small occasions he appears self-retiring; his services are difficult to get and difficult to keep while he appears gentle and weak. Such is his appearance!

> "A *Ju* may be approached by gentle manners but may not be cowed by force; he is affable but he cannot be made to do what he doesn't want; and he may be killed, but may not be humiliated. He is simple and frugal in his living, and his faults or mistakes may be gently explained but not abruptly pointed out to his face. Such is his strength of character!

> "A *Ju* lives with the moderns but studies the ancients. What he does today will become an example for those in the generations to follow. When he lives in times of political chaos, he neither courts favors from those in authority, nor is boosted by those below. And when the petty politicians join hands to defame or injure him, his life may be threatened, but the course of his conduct may not be changed. Although he lives in danger, his soul remains his own, and even then he does not forget the sufferings of the people. Such is his sense of responsibility!

> "A *Ju* is broad in his knowledge and not narrow-minded; he cultivates his conduct without cease; and in his private life he does not abandon himself. When he is successful, he does not depart from the truth. In his personal manners he values living in peace and harmony with others. He maintains the beauty of his inner character and is leisurely in his ways. He admires those cleverer than himself and is generous toward the masses, and is flexible in principle. Such is his ease of mind and generosity of character!"

Against this background of international anarchy and a collapsing ancient feudal order, the different essential tenets of Confucian teachings will be more readily understood and appreciated, particularly Confucius' efforts to restore an ancient feudal order through ritual and music. The characteristic ideas of this body of teachings are, to my mind, five in number, and since these are also the ideas constantly to be met with in the following translations, an examination of their exact import is essential to a true understanding of Confucianism.

1. The identification of politics and ethics:

The whole emphasis of Confucianism upon ritual and music and its apparent preoccupation with moral platitudes usually strikes the Western readers as queer and almost unintelligible. And yet, nothing is clearer than the fact that the so-called "ritual and music" embody better than any other phrase, the entire aim of the

Confucian social order. It sounds almost childishly naive to hear Confucius say, in reply to a question about government by his disciple: "Ah Shih, didn't I tell you before? All that one needs to do is simply for the gentleman to fully understand ritual and music and then apply them to the government! (*Liki,* Ch. XXVIII)." This is easily understood, however, from the Confucian point of view, if we remember the Confucian definition of government as merely an effort to "put things right" or "put things in order." In other words, Confucius was aiming at the moral basis for peace in society, out of which political peace should naturally ensue. The *Analects* reports a conversation as follows: Someone asked Confucius, "Why don't you go into the government?" And Confucius replied, "Is it not said in the *Book of History* concerning filial piety that the King of Chen was a good son and a good brother and then he applied the principles to the government of things? This is also being in the government. Why, therefore, should I go into the government?" In other words, Confucius was almost an anarchist, believing as his highest political ideal in a society of people living in moral harmony which should make government itself unnecessary. This is implied in his saying that "In acting as a judge at lawsuits, I am as good as anyone. But the thing is, to aim so that there should not be any lawsuits at all (*Analects,* XII)." How this is to be achieved will be made clear in the following paragraphs. But it is unmistakable that Confucius held the final aim of government and the criminal law and ritual and music to be identical: "The final goals of ritual and music and the criminal law and government are the same, namely, to bring about a community of the people's aspirations and to result in social and political order" (see Chapter X "On Music"). Confucius was never quite satisfied with the kind of political order achieved by a rigorous administration or enforcement of the criminal law. "Guide the people by governmental measures," he said, "and regulate them by the threat of punishment, and the people will try to keep out of jail, but will have no sense of honor or shame. Guide the people by virtue and regulate them by *li* (sense of propriety) and the people will have a sense of honor and respect." There are then two kinds of political order, and it is in this sense that Confucius once said, "When the kingdom Ch'i moves a step forward, it will have reached the culture of the kingdom of Lu (his own country), *i.e.,* the first stage of peace that he spoke of; and when the kingdom of Lu moves a step forward, it will have reached the stage of true civilization, *i.e.,* the second stage."

2. *Li,* or the rationalized social order:

Confucianism, besides being known in China as "the religion of Confucius" and "the religion of the *Ju,*" is further known as "the religion of *li,* or ritual." It will at once be sensed by Western readers, that there is much more to this conception of *li* than merely ritualism itself, or the entire Confucian system is a sham and a fake. We have to meet this fact squarely, for the phrase "ritual and music" occurs again and again in the Confucian texts and seems to embody the entire Confucian system of outward social order, as the conception of "true manhood" seems to embody the essence of Confucian teachings regarding personal conduct. The importance and exact meaning of the phrase "ritual and music" will be made amply clear in the Three Confucian Discourses (Chs. VI, VII, VIII). Here it is only necessary to point out that Confucius' own definitions of government and of *li* exactly coincide. Government is defined as putting things or people in order, but *li* is also defined as "the order of things" (*Liki,* XXVIII). The Chinese word *li* therefore cannot be rendered by an English word. On one extreme, it means "ritual," "propriety"; in a generalized sense, it simply means "good manners"; in its highest philosophic sense, it means an ideal social order with everything in its place, and particularly a rationalized feudal order, which was breaking down in Confucius' days, as I have already pointed out.

To adhere to the philosophic meaning, Confucius was trying to restore a social order, based on love for one's kind and respect for authority, of which the social rites of public worship and festivities in ritual and music should be the outward symbols. Of course, the rituals of worship lead straight back to primitive religious rites and ceremonies, and it is clear that this so-called "religion of *li*" was truly semi-religious in character, being related to God at one end in the sacrifice to heaven by the Emperor, and related to the common people at the other end by the teachings of affection and discipline and respect for authority in the home life. There have existed different religious sacrifices to heaven or God, to the ancestors of the rulers, to the spirits of the earth and the mountains and rivers. Confucius, as reported several times in the *Analects* and the *Liki,* said that he did not know of the meaning of these particular sacrifices to God and the Imperial Ancestors, known as *chiao* and *t'i,* and that if he did, it would be as easy to rule the world as to turn over one's hand. In this aspect, the body of Confucian thought resembles most the laws of Moses, and it is easier to compare Confucius in the *scope* of his teachings to Moses than to any other philosopher. The *li* of Confucius, like the laws of Moses, covers both religious laws and laws of civil life and considers the two as integrated parts of a whole. After all, Confucius was a product of his times, living in what Comte calls the "religious" era.

Furthermore, Confucius would undoubtedly have been a High Churchman in temperament, an Episcopalian or a Roman Catholic, if he were a Christian. He loved the rituals of worship, certainly not as merely ceremonial acts without meaning, but with his clear knowledge of human psychology, he saw that the proper rituals brought about in the worshipper a respectful or God-fearing state of mind. Furthermore, he was a conservative, like all Episcopalians or Roman Catholics, and believed in authority and in continuity with the past. Personally, his artistic sense was too keen for him not to be moved by the appeal of ceremonies and music, of which we have ample evidence in the *Analects* (see Ch. V, Sec. 2, "The Emotional and Artistic Life of Confucius"). And as the worship of God and the ancestors of the rulers was to bring about a state of true piety, so the ceremonies of drinking festivals and archery contests in the villages, accompanied with song and dance and kowtowing, teaching the villagers to observe form and order in their festivities, were also to bring about a sense of general order and courtesy among the masses.

Psychologically, therefore, the functions of ritual and music are the same. Confucianism gave a sort of philosophic and even poetic meaning to ritual and music and dance. This is nothing surprising, considering that Confucius himself was a great lover of music, learned to play on musical instruments from a master of music at the age of twenty-nine, and constantly sang and played on the *ch'in* (a string instrument) even amidst his troubles. It is definitely stated that the six branches of study in Confucius' time were: ritual, music, archery, carriage driving, writing and mathematics. Confucius himself edited the *Book of Songs* at the age of sixty-four, and it is said that after this job of editing, the different songs were first shifted and properly classified with respect to their accompanying music. In fact, Confucius' own school, according to reports, seemed continually to echo with the sounds of song and music, and Tsekung, when placed in charge of a town, began to teach the people to sing, which induced a smile and a joke from Confucius (Ch. V, Sec. 3). The philosophic meaning of ritual and music is fully developed in Chapter X. The gist of it is: "when you see a nation's dance, you know the character of the people"; "music comes from the heart, while ritual comes from the outside"; "music is a sense of joy— what cannot be restrained or replaced from the human heart"; "the different kinds of music in different countries are an indication of the different *mores* of the different peoples"; "music harmonizes the community, while ritual draws its social distinction"; "music represents heaven or the abstract, while ritual represents the earth or the concrete"; finally "therefore the ancient kings instituted ritual and music not only to satisfy our desires of the ear and the eye and the mouth and the stomach, but in order to teach the people to have the right taste or the right likes and dislikes and restore the human order to its normalcy."

Naturally, the whole system of *li* embodies also a concrete plan of a social hierarchy, concluding with a prodigious amount of scholarship regarding rules and ceremonies for the religious sacrifices, the festivities

of drinking and archery and the conduct of men and women and children and the taking care of old people. This branch of Confucian historical scholarship was best developed by Hsuntse, a great philosopher whose books still exist and who was a contemporary and rival of Mencius, while its philosophic meaning is also fully developed in the *Liki* (see the Three Confucian Discourses, Chapters VI, VII, VIII), which largely reflect Hsuntse's interpretations.

This understanding of the importance of *li* helps us also to understand another corollary of Confucius' doctrines, the importance of terminology, that is, everything should be called by its right name. Therefore, when Confucius wrote the political annals of his time and the two preceding centuries, called the *ch'uch'iu* or *Spring and Autumn,* his intention was largely to restore the social order by sharp distinctions in terminology. A ruler killing a rebellious general would be called *sha,* while a prince or a minister killing his ruler would be called *shih.* When the Baron of Wu assumed the title of "king," Confucius merely wrote down "Baron Wu," thinking that he had degraded him by that single word in his Chronicles.

3. Humanism:

The finest philosophic perception of Confucius, it seems to me, is his recognition that "the measure of man is man." If it were not so, the whole system of Confucian ethics would fall to pieces, and would immediately become impracticable. The whole philosophy of ritual and music is but to "set the human heart right," and the kingdom of God is truly within the man himself. The problem for any man intending to cultivate his personal life is merely to start out on a hunt for the best in his human nature and steadfastly to keep to it. That is practically the essence of Confucian ethics. This results in the doctrine of the Golden Rule, and is best explained in Chapter III, "Central Harmony." Of course as a part of this humanism, there is a high and fine conception of *jen* or "true manhood," about which Confucius constantly talked, but which, as a qualification, he consistently refused to allow to all except two of his disciples and three great men in history. Confucius was constantly reluctant to fix this concept of a "true man," and when he was asked whether such and such a good man was a "true man," in nine cases out of ten he refused to apply that epithet to a living man. But, as is made clear in the chapter on "Central Harmony," Confucius also pointed out that in order to climb high, one had to begin from the low ground, and in order to reach a distant place, one had to begin by making a first step, and once he said, "Being a good son and a good younger brother provides already the basis for being a true man."

The conception *jen* (true manhood) is as difficult to translate as the conception of *li.* In Chinese writing, this character is composed of "two" and "man," signifying the relationship between men; in its present pronunciation, it is identical with the sound for "man," but in the ancient language it had a pronunciation which was identical to that of "man" in a particular phrase, quoted by a Han commentator, but unrecognizable today. In certain instances in Confucian books, the word for "true manhood" is actually used interchangeably with the common word for "man," the clearest instance of which occurs in the **Analects,** where a disciple speaks about "a man falling into a well," the word for "man" being written with the word for "true manhood," usually translated as "kindness" or "benevolence." Anyway the association of ideas is clear. In the English language in different words, such as *human, humane, humanitarian,* and *humanity,* the last word has a double meaning of "mankind" and "kindness." Both Confucius and Mencius also once defined "true manhood" as the "love of man." But the matter is not so simple. In the first place, as I have pointed out, Confucius refused to give a concrete example of a true man, whereas certainly he would not have refused to give a concrete example of merely "a kind man." In the second place, this "true manhood" is often described as a state of mind, a state that one "searches for," "attains," "feels at peace in," "departs from," "is based upon," and (Mencius) "dwells in," as in a house.

The essential idea of *jen* is therefore a conception of the state when man is truly himself, and from this point on, Mencius starts out on his whole philosophy about the essence of human nature, and finds that "human nature is good," while Hsuntse, believing that human nature is bad and taking up the other end of Confucian teachings regarding education and music and the system of social order and outward forms of moral conduct, develops the idea of *li,* with emphasis on restraint. In common English phraseology, we speak of certain people among our acquaintances as "a real man" or "a real person," and this seems to come closest to the Confucian conception of *jen.* On the one hand, we begin to understand why Confucius refused to give so many good men of his day that label, as we can see today how many men or women we would be willing to call "a real person," in its most ideal sense. (Abraham Lincoln certainly was one.) On the other hand, we do find that the approach to being a real man is after all not so difficult, and that anyone can be a real person if he keeps his heart right and has some contempt for the artificialities of civilization—in other words, every common person can be a real man if he wants to. This fully fits in with the Confucian and Mencian statement that to be a real man, one merely needs to start out by being a good son or daughter or brother or sister, or a good citizen. I consider, therefore, my translation of *jen* as "true manhood" fully accurate and adequate. In certain places, it will have to be rendered merely as "kindness," just as the word *li* in certain places will

have to be rendered merely as "ritual" or "ceremony" or "manners."

Actually, Mencius arrived at the position that men are all created equal in goodness of heart, and that "all men can be like the Emperors Yao and Shun" (the Confucian models of perfect virtue). It is this humanistic approach of climbing high from the low and reaching the distance from the nearby, and of making an easy start in virtue or the development of character that accounts for the great fascination of Confucianism over the Chinese people, as distinguished from the much more idealistic doctrine of Motse, teaching actually the "fatherhood of God" and "universal love," so akin to Christianity. The humanistic idea of measuring man by man not only forces one to discover the true self, but naturally also results in the Golden Rule, known in Chinese as *shu,* namely, as Confucius repeatedly said, "Do not do unto others what you would not have others do unto you." Confucius not only gave this as a definition of the "true man," but also said that it was *the* central thread of all his teachings. The word for *shu* (meaning "reciprocity") is written in Chinese with the two elements "a heart" and "alike." In modern Chinese, it usually means "forgiveness," but the transition is easy to understand, for if you assume that all men's reactions are the same in a particular circumstance, and if you place yourself in the other man's position, you would naturally forgive. Confucianism, therefore, constantly reverted to the personal test of how would you feel yourself or "finding it in yourself." The best analogy, as given in Chapter III, is that of a carpenter trying to make an axe-handle—all he needs to do is to look at the handle of the axe in his own hand for a model. He will not have to go far. The measure of man is man.

4. Personal cultivation as the basis of a world order:

The ethical approach of Confucianism to the problems of politics has already been made clear. Put in the plainest terms, Confucius believed that a nation of good sons and good brothers could not help making an orderly, peaceful nation. Confucianism traced back the ordering of a national life to the regulation of the family life and the regulation of the family life to the cultivation of the personal life. That means very much about the same thing as when modern educators tell us that the reform of the present chaotic world after all must ultimately depend on education. The logical connections between a world order as the final aim and the cultivation of the personal life by individuals as a necessary start are made perfectly plain in the chapter, "Ethics and Politics" (Chapter IV) and also in Chapter III, Sec. 6, and throughout the Chapters VI, VII, VIII. The Chinese preoccupation with moral maxims and platitudes becomes then intelligible, for they are not detached aphorisms, but are part of a well-rounded political philosophy.

Interpreted in the light of modern psychology, this doctrine can be reduced easily to two theories, the theory of habit and the theory of imitation. The whole emphasis on "filial piety," more clearly translated by myself as "being a good son," is psychologically based on the theory of habit. Confucius and Mencius literally said that, having acquired the habits of love and respect in the home, one could not but extend this mental attitude of love and respect to other people's parents and elder brothers and to the authorities of the state. As stated in Chapter IV, "when the individual families have learned kindness, then the whole nation has learned kindness, and when the individual families have learned courtesy, then the whole nation has learned courtesy." The teaching of young children to love their parents and brothers and to be respectful to their superiors lays the foundation of right mental and moral attitudes for growing up to be good citizens.

5. The intellectual upper class:

The theory of imitation, or the power of example, results in the doctrine of the intellectual upper class and of "government by example." The intellectual upper class is at the same time a moral upper class, or it fails in its qualifications to be considered the upper class at all. This is the well-known conception of the Confucian "gentleman" or "superior man" or "princely man." This princely man is not at all a super man of the Nietzschean type. He is merely a kind and gentle man of moral principles, at the same time a man who loves learning, who is calm himself and perfectly at ease and is constantly careful of his own conduct, believing that by example he has a great influence over society in general. He is perfectly at ease in his own station of life and has a certain contempt for the mere luxuries of living. All the moral teachings of Confucius are practically grouped around this cultivated gentleman. The Chinese word for this, *chuntse,* was a current term given a new meaning by the usage of Confucius. In many places, it definitely meant "the sovereign" and could not be translated as "gentleman" and still make sense; in other places, it obviously meant only a cultivated "gentleman." With the existence of an intellectual upper class of rulers, the two meanings merged into one another, and formed a concept very similar to Plato's "philosopher king." The theory of the power of example is fully developed in Chapter XII of the *Analects.* . . . Confucius had an overweening confidence in the power of moral example. When a rapacious rich official, Chik'angtse, told Confucius that he was worried about the prevalence of robbers and thieves in his country, Confucius bluntly replied, "If you yourself don't love money, you can give the money to the thieves and they won't take it."

II. A BRIEF ESTIMATE OF THE CHARACTER OF CONFUCIUS

The great prestige of Confucius and Confucian teachings during the centuries immediately after his death, as well as in subsequent Chinese history, must be ascribed to three factors: first, the intrinsic appeal of Confucian ideas to the Chinese way of thinking; second, the enormous historical learning and scholarship accumulated and practically monopolized by the Confucianists, in contrast to the other schools which did not bother with historical learning (and this body of scholarship carried enough weight and prestige of its own); and thirdly, the evident charm of personality and prestige of the Master himself. There are in this world certain great teachers, whose personality seems to account for their influence more than their scholarship. We think of Socrates, or of St. Francis of Assisi, who themselves did not write any books of account, but who left such a tremendous impress on their generation that their influence persisted throughout the ages. The charm of Confucius was very much like the charm of Socrates; the very fact that the latter commanded the affection and respect of Plato is sufficient evidence of the power of his personality and his ideas. It is true Confucius edited the **Book of Songs,** and it is also true that he wrote the bare skeleton of events, chronicled in the ***Spring and Autumn,*** but after all the great tradition of his teachings was put down by his disciples and future followers.

There are, of course, many characterizations of Confucius' personality in the various Confucian books. We get a foretaste of it at the end of Chapter III, on "Central Harmony." His disciple Yen Huei also lauded him to the skies, comparing him to a great mysterious something: "You turn up your head and look at it and it seems so high; you try to drill through it and it seems so hard; it appears to be in front of you and all of a sudden it appears behind you." Some of the best characterizations, however, are the following: It was said that he was "gentle but dignified, austere, yet not harsh, polite and completely at ease." Confucius' self-characterizations were still better. Once a king asked one of his disciples about Confucius and the disciple could not make an answer. The disciple then returned to tell Confucius of the incident, and Confucius replied, "Why didn't you tell him that I am a man who forgets to eat when he is enthusiastic about something, who forgets all his worries when he is happy, and who is not aware that old age is coming on?" In this statement, we see something of the joy of life, the enthusiasm and the positive, persistent urge for doing something. He also said of himself several times that he was not a "saint," but that he admitted he was tireless in learning and in teaching other people. As an illustration of this positive urge in Confucius, there is also the following record. One of his disciples was putting up for the night at a place, and the gatekeeper asked him where he was from. Tselu replied that he was from Confucius and the gatekeeper remarked, *"Oh, is he the fellow who knows that a thing can't be done and still wants to do it?"* There was a high moral idealism in Confucius, a consciousness of a mission, that made him completely believe in himself.

The charm of Confucius' private character really lies in his gentility, as is so clearly shown in his conversational tone with his disciples. Many of the sayings of Confucius contained in the *Analects* can only be interpreted in the light of a leisurely discourse of a humorous teacher with his disciples, with an occasional shot of witticism. Read in this light, some of his most casual remarks become the best. I like, for instance, such perfectly casual sayings as the following: He remarked one day to two or three intimate disciples talking with him, "Do you think that I have hidden anything from the two or three of you? Really, I have hidden nothing from you. There is nothing that I do that I don't share with the two or three of you. That's I." Another instance: Tsekung loved to criticize people and Confucius said, calling him by his intimate name, "Ah Sze, you are very clever, aren't you? I have no time for such things." Another instance: Confucius said, "I really admire a fellow who goes about the whole day with a well-fed stomach and a vacuous mind. How can one ever do it? I would rather that he play chess, which would seem to me to be better." In one instance, Confucius said something derisively about what one of his disciples was doing. The disciple was puzzled, and Confucius explained that he was merely pulling his leg, implying that really he approved. For Confucius was a gay old soul. His gentility and hospitality toward all desiring to learn are recorded in the following incident, resembling a story in the Bible when Jesus said, "Suffer the little children to come unto me." The people of a certain village were given to mischief, and one day some young people from that village came to see Confucius, and the disciples were surprised that Confucius saw them. Confucius remarked, "Why be so harsh on them? What concerns me is how they come and not what they do when they go away. When a man approaches me with pure intentions, I respect his pure intentions, although I cannot guarantee what he does afterwards."

But Confucius was not all gentility. For he was a "real man." He could sing and be extremely polite, but he also could hate and sneer with the hatred and contempt of a "real man," which was shared by Jesus in his hatred of the Jewish scribes. There was never a great man in this world who did not have some genuine good hatreds. Confucius could be extremely rude and there are recorded in the *Analects* four or five caustic remarks made about people in their presence. He could be rude in a way that no Confucianist dares to be rude today. There was no class of persons that Confucius hated more than the goody-goody hypocrites whom Confucius described as "the thieves of virtue." Once such a person, Ju Pei, wanted to see Confucius, and Confucius sent word to say he was not at home. When

Ju Pei was just outside the door, Confucius took up a string instrument and sang "in order to let him hear it" and know that he was really at home. This passage in the *Analects* has confused all Confucian critics, who proceeded upon the asumption that Confucius was a saint and not a human being, and was always polite. Such orthodox criticism naturally completely dehumanized Confucius. Another passage in the *Analects,* recorded in *Mencius,* also puzzled the critics. A corrupt official, by the name of Yang Ho, presented Confucius with a leg of pork. As the two persons heartily disliked each other, Yang Ho found out when Confucius would not be at home and then presented the leg of pork at his home as a matter of courtesy. Confucius also took the trouble to find out when Yang Ho was not at home and then went to say thanks to him and leave his card. In reply to a question from his disciples concerning the rulers of his day, Confucius remarked, "Oh, those are rice bags!" (i.e., good only for filling themselves with rice). At another time he made this remark about a man who was reputed to have indulged in singing at his mother's death. "As a young boy, you were unruly; when grown up, you have accomplished nothing, and now in your old age you refuse to die. You are a thief!" And Confucius struck his shin with a walking stick.

There was, in fact, a lot of fun in Confucius. He led a full, joyous life, the full human life of feelings and artistic taste. For he was a man of deep emotionality and great sensitive taste. At the death of his favorite disciple, Confucius wept bitterly. When he was asked why he wept so and was so shaken, he replied, "If I don't weep bitterly at the death of such a person, for whom else shall I weep bitterly?" His curious sensitiveness and capacity for shedding tears was shown in an instance when he passed by casually a funeral of one of his old acquaintances. He went in, and moved by the weeping of others, he also wept. When he came out, he asked his disciple to take a part of the accoutrements on his horse as a funeral gift, and said, "Take it in as my formal present. I hated this weeping without reason."

This man, who sang and played musical instruments (*ch'in, seh,* and *hsuan*) and edited a book of songs with accompanying music, was an artist. As I have already pointed out, he was a lover of ritual and music. As an illustration of his Episcopalian temper, there was the following incident which contrasted him sharply with Jesus who had much less respect for the laws and the prophets and all the ritualism that went with them. Jesus allowed a person to save a cow out of a pit on the Sabbath. Confucius might have approved, or he might not. His disciple Tsekung once proposed to abolish the winter sacrifices of lambs, and Confucius replied, "Ah Sze, you love the lamb, but I love the ritual!" Anyway, he wasn't interested in animals. For on hearing that a stable was burnt down by fire, it was

"Master Kung became separated from his disciples and wandered about, a bystander said, 'like a stray dog'."

recorded that he asked whether any persons were hurt but "did not ask about the horses." The artist in him made him say that a man's education should begin with poetry, be strengthened by proper conduct, and "consummated in music." It was also recorded that when he heard another man sing and liked it, he would ask for an *encore* and then join in the refrain. The artist in him also made him very fastidious about his food and his dress. I have already pointed out elsewhere that his fastidiousness about food was most probably the cause of his wife's running away. He refused to eat when anything was not in season, or not properly cooked, or not served with its proper sauce. And he had good taste in matching colors in his dress. A modern modiste could easily understand why he would match a black lamb coat with a black covering, a white faun coat with a white covering, and a fox coat with a yellow covering. (This "covering" corresponds to the "lining" in Western fur coats, for Chinese fur coats are worn with the fur on the inside and the silk on the outside.) He was also something of an inventor in the matter of dress. His bedclothes were longer than his body by half, to avoid cold feet, and he struck upon the beautiful idea of making his right sleeve shorter than his left sleeve for convenience at work, which must have also exasperated his wife and caused this woman to run away from the crazy man. (For all these facts see Chapter X of the **Analects,** or Chapter V, Section 2, in this book. The aristocracy of his taste extended even to divorce. For three successive genera-

tions, the Master, his son, and his grandson were divorced or separated from their wives. On the intellectual lineage (the Master, his great disciple Tsengtse, and Tsengtse's disciple Tsesze), the record of divorce was also unbroken for three and a half generations, it being reported that the intellectual fourth generation, Mencius (who studied under Tsesze), *almost* divorced his wife. So, although none of them was particularly rich, they were undoubtedly aristocrats.

One of the most important characteristics of Confucius which really accounted for his great prestige was simply his scholarship and love of learning. Confucius said this repeatedly of himself. He admitted that he was not one of those "born to know the truth," but that he was an indefatigable reader and teacher, tireless in his search after knowledge and learning. He admitted that in every hamlet of ten families, there were some righteous and honest men as good as himself, but none who loved learning the way he did. He counted as one of the things that would trouble him "the neglect of his studies." In one of his sayings, I note a sigh of regret which is the regret of a modern research scholar. In his efforts to reconstruct the religious practices, ceremonies and customs of the ancient dynasties, he went to the city of Chi to search for survivals of the customs of Hsia Dynasty, and to the city of Sung to learn of the surviving religious practices of the ancient Dynasty of Shang. He said, "I should be able to talk about the religious customs of the Hsia Dynasty, but there are not enough evidences in the city of Chi. I should be able to talk about the religious customs of the Shang Dynasty, but there are not enough evidences in the city of Sung. There are not enough historical documents and evidences left. If there were, I should be able to reconstruct them with evidences." In other words, he was essentially a research scholar in history, trying to salvage from existing customs as well as historical documents the ancient social and religious practices which had decayed and the theocracy which had broken down. Nevertheless, he did his best, and the result of his labors was the collection of the Confucian *Five Classics* which were strictly history (dictum of a Ch'ing scholar, Chang Hsueh-ch'eng), as distinguished from the *Four Books.* I have no doubt that people were attracted to Confucius, less because he was the wisest man of his time, than because he was the most *learned* scholar, the only one of his day who could teach them about the ancient books and ancient scholarship. There was a great body of historical learning concerning the governmental systems of ancient times, and there was still a greater body of historical learning concerning the religious rites and ceremonies of a decaying or decayed theocracy, particularly that of the Shang Dynasty, as we can see from Confucius' *Five Classics.* He was reported to have had three thousand pupils in all, of which number seventy-two were accomplished in the *Book of Songs,* the *Book of History* and the theory and practice of rituals and music. He believed in history and the appeal of history, because he believed in continuity. It will be seen in the chapter on "Central Harmony" (Chapter III), that he regarded as the three essential requisites for governing the world: Character, position of authority, and the appeal to history, and that lacking any one of these things, no one could succeed with a governmental system and "command credence," however excellent it might be. The actual result was that there grew up within the Confucian school a great body of historical learning which the other schools entirely lacked, and personally I believe the victory of the Confucian school over the other schools of Laotse and Motse was as much due to its prestige in scholarship as to its intrinsic philosophic value. The Confucian teachers had something definite to teach and the Confucian pupils had something definite to learn, namely, historical learning, while the other schools were forced to air merely their own opinions, either on "universal love" or on "love of oneself."

A word must be said about the genial humor of Confucius, both because it supports and illustrates what I have said about his living a full, joyous life, so different from the conventional picture of Confucius presented to us by the killjoy Sung doctrinaires, and because it helps us to see his simplicity and greatness. Confucius was not a cheap wit, but occasionally he could not resist turning a clever line, such as the following: "A man who does not say to himself 'What to do? What to do?'—indeed I don't know what to do

with such a person"; or this, "Know what you know and know that you don't know what you don't know— that is the characteristic of one who knows" (or in Chinese fashion, "Know, know; don't know, don't know—that is know"); or this, "A man who knows he has committed a mistake and doesn't correct it is committing another mistake." Sometimes he was also capable of a little bit of poetic humor or occasional license. There was a passage in the *Book of Songs,* in which the lover complained that it wasn't that she did not think of her sweetheart, but that "his house was so far away." Commenting upon this passage, Confucius remarked, "She really did not think of him at all; if she did, how could the house seem far away?"

But the most characteristic humor that we find in Confucius was also the best kind of humor generally, the humor of laughing at his own expense. He had plenty of chance to laugh at his own outward failures or of admitting that other people's criticisms of him were quite correct. Some of this humor was merely casual light raillery between the Master and his disciples. Once a man from a certain village remarked, "Great indeed is Confucius! He knows about everything and is expert at nothing." Hearing this comment, Confucius told his disciples, "What shall I specialize in? Shall I specialize in archery or in driving a carriage?" (In this connection he once admitted jokingly that if wealth could be achieved entirely by human effort, he would achieve it even if he had to be a cab driver.) During the failure of his political career, Tsekung once remarked, "Here is a piece of precious jade, preserved in a casket and waiting for a good price for sale." And Confucius replied, "For sale! For sale! I am the one waiting for a good price to be sold!" Refusal to see humor in Confucius would land the critics and commentators in ridiculous difficulties over such a passage. But as a matter of fact, the Master and his disciples constantly joked back and forth. Confucius was once in difficulties while travelling. Being mistaken for a certain other man who had maltreated the people, he was surrounded by troops. He finally escaped, but his favorite disciple Yen Huei failed to turn up till later, and Confucius said to him, "I thought you were killed." Yen replied, "As long as you live, how dare I be killed!" In another story, once the Master and his disciples had lost track of each other. The disciples finally heard from the crowd that there was a tall man standing at the East Gate with a high forehead resembling some of the ancient emperors, but that he looked crestfallen like a homeless wandering dog. The disciples finally found him and told him about this remark and Confucius replied, "I don't know about my resembling those ancient emperors, *but as for resembling a homeless, wandering dog, he is quite right! He is quite right!"* This is the best type of humor, and what appeals to me most is that passage in *The Life of Confucius* (Chapter II, Section 5), where Confucius was actually singing in the rain. There is a deep pathos about that group of wandering scholars, roaming for three years in the wilds between Ch'en and Ts'ai, having just escaped trouble, all dressed up in their tremendous scholarship and having nowhere to go. These last years of wandering became the turning point of Confucius' career, after which he admitted his full failure in seeking a political career and returned to his native country to devote himself to editing and authorship. He compared himself and his disciples to a nondescript band of animals, "neither buffalos, nor tigers" wandering in the wilds, and began to ask his disciples what was wrong with him. After the third answer, Confucius approved and said to the disciple who made that clever answer, smilingly, "Is that so? Oh, son of Yen, *if you were a rich man, I would be your butler!"* That is a passage that completely won me over to Confucius. Taken as a whole, that passage has a beauty and pathos comparable to Gethsemane, except that it ends on a cheerful note.

III. SOURCES AND PLAN OF THE PRESENT BOOK

I have remarked that the Confucian school practically monopolized the historic scholarship of those days, including the ability to read what was then already an archaic script, and this body of historic learning was handed down as the Confucian *Five Classics*. In the year 213 B.C., the "burning of books" (with the exception of books on medicine, astrology and horticulture) took place, and in the following year, 212 B.C., 460 Confucian scholars were buried alive for criticizing Ch'in Shihhuang, the builder of the Great Wall. It happened, however, that this Emperor's Dynasty, founded for "ten thousand generations," collapsed five years after the massacre and many old Confucian scholars who had committed the classics to memory had survived it. These old scholars thus had salvaged the Confucian classics by an oral tradition and by sheer memory, assisted, I suspect, nevertheless by some inscribed pieces of bamboo that they had hidden away. These people then taught their disciples and had these classics written down in what was then called the "modern script," for Chinese writing went through a great process of simplification during the reign of that great Emperor. In the century following and afterwards, however, there came to light ancient bamboo inscriptions, written in the "ancient script," which had been hidden away and had escaped destruction. The most notable instance was the discovery of ancient texts by a "King of Lu," who had opened up the walls of Confucius' own house and temple and found these preserved. As they were in archaic script, scholars set about to decipher them, a difficult but not impossible job in those times. There grew up, therefore, a separate tradition, known as the "ancient script" tradition, which in part differed from the tradition of the "modern script," notably in regard to the records of the ancient forms of society and

systems of government and concerning the mythological rulers. These two different traditions were noted already in the Han Dynasty, but the greatest commentator, Cheng Hsuan, for instance, tried to harmonize the two. A compromise was effected. Thus throughout the succeeding dynasties, the orthodox version and interpretation of the *Book of Songs* and the *Spring and Autumn* were based upon the "ancient script," while the *Liki,* admitted as one of the *Five Classics,* decidedly belonged to the tradition of the "modern script." The distinction between the two traditions was not sharply drawn until the Ch'ing scholars of the 17th, 18th and 19th centuries set about with their scientific comparative method to restore the tradition of the "modern script." Every available scrap of evidence and every method of historical criticism and philological research was brought to bear upon this question, the most notable achievement being the conclusive proof of forgery of twenty-five out of the fifty-eight existing chapters in the *Book of History,* thus restoring this classic to a collection of thirty-three chapters, representing the tradition of the "modern script." The general position is, not that the archaic script itself was a forgery, but that our present version of the so-called archaic script was a forgery.

The term "Confucian classics" today usually refers to the *Five Classics* and the *Four Books.* The *Five Classics* as I have pointed out formed the body of historical learning edited, taught and handed down by Confucius himself, while the *Four Books* on the whole represented the works of his followers, their records of Confucius' sayings and their interpretations or developments of Confucius' thoughts. Then at other times, we also speak of the *Thirteen Classics. . . .* It should be remembered, however, that in Confucius' own day, there were *Six Classics* instead of *Five,* the additional one being *The Book of Music,* the remaining portions of which survive today as one of the chapters of *Liki. . . .*

The usual approach to the study of Confucian wisdom by directly attacking the *Analects* is a mistake, because it leads nowhere. The *Analects* is a promiscuous and unedited collection of Confucius' sayings, often taken out of their contexts in longer discourses recorded elsewhere, which would make the meaning clearer. There are also duplicate quotations existing in different chapters, of which there are twenty, showing that the work grew by itself in separate hands and was not edited by any one man. Some of the chapters, evidently compiled by the disciples of Tsengtse, would contain more sayings of Tsengtse. The different sayings in any one chapter are not arranged at all in sequence of ideas; sometimes one can detect a main theme, but more often one cannot. There are evident later additions at the end of some chapters, and some lines in the text, for instance those at the end of Chapter X, are clearly incomplete.

But the greatest difficulty for a Western reader in approaching the system of Confucian thought through the *Analects* lies in the Western reader's habit of reading. He demands a connected discourse, and is content to listen while he expects the writer to talk on and on. There is no such thing as reading a line out of a book and taking a day or two to think about it, to chew and digest it mentally and have it verified by one's own reflections and experience. Actually, the *Analects* must be read, if it is to be read at all, by having the different aphorisms spread out on the separate days of a calendar block, and letting the reader ponder over one saying each day and no more. This is the orthodox method of studying the *Analects,* the method of taking a line or two and thoroughly mastering the thought and its implications. This evidently cannot be done with respect to modern readers. Besides, no one can get a well-rounded and consecutive view of the development of Confucius' thoughts by merely reading the *Analects*. . . .

There is the general question as to the validity and accuracy of records of Confucius' sayings in *Liki* and even in the *Analects*. This is the general question of what exactly Confucius or Buddha or Socrates said and to what extent we can believe, for instance, that Plato's accounts of the Socratic dialogue were literally accurate. A synoptic study of the Four Gospels of the Christian Bible reveals discrepancies enough. And we find the same variations of the sayings of Confucius, given in slightly different words in the *Analects,* the *Book of Mencius* and the *Liki*. It was inevitable that Plato colored the sayings of Socrates through his own pen, and the same was true of many of the chapters of the *Liki*. Modern politicians who have the occasion to be interviewed by reporters realize the practical impossibility of obtaining a literally accurate report of what they have said. Nothing short of a dictaphone can convince the politicians of what they actually said themselves.

The *Liki* itself, as I have already said, is only a collection of various records in the possession of the Confucian school, and is definitely of extremely diverse origin. Some of these, including the essay on "Central Harmony" are ascribed to Tsesze, the grandson of Confucius, and some others, particularly a few in the "Great Tai" collection, are undoubtedly handed down by Tsengtse or his disciples. The chapters on education and music doubtless reflect the ideas of the Confucian philosopher Hsuntse, a contemporary of Mencius who spoke of the latter with contempt ("a gutter philosopher" was the phrase used). For the rest, a shocking proportion of the *Liki* is devoted to discourses on funeral ceremonies, while the "Great Tai" collection is devoid of these discussions. A good number of chapters are devoted to the philosophic meaning and actual ceremonial robes and vessels of public worship. There are also chapters on the rules and customs pertaining to all kinds of festivities—marriage, archery contests, dance, village festivals, drinking and games (Chapter XL for instance, describes a game in detail, similar to those we see in shooting galleries). An important chapter, Chapter V, is the basis of the "modern script" school on the ancient system of administration, as the *Chouli* is the basis for the "ancient script" school. There are other chapters dealing with the conduct of women and children and ordinary points of etiquette. The very first chapter, for instance, besides giving the philosophic justification for ritualism, also covers advice such as the following:

> "Do not roll rice into a ball, do not leave rice on the table, do not let your soup run out of your mouth. Do not smack your lips, do not leave a bone dry, do not turn over the fish, do not throw bones to the dog, and do not persist in trying to get a particular piece of meat. Do not turn rice about to let it cool off, and do not take porridge with chop sticks. Do not gulp the soup up, do not stir the soup about, do not pick your teeth, and do not add sauce to your soup. . . . bite off boiled meat with your teeth, but do not bite off cured meat with your teeth."

This reads like Deuteronomy, and it is important that it be understood that the "religion of *Li,*" like Judaism, embraces both religious worship and daily life, down to the matter of eating and drinking.

. . . . .

IV. ON THE METHOD OF TRANSLATION

A little more must be said about the present method of translation. I consider a translation in this case as indistinguishable from paraphrase, and believe that is the best and most satisfying method.

The situation is as follows: The ancient texts were extremely sparing in the use of words, owing of course to the method of inscribing on bamboo sticks. Most of the important ideas and characterizations that covered a whole class of qualities were expressed by monosyllabic words, and in accordance with the general nature of Chinese grammar, the meaning was indicated by syntax or word order rather than by the usual English connectives. Here are two extreme instances in the Chinese form: "Confucius completely-cut-off four— no idea—no must—no *ku*—no I"; "Language expressive only." It is clear that unless connectives are supplied by the translator, the translation would be practically unreadable. The extent to which connectives and amplifying phrases are allowable has by necessity to be left to the discretion of the translator, and for this the translator has no other guide than his own insight into the wisdom of Confucius, assisted, of course, by the commentators.

The first job is of course to determine the scope and connotation of a term in the general classical usage and secondly its particular meaning and shade of meaning in a given sentence. In the above instance of the word *ku*, this word meant several things: "strong," "stubborn," "persistence," "narrow-mindedness," "vulgarity," "limited in knowledge," and "sometimes also." From these different possible meanings, the translator has to make his choice. That is the terrible responsibility and the latitude given to the translator of ancient Chinese texts, and it is clear that a choice of a different word would alter the sense of the line completely. In this particular instance, I have translated the passage as follows: "Confucius denounced (or tried completely to avoid) four things: arbitrariness of opinion, dogmatism, narrow-mindedness and egotism." It is, of course, open to question whether the phrase "no must" should be translated as "don't insist upon a particular course," "don't be persistent," "don't be insistent," or "don't assume that you *must* be right (or don't be dogmatic)." Any of these translations involves as much paraphrasing as the others. In translating the phrase "no idea," I have paraphrased it as meaning "don't start out with preconceived notions," or "don't be arbitrary." That is a sense or shade of meaning won from a knowledge of the general meaning of the word "idea" in the Chinese language, and from an insight into the whole character of Confucius' conduct. But the mere use of the phrase "preconceived notion" or "arbitrariness of opinion" necessarily expresses what at best was only implied in the Chinese word "idea."

In the more fundamental concepts, like *li, jen, hsin, chung,* etc., I have adopted a method of provisionally translating these words in my mind by a certain English concept and going over the body of the texts containing these words to see which one would cover the field of meaning most adequately in the majority of cases, allowing, of course, several meanings for one word. Thus I have come to the conclusion that *li* usually translated as "ritual" or "ceremony" must be translated as "the principle of social order" in the general social philosophy of Confucius, and as "moral discipline" in certain passages dealing with personal conduct. I have also come to the conclusion that the translation of the word *jen* as "kindness," "charity," or "benevolence" is completely inadequate, but represents Confucius' ideal of the "true man," or the "great man" or the "most complete man." Likewise, *hsin* cannot be translated as "honesty" or "keeping one's promise," which latter quality Confucius rather despised and actually didn't care about in his own conduct. Sometimes *hsin* means a condition of "mutual confidence in the state," and sometimes it means "faithfulness."

In the actual act of translation, the translator is faced with two jobs after he has grasped the meaning of the sentence. First he is faced with the choice of one of a number of synonyms, and failure to get at the exact word would completely fail to render the meaning of the remark clear to the reader. I found it impossible, for instance, always to translate the word *teh* as "virtue" or "character," or the meaning would be hopelessly lost for the reader. Thus, Confucius said, "Thoroughbred, don't praise its strength praise its *character*." The meaning becomes clear only when we translate it as follows: "In discussing a throughbred, you don't admire his strength, but admire his *temper*." Now comes this same word for "character" in another passage: "Confucius said, 'One having virtue must have words; one having words not always has virtue.'" The meaning becomes clear only when we translate the word for "character" or "virtue" here by the word "soul" in the English language, as follows: "Confucius said, 'A man who has a beautiful soul always has some beautiful things to say, but a man who says beautiful things does not necessarily have a beautiful soul.'" Then again occurs the same word elsewhere in the phrase *teh yin;* to translate this as "virtuous sounds" may give the impression of scholarly fidelity, but merely hides the lack of understanding on the part of the scholarly translator that it means "*sacred* music." Again Confucius said, "Extravagant than not humble; frugal than *ku* (vulgar or stubborn, etc.). Rather than not humble, be *ku*." The connection between extravagance and lack of humility must be quite vague, and becomes clear only when we realize that people who live extravagantly are liable to be *conceited*. A fully clear and adequate translation must therefore involve a sure choice of words. I believe it should be translated as follows: "Confucius said, 'The people who live extravagantly are apt to be snobbish (or conceited), and the people who live simply are apt to be vulgar. I prefer vulgarity to snobbery (or I prefer the vulgar people to the snobs).'"

In the second place, the translator cannot avoid putting the thought in the more precise concepts of a modern language. The translator does not only have to supply the connectives, but has also to supply a finer definition of ideas, or the English will be extremely bald. Thus in the example given above, "Language expressive only," the modern translator is forced to translate it as follows: "Expressiveness is the only *principle* of language," or "expressiveness is the sole *concern*, or *aim*, or *principle*, of rhetoric." It is clear that there are at least a dozen ways of translating this line in any case. But it is inevitable that the translator would have to slip in a word like "principle" or "aim" or "concern" or "standard." It simply cannot be helped, if the translation is not to become unreadable. . . .

Fung Yu-lan (essay date 1948)

SOURCE: "Confucius, the First Teacher," in *A Short History of Chinese Philosophy,* The Macmillan Company, 1948, pp. 38-48.

[In the excerpt below, Fung remarks on Confucius's life, discusses the concept of righteousness in Confucian thought, and assesses Confucius's ever-changing stature in Chinese history.]

Confucius is the latinized name of the person who has been known in China as K'ung Tzu or Master K'ung. [The word "Tzu" or "Master" is a polite suffix added to names of most philosophers of the Chou Dynasty, such as Chuang Tzu, Hsün Tzu, etc., and meaning "Master Chuang," "Master Hsün," etc.] His family name was K'ung and his personal name Ch'iu. He was born in 551 B.C. in the state of Lu, in the southern part of the present Shantung province in eastern China. His ancestors had been members of the ducal house of the state of Sung, which was descended from the royal house of Shang, the dynasty that had preceded the Chou. Because of political troubles, the family, before the birth of Confucius, had lost its noble position and migrated to Lu.

The most detailed account of Confucius' life is the biography which comprises the forty-seventh chapter of the *Shih Chi* or *Historical Records* (China's first dynastic history, completed ca. 86 B.C.). From this we learn that Confucius was poor in his youth, but entered the government of Lu and by the time he was fifty had reached high official rank. As a result of political intrigue, however, he was soon forced to resign his post and go into exile. For the next thirteen years he traveled from one state to another, always hoping to find an opportunity to realize his ideal of political and social reform. Nowhere, however, did he succeed, and finally as an old man he returned to Lu, where he died three years later in 479 B.C.

Confucius and the Six Classics

. . . [The] rise of the philosophic schools began with the practice of private teaching. So far as modern scholarship can determine, Confucius was the first person in Chinese history thus to teach large numbers of students in a private capacity, by whom he was accompanied during his travels in different states. According to tradition, he had several thousand students, of whom several tens became famous thinkers and scholars. The former number is undoubtedly a gross exaggeration, but there is no question that he was a very influential teacher, and what is more important and unique, China's first private teacher. His ideas are best known through the *Lun Yü* or Confucian *Analects,* a collection of his scattered sayings which was compiled by some of his disciples.

Confucius was a *ju* and the founder of the *Ju* school, which has been known in the West as the Confucian school. . . . Liu Hsin wrote regarding this school that it "delighted in the study of the *Liu Yi* and emphasized matters concerning human-heartedness and righteous-

ness." The term *Liu Yi* means the "six arts," i.e., the six liberal arts, but it is more commonly translated as the "Six Classics." These are the *Yi* or *Book of Changes,* the *Shih* or *Book of Odes* (or *Poetry*), the *Shu* or *Book of History,* the *Li* or *Rituals* or *Rites,* the *Yüeh* or *Music* (no longer preserved as a separate work), and the *Ch'un Ch'iu* or *Spring and Autumn Annals,* a chronicle history of Confucius' state of Lu extending from 722 to 479 B.C., the year of Confucius' death. The nature of these classics is clear from their titles, with the exception of the *Book of Changes*. This work was in later times interpreted by the Confucianists as a treatise on metaphysics, but originally it was a book of divination.

Concerning the relation of Confucius with the Six Classics, there are two schools of traditional scholarship. One maintains that Confucius was the author of all these works, while the other maintains that Confucius was the author of the *Spring and Autumn Annals,* the commentator of the *Book of Changes,* the reformer of the *Rituals* and *Music,* and the editor of the *Book of History* and *Book of Odes*.

As a matter of fact, however, Confucius was neither the author, commentator, nor even editor of any of the classics. In some respects, to be sure, he was a conservative who upheld tradition. Thus in the rites and music he did try to rectify any deviations from the traditional practices or standards, and instances of so doing are reported in the *Lun Yü* or *Analects*. Judging from what is said of him in the *Analects,* however, Confucius never had any intention of writing anything himself for future generations. The writing of books in a private rather than official capacity was an as yet unheard of practice which developed only after the time of Confucius. He was China's first private teacher, but not its first private writer.

The Six Classics had existed before the time of Confucius, and they constituted the cultural legacy of the past. They had been the basis of education for the aristocrats during the early centuries of feudalism of the Chou dynasty. As feudalism began to disintegrate, however, roughly from the seventh century B.C. onward, the tutors of the aristocrats, or even some of the aristocrats themselves—men who had lost their positions and titles but were well versed in the Classics— began to scatter among the people. They made their living, as we have seen in the last chapter, by teaching the Classics or by acting as skilled "assistants," well versed in the rituals, on the occasion of funeral, sacrifice, wedding, and other ceremonies. This class of men was known as the *ju* or literati.

Confucius as an Educator

Confucius, however, was more than a *ju* in the common sense of the word. It is true that in the *Analects*

38

we find him, from one point of view, being portrayed merely as an educator. He wanted his disciples to be "rounded men" who would be useful to state and society, and therefore he taught them various branches of knowledge based upon the different classics. His primary function as a teacher, he felt, was to interpret to his disciples the ancient cultural heritage. That is why, in his own words as recorded in the *Analects,* he was "a transmitter and not an originator." (*Analects,* VII, 1.) But this is only one aspect of Confucius, and there is another one as well. This is that, while transmitting the traditional institutions and ideas, Confucius gave them interpretations derived from his own moral concepts. This is exemplified in his interpretation of the old custom that on the death of a parent, a son should mourn three years. Confucius commented on this: "The child cannot leave the arms of its parents until it is three years old. This is why the three years' mourning is universally observed throughout the world." (*Analects,* XVII, 21.) In other words, the son was utterly dependent upon his parents for at least the first three years of his life; hence upon their death he should mourn them for an equal length of time in order to express his gratitude. Likewise when teaching the Classics, Confucius gave them new interpretations. Thus in speaking of the *Book of Poetry,* he stressed its moral value by saying: "In the *Book of Poetry* there are three hundred poems. But the essence of them can be covered in one sentence: 'Have no depraved thoughts.'" (*Analects,* II, 2.) In this way Confucius was more than a mere transmitter, for in transmitting, he originated something new.

This spirit of originating through transmitting was perpetuated by the followers of Confucius, by whom, as the classical texts were handed down from generation to generation, countless commentaries and interpretations were written. A great portion of what in later times came to be known as the Thirteen Classics developed as commentaries in this way on the original texts.

This is what set Confucius apart from the ordinary literati of his time, and made him the founder of a new school. Because the followers of this school were at the same time scholars and specialists on the Six Classics, the school became known as the School of the Literati.

The Rectification of Names

Besides the new interpretations which Confucius gave to the classics, he had his own ideas about the individual and society, heaven and man.

In regard to society, he held that in order to have a well-ordered one, the most important thing is to carry out what he called the rectification of names. That is, things in actual fact should be made to accord with the implication attached to them by names. Once a disciple asked him what he would do first if he were to rule a state, whereupon Confucius replied: "The one thing needed first is the rectification of names." (*Analects,* XIII, 3.) On another occasion one of the dukes of the time asked Confucius the right principle of government, to which he answered: "Let the ruler be ruler, the minister minister, the father father, and the son son." (*Analects,* XII, 11.) In other words, every name contains certain implications which constitute the essence of that class of things to which this name applies. Such things, therefore, should agree with this ideal essence. The essence of a ruler is what the ruler ideally ought to be, or what, in Chinese, is called "the way of the ruler." If a ruler acts according to this way of the ruler, he is then truly a ruler, in fact as well as in name. There is an agreement between name and actuality. But if he does not, he is no ruler, even though he may popularly be regarded as such. Every name in the social relationships implies certain responsibilities and duties. Ruler, minister, father, and son are all the names of such social relationships, and the individuals bearing these names must fulfill their responsibilities and duties accordingly. Such is the implication of Confucius' theory of the rectification of names.

Human-heartedness and Righteousness

With regard to the virtues of the individual, Confucius emphasized human-heartedness and righteousness, especially the former. Righteousness (*yi*) means the "oughtness" of a situation. It is a categorical imperative. Every one in society has certain things which he ought to do, and which must be done for their own sake, because they are the morally right things to do. If, however, he does them only because of other non-moral considerations, then even though he does what he ought to do, his action is no longer a righteous one. To use a word often disparaged by Confucius and later Confucianists, he is then acting for "profit." *Yi* (righteousness) and *li* (profit) are in Confucianism diametrically opposed terms. Confucius himself says: "The superior man comprehends *yi;* the small man comprehends *li*." (*Analects,* IV, 16.) Herein lies what the later Confucianists called the "distinction between *yi* and *li*," a distinction which they considered to be of the utmost importance in moral teaching.

The idea of *yi* is rather formal, but that of *jen* (human-heartedness) is much more concrete. The formal essence of the duties of man in society is their "oughtness," because all these duties are what he ought to do. But the material essence of these duties is "loving others," i.e., *jen* or human-heartedness. The father acts according to the way a father should act who loves his son; the son acts according to the way a son should act who loves his father. Confucius says: "Human-heartedness consists in loving others." (*Analects,* XII, 22.) The man who really loves others is one able to perform his duties in society. Hence in the *Analects* we see that Confucius sometimes uses the word *jen* not only to denote a special kind of virtue, but also to denote all the virtues combined, so that the term "man of *jen*" becomes synonymous with the man of all-round virtue. In such contexts, *jen* can be translated as "perfect virtue."

Chung *and* Shu

In the *Analects* we find the passage: "When Chung Kung asked the meaning of *jen,* the master said: . . . 'Do not do to others what you do not wish yourself. . . . '" (XII, 2.) Again, Confucius is reported in the *Analects* as saying: "The man of *jen* is one who, desiring to sustain himself, sustains others, and desiring to develop himself, develops others. To be able from one's own self to draw a parallel for the treatment of others; that may be called the way to practise *jen*." (VI, 28.)

Thus the practice of *jen* consists in consideration for others. "Desiring to sustain oneself, one sustains others; desiring to develop oneself, one develops others." In other words: "Do to others what you wish yourself." This is the positive aspect of the practice, which was called by Confucius *chung* or "conscientiousness to others." And the negative aspect, which was called by Confucius *shu* or "altruism," is: "Do not do to others what you do not wish yourself." The practice as a whole is called the principle of *chung* and *shu,* which is "the way to practice *jen*."

This principle was known by some of the later Confucianists as the "principle of applying a measuring square." That is to say, it is a principle by which one uses oneself as a standard to regulate one's conduct. In the *Ta Hsüeh* or *Great Learning,* which is a chapter of the *Li Chi* (*Book of Rites*), a collection of treatises written by the Confucianists in the third and second centuries B.C., it is said: "Do not use what you dislike in your superiors in the employment of your inferiors. Do not use what you dislike in your inferiors in the service of your superiors. Do not use what you dislike in those who are before, to precede those who are behind. Do not use what you dislike in those who are behind, to follow those who are before. Do not use what you dislike on the right, to display toward the left. Do not use what you dislike on the left, to display toward the right. This is called the principle of applying a measuring square."

In the *Chung Yung* or·*Doctrine of the Mean,* which is another chapter of the *Li Chi,* attributed to Tzu-ssu, the grandson of Confucius, it is said: "*Chung* and *shu* are not far from the Way. What you do not like done to yourself, do not do to others. . . . Serve your father as you would require your son to serve you. . . . Serve your ruler as you would require your subordinate to serve you. . . . Serve your elder brother as you would require your younger brother to serve you. . . . Set the example in behaving to your friends as you would require them to behave to you. . . . "

The illustration given in the *Great Learning* emphasizes the negative aspect of the principle of *chung* and *shu;* that in the *Doctrine of the Mean* emphasizes its positive aspect. In each case the "measuring square" for determining conduct is in one's self and not in other things.

The principle of *chung* and *shu* is at the same time the principle of *jen,* so that the practice of *chung* and *shu* means the practice of *jen.* And this practice leads to the carrying out of one's responsibilities and duties in society, in which is comprised the quality of *yi* or righteousness. Hence the principle of *chung* and *shu* becomes the alpha and omega of one's moral life. In the *Analects* we find the passage: "The master said: 'Shen [the personal name of Tseng Tzu, one of his disciples], all my teachings are linked together by one principle.' 'Quite so,' replied Tseng Tzu. When the master had left the room, the disciples asked: 'What did he mean?' Tseng Tzu replied: 'Our master's teaching consists of the principle of *chung* and *shu,* and that is all.'" (IV, 15.)

Everyone has within himself the "measuring square" for conduct, and can use it at any time. So simple as this is the method of practising *jen,* so that Confucius said: "Is *jen* indeed far off? I crave for *jen,* and lo! *jen* is at hand!" (*Analects,* VII, 29.)

Knowing Ming

From the idea of righteousness, the Confucianists derived the idea of "doing for nothing." One does what one ought to do, simply because it is morally right to do it, and not for any consideration external to this moral compulsion. In the *Analects,* we are told that Confucius was ridiculed by a certain recluse as "one who knows that he cannot succeed, yet keeps on trying to do it." (XIV, 41.) We also read that another recluse was told by a disciple of Confucius: "The reason why the superior man tries to go into politics, is because he holds this to be right, even though he is well aware that his principle cannot prevail." (XVIII, 7.)

As we shall see, the Taoists taught the theory of *"doing nothing,"* whereas the Confucianists taught that of *"doing for nothing."* A man cannot do nothing, according to Confucianism, because for every man there is something which he ought to do. Nevertheless, what he does is "for nothing," because the value of doing what he ought to do lies in the doing itself, and not in the external result.

Confucius' own life is certainly a good example of this teaching. Living in an age of great social and political disorder, he tried his best to reform the world. He traveled everywhere and, like Socrates, talked to everybody. Although his efforts were in vain, he was never disappointed. He knew that he could not succeed, but kept on trying.

About himself Confucius said: "If my principles are to prevail in the world, it is *Ming*. If they are to fall to the ground, it is also *Ming*." (*Analects,* XIV, 38). He tried his best, but the issue he left to *Ming*. *Ming* is often translated as Fate, Destiny or Decree. To Confucius, it meant the Decree of Heaven or Will of Heaven; in other words, it was conceived of as a purposeful force. In later Confucianism, however, *Ming* simply means the total existent conditions and forces of the whole universe. For the external success of our activity, the cooperation of these conditions is always needed. But this cooperation is wholly beyond our control. Hence the best thing for us to do is simply to try to carry out what we know we ought to carry out, without caring whether in the process we succeed or fail. To act in this way is "to know *Ming*." To know *Ming* is an important requirement for being a superior man in the Confucian sense of the term, so that Confucius said: "He who does not know *Ming* cannot be a superior man." (*Analects,* XX, 2.)

Thus to know *Ming* means to acknowledge the inevitability of the world as it exists, and so to disregard one's external success or failure. If we can act in this way, we can, in a sense, never fail. For if we do our duty, that duty through our very act is morally done, regardless of the external success or failure of our action.

As a result, we always shall be free from anxiety as to success or fear as to failure, and so shall be happy. This is why Confucius said: "The wise are free from doubts; the virtuous from anxiety; the brave from fear." (*Analects,* IX, 28.) Or again: "The superior man is always happy; the small man sad." (VII, 36.)

Confucius' Spiritual Development

In the Taoist work, the *Chuang-tzu,* we see that the Taoists often ridiculed Confucius as one who confined himself to the morality of human-heartedness and righteousness, thus being conscious only of moral values, and not super-moral value. Superficially they were right, but actually they were wrong. Thus speaking about his own spiritual development, Confucius said: "At fifteen I set my heart on learning. At thirty I could stand. At forty I had no doubts. At fifty I knew the Decree of Heaven. At sixty I was already obedient [to this Decree]. At seventy I could follow the desires of my mind without overstepping the boundaries [of what is right]." (*Analects,* II, 4.)

The "learning" which Confucius here refers to is not what we now would call learning. In the *Analects,* Confucius said: "Set your heart on the *Tao*." (VII, 6.) And again: "To hear the *Tao* in the morning and then die at night, that would be all right." (IV, 9.) Here *Tao* means the Way or Truth. It was this *Tao* which Confucius at fifteen set his heart upon learning. What we now call learning means the increase of our knowledge, but the *Tao* is that whereby we can elevate our mind.

Confucius also said: "Take your stand in the *li* [rituals, ceremonies, proper conduct]." (*Analects,* VIII, 8.) Again he said: "Not to know the *li* is to have no means of standing." (XX, 3.) Thus when Confucius says that at thirty he could "stand," he means that he then understood the *li* and so could practice proper conduct.

His statement that at forty he had no doubts means that he had then become a wise man. For, as quoted before, "The wise are free from doubts."

Up to this time of his life Confucius was perhaps conscious only of moral values. But at the age of fifty and sixty, he knew the Decree of Heaven and was obedient to it. In other words, he was then also conscious of super-moral values. Confucius in this respect was like Socrates. Socrates thought that he had been appointed by a divine order to awaken the Greeks, and Confucius had a similar consciousness of a divine mission. For example, when he was threatened with physical violence at a place called K'uang, he said: "If Heaven had wished to let civilization perish, later generations (like myself) would not have been permitted to participate in it. But since Heaven has not wished to let civilization perish, what can the people of K'uang do to me?" (*Analects,* IX, 5.) One of his contemporaries also said: "The world for long has been without order. But now Heaven is going to use the Master as an arousing tocsin." (*Analects,* III, 24.) Thus Confucius in doing what he did, was convinced that he was following the Decree of Heaven and was supported by Heaven; he was conscious of values higher than moral ones.

The super-moral value experienced by Confucius, however, was, as we shall see, not quite the same as that experienced by the Taoists. For the latter abandoned entirely the idea of an intelligent and purposeful Heaven, and sought instead for mystical union with an undifferentiated whole. The super-moral value which they knew and experienced, therefore, was freer from the ordinary concepts of the human relationships.

At seventy, as has been told above, Confucius allowed his mind to follow whatever it desired, yet everything he did was naturally right of itself. His actions no longer needed a conscious guide. He was acting without effort. This represents the last stage in the development of the sage.

Confucius' Position in Chinese History

Confucius is probably better known in the West than any other single Chinese. Yet in China itself, though always famous, his place in history has changed considerably from one period to another. Historically speaking he was primarily *a* teacher, that is, only one teacher among many. But after his death, he gradually came to be considered as *the* teacher, superior to all others. And in the second century B.C. he was elevated to an even higher plane. According to many Confucianists of that time, Confucius had actually been appointed by Heaven to begin a new dynasty that would follow that of Chou. Though in actual fact without a crown or a government, he had ideally speaking become a king who ruled the whole empire. How this apparent contradiction had happened, these Confucianists said, could be found out by studying the esoteric meaning supposedly contained in the **Spring and Autumn Annals.** This was supposed by them not to be a chronicle of Confucius' native state (as it actually was), but an important political work written by Confucius to express his ethical and political ideas. Then in the first century B.C., Confucius came to be regarded as even more than a king. According to many people of that time, he was a living god among men—a divine being who knew that after his time there would someday come the Han dynasty (206 B.C.-A.D. 220), and who therefore, in the **Spring and Autumn Annals,** set forth a political ideal which would be complete enough for the men of Han to realize. This apotheosis was the climax of Confucius' glory, and in the middle of the Han dynasty Confucianism could properly be called a religion.

The time of glorification, however, did not last very long. Already beginning in the first century A.D., Confucianists of a more rationalistic type began to get the upper hand. Hence in later times Confucius was no longer regarded as a divine being, though his position as that of *the* Teacher remained high. At the very end of the nineteenth century, to be sure, there was a brief revival of the theory that Confucius had been divinely appointed to be a king. Soon afterward, however, with the coming of the Chinese Republic, his reputation fell until he came to be regarded as something less than *the* Teacher, and at present most Chinese would say that he was primarily *a* teacher, and certainly a great one, but far from being the only teacher.

Confucius, however, was already recognized in his own day as a man of very extensive learning. For example, one of his contemporaries said: "Great indeed is the Master K'ung! His learning is so extensive that he cannot be called by a single name." (**Analects,** IX, 2.) From the quotations given earlier, we may see that he considered himself the inheritor and perpetuator of ancient civilization, and was considered by some of his contemporaries as such. By

his work of originating through transmitting, he caused his school to reinterpret the civilization of the age before him. He upheld what he considered to be best in the old, and created a powerful tradition that was followed until very recent years, when, as in Confucius' own time, China again came face to face with tremendous economic and social change. In addition, he was China's first teacher. Hence, though historically speaking he was only *a* teacher, it is perhaps not unreasonable that in later ages he was regarded as *the* teacher.

Liu Wu-chi (essay date 1955)

SOURCE: "K'ung Ch'iu, Founder of the Ju School," in *A Short History of Confucian Philolosophy,* 1955. Reprint by Hyperion Press, Inc., 1979, pp. 13-25.

[*In the following excerpt, Wu-chi focuses on the life and thought of Confucius and contends that Confucius's "greatness lies in his transforming the feudal code of rites and etiquette into a universal system of ethics."*]

Chapter One:

K'ung Ch'iu, Founder of the Ju School

1. *On the Greatness of Ju Philosophy—A Prelude*

The Ju philosophy that has dominated Chinese thought for the last twenty-five centuries had its beginning in the teachings of K'ung Ch'iu (551-479 B.C.), commonly known as Confucius, founder of the Ju school. Because of its long, eminent tradition, Ju philosophy also exerted the greatest influence on Chinese life. It moulded the national character; it touched every corner of human activity; it permeated life in all its aspects, whether moral, political, or social. It also gave continuity to a remarkable old civilization which, far from becoming extinct or stunted in its growth, showed rather a wonderful vitality in its struggle for survival and supremacy.

For one thing, the greatness of Ju philosophy is due to its power of adaptation. Phoenix-like, it has been constantly reborn and reorientated. Like the Chinese race, which conquered not by force, but by assimilation, the Ju philosophy also eliminated its rivals by virtue of absorption until all that was good and useful in the other doctrines became incorporated in its grand melting-pot, which was Chinese culture itself. Originally, these were separate systems of thought like Mohism, Legalism, Taoism, and Buddhism, but they were all pressed upon to contribute generously to the Ju stock, thus saving it from exhaustion.

As a result of this process of development, Ju philosophy to-day is just as different from the original teachings of K'ung Ch'iu as the latter is, for instance, from the teachings of Christ. To be sure, the words of K'ung Ch'iu still form the kernel of the Ju concept, but in the course of its evolution it has acquired so many novel ideas and interpretations that the main bulk of Ju philosophy to-day would be hardly recognizable to its great progenitor himself. This transformation, of course, was obviously healthy. Though there have been many complaints by the orthodox against this admixture of foreign elements, yet considered as a whole, these additions are really what gave impetus and animation to an ancient system of thought, which, but for these injections of new blood, would certainly have become anaemic long ago.

Important because of its tremendous impact upon Chinese life, the evolution of Ju philosophy is as complicated as it is interesting. To trace the various stages of this development and the main ideological trends with which it has come into contact is in fact to write a history of Chinese thought itself. But before we start on this long and arduous historical journey, let us pause first to have a look at the origin of the word Ju as well as at the Ju profession that flourished in the feudal society of the Chou period.

2. *Scholars or 'Weaklings'?*

In current usage, the word Ju means a scholar of the K'ung school. As such he is to be distinguished from the Buddhist or Taoist teacher, who holds an altogether different view of life. The close association between Ju and K'ung has also led Western writers, after they smugly transformed K'ung-fu-tz , or Master K'ung, to Confucius, to call the Ju teaching Confucianism and the Ju followers Confucianists. Though this is un-Chinese, yet in the sense that K'ung Ch'iu was the protagonist of the school, the translation is by no means entirely unacceptable.

But originally, there was also another meaning to the word Ju. Etymology tells us that Ju is a combination of two radicals, 'man' and 'weakness'. Hence the question naturally arises as to who these 'weaklings' were, if there was ever such a class of people. This is indeed a most intriguing question, to which, unfortunately, no clue has been given by the early Chinese writers. It is only in recent years that critics have begun to delve into the subject with apparently rich findings.

So far, two theories have been advanced.[1] According to the first, these 'weaklings' were actually descendants of the Shang people, whose dynasty had been overthrown by the Chou people in the twelfth century B.C. Being the survivors of a subjugated race, they extolled the virtue of weakness, or rather, the strength of weakness, as the best means of self-preservation. Degraded and dispossessed, but nevertheless rich in ceremonial knowledge, they made a living among their conquerors by assisting in funerals, marriages, and other occasions in the households of the Chou overlords. Because of their humble manners and occupation, so it is asserted, these Shang descendants earned for themselves the contemptible name of 'weaklings'.

Another theory, which we hold, is that these 'weaklings' were not the remnants of the once great but now degenerated Shang race, but disinherited members of the Chou aristocracy, who, in spite of their blue blood, had drifted into commonalty during the long centuries of the Chou dynasty. They were either offspring of the cadet branches of some noble family far removed from its great founder, or aristocrats who had been degraded into commoners. In either case, they had lost their rank and revenue as well as their special privileges. Though not as helpless as the ignorant peasants, who toiled all their lives on the soil, they were nevertheless so reduced in their circumstances that they had to employ whatever talents they might have acquired in the good old days to make a living. They thus became a new middle class between the patricians and the plebeians.

The number of such dispossessed nobles increased rapidly in the decades shortly before the advent of K'ung Ch'iu in the sixth century B.C. The feudal structure of Chou society built up by the great Duke of Chou[2] had been steadily crumbling since the removal of the Chou capital eastward to Lo in 770 B.C., but the process of deterioration did not assume alarming proportions until a century later. There emerged from this social transformation a new group of people, intelligent, resourceful, and eager to carve out a worthy career for themselves. But their inborn nobility and ambition notwithstanding, they were poor and powerless, and the best they could do was to become potential office-seekers.

What kind of talents did these people possess with which to earn a living? As former aristocrats, they must have been familiar with some or all of the six arts that were the hallmark of a noble education, namely, ceremonials and music, history (or writing) and numbers, archery and charioteering. As we can easily see, these were also good practical subjects, a knowledge of which would render a man useful to his feudal superiors. A knowledge of archery and charioteering, for instance, would qualify one to be a military commander or governor of a walled town, while a knowledge of writing and numbers would make one a good steward in the ministerial families. Likewise, as an expert in music and rituals, one could either become a tutor to the fledgling aristocrats or serve as a functionary on solemn ceremonial occasions. The rôles indeed were many in which these impoverished, disinherited nobles could employ their parts to advantage.

43

At the same time, their rank and file was further swelled by a large number of diviners, historiographers, and ceremonial and music masters, who were originally attached to the court, but who had lost their positions because of the dissolution of the feudal system and the decline and fall of the small principalities. Since their offices were formerly hereditary, they had been for many centuries custodians of Chinese culture, which, like the Promethean fire, had been jealously kept from the common people. But now, commoners themselves as a result of the great social upheaval, these forlorn intellectuals began to dole out their Olympian knowledge to all and sundry who had the means and the desire to learn. Thus was ushered in a new era noted for its wide diffusion of learning.

In the very beginning, we suspect, no name was given to this intellectual professional group. Apparently, their interests were greatly varied, and their jobs, now no longer hereditary, of a miscellaneous nature. No one word, indeed, could cover the multitudinous activities in which they were severally engaged. But for one of these professions a term had been coined, though it was by no means frequently used in K'ung Ch'iu's time. This was the word Ju, denoting a soft-spoken, genteel intellectual, whose job it was to assist at the ceremonies in the noble households. As the aristocratic society of the Chou period was extremely ritualistic, and its code of etiquette, known as *li,* highly elaborate, no ordinary man could conduct with propriety and proficiency such family ceremonies as capping and coiffure, marriage and funerals; or such stately entertainments as banqueting and archery contests; or the elaborate religious observances in the ancestral temples. Experts were needed for such occasions, and there soon appeared a group of people who specialized in all these branches of ritual and who were at the beck and call of any noble patron. To distinguish themselves, they were dressed in special costumes that bespoke their profession. Thus, wearing broad-sleeved robes girdled with silk sashes and trimmed with jade tablets, high round feather hats and square shoes, these men of *li* must have walked demurely, bowed deeply, and acted decorously—all of which earned for them the nickname of 'weaklings'.

3. *A Great Ju Rises in the East*

Just about this time there rose in Lu, one of the eastern states in the Chou kingdom, a remarkable young man by the name of K'ung Ch'iu. He was one of those disinherited nobles who claimed their ancestry from the ducal house of Sung, and thence from the fallen house of Shang. But by this time the royal blood had been so diluted that little of it was left in him except that which showed in the superior intelligence of the young man. This was in fact the only patrimony he had received from his great ancestors, or from his own father, a minor military official, who had died a few years after the boy's birth, leaving him and his mother to take care of themselves as best they could. Faced with the problem of making a living, young K'ung Ch'iu first took office as overseer of the granary and later of the herds.

This was in line with the tradition of his people, who, as dispossessed aristocrats, had to seek miscellaneous jobs for a living. Since he had had no formal instruction in the useful arts, what else could K'ung Ch'iu do but take up this mean employment? Just as his father before him had become an army officer, so K'ung Ch'iu became a state employee. As such, he was known to have been a hard, conscientious worker, who always kept a correct account of the grain and fed his oxen and sheep so well that they grew fat and strong and multiplied. It was no doubt in recognition of these services that, when a male child was born to K'ung Ch'iu, the Duke of Lu sent him the ceremonial present of a carp. One can well imagine the excitement which the gift created in the humble K'ung family. Indeed, in token of this great honour, the boy was named Li, or carp!

But, if circumstances had forced him to accept these petty positions, the ambitious and idealistic K'ung Ch'iu was by no means satisfied. He was looking forward to employment more congenial to his nature and worthier of his talents. The break came when his mother died and he was forced to go into seclusion for three years in accordance with the previaling custom. Great thoughts, it seems, were then agitating his breast, and he began to make preparations for launching out into a brave new world hitherto unexplored.

4. *The Brave New World of Education*

When at the age of thirty-four K'ung Ch'iu next emerged into public notice, he was already a distinguished teacher of ceremony. We know practically nothing about his life in the intervening years except that during this period he had been exploring all the avenues of learning in order to improve himself. There is no doubt, however, that he became, through sheer diligent study, an expert in the code of *li.* The period of mourning over, this self-made scholar soon started as a public teacher, gathering to his door young men interested in acquiring training for a profession. Even though his father had been an army officer and he himself was familiar with archery and charioteering, K'ung Ch'iu, it seems, did not include military science in his curriculum. What he taught was *li,* his main subject, as well as writing, numbers, and oratory. All these qualified his students for government jobs and stewardships in aristocratic households.

There was nothing startling in this educational programme. But what was original was the way in which K'ung Ch'iu enlisted his students. In former days there had been official teachers, whose duty it was to educate the scions of the overlords in the six arts. These hereditary pedagogues were part of the aristocratic appanage, and their learning was available only to the rulers and their sons. Besides, there might have been in K'ung Ch'iu's time private tutors who could be hired by anyone. But, to set up a sort of school for young men of all classes was something unheard of in history; at least, there is no record of such a practice before the sixth century B.C. It was a daring experiment first made by K'ung Ch'iu, and his success led to the rapid development of the system in the decades after him.

The new schoolmaster, moreover, was a man of great vision. Tuition, of course, he had to charge in order to carry on his work, but it was so nominal—just a bundle of dried meat—that it was within the means of the humblest. Scions of noble families, who were able to pay liberally, were welcome, but no intelligent young man who had the desire to learn ever found the door of the K'ung school closed to him. This democratic basis of admission was the more remarkable when we remember that K'ung Ch'iu lived in the feudal period when there was still a great dividing line between aristocracy and commonalty. But to K'ung Ch'iu, the first teacher, such distinctions did not exist; certainly, they were overlooked in his school-room. Very proudly he announced to his students: 'There is no class in education.'[3]

Master K'ung's educational policy being such, all sorts of young men flocked to his schoolroom. There was Tzǔ-lu, once a swashbuckling bravado, who died a loyal official and a martyr to the cause of *li*; there was Yen Hui, a poor but industrious scholar, who was satisfied with his bamboo bowl of rice and his gourd cup of water; there was Ssǔ-ma Niu, in constant fear of persecution by his elder brother, a wicked minister of Sung; there was Kung-yeh Ch'ang, who, while studying with the Master, was thrown into jail; there was Tsai-yü, who fell to day-dreaming during the Master's lecture; there was Fan Chi, who seemed to be more interested in gardening and farming than in literature and politics; there was Kung-hsi Chih, a ceremonial expert in the great ceremonial school; and many others from every walk of life, equally rich and diversified in their personality. What a galaxy of wits these were that enlivened the happy atmosphere of the K'ung school!

As a result of Master K'ung's indefatigable teaching, a number of his students became ritual experts, stewards of ministerial families, governors of walled towns, officials, courtiers, as well as teachers. By this time, K'ung Ch'iu, who had started as a teacher of ceremonies, had greatly widened his scope of instruction to include in his curriculum history and poetry, ethics and politics, all of which were essential to a successful public career. The importance of historical knowledge to government officials is readily understood; but, in those days, poetry too played a vital part in diplomatic intercourse, in which ancient odes were often quoted not only to show the speaker's good breeding, but also to illustrate and support by subtle implication the argument to be advanced. Especially among his younger students, both these subjects were studied with increasing interest, and the literary tradition of the K'ung school was thus established.

In the meantime, Master K'ung had grown more experienced in human affairs, just as he had become more advanced in learning. Desiring to study its culture at first hand, he had visited Lo, the Chou capital. There he had learned from Lao-tan, the great ceremonialist and keeper of the royal archives. Next, he had visited Ch'i, where he had become acquainted with its divine music, which so engrossed him that he is said to have forgotten the taste of meat for three months. He had also filled responsible administrative positions in Lu, first as magistrate, then as minister of crime and, possibly, as acting premier. He had taken part in the diplomatic conference between Ch'i and Lu, in which his supreme knowledge of ritual had won for his state a great moral triumph. Later, when he had had to give up his office in Lu, he had spent thirteen or fourteen years abroad, travelling, teaching, and visiting the feudal rulers of his time. When at last he was recalled to Lu, he was already an old man, an elder statesman, whose advice was constantly sought after by both the reigning duke and his chief minister. The humble overseer of herds, who had turned schoolmaster, was now the most honoured man in his native state; he was also the most learned scholar of the Chinese world.

5. A Happy Innovation

A new inspiration seized K'ung Ch'iu in the last years of his life. He must have then realized that his days were fast running short, and that, if he had successfully initiated a noble profession, he was by no means sure that his doctrines would be handed down intact through mere oral tradition. Something, it seemed, should be done to insure their preservation in future years. Hence, thoughts like these led ultimately to his becoming a literary editor and anthologist.

K'ung Ch'iu, an authority on Chou culture, was also its preserver. For many years he had industriously gathered all the literary materials that he could lay his hands on. In this attempt he was more than fortunate, for at that time many of the official documents formerly kept in the court archives and ancestral temples had begun to leak out to the public. In addition, he must have obtained a large part of his materials through his connexions with the feudal courts. In Lu, which had long been the centre of Chou culture, he had had direct access to valuable sources hitherto not available to the common people. His trip to the Chou capital must also have yielded a rich harvest, as undoubtedly did his visit to the other states. What he had collected, however, was mostly unedited material in bundles of bamboo tablets that had to be strung together with leather thongs. Books in the modern sense of the word did not exist; and Master K'ung, the pedagogue, soon became China's first book-maker.

K'ung Ch'iu's contribution to Chinese literature can never be over-estimated. He it was who first brought together the Chou classics under the name of his school. It is possible, of course, that portions of the *Classic of Poetry* and the *Classic of History* had been in circulation long before K'ung Ch'iu's time. But it is doubtful whether they ever existed in the form left to us by him, who was in this sense their 'sole begetter'.[4] To be sure, what he actually did was merely to collate and edit, but even so, this work that seems so conventional and simple to us, was in those days certainly an epoch-making innovation.

Unfortunately, Anthologist K'ung's labour on rituals and music has been lost to posterity. The *Record of Rites* that we have is a compilation of the Han dynasty, though it may retain much of the original material as well as many of the Master's observations on these subjects.

The *Classic of Change,* a manual of divination, said to have been written by King Wen, founder of the Chou dynasty, and the Duke of Chou, is probably the earliest Chinese book extant. Its mysterious contents seem to have fascinated K'ung Ch'iu in his last years, but his share in this work is rather uncertain. According to some critics, even the philosophical interpretation given it in the ten 'Wings' or 'Appendices' traditionally attributed to Master K'ung might have come from another pen.

So far, in all the works we have mentioned, K'ung Ch'iu was satisfied to play the rôle of a transmitter.[5] It was a great rôle without doubt, for what he transmitted was none other than the main bulk of ancient Chinese culture. But that was not all. To K'ung Ch'iu also belonged the honour of being the first Chinese author, a great honour indeed.

As a writer, K'ung Ch'iu is chiefly remembered for his *Spring and Autumn,* annals of Lu covering the reigns of its twelve dukes from 722-481 B.C. It was probably the last literary work that he undertook. As the first Chinese book written by a private individual,[6] it had an immense historical interest. As a matter of fact, K'ung Ch'iu himself entertained such a high opinion of this unprecedented adventure that he staked his reputation on it. Said he: 'If anyone recognizes my greatness in future generations, it will be because of the *Spring and Autumn.* If any one condemns me in fu-

ture generations, it will likewise be because of the *Spring and Autumn*.'[7]

Such being the author's opinion of the *Spring and Autumn,* it comes as a surprise that the book contains merely a list of dry, uninspiring entries under the reign of each of the twelve dukes. But we have an explanation for this. In K'ung Ch'iu's time the Chinese language, as we know, had not attained that flexibility, eloquence, and richness which characterize the historical and philosophical writings of a later period. K'ung Ch'iu's style, therefore, was simple, straightforward, and factual. This, too, was natural enough, because it was only the facts, the bare historical events of his native state and the confederated Chou world, in which he was primarily interested. But even here little credit was due to the writer, who did not first record these events, but took them from the official chronicles of Lu. Hence K'ung Ch'iu's originality consisted merely in his arrangement of the entries, his wording, his style, and his purpose, which was to use the past to mirror the present and the future.[8] If this first historical book by a private individual fails to meet our expectation as a great work of literature, we must bear in mind that it is after all only an innovation.

6. *Short of a Miracle: the Professionals turned Philosophers*

When K'ung Ch'iu died in 479 B.C. at the age of seventy-three, his mission of embodying in himself and his school the best of orthodox Chou culture had been accomplished. As we remember, he started his career as a ritual expert, vaguely known in those days as Ju, but soon became famous as a scholar of wide learning. Though a Ju by profession, he seemed to have used the word rather gingerly in his recorded sayings. In fact, only once did he mention it, and that was when he advised Tzŭ-hsia, one of his younger pupils, to become a noble, and not a lowly, Ju. Here, however, the meaning is somewhat equivocal. Since Tzŭ-hsia has never been known as a ritual practitioner, we might infer that the Master was using the word in the broader sense of a scholar rather than in its original sense of a mild-dispositioned man of *li*. Anyway, the Ju class, from which K'ung Ch'iu sprang, and of which he was the greatest representative, had been so closely identified with him that Ju and K'ung soon became synonymous. Meanwhile, the word Ju began to assume its new meaning, as Master K'ung had used it in reference to Tzŭ-hsia, as a scholar of the K'ung school. And, most important of all, amidst all these changes, a Ju philosophy had been developed.

It all came about like this. While basing his teaching on the authority of the sage kings of antiquity[9] and the orthodox feudal concepts of his time, K'ung Ch'iu, the great originator, soon evolved a new ethical and political philosophy of his own. In politics he contributed the idea of paternal government, in which the ruler should govern his people benevolently, as a patriarch his family. And just as a father is bound to his children by the tie of blood, which accounts for their attachment to one another, so should a prince be bound to his subjects by the same inalienable tie of love and kindness. Hence to a ruler the most important consideration was the welfare of the people. To summarize, according to Master K'ung, the three fundamental requirements of a state are that its sovereignty be safeguarded by adequate military strength, its welfare by sufficient food, and its government by the confidence of the people; of which the last is the most important. When we remember how the peasants of those days were oppressed by the autocratic rulers, we can see very well why Master K'ung's principle of benevolent government, though to us trite and old-fashioned, was, when viewed historically, highly significant.

But K'ung Ch'iu's real greatness lies in his transforming the feudal code of rites and etiquette into a universal system of ethics. It is wonderful that the humble practitioner of *li* should have become ultimately the greatest teacher of morality; but what is even more wonderful is that that morality, though 2,500 years old, is in its fundamental concept strikingly up to date and still aspiring. Here we are not referring to his observations on family relationship, which have failed to harmonize with modern trends owing to the great social changes of the past centuries. But what impresses us most is his lofty conception of the basic virtues of *chung* (faithfulness to oneself and others), *shu* (altruism), *jen* (human-heartedness), *yi* (righteousness), *li* (propriety), *chih* (wisdom), *hsin* (realness or sincerity), all of which the Master preached so forcibly and exemplified in himself so worthily that they have since become an ethical creed of the Chinese people. In fact, it was this insistence on man's moral cultivation, irrespective of rank and class, that has made K'ung Ch'iu such an immortal teacher. Thus, though living in the medieval society of the sixth century B.C., he was able to transcend the limitations of his age and profession to develop a far-reaching philosophy with moral perfection as its ultimate aim. As he himself had constantly asserted, he was all his life championing a way of life, or truth, which he called *tao;* and he would not be satisfied until it had been adopted by mankind.

The pursuit of this *tao* was therefore the greatest endeavour of Master K'ung's life. He also taught it to his pupils, no matter what personal ambitions they might have. In studying with him, they might seek training as ritual functionaries, family stewards, courtiers, governors, or teachers, but no one could leave the door of the K'ung school without being instilled with a lofty sense of morality. The Master's enthusiasm was so intense that a number of his devoted disciples were fired by it. Thus these men who had come to him to learn a profession turned out to be the torch-bearers of

a grand new philosophy, the Ju philosophy, whose ultimate achievement was the superior man.

Notes

[1] Page 15. For a discussion of this subject, see Hu Shih, 'On the Ju,' in his *Recent Essays on Learning* (Chinese), Shanghai, 1935, 3-102; Fung Yu-lan, *A History of Chinese Philosophy* (Chinese), II, Appendix, 1-61; Ch'ien Mu, *An Interlinking Chronology of the Ante-Ch'in Philosophers* (Chinese), 85-8, 92; and Ch'ien Mu, *An Outline of Chinese National History* (Chinese), Shanghai, 1948, I, 65-6.

[2] Page 15. The Duke of Chou (12th century B.C.), one of the great figures in ancient Chinese history, was highly praised by Master K'ung as a model statesman. He helped his father, King Wen, and his brother, King Wu, to establish the Chou dynasty and to institute the feudal system that lasted for many centuries.

[3] Page 19. *Lun-yü (The Analects)*, Bk XV, Ch. 38.

[4] Page 22. In the course of the Ch'in fire, as told later in Ch. VII, most of the K'ung classics were destroyed. But they were restored later by the Han scholars. It is believed that these Han versions are substantially the same as those handed down by Master K'ung himself.

[5] Page 22. Master K'ung once called himself a transmitter who believed in and loved the ancients. (*Lun-yü,* VII, 1.)

[6] Page 23. The *Chou Li (The Ritual of Chou)* was supposed to have been written by the Duke of Chou, but his authorship has been generally discredited by scholars, and the book itself is now considered as a much later work, probably at the time of the Warring States (5th-3rd century B.C.). Also of dubious origin are the *Kuan-tzŭ (The Works of Master Kuan)*, a Legalist book attributed to Kuan Chung, a great statesman of the 7th century B.C. and the *Tao Teh Ching (The Classic of Tao)*, attributed to Lao-tan, a senior contemporary of Master K'ung. After such elimination, the *Ch'un Ch'iu (Spring and Autumn)* becomes the first Chinese book written by a known author.

[7] Page 23. *Meng-tzŭ (The Works of Master Meng)*, Bk III, Pt ii, Ch. 9.

[8] Page 23. Cf. Meng K'o's somewhat exaggerated claim that 'When Master K'ung completed the *Spring and Autumn* rebellious ministers and villainous sons were struck with terror.' *Ibid.* These words, however, make a good testimony to the significance of the book which, though unimportant to us, had nevertheless a great influence in its time when the lessons of history it contains were still fresh in the minds of its readers.

[9] Page 24. For a list of the sage kings and their periods, see Appendix 1. All these kings were noted for their great virtue. Yao and Shun were model rulers who, instead of leaving the throne to their lineal descendants, yielded it to their sage ministers, i.e. Yao to Shun, and Shun to Yü. Yü, the founder of Hsia, the first Chinese dynasty, was the saviour of the Chinese people from a devastating flood that had overrun the land. When the last of the Hsia kings, who came to the throne some 400 years later, proved to be a tyrant, he was overthrown by the virtuous Tang, who established the Shang dynasty. Likewise, after some 600 years, the Shang came to an end during the reign of Chou Hsin, another tyrant, and it was succeeded by the Chou dynasty, whose founders, as we have already noted, were King Wen, King Wu, and the Duke of Chou. Some modern critics, however, doubt the existence of Yao, Shun, and Yü as well as the historicity of the Hsia dynasty. Still others believe that the entire story of these sage kings was invented by the Confucianists to give authority to their political teachings.

Wing-tsit Chan (essay date 1963)

SOURCE: "The Humanism of Confucius," in *A Sourcebook in Chinese Philosophy,* Princeton University Press, 1963, pp. 14-48.

[*In the following excerpt, Chan argues that Confucius's ideas on humanism greatly influenced the development of Chinese philosophy and that Confucius's belief in "the perfectibility of all men" radically altered the traditional concept of the "superior man."*]

Confucius (551-479 B.C.) can truly be said to have molded Chinese civilization in general. It may seem far-fetched, however, to say that he molded Chinese philosophy in particular—that he determined the direction or established the pattern of later Chinese philosophical developments—yet there is more truth in the statement than is usually realized.

Neo-Confucianism, the full flowering of Chinese thought, developed during the last eight hundred years. Its major topics of debate, especially in the Sung (960-1279) and Ming (1368-1644) periods, are the nature and principle (*li*) of man and things. (For this reason it is called the School of Nature and Principle, or *Hsing-li hsüeh*.) Supplementary to these topics are the problems of material force (*ch'i*); yin and yang (passive and active cosmic forces or elements); *T'ai-chi* (Great Ultimate); being and non-being; substance and function; and the unity of Nature and man. Confucius had nothing to do with these problems, and never discussed them. In fact, the words *li, yin, yang,* and *t'ai-chi* are not found in the **Lun-yü** (Discourses or **Analects**). The word *ch'i* appears several times, but is not used in the sense of material force.[1] And Confucius' pupils said that they could not hear the Master's views on human nature and the Way of Heaven.[2] He did not talk about human nature except once, when he said that "by nature men are alike. Through practice they have become far apart,"[3] but the theory is entirely different from the later orthodox doctrine of the Confucian school that human nature is originally good.

The present discussion is based on the **Analects,** which is generally accepted as the most reliable source of Confucius' doctrines. The subject of "the investigation of things" originated in the *Great Learning* and most of the other topics are mentioned in the **Book of Changes**. But these two Classics are not generally regarded as Confucius' own works. Furthermore, even if they were, the subjects are only briefly mentioned without elaboration. It is correct then to say that the Neo-Confucianists drew their inspiration from them or made use of them to support their own ideas, but it would be going too far to suggest that they provided an outline or framework for later Chinese philosophy.

However, judging on the basis of the **Analects** alone, we find that Confucius exerted great influence on Chinese philosophical development in that, first of all, he determined its outstanding characteristic, namely, humanism.

As pointed out in the previous chapter, the humanistic tendency had been in evidence long before his time. But it was Confucius who turned it into the strongest driving force in Chinese philosophy. He did not care to talk about spiritual beings or even about life after death. Instead, believing that man "can make the Way (Tao) great," and not that "the Way can make man great,"[4] he concentrated on man. His primary concern was a good society based on good government and harmonious human relations. To this end he advocated a good government that rules by virtue and moral example rather than by punishment or force. His criterion for goodness was righteousness as opposed to profit. For the family, he particularly stressed filial piety and for society in general, proper conduct or *li* (propriety, rites).

More specifically, he believed in the perfectibility of all men, and in this connection he radically modified a traditional concept, that of the *chün-tzu,* or superior man. Literally "son of the ruler," it came to acquire the meaning of "superior man," on the theory that nobility was a quality determined by status, more particularly a hereditary position. The term appears 107 times in the **Analects**. In some cases it refers to the ruler. In most cases, however, Confucius used it to denote a morally superior man. In other words, to him nobility was no longer a matter of blood, but of character—a concept that amounted to social revolution. Perhaps it is more correct to say that it was an evolution, but certainly it was Confucius who firmly established the new concept. His repeated mention of sage-emperors Yao and Shun and Duke Chou[5] as models seems to suggest that he was looking back to the past. Be that as it may, he was looking to ideal men rather than to a supernatural being for inspiration.

Not only did Confucius give Chinese philosophy its humanistic foundation, but he also formulated some of its fundamental concepts, five of which will be briefly commented on here: the rectification of names, the Mean, the Way, Heaven, and *jen* (humanity). In insisting on the rectification of names, Confucius was advocating not only the establishment of a social order in which names and ranks are properly regulated, but also the correspondence of words and action, or in its more philosophical aspect, the correspondence of name and actuality. This has been a perennial theme in the Confucian school, as well as in nearly all other schools. By the Mean, Confucius did not have in mind merely moderation, but that which is central and balanced. This, too, has been a cardinal idea in Chinese thought. In a real sense, the later Neo-Confucian ideas of the harmony of yin and yang and that of substance and function did not go beyond this concept. In his interpretation of Heaven, he departed from traditional belief even more radically. Up to the time of Confucius, the Supreme Power was called *Ti* (the Lord) or *Shang-ti* (the Lord on High) and was understood in an anthropomorphic sense. Confucius never spoke of *Ti*. Instead, he often spoke of *T'ien* (Heaven). To be sure, his Heaven is purposive and is the master of all things. He repeatedly referred to the *T'ien-ming,* the Mandate, will, or order of Heaven. However, with him Heaven is no longer the greatest of all spiritual beings who rules in a personal manner but a Supreme Being who only reigns, leaving his Moral Law to operate by itself. This is the Way according to which civilization should develop and men should behave. It is the Way of Heaven (*T'ien-tao*), later called the Principle of Heaven or Nature (*T'ien-li*).

Most important of all, he evolved the new concept of *jen* which was to become central in Chinese philosophy. All later discussions on principle and material force may be said to serve the purpose of helping man to realize jen.[6] The word *jen* is not found in the oracle bones. It is found only occasionally in pre-Confucian texts, and in all these cases it denotes the particular virtue of kindness, more especially the kindness of a ruler to his subjects. In Confucius, however, all this is greatly changed. In the first place, Confucius made *jen* the main theme of his conversations. In the **Analects** fifty-eight of 499 chapters are devoted to the discussion of *jen,* and the word appears ·105 times. No other subject, not even filial piety, engaged so much attention of the Master and his disciples. Furthermore, in-

stead of perpetuating the ancient understanding of *jen* as a particular virtue, he transformed it into general virtue. It is true that in a few cases *jen* is still used by Confucius as a particular virtue, in the sense of benevolence. But in most cases, to Confucius the man of *jen* is the perfect man. He is the true *chün-tzu*. He is a man of the golden rule, for, "wishing to establish his own character, he also establishes the character of others, and wishing to be prominent himself, he also helps others to be prominent."[7] In these balanced and harmonized aspects of the self and society, *jen* is expressed in terms of *chung* and *shu,* or conscientiousness and altruism, which is the "one thread" running through Confucius' teachings, and which is in essence the golden mean as well as the golden rule. It was the extension of this idea of *jen* that became the Neo-Confucian doctrine of man's forming one body with Heaven, or the unity of man and Nature, and it was because of the character of *jen* in man that later Confucianists have adhered to the theory of the original good nature of man.

It is clear, therefore, that Confucius was a creator as well as a transmitter. He was not a philosopher in a technical sense, but Chinese philosophy would be quite different if he had not lived. He was born in 551 (or 552) B.C. in the state of Lu in modern Shantung. His family name was K'ung, private name Ch'iu, and he has been traditionally honored as Grand Master K'ung (K'ung Fu-tzu, hence the Latinized form Confucius). He was a descendant of a noble but fairly poor family. His father died when Confucius was probably three years old. Evidently a self-made man, he studied under no particular teacher but became perhaps the most learned man of his time.

He began his career in his twenties or thirties. He was the first person in Chinese history to devote his whole life, almost exclusively, to teaching. He sought to inaugurate private education, to open the door of education to all, to offer education for training character instead of for vocation, and to gather around him a group of gentlemen-scholars (thus starting the institution of the literati who have dominated Chinese history and society).

In his younger years Confucius had served in minor posts in Lu. At fifty-one he was made a magistrate, and became minister of justice the same year, perhaps serving as an assistant minister of public works in between. At fifty-four, finding his superiors uninterested in his policies, he set out to travel (for almost fourteen years) in a desperate attempt at political and social reform. He took some of his pupils along with him. Eventually disappointed, he returned, at the age of sixty-eight, to his own state to teach and perhaps to write and edit the Classics. According to the *Shih chi* (Records of the Historian),[8] he had three thousand pupils, seventy-two of whom mastered the "six arts."[9] He died at the age of seventy-three.

Many Chinese scholars, especially in the last several decades, have debated such questions as whether he actually made a trip some time in his forties to see Lao Tzu to inquire about ancient rites and ceremonies, whether he wrote the ***Ch'un-ch'iu (Spring and Autumn Annals),*** edited the other ancient Classics, and wrote the "ten wings" or commentaries of one of them, namely, the ***Book of Changes***. After having once rejected these claims, many scholars are now inclined to believe them. The controversy has by no means ended. At the same time, the fact that the ***Analects*** is the most reliable source of Confucius' teachings is accepted by practically all scholars. For this reason, the following selections are made entirely from this book.

> Ceremonies and Music: 1:12; 2:5; 3:3-4, 17, 19; 6:25; 8:8
>
> Confucius: 2:4; 5:25; 6:26; 7:1, 2, 7, 8, 16, 18-20, 37; 9:1, 4; 10:9, 14; 14:30, 37, 41; 18:6; 19:24
>
> Education and Learning: 1:1, 6, 8, 14; 2:11, 15; 6:25; 7:7, 8, 24; 16:9; 17:8; 19:6
>
> Filial piety: 1:2, 6, 11; 2:5, 7; 4:18, 19, 21
>
> Government: 2:1, 3; 3:19; 8:9, 14; 12:7, 11, 17, 19; 13:3, 6, 16, 29, 30; 14:45; 15:4; 16:1
>
> Heaven, Spirits, Destiny: 2:4; 3:12, 13; 5:12; 6:20, 26; 7:20, 22, 34; 9:1, 5, 6; 11:8, 11; 12:5; 14:37; 16:8; 17:19
>
> Humanism: 6:20; 10:12; 12:22; 15:28; 18:6
>
> Humanity (*jen*): 1:2, 3, 6; 3:3; 4:2-6; 6:20, 21, 28; 7:6, 29; 8:7; 12:1, 2, 22; 13:19, 27; 14:30; 15:8, 32, 35; 17:6, 8; 19:6
>
> Knowledge and Wisdom: 2:17, 18; 4:2; 6:18, 20, 21; 7:27; 12:22; 14:30; 15:32; 16:9
>
> Literature and Art: 1:15; 6:25; 7:6; 8:8; 9:5; 15:40; 17:9
>
> Love and Golden rule: 4:2, 15; 5:11; 6:28; 12:2, 5; 14:36, 45; 17:4
>
> Mean and Central thread: 4:15; 15:2
>
> Nature, human: 5:12; 6:17, 19; 16:9; 17:2, 3
>
> Rectification of names: 12:11, 17; 13:3, 6
>
> Righteousness: 2:24; 4:16; 13:3, 6; 15:17
>
> Superior man: 1:2, 8, 14; 2:11, 13; 4:5, 24; 6:16; 9:13; 13:3; 14:30; 15:17, 20, 31; 16:8, 10; contrasted with inferior man: 2:14; 4:11, 16; 8:6; 12:16; 13:23, 26; 14:24; 15:20; 17:23
>
> Virtue: 1:4, 6, 8; 4:12; 7:6; 8:5, 7, 13; 9:4; 13:18, 19; 14:33; 15:8, 17; 16:4, 10; 17:6, 8
>
> Way (Tao): 4:5, 8; 7:6; 15:28, 31; 17:4
>
> Words and Acts: 2:13, 18; 4:24; 13:3; 14:29

THE ANALECTS[10]

1:1. Confucius said, "Is it not a pleasure to learn and to repeat or practice from time to time what has been learned? Is it not delightful to have friends coming from afar? Is one not a superior man if he does not feel hurt even though he is not recognized?" *Comment.* Interpretations of Confucian teachings have differed radically in the last 2,000 years. Generally speaking, Han (206 B.C.-A.D. 220) scholars, represented in Ho Yen (d. 249), *Lun-yü chi-chieh* (Collected Explanations of the *Analects*),[11] were inclined to be literal and interested in historical facts, whereas Neo-Confucianists, represented in Chu Hsi (1130-1200), *Lun-yü chi-chu* (Collected Commentaries on the *Analects*) were interpretative, philosophical, and often subjective. They almost invariably understand the Confucian Way (Tao) as principle (*li*), which is their cardinal concept, and frequently when they came to an undefined "this" or "it," they insisted that it meant principle. This divergency between the Han and Sung scholars has colored interpretations of this passage. To Wang Su (195-265), quoted in Ho, *hsi* (to learn) means to recite a lesson repeatedly. To Chu Hsi, however, *hsi* means to follow the examples of those who are first to understand, and therefore it does not mean recitation but practice. In revolt against both extremes, Ch'ing (1644-1912) scholars emphasized practical experience. In this case, *hsi* to them means both to repeat and to practice, as indicated in Liu Pao-nan (1791-1855), *Lun-yü cheng-i* (Correct Meanings of the *Analects*). Thus Ho Yen, Chu Hsi, and Liu Pao-nan neatly represent the three different approaches in the three different periods. Generally speaking, the dominant spirit of Confucian teaching is the equal emphasis on knowledge and action. This dual emphasis will be encountered again and again.[12]

1:2. Yu Tzu[13] said, "Few of those who are filial sons and respectful brothers will show disrespect to superiors, and there has never been a man who is not disrespectful to superiors and yet creates disorder. A superior man is devoted to the fundamentals (the root). When the root is firmly established, the moral law (Tao) will grow. Filial piety and brotherly respect are the root of humanity (*jen*)."

1:3. Confucius said, "A man with clever words and an ingratiating appearance is seldom a man of humanity."[14]

1:4. Tseng-Tzu[15] said, "Every day I examine myself on three points: whether in counseling others I have not been loyal; whether in intercourse with my friends I have not been faithful; and whether I have not repeated again and again and practiced the instructions of my teacher."[16]

1:6. Young men should be filial when at home and respectful to their elders when away from home. They should be earnest and faithful. They should love all extensively and be intimate with men of humanity. When they have any energy to spare after the performance of moral duties, they should use it to study literature and the arts (*wen*).[17]

1:8. Confucius said, "If the superior man is not grave, he will not inspire awe, and his learning will not be on a firm foundation.[18] Hold loyalty and faithfulness to be fundamental. Have no friends who are not as good as yourself. When you have made mistakes, don't be afraid to correct them."

> *Comment.* The teaching about friendship here is clearly inconsistent with *Analects,* 8:5, where Confucius exhorts us to learn from inferiors. It is difficult to believe that Confucius taught people to be selfish. According to Hsing Ping (932-1010),[19] Confucius meant people who are not equal to oneself in loyalty and faithfulness, assuming that one is or should be loyal and faithful; according to Hsü Kan (171-218), Confucius simply wanted us to be careful in choosing friends.[20]

1:11. Confucius said, "When a man's father is alive, look at the bent of his will. When his father is dead, look at his conduct. If for three years [of mourning] he does not change from the way of his father, he may be called filial."

> *Comment.* Critics of Confucius have asserted that Confucian authoritarianism holds an oppressive weight on the son even after the father has passed away. Fan Tsu-yü (1041-1098) did understand the saying to mean that the son should observe the father's will and past conduct,[21] but he was almost alone in this. All prominent commentators, from K'ung An-kuo to Cheng Hsüan (127-200),[22] Chu Hsi, and Liu Pao-nan have interpreted the passage to mean that while one's father is alive, one's action is restricted, so that his *intention* should be the criterion by which his character is to be judged. After his father's death, however, when he is completely autonomous, he should be judged by his conduct. In this interpretation, the way of the father is of course the moral principle which has guided or should have guided the son's conduct.

1:12. Yu Tzu said, "Among the functions of propriety (*li*) the most valuable is that it establishes harmony. The excellence of the ways of ancient kings consists of this. It is the guiding principle of all things great and small. If things go amiss, and you, understanding harmony, try to achieve it without regulating it by the rules of propriety, they will still go amiss."

1:14. Confucius said, "The superior man does not seek fulfillment of his appetite nor comfort in his lodging. He is diligent in his duties and careful in his speech. He associates with men of moral principles and thereby

realizes himself. Such a person may be said to love learning."

1:15. Tzu-kung[23] said, "What do you think of a man who is poor and yet does not flatter, and the rich man who is not proud?" Confucius replied, "They will do. But they are not as good as the poor man who is happy[24] and the rich man who loves the rules of propriety (*li*)." Tzu-kung said, "***The Book of Odes*** says:

> As a thing is cut and filed,
> As a thing is carved and polished. . . . [25]

Does that not mean what you have just said?"

Confucius said, "Ah! Tz'u. Now I can begin to talk about the odes with you. When I have told you what has gone before, you know what is to follow."

1:16. Confucius said, "[A good man] does not worry about not being known by others but rather worries about not knowing them."[26]

2:1. Confucius said, "A ruler who governs his state by virtue is like the north polar star, which remains in its place while all the other stars revolve around it."

> *Comment.* Two important principles are involved here. One is government by virtue, in which Confucianists stand directly opposed to the Legalists, who prefer law and force. The other is government through inaction, i.e., government in such excellent order that all things operate by themselves. This is the interpretation shared by Han and Sung Confucianists alike.[27] In both cases, Confucianism and Taoism are in agreement.[28]

2:2. Confucius said, "All three hundred odes can be covered by one of their sentences, and that is, 'Have no depraved thoughts.'"[29]

2:3. Confucius said, "Lead the people with governmental measures and regulate them by law and punishment, and they will avoid wrongdoing but will have no sense of honor and shame. Lead them with virtue and regulate them by the rules of propriety (*li*), and they will have a sense of shame and, moreover, set themselves right."[30]

2:4. Confucius said, "At fifteen my mind was set on learning. At thirty my character had been formed. At forty I had no more perplexities. At fifty I knew the Mandate of Heaven (*T'ien-ming*). At sixty I was at ease with whatever I heard. At seventy I could follow my heart's desire without transgressing moral principles."

> *Comment.* What *T'ien-ming* is depends upon one's own philosophy. In general, Confucianists before the

T'ang dynasty (618-907) understood it to mean either the decree of God, which determines the course of one's life, or the rise and fall of the moral order,[31] whereas Sung scholars, especially Chu Hsi, took it to mean "the operation of Nature which is endowed in things and makes things be as they are."[32] This latter interpretation has prevailed. The concept of *T'ien-ming* which can mean Mandate of Heaven, decree of God, personal destiny, and course of order, is extremely important in the history of Chinese thought. In religion it generally means fate or personal order of God, but in philosophy it is practically always understood as moral destiny, natural endowment, or moral order.

2:5. Meng I Tzu[33] asked about filial piety. Confucius said: "Never disobey." [Later,] when Fan Ch'ih[34] was driving him, Confucius told him, "Meng-sun asked me about filial piety, and I answered him, 'Never disobey.'"[35] Fan Ch'ih said, "What does that mean?" Confucius said, "When parents are alive, serve them according to the rules of propriety. When they die, bury them according to the rules of propriety and sacrifice to them according to the rules of propriety."

2:6. Meng Wu-po[36] asked about filial piety. Confucius said, "Especially be anxious lest parents should be sick."[37]

2:7. Tzu-yu[38] asked about filial piety. Confucius said, "Filial piety nowadays means to be able to support one's parents. But we support even dogs and horses.[39] If there is no feeling of reverence, wherein lies the difference?"

2:11. Confucius said, "A man who reviews the old so as to find out the new is qualified to teach others."

2:12. Confucius said, "The superior man is not an implement (*ch'i*)."[40]

> *Comment.* A good and educated man should not be like an implement, which is intended only for a narrow and specific purpose. Instead, he should have broad vision, wide interests, and sufficient ability to do many things.[41]

2:13. Tzu-kung asked about the superior man. Confucius said, "He acts before he speaks and then speaks according to his action."[42]

2:14. Confucius said, "The superior man is broadminded but not partisan; the inferior man is partisan but not broadminded."

2:15. Confucius said, "He who learns but does not think is lost; he who thinks but does not learn is in danger."

2:17. Confucius said, "Yu,[43] shall I teach you [the way to acquire] knowledge?[44] To say that you know when you do know and say that you do not know when you do not know—that is [the way to acquire] knowledge."

2:18. Tzu-chang[45] was learning with a view to official emolument. Confucius said, "Hear much and put aside what's doubtful while you speak cautiously of the rest. Then few will blame you. See much and put aside what seems perilous while you are cautious in carrying the rest into practice. Then you will have few occasions for regret. When one's words give few occasions for blame and his acts give few occasions for repentance—there lies his emolument."

> *Comment.* The equal emphasis on words and deeds has been a strong tradition in Confucianism.[46] Eventually Wang Yang-ming identified them as one.[47]

2:24. Confucius said, "It is flattery to offer sacrifice to ancestral spirits other than one's own. To see what is right and not to do it is cowardice."

3:3. Confucius said, "If a man is not humane (*jen*), what has he to do with ceremonies (*li*)? If he is not humane, what has he to do with music?"

3:4. Lin Fang[48] asked about the foundation of ceremonies. Confucius said, "An important question indeed! In rituals or ceremonies, be thrifty rather than extravagant, and in funerals, be deeply sorrowful rather than shallow in sentiment."

3:12. When Confucius offered sacrifice to his ancestors, he felt as if his ancestral spirits were actually present. When he offered sacrifice to other spiritual beings, he felt as if they were actually present. He said, "If I do not participate in the sacrifice, it is as if I did not sacrifice at all."

3:13. Wang-sun Chia[49] asked, "What is meant by the common saying, 'It is better to be on good terms with the God of the Kitchen [who cooks our food] than with the spirits of the shrine (ancestors) at the southwest corner of the house'?" Confucius said, "It is not true. He who commits a sin against Heaven has no god to pray to."

3:17. Tzu-kung wanted to do away with the sacrificing of a lamb at the ceremony in which the beginning of each month is reported to ancestors. Confucius said, "Tz'u![50] You love the lamb but I love the ceremony."

3:19. Duke Ting[51] asked how the ruler should employ his ministers and how the ministers should serve their ruler. Confucius said, "A ruler should employ his ministers according to the principle of propriety, and ministers should serve their ruler with loyalty."

3:24. The guardian at I (a border post of the state of Wei) requested to be presented to Confucius, saying, "When gentlemen come here, I have never been prevented from seeing them." Confucius' followers introduced him. When he came out from the interview, he said, "Sirs, why are you disheartened by your master's loss of office? The Way has not prevailed in the world for a long time. Heaven is going to use your master as a wooden bell [to awaken the people]."

4:2. Confucius said, "One who is not a man of humanity cannot endure adversity for long, nor can he enjoy prosperity for long. The man of humanity is naturally at ease with humanity. The man of wisdom cultivates humanity for its advantage."

4:3. Confucius said, "Only the man of humanity knows how to love people and hate people."[52]

4:4. Confucius said, "If you set your mind on humanity, you will be free from evil."[53]

4:5. Confucius said, "Wealth and honor are what every man desires. But if they have been obtained in violation of moral principles, they must not be kept. Poverty and humble station are what every man dislikes. But if they can be avoided only in violation of moral principles, they must not be avoided. If a superior man departs from humanity, how can he fulfill that name? A superior man never abandons humanity even for the lapse of a single meal. In moments of haste, he acts according to it. In times of difficulty or confusion, he acts according to it."

4:6. Confucius said, "I have never seen one who really loves humanity or one who really hates inhumanity. One who really loves humanity will not place anything above it.[54] One who really hates inhumanity will practice humanity in such a way that inhumanity will have no chance to get at him. Is there any one who has devoted his strength to humanity for as long as a single day? I have not seen any one without sufficient strength to do so. Perhaps there is such a case, but I have never seen it."

4:8. Confucius said, "In the morning, hear the Way; in the evening, die content!"

4:10. Confucius said, "A superior man in dealing with the world is not for anything or against anything. He follows righteousness as the standard."

Comment. This is a clear expression of both the flexibility and rigidity of Confucian ethics—flexibility in application but rigidity in standard. Here lies the basic idea of the Confucian doctrine of *ching-ch'üan,* or the standard and the exceptional, the absolute and the relative, or the permanent and the temporary. This explains why Confucius was not obstinate,[55] had no predetermined course of action,[56] was ready to serve or to withdraw whenever it was proper to do so,[57] and, according to Mencius, was a sage who acted according to the circumstance of the time.[58]

The words *shih* and *mo* can be interpreted to mean being near to people and being distant from people, or opposing people and admiring people, respectively, and some commentators have adopted these interpretations.[59] But the majority follow Chu Hsi, as I have done here. Chu Hsi was thinking about the superior man's dealing with things. Chang Shih (Chang Nan-hsien, 1133-1180), on the other hand, thought Confucius was talking about the superior man's state of mind.[60] This difference reflects the opposition between the two wings of Neo-Confucianism, one inclining to activity, the other to the state of mind.[61]

4:11. Confucius said, "The superior man thinks of virtue; the inferior man thinks of possessions.[62] The superior man thinks of sanctions; the inferior man thinks of personal favors."

4:12. Confucius said, "If one's acts are motivated by profit, he will have many enemies."

4:15. Confucius said, "Ts'an,[63] there is one thread that runs through my doctrines." Tseng Tzu said, "Yes." After Confucius had left, the disciples asked him, "What did he mean?" Tseng Tzu replied, "The Way of our Master is none other than conscientiousness (*chung*) and altruism (*shu*)."

Comment. Confucian teachings may be summed up in the phrase "one thread" (*i-kuan*), but Confucianists have not agreed on what it means. Generally, Confucianists of Han and T'ang times adhered to the basic meaning of "thread" and understood it in the sense of a system or a body of doctrines. Chu Hsi, true to the spirit of Neo-Confucian speculative philosophy, took it to mean that there is one mind to respond to all things. In the Ch'ing period, in revolt against speculation, scholars preferred to interpret *kuan* as action and affairs, that is, there is only one moral principle for all actions.[64] All agree, however, on the meanings of *chung* and *shu,* which are best expressed by Chu Hsi, namely, *chung* means the full development of one's [originally good] mind and *shu* means the extension of that mind to others.[65] As Ch'eng I (Ch'eng I-ch'uan, 1033-1107) put it, *chung* is the Way of Heaven, whereas *shu* is the way of man; the former is substance, while the latter is function.[66] Liu Pao-nan is correct in equating *chung* with Confucius' saying, "Establish one's own character," and *shu* with "Also establish the character of others."[67] Here is the positive version of the Confucian golden rule. The negative version is only one side of it.[68]

4:16. Confucius said, "The superior man understands righteousness (*i*); the inferior man understands profit."

> *Comment.* Confucius contrasted the superior man and the inferior in many ways,[69] but this is the fundamental difference for Confucianism in general as well as for Confucius himself. Chu Hsi associated righteousness with the Principle of Nature (*T'ien-li*) and profit with the feelings of man, but later Neo-Confucianists strongly objected to his thus contrasting principle and feelings.

4:18. Confucius said, "In serving his parents, a son may gently remonstrate with them. When he sees that they are not inclined to listen to him, he should resume an attitude of reverence and not abandon his effort to serve them. He may feel worried, but does not complain."

4:19. Confucius said, "When his parents are alive, a son should not go far abroad; or if he does, he should let them know where he goes."

4:21. Confucius said, "A son should always keep in mind the age of his parents. It is an occasion for joy [that they are enjoying long life] and also an occasion for anxiety [that another year is gone]."

4:24. Confucius said, "The superior man wants to be slow in word but diligent in action."

5:11. Tzu-kung said, "What I do not want others to do to me, I do not want to do to them." Confucius said, "Ah Tz'u! That is beyond you."[70]

5:12. Tzu-kung said, "We can hear our Master's [views] on culture and its manifestation,[71] but we cannot hear his views on human nature[72] and the Way of Heaven [because these subjects are beyond the comprehension of most people]."

5:25. Yen Yüan[73] and Chi-lu[74] were in attendance. Confucius said, "Why don't you each tell me your ambition in life?" Tzu-lu said, "I wish to have a horse, a carriage, and a light fur coat[75] and share them with friends, and shall not regret if they are all worn out." Yen Yüan said, "I wish never to boast of my good qualities and never to brag about the trouble I have taken [for others]."[76] Tzu-lu said, "I wish to hear your ambition." Confucius said, "It is my ambition to comfort the old, to be faithful to friends, and to cherish the young."[77]

5:27. Confucius said, "In every hamlet of ten families, there are always some people as loyal and faithful as myself, but none who love learning as much as I do."

6:5. Confucius said, "About Hui (Yen Yüan), for three months there would be nothing in his mind contrary to humanity. The others could (or can) attain to this for a day or a month at the most."[78]

> *Comment.* On the basis of this saying alone, some philosophers have concluded that Yen Yüan was a mystic and that Confucius praised mysticism!

6:16. Confucius said, "When substance exceeds refinement (*wen*), one becomes rude. When refinement exceeds substance, one becomes urbane. It is only when one's substance and refinement are properly blended that he becomes a superior man."

6:17. Confucius said, "Man is born with uprightness. If one loses it he will be lucky if he escapes with his life."

> *Comment.* Although the Confucian tradition in general holds that human nature is originally good, Confucius' own position is not clear. We have read that his doctrine of nature could not be heard,[79] and we shall read his statement that by nature men are alike.[80] But how they are alike is not clear. The saying here can be interpreted to mean that man can live throughout life because he is upright. This is the interpretation of Ma Jung (79-166),[81] which is followed by Wang Ch'ung (27-100?).[82] Most people followed Chu Hsi. He had the authority of Ch'eng Hao (Ch'eng Ming-tao, 1032-1085),[83] who echoed Cheng Hsüan's interpretation that Confucius said that man is *born* upright. This means that Confucius was not only the first one in Chinese philosophy to assume a definite position about human nature, but also the first to teach that human nature is *originally* good.

6:18. Confucius said, "To know it [learning or the Way] is not as good as to love it, and to love it is not as good as to take delight in it."

6:19. Confucius said, "To those who are above average, one may talk of the higher things, but may not do so to those who are below average."

6:20. Fan Ch'ih asked about wisdom. Confucius said, "Devote yourself earnestly to the duties due to men, and respect spiritual beings[84] but keep them at a distance. This may be called wisdom." Fan Ch'ih asked about humanity. Confucius said, "The man of humanity first of all considers what is difficult in the task and then thinks of success. Such a man may be called humane."

> *Comment.* Many people have been puzzled by this passage, some even doubting the sincerity of Confucius' religious attitude—all quite unnecessarily. The passage means either "do not become improperly informal with spiritual beings,"[85] or "emphasize the way of man rather than the way of spirits."[86]

6:21. Confucius said, "The man of wisdom delights in water; the man of humanity delights in mountains. The man of wisdom is active; the man of humanity is tranquil. The man of wisdom enjoys happiness; the man of humanity enjoys long life."

Comment. In the Confucian ethical system, humanity and wisdom are like two wings, one supporting the other.[87] One is substance, the other is function. The dual emphasis has been maintained throughout history, especially in Tung Chung-shu (c.179-c.104 B.C.) and in a certain sense in K'ang Yu-wei (1858-1927). Elsewhere, courage is added as the third virtue,[88] and Mencius grouped them with righteousness and propriety as the Four Beginnings.[89]

6:23. Confucius said, "When a cornered vessel no longer has any corner, should it be called a cornered vessel? Should it?"

Comment. Name must correspond to actuality.[90]

6:25. Confucius said, "The superior man extensively studies literature (*wen*) and restrains himself with the rules of propriety. Thus he will not violate the Way."

6:26. When Confucius visited Nan-tzu (the wicked wife of Duke Ling of Wei, r. 533-490 B.C.) [in an attempt to influence her to persuade the duke to effect political reform], Tzu-lu was not pleased. Confucius swore an oath and said, "If I have said or done anything wrong, may Heaven forsake me! May Heaven forsake me!"[91]

6:28. Tzu-kung said, "If a ruler extensively confers benefit on the people and can bring salvation to all, what do you think of him? Would you call him a man of humanity?" Confucius said, "Why only a man of humanity? He is without doubt a sage. Even (sage-emperors) Yao and Shun fell short of it. A man of humanity, wishing to establish his own character, also establishes the character of others, and wishing to be prominent himself, also helps others to be prominent. To be able to judge others by what is near to ourselves may be called the method of realizing humanity."[92]

Comment. The Confucian golden rule in a nutshell.

7:1. Confucius said, "I transmit but do not create. I believe in and love the ancients. I venture to compare myself to our old P'eng."[93]

Comment. This is often cited to show that Confucius was not creative. We must not forget, however, that he "goes over the old so as to find out what is new."[94] Nor must we overlook the fact that he was the first one to offer education to all.[95] Moreover, his concepts of the superior man and of Heaven were at least partly new.

7:2. Confucius said, "To remember silently [what I have learned], to learn untiringly, and to teach others without being wearied—that is just natural with me."

7:6. Confucius said, "Set your will on the Way. Have a firm grasp on virtue. Rely on humanity. Find recreation in the arts."

7:7. Confucius said, "There has never been anyone who came with as little a present as dried meat (for tuition)[96] that I have refused to teach him something."

7:8. Confucius said, "I do not enlighten those who are not eager to learn, nor arouse those who are not anxious to give an explanation themselves. If I have presented one corner of the square and they cannot come back to me with the other three, I should not go over the points again."

7:15. Confucius said, "With coarse rice to eat, with water to drink, and with a bent arm for a pillow, there is still joy. Wealth and honor obtained through unrighteousness are but floating clouds to me."

7:16. Confucius said, "Give me a few more years so that I can devote fifty years to study Change.[97] I may be free from great mistakes."

7:17. These were the things Confucius often[98] talked about—poetry, history, and the performance of the rules of propriety. All these were what he often talked about.

7:18. The Duke of She[99] asked Tzu-lu about Confucius, and Tzu-lu did not answer. Confucius said, "Why didn't you say that I am a person who forgets his food when engaged in vigorous pursuit of something, is so happy as to forget his worries, and is not aware that old age is coming on?"[100]

7:19. Confucius said, "I am not one who was born with knowledge; I love ancient [teaching] and earnestly seek it."

7:20. Confucius never discussed strange phenomena, physical exploits, disorder, or spiritual beings.

7:22. Confucius said, "Heaven produced the virtue that is in me; what can Huan T'ui[101] do to me?"

7:24. Confucius taught four things: culture (*wen*), conduct, loyalty, and faithfulness.

7:26. Confucius fished with a line but not a net. While shooting he would not shoot a bird at rest.[102]

7:27. Confucius said, "There are those who act without knowing [what is right].[103] But I am not one of them. To hear much and select what is good and follow it, to see much and remember it, is the second type of knowledge (next to innate knowledge)."

7:29. Confucius said, "Is humanity far away? As soon as I want it, there it is right by me."

> *Comment.* This is simply emphasizing the ever-present opportunity to do good. There is nothing mystical about it. The practice of humanity starts with oneself.[104]

7:34. Confucius was very ill. Tzu-lu asked that prayer be offered. Confucius said, "Is there such a thing?" Tzu-lu replied, "There is. A Eulogy says, 'Pray to the spiritual beings above and below.'" Confucius said, "My prayer has been for a long time [that is, what counts is the life that one leads]."

7:37. Confucius is affable but dignified, austere but not harsh, polite but completely at ease.

> *Comment.* The Confucian Mean in practice.

8:5. Tseng Tzu said, "Gifted with ability, yet asking those without ability; possessing much, yet asking those who possess little; having, yet seeming to have none; full, yet seeming vacuous; offended, yet not contesting—long ago I had a friend [Confucius' most virtuous pupil Yen Yüan?][105] who devoted himself to these ways."

> *Comment.* The similarity to Taoist teachings is striking.

8:6. Tseng Tzu said, "A man who can be entrusted with an orphaned child, delegated with the authority over a whole state of one hundred *li,*[106] and whose integrity cannot be violated even in the face of a great emergency—is such a man a superior man? He is a superior man indeed!"

8:7. Tseng Tzu said, "An officer must be great and strong. His burden is heavy and his course is long. He has taken humanity to be his own burden—is that not heavy? Only with death does his course stop—is that not long?"

8:8. Confucius said, "Let a man be stimulated by poetry, established by the rules of propriety, and perfected by music."

8:9. Confucius said, "The common people may be made to follow it (the Way) but may not be made to understand it."

> *Comment.* Confucianists have taken great pains to explain this saying. Cheng Hsüan said "the common people" refers to ignorant people and Chu Hsi said that ordinary people do things without understanding

why. There can be no denial that Confucius reflected the feudal society in which it was the duty of ordinary people to follow the elite.

8:13. Confucius said, "Have sincere faith and love learning. Be not afraid to die for pursuing the good Way. Do not enter a tottering state nor stay in a chaotic one. When the Way prevails in the empire, then show yourself; when it does not prevail, then hide. When the Way prevails in your own state and you are poor and in a humble position, be ashamed of yourself. When the Way does not prevail in your state and you are wealthy and in an honorable position, be ashamed of yourself."

8:14. Confucius said, "A person not in a particular government position does not discuss its policies."[107]

9:1. Confucius seldom talked about profit, destiny (*ming* or the Mandate of Heaven), and humanity.

> *Comment.* Few passages in the **Analects** have given commentators as much trouble as this one. It is true that the topic of profit is mentioned in the **Analects** only six times and destiny or fate only ten times, but fifty-eight of the 499 chapters of the **Analects** are devoted to humanity and the word *jen* occurs 105 times. Confucianists have tried their best to explain why Confucius can be said to have seldom talked about them. Huang K'an said these things are so serious that Confucius seldom expected people to live up to them. This line of thought was followed by Juan Yüan (1764-1849).[108] Ho Yen thought that Confucius seldom talked about them because few people could reach those high levels. Hsing Ping, who commented on Ho's commentary, repeated it. Chu Hsi, quoting Ch'eng I, said that Confucius seldom talked about profit, for example, because it is injurious to righteousness, and seldom talked about the others because the principle of destiny is subtle and that of humanity is great.

Other scholars have tried to change the meaning of the passage. Shih Sheng-tsu (fl. 1230) in his *Hsüeh-chai chan-pi* (Simple Observations) interpreted *yü* not as "and" but as "give forth," thus making the sentence say that Confucius seldom talked about profit but gave forth [instructions] on destiny and humanity. Bodde accepts this view.[109] Laufer thinks it should be read: "The Master rarely discussed material gains compared with the will of Heaven and compared with humaneness."[110] Chiao Hsün (1763-1820), in his *Lun-yü pu-shu* (Supplementary Commentary on the *Analects*) said that when Confucius occasionally talked about profit, he spoke of it together with destiny or humanity, that is, in the light of either of them. Han Yü (768-824) thought that what Confucius seldom talked about was the *men* of profit, destiny, or humanity, not the three subjects themselves (*Lun-yü pi-chieh,* or Explanations of the *Analects*). According to Huang Shih-nan's *Lun-yü hou-an* (Recent Examinations of the *Analects,* 1844), the word *han* does not mean "seldom," but is an alternate for *hsien,* "elucidation." While this is possible, it seems to be going too far. Most scholars leave the difficulty alone. As K'ang Yu-wei, in his *Lun-yü chu,* says, Confucius talked about the three subjects a great deal, since they are inherently important subjects for discussion.

9:3. Confucius said, "The linen cap is prescribed by the rules of ceremony (*li*) but nowadays a silk one is worn. It is economical and I follow the common practice. Bowing below the hall is prescribed by the rules of ceremony, but nowadays people bow after ascending the hall. This is arrogant, and I follow the practice of bowing below the hall though that is opposed to the common practice."

9:4. Confucius was completely free from four things: He had no arbitrariness of opinion, no dogmatism, no obstinacy, and no egotism.

9:5. When Confucius was in personal danger in K'uang,[111] he said, "Since the death of King Wen,[112] is not the course of culture (*wen*) in my keeping? If it had been the will of Heaven to destroy this culture, it would not have been given to a mortal [like me]. But if it is the will of Heaven that this culture should not perish, what can the people of K'uang do to me?"

9:6. A great official asked Tzu-kung, "Is the Master a sage? How is it that he has so much ability [in practical, specific things]?" Tzu-kung said, "Certainly Heaven has endowed him so liberally that he is to become a sage,[113] and furthermore he has much ability." When Confucius heard this, he said, "Does the great official know me? When I was young, I was in humble circumstances, and therefore I acquired much ability to do the simple things of humble folk. Does a superior man need to have so much ability? He does not." His pupil Lao said, "The Master said, 'I have not been given official employment and therefore I [acquired the ability] for the simple arts.'"[114]

9:13. Confucius wanted to live among the nine barbarous tribes of the East. Someone said, "They are rude. How can you do it?" Confucius said, "If a superior man lives there, what rudeness would there be?"

9:16. Confucius, standing by a stream, said, "It passes on like this, never ceasing day or night!"

Comment. What was Confucius thinking about? Was he thinking of the unceasing operation of the universe (Chu Hsi and Ch'eng I)? Was he lamenting over the fact that the past cannot be recovered (Hsing Ping)? Was he comparing the untiring effort of a superior man's moral cultivation (Liu Pao-nan)? Was he praising water because its springs continuously gush out (Mencius[115] and Tung Chung-shu[116])? Was he praising water because it has the qualities of virtue, righteousness, courage, and so forth (Hsün

Tzu, fl. 298-238 B.C.)?[117] One thing is fairly sure: water to him meant something quite different from what it meant to Indian and Western philosophers, and to some extent to Lao Tzu.

9:25. Confucius said, "The commander of three armies may be taken away, but the will of even a common man may not be taken away from him."

10:9. When his mat was not straight [Confucius] did not sit on it.

10:12. A certain stable was burned down. On returning from court, Confucius asked, "Was any man hurt?" He did not ask about the horses.

10:14. On entering the Ancestral Temple, he asked about everything.

11:8. When Yen Yüan died, Confucius said, "Alas, Heaven is destroying me! Heaven is destroying me!"

11:11. Chi-lu (Tzu-lu) asked about serving the spiritual beings. Confucius said, "If we are not yet able to serve man, how can we serve spiritual beings?" "I venture to ask about death." Confucius said, "If we do not yet know about life, how can we know about death?"

Comment. A most celebrated saying on humanism.

11:15. Tzu-kung asked who was the better man, Shih[118] or Shang.[119] Confucius said, "Shih goes too far and Shang does not go far enough." Tzu-kung said, "Then is Shih better?" Confucius said, "To go too far is the same as not to go far enough."

11:21. Tzu-lu asked, "Should one immediately practice what one has heard?" Confucius said, "There are father and elder brother [to be consulted]. Why immediately practice what one has heard?" Jan Yu (Jan Tzu) asked, "Should one immediately practice what one has heard?" Confucius said, "One should immediately practice what one has heard." Kung-hsi Hua[120] said, "When Yu (Tzu-lu) asked you, 'Should one immediately practice what one has heard?' you said, 'There are father and elder brother.' When Ch'iu (Jan Yu) asked you, 'Should one immediately practice what he has heard?' you said, 'One should immediately practice what one has heard.' I am perplexed, and venture to ask you for an explanation." Confucius said, "Ch'iu is retiring; therefore I urged him forward. Yu has more than one man's energy; therefore I kept him back."

11:25. Tzu-lu, Tseng Hsi,[121] Jan Yu, and Kung-hsi Hua were in attendance. Confucius said, "You think that I am a day or so older than you are. But do not think so. At present you are out of office and think that you are denied recognition. Suppose you were given recognition. What would you prefer?" Tzu-lu promptly replied, "Suppose there is a state of a thousand chariots, hemmed in by great powers, in addition invaded by armies, and as a result drought and famine prevail. Let me administer that state. In three years' time I can endow the people with courage and furthermore, enable them to know the correct principles." Confucius smiled at him [with disapproval].

"Ch'iu, how about you?" Jan Yu replied, "Suppose there is a state the sides of which are sixty or seventy *li* wide, or one of fifty or sixty *li*. Let me administer that state. In three years' time I can enable the people to be sufficient in their livelihood. As to the promotion of ceremonies and music, however, I shall have to wait for the superior man."

"How about you, Ch'ih?" Kung-hsi Hua replied, "I do not say I can do it but I should like to learn to do so. At the services of the royal ancestral temple, and at the conferences of the feudal lords, I should like to wear the dark robe and black cap (symbols of correctness) and be a junior assistant."

[Turning to Tseng Hsi,] Confucius said, "How about you, Tien?" Tseng Hsi was then softly playing the zither. With a bang he laid down the instrument, rose, and said, "My wishes are different from what the gentlemen want to do." Confucius said, "What harm is there? After all, we want each to tell his ambition." Tseng Hsi said, "In the late spring, when the spring dress is ready, I would like to go with five or six grownups and six or seven young boys to bathe in the Ch'i River, enjoy the breeze on the Rain Dance Altar, and then return home singing." Confucius heaved a sigh and said, "I agree with Tien."

> *Comment.* Why did Confucius agree with Tseng Hsi? The field is wide open for speculation, and most Confucianists have taken the best advantage of it. Thus it was variously explained that Tseng Hsi was enjoying the harmony of the universe (Wang Ch'ung),[122] that he was following traditional cultural institutions (Liu Pao-nan), that he was wisely refraining from officialdom at the time of chaos (Huang K'an), that he was thinking of the "kingly way" whereas other pupils were thinking of the government of feudal states (Han Yü), that he was in the midst of the universal operation of the Principle of Nature (Chu Hsi), and that he was expressing freedom of the spirit (Wang Yang-ming, 1472-1529).[123] It is to be noted that the last two interpretations reflect the different tendencies of the two wings of Neo-Confucianism, one emphasizing the objective operation of the Principle of Nature, the other emphasizing the state of mind.

12:1. Yen Yüan asked about humanity. Confucius said, "To master[124] oneself and return to propriety is humanity.[125] If a man (the ruler) can for one day master him-self and return to propriety, all under heaven will return to humanity.[126] To practice humanity depends on oneself. Does it depend on others?" Yen Yüan said, "May I ask for the detailed items?" Confucius said, "Do not look at what is contrary to propriety, do not listen to what is contrary to propriety, do not speak what is contrary to propriety, and do not make any movement which is contrary to propriety." Yen Yüan said, "Although I am not intelligent, may I put your saying into practice."

12:2. Chung-kung[127] asked about humanity. Confucius said, "When you go abroad, behave to everyone as if you were receiving a great guest. Employ the people as if you were assisting at a great sacrifice.[128] Do not do to others what you do not want them to do to you.[129] Then there will be no complaint against you in the state or in the family (the ruling clan)." Chung-kung said, "Although I am not intelligent, may I put your saying into practice."

12:5. Ssu-ma Niu,[130] worrying, said, "All people have brothers but I have none."[131] Tzu-hsia said, "I have heard [from Confucius][132] this saying: 'Life and death are the decree of Heaven (*ming*); wealth and honor depend on Heaven. If a superior man is reverential (or serious) without fail, and is respectful in dealing with others and follows the rules of propriety, then all within the four seas (the world)[133] are brothers.'[134] What does the superior man have to worry about having no brothers?"

12:7. Tzu-kung asked about government. Confucius said, "Sufficient food, sufficient armament, and sufficient confidence of the people." Tzu-kung said, "Forced to give up one of these, which would you abandon first?" Confucius said, "I would abandon the armament." Tzu-kung said, "Forced to give up one of the remaining two, which would you abandon first?" Confucius said, "I would abandon food. There have been deaths from time immemorial, but no state can exist without the confidence of the people."

12.11. Duke Ching of Ch'i[135] asked Confucius about government. Confucius replied, "Let the ruler *be* a ruler, the minister *be* a minister, the father *be* a father, and the son *be* a son." The duke said, "Excellent! Indeed when the ruler is not a ruler, the minister not a minister, the father not a father, and the son not a son, although I may have all the grain, shall I ever get to eat it?"

12:16. Confucius said, "The superior man brings the good things of others to completion and does not bring the bad things of others to completion. The inferior man does just the opposite."

12:17. Chi K'ang Tzu[136] asked Confucius about government. Confucius replied, "To govern (*cheng*) is to rectify (*cheng*). If you lead the people by being recti-fied yourself, who will dare not be rectified?"[137]

12:19. Chi K'ang Tzu asked Confucius about govern-ment, saying, "What do you think of killing the wicked and associating with the good?" Confucius replied, "In your government what is the need of killing? If you desire what is good, the people will be good. The character of a ruler is like wind and that of the people is like grass. In whatever direction the wind blows, the grass always bends."

12:22. Fan Ch'ih asked about humanity. Confucius said, "It is to love men." He asked about knowledge. Confucius said, "It is to know man."

> *Comment.* As a general virtue, *jen* means humanity, that is, that which makes a man a moral being. As a particular virtue, it means love. This is the general interpretation during the Han and T'ang times. Later in Neo-Confucianism, it was modified to mean man and Nature forming one body. The doctrine that knowledge of men is power has been maintained throughout the history of Confucianism. This humanistic interest has to a large degree prevented China from developing the tradition of knowledge for its own sake.

13:3. Tzu-lu said, "The ruler of Wei is waiting for you to serve in his administration. What will be your first measure?" Confucius said, "It will certainly concern the rectification of names." Tzu-lu said, "Is that so? You are wide of the mark. Why should there be such a rectification?" Confucius said, "Yu! How uncult-vated you are! With regard to what he does not know, the superior man should maintain an attitude of re-serve. If names are not rectified, then language will not be in accord with truth. If language is not in accord with truth, then things cannot be accomplished. If things cannot be accomplished, then ceremonies and music will not flourish. If ceremonies and music do not flour-ish, then punishment will not be just. If punishments are not just, then the people will not know how to move hand or foot. Therefore the superior man will give only names that can be described in speech and say only what can be carried out in practice. With regard to his speech, the superior man does not take it lightly. That is all."

> *Comment.* Most ancient Chinese philosophical schools had a theory about names and actuality. In the Confucian school, however, it assumes special importance because its focus is not metaphysical as in Taoism, or logical as in the School of Logicians, or utilitarian as in the Legalist School, but ethical. This means not only that a name must correspond to its actuality, but also that rank, duties, and functions must be clearly defined and fully translated into action. Only then can a name be considered to be correct or rectified. With the ethical interest predominant, this is the nearest the ancient

Confucianists came to a logical theory, except in the case of Hsün Tzu, who was the most logical of all ancient Confucianists.

13:6. Confucius said, "If a ruler sets himself right, he will be followed without his command. If he does not set himself right, even his commands will not be obeyed."[138]

13:16. The Duke of She asked about government. Confucius said, "[There is good government] when those who are near are happy and those far away de-sire to come."[139]

13:18. The Duke of She told Confucius, "In my coun-try there is an upright man named Kung.[140] When his father stole a sheep, he bore witness against him." Confucius said, "The upright men in my community are different from this. The father conceals the mis-conduct of the son and the son conceals the miscon-duct of the father. Uprightness is to be found in this."

13:19. Fan Ch'ih asked about humanity. Confucius said, "Be respectful in private life, be serious (*ching*)[141] in handling affairs, and be loyal in dealing with others. Even if you are living amidst barbarians, these prin-ciples may never be forsaken."

13:23. Confucius said, "The superior man is concilia-tory but does not identify himself with others; the in-ferior man identifies with others but is not concilia-tory."[142]

13:26. Confucius said, "The superior man is dignified but not proud; the inferior man is proud but not digni-fied."

13:27. Confucius said, "A man who is strong, reso-lute, simple, and slow to speak is near to human-ity."

13:29. Confucius said, "When good men have in-structed the people [in morals, agriculture, military tactics][143] for seven years, they may be allowed to bear arms."

13:30. Confucius said, "To allow people to go to war without first instructing them is to betray them."

14:2. [Yüan Hsien][144] said, "When one has avoided aggressiveness, pride, resentment, and greed, he may be called a man of humanity." Confucius said, "This may be considered as having done what is difficult, but I do not know that it is to be regarded as human-ity."

14:24. Confucius said, "The superior man understands the higher things [moral principles]; the inferior man understands the lower things [profit]."[145]

14:29. Confucius said, "The superior man is ashamed that his words exceed his deeds."

14:30. Confucius said, "The way of the superior man is threefold, but I have not been able to attain it. The man of wisdom has no perplexities; the man of humanity has no worry; the man of courage has no fear." Tzu-kung said, "You are talking about yourself."

14:33. Confucius said, "He who does not anticipate attempts to deceive him nor predict his being distrusted, and yet is the first to know [when these things occur], is a worthy man."[146]

14:36. Someone said, "What do you think of repaying hatred with virtue?" Confucius said, "In that case what are you going to repay virtue with? Rather, repay hatred with uprightness and repay virtue with virtue."

> *Comment.* The word for uprightness, *chih,* is not to be understood as severity or justice, which would imply repaying evil with evil. The idea of repaying hatred with virtue is also found in the *Lao Tzu,* ch. 63, and some have therefore theorized that the questioner was a Taoist or that the saying was a prevalent one at the time. In any case, by uprightness Confucianists mean absolute impartiality, taking guidance from what is right instead of one's personal preference, however admirable. Obviously this does not satisfy followers of the Christian doctrine of loving one's enemy. As to the golden rule, see above, comment on 4:15.

14:37. Confucius said, "Alas! No one knows me!" Tzu-kung said, "Why is there no one that knows you?" Confucius said, "I do not complain against Heaven. I do not blame men. I study things on the lower level but my understanding penetrates the higher level.[147] It is Heaven that knows me."

14:41. When Tzu-lu was stopping at the Stone Gate[148] for the night, the gate-keeper asked him, "Where are you from?" Tzu-lu said, "From Confucius." "Oh, is he the one who knows a thing cannot be done and still wants to do it?"

14:45. Tzu-lu asked about the superior man. Confucius said, "The superior man is one who cultivates himself with seriousness (*ching*)." Tzu-lu said, "Is that all?" Confucius said, "He cultivates himself so as to give the common people security and peace." Tzu-lu said, "Is that all?" Confucius said, "He cultivates himself so as to give all people security and peace. To cultivate oneself so as to give all people security and peace, even Yao and Shun found it difficult to do."[149]

15:2. Confucius said, "Tz'u (Tzu-kung), do you suppose that I am one who learns a great deal and remembers it?" Tzu-kung replied, "Yes. Is that not true?"

Confucius said, "No. I have a thread (*i-kuan*) that runs through it all."[150]

15:4. Confucius said, "To have taken no [unnatural] action[151] and yet have the empire well governed, Shun was the man! What did he do? All he did was to make himself reverent and correctly faced south [in his royal seat as the ruler]."

15:8. Confucius said, "A resolute scholar and a man of humanity will never seek to live at the expense of injuring humanity. He would rather sacrifice his life in order to realize humanity."[152]

15:17. Confucius said, "The superior man regards righteousness (*i*) as the substance of everything. He practices it according to the principles of propriety. He brings it forth in modesty. And he carries it to its conclusion with faithfulness. He is indeed a superior man!"

15:20. Confucius said, "The superior man seeks [room for improvement or occasion to blame] in himself; the inferior man seeks it in others."[153]

15:22. Confucius said, "The superior man (ruler) does not promote (put in office) a man on the basis of his words; nor does he reject his words because of the man."

15:23. Tzu-kung asked, "Is there one word which can serve as the guiding principle for conduct throughout life?" Confucius said, "It is the word altruism (*shu*). Do not do to others what you do not want them to do to you."

15:28. Confucius said, "It is man that can make the Way great, and not the Way that can make man great."

> *Comment.* Humanism in the extreme! Commentators from Huang K'an to Chu Hsi said that the Way, because it is tranquil and quiet and lets things take their own course, does not make man great. A better explanation is found in the *Doctrine of the Mean,* where it is said, "Unless there is perfect virtue, the perfect Way cannot be materialized."[154]

15:31. Confucius said, "The superior man seeks the Way and not a mere living. There may be starvation in farming, and there may be riches in the pursuit of studies. The superior man worries about the Way and not about poverty."

15:32. Confucius said, "When a man's knowledge is sufficient for him to attain [his position][155] but his humanity is not sufficient for him to hold it, he will lose it again. When his knowledge is sufficient for him to attain it and his humanity is sufficient for him to hold it, if he does not approach the people with dignity, the people will not respect him. If his knowledge is sufficient for him to attain it, his humanity sufficient for him to hold it, and he approaches the people with dignity, yet does not influence them with the principle of propriety, it is still not good."

15:35. Confucius said, "When it comes to the practice of humanity, one should not defer even to his teacher."

15:39. Confucius said, "In education there should be no class distinction."

> *Comment.* Confucius was the first to pronounce this principle in Chinese history. Among his pupils there were commoners as well as nobles, and stupid people as well as intelligent ones.[156]

15:40. Confucius said, "In words all that matters is to express the meaning."

16:1. Confucius said, " . . . I have heard that those who administer a state or a family do not worry about there being too few people, but worry about unequal distribution of wealth. They do not worry about poverty, but worry about the lack of security and peace on the part of the people. For when wealth is equally distributed, there will not be poverty; when there is harmony, there will be no problem of there being too few people; and when there are security and peace, there will be no danger to the state. . . ."[157]

16:4. Confucius said, "There are three kinds of friendship which are beneficial and three kinds which are harmful. Friendship with the upright, with the truthful, and with the well-informed is beneficial. Friendship with those who flatter, with those who are meek and who compromise with principles, and with those who talk cleverly is harmful."

16:8. Confucius said, "The superior man stands in awe of three things. He stands in awe of the Mandate of Heaven; he stands in awe of great men;[158] and he stands in awe of the words of the sages. The inferior man is ignorant of the Mandate of Heaven and does not stand in awe of it. He is disrespectful to great men and is contemptuous toward the words of the sages."

16:9. Confucius said, "Those who are born with knowledge are the highest type of people. Those who learn through study are the next. Those who learn through hard work are still the next. Those who work hard and still do not learn are really the lowest type."[159]

16:10. Confucius said, "The superior man has nine wishes. In seeing, he wishes to see clearly. In hearing, he wishes to hear distinctly. In his expression, he wishes to be warm. In his appearance, he wishes to be respectful. In his speech, he wishes to be sincere. In handling affairs, he wishes to be serious. When in doubt,

he wishes to ask. When he is angry, he wishes to think of the resultant difficulties. And when he sees an opportunity for a gain, he wishes to think of righteousness."

17:2. Confucius said, "By nature men are alike. Through practice they have become far apart."

> *Comment.* This is the classical Confucian dictum on human nature. Neo-Confucianists like Chu Hsi and Ch'eng I[160] strongly argued that Confucius meant physical nature, which involves elements of evil, for since every man's original nature is good, men must be the *same* and therefore cannot be *alike*. Others, however, think that the word *chin* (near or alike) here has the same meaning as in Mencius' saying, "All things of the same kind are similar to one another."[161] However, on the surface this saying is indisputably neutral, but all of Confucius' teachings imply the goodness of human nature.[162]

17:3. Confucius said, "Only the most intelligent and the most stupid do not change."

> *Comment.* Advocates of the theory of three grades of nature, notably Wang Ch'ung, Chia I (201-169 B.C.),[163] and Han Yü, have drawn support from this saying by equating the most intelligent with those born good, the most stupid with those born evil, and the rest born neutral. They overlooked the fact that this passage has to do not with nature but only with intelligence. Practically all modern Confucianists are agreed on this point. As Ch'eng I,[164] Wang Yang-ming,[165] Tai Chen (Tai Tung-yüan, 1723-1777),[166] and Juan Yüan[167] all pointed out, it is not that they cannot change. It is simply that they are too intelligent to change downward or too stupid to change upward.

17:4. Confucius went to the city of Wu [where his disciple Tzu-yu was the magistrate] and heard the sound of stringed instruments and singing. With a gentle smile, the Master said, "Why use an ox-knife to kill a chicken [that is, why employ a serious measure like music to rule such a small town]?" Tzu-yu replied, "Formerly I heard you say, 'When the superior man has studied the Way, he loves men. When the inferior man has studied the Way, he is easy to employ.'" Confucius said, "My disciples, what I just said was only a joke."

17:6. Tzu-chang asked Confucius about humanity. Confucius said, "One who can practice five things wherever he may be is a man of humanity." Tzu-chang asked what the five are. Confucius said, "Earnestness, liberality, truthfulness, diligence, and generosity. If one is earnest, one will not be treated with disrespect. If one is liberal, one will win the hearts of all. If one is truthful, one will be trusted. If one is diligent, one will be successful. And if one is generous, one will be able to enjoy the service of others."

17:8. Confucius said, "Yu (Tzu-lu), have you heard about the six virtues[168] and the six obscurations?" Tzu-lu replied, "I have not." Confucius said, "Sit down, then. I will tell you. One who loves humanity but not learning will be obscured by ignorance. One who loves wisdom but not learning will be obscured by lack of principle. One who loves faithfulness but not learning will be obscured by heartlessness. One who loves uprightness but not learning will be obscured by violence. One who loves strength of character but not learning will be obscured by recklessness."

17:9. Confucius said, "My young friends, why do you not study the odes? The odes can stimulate your emotions, broaden your observation, enlarge your fellowship, and express your grievances. They help you in your immediate service to your parents and in your more remote service to your rulers. They widen your acquaintance with the names of birds, animals, and plants."

17:19. Confucius said, "I do not wish to say anything." Tzu-kung said, "If you do not say anything, what can we little disciples ever learn to pass on to others?" Confucius said, "Does Heaven (*T'ien*, Nature) say anything? The four seasons run their course and all things are produced. Does Heaven say anything?"

> *Comment.* This is usually cited to support the contention that Confucius did not believe in an anthropomorphic God but in Heaven which reigns rather than rules. In Neo-Confucianism, Heaven came to be identified with principle (*li*).[169]

17:23. Tzu-lu asked, "Does the superior man[170] esteem courage?" Confucius said, "The superior man considers righteousness (*i*) as the most important. When the superior man has courage but no righteousness, he becomes turbulent. When the inferior man has courage but no righteousness, he becomes a thief."

17:25. Confucius said, "Women and servants are most difficult to deal with. If you are familiar with them, they cease to be humble. If you keep a distance from them, they resent it."

> *Comment.* From Confucius down, Confucianists have always considered women inferior.

18:6. Ch'ang-chü and Chieh-ni were cultivating their fields together. Confucius was passing that way and told Tzu-lu to ask them where the river could be forded. Ch'ang-chü said, "Who is the one holding the reins in the carriage?" Tzu-lu said, "It is K'ung Ch'iu (Confucius)." "Is he the K'ung Ch'iu of Lu?" "Yes." "Then he already knows where the river can be forded!" Tzu-lu asked Chieh-ni. Chieh-ni said, "Who are you, sir?" Tzu-lu replied, "I am Chung-yu (name of Tzu-lu)." "Are you a follower of K'ung Ch'iu of Lu?"

"Yes." Chieh-ni said, "The whole world is swept as though by a torrential flood. Who can change it? As for you, instead of following one who flees from this man or that man, is it not better to follow those who flee the world altogether?" And with that he went on covering the seed without stopping. Tzu-lu went to Confucius and told him about their conversation. Confucius said ruefully, "One cannot herd with birds and beasts. If I do not associate with mankind, with whom shall I associate? If the Way prevailed in the world, there would be no need for me to change it."[171]

19:6. Tzu-hsia said, "To study extensively, to be steadfast in one's purpose, to inquire earnestly, and to reflect on what is at hand (that is, what one can put into practice)—humanity consists in these."

19:7. Confucius said, "The hundred artisans work in their works to perfect their craft. The superior man studies to reach to the utmost of the Way."

19:11. Tzu-hsia said, "So long as a man does not transgress the boundary line in the great virtues, he may pass and repass it in the small virtues."

> *Comment.* Even Chu Hsi quoted someone who pointed out that this passage is not free from defect.

19:13. Tzu-hsia said, "A man who has energy to spare after studying should serve his state. A man who has energy to spare after serving his state should study."[172]

19:24. Shu-sun Wu-shu[173] slandered Chung-ni (Confucius). Tzu-kung said, "It is no use. Chung-ni cannot be slandered. Other worthies are like mounds or small hills. You can still climb over them. Chung-ni, however, is like the sun and the moon that cannot be climbed over. Although a man may want to shut his eyes to the sun and the moon, what harm does it do to them? It would only show in large measure that he does not know his own limitations."

Notes

1 *Analects,* 8:4; 10:4 and 8; 16:7. In the rest of this introduction, references to the *Analects* are given only in specific cases. For references on general subjects, see the analytical list at the end of this introduction. For discussion of the *Analects,* see below, n.11.

2 *Analects,* 5:12.

3 *ibid.,* 17:2. . . .

4 *Analects,* 15:28.

5 Yao was a legendary ruler of the 3rd millennium B.C. Shun was his successor. Duke Chou (d. 1094) helped the founder of the Chou dynasty to consolidate

the empire and establish the foundations of Chinese culture.

[6] For this concept, see Chan, "The Evolution of the Confucian Concept *Jen*," *Philosophy East and West,* 4 (1955), 295-319; also, see below, comment on *Analects* 12:22, and comments on the following: ch. 30, A; ch. 31, secs. 1, 11; ch. 32, sec. 42; ch. 34, A, treatise 1.

[7] *Analects,* 6:28.

[8] These accounts are found in the first—and still the standard—biography of Confucius, ch. 47 of the *Shih chi.* See French translation by Chavannes, *Les mémoires historiques,* vol. 5, pp. 299-300, 391-403, 420; or English translation by Lin Yutang, *The Wisdom of Confucius,* pp. 57, 88-91, 95.

[9] Traditionally believed to refer to the Six Classics, i.e., the Books of *History, Odes, Changes, Rites,* and *Music,* and the *Spring and Autumn Annals.* The *Book of Music* is now lost. For three of the others, see above, ch. 1, nn.4-6. The "six arts" are also understood to mean ceremonies, music, archery, carriage-driving, writing, and mathematics.

[10] The *Analects* is a collection of sayings by Confucius and his pupils pertaining to his teachings and deeds. It was probably put together by some of his pupils and their pupils. The name *Lun-yü* did not appear until the 2nd century B.C. At that time there were three versions of it, with some variations. Two of these have been lost. The surviving version is that of the state of Lu, where it circulated. It is divided into two parts, with ten books each. In the *Ching-tien shih-wen* (Explanation of Terms in the Classics) by Lu Te-ming (556-627), ch. 24, it is divided into 492 chapters. Chu Hsi combined and divided certain chapters, making a total of 482, one of which is divided into eighteen sections. In translations like Legge's *Confucian Analects,* and Waley's *The Analects of Confucius,* these divisions are taken as chapters, making 499. The same numbering is used in the following selections.

The material is unsystematic, in a few cases repetitive, and in some cases historically inaccurate. However, it is generally accepted as the most authentic and reliable source of Confucian teachings. Chu Hsi grouped it together with the *Book of Mencius,* the *Great Learning,* and the *Doctrine of the Mean* as the "Four Books." Thereupon they became Classics. From 1313 to 1905, they served as the basis for civil service examinations, replacing the earlier Classics in importance.

[11] In the *Lun-yü chu-shu* (Commentary and Subcommentary on the *Analects*) in the Thirteen Classics Series.

[12] See below, comment on *Analects,* 2:18.

[13] Confucius' pupil whose private name was Jo (538-c.457 B.C.), thirteen years (some say thirty-three years) Confucius' junior. In the *Analects,* with minor exceptions, he and Tseng Ts'an are addressed as Tzu, an honorific for a scholar or gentleman, giving rise to the theory that the *Analects* was compiled by their pupils, who supplemented Confucius' sayings with theirs.

[14] Cf. below, 13:27.

[15] Tseng Ts'an (505-c.436 B.C.), pupil of Confucius, noted for filial piety, to whom are ascribed the *Great Learning* and the *Book of Filial Piety.*

[16] Ho Yen's interpretation: Whether I have transmitted to others what I myself have not practiced. This interpretation has been accepted by many.

[17] *Wen,* literally "patterns," is here extended to mean the embodiment of culture and the moral law (Tao)— that is, the Six Arts of ceremony, music, archery, carriage-driving, writing, and mathematics.

[18] To K'ung An-kuo (fl. 130 B.C.), quoted by Ho Yen, *ku* means "obscure," not "firm." The sentence would read, "If he studies, he will not be ignorant."

[19] *Lun-yü shu* (Subcommentary on the *Analects*). This is part of the *Lun-yü chu-shu.*

[20] *Chung lun* (Treatise on the Mean), pt. 1, sec. 5, SPTK, 1:21b.

[21] Quoted in Chu Hsi's *Lun-yü huo-wen* (Questions and Answers on the *Analects*), 1:20a, in *Chu Tzu i-shu* (Surviving Works of Chu Hsi).

[22] *Lun-yü chu* (Commentary on the *Analects*).

[23] Confucius' pupil, whose family name was Tuan-mu, private name Tz'u, and courtesy name Tzu-kung (520-c.450 B.C.). He was noted for eloquence and was thirty-one years younger than the Master. See *Analects,* 5:8 about him.

[24] An old edition has "happy with the Way."

[25] Ode no. 55. Describing the eloquence of a lover, but here taken by Tzu-kung to mean moral effort.

[26] Similar ideas are found in *Analects,* 14:32; 15:18, 20.

[27] See Ho Yen's *Lun-yü chi-chieh* and Chu Hsi's *Lun-yü chi-chu.*

[28] Cf. *Analects,* 15:4 and *Lao Tzu,* ch. 57.

[29] *Odes,* ode no. 297. Actually there are 305 odes in the book. The word *ssu* means "Ah!" in the poem but Confucius used it in its sense of "thought." For discussion of the *Book of Odes,* see above, ch. 1, n.5.

[30] The word *ko* means both to rectify (according to Ho Yen and most other commentators) and to arrive (according to Cheng Hsüan). In the latter sense, it can mean either "the people will arrive at goodness" or "the people will come to the ruler.". . .

[31] See Ch'eng Shu-te *Lun-yü chi-shih* (Collected Explanations of the *Analects*), 1943.

[32] Chu Hsi, *Lun-yü chi-chu.*

[33] A young noble, also styled Meng-sun, once studied ceremonies with Confucius.

[34] Confucius' pupil, whose family name was Fan, private name Hsü, and courtesy name Tzu-ch'ih (b. 515 B.C.).

[35] Not to disobey the principle of propriety, according to Hsing Ping; not to disobey moral principles, according to Chu Hsi; or not to obey parents, according to Huang K'an (448-545), *Lun-yü i-shu* (Commentary on the Meanings of the *Analects*).

[36] Son of Meng I Tzu.

[37] Another interpretation by Ma Jung (79-166), quoted by Ho Yen: A filial son does not do wrong. His parents' only worry is that he might become sick. About half of the commentators have followed him.

[38] Confucius' pupil. His family name was Yen, private name Yen, and courtesy name Tzu-yu (b. 506 B.C.).

[39] Alternative interpretations: (1) Even dogs and horses can support men; (2) Even dogs and horses can support their parents.

[40] Literally "an implement or utensil," *ch'i* means narrow usefulness rather than the ability to grasp fundamentals.

[41] Cf. below, 9:6.

[42] Cf. below, 4:22, 24; 14:29.

[43] Name of Confucius' pupil whose family name was Chung and courtesy name Tzu-lu (542-480 B.C.). He was only nine years younger than Confucius. He was noted for courage.

[44] The sentence may also mean: "Do you know what I teach you?"

[45] Courtesy name of Confucius' pupil, Chuan-sun Shih (503-c.450 B.C.).

[46] See also *Analects,* 4:22, 24; 5:9; 13:3; 14:29; 15:5; 18:8; and *The Mean,* chs. 8, 13.

[47] See below, ch. 35, B, sec. 5.

[48] A native of Lu, most probably not a pupil of Confucius.

[49] Great officer and commander-in-chief in the state of Wei.

[50] Tzu-kung's private name.

[51] Ruler of Confucius' native state of Lu (r. 509-495 B.C.).

[52] Hate here means dislike, without any connotation of ill will. See *Great Learning,* ch. 10, for an elaboration of the saying.

[53] The word *e,* evil, can also be read *wu* to mean hate or dislike, but it is hardly ever done.

[54] It is possible to interpret the phrase to mean "will not be surpassed by anyone," but few commentators chose it. . . .

[55] *Analects,* 9:4.

[56] *ibid.,* 18:8.

[57] *Mencius,* 2A:2.

[58] *ibid.,* 5B:1.

[59] See Liu Pao-nan, *Lun-yü cheng-i.*

[60] See Chu Hsi, *Lun-yü chi-chu,* and Chang Shih, *Lun-yü chieh* (Explanation of the *Analects*).

[61] See Ch'eng Shu-te, *Lun-yü chi-shih,* on this point.

[62] Literally "land," or one's shelter, food, etc.

[63] Private name of Tseng Tzu.

[64] The Ch'ing viewpoint is best represented in Wang Nien-sun (1744-1832), *Kuang-ya shu-cheng* (Textual Commentary on the *Kuang-ya* Dictionary).

[65] Chu Hsi, *Lun-yü chi-chu.* For discussion of *chung-shu,* see Appendix.

[66] *I-shu* (Surviving Works), 21B:1b, in ECCS.

[67] *Lun-yü cheng-i.* He is referring to *Analects,* 6:28.

[68] See other positive versions in *Analects*, 14:45; *The Mean*, ch. 13; *Mencius*, 1A:7. The negative version is found in *Analects*, 5:11; 12:2; 15:23; in *The Mean*, ch. 13; and in the *Great Learning*, ch. 10.

[69] See *Analects*, 2:14; 4:11, 16; 6:11; 7:36; 12:16; 13:23, 25, 26; 14:7, 24; 15:1, 20, 33; 17:4, 23.

[70] Cf. *Great Learning*, ch. 10.

[71] The term *wen-chang* can also mean literary heritage or simply the ancient Classics.

[72] The word *hsing* (nature) is mentioned elsewhere in the *Analects* only once, in 17:2.

[73] Confucius' favorite pupil, whose family name was Yen, private name Hui, and courtesy name Tzu-yüan (521-490 B.C.). He died at 32.

[74] Tzu-lu.

[75] The word "light" does not appear in the stone-engraved Classic of the T'ang dynasty and is probably a later addition.

[76] Another interpretation: For his own moral effort.

[77] This is Chu Hsi's interpretation. According to Hsing Ping, it would mean this: The old should be satisfied with me, friends should trust me, and the young should come to me.

[78] We don't know whether this was said before or after Yen Yüan's death.

[79] *Analects*, 5:12.

[80] *Analects*, 17:2.

[81] Quoted by Ho Yen.

[82] *Lun-heng* (Balanced Inquiries), ch. 5, SPPY, 2:2a. For English translation, see Forke, *Lun-heng*, vol. 1, p. 152.

[83] See *Lun-yü chi-chu*.

[84] Meaning especially ancestors.

[85] According to *Lun-yü chi-chieh*.

[86] According to Cheng Hsüan, Chu Hsi, and most commentators.

[87] See also *Analects*, 4:2; 12:22; 15:32. . . .

[88] See *Analects*, 9:28; 14:30; *The Mean*, ch. 20.

[89] *Mencius*, 2A:6; 6A:6.

[90] For the Confucian doctrine of the rectification of names, see below, comment on 13:3.

[91] This episode took place when Confucius was 57.

[92] See above comment on 4:15.

[93] An official of the Shang dynasty (1751-1112 B.C.) who loved to recite old stories.

[94] *Analects*, 2:11.

[95] See Fung, *History of Chinese Philosophy*, vol. 1, pp. 46-49.

[96] Cheng Hsüan's interpretation: From young men fifteen years old and upward. Cf. *Analects*, 15:38.

[97] The traditional interpretation of the word *i* (change) is the *Book of Changes*. The ancient Lu version of the *Analects*, however, has *i* (then) instead of *i* (change). Some scholars have accepted this version, which reads " . . . to study, then I may be. . . ." Modern scholars prefer this reading because they do not believe that the *Book of Changes* existed at the time. However, the fact that Confucius was thinking of the *system* of Change instead of the *Book* should not be ruled out.

[98] The word *ya* (often) was understood by Cheng Hsüan as standard, thus meaning that Confucius recited the Books of *Odes*, *History*, and *Rites* in correct pronunciation.

[99] Magistrate of the district She in the state of Ch'u, who assumed the title of duke by usurpation.

[100] According to *Shih chi* (Records of the Historian), PNP, 47:18a, Confucius was 62 when he made this remark. See Chavannes, trans., *Les mémoires historiques*, vol. 5, p. 361.

[101] A military officer in the state of Sung who attempted to kill Confucius by felling a tree. Confucius was then 59 years old.

[102] He would not take unfair advantage.

[103] Other interpretations: Act without the necessity of knowledge; invent stories about history without real knowledge of it; write without knowledge.

[104] See *Analects*, 12:1.

[105] According to Ma Jung, quoted by Ho Yen, Yen Yüan had died long before.

[106] About one-third of a mile.

[107] The same idea is expressed in 14:27-28.

[108] "Lun-yu lun jen lun" (A Treatise on *Jen* in the *Analects*), *Yen-ching-shih chi* (Collected Works of the Yen-ching Study), 1st collection, 8:21a.

[109] "Perplexing Passage in the Confucian Analects," *Journal of the American Oriental Society,* 53 (1933), 350.

[110] "Lun Yü IX, 1," *ibid.,* 54 (1934), 83.

[111] The people of K'uang, mistaking Confucius for Yang Hu, their enemy whom Confucius resembled in appearance, surrounded him. This happened when Confucius was 56.

[112] Founder of the Chou dynasty.

[113] The term *chiang-sheng* is also understood to mean a great sage, or almost a sage.

[114] Cf. *Analects,* 2:12.

[115] *Mencius,* 4B:18.

[116] *Ch'un-ch'iu fan-lu* (Luxuriant Gems of the Spring and Autumn Annals), ch. 73, SPTK, 16:3a.

[117] *Hsün Tzu,* ch. 28, SPTK, 20:5b-6a. . . .

[118] Name of Confucius' pupil, Tzu-chang.

[119] His family name was Pu and courtesy name Tzu-hsia (507-420 B.C.). Also Confucius' pupil.

[120] Confucius' pupil. His private name was Ch'ih and courtesy name Tzu-hua (b. 509 B.C.). Jan Yu (522-c. 462), whose private name was Ch'iu and courtesy name Jan Tzu, was also a pupil.

[121] Tseng Tzu's father, whose private name was Tien and courtesy name Hsi. He was also a Confucian pupil.

[122] *Lun-heng,* ch. 45; SPPY, 15:10a. Cf. Forke, *Lun-Heng,* vol. 2, p. 235.

[123] *Ch'uan-hsi lu* (Instructions for Practical Living), sec. 257. See Chan, trans., *Instructions for Practical Living.*

[124] The word *k'o* was understood by Ma Jung as "to control" but Chu Hsi interpreted it to mean "to master," that is, to conquer the self since it is an embodiment of selfish desires. Here is another example of the sharply different approaches to the *Analects* between the Han Confucianists and the Sung Neo-Confucianists. The Ch'ing Confucianists, such as Juan Yüan, violently opposed Chu Hsi, as is to be expected.

[125] An old saying. Other interpretations: (1) To be able to return to propriety by oneself; (2) to discipline oneself and to act according to propriety.

[126] Other interpretations: (1) Ascribe humanity to him; (2) will follow him.

[127] Confucius' pupil, whose family name was Jan, private name Yung, and courtesy name Chung-kung. He was noted for excellent character.

[128] Paraphrasing two ancient sayings.

[129] See above, comment on 4:15.

[130] Confucius' pupil, whose family name was Hsiang.

[131] Meaning that his brother Huan T'ui (see above, 7:32) was not worthy to be a brother.

[132] Insertion according to Liu Pao-nan.

[133] Ordinarily meaning China, none doubts that here it means the entire world.

[134] Some say that the last sentence is Tzu-hsia's utterance.

[135] He reigned from 546 to 489 B.C.

[136] A great official of the state of Lu. He assumed power of government by usurpation in 492 B.C.

[137] Cf. below, 13:6.

[138] Cf. above, 12:17.

[139] See below, 16:1.

[140] According to Kung An-Kuo, *kung* is not the name but is used as a noun, meaning the body, and that the man walked erect.

[141] The word *ching* here does not mean reverence, which assumes an object, but seriousness, which is a state of mind. See Appendix.

[142] Cf. above, 2:14.

[143] This is Chu Hsi's understanding, which has been satisfactory to most readers.

[144] Confucius' pupil.

[145] This is the general interpretation, based on Huang K'an and commonly accepted before the Sung times.

According to Ho Yen, higher things mean the fundamentals and the lower things mean secondary things. Chu Hsi, consistent with his own philosophy, interpreted the word *ta* not to mean to understand but to reach, and said that the superior man reaches the higher level because he follows the Principle of Nature while the inferior man reaches the lower level because he is carried away by selfish human desires. Cf. below, 14:37.

[146] See Wang Yang-ming, *Ch'uan-hsi lu,* in Chan, trans., *Instructions for Practical Living,* secs. 171 and 191 for his discussion of this topic.

[147] There is a general agreement that the higher level refers to matters of Heaven, such as Heaven's decree (K'ung An-kuo and Huang K'an) and the Principle of Nature (Chu Hsi), and that the lower level refers to mundane matters. Cf. above, 14:24.

[148] The outer gate of the city of Lu. Cf. below, 18:6.

[149] See above, comment on 4:15.

[150] For the idea of a central thread, see above, 4:15.

[151] The term is the same as in Taoism, *wu-wei.* See above, comment on 2:1

[152] Cf. *Mencius,* 6A:10.

[153] Cf. *Great Learning,* ch. 9.

[154] *The Mean,* ch. 27.

[155] According to Pao Hsien (6 B.C.-A.D. 65), quoted by Ho Yen.

[156] Cf. above, 7:7.

[157] The historical background in this chapter may be inaccurate, but the teaching in this selection has never been questioned.

[158] Variously interpreted as sages or rulers. It is more likely a Platonic philosopher-king, for in the Confucian system, the sage should be a ruler and the ruler should be a sage.

[159] Cf. *The Mean,* ch. 20.

[160] *I-shu,* 8:2a.

[161] *Mencius,* 6A:7.

[162] See above, comment on 6:17. . . .

[163] *Hsin-shu* (New Treatises), ch. 5, sec. 3, SPPY, 5:7a. . . .

[164] *I-shu,* 18:17b.

[165] *Ch'uan-hsi lu,* sec. 109. See Chan, trans., *Instructions for Practical Living.*

[166] *Meng Tzu tzu-i shu-cheng* (Commentary on the Meanings of Terms in the *Book of Mencius*), sec. 22.

[167] *Hsing-ming ku-hsün* (Classical Interpretations of Nature and Destiny), in *Yen-ching-shih chi,* 1st collection, 10:16b.

[168] The word *yen,* ordinarily meaning saying, here refers to the virtues mentioned below.

[169] Cf. *Lao Tzu,* ch. 23.

[170] In the *Analects* sometimes "superior man" means a ruler and "inferior man" means a common person. It is not clear which is meant here. But the moral is the same.

[171] This episode took place when Confucius was 64. Cf. above, 14:41.

[172] Cf. above, 1:6.

[173] Official-in-chief of Lu.

Wing-tsit Chan (essay date 1975)

SOURCE: "Chinese and Western Interpretations of Jen (Humanity)," in *Journal of Chinese Philosophy,* Vol. 2, No. 2, March, 1975, pp. 107-128.

[*In the following essay, Chan compares Chinese and Western interpretations of* jen, *the idea of humanity or humaneness, which is a central concept in Confucian thought.*]

The concept of *jen* (humanity, love, humaneness; pronounced *ren*) is a central concept of Confucian thought and has gone through a long evolution of more than 2000 years. The story of that evolution has been told elsewhere.[1] The purpose here is to see how the Chinese have understood the concept and how the West has interpreted it. We shall discuss the Chinese understanding under seven headings.

(1) *Confucius (551-479 B.C.) the First to Conceive of Jen as the General Virtue.* The word *jen* is not prominent in pre-Confucian Classics. It does not appear in the 'Book of Yü' or the 'Book of Hsia' in the ***Book of History*** and only twice in its 'Book of Shang' where the word was originally *JEN* (man) and three times in its 'Book of Chou'. It is not found in the three 'Eulogies' of the ***Book of Odes*** and only twice elsewhere in the book besides once written *Jen.*[2] It is found in eight

passages in the **Book of Changes,** all in the Appendixes which are generally regarded as post-Confucian and none in the text itself which is believed to be pre-Confucian. In sharp contrast to these pre-Confucian Classics, the Confucian **Analects** mentions *jen* 105 times in 58 out of 499 chapters. Thus more than ten percent of the **Analects** is devoted to the discussion of *jen,* more than those on filial piety, Heaven, or rules of propriety.[3]

What is more important, Confucius looked at *jen* in a new light. In pre-Confucian Classics, whether the word is written *jen* or *JEN,* it means benevolence, a particular virtue, along with other particular virtues like wisdom, liberality, etc. Until the time of Confucius, the Chinese had not developed a concept of the general virtue which is universal and fundamental from which all particular virtues ensue. But Confucius was propagating a comprehensive ethical doctrine which must have a basic virtue on which all particular virtues are rooted. In this respect Confucius not only took a great step forward but also built Chinese ethics on a solid foundation. It is true that in a number of cases Confucius still treated *jen* as a particular virtue. When he said, "The man of *jen* is naturally at ease with *jen:* the man of wisdom cultivates *jen* for its advantage" (**Analects,** 4:2) and "The man of wisdom delights in water; the man of *jen* delights in mountains," (6:12), *jen* is coupled with wisdom. When he said, "A man of *jen* necessarily possesses courage but a man of courage does not necessarily have *jen*", (14:5) *jen* and courage are considered as two separate virtues. In his famous saying. "The man of wisdom has no perplexity; the man of *jen* has no worry; the man of courage has no fear", (9:28, 14:30) *jen* is one of three 'great virtues'. And in talking about the six virtues and six obscurations, (17:8) *jen* is one of the six. In all these cases, Confucius was following tradition in understanding *jen* as a specific virtue. In this sense, *jen* may be translated as 'benevolence', 'kindness', or even 'love' or 'humanity' so long as it is understood as a particular virtue.

The great majority of Confucius' sayings on *jen* in the **Analects,** however, goes beyond this idea of particularity. When he said, "A man who is strong, resolute, simple, and slow to speak is near to *jen*", (13:27) he obviously meant that *jen* involves many moral qualities. The same is true of his utterance, "One who can practice five things wherever he may be is a man of *jen*—earnestness, liberality, truthfulness, diligence, and generosity", (17:6) or "When one has avoided aggressiveness, pride, resentment, and greed, he may be called a man of *jen*", (14:2) or "To study extensively, to be steadfast in one's purpose, to inquire earnestly, and to reflect on what is at hand—*jen* consists in these". (19:6) In saying that "A man of *jen* is respectful in private life, is serious in handling affairs, and is loyal in dealing with orders" (13:19) he clearly thought of

jen as the moral standard governing one's entire life. He also said, "If a man is not *jen,* what has he to do with ceremonies? If he is not *jen,* what has he to do with music?" (3:3) Thus *jen* even embraces ceremonies and music. The most important sayings on *jen,* however, are these: When a pupil asked about *jen,* Confucius answered, "Do not do to others what you do not want them to do to you". (12:2) When another pupil asked about *jen,* he said, "To master oneself and to return to propriety is *jen*". (12:1) And when a third pupil asked him about *jen,* he replied, "A man of *jen,* wishing to establish his own character, also establishes the character of others, and wishing to be prominent himself, also helps others to be prominent". (6:28) To master oneself and to establish one's character means self-perfection, and to return to (or restore) propriety and to establish the character of others mean to bring about a perfect society. Undoubtedly the virtue of *jen* involves the perfection of others as well of oneself. Significantly the word *jen* is written in two parts, one a figure of a human being, meaning oneself, and the other with two horizontal strokes, meaning human relations. *Jen* is therefore the moral ideal whether the self or society is concerned. In fact, one involves the other. In short, *jen* is the general virtue which is basic, universal, and the source of all specific virtues. "If you set your mind on *jen*", Confucius said, "you will be free from evil". (4:4) "Only the man of *jen* knows how to love people and hate people", (4:3) for he has reached the highest level of morality. Needless to say that 'hate' here does not mean ill will but the refusal to tolerate evil. With the general virtue established, Chinese ethics entered upon a higher stage, for virtue as a whole can now be understood and particular virtues can now have a foundation.

(2) *Jen as Love.* Although Confucius' concept of *jen* as the general virtue is unmistakable, he never defined it. This responsibility fell upon his followers. In the *Doctrine of the Mean* traditionally attributed to his grandson Tzu-ssu (492-431 B.C.), it is said, "*Jen* is *JEN*", (Ch. 20) that is, *jen* is simply man, or rather the distinguishing characteristic of man. Mencius (372-289 B.C.?) expanded it by saying, "*Jen* is *JEN*. When embodied in man's conduct, it is the Way (Tao)." (*Mencius,* 7B:16) He also said, "*Jen* is man's mind". (6A:11) Commentators generally agree that by the mind of man he meant man's feeling of love.

The idea that *jen* means love began with Confucius. When a pupil asked him about *jen.* Confucius answered by saying that "It is to love men". (**Analects,** 12:22) This line of thought was continued by Mencius who said, "The man *jen* loves others". (*Mencius,* 4B:28) He said further, "A man of *jen* extends his love from those he loves to those he does not love". (7B:1) Again, "The man of *jen* loves all". (7A:46) Generally speaking, from the time of Confucius through the Han Dynasty (206 B.C.-A.D. 220), *jen* was understood in the sense of love. According to Mo Tzu (468-376 B.C.?) "Jen is to love" and to "embody love".[4] To Chuang Tzu (c. 369-286 B.C.), "To love people and benefit things is called *jen*".[5] According to Hsün Tzu (313-238 B.C.?), "*Jen* is love".[6] In the words of Han Fei Tzu (d. 233 B.C.), "*Jen* means that in one's heart one joyously loves others".[7] In the **Book of Rites,** it is said, "*Jen* is to love".[8] In the *Kuo-yü* (Conservations of the states), it is said, "To love people is to be able to be *jen*".[9] Tung Chung-shu (176-104 B.C.) was more explicit when he said, "*Jen* is the name for loving people" and "*Jen* is to love mankind".[10] A little later, Yang Hsiung (53 B.C.-18 A.D.) said, "*Jen* is to see and love" and "To love universally is called *jen*.[11] From all these it is clear that the interpretation of *jen* as love was a consistent tradition in ancient Confucianism. It is for this reason, no doubt, that the *Shuo-wen* (Explanation of words) of 100 A.D. equated *jen* with *ch'in* (affection, endearing).

The above quotations show that not only the Confucian School understood *jen* as love but the Moist, Taoist, and Legalist Schools as well. However, love to Mo Tzu was universal love, whereas love in the Confucian School meant love with distinctions, degree, or grades. On this score the two schools stood diametrically opposed and engaged in one of the most bitter debates in the history of Chinese thought. In Mencius' eyes, the Moist doctrine was "a great flood and ferocious animals". He cried, "Mo Tzu advocated universal love, which means a denial of the special relationship with the father". (3B:9) To the Confucianists, *jen* must rest on the foundation of affection to relatives. According to a Confucian pupil, "Filial piety and brotherly respect are roots of *jen*". (*Analects,* 1:20) After the *Doctrine of the Mean* describes *jen* as the distinguishing characteristic of man, it immediately continues to say that "The greatest application of it is in being affectionate toward relatives". (Ch. 20) This is why Mencius said, "The actuality (or substance) of *jen* consists in serving one's parents". (4A:27) The result is his well-known formula:

> In regard to [inferior] creatures, the superior man loves them but is not humane (*jen*) to them (that is, showing them the feeling due human beings). In regard to people generally, he is humane to them but not affectionate. He is affectionate to his parents and humane to all people. He is humane to all people and feels love for all.

> (7A:45)

Put briefly, this is the Confucian doctrine of love with distinctions or grades. From Mencius' point of view, when the Moists regarded people's parents as their own parents, they had two foundations, (3A:45) for he believed that "Heaven produced creatures" in such a way as to provide them with one foundation (such as parents being the foundation of men) but the Moists would have two foundations, that is, parents and other people. He argued that "It is the nature of things to be unequal". (3A:4) Applied to human relations, some are close and others are remote, and therefore the intensity of feeling varies. From the one foundation, that is, one's parents, one's love extends to other relatives, other people, and finally to all creatures. The point is that love is the same for all but its application varies with different relations. Confucianists start with parents because the relationship with parents is the first relationship in human life and the indispensable one, for one could be without other relations. From the practical point of view, it is also the nearest. As a matter of common practice, although one should have good will toward all, one greets first of all those nearest to him. It is the application that has degrees or grades, not love itself, for it is unthinkable to have half love or quarter love. The repeated sayings by the Confucianists that *jen* is to love all should make the all-embracing character of *jen* perfectly clear.

Partly because Mencius had to clarify why application must vary while love is the same, he advocated the doctrine of righteousness (*i*), or what is correct and proper, along with *jen*. He spoke of *jen* and *i* together many times.[12] He said, "Humanity is man's mind and righteousness is man's path". (6A:11) He also said, "Humanity is the peaceful abode of man and righteousness is his straight path". (4A:10) In other words, the general virtue of humanity has to be carried out in a proper way. This does not mean that humanity is internal whereas righteousness is external, an issue on which Mencius debated vigorously with Kao Tzu. (6A:4) Rather, humanity is the substance while righteousness is the function. In the functioning of anything, there is necessarily priority in time or degree in intensity. The substance does not vary but its operations differ in different situations. The major conflict between Moist universal love and Confucian love for all does not lie in the substance of love but in whether or not there should be differences in application. For the Moists there should be none but the Confucianists insisted that there should and must be. This has been a persistent theme in the Confucian tradition. The upshot of Moist universal love is universalism in which no distinction is made between one's own parents and other people's parents, thus denying any special relationship with one's own parents. When Mencius attacked Mo Tzu and his followers as having no parents he was not merely rhetorical. Instead, he was defending a central Confucian doctrine on human relations.

(3) *Jen as Universal Love.* As a result of the Burning of Books by the Ch'in rulers in 213 B.C., the Moist School virtually disappeared. After Buddhism entered China, its doctrine of universal salvation for all eventually became prevalent. It reached its climax in the T'ang Dynasty (618-907). Scholars who talked about Tao, virtue, humanity, and righteousness followed either the

Taoists or the Buddhists. Being greatly alarmed, the most outstanding Confucianist of the dynasty, Han Yü (768-824), took it upon himself to "clarify the Way of ancient kings". In his *Inquiry on the Way* he loudly declared, "Universal love is called humanity". And he advocated 'burning the books' of the Taoists and Buddhists and "made their lodgings (monasteries) human abodes again".[13] Some writers have claimed that Han Yü's doctrine of universal love is the same as the universal love of the Moists and the doctrine of universal salvation of the Buddhists. If so, what is the difference and why did Han Yü feel he had to attack them?

It should be made clear that the translation of 'universal love' in the case of Han Yü is from the Chinese term *po-ai*. The Moist term is *chien-ai*, literally 'mutual love'. Since the Moist concept is intended to cover all mankind, the translation 'universal love' is perfectly proper. However, although the translation 'universal love' has been used by practically all translators for both Han Yü's *po-ai* and Mo Tzu's *chien-ai*, Mo Tzu repeatedly emphasized the idea of "mutual love and mutual benefit".[14] There is no question that for Mo Tzu the practical benefit is a key factor in mutual love. This utilitarian motive is utterly different from that of Confucianism where humanity is the natural unfolding of man's nature.

The term *po-ai* comes from the *Kuo-yü* where a note to the 'Conversations of Chou' says, "*Jen* is universal love for men".[15] It also appears in the *Classic of Filial Piety* (Ch. 7). It is also found in the *Chung-lun* (Treatise on the Mean) by Hsü Kan (170-217), where it is said, "By the exercise of humanity the superior man loves universally".[16] Thus the concept of universal love is originally Confucian and there was no need to borrow from the outside. Han Yü did not attack the Buddhists and Taoists only but also Mo Tzu and Yang Chu (440-360 B.C.?). The reason he attacked them is that while they taught humanity, they neglected righteousness. This is why he began his *Inquiry on the Way* by saying, "Universal love is called humanity. To practice this in the proper manner is called righteousness". What is proper involves the question of method, a sense of propriety, and a relative degree of intensity. Han Yü granted the Taoists and the Buddhists the feeling of love but he insisted that the lack of righteousness led to the neglect of specific human relations and culminated in neglecting society in favor of a life of quietude and inactivity with the result that economic production was undermined and life itself was endangered. In his view, the Buddhist doctrine of universal salvation is empty and therefore negative whereas the Confucian doctrine is concrete and therefore positive. Actually Han Yü did not contribute much to the development of the Confucian concept of *jen*, but in affirming both the universal and particular aspects of *jen* and in stressing its solid and active character, he did much to strengthen the tradition.

(4) *The Identification of Jen with Nature and Principle and the Doctrine of 'Principle is One but Its Manifestations are Many' (li-i fen-shu).* Both Mencius and Han Yü spoke of humanity and righteousness together because they wanted it to be clear that while humanity is universal in nature, being extended to the entire human race, its applications in different relations and circumstances require specific expressions. However, they did not provide a philosophical basis for this doctrine. For this we have to wait for the Neo-Confucian philosopher Chang Tsai (1020-1077). The philosophical basis of *jen* may be traced to the saying in the *Doctrine of the Mean,* "Humanity is [the distinguishing characteristic of] man" (20) and Mencius' saying, "Humanity is the mind of man". (6A:11) Mencius also described humanity as the "The mind that cannot bear [to see the suffering of] others, that is, "the feeling of commiseration" which is "the beginning of humanity"". (2A:6) Here humanity is identified with the nature of man. Han Dynasty Confucianists generally considered humanity to belong to the nature of man and love to belong to man's feeling. For example, in the *Po-hu t'ung* (The comprehensive discussion in the White Tiger Hall), it is said that "In man's nature there is humanity", but love is considered as one of six feelings.[17] In his *Inquiry on Human Nature,* Han Yü also considers humanity as nature and love as feeling.[18] To Neo-Confucianists of the Sung Dynasty (960-1279), Humanity, principle, and nature are three in one.

The relationship among these three as well as between them and the doctrine of principle being one but its manifestations being many is best expressed, though only implicitly, in Chang Tsai's *Western Inscription*. It reads:

> Heaven is my father and Earth is my mother. . . . Therefore that which fills the universe I regard as my body and that which directs the universe I consider as my nature. All people are my brothers and sisters and all things are my companions. . . . The sage identifies his character with that of Heaven and Earth. . . . He who disobeys [the Principle of Nature] violates virtue. He who destroys humanity is a robber. . . . One who knows the principle of transformation will skillfully carry forward the undertakings [of Heaven and Earth]. . . . [19]

Though a short essay, the *Western Inscription* is one of the most important writings in Neo-Confucianism. As Yang Shih (1053-1135) told us, Chang Tsai's purpose in writing the essay was to urge us to seek humanity.[20] Yang Shih said,

> The meaning of the *Western Inscription* is that principle is one but its manifestations are many. If we know that principle is one, we understand why there is humanity and if we know manifestations are many, we understand why there is righteousness. By manifestations being many is meant, as Mencius

has said, to extend affection for relatives to humaneness for people and love for all creatures. Since functions are different, the application [of humanity] cannot be without distinctions. Some may say that in this case substance (one principle) and function (many manifestations) are two different things. My answer is that function is never separate from substance. Take the case of the body. When all members of the body are complete, that is substance. In its operation, shoes cannot be put on the head and a hat cannot be worn by the feet. Thus when we speak of substance, functions are already involved in it.[21]

Chu Hsi (1130-1200) made it clearer. He said:

There is nothing in the entire realm of creatures that does not regard Heaven as the father and Earth as the mother. This means that the principle is one. . . . Each regards his parents as his own parents and his son as his own son. This being the case, how can the principle not be manifested as the many? When the intense affection for parents is extended to broaden the impartiality that knows no ego, and when sincerity in serving one's parents leads to the understanding of the way to serve Heaven, then everywhere there is the operation that the principle is one but its manifestations are many.[22]

(5) *The Man of Humanity Regards Heaven and Earth and the Ten Thousand Things as One Body.* Chang Tsai said in his *Western Inscription,* "That which fills the universe I regard as my body and that which directs the universe I consider as my nature". The meaning of this is that one extends his affection for parents and relatives to all things until one, Heaven, Earth, and all things form one body. In his essay *On Understanding the Nature of Jen,* Ch'eng Hao (1032-1085) said, "The student must first of all understand the nature of *jen.* The man of *jen* forms one body with all things without any differentiation".[23] Elsewhere he said,

A book on medicine describes paralysis of the four limbs as absence of *jen.*[24] This is an excellent description. The man of *jen* regards Heaven and Earth and all things as one body. To him there is nothing that is not himself. Since he has recognized all things as himself, can there be any limit to his humanity? If things are not parts of the self, naturally they have nothing to do with it. As in the case of paralysis of the four limbs, the vital force no longer penetrates them, and therefore they are no longer parts of the self. . . . Therefore, to be charitable and to assist all things is the function of the sage. It is most difficult to describe *jen.* Hence Confucius merely said that the man of *jen,* "wishing to establish his own character, also establishes the character of others, and wishing to be prominent himself, also helps others to be prominent."[25]

This doctrine of forming one body with all things is a cardinal one in the Neo-Confucianism of the Sung and Ming (1368-1644) Dynasties. From Ch'eng Hao, his brother Ch'eng I (1033-1107), to Chu Hsi, Lu Hsiang-shan (1139-1193) and Wang Yang-ming (1472-1529), they all advocated it. In Wang Yang-ming, the relationship between the concept of *jen* and this doctrine is the most direct. He said,

The great man regards Heaven and Earth and the myriad things as one body. . . . That the great man can regard Heaven, Earth, and the myriad things as one body is not because he deliberately wants to do so, but because it is natural to the humane nature of his mind that he does so. . . . Therefore when he sees a child about to fall into a well, he cannot help a feeling of alarm and commiseration.[26] This shows that his humanity forms one body with the child. . . . Even when he sees tiles and stones shattered and crushed, he cannot help a feeling of regret. This shows that his humanity forms one body with tiles and stones. This means that even the mind of the small man necessarily has the humanity that forms one body with all. Such a mind is rooted in his Heaven-endowed nature and is naturally intelligent, clear, and not beclouded.[27]

In Ch'eng Hao's thinking, *jen* is similar to the vital power of the body which penetrates the entire body while in the thinking of Wang Yang-ming, in the clear character of *jen* there is neither division nor obstruction. In both cases, there is in *jen* the natural power of spontaneous flowing to the point of filling the entire universe. Implicit in this idea is that *jen* is a creative force, a power to grow and to give life.

(6) *Jen and the Process of Production and Reproduction (Recreation and Re-creation, sheng-sheng).* The principle of production and reproduction is a long tradition in the history of Chinese thought. The idea of production goes back to the **Book of Changes** where it is said, "The great virtue of Heaven and Earth is production".[28] In the *Comprehensive Discussion on the White Tiger Hall,* productivity is ascribed to *jen.* "The man of *jen* loves productions", it says.[29] Chou Tun-i said, "To grow things is *jen*".[30] However, the Ch'eng brothers were the ones who definitely interpreted *jen* as the power to produce. To Ch'eng Hao, "The will to grow in all things is most impressive. . . . This is *jen*".[31] And according to his brother Ch'eng I, "The mind is like seeds. Their characteristic of growth is *jen*".[32] Here the interpretation of *jen* is based on its common meaning as seeds. It is not to be taken as merely a pun. Rather, it is an extension of the meaning of *jen* as love or commiseration to include the characteristic of growth, for only with the creative force of growth can one gradually embrace all things and form one body with the universe. Hence their pupil Hsieh Liang-tso (1050-1103) said, "The seeds of peaches and apricots that can grow are called *jen.* It means that there is the will to grow. If we infer from this, we will understand what *jen* is."[33] For this reason, Ch'eng I said,

Origination in the Four Characters (of Origination, Flourishing, Advantage, and Firmness in the process of Change) is comparable to humanity in the Five Constant Virtues (of humanity, righteousness, propriety, wisdom, and faithfulness). Separately speaking, it is one of the several, but collectively speaking, it embraces all the four.[34]

Jen naturally gives rise to the other Constant Virtues just as Origination in the spring naturally leads to the successive stages of Flourishing in the summer, Advantage in the autumn, and Firmness in the winter. Hence philosopher Ch'eng said, "*Jen* is the whole body whereas the other four Constant Virtues are the four limbs".[35] Because of the characteristic to grow and to produce, there is the sense of commiseration that cannot bear the suffering of others, the desire to establish the character of others as well as that of oneself, the extension of affection for parents to the love of all creatures, and the goal to form one body with Heaven, Earth, and all things. This is why Wang Yang-ming said that the man of *jen* does not deliberately form one body but it is because of the nature of his *jen* that he does so. From this, it is clear that *jen* is creative and as such is active.

Jen was interpreted as impartiality by Chou Tun-i (1017-1073)[36] but impartiality is merely an attitude; its nature is passive. For this reason, Ch'eng I said,

> Essentially speaking, the way of *jen* may be expressed in one word, namely, impartiality. However, impartiality is but the principle of *jen;* it should not be equated with *jen* itself. When one makes impartiality the substance of his person, that is *jen*. Because of his impartiality, there will be no distinction between him and others.[37]

Hsieh Liang-tso understood *jen* as consciousness or awareness. He said, "When there is the consciousness of pain in the case of illness, we call it *jen*".[38] This theory sounds like that of Ch'eng Hao who considered the paralysis of the four limbs as an absence of *jen*. However, Hsieh's emphasis is on the state of mind. This can be seen from his saying, "*Jen* is the awareness of pain (in case of illness). The Confucianists call it *jen* while the Buddhists call it consciousness."[39] By equating *jen* with Buddhist consciousness, it is obvious that Hsieh's emphasis is on tranquillity. Such a Buddhistic doctrine can hardly be attractive to Neo-Confucianists. In criticism of it, Ch'eng I said, "One who is not *jen* is not conscious of anything. But it is incorrect to consider consciousness as *jen*."[40] Later Chu Hsi frankly stated, "In over-emphasizing the concept of consciousness, Heieh Liang-tso seems to be expounding the doctrine of the Buddhist Meditation School".[41] The main defect of the interpretation of *jen* as impartiality or consciousness is that it lacks the creative character of *jen* as the process of production and reproduction.

(7) *Jen as 'the Character of the Mind and the Principle of Love'.* As to how *jen* can produce and reproduce, the answer has been provided by Chu Hsi. This is what he said:

> The mind of Heaven and Earth is to produce things.[42] In the production of man and things, they receive the mind of Heaven and Earth as their mind.[43] Therefore, with reference to the character of the mind, although it embraces and penetrates all and leaves nothing to be desired, nevertheless, one word will cover all, namely, *jen*. . . . In discussing the excellence of man's mind, it is said, "Jen is man's mind".[44] . . . What mind is this? In Heaven and Earth it is the mind to produce things infinitely. In man it is the mind to love people gently and to benefit things. . . . In my theory, *jen* is described as the principle of love.[45]

What Chu Hsi meant by the 'character of the mind' and 'principle of love' is that the human mind is endowed with the principle of production and reproduction. That is its nature and its substance. When that principle is expressed in love, respect, etc., these are the feelings and the function of the mind. When the mind to produce things is extended throughout the universe, one will form one body with Heaven, Earth, and all things. The various concepts of *jen* are here synthesized and the Neo-Confucian doctrine of *jen* reaches its climax.

From the survey above, it can readily be seen that the concept of *jen* is very profound and extensive. Western studies of it may be said to have begun in 1662 when the *Great Learning* was translated. The *Doctrine of the Mean* was translated in 1667 and the **Analects** in 1687, all in Latin. The three Classics were rendered into English in 1688 and into French three years later. When in 1711 the *Book of Mencius* was translated into Latin, the Four Books began to attract the attention of Western intellectuals. In 1881, the English missionary James Legge translated the Four Books into English and published them in Hong Kong. He secured the help of Confucian scholar Wang T'ao (1828-1897) and consulted the commentaries of Chu Hsi. Inevitably Chu Hsi's interpretation of the Confucian Classics dominated the translation. Legge's work is scholarly and generally accurate and after a hundred years is still considered as a standard work. Its influence in England and America has been great. In other words, the West has been reading and studying to some extent the Confucian doctrine of *jen* for some three hundred years. What has been its understanding? What has been its appraisal? And what is its tendency? From the survey above, we may roughly draw these conclusions: (1) Although *jen* as the general virtue was understood from the very early days, the fact that *jen* is a central concept in Confucianism is beginning to be appreciated only recently. (2) The West had always considered the Confucian Golden Rule as negative, contrasted with that of Christianity which is considered to be positive. There has been a turn around but not quite complete. (3) The West has been favorable to the Moist doctrine of universal love and critical of the Confucian doctrine of love with distinctions. The reason for this is that the West has not studied the Neo-Confucian doctrine of principle being one and manifestations being many. (4) In the last thirty years, Western scholars have gradually analyzed the concept of *jen* in its various meanings. This is a most encouraging development. Nevertheless, because Western study of Neo-Confucianism developed only after World War II, there are still misunderstandings that need to be corrected and important aspects of *jen* that need to be expounded. These may be discussed as follows:

(1) *Jen and the General Virtue.* From the very early days, Catholic fathers had translated *jen* as 'humanitas', probably based on the saying in the *Doctrine of the Mean* and in the *Book of Mencius* that "*Jen* is [the distinguishing characteristic of] man". In his translation, Legge took great care to distinguish *jen* as a special virtue and *jen* as the general, basic virtue, rendering the former as 'benevolence' and the latter as 'perfect virtue', 'true virtue', and 'the good'. Clearly the Catholic fathers and Legge knew that *jen* denoted a universal virtue. However, in the last hundred years, few Western scholars understood *jen* in this sense but mostly as a particular virtue in the sense of benevolence or kindness. Consequently 'benevolence' has been almost the standard translation. Even as late as 1958, in his excellent work on the Ch'eng brothers entitled *Two Chinese Philosophers: Ch'eng Ming-tao [Ch'eng Hao] and Ch'eng Yi-ch'uan* [Ch'eng I], A.C. Graham chose to translate *jen* as 'benevolence'.[46] There are two reasons for the failure to understand *jen* as the general virtue. On the one hand, the West has not yet recognized that *jen* is a center, or rather the center, of Confucian ethics and has regarded Legge's translation of *jen* as 'perfect virtue', etc. as merely general descriptions. The upshot is that *jen* as a particular virtue has been prominent whereas *jen* as the universal virtue has remained in the background at best. Another reason is that Neo-Confucian discussions and debates on the concept have not been well known in the West. Graham's discussion of the basic concepts of the Ch'eng brothers is penetrating. He may have had in mind benevolence as a general virtue, but to him benevolence "covers those virtues which distinguish first the gentleman from the peasant, later the civilized man from savages and beasts".[47] This is good as far as Mencius' doctrine of *jen* is concerned but Neo-Confucian discussions on *jen* as production and reproduction and *jen* as seeds have been overlooked. In his translation of the **Analects** in 1938, Arthur Waley translated *jen* as 'Goodness' with a capital letter and carefully noted that "*Jen* in the **Analects** means 'good' in an extremely wide and general sense."[48] Undoubtedly he meant that *jen* is the general virtue embracing all other

particular virtues. However, he also said that *jen* in the sense of humanity is totally absent from the **Analects**. What happened was that Waley opposed Chu Hsi's interpretation of Confucianism and refused to accept Chu Hsi's interpretation of *jen* as the character of the mind and the principle of love. Thus Waley's understanding of *jen* is still onesided.

In the last ten years or so the most popular translations of *jen* have been 'human-heartedness' and 'love'. No doubt the former is based on Mencius' dictum that "*Jen* is man's mind (or heart)" and the latter on pre-Neo-Confucian interpretations. To the extent that both 'human heartedness' and 'love' indicate the general character of *jen,* they are acceptable. However, the description of *jen* as human heartedness represents only the interpretation of Mencius and ignores later interpretations. What is more important, human-heartedness is merely a state of mind, whereas the Confucian tradition emphasizes *jen* as an activity. As to the rendering of 'love', the word should be reserved for the Chinese word *ai* which means love. Besides, as the Ch'eng brothers said, "Love is feeling while *jen* is nature",[49] and the two should not be confused. This, I believe, was why Chu Hsi said that *jen* is "the principle of love" but not love itself. From all these considerations, I believe if we have the entire history of Confucian thought in mind and take care of all important ideas involved in the concept of *jen,* the best translation for it is 'humanity' of 'humaneness'. That is to say, use 'benevolence' for *jen* as a particular virtue and 'humanity' for *jen* as the general virtue. In this way the homonym of *jen* as virtue and *JEN* as man, both in pronunciation and in meaning, will be preserved. This will take in the idea that *jen* is both nature and principle as taught by Sung and Ming Neo-Confucianists. When Lin Yutang rendered *jen* in the **Analects** as 'true manhood',[50] and when Peter Boodberg, noting that the word *jen* consists of two parts, one meaning an individual man and the other meaning two (human relations), rendered it as 'co-humanity',[51] they expressed the essential meaning.

(2) *The Golden Rule and the Silver Rule.* Before the twentieth century, the introduction of Confucianism into the West and its study were almost completely done by Christian missionaries. They liked to contrast Confucianism and Christianity, naturally in favor of the latter. Again and again they declared that the Confucian Silver Rule was not as good as the Christian Golden Rule because, they contended, the Confucian rule was negative. When a pupil asked about *jen,* Confucius replied, "Do not do to others what you do not want them to do to you". (**Analects,** 12:2, 15:23) When another pupil said, "What I do not want others to do to men, I do not want to do to them", Confucius remarked that it was beyond him. (5:11) In the *Doctrine of the Mean* it is said, "What you do not wish others to do to you, do not do to them". (Ch. 13) And

in the *Great Learning,* it is said, "what a man dislikes in his superiors let him not show it in dealing with his inferiors". (Sec. 10) All these sayings are in negative expressions. Hence the Confucian rule was called a negative Golden Rule or simply Silver Rule to show that it is inferior to the Christian Golden Rule of loving all others as oneself. Before World War II, this interpretation was virtually standard.

No one doubts the positive character of the Christian teaching, but to think that the Confucian teaching is negative is to overlook several things. The first is that negative expressions such as 'infinite' are often most positive. Secondly, Chinese commentators on the Confucian Classic have never taken the saying to be negative in content. No one understood the Confucian saying, "Do not do to others what you do not want them to do to you" better than Mencius. He said, "And there is a way to win their (people's) hearts. It is to collect for them what they want and do not do to them what they do not like, that is all." (4A:10) There is no question that 'want' and 'not like' are direct borrowings from the Confucian saying. The significant point here is Mencius expressed the doctrine in both positive and negative terms. In commenting on the Confucian saying, the *Han-shih wai-chuan* (Han's commentary on human events with quotations from the **Book of Odes**) says, "If one hates cold and hunger, one knows that the world wants clothing and food. If one hates toil and pain, one knows that the world wants comfort and ease. If one hates poverty, one knows that the world wants riches."[52] A modern commentator, Liu Pao-nan (1791-1855), perhaps the most authoritative on the **Analects** since Chu Hsi, elaborated on the Confucian saying by remarking that "Since one does not do to others what he does not want others to do to him, this means that he will surely do to others what he wants others to do to him".[53] Throughout Chinese history no one has understood the Confucian saying in the negative sense.

In the third place, those who have regarded the Confucian doctrine as negative have failed to understand the real meaning of the word *jen.* In discussing the meaning of *jen,* we have quoted the Confucian saying that "To master oneself and to return to propriety is humanity" (12:1) and that "A man of humanity, wishing to establish his own character, also establishes the character of others, and wishing to be prominent himself, also helps others to be prominent". (6:28) Restoring propriety means restoring social order. In both sayings, the idea is that both the self and society are to be perfected. There is nothing negative in this teaching. When Confucius taught his pupil not to do to others what he does not want others to do to him, it merely means to apply to others the standard one sets for oneself. That is why wishing to establish one's own character, one also helps others to establish their character. It is significant that following the utterance

on this, Confucius continued to say, "To be able to judge others by what is near to oneself may be called the method of realizing humanity". In the *Doctrine of the Mean,* preceding the sentence "What you do not wish others to do to you, do not do to them", it says, "Conscientiousness (*chung* loyalty) and altruism (*shu* reciprocity) are not far from the Way". (Ch. 13) Traditionally, these two moral qualities, conscientiousness and altruism, have been considered as the two inseparable aspects of *jen.* As Chu Hsi described them, "Conscientiousness means exercising one's mind to the utmost and altruism means to extend to others what one holds for oneself".[54] The mind of course refers to the moral mind. This saying, which has served as the standard description of *jen* in the last six or seven hundred years, is derived from Ch'eng Hao. This is what Ch'eng Hao said:

> *Jen* means to devote oneself to the benefit of other people and things. Altruism means putting oneself in their place. Conscientiousness and altruism form the central thread running through all conduct. Conscientiousness is the Principle of Nature whereas altruism is the way of man. Conscientiousness is unerring and altruism is the way to practice that conscientiousness. Conscientiousness is substance while altruism is function. They are the great foundation and universal way of life.[55]

It is clear that the Confucian doctrine of *jen* covers both the self and others and aims at both complete self-realization and full development of society. Only with this understanding can we get the full meaning of such Confucian sayings as "He (the ruler) cultivates himself so as to give the common people security and peace" in the **Analects,** (14:45) "To serve my father as I would expect my son to serve me" in the *Doctrine of the Mean* (Ch. 13), and "Treat with respect the elders in my family, and then extend that respect to include the elders in other families" in the *Book of Mencius.* (1A:7) *Jen* is indeed the one principle that penetrates through Confucian teachings.

Many Western writers have also been bothered with the Confucian saying, "Repay hatred with uprightness". (*Analects,* 14:36) Surely, they say, this is negative ethics, especially contrasted with the Christian teaching of treating enemies as friends. It has been suggested that the saying was a response to the Taoist theory. The person who asked Confucius, "What do you think of repaying hatred with virtue?" may have been a Taoist or at least had in mind Lao Tzu's saying, "Repay hatred with virtue".[56] In reply to that question, Confucius said, "In that case what are you going to repay virtue with? Rather, repay hatred with uprightness and repay virtue with virtue". The key to the understanding of the Confucian teaching lies in the word *chih.* It is generally understood to mean reciprocity or severity, but these interpretations are wrong. The word has always been understood by Chinese commentators to mean uprightness, the same sense as in the Confucian saying, "Man is born with uprightness". (6:17) It means that in response to evil, one should be morally correct and not be swayed by emotion or to return evil with evil. In dealing with people, for example, the ruler should seek to educate those who did wrong rather than punish them. (2:2) Fortunately, the negative interpretation of the Confucian Golden Rule has been declining since World War II. The chief reason for this is that more and more interpreters of Confucian thought are scholars who know the Confucian texts. Still, while conceding that "Confucius formulated a law of human relationship identical with the Golden Rule of the New Testament", one writer said that Confucius "limited the operation of the law of reciprocity, in its complete sense, to the circle of the good, because evil persons were judged unworthy of the mutual consideration prompted by fellow-feeling".[57] Where this writer could have found such teaching in Confucianism is beyong one's imagination.

(3) *Universal Love and Love with Distinctions.* Because Mo Tzu advocated universal love, many Western scholars have regarded Moist ethics as more progressive than the Confucian which insists on distinctions in love. It was argued that this Confucian teaching is ethically deficient and contributed to the downfall of dynasties. According to the argument, it was for the purpose of amending this deficiency that Han Yü taught universal love. In this, it was said, Han Yü was influenced by Buddhism and Mo Tzu. It was further claimed that when several hundred years later Chou Tun-i advocated impartiality and Chang Tsai taught that "All people are my brothers", their goal was to remove the deficiency of the Confucian doctrine.[58] Since Han Yü strongly attacked Mo Tzu along with Buddhism and Taoism, it is difficult to see how he could have accepted a Moist doctrine. In regard to Chang Tsai, we have pointed out that implicit in his *Western Inscription* is the doctrine that principle is one but its manifestations are many. If this doctrine is understood, there won't be any difficulty to see why Mencius, then Han Yü, and later all Neo-Confucianists criticized Mo Tzu and Yang Chu at the same time. According to the Neo-Confucianists, Mo Tzu was sound in teaching universal love for all but he neglected specific human relations such as one's special relation to one's own parents. Similarly, Yang Chu was justified in teaching self-preservation but he ignored society. In either case, the teaching is one-sided. Mo Tzu was right in concentrating on the many, that is, society, but he neglected the one or the particular, that is, one's particular relation with parents, whereas Yang Chu concentrated on the one or the self at the expense of the many. In Confucianism, both the self and society are equally emphasized. This is what *jen* means, whether in its etymological sense of 'man' plus 'two' or in its elaborate sense as conscientiousness with oneself and altru-

ism toward others. It turns out that the doctrines of Mo Tzu and Yang Chu are deficient rather than the Confucian. To understand the Confucian doctrine of love with distinctions, we need to appreciate the teaching of principle being one while its manifestations are many.

(4) *Jen as the Principle of Production and Reproduction.* Only in recent years has the Neo-Confucian doctrine of *jen* as production and reproduction been brought into the discussion of *jen* in the West. In an article on the Neo-Confucian solution of the problem of evil, the present writer devoted a special section to the Ch'eng brothers and their concepts of *jen* and *sheng* (production, creation) and another section to the sources of the idea of *sheng*. The question was asked whether the Neo-Confucian idea of *jen* as seeds could have been borrowed from Buddhism. According to the Consciousness-Only School of Buddhism, consciousness consists of 'seeds'. The 'seeds' or effects of good and evil deeds are stored in the 'store-consciousness'. These seeds have existed from time immemorial and become the energy to produce manifestations. This Buddhist school was very active in Loyang where the Ch'eng brothers lived. Both of them had studied Buddhism. Moreover, their pupil Hsieh Liang-tso came very close to Buddhism in his ideas and actually equated the Confucian *jen* with Buddhist consciousness.[59] Ch'eng I himself said, "The mind is like seeds. Their characteristic of growth is *jen*."[60] However, these Neo-Confucianists were very critical of Buddhism. Besides, the Buddhist idea of seeds, working in a circular way as seeds perfuming or influencing manifestations and manifestations in turn perfuming seeds, leads ultimately to emptiness, whereas the Confucian *jen* as seeds is a progressively creative force that leads to development and fulfillment. The source of the idea of *sheng* has been traced earlier in the discussion of *jen* as production and reproduction. It was pointed out that the idea of production, growth, etc., has been a long tradition in Confucianism. An additional factor that influenced the Ch'eng brothers was probably the influence of their teacher Chou Tun-i. After studying with him, they gave up hunting.[61] Master Chou did not cut the grass outside his window. When Ch'eng Hao was asked about it, he replied, "He felt toward the grass as he felt toward himself".[62] Ch'eng Hao also said, "Feeling the pulse is the best way to embody *jen*" and "Observe the chickens. One can see *jen* this way."[63] With this feeling for life, the sense of production and growth is inevitable.

As a creative force, *jen* is definitely active in character. However, some Western scholars have chosen to see *jen* as a quality of weakness. Waley, for example, who understood *jen* correctly as the general virtue, regarded *jen* as passive in character. He based his contention on the Confucian saying that "The man of humanity delights in mountains". (*Analects,* 6:21) As Waley put it, *jen* "is passive and therefore eternal as the hills". No wonder he concluded that "*Jen* is a mystic entity not merely analogous to but in certain sayings practically identical with the Tao of the Quietists (Taoists)".[64] One is at a loss to find another Confucian saying to support this conclusion. On the contrary, one reads in the **Analects:** The man of *jen*, "after having performed his moral duties, employs his time and energy in cultural studies" (1:6); he "applies his strength to *jen*" (4:6); he "confers benefits upon and assist all" (6:28); he "devotes his strength to *jen* for as long as a single day" (4:6); and he helps others to establish their character and be prominent. Also, "A man who is strong, resolute, simple and slow to speak is near to *jen*". (13:29) All these sayings indicate an active character. Of course an element of tranquillity is present in *jen* but that means calmness and is not to be equated with passivity or weakness.

In a penetrating study, Peter Boodberg pointed out that in ancient Chinese pronunciation, forty or fifty of those words beginning with *j* have the quality of weakness, notably words like *jao* (weak), *jang* (to yield), *juan* (soft), *jo* (weak), *ju* (weakling, scholar). He therefore concluded that *jen* also possesses the meaning of weakness or softness.[65] Boodberg has statistics on his side. However, there are words beginning with *j* that mean strength such as *jan* (to burn) and *jui* (sharp). If statistics is the only guide, then in the **Analects** at least, it is on the side of *jen* as strength.

Along with the supposed element of passivity, some writers have asserted that *jen* is mystical, citing the Confucian saying, "Is *jen* far away? As soon as I want it, there it is right by me." (7:29) They have asserted that this is mysticism. Confucius once praised his most favorite pupil Yen Hui (521-490 B.C.), saying, "About Hui, for three months there would be nothing in his mind contrary to *jen*". (6:5) On the basis of this, some writers, both Chinese and Western, have concluded that Yen Hui was a mystic and that Confucius praised mysticism. To me all this is far-fetched. In the last ten years Western studies have been less speculative and far more analytical as well as comprehensive. In 1966, Takeuchi Teruo traced the evolution of the meaning of *jen* as external beauty to internal morality in ancient times,[66] and Hwa Yol Jung discussed *jen* as practical activity, as sociality, and as love or the feeling of commiseration which is also relational.[67] Two years later, Wei-ming Tu examined the dynamic process between *jen* and *li* (propriety, ceremonies) with *li* as an externalization of *jen,* its concrete manifestation. Thus *jen* is actualization of inner strength and self cultivation in social context.[68] Antonia S. Cua expounded on the same theme in 1971 but considered *jen* as an internal criterion of morality whereas *li* as external, the two being interdependent.[69] A year later, Timothy Tian-min Liu, based on the **Analects,** compared the Confucian concept of *jen* with the Christian concept of love.[70] In 1973, Lik Kuen Tong undertook a comparative study

of Confucian *jen* and Platonic *eros*, regarding both as rational love but thought that Plato emphasized the object of love whereas Confucius stressed the subject.[71] In 1974, Thaddeus T'ui-chieh Hang discussed the choice of *jen, jen* as existential actualization, and the cosmic and metaphysical meanings of *jen*, including a comparison with Western interpretations.[72] By far, the most important and most extensive contribution to the subject is that of Father Olaf Graf who in rendering Chu Hsi's *Chin-ssu lu* (Reflections on things at hand) into German in 1953 had greatly advanced Western studies of Neo-Confucianism.[73] In his *Tao und Jen, Sein und Sollen im sungchinesischen Monismus* of 1970[74], he surveys the concepts of *jen* from ancient Confucianism to Neo-Confucianism, especially Chu Hsi. He examines the various aspects of Confucian ethics and Neo-Confucian philosophy in relation to *jen*. And he compares *jen* with the ethics of Plato, Thomas Aquinas, Spinoza, and the New Testament, among others. With all this informative and instructive material, Western studies of *jen* should develop at a rapid pace.

Notes

[1] Wing-tsit Chan, 'The Evolution of the Confucian Concept *Jen*,' *Philosophy East and West* 4 (1955), 295-319; reprinted in *Neo-Confucianism, Etc.,* pp. 1-44.

[2] *Book of Odes,* odes Nos. 77, 103, 204.

[3] On whether Confucius really "seldom talked about *jen*," see my discussion in work cited in Note 2, pp. 296-297.

[4] *Mo Tzu,* Ch. 40 and 42, *Ssu-pu ts'ung-k'an* (Four Libraries series), ed., 10:1a, 6b.

[5] *Chuang Tzu,* Ch. 12, *Ssu-pu pei-yao* (Essentials of the Four Libraries series) ed. entitled *Nan-hua chen-ching* (True classic of Nan-hua), 5:2b.

[6] *Hsün Tzu,* Ch. 27, *Ssu-pu pei-yao* ed., 19:5a.

[7] *Han Fei-Tzu,* Ch. 20, *Ssu-pu pei-yao* ed., 6:1a.

[8] *Book of Rites,* Ch. 19.

[9] *Kuo-yü* 'Conversations of Chou' *Ssu-pu pei-yao* ed., 3:3b.

[10] Tung Chung-shu, *Ch'un-ch'iu fan-lu* (Luxuriant gems of the *Spring and Autumn*), Ch. 29 and 30, *Ssu-pu pei-yao* ed., 8:9a, 12b.

[11] Yang Hsiung, *T'ai-hsüan ching* (Classic of the supremely profound principle), Ch. 9, *Ssu-pu ts'ung-k'an* ed., 7:8b, 9a.

[12] In the *Analects, jen* and *i* are not spoken together. However, Confucius is quoted in many ancient works as speaking of *jen* and *i* together.

[13] Han Yü, *Yüan tao* (Inquiry on the Way), in *Han Ch'ang-li ch'üan-chi* (Complete works of Han Yü), *Ssu-pu pei-yao* ed., 11:1a, 5a. For a translation of the essay, see Wing-tsit Chan. *A Source Book in Chinese Philosophy*, Princeton University Press, Princeton, New Jersey, 1973, pp. 454-456.

[14] *Mo Tsu*, Ch. 15.

[15] *Kuo-yü*, Ch. 3 (3:3b).

[16] Hsü Kan, *Chung-lun*, Ch. 9, *Ssu-pu ts'ung-k'an* ed., 1:34a.

[17] Pan Ku (32-92), *Po-hu t'ung, Ssu-pu ts'ung-k'an* ed., 8:1a-b.

[18] Han Yü, *op. cit.*, 11:6a. For a translation, see Chan, *Source Book*, pp. 451-453.

[19] *Chang Tzu ch'üan-shu* (Complete works of Master Chang), Ch. 1. For a translation, see Chan, *Source Book*, pp. 497-498.

[20] *Kuei-shan yü-lu* (Recorded sayings of Yang Shih), *Ssu-pu ts'ung-k'an* ed., 2:18a, 3:28a.

[21] *Ibid.*

[22] Commentary on the *Western Inscription* in the *Chang Tzu ch'üan-shu.*

[23] *I-shu* (Surviving works), 2A:3a, in Ch'eng Hao and Ch'eng I, *Erh-Ch'eng ch'üan-shu* (Complete works of the two Ch'engs), *Ssu pu pei-yao* ed.

[24] *Su-wen* (Questions on original simplicity), Sec. 42.

[25] *I-shu*, 2A:2a-b.

[26] Referring to the *Book of Mencius*, 2A:6.

[27] *Wang Wen-ch'eng Kung ch'üan-shu.* (Complete works of Wang Yang-ming), *Ssu-pu ts'ung-k'an* ed., 26:1b-3a.

[28] *Hsi-tz'u* (Appended remarks), Pt. 2, Ch. 1.

[29] *Po-hu t'ung*, 8:2a.

[30] *T'ung-shu* (Penetrating the *Book of Changes*), Ch. 11.

[31] *I-shu*, 11:3a-b.

[32] *Ts'ui-yen* (Pure words), 1:4b, in the *Erh-Ch'eng ch'üan-shu.*

[33] *Shang-ts'ai yü-lu* (Recorded sayings of Hsieh Liang-tso), Pt. 1, p. 2b.

[34] *I chuan* (Commentary on the *Book of Changes*), 1:2b, in the *Erh-Ch'eng ch'üan-shu.*

[35] *I-shu*, 2A:2a. It is not known which brother said this. The two brothers shared many ideas in common.

[36] *T'ung-shu*, Ch. 21 and 37.

[37] *I-shu*, 15:8b.

[38] *Shang-ts'ai yü-lu*, Pt. 1, 11a.

[39] *Ibid.*, Pt. 2, p. 1a.

[40] *Ts'ui-yen*, 1:4a.

[41] *Chu Tzu yü-lei* (Recorded conversations of Master Chu), 1880 edn., 6:19b.

[42] Quoting the Ch'eng brothers, *Wai-shu* (Additional works), 3:1a, in the *Erh-Ch'eng ch'üan-shu.*

[43] *Chu Tzu yü-lei*, 1:4a.

[44] *Book of Mencius*, 6A:11.

[45] *Chu Tzu wen-chi* (Collection of literary works by Master Chu), *Ssu-pu pei-yao* ed. entitled *Chu Tzu ta-ch'üan* (Complete works of Master Chu), 67:20a-21a.

[46] Lund Humphries, London, 1958, Pt. 2, Sec. 1.

[47] *Two Chinese Philosophers*, p. 96.

[48] *The Analects of Confucius*, Allen and Unwin, London, 1938, p.28.

[49] *I-shu*, 18:1a.

[50] Lin Yutang, *The Wisdom of Confucius*, Joseph, London, 1948, p. 184ff.

[51] 'The Semaisiology of Some Primary Confucian Concepts'. *Philosophy East and West* 2 (1953), 330.

[52] Han Ying (fl. 160-130 B.C.), *Han-shih wai-ch'uan, Ssu-pu pei-yao* ed., 3:24a-b.

[53] *Lun-yü cheng-i* (Correct meanings of the *Analects*), 12:2.

[54] *Chung-yung chang-chü* (Commentary on the *Doctrine of the Mean*), Ch. 13.

[55] *I-shu,* 11:5b.

[56] *Lao Tzu,* Ch. 63.

[57] John B. Noss, *Man's Religion,* Macmillan, New York, 4th edn., 1969, p. 285.

[58] Homer H. Dubs, 'The development of Altruism in Confucianism'. *Philosophy East and West* 1 (1951), 48-55.

[59] *Shang-ts'ai yü-lu,* Pt. 2, p. 1a.

[60] *I-shu,* 18:2a.

[61] *Ibid.,* 7:1a.

[62] *Ibid.,* 3:2a.

[63] *Ibid.,* 3:1a.

[64] *The Analects of Confucius,* pp. 28-29.

[65] Boodberg, *op cit.,* pp. 328-330. (Note 52)

[66] 'A Study of the Meaning of Jen Advocated by Confucius', *Acta Asiatic* 9 (1966) 57-77.

[67] '*Jen:* an Existential and Phenomenological Problem of Inter-subjectivity', *Philosophy East and West* 16 (1966), 169-188.

[68] 'The Creative Tension between *Jen* and *Li*', *ibid.,* 18 (1968), 29-39.

[69] 'Reflections on the Structure of Confucian Ethics', *ibid.,* 21 (1971), 125-140.

[70] 'The Confucian Concept of *Jen* and the Christian Concept of Love', *Ching Feng* 15 (1973), 162-172.

[71] 'Confucian *Jen* and Platonic *Eros:* a Comparative Study', *Chinese Culture* 14 No. 3 (September, 1973), 1-8.

[72] '*Jen* Experience and *Jen* Philosophy', *Journal of the American Academy of Religion* 17 (1974), 53-65.

[73] Chu Hsi, *Djin-si lu* 3 vols., Sophia University Press, Tokyo, 1953.

[74] Otto Harrassowitz, Wiesbaden, 1970, 429 pp. xx

Jeffrey K. Riegel (essay date 1986)

SOURCE: "Poetry and the Legend of Confucius's Exile," in *Journal of the American Oriental Society,* Vol. 106, No. 1, January-March, 1986, pp. 13-22.

[*In the essay below, Riegel analyzes three poems about Confucius's time of exile.*]

Among the many stories and tales which constitute the legends of Confucius's life, the most well-known and dramatic involve the Master's suffering and hardships during his exile from Lu. . . . According to the account set forth in the *Tso chuan . . .* and *Shih chi . . . ,* Confucius departed, or perhaps was banished, from his homeland in 497 B.C., after a failed attempt, supported by him, to dismantle the defensive walls around the cities controlled by the powerful Chi . . . , Meng . . . , and Shu . . . families.[1] Along with a small group of followers, he wandered for thirteen years, travelling through Wei . . . , Ch'en . . . , Ts'ai . . . and other states which lay to the west and southwest of Lu.[2]

Tales of his trials, usually introduced with such conventional phrases as, "When the Master was in Wei" or "When Confucius was in danger somewhere between the states of Ch'en and Ts'ai . . . ," are found in numerous ancient sources including his collected sayings, the **Lun yü** . . . , as well as the *Meng tzu . . . , Mo tzu . . . , Chuang tzu . . . ,* and, of course, the *Shih chi* chapter which Ssu-ma Ch'ien . . . (ca. 145-90 B. C.) devoted to Confucian lore, the "K'ung tzu shih chia". . . .[3] It is conventional among those who have made a careful study of Confucius's biography to accept the accounts of the **Lun yü** and *Meng tzu* as "true" while dismissing the hostile *Mo tzu* and *Chuang tzu* stories as fictive hyperboles. Since the "K'ung tzu shih chia" is eclectic and its contents confused by Ssu-ma Ch'ien's attempts to fashion his materials into a consistent chronological whole (and perhaps by subsequent textual tampering as well), its versions have been judged unreliable unless attested by the **Lun yü** and *Meng tzu.*[4]

There can be little doubt that, because works such as the *Chuang tzu* and *Mo tzu* are openly hostile to Confucian teachings, their authors took great liberties with the received tradition, creating a Confucius to serve as the butt of their criticisms. It can at least be allowed that, in contrast to these, the books of the **Lun yü** are, with certain notable exceptions, friendly to Confucius, as is the *Meng tzu,* and hence may be more faithful representations of the earliest versions of the Master's years of exile. Yet, while Confucius's exile may have been an actual historical occurrence, it is doubtful that a claim of strict historicity can be attached to any of the accounts which relate it. All are complex and highly crafted literary pieces involving what we would label, from our perspective, fact and fiction. All exhibit the ingredients of "historical romance."[5] I propose to demonstrate this by showing that some of the literary remains of Confucius's life consist of bits and pieces of ancient poetry which in their origins had nothing to do with Confucius and even predated him.

"A river, like truth, will flow on for ever and have no end."

Among the *Pei feng* . . . of the **Shih ching** . . . is a group of three songs—No. 34: "P'ao yu k'u yeh" . . . , No. 36: "Shih wei" . . . , and No. 37: "Mao ch'iu" . . .[6]—which share striking thematic similarities with some of the lore surrounding Confucius's famous thirteen-year exile from Lu. More specifically, the language and structure of these three early songs are similar to, and in some cases identical with, the language and structure of certain later anecdotes about the exile now found primarily in the **Lun yü** and the "K'ung tzu shih chia," and, to a lesser extent, in the other sources of exile lore mentioned above. It is proposed that the parallels are close enough to warrant our regarding the songs as the models, or thematic archetypes, for the Confucian tales. It will be argued that because of their provenance in a literary compendium which according to scholastic traditions was much admired by Confucius, though remote from him in their original purposes, such literary sources were nevertheless judged, by those who would define the pattern of the Master's life, to be suitable examples of his behavior and teachings. By examining these songs in their original settings and then comparing them with the stories they have influenced, it is possible to provide a relatively detailed example of how Confucian legends utilized such ancient materials.

Together with the *Wei feng* . . . , all of the *Pei feng* and *Yung feng* . . . have long been identified as songs about the ancient state of Wei. . . .[7] This is in part due to the tradition that Pei . . . and Yung . . . were appanages of Wei. More importantly, their association with Wei is drawn from the observation that, along with the *Wei feng,* many of the Pei and Yung songs refer to place names in Wei while some allude to historical personages who can with some certainty be identified with Wei figures known from other accounts. (Although Marcel Granet, Bernhard Karlgren, Arthur Waley, and other **Shih ching** authorities of European training have tended to discount the significance of regionalism within the *Kuo feng* songs in general, other scholars, most notable among them Shirakawa Shizuka . . . , have emphasized the regional origins of the *Kuo feng* as an important feature that should not be ignored.[8]) It is in any case the concern of the various "Small Prefaces" which introduce the songs, of Mao Heng . . . , patriarch of the Mao School version of the **Shih ching** and supposed author of the *Ku hsün chuan* . . . commentary, and of the great Han scholiast, Cheng Hsüan . . . (A.D. 127-200), to explain the meaning of the three songs and reconstruct their original settings in terms of people, places, and events, in Wei. They are naturally unconcerned with the purposes to which the songs may have later been put and we should not expect from them any notice of the songs' influence on Confucian lore.

It should also be noted that the numerous studies of the legends of Confucius, including the monumental works of Ts'ui Shu . . . (1740-1816) and (somewhat more recently) Fujiwara Tadashi . . . , do not mention the contribution of the three songs to Confucian traditions.[9] To the extent that I try to expose this unappreciated connection between later lore and its literary antecedents in the *Shih ching* as well as to formulate the reasons why the connection was made, the study to follow represents a new, and perforce tentative, method of considering and evaluating the nature of the stories of Confucius.

* * *

In the analysis of the three songs, each will be taken up in the order in which it appears in the *Shih ching*. Each song is translated, its meaning paraphrased, and its connection to stories about Confucius's exile examined.

Song 34: "The Gourd Has Bitter Leaves"

"'The gourd has bitter leaves,'
   the ford is deep to cross."
"Where deep step on stones;
   where shallow wade."

"How fully the ford swells,
   'Evil!' the pheasant cries."
"The swelling ford will not wet your axle;
   the pheasant cries out to seek her mate."

"How harmoniously honk the geese,
   when the genial sun first rises.
If a knight goes to take a wife,
   he acts before the ice breaks."

"Beckoning, beckoning, is the boatman,
   Others cross, not I!
   Others cross, not I!
   I await my friend."

Song 34 tells of a man who is hesitant to take a wife. The story is presented as an elliptical dialogue between the man and another person, perhaps his betrothed or a go-between, who tries, without success, to convince him to act.[10] The song opens with the first person referring to himself metaphorically as "a gourd with bitter leaves." Because such gourds, when old, were inedible and merely ornamental, the speaker is casting himself as a useless old man.[11] The same person adds another figurative aphorism about a ford (*chi* . . .) in the river being too deep to cross. In the *Shih ching*, various tropes which have in common the image of crossing a river occur with some frequency in love songs where they express great passion or are euphemistic for seduction. For the first person of Song 34 to say figuratively that the river is too deep to cross means that he is, perhaps out of some unnamed fear, unwilling or reluctant to marry. A second person answers the first by refuting the figure of speech about crossing the river, with terms suitable to its imagery:

"Where deep, step on the stones / where shallow, wade."[12] In this way the second person encourages the first to ignore the dangers and be brave and persistent. [13]

In the opening of the second stanza the first person continues to resist. Now to his earlier saying about the depth of the river he adds the expansiveness of the water, in order to emphasize figuratively his fear that he is not meet for marriage. To this he couples a line about the baleful cry of a pheasant—the pheasant's call is given as *yao* . . . which sounds like the words *yao* . . ."die young" and *yao* . . ."calamity"—which is meant to say that the times are not right. But again he is refuted in the terms of the tropes he has chosen. For, in response, the second person claims that the first has misunderstood the pheasant—*yao* . . . also sounds like *yao* . . . , the desirous call of the cricket in Song 14, "The Grass Bug"[14]—and that its call means that it is seeking its mate. He assures, moreover, that, as deep as the water may appear, it will in fact not even wet his axles.[15]

The second person continues to encourage the first to go (stanza 3), exhorting him, through two bright sayings about overcoming timidity and seizing the moment: if he waits, the friendly circumstances are bound to change, just as the geese honk harmoniously in the morning but not later in the day; if he delays, he will not be able to go, just as a knight seeking a bride will not be able to fetch her once the winter ice melts and the rivers flood. The first person remains unconvinced (stanza 4) and, in keeping with his earlier metaphors about fording the river, sadly portrays himself as one left behind on a shore awaiting a friend while the boatman ferries others across to happiness.

The language of the song, its structure as a dialogue, and its theme of indecision all closely parallel an episode in the account of Confucius's exile in Wei, as preserved both in the *Lun yü*—but in the disparate fashion typical of that book—and more completely and coherently in the "K'ung tzu shih chia."

Sometime toward the end of Confucius's first sojourn in Wei, roughly between the years 493 and 490 B.C. according to the traditional chronology, the Chin nobleman, Chao Chien Tzu . . . initiated an attack on his enemies, the Fan . . . and Chung-hang . . . families. Pi Hsi . . . , Steward of the Fan family stronghold of Chung Mou . . . located in Chin north of the Yellow River, rebelled and took the fortress, apparently as an expression of his alliance with Master Chien of the Chao.[16] He then sent an envoy to Wei, inviting Confucius to join him. The passage describing Confucius's response is found at *Lun yü* 17.7 and in the "K'ung tzu shih chia."[17]

Confucius wished to go. His disciple Tzu Lu said, "I learned from you that, 'Into the company of any man who personally commits evil, the gentleman will not enter.' Now, Pi Hsi is personally holding Chung Mou in revolt. How can you consider going there?" Confucius replied. "There is indeed such a saying. But is it not also said of the truly hard that 'No grinding will ever wear it down'? Is it not also said of the truly white that 'No steeping will ever make it black'?"

Confucius then uttered words which closely mirror the opening metaphor of Song 34: "How is it that I am a gourd? How can I be merely hung as an ornament and not eaten." With these words Confucius expresses his great desire to join Pi Hsi. Yet he does not act. According to a passage immediately following the preceding in the "K'ung tzu shih chia" but occurring in a completely separate chapter in the **Lun yü,** Confucius retires to his home and plays the stone chimes to give expression to his feelings on the matter.[18] A passerby carrying a basket—a man identified by all commentators as an unrecognized sage—declares upon hearing the music: "With such passion does he strike the chimes!" But when the music was over the listener did not care for what it expressed of Confucius's decision. "How stupid he is! How stubborn he is! Since no one recognizes him he just quits! Where deep, step on stones. Where shallow, wade it."

With these last words, identical with the last couplet of the first stanza of Song 34 and intended to encourage Confucius to be brave and persistent, the stranger succeeds in changing Confucius's mind: "The Master said, 'That is resolute indeed. Against such resoluteness there can be no argument.'"[19] There occurs at this point in the "K'ung tzu shih chia" another, unrelated, passage on music occasioned by the story of Confucius playing the chimes. Immediately following it, the story resumes (the passage is not found at all in the **Lun yü**) with Confucius going to the banks of the Yellow River, intending to cross it and join with the Chao family of Chin.[20] In this way, the figurative line in Song 34 about crossing a ford has become in the Confucian legend a literal element of the story: we are meant to suppose that Confucius actually travelled to the river. At the very edge of the river, however, he "hears" the news that two virtuous ministers have been murdered by Chao Chien Tzu. Because of this, Confucius changes his mind once again and, in words which echo the sentiments of the first persona in the last stanza of Song 34, declares his decision not to cross the river: "How beautiful is the river! How very immense it is! That I, Ch'iu, do not ford (chi . . .), is fate." When asked why he did not go, Confucius explains that the murders are an example of yao . . ."perverse murders of the young and innocent," and that a virtuous man will not travel to places where such things occur. His calling the murders yao is significant for it reveals that the episode of having Confucius hear the baleful news is based on the Song 34 figurative saying about the ominous

cry of the pheasant which is cited by the persona of the song to say that the times are not right for marriage.

In summary, in both Song 34 and the foregoing Confucian anecdote the main theme is indecision as expressed in someone's hesitation to cross a ford. At several points in the extended tale Confucius is made to say or do something which either identically repeats or closely paraphrases the imagery of Song 34—especially noteworthy are the mention of the gourd, the allusions to crossing a river, the identical couplet about fording it no matter the depth, the reference to baleful news heard at a river's edge, the vastness of the river, and the final decision not to cross. In a manner similar to Song 34, the anecdote consists of a series of dialogues. Moreover, the order of Confucius's actions and utterances, as they are recorded in the more complete "K'ung tzu shih chia" version, follows that of the Song 34 narrative.

Song 36: "One so reduced!"

Oh, One so reduced, so reduced!
  Why not return?
If it were not for the lord's misfortune,
  why would we be here in the open?

Oh, One so reduced, so reduced!
  Why not return?
If it were not for the lord's impoverishment,
  why would we be here in the mire?

Song 36 is addressed to an exile by his followers. Both the "Small Preface" and Cheng Hsüan agree that this piece and Song 37 are a pair which refer to the exile of a certain Lord Li . . . who was driven from his territory by the Ti barbarians and fled to Wei. . . . Aside from their commentary, there is in the *Tso chuan* a brief mention of how, in 594 B.C., a Lord Li was established by the Chin army in Ti lands.[21] But nothing is said of his having been driven out by the Ti nor is there mention of his having gone to Wei. Still, it is significant that Songs 36 and 37 were recognized by **Shih ching** scholars as a pair, for it is as a pair that they influenced Confucian lore.

We may summarize generally what Song 36 reveals about the character of the exile and his relationship with his followers who address the song to him. Their calling him *Shih Wei* . . . , "One Most Reduced," identifies him as a once-prominent figure who has lost his prestige and is living in humble circumstances.[22] The question "Why not return?" reveals that the man could give up his exile if he chose to do so, but that he is perhaps stubbornly resisting repatriation and thus causing his followers to exhort him. His companions blame his "misfortune" and "impoverishment"[23] for their being "exposed" and "in the mire," hyperbolic metaphors for abject circumstances.[24]

The theme of the stubborn exile accompanied by unhappy followers is also found in the account of an incident that took place during Confucius's time of homeless wandering, when he was in the small state of Ch'en. In 489 B.C., Wu . . . attacked Ch'en and it may be that Confucius and his followers were in fact caught in the crossfire. According to the legend, as embroidered in numerous sources, the small band was starving and near death. There is no specific mention of these troubles in the "K'ung tzu shih chia," only an elliptical reference to how Ch'en was, at the time, plagued by bandits. A story in the *Hsün tzu* . . . refers to Confucius's impoverishment when in the area of Ch'en and Ts'ai and has Tzu Lu wondering why it is that Heaven has rewarded Confucius's merits with such catastrophe.[25] The use of the terms "impoverishment" (*o* . . .) and "catastrophe" (*huo* . . .) may reflect the influence of Song 36.[26] The equally fictive **Lun yü** 15.1 says of Confucius's disciples that, when their food ran out, they were so ill "none could rise to his feet," a phrase reminiscent of the Song 36 followers complaining metaphorically of being exposed and "in the mire." The passage relates that Tzu Lu then came to the master and asked indignantly, "Does the gentleman suffer impoverishment?"—a question which appears to take its inspiration from the Song 36 reference to the impoverishment of the exile portrayed in that song.[27]

Song 37: "Long Hair Hill"

'The kudzu on Long Hair Hill,
  how long its joints extend.'
Oh, my brethren!
  how many have been the days?

Wherever I have rested,
  I have always had friends.
Wherever I have tarried,
  I have always had helpers.

The fox-furs, crazed and confused,
  complain that chariot comes not to the east.
Oh, my brethren!
  I am without friends or comrades.

Oh, my pretty little things!
  sons of the vagabond bird.
Oh, my brethren!
  billowing sleeves and ear-plugs.

Song 37 records the sad, embittered words of an exile—again the "Small Preface" and Cheng Hsüan identify him as Lord Li—whose followers have tired of his cause and are abandoning him for a life of convenience and prestige. He begins by comparing himself to Mao Ch'iu . . . ."Long Hair Hill,"[28] an oddly shaped mound—Mao says of it that "it is high in the front with a depression at the rear"—on which there hangs a mass of dangling kudzu vines (the hill's "hair") whose length symbolizes how the persona's followers have distanced themselves from him. Observing aloud to his followers—whom he calls throughout his "brethren" (*shu po* . . .)—that his exile has been long, he claims for himself that wherever he has chosen to visit or remain he has been able to have with him men who share his values and are meritorious.[29]

But his situation has changed and thus, in stanza three, the persona quotes a saying, "The fox-furs are crazed and confused."[30] "Fox-furs" is a metonymy for noblemen; to say that they are "crazed and confused" (*meng jung* . . .) refers to their acting wild and abandoned, as if their heads were hooded and they could not see.[31] The line alludes metaphorically to the persona's adherents abandoning him. Following this is a problematic line in which the persona appears to relate how his followers, dissatisfied as they are with him and his cause, complain[32] that a chariot has not come to the east, which presumably refers to the fact that there has been no invitation from his homeland to return.

After further lamenting the disloyalty of his "brethren," the exile, in stanza four, brands them "turncoats." Calling them "pretty little things" (*so wei* . . .),[33] a name which figuratively labels them junior and may convey some measure of contempt as well, he condemns them as traitorous and duplicitous by metaphorically identifying them as "sons of the vagabond bird," birds which, as Mao points out, are, "pretty when young but ugly when old."[34] In the closing couplet of the song the "brethren" are described as having "billowing sleeves and ear-plugs," the elegant and elaborate insignia of a high official, and thus they are identified as having accepted office somewhere.

The theme of the exile who expresses his need for loyal friends while criticizing and lamenting the waywardness and disloyalty of his followers is also to be found in an account of an episode during the exile of Confucius. Sometime after the near starvation suffered by Confucius and his small band, referred to above, his companions began to break ranks with him. According to the "K'ung tzu shih chia" account of Confucius's wanderings, when Confucius and his party were still in Ch'en, Chi K'ang Tzu . . . , the newly empowered dictator of Lu, contemplated inviting him to return to his native state.[35] Warned by one of his advisers of Confucius's difficult personality, Chi K'ang Tzu decided instead to invite into his service one of Confucius's followers, Jan Yu. . . . Jan Yu immediately accepted. Confucius worried aloud that the invitation meant that Chi K'ang Tzu intended to employ Jan Yu in some grand office. But when Confucius saw Jan Yu, the disciple's dress and pretentious manner elicited from Confucius an acid comment also found in **Lun yü** 5.22 but without the introduction and setting provided by the "K'ung tzu shih chia".[36]

Shall we return home? Shall we return home? The young boys of my party are wild and brazen. They show off their replete insignia of office without knowing how properly to cut them.

Confucius's question, "Shall we return home?" is a purposeful echo of the exhortation to the exile of Song 36 by his dissatisfied companions. The pleonasm *k'uang chien* . . . "wild and brazen" by which Confucius refers to Jan Yu is but a prosaic gloss on the rarer binom *meng jung*, "crazed and confused," used in the Song 37 saying about disloyal noblemen. Having Confucius refer to Jan Yu as one of the "young boys," an epithet used elsewhere by Confucius to address his disciples, parallels the "pretty little things" of the song. The "billowing sleeves and ear-plugs" of Song 37 become, in the prose anecdote, the less figurative "replete insignia" of Jan Yu.

The contents of *Lun yü* 5.22 also occur in the *Meng tzu* where Confucius is made to say: "My young sons are wild and brazen in entering and taking office. Have they not forgotten their beginnings?"[37] For reasons which are not entirely clear, the "K'ung tzu shih chia" treats *Lun yü* 5.22 and the corresponding *Meng tzu* passage as two separate entries.[38] Numerous authorities have recognized that this must be a mistake and that Confucius should be considered to have uttered his condemnation of his "young sons" only once.[39] It has not been noted, however, that the "K'ung tzu shih chia" places the *Meng tzu* version immediately following its elliptical reference to banditry in Ch'en. This pairing duplicates exactly the traditional coupling of Songs 36 and 37. If the two songs did indeed serve as a source for the anecdotes, this sequence of events in the "K'ung tzu shih chia" is perhaps the one intended by those who formulated the legend. Thus the story of Jan Yu's disloyalty and ambitiousness which parallels Song 37 should be joined with and viewed as a sequel to the tales of Confucius's earlier impoverishment which derive from Song 36.

One initial point suggested by the foregoing analysis of the literary origins of Confucian legend is that, in terms of coherence and completeness as defined by their relative closeness to the language and structure of the songs, the versions of the stories preserved in the "K'ung tzu shih chia" are often preferable to those of the *Lun yü*. This is especially clear in the case of the story of Confucius's indecision about fording the river to go to Chin. What appears in the "K'ung tzu Shih Chia" as a single narrative that parallels Song 34 is divided in the *Lun yü* into two separate passages, with the climax found in the "K'ung tzu shih chia" version omitted entirely. I am not suggesting that the "K'ung tzu shih chia" is a more reliable source for Confucius than the *Lun yü*. Nor am I discounting the distortions of the original lore which apparently resulted from Ssuma Ch'ien's passion for a chronologically connected

narrative. I am claiming for the "K'ung tzu shih chia" that, in the instances studied above and in others as well, its arrangement and presentation of the anecdotes it shares with the *Lun yü* may be closer to earlier forms of the legend than that of the *Lun yü*.

We need not, because of some misguided faith in their antiquity, be wed to the disposition and division of passages in the *Lun yü*. While that book certainly had something like its present form as early as the time of Cheng Hsüan, who wrote the classical commentary for it, we cannot know how long before him this was true. Quotations of the *Lun yü* by title in the "Fang chi" . . . opuscule of the *Li chi* . . . and in the *Han shih wai chuan* . . . are not sufficient evidence in this regard, not only because they do not testify to the overall contents and division of passages of the *Lun yü*, but also because the dates of these sources are themselves problematic. They certainly do not prove that the extant recension of the *Lun yü* predates the compilation of the "K'ung tzu shih chia."[40]

Since there are many quotations of Confucian sayings in the *Meng tzu* which do not appear in the *Lun yü*, it may be, as Arthur Waley seems to suggest, that during the late Chou, the body of Confucian sayings and lore was much larger than and of a rather different nature from the *Lun yü*.[41] The "K'ung tzu shih chia" may adumbrate an alternate arrangement of Confucian tales found in this earlier body of lore, now lost but perhaps similar to the chronological presentation of the first two books of the *Meng tzu,* in which indications of chronology and concern for the coherence and completeness of the narrative were more in evidence than they are in the present *Lun yü*.

I would propose that this early body of Confucian sayings and lore was not only extensive but also enjoyed wide and perhaps even popular circulation. This is already suggested, at least for the Han dynasty, by the incorporation of numerous rather simplistic cautionary tales involving the Master and his disciples in the *Shuo yüan* . . . , *Hsin hsü* . . . , and other eclectic collections of moralistic anecdotes gathered by Liu Hsiang . . . (ca. 79-76 B.C.). The *K'ung tzu chia yü*. . . , which purports to be a collection of ancient Confucian tales, might be another useful reflection of the extent and popularity of Confucian lore during the Warring States and early Han, were it not made suspect by what appear to be numerous interpolations and distortions added to the text to serve the selfish scholarly interests of Wang Su . . . (195-256) in his attempts to denigrate the authority of Cheng Hsüan.[42]

It is thus significant in this regard that in the Fu-yang . . . , Anhwei, tomb of Hsia-hou Tsao . . . (d. 165 B.C.), the second Lord of Ju-yin . . . , there was discovered, among other very fragmentary manuscript remains, a board on both sides of which was written the table of contents of a collection of forty-six stories about Confucius and his disciples.[43] Though the text itself was unfortunately not found—if placed in the tomb it disappeared through deterioration—the table of contents gives the titles of its stories and these suggest that the work had much in common with the present *K'ung tzu chia yü* and was the sort of collection upon which the latter may have been based. In any case, this shred of evidence, found as it was in an area which in Han times was a cultural outpost remote from the centers of learning, does provide some indication of the wide circulation of Confucian tales. We learn by the serendipity of Chinese reporting on the find that one of the anecdotes had the title, "Confucius Wails upon Approaching the River" (*K'ung tzu lin ho erh t'an* . . .).[44] Even if we cannot know in detail this early version of the story of Confucius's decision not to join the Chao family upon learning, at the edge of the Yellow River, of Chao Chien Tzu's crimes, it is gratifying to have some confirmation of its popularity.

That there should have been discovered in the songs of the *Shih ching* models and patterns upon which to base accounts of Confucius's life is not in itself anomalous. Even in antiquity the ancient canon of songs was highly admired as a mirror of proper words and behavior. According to numerous *Lun yü* passages, Confucius himself regarded the songs as a rich catalogue of sentiments, deeds, and expressions which should be emulated. This attitude toward the text is also seen in the frequent quotation of the *Shih ching* to illustrate a point of morality or decorum, a practice much in evidence in the ancient philosophical, historical, and ritual literature.

In the examples we have studied, however, the songs are not merely quoted but reworked and transformed into the skeletons of prose anecdotes. They serve as frameworks of plot and terminology which are then considerably expanded with other materials to fit what the author wishes to say about Confucius and his times. Perhaps the most notable aspect of this exploitation of *Shih ching* imagery is the way in which aphorisms and maxims, figures of speech typical of *Shih ching* style and clearly critical to the rhetorical function of ancient poetry more generally, become literal narrative in the legend. Thus, for example, the fear of fording a river in Song 34, figurative for a man's hesitation to take a wife, serves as a crucial element in the plot of whether Confucius will ford the Yellow River and join the morally suspect government of Chin; and the Song 36 use of "exposed" and "in the mire" as metaphors for abject suffering becomes a literal description of the crawling of Confucius' sick disciples. In Song 37, moreover, we have examples of how the more flowery examples of poetical tropes, e.g., "The fox-furs are crazed and confused" or "billowing sleeves and ear-plugs," are translated into more commonplace expressions.

Though transmuted by literal interpretation and paraphrase, the songs are still recognizable in the language and structure of the legend. This provides a subtle but explicit connection between Confucius and his spiritual forebears, the personae of the *Shih ching* songs. The weavers of the Confucian legend, his "biographers," have Confucius relive the songs by having him say their lines, think their intentions, and act out the gestures portrayed in them. It would be to miscast and underestimate their achievements, however, to say of these "biographers" that they have merely borrowed prestigious materials, or to accuse them of fabricating and fictionalizing Confucius's biography. What they have done is to discover in the *Shih ching* the ancient patterns of proper behavior which Confucius admired and to show how in his life the Master, too, adhered to them. The life of Confucius is made the summation of the *Shih ching* lessons he so revered; or, in the words of *Lun yü* 2.11, he has "reanimated the past" (*wen ku* . . .).

Moreover, according to one ancient literary theory, the *Shih ching* songs should be counted among the great literary works created by those wrongfully banished, punished, or otherwise disaffected, to protest their fate and the circumstances of their age. Ssu-ma Ch'ien says:[45]

> In the past, when Hsi Po . . . (i.e., Wen Wang) was caught in Yu-li he lectured on the *Chou i*. When Confucius was impoverished in Ch'en and Ts'ai he made the *Ch'un ch'iu*. When Ch'ü Yüan was banished he wrote the *Li sao*. When Tso Ch'iu . . . lost his sight (?) he possessed the *Kuo yü*. When Sun Tzu . . . was defooted he discoursed on the *Ping fa*. . . . When [Lü] Pu-wei . . . was demoted to Shu he transmitted the *Lü lan* . . . (i.e., *Lü shih ch'un ch'iu*) to his age. When Han Fei was imprisoned in Ch'in [he wrote] "The difficulties of persuasion" and "Lonely anger." The three hundred songs of the *Shih* are fundamentally works composed by the worthies and sages to express anger.

To some extent this is a self-serving judgment on the part of Ssu-ma Ch'ien, for it provides him with antecedents to his own decision to continue his work on the *Shih chi* in spite of his disgrace at the hands of Han Wu Ti. It is of course most doubtful that the *Chou i,* *Ch'un ch'iu,* and *Kuo yü* were compiled under anything like the circumstances he describes.[46] Moreover, there are other accounts (some of them provided elsewhere in the *Shih chi*) of when and where the *Lü shih ch'un ch'iu, Ping fa,* and the discourses of Han Fei were composed. While the historical details of these characterizations are questionable, yet Ssu-ma Ch'ien is not greatly distorting the motivations that led to most of the works he cites. Certainly prominent among the intentions of those who authored the philosophical treatises he mentions was a passionate and often frustrated desire to reform what were perceived as the ignorant evils and mistakes committed by ancient rulers. The persona of the *Li sao* has undoubtedly suffered banishment. Reading the **Shih ching** one cannot escape the feeling that many, if not most, of its songs are the resentful expressions of the outcast and unhappy who were thwarted by the unresponsiveness of indifferent lovers, rulers, and gods.

It may have seemed to those who have given us the legend of Confucius's exile that the songs, as the expressions of the worthies of antiquity who had undergone similar deprivations, contained the proper prescriptions for the portrayal of the Master whose sufferings had inspired him to literary efforts: Ssu-ma Ch'ien claims that Confucius composed the **Ch'un ch'iu** . . . at that critical moment when he and his disciples were stranded and starving. Seen in this light, the songs defined the proper ways of portraying those special individuals, like Confucius, who were believed to have inherited the predicaments and sensitivities of the **Shih ching** poets. In this way these literary antecedents predetermine the circumstances and characterization as presented in the account of Confucius's life. They are the essential fundamental upon which the miscellaneous details of time, place, and personality—what we would call the real facts of Confucius's life—must rest. The process and its effects are not unlike the use by later Chinese historians of conventional sayings or formulaic characterizations—*topoi*—to introduce and identify the subject of a biography in terms of the classically prescribed roles, as well as to organize and give meaning to the more individualistic details of his life.[47]

The occurrence in Confucian lore of influence from the **Shih ching** goes beyond historiographical practices, however, and is an example of a more broad-based and important phenomenon in Chinese literary history. The harking back to the language and imagery of the **Shih ching** occurs so commonly in later literature, especially of course in poetry, that it deserves to be identified as a literary convention which distinguishes and typifies the Chinese tradition. The significance of these occurrences often escapes due recognition. This oversight is prompted, perhaps unintentionally, when borrowings from the **Shih ching** are labelled mere "allusions." This is an empty term which unfortunately obscures the active and determining influence of the old songs on later literary expression by casting the **Shih ching** as somehow inert or by viewing it as an archaic touchstone or storehouse and the later author who makes reference to it as merely traditional or pedantic. If the examples of the use to which the **Shih ching** songs are put in Confucian lore are typical, they suggest that in literary studies more efforts should be directed toward uncovering the details of how the **Shih ching** and other canonical sources not only influenced the lexicon of later literature but also shaped its themes and content.

Finally, it should be emphasized that the selection of songs to serve in the capacity of models for Confucian legends was not haphazard. Since Songs 34, 36, and 37, but no others, were selected, this choice must have been due to features inherent in the songs which were concordant with what Confucius's biographers already believed to be facts about his life and character. It was undoubtedly important, for example, that the three songs were about Wei, the place where tradition said Confucius spent much of his exile, and that two of them, Songs 36 and 37, were already identified as a pair of songs about someone exiled from his home. More specifically, the hesitation and scrupulousness communicated by Song 34 are traits for which Confucius was well known, and sometimes mocked, elsewhere in the ancient accounts of him. Similarly the "misfortune" and "impoverishment" of which Song 36 speaks are leitmotifs which occur throughout Confucian legend.

More than either Songs 34 and 36, Song 37 seems to exhibit features which may have marked it as an especially fitting archetype for Confucian lore. Most striking is the song's opening metaphor about kudzu growing upon what is called Mao Ch'iu, "Long Hair Hill," for Confucius's given name was Ch'iu . . . , "Hill," and tradition said of him, similar to what Mao said of "Long Hair Hill," that he had a depression atop his head.[48] The song's persona refers to his followers as *shu po*, "brethren," a familial term similar to *ti tzu* . . . , "younger brothers," the name by which Confucius's corps of disciples was known. In Song 37 there is a complaint that no chariot returns to take the persona home, a detail which uncannily anticipates the fact that Chi K'ang Tzu decided not to invite Confucius to end his exile and return east to Lu. Moreover, the claim of the song's persona that he had always been able to attract and associate with like-minded people closely resembles several Confucian sayings—for example, **Lun yü** 4.25: "Virtue never lives alone; it always has neighbors." A song so replete with characteristic "Confucian" images and teachings may have seemed to the composers and compilers of Confucian lore not a mere literary mode but a magical precursor which prefigured and portended Confucius's fate.

Notes

It is a privilege and an honor to dedicate this study to Edward H. Schafer, Agassiz Professor of Oriental Languages and Literature, Emeritus, of the University of California, Berkeley. All citations of the Thirteen Classics of the Confucian Canon are to the edition prepared under the supervision of Juan Yüan . . . (1764-1849) and printed in Nan-ch'ang, Kiangsi, in 1816. For the *Shih ching* I also give the "Mao Number" and for the *Lun yü* and *Meng tzu* I also provide the chapter and section numbers used in the Harvard-Yenching Concordances. References to the *Shih chi* . . . are to the edition included in the *Erh shih wu shih* compiled by the I-wen Press of Taiwan. Unless otherwise indicated, the editions of all other Chinese sources consulted are those of the *Ssu pu pei yao.* My thanks to Paul W. Kroll for his comments on an earlier draft of this article.

[1] For the events leading up to Confucius's exile, see *Tso chuan,* Ting 10, 56.5a-6b and Ting 12, 56.9b-10b. *Kung-yang chuan.* . . , Ting 12, 26.11a, claims Confucius originated the plan to dismantle the cities. The *Tso chuan,* however, credits his disciple, Tzu Lu. . . . A further discussion of this material may be found in Homer Dubs, "The Political Career of Confucius," *JAOS* 66 (1946), 273-82.

[2] A convenient chronological account of Confucius's wanderings, based on *Lun yü* and *Meng tzu,* is provided in D.C. Lau, tr., *The Analects* (Harmondsworth, 1979), 170-77.

[3] H. G. Creel, *Confucius and the Chinese Way* (New York, 1960), 7-11 and 291-94, discusses these sources.

[4] Ibid., 10.

[5] The classic study of the *roman* in ancient Chinese literature is Henri Maspero, "Le Roman de Sou Ts'in," in *Etudes Asiatiques publiées par l'Ecole Française d'Extrême-Orient à l'occasion de son 25e anniversaire,* Volume II (Paris, 1925), 127-42. See also Maspero's *China in Antiquity,* tr. F. A. Kierman (Amherst, 1978), 357-65. In these studies Maspero attempts to show that much of what is said in early sources of the Warring States political strategist, Su Ch'in . . . , is the product of "pure imagination." He believes that the fragmentary stories of Su Ch'in derive not from a work of history but from the now-lost *Su tzu* . . . which he calls a novel or "a work of political philosophy in the form of a novel." Maspero argues not from the origins of the Su Ch'in legends but from chronological inconsistencies and internal contradictions. His conclusion, that Su Ch'in was fictional, should be regarded with some tentativeness, as Maspero himself seems to have done. Moreover, Maspero seems not to have fully appreciated how the competition of cults which grow up about a figure lead to great diversity in the sources for them which have come to us. This was certainly the case with the traditions surrounding Confucius. These and related questions are discussed by David Johnson in connection with the cult of Wu Tzu-hsü which grew and influenced legends about the great hero of the kingdom of Wu during ancient as well as medieval times. See his "The Wu Tzu-hsü *Pien-wen* and Its Sources," *HJAS* 40.1 (1980), 93-156, and 40.2 (1980), 465-505.

[6] The three songs would form a single series were it not for Song No. 35, "Ku feng" . . . , which has nothing to do with the others. That song should instead be read together with three other *Pei feng* songs, Nos. 30, 32, and 41, which form a set having to do with the winds of the four cardinal directions.

[7] On the very fragmentary remains of a manuscript of the *Shih ching,* dating to ca. 185-165 B.C., and quite different in significant details from the Mao School version, there appears the state name *Pei kuo.* . . . This certainly suggests that the division of the Wei songs among three different states was not exclusive to the Mao School version, as was argued by some Ch'ing dynasty authorities, but instead was an ancient feature inherited by the various Han dynasty *Shih ching* traditions. (The manuscript was one of several discovered in 1977 in one of a pair of Former Han tombs located near Fu-yang . . . in Anhwei province. Another text from the cache is discussed below. For details on the *Shih ching* manuscript see *Wen wu,* 1984.8, pp. 1-21.)

[8] See Shirakawa Shizuka, *Shikyō kenkyū:* tsuronhen . . . (Kyoto, 1981), 51-177.

[9] Ts'ui Shu does, however, treat the legendary accounts discussed below in terms of their relative historicity in his *Chu Ssu k'ao hsin lu . . . (TSCC),* 2.47-51, 3.63-70. Fujiwara's useful two-volume study is entitled *Kōshi zenshū . . .* (Tokyo, 1931).

[10] Arthur Waley, *The Book of Songs* (New York, 1960), 54, already renders the song as a dialogue.

[11] Mao says that the bitterness of the leaves of the *p'ao* . . ."gourd" means that they cannot be eaten. The leaves evidently became inedible only very late in autumn when the gourd was old because the leaves of the *hu* . . ."calabash", with which Mao equates the *p'ao,* were delicacies offered the ancestors, according to Song 231, *Shih ching* 15C.3b. The Ho Yen . . . commentary at *Lun yü* 17.4a says that because the gourd cannot be eaten it is regarded as useless and thus hung on a wall where it remains.

[12] *Shuo wen chieh tzu . . .* 11A(2).15b defines *li . . .* as "stepping on stones to ford a stream." *Ch'i . . .*"wading" is defined more specifically by Mao and *Erh ya . . . ,* 7.21a-b as "lifting the skirts." Because of these and other lines in the song which encourage the reluctant first person to act, the song is often taken as an expression of resoluteness.

[13] At *Tso chuan,* Hsiang 14, 32.11a-b, and *Kuo yü . . . ,* "Lu yü," 5.2b-3a, there is an anecdote in which Song 34 is recited by a man to illustrate his resolve to ford a river and pursue the enemy.

[14] *Shih ching* 1D. la.

[15] For *kuei* . . ."axle." see B. Karlgren, *Glosses on the Book of Odes* (Stockholm 1970). p. 118, loss 91.

[16] For proof that Chung Mou was at this time a Fan family possession and not, as some old interpretations have held, already one of the Chao fortresses, see the comments of Huang Shih-san . . . , quoted in *Shikikaichū kōshō* . . . , ed., Takigawa Kametarō . . . (Kyoto, 1958), 47.46-47.

[17] The quote is found at *Lun yü*, 17.3b-4a and *Shih chi*, 47.14b. For a full translation of the latter, see E. Chavannes, *Les mémoires historiques de Se-Ma Ts'ien* (Paris, 1905), V, 347-48.

[18] See *Lun yü*, 14.39 (=14.15b) and *Shih chi*, 47.14b-15a, Chavannes, op. cit., 348-49.

[19] The quote from Song 34 and Confucius's reply to it appear in *Lun yü*, 14.39 but have dropped from the "K'ung tzu shih chia."

[20] *Shih chi*, 47.15a-b; Chavannes, 351-53.

[21] *Tso chuan*, Hsüan 15, 24.11b-12a.

[22] *Wei* . . . occurs in two senses in Song 36. It is in the first line of each stanza the noun, "obscure one, humble one." In the second line it is the negative, "if it were not for. . . ." The word *shih* . . . in general has two meanings in the *Shih ching*. Before verbs it is a modal. This aspect of the word has been studied in Ting Sheng-shu . . . , "*Shih ching* 'shih' tzu shou" . . . , *Bulletin of the Institute of History and Philology* 6.4 (1936), 487-95. When it occurs before nouns I take it to be an emphatic, related to other ancient words whose old pronunciations are similar to it. This seems to be what is suggested by Kuo P'u . . . , at *Erh ya*, 4.12a, who explains *shih wei* . . . as *chih wei* . . . , a gloss I have followed in my translation.

[23] Ma Jui-ch'en . . . , *Mao shih chuan chien t'ung shih* . . . , 4.26b-27b demonstrates that *ku* . . . should be understood as "calamity" or "misfortune" and that *kung* . . . is a short form for *ch'iung* . . . , "impoverishment."

[24] When Mao identifies *chung lu* . . ."in the open" and *ni chung* . . ."in the mire" as fortresses in Wei he is not defining the terms as toponyms but merely associating the scene of distress with strongholds in Wei.

[25] *Hsün tzu*, "Yu tso," 20.4b. At *Mo tzu*, "Fei Ju," 9.15b-16a, a passage with an almost identical formulaic introduction but intended to mock Confucius's hypocrisy claims that Confucius, who was usually scrupulous about his meals, ate meat given him by Tzu Lu even though he had reason to believe Tzu Lu had stolen it.

[26] Cf. note 23 above.

[27] *Lun yü*, 15.1b.

[28] *Mao* . . . should be read *mao*. . . .

[29] Following Mao's paraphrase.

[30] For another instance of the saying, see *Shih chi*, "Chin shih chia," 39.8b, where it refers to the confusion of the Chin nobility when the three families usurped power and there was no single leader.

[31] *Meng jung* . . . , or its variant *meng jung* . . . given in the Fu-yang *Shih ching* (see note 7 above), describes something completely covered over and concealed by a dense growth of vegetation and, by extension, the wild movements of those thus blinded. Because earlier scholars did not appreciate that "fox-furs" (*hu ch'iu* . . .) is a metonymy for the noblemen who wear them, *meng jung* has been mistakenly understood as descriptive of messy and unkempt fur.

[32] I follow the Fu-yang *Shih ching* (see note 7 above) and read *fei* . . ."complain" rather than the negative *fei* . . . given in the Mao School version. The Mao reading has long been recognized as problematic. Ma Jui-ch'en, op. cit. 4.29b, for example, argued that the graph . . . did not here stand for the negative but for a homophonous demonstrative pronoun.

[33] *So wei* . . . is but a variant of *shao wei*. . . .

[34] The bird gets the name *liu li* . . . , "vagabond," from the way it rides about on the wind and does not perch. The identity of the tiny bird is uncertain, though it is probably related to the siskin and, as Ma Jui-ch'en, 4.29b-30a points out, not the owl.

[35] *Shih chi*, 47.16a/b; Chavannes, 357-59.

[36] *Lun yü* 5.10a/b. The passage has been taken to be a comment about some anonymous disciples who remained home during Confucius's exile, but the *Shih chi* makes it clear that it is Jan Yu whom Confucius is criticizing.

[37] *Meng tzu*, 7B.37 (=14B.8a). The last sentence, which begins with the negative *pu* . . . , should be read as rhetorical question, a usage attested at *Meng tzu* 2A.2 and elsewhere.

[38] The *Meng tzu* passage is repeated at *Shih chi*, 47.13b.

[39] Liang Yü-sheng . . . , *Shih chi chih i* . . . (Kuang ya shu chü, 1887), 25.18b-19a.

[40] There is an ancient tradition which ascribes the "Fang chi" to Confucius's grandson, Tzu Ssu. . . . This led

numerous Ch'ing authorities to identify the "Fang chi" as a fragment of the latter's lost writings. In my doctoral dissertation, "The Four 'Tzu Ssu' Chapters of the *Li Chi*" (Stanford, 1978), I show that the ancient traditions are mistaken and propose that the "Fang chi" cannot be dated to much before the first century B.C.

[41] Arthur Waley, *The Analects of Confucius* (New York, 1952), 22-23.

[42] For the authoritative discussion of the problems surrounding the *K'ung tzu chia yü* as well as the differences between the Wang Su and Cheng Hsüan camps, see Gustav Haloun, "Fragmente des Fu-tsi und des Tsin-tsi," *Asia Major* 8 (1932), 456-61.

[43] The Fu-yang cache, first discovered in 1977, is reported in some detail in *Wen wu*, 1983.2, pp. 21-23. (It included the *Shih ching* MS discussed above in note 7.)

[44] *Wen wu*, 1983.2, p. 23, lists the titles of three of the stories and happens to include this one. One imagines that in some future publication we will learn the other forty-three titles included on the board.

[45] *Shih chi*, "T'ai Shih Kung tzu hsü," 130.12a.

[46] The line about the *Kuo yü* is garbled. Historical inconsistencies in the passage's other characterizations of the authorship of the texts it mentions are discussed in the commentary at *Shikikaichū kōshō*, 13.28-29.

[47] See Herbert Franke, "Some Remarks on the Interpretation of Chinese Dynastic Histories," *Oriens* 3 (1950), 113-22, esp. 120-21.

[48] *Shih chi*, "K'ung tzu shih chia," 47.2a.

David L. Hall and Roger T. Ames (essay date 1987)

SOURCE: "Some Uncommon Assumptions," in *Thinking Through Confucius,* State University of New York Press, 1987, pp. 11-25.

[*In the following excerpt, Hall and Ames comment on distinctions between Confucius's original teachings and later interpretations of them.*]

In this essay we have been bold enough to challenge both the principal understandings of Confucian thought and the traditional methods of articulating them. It behooves us, therefore, to begin by discussing certain of the fundamental background assumptions which characterize what we consider to be an appropriate interpretive context within which Confucius' thought may be clarified. The primary defect of the majority of Confucius' interpreters—those writing from within the Anglo-European tradition as well as those on the Chinese side who appeal to Western philosophic categories—has been the failure to search out and articulate those distinctive presuppositions which have dominated the Chinese tradition.

The assumptions we shall be considering are precisely those not shared by the mainstream thinkers of our own tradition. It should be of some real assistance to our Anglo-European readers if they have ready to hand some important cultural contrasts as a means of avoiding the unconscious translation of Chinese Confucian notions into an idiom not altogether compatible with them. We should caution, as well, Chinese thinkers trained within the Neo-Confucian tradition to keep in mind that we are here primarily attempting to explicate the thought of Confucius as it appears in the *Analects,* and not as his Neo-Confucian disciples, however distinguished, have envisioned it.

We must attempt to be as clear as possible at the outset concerning the nature and applicability of these uncommon assumptions. By "assumptions" we mean those usually unannounced premises held by the members of an intellectual culture or tradition that make communication possible by constituting a ground from which philosophic discourse proceeds. By calling attention to contrasting assumptions of classical Chinese and Western cultures, we certainly do not wish to suggest that the conceptual differences we chose to highlight are in any sense absolute or inevitable. The richness and complexity of the Chinese and the Western traditions guarantee that, at some level, the cultural presuppositions dominant in one culture can be found—if only in a greatly attenuated form—in the other milieu as well. Thus, our claims with respect to the assumptions uncommon to Chinese or Anglo-European cultures are to be understood as assertions as to their differential importance within the two cultures.

When we discuss the "uncommon assumptions" in the following pages we shall take the conceptual contrasts from the inventory of Anglo-European philosophy, but the meanings of these contrasts will be shaped in part by the fact that we are employing them to engage Confucius with the Western tradition. This is only to say that we shall often be employing our philosophic vocabulary in a fashion that stretches its traditional connotative bounds.

As we noted in our consideration of the necessary resort to cross-cultural anachronism in the Apologia above, by discussing concepts that Confucius did not explicitly entertain or by representing him as a defender of one of two contrasting assumptions grounded in a distinction he might not explicitly have recognized, we are attempting to provide an assessment of Confucian thought that openly accepts as inevitable that one always begins to think *where one is*. The naive assumptions that one can find a neutral place from which to compare different cultural sensibilities or that one can easily take an objective interpretive stance within an alternative culture, while comforting to those compulsively attached to the external trappings of objective scholarship, have led to the most facile and distorted accounts of exoteric thinkers.

1 An Immanental Cosmos

Perhaps the most far-reaching of the uncommon assumptions underlying a coherent explication of the thinking of Confucius is that which precludes the existence of any transcendent being or principle. This is the presumption of radical immanence. Our language here is somewhat misleading, since, in the strict sense, the contrast of transcendence and immanence is itself derived from our Anglo-European tradition. At any rate, it will become clear as we discuss Confucius' thinking in subsequent chapters that attempts to articulate his doctrines by recourse to transcendent beings or principles have caused significant interpretive distortions. Employing the contrast between "transcendent" and "immanent" modes of thought will assist us materially in demonstrating the inappropriateness of these sorts of transcendent interpretations.

Given the complexity surrounding the several applications of the term "transcendence" in the development of Western thought, it is essential that we be as precise as possible in what we intend by it. Strict transcendence may be understood as follows: a principle, *A,* is transcendent with respect to that, *B,* which it serves as principle if the meaning or import of *B* cannot be fully analyzed and explained without recourse to *A,* but the reverse is not true. The dominant meanings of principles in the Anglo-European philosophic tradition require the presumption of transcendence in this strict sense.

The prominence of the language of transcendence in considering the basic principles of Western philosophers tempts Anglo-European interpreters of Confucius' thinking to employ such language in their analyses of the ***Analects***. This has been particularly true to the extent that the major burden of introducing the Chinese classics to the non-Chinese world fell initially to Christian apologists with an inescapable commitment to the notion of transcendence. The necessity to employ transcendent principles is, of course, quite obvious in the Platonic and Aristotelian traditions. In Plato's *Timaeus,* the ideas or forms are independent of the Cosmos and provide the models in accordance with which the Cosmos is made. Aristotle's Unmoved Mover is the primary substance which, as the eternal, immu-

table, immaterial source of all other things, is the principle that accounts for all change and motion and grounds our understanding of the natural world. This principle, by its very definition, remains undetermined by the Cosmos or any element in it.

Classical forms of materialism, drawn from the philosophies of Democritus and Lucretius, construe the world in terms of "atoms" as the independent and unchanging units of which everything else is comprised. In the strictest sense the atoms of classical materialism transcend the things of the world which they comprise since they are the determinants of these things while themselves remaining unaffected by that which they determine.

A fourth alternative source of philosophical categories among the traditions of Western philosophy is associated with the dominant forms of the existentialist or volitional perspective. Here principles have their ultimate origin in human agents. "Princes" provide principles; rules come from "rulers." In the most general sense the human world is an array of artificial constructs which places upon each individual the burden of achieving "authenticity" by making this world his own through acts of reconstruction and valuation. Although this characterization of the existentialist perspective may seem to echo the sort of human-centered contextual ethics that we choose to associate with Confucius, these are false resonances to the extent that, in the Anglo-European tradition, existentialists have tended to be less concerned with interdependence than with the independent realization of excellence. According to this view, individuals at the peak of self-actualization become transcendent principles of determination, independent of the world that they create.

The existentialist perspective can be adjusted toward classical Confucianism only to the extent that it recognizes the relativity of the individual with respect to the society that determines, as well as is determined by, him. Furthermore, this interaction with the social context cannot be in the form of a "war of each against all" but must be grounded in deferential relations within interdependent contexts.

In the project of comparative philosophy, we have no choice but to attempt to articulate the other tradition by seeking out categories and language found in our own tradition that, by virtue of some underlying similarity, can be reshaped and extended to accommodate novel ideas. The thought of Confucius can only make sense to the Western reader by appeal to analogous structures within the purview of his own cultural experience that, however inadequate, can provide some basic similarity through which to deal with the differences. Difference cannot be taken on wholesale. What we are at a loss to find in the classical Anglo-European philosophic tradition is any fully developed position within which the principles of order and value are themselves dependent upon and emerge out of the contexts to which they have intrinsic relevance. An appropriate and adequate explication of the meaning of Confucius' thought requires a language of immanence grounded in the supposition that laws, rules, principles, or norms have their source in the human, social contexts which they serve.

If contemporary comparative philosophic activity is any indication, it might be the pragmatic philosophies associated with Peirce, James, Dewey, and Mead, and extended toward a process philosophy such as that of A.N. Whitehead, that can serve as the best resource for philosophical concepts and doctrines permitting responsible access to Confucius thought. This presumption, in fact, will be tested in the following chapters. This is hardly a controversial move, of course, since many from both the Chinese and Western contexts have pointed out the similarities between pragmatism and process philosophy, on the one hand, and classical Chinese philosophy, on the other.[1]

This immanental language necessary in the explication of Confucius' thought is of peculiar importance in articulating the Confucian concept of the self as an ethical agent. For there is a direct relationship between the Anglo-European language of transcendence and the necessity to construe the world, and *a fortiori* the *social* world, in terms of substances. Thus any recourse to transcendent principles inevitably leads to a substance view of the self. If the meaning of an agent or an action is to be discerned by recourse to a transcendent principle, then it is that principle which defines the essential nature of both person and context. Rational principles require rational beings to implement them. Moral principles require moral beings to enact them. Such beings are agents characterized respectively in terms of "rationality" and of "morality." And it is such characterization that renders the agent into a substantial being—that is, a being with an essence, an essential "nature."

Confucian philosophy, on the other hand, entails an ontology of events, not one of substances. Understanding human events does not require recourse to "qualities," "attributes," or "characteristics." Thus in place of a consideration of the essential nature of abstract moral virtues, the Confucian is more concerned with an explication of the activities of specific persons in particular contexts. This does not involve a mere shift of perspective from the agent to his acts, for such would still require the use of the substance language we have deemed inappropriate. Characterizing a person in terms of events precludes the consideration of either agency or act in isolation from the other. The agent is as much a consequence of his act as its cause.

The defense of the substantial self so prominent in the Judaeo-Christian tradition is to be contrasted with articulations of more diffuse senses of "self" in the Buddhist, Taoist, and Confucian schools of classical Chinese philosophy. The fact that these two disparate traditions have begun to interact constructively by dint of the recent growth of comparative philosophy raises some extremely interesting questions with regard to the distinctions within the various traditions. Criticisms of the notion of substantial selfhood within Anglo-European philosophy, beginning perhaps with Nietzsche and emerging most distinctively in the twentieth-century process philosophies of James, Bergson, and Whitehead, altered the problematic that had been presumed fundamental to the understanding of persons. The resort to exoteric cultures was therefore almost inevitable, for the theoretical context of Anglo-European thought was not conducive to the optimal expression of the nonsubstantialist insights.

The ontology of events underlying Confucius' thought is a most important implication of the immanental cosmos. Two other implications should be highlighted. These are the altered meanings of "order" and "creativity" in an immanental universe. Two fundamental understandings of order are possible: one requires that order be achieved by application to a given situation of an antecedent pattern of relatedness. This we might call "rational" or "logical" order.[2] A second meaning of order is fundamentally aesthetic. Aesthetic order is achieved by the creation of novel patterns. Logical order involves the act of closure; aesthetic order is grounded in disclosure. Logical order may be realized by the imposition or instantiation of principles derived from the Mind of God, or the transcendent laws of nature, or the positive laws of a given society, or from a categorical imperative resident in one's conscience. Aesthetic order is a consequence of the contribution to a given context of a particular aspect, element, or event which both determines and is determined by the context. It would be an error to suppose that order in Confucius' thinking meant anything like the rational order that results from the imposition of an antecedently entertained pattern upon events. As strange as this may seem to those still persuaded by the rigid stereotypes foisted on us by our received tradition, for Confucius order is realized, not instantiated.

It is also important that the Confucian sense of "creativity" be noted. In the Western philosophic tradition, informed by the Judaeo-Christian notion of *creatio ex nihilo,* creativity is often understood as the imitation of a transcendent creative act. In Confucian terms, creative actions exist *ab initio* within the world of natural events and are to be assessed in terms of their contributions to the order of specific social circumstances. In no sense are creative actions modeled after the meaning-closing actions of an extra-mundane creative event. Creativity in a Confucian world is more closely associated with the creation of *meaning* than of *being*.

2 Conceptual Polarity

The ubiquity of the concept of transcendence in the Western tradition has introduced into our conceptual inventory a host of disjunctive concepts—God and the world, being and not being, subject and object, mind and body, reality and appearance, good and evil, knowledge and ignorance, and so forth—which, although wholly inappropriate to the treatment of classical Chinese philosophy, nonetheless have seriously infected the language we have been forced to employ to articulate that philosophy.[3] The mutual immanence of the primary elements of the Confucian cosmos—heaven, earth and man—precludes the use of the language of transcendence and therefore renders any sort of dualistic contrast pernicious. The epistemological equivalent of the notion of an immanental cosmos is that of conceptual polarity. Such polarity requires that concepts which are significantly related are in fact symmetrically related, each requiring the other for adequate articulation. This is a truistic assertion about Chinese thinking, of course, and is usually illustrated with regard to the concepts of *yin* . . . and *yang*. . . . *Yin* does not transcend *yang,* nor vice versa. *Yin* is always "becoming *yang*" and *yang* is always "becoming *yin*," night is always "becoming day" and day is always "becoming night." But having said as much, most commentators on the Chinese tradition simply leave it at that, without spelling out precisely the character of the presupposition that underlies the mutual immanence and symmetrical relatedness of classical Chinese notions.

The presupposition, abstractly stated, is simply this: the Confucian cosmos is a context that both constitutes and is constituted by the elements which comprise it. But an important clarification is necessary. An organism is generally conceived as a whole with parts that functionally interrelate in accordance with some purpose or goal. In the West, Aristotelian naturalism is the most representative example where in an important sense the end or aim that characterizes the highest purpose or purposes transcends the natural world. The Unmoved Mover is an unconditional aim or goal. Where "organism" might be applied to the Confucian cosmos, an important distinction is that there is no element or aspect that in the strictest sense transcends the rest. Every element in the world is relative to every other; all elements are *correlative.*

If there is a true lack of correlativity even in naturalistic cosmologies such as the Aristotelian, then *a fortiori* there will be this same lack in philosophic systems influenced by cosmogonies of the *creatio ex nihilo* variety. Since the convergence of the Hebraic and Hellenic traditions in the West, *creatio ex nihilo* doctrines have had a profound influence in encouraging the language of transcendence and the dualistic categories which perforce must be employed to instantiate this language.

A dualism exists in philosophic vocabularies influenced by *ex nihilo* doctrines because in these doctrines a fundamentally indeterminate, unconditioned power is posited as determining the essential meaning and order of the world. This dualism involves a radical separation between the transcendent and nondependent creative source, on the one hand, and the determinate and dependent object of its creation on the other. The creative source does not require reference to its creature for explanation. This dualism, in its various forms, has been a prevailing force in the development of Western-style cosmogonies, and has been a veritable Pandora's box releasing the elaborated pattern of dualisms that have framed Western metaphysical speculations.

Polarity, on the other hand, has been a major principle of explanation in the initial formulation and evolution of classical Chinese metaphysics. By "polarity," we wish to indicate a relationship of two events each of which requires the other as a necessary condition for being what it is. Each existent is "so of itself" and does not derive its meaning and order from any transcendent source. The notion of "self" in the locution "so of itself" has a polar relationship with "other." Each particular is a consequence of every other. And there is no contradiction in saying that each particular is both self-determinate and determined by every other particular, since each of the existing particulars is *constitutive* of every other as well. The principal distinguishing feature of polarity is that each pole can only be explained by reference to the other. "Left" requires "right," "up" requires "down," and "self" requires "other."

Dualistic explanations of relationships encourage an essentialistic interpretation in which the elements of the world are characterized by discreteness and independence. By contrast, a polar explanation of relationships requires a contextualist interpretation of the world in which events are strictly interdependent.

Not only are the dualistic categories mentioned above inappropriate to the orientation of polar metaphysics, they can be a source of distorted understanding. Polarity requires correlative terminologies in order to explain the dynamic cycles and processes of existence: differentiating/condensing, scattering/amalgamating, dispersing/coagulating, waxing/waning, and so forth. Further, since everything that exists falls on a shared continuum on which they differ in degree rather than in kind, the distinctions that obtain among them are only qualitative: clear (*ch'ing* . . .)/turbid (*cho* . . .); correct (*cheng* . . .)/one-side (*p'ien* . . .); thick (*hou* . . .)/thin (*po* . . .); hard (*kang* . . .)/soft (*jou* . . .); genial (*wen* . . .)/ overbearing (*pao* . . .).

The polar character of early Chinese thought discouraged the interpretation of creativity in terms of *creatio ex nihilo*. The historian, Michael Loewe, goes so far as to assert that in the classical Chinese context, "in neither mythology nor philosophy can there be found the idea of *creatio ex nihilo*."[4] The *Chuang Tzu*, as an example of this tradition, explicitly challenges the principle of an absolute beginning:[5]

> There is a beginning. There is not yet begun to be a beginning. There is not yet begun to not yet begin to be a beginning. There is being. There is nonbeing. There is not yet begun to be nonbeing. There is not yet begun to not yet begin to be nonbeing. Suddenly there is being and nonbeing. And yet I don't know what follows from there "being" nonbeing. Is it "being" or is it "nonbeing"?

The implications of this dualism/polarity distinction are both many and important in the kinds of philosophical questions that were posed by the Chinese thinkers, and in the responses they provoked. For example, Loewe suggests that in that culture, "no linear concept of time develops from the need to identify a single beginning from which all processes followed."[6] The process of existence is fundamentally cyclical. There is no final beginning or end in this process; instead, there is cyclical rhythm, order and cadence.[7]

Again, the notion of a purposeful, anthropomorphic creator is certainly found in the classical tradition—the *tsao wu che* . . . of the Taoists, for example. However, the polar commitment which does not allow for a final distinction between creator and creature rendered this idea stillborn.[8]

If the Chinese tradition is grounded in conceptual polarities, a reasonable expectation is that this fact would be manifested in the main areas of classical Chinese thought: social and political philosophy. Benjamin Schwartz among others has observed that this is indeed the case. Schwartz identifies several "inseparably complementary" polarities which are grounded in classical Confucianism and which pervade the tradition: personal cultivation (*hsiu shen* . . .) and political administration (*chih kuo* . . .), inner (*nei* . . .) and outer (*wai* . . .), and the familiar knowledge (*chih* . . .) and action (*hsing* . . .).[9]

One of the most significant implications of this dualism/polarity distinction lies in the perceived relationship between mind and body. The dualistic relationship between *psyche* and *soma* that has so plagued the Western tradition has given rise to problems of a most troublesome sort. In the polar metaphysics of the classical Chinese tradition, the correlative relationship between the psychical and the somatic militated against the emergence of a mind/body problem. It is not that the Chinese thinkers were able to reconcile this dichotomy; rather, it never emerged as a problem. Because body and mind were not regarded as essentially different kinds of existence, they did not generate different sets of terminologies necessary to describe them. For this reason, the qualitative modifiers that we usually associate with matter do double duty in Chinese, characterizing both the physical and the psychical. *Hou* . . . for example, can mean either physically thick or generous, *po* . . . can mean either physically thin or frivolous. Roundness (*yüan* . . .) and squareness (*fang* . . .) can characterize both physical and psychical dispositions. In fact, the consummate person in this tradition is conventionally distinguished by his magnitude: great (*ta* . . .), abysmal (*yüan* . . .), and so forth. Similar yet perhaps less pervasive metaphors in the Western languages might hark back to a pre-dualistic interpretation of person. At the least, they reflect an interesting inconsistency between theory and metaphor, reason and rhetoric, in our tradition.

3 Tradition as Interpretive Context

The final assumption that gives access to the thinking of Confucius concerns the character of tradition as the interpretive context within which the foregoing presuppositions receive their literary and philosophic expression. As in the case of the two former assumptions, it will be helpful to characterize the Confucian position in terms of a conceptual contrast.[10]

History may be understood in distinctively different ways, of course, but there is a rather broad agreement concerning the centrality of the concept of *agency*. Whether history is construed directly in terms of efficient causal factors of an above all economic or military sort or is interpreted as the history of ideas, the concept of agency is indeed crucial. Ideas have consequences, if not in the same manner then certainly to the same degree as the arrangement of economic variables, for example. Even so, it would appear that neither idealist nor materialist conceptions of history would promote the notion of human agency to the same extent that, for example, volitional or heroic notions would. But there is little doubt that the materialist and idealist understandings are themselves constructions of individuals who lay claim to greatness. If not the historical figures themselves, then historians and philosophers, as authors of texts, become the efficacious agents determining the meaning of events. One has but to recall the manner in which the history of science, grounded in a materialist paradigm for most of its history, is celebrated in terms of the "great" scientists.

The situation is certainly no different with regard to intellectual history. We are still concerned with the import of our historical past construed almost exclusively in terms of the great minds. Ideas have discoverers, inventors, champions, and caretakers. And these individuals have names and careers. Their stories can be told.

All this is truistic and so much a part of our self-understanding as to be wholly taken for granted. Is there, after all, an alternative? The alternative that most readily contrasts with that of the preeminence of history as the defining context of cultural experience is one which finds tradition to be central. The terms "history" and "tradition" certainly have overlapping significances, but it is usually the case that one of these notions is more fundamental to a given social context. History is *made* by personages or events. Traditions possess a kind of givenness that defies or is at least resistant to the questions of originators and creators. History is rational and rationalizable in the sense that reasons and causes can be demonstrated for any given event or sets of events even though the whole complex of events may seem chaotic and irrational. With tradition just the reverse is true: it may be impossible to defend the rationality of this or that tradition, ritual or custom, but the rationality of the whole complex of traditions can usually be well-defended in terms of, for example, social solidarity and stability.

The different sorts of rationality associated with history and tradition indicate a great deal about the nature of the relationships that are most viable between them. Traditional cultures are ritualistic in the sense that the ritual forms associated with public and private praxis are employed in large measure as ways of maintaining institutional and cultural continuity with a minimum of conscious intervention. Those societies conditioned less by tradition and more by conscious history must resort to positive laws and sanctions to a greater degree.

This obvious and much advertised distinction between historical and traditional cultures is, of course, related to the fact that the former tend to stress morality in the sense of obedience and disobedience to principles and laws while the latter stress the aesthetic character of ritualistic participation. Rules are normative in the sense of external ordering principles with respect to historical cultures, while in traditional cultures rules are constitutive and immanent in the sense that, as ritualistic forms, they constitute the being or agent in the performance of the ritual. Also, given that a necessary and defining condition of ritual action is that it be personalized, there is a closer relationship between rituals and persons than between principles and individuals.

Rituals performed in accordance with tradition are readily contrasted with rules obeyed out of either rational deliberation or prudent self-interest. And the weight of this contrast is to be grasped in terms of the consequences it has for the exteriority of the person with respect to grounding principles characterizing his

social matrix. As a constituting activity, ritual action provides form to the person and the means of his or her expression. On the other hand, laws, which transcend the individual, provide guidelines for actions since they serve as guiding norms which measure, and standardize. They are to be obeyed. As such, one may (indeed must) feel "outside" the laws and alienated to however slight a degree by them and from them.

In the West, the strength with which one feels one's individuality is a function of the exteriority of norms. Unless one exists over against and in tension with the norms of society, there can be little in the way of ego-centered existence. The blending with one's ambience associated with aesthetic, ritualized life does little to promote intense forms of individuality. One can easily understand this by recourse to the contrasting senses of individuality in Western and Chinese cultures.

The distinction between Western forms of individualism and the Confucian concept of the person lies in the fact that difference is prized in Western societies as a mark of creativity and originality, while in China the goal of personality development involves the achievement of interdependence through the actualization of integrative emotions held in common among individuals. Such an ethos is based upon a rejection of those idiosyncratic emotions and actions that are not expressible through immanent norms of custom and tradition. The actions of individuals who dare to stand away from and challenge tradition and the visions of the past are interpretable by the Confucian as consequences of self-serving effrontery in the face of the legitimate continuities of a received tradition.

The dominance of tradition as the source of practical and affective norms leads to a restriction of the novel contributions of persons as individuals who would break the continuities of the past and establish new directions in thought or institutional practice. History thrives on the actions of rebels, idiosyncratic creators and innovators. Traditional societies prize continuities as embodiments and elaborations of the thinking and action of the past. The history of theoretical disciplines in China and Europe illustrates this distinction extremely well. In Chinese philosophy, the mark of excellence is found in the manner in which the wisdom of the originating thinkers of the past is appropriated and made relevant by extension to one's own place and time. In the West, the history of philosophy may be read as a series of revolutionary visions forwarded by (to limit ourselves merely to modern times) Descartes, Hume, Kant, Hegel, Marx, Nietzsche, and so forth.

Tradition-oriented societies, like the persons who comprise them, do not tend to initiate dramatic cultural changes. Of course, this is not to deny change. On the contrary, the continued appeal to the authority of

Confucius as sage in the Chinese tradition has masked a great deal of novelty. Doctrines significantly at variance with those of Confucius have been credited to him by virtue of the tendency to promote the continuity of traditional values. For example, although Confucius seems repeatedly to eschew the explicit treatment of metaphysical questions in the **Analects,** the profoundly metaphysical *Chung-yung* is nonetheless "attributed" to him via his grandson, Tzu-ssu. And Hsün Tzu, consciously flying under the banner of Confucius, does in fact represent a radical paradigmatic shift from his original teachings. Tung Chung-shu, the ranking Confucian scholar of the Western Han, is arguably more representative of Han syncretism than of Confucius or even pre-Ch'in Confucianism. And so on.

This relationship between the original teachings of Confucius and later interpretations can be understood in two ways. Either Confucius, for whatever reason, has been used as a medium to conceal the novel ideas of innumerable creative individuals, or he is in fact a "corporate" person who is continually being seen in a new way by virtue of the participation of later thinkers in the ongoing transmission of cultural values. Thus viewed, "Confucius" is a community, a society, a living tradition. . . .[11]

It is interesting in this connection to note the degree to which important historical changes in China have been occasioned by external forces. The so-called "Westernization" of China, particularly in its late nineteenth- and early twentieth-century phases, is a perfect example of such seeming historical passivity. This very historical passivity, however, masks the novelty and discontinuity of Chinese society. When Liang Souming, one of the principal theoreticians of the Chinese May Fourth Movement, spoke of China's "accommodating will" in contrast to the "aggressive will" of the West, he was alluding to this characteristic of many traditional societies. Such accommodation is a process of absorption taking place over a long period of time. It is, likewise, a process of transformation in which what is in its inception a novel element is provided a traditional interpretation. . . . [One] must avoid the temptation to interpret Confucius' thought from a strictly historical rather than a traditional perspective. To do so would make of him an originator, a "great man," instead of the "transmitter" that he understood himself to be. On the other hand, unless one remains sensitive to the meaning of creativity in Confucianism, the understanding of Confucius as a transmitter of tradition will lead one to mistake him for a mere transmitter, and not the sage that he indeed is.

Notes

[1] See, for example, Hall (1), pp. 169-228 for a discussion of some of the relations between classical Chinese thought and Anglo-European process philosophy.

[2] The distinction we are insisting upon between "logical" and "aesthetic" order will be discussed in some detail at the beginning of Chapter III, below.

[3] Indeed, one may question the appropriateness of dualistic categories in Western thought, as well. See Hall (1), Chapter 3, "What 'God' Hath Wrought," for a consideration of some of the cultural consequences of conceptual dualism.

[4] Loewe, p. 63.

[5] *Chuang Tzu,* 5/2/49.

[6] Loewe, pp. 63-64.

[7] Relative to this observation, it is significant that the notions of "birth" and the process of "growth" (or "life") are not clearly differentiated in Chinese; both are denoted by the character, *sheng.* . . . Since reality in the early Chinese tradition is conceived in terms of cyclical process, the absence of cosmogony is compensated for by an elaborate cosmological tradition, to which the *Yi-ching* and the Taoist, *Yin-yang* and *Wu-hsing* (Five Phases) schools bear witness.

[8] Loewe, p. 68.

[9] Schwartz, pp. 50-62.

[10] We should again stress that our employment of contrasting terms such as "transcendence and immanence," "polarity and dualism," and, in this section, "tradition and history" is not to be construed as descriptive of contrasts existing within the Confucian culture itself. On the contrary, these contrasts are couched in terms more congenial to the Anglo-European intellectual tradition and, as such, have the sort of dualistic associations supported by that context. Freed from these dualistic associations, the concepts of immanence, polarity, and tradition as stipulated here, are the most pertinent we have been able to discover in order to illumine the Confucian world view from a comparative perspective. The proof of their value, however, must be realized pragmatically as one attempts to use these uncommon assumptions in order to understand the discussions in the body of this work.

[11] See de Bary, (1) vol. II, pp. 188-91. Even the term *ju* . . . , typically rendered "Confucian" and taken as the emblem of Confucian thinkers, has the etymological association with *ju* . . . (weakness, servility). . . .

Works Cited

Chang Tzu. Harvard-Yenching Institute Sinological Index Series, Supp. 20. Peking: Harvard-Yenching Institute, 1947.

de Bary, Wm. Theodore. *Sources of Chinese Civilization.* New York: Columbia University Press, 1960.

Loewe, Michael. *Chinese Ideas of Life and Death.* London: Allen and Unwin, 1982.

Schwartz, Benjamin I. "Some Polarities in Confucian Thought." In *Confucianism in Action,* ed. David S. Nivison and Arthur F. Wright. Stanford: Stanford University Press, 1959.

Philip J. Ivanhoe (essay date 1990)

SOURCE: "Reweaving the 'One Thread' of the Analects," in *Philosophy East and West,* Vol. XL, No. 1, January, 1990, pp. 17-33.

[*In the following excerpt, Ivanhoe discusses the Golden Rule, which, in Confucian thought, is described in the notions of* chung *and* shu.]

INTRODUCTION

The Golden Rule—the notion that one's own desires can serve, by analogy, as a guide for how one should treat others—is found in various forms, in cultures throughout the world.[1] It seems that something like it must exist if there is to be any kind of society at all. One cannot have a friend, a tribe, or a civilization without the fundamental recognition that there are others who share at least *some* of one's central desires and that one can know what these are by reflecting on one's own desires. If this notion is joined with a concern for others, one has taken the first halting steps toward a moral life. One sees that one's actions should be *reversible*— that I should treat others as I would want to be treated by them, were we to exchange our positions.

The version of the Golden Rule found in the **Analects** is generally recognized as one of the oldest recorded statements of the notion of reversibility. It has been studied by several prominent scholars, who agree on at least one point: it is a notion of central importance to Confucius' thought.[2] In this article, I will present interpretations of the Confucian Golden Rule by four scholars: Fung Yu-lan, D. C. Lau, Herbert Fingarette, and David S. Nivison. Their respective studies all have contributed significantly to our understanding of this aspect of Confucius' thought. But I believe each of their interpretations leaves certain important difficulties unresolved. After presenting my views on what these difficulties are, I will offer my own interpretation.

REVIEW OF EARLIER INTERPRETATIONS

The Confucian version of the Golden Rule is usually described as consisting of two notions: *chung* and *shu.*

Confucius refers to these as the "one thread" running through his Way.

> The Master said, "Shen! My Way has one thread passing through it."
>
> Tseng-tzu replied, "Yes!"
>
> After the master had left, the other disciples asked, "What did he mean?"
>
> Tseng-tzu replied, "Our master's Way is *chung* and *shu,* nothing more."[3]

What these two words mean and how they fit together as two strands to form the "one thread" of Confucius' Way is our central problem.

Fung Yu-lan presents his interpretation in his book, *A Short History of Chinese Philosophy.*[4] He understands the two concepts *chung* and *shu* as representing "positive" and "negative" aspects of the notion of reversibility. That is, *chung* describes those things that I should do to others because I would like to have them done to me, and *shu* describes those things I should not do to others because I would not like them done to me. They are two aspects of the same principle and together form the "one thread" running through Confucius' Way.

The major strengths of Fung's analysis are that he is able to account in a systematic way for a variety of passages which seem to be connected to the problem of the Golden Rule and that his analysis explains both *chung* and *shu* in terms of the single notion of reversibility. Thus the two strands of the Golden Rule are woven tightly together to form what Confucius describes as his "one thread." Fung says:

> In the **Analects** we find the passage: "When Chung Kung asked the meaning of *jen,* the master said: ' . . . Do not do to others what you do not wish yourself. . . . '" (XII, 2) Again, Confucius is reported in the **Analects** as saying: "The man of *jen* is one who, desiring to sustain himself, sustains others, and desiring to develop himself, develops others. To be able from one's own self to draw a parallel for the treatment of others; that may be called the way to practice *jen.*" (VI, 28)

Thus the practice of *jen* consists in consideration for others. "Desiring to sustain oneself, one sustains others; desiring to develop oneself, one develops others." In other words: "Do to others what you wish yourself." This is the positive aspect of the practice, which was called by Confucius *chung* or "conscientiousness to others." And the negative aspect, which was called by Confucius *shu* or "altruism," is: "Do not do to others what you do not wish yourself." The practice as a whole is called the principle of *chung* and *shu,* which is "the way to practice jen."[5]

This is an interesting interpretation, but it presents several difficulties. First, there is simply no logical difference between the "positive" and "negative" statements of the principle of reversibility, which Fung has equated with the concepts *chung* and *shu*, respectively. Any action I might recommend that one do would, under an alternative description, be something I would recommend that one avoid doing. For example, the imperative "One should keep one's promises" goes over without remainder to the prohibition "Do not break one's promises." The statements of the Golden Rule in the *Analects* are almost all "negative," and Fung is right to point out this feature of the concept *shu* as significant. But his claim that this is complemented by a "positive" statement of the principle of reversibility seems problematic.[6]

Another difficulty is Fung's reading of key passages in the *Analects*. In the passage above, Fung quotes from *Analects* 12.2 and 6.28 to provide examples of the "negative" and "positive" versions of the Golden Rule. He then equates these with *chung* and *shu*, respectively. But neither term is mentioned in either of the passages he quotes. There is ample evidence to sustain the claim that *Analects* 12.2 concerns the notion of *shu*.[7] But even here, Fung leaves out an important part of this passage, a part which contains recommendations for "positive" action.[8] More damaging to Fung's interpretation is his understanding of the notion of *chung*. For while there are several passages in the *Analects* which show that *shu* involves the notion of reversibility, there is not a single passage which describes *chung* as a case of reversibility—positive or negative.

In making his case for *chung* as the "positive" version of the notion of reversibility, Fung relies on material from a different and later text, the *Chung Yung*.[9] This significantly alters the interpretive project. Looking at other, later Confucian texts can often be helpful for understanding the *Analects*, but such material should not serve as the primary evidence for an interpretation of concepts within the *Analects*. We should turn to such material only when we cannot make sense of some concept by relying solely on the evidence within the *Analects*. But even if we allow all the material Fung quotes to be admitted as evidence, we still find no examples of the term *chung* being described as a "positive" case of reversibility.

The next interpretation is that of D. C. Lau.[10] He sees the two concepts, *chung* and *shu*, related in a different way. According to Lau, *shu* is the method of drawing an analogy between oneself and others. It tells us both what we should do and what we should not do. Lau expresses the idea of *shu* with the words from *Analects* 6.30: it is "taking oneself—'what is near at hand'—as an analogy."[11] As for *chung*, Lau says:

> As the way of the Master consists of *chung* and *shu*, in *chung* we have the other component of benevolence. *Chung* is the doing of one's best and it is through *chung* that one puts into effect what one had found out by the method of *shu*.[12]

One of the great strengths of Lau's interpretation is the fact that he does not need to rely on texts beyond the *Analects* for support. But there is a difficulty with Lau's interpretation which involves a problem at the very heart of the notion of reversibility. Lau seems to say that *shu* is using one's intuitions about what is right and wrong as the standard for one's treatment of others.[13] But this moral "principle" can lead one into severe difficulties. For if people are guided solely by their own intuitions about what is right, it seems that the Golden Rule might end up providing warrants for doing many things that are unacceptable—at least to a Confucian gentlemen. For example, following this "Way" would have the unhappy consequence of encouraging masochists to become sadists.[14] In order to avoid such difficulties, the notion of drawing an analogy from oneself must include the qualification "if one were acting as an ideal moral agent." But if this is the case, then one's contribution to this imaginative exercise is at best obscure. One should just follow the imperative "behave like an ideal moral agent."

One way out of this difficulty is to argue for a well-articulated human nature which is shared by all people. Essentially, this packs the objective moral standards into each person's nature. This is the view of later Confucians, such as Chu Hsi. Mencius holds a related but less radical version of this view.[15] But we find no clear statement of such a view in the *Analects*. Confucius' only recorded statement on human nature is, "By nature human beings are close, but through practice they grow apart."[16] The point of this remark would seem to be that a common human *practice* is needed to keep human beings close to each other as they mature.

I find no evidence in the *Analects* to support the claim that Confucius advocated any strong form of innate moral intuitionism. Confucius seems to recommend something quite different. Rather than encourage us to rely upon our innate intuitions, he urges us to be guided by li, "rituals." But he does not advocate blind obedience to ritual. We must develop the ability to follow rituals informed by certain intuitions, but we only develop these intuitions through the intelligent practice of rituals. The case is not unlike that of skill acquisition in general, which relies on intuitions acquired through reflective training.[17] *Shu* is a principle we use *in the application of rituals;* it does not provide us with a moral guide apart from the matrix of rituals.

Another difficulty with Lau's interpretation concerns his understanding of *chung*. He claims that *chung* means "doing one's best" (in doing those things indicated by the imaginative act of *shu*). Understanding *chung* in this way may be plausible, but it is unusual, and one would like to see an argument for this sense of the word. Its basic meaning—the meaning it seems to have throughout the **Analects** and the one that most translators recognize—is "loyalty."[18]

But let us, for the time being, accept Lau's reading; it does bring into relief several important features of the Golden Rule. Understanding *chung* as "doing one's best" would work well if Confucius believed, as most Neo-Confucians did, that we all, in some deep sense, possess complete moral knowledge. *Shu* would reveal to us what we ought to do, and then we must *chung*, "do our best," to carry this out. The problem is that there are no passages in the **Analects** which link *chung* and *shu* in this way. The individuals who are described as being *chung* are not putting into practice actions revealed by the imaginative act of *shu*. As I will show in the presentation of my own interpretation, those described as *chung* are people who scrupulously follow *li*. What is needed, and what I believe my interpretation supplies, is an explanation of the relationship between *chung* and *li* which reveals how these two notions are mediated by *shu*.

Herbert Fingarette presents his analysis of the Confucian Golden Rule in his article, "Following the 'One Thread' of the **Analects**."[19] He believes a revealing analogy can be drawn between the Confucian Golden Rule and the Biblical version found, among other places, in Matthew 22: 35-40, in which Jesus is asked,

> "What is the greatest commandment of the law?" Jesus replied, "Love thy Lord your God with all your soul and with all your mind. That is the greatest commandment. It comes first. The second is like it: Love your neighbor as yourself. Everything in the Law and prophets hangs on these two commandments."[20]

According to Fingarette, the "greatest commandment," *Love thy Lord your God with all your soul and with all your mind,* corresponds to *chung,* and the "second commandment," *Love your neighbor as yourself,* corresponds to *shu.*

For Fingarette, the notion of imaginatively putting oneself in another's place only involves the second concept, *shu. Chung* is a kind of interpersonal good faith and loyalty, mediated by the *li* "rituals." It is one's personal loyalty to—one's love of—the Tao and corresponds to the Christian's loyalty to—love of—God. Fingarette sums up his interpretation:

> Let there always be good faith and loyalty of one person to another, as specified for various circumstances and persons by the *li;* and let this

always be conditioned by direct analogizing of self with other, rather than being solely a matter of conventions and rules and laws.[21]

Like Lau, Fingarette sees the notion of reversibility evident only in *shu,* and he seems basically to share Lau's interpretation in this respect.[22] But they part company on the issue of *chung.* Lau sees it as the implementation of the revelations of *shu,* while Fingarette sees it as interpersonal good faith mediated by the *li.*

Fingarette's analysis reveals important features of the thought we find in the **Analects**. But it suffers from being based on a misunderstanding of the concept of *chung.* He claims that in the **Analects** there is a kind of hybrid notion, *chung-hsin,* which means something like "interpersonal good faith." But this interpretation obscures the very specific and clear use of the term *chung* in the **Analects.** *Chung* always means, "doing one's duty in service to another."[23] To be *chung* is to be the kind of person who fulfills one's public obligations as defined by the *li. Hsin* has various related meanings. Its root sense is to be true to one's word. Related meanings include "being trustworthy" or "having trust in." When the two graphs are combined they describe a person who is reliable and worthy of trust. Fingarette has conflated these distinct senses and claimed that this is what Confucius intended by *chung* in the passages in which it relates to the Golden Rule. If indeed Confucius entertained such a notion, it seems odd that he did not use the purported combination *chung-hsin* in those critical passages relating to the Golden Rule.

The fourth and final interpretation is by David S. Nivison, as presented in his paper, "Golden Rule Arguments in Chinese Moral Philosophy."[24] This study contains a wealth of information about the Golden Rule; Nivison traces this notion throughout the course of Chinese history. But I will restrict my discussion to his understanding of its meaning in the **Analects**.

Nivison's analysis turns on his noticing a very important fact: there is an explicit hierarchical structure in the concepts *chung* and *shu.* Nivison understands *chung* as a guide for personal conduct in regard to one's social equals or superiors. It is the act of imaginatively placing oneself in the position of one's equal or superior and, in light of the *li,* seeing, from this perspective, how one would want one's equal or subordinate to behave toward one. One then uses this insight as a guide for judging what actions are appropriate for one to perform toward one's equal or superior. This process reveals to me my duty toward them, and I can then set about exerting myself to fulfill that duty as so revealed. This interpretation understands the term *chung* in a sense closely related to its basic meaning of "loyalty." As Nivison points out, the loyalty of a person who is *chung* is not just obedience. For Confucius believed that we should be loyal to the spirit of the *li*. This may require one to remonstrate with an errant friend or bad superior. In extreme cases it may compel one to refuse to serve an evil ruler altogether—preferring to starve in the hills rather than aid a corrupt cause.

Shu forms the other half of the Confucian Golden Rule and is directed toward the opposite end of the hierarchical spectrum. It is the feeling of benevolence one should adopt—to one's equals and one's social subordinates—when in a position of authority. *Shu* is the feeling of care and concern one should exercise toward these people. It is the feeling of *jen*, "benevolence," which Confucius once defined as "loving the people."[25] The *li* prescribe what is proper for every person in every situation, but the notion of *shu* insists that in exercising the prerogatives of our position, we temper our application of the rules when applying them to our social equals and subordinates. We are to be kind and considerate in what we demand from others. Nivison sums up his interpretation of *chung* and *shu* in the following way:

> *Chung* then is the quality of reliably following one's duties towards superiors or equals. *Shu* on the other hand is a quasi-supererogatory virtue—that is, it had to do with things that are not strictly required of one; it will mean that in dealing with equals or inferiors as our respective roles may require, I will be polite and considerate. The distinction is implicit again in a familiar early text, **Analects** III.19, not usually brought into this discussion: "The ruler employs his subordinates according to the 'rites'; the subordinate serves his ruler with *chung*, "loyalty."[26]

Nivison has revealed a number of important features of the concepts *chung* and *shu*. But, like Fung Yu-lan, he relies on passages outside of the **Analects** to make his case, specifically, for his interpretation of the notion *chung*. As I noted earlier, this alters the interpretive task. Also like Fung, Nivison claims that *chung* involves the notion of reversibility. But there is not a single passage in the **Analects** in which the notion *chung* is described as a case of imaginatively putting oneself in another's place. Nivison is correct to point out that *chung* consists of doing one's duties (as prescribed by *li*) in regard to one's social peers and superiors. But in no case does this involve the notion of reversibility.[27] As I will show below, *chung* is to do one's duty in service to others, to fulfill one's obligations as prescribed by the *li*. This is why the translation "loyalty" is everywhere appropriate. Such loyalty must contain the important qualification, pointed out by both Lau and Nivison, that it is not blind obedience to an individual. But this is accomplished in principle by being dedicated to the *li*. One's loyalty is to the explicitly social Way described by the *li*, not to some hidden private agenda or individual.

A NEW INTERPRETATION

Before I present my interpretation of the Confucian Golden Rule, I would like to examine briefly some important features of the notion of reversibility in ethical philosophy. Reversibility might be regarded as a *formal principle* which guides me, in the performance of specific actions, to only proper actions—that is, if before I perform a given action, I first conduct a kind of "thought experiment" and imagine how I would feel if I were in the place of the person or persons who will be affected by my proposed action. If I would be willing to be treated in the way I imagine, then I can act in the proposed way. If I follow this principle in every action I take, I can be assured of performing only proper actions.

But the principle of reversibility seems to degenerate in one of two ways. First, it can end up being a disguised way of advocating the adoption of one's personal preferences. For example, as I mentioned earlier, the principle of reversibility would seem to urge a masochist to become a sadist—to adopt the motto: "hurt others as you would have others hurt you." It would also urge those who enjoy hamburgers and beer to offer these to their vegetarian, teetotaler friends. Taken in this direction, the principle seems fatally flawed. It seems to amount to nothing more than a thinly veiled way of saying, "What I like is right, and you should like it too."

Taken in the opposite direction, the principle of reversibility can become a convoluted way of advocating the adoption of a set of unjustified prescriptions for action. It moves in this direction as soon as one realizes the difficulties of the overly subjective interpretation which we have examined above. If the principle of reversibility is to survive, it seems it must be part of a larger, objective ethical system. When I judge how I should treat others by imagining how I would like to be treated, I must accept the premise "If I were in their place *and acting properly*." Following this interpretation, when the Bible tells us, "And as ye would that men should do unto you, do ye also to them likewise,"[28] it is not saying we should use our personal preferences as a standard. By itself, it does not tell us what things we should do. At most it is providing us with a way to judge proposed courses of action. But it will yield the desired results only if one assumes—when imaginatively placing oneself in another's place—that the *you* of your imagination is an ideal Christian.[29]

But if this is what the principle of reversibility accomplishes, then it offers very little. For, as we go on to describe, objectively, what it is to be an "ideal Christian," we cannot seem to avoid providing a set of prescriptions for action. The Golden Rule then appears to be nothing more than a way to hide these rules from plain view. The person following the Golden Rule is simply following a set of prescriptions for action, and rather than invoke the Golden Rule, one might simply urge others to "be good Christians."

It seems that the notion of reversibility, by itself, is inert. On the first interpretation, it elevates mere subjective opinions to universal prescriptions for action and hence provides no moral guidance at all. On the second interpretation, it simply camouflages an imperative to follow a set of unjustified prescriptions for action. It seems that reversibility can at best function as a way to remind one to act as an imaginative ideal agent (of an explicitly defined ethical system). It does not provide us with actions to perform, and it does not work unless it is embedded in a surrounding ethic.

In the absence of a set of explicit prescriptions for action, the only way the principle of reversibility can work successfully to guide moral action is if one accepts the premise that there is something called human nature which is shared among human beings and which will incline them to perform a certain class of actions. In this way, the needed justifications can be found, at some level, in basic human intuitions.[30]

I believe that in the **Analects** we find a case of the Golden Rule which combines an explicitly defined set of moral guidelines with a subtle appeal to *developed* human intuitions. It is an interesting case; it has difficulties of its own, but it seems to avoid the two problems I have described above.[31] It avoids the merely subjective by advocating a set of prescriptions—the *li* "rituals"—which are regarded as the best possible set of rules for governing human life. Under normal circumstances, these prescriptions for action will lead one to act morally. But obedience to the rules is not the final goal. Rituals have an additional function; they guide one *to develop a sense* for what is right. This sense is necessary for a refined understanding of ritual. One develops this sense by continually reflecting upon the ultimate goal of ritual, the harmonious functioning of a society of human beings. In time, such reflection will reveal the spirit behind the letter of these "rules" and will show one that occasionally this spirit compels one to amend, bend, or suspend the "rules."

The first and primary notion in the Confucian Golden Rule is *chung. Chung* is one's loyalty to the Way; it is the personal virtue which assures others that one will do one's duty, as prescribed by the *li,* in service to others. Confucius taught his disciples, first of all, to adhere to a traditional creed of personal conduct described by the *li.* These rituals provided the initial direction and preliminary shape for their moral cultivation.

> The gentleman studies culture extensively and restrains himself with the rites. In this way he makes no transgressions.[32]

Confucius

Confucius' creed involved a strict set of rules, the *li.* He taught his disciples to submit to these prescriptions for action; he did not urge them merely to act in accordance with their innate intuitions.[33] But he also insisted that there was much more to his way than simply following these rules.

> They talk about ritual! They talk about ritual! Are gems and silks all that there is to ritual?[34]

One was not fully following the *li* until one performed each ritual with the appropriate attitude, but one could only develop these attitudes by practicing the *li.* One who had cultivated these proper attitudes and developed them into dispositions for ritual action would see that the traditional rituals provided the best way to give expression to human life. Such an individual would begin to acquire the cultivated sense of ritual which would allow him or her to depart from the mere practice of ritual and begin to apply the *li* with moral sensitivity. But one could make such judgments only at advanced levels of moral development. For example, when one is first introduced to the traditional rituals for mourning, one must begin by mastering a set of prescribed actions. As one masters the rudiments of these actions one becomes aware of the corresponding emotional states one is to adopt in each case. One comes to see how each facet of the ritual relates to and reflects every other and how its various parts fit together to form a pattern which gives beautiful expression to the deep and troubling emotions that accompany the loss of a loved one. One then fully understands the rationale for the various parts of the ritual. One sees that this ritual is the best way to give form to this aspect of human life, and one begins to see when and how the ritual is to be interpreted and applied in actual situations.

The first step in this process is simply to *practice* the *li*. One must learn to do one's duty in service to others, to take one's place and participate in society. *Chung* is one's commitment to do one's duty, as prescribed by the *li*, in service to others.

Confucius regarded government service as the highest calling a morally cultivated individual could follow. Throughout his life he sought for a position from which he could put the Way into practice, and he taught his disciples always with this goal in mind. Government service places one in a situation where the different senses of "loyalty" are put to the test. This is why Confucius proposed the example of a minister's service to his ruler as a paradigmatic case for *chung* behavior:

> Lords employ their ministers according to ritual. Ministers serve their lords with loyalty (*chung*).[35]

In this passage, we clearly see the hierarchical nature of the concept *chung*.[36] *Chung* is following the rituals *in service to others*. A person can never be *chung* to a subordinate (just as it would be odd for us to say one is "loyal" to a subordinate).

In these and other passages, *chung* implies a morally charged sense of loyalty. It has the sense of "integrity" rather than "obedience." *Chung* is the commitment (and eventually the disposition) to follow the *li*. And since following the *li* consists of working in concert with others, there is an additional aspect to being *chung*. One who is *chung* will advise and instruct those he or she serves whenever they are failing to perform *their* ritual obligations.

> Tzu-kung asked about friendship. The master said, "Loyally (*chung*) advise and skillfully lead them (to do what is proper). If they do wrong, do not join them in it. Do not disgrace yourself."[37]

A true friend or faithful subordinate does what is in one's "best" interest. And for Confucius, this means that this person helps one to stay on the Way. The loyalty of the *chung* person is not morally blind. As Confucius says, "Can there be loyalty without instruction?"[38]

But if this were all there was to Confucius' Way, his disciples would have been little more than moralizing martinets. They would have lost sight of—perhaps never even seen—the underlying rationale for the rituals: to produce a harmonious and humane society. They would never have developed the overarching concern for their fellow human beings, Confucius' premier virtue, *jen*, "benevolence."

Being perfectly *chung* does not constitute being *jen*. We see this in another passage, which also describes the behavior of an official.

> Tzu-kung asked, "The prime minister Tzu-wen was appointed to office three times without manifesting joy and was dismissed three times without manifesting sadness. (In each case), he duly informed the incoming prime minister concerning the affairs of government. What can one say of him?"
>
> The master said, "He was loyal (*chung*)."
>
> "Was he benevolent (*jen*)?"
>
> "I do not know. How can he be pronounced benevolent (*jen*)?"[39]

Tzu-wen did his duty in service to his lord, strictly adhering to *li*, and so he qualified as *chung*, "loyal." But Confucius declared that there was as yet no evidence to warrant calling Tzu-wen *jen*.[40] What was missing? It was the other strand of Confucius' "one thread"—the moral sensitivity of *shu*. *Shu* is specifically defined in the **Analects**:

> Tzu-kung asked, "Is there a maxim which one can follow all one's life?"
>
> The master said, "Is it not the maxim of *shu*: do not bestow upon others what you do not want for yourself?"[41]

I noted earlier, as have others, that the maxim is stated "negatively"; it tells one what one should *not* do.[42] I believe this is significant. It shows that *shu* is primarily concerned with mediating the application of rules—specifically the application of *li*. *Shu* is the governor of *chung*. It tells me when I should relax or suspend the rules of *li*, and when I should go beyond what *li* strictly prescribes. It gives me a way to know when I should not go strictly "by the book."

Shu consits of imaginatively placing oneself in the position of those who will be affected by one's proposed actions and considering whether or not one would accept such treatment oneself. It ensures that one will run the rules and not be run by the rules. Only through the sensitivity gained by the exercise of imaginatively placing oneself in another's place can one keep before one the ultimate goal of ritual—the harmonious, humane society. This is why Confucius regarded *shu* as "the method of *jen*, 'benevolence'."

> . . . One who is *jen*, wishing to be established helps others to be established and wishing to advance helps others to advance. To be able to draw the analogy from oneself can be called the method of *jen*.[43]

Above, I quoted the passage in which Confucius refers to *shu* as the one maxim one could follow throughout one's life. Why did he single out *shu* over *chung*? Perhaps we can find the answer if we keep in mind Confucius' primary task: the cultivation of young men for service in a benevolent government. Is it not reasonable to assume that he found it easier to find zealous disciples than morally sensitive ones?

In particular, consider Tzu-kung, the disciple to whom Confucius gave this advice. There is clear evidence to show that he was a young man who had the letter but not quite the spirit of the *li*. In a well-known passage, Confucius describes Tzu-kung as a *ch'i*, "vessel" or "tool," one of limited capacity or ability.[44] But Tzu-kung was no common "tool"; he was a tool for ritual, a "sacrificial vessel." He could serve another in performing his duties according to ritual, but he lacked the moral sensitivity necessary for fine-tuning their application. He still employed a kind of "cook book" approach to the *li*. He was not yet a moral connoisseur. Tzu-kung was strict with himself, but he was too strict with others.[45] He did not know when and how to amend, bend, or suspend the *li* when they adversely affected others. He was a bit of a moral martinet. One of the most insidious forms of such overzealous righteousness is believing in one's own selfless devotion to the moral ideal. And this is precisely what Tzu-kung does. He claims to be *shu*, which is what he is not.

> Tzu-kung said, "What I do not want others to do to me, I do not do to others."
>
> The master said, "Oh Ssu! That is something you have not yet attained."[46]

Confucius' most difficult task was to instill in his disciples the sensitivity needed to implement the rituals in a humane manner. It is far easier to train people to follow a set of rules mechanistically than to apply them with sensitivity; the latter requires the consummate skill that comes only with reflective experience, if it comes at all. It requires wisdom as well as knowledge. Confucius' general emphasis on culture perhaps should be seen as an effort to refine his disciples' humanistic sensitivity in an effort to avoid the often horrible self-righteousness that accompanies moral education.[47]

We can now see how *chung* and *shu* are woven together to form the "one thread of Confucius' Way."

Confucius was offering practical moral guidance to his young disciples, not a formal ethical theory. The *locus classicus* for this notion—the *only* passage in which the two terms of *chung* and *shu* are mentioned together and referred to as "Confucius' one thread"—is a record of Confucius in the act of such teaching.[48]

Confucius' Way was a refined traditionalism. He did not invent the *li* nor did he derive them from some set of underlying moral principles. Questions about what *constituted* the right or the good were, for him, already answered. He never questioned the legitimacy of the traditional rituals.[49] He regarded the culture of the Chou—the culture described by the traditional rituals which he followed—as both inspired and protected by Heaven. Confucius was engaged in *practical* moral education. The first thing he taught was allegience to the *li*. *Chung* called on his disciples to do their ritual duty, to follow the *li*.

By being *chung*, Confucius' disciples would prove themselves capable and loyal subordinates to any ruler who followed the Way. But Confucius wanted more. He taught his disciples to be charitable in their demands and generous in their service. One was not to require strict ritual compliance from others, regardless of the consequences. And one was not to be satisfied with oneself in merely discharging one's duties in a perfunctory manner. One was to cultivate and use one's judgment to determine what was proper on a case-by-case basis. With enough experience and practice, one could learn when it was appropriate to amend, bend, or suspend the *li*. Sometimes one should not require strict compliance from others, and sometimes one should go beyond what was strictly required of oneself. One made such judgments by employing the imaginative act of putting oneself in the other person's place and determining what one should do by seeing how one would like to be treated. This is *shu*, the second strand of Confucius' "one thread."

Shu helps one avoid becoming a slave to the *li*. It insures that individuals will have an active sense of their co-humanity with others. It guarantees that people will run the rules and not be run by the rules. One is to see oneself as dedicated to serving others according to the rituals, but one is also to see oneself as responsible for the well-being of others. One is to be strict with oneself, but one is to be kind to others. Both of these imperatives are mediated through the rituals. Without a firm commitment to *li*, the "kindness" of *shu* can collapse into vague, formless sentimentality and the "loyalty" of *chung* can degenerate into blind, mechanistic obedience. Neither *chung* nor *shu* can be understood apart from the *li*, and only in support of each other do they constitute *jen*.

There is a passage in the ***Analects*** in which both strands of this "one thread" are clearly visible, though neither term is used. One of Confucius' disciples asks about *jen* (again, Confucius is giving practical moral guidance to a disciple who aspires to serve as a government official). Confucius responds by saying one should always act as if one were performing an important ritual (that is, one should be *chung*), and one "should not do to others what one does not want for oneself" (that is, one should be *shu*).

> Chung-kung asked about *jen*. The master said, "Outside your home, act as if you were hosting a grand reception (a ritual performed by a lord, who hosts his vassals). Employ the people as if you were officiating at a great sacrifice (another important ritual observance). What you do not want for yourself, do not do to others. . . ."[50]

Here we see both strands of the "one thread" which runs through Confucius' Way. It urges one to be disposed to carry out one's role-specific duties, as prescribed by *li*, but to insure that the performance of one's duties is informed by an overarching concern for others as fellow human beings.

CONCLUSION

In conclusion, I would like to illustrate my understanding of the notions *chung* and *shu* by looking at an interesting example proposed by Herbert Fingarette.[51] Fingarette describes the case of a student who comes asking for a higher grade, in order to help him get into law school. In arguing for the higher grade, the student challenges his teacher to "put yourself in my place." Of course, to give the unwarranted grade clearly is wrong. And Fingarette claims that he comes to see this by placing himself in the student's position. This he says is an example of *shu*.

But there is no need to introduce the idea of imaginatively putting oneself in the student's place in order to see that giving the unwarranted grade would be wrong. It is self-evident that such a course of action is wrong. One is tempted to grant the higher grade only if one forgets where one's role-specific duty—as a teacher—lies. *Chung* helps one keep this duty clearly in mind.

Chung urges one to be a strict rule follower. It helps one to do what is right, according to *li*, especially when one might be inclined to be remiss or lax in the performance of one's duties. It helps one cultivate a sense of "loyalty" and "integrity," a virtue which insures others that one can be relied upon to fulfill one's role-specific duties. If one were to grant this student's request, one would not be loyal to one's colleagues, chairman, dean, and president. One would stray from the teacher's Tao. Fingarette's example is a perfect case of *chung,* not *shu*.

But one cannot fulfill the teacher's Tao by being *chung* alone. One must also be *shu. Shu* urges one to be a

benevolent rule enforcer. It tells one that it is absurd to require an ill student to sit for a scheduled exam and cruel to insist that a student turn in a paper on time, if it means that she will not be able to attend her grandmother's funeral. *Shu* tells one to be alert for those students who might need a bit more encouragement, understanding, or guidance in order to do well. It urges one to keep before one the ultimate goal of assignments and deadlines—educating young men and women—and reminds one this cannot be done well if one is not concerned with these students as fellow human beings. By the imaginative act of putting oneself in their place, one can see those cases when one should amend, bend, or suspend the rules. In some situations, one will require a little less of them; in other situations, one will require much more of oneself. And in the process, both teacher and student may learn something critically important about being human.

Notes

References to the text of the *Analects* follow the section numbers in James Legge, trans., *Confucian Analects,* in *The Chinese Classics* (Reprint, Hong Kong: University of Hong Kong Press, 1970).

[1] For a survey of the Golden Rule in various cultures, see Bruce Alton, *An Examination of the Golden Rule* (Ann Arbor: University Microfilms, 1966). For a modern Western philosophical analysis which discusses the notion of the Golden Rule in contemporary moral theory, see R. M. Hare, *Freedom and Reason* (Oxford University Press, 1963).

[2] In addition to the analyses which I consider here, see Robert E. Allison, "On the Negative Version of the Golden Rule as Formulated by Confucius," *New Asia Academic Bulletin* 3, Thematic Issue on Confucianism (Hong Kong, 1982): 223-232; also see David L. Hall and Roger T. Ames, *Thinking Through Confucius* (Albany: State University of New York Press, 1987), pp. 283-290.

[3] *Analects* 4.15.

[4] Fung Yu-lan, *A Short History of Chinese Philosophy,* trans., Derk Bodde (New York: The Macmillan Co., 1953), pp. 43-44.

[5] Ibid., p. 43.

[6] As will be clear when I present my own interpretation, I do believe that the "negative" aspect of *shu* is significant: *shu* functions to *limit* one's allegience to the rituals. This explains why it is most often expressed in terms of what one *Should not* do. A similar view is presented by Hall and Ames in *Thinking Through Confucius* (pp. 289-290). However, they interpret *shu*

as much more open-ended. It is difficult to discern the relationship, on their analysis, between *chung* and *shu* and the traditional rituals which Confucius so closely followed and so strongly advocated. They seem to see *shu* as the overriding notion in the Confucian Golden Rule, as they say, " . . . Confucius believed *shu* to be the single thread that served as the unifying theme of his thinking . . ." (p. 200). But, as is seen clearly in their own translation of *Analects* 4.15 (p. 285), the unifying thread of Confucius' Tao "is *chung* and *shu*"—not just *shu*.

7 In *Analects* 15.23, *shu* is defined as "not doing to others what one does not want for oneself."

8 I discuss this more fully below, in presenting my own interpretation.

9 Fung also relies on evidence from another later text, the *Ta Hsüeh* "Great Learning." In this latter case, the material he quotes is not ascribed to Confucius.

10 Lau presents his interpretation in the introduction to his translation of the *Analects*. See D. C. Lau, trans., *The Analects* (New York: Dorset Press, 1979).

11 Ibid., p. 16.

12 Ibid.

13 Lau does not use the word "intuitions," but this seems to be what he intends by " . . . taking oneself—'what is near at hand'—as an analogy and asking oneself what one would like or dislike were one in the position of the person at the receiving end" (p. 16).

14 For a more detailed discussion of this and related problems with the notion of reversibility, see the opening section of the presentation of my own interpretation, below.

15 Mencius believes we have a nascent moral sense which can guide us in making moral judgments. But until one has developed this nascent sense, it seems one cannot fully rely upon it to make difficult moral decisions. However, versions of Mencius' position can provide powerful and provocative arguments for such an appeal.

16 *Analects* 17.2.

17 A given individual may have a greater innate ability to acquire the intuitions needed to perform a certain skill, but until this person has *mastered* the skill, he or she cannot be said to possess the needed intuitions. The intuitions of a master are *acquired* through the reflective *practice* of an art.

18 In his introduction (p. 16, note 6), Lau points out that "loyalty" is the usual translation of *chung* but asserts this is wrong. He is correct to note that in the *Analects, chung* does not mean blind "devotion"; this is not the only sense of the word "loyalty." A loyal subordinate has one's *true* interests at heart, and this may require him or her, in certain situations, to disagree with one's behavior. In the *Analects, chung* is never directed at one's social subordinates and so "loyalty"—in the sense of a morally informed dedication—seems like the best translation. Lau's suggested alternative seems not to work well at all in *Analects* 14.8. Hall and Ames provide an argument for Lau's reading in *Thinking Through Confucius* (p. 285). But their evidence, while interesting, is not conclusive. I believe it can just as easily be read to support the interpretation I present below.

19 Herbert Fingarette, "Following the 'One Thread' of the *Analects,*" *Journal of the American Academy of Religion* 47, no. 35, Thematic Issue S (September 1979): 373-405.

20 Ibid., p. 374.

21 Ibid., p. 397.

22 Fingarette believes that the qualification problem, mentioned in my discussion of Lau's notion of *shu,* is avoided by a special feature of the imaginative act: "I must not imagine *myself* being in your situation; I must imagine *being you*" (Ibid., p. 384). I do not fully understand what he means by this.

23 In other words, to be *chung* is to serve others according to *li*. As I will show below, this is the meaning throughout the *Analects*. Fingarette's description of *chung* obscures the very important fact, first noted by Nivison (see below), that *chung* always refers to relationships with one's social peers or superiors. It is not simply "interpersonal good faith." For the meaning of *hsin*, "trust," see the article discussing this character by David S. Nivison in *The Encyclopedia of Religion,* ed., Mircea Eliade (New York: Macmillan Publishing Company, 1987), vol. 6, p. 477.

24 David S. Nivison, *Golden Rule Arguments in Chinese Moral Philosophy* (Presented as the inaugural address of the annual Walter Y. Evans-Wentz Professorship in Oriental Philosophies, Religions and Ethics, Stanford University, 13 February 1984).

25 *Analects* 12.22.

26 Nivison, *Golden Rule Arguments,* p. 9.

27 In the passage I quoted above, Nivison cites *Analects* 3.19 as evidence for his interpretation. But if he is correct—if *chung* and *shu* are parallel concepts—we would expect the first half of the line he quotes to say, "A ruler employs his subjects with *shu.* . . ."

[28] Luke 6.31.

[29] This seems to me to be the flaw in Fingarette's proposed solution to the qualification problem, mentioned earlier.

[30] As I mentioned earlier, I believe some version of this position offers the best hope for the Golden Rule and for moral philosophy in general. Strong versions of this claim cannot be defended, but weaker versions are not at all trivial. Human beings seem to share an important set of recognized "goods." Life, freedom, the opportunity to form and sustain interpersonal relationships, and health are just a few examples of "goods" which seem to be highly valued by reflective people in every culture. Such a view would recognize a great deal of what some regard as moral issues as really matters of taste. But some important moral issues might be decided and others made more clear by such an approach.

[31] The primary difficulty is providing a convincing justification for the traditional rituals which Confucius followed and advocated. Confucius' allegiance to tradition was largely unexamined, motivated by his belief in a past Golden Age which relied upon a cultural system sanctioned by Heaven. Granting that such a justification could be found, several issues remain; for example, could rituals be modified, added, or abandoned? If rituals are flexible to this extent, how would such decisions be made and implemented?

[32] *Analects* 6.25. See also 12.1 and so forth. It is easy to see why the young men Confucius trained made attractive subordinates. In addition to their administrative competence, they were politically known quantities. They were not out for personal gain. Their allegience and agenda were public knowledge.

[33] Had Confucius held a naïve belief in the innate goodness of human beings, he would simply have urged his disciples to follow their natural impulses. There would have been no need for him to preserve and promote the *li*. Clearly, he taught something quite different. One was to "Subdue oneself and submit to rituals" (*Analects* 12.1), at least in the initial stages of self-cultivation.

[34] *Analects* 17.11. See also 2.7, 3.3, etc.

[35] *Analects* 3.19. See also 2.20, 5.18, and 12.14.

[36] Nivison is the first to notice this feature of the concepts *chung* and *shu*. See Nivison, *Golden Rule Arguments*.

[37] *Analects* 12.23.

[38] *Analects* 14.8.

[39] *Analects* 5.18.

[40] There are other clear examples of people who are *chung* but not *jen*. In *Analects* 5.7, Confucius describes disciples who are competent in government service (*chung*) but are not *jen*. In *Analects* 14.2, we see that even one who is scrupulous in personal conduct (*chung*) does not, on that basis alone, qualify as *jen*.

[41] *Analects* 15.23.

[42] See note 6, above. Note however that sometimes the "limit" placed upon one's allegience to the *li* calls on one to go *beyond* what they strictly require one to do. Knowing when and how to do this distinguishes the *jen* person from one who is merely *chung*. In this aspect, *shu* is expressed "positively." See, for example, *Analects* 6.28.

[43] *Analects* 6.28.

[44] *Analects* 5.3. This goes against Confucius' ideal. A gentleman is not restricted to any single skill or vocation. He says explicitly, in *Analects* 2.12, "A gentleman is not a vessel (or tool)."

[45] Confucius once upbraided Tzu-kung for constantly criticizing others. See *Analects* 14.31.

[46] *Analects* 5.11. Ssu is Tzu-kung's personal name. Confucius seems amused at Tzu-kung's presumption.

[47] Confucius' genuine concern for his fellow human beings too often gets obscured by the picture of Confucius we get from his later followers and from modern attempts to read into his thought too much formal philosophy. The profound appeal of Confucius is as an example of an excellent human being doing his best to make the world a better place in which to live. He is not a very good philosopher (arguably he is not a philosopher at all). He *is* a wise and compassionate human being, something not every philosopher can claim to be.

[48] *Analects* 4.15.

[49] In all of the *Analects,* there are only two passages which can be construed as evidence that Confucius had a flexible attitude toward the *li*. The first is *Analects* 2.23, which describes the evolution of the *li* from the Hsia dynasty down to the Chou. But Confucius' concluding remark seems to say that the *li* have now reached perfection and hence can be known "for a hundred generations to come." The other passage is *Analects* 9.3. This is sometimes cited as a case (it would be the only case) of Confucius *modifying* a ritual. First of all, it must be admitted that the change Confucius condones is quite trivial. Second, Confucius is not *initiating* this change. He says, "I follow the common

practice." It seems that he is making a temporary concession to a current practice in order to insure the preservation of most of an important ritual; he does not modify or abandon the traditional *li*. I discuss this issue more thoroughly and offer suggestions for how this general question about the *li* might be dealt with in an as yet unpublished paper, "Chess, Checkers and Change: Traditional Confucianism and Its Modern Possibilities."

[50] *Analects* 12.2. Nivison was the first to point out the importance of this passage (see Nivison, *Golden Rule Arguments,* p. 8.). My interpretation differs slightly from his. For another example of this dual orientation, see 15.14.

[51] For the example, see Fingarette, "Following the 'One Thread'," p. 387.

FURTHER READING

Boodberg, Peter A. "The Semasiology of Some Primary Confucian Concepts." *Philosophy East and West* 2, No. 4 (January 1953): 317-32.
> Discusses translations for several Chinese idioms that appear in Confucius's teachings.

Cleary, Thomas. Introduction to *The Essential Confucius: The Heart of Confucius' Teachings in Authentic I Ching Order,* translated by Thomas Cleary, 1992, pp. 1-11.
> Provides an overview of Confucius's ideas on education and society as well as an examination of the historical background to Confucius's teachings.

Creel, H. G. *Confucius, The Man and the Myth.* New York: John Day Company, 1949. 363 p.
> Standard study by highly respected scholar. Three separate sections address historical background, biography, and Confucianism as a general phenomenon.

——. "Confucius and the Struggle for Human Happiness." In *Chinese Thought from Confucius to Mao Tse-tung,* The University of Chicago Press, 1953, pp. 25-45.
> Examines Confucius's ideas on religion and politics and argues that as a teacher, Confucius was concerned with turning his students into gentlemen regardless of their social rank at birth.

Crow, Carl. *Master Kung: The Story of Confucius.* New York: Harper & Brothers, 1938.
> Describes Confucius's life and philosophies in accessible narrative.

Do-Dinh, Pierre. *Confucius and Chinese Humanism.* Trans. by Charles Lam Markmann. New York: Funk and Wagnalls, 1969. 217 p.
> Places Confucius's life and doctrines in a broad overview of Chinese culture. Contains numerous photographs of relevant artifacts.

Fingarette, Herbert. "Human Community as Holy Rite." In *Confucius—the Secular as Sacred,* Harper & Row, 1972, pp. 1-17.
> Discusses Confucius's ideas on human nature and the ritualistic aspects of *li*, Confucius's concept of social forms.

Hsü, Leonard Shihlien. *The Political Philosophy of Confucianism.* London: George Routledge and Sons, 1932. 258 p.
> Asserts that Confucius envisioned a political structure that would be "at once paternal and democratic."

Kaizuka, Shigeki. *Confucius.* Trans. by Geoffrey Bownas. New York: Macmillan, 1950. 192 p.
> Respected biography by Japanese scholar. Presents Confucius's life in the context of Chinese history and philosophy, both his own and in general.

Kieschnick, John. "*Analects* 12.1 and the Commentarial Tradition." *Journal of the American Oriental Society* 112, No. 4 (October-December, 1992): 567-76.
> Analyzes various interpretations of chapter twelve of the *Analects.*

Kupperman, Joel J. "Confucius and the Nature of Religious Ethics." *Philosophy East and West* XXI, No. 2 (April 1971): 189-94.
> Argues that Confucius's ethics are religious.

Liu Wu-chi. *Confucius, His Life and Time.* New York: Philosophical Library, 1955. 189 p.
> Presents biography and study of Confucius's philosophies together, former in first seven chapter and latter in last five.

Sim, Luke J. and Bretzke, James T. "The Notion of Sincerity (*Ch'eng*) in the Confucian Classics." *Journal of Chinese Philosophy* 21, No. 1 (June 1994): 197-212.
> Examines the Confucian understanding of sincerity and humanity as expressed in the *Great Learning* and the *Doctrine of the Mean.*

Tu Wei-Ming. "Jen as a Living Metaphor in the Confucian *Analects.*" In *Confucian Thought: Selfhood as Creative Transformation,* State University of New York Press, 1985, pp. 81-92.
> Discusses the rhetorical structure of the *Analects* and the semiotics of *jen.*

Waley, Arthur. *Three Ways of Thought in Ancient China.* London: George Allen & Unwin, 1939. 275 p.
> Provides selections and translations from three texts central to Chinese philosophy. The first, *Chuang Tzu,* includes many stories of Confucius and his sayings.

Additional coverage of Confucius's life and career is contained in the following sources published by Gale Research: DISCovering Authors.

Sir John Mandeville

mid-fourteenth century

Travel writer whose precise identity is unknown.

INTRODUCTION

Mandeville's Travels, most likely written in 1356 or 1357, purports to chronicle the travels of English knight Sir John Mandeville. In the years immediately following the return to Europe of such famous travelers as Marco Polo and Friar John of Plano Carpini, accounts of travel in the Middle East and Far East were in demand. More than 270 manuscripts of the book, in ten European languages, survive today, attesting to its immense popularity. In addition, authors of subsequent travel books retold Mandeville's stories, and his accounts influenced thought and literature until the mid-1500s, when settlement of the New World shifted interests.

Biographical Information

Scholars originally believed that Sir John Mandeville was an English knight who had traveled extensively throughout his life and in his old age settled in England to write an account of his jpurneys. Nineteenth-century commentators, however, discovered that the author of the book had plagiarized accounts from other travel writers. The sources include the works of William of Boldensele and Odoric of Pordenone, published in the 1330s, the Letter of Prester John (published in the late twelfth century), the encyclopedia of Vincent of Beauvais (1250s), and William of Tripoli's description of Muslim culture (1273). What is more, the scholars argued, an author with such an extensive reading background could not have had time to travel himself. The author of *Mandeville's Travels* also placed events out of chronological sequence, further proof that the author did not actually experience the events described. Scholars have offered several theories as to the identity of Mandeville: Jean de Bourgogne, a physician from Liège; Jean d'Outremeuse, a romance writer from Liège; Brother Jean le Long, a Benedictine monk; an anonymous Continental author; or an Englishman, perhaps named John Mandeville and perhaps also a knight. In addition, commentators have been unable to determine whether the work was written originally in Latin, English, or French, although most scholars now support the view that the work was written in French.

Major Works

Mandeville's Travels chronicles the experiences of Sir John Mandeville, an English knight who traveled for

more than thirty years through Europe, Northern Africa, and Asia. The text is divided into two parts. The first describes a number of routes from Europe to the Holy Land and discusses important historical and religious sites that he encountered along the way. In the prologue, Mandeville states that the book is intended as a guide for religious pilgrims planning to travel to Jerusalem. The second half of the narrative describes the world to the East beyond the Holy Land. At the center of Mandeville's adventure is the Earthly Paradise, which he describes in great detail but claims not to have entered because he believes himself unworthy. Mandeville describes the customs and cultures of the people he encounters, including the Chinese and the Muslims, as well as the geography and physical characteristics of the Middle and Far East. Included in the narrative are descriptions of headless giants, mute pygmies, and mythical beasts, as well as anecdotes about Mandeville himself, including stories about his passage through the Far Eastern Valley Perilous and his military service to the sultan of Egypt and the khan of Cathay. Although the original manuscript of *Mandeville's Travels* is not extant, most scholars believe that it was written by someone living in northern France and that three of the French manuscripts—The Continental Version, dated 1371; The Liège Version; and The Insular Version—are independent derivatives of the original. There are four principal English versions of *Mandeville's Travels* in manuscript: the Bodley, Cotton, Defective, and Egerton versions. The Bodley Version was translated from a Latin source, while the Egerton Version is a revision of either the Cotton or Defective versions. Scholars believe that one of the latter was translated from a French text shortly before 1400 and that the other was a revision of the earlier translation. Two renditions in English verse—one metrical, the other stanzaic—have also been discovered, although the stanzaic version exists only as a fragment. Although the Defective Version was the first English edition to be printed (c. 1496), the Cotton Version, first printed in 1725, has enjoyed a wider popular and scholarly influence on the narrative's history in English than the other three versions.

Critical Reception

Mandeville's Travels enjoyed wide popular appeal from the late fourteenth century through the mid-1500s. It was respected among scholars, who at one time considered Mandeville the "Father of English prose"; explorers, including Christopher Columbus; and cartographers, who consulted it as a reliable source on the Far East. During the nineteenth century, a number of scholars attacked *Mandeville's Travels* as a hoax, charged the author with plagiarism, and found evidence to suggest that the author was not an English knight but a Continental writing under an assumed name. During the twentieth century, however, *Mandeville's Travels* has enjoyed a revival. Commentators have noted that "plagiarism," as it applies to *Mandeville's Travels,* was not an uncommon practice in the Middle Ages. Other commentators have argued that *Mandeville's Travels* should be approached as a work of imaginative literature and argue its importance to the development of the novel. Josephine Waters Bennett, for instance, has written that the *Travels* "is incomparably richer than the materials out of which it was made because the imagination of a writer of genius has shone upon those materials and brought them to life. Mandeville is neither a plagiarist nor a 'forger,' but the creator of a romance of travel." Others have argued that Mandeville was approaching his subject as a scholar, a compiler of an encyclopedia of knowledge, and that his mode of presentation was intended to be interesting rather than deceptive. As C.W.R.D. Moseley has stated: "The huge number of people who relied on the *Travels* for hard, practical geographical information in the two centuries after the book first appeared

demands that we give it serious attention if we want to understand the mental picture of the world of the late Middle Ages and the Renaissance."

PRINCIPAL WORKS

*The Book of John Mandeville [*Mandeville's Travels*] (travel) c. 1356

*This work was originally written in French and circulated in numerous translations and editions.

CRITICISM

Malcolm Letts (essay date 1949)

SOURCE: "The Times," in *Sir John Mandeville: The Man and His Books*, The Batchworth Press, 1949, pp. 23-40.

[*In the excerpt below, Letts describes the historical context in which Mandeville wrote and remarks on his critical reception and influence on other writers.*]

Before we come to the journey itself, it may be well to sketch in outline the historical background against which Mandeville lived and wrote. During practically the whole period covered by the so-called travels England and France were at war. The Hundred Years' War broke out in 1338. Crécy was won in 1346, Calais was taken in 1347, and at Poitiers, in 1356, the French King was taken prisoner. Mandeville speaks in his Epilogue of the destruction and slaughter and the accumulations of evils produced by the war, and of the two kings having made peace, but writing, as he appears to have done, in his library at Liége, the struggle, under God's protection, left him untouched. Liége cannot, however, have been always a haven of rest. The town went through much the same domestic upheavals as other Flemish towns, and local disturbances must have figured largely in the daily life of the people, even if they left our author in peace.

During the whole of the century the hope of recovering the Holy Land was never absent from men's minds. The Crusade of 1270 led by Louis IX of France had ended in disaster, and Mandeville, like others, must have viewed the growing power of Islam with dismay. He refers again and again to the need for a new crusading spirit, but he realised that, unless Christian princes composed their differences and presented a united front with the Church, there was no hope of success. The Holy Land was lost by sin and could only be recovered by righteousness. But quite apart from the quarrels of princes, the affairs of the Church were in such disorder that no joint effort was possible. Between 1305 and 1378 the popes were at Avignon. The Franciscans were demanding evangelical poverty for the pope and all churchmen. They denounced the wealth and splendour of the papal court and were preparing the way for Wycliffe. Mandeville makes no effort to conceal his feelings about the papacy, but he was probably only reflecting the views of thousands of others. There is no reason to believe that his anti-papal feelings affected his general outlook or disturbed his peace of mind.

There was one event, however, which must have gravely affected our author's tranquility—the Black Death, which decimated Europe from 1347 onwards. There is no reference to this in the **'Travels,'** but Mandeville, alias de Bourgogne, lived through it. He speaks of himself in his *de Pestilentia* as having practised medicine for forty years, and refers to his experiences at Liége during one outbreak which raged there in 1356.

Mandeville knew what he was doing when he sat down to write a book of travels, for during the first part of the fourteenth century, travel was in the air.[1] The Polos had returned to Venice in 1295 from their long sojourn in Asia, and for the next fifty years, that is roughly between 1290 and 1340, a steady stream of travellers took the eastern road. The Tartar conquests of the first part of the thirteenth century had accomplished one of the most striking revolutions in history, by bringing the East into touch with the West. In 1214 the Tartars swept from Mongolia upon China, taking Peking and conquering most of Eastern Asia. They then turned westward, spread across Asia and over a large part of Russia, into Poland, Hungary and Persia, so that by 1259 one empire extended from the Yellow River to the banks of the Danube, and from the Persian Gulf to Siberia. At first Europe was horror-struck by the invasion. It seemed as if the end of the world was at hand, and that Gog and Magog and the armies of anti-Christ had at last burst forth from their mountain fastnesses to destroy Christianity and overrun the whole world. Then, after much hesitation and confusion of mind, it dawned upon the West that, horrible and brutal as the conquerors were, they might be useful as allies in breaking down the power of Islam. The Tartars were known to be tolerant of all creeds. The first thing was to convert them to Christianity, and then, with their help, to recover the Holy land. It was a vain hope, but it produced a wave of missionary zeal which is one of the glories of the medieval Church—the episode of the missionary friars. There are few brighter or more romantic stories in history than the tale of the journeys, successes and failures of the Christian pioneers in Asia. But, although the best travel-books were written by missionaries—Mandeville makes use of two of them—the real impetus to travel was given by trade, and it was by the trade-routes that merchants took the road to Cathay. The journey must have been hazardous enough,

according to modern ideas, but the merchants seem to have made light of it. They appear to have penetrated everywhere in the East. Luckily, we know a good deal about their journeys and the difficulties they had to face from the *Pratica della Mercatura*,[2] a kind of merchants' handbook, written about 1340 by Pegolotti, an agent of the great Florentine house of Bardi. The book deals with the trade between the Levant and the East, and describes the route from Tana to Peking, with all kinds of practical suggestions for the novice. He must let his beard grow and hire a dragoman at Tana. His servants must speak Kuman and he would be wise to take a Kuman woman with him if he wished to study his comfort, although comfort is a strange word to use when one realizes that the journey was likely to take some six or seven months (Mandeville says eleven or twelve months from Venice or Genoa to Cathay), travelling at times with ox-wagons, camel-carts and pack-asses, with only outlying and remote halting places for rest and refreshment. One of the most striking commentaries on medieval commercial intercourse is the statement by Pegolotti that the road from Tana to Peking was perfectly safe whether by day or night, but this must surely be an overstatement. Mandeville has several references to merchants, but he never makes light of their difficulties.

Mandeville's ideas of geography were those of his age. By his time geography had lost its character of a science and had become once more the subject of myth and fancy. In the Middle Ages there were two schools of geographical thought, the ecclesiastical or patristic, and the Arabic. The Arabs' approach to geography was scientific, speculative and progressive. The ecclesiastical outlook was traditional, stereotyped and hidebound by authority, and it is with this school that we are concerned. The Fathers of the Church would have nothing to do with original thought. For them the Ptolemaic writings and the studies of Arabic geographers might never have existed. Nothing could be sanctioned which had not the authority of Holy Writ. This clerical hold on scholarship was responsible, among others, for two conspicuous features of medieval geography—the belief that Jerusalem was the centre of the earth—'I have set it in the midst of the nations' (Ezekiel V. 5)—and the situation of the Earthly Paradise. Both the Earthly Paradise and Jerusalem as the centre of the earth figure largely in Mandeville, as they do in all the medieval picture maps, and in the pilgrim and other geographical literature of the Middle Ages.

Taken as a whole, Mandeville's world was a circle enclosing a sort of T-square. The east was at the top. Jerusalem was plumb in the centre. The Mediterranean sea straggles across the lower half, which was divided between Europe and Africa. The top was devoted to Asia, which was expanded to an enormous extent, and, as very little was known about it, the medieval map-makers filled up the blanks with monsters and other strange creatures which they took from the Bible, Crusaders' tales and other sources. If we want to know what Mandeville's world looked like we have only to examine the great *Mappa Mundi* in Hereford Cathedral which was made about 1300. The T-square fits into it perfectly. The Earthly Paradise is at the top. Jerusalem is in the centre, and here and there, particularly in Africa, are pictures of all the strange monsters described by Mandeville, with their idiosyncracies pithily set forth in crabbed Latin legends. I shall have more to say about this map later, but the resemblance between it and Mandeville's notion of geography is too marked to be overlooked.

Mandeville had no doubt that the world was round, that its circumference was 20,425 miles (or more) and that in the heart and midst of it was Jerusalem. There could be no doubt about this, for men could prove and shew it 'by a spear that is pight into the earth, upon the hour of midday, when it is equinox, that sheweth no shadow on no side,' which seems to imply that the Holy City was on the equator! Mandeville was concerned about the antipodes because of the suggestion (by the supporters of the flat-earth theory) that, if the earth were in fact a sphere, the men on the sides and lower surface would be living sideways or upside down, even if they did not fall off into space, and, if men could fall off the earth, there was no reason why the great globe itself (being so great and heavy) should not topple over into the void, which was of course unthinkable. 'But that may not be, and therefore saith our Lord God, *Non timeas me, qui suspendi terram ex nihilo*.' Moreover, as Mandeville implies, if a man thinks he is walking upright he is in fact walking the right way up, as God meant him to do, and that is all that matters. As to the roundness of the earth, it was beyond all question, for in his youth Mandeville had heard tell of a worthy man who went so far by sea and land that he came at last to an island where, to his amazement, he heard a ploughman calling to his beasts in his own language. The traveller had encompassed the whole earth without knowing it.

To these observations the author adds some sensible remarks on the way in which astronomers apply mathematical reasoning to the mapping of the firmament and the earth. These observations, and his familiarity with the use of the astrolabe, suggest that he was not only abreast of, but actually at times in advance of, the scientific knowledge of his time. . . .

. . . . .

It is not easy to trace the development of modern criticism concerning Mandeville, and it is strange how the pendulum swings to and fro. An air of verisimilitude was undoubtedly given by the statement in the English versions that Mandeville, on his way home, submitted his book to the pope at Rome, and that the holy father

approved of it, but this passage does not appear in any of the French manuscripts and is clearly an interpolation. For most contemporary readers the book had to rest on its own foundations, and as the marvels which Mandeville sets down as sober facts can be capped and even outrivalled by other writers—the author of Prester John's Letter, for instance—the reading public of the fourteenth and fifteenth centuries probably swallowed their Mandeville whole. Bale, who published his *Catalogue of British Writers* in 1548, had no doubt about the authenticity of the **'Travels,'** and his contemporary Leland (who died in 1552), goes even further, for he placed Mandeville above Macro Polo, Columbus, and Cortez and other travellers (*nemo tamen illorum tamdiu labori insistebat, quam noster Magnovillanus*), and he compares Mandeville with Mithridates for his knowledge of foreign languages.[3] Leland tells us that as a boy he heard much about Mandeville from an old man called Jordan, and that at Canterbury he had seen among the relics at Becket's shrine a crystal orb containing an apple, still undecayed—an offering, so he was told, from Mandeville himself.

Purchas[4] thought Mandeville 'the greatest Asian Traveller that ever the World had,' and accused some other writer (probably a friar) of having stuffed his book full of fables. He placed Mandeville next (if next) to Marco Polo, and accused Odoric, who really was a great Asiatic traveller, of thieving from Mandeville, whereas in fact the substance of Mandeville's travels in India and Cathay was stolen without acknowledgement from Odoric. As we shall see, Mandeville, in his account of his adventures in the Valley Perilous, states that among his companions were two friars minor from Lombardy. The whole passage is worked up from Friar Odoric, and the reference to the two friars may well have been intended to anticipate a possible charge of plagiarism, and to suggest that Mandeville and Odoric travelled together. The result can be seen in a manuscript at Wolfenbüttel of the *Liber de Terra Sancta*, attributed to Odoric, which begins: 'Itinerarius fidelis fratris Oderici, *socii militis Mandavil*, per Indiam, licet hic prius et alter posterius peregrinationem suam descripsit.'[5] As Sir George Warner points out, the friar is doubly wronged here by the assertion that Mandeville's work was written first, whereas Odoric's was written in 1330. It may be noted that in the Antwerp (Gouda) Latin edition of Mandeville, printed in 1485 (and reprinted in the first edition of Hakluyt), frequent references to Odoric have been inserted in the text, and the description of the Valley Perilous ends with a statement that Odoric did not suffer as much there as Mandeville. The whole subject is discussed later (p. 89).

But poor Odoric was to suffer still greater indignities at a later date. In the collection of travels called 'Astley's Voyages' published in 1745-7 Odoric's narrative is described as superficial and full of lies, and in the index he fares even worse, his name being entered as 'Odoric, Friar, Travels of, IV, 620. A great Liar.'

There is a curious Mandeville reference in the English translation of Estienne's *Apology for Herodotus,* 1607, by R. Carew. In his Introduction to the Reader, the translator writes: 'imagine not that thou hast either . . . Goularts Admiranda, or Wolfius his Memorabilia, or Torquemeda's Mandevile of Miracles, or any such rhapsodie of an indigested history.' This last reference is to the "Jardin de Flores Curiosas" by Antonio de Torquemada, 1570 translated by Ferdinando Walker as "The Spanish Mandevile of Miracles," 1600.'

But the English title is not quite fair either to the Spanish author or to Mandeville. The book is a curious but amusing hotch-potch of monsters, the vagaries of fortune, strange countries, dreams, spirits, witches and hags, mostly from Spanish sources, such as Robert Burton would have loved. There is a good deal about the Earthly Paradise, Cathay and Prester John. Mandeville is mentioned here and there, and we learn with interest, what Sir John does not tell us, that he received wages and a pension from the Great Chan, but most of the eastern stories come from Marco Polo. The translator seems to have done his work well and does not appear to have added anything of his own, nor is there anything in his Dedication to explain the title-page. All we can say is that he must have been reflecting the views of his contemporaries.

Neither Robert Burton nor Sir Thomas Browne subscribed to Purchas's opinion of Mandeville. The former dismisses Mandeville quite briefly as a liar.[6] It does not appear from the list of Burton's books at the Bodleian and Christ Church that he even possessed a copy of the **'Travels.'**[7]

Sir Thomas Browne says much the same but in more temperate language.[8] The writer on Mandeville in Chalmer's *Biographical Dictionary* (1815), asserts that many things in the book, which were looked on as fabulous for a long time, had then been verified beyond all doubt, but giving up his giants of fifty feet high, there did not appear to be any very good reason why Sir John should not be believed in things that he relates from his own observation, and this seems to be the line taken generally in the eighteenth century. But it is difficult to know what is meant by personal observation. Mandeville claims in his Prologue to have visited all the countries he mentions, and the not infrequent interjections—'This I saw not': 'I was not there' and so on—imply that he saw and experienced whatever else he describes; but in Pollard's edition, containing 209 pages, I have counted only twenty-three specific personal statements—I saw, I dwelt, I came, I departed, I asked, and so on. And of these, one at least, the passage through the Valley Perilous, required a good deal of justification at the hands of the German

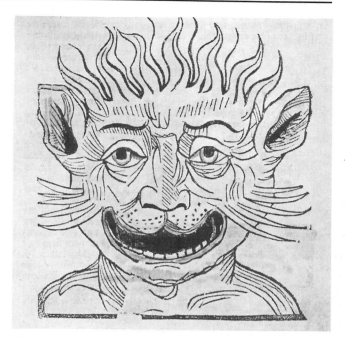

The Devil's head in the Valley Perilous, from the 1484 translation of Mandeville's Travels.

translator, Velser, before it could be presented to his readers.[9] Hugh Murray, in the early nineteenth century, was shrewd enough to realise that much of Mandeville was lifted from Odoric and others and had no hesitation in pronouncing the work to be pure and entire fabrication—'What he added of his own consists, I think, quite exclusively of monstrous lies.'[10] We can cap this with a quotation from an old Play:[11]

Drake was a didapper to Mandevill.
Candish and Hawkins, Frobisher, all our
  Voyagers
Went short of Mandevill.

But shortly after Murray's indictment an anonymous writer was busy compiling a long justification of Mandeville, which appeared in the *Retrospective Review* for 1821, vol. III, part II, p. 269. The writer protests in no uncertain terms against the great outcry of fraud which had been raised against Mandeville. There was no question of falsehood. All that could be charged against him was want of judgment. The writer's concluding words are worth quoting. 'The literature of the middle ages has scarcely a more entertaining and interesting subject; and to an Englishman it is doubly valuable, as establishing the title of his country to claim as its own the first example of the liberal and independent gentleman, travelling over the world in the disinterested pursuit of knowledge unsullied in his reputation; honored and respected wherever he went for his talents and personal accomplishments.' Curiously enough, this is much the line taken by Halliwell in his Introduction to the 1839 reprint of the **'Travels.'** And so matters remained until the 1870's when Nicholson laid the foundations for a new approach to the whole subject in his letter to *The Academy* on 11 November, 1876. His subsequent letters appeared in that journal on 12 February, 1881 and 12 April, 1884.

But whether truth or fiction, Mandeville's influence on the literature of the sixteenth century was profound. Many of his stories and most of his monsters, as depicted by his artists, found their way into the *Nuremberg Chronicle,* and Münster's *Cosmographia* (1544). Like the *Nuremberg Chronicle,* Münster's book was extremely popular, there having been as many as forty-seven editions in seven languages before 1650.

Münster was a very learned person. He had 120 collaborators to help him in his work, and when he wrote there was already a considerable literature in existence with which he was perfectly familiar, and to which he could have turned for an accurate and sober account of late geographical discovery. But, so far as Asia, India and Africa are concerned, he made little use of this material. Instead, we have the old stories and pictures of cannibals, one-eyed, one-legged and headless men, Amazons, pigmies and Brahmans, dragons, unicorns, gold-digging ants and griffins. Münster does not mention Mandeville by name (he acknowledges his debt to Marco Polo and Haiton, the Armenian), but it was Mandeville who created the popular demand for stories of this kind, and it was a demand which had to be met.

There can be no doubt that this demand was increased by the great discoveries of the fifteenth and sixteenth centuries. Eastward and westward by 1530, the route lay open to the Indies, and although the English at first had troubled little about conquest and the planting of colonies, the foreign press teemed with accounts of the New World and the East, and each returning traveller added something fresh. Münster's *Cosmographia* was abridged and translated into English in 1552, and in 1564 appeared a curious and interesting book which showed that the English were not to be outdone in the hue and cry after wonders and marvels. This was *A Dialogue against the Fever pestilence* by Wm. Bullein, a man of learning and a physician. Bullein had obviously read and studied Mandeville, Münster and any other books of travel he could come across, and he disliked and distrusted what he read—and a good many other things as well. But he did a very dangerous thing. He satirised travel literature as a whole.

The result, which Bullein cannot have foreseen, is that his book owed any popularity it may have had, not to his attacks on usury, lawyers, legacy-hunters and the Church of Rome, not even to his timely and suitable remarks on fresh air, diet, and herbs as remedies for the plague, but to the introduction into his dialogues of a traveller called Mendax, one of the most amusing

and attractive liars in literature. The name Mendax, we learn, signifies 'in the Ethiope tongue, the name of a great Citie, the mother of holie religion and truth,' and once the reader has met Mendax his interest never flags. It would be out of place here to follow Mendax in his travels in the East, diverting as they are, but it is sufficient to say that, among other adventures, he was turned into a dog (only temporarily), whereas his boy, a gentleman of good house, and would have married with one Jone Trim, was so strongly bewitched that he was a dog still. Most of Mandeville's stories re-appear, including the loadstone rocks, which Mandeville saw afar off, but on which Mendax and his companions were wrecked, escaping with their lives but losing their treasure.

Mandeville has much to say about the Antipodes. It was reserved for Mendax to discover there, foot against foot, another England, where were 'Gaddes Hill, Stangate Hole, Newe Market Heath, like ours in all points,' with this exception that, whereas there one found honest men, here there were none at all. We read of dancing geese, of parrots playing chess with apes and discoursing in Greek or singing descant, of Solomon and the Queen of Sheba seen in a magic mirror, attended by 14,000 ladies, and a race of men who cast their skins like snakes: 'Marie,' says he, 'they were full of hooles.' Here we have lying reduced to a fine art, but what Bullein did not realise was that the English have always loved a good liar and that satire is a two-edged weapon. It is possible that his book actually increased the demand for tall stories instead of killing it. In any event Mandeville continued to sell. A popular English edition with wooducts appeared in 1568. In the eighteenth century the **'Travels'** appeared as a chap-book. The sales went on all through the nineteenth century and its popularity has never waned, whereas Bullein's satire is now almost entirely forgotten.

Notes

[1] On the whole subject see the brilliant chapter by the late Eileen Power, 'Routes to Cathay' in *Travel and Travellers of the Middle Ages* (1926), ed. Newton.

[2] Extracts in Yule's *Cathay and the Way Thither,* Hakluyt Society, second ed. vol. III.

[3] Bishop Tanner's *Bibliotheca Britannico-Hibernica* (1748), p. 505, quoted by Warner, p. 31.

[4] *His Pilgrimes* (1625), reprint XI, pp. 188, 364.

[5] Warner, p. 22. Cf. Yule, *Cathay and the Way Thither,* II, p. 45, who refers to another MS at Mainz with the same opening statement.

[6] *Anatomy of Melancholy,* ed. Shilleto, II, p. 46. But then Burton also calls Marco Polo a liar.

[7] Oxford Bibliographical Society, *Proceedings,* I pt. III, 1925, p. 224 ff.

[8] 'Vulgar Errors,' in *Works,* ed. Wilkin, II, p. 236.

[9] See below, p. 92.

[10] *Historical Account of Discoveries and Travels* (1820), I, ch. iv.

[11] Quoted by Beazley, *Dawn of Modern Geography,* III, p. 322.

Zoltán Haraszti (essay date 1950)

SOURCE: "The Travels of Sir John Mandeville," in *The Boston Public Library Quarterly,* Vol. 2, No. 4, October, 1950, pp. 307-16.

[*In the following essay, Haraszti provides an overview of* Mandeville's Travels, *remarking on the subjects treated in the account, the identity of its author, and the work's sources and textual history.*]

At the Kreisler Sale held in New York on January 1949 the Boston Public Library acquired a number of extremely valuable fifteenth-century and other early printed books. One of the most valuable among them was a copy of the German translation of the **Travels of John Mandeville—*Reysen und Wanderschafften durch das Gelobte Land*—**printed by Anton Sorg in Augsburg in 1481.[1] This was believed to be the first appearance of the German text in print until Professor Schramm called attention to an earlier, undated edition by Sorg, probably printed in 1478, an imperfect copy of which he had discovered at Munich.[2]

The volume is printed in small folio format, comprising ninety-one unnumbered leaves. The type is that round Gothic characteristic of the work of most of the Augsburg printers. The text is illustrated by 117 woodcuts, each enclosed in a double border. Most of these measure 76 x 78 mm., but some, 74 x 118 mm. There are two full-page cuts, of the size of 118 x 197 mm. The first, which serves as frontispiece, represents a young knight with a sword on his left side and holding a banner in his right hand; through the open door a landscape with a church is visible, and above a scroll is inscribed "Johannes Montevilla," the Latin form of the author's name. The second large cut shows the Emperor of Cathay, seated at his table with his three wives, his scribes recording his words. In the Library's copy the first leaf with the frontispiece is supplied in facsimile; otherwise the copy is in excellent condition—the pages are clean, the woodcuts are uncolored, and the binding (oak-boards, half-covered with tooled leather) is original.

"I, John Mandeville, Knight," the narrative begins, "that was born in England, in the town of St. Albans, passed the sea in the year of our Lord Jesu Christ, 1322, in the day of St. Michael; and hitherto have been long time over the sea, and have seen and gone through many diverse lands, and many provinces and kingdoms and isles and have passed throughout Turkey, Armenia the little and the great; through Tartary, Persia, Syria, Arabia, Egypt the high and the low; through Lybia, Chaldea, and a great part of Ethiopia; through Amazonia, Ind the less and the more, a great part; and throughout many other Isles, that be about Ind; where dwell many diverse folks, and of diverse manners and laws, and of diverse shapes of men. Of which lands and isles I shall speak more plainly hereafter . . ."[3] The work ends with the return of the knight, now suffering from gout and "artetykes," thirty-four years later. On his way back he visited the Pope, who absolved him of all that weighed on his conscience. "Amongst all," the author writes, "I shewed him this treatise, that I had made after information of men that knew of things that I had not seen myself, and also of marvels and customs that I had seen myself, as far as God would give me grace . . ." Upon his request, the Pope had the book examined by his council which proved it for true.

The marvels which Mandeville reported were remarkable indeed. He knew of giants thirty feet tall who ate nothing but raw flesh and fish; of people who had no heads and whose eyes were in their shoulders; of others who had a flat face, without nose and mouth; and of pygmies who could not speak but made signs to one another, and who lived by the smell of wild apples. Some islands were inhabited by a folk with horses' feet, or by evil women who had precious stones in their eyes, slaying men with their glances as do the basilisks. He could tell endless stories of the great Chan of Cathay—of his prodigious palace dubbed with precious stones and pearls; of his sumptuous private banquets and magnificent public feasts; of his journeys from country to country, riding in a chariot drawn by four elephants and accompanied by innumerable kings and lords. He could not miss, of course, gathering first-hand information about the Christian Emperor of the Inds, Prester John, who dwelled in the Isle of Pentexoire. Prester John's domains were full of splendor and abounded in all kinds of goods, but they also had deserts peopled with wild men who were horned and grunted like pigs. Mandeville passed through the whole length of the Empire. He drank of the Well of Youth at Polombe; descended into the Vale Perilous which was guarded by a horrible devil, and where the ground was strewn with gold, silver, and jewels. He had not visited the Earthly Paradise, the Garden of Eden, so modestly he told only what he had heard about it from wise men. In the islands of the Sea of Java he met hordes of vicious cannibals, yet in that sea was located also the Land of Faith. The happiness of the Isle of Bragman was marred by no thief, murderer, loose woman, or beggar; its people prized no wealth, but lived soberly and long. "And albeit that these folk," the English traveller observed, "have not the articles of our faith, natheles, for their good faith natural, and for their good intent, I trow fully that God loveth them." On the other island he found that the king was chosen not for his riches but for his good manners and could not doom any man to death without the assent of his councillors.

Of all the wonderful descriptions of the world, **Mandeville's Travels** was the most fabulous. It was natural, therefore, that it was read avidly by all the nations of the West. The blending of the personal element with the mass and variety of information added to the fascination of the book. The public of Marco Polo was limited compared with the multitudes who read Mandeville; and not one out of a thousand of his devotees ever heard of the voyages of William of Boldensele or of Odoric of Pordenone, whose narratives, taken over verbatim and then embellished by fables, constitute the larger portion of the **Travels.** Well over three hundred manuscripts of the work exist, and the fifteenth-century printed editions alone—in Latin, French, English, Dutch, German, and Italian—number at least thirty-five.

To be sure, the value of the work was questioned even by some of the earlier writers. Jean-Pierre Niceron, for instance, remarked in his *Memoires* of 1734 that the book was rare, which however, was no great loss, for it was "a mass of fables and little else." Yet Dibdin still spoke of Mandeville with his customary enthusiasm as "a venerable English author"; and J. O. Halliwell, in reprinting the 1725 English edition of the Cotton manuscript, regarded the suggestion that Mandeville might never have gone to the East at all but had compiled his book out of previous journals as a "wholly unjustifiable conclusion."

Mandeville's trustworthiness was first seriously attacked after the middle of the nineteenth century. In his *Bibliographia Geographica Palaestinae,* published at Leipzig in 1867, Titus Tobler explained the small number of the Latin editions by the fact that "the adventures and lying stories with which the author tried to win readers did not particularly appeal to learned people, and therefore in every country the work assumed the character of a folk-book." Finally Sir Henry Yule, an eminent geographer, and Edward B. Nicholson, librarian of the Bodleian, demolished all belief in Mandeville's veracity and good faith. In a joint article published in the ninth edition of the *Encyclopaedia Britannica,* in 1883, they called attention not only to Mandeville's dependence upon Boldensele and Friar Odoric, but also showed that the rest of his story was mainly taken from Vincent de Beauvais's *Speculum Historiale* and *Naturale* and from Voragine's *Golden Legend.* Since then the ori-

gin of every passage of the **Travels** has been investigated by two scholars working independently— Albert Bovenschen, of the University of Leipzig,[4] and George F. Warner, of the British Museum.[5] Indeed, with the exception of one or two sections, the entire work has been proved to be a patch-work of various narratives, a compendium of plagiarisms—a rank literary imposture.[6]

The first part of the **Travels** treats of the Holy Land and the routes to it, together with Egypt and Sinai. "If any of the matter was drawn from personal knowledge and observation," Warner writes, "it is contained within the first fifteen chapters only."[7] It has been thought probable that Mandeville had really travelled as far as Palestine and Egypt, although the description of the route to Constantinople, through Hungary, has nothing in it of a personal nature. "Troweth not," the reader is warned, "that I will tell you all the towns and cities and castles that men shall go by, for then should I make too long a tale; but only some countries and most principal steads . . ."—and these latter were taken from the history of the First Crusade by Albert of Aix. In the chapter on Constantinople, which the author pretends to know intimately, he copied verbatim William of Boldensele, and in that on the routes from Constantinople to Jerusalem, the twelfth-century Latin Itineraries. The account of Egypt, for which no sources have been found, may be the most important part of the work. Mandeville claims to have spent a long time in the service of the Sultan, fighting in his war against the Bedouins. "And he would have married me full highly," he writes, "to a great prince's daughter, if I would have forsaken my law and my belief; but I thank God, I had no will to do it, for nothing that he behight me."[8] Even Sir Henry Yule, among the first to brand Mandeville a "profound liar," saw here evidences of personal experience.

The larger part of the work, all that comes after Palestine, was appropriated from Friar Odoric and then from the Voyages of Joannes de Plano Carpini, Hayton (Hetoum) the Armenian, and other writers, the whole "swollen" with interpolated fables. Yet Mandeville never mentions Odoric; nor does he give any hint about his other sources. As to his use of Pliny, Solinus, Jerome, and Isidore of Seville, Dr. Warner remarks that he may have consulted these authorities directly or he may have derived his information from Vincent de Beauvais's excerpts.[9]

However, one should not deny Mandeville his due. He insists that Jerusalem is in the midst of the world, where a spear stuck into the earth has no shadow on shadow on either side at midday in the time of the equinox; yet some of his astronomical notions were correct. He knew that latitude could be ascertained by the observation of the lode-star, and that there were antipodes. "Men may well perceive," he wrote, "that the land and the sea be of round shape and form; for the part of the firmament sheweth in one country that sheweth not in another country. And men may well prove by experience and subtle compassment of wit, that if a man found passages by ships that would go to search the world, men might go by ship all about the world and above and beneath."[10]

The deceitfulness of the author, made even more obvious through his constant reiteration of minute personal knowledge, has led to doubts about the existence of Mandeville himself. The name is not rare in English records of the period; however, no connection of it with St. Albans has been discovered as yet. John Bale's catalogue of British writers, first published in 1548, contained a lengthy notice of Sir John Mandeville, but this was based entirely upon statements found in the work.[11] Mandeville's tomb at Liége has been described by several early historians, who note that he was a physician, died in 1372, and was also called "John with the Beard." The contemporary Liége chronicler Jean d'Outremeuse, however, offers the surprising information that there died in the city in that same year a certain Jean de Bourgogne "with the Beard," who on his deathbed had revealed himself to him as Jean de Mandeville, knight, seigneur of Montfort, lord of the isle of Campdi and Perouse, who, having killed a count, was forced to leave his country. It should be noted that, in the common Latin version, Mandeville relates that he met at Cairo, at the court of the Sultan, a venerable and skillful physician who was "sprung from our own parts"; and that long afterwards at Liége he wrote his **Travels** at the advice and with the help of the same man. It was by chance that they met again. Mandeville, confined by his gout, was treated by several physicians, in one of whom, "Master John with the Beard," he recognized his old acquaintance.

Dr. Warner suggests that the bearded doctor's real name was, and always had been Jean de Bourgogne; and that, "having written his book of travels under the assumed name of Mandeville, he was tempted by its success to secure himself a posthumous fame by reversing the facts and claiming as his veritable name that which was fictitious."[12] The same writer also found that there was in England a certain John de Bourgoyne, chamberlain to John de Mowbray, who in 1322, after the execution of his patron, was banished—the date agreeing with that of Mandeville's departure for his voyages.

The identification is based, admittedly, on mere speculation; and the problem is becoming more and more complicated by the discovery of new candidates. Thus more recently a John Mangevilayn has been put forward, a man who was similarly embroiled with Mowbray in Thomas of Lancaster's revolt. The name may be a variant of Magnevillaine, meaning "of Magneville"; and it has been pointed out that the Mandevilles, Earls of Essex, were originally styled "de Magneville." Endless variations of the name seem possible. The situation has been summed up with fairness by Dr. Warner:

> The last word on the subject has doubtless not yet been spoken; but after all, now that the work is known for what it is, the question of its authorship is of greatly diminished importance. Whether it was written by a real or fictitious Mandeville, whether the Liége physician's story was more or less true or wholly false, or whether it was a mere invention by its reporter, the belief in the great English traveller who spent the best part of his life in wanderings through the known world from England to China and returned home in old age to write an account of them—this still lingering belief must be finally abandoned as an exploded myth. The **Travels** indeed remain, and it is to be hoped, will always be read, both for curiosity of matter and certain indefinable charm of style; but to quote them as possessing any authoritative character, and to count Sir John Mandeville among our English worthies as a foremost pioneer of travel and adventure is utterly unwarrantable.[13]

The prologue of the English version contained in the Cotton Manuscript (British Museum) ends with the assertion: "Ye shall understand, that I have put this book out of Latin into French, and translated it again out of French into English, that every man of my nation may understand it." The other prominent English version, that of the Egerton manuscript (also in the British Museum), has no such passage; but the French version from which it was derived states: "Know that I should have put this book into Latin to be more concise; but seeing that many understand Romance better than Latin, I have put it into Romance . . ." The priority of the French version was, indeed, conclusively proven from internal evidence by Carl Schönborn, who also made it clear that none of the Latin texts originated with Mandeville.[14] In fact, there are no less than five distinct Latin versions, each with errors of its own and each pointing to a French original.[15]

The Cotton manuscript's ascription of the authorship of the English translation to Mandeville himself is without foundation. Both the Cotton and Egerton manuscripts, dating from 1410-1420, contain a number of glaring errors which prove that the translators often completely misunderstood their texts. (For example, the Cotton MS. renders *montaignes* as "hille of Aygnes" and *signes du ciel* as "swannes of heuene," and the Egerton Ms. calls *ly Comainz*—that, is, the "Cumani"—"comoun pople.") The seven other English manuscripts in the British Museum have a big gap, lacking a part of the section on Egypt as well as chapters on Sicily, Mount Sinai, and the Church of Saint Catherine. Dr.

Warner assumed the existence of a similarly defective common ancestor of the Cotton and Egerton MSS., both of which, he thought, were filled out later from a complete French manuscript. On the other hand, J. Vogels, who was the first to compile a census of all the English manuscripts, maintained that the Cotton manuscript was the original English version, and that the Egerton manuscript, which made use also of a new Latin translation of the French text, was a mere re-editing of it.[16] In any case, the anonymous author, whoever he was, produced one of the earliest prose works in English.

The German version published by Sorg was made by Michel Velser (Michelfeld), probably a native of Bavaria. He must have finished his work before 1409, for there is a German manuscript in Munich which is dated of that year. Little is known of the translator, except that he had travelled in Italy, visiting Pavia and Genoa. He used a French text, which he faithfully followed, apart from a few abbreviations and explanatory sentences. The language is simple, yet indicative of an intimate understanding of the text. The manuscript has often been copied; in Munich alone there are five codices. It is illustrated with pictures which served as models for the woodcuts of the first printed edition.[17] About the same time, Otto von Diemeringen, a prebendary of the cathedral of Metz in Lorraine, prepared another version, also based on a French original, which however omits many of Mandeville's adventures.[18] This version was first printed at Basel, probably in 1481.[19]

Muther described the woodcuts as "naive," adding that the nudes are "not unskillfully depicted." Schreiber finds them "done with ability, and their engraving carefully executed," so that "the work occupies an important place among the Augsburg imprints of the period." He also notes that the *Nuremberg Chronicle* of 1493 copied many of the monsters and curious animals. This is, however, a mistake. Folio xii of the Chronicle contains twenty-one such pictures, none of which resembles the woodcuts of Mandeville. They are illustrations of stories of Pliny, Augustine, and Isidore—the common sources of inspiration of both the Chronicle and the **Travels.**

All the printed editions of Mandeville are extremely rare. The one issued by Sorg exists in two other copies in America.

Notes

1 Hain *10647; Muther 166; Schreiber 4798; Klebs 651.1; Stillwell M142; Schramm iv, 579-698.

2 Albert Schramm, *Der Bilderschmuck der Frühdrucke,* Leipzing 1921, 11.

3 Quoted from A. W. Pollard's version of the Cotton Manuscript in modern spelling, *The Travels of Sir John*

Mandeville, London 1915, 5. This epilogue is not included in the German text as printed by Sorg, which ends with the brief statement: "I Johannes de Montevilla . . . returned and had to rest because of my illness, although I would have gladly experienced more wonders; and I was away twelve years." The difference of the duration of the travels is especially noteworthy.

4 *Die Quellen für die Reisebeschreibung des Johann von Mandeville,* Berlin 1888.

5 *The Buke of John Maundeuill,* Printed for the Roxburghe Club, Westminister 1889.

6 Characteristically enough, C. Raymond Beazley's comprehensive work *The Dawn of Modern Geography,* Oxford 1897-1906, devotes only four pages to Mandeville as against 144 to Marco Polo and 37 to Odoric. "As a masterpiece of plagiarism," the author writes, "the work will always deserve attention; but, except for the student of geographical mythology and superstition, it has no importance in the history of Earth-Knowledge." (III, 320.)

7 Warner, *op. cit.,* xv.

8 Pollard, *op. cit.,* 24.

9 Warner, *op. cit.,* xxiii.

10 Pollard, *op. cit.,* 120.

11 *Illustrium Majoris Britannae Scriptorum . . . Summarium,* Ipswich 1548, f. 149b. An English translation was printed in the preface to the 1727 edition, and also reprinted by Halliwell.

12 Warner, *op. cit.,* xxxix.

13 Warner, *op. cit.,* xli.

14 *Bibliographische Untersuchungen über die Reise-Beschreibung des Sir John Maundevile,* Breslau 1840.

15 J. Vogels, *Die Ungedruckten Lateinischen Versionen Mandeville's,* Crefeld 1886. Quoted by Warner, *op. cit.,* vi.

16 *Handscriftliche Untersuchungen über die Englische Version Mandeville's,* Crefeld 1891, 35, 41. Yule and Nicholson regard Vogels's explanation "labored and improbable."

17 *Allgemeine Deutsche Biographie,* Leipzig 1895, XXXIX, 576.

18 Francis Edward Sandbach, *Handschriftliche Untersuchen über Otto von Diemeringen's Deutsche Bearbeitung der Reisenbeschreibung Mandeville's,*

Noah's Ark on Mount Ararat, from the Bibliothèque Nationale manuscript of Mandeville's Travels.

Strassburg 1899, 7-8, enumerates eighteen such passages.

[19] The annotation for No. 283 in the *Fairfax Murray Catalogue* is altogether confused: "Second (?) edition of the first German translation, by Otto von Diemeringen, canon of Metz cathedral, but it is not at all certain that it might not precede Sorg's edition of 1481 (Augsburg), considered the first, though it certainly seems more probable that the book was first published in Germany."

Josephine Waters Bennett (essay date 1954)

SOURCE: "The Transformation of the Materials" and "The Romance of Travel," in *The Rediscovery of Sir John Mandeville,* The Modern Language Association of America, 1954, pp. 26-38, 39-53.

[*In the following excerpt, Bennett compares* Mandeville's Travels *with the account of Odoric of Pordenone's travels, from which Mandeville borrowed extensively, and argues that Mandeville's text is far richer because his imagination and literary skills brought the materials to life.*]

Mandeville has been called a forger, a "mere plagiarist," and even a "mere translator." His debt to William of Boldensele has been somewhat exaggerated, although it is real enough; but his borrowings from Odoric of Pordenone are not only extensive but continuous, and therefore they will serve best to illustrate how skillfully he transformed his materials to build up the illusion of reality which is the foundation of successful fiction. The comparison is easily made, because he follows Odoric's itinerary step by step. But he adds, deletes, revises, and changes the character of the whole, including the personality of the traveler, in a way which strikingly demonstrates his conscious artistry.

The two begin their journey together at Trebizond,[1] about which city Mandeville borrows some of Odoric's very words. He omits, however, Odoric's simple marvel of some partridges which followed a man like so many chickens. Instead he elaborates what Odoric has to say of St. Athanasius: that he "made the Creed," and is buried at Trebizond. Mandeville adds to this bare statement the story that the saint was put in prison for heresy and while there wrote a psalm which embodied his faith. He sent it to the Pope, who was thereby convinced that he was a true Christian and ordered his release.[2]

Next Odoric says that he went to Armenia, to a city called Erzeroum (Erzrum). The mention of Armenia reminds Mandeville of a good story, and he proceeds to tell of the castle of the sparrowhawk—a story which accounts for the sorrows of that land. This is a beautifully proportioned little folktale, involving three men and three trials with different results. Whether Mandeville invented it, or not,[3] apparently he was responsible for the attachment of this story to the legend of the house of Lusignan. The king of Armenia, when the *Travels* was being written, was a member of the house of Lusignan (1342-75), as Mandeville undoubtedly knew.

Next Mandeville repeats, verbatim, what Odoric has to say of Erzrum, amplifying a little the account of the Euphrates.[4] Then Odoric mentions "Sarbisacalo,".the "mountain whereon is Noah's Ark. And," he says boastfully, "I would fain have ascended it, if my companions would have waited for me," although the people of the country reported that no man could ever ascend it because it was not "the pleasure of the Most High."[5] Mandeville changes the whole spirit of the account and enriches it with graphic details. He says, first of all, that the mountain is also called "Ararat," and by the Jews "Taneez"; that it is seven miles high; and then, to Odoric's statement that Noah's Ark rests on its summit, he adds, "And men may see it afar in clear weather." In reporting the inaccessibility of the summit, he converts Odoric's futile boast into an impersonal but graphic explanation: "And that mountain is well a seven mile high. And some men say that they have seen and touched the ship, and put their fingers in the parts where the fiend went out, when that Noah said, *Benedicite*. But they that say such words, say their will. For a man may not go up the mountain, for great plenty of snow that is always on that mountain, neither summer nor winter" (p. 100). So no man since Noah's time has been up, except one monk who brought away a plank from the ark which is preserved in the monastery at the foot of the mountain. Marco Polo, Hayton, and Friar Jordanus all mention the snow, and the inaccessibility, and Rubruquis tells the story of the plank, although not in quite the same form. Warner found no source for the height of the mountain, for the Jewish name for it, or for the hole in the ark where the fiend went out.[6] The last sounds like an episode in a Noah play.

Mandeville has not only changed the whole tone and spirit of Odoric's account, but he has created a visual image by adding details of sense impression—the ark can be seen afar in clear weather. He also injects a reassuring note of scepticism by his disbelief that anyone has been up to touch the ark, and he gives a characteristically reasonable explanation why it is impossible. Then he makes the difficulty of the ascent vivid by telling the story of the monk who got to the

top only with the help of an angel. The economy of the whole episode, fifteen lines in Pollard's text, is perfect in its kind, and as far above Odoric as the work of a master artist is above that of an ordinary reporter.

Next, both Odoric and Mandeville speak of Tauris (Tabriz), where Odoric reports the famous "dry tree." Since Mandeville has other and more effective use for this marvel, he omits it here. He also omits Odoric's comment, "And there are many things else to be said of that city, but it would take too long to relate them."[7] The wandering friar often expresses his impatience with his task and lets the reader down in this way, as Marco Polo does also. Mandeville seldom, or never, resorts to generalization, and one of his charms is that he has no set phrases.[8]

He follows Odoric past the summer palace of the Emperor of Persia, at Sultânieh, and on to Cassan (Kashan), which, Odoric remarks, is the city of the Magi. Mandeville drops out the "bread and wine, and many other good things," which interested Odoric, and concentrates his whole attention on the story of the three Magi. Neither does he stop here to describe the dry sea, to which Odoric devotes a sentence. Mandeville saves this marvel until near the end of his book, and then he draws upon the more imaginative *Letter of Prester John* for his materials.[9]

Odoric is fond of such flat and colorless generalizations as "And there are many other matters there" or "It aboundeth in many kinds of victual." Mandeville regularly omits such statements. For example, Odoric says, "At length I reached the land of Job called Hus which abounds in all kinds of victuals." Mandeville omits the victuals and concentrates on the story of Job.[10] Odoric next mentions some mountains good for pasturing cattle. Then he says, "There also is found manna of better quality and in greater abundance than in any part of the world. In that country also you can get four good partridges for less than a Venetian groat." Mandeville wastes no time on the cattle or the partridges, but he writes (out of Vincent of Beauvais) as if he had seen and tasted the manna: "In that land of Job there ne is no default of no thing that is needful to man's body. There be hills, where men get great plenty of manna in greater abundance than in any other country. This manna is clept bread of angels. And it is a white thing that is full sweet and right delicious, and more sweet than honey or sugar. And it cometh of the dew of heaven and falleth upon the herbs in that country. And it congealeth and becometh all white and sweet. And men put it in medicines for rich men to make the womb lax, and to purge evil blood. For it cleanseth the blood and putteth out melancholy" (p. 102).

Surely it is no wonder that there are four or five times as many manuscripts of Mandeville's *Travels* as there are of Odoric's. Mandeville knew how to select and develop his material. He takes the reader with him, giving a sense impression of what he describes, so that we can see and feel and taste it. As Lowes said of the later voyagers, he has a way "of clothing the very stuff and substance of romance in the homely, direct, and everyday terms of plain matter of fact."[11] He knows also the trick of comparing the strange with the familiar, cultivated to such good advantage by Hakluyt's worthies, two centuries later. Odoric says of the women of Chaldea that they wear short gowns with long sleeves that sweep the ground. Mandeville adds, "like a monk's frock."

Next Odoric describes inland India as a place where men live almost entirely on dates, "and you get forty-two pounds of dates for less than a groat; and so of many other things."[12] Here Mandeville, impatient at this dull commercial stuff, leaves him (pp. 102-108) to return to Ur of the Chaldees, and to remind us that here Abraham was born, and here Ninus, who founded Ninevah, was king, and Tobet lies buried. He speaks of Abraham's departure with Sarah to the land of Canaan, and of Lot and the destruction of Sodom and Gomorrah, and he says that beyond Chaldea is Scythia, the land of the Amazons, to whose history he devotes a page, mentioning Tarmegyte (Merv?), where Alexander built cities, and Ethiopia and Mauritania, where live the men who have only one foot and use it for a sunshade.[13] Then he passes to India to tell, not of dates, but of diamonds. He gives us a wonderful story of how diamonds breed and grow like animals, and of how, in the far North, ice turns to crystal, and on the crystal grow the good diamonds. He goes on more soberly to the various uses and kinds of diamonds, ending with practical suggestions about how to tell a good diamond from an inferior one.

Nor is he ready, even yet, to rejoin Odoric. First he must tell of the Indus with its great eels "thirty foot long and more" (according to Pliny and his successors), and of the vast population of India which travels but little because it is ruled by Saturn, whereas "in our country is all the countrary; for we be in the seventh climate, that is of the moon. And the moon is of lightly moving . . . , and for that skill it giveth us will of kind for to move lightly and for to go divers ways, and to seek strange things and other diversities of the world" (p. 109).[14]

At last Mandeville is ready to rejoin Odoric at Ormes (Hormuz), where he repeats Odoric's surprising information that the great heat makes *ly perpendicles del homme, i.e. testiculi* hang down to their knees.[15] He adds, from Marco Polo or the *Letter of Prester John,* that "in that country and in Ethiopia, and in many other countries, the folk lie all naked in rivers and waters" to escape the heat.[16] Then, apparently of his own invention, comes the further detail that "men and

women together . . . they lie all in the water, save the visage . . . and the women have no shame of the men, but lie all together, side by side, till the heat be past" (p. 109). Mandeville actually describes what he had not seen but only imagined, while Marco Polo, who had seen it perhaps, reports without attempting to describe.

Both Odoric and Mandeville speak of the ships built without nails (a procedure for which Mandeville supplies a reasonable explanation), and of the great rats at Thana. But next Odoric gives us a long, pious tale of four friars who got into trouble with the authorities and were slain. They were able to stand unharmed in fire, so their heads were cut off. Then their flesh refused to rot, and they were finally buried by the Christians. Odoric claimed that he gathered up their bones and carried them all the way to China (by sea), performing miracles with them along the way.[17] Mandeville shows no interest whatever in this typical medieval miracle. The only trace of the martyred friars in the *Travels* is the remark (borrowed from the midst of Odoric's recital) that at Thana the dead are not buried because the sun soon dries up dead bodies.[18] The comment is oblique but revealing, both of the personality of Mandeville and of his attitude toward Odoric. In place of the long account of the martyred friars, he devotes his attention to the strange religions of India. Odoric says, "The people thereof are idolaters, for they worship fire, and serpents, and trees also."[19] He is not interested in the how or the why. Mandeville is interested in both, because he recognizes that these people of strange lands are human beings like himself. His attempts to understand them gives his narrative the human interest which vitalizes it and makes his imaginary travel more real than the actual peregrinations of Odoric, or even of Marco Polo.

He elaborates the account of the religion of these people, crediting them with natural religion, "for they know well that there is a God of kind [nature] that made all things, the which is in heaven" (p. 110). They worship the sun because it is so profitable that they know "God loveth it more than any other thing," and they worship the ox because it is the most patient and profitable of beasts. He is attempting to rationalize what Odoric and others have merely reported. He adds, moreover, an account of their superstitions, mentioning similar superstitions among Christians, and adding the charitable comment that, since Christians who are well instructed have such beliefs, it is no marvel that the pagans "that have no good doctrine but only of their nature, believe more largely for their simpleness." He has seen augurs foretell the future by the flight of birds, but nevertheless "therefore should not a man put his belief in such things, but always have full trust and belief in God our sovereign Lord" (p. 112).

Mandeville's tolerance and charity are in striking contrast to Odoric's rigid orthodoxy. To Odoric the heathen are simply "idolaters" and the Nestorian Christians, who befriended the Roman missionaries in all parts of Asia, are "schismatics and heretics," or "vile and pestilent heretics."[20] Mandeville, on the other hand, includes nine Nestorians among the fifteen men who went with him into the Valley of Devils, a feat which Odoric considered evidence of his own special holiness. Mandeville is sure that "all the divers folk, that I have spoken of . . . have certain articles of our faith and some good points of our belief . . . But yet they cannot speak perfectly (for there is no man to teach them), but only that they can devise by their natural wit" (p. 206). His tolerance and charity give an impression of urbanity which dignifies and enlarges the mind of the author. The field of his interests is much above Odoric's.

The divergence in the account of the pepper forests of Minibar (Malabar) shows another facet of the contrast. Odoric says that the pepper forests are full of snakes which must be burned out before men can gather the pepper.[21] Mandeville says that "some men say" fire is used to drive out the snakes, but it is not so, for fire would burn up the pepper. What they really do, he says, is to anoint themselves with the juice of lemons (the Cotton text mistranslates "snails"), and the snakes dislike the smell and do not trouble them (p. 113). Odoric's remedy for snakes in the pepper can be found in Isidore of Seville. Mandeville apparently invented his, taking a hint from another part of Odoric's Itinerary, where Odoric says that lemon juice is used in Ceylon to keep off leeches.[22] Neither man is reporting from first-hand observation. Both are dependent upon "the authorities," but Mandeville creates the impression of careful observation and good sense by saying, "For if they burnt about the trees that bear, the pepper should be burnt, and it would dry up all the virtue, *as of any other thing.*" Friar Jordanus denies the use of fire,[23] but it was not until John of Marignolli published his report, the same year the **Travels** was finished, that Europeans were told pepper did not grow in forests at all, but in gardens.[24] The passage illustrates Mandeville's tendency to disagree with his authorities and to look for a reasonable explanation which does not violate the laws of nature.

After the pepper forests, Odoric describes Polumbrum (Quilon, in Malabar) and reports the worship of the ox and the "abominable superstition" of anointing with its ordure. He also reports the sacrifice of children, the practise of suttee, and he says, "there be many other marvelous and beastly customs which 'tis just as well not to write."[25] Mandeville, in repeating all this, raises it from a depressing kind of anthropology to high romance. He begins by interpolating an account of the Fountain of Youth, which he borrows from the *Letter of Prester John* and locates at Polumbrum. He says, by

way of authentication. "I have drunken there of three or four sithes, and yet me thinketh I fare the better" (p. 113)—surely a modest way of making a wild boast! Next he describes the worship of the ox, borrowing the name of the priest who officiates, the "archiprotopapaton," out of the *Letter of Prester John,* and making an elaborate religious ceremony out of Odoric's "abominable superstition."[26]

So this ill-sorted pair journey uneasily together, like the two horses of Plato's chariot of the soul, one all fire and spirit, the other pedestrian and earthy, interested chiefly in the quality of the victuals and the wickedness of the heathen. Both report the worship of the Juggernaut, but Mandeville alone is moved to say: "And them thinketh that the more pain, and the more tribulation that they suffer for love of their god, the more joy they shall have in another world. And, shortly to say you, they suffer so great pains, and so hard martyrdoms for love of their idol, that a Christian man, I trow, durst not take upon him the tenth part the pain for love of our Lord Jesu Christ" (p. 117). Odoric traveled in the flesh, but how much more truly Mandeville traveled in the spirit!

Odoric, following Marco Polo, remarks that at Lamary (Sumatra) "I began to lose sight of the north star, as the earth intercepted it."[27] Mandeville picks up this sentence and elaborates it into his famous account of the roundness of the earth and the practicability of circumnavigation. Indeed, at every step of the way, Mandeville illuminates and vivifies and humanizes Odoric's account of his journey. He adds details which are picturesque, as in the case of the king of Campa (Cochin China), whose fourteen thousand elephants Odoric mentions.[28] Mandeville equips them with "castles of tree" which he says are put on their backs for fighting.[29] Both report the fish which come up onto the land every year, and Odoric says that the natives claim they come to pay homage to their emperor. Mandeville repeats this explanation, and then suggests that perhaps the real reason is that they come to feed the offspring of this king, who has a thousand wives (according to Odoric), and so obeys the commandment given to Adam and Eve: *Crescite et multiplicamini et replete terram.* Then he adds, more soberly: "I know not the reason why it is, but God knoweth; but this, meseemeth, is the most marvel that ever I saw. For this marvel is against kind [i.e., natural law] and not with kind . . . And therefore I am siker that this may not be, without a great token [i.e., miracle]" (pp. 128-129).[30] He never loses sight of the principle that God is also the creator and God of the heathen, though he has only revealed Himself to them through His works. Mandeville's assumption that the laws of nature operate even on the other side of the world is a fundamental part of his belief that it is possible to sail all the way around it. In fact, his conception of natural law as universal makes it highly improbable that he believed at all in the unnatural marvels which he retold from Odoric and Solinus and the *Letter of Prester John*.

Twice, into Odoric's sufficiently fanciful account of the islands of the Indies, Mandeville inserts additional marvelous islands. After Odoric's account of the dog-headed men of Nacumera[31] he has some additions, and again after Odoric's Dondin, where men kill and eat the sick. After Dondin, Odoric goes directly to Manzi (Marco Polo's name for China), merely remarking that there are "a good twenty-four thousand islands" which he will omit. Mandeville says, at this point, that the king of Dondin has fifty-four (note the modest number) great isles in subjection, each with a king who paid him tribute. He populates these islands with a whole list of marvels collected out of Pliny by Solinus and incorporated in Isidore of Seville, Vincent of Beauvais, and others. Here are the islands of cyclops, men without heads, men with mouths in their backs, men without faces, men with upper lips so large they used them for sunshades, pigmies with mouths so small they had to eat through a pipe, men with ears that hang down to their knees, centaurs, men who go on all fours, hermaphrodites, men with eight toes, and "many other divers folk of divers natures" (pp. 133-135).

This perfect spate of absurdities, all crammed into a single page (fol. 191 of the MS. written in 1371), perhaps was brought on by Odoric's protest that "there be many other strange things in those parts which I write not, for unless a man should see them he never could believe them. For in the whole world there be no such marvels as in that realm. What things I have written are only such as I was certain of, and such as I cannot doubt but they are as I have related them."[32] Mandeville's outburst fills this omission in Odoric's text. Evidently he did not want to omit any marvels, but we might well ask ourselves whether he actually believed in them, or expected his readers to believe. John de Marignolli, in his account of his embassy to the Great Khan, explains that while freaks do occur in nature, such as six-legged calves and two-headed birds, whole races of them do not exist anywhere.[33] Marignolli was a learned man, but not an intellectual giant. He denied the possibility of circumnavigation, which Mandeville argued in favor of, and he confused the great rivers of Asia in an absurd way. But he was not simple and credulous, like Friar Odoric.

Odoric reported more marvels than Marco Polo, who reported enough to discredit him with such practical men as King John of Portugal in the days of Christopher Columbus. Mandeville certainly knew Marco Polo's book, but he elected to follow Odoric, whose account of the East was much briefer and full of marvels. Odoric's contemporaries found his report hard to credit. Sir Henry Yule calls attention to the affidavit which Odoric was called upon to append to his narrative, and he mentions also the apologies made by

Odoric's ecclesiastical biographers. Henry of Glatz, Odoric's contemporary, declares, "that if he had not heard such great things of Odoric's perfections and sanctity, he could scarcely have credited some of his stories."[34] Mandeville, in following and improving upon Odoric, was writing the first romance of travel in modern times.

. . . . .

The step by step comparison of Mandeville's **Travels** with Odoric's Itinerary shows most clearly the differences between the two works. Odoric records, without selection, whatever came to his attention along the way; or rather, since he dictated his account after his return, whatever he happened to remember. Mandeville's is a literary undertaking, the product of much reading and of literary rather than purely geographical interests. He everywhere substitutes local history for Odoric's comments on the food supply. The two accounts differ in form, in substance, and in purpose.

Mandeville was writing in a literary genre which has a long history, from the *Odyssey* and the lost *Arimaspeia* of Aristeas, through Ctesias, Megasthenes, and parts of Herodotus, Strabo, Aelian, Photius, and the lost novel of Antonius Diogenes about the wonders beyond Thule. Pliny collected these travelers' tales indiscriminately, and Solinus, perhaps Mandeville's closest forerunner, made a selection from Pliny of choice geographical wonders. Lucian travestied the genre in his *True History*, but St. Augustine included a chapter on the fabulous races of men in his *City of God*. In his day, the romance of Alexander was beginning its long history with the *Pseudo-Callisthenes* and the Epistle of Alexander to Aristotle about the marvels of India. In the seventh century Isidore of Seville repeated much of this lore, and shortly afterwards the pseudo-Aethicus produced his *Cosmographia,* which shows the same disregard for the changes wrought by time, and the same appropriation of other people's experiences complained of in Mandeville. In the Renaissance the popularity of Solinus and Aethicus tended to eclipse Mandeville!

Sometime between the third and seventh centuries a letter was invented which purported to be from "Fermes" to the Emperor Hadrian, describing a journey to the East on which the writer saw all the traditional marvels of strange beasts and stranger men. A book of *Marvels of the East* was made, mostly out of "Fermes." It is preserved in both a Latin and an Anglo-Saxon text.[35] At the opening of the thirteenth century, Gervase of Tilbury included all of "Fermes" in his *Otia Imperialia.* Meanwhile, about 1165, the *Letter of Prester John* appeared and circulated widely. In the thirteenth century, when Europeans had an opportunity to visit China, they reported not only what they saw, but what they expected to see.

As a result, they merely added some fresh marvels to the old ones, and the better educated or more sceptical regarded all alike as "great liars." Marco Polo's difficulties with the incredulous are well-known, and even Friar Odoric's sanctity did not entirely protect him from the sceptics. Mandeville was free, therefore, to add and subtract, to polish, change, and interpret what he found in his sources. He does not omit the best of the traditional wonders of the earth, but he found, in the newer reports of the Orient, things more marvelous than in the old. For example, he took from Odoric the lake at Sylan (Ceylon) formed by the repentant tears of Adam and Eve. Marco Polo reported that the king of Nicoveran had a necklace of one hundred and four great pearls and rubies, which he used, like a rosary, to say his prayers.[36] Odoric raises the number to three hundred pearls,[37] and Mandeville follows Odoric. This same king had a famous ruby, which Marco Polo said was "a large palm long and quite as thick as the arm of a man."[38] Odoric makes it "a good span in length and breadth," and Mandeville reports it "a foot of length and five fingers large" (p. 131). Modern critics have called Marco Polo's statement "hearsay," Odoric's "gullibility," but Mandeville's "sheer mendacity." It was, rather, pure fiction.

In his account of Manzi, or China, Mandeville shows much less dependence on Odoric than in the earlier part of the journey. He omits the visit to Zaiton, where Odoric left the bones of the four friars; and he omits some of Odoric's cruder marvels, such as the mountain on one side of which everything is black, while on the other everything is white.[39] He uses other sources of information, as when he substitutes otters for the birds which, according to Odoric, are trained to catch fish for their masters.[40] Both otters and cormorants were actually used, but, perhaps because birds were used for hunting in Europe, the otter seemed the greater marvel. He does not approve of crude exaggeration, however. Where both Marco Polo and Odoric say that Cansay (Hang-chow) is a hundred miles in compass, Mandeville says it is fifty-one miles.

He is much interested in the monastery, reported by Odoric, where the monks feed animals which have human faces, and which they believe are the souls of men. Odoric claimed that he argued with the monks that they were only animals.[41] Mandeville substitutes a characteristic suggestion: "And I asked them if it had not been better to have given that relief to poor men, rather than to those beasts. And they answered me and said, that they had no poor men amongst them in that country; and though it had been so that poor men had been among them, yet were it greater alms to give it to those souls that do there their penance" (p. 137). The point of view which he is attributing to the Chinese monks is the same as that taken by many Christian churchmen of his day about masses for the dead, but if his intention is ironic, it is gently and subtly so.

Such implications as this constitute his commentary on mankind, and on the life of his time. He describes the strange customs of other lands and lets his reader draw what parallels he will. But we should observe that he has turned Odoric's reaction into something entirely different. He constantly assumes that human nature is the same everywhere, and he uses the familiar to explain the strange, and the strange to suggest comment on the familiar. Yet he is content to observe, clearly and simply, with the full, sympathetic, and imaginative understanding which is true charity.

The pigmies, whom Odoric reported,[42] interested Mandeville, and he adds to every statement that Odoric makes about them, adding also their war against the cranes, which had been traditional since Homer. His greatest contribution to the literature of the pigmies, however, is his account of their relationship to men of normal size. Here, it has been suggested, he set the model for Swift. He says that the pigmies do the finer work, such as weaving, while men of normal size do the farming, "And of those men of our stature have they as great scorn and wonder as we would have among us of giants, if they were amongst us" (p. 138). So Gulliver found it.

Mandeville's descriptive skill is beautifully illustrated by his account of the palace of the Great Khan. He turns Odoric's red leather walls[43] into panther skins which exude a sweet smell, are red as blood, and shine in the sun (p. 141). They are prized, he says, more than fine gold.[44] Odoric mentions next some mechanical peacocks, operated "by diabolic art, or by some engine underground."[45] He gives them about six lines. Mandeville, with a better sense for creating a word-picture, sets the stage first by describing the jeweled throne of the Khan with its three "seges" of graduated heights for his three wives. Next he explains how the Khan is served at table, and how his secretaries write down every word he utters. Then he is ready to tell how, at solemn feasts, mechanical peacocks are displayed in motion. The story is much more impressive at this point. He says that the peacocks "dance and sing, clapping their wings together . . . and whether it be by craft or by necromancy I wot never; but it is a good sight to behold, and a fair; and it is great marvel how it may be." Then he dramatizes his own curiosity and the cleverness of the Chinese by claiming, "I did great business for to have learned that craft, but the master told me that he had made a vow to his god to teach it to no creature, but only to his eldest son" (pp. 142-143).

Next he adds the famous vine, with leaves of gold and fruit of precious stones, out of the Epistle of Alexander, *De Situ Indiae,* and some cups of emerald, sapphire, and topaz, from which the Emperor is served, and then he mentions the practical detail of guards kept in the hall, and explains how he came to see it all: "And ye shall understand, that my fellows and I with our yeomen, we served this emperor, and were his soldiers fifteen months against the King of Mancy, that held war against him. And the cause was for we had great lust to see his noblesse and the estate of his court and all his governance, to wit if it were such as we heard say that it was" (pp. 143-144). Here he is adapting a story of Marco Polo's to his own use, but the suggestion of scepticism effactually reassures the reader and makes it possible for Mandeville to find everything more wonderful than he had heard that it was, "insomuch that we would never have lieved it had we not seen it. For I trow that no man would believe the noblesse, the riches ne the multitude of folk that be in his court, but he had seen it." Then he adds the comparison with things familiar which distinguishes his narrative from that of his sources. He says, "it is not there as it is here. For the lords here have folk of certain number as they may suffice; but the great Chan hath every day men at his costage and expense as without number. But the ordinance, ne the expenses in meat and drink, ne the honesty, ne the cleanness, is not so arrayed there as it is here; for all the commons there eat without cloth upon their knees, and they eat all manner of flesh and little of bread, and after meat they wipe their hands upon their skirts, and they eat not but once a day. But the estate of lords is full great, and rich and noble" (p. 144).[46] The comparison not only creates the air of simple candor which is Mandeville's specialty, but it also saves the pride of his readers and sets the seal of apparent authenticity on his work.

Having drawn the picture of the Great Khan, he turns next (Chapters XXIV-XXVII in the Cotton text) to a sketch of the origin and history of the Tartars, out of Hayton, Vincent, and others. Odoric has very little to say on these subjects, but he was apparently the first to bring to Europe the wonderful Chinese story of the vegetable lamb, which Mandeville could not possibly omit.[47] He has no use, however, for Odoric's unimaginative account of Tibet, the land of Prester John. Odoric says that not a hundredth part of the stories about it are true[48] (Carpini says not a tenth part). Here Mandeville turns to the *Letter of Prester John* and gives his readers what will delight them.

He makes use of both Odoric[49] and Marco Polo in his story of the Old Man of the Mountain, but as usual the interpretation is his own. Probably from Marco Polo, he got the "fair halls and fair chambers depainted all with gold and azure,"[50] but Marco Polo locates the garden in a valley between two mountains. Odoric puts the wall around two mountains. Mandeville is reminded of the Christian traditions of the Earthly Paradise, so he puts it on top of a mountain on an island (where Tasso put his garden of Armida).[51] Marco Polo says that it is in Saracen country, and that the Old Man represents it to his followers as the paradise promised by Mahomet. Odoric calls it simply "a paradise."

Mandeville represents the Old Man as quoting the Bible on a land flowing with milk and honey—a concept which Coleridge caught up in the line, "For he on honey-dew hath fed, / And drunk the milk of Paradise." Mandeville even has the Old Man hint of the higher, heavenly paradise, which also belonged in the medieval Christian tradition (p. 184). Marco Polo mentions four conduits flowing with wine, milk, honey, and clear water.[52] Mandeville mentions these, but he adds three wells, "fair and noble, and all environed with stone of jasper, of crystal, diapered with gold, and set with precious stones and great orient pearls," which could, at will, be made to run with wine, milk, and honey. Like Marco Polo, he mentions the fruits and flowers, but he adds mechanical beasts and birds "that sung full delectably and moved by craft, that it seemed that they were quick." Perhaps he was remembering the mechanical peacocks, or similar mechanisms of the romances.[53] At any rate, he is probably responsible for the mechanical birds which appear in the artificial paradise described by Spenser.

Mandeville owes to Odoric much of his account of the Valley of Devils, which follows next, but here Odoric is especially vainglorious, saying, "all the Saracens, when they heard of this [that he had traversed the valley], showed me great worship, saying that I was a baptized and holy man."[54] Mandeville, on the other hand, remarks whimsically of his courage at this point in the journey, "I was more devout then, than ever I was before or after" (p. 187). He says (in the French, but not in the English text) that his party consisted of fourteen: nine Nestorians, two Greeks, and three Spaniards. Only nine passed through, but some, he says, went around another way. He describes how the party debated whether they should go through, or not, and he says that they were "shriven and houseled" by two friars minor of Lombardy that were in their company. Odoric was a Franciscan friar of Lombardy, and he traveled with a single companion! It is characteristic of Mandeville's sly humor that he should imply that Odoric was his confessor in this tall tale he is borrowing from him.

His description is far better than Odoric's, however. Odoric says that the devils that infest the valley play "nakers" and make sweet harmonies to allure travelers.[55] Mandeville turns this into "great tempests and thunders, and . . . great noise, as it were sound of tabors and of nakers and of trumps, as though it were a great feast" (p. 185). Odoric says the place was full of dead bodies. Mandeville marvels at the freshness of the bodies, and the great multitude of them, "as though there had been a battle between two kings, and the mightiest of the country, and that the greater part had been discomfited and slain." If he was not thinking of the fields of Crécy and Poitiers, his readers must have been reminded of them, and perhaps have drawn an inference from the fact that he makes the valley a test of covetousness. Here again, by comparing the strange with the familiar, a literary device which he did not find in his sources, he has enabled his readers to create a visual image.

After his account of the Valley of Devils, Odoric ends abruptly with profuse protestations of the truth of everything he has recounted. How he got home he does not say. Obviously he had been in the land of hearsay and pure fantasy for some time. Mandeville ends in a more orderly way, bringing his reader home through India, past the land of the Bragmans which Alexander failed to conquer, and Taprobane with its hills of gold protected by ants (out of Herodotus via Vincent of Beauvais). He tells of the four rivers of Paradise, and of the land of darkness.[56] He makes skillful use of bits from Odoric, omitted earlier, such as the funeral service in Tibet where birds are fed the flesh of the dead, and a cup is made out of the skull.[57] From Odoric's account of China he is now ready to tell the story of the rich epicure who lives "in ease as a swine that is fed in a sty for to be made fat" (p. 205). Odoric follows this by a mention of the Chinese fashion of wearing long fingernails. Mandeville puts the two together, using the nails as the reason that the man has to be fed by others, the inconvenience of long nails immediately occurring to him.

He ends with a defense of the beliefs of the heathen, and of his own. He says that they all have "some articles of our faith," but imperfectly, because they have only natural religion, and not the revelations of the Bible, to guide them. He defends the Christian use of "simulacres," which he distinguishes from idols, saying, "we worship not the images of tree or of stone, but the saints in whose name they be made after." Then, with characteristic humor (since what he is writing is fiction), he leaves the door of adventure open to his successor. He says that he has not told all of the marvels of the world, but only what he has seen (sic!); and he has not told all of those, so that other men who go thither may, as a reward for their labors, find enough that is new to tell of.

How much the travelers of the next two centuries found to tell can be read in the compilations of Hakluyt and Purchas, but in these later accounts we keep coming upon reminders that these men, in their youth, had read Mandeville as well as Pliny, Solinus, and Strabo and the more "authoritative" ancients. They could have learned some of their narrative art from Mandeville, for much that Lowes describes as the art of the voyagers—their simple, lucid style, their conveying of sense perceptions, their expression of the unknown by homely comparisons with the familiar—all these elements are characteristic of Mandeville.

There are other things which Mandeville did not borrow from Odoric or from Marco Polo. Odoric piles on

his marvels indiscriminately, the bad with the good, without proportion or arrangement. Mandeville, like a careful gardener, weeds, prunes, transplants, and arranges his materials to insure variety, harmony, and continued interest. Obviously those who call Mandeville a "mere plagiarist" have not compared the two. Nor is he to be compared to Marco Polo, for Polo, as his most recent editors point out, was not writing a narrative of his travels, but a description of the world. He takes up China, province by province, and city by city, giving for each the location, size, government, religion, currency, taxes, measures, products, and the things which a merchant might want to know. His descriptions are informative catalogues, always expressed in general terms, never in pictorial detail. It has been said of him that he had "looked at everything and seen nothing."[58] His stories are artless and long-winded in a fashion which suggests that his amanuensis, the romance writer, Rusticiano de Pisan, was largely responsible for his literary form.[59] Mandeville, on the other hand, gains his effects by the proper selection and arrangement of details and the apt use of simile, in a way which could, and probably did, give lessons to such moderns as Defoe and Swift.

He writes like a man of reading and social experience, who brings to his travels more than he finds in books. He looks through the eyes of others and sees more than they have recorded. He was writing, at least in his account of Asia, entirely out of his reading; but he had read so widely that the source-hunters, intent on proving that he had not traveled at all, have succeeded in proving that he had read most geographical works from Pliny to Marco Polo. What is more important, he read with his imagination. In the school of Solinus and Aethicus he was writing an epitome of the new travel literature of his own time. He was writing literature, not a dishonest travel book.

He does not pretend to confine himself to the experience of an actual traveler. He enriches his narrative, wherever he can, by telling of the religious and literary associations of whatever place he is describing. In the first part of the book, he reports not only the religious associations of the Holy Land, but the classical and romance associations as well. He understands the use of literary allusion, and he combines the pleasures of novelty and of recognition.

He is artist enough to go a step further and create literary associations. He succeeded in attaching folk tales to new places. He has an unfailing instinct for what is appropriate. Warner remarks that his folklore is always right for the region to which it is assigned.[60] Perhaps he has had a larger share than has been recognized in forming our concepts of what is appropriate to various regions. At any rate he localized the castle of the watching of the sparrowhawk in Armenia, where it took its place quite naturally in the folklore of the

East. He borrowed the story of the perilous kiss, perhaps from the romance of *Le Bel Inconnu* (the English version, *Libeaus Desconus,* by Thomas Chester, was written 1325-50), localizing it at Lango, or Cos, making the dragon-woman a daughter of Hippocrates. The association is plausible, because Hippocrates was born at Cos, was associated with the serpent cult of Aesculapius, and had a son or grandson named Draco. Whether Mandeville knew all this, or whether his invention was merely a fortunate one, its effectiveness is shown by the fact that it was adopted into both the romances and the local histories.[61] The dragon-woman of Cos is referred to in Bondelmonti's *Liber Insularum* (ca. 1420), in Porcacchi's *L'Isole più Famose* (Venice, 1576), and as late as Boschini's *L'Arcipelago* (Venice, 1658). Mortorelli incorporated it verbatim into his fifteenth century romance of *Tirante lo Blanch*.[62] Evidently Mandeville had the same power to localize folklore which Washington Irving displayed so notably. It is a literary gift of great value.

Mandeville was not responsible for localizing the tale of the Gorgon's head at the Gulf of Adalia, or Satalia. It had been traditional there from the time of the early crusades,[63] but he modified the story in several ways. Where others say that the head was thrown into the gulf and made it dangerous, Mandeville says that because of it the city sank into the sea and the gulf was formed. He also suppressed the cruder elements of magic in the story, converting it into a romance of a lost city,[64] and created a more polished narrative without violating the nature of the folktale he was revising.

Perhaps the best example of his instinct for what is right in folklore appears in the case of the orb which he says has fallen from the hand of the statue of Justinian at Constantinople. He says that it will not stay when it is put back, because it "betokeneth the lordship that he had over all the world," much of which had been lost by the Eastern Empire. A careful checking of the reports of other travelers indicates that the orb was still in the statue's hand in Mandeville's day,[65] but symbolism required that it should have fallen out. A similar tale of a giant idol on the shore at Cadiz, said to have been erected by Mahomet, told of a key destined to fall out of the idol's hand when a king should be born in France who should restore Christianity to Spain.[66] Mandeville may have been imitating this story in his account of the statue of Justinian. At any rate he knew what was appropriate.

Warner comments on the aptness of his mention of St. Nicholas in juxtaposition with the Greek Sea, because the Greek islanders of the Middle Ages attributed to St. Nicholas what their forefathers had fabled of Poseidon.[67] On the other hand, sometimes Mandeville may make a bold transfer of a bit of folklore; for example, he attributes to a tribe in India a superstition about the breaking of maidenheads which Julius Cae-

sar had attributed to the Britons. The historians of travel literature have been particularly outraged by this transposition, but Mandeville was certainly right in putting the belief in a far country. In fact, he may not have been following Caesar at all, but Solinus, who tells a slightly different version of the story about the Augyles, who live next to the Troglodites in Ethiopia (which in the Middle Ages was considered to be a part of India.)[68] He has been accused of transferring the castle of the sparrowhawk from Arles to Armenia, but there is no evidence that the watching test was a part of the *Mélusine* legend before Jean d'Arras borrowed it from Mandeville and added it to the end of his romance of *Mélusine* by calling the fairy mistress of the sparrowhawk Melior (Mandeville does not name her), and making her a sister of Mélusine.

Mandeville's dependence on his authorities, and especially on Odoric of Pordenone, is so great that it does not seem possible that he had traveled in the Far East. But if he did not travel with Odoric, neither did he merely plagiarize from him. He made of the bald and undiscriminating Itinerary of the Friar what is, indeed, another book, as different from Odoric's as the personality and education of Mandeville are different from Odoric's. The *Travels* is incomparably richer than the materials out of which it was made because the imagination of a writer of genius has shone upon those materials and brought them to life. Mandeville is neither a plagiarist nor a "forger," but the creator of a romance of travel, a field in which he holds his place with the best.

Notes

[1] For his account of the Holy Land, from Bethlehem on, Mandeville drew heavily on a *De Terra Sancta* which was attributed to Odoric; see Warner's notes to pp. 35 ff.

[2] The story seems to be a confused reflection of the troubles St. Athanasius had with various Roman emperors, and was probably not original with Mandeville. Warner, note to p. 73, 1. 4, comments on the confusion of two bishops named Athanasius. I quote the translation of Odoric in Sir Henry Yule's *Cathay and the Way Thither,* II, 97 ff.

[3] . . . Jean d'Arras added the story to the Melusine legend by making the heroine, Melior, a sister of Melusine. Leo Hoffrichter, "Die ältesten französischen Bearbeitungen der Melusinensage," *Romanistische Arbeiten,* XII (1928), 33-34, points out that the last king of Armenia of the Lusignan line died in Paris in 1393, *after* the romance of Melusine was completed, but the fairy curse falls on Armenia and the whole line of kings, not on any particular one. Hoffrichter says that the transfer of the castle from Arles to Armenia is probably due to the Lusignan connection, and R. S.

Loomis agrees: *Arthurian Tradition and Crétien de Troyes* (New York, 1949), pp. 89-95.

[4] Pollard's ed., p. 100.

[5] *Cathay,* II, 102.

[6] Notes to p. 74, ll. 17 and 23; and see Letts, p. 53 n.

[7] *Cathay,* II, 104.

[8] Some of the later, but not the early MSS., begin almost every paragraph with the word "Item," and call every country an "isle," but it is not so in the original.

[9] Pollard, p. 180; and Zarncke, *Der Priester Johannes,* VII, 914.

[10] The story of Job, Warner's French text, p. 76, ll. 29-34, beginning "Iob fuist paen . . ." and ending "quant il Morust, CCXLVIII ans," is omitted in the 1371 MS., but appears on fol. 48 of the better text of this redaction, Bibl. Nat. MS. nouv. acq. fr. 10723. . . .

[11] J. L. Lowes, *The Road to Xanadu* (Boston, 1927), p. 313.

[12] *Cathay,* II, 111-112.

[13] They are described by Pliny, Solinus, Isidore, Vincent, Higden, and even St. Augustine; see Warner's note to p. 78, l. 22.

[14] Warner, note to p. 81, l. 5, quotes a similar passage from Gower (ed. 1857, III, 109). Hamelius hastens to point out that both England and Liège are in the seventh climate; see his note to p. 108, l. 6.

[15] See Cordier's note 4, in Yule's *Cathay,* II, 112-113.

[16] This passage is cited by Warner, note to p. 81, l. 17, and Sir Henry Yule, "Mandeville" in the *Encyclopaedia Britannica,* as the only borrowing from Marco Polo in Mandeville, but there are others: the mark made by the crocodile's tail in the sand, details of the garden of the Assassins, etc. . . . The detail of the crocodile is not in Odoric, or in Vincent, as Warner notes on p. 98, l, 4. Marco Polo does not make the statement about the sexes; see A. C. Moule and Paul Pelliot, *Marco Polo: The Description of the World* (London, 1938), I, 124-125, and, on the mark of the Crocodile's tail, I, 279.

[17] Marco Polo also records miracles of this type, such as the moving of a mountain by prayer, and the existence of a church in which the roof is supported by pillars which do not touch the ground: Moule, I, 105-112, 144-146.

[18] *Cathay,* II, 137. Pollard, p. 112.

[19] *Cathay,* II, 114.

[20] *Cathay,* II, 117, 142. On the importance of the Nestorians in China in the 13th and 14th centuries, see Budge, *The Monks of Kûblâi Khân,* pp. 36 ff.; and A. C. Moule, *Christians in China before the Year* 1550 (London, 1930).

[21] *Cathay,* II, 136.

[22] *Cathay,* II, 171.

[23] *The Wonders of the East,* trans. and ed. Sir Henry Yule, Hakluyt Soc., No. 31 (1863), p. 27. Friar Jordanus was in India just before Odoric.

[24] Marignolli's Itinerary is translated in Yule's *Cathay,* III (Hakluyt Soc. 2d Ser. No. 37 for 1914), see p. 217; and see Warner's note to p. 83, ll. 17, 18.

[25] *Cathay,* II, 140.

[26] See Warner's note to p. 84, l. 18. The Zoroastrians of India use the urine and ordure of the bull in their lustrations.

[27] Moule, I, 371, 373; *Cathay,* II, 146-147.

[28] *Cathay,* II, 164.

[29] Marco Polo mentions these "castles" on the elephants of Zanzibar; Moule, I, 433; and of Tibet and India, I, 287.

[30] Warner, in his note to p. 95, l. 24, cites records of the similar behavior of fish. Many fish, such as salmon and carp, spawn in shallow water, and one species actually buries its eggs in the sand at high tide.

[31] *Cathay,* II, 167. Odoric created them by combining what Marco Polo says about three different islands, "Necuveran," where the men behave like dogs (Moule, I, 377-378), and "Angerman," where the men have heads like mastiffs (Moule, I, 378), and "Maabar," where a miniature of the ox is worn on the forehead (Moule, I, 404); see Warner's note on p. 97, l. 13.

[32] *Cathay,* II, 176.

[33] *Cathay,* III, 254-256.

[34] *Cathay,* II, 24.

. . . . .

[35] Edited by M. R. James for the Roxburghe Club (1929). In his Introduction (p. 25), James gives a brief summary of the genre. The letter to the Emperor Hadrian is discussed also by E. Farel, "Une Source

Latine de L'Histoire D'Alexandre: La Lettre sur les Merveilles de L'Inde," *Romania,* XLIII (1914), 199-215, 353-370. On Solinus and Aethicus see C. R. Beazley, *The Dawn of Modern Geography* (London, 1897-1906), I, 250 ff., and 360 ff.

[36] Moule ed., I, 383-384.

[37] *Cathay,* II, 169. Mandeville and Marco Polo, but not Odoric, say that the king uses the jewels "as our ladies wear paternosters."

[38] Moule ed., I, 380. Jordanus says much the same, op. cit., p. 30.

[39] *Cathay,* II, 187.

[40] Ibid., p. 190.

[41] Ibid., pp. 201-203.

[42] Ibid., p. 207.

[43] Ibid., p. 220.

[44] Warner suggests confusion with the stone *pantheros* which was described as red and shining; note to p. 106, 1. 1. Letts (p. 66) cites Vincent of Beauvais, who mentions the sweet odor.

[45] *Cathay,* II, 222.

[46] Warner gives Carpini as the source; note to p. 108, 1. 5. Jordanus gives a similar account of the eating habits of the Persians, op. cit., p. 10.

[47] See Warner's note on pp. 212-213, and *Cathay,* II, 240-241. Bot Odoric and Mandeville compare this lamb which grows on a tree to the barnacle goose.

[48] *Cathay,* II, 244-245.

[49] Ibid., 257-260. Mandeville changes the name of the Old Man from Marco Polo's Alaodin (Ala-ed-din), the name of the last leader of the Assassins of Persia, destroyed in 1256, to Gatholonabes, and the name of the place from Marco Polo's Mulecte and Odoric's Millestorte to Mistorak. A recent account of the assassins is C. E. Nowell, "The Old Man of the Mountain," *Speculum,* XXII (1947), 497-519. The name of the place was Alamut in the Mulihet Mountains, according to Rubruquis. The story of the assassins was well-known in Europe by Mandeville's time, but the legend of the garden paradise does not go back of Marco Polo in Europe and seems to be of oriental origin: F. M. Chambers, "The Troubadours and the Assassins," *Modern Language Notes,* LXIV (1949), 245-251.

[50] Moule ed., I, 129. Lois Whitney, "The Literature of Travel in the 'Faerie Queene'," *Modern Philology,* XIX (1921-1922), 165, notes that the *Romans de Bauduin de Sebourc* has an account of the Old Man of the Mountain, out of Marco Polo, which includes the gold and azure palace and streams of claret, honey, and another wine.

[51] . . . On traditions of the earthly and heavenly paradise see H. R. Patch, *The Other World* (Cambridge, Mass., 1950).

[52] Odoric mentions briefly a fountain of water, two conduits, girls, and *horses.*

[53] Earlier instances of singing metal birds are noted by Otto Söhring, "Werke bildender Kunst in altfranzösischen Epen," *Romanische Forschungen,* XII (1900), 582-586; and Frederic E. Sweet, in his edition of Johann von Konstanz, *Die Minnelehre* (Boston, n.d., ca. 1934), pp. lxxii-lxxiii.

[54] *Cathay,* II, 266.

[55] Ibid., p. 264. J. L. Lowes suggests that Odoric's valley derives from Marco Polo's account of the desert of Lop, or Gobi, where also strange, alluring music is mentioned: *The Road to Xanadu,* pp. 489-490, n. 4, and "The Dry Sea and the Carrenare."

[56] Marco Polo puts it in the far north: Moule ed., I, 472-473. He attributes the darkness to magic employed to rob the natives of their furs. He says the Tartars get in and out by using mares, since they will return to their colts without guidance.

[57] *Cathay,* II, 254. This Zoroastrian custom is still being reported: see Lt. Col. Ilia Tolstoy, "Across Tibet from India to China," *National Geographic Magazine,* XC (1946), 181. He does not mention the skulls.

[58] Moule ed., 1, 40.

[59] P. Paris suggested that Marco Polo's companion in prison, who wrote down his account of his travels, was Rusticiano, or Rustichello de Pisan, compiler of the *Table ronde,* and grandfather of Christine de Pisan: "Extrait d'une notice sur la relation originale de Marc-Pol, Vénitien," *Journal Asiatique,* 2d Ser., XII (Sept. 1833), 244-254, extracted from the *Bulletin de la Société de Géographie,* 1st Ser., XIX (1833), 23-31. L. F. Benedetto, *Marco Polo: Il Milione* (Florence, 1928), pp. xiii-xxxiii, has demonstrated the truth of this theory, and Moule and Pelliot, in their edition, accept the identification, 1, 40-43.

[60] Note on p. 12, 1. 16.

[61] Ibid. A discussion of Mandeville's source, with references to other discussions, is G. Huet's "La Légende

de la Fille d'Hippocrate à Cos," *Bibliothèque de l'Ecole des Chartes,* LXXIX (1918), 45-59. Huet argues that it was a local legend at Cos.

[62] Warner, note on p. 12, l. 16.

[63] It is reported in detail by Benedict of Peterborough, Roger of Hoveden, Gervase of Tilbury, Walter Map, and others. Warner's note on p. 14, l. 6, gives references and also notes that the story figures in the Vulgate version of the *Livre d'Artus.* See also Hamelius' note, 11, 33-34.

[64] Several hundred local legends of engulfed cities, monasteries, etc., were recorded by René Basset, "Les Villes Englouties," *Revue des Traditions populaires,* V-XXXIV (1890-1919). The cities are usually under lakes, and were often engulfed because of sins or curses, but none of the stories resembles Mandeville's significantly. H. M. Smyser, "The Engulfed Lucerna of the *Pseudo-Turpin,*" *Harvard Studies and Notes in Philology,* XV (1933), 49-73, summarizes Basset.

[65] Warner, note on p. 4, l. 16, says that the *cross* on the orb was blown down in 1317 and repaired in the same year. Boldensele does not mention the loss of the orb, nor does Bondelmonti in 1422. Stephen of Novgorod (1350), Zosimus (1420), and Clavijo (1403) describe it as still in place. Schiltberger (1427) repeats Mandeville's story, but he also tells Mandeville's story of the watching of the sparrowhawk, and several others of his fictions. His learned editor, evidently unaware of his debts to Mandeville, has some amusingly puzzled notes on these points: see *The Bondage and Travels of Johann Schiltberger,* trans. J. Buchan Telfer with notes by P. Bruun, Hakluyt Society, Vol. 58 (1879), Chaps. 30, 31, 38, and 57, with the note on pp. 228-229. *Clavijo: Embassy to Tamerlane, 1403-1406,* translated by Guy Le Strange, is in the Broadway Traveler Series (London, 1928), see p. 72. Robert Fazy, "Jehan de Mandeville: Ses Voyages et son séjour discuté en Egypte," *Asiatische Studien,* 1-4 (1950), 30-54, argues that this and other details of the account of the Near East are authentic and show that Mandeville had been there.

[66] C. Meredith-Jones, *Historia Karoli Magni et Rotholandi ou Chronique du Pseudo-Turpin* (Paris, 1936), Chap. IV, pp. 100-102; R. N. Walpole, *Philip Mouskés and the Pseudo-Turpin Chronicle* (Berkeley, 1947), pp. 327-433, provides a source study; and another text in "The Burgundian Translation of the Pseudo-Turpin Chronicle in Bibliothèque Nationale (French MS. 25438)," *Romance Philology,* 11 (1949), 177-215; also edited by H. M. Smyser, *The Pseudo-Turpin,* Mediaeval Academy of America Publications, 30 (1937), see p. 60 and p. 20 and note.

[67] Note on p. 11, l. 16.

[68] See Chap. 31 of the *Polyhistor,* ed. Th. Mommsen (Berolini, 1864); or A. Golding's translation (London, 1587), Chap. 34.

M. C. Seymour (essay date 1967)

SOURCE: An introduction to *Mandeville's Travels,* Oxford at the Clarendon Press, 1967, pp. xiii-xxi.

[*In the excerpt below, Seymour comments on style and structure in* Mandeville's Travels *and places the work in the context of medieval literature.*]

Mandeville's Travels was written in French on the Continent, possibly at Liège and probably not by an Englishman, about 1357. Nothing else is known, and little more can be inferred, about the immediate origins of the book. None of the various attempts to pierce the author's anonymity, which began in the fourteenth century at Liège and which have successively associated the book with Jean de Bourgogne, a Liège physician (d. 1372), and Jean d'Outremeuse, a Liège notary (d. 1399), as well as with the author's adopted name, will bear critical examination.

The book was immediately successful. Approximately 250 manuscripts survive to attest its tremendous popularity. Within a hundred years it had been translated, often many times, into Latin, English, High and Low German, Danish, Czech, Italian, Spanish, and Irish; it had been abridged and epitomized for widely differing audiences, and even turned into an English metrical romance; and in almost every part of Europe successive editions began to appear as soon as printing presses were set up. In England alone five distinct versions are known to have circulated in manuscript, alongside one French and four independent Latin versions, and Richard Pynson and Wynkyn de Worde printed at least four separate editions in the reign of Henry VII.

The fascination of ***Mandeville's Travels*** is not hard to understand. In an easily digestible form it made available the newly discovered wonders of the East and, plentifully supplied with fable, it satisfied without wearying both the seeker of knowledge and the lover of marvels; as the author rightly claimed (p.228), 'men seyn alleweys that newe thinges and newe tydynges ben plesant to here'. Moreover, a large part of the book is concerned with a description of the Holy Land, a perennial source of interest as the author noted (p. 3), and his essential catholicism, at once pious and tolerant in the best medieval tradition, must have seemed especially attractive to a world divided by self-interest and heresy. This many-sided appeal is reflected in the various abridgements which appeared in the fifteenth century; for some the book was a fascinating storehouse of fable, for others an apparently genuine guide to the Holy Land, for others a theme for moral exhortation, while in England especially the romantic interest attaching to a seemingly historical knight adventurer (who perhaps served as the model for Chaucer's *verray parfit gentil knyght*) rivalled the popularity of the traditional heroes of romance. At all points the book touched contemporary life—indeed, in a very real sense, it is itself an epitome of the later Middle Ages—and it furnished a splendid and spectacular example of God's plenty.

It is perhaps ironical that this exotic book should overshadow the popularity of Marco Polo's *Divisament dou Monde,* and that the genuine and truthful traveller should be dubbed *Il Milione,* a liar who described everything in millions, while the fictitious 'Mandeville' should be believed by all. For **Mandeville's Travels** is a compilation at second-hand of other mens' travels and contains a sufficient number of inaccuracies and inconsistencies to make it extremely improbable that its author ever left his native Europe.

The chief source of **Mandeville's Travels** was a series of French translations of genuine itineraries, completed by Jean le Long, monk of St. Omer, 150 miles from Liège, and justly styled 'the Hakluyt of the Middle Ages', in 1351. The major works in this huge compilation were the account of the Holy Land by William of Boldensele (1336), the description of the East by the Franciscan missionary Odoric of Pordenone (1330), and Haiton's *Fleurs des Histoires d'Orient* (before 1308); of which Jean le Long followed Nicholas Falcon's Latin translation. These travellers were factual and accurate observers and 'Mandeville' copied large extracts from their writings (slightly distorted by scribes and translators) into his own book.

'Mandeville' used several other sources, particularly the medieval encyclopedia of Vincent of Beauvais (c. 1250), which was based on earlier compilations (such as those of Solinus and Isidore of Seville) and preserved verbatim lengthy quotations from classical and earlier medieval writings. The reverence for the written word was such that virtually any account could be uncritically transcribed and believed, and thus the monsters of classical antiquity (the dog-headed men, the basilisk-eyed women, and the rest) found their way into **Mandeville's Travels**. Perhaps the most curious example of this uncritical repetition is the description of the 'isle' in the land of Prester John (p. 208) where the incestuous inhabitants derive, by way of Vincent of Beauvais, from the ancient Britons described by Caesar. And elsewhere this unwary approach is responsible for two descriptions of Ceylon, variously called *Silha* (p. 144) and *Taprobane* (p. 218) in different sources.

Yet, given the intellectual climate of the time, 'Mandeville' himself cannot be harshly criticized for

Monsters worshipping an idol. From the 1507 Strasbourg edition.

reproducing these absurdities. And when due allowance is made for such exceptions and for those scribal contaminations which distort all medieval books, it may be fairly claimed that **Mandeville's Travels** accurately incorporates much, indeed most, of medieval knowledge of the world. The belief that the world is round, for example, a doctrine that had been reborn in the University of Paris in the thirteenth century, and which 'Mandeville' did much to popularize, is explained in great detail (pp. 132-7), and many of the marvels which more cynical generations have mocked, such as the annual running of spawning fish (p. 141), have a substantial basis of fact. Thus, the reputation of the father of lies' which 'Mandeville' has enjoyed since the eighteenth century is misleading. Though there is much in the book which may not be credited, such as the author's statement that he drank at the miraculous Well of Youth (p. 124), it is incontrovertible that 'Mandeville' himself and his contemporaries believed implicitly in the wonders that he recorded.

To support this structure of marvellous fact 'Mandeville' chose to erect an entirely fictitious framework. He tells us that he was born and bred at St. Albans, that he left England on Michaelmas Day (29 September) 1322, and that, having served both the Sultan and the Great Khan and visited most of the known world, he wrote his book from memory while incapacitated by arthritic gout. And throughout the work this engaging fiction is supported by a number of personal avowals, disclaimers, and protestations, most notably perhaps his acceptance of the justice of the Sultan's strictures on evil-living Christians (pp. 100-1). None of this is true. The date of departure is taken from William of Boldensele's letter of dedication to his patron, Cardinal Talleyrand-Périgord; the name 'Mandeville' is probably borrowed from the satiric French romance *le Roman de Mandevie,* written about 1340; the service in the court of the Great Khan is copied from Odoric; and so on. The pretence is skilfully maintained by brief references to England, and even today exercises its force on the unwary. In its own day scribes and translators felt its fascination and cheerfully interpolated a horde of spurious detail, such as a dedication to Edward III and the story of the visit to the Pope at Rome (pp. 228-9).

This marrying together of medieval fact and fiction seems at first sight a monstrous paradox, which critics have been at pains to explain. Some have seen 'Mandeville' as a deep and mocking satirist, others as an arch/heretic seeking to undermine the power of the Pope, others as a consummate artist bent on creating a literary masterpiece, others as the creator of prose fiction, and others as the perpetrator of the biggest literary hoax in history. All these views are purblind. Any critic who ignores the essential accuracy of the book betrays a naïveté more than medieval. The spur of fame and prosperity is not relevant to the writing of an anonymous work in the Middle Ages, and though it is possible that the author was inspired by the example of some genuine traveller, Marco Polo for instance, it seems most probable that *Mandeville's Travels* was designed as a popular encyclopaedia where the narrator should, like the Dreamer in *Piers Plowman* or Dante Alighieri, hold together the various threads of knowledge. The idea of the fictional narrator was slowly maturing in the European consciousness and in the later Middle Ages was used increasingly, in and out of the pulpit, to teach wayward man the road to wisdom. As the Nun's Priest says, in a pointed paraphrase of Romans xv. 4,

> For Seint Poul seith that al that written is
> To oure doctrine it is ywrite, ywis,

and however personal his immediate motives might be, every medieval writer was vividly aware of this essential purpose.

In such a context the problem of the anonymity of *Mandeville's Travels,* which has bedevilled literary criticism of the work for far too long, is no longer crucial. In a medieval community to make available a vernacular and easily read abridgement of diverse accounts of the wonders of the world was a charitable office which was its own reward, and there is no reason to doubt the sincerity of the author's final prayer: 'Wherefore I preye to alle the rederes and hereres of this boke, yif it plese hem, that thei wolde preyen to God for me.' A close and illuminating parallel is provided by Caxton, whose Preface to *Le Morte Darthur,* for example, attests both the piety and the concern for the common good, expressed by the same quotation of

St. Paul, which are the hallmarks of medieval literary endeavour.

The structure of *Mandeville's Travels* is eminently suited to an edited selection of other men's writings. The book has an obvious autobiographical beginning and end, and there is a sufficient number of cross-references and statements about the need for conciseness to show that the author was working to a general design. There are even moments of sustained personal drama, in the colloquy with the Sultan and the journey through the Valley Perilous (pp. 100-1, 203-5) for example. But over all there is no intense preoccupation with the form of the book. The author's sense of control is easy and unobtrusive, perhaps for the most part even unpremeditated. He chose from his sources what seemed to him to be of most interest; the routes to the Holy Land, for example, are described in much more detail than those to the East; and the final impression of the book is one of natural selection. To praise this naturalness as consummate artistry, as some have done, is misleading. The author frequently copies lengthy verbatim extracts from his sources and rarely, if ever, moves far from his authorities, even though this restriction leads him at times into repetition and confusion. If the book pleases, it is because its contents appeal to the reader in exactly the same way as they appealed to the educated and gentle author. There is no more studied artistry in *Mandeville's Travels* than there is in, say, Johnson's *Lives of the Poets.* Both are, within their general framework, and *mutatis mutandis,* the spontaneous productions of lively minds, which speak across the centuries with an engaging and stimulating freshness.

The style of *Mandeville's Travels* reflects this ease and unobtrusiveness. Just as the author journeys from land to land and from story to story with little more than geographical direction, so he writes in a simple, unselfconscious manner, entirely free from rhetorical ornament and stylistic device; in both cases offering a close parallel to Huckleberry Finn adrift on the Mississippi. Where the reader finds 'Mandeville' obscure or contorted, even in passages like the calculations of astrology which determine the size of the globe (pp. 133-7) by concepts and terms unfamiliar today, it is always because of distortion by scribe or translator. Yet here also it is misleading to think in terms of a conscious and independent artist deliberately reshaping his material. 'Mandeville' wrote in the familiar descriptive idiom of his time, the *doulz franceys* justly admired throughout fourteenth-century Europe for its precision and grace, and he was untrammelled by, and probably unaware of, any need for allegorical or stylistic conceit. He was, it is true, always concerned with an immediate clarity, at pains to explain the unfamiliar, and carefully glossing exotic words and phrases; but his explanations are exactly phrased in the terms of his sources (themselves often derivative and generally in translation). Thus, when he appears most vivid, for example in the description of the crocodile (p. 144)—'and whan thei gon be places that ben grauelly, it semeth as though men hadde drawen a gret tree thorgh the grauelly place'—he is most derivative. In the same manner as Robert Burton, whose habit of incorporating extensive and unacknowledged quotation from earlier writers into the *Anatomie of Melancholy* has betrayed more than one critic into absurdity, 'Mandeville' sweeps his drag-net across the styles of many men and many centuries. The clarity and freshness of *Mandeville's Travels* are undeniable and are often reflected in the many non-French versions of the book, but they are essentially the characteristics not so much of the author as of his age.

In England this *caveat* is especially necessary. Though he is no longer praised as 'the father of English prose', 'Mandeville' is still in some quarters held in high repute as a stylist. In fact, the earliest English translation (an abridged text known as the Defective Version) is a workmanlike rendering made before 1400, but in no way superior to any other contemporary translation from the French, such as the *Book of the Knight of the Tour Landry*; and the conflation based on it, the Cotton Version (which has held the field since 1725, and is printed in this edition), is decidedly inferior. The conflator had an unhappy command of French idiom and produced more mistranslations and clumsy renderings of gallicisms (as the Textual Commentary shows) than any of his contemporaries whose work is still extant.

None the less, *Mandeville's Travels* is a deservedly popular and entertaining book. More than any other work, it popularized many of the facts and fictions of our classical inheritance—the representation of the True Cross in the banana, the weeping crocodile, 'the men whose heads do grow beneath their shoulders', and a hundred other colourings of popular imagination, draw their strength from *Mandeville's Travels*; and in Thomas East's 1568 edition of the Defective Version, which maintained its dominance for two centuries, it fertilized the minds and kindled the hearts of generations of poets and playwrights. Inevitably and perhaps reluctantly men have had to bid farewell to the griffon and the hippocentaur and the other monstrous inhabitants of the isles in the Great Ocean Sea, and *Mandeville's Travels* has become something of a fairy tale in consequence. It is a sad fate. The great Eastern travellers of the Middle Ages, Marco Polo and Friar Odoric and their fellows, made possible the great sea voyages of the Renaissance, and 'Mandeville' was, more than any other, their trumpeter. When the *Santa Cruz* sighted land on 12 October 1492, a copy of *Mandeville's Travels* lay beside Marco Polo's book in the admiral's day-cabin, a not ignoble destiny for a work designed as a popular encyclopaedia, and one which might well give pause to those tempted to dismiss it as 'a fanciful narrative of superstitious ignorance'. For as in its own

day *Mandeville's Travels* was the most popular secular book in circulation, so it remains one of the most endearing monuments of medieval civilization.

Christian K. Zacher (essay date 1976)

SOURCE: "The Pilgrim as Curious Traveler: Mandeville's *Travels*," in *Curiosity and Pilgrimage: The Literature of Discovery in Fourteenth-Century England*, The Johns Hopkins University Press, 1976, pp. 130-57.

[*In the following excerpt, Zacher presents an overview of* Mandeville's Travels, *focusing on Mandeville's treatment of the Holy Land, and argues that the work is worth interest because of "its peculiar attitude toward pilgimage and exploration, its intricate sturcture, and its sophisticated point of view."*]

Mandeville's *Travels* was internationally popular in the fourteenth and fifteenth centuries (over 250 manuscript versions of it survive): it influenced contemporary writers like Chaucer and the *Gawain*-poet,[1] and Columbus, among other explorers, turned to it for advice before making his ocean voyages.[2] In our time, however, it is largely unread and seldom discussed by medievalists. There may be some excuse for this neglect. The complicated manuscript tradition of the *Travels* has long demanded most of the attention scholars have given the work (there are, for example, three modern editions of the Cotton MS English version alone, which dates from about 1400[3]). Debate about the provenance of the book has led to a concentration on the date of composition, the author's still-uncertain identity and nationality, and his reading and sources.[4] New discoveries about these matters will surely be made, but more attention should begin to be given to the *Travels* as imaginative literature and to its contribution toward modern understanding of certain intellectual concerns of its time. Except for an occasional remark in commentaries to editions and in some portions of two book-length studies of the work, there has been little discussion of the literary worth of the *Travels*.[5] Readers have long been fascinated by its revelations about Asia, but the book—a "romance of travel," in Josephine Bennett's view[6]—ought to interest us also because of its peculiar attitude toward pilgrimage and exploration, its intricate structure, and its sophisticated point of view. And what should intrigue us above all is the insistent presence of a narrator who interests us in him and his travel book because *he himself* is so curiously interested in the world. The mind of its author is at once naive, inquisitive, ironic, self-deprecating, and serious; it is a mind that intelligently speculates about the differing mores and values of late medieval Christian and pagan cultures. Approaching the book with this in mind at least would enable us to shunt aside what seems an irrelevant issue: the longstanding assertion of historians, geographers, and textual scholars that the work is an unoriginal mixture of half-truths mostly borrowed from other sources, a fraud, a hoax.[7] These, in substance, are the opinions Mandeville's readers have untiringly rendered—and the application of a term like "fraud" to both the identity claimed by the author and the veracity of what he reports has accounted for confusion and harshness and misunderstanding in many of these judgments.

Mandeville's *Travels* is in part the record of a pilgrimage to the Holy Land, but it is in greater measure the account of a curious man's exploration of the earth. And the book is not simply a diary-like summary of successive experiences, composed seriatim (as, for example, Marco Polo's), but a consciously arranged sequence of adventures. Structurally, the book breaks into two parts, and these reflect the differing motivations of the traveler.[8] The first part recounts the pilgrimage routes through the known world from Europe to Palestine; the second and slightly longer part describes the marvels of the unknown world that stretches beyond Jerusalem to the lands of Prester John, the Great Chan of China, and the Terrestrial Paradise. The changing nature of Mandeville's itinerary corresponds to (and indeed demonstrates) the author's actual motives for traveling. In the linear narrative of the book, the devout pilgrim metamorphoses into the wide-eyed curious wanderer. But at the same time, in a number of other ways Mandeville shows himself to us, from the moment of departure from "the west syde of the world," as an incorrigible *curiosus,* made so in part by the thirty-four years he spent "longe tyme ouer the see." Furthermore, Mandeville's book reveals that for him, as for humanists like de Bury, *curiositas* was rather a happy condition of mind than a moral fault. Unlike the Chaucer of the *Tales,* Mandeville viewed pilgrimage not as an ideal spiritual practice become desiccated but as only one form of travel, which can and must be supplemented by a further, worldly kind of travel. I wish to show that in the *Travels* we are witnessing, as it were in a compressed form, the shifting motivations that distinguish the medieval pilgrim from the Renaissance voyager. Within this one book pilgrim piety is replaced by confessed curiosity. And that curiosity leads Mandeville to a perception of the cultural and religious diversity of the world—a world gradually seen to be larger, stranger, and more deserving of investigation, the world that in the fifteenth and sixteenth centuries thinkers and travelers (often inspired by this book) began to uncover.[9]

Mandeville's Prologue explains why Christians should go to the Holy Land and why he has chosen to describe this pilgrimage route. Christians journey to the "Lond of Promyssioun" because Christ selected it over all other lands inasmuch as it is "the herte and the myddes of all the world" (1).[10] Aristotle had said "The vertue of thinges is in the myddes," but common sense also teaches that anyone wishing to make public an

announcement "wil make it to ben cryed and pronounced in the myddel place of a town," as Christ wished his Word to become known "euenly to alle the parties of the world" (2).[11] Throughout the first portion of the *Travels,* as he moves toward Jerusalem, Mandeville often reminds us that Christ's home is the focal point of every pilgrim's journey, and once in the city he will allude to the exegetical and mystical beliefs that pictured Jerusalem as the navel of the world. All good Christians also need to make the "holy viage" to "chacen out alle the mysbeleeuynge men" (2). Earlier *itineraria* to the Moslem-beseiged Holy Land normally began with this call to crusade, and Mandeville, though somewhat less vigorously, follows suit.[12] Aziz Atiya would have us understand Mandeville's *Travels* as "paramountly a work of propaganda," an exhortation to the nobility to put aside vice and unite to repel the Saracens.[13] However, unlike contemporary crusade propagandists, Mandeville is eager to describe the wonders of the East, and he displays little serious interest in the military stance of the enemy aside from estimating Saracen fighting strength (26). He does worry that pride, covetousness, and envy have made fourteenth-century European lords "more besy for to disherite here neyghbores more than for to chalenge or to conquere here right heritage" (2-3). The immorality of a lax nobility—a perennial topic with homilists of the time—is a recurrent theme in the *Travels,* and it may partly account for the frequent inclusion of Mandeville's book in collections of moral treatises.[14]

But having made the standard plea for lords and "comoun peple" to go and disperse the heathens, Mandeville turns to his real motives for writing the book. He writes, he says, for the "many men" who "desiren for to here speke of the Holy Lond" but have been deprived of news because there has been for a "longe tyme . . . no generalle passage ne vyage ouer the see" (3); he also, of course, is writing a guidebook for pilgrims planning to visit the region. In between these brief statements of intention, Mandeville tells us his name, says he was born in England at St. Albans, and notes that he went to sea in 1322. His credentials as a world traveler are more imposing than Chaucer's Knight's. He has journeyed through "Turkye, Ermonye the Lityle and the Grete, thorgh Tartarye, Percye, Surrye, Arabye, Egypt the High and the Lowe, thorgh Lybye, Caldee, and a gret partie of Ethiope, thorgh Amazoyne, Inde the Lasse and the More a gret partie, and thorghout many othere iles that ben abouten Inde." Clearly he is going to give us more than a guide to the Holy Land. His assumed audience includes all *curiosi* waiting to be transported from the known to the unknown world. Mandeville wants us to believe he is no vicarious encyclopedist; he everywhere makes us feel he has been there, seen it all, and returned home to take us back with him; and he has taken pains to convince us that what follows are his own observations, his own experiences. Indeed, not until the last chapter is there any explicit admission that he has also used "informacoun of men that knewen of thinges that I had not seen myself" (228). With a further reminder that he has traveled East "often tymes," much as Chaucer's Knight had "riden, no man ferre, / As wel in cristendom as in hethenesse," Mandeville calls upon other competent authorities to correct or add to his book and begins "To teche you the weye out of Englond to Constantynoble."

Through chapters I-XIV Mandeville sketches the pilgrimage routes on a map that extends from "the west syde of the world"—specifically England, Ireland, Wales, Scotland, and Norway—to Palestine. He describes not the whole network of pilgrimage roads but only the "most princypalle stedes," because to name them all would (as he has occasion to say so often during the book) "make to long a tale" (5); and, besides, for Christians "the weye is comoun and it is knowen of many nacyouns" (39). Since the book is meant to entertain curious readers who like "to here speke of straunge thinges of dyuerse contreyes" (15) as much as to instruct potential pilgrims, these chapters offer a mixture of local history, mileage estimates (given in terms of "iourneyes"), and descriptions of cities, shrines, and relics. This initial decision to write for two audiences, the pilgrim and the expectant armchair reader, proved to be Mandeville's guarantee of popular success. As an incessant *curiosus* he was naturally equipped for the task.

His first pause along the road to Jerusalem is in Constantinople at Saint Sophia, "the most fayr chirche and the most noble of alle the world" (6). In front of the church stood a gold statue of Emperor Justinian on horseback; a round gold apple he once held in his hand, Mandeville observes, "is fallen out therof. And men seyn there that it is a tokene that the emperour hath ylost a gret partie of his londes and of his lordschipes. . . . This appulle betokeneth the lordschipe that he hadde ouer alle the world that is round." Bennett says "symbolism required that it should have fallen out," agreeing with other commentators that the apple, in Mandeville's time, was still in place, not fallen.[15] Mandeville mentions the statue, of course, because it was a pilgrims' landmark and because the moral *sentence* echoes what he says elsewhere about lords who grow too fond of the world. He understood the fallen apple as a sign of Justinian's lost empire; and the world where fallen man has lived since Adam "ete the appulle" (8) was commonly enough symbolized by that fruit in the late Middle Ages.[16] But it is clear Mandeville is also very much interested in the *roundness* of the apple; the object is not only a symbol but also the first of a series of spherical images he will discover in surveying the religious geography of the Christ-centered pilgrim world that wheels about Jerusalem. In chapter X he describes in detail the various circular structures in and around the city lying in the middle of

the world. And he finds in Egypt a temple "made round after the schappe of the temple of Ierusalem" (34); the apple tree of Adam (35), whose seed produced the tree later used to make Christ's cross (8)[17]; and a fruit (in actuality the banana) the Egyptians call the apple of Paradise, which, when cut open, reveals in its core "the figure of the holy cros of oure lord Ihesu" (35).

Mandeville's eye lighted on the round object Justinian held because it suggested all this. The *mappamundi* he will tell us he saw in the Pope's chambers on his way home to England (229) (a map probably similar to the Ebsdorf and Hereford T-O maps) might have represented the earth as round and two-dimensional and depicted Jerusalem (a round or square emblem at the center), the circular maze at Crete (usually moralized as the labyrinth of this world), the garden of Eden at the top circled by a wall, and Christ's head, hands, and feet visible at the four sides of the map as though He were crucified on the globe.[18] While Mandeville generally adheres to this conception of a Jerusalem-centered world, there is a further implication in the nature of the world's roundness—but he saves that till later. The world, he will say, is round in three dimensions, not just two; a man might go all the way around it; and, strangest of all, he will probably find other men living all over it.[19] All these ideas are withheld at this early point in the book because the pilgrims are merely going to the Holy Land; it is the *curiosi* who think about circumnavigating the earth.

Only in Jerusalem could pilgrims visit the site of their Savior's crucifixion, but they might receive a foretaste of the experience in Constantinople, where the cross Saint Helen found, Christ's coat, the sponge of gall, and one of the nails were preserved. Mandeville in passing warns pilgrims against believing the monks of Cyprus, who, in order to defraud visitors, wrongfully pretend to possess half of the cross (7, 20), then describes the four kinds of precious wood used to fashion the cross. He notes, perhaps for the benefit of English readers, that Saint Helen's father and son were English kings. As for the crown of thorns, half of it is in Constantinople and the other half in Paris. Mandeville brags a bit by confiding that he has "on of tho precyouse thornes," and says, almost as if all eyes are on him and he is still examining it, that it "semeth liche a white thorn, and that was youen to me for gret specyaltee" (9). Continuing on through Greece, Mandeville informs us that men honor Aristotle at his tomb "as though he were a seynt" (12), and this reminds him that back in Saint Sophia the body of another ancient pagan, Hermogenes, was unearthed along with a tablet on which he proclaimed his belief in the Savior who would be born to Mary (12-13). He assays a short explanation of the doctrinal differences between the Greek and western churches and cheekily repeats the Greek patriarch's curt reply to Pope John XXII's demand for obedience, a reply that ended with the taunt, "*Dominus tecum quia dominus nobiscum est. . . .* Lord be with the, for oure lord is with vs" (13). Mandeville refrains from criticizing the autonomous stand of the Greeks; even when he sees that they "sellen benefices of Holy Chirche," he wryly mentions that "so don men in othere places" (14).

Sacred and worldly marvels are as numerous in the islands and seaports of the Mediterranean as on the continent. At Ephesus one can visit the grave of John the Apostle and watch it "steren and meuen as there weren quykke thinges vnder" (16). Not far off is the isle of Lango (here we are in romance territory) where a fair lady in the shape of a dragon waits for the brave knight who will kiss her and thus become lord of the region (16-18). There is Tyre, where Christ preached, and, eight miles away at Sidon, the home of Dido "that was Eneas wif" (21). After arriving at the port of Jaffa (named for Japhet, son of Noah), pilgrims can proceed directly to Jerusalem; but Mandeville interrupts to say that some pilgrims may go first to Mount Sinai through the wilderness, up to Babylon, before going to Jerusalem—and this means meeting the Saracens.

Babylon is the seat of Saracen rule, and Mandeville rehearses the history of its rulers, customs, and military conquests at some length, for the account would have interested still-hopeful crusaders as well as pilgrims wandering by the way. He gained his thorough familiarity with Islam, we are to believe, during long service at the sultan's court "as soudyour in his werres a gret while ayen the Bedoynes" (24); the sultan even offered Mandeville the chance to marry a prince's daughter, but (unlike Constance in the *Man of Law's Tale*) he refused the proprosal since it would have meant forsaking "my lawe and my beleue" (24). As an afterthought, he tells us that this city of Babylon (present-day Cairo) is distinct from that other Babylon "where the dyuersitee of langages was first made for vengeance by the myracle of God, whan the grete tour of Babel was begonnen to ben made" (28). The "tour of Babiloyne," now surrounded by desert, dragons, and serpents, was built by Nimrod, "the firste kyng of the world," the same man responsible for inventing "the ydoles and the symulacres" (28).

Mandeville guides us back from old Babylon to the new one and the pilgrim's road, though not before mentioning the awesome names of the Great Chan and Prester John, whose distant realms he promises to speak of later. In a quick survey of the sweep of the Arabian desert from east to west, he identifies Mecca ("where Machomet lyth") and, again mindful of English and French legendary ancestry, the city of Carthage "that Dydo that was Eneas wif founded, the whiche Eneas was of the cytee of Troye and after was kyng of Itaylle" (30). Egypt would have been the major attraction for pilgrims taking the southern route to go up through Sinai, and Mandeville devotes a long chapter to this

country, combining edifying tales about a deformed desert beast that believed in Christ and the phoenix bird who is like the resurrected Lord with practical advice on how not to get duped when buying balm from Saracens and his sure opinion (one very few actual travelers disputed) that the pyramids were once Joseph's grain garners and not, as "sum men seyn," tombs.[20]

The nearer the *peregrini* are brought to the Holy Land, the more their progress is slowed by the increasing number of shrines and holy places lying in their way. Mandeville has so far described two prominent overland routes from western Europe, one leading through Egypt and the other bypassing it, and now, in chapter VIII, he pauses to insert an alternate itinerary for pilgrims who desire a speedier journey. This route leads by sea from Italy and includes stopovers at Sicily (the site of Mount Etna and volcanoes that "ben weyes of Helle"), Crete, Rhodes, Cyprus, Constantinople, Alexandria, and finally the new Babylon. Here pilgrims who have arrived by ship join others to go through the Arabian wasteland where "Moyses ladde the peple of Israel" (41) on an earlier and more memorable pilgrimage. Mandeville misses none of the historic spots along the way, he is careful to note the exact lengths of various legs of the journey, and he adds an occasional bit of factual information (the Red Sea, for instance, "is not more reed than another see"). We are made to notice several monasteries in the desert, particularly one lying at the foot of Mount Sinai. It adjoins the Church of Saint Catherine, where men may go to see the burning bush of Moses. Indeed, says Mandeville, since all the birds of the country come there annually "as in pilgrymage" to honor the virgin Catherine and do so lacking "kyndely wytt ne resoun," therefore "wel more oughten men than to seche hire and to worschipen hire" (43). With the slyness Chaucer's Pardoner might have appreciated, Mandeville the *curiosus* has here quietly rebuked the impiety of Christian pilgrims; but no reader could have done less than nod in pious agreement, since he would not learn until much later that Mandeville is ultimately concerned more with terrestrial than spiritual observations. The final stage of the trek through the desert brings the pilgrims, in succession, through Beersheba and Hebron—where Adam wept one hundred years over the death of Abel—past the dry tree that will grow green again only when "a lord, a prince of the west syde of the world" wins back the Holy Land, through Bethlehem and, then at last, only two miles farther on (about as far as Canterbury lay from Harbledown), into Jerusalem.

That city has been the reader-pilgrim's destination all along, but it would be wrong to make too abrupt an entry. Thus, Mandeville spends four chapters (X-XIII) showing pilgrims and readers the abundant sacred wonders of the Holy Land.[21] The shrines and miracles that may have edified pilgrims up to this point were merely stimuli urging them on along over the many ways that, like spokes of a wheel, "comen to on ende," Jerusalem. Nearly everything Mandeville describes in these chapters underscores that major consideration of traditional Christian geography, the actual and symbolic location of Jerusalem at the center of the world, the *orbis terrarum* comprising Europe, Africa, and Asia.[22] The lands surrounding Judea, the country about Jerusalem, exist at the four points of a compass whose center is Jerusalem: Arabia lies east, Egypt south, the Great Sea and Europe on the west, and Syria on the north (54). Within a smaller circuit lie the cities of the Holy Land, described here in terms of their distances from the city of peace.

And there are holy spots within spots in the central city of Christendom. Men's "first pilgrymage" in the city is to the Church of the Holy Sepulchre, a building "alle rownd," in the middle of which rests the tabernacle enclosing Christ's tomb. Inside the church pilgrims will also find the rock of Golgotha, on which is written in Greek and Latin, "This God oure kyng before the worldes hath wrought hele in myddes of the erthe" (Psalm 74:12). As men "gon vp to that Golgatha be degrees" they can find wonders of history miraculously condensed in a small space: the head of Adam, discovered on the rock after Noah's flood, the place of Abraham's sacrifice, and the tombs of crusaders Godefroy de Bouillon and Baldwin and other Christian kings of Jerusalem (56). By this point in the description, none of Mandeville's readers would be amazed to learn that "in myddes of that chriche" a "compas" or circle in which Joseph of Arimathea laid Christ's body was also "the myddes of the world" (58).

It is a short walk from the Holy Sepulchre to the Temple of Jerusalem, which is similarly "alle round." Mandeville takes a moment to boast that while the Saracens usually forbade Christians to enter the temple, the sultan gave him a special pass and instructed subjects that he be allowed to "seen alle the places" throughout the country and be shown "alle the mysteries of euery place" (60). As one might expect, there are some places the pilgrim cannot go that the curious man with the right connections can. We are given the history and dimensions of the temple and the names of its builders and protectors. The remains of Biblical history to be seen around it on every side overwhelm the pilgrim: the ark containing the Ten Commandments; Aaron's rod and Moses' staff; the rock of Jacob's ladder (in Christian mystical thought, a means of ascent to heaven usually located at the navel of the earth, along with Mount Tabor, the rod of Jesse, and the cross[23]); the headquarters of the Knights Templar; Herod's house; Mount Sion; the innumerable scenes from Christ's life and passion (67-72). Mandeville concludes his tour of the Holy Land in the next two chapters (XII-XIII), offering the long-suffering pilgrim-reader a visit to the Dead Sea and towns along the

Jordan, a summary of the arguments over the authenticity of a head of John the Baptist kept in Samaria, a prediction of what the Last Judgment will be like, and the information that Cain lived two thousand years before being slain by Noah's father.

In chapter XIV Mandeville closes the portion of his book devoted to the *itineraria hierosolymitana*. He admits that the routes he has shown us from England to Jerusalem are the "farrest and longest" ones, and in short order he lists three other faster and more direct routes. It is worthwhile knowing these ways, because

> some men will not go the other; some for they have not spending enough; some for they have no good company, and some for they may not endure the long travel, some for they dread them of many perils of deserts, some for they will haste them homeward, desiring to see their wives and their children, or for some other reasonable cause that they have to turn soon home.[24]

We are not halfway through his book, yet already we sense that Mandeville would not count himself among those travelers who might choose safer and quicker routes. Here and there in the **Travels** he implies that he journeyed in a style befitting a knight, a friend of sultans, and at times a mercenary. He enjoyed traveling in the "gode companye of many lordes" (3) and had an unusual liking for "long travel," as his thirty-four years of journeying testifies. Later we will watch him risk not only the "perils of deserts" but a valley full of devils, "on of the entrees of Helle" (203). And at the end we will hear him grudgingly confess to having returned home not in haste but "mawgree myself . . . ayenst my wille, God knoweth" (229).

John Mandeville was no ordinary pilgrim, but a far-traveler whose guide to the Holy Land was only the preamble to an account of the longer excursions that dominate the **Travels**. He wrote a book of travels, not just another *itinerarium,* and pilgrimage was to him but one form of travel, undertaken, he realized, for various spiritual reasons and with particular destinations in mind. Pilgrims gloried in hearing saints' stories and in learning of the world symbolically fallen from an emperor's hand as they journeyed on toward Jerusalem, the city symbolic of the higher world. But Mandeville's book effectively subordinates pilgrimage to a form of travel motivated by love for this world. Ultimately, though Mandeville speaks of the divided earth as if it were two equal halves, his greater interest is not in the commonly known Christian world but in the vast, unknown, non-Christian sphere lying beyond; not in the familiar tales of saints but in anecdotes about Alexander and the Chan; not in moral significances but in empirical speculations about the round earth diverse races of men inhabit. At chapter XV Mandeville left the pilgrim to retrace his way home, while he pushed past Jerusalem. In his narrative he goes on to do what cartographers like Fra Mauro and Bianco a few generations later began to do: he decentralizes Jerusalem (and the objectives of pilgrimly travel) because his mental map of the world is much larger and his reasons for travel are other than spiritual.[25] He is eager to tell "of the marches and iles and dyuerse bestes and of dyuerse folk" in the East—"yif it lyke you," he adds, playing with our curiosity as Chaucer, turning from the solemn *Knight's Tale,* playfully apologized for the *Miller's Tale* to "whoso list it nat yheere."

Since Mandeville's exact itinerary in the rest of the book would have been of little practical use to readers, we do best to discontinue following his progress from one place to another. Besides, his *curiositas*—as I have already suggested—is really discernible from the very start of the *Travels,* not just in the second part of the book. To expose this *curiosus* disguised in pilgrim's clothing we must look all over his book at once.

At the beginning and end of the *Travels* Mandeville quite openly admits that he has written the book for people like himself who enjoy seeing and hearing about strange new things; but it is not until midway through the work that he takes the occasion to explain why he and kindred *curiosi* are the way they are. His reaction to the enormous population of Ind prompts him to remark that the people there

> han this condicoun of kynde, that thei neuere gon out of here owne contree, and therefore is ther gret multitude of peple. But thei ben not sterynge ne mevable because that thei ben in the firste clymat, that is of Saturne; and Saturne is slough and litille mevynge, for he taryeth to make his turn be the xii. signes xxx. yeer, and the mone passeth thorgh the xii. signes in o moneth. And for because that Saturne is of so late sterynge, therfore the folk of that contree that ben vnder his clymat han of kynde no wille for to meve ne stere to seche strange places.

But sloth and inertia have no such hold on Mandeville's countrymen:

> [for] in oure contrey is alle the contrarie, for wee ben in the seuenthe clymat that is of the mone, and the mone is of lyghtly mevynge and the mone is *planete of weye.* And for that skylle it yeueth vs wille of kynde for to meve lyghtly and for to go dyuerse weyes and to sechen strange thinges and other dyuersitees of the world, for the mone envyrouneth the erthe more hastyly than ony other planete. (119-120)

Mandeville's explicit coupling of curiosity with travel and of both preoccupations with Englishmen seems to have hardened into a conviction among English writers by the fourteenth century.[26] Ranulph Higden, the historian, observed that the English are

curious, and kunneth wel i-now telle dedes and wondres that thei heueth i-seie. Also they gooth in dyuers londes, vnnethe beeth eny men richere in her owne londe othere more gracious in fer and in straunge londe. They konneth betre wynne and gete newe than kepe her own heritage; therefore it is that they beeth i-spred so wyde and weneth that euerich other londe is his owne heritage.[27]

The ever-restless palmers, said Chaucer, "longen . . . for to seken straunge strondes, / To ferne halwes, kowthe in sondry londes." In *Confessio Amantis* Gower accounted for the Englishman's wanderlust with the same astrological evidence Mandeville used:

> . . . he schal his places change
> And seche manye londes strange:
> And as of this condicion
> The Mones disposicion
> Upon the lond of Alemaigne
> Is set, and ek upon Bretaigne,
> Which nou is cleped Engelond;
> For thei travaile in every lond.[28]

This influence of the moon, which, as C.S. Lewis said, was thought to produce wandering of two kinds, traveling and lunacy,[29] also occurred to Caxton as an explanation for the wide variance of English dialects. "For we englysshe men / ben borne vnder the domynacyon of the mone which is neuer stedfaste but euer wauerynge / wexynge one season / and waneth & dyscreaseth another season / And that comyn englysshe that is spoken in one shyre varyeth from a nother."[30] Ruled by the moon and "this condicioun of mynde"— curiosity, manifested by ceaseless travel—Mandeville went forth to search the world. He could have wished it said of him as it was said of Marco Polo, that he "observed more of the peculiarities of this part of the world than any other man, because he travelled more widely in these outlandish regions than any man who was ever born, and also because he gave his mind more intently to observing them."[31]

Mandeville is the main character of the *Travels* as well as its author; he is present at the center of every experience. Sometime after 1400, in fact, the book was recast into an English metrical romance, centering on the adventures of "Sir Iohn Mavndevile."[32] Indeed, "I, John Mandeville"[33] resembles that other popular medieval hero, Alexander the Great, whose reputation in the romances as a curious wanderer may explain in part his conspicuous presence in the *Travels*. In one well-known episode from Alexandrian romance, the young king voyaged as far as the garden of Eden but was prevented from entering by gatekeepers who gave him an eye as a sign "that thine eye is not satisfied with riches, nor will thy desire be satisfied by thy roaming over the earth."[34] In one of Mandeville's own tales, Alexander's combination of curiosity and pride earns him a rebuke from the islanders of Gynosophe who cannot understand why he is "so besy for to putten alle the world vnder his subieccoun" (213). To be "busy" is one delight of the *curiosus,* and Mandeville himself is always "busy"; for example, he stresses that he "did gret besyness" at the Chan's court to learn the trick of making metal birds dance and sing (157). The magicians there refused to teach him, claiming that Chinese could "seen with ii. eyen, and the Cristene men see but with on, because that thei ben more sotylle than thei" (157). Most Christians, knowing what thinkers like Augustine and Bernard had said about lust of the eyes, might meekly accept that remark as a compliment. But to Mandeville it must have been as painful a rebuff as any teacher could give an aspiring student.

However, Chinese opinion to the contrary, Mandeville in various ways everywhere exhibits a curious eye. In the *Travels* we have "one of the few descriptions of Islam in the literature of medieval Europe"[35] only because Mandeville obtained permission from the sultan to see and learn "alle the mysteries of euery place." He prided himself on witnessing things at first hand. He assures us he saw the spear that killed Christ (10), that he had "often tyme seen and radd" the Koran (96) (an unusual and questionable activity for any European of his day), and that he personally observed the efficacy of pagan auguries and prognostications (though, naturally, a Christian should not "putten his beleeve in suche thinges") (123). He vouches for the existence of Asian reeds thirty fathoms long (perhaps bamboo shoots or else the redwood-sized reed trees mentioned in earlier Alexander sagas) and fish that cast themselves out of the sea in homage to a king (140-42) by stressing that he saw them "with myn owne eyyen" (140). He takes a special detour to visit the castle of the sparrowhawk in Armenia, explaining that "This is not the right weye for to go to the parties that I haue nempned before, but for to see the merueyle that I haue spoken of" (108). As we are wondering whether Mandeville actually saw all these marvels, he abruptly disarms us with candid admissions that there are some other places he has not been to. As for the dragon-lady of Lango, "I haue not seen hire" (16); he heard of, but never saw, the trees of the sun and moon that conversed with Alexander (36, 215). Yet Mandeville often credited reports of things he had never set eyes on. As he tells us, he was just as skeptical of the Chan's power and riches as we might be, "til I saugh it" (159); and once he had actually experienced fear in the valley of the devils "I was more deuout thanne than euere I was before or after" (205). For the curious, most of the time anyway, seeing is believing.

In other ways, Mandeville keeps reminding us that he conscientiously sought out and investigated all phenomena, both the marvelous and the more strictly miraculous (Mandeville equates these two things, in fact, throughout the book, just as de Bury treated holy and secular books as companionable storehouses of learning). He examines the crown of thorns at Constantinople to check its authenticity and verifies the Jewish plot to poison all Christianity by listening in on Jews' confessions (139). He learns that Saracens counterfeit balm and Indians falsify diamonds, figures out how to tell the genuine article in both cases, and passes along the information for other travelers (36-37, 117-18). Though at times he accepts a rumor or story because it is supported by authority, at other times he makes a point of testing opinions by his own experience. The land Christ chose to dwell in naturally sits in the middle of the world because, as Aristotle said, virtue lies in the middle way, and because a message is best spread equally to all men from the center of population. But, as Mandeville confidently adds, the centrality of Jerusalem can also be "preuen" by placing a spear into the ground there at noon and observing that it casts no shadow (134). As a *curiosus,* Mandeville always keeps an eye out for matters of scientific interest. Egypt, he says, is an ideal place for astronomers to work, since "the eyr is alwey pure and cleer" (32). He twice mentions the ingenuity of the Chinese magicians and astrologers, whose ruling authority is second only to the Chan's (157, 169-70). With apparent seriousness (we can never be sure) he claims to have taken the "smale children" engendered by "male and femele" diamonds and watered them with May dew until they grew (116). In a more practical vein, he argues after long thought, experimentation with the astrolabe, and "sotyle compassement of wytt," that "yif a man fond passages be schippes that wolde go to serchen the world, men myghte go be schippe alle aboute the world and abouen and benethen" (132).

The curious man betrays an unflagging desire to examine all that he sees; he also reveals himself by telling tales that are strange, or unbelievable, or both. Putting aside for the moment the possibility that Mandeville's *Travels* is one gigantic tale-in the sense of a fiction, or even in the sense Mandeville's modern critics mean when they call it plagiarism—it is feasible to read the book as if it were a miscellany of tales. Pilgrims were expected to be tale-tellers (Chaucer and his Canterbury folk knew that), and the individual stories John Mandeville offers us are often as unusual as this curious book as a whole. To define what he meant by "tales," or to classify them as legends, fables, saints' lives, and romances, is unnecessary. As a *curiosus* and a believer in the heterogeneity of earthly inhabitants, Mandeville found all varieties of stories useful, and for two purposes: to amaze, but finally to enlarge his readers' outlook on the familiar and the unfamiliar worlds.

There are all sorts of tales about his new-found wondrous world that need to be recorded. He writes about an abbot's lamp that lights and quenches itself (and expresses annoyance at the monks' refusal to tell him how it happens); he describes the sea off Java that seems higher than the land and the perpetual zone of darkness in Persia that once protected Christians from heathens; but in each instance he eventually accounts for the wonder by quoting relevant passages from the Psalms about God's *mirabilia* (44, 145, 188). For a far-traveler who sees exploration as an inevitable extension of pilgrimage, God's miracles and the inexplicable marvels of God's creation are one. Mandeville satisfies the pilgrim audience's liking for anecdotes about the saints, then enthralls them with a story of the woman in the shape of a dragon who has killed two knights that feared to kiss her and, like Joyce's Earwicker, still sleeps, waiting to be restored to human form (16-18). In between a capsule life of Saint Athansius (106-7) and a skeptical report about a monk who said he climbed Mount Ararat (109) Mandeville's readers could find a tale—so far traceable to no known literary source—about "a faire lady of fayrye" who would grant men "wyssche of erthely thinges." To a rich lord who asked for her body she gave instead poverty and strife, to a Knight Templar she gave riches that eventually destroyed his Order, but to a poor boy she gave fame and wealth (107-8). The *Travels* also offered readers a selection of extracts from the romances about Alexander,[36] a tale of trees that grow and disappear in a day—truly "a thing of fayrye" (198)—and a story of the insidious Gatholonabes, the original Assassin, who lured "lusty bacheleres" into an enclosed garden that he called Paradise (200-202). Mandeville could usually match these wonders with an invention or two of his own, most notably the intriguing story "I haue herd cownted whan I was yong" about a precocious medieval Magellan who traveled all around the world till he reached home again (135). The fact that manuscripts of the *Travels* were often bound together with romances suggests one effect all these disparate tales had on readers' understanding of the book.[37] Mandeville realized perfectly well that "men han gret likyng to here speke of straunge thinges" and that "newe thinges and newe tydynges ben plesant to here" (228). Chaucer, like his curious pilgrims, knew it too. And one must wonder where on his eclectic shelves de Bury would have placed this incredible book, had he lived long enough to purchase it.

The audience's curiosity, as much as the author's, fed on novelty and strangeness. This appetite extended beyond the assorted tales of unusual human behavior and supernatural happenings to the beasts that, having escaped from maps and other manuscripts' margins, romp across the pages of the *Travels* and to Mandeville's stories about that fantastic Christian ruler in Asia, Prester John. Bestiaries must have provided Mandeville with models for many of the strange animals that dot his African and Asian landscapes, but except for the phoenix, which was undeniably "lykne . . . vnto God" (34), most of his creatures amble by without symbolic trappings. Like the pictorial zoos that

crowded the medieval world maps, and like the vulgar oddities Bernard objected to, Mandeville's beasts no doubt had the straightforward appeal "of the strange and the wonderful, the appeal to the imagination of men who . . . had not ceased to dream of marvels at the far corners of the earth."[38] The legendary Prester John, whose mighty armies European Christians once expected to crush the Saracens boldly from the rear, had the same imaginative appeal. Karl Helleiner has suggested, in fact, that stories about this figure affected medieval readers much as science fiction affects modern readers; both audiences "derived vicarious pleasure from visualizing fantastic accomplishments and experiences of a race of superior beings."[39] If so, then Mandeville's further speculations about the inhabitable lands lying eastward beyond Prester John's domain (chapters XXXIII, XXXIV) would have been all the more appealing to the imagination.

Mandeville's tale-telling, added to his interest in exotic animal life and in the lore surrounding Prester John, reflects the same "awakening desire to know more of the great world and its secrets beyond the limits of the local *patria*" that G. R. Owst has documented in English sermon materials of the fourteenth and fifteenth centuries.[40] (Mandeville would have well understood the plan of a later Jerusalem-bound English pilgrim, the humanist John Tiptoft, to take an artist along on board to make accurate drawings of any strange birds, animals, and scenes he might encounter in the East[41]— the kind of project naturalists of later centuries routinely carried out on voyages.) A passion for the strange or new identical to Mandeville's pervaded the writings of the important group of fourteenth-century English friars whom Beryl Smalley considers incipient humanists. *Curiositas* "was devouring the minds of educated clergy and laity alike"; it led scholars like Thomas Waleys and Robert Holcot to indulge their taste for tales from history and mythology with such enthusiasm that the sacred matters under consideration became obscured by all the profane embroidery. To these men of Mandeville's generation, almost anything "nova et inusitata" was worth repeating.[42]

Storytellers like Mandeville thrive on novelty, and as the range of their experience widens, their repertoire becomes richer. But at the same time their sense of the differences among the accumulated items of that experience forces them to examine the meaning of human diversity. "Undoubtedly Philosophers are in the Right," Gulliver comes to realize (for a time, anyway), "when they tell us, that nothing is great or little otherwise than by Comparison."[43] From the very beginning of his book Mandeville is aware that the world is composed of "dyuerse folk and of dyuerse maneres and lawes and of dyuerse schappes of men" (3). This fascination with diversity is present all through the *Travels*; the curious man who makes his home in the climate of the moon feels compelled to immerse himself in the

Manuscript page of Mandeville's Travels.

"dyuerse weyes and to sechen strange thinges and other dyuersitees of the world" (120). Toward the end of the *Travels* Mandeville will speak of the fundamental unity of all men; but, being curiously disposed, he is at first more concerned to make discriminations between cultures and religions. He appreciates the diversity of languages (as did Chaucer), and he senses the need (as did Bacon and de Bury) for all westerners, not just pilgrims, to become more aware of them. Patiently, although not too accurately, Mandeville describes the alphabets of the Greeks (14), Egyptians (38), Hebrews (79), and Arabs (104), treating us in the last instance with a short lecture on linguistics:

> And iiii. lettres thei haue more than othere for dyuersitee of hire langage and speche, for als moche as thei speken in here throtes. And wee in Englond haue in oure langage and speche ii. lettres mo than thei haue in hire abc, and that is þ and ȝ, the whiche ben clept *thorn* and *yogh*.

An English traveler of the fifteenth century, William Wey, compiled handy (and more reliable) English-Greek, Greek-Latin, and Greek-English glossaries for pilgrims going to the Levant, but Mandeville's alphabets would have been of less real value to pilgrims.[44] They were, in both the medieval and modern senses, curiosities, and Mandeville put them in for anyone who wished merely to "knowe the difference of hem and of othere" (38).

Morton Bloomfield has pointed out that Mandeville's sense of cultural diversity—shared by Chaucer and by very few other English contemporaries—owed something to the thirteenth-century schoolmen's attempt to prove that a belief in the existence of God was implanted in all men by the light of natural reason. "The far-reaching implications of this attempt led to the belief that all men could arrive at some concept of the truth. This in turn involves the belief that to some extent other cultures are worth some consideration."[45] In a passage Bloomfield singles out, Mandeville writes:

> And yee schulle vndirstonde that of alle theise contrees and of alle theise yles and of alle the dyuerse folk that I haue spoken of before and of dyuerse lawes and of dyuerse beleeves that thei han, yit is there non of hem alle but that thei han sum resoun within hem and vnderstondynge-but yif it be the fewere-and that han certeyn articles of oure feith and summe gode poyntes of oure beleeve; and that thei beleeven in God that formede alle thing and made the world and clepen Him God of Nature . . . (227)

In a slightly earlier passage Mandeville makes the same point but with even more feeling.

> And therefore alle be it that there ben many dyuerse lawes in the world, yit I trowe that God loueth

alweys hem that louen Him and seruen Him mekely in trouthe, and namely hem that dispysen the veyn glorie of this world, as this folk don and as Iob did also. . . . no man scholde haue in despite non erthely man for here dyuerse lawes, for wee knowe not whom God loueth ne whom God hateth" (214).

It is wrong, I think, to argue from these sentiments, as some have, that Mandeville doubted Christianity's superiority over other religions.[46] Rather, it seems that in these moments of reflection and summary his aim is to remind other Christians that they should love their neighbors—and also tolerate and try to understand them, Moslems and Mongols as well as Greek Orthodox. As Chaucer put it in the *Troilus,* "ecch contree hath his lawes" (II, 42). At any rate, Mandeville's interest in the strangeness of other religions follows as a corollary from his perception of cultural diversity.

This broad moral viewpoint rests heavily on Mandeville's firm belief that the earth is not only round but inhabitable "vnder as above," and is inhabited everywhere. His lengthy proofs for this idea, which are set forth in chapter XX, spring, he says, from observation, scientific calculation, and intuition. First, he asserts what most knowledgeable men had believed since classical times, that "the lond and the see ben of rownde schapp and forme" (132).[47] For Mandeville it follows that if men found the right passages they could "serchen the world . . . be schippe alle aboute the world."[48] So positive an assertion was astounding for a mid-fourteenth-century man. Nicole Oresme in the 1370s went only as far as to say that a man *might* be able to circumnavigate the earth (though he was quite sure of the time it would take: four years, sixteen weeks, and two days).[49] Mandeville says he would have been curious to undertake such a voyage himself "yif I hadde had companye and schippynge for to go more beyonde" (133). He may also have felt that inquisitive men could go around the world as easily as their governing planet the moon "envyrouneth the erth."

But having said the round earth is circumnavigable, a statement that had a profound impact on Renaissance voyagers[50] and on Renaissance geographers like Toscanelli,[51] Mandeville cannot escape the theologically unsettling conclusion: sailing around the earth one "alleweys . . . scholde fynde men, londes, and yles als wel as in this contree [Lamary]" (134).[52] Few men before or during his time would have suggested that the earth was inhabited all over or expressed the opinion so forthrightly. In 1410 Pierre d'Ailly was still reluctant to deny the authority of the Bible and Augustine and admit the antipodes were populated; and that curious pilgrim, Felix Fabri, expressed the same reservations in the 1480s.[53] Such hesitation was understandable, for all humankind, it must be remembered, was thought to reside only on the three joined continents, which were surrounded by the wide Ocean Sea and cut off from any other hypothetical land masses. Mandeville's notion thus undercut the traditional belief that all peoples were descended from Adam and Eve and, furthermore, that the Gospel of Jesus had been able to reach all men (Romans 10:18).[54] Mandeville does not grapple with the theological implications of what he has just said; instead, he proceeds to support his theory with an anecdote about a man who *did* circumnavigate the globe-twice.[55] The inference he draws is really an observation on human nature that will become the foundation for his ideas about diversity and tolerance. "For fro what partie of the erthe that man duelle, outher abouen or benethen, it semeth alweys to hem that duellen that thei gon more right than any other folk" (135). Good Christians, especially pilgrims, rightly focus their eyes on Jerusalem, the sacred midpoint of the world; but explorers who look with care and curiosity to the world beyond Christendom come to adopt a perspective on the ways men live and worship that the true Christian pilgrim would be uninterested in sharing.

Mandeville's recognition that there is great diversity and contrariety between "this half and beyond half" is important because it underlies the total principle of organization in the ***Travels***. M. C. Seymour has allowed that the work "has an obvious autobiographical beginning and end, and there is a sufficient number of cross-references and statements about the need for conciseness to show that the author was working to a general design," but his opinion is that "overall there is no intense preoccupation with the form of the book."[56] Intense it may not have been, but Mandeville did have a definite sense of the form of the book, a conception of its organization that depended chiefly on his dual role as pilgrim and explorer. Structurally, he separates the goal of pilgrimage from the other distant goals of exploration.

So the book divides easily into two sections: the first comprises the principal and secondary pilgrimage routes from England to the Holy Land, and the second is a longer account of travels through other parts of the world. En route and at its destination, the pilgrimage of chapters I-XIV pauses at points of Christian worship, while the wanderings of the rest of the book take Mandeville and the reader through regions made marvelous by secular and non-Christian news. Pilgrims find their goal at Jerusalem where they adore the land their Savior favored as the center of the world; their pilgrimage done, these men are free to "turn soon home." After a chapter (XV) full of information about the crusaders' enemy, Mandeville invites us to follow him on a journey to other destinations. In the words of a thirteenth-century traveler to Asia, it is like "stepping into another world."[57] By chapter XXII we are among one-eyed, headless, and flat-faced peoples; in this looking-glass land, as Gulliver later found, there is a race of pygmies who employ normal-sized humans

to labor for them. "And of tho men of oure stature han thei als grete skorn and wonder as we wolde haue among vs of geauntes yif thei weren amonges vs" (152). Farther on in this topsy-turvy region we meet the most powerful king on earth, the Chan, whose round and walled palace-city contains inside it other palaces and a hill on which sits still another palace (154-55). Going still farther, we encounter the gloriously Christian Prester John. And, at last, somewhere near the extreme eastern edge of the Asian continent, we approach the Terrestrial Paradise.

If Prester John's existence was thought miraculous and the Chan's domain unbelievably marvelous (159), then Eden is both at once. It is protected by fire "so that no man that is mortalle ne dar not entren" (220); surrounded by a wall (depicted as a golden O in the duc de Berry's *Tres riches heures*[58]); it rests on the highest point of the earth—"like a woman's breast," thought Columbus, who believed he had found it in South America and tried to enter.[59] For Mandeville the moon-driven traveler, the earthly paradise—which "toucheth nygh to the cercle of the mone, there as the mone maketh hire torn" (220)—has turned out to be his true destination. With other Christian pilgrims he went to Jerusalem, and of course he hoped some day to reach the heavenly paradise. But being an earth-bound *curiosus* he also sought, like Alexander before him, to find the terrestrial one: a place located (medieval tradition had it) at the pole exactly opposite Jerusalem.[60] Mandeville never gets inside the garden, but even in defeat his curiosity prevails:

> Of Paradys ne can I not speken propurly, for I was not there. It is fer beyonde, and that forthinketh me, and also I was not worthi. But as I haue herd seye of wyse men beyonde, I schalle telle you with gode wille. (220)

Mandeville's inquisitiveness produced not the promised guidebook "specyally" for pilgrims but a small compendium concerned mainly with earthly regions most pilgrims would never enter. The Prologue advertises a pilgrimage and something more, but by the final chapter it is the curious journey and Mandeville's curious speculations that have dominated the book. One last time he affirms that all he has written is true and that he has told it all because men enjoy hearing strange new things. Indeed, his desire to obtain a papal imprimatur and have his confession heard by the pope (228-29) may reflect some momentary worry about much of what he put in this unusual book.[61]

Mandeville's curiosity asserted itself most noticeably once he advanced beyond the Holy Land. All the concomitants of the explorer's curiosity—his pilgrim fondness for tales, his appreciation of human diversity, and his acceptance of cultural relativity—became increasingly evident with each stride into the unknown. Along the pilgrimage roads he only occasionally doubted the veracity of miracles; for the most part he held his tongue and took on faith what a Christian had no business questioning. Beyond the Christian pale, however, he allowed his speculative urges fuller rein, continually testing with his senses the workings of magic, the inferences to be drawn from the sphericity of the globe, all the phenomena of nature. His accounts of saints, relics, and events of Christian history mostly echoed received opinion, but his narration of Asian experiences depended on the claim of having seen and heard everything at first hand. There was no end of the tales to be collected and passed on about the lands of the East, and indeed the climate there brought out the best in Mandeville. Informed by the natives of Caldilhe that a particular fruit contained edible animals, he matched them with "als gret a merueyle," a description of the fruit in "oure contree" that becomes flying birds that men catch and eat. He seems to have won that exchange, for the natives thought his story so amazing "that summe of hem trowed it were an inpossible thing to be" (191). Medieval and Renaissance travelers consistently worried that readers would not believe some of their stories or discoveries, and in the process of denying that they were lying they often only confirmed the wary audience's opinion. In responding to the Caldilheans with his own barnacle geese tale, Mandeville offers us a little parable about this whole problem of credulity toward the unfamiliar. The reader may believe or disbelieve the natives' story, or Mandeville's, or both; the final effect is to broaden the mind, to encourage westerners to become as open as curious Mandeville is to the possibility of the improbable—in short, to share Mandeville's sense of the cultural diversity of man. The *curiosus* thrives on the implications of multiple points of view. Two hundred years later, Walter Ralegh reported that he had located a tribe of people in Guiana with eyes in their shoulders and mouths in their chests: just such a people as Mandeville imagined in the *Travels*. Ralegh was forced to admit that "Such a nation was written of by *Mandeville,* whose reports were holden for fables many years; and yet since the *East Indies* were discovered, we find his relations true of such things as heretofore were held incredible."[62] Ralegh tried; Mandeville—by trading the flying birds for the animal fruits and making us decide—succeeded.

Mandeville's strange, improbable world, the unknown half of the globe, however, has meaning only when gauged against the known. The pilgrimage in the first fourteen chapters of the book must of necessity come first because it provides, as it were dramatically, the background and norms against which any intelligible judgments about the non-Christian world can be made. To make a convincing case for the plenitude of the world and for his forward-looking belief that the world is more mysterious and exciting than most of his contemporaries thought, Mandeville chose to prepare them to accept the improbable by reminding and summarizing for them the understood Christian world. Thus, for example, unfamiliar eastern religious practices can be explained in terms familiar to the western Christian audience: the pagans chant prayers like ours (143, 225), they have orders of holy men and leaders corresponding to our monks (148), friars (150), bishops (103), and pope (224). Saracens kneel before the sultan's signet-ring as Christians genuflect before the "*corpus domini*" (60-61), and the people of Milke—one of the several cannibalistic nations Mandeville visits—gladly drink human blood "whiche thei clepen *dieu*" (143). Sometimes Mandeville compares non-Christians with Christians to criticize failings of the latter. The natives of Calamye in India revere the arm and hand of Saint Thomas the Apostle and let it adjudicate all "doubtable causes"; they also make pilgrimages to a gilded idol "with als gret deuocoun as Cristene men gon to Seynt Iames or other holy pilgrimages" and endure so much self-inflicted punishment "for loue of hire god. . . . that a Cristene man, I trowe, durst not taken vpon him the tenthe part the peyne for loue of oure lord Ihesu Crist" (128-29). The familiar world of Christian pilgrimage must precede the new, unpredictable, curiously seen world which follows.

Medieval readers and librarians variously responded to Mandeville by shelving his book with other works on eastern travel, or with romances, or with moral treatises and social criticism. It was bound once with Chaucer's *A Treatise on the Astrolabe* (which opens with remarks on the diversity of speech and learning in the world before describing the workings of Mandeville's favorite instrument); once it was put with the book of another *curiosus,* Richard de Bury's *Philobiblon.*[63] The **Travels** had a many-sided appeal. Moreover, it gave evidence of having been shaped out of older materials for a particular reason. Mandeville's readers could have learned much of what he told them by turning to Vincent of Beauvais or any number of Holy Land itineraries or eyewitness reports of travelers like Polo, Odoric, Carpini, and Rubroek—as in fact we know Mandeville had turned to them. But Mandeville's ingenious yoking of the two kinds of journeys offered his countrymen a different perspective on the "newe thinges and newe tydynges" they enjoyed hearing. As far as I know, it is the first "travel book" of its kind to combine a pilgrimage itinerary with an account of worldly exploration. The two worlds, two sorts of journeys, and two kinds of travelers embraced by the **Travels** and its author finally complement rather than oppose each other. Pilgrims, inevitably and historically, develop into curious wanderers: pilgrimage converts to exploration.

Christopher Columbus, the last medieval traveler, consulted his copy of Mandeville before sailing out to find China; Ralegh had it in mind while writing about Guiana; and Frobisher took along a copy of the book on his search for the northwest passage in 1578.[64] Throughout the centuries the *Travels* continued to be read, though less as an authority on Asia and more as a source of entertainment—for what Thomas Browne called its "commendable mythologie"[65] or for what one dull contemporary of Browne's called an idle man's waste of time.[66] Thomas More and Jonathan Swift were influenced by the book; Renaissance travelers quoted from it, authors of Renaissance romances and plays drew on it.[67] Samuel Johnson, facetiously or not, recommended Mandeville as a valuable guide for a friend going to China in 1784.[68] It is likely that medieval audiences read it for both amusement and instruction. As the curious John Leland said, John Mandeville was England's greatest traveler: Britain's "Ulysses," he called him.[69] Scholars of this century and the last, suspicious that "I, John Mandeville" may not have been the actual historical person he claimed to be and irritated by his unmodern habit of "plagiarizing" from earlier writers, have generally judged the book and its author to be frauds.[70] If the mysteries of "John Mandeville's" identity are ever cleared up, the facts may turn out to be of some interest. Such investigations could substantiate the theory that the *Travels* was written by someone with a different name or prove that a real John Mandeville was a great traveler. But would it not be as easy to argue that the "I" of the narrative had simply an intended fictional existence: that he was a character, a persona, like Chaucer the pilgrim, or the "I" of *Troilus and Criseyde,* or the "I" of another book of travels, Lemuel Gulliver?[71] It does not matter what the author's name was, for, finally, it is our awareness of this narrator's presence that holds us to the book, and what we sense is his inquisitive fascination with a world he wants to make us imagine. Mandeville was a reader (and perhaps, to an extent, a traveler) who wrote for other readers, not really a returned world traveler, immobilized by "gowtes artetykes," writing for other travelers. Even the tactic of worrying about whether his audience will believe his accounts (159, 191, 229 *et alia*)—whether the worry was serious or playful—works to keep us alert, to keep the readers (like Ralegh) as curious as the writer about what is possible and imaginable. Should a historical "John Mandeville" be turned up one day, it might happen that in discovering him we will lose another, equally valuable Mandeville.

The modern resolve to discount the factuality of the *Travels* is, moreover, a condescension to the medieval reader as much as a rebuke to the author. To say Mandeville was a deceiver is to imply that his readers were gullible and that he somehow possessed an intellect superior to theirs. In truth, Mandeville's book is no more susceptible to the charge of untruthfulness than Isidore's etymologies, or the bestiary's zoology, or the oddly outlined medieval maps of the world, or the selective techniques of medieval chroniclers. His and their conception of history and truth was different

from ours, and not as rigorous. Etymologies, Mandeville knew, were intended to convey more than linguistic origins (and therefore "Ham" gives us "Chan"), animals had symbolic meanings that were sometimes more important than the factual ones, *mappaemundi* were artistic enjoyments for the eye and not charts meant for navigators,[72] and interest more than relevance was the criterion historians normally abided by in arranging their materials.[73] So for the same reasons that Mandeville made no solid distinctions between what we would think of as fact and fiction, his readers would have been unperturbed by the thought that the author might not really have been everywhere he claimed and might have written it all out of other men's books. He was, as John Updike somewhere says of Marco Polo, a "mental traveller," and he dreamed a world more and more medievals were ready to realize. As one medievalist has remarked in explaining the attitude toward fact and fiction shared by a contemporary of Mandeville's,

> If Holcot could attach *exempla* to real authors with no justification, may he not have invented authors as well as *exempla*? He used a medley of classical and medieval sources, medieval commentaries on classical texts in particular. The borderline between what he read and what he invented must have been thin. . . . Holcot not only pillaged antiquity and improved on it, but invented ancient tales and ancient authors when it suited him. He had the qualities of a historical romancer.[74]

Whether Mandeville copied his book from other men's books or whether he traveled as he said (and, of course, he could have done both) remains a partial mystery, but it does not pose an obstacle to our understanding of the *Travels*. The narrator and character John Mandeville had been to all those places, as much as Gulliver had been to Lilliput, risked devils in the Valeye Perilous, measured the earth, and come home to tell about it; his story would be read alongside other romances, for his exploits were as entertaining as any romance hero's. And then, as for the unknown author who must lie behind this adventurer, we still know very well what kind of man he was. Like de Bury inside his study and Chaucer inside his book of fictive pilgrimage, Mandeville was the armchair *curiosus,* whose satisfaction was gotten vicariously. Like Petrarch, who rejected an offer to accompany a friend on a Palestine pilgrimage but agreed to write a guidebook for the man (a nobleman with the curious name of Giovanni di Mandello), Mandeville chose "not to visit those countries a single time by ship, on horseback, or on foot—interminable journeys!—but to make many brief visitations with maps, and books, and imagination."[75]

It is odd that scholars have labored so long to prove that Mandeville's *Travels* was not a tale of an actual journey, that its author was a fake; and that at times other scholars, hoping to discover Chaucer's interest in pilgrimage, have stressed that Chaucer lived in Kent, must have been to Canterbury, knew the route well, and so forth. One almost wishes the facts of Chaucer's life were unknown and that a full biography of a Sir John Mandeville of St. Albans existed. What is important is that both men knew what pilgrimage had meant traditionally; and although they seem to have had different opinions on the matter, both knew that pilgrimages in their day had become vehicles for curiosity— an urge that could be socially and institutionally detrimental *or* valuably enlightening. And what is important in reading the ***Travels*** is to be able to see the world, a new world, through the eyes of a blissfully curious pilgrim-explorer. Mandeville's broad humanist perspective on this world is finally that of the following generations of thinkers and voyaging discoverers; as Elisabeth Feist Hirsch has said of them, "The humanists, it becomes clear, thought of Christian unity in different terms than did the men of the Middle Ages. For them the idea of one Christendom exploded; they put in its place a Christian world composed of varied elements."[76]

The fellowship de Bury shared with his beloved books and colleagues is not unlike the larger fellowship Mandeville encourages his audiences to see among the "varied elements" of east and west, a fellowship of understanding and tolerance based on the love God holds for all creatures on the water-linked land mass. Chaucer's pilgrims lack fellowship, partly because of their individual curious urges; but perhaps each one of them, given the chance to travel alone and as far as Mandeville, would reach the goals de Bury, Mandeville, and Chaucer himself sought in their separate intellectual endeavors, in their readings and writing, in their travels and intersecting associations with Italy, St. Albans, and Avignon. Possibly one more Chaucerian invention—say, an unthinkable hybrid of learning and wayfaring called "The Clerk of Bathe"—would best typify the feeling for nature, interest in new scientific discoveries, sense of the past, and curiosity about new lands and peoples that characterize the kind of fourteenth-century English world the humanist bishop, the poet, and the explorer reveal to us. With them we are in the great age of poetry, learning, and discovery that has already dawned.

Notes

[1] Hugo Lange, "Chaucer und Mandeville's Travels," *Archiv für das Studium der neueren Sprachen,* 173 (1938), 79-81; Josephine Waters Bennett, "Chaucer and *Mandeville's Travels,*" *MLN,* 68 (1953), 531-34. These articles were superseded by the discussion of Chaucer's and the *Gawain*-poet's debt to Mandeville in Josephine Waters Bennett's *The Rediscovery of Sir John Mandeville* (New York: MLA, 1954), pp. 221-27.

Bennett's book, for a time out of print, has been reissued (New York: Kraus Reprint Co., 1971).

[2] Marianne Mahn-Lot, *Columbus,* trans. Helen R. Lane (New York: Grove Press, 1961), p. 54.

[3] The Cotton version of the *Travels* is found in British Museum MS Cotton Titus C. xvi. It was first printed in 1725 and has been edited in modern times by A. W. Pollard (1900; rpt. New York: Dover, 1964; modernized spelling); by P. Hamelius, EETS, O.S. 153 and 154 (London: Oxford Univ. Press, 1919 and 1923); and by M.C. Seymour (Oxford: Clarendon Press, 1967). Seymour, who has become the current authority on the textual problems associated with the *Travels,* is presently preparing an edition of the so-called Defective Version, which was made in England before the Cotton version. The fullest treatment of manuscripts and editions is to be found in Bennett, *Rediscovery,* pp. 265-385; Seymour, pp. 272-78, condenses Bennett's enormous amount of information into a convenient list. See also Seymour's "The English Manuscripts of *Mandeville's Travels,*" *Edinburgh Bibliographical Society Transactions,* 4 (1966), 169-210.

[4] In his edition (p. xiii) Seymour says that the *Travels* was written originally in French on the Continent and "probably" not by an Englishman; in his introduction and notes and in articles on various manuscript versions of the *Travels* he has discussed his reasons for believing "Mandeville" was a name made up by the author, who (for some reason Seymour has not yet divulged) wanted to convince people he was English. Bennett, who believes that Mandeville was probably English, discusses earlier theories of the author's identity and nationality, pp. 89 ff. J. D. Thomas, "The Date of *Mandeville's Travels,*" *MLN,* 72 (1957), 165-69, concludes that the work was composed between 1356 and 1366. Arpad Steiner, "The Date of Composition of *Mandeville's Travels,*" *Speculum,* 9 (1934), 144-47, had put it slightly later, between 1365 and 1371. Seymour, in his new edition of *The Metrical Version of Mandeville's Travels*, EETS, 269 (London: Oxford Univ. Press, 1973), p. xvi, repeats his belief that the book was first composed on the Continent, c. 1357, and that the first copy of the work probably appeared in England about 1375. On the sources of the *Travels,* see Bennett's plentiful treatments, Seymour's commentaries in his 1967 edition, and Malcolm Letts, *Sir John Mandeville: The Man and His Book* (London: Batchworth Press, 1949), esp. pp. 29-33.

[5] In addition to Bennett's and Letts's books, see Donald R. Howard, "The World of Mandeville's *Travels,*" *YES,* 1 (1971), 1-17; and C. W. R. D. Moseley, "The Metamorphoses of Sir John Mandeville," *YES,* 4 (1974), 5-25.

[6] *Rediscovery,* p. 53.

[7] Hamelius's notes to his edition are replete with suggestions that Mandeville merely copied from other travel writers. The remark by C. Raymond Beazley, *The Dawn of Modern Geography* (1897, 1901, 1906; rpt. New York: Peter Smith, 1949), III, 320, is rather typical of the way geographers and historians of travel have viewed the *Travels:* " . . . except for the student of geographical mythology and superstition, it has no importance in the history of Earth-Knowledge." Zoltan Haraszti, "The Travels of Sir John Mandeville," *The Boston Public Library Quarterly* 2 (1950), 306-16, speaks of "the deceitfulness of the author." J. H. Parry, *The Age of Reconnaissance* (New York: Mentor Books, 1964) admits that the book "did more to arouse interest in travel and discovery, and to popularize the idea of a possible circumnavigation of the globe" than any other medieval travel book, but it was still a collection of "lying wonders" which had little value for serious explorers (p. 24).

[8] Various scholars have commented on the two-part structure of the book, usually to stress that the pilgrimage portion is worthwhile and credible while the rest of the book is fanciful nonsense; see, for example, Kenneth Sisam, ed., *Fourteenth Century Verse & Prose* (1921; rpt. Oxford: Clarendon Press, 1967), p. 94. But Howard, "The World of Mandeville's *Travels*," has detected significant, purposeful reasons for the author's decision to juxtapose the two parts.

[9] Parry, p. 24. C. W. R. D. Moseley is currently preparing a lengthy study of the strong influence Mandeville had on Renaissance voyagers.

[10] I use Seymour's edition (Oxford: Clarendon Press, 1967) and cite page references (in Arabic numerals) and chapter references (in Roman numerals) within parentheses in the body of my text.

[11] B. G. Koonce, *Chaucer and the Tradition of Fame: Symbolism in The House of Fame* (Princeton: Princeton Univ. Press, 1966), pp. 152-53, treats some of the medieval associations between Jerusalem and the *centrum* or *medium* of the world. He cites Bersuire's gloss on Joel 3 which sounds very much like Mandeville's remark about publishing news from the middle of a town.

[12] Aziz S. Atiya, *The Crusade in the Later Middle Ages* (1938; rpt. New York: Kraus Reprint Co., 1965), ch. VIII.

[13] Ibid., p. 163.

[14] The popularity of such criticisms is demonstrated by G. R. Owst, *Literature and Pulpit in Medieval England,* 2nd ed. (Oxford: Basil Blackwell, 1961), pp. 287-331. Mandeville berates the nobility for their sinful lives often in the book, but the sermon he says he heard from the sultan (100-102) is probably the strongest statement of this sort in the work. And when the sultan has finished, Mandeville adds some more complaints of his own. For evidence that the *Travels* was looked upon as a moral treatise and was often bound with such works, see Bennett's appendix on MSS and editions, pp. 265 ff.; and Seymour, "The English Manuscripts," 172-75.

[15] *Rediscovery,* pp. 51-52. In their critical notes, Hamelius and Seymour cite reports of eye-witnesses who saw the apple in the statue's hand; also see the long note on the matter in *The Buke of John Maundevill,* ed. George F. Warner, Roxburghe Club (Westminster: Nichols and Sons, 1889), p. 158. The notes in Warner's edition of the Egerton MS are invaluable.

[16] It is difficult to say when the Latin words *malum* and *pomum* began to mean apples specifically and not just fruit in general; at least by the twelfth century the forbidden fruit had been translated as meaning apple (as in the sculpture of Eve in St. Lazarus Cathedral at Autun). The metaphor of the fallen world as an apple could only occur once the fruit Eve and Adam ate had been understood to be an apple. Richard of St. Victor relates lust of the eyes to the apple (*Sermo 43, PL* 177: 1015). Nicholas Bozon (c. 1300) says the world is like a cedar-apple-sweet on the outside but bitter within; see *Les Contes Moralisés de Nicole Bozon Frère Mineur,* ed. L. T. Smith and P. Meyer (Paris: Firmin-Didot, 1889), p. 109. *The Book of Vices and Virtues,* ed. W. Nelson Francis, EETS, O.S. 217 (London: Oxford Univ. Press, 1942) equates the apple with the world and opposes it to heaven (p. 80). Mandeville, like Bozon, mentions the apple that is bitter within from the cinders God rained down on Sodom (74). In *Piers Plowman* we are told that "Adam and Eue eten apples vnrosted" (B, V, 612); see also *St. Erkenwald,* 1. 295; *Cleanness,* 1. 241; and *Pearl,* 1. 640.

[17] There is a succinct explanation of the growth of this popular medieval legend by Hugo Rahner, "The Christian Mystery and the Pagan Mysteries," in *The Mysteries: Papers from the Eranos Yearbooks,* ed. Joseph Campbell, Bollingen Series XXX, Vol. 2 (New York: Pantheon Books, 1955), pp. 369 ff., esp. 384-85.

[18] These features are found variously on the Ebsdorf and Hereford maps. Seymour (Cotton edition, p. 258) mentions some other maps that may have been available to Mandeville in Rome during his supposed visit there. There are good reproductions of the Ebsdorf and Hereford maps in Leo Bagrow, *History of Cartography,* rev. by R. A. Skelton (London: C.A. Watts, 1964), plates E and XXIV. Letts, *Sir John Mandeville,* ch. xi, has drawn a number of parallels between pictures on the Hereford map and certain descriptions found in Mandeville.

[19] Mandeville's preoccupation with round objects and the roundness of the earth may have been an esoteric concern of some significance to him. There is a strange story that comes down from the sixteenth-century antiquarian, John Leland: he said that he saw an undecayed apple enclosed within a crystal orb among the relics at Becket's shrine at Canterbury and was told it had been a gift from Mandeville (*Commentarii de Scriptoribus*, ed. Antonius Hall [Oxford, 1709], I, 368).

[20] In his edition (p. 236) Seymour says Mandeville was sharing a popular European "credulity" which genuine travelers (who reported the pyramids to be tombs) did not hold to. However, in my reading I find that a great number of medieval and Renaissance travelers, many of them otherwise reliable observers, called the pyramids the granaries of Joseph; among them were an anonymous 1350 traveler, Marino Sanuto, Frescobaldi, Sigoli, and Pero Tafur.

[21] For a summary of the places usually visited in the Holy Land, see John G. Demaray, *The Invention of Dante's* Commedia (New Haven: Yale Univ. Press, 1974), ch. 1.

[22] On the various associations of the three known continents with the Trinity, see George H. Williams, *Wilderness and Paradise in Christian Thought: The Biblical Experience of the Desert in the History of Christianity and the Paradise Theme in the Theological Idea of a University* (New York: Harper, 1962), pp. 169-71. G. R. Crone, *The World Map by Richard of Haldingham in Hereford Cathedral circa A.D. 1285* (London: Royal Geographical Society, 1954), p. 24, says the tripartite division of the earth was not a biblical concept but began with the Romans, perhaps Sallust.

[23] See Eleanor Simmons Greenhill, "The Child in the Tree: A Study of the Cosmological Tree in Christian Tradition," *Traditio,* 10 (1954), 323-71, and esp. 335-37 on the idea of Jerusalem as the navel of the world; and Mircea Eliade, *Images and Symbols: Studies in Religious Symbolism,* trans. Philip Mairet (New York: Sheed and Ward, 1961), ch. 1.

[24] Half of this passage is missing from the Cotton MS and what I have quoted here appears in another version of the *Travels*, the Egerton MS. I quote from Pollard's edition, which includes it (p. 83); the spelling has been modernized.

[25] Fra Mauro's world map dates from the mid-fifteenth century; in placing Jerusalem off-center, he apologized for abandoning the ancient tradition; see G. R. Crone, *Maps and Their Markers: An Introduction to the History of Cartography* (1962; rpt. New York: Capricorn Books, 1966), pp. 54-55. On Bianco's map and its implications, see R. E. Skelton, Thomas E. Marston, and George D. Painter, *The Vinland Map and the Tartar Relation* (New Haven: Yale Univ. Press, 1965), pp. 124-26.

[26] Bennett, *Rediscovery* (p. 9 n. 14), says "Wyclif, Gower, and Higden all comment on the Englishman's love of travel, and Chaucer gives his knight that characteristic, but all of these comments were written after the *Travels* had begun to circulate." She does not describe the love of travel as *curiositas*.

[27] *Polychronicon*, ed. Churchill Babington, Rolls Series (London: Longman and Co., 1869), II, 169. I quote from Trevisa's translation of Higden.

[28] *The English Works of John Gower*, ed. G. C. Macaulay, EETS, E.S. 81-82 (London: K. Paul, Trench, Trübner, 1900-1901), II, 253.

[29] C. S. Lewis, *The Discarded Image: An Introduction to Medieval and Renaissance Literature* (Cambridge: Cambridge Univ. Press, 1964), p. 109.

[30] *The Prologues and Epilogues of William Caxton*, ed. W. J. B. Crotch, EETS, O.S. 176 (1928; rpt. Oxford: Oxford Univ. Press, 1956), p. 108.

[31] *The Travels of Marco Polo*, trans. Ronald Latham (Baltimore: Penguin Books, 1965), p. 10.

[32] M. C. Seymour's edition; see note 4 above.

[33] C. W. R. D. Moseley notes that the inclusion of phrases like "I John Mandeville" occurred with more frequency as the work became more popular and more copied—although he admits that the sense of an authority addressing us is present already in the earliest versions; see "Sir John Mandeville's Visit to the Pope: The Implications of an Interpolation," *Neophilologus*, 54 (1970), 79.

[34] Mary Lascelles, "Alexander and the Earthly Paradise in Mediaeval English Writings," *MÆ*, 5 (1936), 39.

[35] Atiya, p. 165.

[36] On Mandeville's familiarity with Alexandrian romances, see the notes in Seymour's edition (1967), pp. 209, 211, and 254.

[37] Bennett, *Rediscovery,* pp. 83-84. Polo's travel account was composed with the aid of a professional romance-writer, who may have added romance material to Polo's factual record.

[38] Grover Cronin, Jr., "The Bestiary and the Mediaeval Mind-Some Complexities," *MLQ,* 2 (1941), 196.

[39] "Prester John's Letter: A Mediaeval Utopia," *Phoenix,* 13 (1959), 56-57. The best recent study of the impact Prester John had on the medieval European consciousness is Vsevolod Slessarev, *Prester John: The Letter and the Legend* (Minneapolis: Univ. of Minnesota Press, 1959).

[40] *Literature and Pulpit,* pp. 173-76.

[41] R. J. Mitchell, *The Spring Voyage: The Jerusalem Pilgrimage in 1458* (London: John Murray, 1964), p. 42.

[42] "Thomas Waleys O.P.," *Archivum Fratrum Praedicatorum,* 24 (1954), 74-76. The phrase "nova et inusitate" occurs in a fourteenth-century moralist's attack on *curiositas* in sermons; see Th.-M. Charland, *Artes Praedicandi: Contribution à l'Histoire de le Rhétorique au Moyen Age* (Paris: J. Vrin, 1936), p. 316.

[43] *Gulliver's Travels,* in *The Prose Works of Jonathan Swift,* ed. Herbert David (Oxford: Basil Blackwell, 1941), II, 71.

[44] *The Itineraries of William Wey,* ed. G. Williams, Roxburghe Club (London: J. B. Nichols and Sons, 1857), I, appendix.

[45] Morton W. Bloomfield, "Chaucer's Sense of History," *JEGP,* 51 (1952), 310-11.

[46] Hamelius was convinced that Mandeville's book embodied a running attack on the papacy, and he argued that Mandeville was possessed of a covert unorthodoxy; see his commentary and notes, passim. Margaret Schlauch, *English Medieval Literature and Its Social Foundations* (Warsaw: Panstwowe W. Naukowe, 1956), p. 196, finds in the *Travels* a deliberate burlesquing of the Christian religion. See Howard, "The World of Mandeville's *Travels,*" for another theory of what Mandeville was trying to do in polarizing Eastern and Western religions.

[47] For a short summary of classical and medieval opinion on the shape of the earth, see Charles W. Jones, "The Flat Earth," *Thought,* 9 (1934), 296-307.

[48] Bennett observes: "Mandeville's assumption that the laws of nature operate on the other side of the world is a fundamental part of his belief that it is possible to sail all the way around it" (*Rediscovery,* p. 36).

[49] *Nicole Oresme le livre du ciel et du monde,* ed. Albert D. Menut and Alexander J. Denomy, trans. Albert D. Menut (Madison: Univ. of Wisconsin Press, 1968), pp. 576-77.

[50] See Parry, *The Age of Reconnaissance,* p. 24, Bennett,

ch. 15, and Moseley's forthcoming study.

[51] Toscanelli corresponded with Columbus (who read Mandeville); Columbus also was stirred by d'Ally's remarks (c. 1414) that the ocean might be navigable, if winds were fair. On the indirect influence of Mandeville and late-medieval geographical thinkers on those of Columbus's generation, see Thomas Goldstein, "Geography in Fifteenth-Century Florence," in *Merchants and Scholars: Essays in the History of Exploration and Trade,* ed. John Parker (Minneapolis: Univ. of Minnesota Press, 1965), pp. 9-32.

[52] See Arthur C. Cawley, "'Mandeville's Travels': A Possible New Source," *N&Q,* N.S. 19 (1972), 47-48; he finds in Macrobius a likely source for Mandeville's comments on the antipodeans (ch. XX).

[53] *Imago Mundi by Petrus Ailliacus,* trans. Edwin F. Keaver (Wilmington, N.C., 1948), ch. 7; *The Wanderings of Felix Fabri* (London: Palestine Pilgrims' Text Society, 1897), III, 376.

[54] For a full explanation of this problem, see Edmundo O'Gorman, *The Invention of America: An Inquiry into the Historical Nature of the New World and the Meaning of Its History* (Bloomington, Ind.: Indiana Univ. Press, 1961), pp. 54-55; Don Cameron Allen, *The Legend of Noah: Renaissance Rationalism in Art, Science, and Letters* (Urbana: Univ. of Illinois Press, 1949), pp. 113 ff.; and Bennett, *Rediscovery,* pp. 233 ff.

[55] Scholars have not pinned down the source of Mandeville's tale of the Norwegian who twice circumnavigated the globe, although it has been suggested that Adam of Bremen (or some other writer who mentioned accounts of early voyagers) could have reminded Mandeville of Viking sailors. Any number of sources, oral or written, might exist. I am currently preparing a study on the probable influence of Gautier de Metz's *Image du Monde* on Mandeville's notions and especially on Mandeville's anecdote. It may be that the now lost *Inventio Fortunatae,* a written account of a voyage by an Englishman (possibly Nicholas of Lynne) to the Arctic area during the mid-fourteenth century, was known to Mandeville and influenced him on this whole issue of circumnavigation.

[56] Seymour, introduction, p. xvii.

[57] The phrase occurs in an account contained in *The Mongol Mission: Narratives and Letters of the Franciscan Missionaries in Mongolia and China in the Thirteenth and Fourteenth Centuries,* ed. Christopher Dawson (London: Sheed and Ward, 1955), p. 93.

[58] For a convenient representation, see plate 89 in D. W. Robertson, Jr., *A Preface to Chaucer: Studies in*

Medieval Perspectives (Princeton: Princeton Univ. Press, 1962).

[59] _Relations des Quatre Voyages Entrepris par Christophe Colomb_ . . . , ed. M. F. de Navarrete (Paris: Treuttel et Wurtz, 1828), III, 32.

[60] On the tradition that Eden lay opposite Jerusalem, see Charles S. Singleton, "A Lament for Eden," in _Journey to Beatrice: Dante Studies 2_ (Cambridge, Mass.: Harvard Univ. Press, 1958), pp. 141-58. For a summary of traditional views about Eden as a remote or nonexistent spot, see A. Bartlett Giamatti, _The Earthly Paradise and the Renaissance Epic_ (Princeton: Princeton Univ. Press, 1966), ch. 1; and on Mandeville as representative of the medieval view about terrestrial Eden, see Howard Rollins Patch, _The Other World According to Descriptions in Medieval Literature_ (Cambridge, Mass.: Harvard Univ. Press, 1950), pp. 164-73.

[61] See Moseley, note 33 above. Whatever the "tretys" was that Mandeville says he showed the pope on the way home-and assuming he might have stopped at Avignon, if not Rome-it obviously was not the finished version of the _Travels_. It is clear from the Prologue and the last chapter that while the work may have been sketched out by the man during his journeys (and perhaps shown to the pope in some rough draft), the complete book was, as Mandeville says at the end, "fulfilled" later. Of course, if the author never traveled or never visited the pope, all this is just more of the apparatus of the fiction.

[62] _The Discovery of Guiana,_ in _Voyages and Travels Ancient and Modern,_ ed. Charles E. Eliot (Boston: The Harvard Classics, 1920), pp. 359-60. See Bennett, _Rediscovery,_ p. 245.

[63] Bennett, _Rediscovery,_ pp. 82-84; Seymour, "The English Manuscripts of _Mandeville's Travels,_" 200 (the _Travels_ bound with Chaucer's _Astrolabe_); and Bennett, _Rediscovery,_ p. 299 (the _Travels_ bound with the _Philobiblon_).

[64] _The Three Voyages of Martin Frobisher,_ ed. Vilhjalmur Stefansson (London: The Argonaut Press, 1938), II, 77.

[65] _Pseudodoxia Epidemica,_ in _The Works of Sir Thomas Browne,_ ed. Geoffrey Keynes (Chicago: Univ. of Chicago Press, 1964), II, 54.

[66] See Louis B. Wright, _Middle-Class Culture in Elizabethan England_ (1947; rpt. Ithaca: Cornell Univ. Press, 1958), p. 86.

[67] See Bennett, _Rediscovery,_ pp. 237-38 (on More), pp. 255-56 (on Swift); see W. T. Jewkes, "The Literature of Travel and the Mode of Romance in the Renais-

sance," in _Literature as a Mode of Travel_ (New York: The New York Public Library, 1963), pp. 13-30; C. W. R. D. Moseley, "Richard Head's 'The English Rogue': A Modern Mandeville?" _YES,_ 1 (1971), 102-7; and Moseley's "The Lost Play of Mandeville," _The Library,_ Series 5, 25 (1970), 46-49.

[68] _Johnsonian Miscellanies,_ ed. George B. Hill (New York: Harper & Bros., 1897), II, 387.

[69] _Commentarii,_ pp. 366-67.

[70] The name "Mandeville" and the various dates mentioned in the manuscript versions continue to be major targets for those intent on figuring out the author's identity. Beazley (III, 320-21)-apparently following a suggestion of Warner's-remarked that perhaps the name Mandeville was derived from a satirical French romance, _Mandevie,_ written by one Jean du Pin about 1340. Seymour repeats this idea and also notes that the date Mandeville gives as his time of departure from England—Michaelmas Day (September 29), 1322—was probably taken from the itinerary of William of Boldensele, another fourteenth-century traveler (introduction, p. xvi).

[71] Letts, _Sir John Mandeville_ (p. 125), notes that in one eighteenth-century edition of the _Travels_ the date 1372, which appears in some fourteenth-century versions of the work, was inadvertently altered to read 1732; and there is a remark in that edition to the effect that "Mandeville is turned into another Gulliver." _Gulliver's Travels_ was published in 1726, the year after the famous first printing of the Cotton MS version of Mandeville.

[72] Lewis, p. 144.

[73] On this point see William J. Brandt, _The Shape of Medieval History: Studies in Modes of Perception_ (New Haven: Yale Univ. Press, 1966), ch. 2.

[74] Smalley, "Robert Holcot O.P.," _Archivum Fratrum Praedicatorum,_ 26 (1956), 82.

[75] _Letters from Petrarch,_ trans. Morris Bishop (Bloomington, Ind.: Indiana Univ. Press, 1966), p. 261.

[76] "The Discoveries and the Humanists," in _Merchants and Scholars,_ p. 40.

C. W. R. D. Moseley (essay date 1982)

SOURCE: An introduction to _The Travels of Sir John Mandeville,_ Penguin Books, 1982, pp. 9-39.

[_In the following excerpt, Moseley discusses the work's author, reputation, values, and sources. The critic_ *contends that the popularity of* Mandeville's Travels *demands that the work be given serious attention if scholars want to understand the world view of the Middle Ages and the Renaissance.*]

When Leonardo da Vinci moved from Milan in 1499, the inventory of his books included a number on natural history, the sphere, the heavens—indicators of some of the prime interests of that unparalleled mind. But out of the multitude of travel accounts that Leonardo could have had, in MS or from the new printing press, there is only the one: Mandeville's **Travels.** At about the same time (so his biographer, Andrés Bernáldez, tells us) Columbus was perusing Mandeville for information on China preparatory to his voyage; and in 1576 a copy of the **Travels** was with Frobisher as he lay off Baffin Bay. The huge number of people who relied on the **Travels** for hard, practical geographical information in the two centuries after the book first appeared demands that we give it serious attention if we want to understand the mental picture of the world of the late Middle Ages and the Renaissance. Yet soon after 1600 Bishop Joseph Hall can speak of 'whetstone leasings of old Mandeville', Richard Brome can hang an entire satiric comedy (*The Antipodes*) on the book and its author—which suggests just how widespread was knowledge of the book—and assume (rightly) that virtually nobody then would regard the work at all seriously. The modern dismissive attitude to the book is heir to this later tradition; yet its astonishing popularity (which continued even after it had ceased to command respect as a work of information) can be shown to depend on genuine merits. Ironically, both the earlier attitude of uncritical acceptance and the later rejection are based on a distorted view of what the author was trying to achieve.

1 *The Book and its Author*

The **Travels** first began to circulate in Europe between 1356 and 1366. Originally written in French (quite possibly in the Anglo-Norman still current in English court circles), by 1400 some version of the book was available in every major European language; by 1500, the number of MSS was vast—including versions in Czech, Danish, Dutch and Irish—and some three hundred have survived. (For comparison, Polo's *Divisament dou Monde* is extant in only about seventy.) The very early printed editions testify at once to the importance attached to it and to its commercial appeal. The MS history is extremely complicated; briefly, the MSS divide into two broad groups, a Continental and an Insular version. The latter—circulating, so far as one can see, mainly in England and mainly preserved in British libraries—makes no mention of a peculiar story in the Continental version which connects the author with a certain Dr Jean de Bourgogne (author of an extant treatise *De Pestilentia*) and a dull, wordy and industrious Liège notary, Jean d'Outremeuse. There is

no serious doubt that d'Outremeuse handled a text and influenced the scribal tradition considerably, but there is not a shred of evidence which would compel the conclusion that 'Mandeville' was either de Bourgogne's or d'Outremeuse's *nom de plume,* as was first suggested at the end of the nineteenth century. If d'Outremeuse is an unreliable witness (as we know from elsewhere he is) and if the references to de Bourgogne depend on d'Outremeuse, one would be inclined to regard the MSS of the Insular version as the less contaminated. But here is not the place to go into this complex matter fully[1]—and what I have just said makes the cutting of the Gordian knot look diffident by comparison; the text I have chosen for this edition is one of the three (I think the best) early English translations from the Anglo-Norman of the Insular version (all extant in MSS of the late fourteenth and early fifteenth centuries). Its relation to the others is briefly indicated in the note preceding the text.

Despite the ingenuity of scholars, then, nothing is known of the author apart from what he tells us in his book, and he may, of course, be creating to a greater or lesser degree a fictional *persona.* He tells us that he was an English knight, that he travelled from 1322 to 1356 (1332 to 1366 in some texts) during which time he saw service with the Sultan of Egypt and the Great Khan. He may indeed have been one of the Mandevilles of Black Notley in Essex, but the evidence is again inconclusive. Nevertheless, the case for an English author is quite good: the narrative is wholly consistent in its references to 'this country', 'our country', the discussion of the peculiarly English letters ȝ and þ, the barnacle geese reputed to breed in Britain, and so on. The unsystematic consistency of such little details is persuasive.[2] Moreover, the chronicler Thomas Walsingham, writing probably between 1370 and 1396, in his discussion of famous people connected with St Albans, as Mandeville is reputed to have been, clearly accepted the story of the English authorship, and the Abbey of St Albans seems to have been something of a centre of dissemination for MSS of the **Travels.** But the really crucial question, as yet unanswered, is, if the author was not English, what conceivable motive had he in so cleverly pretending to be? (And if he was not, then our opinion of his book must be the higher because of the brilliant and convincing fiction.) The original's being in French is no argument, for the natural language for literary endeavour of a secular (non-religious and non-scholarly) nature for an Englishman born in the early 1300s would be Anglo-Norman French —even if, like Henry of Lancaster (or John Gower) he felt the need to apologize for his handling of it.[3] There is nothing in the early texts against our accepting the author's own account of himself as an Englishman.

How far he travelled (if at all) is a similar question. The post–Renaissance view of Mandeville is to see him as the archetypal 'lying traveller'. He claims to have travelled as far as China, though not, interestingly, as far as the Japan visited by Marco Polo. Though very unusual, such journeys were not in themselves improbable. The Franciscans, like Odoric of Pordenone or John of Plano de Carpini, and a few merchants, like the Polos and Balducci Pegolotti, penetrated in some numbers during the period of Tartar hegemony—roughly the century after 1220—to the Far East and lived to write their memoirs. But two factors have severely damaged Mandeville's credit. First, since the European voyages of discovery, we have a completely different picture of the world and no longer accept the stories of monstes and marvels that descended to the medieval mind from Pliny, Aethicus, Solinus and Herodotus. If Mandeville reported them, then he was a liar. But this is not an entirely valid argument; for what you see (and can write about) depends to a large extent on the conceptual and methodological structures you have in your mind; the fact that we see lepers as victims of a disease while the ancient writers saw them as 'flatfaces' (or, similarly, sufferers from elephantiasis as sciapods) depends on our respective assumptions. The cargo cults of the Pacific provide an illustration: to us, a prosaic aeroplane, yet to a different mind—and equally 'truly'—a great silver bird which brings gifts from the gods. The second factor is the convincing demonstration of Mandeville's vast dependence on a large number of earlier accounts of the East. This has led one critic to say roundly that Mandeville's longest journey was to the nearest library. But this again is far from conclusive. The medieval convention - not only accepted but admired—of reworking 'olde feeldes' for 'newe corne', 'olde bokes' for 'newe science', the reliance on *auctoritas,* would make a book that did not rely on others unusual in the extreme. Plagiarism is a charge beside the point; borrowing is an accepted artistic norm. Marie de France, for example, can rework Robert of Flamborough's *Poenitentiale,* using the first person and thus claiming experiences she could not have had, without any unease. Likewise, Mandeville's claim to have lived with the Great Khan at Manzi (p. 144)—an imitation of his source Odoric of Pordenone—is impossible as it stands since the kingdom of Manzi fell at the end of the Sung dynasty in 1278. So far, then, Mandeville is working within a normal pattern. But, more to the point, later travellers, like Johann Schiltberger, captured after Nicopolis in 1396, and about whose wanderings there is absolutely no doubt, can be shown to have borrowed freely from Mandeville to flesh out their own accounts. Even the estimable Polo, like Herodotus before him, repeated hearsay. Neither of these factors, then, disproves Mandeville's having travelled. Indeed, there are some elements and details, inexplicable in terms of sources, which just could be firsthand reporting. The story of 'Ypocras'' daughter at Cos, for example, has no known source; yet the reliable Felix Fabri found it current in the island when he visited it in 1483. Again, Mandeville says the walls of the Great Khan's palace were cov-

ered with the sweet-smelling skin of 'panthers' (p. 142), a detail not in his source Odoric, who mentions only leather. The detail is included for no obvious reason. The commentators have discoursed about the sweet smell the Bestiaries attached to the panther; but the red panda does smell of musk, and the Nepali word 'panda' could easily be misheard as the Latin *'panthera'*. Finally, it would be very odd indeed if a man with so great an interest in far countries should have found no way of getting at least as far as the Holy Land in a century when (just as on the Muslim Hajj to Mecca) relatively large numbers of people of all social classes took advantage of the pilgrim routes thither; these were organized almost as comprehensively as the modern package tour—even to the hiring out of sleeping rolls for the sea voyage by a man who worked from the Piazza San Marco in Venice. The motives for going, then as now, were never entirely pure. Some just liked 'wandringe by the weye'—whatever Chaucer may have meant by that; some went out of genuine devotion; all looked for souvenirs. It is entertaining that Mandeville reports a Saracen solution to problems of tourist pressure on ancient monuments identical to that adopted by the Department of the Environment (p. 77). Now none of this proves Mandeville travelled; but equally it is not possible to dismiss his claim entirely. If this man did not travel at all, our opinion of his literary ability must be the higher: his book conveys a superbly coherent illusion of a speaking voice talking of firsthand experience, even to the important (and often amusing) disclaimers when he is unable to tell us something: 'Of Paradise I cannot speak properly, for I have not been there; and that I regret' (p. 184). The irony is that the more one questions Mandeville's truthfulness, the higher one has to rate his literary artistry.

But these questions, though interesting, are relatively side-issues. Many people wrote travel books; only this one achieved an enormous and lasting popularity.[4] The reasons for that popularity and the considerable influence it exerted must be sought in the nature of the book and its treatment of its material—and in the handling of the audience's assumptions. To a modern reader, the form seems loose and inconsequential. This is deceptive. The journey narrative has the great advantage of being inclusive of many diverse elements (a quality beloved of the medieval mind) and provides a basic structuring for the material against a landscape (in the first half of the book at least) geographically and politically recognizable to fourteenth-century eyes. At least in part, too, the narrative caters for the same sort of taste as the *Alexander Romances* and Prester John's letter (which latter had lost, by the time Mandeville was writing, some of its initial political urgency). Mandeville uses elements of both. The language and form are accessible to a wide audience, and thus provide an ideal medium for a *haute vulgarisation* of authoritative 'geographical' thought. Mandeville was a serious writer, taking his matter from sources he believed (generally correctly) to be accurate; his book was as accurate and up to date and account of knowledge of the world as he knew how to make it. He deliberately draws together—remember the medieval delight in the *summa* and the compendium—material of very different kinds that could not so readily be found elsewhere; but unlike the compendium writer— for example, Vincent of Beauvais, whose *Speculum Naturale* and *Speculum Historiale* he used—he does not just compile. One of his most remarkable and interesting achievements is to have synthesized so many sources so that the joins do not show. He adapts and shapes to fit his plan, unifying all with the stamp of a valuing subjectivity. The medieval ideal of *lust* and *lore*—pleasure and instruction—seems to be the goal. We must not forget, either, the medieval (and indeed Renaissance) assumption that all writing must have a serious moral intent which is discoverable by intellectual understanding penetrating the surface of the text. The earth, likewise, is to be understood as a factual place first; therefore we have the careful and authoritative account of the size and shape of the earth; but it is also to be understood morally, and so we have a pleasant story of the reproduction of the diamond followed by its moral significance from the lapidaries (pp. 118-19), or an emphasis on there being a *significacio* for fish coming to land to be caught (p. 133). It is also a place where we must judge experience: 'Let the man who will, believe it; and leave him alone who will not' (p. 144). The medieval view of the world, as of literature, was polysemous, carrying many meanings; the physical world itself was the *umbra* from which Faith could be supported by Reason:

> Yit nevertheless we may haif knawlegeing
> Off God Almychtie, be his Creatouris . . .
> (Robert Henryson, *The Morall Fabillis*
> *of Esope the Phrygian,* ll. 1650ff.)

'All that is written is written for our profit.' And so Mandeville's impeccable geographical thought (in the sense in which we use the term 'geographical' in our methodology), despite its intrinsic interest for us as the picture of the world that a well-educated medieval man would have held, is only part of the importance of the **Travels,** just as is the delight in strange things (p. 44) that Mandeville assumes in his reader or hearer (p. 189).

It is really the difference in our mental maps and assumptions governed by them that makes a just assessment of Mandeville's impact in his time so hard. We simply do not look at the world in the same way. The precise spatial relationships of, for example, Dante, are almost unique in the writing of this period, and even those are moral and philosophical metaphors drawing heavily on a Thomist world model. The physical face of the earth is never, in my experience, as concretely articulated as Dante's universe. The landscape

of the romance *King Alisaunder,* or the *Roman de toute chevalerie* of Thomas of Kent, is completely lacking in physical sequence and detail. The spatial vagueness and mysteriousness of descriptions of the earth in this period is more akin to a kind of description found only in fiction and fantasy now—the sort of setting in E. R. Eddison's *The Worm Ourobouros* or Ursula le Guin's *A Wizard of Earthsea.* But these two latter are the result of choice. Mandeville's, or anybody else's, was not. Thus it is meaningless to attempt, as some editors have done, to plot Mandeville's places and journey on a modern map outline, for the rigid spatial relationships of the modern map, for us so important a part of the meaning of map conventions, are conceptually incompatible. Even direction is vague to the medieval mind. We easily forget how much the relatively modern inventions of coordinates and the compass rose have altered our modes of understanding our world. But that we see the world differently does not imply that the medieval idea was in its time unworkable—it clearly was not—nor that we are more 'right' than they were. Indeed, it is the root from which our way of thinking has grown. Mandeville's insistence that had he found company and shipping he too could have girdled the entire globe (and it is, incidentally, a modern slander that the medievals believed the earth to be flat) played, with his discussion of the Pole star, some part in the dissemination of important geographical concepts and in preparing for the great voyages of the next century on which our world-view is partly based.

Learned though it is, 'a compendium' is not the only key to the nature of the book. It also includes Romance elements and stories, which I discuss below. It shares to some degree that element, easily forgotten by us, in all western writing about the East that is not pure romance, of political interest in a strategic linking with the Tartars and Prester John against a menacing Islam. (This strategic concern was one of the three chief motives that spurred Prince Henry of Portugal to his sponsoring of the voyages of discovery—and it is one of the reasons he was so interested in Mandeville.) It provides a moral and political perspective (quite deliberately) for Europe (for example, pp. 149, 156). European's assumptions about their superiority in politics, law, virtue and religion are either directly or ironically challenged. And last, it is, at least in part, a quite careful and genuine pilgrim's devotional manual for the journey to the Holy Land. One owner of the Cotton text apparently so used it (see p. 23). Now these different genres, homogenized by the journey narrative, result in a complex and subtle book which can very easily make a fool of an inattentive or incautious reader. These elements, including the handling of sources, will need some discussion later, after we have looked in more detail at the structure and control of the book.

The tight categorical and proportional structuring of narrative, where everything relates to everything else, where balanced structure is an important clue to meaning, that we find in, for example, Dante, Gower or Chaucer, is largely lacking. There are, however, certain topics Mandeville refers to frequently—the insistence on Christians' unworthiness to possess Palestine, the corruption and complacency of the Western Church, the goodness in works of non-Christians. These could be said to be the thematic keys of the work. Almost exactly half-way through, the division is clearly marked between the parts dealing with the Holy Land and the Far East. Both these parts open and close with a repeat of their first ideas—the ways to the Holy Land, and the division of the world by the four rivers of Paradise. The last pages echo the ideas of the prologue. The narrative is clearly signposted, the signposts marking divisions of the matter (for example, pp. 44, 103, 111, 188). I also see a certain almost 'typical' linking between the repeated insistence on the inability of the Christians to take Palestine (not recognizing their need for moral and social reform before so doing) and the impossibility of Mandeville himself reaching the balm near Alexander's Trees of the Sun and Moon (p. 181, cf. p. 66), or the impossibility of great lords with all their power attaining to the Earthly Paradise (p. 185) because of the opposition presented by the very nature of the world. So a simple formal structure is supported by a thematic one.

The response of the audience is controlled in crucial places by the device of a *persona*. Though nowhere near as complex or as developed as, for example, Chaucer's or Langland's, nevertheless Mandeville's *persona* is significant. It is set up as a somewhat sceptical reporter, firmly rooted in experience—the 'first-hand' convention. It is very noticeable that in the early versions the *persona* is carefully made to question and to refuse to give an opinion, as well as, occasionally, to affirm the truth of the material; later redactions are marked by a multiplication of asseveration, often in a style much more emphatic than what we find in the earlier—'I, John Mandeville, saw this, and it is the truth.' The building up of this figure is interestingly oblique. He introduces himself, with an engagingly modest protestation of this unworthiness, as an experienced pilgrim who travels in good company (p. 45); he possesses a thorn from the Crown of Thorns (a king's ransom!) and *implies* he was given it by the Byzantine Emperor; he served as a soldier with the Sultan, and was offered a princess in marriage—'but I did not want to' (p. 59); he is experienced in the tests for good balm, and shows a sturdy independence of mind at the monastery of Saint Katherine on Sinai (pp. 66, 71). The Sultan gave him special letters of introduction ('to me he did a special favour', p. 80) to the Temple authorities. He has a 'private' talk with the Sultan (p. 107). He is ready to disclaim knowledge ('I never followed that route to Jerusalem, and so I cannot talk about it', p. 103). He is very plausible in relating

what is supposedly his own experience in seeing the southern stars (p. 128). The boasting is amusing; but gradually his trustworthiness as a guide for us in our response is built up. He is made to be detached about his own job as a reporter or narrator; he is cautious about the Ark on Ararat (pp. 113-14), and about the supposed cross of Dismas in Cyprus and other relics (pp. 46, 55). He is sensible about the pepper forests (in fact he contradicts his source, p. 123, because it is talking patent nonsense) and reflective about the problems of belief in unfamiliar material (p. 144). When going through the Vale Perilous, there is a linguistic emphasis on seeming, illusion, fantasy—a distrust of his own cognition (p. 173)—and, by implication, ours, and our response to his material. Almost the last remark in the book is deliciously ironic: 'I shall cease telling of the different things I saw in those countries, so that those who desire to visit those countries may find enough new things to speak of for the solace and recreation of those whom it pleases to hear them' (p. 188). This *persona* is also used for comic or evaluative effect. Sometimes this is done by tone, or by the positioning of a clause. I have already quoted his apology for not telling us about Paradise, but he did drink of the Well of Yough, and characteristically claims not the instant rejuvenation one would expect from the (interpolated) *Letter of Prester John,* but 'ever since that time I have felt the better and healthier'. Going through the Vale Perilous (one of the stimuli, by the way, for Bunyan's Valley of the Shadow) he and his companions were much afraid: 'We were more devout then than we ever were before or after' (p. 174). In Lamory, he reports the 'evil custom' of fattening children for the table; but our expected horror is pointed by the deadpan, sardonic positioning at the end of the paragraph of the simple remark: 'They say it is the best and sweetest flesh in the world' (p. 127). The statement that '[Hippopotami] eat men . . . no meat more readily', is carefully booby-trapped by the insertion of the clause 'whenever they can get them' (p. 167). But most important are the occasions when the *persona* involves himself in dialogue. During his confidential talk with the Sultan his laconic unease introduces the Sultan's fluent indictment of Christian conduct, and he is wrong-footed at every turn (p. 108). This episode is comic in precisely the same way as the *persona* Gulliver is comic when talking to the King of Brobdingnag. But he can also be used not only to trigger a moral assessment of his own culture but to point out false values in others'—for example, his expostulation at the obscurantism of the monks on Mount Sinai (p. 71). Or he can modify our initial reactions in the direction of sense and understanding; for instance, when he asks Judas's question of the monk of Cassay (p. 139) who is feeding the animals, it elicits two things: the good organization of a state so that the poor do not exist and the fact that there is a rational explanation for a very odd act. (His source, Odoric, merely 'laughed heartily' at this pagan piety). And is not that act exactly parallel to the European custom of Masses for the dead? At the court of the Great Khan, the *persona* is confident that the marvels are not 'diabolic' as Odoric said, but capable of rational explanation on terms he can understand. And, finally, the *persona* can direct our moral response in a quite unambiguous way. The approval and admiration for the Gymnosophists is supported by a second reference to the important figure of Job (p. 180, cf. p. 115). All the accumulated authority of this figure is behind the remark 'we know not whom God loves nor whom He hates'—a generalized statement subsuming all the hinted warnings against too uncritical a judgement or too ready an acceptance of the unusual and strange. The handling of the *persona*, therefore, is the key to the book's success.

2 *The Use of the Sources*

We must now look at the handling of sources and the genres used in the book. Apart from those I mentioned above (p. 12) there are important elements for which no source is known. Some of these are Romance elements like the story of the Castle of the Sparrowhawk, or the story of the circumnavigation of the world. But the list of discovered sources is large:

> Albert of Aix, *Historia Hierosolomitanae Expeditionis*
> Jacopo de Voragine, *The Golden Legend*
> William von Boldensele, *Itinerarius*
> Jacques de Vitry, *Historia Hierosolomitana*
> Haiton of Armenia, *Fleurs des Histors d'Orient*
> William of Tripoli, *De Statu Saracenorum*
> Odoric of Pordenone, *Itinerarius*
> pseudo-Odoric, *De Terra Sancta*
> Caesarius of Heisterbach, *Dialogus Miraculorum*
> Pilgrims' manuals
> *The Letter of Prester John*
> *Alexander Romances,* including Alexander's letter to Aristotle
> Vincent of Beauvais, *Speculum Historiale* and *Speculum Naturale,* including extracts from John of Plano de Carpini, Pliny and Solinus

and possibly:

> Burchard of Mount Sion, *Descriptio Terrae Sanctae*
> John of Sacrobosco, *De Sphaera*
> Brunetto Latini, *Livre dou Tresor*

Quite a reading list. Even allowing for the fact that several are anthologized in Vincent of Beauvais, and that many of the travel accounts occur conveniently in the compendium of travels made by Jean le Lonc of Ypres (which Mandeville quite possibly used), Mandeville still did a good deal of research. But the sources are used with quite remarkable assurance: there are certainly verbatim liftings (as there are in Shakespeare) but one is never conscious of where

Mandeville leaves one source and moves to another. He moves backwards and forwards between them with complete confidence, dovetailing Haiton into Odoric and mixing in Vincent exactly as he requires.[5] This, however, suggests a mere scissors-and-paste job; the impressive thing is the freedom with which the source has been altered and shaped. Reported speech is transposed into the much more arresting direct—for example, when Mandeville reworks Haiton's story of the advice of the dying Great Khan (p. 148). Many elements are amplified with considerable ingenuity. Three examples will show the different levels on which this is done.

First, Odoric,[6] that homespun Odysseus, has one sentence (Yule, p. 114) on his trip on one of the stitched ships (which, incidentally, still exist in the Gulf region). Mandeville uses the story twice: once, briefly, in describing Ormuz (p. 120)—the right region for them, in fact; again, as a result of one of the many perils of the sea off Prester John's land. Odoric's sentence is blown up into a circumstantial account, full of personal observation. It is vastly more interesting.[7] Second, Odoric's story of the Vegetable Lamb of Tartary (Yule, p. 240f.): Mandeville again expands, and alters the whole tone of the incident. Odoric merely mentions an unusual 'melon' he has been told of, which story (he feels) may be true, as there are trees in Ireland which produce birds. Mandeville's account is much more circumstantial, both of the fruit and his reaction:

> There there grows a kind of fruit as big as gourds, and when it is ripe men open it and find inside an animal of flesh and blood and bone, like a little lamb without wool. And the people of that land eat the animal, and the fruit too. It is a great marvel. Nevertheless I said to them that it did not seem a very great marvel to me, for in my country, I said, there were trees which bore a fruit that became birds that could fly; men call them barnacle geese, and there is good meat on them . . . And when I told them this they marvelled greatly at it. (p. 165)

The *persona*'s intervention emphasizes by implication one of Mandeville's key ideas—that the same Nature rules everywhere and what is impossible in Europe is impossible in Cathay. If the impossible seems to happen, either our knowledge or our interpretation is at fault. He hints that just as the East looks odd to the West, the West looks odd to the East.

Finally, Odoric's journey through the Vale Perilous. His account demonstrates both the problem of assimilating new experience outside normal conceptual patterns, as mentioned above, and the essential qualities of his narrative. Odoric was undoubtedly a truthful reporter and a man of considerable courage. The singing sands of the deserts of Asia are quite beyond his previous experience, but the idea of devils is not; and so the noises and appearance of the Valley become supernatural and threatening:

> I went through a certain valley which lieth by the River of Delights. I saw therein many dead corpses lying. And I heard also therein sundry kinds of music, but chiefly nakers (drums) which were marvellously played upon. And so great was the noise thereof that very great fear came upon me. Now, this valley is seven or eight miles long; and if any unbeliever enter therein he quitteth it never again, but perisheth incontinently. Yet I hesitated not to go in that I might see once for all what the matter was. And when I had gone in I saw there, as I have said, such numbers of corpses as no one without seeing it could deem it credible. And at one side of the valley, in the very rock, I beheld as it were the face of a man very great and terrible, so very terrible indeed that for my exceeding great fear my spirit seemed to die within me. Wherefore I made the sign of the cross . . . I ascended a hill of sand and looked about me. But nothing could I descry, only I still heard those nakers play which were played so marvellously. And when I got to the top of that hill I found there a great quantity of silver heaped up as it had been fishes' scales, and some of this I put into my bosom. But as I cared nought for it, and was at the same time in fear lest it should be a snare to hinder my escape, I cast it all down again to the ground. And so by God's grace I came forth scathless. Then all the Saracens, when they heard of this, showed me great worship, saying I was a baptized and holy man. But those who had perished in that valley they said belonged to the devil. (Yule, pp. 262-6)

Now compare Mandeville's version (pp. 173-4). This is obviously much expanded and much more vivid, particularly in the development of details. But, crucially, Mandeville has made the crossing of the Vale a test of covetousness; he develops Odoric's picking up and then casting away of the silver into a warning—for some fail the test. Odoric, somewhat complacently, relies for safety merely on his profession of faith; Mandeville insists that to be safe even Christians must be 'firm in the faith . . . be cleanly confessed and absolved' and must 'bless themselves with the sign of the Cross'. Mandeville not only questions the evidence of the senses and judgement based on them—a serious enough issue in itself, and one not insignificant as a motif in the whole book; he also, with some finesse, suggests that he was accompanied by two Franciscans who sought safety in numbers! Mandeville tempers Odoric's seriousness with a wry humour. Clearly the passage is the work of an extremely competent writer, who knew exactly what he wanted.

This shrewd judgement in the handling of sources cannot, of course, be separated from the use of the *persona*. Too emphatic a commitment to the personal experience of everything would diminish returns rap-

idly; and Mandeville knew that. So the sources are not only shaped by *amplificatio* but sometimes, as in the case of Haiton's personal experience of the Land of Darkness, abbreviated and objectified. Generally, then, the sources are unified and the key ideas controlled by the device of the *persona* and the journey framework.

3 *Modes and Values*

The modes (and the expectations they arouse) used in this book are an interesting and unusual mixture. The hearer or reader coming to the book for the first time might easily assume he is embarking on a devotional guide, a manual of the pilgrim voyage to the Holy Land, like many others of the period. There are striking methodological and stylistic parallels between Mandeville's description of Jerusalem's relics and places and the description of those of Rome and Jerusalem in the pilgrims' manuals, like *The Stacions of Rome* or the *Informacōn for Pylgrymes into the Holy Londe,* printed by de Word in 1498. This sort of book was useful as a reminder to the returned pilgrim, a guidebook for the new, and an armchair voyage for the sedentary. In all three cases there was some devotional response—at the lowest level, the detailed recalling of the events and places that witnessed the individual reader's salvation. The concrete place is frequently used as a mnemonic stimulus for a biblical text and for a figuring of the Passion.[8] Wherever Mandeville is dealing with the Holy Land or the Saints of the Church and their miracles, this stylistic mode is used. Sometimes, indeed, the details are so vividly filled in—as in the story of Samson, or the detail about the auger hole in the Ark whence the Devil escaped (pp. 57, 113)—that one wonders whether Mandeville is drawing on another religious mode as well, the mystery play. Just as Mandeville certainly used pilgrims' manuals, so a number of later works—some much later—borrowed Mandeville's remarks and incorporated them into devotional guides. (For example, the *Pylgrymage of Sir Richard Guylford to the Holy Land A. D. 1506,* and the forgery based on it, the *Pylgrymage of Sir Richard Torkyngton, 1517.*) One owner of the Cotton text of the **Travels** tore out those pages that could be used as a pilgrim guide—one suspects in order so to use them. (The mode itself is astonishingly durable, still being traceable in Henry Maundrell's *A Journey from Aleppo to Jerusalem at Easter, 1697.*) The pilgrimage motif is itself a metaphor for the life of man on earth as a journey to the Heavenly Jerusalem, specifically picked up in the last words of the book, and this casts an ironic light on Mandeville's claim to be writing in furtherance of a crusade. The 'Land of Promise'—earthly or heavenly—can only be won if Christians reform themselves according to the truth they profess. (The alert reader will notice an ironic backward glance at Christian pilgrimage when Mandeville speaks of the devout pilgrims to the shrine of the Juggernaut, pp. 125-6.) And when the need arises, he can adopt the quite recognizable style of the sermon (for example, p. 180, with its careful array of biblical texts). With this devotional interest is mingled a deal of practical advice on the various routes, of modern observations on tourist attractions and on a tourist vandalism familiar to us today (pp. 77, 99). A choice of pilgrimage could quite sensibly be based on Mandeville's description of the different journeys.

But the first half of the book, on the ways to Jerusalem, does not deal only with devotional material. Here, as later, the narrative is frequently suspended by digressions into other modes. Mandeville is fond of a good story, and he took them from other places as well as the appropriate *Golden Legend*. They rarely remain only stories. The lurid mixture of necrophilia and disaster in the story (current in the chroniclers) of the 'Bane of Satalye', near Adalia in Turkey (p. 55) is used not simply to account for the *ville engloutie* which fascinated many pilgrims but to make a moral point about the consequences of man's sin in the macrocosm. The charming story of the Field of Flowers is similar to one told of Abraham's daughter; it is paralleled in Machaut's *Dit du Lion* (1342) and the Apocryphal legend of Susanna; Mandeville, however, uses it rather like a *Golden Legend* story, to account for the existence of roses and to demonstrate the saving grace of God. The Watching of the Sparrowhawk (pp. 112-13) is a splendidly told story (which reappears in the Mélusine romance which was thus linked to the House of Lusignan) which is concerned not just with sensation but with personal moral and ethical choice and behaviour. Later, the Old Man of the Mountains is worked up from Odoric to emphasize the conscious and mechanically engineered deceit of his fake Paradise. Europe had heard enough of that medieval Mafia boss to be fascinated by *how* he got his assassination squads to work. Similarly, the long-nailed Mandarin, whom he took from Odoric again, is made much more voluptuous and then is 'placed' as an icon of gluttony. (He reappears in *The Further Adventures of Robinson Crusoe*.) So the stories generally are used to demand a moral response from the audience. Some actually do not need overt moralizing; the well-known ones, like the story of the 'hills of gold that pismires [ants] keep' (p. 183) are automatically a symbol of the foolish industry of men working to gather for themselves what they cannot possess and another enjoys. The digressions, then, are not only enjoyable diversions but functional supporters of the central ideas of the book.

Those central ideas spring essentially from two concerns: the moral state of Christendom, and the nature of the world we inhabit. Some critics have been so impressed by the remarks about Christendom that, like the late Professor Hamelius, they have seen the *Travels* as no more than 'an anti-papal pamphlet in disguise'. This is going too far, despite the demonstrable coolness towards the papacy, and oversimplifies a very

complex book. Nevertheless, the amount of moral comment and how it is achieved demands our attention.

I have already referred to the way Mandeville insistently reiterates the need for moral reform before Christians can hope to possess the holy places. First, it is set out clearly in the prologue: the scheme of salvation has been set up, yet 'pride, envy and covetousness have so inflamed the hearts of lords of the world that they are more busy to disinherit their neighbours than to lay claim to or conquer their own rightful inheritance'. The common people are left leaderless, like sheep without a shepherd. Social divisions have a moral origin. The same note is sounded again, briefly, as a hope for eventual reform, in the most appropriate place, the chapter on Jerusalem (p. 77). Then Mandeville attacks from a different angle. The *persona* is made to suffer the Sultan's comprehensive and systematic attack on the gap between profession and practice; all the sins are noted and the behaviour of the estates castigated (p. 107). The force of this is increased by having it in direct speech, and by making the speaker a Muslim who condemns Christians on Christian terms. We are made to see the attack as an objective appraisal from outside the Christian sensibility and *données* of the *persona*—in fact, we partly identify with the *persona*. Europocentric confidence in moral and religious superiority is challenged often. The Saracens, benighted as they are, administer justice better than Christians: 'They say that no man should have audience of a prince without leaving happier than he came thither' (p. 61).[9] The pagan monk of Cassay indicates a social system more efficient in preventing poverty than a religion that specifically honours the poor. The Bragmans (Brahmins) take the idea further; here is a detailed account of a people not Christian yet living lives which, in terms of works, Christians ought to envy. The passage (pp. 178-9) is full of echoes of Dominical injunctions. Alexander is said to have wanted to conquer them, and Mandeville uses their traditional reply to attack the vainglory and deceitfulness of Western values. Alexander, like the *persona* earlier, is sent away with his tail between his legs. Mandeville is deliberately setting up more or less differing mirror societies as a commentary on Christian practices and failings—just as, indeed, Utopian fiction was later to be employed, often using Mandeville's own travel motif (for example, *Utopia* itself, or Bishop Hall's *Mundus Alter et Idem*). The attack starts destructively but gradually becomes more and more idealistic, finally culminating in the deliberate repetition of the account of the virtuous Bragmans in the paradisal innocence (symbolized by nakedness) of Gynoscriphe (the land of the Gymnosophistae; pp. 179-80). In the process, the good, peaceful government of the Chinese is used as a contrast to the internecine quarrels of Europeans; Prester John's kingdom is the ideal Christian state; the almsgiving of the Saracens challenges the moral superiority of Europe. The account of suttee is used to show that pagans take Heaven more seriously than Christians, and the horrific piety of the pilgrims to the Juggernaut (pp. 125-6) first shocks by its violence, and then by its direct moral: 'And truly they suffer so much pain and mortification of their bodies for love of that idol that hardly would any Christian man suffer the half—nay, not a tenth—for love of Our Lord Jesus Christ.'

This general critique is not unsupported by detailed complaint. Hamelius was right to detect an anti-clerical note—virtually every writer in this century (even the churchmen) forcefully attacks the abuses of the Church. Those who should be the shepherds are specifically criticized. The manner can vary from the open 'For now is simony crowned like a king in Holy Church' to the more oblique suggestion whose thrust is pointed by the positioning of the clause and the falter in the rhythm: 'They sell benefices of Holy Church, and so do men in other places.' Both these examples come from the generally accurate account of Greek Orthodoxy, the first of many descriptions of different rites and religions. The summary of the Greek position is remarkably neutral at a time of strained relations with Byzantium. Mandeville quotes without comment a letter of the Greeks to Pope John XXII damning the claims of the papacy and accusing it of avarice. His silence suggests approval and enjoyment of the Pope getting his comeuppance. The Jacobite Christians practise a real devotion, despite their not using 'the additions of the popes, which our priests are accustomed to use at Mass' (p. 79). The Tibetans have a religious leader (p. 186), 'the Pope of their religion, whom they call Lobassi . . . and all the priests and ministers of the idols are obedient to him'; the sentence and the paragraph close with the deliciously sardonic phrase, 'as our priests are to our Pope'—this, in the century of the Babylonish Captivity when the respect for the papacy reached probably its lowest ever level of respect![10]

The consequence of this cool look at western Christendom is apparent in the attitude to other sects, religions and societies. His accounts of the Eastern Churches and Islam are quite untypical of the period in their accuracy and lack of animus. Despite centuries of contact and trade, it was not only in 'popular' writing that the Saracens were seen, with a total ignorance of their theology, as virtual devils incarnate. The miracle plays, and romances like *The Sowdone of Babyloine,* echo the standard idea Lydgate repeats of Muhammad as a false prophet, glutton, and necromancer (*Fall of Princes,* IX, 53ff.). The scholars (some Mandeville's sources), despite odd exceptions like Abélard, William of Malmesbury and Roger Bacon, are no better. Few men studied Islamic books at all deeply; those who did, like Ramon Lull and Ricold of Monte Croce (both of whom preached in Arabic), either carried little weight or confirmed the prejudices of their audience. Lull's agonized vision of a vast army of souls trooping down

to Hell for want of Christian doctrine led him to plead in 1315 at the Council of Vienne for centres of Islamic study; the plea was ignored, and even Lull comes round to advocating military force. Ricold used his learning to seek points of difference, merely writing polemic. A bishop of Acre, Jacques de Vitry, shows complete misunderstanding of Muslim theology; even the remarkably fair-minded Burchard of Mount Sion gives a far less neutral account than Mandeville. The same intolerant ignorance extends to other religions and peoples; John of Plano de Carpini, Mandeville's source on the Tartars, clearly loathed them; Ricold, despite wide travels, only abuses them, and William of Rubruck saw all eastern religions as diabolic aberrations. The politic Greek was distrusted (not without reason); nevertheless it is chilling to find the gentle Burchard recommending the seizing of Constantinople and the burning of all dubious books. Ludolf von Suchem emphasizes that the Pope has given full permission for the forcible dispossession of Greeks from their lands and for their being sold as cattle. Now it is fair to object that all these writers are clerics and have, to some extent necessarily, a *parti-pris* position; but elsewhere it is clear from the silence that tolerant understanding is not even considered. Gower, perhaps, reveals moral unease at the idea of a crusade (*Confession Amantis,* III 2488-96), as did Wiclif; and Langland's Anima hopes that Saracens and Jews will alike be saved (*Piers Plowman,* B, 382ff., 488ff., 530ff). But that is as far as it goes. There is nothing comparable to the Muslim Averroës' assertion that God is worshipped satisfactorily in many ways.

The importance of Mandeville's treatment of these topics has been largely overlooked. The imaginative leap necessary for his tolerance is itself remarkable; and because the book was so widely read, many would get their first reasonably accurate account of the Koran from it. His summary of Muslim attitudes to Jesus and Muhammad is fair, sensible and detailed. (It is noticeable how this balance and openness was coarsened and indeed cancelled in later reworkings of the *Travels.* The norms reassert themselves.) Similarly, he treats the Greeks, the Muslims, the Jacobites and the Bragmans as interesting and honourable and worthy of sympathetic respect, not merely as sticks to beat European complacency with. He not only diverges from his source, de Vitry, on the Jacobites and Syrians. He describes their rites neutrally, supports their doctrine of confession with a goodly array of biblical texts (pp. 97-8) and he concludes merely with the sentence—astonishing in its period—'all their differences would be too much to relate'. Most of his contemporaries would have revelled in the castigation of such variance.

The same tendency radically to redirect his source is apparent in the descriptions of Far Eastern cults and societies. Odoric's sensibilities were particularly upset by the cannibalism and sexual promiscuity of Lamory: 'It is an evil and a pestilent generation', he cries (Yule, p. 127). But Mandeville delights in expanding the details and provides a biblical text to justify the sexual licence—'Increase and multiply and fill the earth' (p. 127). Thus he forces his audience to justify the opposite standards they take for granted. He can so easily climb inside the skin of a man brought up in a totally different, if invented, culture that the preconceptions of Europe must necessarily be questioned. Perhaps the best example of this redirection of material and consequent upending of European assumptions is Mandeville's interpolation (drawing, possibly, on Isidore of Seville) in Odoric's account of Tana; where he saw only 'idolaters', Mandeville saw 'a variety of religions' (p. 121) and introduces a long discussion of the philosophical and cult difference between an image (simulacre) and an idol. It is conducted resourcefully and intelligently, and allows him to 'place' the worship of the ox, and human sacrifice. His implication is that intention to worship is more important than any failing in *cultus*. Odoric's marvellous and beastly customs' hide universal man.

The crucial idea, that men behave rationally according to their lights, is the key to understanding how Mandeville treats all other strange societies. Just because the society of Amazons reverses our social norms, it does not mean it will not work. Just because we are revolted by Jainism, or necrophagy, or the strange use of one's ancestors' skulls in Tibet, does not mean that there is not real piety in the actions. All these threads of tolerance, understanding, charity and questioning are woven together in a crucial passage linking those Bragmans who live well by works with the virtuous pagan Job (p. 180): 'And even if these people do not have the articles of our faith, nevertheless I believe that because of their good faith that they have by nature, and their good intent, God loves them well and is well pleased by their manner of life, as He was with Job, who was a pagan . . . For we know not whom God loves nor whom He hates.' And notice that in the passage is a warning of the fallibility of human judgment.

The diversity of the world we inhabit, then, is comprehensible by reason. The final topic we must briefly mention is Mandeville's idea of nature. Nature is a mirror of providence, a reliable guide to understanding. The Dead Sea (p. 89) has qualities that are apparently 'against nature', yet those qualities are consequences of sin 'against nature', and designed by God so that man's mind by contemplation of the marvel will understand the sterile denial of nature implicit in all sin. (The *Gawain* poet uses the Dead Sea in this way too.[11]) First appearances are a dubious basis for judgement; the pygmies (p. 140) cannot be dismissed as the freaks their appearance might suggest; they are 'very clever, and can judge between good and evil'.

Throughout the book there is the implication that nature is ultimately rational, if one looks far enough. A necessary consequence of this insight that the marvellous is explicable is that men may have confidence in the world behaving according to the same rules wherever they travel. And, if they have company and shipping, they can travel everywhere.

The *Travels,* then, is a complex and thoughtful book, executed with skill of a high order. The diverse material that has been gathered into it has been drawn into the service of a unified purpose, controlled successfully by a clever manipulation of the reader's response. Its immediate popularity rested on its meeting a number of tastes—the interest in the mysterious East, the desire for devotional Baedekers, and its provision of a very considerable amount of information. But that popularity could not have been achieved and sustained had the book not had that indefinable quality, that *quidditas,* which distinguishes the outstanding from the merely competent. I think much of that continuing attraction lies in the credibility of the *persona*'s good sense and good nature. Mandeville, whoever he was, old, infirm and travel-worn, deserves the prayers he asks for.

4 *The Career of the* Travels

All old authors suffer from the vicissitudes of reputation. The differing estimates held of a book reveal quite as much about the readers as they do of the book, and thus almost any significant work can be used as a tool to diagnose the values and emphases (and blind-spots) of a culture. Up to 1750 only Chaucer among other fourteenth-century English works has a comparably large and constant body of readers; and Mandeville's was a more heterogeneous body than Chaucer's and his reputation much more complex. The response to and use of the *Travels* can be used as a kind of intellectual litmus to test the assumptions, values and perceptions of a given period. There is, unfortunately, not space to go into this entertaining question here. It is only worth mentioning in order to emphasize that significant shifts in the reputation and use made of the *Travels* need seeing in a wider context. All we can do is sketch the importance of the *Travels* in Renaissance geographical thought and discovery, and its literary influence.

The happy accident of its being written first in French ensured that it immediately acquired a European readership as well as an English one. Within a hundred years of its writing the rapid proliferation of MSS made it available in most countries of Europe; the early translation into Latin—the language, significantly, of scholarship, and thus an indicator of how some early readers felt about its material—allowed it to cross any remaining linguistic boundaries. These MSS do, of course, show a greater or lesser degree of adaptation and contamination. Some of them are not so much copies as versions, made for special interests. The spread of the printing press probably tended to standardize the text in general circulation on a copy text; thus in England after Pynson's edition of Defective (1496) (see p. 38), all subsequent printed editions known in English of the *Travels* in the sixteenth century are offshoots of Defective, and the same process is repeated after the 1478 and 1481 Augsburg editions of Anton Sorg, or the 1480 Milan edition of Comeno. The earliness of these printings is remarkable: before 1500 eight German printings are known, seven French, twelve Italian, four Latin, two Dutch and two English. There are Czech and Spanish editions before 1520. Clearly there was money as well as interest in Mandeville.

Very early on in its manuscript career, the *Travels* was included in the compendia, collections of important texts on a particular area. It was included, with Odoric of Pordenone, in the *Livre de Merveilles* of 1403, an authoritative collection of material on the East. Michel Velser's German translation, made about 1393, is included in an MS miscellany of astronomical works, presumably because the compiler thought the account of the Pole star important. A couple of centuries later, this still goes on. Hakluyt's first edition of the *Principall Navigations* (1598) was specifically gathered to provide a ready fund of information for his countrymen aspiring to commercial exploits in the Orient—the book is both commercial inducement and geographical information; it includes Mandeville in the version known as the Latin Vulgate (a Continental text). Hakluyt extolled the scholarship and good sense of Sir John, yet is aware that the text has been corrupted by scribes and printers—blanket acceptance or rejection of the text as fact will not do and only the discerning mind will find it useful. Hakluyt's view of Mandeville's usefulness changed radically as the next ten years saw a flood of information about the New World reaching England from English travellers and translated Spanish sources, and he dropped Mandeville from his second edition. But Samuel Purchas, a most eager Elisha, clawed Hakluyt's mantle down on himself in his publication of *Purchas his Pilgrimes* (1625)—a text which Coleridge loved. His collection is less concerned with trade statistics and discovery than with picturesque descriptions and theological and missionary musings. A heavily cut Mandeville appears, and his portrait appears on the title page with Columbus and King Solomon and others. It is important that two writers, one ostensibly following the other, should, in so short a time, use Mandeville for such different purposes. The *Travels* was also pillaged, extracted, or epitomized in such seminal books as the *Nuremberg Chronicle* (1493), and Münster's *Cosmographia* (1544), chiefly for its information on the East. Much of Mandeville's material then flows indirectly through these conduits, as well as directly,

into the sum of European knowledge in the Renaissance.

The practical importance of this sort of dissemination cannot be discounted. The *Travels* was anthologized because it was authoritative; it was given new authority by being anthologized, and so it gets into the hands of men who over two centuries were responsible for the European discovery of the East and of America. The *Travels* was used as a source in the outstanding Catalan Atlas of 1375. Abraham Cresques made this atlas for Peter III of Aragon, who was very interested indeed in reports of the East and Prester John. It incorporates the very latest geographical knowledge. The *Travels* again seems to have been used (as Polo was not) in the Andrea Bianco map of 1434. And the so-called 'Behaim' globe made in Nuremberg in 1492—the earliest to have survived—quotes Mandeville wholesale, with great respect. Now this is crucial; these maps represent the picture of the world the explorers took with them and the basis on which their backers financed them.

Prince Henry of Portugal is not unique in being interested strategically, commercially and religiously in the East, nor in having his agents scour Europe for information on the East; the hard-headed German commercial empire of the Fuggers put money into these voyages, and one wonders whether the Augsburg editions of the *Travels* may have some connection with Fugger interest. (It is indeed a curious coincidence that right up to the end of the sixteenth century there are noticeable increases in the frequency of editions of the *Travels* coinciding with major voyages of exploration.) Several important explorers are known to have used Mandeville as one of their sources of information—for example, the principal sources of Columbus's ideas were Polo, Mandeville and Ptolemy. It may indeed be that Columbus's determination to sail west to Cathay was fuelled by Mandeville's story of circumnavigation. Frobisher, in his attempt on the Northwest passage, took with him a copy of Mandeville for its information on China. The expectations aroused by Mandeville led the first discoverers to see the New World not objectively but in preconceived terms: Columbus seems, from surviving letters, to have died believing he had found islands off Mandeville's Cathay. Even after America was known to be a new continent, the old legends were still operative, merely being transferred to the unknown interior. When the native Amerindian myth of the regenerative land of Bimini reached the ears of the first Spanish settlers, they eagerly grafted on to it the story of Mandeville's Well of Youth, of which Mandeville had drunk, and Ponce de Leon led two expeditions, in 1513 and 1521, to look for it. The result was the finding of Florida. The English descriptions of the Roanoke voyages, again, are full of the *topoi* of the travel literature of the past, and (probably unconsciously) exploit the conceptual and semantic parameters of the icons of innocence from the Bragmans to the Earthly Paradise. Sir Walter Raleigh's *Discoverie of Guiana* shows clearly his heavy conceptual dependence on these old accounts of the wonders of the East, and, indeed, he quotes Mandeville by name. Once again, the new is misunderstood in terms of the old, as we see with Odoric; and seeking Cathay to satisfy the dream of their fathers, the voyagers found an image of Paradise for their children.

It is somewhat oversimple to look at the geographical influence of Mandeville in this way. It is nevertheless doubly useful; first, it shows a deliberate and widespread use of only a *part* of what we saw above as the totality of meaning of the *Travels;* secondly, the effect of the explosion of geographical knowledge resulting partly from Mandeville and his confident and unusual insistence that the world was everywhere traversable radically altered the esteem in which the book was held and the uses to which it could be put. Although Richard Willes, in his *Historie of Travaile* (1577) can still treat Mandeville as a prime authority, this is becoming less and less possible. Gerard Mercator in that same year, in a letter, accepted Mandeville's story of his circumnavigation (and used him as a source for his map) but seriously questioned his judgement in reporting what he saw—an unease felt, as noted above, by Hakluyt. Although Mandeville's material still found its way into scientific compilations, it did so less and less frequently. By about 1600, his reputation has fallen sharply; he is now outdated by new knowledge and his work often treated with contempt. There are however, supplementary reasons for this.

Just as the *Travels'* real nature had been distorted to serve the interests of the learned, so it was reworked for other partialities. At the same time that Prince Henry was using it for political and commerical information, it was available in re-editings as a book merely of wonders, as a devotional guide, as a romance. Part (much cut) was put into heavy-footed octosyllabic verse at about the end of the fifteenth century, as a popular account of the East, strongly pointed with a muscle–bound Christianity; another late-fifteenth-century ancestor of McGonagall made a nearly complete version in coarse octosyllabics, as a sort of popular Romance (the *Metrical Version*) incorporating many other legendary wonders. Everything is sensationalized, and the original delicate balance between matter and treatment has completely gone. The *Metrical Version* points firmly to the much later career of the book as a chapbook for children; it is the nearest thing to the 'film of the book' (complete with regular stars like Alexander and the Nine Worthies) that the Middle Ages could manage.

So, by the end of the fifteenth century, 'Mandeville' could mean many different things to different people— or to the same person at the same time. The process

intensifies. William Warner in 1586 published in *Albion's England* an account in fourteener verse of mythical English history down to the voyages of his time, and in Books XI and XII interlards it with a surgary romance in which Mandeville's travels are reduced to knight errantry resulting from an unhappy love affair. *Albion's England* seems to have been an influential source for the Elizabethan dramatists and also for Milton. It must have been difficult to have taken Mandeville seriously as a source of information or anything else when Warner's bland fourteeners plodded into your consciousness.

It would be even more difficult if you had seen the play of Mandeville which ran fairly successfully in the 1590s; if, as I suspect, the source was Warner and it is to this play Nashe refers in his *Nashes Lenten Stuffe* (1599), the prospect of such vapid drama is alarming. Clearly, by the end of the century, the knight is an almost mythical figure, the archetypal traveller, the grandfather of lies that are like truth. It is exactly in this way that Richard Brome's comedy *The Antipodes* (1636) regards him. Significantly, his name can even be used in a book title: *The Spanish Mandeuile of Miracles* (1600), the title given to the translation of Antonio de Torquemada's *Jardin de Flores Curiosas* (1570). The multiple Mandeville tradition plus the revolution in knowledge of the world finally killed the book's serious career as a work of information—even though as late as the eighteenth century we find the odd anomalies of Dr Johnson recommending it to a friend for information on China, and a catchpenny re-editing (claiming Mandeville set out in 1732!) with the travels of the excellent Jonas Hanway and Lionel Wafe issued about 1760 by a consortium of London publishers. Nevertheless, illustrated printed editions and chap-book versions still continue to be made and sold. The knowledge of the *Travels* remains general; the attitude to it changes irrevocably.

It is a labour of very doubtful value to seek out specific borrowing from Mandeville in other authors. It can be done, and a list of Man deville's debtors, from the *Gawain* poet to Coleridge, is huge. The really interesting thing, which can here be touched on only briefly, is how the *Travels* as a whole fertilized something already in a writer's mind and helped it to fruit. For example, the development of Mandeville's use of 'mirror' societies was clearly a most useful tool for Saint Thomas More whose *Utopia* is the parent of all subsequent writing in that important mode. It is significant how often satiric or moral Utopias of the sixteenth or seventeenth century borrow details and techniques from the *Travels*. Again, Mandeville is the first fully to develop the travel-fiction form; it was enthusiastically adopted by Rabelais, by Joseph Hall, by Richard Head—whose debt in *The English Rouge* to Mandeville is very large—and by Defoe and Swift. (Oddly enough, the 'I' of *Robinson Crusoe*—especially in *The Further Adventures*—and of

Gulliver's Travels both seem close to the *persona* of the ***Travels; Robinson Crusoe*** was published in 1719, *Gulliver* in 1725 and the Cotton text of Mandeville in 1725.) Interestingly, these uses (particularly the latter) depend on both reader and author taking for granted that what is consistenth presented as truth is in fact fiction. Such a sophistication is, I feel, present in some degree in the ***Travels*** and is not framed by the usual suspenders of disbelief we find commonly in medieval poetry. The final example of this curious symbiosis between the ***Travels'*** nature and the mood, interests and assumptions of various ages is in fact the beginning of a totally new development in the reading of the ***Travels*** in the eighteenth century. In the 6 November 1711 issue of the *Spectator*, Addison sounds for the first time the note that will resound in *La Natchez* and, modulated, in *Ivanhoe,* the 'delight in contemplating those Virtues which are wild and uncultivated'. Steele, in *The Tatler* No. 29 (1710), connects this half-moralizing taste for the outlandish with an escapist delight in 'unscientific' travel-books—especially Mandeville 'all is enchanted ground and Fairyland'.[12]

Here is a revolution indeed! No moral disapproval of the lying traveller, only a delight in fiction as a safe escape. Here is the germ of that curiously sentimental and patronizing early-eighteenth-century delight in old books simply because they are old—a germ that developed into the foundations of serious medieval scholarship as we know it. The publication of the Cotton text in 1725—the first scholar's text—could hardly have happened without this taste being present; and it is extremely significant in itself. In an entirely new way, Mandeville is now in the province of the scholar and the dilettante; the chapbooks and the continuing Defective versions are clearly to be distinguished from an authoritative old text, and gradually we meet a growing surprise at the quality revealed when the ***Travels*** are read in a good text. But that very change in taste and attitude ensures that from then on the lively luxuriation of Mandevilliana will stop; as the integrity of the book was at last guaranteed, its power to change and inform imaginative thought was almost killed. Nothing grows in formalin.

And I, like John Mandeville, 'am now come to rest, as a man discomfited for age and travel and feebleness. I must now cease telling of diverse things so that those who follow may find things enough to speak of.' . . .

Notes

[1] The most helpful discussions of this tangled matter are in the works by Drs de Poerck and Seymour and by Mrs Bennett. . . . Mrs Bennett's book contains a list with descriptive details of the known extant MSS.

[2] When authors try to assume the character of a national of a country not their own it is very common to find slips which betray them. For example, in 1708 the *London Monthly Miscellany* published a 'Letter from Admiral Bartholomew da Fonte', purporting to describe a voyage from the Pacific to the Atlantic in 1640. The circumstantial detail is good. But the fictious da Fonte's credibility is destroyed by having him reckon his dates from the accession of Charles I of England. (Reprinted in H. R. Wagner, 'Apocryphal Voyages to the West Coast of America', *Proceedings of the American Antiquarian Society* 41 (1931), pp. 179-234.) Similarly, George Psalmanazar (1679?-1763) was unable to maintain his assumed Formosan nationality and passed from ridicule to obscurity, despite the friendship of Dr Johnson.

[3] 'Jeo doie estre escusee, pur ceo qe jeo sui engleis et n'ai pas moelt hauntee le franceis' (*Livre de Seyntz Medecines,* ed. E. J. Arnould (Oxford, 1940), p. 239). The rhetorical figure of *diminutio*—a polite apology for one's real or potential inadequacy—may be behind Henry's and Gower's remarks. But it is just possible that both are aware of the growing fashionableness at this period of the Paris French dialect as a literary language. Chaucer's cutting remark about his Prioress's Flemish French suggests that one so conscious of what is *comme il faut* ought to have been more up to date in the matter of a polite language.

[4] This and the previous point are highlighted by comparing the *Libro del Conoscimiento* (*ca.* 1350) written by a Spanish Franciscan (translated for the Hakluyt Society by C. Markham, 1912). This man did go all over Africa and the East, and did not just compile; yet he includes all the fabulous monsters and stories of the ancient tradition. His ineffable dullness and lack of detail underline how vastly more informative and entertaining Mandeville is.

[5] This does not mean that there are not occasional awkwardnesses, which modern filing systems and methods of writing books would have sorted out. Sometimes the sources are not fully digested, and very occasionally two conflicting versions of the same event happen—for instance, the two stories of Muhammad's prohibition of wine, Chapters 9 and 15. Sometimes one single ultimate source comes to Mandeville by two routes, and is thus doubleted—for for instance, the double account of Silha and then Taprobane (chapters 21 and 33). But this last is in no way Mandeville's fault.

[6] Translated by Sir Henry Yule, in Vol. II of *Cathay and the Way Thither,* an invaluable collection of accounts of the East. . . .

[7] One might here just note how different Polo, Odoric and Mandeville are: Odoric plods worthily on his way, Polo is a keen and accurate observer, and Mandeville

is the creator of a memorable fanciful trope. See *The Travels of Marco Polo* (Penguin Books, London, 1958), p. 66.

[8] The strong devotional interest in the book is borne out by the way it was illustrated, among other things. The early-fifteenth-century MS, Addit. 24189, in the British Library, is simply a picture-book Mandeville, without text; it has a picture for each of the Crownings of Our Lord, and the first five chapters are expressed in twenty-eight superb illustrations. Another illustrated Mandeville appears in the compendium MS Addit. 37049, which is entirely composed of devotional material.

[9] This may be deliberate irony: Pope Clement VI used to say this of his own role.

[10] The story of the book's having been authorized as true by the Pope is an interpolation, found only in the English versions, that must date from after 1377, when Gregory XI returned the papal seat to Rome.

[11] Compare *Clannes* 977-1052, and below, p. 34. See also the comments in Gollancz and Day, *Clannes: Glossary and Illustrative Texts* (Oxford, 1933), pp. 75, 91-2, and 96-8, and in R.J. Menner, *Yale Studies in English* 61 (New Haven, 1920), p. xlff. It has long been recognized that the *Gawain* poet knew the *Travels,* and I have argued elsewhere that Chaucer and the poet of the Alliterative *Morte Arthur* did too.

[12] See p. 37. Mandeville is here well on the way to being bracketed with Münchausen in most people's minds—yet they make a pair only in the alliteration of their names.

Mary B. Campbell (essay date 1988)

SOURCE: "'The Other Half': Mandeville Naturalizes the East," in *The Witness and the Other World: Exotic European Travel Writing, 400-1600.* Cornell, 1988, pp. 122-61.

[*In the excerpt below, Campbell argues that* Mandeville's Travels *was a parody and an early precursor of the modern novel.*]

With **Mandeville's Travels,** the developing genre of travel literature in the West reaches a complicated and long-sustained climax. The book's popularity has been greater than that of any other prose work of the Middle Ages, and its practical effects farther reaching.[1] To investigate the reach and nature of its artistic effects, it will be necessary first to stand back and take the long view of the tributaries that feed it and the genre for which it helped carve a new bed.

Although his most important modern critic, Josephine Waters Bennett, calls Mandeville's book a "travel romance," that is precisely the term I hope to avoid in sketching Mandeville's literary context. The capacity to conceive and construct romance out of the materials of history is an accomplishment for which medieval writers had long been sitting on their laurels. Mandeville was up to something more novel. In a sense crucially qualified by the nature and degree of his readers' imaginative receptivity, he was writing realistic prose fiction—for the first time since Petronius. Fiction was not of course entirely foreign to prose in the fourteenth century. Prose romances such as the thirteenth-century French *Lancelot* had kept alive the possibility of fictional meaning for secular prose narrative, but in the safe confines of material too unremittingly marvelous ever to be mistaken for actuality. (According to Auerbach's scathing dictum, "the courtly romance is not reality shaped and set forth by art, but an escape into fable and fairy tale"; *Mimesis,* 138). But Mandeville's realism was a challenge to an ancient dichotomy between the "fables" of poets and the "truth" of science and history which was still seen as nearly identical with the rhetorical opposition of verse and prose. From the beginning, the question of his creation's epistemological status has confused its most perceptive readers. The controversy over the "truth" of Mandeville's document suggests that in it may be found one seed of the crisis over historicity and significance which signaled the birth trauma of the modern novel.

The generally acknowledged complicity of romance in the genesis of the novel is a peculiarity perhaps insufficiently appreciated as peculiar. To begin with, romance is a genre characterized by its material, while the novel is characterized by its technique. And to whatever extent the novel *could* be said to have a generic material, it lies at the furthest extreme from that of romance: where romance wanders among marvels in distant or otherworldly places, the novels of "the Great Tradition" tend to play themselves out in the intimate and familiar settings of bedrooms, kitchens, and parlors. (Under the influence of this tradition, Hawthorne called "romances" those of his novels set in the past or in Europe.) Ultimately, though, we recognize a novel more by its delivery than by its setting. Its earliest protagonists *are* in fact wanderers, and many of them wander far from home. Robinson Crusoe and his island are the stuff of romance, but *Robinson Crusoe* is emphatically not. The palpability of its presentation works against the marvelous elements in it, and out of nameless, exotic flora Crusoe constructs a bedroom, a kitchen, a parlor—in exhaustive, gratuitous detail.

Concern with the details of the phenomenal world once belonged most properly to the prose of history and "natural philosophy." But an aerial view of the novel's prehistory in medieval narrative and prose will disclose a vast, slow shift in consciousness which redefined the mutual boundaries of history, geography, and romance and thus helped set the stage for *Robinson Crusoe*. **Mandeville's Travels** was an important enabling factor in this process, but its precocious realism is not historically inexplicable. By Mandeville's time the fabulous and romantic Matter of the East had already begun to intersect with the more or less documentary forms of chronicle and *itinerarium*. The Crusades had domesticated the Levant, bringing it closer to the sphere of the mundane and merely natural (and at the same time pushing back the threshold of the "fabulous" East so far that, in the end, men like Columbus could begin to think of sailing *west* to reach it). That foothold in the mundane essential even to "magical realism" was at last available to a man who wanted to write about Elsewhere.

The demystification of the actual East begins as early as Fulcher of Chartres's eyewitness account of the First Crusade, the *Historia Hierosolymitana* (finished c. 1127). After describing an eclipse of great beauty, Fulcher expostulates over God's power to create wonders and says:

> Consider, I pray, and reflect how in our time God has transformed the Occident into the Orient.
>
> For we who were Occidentals have now become Orientals. He who was a Roman or a Frank has in this land been made into a Galilean or a Palestinean. . . . We have already forgotten the places of our birth; already these are unknown to many of us or not mentioned any more. . . . Indeed it is written 'the lion and the ox shall eat straw together' [Isa. 62:25]. He who was born a stranger is now as one born here; he who was born an alien has become a native. (III.xxxvii).[2]

Fulcher at least finds this conflation of Occident and Orient a matter for wonder. The process of demystification has gone even further by the time of the Fourth Crusade, when Villehardouin can speak this matter-of-factly of Constantinople's Hagia Sofia (traditionally a catalyst for expressions of solemn awe and wonder): "And then [Dietrich] went back with a great party of the emperor Henry's men; and found that the castle was pulled down, and he closed up and fortified the church Sainte Sophye, which building is high and fine, and held it to use for the war" (*La conquête de Constantinople,* 2:271).[3]

The opening up of China by missionaries and merchants in the thirteenth century and the annexing of Palestine by European powers during the period of the Crusades had enlarged the *oikumene* of Europe and allowed for significant overlap of this world and the Other World of the imagination. Mandeville's terms for West and East are "on this half" and "in that half." Halves of what? Of one physical, spherical

whole in which the laws of nature operate unilaterally and where if one sails far enough one ends up back at home:

> And therefore hath it befallen many tymes of o thing that I have herd cownted whan I was 9ong, how a worthi man departed somtyme from oure contrees for to go serche the world, And so he passed ynde and the yles be9onde ynde . . . And so longe he wente be see & lond & so enviround the world be many seisons, that he fond an yle where he herde speke his own langage, callynge on oxen in the plowgh such wordes as men speken to bestes in his own contree, Where of he hadde gret mervayle. (XXI, 122)[4]

It may not be too farfetched to see reflected in this little tale the peregrinations of fiction itself, from the wanderings of Odysseus across what Joseph Campbell calls "the Threshold of the Known" to the wanderings of Leopold Bloom among the transformed streets of his hometown, "where of he hadde gret mervayle."[5] For eventually the Threshold of the Known was pushed past even far Cathay, to the Caribbean, to Roanoke, to New Jersey, and the Earthly Paradise filled up with farms and cabins and post offices and, in the end, with shopping malls.

By the time of Mandeville (in the Cotton text, the **Travels** is dated 1356 by its author), travel to the once sacred or fabulous places of the East had dropped off sharply: the Crusades were over, and the relatively gregarious Mongol Empire had been overthrown in China and was being absorbed by hostile Saracen Turks closer to home.[6] But the chronicles of crusaders and travel accounts of missionaries had familiarized both the Near and Far Easts for Europe's reading public and themselves had grown even a little stale.

It was the perfect moment for a literary hoax (though Mandeville made something more than that). With actual contact slowed to a trickle, "news" of the East was out of the question and the Matter was going stagnant again. The forms in which the Matter was contained were widely familiar and, because they were infrequently used, had rigidified in their conventions. And with so few Eastern travelers around, verifiability was not a pressing restriction on the writer's art.

The "hoax" worked because it imitated something recognizable. There is evidence that at least some people believed in the **Travels** for a long time. Ralegh, Frobisher, and (apparently) Columbus all read it earnestly—Frobisher even brought it with him to Baffin's Bay in 1576. Mercator and Ortelius cite Mandeville as an *auctoritas* in their world atlases. Hakluyt included it in the first edition of his *Principall Voyages* (from which he excluded the probably authentic *Relation* of David Ingram for lack of "credibility").[7]

Since we now know that Mandeville's credibility was founded neither in personal experience nor for the most part in the transmission of accurate facts, it must be a literary credibility, a sort of intertextual verisimilitude.[8] Mandeville must be received as truth (where he is so received) because he sounds like truth. A close look at the *Travels,* then, will be in part a close look at its genre in little, as the genre had come to be understood by the time of its first great parody (since Lucian). That the *Travels is* in part a parody, however, cannot be forgotten: it discards and subverts and extends the possibilities of many of its inherited characteristics. And the spirit that shapes it is almost wholly new.[9]

We have already taken note of most of the main currents feeding the *Travels'* stream: the eyewitness pilgrimage narratives, the Alexander romances and their spin-offs, the mercantile and missionary accounts of India and Cathay. But there are other, newer sorts of texts around by 1356 which also convey the reader to places I have been calling Elsewhere. Accounts of the Holy Land best termed guidebooks (foreshadowing the degradation of eighteenth-century Grand Tour accounts into nineteenth-century Baedekers) are a flourishing subliterary genre, and of course the Crusades have been thoroughly chronicled. Neither kind of book contributed much directly in the way of style or topics to the *Travels,* but both form part of its literary context and helped shape Mandeville's opportunity.

The guidebooks are the sadly degenerated offspring of Egeria's letter to her Venerable Sisters—not quite a return to the itineraries of late antiquity, but lifeless and depersonalized. Some features of the style of a representative fourteenth-century account are identical with some of Egeria's. Almost all the places described are "places where" some scriptural (or, by this time, apocryphal) event took place; miraculous features are qualified by "it is said"; transitions from one description to another announce distances: "Thence you shall go forty miles to Gaza." But in place of Egeria's experienced pauses for prayers and readings at the holy places, we are confronted with the formulas "and there is an indulgence for seven years and seven Lenten seasons" and "there is absolution from pain and guilt." The work is completely nonnarrative in structure and, most importantly, voiceless. No particular person administers or receives the absolutions and indulgences. No one judges among the marvels, hikes up the mountains, chats with a bishop: no one even writes the book—at least half of it is plagiarized from a thirteenth-century guidebook and seamlessly so. In the following extract, section 40 is plagiarized and section 41 is new:

> (40) Thence you come to the doors, and in the midst of the choir is the place called the Centre of the World, where our Lord Jesus Christ laid his finger,

saying, 'This is the centre of the world.' And there is an indulgence for seven years and seven Lenten seasons.

> It should also be known that at the great altar is an indulgence for seven years and seven Lenten seasons, and at all the altars constructed within the church.

> (41) Thence you come to a pillar near the chamber of the holy sepulchre, above which it is said that the following miracle took place. A certain Saracen entered the Church of the Holy Sepulchre, and looking round saw the aforesaid image painted above the pillar. Then he tore out the eyes of the image, and straightway his own eyes fell out on the ground. (Bernard, "Guidebook to Palestine," 8-9)[10]

But although the structure of the work is nonnarrative, it is full of stories: some from Scripture, some from the Apocrypha, some from martyrologies, some from legend. Egeria and Arculf retold stories as well, but for the most part far more briefly. Of the mountain Agrispecula, for instance, Egeria says: "This is the mountain on which Balac, son of Beor, put the soothsayer Balaam to curse the children of Israel and God, as it is written, was unwilling to permit that" (XII.10). Egeria's micronarratives are reminders of stories told in full in the Scriptures and function chiefly to identify the places she describes. In the fourteenth-century guidebook they are amplified in both length and number, and drawn from almost every possible source. Like the epic simile, they function far beyond the limits of their apparent task:

> (66) As you go down Mt. Sion is the place where the Apostles, as they bore the body of the Blessed Virgin to burial in the valley of Jehoshaphat, laid down the bier. And the Jews who lived in the village hard by collected at the spot, that they might carry off the body to burn it. Then the chief priest of the Jews, more bold and imprudent than the rest, laid his hand on the bier, whereupon his hands were withered. Then he besought blessed Peter to pray for him, and to restore his hands to him. To whom blessed Peter said, 'If thou believest that this is the mother of Christ, and art willing to be baptized, thou shalt be made whole.' And he believed, and was restored to his former health. And there is an indulgence for seven years and for seven Lenten seasons.

> (78) Then you come to a declivity of Mount Olivet, two furlongs eastward, to Bethphage, which is, being interpreted, the House of Figs. There our Lord sent two of his disciples, viz., Peter and Phillip, for the ass and her colt on Palm Sunday, saying, 'Go into the village over against you, and straightway ye shall find an ass tied, and a colt with her; and they, having gone, brought the ass and the colt, and they set Him thereon.' [Matt. 21:2, 7] And He was led

Reproduction from a manuscript of The Travels of Sir John Mandeville.

upon the ass from that place to Jerusalem with hymns and praises, and was received with honour by the children of the Hebrews bearing palm branches. And there is an indulgence for seven years and seven Lenten seasons. ("Guidebook to Palestine," 13-14, 16)

About two-thirds of the length of each of the two representative sections quoted above is given over to anecdote, narrated at much greater length than the needs of identification would require. The stories are not new or otherwise difficult of access: their charm is the unadorned charm of narrativity itself. They compensate for the guidebook's lack of structural narrativity—a necessary absence in an *itinerarium* without an itinerant.

Not all the guidebook's narrative excurses qualify as full stories, but the urge toward amplification is evident everywhere, even in the briefest of notices: "(107) Also near the church, it is said, was the palace of King Herod; and near there was the house of Judas the traitor, *where he lived with his wife and children*" (II,

emphasis mine). This development from Egeria's mere identifications to a framework literally "stuffed" with tales has a musical analogy in the thirteenth century's development of the motet from the *clausula:* the brief phrase of the *clausula* acquired a full and usually secular text in its ornamental upper part, which resulted ultimately in a new and self-contained musical form, the motet.[11]

Such hypertrophy of an ornament is surely a sign of exhaustion in the host form, as is the extensive plagiarism among the later accounts of the Holy Land. But why *not* plagiarize? With the closing of the Crusades there was little new information to bring back, at least under the traditional heads, and the pilgrimage routes were almost as old and established as the Gospels that had inspired them. The guidebook is the detritus of a tradition a millennium old, and in a literary culture bound by a rhetoric of set topoi, figures, and arguments, the notion of plagiarism is almost beside the point. Tradition dictates not just the loci to be described, and their relative importance, but even their characterizing details. Of Mt. Olivet: "and the stone which He had under His feet still retains their impression, and it is visible to this day" ("Guidebook to Palestine," 15); "Within this [chapel] may be seen the mark of Christ's left foot, which He imprinted on the stone when He ascended into heaven" (Poloner, *Description of the Holy Land,* 9); "Know that on Mt. Olivet Jesus Christ went up to heaven on the day of the Ascension, where the form of his right foot appears yet in a stone" ("City of Jerusalem," 40).

What there was to be seen, even the order in which it ought to be seen, had been so extensively codified that an autobiographical account could offer only the addition of the author's own personality. Necessary as this may seem from a literary viewpoint, it was of course problematical from the devotional angle. Hundreds of years had passed since the times of tentative and scanty travel in which Egeria's and Arculf's personalizations of their accounts were justified. It still happened now and again—for instance in Ludolph von Suchem's account, almost exactly contemporaneous with Mandeville's, and to some extent in that of his traveling companion, Wilhelm von Boldensil, from whom Mandeville plagiarized parts of his work. But the guidebooks were the rule, a rule that called out to be broken with the flamboyant magnificence Mandeville expended on his task.

One of the few original conceptual features of the *itineraria* of the later Middle Ages is found in their occasional reference to the scriptural future and to the present as marking the fulfillment of old prophecies. This is even more notable, naturally enough, in the Crusade chronicles: on the arrival of the army of the First Crusade at Nicaea, Fulcher says:

What then shall I say? The islands of the seas and all the kingdoms of the earth were so moved that one believed the prophecy of David fulfilled who said in his Psalm "All the nations whom thou has made shall come and worship before Thee, O Lord" [Ps. 85:9], and what those who arrived later deservedly said "We shall worship in the place where His feet have stood" [Ps. 131:7]. Of this journey moreover we read much more in the prophets which it would be tedious to repeat. (*History of the Expedition,* I.xlix)

How like and yet unlike Egeria's instructions to her Venerable Sisters to read further in Numbers about the place she has mentioned, as she is too pressed for time to describe it herself. The peculiar relationship of text and Scripture, by way of a geographical *materia* that is itself a figure or a sign, remains the same, but present time as well as present space seem now to participate in the reality to be transcribed.

Time and its events provide the backbone of the Crusade chronicle, and the form is for that reason important to the development of a fully narrative genre of travel writing. But to the extent that public reality is more important in the chronicle than private experience, and topography only significant from a military perspective, it is at most tangentially related to the still spatially oriented, descriptive, and (potentially) subjective genre on which we are focused. Traveling with an army into occupied territory certainly insulates the eyewitness chronicler from immersion in the alien: still, in its reintroduction of the first-person narrative to the mise-en-scène of the Eastern world, the form in its rhetorical aspect demands some commentary here.

Justifying a first-person narration in the chronicle form is no trouble—most of the chronicles were written by real movers and shakers whose experience was indeed history. But this history was taking place on ground until now the province of the pilgrimage narratives and biblical commentaries, in which description and identification of the Holy Places were a matter of course. Under the influence of this literary heritage, the chroniclers bring together again the separated functions of autobiography and geographical description, or at least make them visible between the covers of a single book. This fortuitous intersection may have helped pave the way for the resurgence of autobiographical matter in the pilgrimage accounts, and certainly it nourished the art of prose narrative. (At the end of the fourteenth century, Philippe de Mézières produced the weird hybrid *Le songe du vieil pèlerin,* a fictional, allegorical, autobiographical prose *itinerarium* propagandizing for a new crusade. As a prose fiction set in historical time and geographical space for serious moral purposes, it deserves at least a mention in the history of the novel. But as allegory and propaganda, its fictionality is too blatant and its structure too antimimetic to provide a really new experience for the imaginations of its first readers.)

As I have said, the result of the domestication of the East by the crusaders and their chroniclers was to push back its border, toward India and China. The fabulous place is still there, and it is still Elsewhere. At home in Palestine for twenty years, Fulcher, during a lull in the crusading action of which his chronicle has become a running commentary, undertakes to summarize the flora, fauna, and ethnography of his new country. He takes almost all of his data from Pliny's third-century epitomizer, Solinus, and it is mostly about the animals of Egypt and India: "The very little that I have said I have excerpted as far as possible from that most sagacious investigator and skillful writer Solinus. What Alexander the Great likewise found in India and saw there I shall relate later on" (III.xlix).

This borrowing suggests that what has come to be called the "marvels material" is so intimately a part of any account of the East that it finds its way perfunctorily into even a work written in a nondescriptive, historical genre, by the magnetic virtue of the setting. It is on every level a digression from the business at hand as it appears in Fulcher, and as such testifies to an overwhelming impulse of confused literary decorum. Fulcher is one of the very first Crusade chroniclers, and as I have said, the literary heritage on which he must draw includes not only previous chronicles of other historical events, but the existing literature on the East. But the displacement of his attention from the part of the East in which he lives into other parts of which he is conscious of having no authority to speak is a telling gesture. Coming as it does toward the end of a relentlessly autobiographical eyewitness account, it is a particularly clear sign of the link between the ideas "marvels" and "Elsewhere." Busy in the work of sacking and fortifying cities, he has seen no marvels here in Palestine. If, as he puts it, the Occident has become the Orient, then the imperative Orient of the mind's geography must lie farther to the East, and to the South. Since he is writing about the East, he must include the marvels material, but since the East has become Home, that material must belong elsewhere.[12]

That this tortuous logic directs his pen instead of the urge to describe what flora and fauna he has actually become familiar with is also suggestive. The title of the chapter on animals is "The Different Kinds of Beasts and Serpents in the Land of the Saracens.". . . India, Ethiopia, and Scythia do not really qualify as Saracen lands, and he has not even visited them. The duty of the travel writer, which for a moment he has become, must then be, at least in Fulcher's eyes, to reiterate the existence of Nature's "fringe elements," to reassure the homebound that Nature is indeed more healthy at the center and more exciting on the edges.

In "Geography, Phenomenology, and the Study of Human Nature," Yi-fu Tuan speaks of the importance of the binary opposition "home-journey" to the continued felt identity of the term "home": "Home has no meaning apart from the journey which takes one outside of home" (188). That this opposition has been unsettled in Fulcher's colonial experience is clear from the slightly pensive extract, quoted earlier in this chapter, on God's miraculous transformation of Occidentals into Orientals. This later reinstatement of the characteristically bizarre Elsewhere may function in part to steady the writer's own nerves.

The Lord of Joinville inserts a similarly parenthetical account of the lands farther East in his hagiographical *Vie de Sainte Louis* (finished c. 1207), a chronicle of the Seventh Crusade, during which Joinville acted as a special adviser (and close friend) to the king. Envoys sent to the khan to negotiate an alliance against the Saracens have returned with bad news, and Joinville takes the opportunity to report other "news" they have brought back, chiefly ethnographical and historical, about the Tartars, Prester John, and Gog and Magog. Outside of a passage on the cult of the Assassins, it is the only such reporting in the book; the rest focuses entirely on the deeds of Louis, the events of the Crusade, and Joinville's personal relationship with the king.

The *Vie de Sainte Louis* is a beautiful book and difficult to pass over without a little further comment. In it is advanced to the highest degree since perhaps Augustine's *Confessions* the technique Richardson was to call "writing to the moment" and which was to prove so central to the technique of the sentimental novel. In the following extract, the passage of narrative time is so minutely detailed as almost to replicate the real duration of the incident recounted, and this reverence for the minutiae of time is essential to the concerns of the novel:

(431) While the king heard grace, I went to an open window which was in an embrasure next to the head of the king's bed. And I passed my arms through the bars of the window. And I thought that if the king went into France that I would go to the prince of Antioch, who thought of me as a father and who had sent to ask for me, until such time as another expedition came to the country by which the prisoners might be delivered, according to the counsel that the lord of Boulaincourt had given me.

(432) While I stood there, the king came and leaned on my shoulders, and held my head in his two hands. And I thought that this was my lord Phelippe d'Anemos, who had irritated me enough already that day because of the counsel I had given. And I said thus: "Leave me in peace, my lord Phelippe." Unfortunately, as I turned my head the hand of the king fell across my face and I knew that this was the king by an emerald that he had on his finger.

And he said to me: Keep quite still. Because I want to ask how you could be so bold, that you who are a young man dare advise me to remain, against all the great men and the sages of France who advised me to go.

(433)—Sir, I said, even if I had the cowardice in my heart, still I would not for anything advise you to do it.—Are you saying, said he, that I would be doing wrong if I went away?—So help me God, sir, said I, yes. And he said to me: "If I remain, will you remain?" And I told him yes, "if I can, either at my own or at someone else's [expense]."—Then rest easy, said he. Because you are in my good graces for what you have advised me. But don't say it to anyone all this week. (*La vie de Sainte Louis*, pars. 431-33)

There is nothing like this in Mandeville; indeed, European prose will wait long for another such detail as the king's hand sliding down his vassal's face until Joinville recognizes the emerald ring. But the amplification of detail to render an object or event both credible and accessible is a technique Mandeville will put to important use, as will be seen later in this chapter. Its appearance in an account of distant travel marks a crucial shift in the nature of the genre's attention to its subjects. Wonder is brief; sympathy is ample.

The chronicles display a number of novelistic features: in particular the use of suspense and the depiction of character over time (as opposed to the iconographic *effictio* prevalent in romance and more detached historical writing). But their major contribution to travel writing itself, as it then stood, conditioned by the status of its most typical subject matter, the Near East, lay in their focus on present time. For Egeria and her descendants, events were over, sealed into places, and already recorded in Scripture. Fulcher's events are fulfillments of scriptural hints and prophecies, and many of his "places" are in the process of becoming sacred almost as he speaks. (Even Joinville's essentially biographical "chronicle" is *hagiographical*, intent on rendering its crusader-king as a saint, an agent of divine history.) The Crusades are seen as a chapter in eschatological history, taking place on the same soil as the history recounted in the Bible. With this perception, their chroniclers can and do speak of events in the Holy Land, at last, in the present tense. It remains for the *curiositas* of the later Middle Ages to secularize this present tense, to detach it from the eschatological frame so that it can carry the events of a private man's excursion across the "Threshold of the Known."

Mandeville and Fiction

In his *Manual of English Prose Literature* (1872), William Minto grandly called Mandeville the "father of English prose." M. C. Seymour, Mandeville's most recent editor, is convinced that he was French, but convinced of little else—he refers to him in the notes as "Mandeville," inside quotation marks. Robert Burton denounced him (in the same breath as Marco Polo) as a "Liar"; recently, Donald Howard and Christian Zacher have published elegant close readings that implicitly issue him a poetic license to "call the sun a rush candle if it pleases him."[13] But Mandeville was neither simply a liar nor simply a poet, and if it is true enough that he fathered English prose, it is also true that his book was written originally in French.[14] Even looked at in the light of its genre and its time, the book is singular and, beneath its dazzle, baffling. But the standoffs between its critics are perhaps unnecessary; at least in part they stem from incomplete consideration of the issues and conventions of its literary and "scientific" genealogy, as they were understood to function in Mandeville's own era.

The world owes the rediscovery of *Mandeville's Travels* as a work of art primarily to three people: Josephine Waters Bennett, Donald Howard, and Christian Zacher.[15] They have performed an important imaginative task in realizing and publicly re-presenting the beauty and delicacy of the book. But they have perhaps leapt too quickly over old-fashioned problems of authorial intention and audience reception and in the process misrepresented some of its beauty. In his letter to Can Grande, Dante, Mandeville's near contemporary, reiterates the old list of points to consider in interpreting a work of literature; "form" and "purpose" are two of them.[16] Neither can be understood rightly from the vantage point of a literary culture in which the words *science* and *art* refer to activities opposed in both method and language.

Bennett argues that the *Travels* has been received from the very beginning as a work of what we now call art:

> He is free to mix truth with fantasy because he can trust his readers to distinguish between them. He is free to decorate the borders of his moral earnestness with delicate (and indelicate) grotesques without fear that those for whom he is writing will be unable to distinguish between the text and the decoration. The decoration is intended to amuse, just as the impish monsters and absurd postures in the borders of the fourteenth century missals and psalters were intended to amuse, without detracting from the seriousness of the text they illuminated. (*Rediscovery of Mandeville,* 78)[17]

A presupposition lurks here with which one must agree—that we have no business discussing the *Travels* as an object constructed to stimulate imaginative pleasures if it could not have so stimulated its original readers. But a number of more careless assumptions lurk with it about that readership and about the nature of "truth" in the fourteenth century

It is true that Dante mixed "truth" with fantasy for a receptive audience at about the same time. According to Curtius, the long tradition of Homeric and Virgilian allegoresis allowed him to do so with impunity—though even so, there were complaints.[18] But Dante, like Homer and Virgil, wrote in verse, which gave his audience a necessary rhetorical cue. Mandeville wrote in the vernacular prose of a scientific popularizer, and there are no borders or margins in such discourse to make the separation obvious between "moral earnestness" and "delicate grotesque." Nor was the level of geographic and ethnographic knowledge high enough in the fourteenth century to permit even the most sophisticated reader to dismiss the Acephali (still being "earnestly" reported by Ralegh two and a half centuries later), while attaching his belief to the historical but almost equally bizarre "Old Man of the Mountains."

Mandeville himself knew when he wrote, as we know now, that he was in many instances lying, plagiarizing, fictionizing. But he was making use of a form devised to transmit facts and never previously used with any antifactual intent. It is also important to remember that many of his "delicate grotesques" had claimed the status of fact for at least two millennia and would continue to do so well into the eighteenth century.

A fact and its linguistic representation are clearly separable entities in a culture long possessed of experimental science. Nor is *descriptio* any longer the only method of representing facts: facts are now displayed in the forms of graphs, charts, statistical columns, photographs, their significance discernible without much linguistic mediation to anyone familiar with the conceptual systems that provide their contexts. Before the advent of museums and the taxonomic organization of such sciences as botany, zoology, ethnology, and geology, men were dependent for their knowledge of the visible world on the prose descriptions of select eyewitnesses and their epitomizers. (Astronomy presents an obvious exception: a significant portion of the night sky is visible to anyone.) A fact and the words in which it was encapsulated were much more clearly identical than they are now: for all practical purposes a change in wording was a change in fact, a mistranslation could alter the world. What Margaret Hodgen, in *Early Anthropology,* sees as a stubborn, paralytic resistance to new knowledge could be seen more generously as a linguistic conservatism motivated by the need literally to conserve what data were already available.[19] Iconographic representation (the characteristic method) simplifies and restricts knowledge. It also preserves it, or at least preserves a fuller spectrum of possibility than would otherwise be visible. In the form of the conventional unicorn, memory of the rhinoceros was preserved in western Europe for thousands of years. The manticore memorialized the man-eating tiger, the Gymnosophists the habits and habitat of the Yogis.[20]

167

The presence in the *Travels* of the formulaic marvels material suggests neither a scorn for facts nor a mere delight in the picturesque. The material is not our clue to the fictive nature of the *Travels,* nor was it likely to have been separated out by the men of that time. Subsequent redactions, epitomes, and chapbook descendants of the original isolate parts of its material on the basis of subject matter, devotional or sensational appeal, but not according to truth value.[21]

The facts and data of the Middle Ages were not just wrong, they were literary or at least linguistic objects, attributable in that aspect to the specific authors who first promulgated them. Thus Fulcher carefully quotes Solinus even to describe the one animal he *is* likely to have seen, the crocodile (III.xlix). In the twentieth century we are continually trying to alter and refine our descriptions of facts, while at the same time trying to stabilize literary texts in "definitive" editions. The description of a fact has no acknowledged literary value and becomes disposable at a moment's notice. The description of a fantasy, once canonized as literature, becomes immutable.

It is therefore a task requiring some care from us to avoid anachronism in imagining the "form" and "purpose" of a literary work of the fourteenth century which sets out to describe "sum partie of thinges that there ben." Knowledge was scarce, reverenced, and largely inseparable from the particular texts that transmitted it. At the same time, texts themselves were fluid: plagiarized, misquoted, mistranslated, interpolated upon, bowdlerized, epitomized, transformed, and transformable at every stage of their complex dissemination. When new knowledge did arrive it was easily enough corrupted into older images, particularly in the process of translation. Marco Polo's information about the short days and long nights of the Russian winter had regressed into the year-round "Land of Perpetual Darkness" by the time of the "Geographic Text."[22] The authors of the encyclopedias and cosmographies that perpetuated the scientific misinformation of the Middle Ages were shoring fragments against a ruin: in their manic comprehensiveness can be seen an attempt to halt the endless fluctuation and circulation of verbal data-ions by cramming them all together in a small container. Without articulated taxonomies this attempt was bound to fail: proximity does not necessitate bonding.

Mandeville's book can be seen as part of this same serious struggle and the learned plagiarist as confronted by the same debilitating array of disconnected data that inspired the encyclopedists. Mandeville did not invent a taxonomy; instead, he shaped a fiction. His building blocks were those peculiar entities impossible for us to define either simply as data or simply as passages from other works. For him they were above all building blocks; his aim and his contribution were

(at last) to build something with them. What he built was true because coherent; like any good building, it was used and it lasted.

Unlike most good buildings, though, it was subversive. Its coherence lent authority to the misinformation included in it, and its prose assertiveness disturbed, for some, the conventional credibility of prose. (Not that travel accounts had not always strained credulity: the anxious, even florid, claim to veracity and reliability is a conventional feature of any premodern, first-person narrative of travel and is parodied in the very title of Lucian's *A True Story*.) But most subversive of all is Mandeville's aesthetic attitude toward fact: he is a hedonist of knowledge. Unable to test the truth of his materials, he settled for arranging them, as if they were in fact just so many words, as if "everything possible to be believ'd is an image of truth," as if beauty were truth, truth beauty—Keats never wrote a geography.

Although Mandeville's prologue has a familiar feel to it, many of the conventions and topoi we might expect are absent from it or subverted. There is no address to the reader and no dedication. There is no *occupatio* in which the traveler claims only a humble style and an incapacity for the task ahead. There is only the most deliciously ambiguous of truth claims, and the long sentences that promise to explain why the writer should write, or the reader read, yet another account of "the lond of promyssioun" drift to an end without delivering.

But it elaborately amplifies a topos hinted at in the first chapters of Fulcher's *History of the Expedition to Jerusalem,* in Burchard of Mt. Sion's splendid thirteenth-century *Descriptio,* and in Ludolph von Suchem's *Itinerarium* (c. 1350):[23] the contrast between the decadent West, where lawlessness and faithlessness are rampant, and the sacredness of the Holy Land, which the West has allowed to fall into the hands of the infidels. Ludolph and Mandeville both refer to the Holy Land as "the Promised Land"—Mandeville in his very first sentence. Desire to possess, or repossess, has become a new face of the West's desire for the East and a breach opened for an earthly utopianism to replace the old quandary of the pilgrim who found in Jerusalem only the shadow of his celestial goal.

> That lond he [Jesus] chees before all other londes as the beste & most worthi lond & the most vertuouse lond of all the world. . . . Wherefore every gode cristene man that is of powere & hath whereof scholde peynen him with all his strengthe for to conquere oure right heritage and chacen out all misbeleevynge men. . . . But now pryde couetyse and enuye han so emflawmed the hertes of lordes of the world that thei are more besy for to disherite here neyghbores more than for to chalenge or to conquere here right heritage before seyd. (Prologue, 1-3)

This sort of thing is very earnest in Fulcher and the others, but in Mandeville a little less so, since we find him later employed by "misbeleevynge men" as a mercenary (xxiv, 144), and putting an eloquent speech of moral wisdom and rebuke into the mouth of the Saracen "soudan" (xvi, 88-90).

There are two conventional reasons for writing an account of the Holy Land: because men want to hear about it who cannot go there ("possessed by a desire to picture to their minds those things which they are not able to behold with their eyes"; Burchard, *Description of the Holy Land,* 4), and because the author is an eyewitness ("I have dwelt in those parts for an unbroken space of five years"; Ludolph, *Description and the Way Thither,* 1). Two long, unfinished sentences in Mandeville's prologue hint at these topics but do not deliver. The dependent clauses become so enthusiastic and thus so long that they end at last without result clauses:

> For als moche as the londe beʒonde the see that is to sey the holy londe that men callen the lond of promyssioun or of beheste passynge all othere londes it is the most worthi lond most excellent and lady and souereyn of all othere londes & is blessed & halewed of the precyous body & blood of oure lord jhesu crist; in the whiche land it lykede him to take flesch & blood of the virgyne marie to envyrone that holy lond with his blessede feet; And there he wolde of his blessedness enoumbre him in the seyd blessed & gloriouse virgine marie & become man & worche many myracles and preche and teche the feyth & the lawe of crystene men vnto his children. (Prologue, 1)

> And for als moche as it is longe tyme passed that ther was no generall passage ne vyage ouer the see and many men desiren for to here speke of the holy lond and han there of gret solace & comforte, I John Maundevylle knyght all be it I be not worthi that was born in Englond, in the town of seynt Albones & passed the see in the ʒeer of oure lord jhesu crist Mill ccc & xxij. in the day of seynt Michell & hiderto haue ben longe tyme ouer the see & haue seyn & gon thorgh many dyuerse londs & many prouynces & kyngdomes & jles And haue passed thorghout Turkye Ermonye the lityll & the grete [the sentence continues without grammatical resolution for several more lines]. (Prologue, 3)

It could be that Mandeville cannot handle so complex a syntax as he initiates in these two sentences and, intoxicated with his *amplificationes,* forgets about the claims of grammar and sense. If so, it is his last spate of such weakness. On the other hand, these highly conventional rhetorical moments are perfect opportunities for a quasi-parodic abandonment of sense. The reader should know what sentiments and justifications lurk in the wings.

It is even easier to put these deliriously collapsed sentences down to artfulness when we encounter the coy and suggestive truth claim that concludes the prologue:

> And ʒee schull vndirstonde that I haue put this boke out of latyn in to frensch and translated it aʒen out of frensch in to Englyssch that euery man of my nacioun may vnderstonde it. But lordes & knyghtes and othere noble & worthi men that conne not latyn but lityll & han ben beʒonde the see knowen & vnderstonden ʒif I seye trough or non. And ʒif I err in deuising for forʒetynge or ell that their mowe redresse it & amende it. For thynges passed out of longe tyme from a mannes mynde or from his syght turnen sone in to forʒetynge because that mynde of man ne may not be comprehended ne with holden for the freeltee of mankynde. (4)

It is true that some of the more suggestive touches in the English version may be the results of mistranslation or interpolation by the Englisher (although Mandeville may have been the Englisher himself). In good medieval fashion, **Mandeville's Travels** (like the far earlier *Wonders of the East* or the more recent **Travels** of Marco Polo) is the product of more than one consciousness, and a certain amount of unconsciousness as well. But in general drift, the French and English versions agree: in place of the anxious vow to tell the truth, the whole truth, and nothing but the truth, Mandeville leaves it up to the traveled among his readers to gauge his veracity. This is cagey in two ways: first, it begs the question of whether or not he has been the eyewitness his "I John Maundevylle" sentence implies he was—his work can contain nothing but "facts" and remain "untrue" by virtue of its fictional narrative frame. Second, in the very first chapter he comes out with a lie that a traveled reader would probably recognize as such: describing the famous golden statue of Justinian that stood before the Hagia Sofia, he falsely claims that the "round appell of gold in his hond" has fallen out (and when replaced will not remain) because "this appull betokeneth the lordschipe that he hadde ouer all the world that is round"—which lordship has been broken.[24]

The imagined traveled reader thus knows early on "ʒif I seye trouthe or non." At this point the traveled reader is confronted with a new twist to the reading experience, the aesthetically justified "lie." The lie does a number of things for the book that mere truth could not accomplish. It allows Mandeville to emphasize the presence of the "fallen West" as a starting point in both space and time—this is of enormous structural importance in a work that takes us eventually to the gates of the Earthly Paradise in the farthest East, takes us back to an *unfallen* place and time as it takes us to the cardinal point geographically opposed to England in the extreme West. And it ties this theme of the fallen world to his theme of the round world. The "round appell of gold . . . betokeneth the lordschipe that he hadde ouer all the world that is round." Both the hope and the pessimism of the writer are bound together in this image of the fallen golden orb, to bear fruit in the peculiarly passionate chapter on "the roundness of the erthe" and all that that implies.

But how about the untraveled reader, who may also "conne not latyn but lityll" and therefore be unable to compare Mandeville with his sources and contemporaries? This more likely reader has had a marvel thrust upon him that is perhaps even more striking as "fact" than as pure symbol. Fortuitous congruences of matter and significance had (and still have) a hold over the Christian imagination, anchored as it is by the Incarnation and nurtured on allegoresis. For this reader, Mandeville is not the artist, God is. Mandeville merely reports His artistry. While Mandeville was writing in an age without extended prose fiction, it was also an age that saw symbolic meaning everywhere—in letters, comets, stones, and maps, in the number of the fixed stars and the quills of the porcupine. In an Age of Faith, the symbolic nature of Christ's life on earth allowed for a conception of life in which reality need not be restructured by the literary artist for significant pattern to inhere in it. Even such a random event as the hooting of an owl in the night could carry symbolic overtones of a restricted kind. The history of the earth itself was seen as a fiction created by God, and . . . the geography of the earth was a physical figure of spiritual realities. In this atmosphere, even the naïve reader who accepted the book as "factual" could have and would have seen beyond concrete detail. If life was allegorical, then so was a record of it. We are looking back to a vanishing point where not only fact and text, but fact and fiction partake more of each other's natures than they are now felt to do. But by consciously constructing the "facts" himself, Mandeville is taking a step in our direction.

Of course, in between these two readers, the traveled and the naïve, there must have been a skeptical third who recognized the anatomy of marvel formation and suspected the traveler's traditional impulse to overshape his rendering of the exotic. The skeptical third was to inherit the earth; in his eyes, all the language strategies with which the medieval traveler converted the Unknown into the knowable were fictions in the meanest sense.[25] But Mandeville does not write for him: "And tho that han ben in tho contrees and in the gret Canes household knowen wel that I seye soth And therfore I will not spare for hem that knowe not ne beleue not but that thei seen for to tell ʒou a partie of him and of his estate" (XXIV, 145). To Mandeville the skeptical reader is a Doubting Thomas whose failure of imagination makes him dismissable. He wants belief, but this may include the special kind Coleridge called suspension of disbelief: "And whoso that wole may leve [believe] me ʒif he will, And whoso will not may leue also" (XXIV, 145).

Mandeville's fictionality is not to be gauged by the truth value of his inherited data: he is not a liar whose charm has cozened a later age into dubbing him a poet. In undermining the reader's desire and ability to simply believe or disbelieve his account, he is creating an imaginative freedom for his reader and himself, and directing our attention toward a realm in which faith— the active form of belief—is required of us, and contemplation matters more than the acquisition of knowledge. At the root of fiction is a magical gift, like the shield of invisibility or the shoes of flight: we are released by this mode of discourse from having to deal responsibly with new knowledge. We can view and consider data that we need not integrate into our survivalist map of the actual. There are of course facts in every fiction; historians piece together pictures of the daily lives of past peoples from their poems and novels, no doubt fairly accurately. But when fiction functions as itself it is precisely to allow us a sabbatical from the hunting and gathering of information. the most obvious device for signaling our freedom to us is the introduction of the impossible, the presence of the unreal—the magic ring, the flying horse, the one-eyed giant. Travel writing, then, hovers at the brink of the fictional abyss. In the days before travel was common and photographs offered conclusive documentation, travel writing presented its readers with an inherently problematic experience. A marvel in any other context signals the freedom I have been talking about. But here it may provoke the attempt to alter radically one's map of the actual and possible. In fact it did, as Augustine's struggle with the monostrous races gives evidence.

The customary claim to veracity with which medieval travel narratives open (or close, or both) is a response to this problem—a problem inherent not only in the material but in the formulas through which much of it was characteristically transmitted. The much later *Pilgrim's Progress* opens with the defensive epigraph (taken from Hosea), "I have used similitudes." The Bible's use of similitudes, as Curtius clearly outlines, occasioned a whole literary apologetics among medieval churchmen, for similitudes are figures, and figures are "*mendacia poetarum*."[26] The Bible, it was decided, uses similitudes to hide its wisdom from the vulgar. The travel writer has no such motive; in fact his use of similitudes has precisely the opposite intention—to convey his knowledge to the vulgar. The defensiveness of Bunyan's loud announcement indicates a still vivid sense in his readership that figures are lies and lead away from, not toward, the truth.

How much more vivid must have been Mandeville's sense of mendacity, an author who was not writing an obvious allegory and who was using a traditionally documentary form. The absence of an unambiguous truth claim in his prologue, then, is a matter of real importance in our assessment of his literary intention, and his intention a matter of inspired illumination concerning the nature and potential of his chosen genre. He has taken the doubt with which the reader may greet the figural encoding of the alien and exotic and transformed it into the potential experience of free imaginative contemplation. And the total object that he gives us for that contemplation is a redeemed world, a world he insists is round and human, where God is present "in alle places" and worshiped in most of them.

Mandeville and Travel Writing

So far I have been dealing chiefly with Mandeville's relation to the development of fiction. That an analysis of this most glorious of all premodern travel works should entail a discussion of fiction is significant, but it is time now to look at the work under the rubric of travel writing per se. Although we will uncover a structure that has significance of the sort that the structures of fiction do, the flesh of the *Travels* is the same stuff of which Odoric, Burchard, Ludolph, and William made their *itineraria*—often quite literally the same.

William of Boldensil provides much of the flesh of part 1, the account of the Holy Land. Odoric of Pordenone, who journeyed as a missionary to the khan between 1316 and 1330, is the primary source for part 2, the excursion into the Utter East.[27] Marvelous information from Vincent of Beauvais's *Speculum historiale* and *Speculum naturale* is scattered strategically throughout, as are motifs from legend and romance belonging more or less to the public domain. If Mandeville had done nothing but combine William's and Odoric's accounts into one journey, he would still have made a notable breach in the consciousness of his age. The journey to Palestine was always formally motivated by the central religious purpose of pilgrimage (the Crusades, called "general passages," were considered large-scale pilgrimages). The journey farther East was of two types, mercantile or missionary, and as we have seen in the last chapter these purposes provided characteristic organizing criteria for the writer as well. Mandeville-the-narrator emerges from his conflation of these subgenres as a pure wanderer, and travel as an activity in and of itself. Thus, if we are naming fathers, we can call Mandeville not only the "father of English prose" but the father of modern travel writing.[28] It is a felicity of history that the first such traveler did all (or most) of his travel in his head and that the first such account was essentially a fiction. The form and attitude of this fiction were so prophetic of those of later "true stories" that, as late as 1866, Sir Henry Yule (no mean traveler himself) was making use of Mandeville to corroborate or explicate details in Odoric.

Mandeville starts us at Home and takes us back there at the end; the first chapter is called "To teche you the weye out of Englond," and in the last he tells us "now

I am comen home mawgree myself to reste for gowtes Artetykes that me distreynen, that deffynen the ende of my labor aȝenst my will god knoweth" (XXXV, 210). Thus the Other World is drawn into some contiguity with this one, and though there is no overt description of home (such as begins Bruce Chatwin's *In Patagonia* or ends Robert Byron's *The Road to Oxiana*), there is a marvelously covert inclusion, in a late chapter on the Vale Perilous, of Tacitus's description of Britain. The multiple ironies of Mandeville's plagiarism of a depiction of his own people, as seen through the eyes of a more civilized foreigner of antiquity, inserted at the proverbially wildest margin of the earth, belong to the history of fiction in the way they complicate the relation of prose statement to meaning. But the coming to consciousness of travel writing as a vehicle for irony is also a notable event in itself.

Donald Howard has already commented on the irony that structures and flavors the *Travels,* and says about the link between travel and irony: "If his book is ironic, it is because travel itself is ironic: things are other than what we expect at home, and the contrast turns us back upon ourselves" ("World of *Mandeville's Travels,*" 10). He also notes in passing that Mandeville "grasped this instructive feature of traveling better than previous authors" and speculates that this is because "he saw from afar, through a world of books." But if "travel itself is ironic," why should the untraveled Mandeville be the first to notice it? And to what extent do the pilgrimage and missionary accounts betray any sense of expectations surprised? (William of Rubruck does in fact convey that sense: his eye was keen and his disillusionment deep. But his tone is anomalous within the genre up to this point.) The continued and central presence of the marvels material in accounts of the Far East, and the mutual repetitiveness of the pilgrimage accounts, argues that travel as an experience may have been a quite different thing for Mandeville's predecessors from what it is for Naipaul, Rabin, Chatwin, Theroux, and their confederates. We have observed moments of change in the painfully slow opening up of perception in Western travelers over the millennium between Egeria and Mandeville, but the breaches have been small and induced by the kinds of cataclysmic historical events that require readjustment in even the most rigid dynamic of perception. It is as if the mentality of the West rejected the possibility of real surprise in the experience of travel, and it may be that that rejection was designed to protect an archetypal *imago mundi* of the sort described in chapter 2 and revealed so clearly in medieval world maps. The desire for a world that contains both text and border, Home and Elsewhere, mundane and sacred territory, and that contains them as somehow polar and unmixed, opposed and absolute, is a desire served admirably by the imperturbable repetitions of Pliny and Solinus and the ethnographic bareness that preceded Mandeville.[29]

It may also be that the world's love-hate relationship with the *Travels* stems from the irony with which it subverts the image of that desire. Perhaps Mandeville was hailed as a liar because his ultimately round and human world was too mixed and contingent to satisfy the requirements of the ancient dream, and perhaps he was loved and believed because it was getting to be time for one of those brief periods of wakefulness in which history prods itself into continuing.

The chapters themselves may seem, to modern eyes, to have been constructed "dream-wise." This is partly the result of the book's category-shattering scope: it is not the record of a journey (except intermittently), nor is it the strict verbal map Burchard had produced, nor is it focused by a purely spiritual or purely mercantile interest in one specific territory. It is determined to be encyclopedic, but nothing like the modern encyclopedia's formal set of subheadings has yet been generated, and what has is insufficient to the task at hand. The bonds between the pieces of data conveyed in any one chapter are usually eidetic, contributing enormously to our overall sense of being presented with an "image of truth"—an image that, qua image, is more amenable to interpretation than simple belief.

Chapter 5, untitled in the Cotton manuscript, seems at first glance a mere grabbag of information in which the reader's consciousness is asked to skip not only from topic to topic, but from mode to mode—from fable to history to flat topographical description—without transitions. And yet there is clearly something like the "concatenation" we saw in *Wonders* at work here, and something more. The chapter begins with the tale of a fallen city, "Cathaillye"—"lost thorgh folye of a ʒonge man." When this young man's paramour died, he climbed down into her marble tomb and "lay be hire," from which union was begotten a hideous adder "the whiche als swithe fleigh aboute the cytee & the contree & sone after the cytee sank down." Besides rearranging the motifs of the previous chapter's tale (of a serpent-woman under Diana's curse who can only be freed of her monstrous form by the kiss of a knight), this story leads us on to a number of other linked images.

"In the castell of amoure lyth the body of Seynt Hyllarie & men kepen it right worschipfully." "In Cipre is the manere of lordes & all othere men all to eten on the erthe, for thei make dyches in the erthe all aboute in the hall depe to the knee and thei do paue hem." "And there is the welle of the whiche holy writte speketh offe & seythe: FONS ORTORUM & PUTEUS AQUARUM VIUENCIUM, that is to seye the welle of gardyns and the dych of lyuinge waters. In this cytee of Thire seyde the womman to oure lord: BEATUS VENTER QUI TE PORTUIT & UBERA QUE SUCCISTI, that is to seye: Blessed be the body that the baar & the pappes that thou sowkedest. And there oure lord forʒaf the womman of Chananee

hire synnes." Then, in connection with the "port Jaff," we hear about Noah's Flood, and the rock where "Andromade a gret Geaunt was bounden & put in prisoun before Noes flode." Then by the river of Belon (at the site of an ancient glassworks sometimes mentioned by pilgrims on account of its glassy sand) we have the bottomless sea of "gravel schynynge brighte" which, like the "dych of lyuynge watres" or "the pappes that thou sowkedest," "be neuere so meche taken awey there of on the day at morwe it is as full aʒen as euere it was." Finally we are reminded of the story of the "tresoun of Delida" and Sampson's entombment of himself, "his paramour," and the Philistines in their "gret halle whan thei were at mete." We are led out of this chapter by way of a "wyldernesse and desert" where "all weys men fynden god jnnes & all that hem nedeth of vytaylle" (v, 16-20).

Although other images are scattered throughout which bear superficial connections to one or another of these cited above, the major cluster is tomb/ditch/pit/well/breast/flood: earth and water, body and spirit, fecundity and carnality and necrophilia. Paradox is the major arrangement: the sea of gravel, the desert full of "vytaylles," impregnation of a dead body, entombment in the dining hall, the saint's body kept "ryght worschipfully" in the "castell of amoure."[30]

The East remains a kind of mantra in Mandeville's hands, or a setting for dreams. But this chapter does not dream *about* the East as a simple object of wish-fulfillment fantasy, as Marco Polo's chapters do. These "dream thoughts" are about the body, which is made of earth and eats in tombs, and the spirit, which drinks from a well of living waters, and this world, in which the Word was made flesh, in which women give birth to both beasts and gods, and the desert is full of "vytaylles" (for those who know where to look). The East remains a convenient screen for imaginative projection, as it was for earlier pilgrims and merchants of our acquaintance. But even this isolated chapter suggests that what is being projected is not so much a starved or hidden aspect of a culture's personality as it is a whole self. The issues that unify the concatenations are not necessarily galvanized by concentration on the East, Elsewhere, the Other World—they unify the *Vita nuova,* the *Roman de la rose,* the *Canterbury Tales,* the great poems and fictions of the later Middle Ages.

This is not to suggest that the overt charm of Mandeville's opus is not what it has always seemed to be. It is a book of marvels, it is a book about Elsewhere, its atmosphere is both grotesque and otherworldly. Overtly, it is a fitting culmination to a tradition reaching back to the *Odyssey* (and lingering into our time in Alexandra David-Neel's *Magic and Mystery in Tibet*).[31] And without this tradition (and the scarcity of data that underlies it) Mandeville would not have had the freedom to put his pieces together "dreamwise," nor to exploit in us the freedom of fictional contemplation. It is a moment of deeper change I am charting here, a change of attitude and understanding, clothed in the conventions and formulas and even the very words of what came before it. Mandeville is not averse to supplying his readers with a khan every bit as splendid as Marco's or Odoric's, and he is more willing than Marco to supply marvelous beasts and plants, more willing than Odoric to supply monsters. As usual, the farther we penetrate into the East, the weirder it gets, and the comparisons and similes used to help us visualize what we hear about have the usual alienating effect. Every ripple on the surface of this stream is familiar; it is the current that has shifted.

Some attention to the ways in which Mandeville fiddles with Odoric's account of the Far East, even when he is most clearly following it, will be revealing in the latter regard. Many of these instances have been pointed out before, by stern editors and admiring critics, usually as evidence of mendacity or broadmindedness in the author (which they are). Perhaps most problematic for current critics is Mandeville's inclusion of almost the whole gamut of the Plinian monstrous races at precisely that point in Odoric's account of "the gret yle that is clept DONDUN" where the friar disdains to report marvels that no one could believe. As this seems an obstacle to the prevailing desire to see Mandeville as enlightened beyond his era and a believer in natural law as geographically universal, Bennett says: "It is highly improbable that he believed at all in the unnatural marvels which he retold from Odoric and Solinus and the *Letter of Prester John*" (*Rediscovery of Mandeville,* 36). Moseley goes even further, into flat-out untruth: "Comparison of **Mandeville's Travels** with its sources shows that the author deliberately edited so as to *reduce* the incidence of 'wonders'" ("Metamorphosis of Mandeville," 6). Hamelius, in his notes to chapter 23, refers at this juncture to Mandeville's "licentious imagination" (**Mandeville's Travels,** 2: 110).

But Mandeville's context is at every point denser, richer, more constraining than has been possible in previous, less nearly metaphysical works. He may or may not believe in the monstrosities (or he may have an apprehension of them conforming to their previously discussed status as part fact/part text). What matters more is that they operate in the service of some truths unfolding beneath the surface of their chapter. This is the chapter of the Cornucopia, the prelude to the long, conventionally superlative treatment of the khan—a locus for the theme of plenitude since Marco Polo's initial swoon.[32]

The diversity and plenitude of human forms and customs manifested in the list of mostly monstrous races are followed immediately by a discussion of "Mancy": "And it is the beste lond & on the fairest that may ben

in all the world, and the most delectable & and the most plentifous of all godes that is in power of man. . . . And there is more plentee of peple there than in ony other partie of ynde. . . . In that contree is no nedy man ne non that goth beggynge" (XXIII, 135). And so on. Then we come to the idols (stripped of Odoric's gleeful hooting at the way they receive only the smoke of sacrifices while the worshipers get the meat), the abbey where the monks feed "Apes, Marmozettes Babewynes & many other dyuerse bestes," and, at the gateway of "the gret Chans" domain, the "PIGMEYES."

Mandeville in this chapter compresses into smaller compass and neater geographical organization a particularly meandering and xenophobic stretch of Odoric's text, as well as adding from other sources the account of the Plinian races.[33] His most obvious amplifications and changes are in the direction of tolerance and understanding: he omits to tell us, as Odoric did not, that DONDUN means "unclean" or that the cannibalistic funeral rite of its people is "foul," and he leaves out the anecdote of Odoric's berating them over it. In place of Odoric's dogmatic conversation with the monks who feed apes, about whether or not the apes are reincarnated men, Mandeville questions, with far more humanity, the justice of feeding animals instead of the poor: "And their answerde me & seyde that thei hadde no pore man among hem in that contree" (XXIII, 137). From one sentence in Odoric—"But these pygmies have rational souls like ourselves" ("habent autem animam rationalem sicut nos"; 316)—he develops a whole cultural being for the pygmies, and one that includes an irony so pungent in relation to Odoric that one must wonder if Mandeville's text is at open war with its source: "This lityll folk nouther labouren in londes ne in vynes but thei han grete men amonges hem of our stature that tylen the lond & labouren amonges the vynes for hem. And of tho men of oure stature han thei als grete skorn & wonder as we wolde haue among us of geauntes ʒif thei weren amonges us" (XXIII, 138).[34] Touché!

But Mandeville's understanding goes beyond the rejection of Odoric's offensive xenophobia. He has explained idol worship in a previous chapter, and the difference between idols and *simulacra:* "For symulacres ben ymages made after lykness of men or wommen or of the sonne or of the mone or of ony best or of ony kyndely thing, & ydoles is an ymage made of lewed will of man that man may not fynden among kyndely thinges" (XIX, 109). He (or else a scribal interpolator) has also told us what a monster is: "a thing difformed aʒen kynde bothe of man or of best" (VII, 30). Here we find idols and monsters in the same chapter, a chapter suffused with a spirit of toleration and organized around the theme of plenitude. Mandeville's examples of idols given in the earlier chapter include "an ymage that hath jiii hedes" and one that is "of an ox the on parte & the other halfondell of a man." Among the monsters in chapter 23 we find "folk that han non hedes" and "folk that han hors feet." (See fig. 6 for an illustration of monsters worshiping an idol.) He has been kind toward the idol worshipers, and kind toward Pliny and Solinus, and made an astonishing identification of our emotions with those of the pygmies. Is it too much to claim for this characteristically ironic and generous sensibility that he has sensed a strain of idol worship in the West's tenacious attachment to its geographically displaced monsters, and forgiven it in the same breath with Odoric's "idolators" (who become, in Mandeville's words, "gode religious men after here feyth & lawe"; XXIII, 137)?

At any rate, the monsters were a part of his "data,' part of the total but till now fragmented image of the world he had set out to make coherent and redemptively significant. He has included them in such a place that certain of his readers' braces must relax. If there are monsters, then the idols that resemble them are no worse than the benign *simulacra*. If there are not, then our belief in them is little better than the "ymages" of the gently tolerated idolators. And whether God's creation or our own, they form part of the plenitude of this "fairest . . . & most delectable" of lands. "And whoso that wole may leve me ʒif he woll, And whoso will not may leve also."

One notable aspect of the pageant of monsters in Mandeville is its iconographic mode of presentation— notable in that this is *not* usually Mandeville's way. Perhaps he has fooled Moseley into believing that he edited "so as to reduce the incidence of monsters" by his more characteristic amplitude. Scorning as he does, with effects already discussed, the conventional strategies of inducing belief in his readers (truth claims, refusal to report what will be too hard to credit, reliance on the *auctoritas* of his sources), he is forced to rely on a kind of proto-verisimilitude. One of his many techniques (among which might be numbered his growing presence as an actor on the scene, in the second and more incredible part of the book) is the amplification of his inherited iconographic images. The sheer length of his treatment of the pygmies, as compared to Odoric's, makes them more vivid and thus "realer" to the imagination. Of course this method extends and emphasizes the marvels, but it also rationalizes them and "naturalizes" them. Odoric's pygmies are conveyed in the usual fashion: in five sentences, five disconnected features of their physical nature, habitat, and custom are listed, and then we are off to another topic. Mandeville, while exaggerating one marvelous aspect— Odoric's pygmies procreate at age five, Mandeville's "whan they ben half ʒere of age"—invents another marvelous aspect to rationalize the first: "thei lyuen not but .vi ʒeer or .vij at the moste." Mandeville's pygmies are not only more detailed, their details complement and make sense of one another. In the

world of nature as it operates in England, life span and body size are logically related. So they must be in "the lond of PIGMANS."[35]

It is a feature of the iconographic mode that its selectivity of detail can make a marvel out of anything unfamiliar.[36] It is also the case that a detailed enough description, provided there be usefully interrelated categories in which to anchor the details, can demystify a marvel, unfold the data hidden within. Mandeville's unusually long descriptions are part of a literary step forward toward the establishment of a scientifically usable fund of information. The other major steps— development of the "scientific method" and taxonomies—were the task of natural philosophy. Slow refinements in the rhetorical conventions of travel literature were to prove useful to the philosophers in their task.

But so far as he is concerned, Mandeville's method is a literary device in the service of imaginative, not philosophical, truth. Another of his devices for establishing verisimilitude is to claim that he has *not* been somewhere, *not* seen something with his own eyes, and cannot necessarily vouch for the truth of other men's reports. This device is put to particularly poignant use at the end of part 2, when after transforming Odoric's final story, of a perilous valley fraught with devils (Mandeville calls it "on of the entrees of helle"), geographical logic leads him to "paradys terrestre . . . towardes the EST at the begynnynge of the erthe" (XXXIV, 202).

Odoric's narrative ends with the Vale Perilous, from which he "came forth scathless" because he was "a baptized and holy man" (*Cathay,* 262-66). His account is almost criminally self-congratulatory; it is tempting to see behind Mandeville's inclusion of a complementary sacred place, unvisited because "I was not worthi," an intentional corrective. But there are a number of broader considerations. Mandeville has aimed for an unprecedented totality in his coverage of the lands beyond, and to leave out the Earthly Paradise would be to place a black hole on the *mappa mundi*. On the other hand, he is writing in a cultural climate that considers *curiositas* a sin and the limiting of intellectual greed a matter of moral propriety.[37] There is an angel at the gate of paradise with a sword of flame: what better place to be brought up short? The traditional mode of presentation for paradises is what Patch calls the "negative description": it is appropriate to the increasingly narrative method of the ***Travels*** at this point that "paradys terrestre" be present as a place not visited.[38]

But present it must be, as a redemptive complement to the "entree of helle," as the ironically located birthplace of the human race (the point furthest from what we now call Home), as the primitive and original place in which Mandeville's backward journey through historical time (elegantly traced by Donald Howard) can find a fitting climax.[39]

And as Christian Zacher points out, "for Mandeville the moon-driven traveler, the earthly paradise—which 'toucheth nygh to the cercle of the mone, there as the mone maketh hire torn' . . . —has turned out to be his true destination" (*Curiosity and Pilgrimage,* 151). Mandeville has earlier pinned his predilection for travel on his national origin and its climatic influence: "For in our contrey wee ben in the seuenthe clymat that is of the mone. And the mone is of lyghtly mevynge & the mone is planete of weye. And for that skyll it ʒeueth vs will of kynde for to meve lyghtly & for to go dyuerse weyes & to sechen strange thinges & other dyuersities of the world, For the mone envyrouneth the erthe more hastyly than ony other planete" (XIX, 108). How right and lovely that his destination should be paradise, like that of the pilgrims before him, and like theirs one he cannot enter. And how true to what appears to be an essential paradox of travel—that "you can't get there from here" (or, as Joyce puts it in *Ulysses,* "the longest way round is the shortest way home").

Elsewhere has been moving steadily East for some time, as Home has expanded its borders. It was Mandeville's last move to place it ultimately out of man's reach, beyond the "derke Regyoun" (descended from Marco's Russian "Land of Darkness") on the "highest place of erthe" and "enclosed all aboute with a wall." The Elsewhere of sub- or supernature, into which the West had so long projected the other halves of its divided self, is *not* accessible to the earthly traveler, and Mandeville has rendered the places and peoples that once belonged to it as "part of nature, part of us." He has rolled all that truly Otherworldly sweetness up into one ball and perched it at "the begynnynge of the erthe," beyond a veil of darkness, at the place where time began for us, and all our woe—at the place and moment of our birth.

It is precisely at this point that he reminds us of the "roundeness of the erthe, of the whiche I haue towched to you of before." The inaccessible paradys terrestre is really only temporally "at the begynnynge of the erthe." For "that is not that EST that we clepe oure EST on this half, where the sonne riseth to us, for whanne the sonne is EST in tho partyes toward paradys terrestre, it is thanne mydnyght in oure parties on this half for the roundeness of the erthe."

It is in his avoidance of the absolute and its closure that Mandeville is perhaps most new. His paradise is many things, including—figuratively—his destination. But it is not the end, nor even the end of the book. Geography, shapeless and real, must here part company with the shapely hierarchy of the theological map. The center of a spherical world cannot be found on its surface, and the edge cannot be found at all. Mandeville has used his geography symbolically, as did the makers of the *mappae mundi* and the biblical commentaries. But his method is an inversion of theirs: they imagined a geography expressive of preordained ideas. He shaped ideas out of the geography of the real.

Mandeville the artist was indeed "ahead of his time," ahead, as good artists are, of any time. The climate and conditions of his moment permitted him his emotional and intellectual lucidity; the quasi-scientific, quasi-imaginative status of his genre permitted his balancing act with two kinds of truth. But as the later history of his book reveals, he was soon to be romanticized and literalized, as the intellectual realms that coalesced in the ***Travels*** began to draw apart. Columbus may have been both his best and worst reader, who sailed West over "the roundeness of the erthe" to reach, not America, but that high place from which "the iiij flodes" flow. And all our woe.

Notes

[1] Josephine Waters Bennett lists about 250 surviving manuscripts in Appendix 1 of *The Rediscovery of Sir John Mandeville.* The book was first printed in 1470, one of the earliest of all printed books. According to George Sarton (in "The Scientific Literature Transmitted through the Incunabula"), Mandeville is the eighth most popular author on Arnold Kleb's list of the incunabula; none of the leading seven is a medieval prose writer.

[2] All quotations from Fulcher will be cited, by volume and chapter numbers, from Frances Rita Ryan's translation, *A History of the Expedition to Jerusalem.* Ryan's translation is based on Heinrich Hagenmeyer's definitive text, *Fulcheri Carnotensis historia Hierosolymitana* (1913).

[3] "Et cil s'en rala a grant partie de la gent l'empereor Henri; et trova que li chastiaus ere abutez et ferma et horda le moutier Sainte Sophye, qui mult ere halz et biels, et retint iqui endroit la guerre."

[4] This and all further quotations are indicated by chapter and page number, and are taken from the Early English Text Society edition of Hamelius (1919). This is a documentary edition of MS Cotton Titus Cxvi. Although the Cotton manuscript is not the version Hakluyt disseminated so importantly in the first edition of his *Voyages,* and in fact did not reach print until 1725, I have chosen it as my chief text of the *Travels* because it is closer to the French original than the once prominent "Defective Version," and I am as much interested in the author's conscious artistry as in the wider influence of the work in its many abridged versions. References to Hamelius's notes will be cited by volume and page number of the EETS edition.

[5] The terms of Joseph Campbell's Jungian analysis of what he calls the "monomyth" of the heroic journey (in *The Hero with a Thousand Faces*) can be applied with some usefulness to accounts of actual travel to the East and to the New World, although Campbell is talking about myths, folktales, and dreams. The connection lies in the fact that the travelers whose accounts we are looking at had themselves a mythic understanding of their activity: they were on pilgrimage to the World Navel, or, in going farther East or sailing to the New World, they were leaving the *oikumene* behind them and entering "a dream landscape of curiously fluid and ambiguous forms."

[6] Shortly after the fall of Acre in 1291, the Persian khan Oljaitu converted to Islam. The Mongols in Persia, Russia, and Turkestan were quickly absorbed into the Moslem cultures around them, and relations with the West broke down. A Christian mission remained in China, but fell with the fall of the Mongols there: the last Western missionary, John of Marignolli, left China in 1347, and the Christians were expelled in 1369 by Chinese nationalists.

[7] Hakluyt's successor, Samuel Purchas, admits that he "smell[s] a Friars (Lyars) hand in this," but hints that it was Odoric—the real traveler from whom Mandeville adapted much of the second half of his book—who later "stuffed" it full of "Fables" (Purchas, *Purchas His Pilgrimes,* 11:363-64). For the story of Ingram see Adams, *Travelers and Travel Liars,* 133-34.

[8] The credit for first bringing to light the extent of Mandeville's plagiarisms belongs to two nineteenth-century scholars: Albert Bovenschen, whose dissertation "Die Quellen fur die Reisebschreibung des Johann von Mandeville" was published in Berlin in 1888, and Sir George Warner, who edited the Egerton manuscript for the Roxburghe Club in 1889. It is difficult to believe that some of this was not noticed far earlier, as the *Travels* was often bound in manuscripts together with some of its sources. (See Bennett, *Rediscovery of Sir John Mandeville,* Appendix 1.)

[9] Iain Higgins (currently working at Harvard University on a dissertation about *Mandeville's Travels*) has suggested that I qualify my use of the word *parody* in connection with the *Travels,* since current usage restricts its meaning to a kind of stylistic joke. The word in its older, etymological, sense suggests a text that stands alongside other texts in critical or ironic imitation of them, and it is in that sense that the *Travels* is parodic. Higgins's wide-ranging and sensitive study of the *Travels* did not reach my attention until this book was in press; it will be a valuable addition to Mandeville scholarship.

[10] Section 40, according to Bernard, is one of many in the work stolen from the thirteenth-century account of Phillipus Brusserius Savonensis.

[11] Pope John XXII's encyclical of 1322 (quoted in chap. 3, n. 20) forbidding the increasingly florid ornamentation of liturgical music, and particularly outraged at the "stuffing" (*inculcare*) that introduced secular texts into the performance of the organa, was effectively an attempt to halt the development of polyphony. And yet the fourteenth century saw the creation not only of the earliest extant polyphonic mass (the "Tournai mass") but also the initial development of the "parody mass," in which all the voice parts were borrowed from another, secular, text. These musical instances of the simultaneous presence of two or more nonconsonant "voices" and/or texts in one extended musical work are nicely analogous to Bakhtin's ideas of "polyglossia" and parody as essential generic features of the novel. Musical and purely verbal "polyglossias" seem parallel in instinct and related as well to the institution of the farce, originally a comic/parodic interlude between acts of a liturgical drama (in fact, the term *farcing* was synonomous as a musical—and culinary—term with *stuffing*). That the structure of Mandeville's book can be illuminated by these terms, in its weaving together of the anecdotes and the very words of such disparate texts as Marco Polo's, Wilhem von Boldensil's, Odoric of Pordenone's, and Vincent of Beauvais's encyclopedias will soon be clear. A feeling for the spirit of polyphony is useful for a full appreciation of Mandeville's art, and a combined analysis of the terms *polyphony* and *polyglossia* might even unearth some suggestive common denominator in the literary and muscial developments of the later Middle Ages.

[12] Olschki observes that Marco Polo tends to push the most extravagant of his descriptions of Oriental splendor into Japan, the Utter East that he has not himself visited: "It is only beyond the boundaries of Cathay that he mentions gold for the first time—in order to evoke the riches of Japan, where he had never set foot" (*Marco Polo's Asia,* 60). Something, obviously, has changed by the time Montaigne can say: "Wee neede not goe to cull out miracles and chuse strange difficulties: me seemeth, that amongst those thing we ordinarily see, there are such incomprehensible rarities, as they exceed all difficulties of miracles" (*Essayses,* 2:509). It is this sentiment that most clearly divides the modern novel from the travel narratives in which it incubated. And it is perhaps something more than a felicitous figure for this development in the scope of literary attention that, as the Renaissance drew near, the marvels crept closer to Home. In his article "The Basilisk" (in *Mythical and Fabulous Creatures*), Laurence Breiner notes "the general shift of the basilisk into a domestic *European* monster," and certainly the crown of necromancy was shifting from Chaldea to Britain during this period.

[13] See Donald R. Howard, "The World of *Mandeville's Travels*" (1971); idem, *Writers and Pilgrims: Medieval Pilgrimage Narratives and Their Posterity* (1980); Christian K. Zacher, *Curiosity and Pilgrimage: The Literature of Discovery in Fourteenth-Century England* (1976), chap. 6.

[14] The controversial point is whether the author did indeed, as the English texts claim, English the book himself. Hamelius finds gross errors in the translation from the French that would be hard to account for if the author had done his own translation. On the other hand, Bennett says "enough manuscripts survive to provide ample evidence that the original version was written in the French of Gower and the English court in the mid-fifteenth [*sic*] century, and that it was written, in all probability, in England, since the best texts are written in English hands and are still preserved in English libraries" (*Rediscovery of Sir John Mandeville*, 176). Howard follows her, citing "the greater subtlety of the English diction" ("World of *Mandeville's Travels*," 4n).

[15] Sir Malcolm Letts preceded them in 1949 with his *Sir John Mandeville: The Man and His Book*. But his treatment of the book is a recapitulation of the most amiable of old attitudes and assumptions, and contributed little to its newly elevated status.

[16] "Sex igitur sunt quae in principio cuiusque doctrinalis operis inquirenda sunt, videlicet subiectum, agens, forma, finis, libri titulus, et genus philosophiae" (Toynbee, *Letters of Dante*, x6.119-22).

[17] Cf. Letts: "For most contemporary readers the book had to rest on its own foundations, and as the marvels which Mandeville set down as sober facts can be capped and even outrivalled by other writers—the author of Prester John's letter, for instance—the reading public of the fourteenth and fifteenth centuries probably swallowed their Mandeville whole" (*Sir John Mandeville*, 34).

[18] See Curtius, *European Literature and the Latin Middle Ages*, chap. 12. In this chapter Curtius quotes from the preface of the *Tractatus de reprobatione monarchie composite a Dante* of Guido Vernani: "In the preface Dante is described as a poetizing visionary and verbose sophist, whose delusive pictures lead the reader away from the truths of salvation ('conducit fraudulenter ad interitum salutiferae veritatis')" (221).

[19] See chap. 2, p. 74, for quotation from Hodgen on this point.

[20] According to Friedman, "even the improbable-sounding Hippopodes may have had a basis in fact. A tribe exists today in the Zambesi valley on the border of Southern Rhodesia among whose members 'lobster-claw syndrome' has become an established characteristic. This condition, which is hereditary, possibly via a single mutated gene, results in feet that are divided into two giant toes instead of five smaller ones—'ostrich feet,' as they are described by neighboring tribes. The remoteness of the region and a considerable amount of inbreeding have encouraged the trait" (*Monstrous Races in Medieval Art and Thought*, 24).

[21] See C. W. R. D. Moseley, "The Metamorphosis of Sir John Mandeville," for a full account of the *Travels'* rich and various *Nachleben*. According to Moseley, subsequent "bastard versions" in both prose and verse tended to flatten "the subtleties and curiosities of (Mandeville's) description" (14), concentrating on the *Travels'* information rather than on Mandeville's arrangement or delivery of it, his readers, he concludes, "used it as a storehouse of *exempla* as well as for entertainment and instruction" (10). Although some redactions turned the *Travels* into a "Wonderbook," real "wonders" were also retained or added, such as descriptions of the khan's court or, in the "Metrical Version," of Rome.

[22] . . . The process of scribal transmission can of course create new marvels as well, in the "curiously fluid and ambiguous" context of accounts of the East. Paul Gibb gives an example of a scribally created bird-centaur in his introduction to *Wonders of the East*: "Loose punctuation, together with the curiously inverted *ut aves leni voce*, 'with a soft voice like birds,' seems to have caused *ut aves* to be reinterpreted as part of the preceding clause in line 17:3, resulting in the untenable corruption *longis cruribus ut aves*, 'with long legs like birds'—a most unusual way of describing Centaurs" (23).

[23] See Fulcher, *History of the Expedition to Jerusalem*, 1.i-v; Burchard of Mt. Sion, *Description of the Holy Land*, 1-3; and Ludolph von Suchem, *Description of the Holy Land*, 3.

[24] "The cross on the orb was blown down in 1317. Boldensele and Bondelmonti (*Liber insularum Archipelagi*, ed. 1824, p. 122) saw the apple in its place. John of Hildesheim . . . also describes the statue as holding its orb and threatening the Saracens in the East with its right hand" (Hamelius, *Mandeville's Travels*, 2:25).

[25] Next to Odoric of Pordenone's name in the index to the eighteenth-century *Astley's Voyages* the editor has written "A great Liar." The eighteenth century in England was the inheritor of the Royal Society's "correspondence instructions" to travelers, and the voluminous travel literature it produced has erected a monolithic norm of "objectivity" behind which it is difficult to see how serious and authentic the reports of earlier travelers might be. The combined amplitude and im-

personality of the eighteenth-century observer's style and its serene assumption that objectivity is possible in the situation of the traveler abroad have reached their own climax in the emergence of the modern "foreign correspondent." The temptation to believe in the self-supposed transparency of such reportage can be overcome by reading an article or two from a Chinese newspaper's coverage of the day's events in Washington.

[26] See Curtius, *European Literature and the Latin Middle Ages,* chap. 12, especially sec. 3.

[27] A scholarly translation of Odoric is available, with copious notes and a Latin and an Old Italian text appended, in volume 2 of Sir Henry Yule's compendium *Cathay and the Way Thither.* Quotations from Odoric will be taken from this edition, cited by chapter number. There is no English translation of William of Boldensil. The most recent printed edition is that of C. L. Grotefend, "Itinerarium Guilielmi de Boldensele," in *Zeitschrift des Historischen Vereins für Niedersachsen* (1852).

[28] As Percy Adams rightly pointed out in a note on the manuscript of this book, "every father has a grandfather." But for the purpose of identifying junctures in the *longue durée,* it is convenient to characterize as a father one who not only broke radically with his genre's stance and structure as they prevailed before him, but who, in so doing, redefined for others that genre's potential. No writer really fathers (or mothers) anything but his own book, but Mandeville is more than just an example of a new trend. His name came to signify "traveler" (as well as "liar") for European culture.

[29] For all its smug "objectivity," the eighteenth century, at least in England, showed signs of a similar stasis in the *imago mundi* preserved by its travel literature. The Grand Tour (primary object of this literature) became so codified, and the writer so fearful of egotism, that it became possible once again to plagiarize seamlessly. (See Adams, *Travelers and Travel Liars,* especially chap. 8, "Peculiar Plagiarisms.") The link between the genre and its essential subject matter is tight enough that it comes to seem part of the travel writer's task to preserve certain root images or necessary fictions, as much as to extend the horizon or intimacy of our knowledge. Annotation of the beloved world image of the English eighteenth century is outside the scope of this book: some of its outline can be gleaned from Charles L. Batten, Jr.'s *Pleasurable Instruction: Form and Convention in Eighteenth-Century Travel Literature.*

[30] Saint Hilarion, for whose life our primary source is Saint Jerome, was a desertdwelling ascetic who lived on fifteen figs a day for years. Inconveniently popular,

especially with women, he was driven from place to place around the Mediterranean in search of solitude. His miracles included stopping a tidal wave, bringing rain to the desert, and making a barren woman fruitful (by supernatural means). In short, his *vita* displays the same themes as Mandeville's chapter, arranged in similar paradoxes.

[31] As Tibet has remained artifically unreachable into modern times, books about it are written under conditions that in some ways simulate those of the travel writers of antiquity and the Middle Ages. David-Neel, a relatively cool-minded Western scholar of Buddhism, went to Tibet to obtain precisely the sorts of information Hodgen berates the medieval writers for not seeking and not receiving. But the title of her book, *Magic and Mystery in Tibet,* is a clue to the kind of information it contains—in large part what Hodgen calls "the abnormal, the monstrous, the trivial." The proportion of lascivious anecdote is as high as in Marco's treatment of Tibetan mores, and her fascination with necromancy as intense as Odoric's, if less horrified. (And like Marco, Odoric, and Mandeville, she is a lot of fun to read.)

[32] The cornucopia is a feature equally of literal and imaginative journey tales—it represents an expectation of the psyche. In his study of the paradises and hells of both folk and "serious" literature, *The Other World,* Howard Patch documents the motif of abundances as essential to the imagination of paradise—abundances of trees, of birds, of colors, of gems, of food, and often of women. (Marco Polo's claim that twenty-thousand prostitutes were living on the outskirts of one of the khan's cities for the convenience "of the foreigners" is a good instance of the last.)

Since Joseph Campbell is ultimately interested in the progress and liberation of the individual human psyche, he concentrates on cornucopian events at the climax of the Hero's journey, rather than on places. In this connection he quotes from the *Jataka* a description of the state of the universe after the Buddha reaches enlightenment under the Bo tree: "Throughout the ten thousand worlds the flowering trees bloomed; the fruit trees were weighed down by the burden of their fruit; trunklotuses bloomed on the trunks of trees; branch-lotuses on the branches of trees; vine-lotuses on the vines; hanging lotuses in the sky; and stalk-lotuses burst through the rocks and came up by sevens" (192).

Mandeville, like Marco before him, scatters the cornucopian largesse all across his East—here a "land of Feminye," there a "welle of ʒouthe"—but as in Marco's book, the khan is its magnetic center. The New World voyagers were perhaps even more obsessed with this image: the cornucopia has become the symbol of the first specifically American holiday, and even before they landed, sailors could smell it in the shore breeze off Roanoke.

[33] See Odoric, *Travels,* chaps. 26-35.

[34] The predictable fact that manuscripts of Mandeville and Odoric were often bound together supports the possibility of their being read in this relation accurately. So too does Mandeville's most whimsical bit of play with Odoric's text, completely lost on anyone not familiar with Odoric: in the episode of the Vale Perilous, a personal anecdote stolen from Odoric, Mandeville mentions that his company for this adventure included two "worthi men Frere Menoures, that weren of lombardye that seyden that ȝif ony mon wolde entren, thei wolde gon in with us" (XXXII, 188). Odoric was a Minorite friar from Lombardy who traveled with a colleague. But in Odoric's self-serving version, "I hesitated not to go in that I might see once for all what the matter was" ("Et quamquam in illa sic omnes moriantur, tamen volui intrare ut viderem finaliter quid hoc esset"; *Cathay,* 2:332).

[35] Mandeville's sense of humor was basically sneaky. Although at first glance his amplification of Odoric has the effect of rationalizing the marvel, he has in part remarvelized the PIGMANS in the same breath. Now that they live only to the age of six or seven, their giving birth at six months is proportionately just as strange as Odoric's pigmies giving birth at five years old.

[36] The Lilliputians' report on the contents of Gulliver's pockets is an instructive inversion of the traveler's perspective. It parodies the results to be expected from the Royal Society's "correspondence instructions" to the travelers of the new scientific age by producing, via the new method, the same old marvel material—out of a pocket watch: "And we conjecture it is either some unknown Animal, or the God he worships" (Swift, *Gulliver's Travels,* 18).

[37] See Zacher, *Curiosity and Pilgrimage,* chap. 2.

[38] See Patch, *Other World,* 12-13.

[39] "The second half of the book, from chapter 16 on, is a voyage into the Orient, but it is integrated with the first part in a remarkable way and differs from other members of its genre precisely because it is cast in the form of a quasi- or anti-pilgrimage through a state of nature. We pass beyond the land of Prester John to a shrine one may not enter: 'Paradise Terrestre, where that Adam our foremost father and Eve were put that dwelled there but little while, and that is towards the east at the beginning of the earth' (33). The pilgrimage to Jerusalem was a journey backward in time: one saw the relics of New and Old Testament times, what the Middle Ages would have called the Age of Grace and the Age of Law (that is, the law of Moses). Mandeville keeps this reverse order: in the second part we learn that Noah's ship is on Mt. Ararat; that each of Noah's sons inhabited one of the three continents, Asia, Africa, Europe; that the round earth was wasted by Noah's flood; that there is a lake in Ceylon where Adam and Eve wept a hundred years. In this world of the distant past lies the dispersal of individuals, peoples, and languages; at the root of all, the expulsion from Paradise. We pass through the leavings of the *first* age of the world, the age before the law of Moses, the Age of Nature" (Howard, *Writers and Pilgrims,* 272).

FURTHER READING

Criticism

Bennett, Josephine Waters. "The Woodcut Illustrations in the English Editions of *Mandeville's Travels.*" *The Papers of the Bibliographical Society of America* 47 (1953): 59-69.

  Discusses the origins of the woodcuts used first in a German and later in English editions of *Mandeville's Travels.*

Burnett, Charles, and Patrick Gautier Dalché. "Attitudes Towards the Mongols in Medieval Literature: The XXII Kings of Gog and Magog from the Court of Frederick II to Jean De Mandeville." *Viator: Medieval and Renaissance Studies* 22 (1991): 153-67.

  Examines the history and sources of a text titled the *Mirabilia mundi,* which links the races of Gog and Magog to the Mongols, and argues that the *Mirabilia mundi* was one of Mandeville's sources.

Cameron, Kenneth Walter. "A Discovery in *John De Mandevilles.*" *Speculeum* 11, No. 3 (July 1936): 351-59.

  Provides an annotated list of people who might have been the author of *Mandeville's Travels.*

Hamelius, P. An Introduction to *Mandeville's Travels,* by Sir John Mandeville, pp. 1-22. London: Oxford University Press, 1961.

  Argues that Jean d'Ourtemeuse, author of *Mirror of Histories,* was the author of *Mandeville's Travels* and discusses the work's political significance.

Howard, Donald R. "The World of Mandeville's Travels." *The Yearbook in English Studies* 1 (1971): 1-17.

  Discusses *Mandeville's Travels* within the context of the Middle Ages and characterizes Mandeville as a scholar and encyclopedist who mastered a large amount of written material and presented it in a thoughtful manner.

Jackson, Isaac. "Who Was Sir John Mandeville? A Fresh Clue." *Modern Language Review* 23, No. 4 (October

1928): 466-68.
Suggests that Mandeville was an Englishman living in Ireland who fled to France after murdering a fellow English nobleman.

Metlitzki, Dorothee. "The Voyages and Travels of Sir John Mandeville." In *The Matter of Araby in Medieval England*, Yale University Press, 1977, pp. 220-39.
Focuses on Mandeville's account of the Assassins and on his descriptions of Muslim customs and manners.

Moseley, C. W. R. D. "Chaucer, Sir John Mandeville, and the Alliterative Revival: A Hypothesis Concerning Relationships." *Modern Philology* 72, No. 2 (November 1974): 182-84.
Argues that Chaucer's work reveals a debt to Mandeville.

————. "The Metamorphoses of Sir John Mandeville." *The Yearbook of English Studies* 4 (1974): 5-25.
Comments on some of the new versions of *Mandeville's Travels* that appeared in England between 1350 and 1750, noting how the changes made in each new presentation reflected the editor's interests and prejudices.

Seymour, M. C. "The Scribal Tradition of Mandeville's *Travels*: The Insular Version." *Scriptorium* 18, No. 1 (1964): 34-48.
Discusses the history of "The Insular Version" of *Mandeville's Travels*. Seymour contends that this version, written in England, is one of the three principal derivitives of the original text.

————. *Sir John Mandeville*. Aldershot, England: Variorum, 1993, 60 p.
Suggests that the author of *Mandeville's Travels* was Jean le Long, a Benedictine monk who lived in northern France.

Additional coverage of Mandeville's life and career is contained in the following source published by Gale Research: *Dictionary of Literary Biography*, Vol. 146.

Origen

c. 185-*c.* 254

Greek theologian.

INTRODUCTION

Considered the father of dogmatic theology, Origen, with the exception of St. Augustine, was the most distinguished and influential theologian of the ancient Church. Origen was critical in the development and final solidification of Christian dogma during the fourth and fifth centuries. This development began two generations before Origen, with Justin, Clement, and others, in an attempt to find an intellectual expression and philosophical basis for the Christian faith. By proclaiming the reconciliation of the best of pagan philosophical wisdom and its highest cultural forms with Christian theology and the Gospel, Origen did more than anyone else of his time to convert the East to Christianity. All of his work has as its premise his unshakable conviction that the sacred truths of Christianity are fully compatible with the ideals of antiquity. It was this conviction that led him into theological speculations founded on pagan Greek philosophical ideas. By the seventh century, however, when Christian doctrine had solidified and speculative theology was no longer welcomed, such theory had become inadmissible. Origen formulated his theological thought in opposition to both the pagan Greek philosophers (the Neoplatonists) and the Christian gnostic heresies, but his ideas nevertheless bear the clear impression of both. Despite his salutary influence upon it, Christian dogma had taken a different direction than that in which he had been directing it. This divergence led in the sixth century to the loss of his orthodox standing in the Church due to his neoplatonist and gnostic thought. During his lifetime, however, Origen enjoyed the highest esteem of the Church as a teacher of Scripture, and a great value was placed on his theological acumen, which was sought by both kings and bishops. Alongside his theological contribution, Origen had also laid the foundations for allegorical exegeses of Scripture that lasted long into the Middle Ages and a system of textual criticism of the Old and New Testaments that still commands respect. Origen's reputation has been somewhat restored by modern scholarship inasmuch as his theology and the significance of its historical contribution to the development of Christian thought is better understood.

Biographical Information

Origen was born in Alexandria of Christian parents in about 185. His father, Leonides, gave him a first-class education, for which he showed an early aptitude. This took place in the catachetical school in Alexandria, which was the only institution at that time where Christian boys were given both a Hellenistic and Christian education, being taught both the Greek sciences and the Holy Scriptures. Alexandria, even in the third century, was still the nexus of East and West, the place where Christian and Greek thought could interact. Consequently, in Alexandria, Christian thinking tended to be more speculative and less dogmatic and was strongly influenced by Greek philosophy, which permeated the intellectual climate there. A persecution arose in 202 in which Origen's father was martyred and the family lost its livelihood. In 203, at the age of 18, Origen launched his career as lecturer and writer, when he was made headmaster by the bishop Demetrius of a catechetical school to provide instruction to young inquirers about the Christian faith. As a teacher, he devoted himself to the study of Greek philosophy and the Scriptures, regularly attending the lectures of a famous neoplatonist, Ammonius Saccus, and acquiring a knowledge of Hebrew to study the Old Testament in the original language. Origen lived an extremely ascetic life, practicing at once the principles of Christian ethics and those of the Stoics. Because he taught many young women, tradition tells us, he had himself surgically castrated in order to prevent rumor and maintain his purity. His school was highly regarded, and both pagans and Christians thronged to it. After a few years, giving the beginning pupils over to the instruction of his colleague Heracles and teaching only the advanced students, Origen freed enough time to begin his textual criticism of the Scriptures. At the same time, he began publishing his many commentaries on the Old Testament and his theological investigations. He labored in these pursuits for the next twenty-eight years. During this period, he also traveled throughout the East and parts of the West for scholarly and ecclesiastical purposes and often by invitation to deliver public lectures in the churches. Even as a layman, Origen was often asked by bishops to teach in their churches, as was the custom in the East. But this was not done in Alexandria, because bishop Demetrius strongly disapproved of Origen's teaching in the Church; in fact, he once called Origen back to Palestine from his teaching engagements to demonstrate his disapproval. When Origen was ordained a presbyter by the bishops in Palestine in 230, Demetrius, believing it an infringement on his rights as the bishop of Alexandria, arranged to have him stripped of his presbytership on grounds that he promulgated objectionable doctrine. Under pressure to leave Alexandria, Origen retired from the city in 232 and traveled to Palestine, where his condemnation was not acknowledged. He eventually settled in Caesarea, where he established a school which flourished and soon rivaled the reputation of that which he left in Alexandria. He also continued his indefatigable labors as a teacher and writer of exegesis and theology and traveled on demand, as his reputation in the East as the Church's greatest teacher remained strong. In 250, the Decian persecution broke out, and Origen was arrested, imprisoned, and tortured. Although he survived, his health had been broken. In 254, Origen died at Tyre, where his grave was on display throughout much of the Middle Ages.

Textual History

Eusebius, Origen's fourth-century biographer, collected and edited more than one hundred of Origen's letters in a series of volumes which he deposited in the library at Caesarea, but all have been lost with the exception of two and a few fragments. Origen's *Hexapla*, the culmination of more than twenty years of textual studies on the Old Testament, was probably never fully transcribed, but large sections survive because excerpts were taken from it by various scholars in the fourth century. His exegeses, covering the Old and New Testaments, were divided into *Scholia*, or brief, grammatical annotations; *Homilies*, or exegetical expositions; and *Commentaries*. Few of these are extant in the original Greek text preserved by his great admirer, St. Jerome, but many more survive in Latin translations, although some were greatly abbreviated and paraphrased by his contemporary Rufinus of Aquileia and by St. Jerome to make them more readable and more orthodox. *Against Celsus*, Origen's major apologetical work, has been preserved completely in the original. Of his many dogmatic writings, only *On First Principles* survives, and only in Rufinus' translation, while *Stomata* and tractates on the Resurrection and free will survive only in fragments. *The Exhortation to Martyrdom*, Origen's work of practical theology written during the Caesarean period, still survives intact. During his lifetime, many forgeries and falsifications were made of his works; many of these are still in existence and remain falsely attributed to him. The most noteworthy is the *Dialogues* of a certain Adamantius whose name was also Origen. After Origen's death, the Cappadocian Fathers Gregory of Nazianzus and St. Basil collaborated on an anthology of Origen's works, the *Philocalia*, which has survived in many editions over the centuries.

Major Works

The writings of Origen consist of letters, textual criticism, exegesis, apologetics, and dogmatic and practical theology. The *Hexapla* and the *Tierapla*, Origen's textual criticism, were undertaken to develop a more

reliable text of the Scriptures by resolving the discrepencies between the Septuagent (the Greek text of the Old Testament) and the Hebrew text. In these works, Origen set the Hebrew side by side with the Greek versions, generally correcting the various Greek versions by the Hebrew. Of his exegetical works— the *Scholia*, *Homilies*, and *Commentaries*—those that have drawn the most attention, largely because they alone survive in any quantity, are the homilies on Jeremiah, the books of Moses, Joshua, and Luke, and the commentaries on Matthew, John, and Romans. In evidence in these texts is Origen's method of grammatical analysis and his allegorical method of interpretation, by which he distinguishes a threefold sense of the Scriptures: a grammatico-historical sense, a moral sense, and a spiritual sense, where the true wisdom of the Scripture is discerned. His principal work of apologetics is *Against Celsus*, a late work in which he answers a famous critique and denunciation of Christianity by a well-known Platonist of the second century. *Against Celsus* is invaluable as a historical source of information about the situation of the Church in the second century in that it contains almost the entire text of Celsus's treatise. Origen's answer reveals clearly the syncretic character of his mind, which bore a close affinity to Celsus's in its fundamental philosophical and theological presuppositions. Origen's major work of dogmatic theology, *On First Principles*, is a relatively early work in which he presents an exhaustive and reflective statement of Christian doctrine that is probably the first example of systematic theology. Its dogmatic intent notwithstanding, *On First Principles* is a speculative work, for Origen's idea of the dogmatic was based on the hypothesis that although every Christian is committed to the Faith as it was handed down by the Apostles, the philosophically trained believer is at liberty to speculate as reason and wisdom directs him. Origen's most important devotional work is *Exhortation to Martyrdom*, a late treatise (c. 235) addressed to two friends who had recently suffered severe persecution under Maximinus I.

Critical Reception

Origen was a highly controversial theologian. Even in his lifetime he came under numerous assaults on what already appeared to be his heterodoxy. He was accused of polluting Christianity with the influence of pagan philosophy and of using allegory to introduce gnostic ideas into the Church's understanding of the Scriptures. He was charged with antitrinitarianism, making the Son inferior to the Father, and he was also supposed to have denied the historical fact or significance of the Resurrection, the existence of Hell, and the entire historical foundation of Christianity. Origen, however, always believed he was propounding orthodoxy and contended that faith and philosophical wisdom were strongly connected. Especially in the East, however, Origen was immensely popular as a teacher and biblical scholar. After his death, he had many powerful defenders, among them St. Athanasius and St. Basil, and great admirers like St. Jerome, who, although he admired Origen, could not defend him. Opposition to Origen culminated in the sixth century, when the Byzantine emperor Justinian I and the Fifth Ecumenical Council at Constantinople in 553 denounced him as a heretic. As recently as the nineteenth century, based on Eusebius's critique of Porphyry's attack on Origen, it was believed that there were two Origens: one a pupil of the neoplatonist Ammonius Saccas and the other the Christian theologian. It is now understood that they are the same man. Among modern scholars there remains considerable disagreement over Origen's true relation to Christian orthodoxy. It is now better understood from a historical perspective, however, that the strong philosophical components which composed the framework of Origen's singular thought exerted their powerful influence at a time and place in which Christian dogma had not yet been permanently formulated and speculation on the meaning of the Faith of the Apostles was at a high pitch.

PRINCIPAL WORKS

Exhortatio as martyrdom (edited by P. Koetschau) 1899

Contra Celsum (edited by P. Koetschau) 1899

De oratione (edited by P. Koetschau) 1899

In Joannem (edited by E. Preuschen) 1903

De principiis (edited by P. Koetschau) 1913

In Genesim, Exodum et Leviticum homiliae (edited by W. Baehrens) 1920

In Numeros, Jesu Nave et Judicum homiliae (edited by W. Baehrens) 1921

In Canticum canticorum (edited by W. Baehrens) 1925

In Canticum canticorum homiliae (edited by W. Baehrens) 1925

In Librum Regnorum, Isaiam et Ezekielem homiliae (edited by W. Baehrens) 1925

In Matthaeum (edited by E. Benz and E. Klostermann) 1933, 1935, 1941, 1955

In Lucam homiliae et fragmenta (edited by M. Rauer) 1959 [2nd ed.]

In Jeremiam homiliae (edited by E. Klostermann with corrections by P. Nautin) 1983

PRINCIPAL ENGLISH TRANSLATIONS

De oratione (edited by P. Koetschau) 1899

Vin Canticum canticorum (translated by P. Koetschau) 1899

In Joannem (edited by E. Preuschen) 1903

Jesu Nave et Judicum homiliae (edited by W. Baehrens) 1921

Commentary on the Gospel of Matthew (translated by J. Patrick) [Books II-XIV only]

Selection from the Commentaries and Homilies of Origen (translated by R. Tollinton) 1929

On First Principles (translated by G. W. Butterworth) 1936

Origen's Treatise on Prayer (translated by E. C. Jay) 1954

The Song of Songs, Commentary and Homilies (translated by R. Lawson) 1957

An Exhortation to Martyrdom (translated by R. Greer) 1979

Contra Celsum (translated by H. Chadwick) 1980

Homilies on Genesis and Exodus (translated by R.E. Heine) 1982

Commentary on the Gospel according to John, Books 1-10 (translated by R.E. Heine) 1989

Homilies on Jeremiah and I Samuel 28 (translated by John Clark Smith) 1996

CRITICISM

Eusebius (essay date *c.* 339?)

SOURCE: "Book VI," in *Ecclesiastical History, Vol. II*, n. p., c. 339? pp. 51-95..

[*In this excerpt, Eusebius, the first historian of the Church, defends Origen's reputation as an orthodox theologian against his detractors while reviewing his life and work.*]

And so accurate was the examination that Origen brought to bear upon the divine books, that he even made a thorough study of the Hebrew tongue, and got into his own possession the original writings in the actual Hebrew characters, which were extant among the Jews. Thus, too, he traced the editions of the other translators of the sacred writings besides the Seventy; and besides the beaten track of translations, that of Aquila and Symmachus and Theodotion, he discovered certain others, which were used in turn, which, after lying hidden for a long time, he traced and brought to light, I know not from what recesses. With regard to these, on account of their obscurity (not knowing whose in the world they were) he merely indicated this: that the one he found at Nicopolis, near Actium, and the other in such another place. At any rate, in the Hexapla of the Psalms, after the four well-known editions, he placed beside them not only a fifth but also a sixth and a seventh translation; and in the case of one of these he has indicated again that it was found at Jericho in a jar in the time of Antoninus the son of Severus. All these he brought together, dividing them into clauses and placing them one over against the other, together with the actual Hebrew text; and so he has left us the copies of the **Hexapla**, as it is called. He made a further separate arrangement of the edition of Aquila and Symmachus and Theodotion together with that of the Seventy, in the **Tetrapla**.

Now as regards these same translators it is to be noted that Symmachus was an Ebionite. Those who belong to the heresy of the Ebionites, as it is called, affirm that the Christ was born of Joseph and Mary, and suppose Him to be a mere man, and strongly maintain that the law ought to be kept in a more strictly Jewish fashion, as also we saw somewhere from the foregoing history. And memoirs too of Symmachus are still extant, in which, by his opposition to the Gospel according to Matthew, he seems to hold the above-mentioned heresy. These, along with other interpretations of the Scriptures by Symmachus, Origen indicates that he had received from a certain Juliana, who, he says, inherited in her turn the books from Symmachus himself.

At this time also Ambrose, who held the views of the heresy of Valentinus, was refuted by the truth as presented by Origen, and, as if his mind were illuminated by light, gave his adhesion to the true doctrine as taught by the Church. And many other cultured persons, since Origen's fame was noised abroad everywhere, came to him to make trial of the man's sufficiency in the sacred books. And numbers of the heretics, and not a few of the most distinguished philosophers, gave earnest heed to him, and, one might almost say, were instructed by him in secular philosophy as well as in divine things. For he used to introduce also to the study of philosophy as many as he saw were naturally gifted, imparting geometry and arithmetic and the other preliminary subjects, and then leading them on to the

systems which are found among philosophers, giving a detailed account of their treatises, commenting upon and examining into each, so that the man was proclaimed as a great philosopher even among the Greeks themselves. And many persons also of a more ignorant character he urged to take up the ordinary elementary studies, declaring that they would derive no small advantage from these when they came to examine and study the divine Scriptures. For this reason he deemed especially necessary even for himself a training in secular and philosophic studies.

Now, as witnesses also to his achievements in this direction, we have the Greek philosophers themselves who flourished in his day, in whose treatises we find frequent mention of the man. Sometimes they would dedicate their books to him, sometimes submit their own labours to him for judgement, as to a master. But why need one say this, when even Porphyry, who settled in our day in Sicily, issued treatises against us, attempting in them to slander the sacred Scriptures, and mentioned those who had given their interpretations of them? And since he could not by any means bring any base charge against our opinions, for lack of argument he turned to deride and slander their interpreters also, and among these Origen especially. He says that in his early manhood he had known him; and he tries to slander the man, but unknown to himself really commends him, telling the truth in some cases, where he could not speak otherwise, in others telling lies, where he thought he could escape detection; and at one time accusing him as a Christian, at another describing his devotion to the study of philosophy.

But hear the very words that he uses: "Some, in their eagerness to find an explanation of the wickedness of the Jewish writings rather than give them up, had recourse to interpretations that are incompatible and do not harmonize with what has been written, offering not so much a defence of what was outlandish as commendation and praise of their own work. For they boast that the things said plainly by Moses are riddles, treating them as divine oracles full of hidden mysteries, and bewitching the mental judgement by their own pretentious obscurity; and so they put forward their interpretations."

Then, after other remarks, he says: "But this kind of absurdity must be traced to a man whom I met when I was still quite young, who had a great reputation, and still holds it, because of the writings he has left behind him, I mean Origen, whose fame has been widespread among the teachers of this kind of learning. For this man was a hearer of Ammonius, who had the greatest proficiency in philosophy in our day; and so far as a grasp of knowledge was concerned he owed much to his master, but as regards the right choice in life he took the opposite road to him. For Ammonius was a

Christian, brought up in Christian doctrine by his parents, yet, when he began to think and study philosophy, he immediately changed his way of life conformably to the laws; but Origen, a Greek educated in Greek learning, drove headlong towards barbarian recklessness; and making straight for this he hawked himself and his literary skill about; and while his manner of life was Christian and contrary to the law, in his opinions about material things and the Deity he played the Greek, and introduced Greek ideas into foreign fables. For he was always consorting with Plato, and was conversant with the writings of Numenius and Cronius, Apollophanes and Longinus and Moderatus, Nicomachus and the distinguished men among the Pythagoreans; and he used also the books of Chaeremon the Stoic and Cornutus, from whom he learnt the figurative interpretation, as employed in the Greek mysteries, and applied it to the Jewish writings."

These statements were made by Porphyry in the third treatise of his writings against Christians. And while he tells the truth about the man's training and erudition, he clearly lies (for what is the opponent of Christians not prepared to do?) where he says that Origen came over from the Greeks, and that Ammonius lapsed from a godly life into paganism. For Origen kept safely the Christian teaching which he had from his parents, as the history above made clear; and Ammonius maintained his inspired philosophy pure and unshaken right up to the very end of his life. To this fact the man's works witness to the present day, and the widespread fame that he owes to the writings he left behind him, as, for example, that entitled On the Harmony of Moses and Jesus, and all the other works that are to be found in the possession of lovers of literature.

Let these things be stated to prove at once the false one's calumny and Origen's great knowledge of Greek learning. With regard to such learning also he writes as follows in a certain epistle, defending himself against those who found fault with him for his zeal in that direction: "But as I was devoted to the word, and the fame of our proficiency was spreading abroad, there approached me sometimes heretics, sometimes those conversant with Greek learning, and especially philosophy, and I thought it right to examine both the opinions of the heretics, and also the claim that the philosophers make to speak concerning truth. And in doing this we followed the example of Pantaenus, who, before us, was of assistance to many, and had acquired no small attainments in these matters, and also Heraclas, who now has a seat in the presbytery of the Alexandrians, whom I found with the teacher of philosophy, and who had remained five years with him before I began to attend his lectures. And though he formerly wore ordinary dress, on his teacher's account he put it off and assumed a philosophic garb, which he keeps to this day, all the while studying Greek books as much as possible."

This, indeed, is what he wrote in defence of his Greek training. But at this time, while he was living at Alexandria, one of the military appeared on the scene and delivered letters to Demetrius, the bishop of the community, and to the then governor of the province of Egypt, from the ruler of Arabia, to the intent that he should send Origen with all speed for an interview with him. He duly arrived in Arabia, but soon accomplished the object of his journey thither, and returned again to Alexandria. But after the lapse of some time no small warfare broke out again in the city, and leaving Alexandria secretly he went to Palestine and abode at Caesarea. And although he had not yet received ordination to the presbyterate, the bishops there requested him to discourse and expound the divine Scriptures publicly in the church. That this is so is clear from what Alexander, the bishop of Jerusalem, and Theoctistus, the bishop of Caesarea, write with reference to Demetrius. They make their defence somewhat as follows: "And he added to his letter that such a thing had never been heard of, nor taken place hitherto, that laymen should preach in the presence of bishops; though I do not know how he comes to say what is evidently not true. For instance, where there are found persons suited to help the brethren, they also are invited to preach to the people by the holy bishops, as, for example, in Laranda Euelpis by Neon, and in Iconium Paulinus by Celsus, and in Synnada Theodore by Atticus, our blessed brother bishops. And it is likely that this thing happens in other places also without our knowing it."

In this way honour was paid to the man of whom we are speaking, while he was still young, not only by his fellow-countrymen but also by the bishops in a foreign land. But since Demetrius once again recalled him by letter, and by men who were deacons of the Church urged him to come back with speed to Alexandria, he returned and continued to labour with his accustomed zeal.

Now there flourished at that time many learned churchmen, and the letters which they penned to one another are still extant and easily accessible. They have been preserved even to our day in the library at Aelia, equipped by Alexander, then ruling the church there; from which also we have been able ourselves to gather together the material for our present work.

Of these Beryllus has left behind him, as well as letters, varied and beautiful compositions. He was bishop of the Arabians at Bostra. And likewise also Hippolytus, who also presided over another church somewhere.

And there has reached us also a Dialogue of Gaius, a very learned person (which was set a-going at Rome in the time of Zephyrinus), with Proclus the champion of the heresy of the Phrygians. In which, when curbing the recklessness and audacity of his opponents in composing new Scriptures, he mentions only thirteen epistles of the holy Apostle, not numbering the Epistle to the Hebrews with the rest; seeing that even to this day among the Romans there are some who do not consider it to be the Apostle's.

But indeed when Antoninus had reigned for seven years and six months he was succeeded by Macrinus; and when he had continued in office for a year, again another Antoninus received the Roman government. In the first year of the latter, Zephyrinus, the bishop of the Romans, departed this life, having held the ministry for eighteen entire years. After him Callistus was entrusted with the episcopate; he survived five years and then left the ministry to Urban.

After this the Emperor Alexander succeeded to the principate of the Romans, Antoninus having continued in office for only four years. At this time also Philetus succeeded Asclepiades in the church of the Antiochenes.

Origen's fame was now universal, so as to reach the ears of the Emperor's mother, Mamaea by name, a religious woman if ever there was one. She set great store on securing a sight of the man, and on testing that understanding of divine things which was the wonder of all. She was then staying at Antioch, and summoned him to her presence with a military escort. And when he had stayed with her for some time, and shown her very many things that were for the glory of the Lord and the excellence of the divine teaching, he hastened back to his accustomed duties.

At that very time also Hippolytus, besides very many other memoirs, composed the treatise *On the Pascha,* in which he sets forth a register of the times and puts forward a certain canon of a sixteen-years cycle for the Pascha, using the first year of the Emperor Alexander as a terminus in measuring his dates. Of his other treatises the following have reached us: *On the Hexaëmeron, On what followed the Hexaëmeron, Against Marcion, On the Song, On Parts of Ezekiel, On the Pascha, Against All the Heresies;* and very many others also might be found preserved by many people.

Starting from that time also Origen's commentaries on the divine Scriptures had their beginning, at the instigation of Ambrose, who not only plied him with innumerable verbal exhortations and encouragements, but also provided him unstintingly with what was necessary. For as he dictated there were ready at hand more than seven shorthand-writers, who relieved each other at fixed times, and as many copyists, as well as girls skilled in penmanship; for all of whom Ambrose supplied without stint the necessary means. Nay further, he contributed to Origen a vast amount of zeal in the earnest study of the divine oracles, a zeal which more than anything else acted as an incentive to him to compose his commentaries.

Such was the state of affairs when Pontianus succeeded Urban, who had been bishop of the church of the Romans for eight years, and Zebennus came after Philetus as [bishop] of the [church] of the Antiochenes. In their day Origen journeyed to Greece through Palestine because of an urgent necessity in Church matters, and received the laying-on of hands for the presbyterate at Caesarea from the bishops there. The agitation that was set on foot concerning him on this account, and the decisions made by those who presided over the churches on the matters agitated, as well as the other contributions that he made as he was reaching his prime to the study of the divine Word, require a separate composition, and we have given a fairly full account of them in the second [book] of the *Apology* that we have written on his behalf.

But to that information it is necessary to add that in the sixth of his ***Expositions on the* [Gospel] *according to John*** he indicates that he composed the first five while he was still at Alexandria; but of this work on the whole of the selfsame Gospel only twenty-two tomes have come our way. And [we must also state] that in the ninth of those ***On Genesis*** (there are twelve in all) he shows that not only were those before the ninth written at Alexandria, but also [his commentary] on the first twenty-five Psalms, and, as well, those on Lamentations, of which there have come to us five tomes. In these he mentions also those ***On the Resurrection,*** of which there are two. Moreover he wrote his ***De Principiis*** before his removal from Alexandria, and he composed the [books] entitled ***Stromateis,*** ten in number, in the same city in the reign of Alexander, as is shown by the annotations in his own hand in front of the tomes.

Now while expounding the first Psalm he set forth the catalogue of the sacred Scriptures of the Old Testament, writing somewhat as follows in these words: "But it should be known that there are twenty-two canonical books, according to the Hebrew tradition; the same as the number of the letters of their alphabet."

Then further on he adds as follows: "These are the twenty-two books according to the Hebrews: That which is entitled with us Genesis, but with the Hebrews, from the beginning of the book, Brēsith, that is 'In the beginning.' Exodus, Ouelle smōth, that is, 'These are the names.' Leviticus, Ouïkra, 'And he called.' Numbers, Ammes phekōdeim. Deuteronomy, Elle addebareim, 'These are the words.' Jesus the son of Nave, Iōsoue ben noun. Judges, Ruth, with them in one book, Sōphteim. Of Kingdoms i, ii, with them one, Samuel, 'The called of God.' Of Kingdoms iii, iv, in one, Ouammelch david, that is, 'The kingdom of David.' Chronicles i, ii, in one, Dabrē iamein, that is, 'Words of days.' Esdras i, ii, in one, Ezra, that is, 'Helper.' Book of Psalms, Sphar thelleim. Proverbs of Solomon, Melōth. Ecclesiastes, Kōelth. Song of Songs (not, as some suppose, Songs of Songs), Sir assireim. Esaias, Iessia. Jeremiah with Lamentations and the Letter, in one, Jeremia. Daniel, Daniēl. Ezekiel, Ezekiēl. Job, Jōb. Esther, Esthēr. And outside these there are the Maccabees, which are entitled Sar bēth sabanai el."

These things he inserts in the above-mentioned treatise. But in the first of his *[Commentaries] on the Gospel according to Matthew,* defending the canon of the Church, he gives his testimony that he knows only four Gospels, writing somewhat as follows: ". . . as having learnt by tradition concerning the four Gospels, which alone are unquestionable in the Church of God under heaven, that first was written that according to Matthew, who was once a tax-collector but afterwards an apostle of Jesus Christ, who published it for those who from Judaism came to believe, composed as it was in the Hebrew language. Secondly, that according to Mark, who wrote it in accordance with Peter's instructions, whom also Peter acknowledged as his son in the catholic epistle, speaking in these terms: 'She that is in Babylon, elect together with you, saluteth you; and so doth Mark my son.' And thirdly, that according to Luke, who wrote, for those who from the Gentiles [came to believe], the Gospel that was praised by Paul. After them all, that according to John."

And in the fifth of his *Expositions on the Gospel according to John* the same person says this with reference to the epistles of the apostles: "But he who was made sufficient to become a minister of the new covenant, not of the letter but of the spirit, even Paul, who fully preached the Gospel from Jerusalem and round about even unto Illyricum, did not so much as write to all the churches that he taught; and even to those to which he wrote he sent but a few lines. And Peter, on whom the Church of Christ is built, against which the gates of Hades shall not prevail, has left one acknowledged epistle, and, it may be, a second also; for it is doubted. Why need I speak of him who leaned back on Jesus' breast, John, who has left behind one Gospel, confessing that he could write so many that even the world itself could not contain them; and he wrote also the Apocalypse, being ordered to keep silence and not to write the voices of seven thunders? He has left also an epistle of a very few lines, and, it may be, a second and a third; for not all say that these are genuine. Only, the two of them together are not a hundred lines long."

Furthermore, he thus discusses the Epistle to the Hebrews, in his *Homilies* upon it: "That the character of the diction of the epistle entitled To the Hebrews has not the apostle's rudeness in speech, who confessed himself rude in speech, that is, in style, but that the epistle is better Greek in the framing of its diction,

will be admitted by everyone who is able to discern differences of style. But again, on the other hand, that the thoughts of the epistle are admirable, and not inferior to the acknowledged writings of the apostle, to this also everyone will consent as true who has given attention to reading the apostle."

Further on, he adds the following remarks: "But as for myself, if I were to state my own opinion, I should say that the thoughts are the apostle's, but that the style and composition belong to one who called to mind the apostle's teachings and, as it were, made short notes of what his master said. If any church, therefore, holds this epistle as Paul's, let it be commended for this also. For not without reason have the men of old time handed it down as Paul's. But who wrote the epistle, in truth God knows. Yet the account which has reached us [is twofold], some saying that Clement, who was bishop of the Romans, wrote the epistle, others, that it was Luke, he who wrote the Gospel and the Acts."

But this must suffice on these matters. Now it was in the tenth year of the above-mentioned reign that Origen removed from Alexandria to Caesarea, leaving to Heraclas the Catechetical School for those in the city. And not long afterwards Demetrius, the bishop of the church of the Alexandrians, died, having continued in the ministry for forty-three entire years. He was succeeded by Heraclas.

Now at this time Firmilian, bishop of Caesarea in Cappadocia, was distinguished; he displayed such esteem for Origen, that at one time he would summon him to his own parts for the benefit of the churches; at another, journey himself to Judaea, and spend some time with him for his own betterment in divine things. Nay further, Alexander, who presided over the [church] of Jerusalem, and Theoctistus, [who presided] at Caesarea, continued their attendance on him the whole time, as their only teacher, and used to concede to him the task of expounding the divine Scriptures, and the other parts of the Church's instruction.

But to resume. When Alexander the Emperor of the Romans had brought his principate to an end after thirteen years, he was succeeded by Maximin Caesar. He, through ill-will towards the house of Alexander, since it consisted for the most part of believers, raised a persecution, ordering the leaders of the Church alone to be put to death, as being responsible for the teaching of the Gospel. Then also Origen composed his work *On Martyrdom,* dedicating the treatise to Ambrose and Protoctetus, a presbyter of the community at Caesarea; for in the persecution no ordinary distress had befallen them both, in which distress it is recorded that these men were distinguished for the confession they made during the period, not more than three years, that the reign of Maximin lasted. Origen has noted this particular time for the persecution, in the twenty-second of his *Expositions of the Gospel according to John,* and in various letters.

Gordian having succeeded to the Roman government after Maximin, Pontianus, when he had been bishop of the church of Rome for six years, was succeeded by Anteros; who exercised his ministry for a month, and was succeeded by Fabian. It is said that Fabian, after the death of Anteros, came from the country along with others and stayed at Rome, where he came to the office in a most miraculous manner, thanks to the divine and heavenly grace. For when the brethren were all assembled for the purpose of appointing him who should succeed to the episcopate, and very many notable and distinguished persons were in the thoughts of many, Fabian, who was there, came into nobody's mind. But all of a sudden, they relate, a dove flew down from above and settled on his head, in clear imitation of the descent of the Holy Ghost in the form of a dove upon the Saviour; whereupon the whole people, as if moved by one divine inspiration, with all eagerness and with one soul cried out "worthy," and without more ado took him and placed him on the episcopal throne.

At that very time also Zebennus, bishop of Antioch, departed this life and Babylas succeeded to the rule; and in Alexandria, Heraclas, having received the ministry after Demetrius, was succeeded in the Catechetical School there by Dionysius, who had also been one of Origen's pupils.

Now while Origen was plying his accustomed tasks at Caesarea, many came to him, not only of the natives, but also numbers of foreign pupils who had left their own countries. Among these as especially distinguished we know to have been Theodore, who was the selfsame person as that renowned bishop in our day, Gregory, and his brother Athenodore. Both of them were strongly enamoured of Greek and Roman studies, but Origen instilled into them a passion for philosophy and urged them to exchange their former love for the study of divine truth. Five whole years they continued with him, and made such progress in divine things that while still young both of them were deemed worthy of the episcopate in the churches of Pontus.

At that time Africanus also, the author of the books entitled *Cesti,* was well known. A letter of his, written to Origen, is extant; he was at a loss as to whether the story of Susanna in the book of Daniel were a spurious forgery. Origen makes a very full reply to it. And of the same Africanus there have reached us as well five books of *Chronographies,* a monument of labour and accuracy. In these he says that he himself made a journey to Alexandria because of the great fame of Heraclas; who, as we have stated, was greatly distinguished for philosophy and other Greek learning, and was entrusted with the bishopric of the church there.

And another letter of the same Africanus is extant, to Aristides, On the supposed discord between the Genealogies of Christ in Matthew and Luke. In it he establishes very clearly the harmony of the evangelists from an account that came down to him, which by anticipation I set forth in the proper place in the first book of the present work.

And Origen too at this time was composing his *Commentaries on Isaiah,* and at the same time those also on Ezekiel. Of the former, thirty tomes have come our way on the third part of Isaiah, up to the vision of the beasts in the desert; and on Ezekiel five and twenty, the only ones that he has written on the whole prophet. And having come at that time to Athens, he finished the commentary on Ezekiel, and began that on the Song of Songs, carrying it forward there up to the fifth book. And returning to Caesarea he brought these also to an end, numbering ten. Why should one draw up the exact catalogue of the man's works here and now, seeing that such would require a special study? And we did record it in our account of the life of Pamphilus, that holy martyr of our day, in which, in showing the extent of Pamphilus's zeal for divine things, I quoted as evidence the lists in the library that he had brought together of the works of Origen and of other ecclesiastical writers; and from these anyone who pleases can gather the fullest knowledge of the works of Origen that have reached us. But we must now proceed with our history.

Beryllus, who, as we have mentioned a little above, was bishop of Bostra in Arabia, perverting the Church's standard, attempted to introduce things foreign to the faith, daring to say that our Saviour and Lord did not pre-exist in an individual existence of His own before His coming to reside among men, nor had He a divinity of His own, but only the Father's dwelling in Him. Whereupon, after a large number of bishops had held questionings and discussions with the man, Origen, being invited along with others, entered in the first place into conversation with the man to discover what were his opinions, and when he knew what it was that he asserted, he corrected what was unorthodox, and, persuading him by reasoning, established him in the truth as to the doctrine, and restored him to his former sound opinion. And there are still extant to this very day records in writing both of Beryllus and of the synod that was held on his account, which contain at once the questions Origen put to him and the discussions that took place in his own community, and all that was done on that occasion. And a great many other things about Origen have been handed down to memory by the older men of our day, which I think it well to pass over, as they do not concern the present work. But all that it was necessary to know of his affairs, these also one may gather from the *Apology* that was written on his behalf by us and Pamphilus, that holy martyr of our day, a work that we were at pains to compose conjointly because of the fault-finders.

When after six whole years Gordian brought his government of the Romans to an end, Philip along with his son Philip succeeded to the principate. It is recorded that he, being a Christian, wished on the day of the last paschal vigil to share along with the multitude the prayers at the church, but was not permitted to enter by him who was then presiding, until he confessed and numbered himself among those who were reckoned to be in sins and were occupying the place of penitence; for that otherwise, had he not done so, he would never have been received by [the president] on account of the many charges made concerning him. And it is said that he obeyed readily, displaying by his actions how genuine and pious was his disposition towards the fear of God.

It was the third year of his reign when Heraclas departed this life, after presiding for sixteen years over the churches at Alexandria; Dionysius took up the episcopal office.

Then indeed, as was fitting, when the faith was increasing and our doctrine was boldly proclaimed in the ears of all, it is said that Origen, who was over sixty years of age, inasmuch as he had now acquired immense facility from long preparation, permitted short-hand-writers to take down the discourses delivered by him in public, a thing that he had never before allowed.

At that time also he composed the treatises, eight in number, in answer to the work against us, entitled *True Discourse of Celsus the Epicurean,* and his twenty-five tomes on the Gospel according to Matthew, and those on the twelve prophets, of which we found only five and twenty. And there is extant also a letter of his to the Emperor Philip himself, and another to his wife Severa, and various other letters to various persons. As many of these as we have been able to bring together, preserved as they were here and there by various persons, we arranged in separate roll-cases, so that they might no longer be dispersed. These letters number more than a hundred. And he wrote also to Fabian the bishop of Rome, and to very many other rulers of churches, with reference to his orthodoxy. You will find these facts also established in the sixth book of the *Apology* we wrote on the man's behalf.

Once more in Arabia at the above-mentioned time other persons sprang up, introducing a doctrine foreign to the truth, and saying that the human soul dies for a while in this present time, along with our bodies, at their death, and with them turns to corruption; but that hereafter, at the time of the resurrection, it will come to life again along with them. Moreover, when a synod of no small dimensions was then assembled together,

Origen was again invited, and there opened a discussion in public on the subject in question, with such power that he changed the opinions of those who had formerly been deluded.

At that time also another perverse opinion had its beginning, the heresy known as that of the Helkesaites, which no sooner began than it was quenched. Origen mentions it in a public address on the eighty-second Psalm, in some such words as these: "There has come just now a certain man who prides himself on being able to champion a godless and very impious opinion, of the Helkesaites, as it is called, which has lately come into opposition with the churches. I shall lay before you the mischievous teachings of that opinion, that you may not be carried away by it. It rejects some things from every Scripture; again, it has made use of texts from every part of the Old Testament and the Gospels; it rejects the Apostle entirely. And it says that to deny is a matter of indifference, and that the discreet man will on occasions of necessity deny with his mouth, but not in his heart. And they produce a certain book of which they say that it has fallen from heaven, and that he who has heard it and believes will receive forgiveness of his sins—a forgiveness other than that which Christ Jesus has bestowed."

But to resume. When Philip had reigned for seven years he was succeeded by Decius. He, on account of his enmity towards Philip, raised a persecution against the churches, in which Fabian was perfected by martyrdom at Rome, and was succeeded in the episcopate by Cornelius.

In Palestine, Alexander, the bishop of the church of Jerusalem, appeared once more for Christ's sake at Caesarea before the governor's courts, and for the second time distinguished himself by the confession he made; he underwent the trial of imprisonment, crowned with the venerable hoary locks of ripe old age. And when after the splendid and manifest testimony that he gave in the governor's courts he fell asleep in prison, Mazabanes was proclaimed as his successor in the episcopate at Jerusalem.

And when at Antioch Babylas, in like manner to Alexander, after confession departed this life in prison, Fabius was made president of the church there.

Now the nature and extent of that which happened to Origen at the time of the persecution, and what was the end thereof; how the evil demon marshalled all his forces in rivalry against the man, how he led them with every device and power, and singled him out, above all others upon whom he made war at that time, for special attack; the nature and extent of that which he endured for the word of Christ, chains and tortures, punishments inflicted on his body, punishments as he lay in iron and in the recesses of his dungeon; and

Justinian I

how, when for many days his feet were stretched four spaces in that instrument of torture, the stocks, he bore with a stout heart threats of fire and everything else that was inflicted by his enemies; and the kind of issue he had thereof, the judge eagerly striving with all his might on no account to put him to death; and what sort of sayings he left behind him after this, sayings full of help for those who needed uplifting—[of all these matters] the man's numerous letters contain both a true and accurate account.

Charles Bigg (lecture date 1886)

SOURCE: "Origen," in *The Christian Platonists of Alexandria: Eight Lectures*, Oxford at the Clarendon Press, 1886, pp. 115-34.

[*In this lecture, Bigg provides an overview of Origen's life and work in its various aspects: textual criticism, exegesis, and religious philosophy.*]

Clement as we have seen is a philosopher of a desultory and eclectic type and so far as the needs of his tranquil spirit led him on. Egypt is his world, Gnosticism his one trouble. Origen had travelled to Rome in the West and Bostra in the East, and had found everywhere the clash of arms. But apart from this he was not one of those who discover the rifts in their harness only on the morning of the battle. His sceptical intelligence pries unbidden into every defect, and anticipates the hostile thrust. He stands to his arms for life or death, like a Dominican theologian of the thirteenth century, or an English divine of the nineteenth. The range of his activity is amazing. He is the first great scholar, the first great preacher, the first great devotional writer, the first great commentator, the first great dogmatist. But he is nothing else. Already we have entered upon the joyless age of erudition. The beauties of Hellenism, in which Clement still delighted, are a withered flower, and Christian art is as yet unborn.

The life of Origen extended from 185 A.D. to 254 A.D., from the reign of Commodus to that of Valerian and Gallienus. During this long and eventful period his activity was constant, varied and distinguished, and friends and enemies, both equally ardent, have left us large materials for his biography. It is impossible here to deal exhaustively with a subject so wide. We must content ourselves with touching upon the most characteristic features[1].

He was 'by race an Egyptian,' a Copt, one of the children of the soil, despised by the Greek colonists for their animal-worship and their petulant turbulence, and treated even by the upright Roman law on the footing of slaves. Son as he was of Christian parents he yet bore the name of one of his country's deities, Origenes, child of Hor, the god of Light[2]. From his blood he drew that fiery ardour which long tribulation softened but could not quench. He was a martyr by race, but a stern schooling was needed before he learned to drink the cup as God had mixed it for him. When his father Leonidas fell a victim to the persecution of Severus, nothing but the womanly sense of his mother prevented Origen, then a boy of seventeen, from drawing destruction on his own head by open defiance of the authorities. The destitute orphan found shelter in the house of a wealthy Alexandrine lady, but neither gratitude nor the sense of a common misfortune could induce him to behave with civility to her Gnostic chaplain. Shortly afterwards, at the age of eighteen, he found independence in the mastership of the Catechetical School, left vacant by the flight of Clement. He breathed his own spirit into his pupils, of whom six at least perished. Nor was it Origen's fault that he did not share their fate. He visited them in prison, he acted as their advocate, and gave them the brotherly kiss in open court. We are not surprised to hear that he narrowly escaped stoning in the streets, or that he was hunted from house to house by the gendarmery. What is remarkable is that he escaped, and even contrived throughout the reign of terror to keep his school to-gether. It is probable that the edict of Severus, which was directed against converts only, did not touch him, and that so long as he abstained from formal defiance he was personally safe[3]. And he had already learned that formal defiance was suicide.

The second path that allures the wilful martyr is that of self-torture. Like Buddha, like Marcus Aurelius, like Wesley, like many another enthusiast in every age and clime and church, Origen flung himself into asceticism only to learn the truth of the old Greek adage, 'He who starts in the race before the signal is given is whipped.' He sold the manuscripts of the Greek classics, which he had written out with loving care, for a trifling pension, in order that he might be able to teach without a fee, and subjected himself for some years to the severest discipline by night and day. This was the time of his bondage to the letter. He would carry out with severest fidelity the precept of the Saviour, 'provide neither gold nor silver . . . neither two coats, neither shoes.' He went, as is well known, even farther than this, and did what was condemned at once by the whole-some severity of the Roman law, and the conscience, if not the actual ordinance of the Church. This error too he learned to renounce, but not wholly nor frankly, for to the last he looked with a sombre eye on the affections of the flesh.

Rebellion is the third temptation of undisciplined zeal, and this charge also may be laid to Origen's account. Here unhappily our materials are too scanty for a clear and dispassionate judgment. The bare facts are that in the year 215 Origen, being then at Caesarea, accepted the invitation of Alexander, Bishop of Jerusalem, and Theoctistus, Bishop of Caesarea, to expound the Scriptures before the assembly of the Church, though as yet a layman, and that in 228 he was ordained at the same place by the same Bishops. We cannot tell how far these acts were in violation of the existing discipline. Both were lawful in Palestine, both were regarded by Demetrius as unlawful. If the rule was more stringent at Alexandria, it was possibly a recent innovation. We do not know how far the dispute was complicated by the character of the Patriarch, by the teaching and conduct of Origen, or by the peculiar position of the Alexandrine Presbytery. But it is significant that the extreme penalty of degradation was carried only by the voices of the newly created suffragan bishops, against the inclination of the priests. These latter could not but sympathise with a victim of the same usurpation that lay so heavy on themselves.

For our present purpose the importance of the incident is that it marks the final renunciation by Origen of that narrow legal spirit, which leads by many paths to the one goal of servitude. He was learning in strange and unexpected ways the true meaning of the Christian sacrifice. He had been willing and eager to 'give his body to be burned,' he had 'given all his goods to feed the poor,' and his reward had been not the martyr crown but the martyr spirit, 'love which beareth all things.' Now, when he had found his true career in indefatigable labour for the Word of God, and sought to sanctify his toil and enlarge his influence by the name and authority of a priest, what he sought was given to him, but at the cost of banishment and obloquy. Such discipline was needed before this high impatient spirit could obey with docility the bridle of God.

Many years before this it had become manifest in what direction Providence was leading him. As a child he had received by his father's care not only a minute knowledge of Scripture, a great part of which he learned by heart, but a thorough training in what was called the encyclic discipline—the grammar, rhetoric and science which formed the ordinary education of a youth of good family. Hebrew, a rare accomplishment, and philosophy[4], he acquired while so absorbed in school work that he could find time for study only by curtailing the hours of sleep. His literary activity began in 223, when he would be thirty-eight years old, and continued incessantly to the end of his life. Like many other men of studious habits he found the labour of composition irksome, but Ambrosius, a wealthy and intelligent man whom Origen had reclaimed from Gnosticism, continually spurred him on, and overcame the physical difficulty by providing him with a number of shorthand writers and copyists. From this time his labours were unremitting. 'The work of correction,' he says in one of his letters, 'leaves us no time for supper, or after supper for exercise and repose. Even at these times we are compelled to debate questions of interpretation and to emend MSS. Even the night cannot be given up altogether to the needful refreshment of sleep, for our discussions extend far into the evening. I say nothing about our morning labour continued from dawn to the ninth or tenth hour. For all earnest students devote this time to study of the Scriptures and reading[5].

Such was his life during the progress of the **Hexapla,** and indeed at all times. The volume of writing thus produced was enormous. But it is evident that no man can accomplish the best work of which he is capable under these conditions, harassed by the demands of pupils, toiling with feverish anxiety to master the ever-growing mountain of minute facts, and in hardly won intervals pouring out the eager flow of extemporaneous thought to nimble-fingered stenographers[6]. The marvel is not that Origen composed so much, but that he composed so well.

And to these professional labours must be added a far-reaching personal influence, with all its responsibilities and engagements. Origen was essentially a man of the student type, but he wielded that powerful charm which attaches to high intellectual gifts when combined with an ardent and sympathetic nature. His pupil

Gregory Thaumaturgus speaks of his 'sweet grace and persuasion mingled with a certain constraining force[7],' and uses towards him that strong Greek word by which Plato describes the love of the soul for its ideal. Such a charm is a practical power, and works with more freedom and pungency in a private station of life. It constituted Origen the unofficial representative, arbiter, peacemaker of the Eastern Church. A provincial governor consults him on affairs of the soul, the Christian or half-Christian Emperor Philip corresponds with him, the Empress Mother Mammaea summons him to Antioch and provides him with a guard of honour[8]. The Churches of Achaea and Arabia make him their umpire, and peace follows his award. In the furnace of affliction he has grown to be one of those magnetic natures that test the capacity for love and veneration in every one that comes within their sphere.

Origen had long learned to acquiesce in the prevalent view of the Easterns that martyrdom involves a high responsibility, that the Christian has no right either to fling away his life or to fix the guilt of blood upon 'the powers ordained of God.' The Church would gladly have restricted this Olympian contest to her chosen athletes. Hence he quitted Alexandria during the Fury of Caracalla, which though not specially directed against Christians, no doubt involved them. Once again he fled from the persecution of Maximin to Caesarea of Cappadocia, where in the house of Juliana he whiled away the stormy days in labour upon the *Hexapla*. What thoughts solaced him during this dry and gigantic task we know from the treatise on Martyrdom, composed at this time for the benefit of his friend Ambrosius, who had been thrown into prison, 'a golden book' it has been called with truth, for it touches not a single false note. At last his own summons came. He was incarcerated in the persecution of Decius, and treated with a severity which shattered his frame already enfeebled by labour and old age.

He was buried in Tyre, where for centuries his tomb, in the wall behind the high altar, formed the chief ornament of the magnificent cathedral of the Holy Sepulchre. Tyre was wasted by the Saracens, but even to this day, it is said, the poor fishermen, whose hovels occupy the site of that city of palaces, point to a shattered vault beneath which lie the bones of 'Oriunus[9].'

We may consider his voluminous and many-sided works under three heads—Textual Criticism, Exegesis, and Religious Philosophy. The first of these does not properly fall within the scope of our enquiry, but a brief notice may be permitted for the sake of the side-light which it throws upon the character of our author.

He devoted much time and labour to the text of the New Testament, which was already disfigured by corruptions, 'some arising from the carelessness of scribes, some from the evil licence of emendation, some from arbitrary omissions or interpolations[10].' Already the records were perverted in numberless passages, not only by Gnostic audacity, but by those minor variations which constitute what are known as the Western and Alexandrine families. Between errors of the latter class and the genuine reading he had no means of deciding except the perilous canon of intrinsic probability, which he applies with much acuteness, but at the same time with severe caution[11]. All that he could hope was to purify his own MS. or MSS.[12] (for he used more than one, and those of different families) from manifest faults of transcription and from recent and obvious depravations. This he effected with care and ability. The *Exemplaria Adamantii* acquired the authority of a standard, and derived additional importance from the fact that a copy was presented by Eusebius to the Emperor Constantine. But Origen's fame as a critic rests chiefly upon the *Hexapla*. In controversy with the Jews the Christian disputant was constantly baffled by the retort, that the passages on which he relied were not found, or were otherwise expressed, in the Hebrew. Several new translations or recensions of the whole or part of the LXX had been produced, in which the discrepancies of the Alexandrine Version from the original were brought into strong relief. Origen saw clearly the whole of the difficulties involved, and with characteristic grandeur and fearlessness determined upon producing an edition of the Old Testament that should exhibit in parallel columns the Hebrew text and the rival versions, thus bringing before the eye of the enquirer in one view the whole of the evidence attainable[13]. At the same time he corrected and supplemented the LXX from the other versions, chiefly those of Theodotion and Aquila. This gigantic and costly scheme was rendered feasible by the munificence, and facilitated by the active cooperation, of Ambrosius.

The *Hexapla,* the first great achievement of Christian erudition, is impressive in many ways, not least as a proof of the intelligence and sincerity of the community to which it was addressed. But with all his devotion and learning Origen was not a consummate master in the higher functions of criticism. His equipment was insufficient. His knowledge of Hebrew was respectable, and for his age remarkable, but not profound. He had a fair acquaintance with the grammar and dictionary, but had not penetrated into the genius of the language[14]. Again he was hampered by prejudice. He regarded the LXX as an independent and inspired authority, and, like Justin, accounted for its variation from the Hebrew by supposing that the latter had been deliberately falsified by the Jews[15]. In this way he explained the absence from the Canon of the Apocryphal Books. On one occasion he had employed in a public debate doctrinal proofs taken from the History of Susanna. This drew upon him an epistle from Julius Africanus, in which it was shown with great force and ingenuity that this addition to the Book of Daniel could not have been composed in Hebrew[16]. Origen with much learning and some little warmth refused to be convinced, but the honour of arms remained with Africanus, whose letter indeed is a signal refutation of the epithets 'credulous' and 'uncritical' so often applied to the age in which, and the men by whom, the Canon of the New Testament was settled.

Of the stately **Hexapla** time has spared us nothing but a gleaning of scattered fragments. The original MS. perished probably when the library of Caesarea was destroyed by the Arabs in the middle of the seventh century, and its immense size—it consisted of not less than fifty great rolls of parchment—must have prevented its ever being copied as a whole, though the revised LXX was circulated separately, and indeed still exists in a Syriac translation[17]. But of the exegetic work of Origen a very considerable mass is still extant, partly in the authentic Greek, partly in Latin translations. The surviving remains cover a large part both of the Old and of the New Testaments, and afford ample material for judging the method and substance of his teaching. Yet they are but a portion of what he accomplished. In the form of Scholia, Homilies or Commentaries he expounded nearly every book in the Bible, and many books were treated in all three ways.

The Scholia[18] were brief annotations, such as are commonly found on the margin of ancient MSS. The Homilies and Commentaries require a fuller notice.

Already the old prophesyings and speaking with tongues, except among the Montanist sectaries, have disappeared before the growing reverence for Scripture and the increasing stringency of discipline. Their place was supplied by the Homily[19] or Discourse, a name derived from the philosophic schools, expressive of the character of Christian eloquence, which was didactic and not rhetorical. In the days of Origen, and in Palestine, (for his priestly activity belongs wholly to the time after his exile from Egypt) public worship was held no longer in the large room of some wealthy brother's house, but in buildings definitely appropriated for the purpose, in which the Bishop and his clergy were seated in a semicircle round the decorated Altar[20]. The service was divided into two portions, corresponding to what were afterwards known as the Mass of the Catechumens and the Mass of the Faithful. To the first, which was held daily, belonged the reading of Scripture, the Sermon, and apparently certain prayers[21]; to the second, celebrated on Sundays and festivals, the prayers properly so called and the Eucharist. At the first catechumens, even heathen, were allowed to be present; from the second all, save the baptised, were rigidly excluded.

The Lessons were often of considerable length, comprising as much as three or four of our modern chapters, and went on in regular order, and the preacher expounded the whole or a portion of each according to

the direction of the presiding bishop[22]. It is probable that the friendly prelate of Caesarea suffered Origen to follow his own plan; hence his Homilies form a continuous exposition of the several books. They were delivered before a mixed, shifting, and not always orderly congregation. The services were daily and long. Some of the brethern would attend only on feast-days, and not always then. Some left the church before the sermon began, or if they remained, gathered in knots in the farther end of the building, the place of the heathen and unbaptised, 'turning their backs on the Word of God and busying themselves with secular gossip.' There were broad differences again in knowledge and morality. Some thought it not inconsistent with their Christian profession to haunt the circus or the amphitheatre; some fluctuated between Gnosticism and the Church; some were still tainted with heathen superstitions; some, sincere but ignorant, interpreted the promises of the Gospel in the most gross and carnal sense, or 'believed of God what would not be believed of the cruelest of mankind.' Hence the duty of Reserve, which Origen everywhere professes, weighs upon him with especial urgency in the Homilies[23].

The Homilies are rather what we should call Lectures than Sermons. His object in the pulpit, Origen tells us, is not the explanation of the letter so much as the edification of the Church; hence he dwells here almost entirely upon the moral and spiritual sense[24]. There is abundance of allegory but little exhortation, still less unction or pathos. Origen does not wind himself into the heart. He has not the blithe geniality of Clement, whose cloistered life seems never to have felt a storm. In Origen there is a subdued fire that reveals the tale of mental suffering and exhausting toil. Hence that austere solemnity, that absolute sincerity, that breadth and dignity of mind, which still grasp and detain the reader with the same spell that was cast upon Gregory. Origen is emphatically 'a man of God,' strong and subtle yet infinitely humble and gentle, a true *Ductor Dubitantium,* because he knew there was much that he did not know and yet was not afraid. His style is almost everywhere loose and prolix, owing to his habit of extemporaneous speech or dictation. This applies to the Commentaries as well as to the Homilies. Where he used the pen it is terser and more collected. But it is always simple and direct, flowing straight from the heart, devoid of every ornament, and owing its force entirely to that glowing fusion of thought and feeling by which it is informed.

The plan which he laid down for himself in the Commentaries[25] was to give first the literal, then the moral, then the spiritual sense of each verse in regular succession. The text is but the threshing-floor on which he pours out all the harvest of his knowledge, his meditations, his hopes. Any word may open up a train of thought extending throughout all Scripture and all time. Hence there is much repetition and confusion. Even here the object is not so much instruction as the deepening of the Christian life. We lose in perspicuity, but we never miss the inspiriting sense of immediate contact with a great character.

To us, though not to himself nor to the men of his time, Origen's merit as an expositor rests mainly upon the skill and patience with which he evolved the real and natural sense of the Bible.[26] He himself saw clearly that this is the foundation of everything. If we measure him by the best modern commentators, we may be struck by his deficiencies. But in relation to his own age his services are extraordinary. He need not fear comparison with the great pagan grammarians. He took great pains as we have seen to ascertain the text; he insists on the necessity of fixing the precise meaning of the words, and for this purpose will hunt a phrase through the whole Bible with a fertility of quotation truly prodigious, when we remember that it rests upon unaided memory. He never slurs a difficulty, raising and discussing every doubt that can by any possibility suggest itself. Hebrew he knew but imperfectly, and this is a fatal defect in dealing with the LXX. But in the New Testament he displays an accurate and intelligent appreciation of Greek grammar. Where he fails it is from preconceived ideas, from the hairsplitting and oversubtlety which are the Nemesis of Allegorism, or from deficiency of that sense of humour which corrects the extravagances of Clement. He cannot understand irony, and the simpler a thing is the more difficult he makes it.[27] Such scientific knowledge as the times could supply is at his call,[28] and he had travelled in Palestine with a keen eye for the geography of the Gospels. Philosophy too was at his command, though he does not rate it so high as Clement.[29] 'Few,' he says, 'are those who have taken the spoils of the Egyptians and made of them the furniture of the tabernacle.' Learning is useful, he tells his pupil Gregory, but the Scriptures are their own best key. 'Be diligent in reading the divine Scriptures, yes, be diligent . . . Knock and the doorkeeper will open unto thee . . . And be not content to knock and to enquire, for the most necessary aid to spiritual truth is prayer. Hence our Saviour said not only "knock and it shall be opened," and "seek and ye shall find," but "ask and it shall be given you."'[30]

Notes

[1] For fuller information about the biography of Origen the reader should consult Thomasius, Redepenning, or Huet. Denis, *Philosophie d' Origène,* is a most valuable aid to the study of his system of doctrine. Dr. Harnack's *Dogmengeschichte* is also very useful. Redepenning, ii. 472, gives a list of editions. The special literature will be found in Möller's article in Herzog, in Nitzsch, *Dogmengeschichte,* or in Ueberweg, *Grundriss der Gesch, der Philosophie.* All my references are to the edition of Lommatzsch, the volume

and page have been noted where it seemed desirable. [2] G.J. Voss was the first who gave the right derivation of the name of Origen; Redepenning, i. 421. Suidas, Erasmus, Halloix, Cave were satisfied with the impossible etymology, 'born in the mountains.' Origen is commonly spoken of by the by-name Adamantius, which, according to Photius, Cod. 118, means the same as Doctor Irrefragabilis. . . , according to Jerome denotes his indefatigable capacity for labour . . . , according to Huet the firmness with which he stood like a rock against Heretics. For the heathen philosopher of the same name see Porphyry, *Vita Plotini,* 20; Eunapius, *Vita Porphyrii,* p. 457; Ruhnken, *Diss. philologica de vita et scriptis Longini,* in his ed. of Longinus, Oxford, 1806. Epiphanius endeavoured to save the reputation of Origen by inventing a second author of the same name, to whom he ascribed the more heterodox articles of Origenism, *Haer.* 1xiii. I; 1xiv. 3. The Praedestinati auctor, *Haer.* 42, calls this phantom heresiarch Syrus sceleratissimus, and adds a third Origen, who denied the Resurrection. See Huet, *Origeniana,* i. 1. 7.

[3] An excellent account of the persecution of Severus will be found in Aubé, *Les Chrétiens dans l'Empire Romain.* See also Münter, *Primordia Eccl. Afr.*

[4] Origen does not name the professor whose lectures he attended. The belief that it was Ammonius Saccas rests upon the statement of Porphyry. Porphyry, who was an excellent man, no doubt spoke in good faith, but he has confused the heathen Origen whom he once knew with the Christian Origen whom he can never have known, and therefore no weight at all can be attached to what he says. The teacher may well have been Ammonius, but it is by no means certain. For even if that distinguished man was already in the chair, it appears from the opening of the *Eunuchus* ascribed to Lucian, that at a great school there were two professors of each of the four sects of philosophy. Their stipend was 10,000 drachmas per annum. See notes in Heinichen on Eusebius, *H. E.* vi. 19.

[5] From the *Epistle to a Friend about Ambrosius,* in Lomm. xvii. p. 5.

[6] Ambrosius, whom Origen calls his $\dot{\epsilon}\rho\gamma o\delta\iota\acute{\omega}\kappa\tau\eta s$, taskmaster, provided him with seven stenographers, and the same number of calligraphists. We may compare them with the staff of a modern lexicographer. But Origen used them for his commentaries and other composition. Thus *In Joan.* vi. 1 (Lom. i. p. 176) he complains that his work has been at a standstill because the $\sigma\upsilon\nu\acute{\eta}\theta\epsilon\iota s\ \tau\grave{\alpha}\chi\upsilon\gamma\rho\acute{\alpha}\phi o\iota$ were not with him. After the year 246 his extemporaneous Homilies were taken down by shorthand writers.

[7] From the *Panegyric* of Gregory Thaumaturgus, 6 (in Lom. xxv). The student of Origen should certainly begin

with this graphic and loving though too rhetorical sketch of the great master. Gregory was on his way to the Roman law school at Berytus, where he was to study for the bar. But by a series of accidents, which he regarded afterwards as divinely ordered, he fell in with Origen at Caesarea, and could not tear himself away. 'It was as if a spark fell into my soul and caught fire and blazed up, such was my love for the Holy Word and for this man its friend and advocate. Stung by this desire I forgot all that seemed to touch me most nearly, my studies, even my beloved jurisprudence, my country, my relatives, my present mission, the object of my travels.' Gregory stayed with Origen for five years, became a bishop, and was famed for his miracles.

[8] The date of the interview with Mammaea is doubtful. Baronius, Tillemont and De la Rue (see Huet) place it in 218. Redepenning, i. 372, in 223; this is Huet's own opinion. Aubé, pp. 306 sqq. throws it forward to 232, on the ground that it was after the ordination of Origen, but I am not aware what reason he has for this statement. On the vexed question of the relation of Philip to Christianity see Huet and Aubé, pp. 470 sqq.

[9] I owe this fact to Dr. Westcott's article, *Origen and the beginnings of Christian Philosophy,* in the Contemporary Review for May, 1879.

[10] *In Matth.* xv. 14 (Lom. iii. 357).

[11] See the *Diss. critica de Cod. IV Evang. Origenis* in Griesbach, *Opuscula Academica,* vol. i. Origen sometimes makes conjectures in his Commentaries, but never admitted them into his text. Thus he thought the words 'thou shalt love thy neighbour as thyself' spurious in Matt. xix. 19 (see *In Matth.* xv. 14), but he does not venture to expunge them. He supports the reading $\alpha\epsilon\rho\gamma\epsilon\sigma\eta\nu\omega\nu$ in Matt. viii. 28 and the parallel passages, but it is doubtful whether he actually inserted it in his MS.; see *In Joan.* vi. 24; Redepenning, ii. 184 note; and Tischendorf. Bethabara he found in some copies. In Rom. v. 14 the majority of his MSS. omitted the $\mu\dot{\eta}$, *In Rom.* v. 1 (Lom. vi. 344). There were bolder critics in his time. Some wished to set aside the story of Dives and Lazarus, *In Joan.* xxxii. 13 (Lom. ii. 447); the words 'to-day thou shalt be with me in Paradise,' *In Joan.* xxxii. 19 (Lom. ii. 481); and the advice given to slaves, 1 Cor. vii. 21, *In Rom.* i. 1 (Lom. vi. 12).

[12] Redepenning, ii. 182 sqq.; Griesbach, p. 240. The latter scholar pointed out that the text of Mark used by Origen for *In Matth.* was Western, while that quoted in the *In Joan.* is Alexandrine. See Gregory, *Prolegomena* to Tischendorf, p. 189; Westcott and Hort, p. 113.

[13] Field, in his magnificent work, *Origenis Hexapla,* xlviii. does not think that Origen had a distinctly controversial purpose in view. But see Redepenning, i. 234. 375; ii. 170. The *locus classicus* is *In Matth.* xv. 14. Partly owing to the plan followed by Origen, partly to the haste and inaccuracy of transcribers, the *Hexapla* caused very serious changes in the text of the LXX. Jerome, *Praefatio in Librum Paral.,* Migne, vol. xxviii. p. 1323; Schürer, p. 701.

[14] Redepenning, i. 367; ii. 166. 198; Ernesti, *Opuscula Philologica et Critica.* There is however some reason for lowering this estimate. *In Num.,* Hom. xiv. 1, Aiunt ergo qui hebraicas literas legunt, in hoc loco Deus non sub signo tetragrammati esse positum, de quo qui potest requirat (Redepenning thinks these words may have been inserted by the translator). . . . Origen does not speak of his own knowledge on this important and much debated point, and the authorities on whom he relied misled him, for the word *almah* is not found in the passage to which he refers, Deut. xxii. 23-26. It is evident from the *Ep. ad Afric.* that Origen could not walk alone in Hebrew. Hence Boherellus inferred 'Origenem hebraice plane nescivisse.' See Rosenmüller, iii. 63. 23. 153.

[15] Justin, *Trypho,* 71; Otto, p. 256.

[16] The chief point urged by Africanus is the play of words. . . . Origen struggles against this cogent argument in the *Ep. ad Afric.* But in a Fragment from *Strom.* x. (Lom. xvii. p. 74) he admits that *if* the paronomasia does not exist in Hebrew the objection is fatal. The *if* is not critical but theological. See Schürer, p. 717.

[17] The Syro-Hexaplar text is probably nearly all in existence, though till all the Fragments have been published it cannot be known what deficiencies may exist. See the articles *Versions* in Dict. of Bible by Tregelles and *Syrische Bibelübersetzungen* by Nestle in Herzog; Field; Ceriani, *Codex Syro-hexaplaris Ambrosianus,* Milan, 1874; Lagarde, *V. T. ab Origene recensiti frag. apud Syros servata quinque,* Göttingen, 1880; Dr. T. Skat Roerdam, *Libri Judicum et Ruth,* Hauniae, 1861; the last-named authority gives full and elaborate prolegomena.

[18] Jerome, Preface to his translation of the *Homilies on Ezekiel,* 'Scias Origenis opuscula in omnem Scripturam esse triplicia. Primum eius Excerpta, quae Graece [scolia] nuncupantur, in quibus ea quae sibi videbantur obscura atque habere aliquid difficultatis summatim breviterque perstrinxit.' In the Preface to his Comm. on Matthew, Jerome calls them 'commaticum interpretandi genus.' The word $\sigma\eta\mu\epsilon\iota\omega\sigma\iota\varsigma$, which also occurs, appears to be used in the general sense of 'notes,' which were sometimes perhaps [scolia], sometimes extracts from the Commentaries or Homilies, *Origeniana,* iii. 1. 4, but see Redepenning, ii. 376; Ernesti, *Opuscula Philologica.* Such are the fragmentary extracts, chiefly from Catenas and of somewhat doubtful authenticity, published as Selecta. See the

monita in De la Rue. Gallandi, vol. xiv., *App.,* has collected many fragments that are not given in Lommatzsch.

[19] Redepenning, ii. 212 sqq. The terms $\sigma\acute{\eta}\rho\nu\gamma\mu\tilde{\alpha}$ and $\delta\iota\acute{\alpha}\lambda\epsilon\xi\iota s$ were also in use.

[20] *In Jesu Nave,* Hom. x. 3 (Lom. xi. 104); *In Judices,* Hom. iii. 2 (Lom. xi. 237); Probst, *Kirchliche Disciplin,* p. 212.

[21] Many of the Homilies end with the admonition to stand up and pray, e.g. *In Luc.* xxxix. Catechumens were addressed *In Luc.,* Hom. vii. Heathen were sometimes present, *In Jerem.,* Hom. ix. 4 (Lom. xv. 210).

[22] The Lesson read before the Sermon on the Witch of Endor included 1 Sam. xxv. xxvi. xxvii. xxviii. . . . There was as yet only one lesson, taken sometimes from the Old, sometimes from the New Testament. At a somewhat later period there were four, divided into two pairs, the first pair from the Old, the second from the New Test., and between the two readings a psalm was sung, *Const. App.* ii. 57, but no trace of this usage is found in Origen, Redepenning, ii. 221 sqq.; Probst, *Liturgie,* 152. Many of Origen's Homilies must have taken an hour and a half in the delivery.

[23] The behaviour of the women was especially troublesome, 'quae tantum garriunt, quae tantum fabulis obstrepunt, ut non sinant esse silentium. Iam quid de mente earum, quid de corde discutiam, si de infantibus suis aut de lana cogitent aut de necessariis domus,' *In Exod.* Hom. xiii. 3: cp. *In Num.* Hom. v. 1; *In Lev.* Hom. ix. 5. 7. 9; *In Gen.* Hom. x. 1; *Philocalia,* i. *ad fin.;* Redepenning, ii. 229.

[24] *In Lev.* Hom. i. 1; *In Num.* Hom. xiv. 1. The reader may acquire a just idea of Origen as a preacher by perusing *In Gen.* viii; *In Lev.* vii; *In Luc.* xiv. The Homilies on *Judges* we know to have been written, though extempore passages were added in the delivery, see Hom. i. 3: 'Sed et illud quod dicentibus nobis occurrit,' &c. Beyond this passage I am not aware of the existence of any positive evidence as to which of his works were written with his own hand, though some, e.g. the *In Joan.,* we know were not. But I cannot think that the *De Principiis,* the *De Oratione,* or the *De Martyrio* belonged to the latter class. Eustathius complains of Origen's $\mathring{\alpha}\mu\epsilon\tau\rho\sigma\phi\lambda\upsilon\alpha\rho\acute{\iota}\tilde{\alpha}$; Theophilus called him 'Seminarium loquacitatis;' Erasmus on the other hand praises his brevity, Huet, *Orig.* iii. 1. 1; Redepenning, ii. 252. Some interesting remarks will be found in Rothe, *Geschichte der Predigt,* Bremen, 1881.

[25] I may recommend to the reader the allegory on the Treasury *In Joan.* xix. 2; the passage on the Death of Christ, *ibid.* xxviii. 14; on Faith, *ibid.* xxxii. 9; the allegory on the Mercy Seat, *In Rom.* iii. 8, and the

Exposition of the Parables in St. Matthew. The latter Commentary is generally superior to that on St. John. But those who wish to see Origen at his best will seek him where he is least allegorical, in the *Contra Celsum,* or the treatises on *Prayer* and on *Martyrdom.*

[26] Perhaps the best instance of Origen's merits and defects in dealing with the literal sense is to be found in his comments on the opening words of St. John's Gospel *In Joan.* i. 16 onwards. In the New Testament he is always excellent, but we must compare him with the ancient commentators on Homer, not, as Rosenmüller practically does, with the best modern divines. I have adhered to Origen's own distinction of the literal from the mystic sense. But it must be remembered that many of the most important passages in the N. T. are figurative, and that it is precisely in the explanation of these that the merit of Origen is to be found. Perhaps his supreme excellence lies in his clearness and courage in pointing out difficulties, the moral anomalies which beset the Gnostic and the ignorant Christian, the apparent non-fulfilment of the Messianic hope which rebuffed the Jew (see for all this the opening of the *Philocalia*); the contradictions of the Evangelists, *In Joan.* x. 3. sqq.; the chronological difficulty involved in the 'four months before harvest,' *In Joan.* xiii. 39; the historical difficulty in the title $\beta\tilde{\alpha}\sigma\iota\lambda\iota\kappa\tilde{\alpha}s$, *In Joan.* xiii. 57. If he often creates perplexities out of insignificant verbal distinctions, this is still a fault on the right side. For details see Redepenning, ii. 200 sqq.; Rosenmüller. Ernesti, *Opuscula Philologica et Critica,* rates him very high as the founder of textual criticism and scientific inductive exegesis.

[27] A good instance of this is this treatment of the gift of Caleb to his daughter Achsa (Joshua xv. 19), 'Et accepit Gonetlam superiorem et Gonetlam inferiorem . . . Videtis quia vere auxilio Dei opus est ut haec explanari queant,' *In Jesu Nave,* Hom. xx. 4.

[28] It did not amount to much. See the account of the different kinds of pearls *In Matt.* x. 7. Origen thought that the popular beliefs that serpents spring from the spinal marrow of dead men, bees from oxen, wasps from horses, beetles from asses, that serpents have a knowledge of antidotes, that the eagle uses the $\mathring{\alpha}\epsilon\tau\acute{\iota}\tau\eta s$ $\lambda\acute{\iota}\theta os$ as an amulet for the protection of its young were possibly true, *Contra Celsum,* iv. 57. 86. But he is no worse than Celsus himself or Pliny. Similar absurdities are to be found in Clement. For Origen's other accomplishments, see *Origeniana,* ii. 1; Redepenning, i. 219. M. Denis, p. 14, rates them very low. Indeed absorbed as Origen was in the drudgery of tuition from his eighteenth year, it is impossible that he can have gone profoundly into any line of knowledge not immediately connected with his special studies.

[29] For the use that he made of philosophy, see the *Panegyric* of Gregory, and the account of his method

of teaching in Lecture II. M. Denis, *Philosophie d'Origène,* p. 30, says: 'Il ne conservait de l'esprit philosophique que l'insatiable curiosité,' and complains, in the chapter on *Anthropologie,* of his neglect of ethics, psychology and politics. The duties of citizens would not have been a safe theme for a Christian writer under the heathen Empire. Psychology again is for another reason an exceedingly difficult subject for a Christian, because he cannot isolate it, because he has to regard above all things the point of junction with metaphysics, and with the metaphysics of Revelation. Clement and Origen were the first to attempt the problem from this point of view. The same difficulty attaches to the theory of Ethics. The practice of Ethics is undervalued both by Clement and Origen, though not so markedly by the latter. Hence it is a just criticism, 'Qu'il y a bien plus à apprendre sur l'observation intérieure non seulement dans Saint Augustin ou dans Saint Jérome, mais encore dans Tertullien.' The remarks of M. Denis are brilliant and in the main accurate, but the plan of his work compels him to approach Origen obliquely, and view him in a false light. Origen is before all things a theologian, but a philosophical theologian. The reader may consult with advantage Harnack, *Dogmengeschichte,* pp. 514 sqq.

[30] From the *Epistola ad Gregorium.* The difference between the attitude of Clement and Origen towards philosophy is well described by M. Denis, *Introduction.*

René Cadiou (essay date 1944)

SOURCE: "Origen the Pagan," in *Origen: Life at Alexandria,* B. Herder Book Co., 1944, pp. 186-208.

[*In this essay, Cadiou explains the purported identification of Origen's thought with pagan Neoplatonism, the problems that follow upon such an identification, and the facts about Origen's reception of Neoplatonism.*]

The comparative study of the two systems of thought justifies us in the assertion that the Platonism which Origen acquired at Alexandria in the beginning of the third century was the decisive factor in the development of his philosophy. Thirsting for its teachings on the origin of the soul, the hierarchy of spirits, the role of providence, and the genesis of created things, he sought from it far more than the ordinary student who was content to find in it a sufficient number of commonplaces for his religious studies. In arriving at this conclusion about the source of his system of thought, we deliberately exclude all problems of biography. Even if he had never attended the classes of Ammonius, we should still have to find a place for him in this preliminary period of the history of Neoplatonism. But then would arise the difficulty of explaining how he be-

came so steeped in this particular version of Platonism. It is revealed in his writings as a doctrine acquired, mastered, and retained for the help he drew from it in his studies of the soul and of God.

PORPHYRY'S TESTIMONY

A contemporary witness asserts that the young Origen followed the lectures of Ammonius Saccas over a period of years. The record is found in the *Treatise against the Christians* which Porphyry wrote in the year 274. "This man, having been a hearer of Ammonius, who had made the greatest proficiency in philosophy among those of our day, with regard to knowledge, derived great benefit from his master." Eusebius does not deny the influence of Ammonius although it lessens the stature of his hero. On the contrary he confirms Porphyry's statement by quoting a letter written by Origen in the days of his exile. In that letter the great Alexandrian scholar acknowledged his debt to Greek learning. He says that he became a pupil of one whom he calls a master of philosophical sciences. He was then older than the ordinary student, for he informs us that he followed the example of Heraclas, his colleague, "who I have found persevered five years with a teacher of philosophy before I began to attend to these studies." This enables us to fix the year 210 as the earliest date when Origen could have joined the classes of Ammonius. At that date Origen was more than twenty-five years old. It is true that Ammonius is not mentioned in this letter, but it is obvious from the context that the school of Ammonius is the locale of the studies which Origen refers to.

A more serious difficulty is created by the fact that the critics have discovered a number of errors in Porphyry's testimony. Porphyry seems to imply that Origen was reared in Greek paganism and was a convert to Christianity. Eusebius is not alone in this interpretation of Porphyry's text, and the conclusion would therefore be inevitable that Porphyry was guilty of confusing two different writers. But the fact is that Porphyry was concerned with nothing more than Origen's ideas and with the sources of the allegorical method of exegesis that made his teachings so well known. He accuses Origen of taking from the Greeks, as an excellent instrument for use in making his commentaries on the Bible, a method of interpretation to which his first years at the catechetical school had introduced him. Of a conversion, properly so called, from Greek paganism to Christianity, there is no question in the quotation given by Eusebius: "But Origen, having been educated as a Greek in Greek literature, went over to the barbarian recklessness. And carrying over the learning which he had obtained, he hawked it about, in his life conducting himself as a Christian and contrary to the laws, but, in his opinions of material things and of the Deity, being like a Greek, and mingling Grecian teachings with foreign fables." It was an appraisal which Origen's history must readily have suggested to a non-Christian writer.

There is nothing in Porphyry's testimony to allow us to accuse him of error or of falsehood in what concerns the personal life of the great Alexandrian. Further, he is correct in implying that Origen was not a member of the brotherhood formed by the disciples of Ammonius, as Heraclas undoubtedly was. Origen was merely a hearer, with the purpose of acquiring a method, a philosophical attitude, and a familiarity with certain problems rather than a definite set of doctrines. There was nothing astonishing in the fact that the Christian catechist should follow the lectures of a philosopher of Christian birth whose spiritual tendencies were well known. Besides, the time had not yet come, as a modern writer remarks, when Neoplatonist philosophy enrolled under the banner of Greek polytheism. If it is desirable to distribute Porphyry's observations among more than one person instead of applying them exclusively to Origen, the head of the Academy at Alexandria, it is not because there are errors in the text, but because other texts seem to indicate that this is the course to be pursued.

Contemporary documents, among which are numbered other references by Porphyry, seem to offer, on this subject of Origen, a number of statements which are in contradiction to what is indubitably certain in our knowledge of his history. In point of date, the earliest passage where we find his name associated with that of Ammonius is a fragment of the treatise *On the End* written by Longinus the rhetorician before the year 268. This author gives us a list of leading scholars whom he had known when he was a young man. The list, covering the years from 230 to 235, includes the Platonists Ammonius and Origen. "I attended their classes for a long time. They were far more intelligent than any of their contemporaries." This man, with the name of Origen, was not considered a genuine writer. He was one of those authorities who did not take the trouble to leave books to posterity or to polish a treatise, but who regarded the writing of books as a matter of secondary importance. He did, however, write one book, a treatise on the demons. Porphyry's testimony confirms this item of information; the reference is found in his biography of Plotinus, written after the year 298 to serve as an introduction to an edition of the *Enneads*. We would have to suppose that Origen received from Ammonius the same grounding in philosophy which had been given to the founder of Neoplatonism, and that he violated the philosophical secret by publishing, in addition to the tract already mentioned by Longinus, a second work, *That the King Alone Is a Poet,* during the reign of Emperor Galienus.

Farther on in Porphyry's biography of Plotinus we read that one day the great man was filled with confusion when he found that Origen was in his audience. The incident took place at Rome, where Plotinus is known to have conducted a philosophical school at some period after the year 244. As Porphyry describes the scene, it is quite in harmony with the sentiments of those Platonists of Alexandria who regarded the lectures of a master as a sort of condescension on the part of the philosophical mind, a diffusion of light in the darkness of less gifted minds: "One day the master blushed and wished to rise from his seat when he perceived that Origen was in the audience. When Origen besought him to proceed with the lecture, he replied that he no longer had a mind to do so since he was sure of addressing people who already understood what he was about to say. After a few brief observations the master rose from his chair and left the gathering."

With regard to this evidence from Longinus and Porphyry, neither the greater part of the alleged facts nor the dates nor the titles of the works mentioned can be brought into agreement with what we know of Origen, the head of the Academy at Alexandria. One way to explain these data is to suppose that they refer to another man of the same name, whether the two authors had such a man in view or merely confused him with the Christian catechist. In any case, the confusion gave birth to the hypothesis of a second Origen, often called Origen the pagan, a hypothesis which is today accepted almost universally by the critics.

The humanists of the Renaissance, however, seem to have been ignorant of any such theory.[1] But the authority of Valesius, editor of the *Historia ecclesiastica,* gave it a certain credibility in the seventeenth century, a period when scholarship, welcoming all kinds of distinctions, was quite ready to accept every notion by which sacred history and profane literature could be kept in watertight compartments. Valesius considered that the treatise written in the reign of Emperor Galienus was a work of flattery addressed to the Emperor, who is known to have composed a number of poems. This, however, was attributing to the Neoplatonists an interest in politics, an alien activity in which they had never shown the slightest concern. Another critic thought that the treatise might have been written in jest, if not in downright irony. It is beyond question that the name of Origen was borne by a well-known contemporary of the Alexandrian catechist, like him an Egyptian, a Platonist, and a rival of Plotinus; it is also unquestionable that Porphyry was acquainted with this second Origen. Huet and Redepenning concur in this opinion. The Tübingen school, however, has rejected it, but for reasons that carry little weight.

CONFUSION OF NAMES

Even as late as the nineteenth century, Origen the pagan was being allowed to usurp the place of honor which history has always given to Origen Adamantius, and this in spite of the fact that Porphyry's statements in the treatise against the Christians apply only to the former. "Porphyry, who was an excellent man, no doubt spoke in good faith, but he has confused the heathen Origen whom he once knew with the Christian Origen whom he can never have known, and therefore no weight at all can be attached to what he says. The teacher may well have been Ammonius, but this fact is by no means certain."[2] On the basis of evidence gathered from a number of different sources, we know, on the contrary, that Porphyry became acquainted with Origen the pagan at Tyre or at Caesarea, probably at each of those towns. Yet he attacks Origen the Christian. He attacks him on the basis of his faith, which was built on a foundation of Alexandrian Platonism and on a number of philosophical works of which his attacker finds it possible to give a list.

It is difficult to understand how a confusion of names can complicate a matter of personal polemics, but in this case an ill-founded hypothesis blotted out evidence of the strongest kind. How such a flimsy hypothesis could have been conceived in the first instance baffles comprehension. In historical fact, its sole support is the mention of the name of Origen, made incidentally by some Neoplatonists. That any such man existed at all is nothing more than a mere inference. The inference has been woven into the history of the life and works of the great Alexandrian. It occurs in no other problem of the period, and no confirmation of it has ever been produced by any independent source.

The Praedestinatus

The temptation arises to recall a similar ancient tradition. The same solution, which historical difficulties suggested to the moderns, had been already offered to the theologians in their concern with difficulties of doctrine. A number of sects, for their own purposes, made use of Origen's name. The noisiest of them was a group of Palestinian ascetics who upheld the reading of the apocryphal books, attacked the administration of the bishops, and even accused them of immoral practices. Discussing this group in his work *Contra haereticos,* St. Epiphanius does not go quite so far as to link them with the great Alexandrian. "They call themselves Origenists, but I do not know because of what author. I have no means of finding out whether they come from Origen Adamantius, who is also called Syntacus, or from any other. The name is all that I have."[3] This was, in itself, a small thing, but we find St. Augustine repeating the remark of St. Epiphanius in a more positive form. The anonymous compiler of the *Praedestinatus* acquired new information about the matter and discovered an additional heresy, if not two heresies, with which to enrich his catalogue. "The forty-second heresy had for its founders the Origenists, called after a certain Origen, not the Origen who is known to almost all of us, but a miserable Syrian of whom St. Epiphanius says that

he taught such shameful doctrines that they must not be preserved for posterity."

The inquiry becomes better as it goes along. Although nothing is known of this first doctrine beyond the fact that it was heretical, we find that there were other Origenists who denied the resurrection from the dead and held that the Holy Ghost was a created being. This heretical sect had been founded by a third Origen. At this stage of his inquiry the author of the *Praedestinatus* encounters the objection that a mere reading of the works of Adamantius, and especially of the four books of the **De principiis,** is sufficient to show the presence therein of the majority of the errors of those different heretics. The objection causes him no dismay. His acquaintance with the **Apology of Origen,** which he had studied probably in the Rufinus translation, furnishes him with a reply. Origen's works have been tampered with, he says, and rags have been sewn on the cloth of gold, as the holy martyr Pamphylius has shown. In this solution the two or three heretical Origens fall into their proper places. The most heterodox passages in the Alexandrian's writings come from those men who bore Origen's name but lacked the Christian faith that inspired him. A manuscript transmits only words and ideas; but if it were possible to see the faces of the writers, the imposture would be unmasked.

Under the sponsorship of St. Epiphanius and of the author of the *Praedestinatus,* Origen the pagan thus makes his entry on the stage of ecclesiastical history, all decked out with a collection of heresies. Nevertheless it is well to note that his existence is, from the very beginning, a matter of mere hypothesis in the mind of St. Epiphanius, a fact that considerably weakens the value of the tradition about him. Certainly we find in Christian antiquity no fact or writing that could be attributed to this hypothetical personage whose history would have been intimately joined with the destinies of Origenism. The tolerant manner of his admission to the franchise of the philosophy of Christian antiquity is, we confess, a definite warning to us to be unusually careful in his regard.

I. THE WORKS
THE COMMENTARIES ON PLATO

All recent study of Neoplatonism establishes the fact that a special trait of its adherents was their care and fidelity in conserving all notes and manuscripts pertaining to their doctrines. From this fact the belief has arisen that Neoplatonist tradition was less careful than usual in the case of this Origen, for he certainly would have been one of its own. Proclus, in his *Commentary on the Timaeus,* quotes a number of Origen's interpretations: modern critics, for the most part, attribute them to a Platonist philosopher of the same name.

Like all his contemporaries, Origen the pagan showed a preference for the myths of Plato. Being an enemy of literalism, he found in them an esoteric doctrine. Those mysterious fables were intended to test the student's mental caliber, to stimulate his thoughts, and finally to flood his soul with an inner experience the beauty of which baffles description. He says of Plato that "assuredly he is not indifferent to beauties of literary style, but the goal he seeks is not the mere entertainment of the reader." This was not the critical verdict of Longinus, who regarded the myths as pretty ornaments. In regard to the other Platonists, such as Numenius and his disciples, they saw everywhere in Plato veils and secrets and interdicts at the threshold of divinity.

The Timaeus

In the work by Proclus, Origen follows his own principles in his interpretation of the perfect city, the great lines of which are drawn in the opening pages of the *Timaeus.* In that outline Plato prepares the reader for the contemplation of the divine plan. "He used this image to produce a harmonious condition of the soul to which his doctrine was about to be presented."4 Origen no longer believed the myths of Atlantis, a matter in which he agreed with Numenius. He regarded the account of the Egyptian soothsayer as a fiction which contained a hidden doctrine, because "Plato was not solicitous about beautiful metaphors but wished that his fictions could persuade spontaneously, with frankness and accuracy. He resorted to this method of expression as befitting one who was a great scholar."5

Symbolism such as this was no common theory, for it was compounded of the accuracy of the learned and the wisdom of the holy. The myth was the touchstone of delicate souls. It put them in a state of grace before giving them a passport to wisdom. Clement had recommended this method in his *Stromata.* He says that the seed must be allowed to germinate "after preparing in this careful way those who are worthy of it." Instead of a truth being at once presented in its austerity, it was at first introduced by a scholarly metaphor that rendered the doctrines more attractive and their possession more agreeable.

The Republic

Origen, being Clement's pupil, had a preference for this method of spiritual instruction, and we know that his opinion of its value was confirmed by his reading of Plato. In the sixth book of his *Stromata,* commenting on the third book of the *Republic,* probably with reference to the *Timaeus,* he makes this observation: "for the benefit of souls it is often necessary to employ a ruse." Like many modern critics but with more success, Origen wished to explain the myths of Plato by the application of this principle. Certain methods of deception are a useful kind of therapeutic knowingly employed by those

who govern. But it is illicit to invent a religion for the people or to employ crude and gross descriptions to render a doctrine acceptable to the illiterate and uneducated. Truth lowers itself to the comprehension of the simple for no other purpose than to lift their hearts to God. In the twilight zone of their belief, allegory excites and stimulates them to further inquiry, myth assumes the semblance of truth, and the entire fiction is adjusted to the temperament of him who hears it. Thus allegory introduces the souls of the simple to a truth too mysterious for them to understand directly. "But if the condition of the hearer demands it, the teacher uses ambiguous words, and brings forth his meaning by way of enigmas, both in order to maintain the dignity of the truth and to ensure that what might be harmful if it were candidly spoken to the illiterate should be uttered in words that conceal something of its full meaning. But let the teacher on whom this necessity falls be careful that, when he uses a fiction in this way, he employs it as a sort of condiment or medicament. Thus he will preserve the right order of things." 6 Understatement and exaggeration are equally alien to a sane method of instruction, and neither technique is ever permitted, even where it seems desirable for the spiritual progress of a beginner.

Outside the most scholarly circles of modern criticism it would not be possible to find as comprehensive a theory of the myths of Plato. Even yet a number of our moderns have much to gain from a study of the ingenuity of Alexandrian methods of interpretation. Origen was wrong on only one point: he desired to apply his method to all myths, especially to those which are called genetic myths, such as those telling of the wars in Atlantis. If he had taken better care to distinguish between fable, which Plato calls mythology, and traditions which are half-didactic and half-historical, his spiritual commentaries would have been more prudent. He especially failed to understand that a recorded fact is not a symbol; the method of interpretation which was suitable to explain certain passages in Plato could not be applied at all, even at the cost of many reservations and of multiple changes, to the historical books of the Bible. The history of the dealings of providence with the affairs of men is the direct opposite of a myth, since the value of that history is to be found primarily in the events themselves.

THE THREE CITIES

By use of this method Origen constructed, in the manner of the Timaeus, his threefold plan of the order of the universe. There are three cities: that of God, that of souls, and that of natural forces. From what city does Socrates wish to speak when he describes the highest form of government? From the first, where gods and angels live the life of contemplation? From the second, where the angels are drawn up in battle array on the frontiers of the visible world, attracting to themselves the best of souls? Certainly not the third, that of the passions, because it is excluded. Origen chose the first, the intellectual city, "because it is there that the sciences are entrusted to the guardians," to those of whom the *Republic* speaks. This heavenly abode is described in Platonist language in the first book of the *De principiis,* Origen's nearest approach to the commentaries of the Greeks. "Certain races of souls are set apart in a city of a special character. . . . On that lofty level types of vice and of virtue are presented to them."[7] The contemplation uniting all those souls to one another surpasses every other knowledge. Even when they leave the higher city to constitute the angelic army, they can still instruct fallen beings by salutary lessons drawn from their own knowledge.

The second city, that of the warlike life, is represented in the account of Atlantis. On this point Proclus writes: "Several commentators interpret it as indicating the rivalry of certain demons or powers, the good demons against the bad demons, the former superior in numbers and the others superior in force, as Origen supposed." The power of the angels is more clearly expressed in a fragment from the *Commentary on Genesis* and is discussed at far greater length in that part of the *De principiis* from the fifth to the eighth chapter of the first book; this entire section is a thorough study of spiritual beings. The angels clarify our powers of decision and help us to vanquish the enemy. Their influence is especially powerful in the city of those souls which occupy an intermediate place between good and evil powers and as yet are placed in a state of struggle and trial.[8] With regard to the heavenly movements, those movements exercise their influence within the bounds of the higher city. Souls conserve there "the delicacy and the blessed movement of their nature because of the whirling of the universe which surrounds them and draws them along in its rotation."[9]

We must now consider some aspects of the scholastic regime at the school of Ammonius. Although it was known as a philosophical school, its curriculum did not give equal value to each of the philosophical sciences. Astronomy, geometry, and even logic were excluded in favor of metaphysics, the reason being that this last-named science alone led to knowledge of the soul and therefore to the study of intelligences. The different parts of philosophy were merely so many different aspects of metaphysics as the supreme necessity. Besides, the method followed in the classes forbade any dallying with topics not immediately connected with metaphysics. The usual analysis of a passage from Plato was as follows: observations based on the science of physics led to a discussion about the history of souls in the world; a kind of transcendent ethics was then applied to the hidden forces involved in the struggle in which the rational conscience is ever engaged; finally, Alexandrian mysticism, which was far removed from magic and the occult sciences, was brought into play to show how the

activity of contemplation may become greater or less in the spiritual beings that are charged with the administration of the divine plan. In addition to this, the text sometimes called for a philological analysis.

The first part of the *Timaeus* was the text usually employed for those commentaries. Advanced students also made use of the *Republic* and especially of the *Phaedrus,* in the study of which they began their researches into a philosophy of the universe, although the destiny of individual souls, a problem more akin to religious ideals, continued during this period to hold the place of primary importance. The *Phaedo* and the *Banquet* were less in evidence in the activities of the school. Belief in immortality was a topic discussed in the elementary classes on Platonism. The question of the ascent of the individual soul belonged preferably to the general cycle of the fall and the re-establishment of souls. Such were the ordinary exercises of the student at the school of Ammonius. Origen spoke of them as the clearly defined highway to knowledge.

Thus far we have found that our Origen bears a striking resemblance to his fellow pupil, Origen the pagan. Indeed, they might be almost mistaken for each other. Origen the pagan breathes the air of the school of Numenius during his early studies but does not adhere to its teachings. He accepts the hierarchy of beings in the form expounded by Clement and Ammonius, but he does so with the reservation that the angelic beings are not far removed from the level of men. His vision of paradise takes note of the signs of combat, a new element unseen by the philosophy of impassibility sponsored by his predecessors. His thought is that even in the world of intelligences virtue is not a natural attribute but rather an acquirement or an attainment that stands midway between merit and sin. He has found in Holy Scripture a number of descriptions of battles, with their alternations of victors and vanquished, and has taken them as the key to certain ineffable mysteries.[10]

Origen the pagan is our best guide for an approach to the first book of the *De principiis*. He not only uses its ideas and expresses them in its phraseology but he also manifests its general tendencies. But his thought is more akin to that of the fragments belonging to the *Stromata* of Origen Adamantius.

The Stromata

Origen's mind was steeped in Greek learning. Greek scholarship never lost its attraction for him. He had a special admiration for the work of Greek philosophers on certain matters of science and morals. The notion came to him to compare Christian teachings with the theories of the Greeks on those points. For this work of comparison the most suitable form appeared to him to be the literary style of Clement's *Stromata;* it was a method eminently fitted for his plan of eclecticism, and Clement's former pupil recognized its value. Its flexibility and its adaptability to varying shades of thought permitted of its being reserved for the outstanding pupils of the Academy. They were capable of deriving profit from it by their own labors without intruding in any appreciable degree on Origen's own researches.

Adopting Clement's conviction that sacred and profane learning ought to blend, Origen quoted, among other authors, Plato and his principal commentator Numenius. Nor did he exclude the Stoics; two representatives of the final phase of that Greek system of thought found a place in his work. These two were Cornutus, the master of the poet Persius, and Cheremon, the librarian of Alexandria. It is probable that he also borrowed from the Neo-Pythagoreans. This great effort to weave into the texture of Christian belief so many different strands of Greek learning was rendered the easier by Origen's fondness for the allegorical method of biblical interpretations. Following the example of Hippolytus, he preferred to apply it to the deuterocanonical books of the Old Testament, in which history was of less importance than doctrine. He used it especially for the elucidation of a number of passages from the Book of Daniel.

The work was completed at Alexandria about the year 221, not long after the accession of Emperor Alexander Severus. Like Clement's similarly named work, it was the fruit of several years' labors, and the young professor made use of it as a way to dispose of the surplus of his progressively increasing store of learning. Its literary form enabled him to discuss all manner of subjects, as long as he maintained a certain unity of tone. Hitherto unused notes found a place in it, especially the commentaries on St. Paul which he had written during his controversy with the Marcionites. Its third book, for example, explained a number of passages from the Epistle to the Romans; and in its fourth book, where he discussed the First Epistle to the Corinthians, he presented virginity as a virtue of the heart, far surpassing the simple purity of the body. Farther on, another commentary on this same Epistle asserted the continual role of Christ in the life of the people of Israel. This same fourth book reminded its readers that superior souls, such as the soul of St. Paul, are not of a different essence from those of the common run of men; they share the weakness of ordinary human beings; as other men are weak, so also are they.

Everywhere throughout this work we find the somewhat bookish scholar of the early commentaries, reaping now with ease and certainty the plenteous harvest of his years of contemplation. Beyond the other benefits with which God had showered him, he feels now that he has been granted, in his possession of the secret of truth, the highest reward, the feeling of physi-

cal and mental integrity which a rational being finds in the due exercise of his intelligence. Prayer is an elevation of the soul rather than a petition. In the great cry of the innocent Susanna are heard again the voices of the pure souls of whom he had already written in the *Commentary on the Psalms*. God hearkens to the cries of His holy ones. Their appeal becomes clearer and stronger on account of the love that glows in their hearts, the uprightness that prevails in their minds, the acknowledgment of the divine greatness which their intelligence offers to God. The temptation of the two elders is described in the manner of the psychology which would later become habitual with Origen. At first a passion is born; or, to speak more accurately, a disturbance. This yields to the weakness of the flesh, and the power of right judgment is blinded. Then there follow the deformation and the denial which are the preliminary to every act of sin: the moral sense is ruined, and the eyes of the intelligence are so utterly blinded that the sinner no longer sees the things of heaven, no longer remembers either God or man or the primal tendency which urges every being in the direction of the Good.

St. Jerome's translation of the section dealing with the Book of Daniel reproduces, in vigorous Latin, those traits of Origen. The accuracy of the translator and his deep love of souls could not fail to preserve the sweet odor of Origen's thoughts and perhaps to add to it, so that those lofty concepts become, as it were, hothouse flowers transplanted into a richer soil. Yet it is still possible to recognize here and there the Alexandrian elegance of the Origen of the *Commentary on the Psalms,* his skill in the choice of words, and his technique of the balanced phrase.

But Origen's great effort was doomed to failure. In all the literature of Christian antiquity we find not a single quotation from it. It meets the fate of all the other efforts of reconcile sacred and profane knowledge. Every such work succeeds only in drawing down upon its author the thunderbolts of both parties. The philosophers, on the one hand, always accuse such a writer of misusing their teachings and of selling them off at second hand. This was, in fact, the charge leveled against Origen by Porphyry, who probably read the work. The Christian theologians, on the other hand, resent the degradation of their doctrines to the level of the profane and feel a sense of outrage at the sight of the dogmas of the Church being compared with the teachings of pagan thinkers like Cornutus and Numenius. The great dogma of the resurrection is unrecognizable to them if Origen declares that it is to be explained simply as a vivifying effect produced in a rational being by a mysterious revelation. Thus, under assaults from both sides, the work falls apart. Each body of critics interprets it with praise for one half of it and blame for the other. Because of this divided reception, the work soon becomes quite unintelligible for posterity. Is this not the entire history of Origen the pagan?

THE PLATONIST TREATISES

We must now consider the two treatises mentioned in Porphyry's biography of Plotinus as having been written by Origen the pagan. Here, in its very cradle, the hypothesis of a second Origen is far from impressing us as being a vigorous and sturdy infant, for the titles of the works in question reflect the philosophical activities with which Origen was preoccupied at that time. In his hands the Alexandrian system of teaching was becoming more dramatic and more ample. The order of the universe was to be realized not only by a system of mutual help and prudent education of souls, but by a warfare. The war was a struggle between righteous spirits and evil spirits, and above all between favorable powers and adverse powers. The purpose of providence in presiding at this combat was to restore fallen intelligences to the angelic state. If the Alexandrian catechist was to complete his philosophical theory of the divine plan, such as he understood it to be taught by the spiritually minded philosophers of his day, it was necessary for him to write a *Treatise on the Demons* or on the powers, as those beings were named at the Academy.

The other great Alexandrian problem of the period was how to unite in one comprehensive theory the doctrine of providence and that of what was called the production of the world; of those two doctrines, one was intellectualist and the other voluntarist. The Ammonius fragment lets us understand what the difficulty was: the will of God is the cause of the subsistence of the universe, and wisdom has the subordinate role of an organizer that establishes the hierarchy of beings by the exercise of a certain discrimination. Origen solved the problem by reconciling the two notions. He argued that an act of will is an act of a spiritual being. For him, intelligence was the primal unity from which all beings proceed. With this tenet Neoplatonism assumed the role it would hold until the emergence of Plotinism, half a century later. The divine intelligence governs all things. It is likewise the principle of all things. And it manifests its operation simultaneously by the demiurge and by providence. Whether He creates or presides at the course of events, "through wisdom, God has power over all things." [11] This doctrine of the intelligence-demiurge, or at least some trace of it, is found in all the representatives of the first period of Neoplatonism, in the writings of Longinus as well as in the early works of Porphyry.

From this philosophy, Origen derived the equipment that enabled him to give a decisive reply to the heterodox. The King is a Creator, he said with the Platonists. Then, turning toward the habitual foes of the Academy, he added: "He is the one and only Creator." In thus giving him assured principles in his controversies with the heretics, the new philosophy did not deceive his hopes. Since the intelligence of God has created the world, it was impossible to see the universe as the half-spoiled work of a poorly equipped artisan or of a worker not adequately conscious of his own idea. It was equally impossible to set limits to the work of providence. The King of intellectual nature, in guiding rational beings, guides also their corporeal nature. The three great cities of the Cosmos proclaim the almighty power of Him who is at once their Creator and their Ruler. Looking at the matter from another angle, is not this the teaching of Scripture when it proclaims the kingship of Christ?[12]

To say that the King is the one and only Creator was an adaptation of early Neoplatonism to the theological studies with which the Academy was engaged. It was the first step in the construction of a philosophical weapon for the defense of orthodoxy. The form in which Origen expressed his great principle was taken from the paradoxes of the Stoics. In such a case he had no objection to incur this small debt.

There is no impossibility in the supposition that the head of the Academy was the author of the two treatises attributed to Origen the pagan. On the contrary, the probabilities for the truth of such a supposition are very strong. It is not impossible that each of these treatises came from a collection of independent essays found somewhere among his works. The supposition is reinforced if we remember that Longinus and Porphyry could have known or quoted from dissertations which originally belonged to the *Stromata* or to other Origenist writings. As a matter of fact, the first book of the *De principiis* contains in the first two chapters a dissertation on intelligence considered as a principle. From chapter five to chapter eight the same book contains a complete essay on the heavenly powers. Further, Origen himself called one of the books of the *De principiis* a treatise. Thus would be explained the failure of Eusebius to include in his catalogue of the writings of Origen the two essays mentioned by Porphyry and Longinus. Those two essays would have been inserted or partially used in Origen's subsequent writings.

Longinus does not say, as has so often been assumed, that the philosopher Origen did not publish any other works. Longinus was a Greek philologist, fastidious in his use of language and ceaselessly urging his pupils to have a care for the susceptibilities of posterity. It was his severe judgment that whatever works Origen may have written outside this particular treatise did not deserve the name of literary productions. Even the paradox treating of the creative intelligence did not seem to him to be worthy of mention. In thus neglecting the contributions of the Alexandrian thinker to the history of philosophical literature, the Athenian philologist ranged himself naturally on the side of the

Hellenists. "Origen lacks what makes masterpieces. His writings are improvisations that should have been condensed or subjected to further and more careful study. In the history of Greek literature he belongs only to the second rank." We may add that a great part of the exegesis, some echoes of which could have reached Longinus, was an esoteric doctrine at the Academy of Alexandria and that students were admitted to the study of it only after a long period of probation.

II. THE FACTS

THE MEETING OF ORIGEN AND PLOTINUS

The real difficulty is not in the titles of the two essays mentioned, but in the alleged facts adduced by Porphyry. In his biography of Plotinus he gives an account of a meeting supposed to have taken place between Origen and Plotinus in Rome at some date after the year 254 while the latter was conducting a philosophical school there. There is no evidence for this second visit of Origen to Rome. Porphyry also asserts that the second of the tracts in dispute, *The King Alone Is a Poet,* was published during the reign of Galienus. This emperor came to the throne in the year 254. Now, no historian would admit that Origen lived very long after the Decian persecution, and the general opinion is that he died about the year 252, at the beginning of the reign of Gallus.[13]

He may have been in Rome at some time during the pontificate of Fabian, for he had tried to justify himself with that Pope by means of a letter addressed to the Bishop and the Church of Rome. His apology was fruitless. If a journey to Rome was made subsequently to the sending of the letter, probably it had a humiliating result, and perhaps Eusebius in his biographical sketch of Origen preferred to pass the whole thing over in silence. If the visit occurred, Origen might have attended one of the lectures of Plotinus. The theories of that great thinker had not yet crystallized into a system, and their only effect on Origen would have been to remind him that he and Plotinus had sat at the feet of the same master.

Quite different is the importance of the second difficulty, which is concerned with the date of the treatise. This alleged fact, and this alone, is in contradiction with the history of Origen Adamantius; and it agrees very little better with the biography of Plotinus. The following is what Porphyry says: "Herennius, Origen, and Plotinus made a joint agreement to keep the teachings of Ammonius secret, as they had heard them expounded with uniform clarity in the lectures delivered to them by their master. Plotinus kept the promise. . . . Herenius was the first to break the agreement, and Origen followed him. . . . For a long time Plotinus continued to abstain from writing anything, but he gave his lectures in accordance with the teaching he had received from Ammonius. This was his practice for

ten whole years." We know from Porphyry that Plotinus began to write about the year 255. This is the earliest date that can be assigned to the essay written by Origen. If the two philosophers were publishing at the same time, Porphyry's anecdote loses all its meaning. It is impossible to believe that Plotinus waited very long to follow the example of his former classmate.

This text, confused and obscure from whatever angle it is examined, was the work of an elderly man who wrote fifty years after the alleged incidents were supposed to have happened. In regard to its references to Origen, does such a text require the creation of a second personage whose sole destiny was to be present at the date vaguely mentioned by Porphyry? Reduced to its elements, this is the problem of Origen the pagan. To reach a simpler solution of the difficulty, is it good historical technique to invent an Origen on whom everybody must agree? Recent historians certainly agree, for they ignore him altogether, except for the document which the hypothesis of his existence is supposed to justify without ever quite succeeding. Are there no possibilities except the clumsiest and costliest hypothesis of all, the gratuitous addition of a name to history?

The critics might feel obliged to accept the hypothesis as long as an imperfect knowledge of the origins of Neoplatonism rendered it impossible to clarify the relations of Origen and Plotinus. But the invention of a hypothetical personage was so easy that a number of critics began to be suspicious of it. Was it necessary to invent even a third Origen because the philosopher Eunapius, confused in his recollections of Porphyry's biography of Plotinus, called Origen one of the outstanding classmates of Porphyry? The scholarly Huet is hesitant before this new element of the problem: "If Eunapius is right, two Origens lived in Rome at the same time and were familiar with Plotinus. One of them was his former classmate, and the other was his pupil." In addition to the danger of this swarming of identities, those doubles, so like the great man that they are almost his second self and, besides having no right whatever to a place in history, they are furnished with documents bearing the surest marks of authenticity. Origen the pagan, whose existence is gratuitously assumed as proved, ends by usurping in the school of Ammonius the place occupied, according to the clearest evidence of the texts, by the one Origen whose history we know.

The one insoluble difficulty seems to be the mention of the name of Emperor Galienus. But the supposition of some mistake in the name or of a slip on the part of a copyist would resolve it. Then these phantoms would disappear, with all the dangers they imply. Origen the pagan would rejoin his contemporary, the second Africanus who was another invention of the infancy of historical criticism, in the realm of shadows, in that dim region where the myths of history sleep in a silence from which they never return. In that repose he would join Seneca the tragedian and a number of other such fabulous beings.

In a problem like this, which has been the subject of discussion from the beginning of historical criticism and which has persisted in its obscurity in spite of the fact that its limits are quite definite, it would be presumptuous to hold that we have finally reached a solution. But, for the history of Origen, it is important that a hypothesis should be debarred from entering the domain of certainty. It is equally important to remember that, when we encounter in that history matters we are not certain of, other conjectures, even mediocre ones, are preferable to the hypothesis which the critics have been in the habit of proposing.

Origen was a pupil of Ammonius. This is a point beyond doubt. It is upheld by two quite distinct traditions, that of the Christians and that of the Neoplatonists. It is known to have been accepted without question by his contemporaries and it was the universal belief up to the end of the period of Christian antiquity. A pupil already mature in years and in learning, he sought in the teachings of Ammonius the confirmation of the doctrine he himself had drawn from his Christian faith. His expectations were richly fulfilled. In this Alexandrian philosophy, with its vigorous ingredients of Judaism and Christianity, he discovered, in a form that was even more logical than his own, the conjectures that he himself had already scattered throughout his commentaries. His notion of a total creation, of no pre-existing matter, of an omnipotent providence that disposes the course of events for the education of souls, and that is a divine idea considered as the cause and guardian of the universe, all found their confirmation in the philosophy of Ammonius.

NEED OF A CHRISTIAN SYSTEM

Under the direction of Ammonius he, in his turn, began a comprehensive study of Plato's works. Parallels flooded in his mind. The King of all things, as Plato sketches Him in the *Philebus* and in the *Laws*, recalled to him the kingship of Christ which he had already found in the Epistles of St. Paul. The parallels were committed to his notes. Some of his discoveries were shared with his classmates, even with the unbelievers among them, for they listened to his account of Er the Armenian and to his analysis of the cosmogony of the *Timaeus*. Among them were found perhaps the Platonists Euclid and Democrites, and probably Herennius. In this association Origen undoubtedly passed three or four years, more time than he could have afforded at a later date. Whenever his labors at the Academy permitted, he would be found in the

school of Ammonius Saccas. The **Stromata** was the principal result, but he found time also for the composition of two little works that were his first steps in the direction of the **De principiis**.

By acquiring the philosophy of Ammonius he strengthened his own views, which now began to fall into a more systematic form. His spiritual life, stimulated in his youth by his desire for martyrdom, was about to justify itself in a theoretical martyrdom by his sufferings from the imperfections that press heavily upon free souls like his. His theology would express the inner bond that holds creatures to the divine thought from which they came. He would lead human reason back to that supreme wisdom in which God is pleased to assemble His perfect ideas. Instead of shutting himself in the dusty cell of the Commentaries, the young head of the Academy would create his own philosophy and develop his own system of thought; but it would be a philosophy founded on the word of God, a body of Christian teaching against which the heretics would hurl themselves in vain. Let us permit Origen the pagan to build up his great work and to use his memories of Platonism. Can he do anything else but develop the message of the Church, the one and only truth which Origen the Christian never ceased to carry within his heart?

The result justified only in part the optimism that inspired the vague and generous plan. In the life of Adamantius these two men were sometimes in opposition to each other, until posterity, startled at the complexity of such a soul, made of him two different persons.

Notes

[1] Baronius, *Annales, ann.* 248.

[2] Bigg, *The Christian Platonists*, p. 156.

[3] Epiphanius, *Haer.*, 63; *P.G.*, XLI, 1062.

[4] Proclus, *In Plat. Tim. Comment.*, Diehl, p. 60.

[5] *Ibid.*, p. 86.

[6] *Strom.*, VI; *P.G.*, XI, 101.

[7] The authenticity of this fragment is doubtful. It is inserted by Koetschau in the *De princip.*, I, viii, 4.

[8] *In Gen.*, III; *P.G.*, XII, 84; *De princip.*, I, v, 1.

[9] Proclus, *Tim. Comm.*; Diehl, p. 162. Cf. *De princip.*, I, viii, 4; III, ii, 5.

[10] Cf. *De princip.*, IV, ii, 8.

[11] *Ibid.,* I, ii, 10: "Through wisdom, which is Christ, God has power over all things." Cf. *ibid.,* II, ix, 7: "All things were created by the word of God and by His wisdom, and were set in order by His justice."

[12] *In Joan.,* I, 30; P.G., XIV, 77.

[13] Bigg, *op. cit.* Valesius places the death of Origen at 252; Redepenning at 254; Baronius at 256.

Jean Daniélou (essay date 1955)

SOURCE: "Origen's Theology of the Spiritual Life," in *Origen,* Sheed & Ward, 1955, pp. 293-309.

[*In this essay, Daniélou examines Origen's contribution to the theology of the spiritual life or mystical theology that had an extensive influence in Western and Eastern monasticism, particularly through Origen's allegorical expositions of the Scriptures in which he traced the soul's pilgrimage back to union with God.*]

Origen occupies a conspicuous position in the history of exegesis and was the most eminent theologian in the early Church. The part he played in working out the theology of the spiritual life is historically no less important. This side of him was for long neglected by students, but it has recently been made the subject of a considerable number of monographs.[1] This is a consequence of the interest now taken in the study of spirituality: the subject has shown how important Origen is. Gregory of Nyssa[2] and Evagrius Ponticus, the two great theorists who wrote on mystical theology in the fourth century, were both disciples of his, and if Gregory went further than Origen in stressing the part played in the mystical union by love without light, he still was closely dependent on him. The line of thought started by Origen was carried on in the spirituality of the east by the Pseudo-Dionysius, who was a disciple of Gregory of Nyssa. Maximus the Confessor depends on him, either directly or through Evagrius and the Pseudo-Dionysius, as Fr. von Balthasar has shown.[3] In addition, his spiritual teaching was transmitted to the west through Evagrius Ponticus, who handed it on to Cassian.[4] The influence Cassian exerted on Western monachism from his monastery at Marseilles is a matter of common knowledge. And although it is not always possible to say whether the influence was direct, it is nevertheless to Origen that we must ascribe at least the remote beginnings of St. John of the Cross's spirituality of the desert, St. Bernard's analogy between mysticism and marriage, St. Bonaventure's devotion to the humanity of Christ and Tauler's devotion to the eternal Word.

So extensive an influence would be inexplicable if Origen himself had not lived the spiritual life to an eminent degree. What exactly, then, was the part he played? He was not the first of the great mystics; there had been others before him. St. ignatius of Antioch and St. Irenaeus had been far advanced in the spiritual life; so too had the martyrs, visited as they were by the Lord in the midst of their torments. There is evidence of deep spiritual experience in these men, but you do not find them giving a systematic account of their experience. The introduction of systematic description was mainly the work of Origen. On that point there is general agreement. In order to achieve this result, Origen made use of some of the concepts found in the Platonist mystical writings in circulation at the time, just as Clement of Alexandria had done before him. That is the side of the question which is usually stressed. But it is not the only side. If it were, his influence would be hard to account for.

If his theology of the spiritual life struck a chord in the hearts of so many Christians, the reason is that it was first and foremost a product of the Bible. In Origen's opinion there was no book to equal Scripture. All dogmatic theology was contained in it, all mystical theology was too—the one coming to light when Scripture was interpreted of the Church, the other when it was applied to the individual. Thus, from that point of view, the whole of Scripture had a bearing on the life of the soul and its relations with Christ. As we have seen, Philo too thought that the spiritual meaning of Scripture was the chief one. It was not the same in Origen's case: he realized that there was a dogmatic meaning as well. Yet he did think that the spiritual meaning was just as essential as the dogmatic. The man who regarded things in a purely natural light—the Israelite—did not look beyond the surface of Scripture; but the spiritually-minded man, the man with a taste for spiritual things, had the veil removed from his eyes by the Holy Spirit and then, beneath the letter of Scripture, he could find food for his soul. This idea that Scripture speaks in symbolical terms of the spiritual life was to play a very prominent part in the mystical writings of later ages. It struck root in Tradition when Origen took it up. He describes the main stages in the soul's journey to God in function of it.

The first stage is that in which a man returns to himself or is converted. A concept much to the fore in the theology of the spiritual life, the idea of the image, comes up in this connection. It originated in the meeting of two great doctrines, the biblical one . . . and the Platonist one that man's perfection depends on his likeness to God. Fr. Festugière has given an illuminating account of the way in which the two themes converged.[5] The concept is first found in Philo.[6] It next occurs in Theophilus of Antioch and Clement of Alexandria. Origen develops it to the full. It gives the theology of the spiritual life a dogmatic basis. God created man in his own image. Man's real being is therefore his inner being, his spiritual being, which in a sense partakes of the nature of God. But man is also involved in the life of the senses, which is foreign to his essence. He loses

God's image in so far as he moulds himself to the pattern of the animal life. The spiritual life will therefore consist of the process by which he returns to his true nature—his efforts first to realize what he is and then to try and recover his real nature by destroying the power of his corrupt animal life. To the extent to which he succeeds, he will recover the image of God that once was in him and in it will see God.

We meet with this theme in the homilies on Genesis:[7] "The man who was made in God's image is the inner man, the incorporeal, incorruptible, immortal one." To be more precise, man was made not just in God's image but in the image of the Logos. "What was the image of God that man was modelled on? It could only have been our Saviour. He is the firstborn of every creature [Col. i. 15]. He said of himself: 'To see me is to see him who sent me' [John xii. 45]: 'Whoever has seen me has seen the Father' [John xiv. 9]. If you see a picture of someone, you see the person the picture represents. Thus, when we see the Word of God, who is God's picture, we see God himself." Man lost his likeness to God when he sinned. "Sin made him like the devil, because he went against his nature and looked at the devil's image. When our Saviour saw that man, who had been modelled on him, had shaken off his likeness to him and acquired a resemblance to the devil, he was filled with pity and made himself like man and came down to man." Ever since then, it has been possible for men to recover their likeness to the Word if they will but consent to turn to him. "All who come to him and strive to be like him are inwardly renewed, day by day, according to the progress they make, in the image of him who made them."[8]

Thus, the spiritual life begins when the soul realizes the dignity that belongs to it as God's image and understands that the real world is the world inside it. Here again a biblical theme—"If thou knowest not thyself, O fairest among women, go forth and follow after the steps of the flocks" (Cant. i. 7)—converges with a Platonist one. . . . Origen links the two quite explicitly.[9] Applying the text: "If thou knowest not thyself, O fairest among women" to the soul, he says: "And perhaps you may not know, either, why you are beautiful, may not realize that because you were made in God's image there is great beauty in you by nature. If you are not aware of this and if you do not know what you were originally, then my orders to you are that you should go out after the flocks" (whose way of life you share, as you live like an animal yourself). We have seen that the idea of the image is found in Philo; so too is the application of the maxim "know thyself" to the spiritual life. After Origen, it occurs in Gregory of Nyssa,[10] Ambrose[11] and William of St. Thierry.[12] After that, the idea of the image is found in mystical theology chiefly in the school of William of St. Thierry and St. Bernard. St. Bernard was also influenced by Gregory of Nyssa, whom he knew through William of

St. Thierry's translation, as Dom Déchanet has so ably shown. We next meet with it in the Rhineland, in Tauler's mystical teaching. It is one of the leading themes in the theology of the spiritual life.

In the form it takes in Origen it possesses the same sort of ambiguity as the one mentioned in connection with his theology of grace. The Platonists held that when the soul entered into itself, it discovered its true essence, which was divine.[13] Origen never quite managed to rid his mind of that belief. It was not until the fourth century that the radical transcendence of the Trinity was strongly emphasized and the image of God in the soul was seen to be a product of grace and not a natural property, a personal gift from God and not the soul's own true nature, which it could recover by ridding itself of all foreign elements. In Origen, the soul's kinship with the divine is still represented as a natural property.

The second stage in the spiritual life is reached when the soul embarks on its passage through the period of purgation. This stage, with its trials and its occasional flashes of light, is figuratively represented by the exodus. Here again Origen's spiritual teaching stands at the confluence of two streams of thought. On the one hand, the traditional view held by all Christians was that the departure of the Israelites from Egypt and the crossing of the Red Sea typified man's deliverance from the tyranny of the devil and his release by Baptism. On the other hand, although we do not find Philo systematically fitting the account of the exodus to the stages of the soul's return to God, as was the case with the lives of the patriarchs, he does at least take certain details of the story, such as the darkness on Mount Sinai, and interpret them of the spiritual life. By uniting these two streams, Origen evolved a whole theory about the route followed in the mystical life from the departure from Egypt to the arrival in the Promised Land. Two things need pointing out in this connection. In the first place, the symbolism does not refer to the sacraments: crossing the Red Sea does not stand for entering the catechumenate, crossing the Jordan does not mean being baptized. In this case, it is Baptism that is the crossing of the Red Sea and the beginning of the soul's journey through the mystical life. Secondly, on Origen's map of the soul's route, the term is not the summit of Mount Sinai but the Promised Land. Sinai does not come in at all. Yet it had played an important part in Philo's theory and in Clement's too, and with Gregory of Nyssa it became important once again. The fact is that Origen's theology of the spiritual life takes no account of the part played by darkness in the life of the soul; it deals only with light. That, perhaps, is where its limitations lie. It is a speculative theory of the way the mind is illumined by the gnosis rather than a description of mystical experience, an account of the way the presence of the hidden God is felt in the darkness by the soul as it reaches out and touches him. It is important to get this point clear.

Origen deals with the theme of the soul's journey in his homilies on Exodus and Numbers. The most important of these is the twenty-seventh homily on Numbers, which gives a summary enumeration of all the stages the soul has to pass through. "The children of Israel were in Egypt, toiling with straw and clay in Pharao's service, until the Lord sent them his Word, through Moses, to lead them out of Egypt. We too were in Egypt—we were in the darkness of ignorance and error, working for the devil and sunk in the lusts of the flesh—but the Lord was sorry to see us in that sad plight and he sent us his Word to set us free."[14] This gives us the starting-point—the soul sunk in sin. With the Bible, Origen regards the soul in that condition as being under the tyranny of the devil; with Plato he thinks of it as sunk in the mire.[15] The spiritual journey begins with the advances made by the Word, the Deliverer. The soul's response is her conversion: she sets out after him as the Hebrews in Egypt did after the pillar of cloud, which was a figure of the Word or of the Holy Ghost. Origen then goes on to describe the successive stages in the journey, the various places where the soul stops and rests. "When we have made the decision and left Egypt, our first resting-place is the one where we stop worshipping idols and honouring evil spirits, the one where we come to believe that Christ was born of the Virgin Mary and the Holy Spirit and that he came into this world in the flesh."[16] The basis of the spiritual life is faith. The point is of the utmost importance and it shows at the outset that the kind of asceticism Origen has in mind is not at all what Plato envisaged. The liturgical equivalent of this initial step is the abjuration of Satan, i.e., of idolatry, and the acceptance of Christ which precede the ceremony of Baptism. This is the first step. "After that, we must strive to go further and pass through the various grades of faith and virtue one after another."[17]

The great event in the three days' journey from Egypt to the Red Sea was the pursuit of the Israelites by Pharao and the Egyptians. Origen comments on it in another of his works. "The Egyptians pursue you," he says, "and try to bring you back into their service. By Egyptians I mean the rulers of this world and the evil spirits you used to serve."[18] Such are the temptations that begin to attack the soul when once she has set out on the road to perfection and strive to make her change her purpose and return to the world. But if she perseveres, the Egyptians will be swallowed up in the Red Sea and the soul will "go from one to another of those resting-places of which, we are told, there are so many in our Father's house [John xiv. 2]. In each one she will acquire a fresh degree of light and little by little will become used to the sight of the true Light, who enlightens every soul born into the world [John i. 9]. She will gradually learn to endure the brightness of his

wonderful majesty."[19] What is happening is that the soul is beginning to cross the desert. In the course of the crossing, she is "trained in the keeping of the Lord's commandments and her faith is tested by temptation. . . . What are called resting-places are the stages of her progress through the various temptations against virtue and faith. The words: 'They shall go from virtue to virtue' [Ps. lxxxiii. 8] apply to them. Such souls will indeed go from virtue to virtue until they come to the highest degree of virtue and cross God's river and receive the inheritance promised them."[20]

This trek across the desert corresponds to the gradual stripping-away of the merely natural life which takes place when the soul awakes to the importance of the spiritual life. Origen begins by pointing out that the people were led by Moses and Aaron. That means that if the soul is to make progress, she will need both action, which is what Moses stands for, and contemplation, which is what is signified by Aaron. "When we leave Egypt, we must have some knowledge of the Law and the faith and we must also bear fruit in the shape of works pleasing to God [cf. Col. i. 10]."[21] That, too, comes from Philo. The stripping-process will begin with renunciation of sin, which is prefigured by the vengeance God took on the gods of Egypt. The next halt is called Ramesses (Exod. xii. 37), which according to Origen, means "violent disturbance". "The first progress the soul makes is that she withdraws from the bustle of earthly things and realizes that like a traveller, she must live in tents: she must be free and unattached and so in a position to face her enemies."[22] After the struggle against sin comes the struggle against the passions, $\pi \acute{\alpha} \theta \eta$, and the acquisition of $\acute{\alpha} \pi \acute{\alpha} \theta \epsilon \iota \alpha$, spiritual freedom, which comes with the practice of detachment and makes recollection possible. The vocabulary here is Hellenistic, Stoic in fact, but diverted into a Christian context.

Two more stages follow. The special characteristic of the first is the practice of penance to a moderate extent, for "excess and lack of measure in abstinence are dangerous to beginners". The second is called Beelsephon (Exod. xiv. 2), which is translated as *ascensio speculae* and means that the soul is beginning to get a dim idea of the good things in store for her and to see that she is making progress. The idea of the *specula* is found in Plotinus as well and it plays a prominent part in Gregory of Nyssa's theology, where it signifies that earthly things recede into the background as God's good gifts come closer to the soul. In the next stage, Mara (Exod. xv. 23), spiritual trials are to the fore: the spiritual life is distasteful to nature, which hankers after the flesh-pots of Egypt. But the soul begins to receive spiritual consolation. This is signified by the springs of water and the palm-trees at Elim (Exod. xv. 27). "You could not have reached the palm-groves unless you had passed through the harsh region of temptation; you could not have come to the fresh water of the springs without first going through

rough, unpleasant country. Not that this is the end; this is not the height of perfection. But as God is the soul's guide in this journey, he has arranged *refrigeria* for her in the midst of her exertions, oases where she can repair her strength and so be able to return with greater fervour to the labours still awaiting her."[23]

The soul then comes to the desert of Sin (Exod. xvi. 1). The word means both "vision" and "temptation". And there are in fact, Origen says, "visions which are also temptations, for sometimes the wicked angel 'transformeth himself into an angel of light' [2 Cor. xi. 14]".[24] It is the time when illusion comes into the spiritual life. Origen analyses it with great insight. "That is why one must be on the alert and try to identify accurately the class to which the vision belongs. The soul that has reached the point where she begins to identify the class to which her visions belong will prove that she is really spiritual when she is able to classify them all. It is for this reason, too, that the gift of the discerning of spirits [1 Cor. xii. 10] is included with the other spiritual gifts among the gifts of the Holy Ghost."[25] The doctrine of the discerning of spirits is worked out at length in the *De Principiis*. It is one of the chief elements Origen studied in the spiritual life. The Fathers of the Desert inherited the doctrine from him. It came to play a considerable part in the spiritual teaching of Evagrius. It has a prominent place assigned to it in the *Life of St. Antony*.

The next stages are taken as relating to the soul's recovery of health and the destruction of concupiscence. Now that she is cured and her strength restored, she begins to enter the specifically mystical region. It will be noticed that Sinai is passed over without mention. The soul arrives at Aseroth, which means "perfect courts" or "blessedness". "Everyone travelling by this road, whoever he may be, should carefully consider the order the various stages come in. First you kill the impulses of corrupt nature and bury them; then you come to the spacious courts, you come to a state of blessedness—for the soul is blessed when she is no longer a prey to the desires of corrupt nature. From Aseroth she goes to Rathma, which means 'perfect vision'. The significance of that must be that the soul grows so strong when she ceases to be disturbed by natural desires that she is granted perfect vision, perfect understanding of things, fuller and deeper knowledge of the reasons why the Word became incarnate and planned things the way he did."[26] That brings us to the gnosis, the object of which is the knowledge of the things of God. In another of his works, Origen defines it as consisting of the "knowledge of divine things and human things and their causes".[27] It bears particularly on created spirits and their various dwelling-places.[28] It also bears on the origin of man and on his end and present lot. Knowledge of the things of God detaches the soul from the fleeting things of earth and admits her to the intelligible world. This is the operation which

is carried out at the next resting-place. The gnosis is essentially a kind of knowledge that transforms the soul and brings her into the heart of the things she knows by means of it.

Yet the fact that the soul has reached these heights does not mean that she escapes temptation. "Temptations are given her to guard her and keep her safe."[29] Several of the resting-places stand for these temptations. They try the soul's patience. At the same time, now that she has so many virtues to serve her as armour, she must of necessity go out and fight with the princedoms, dominions and *cosmocratores*. The battle will take place in the realm of the spirit, but it will also be a matter of doing the work of preaching and teaching. In Origen's view, the end which the man leading a spiritual life must aim at is not mere contemplation. If God fills him with his own light and strength, it is to enable him to undertake the hard battles of the apostolate for his sake. Völker is right in dwelling on this side of the question.[30] "He has made us ministers of the New Testament," Origen says, quoting St. Paul (2 Cor. iii. 6). The battle against the powers of evil is also a means of sharing in the Redemption, whether it be fought by martyrs or by ascetics.

All that now remains is for the soul to pass through the final stages of the contemplative life. "From there we come to Thara, the Greek for which is . . . a word used when the mind is so astonished at something as to be stunned by it. [It], then, occurs when in knowing things great and wonderful the mind is suspended in astonishment."[31] These few lines have given rise to quite a controversy. Völker regards them as a declaration on Origen's part that he had experienced ecstasy himself. He compares the passage, which unfortunately survives only in the Latin translation by Rufinus, with another passage, in which Origen talks about "withdrawing from the things of men, being possessed by God and getting drunk, not in the usual senseless way but divinely."[32] H. C. Puech discusses this interpretation at length in his article on Völker's book.[33] He shows that according to Philo,[34] [it] may mean either excessive astonishment at unexpected events or the annexation of the mind by the divine $\pi\nu\epsilon\tilde{\upsilon}\mu\alpha$ and the expulsion of the $\nu o\tilde{\upsilon}\varsigma$ $\check{\iota}\delta\iota o\varsigma$. The second of these meanings is the one that eventually came to be denoted by the term "ecstasy" in the technical sense. But in the *Commentary on St. John,* the word is obviously used by Origen in the first sense. And the passage where it occurs speaks of passing from the things of men to the things of God and not of that "withdrawal from the self" which is the essence of ecstasy. Fr. Rahner,[35] Fr. Viller[36] and Fr. Hausherr[37] are of the same opinion and do not consider that there is any allusion at all in Origen to ecstasy properly so-called.

These observations seem justified. It is undeniable that at the beginning of the third century ecstatic phenomena of a doubtful nature were regarded with distrust, because of the excesses committed by the Montanists. It is also undeniable that the trend of Origen's mystical theology is more towards intellectual contemplation than towards the experimental awareness of the presence of God and the transformation of the soul by love, such as Gregory of Nyssa was afterwards to describe them. He was always the *didaskalos,* and as his mystical theory was in keeping with this fact, he considered that the highest point attainable in mysticism was the contemplation of the mysteries of Christianity. It was left for Gregory of Nyssa to lay the foundations of mystical theology properly so-called by describing how the soul goes out into the dark and there experiences God's presence, not with the aid of concepts, which she leaves behind her, but by love. Origen stays in the sphere of the gnosis, whereas Gregory goes beyond it. Or at any rate, Origen's description of the mystical life stops short at the gnosis.

Such is Origen's spiritual interpretation of the exodus. It contains a wealth of admirable teaching on the spiritual life. The central theme is the idea of the desert—the journey through the night of the senses, with the taste for the things of God growing as the taste for feeding on the things of earth is mortified. Origen describes the stages of this journey. But there was another thing, to his mind, even more characteristic of the spiritual life. This was an idea he bequeathed to Gregory of Nyssa, the idea that the spiritual life is an affair of continual progress. Thus, the second theme is the one centring round the tabernacle, the desert tent, which is never more than a provisional dwelling-place. "Here we have no abiding city." "If you want to know the difference between houses and tents, this is the distinction. A house has fixed foundations, is made to last and stands on a particular site. Tents are where people live when they are travelling and have not reached their journey's end. . . . Those who devote themselves to the pursuit of knowledge and wisdom have no end to their labours. How could there be an end, a limit, where the wisdom of God is concerned? The nearer a man comes to that wisdom, the deeper he finds it to be, and the more he probes into its depths, the more he sees that he will never be able to understand it or express it in words. Travellers, then, on the road to God's wisdom have no houses, because they have not reached their goal. They have tents, which they carry with them on their perpetual journeys, their never-ending travels; and the further they go, the more the road before them opens out, until it stretches to infinity. Everyone who has made any progress in knowledge or had any experience of it knows that when the soul attains to clear sight or knowledge of spiritual mysteries, she uses it like a tent and stays in it. When another of her discoveries comes up for inspection and she proceeds to consider this other thing, she picks up her tent and goes with it to a higher spot and, leaving her senses at peace, dwells there in spirit. Thus, she

finds fresh spiritual experiences accessible to her in consequence of her previous ones. So it is that pressing forward the whole time, she seems to be always on the road and under canvas."[38] The last words of the passage introduce what was to be the central theme in Gregory of Nyssa's mystical theology—the idea of *epectasis*. The essence of the spiritual life is that non-proprietary attitude towards things which makes the soul refuse to rest in what she has already acquired and keeps her in a state of readiness to receive further gifts. It will be noticed that this brings us back to Origen's idea of the created spirit as a being perpetually advancing towards the good. On this point, his theology of the spiritual life is the practical application of his anthropology.

We now come to the zenith of the spiritual life, the perfect union foreshadowed by the Song of Songs. We possess two homilies by Origen on this book and also a commentary. It is the commentary which is important for his teaching on the spiritual life. Origen's was not the first commentary on the Song of Songs. There had been one by Hippolytus of Rome, but it had treated of the union of the Word with the Church. Origen was the first to regard the Song of Songs as celebrating the union of the soul with the Word. Or rather, he saw it as both these things together: the Word's marriage was at once a union with the whole Church and a union with the individual soul. The ***Commentary on the Song of Songs*** is the most important of Origen's works, as far as getting to know his ideas on the spiritual life is concerned. It is also the one that had the greatest influence on other writers; through Gregory of Nyssa and St. Bernard, it introduced a new method of symbolizing the mystical life.

In it, Origen works out a theory about the three stages of the spiritual life. He took the idea from Philo and Philo in turn had taken it from the Greek philosophers. It was destined to have a very far-reaching influence. Origen begins by reminding his readers that the Greeks reduced the abstract sciences (as distinct from the elementary curriculum) to the three subjects of ethics, physics and "theory". He calls them by the names of morals, physics and contemplation. He then goes on to say that "to distinguish between these three sciences, Solomon treated of them in three separate books, each in keeping with the degree of knowledge it was concerned with. First, in the book of Proverbs, he taught morals and set out the rules for living a good life. Then he put the whole of physics into Ecclesiastes. The aim of physics is to bring out the causes of things and show what things really are, and thus to make it clear that men should forsake all this emptiness and hasten on to what is lasting and eternal. It teaches that everything we see is frail and fleeting. When anyone in pursuit of Wisdom comes to realize that, he will have nothing but scorn and disdain for those things. He will, so to say, renounce the whole world and turn to those invisible, eternal things the Song of Songs teaches us about in figurative terms, with images taken from love-making. Thus, when the soul has been purified morally and has attained some proficiency in searching into the things of nature, she is fit to pass on to the things that form the object of contemplation and mysticism; her love is pure and spiritual and will raise her to the contemplation of the God-head."[39]

The passage is of the greatest importance for the history of the theology of the spiritual life. What it amounts to is, in fact, an account of the three ways, the purgative, the illuminative and the unitive. We may take special note of what Origen says about the second of these, as it is particularly interesting. The essential operation of the illuminative way is the formation of a true estimate of things: the soul must come to realize the nothingness of temporal things and learn to understand that the spiritual world alone is real. What she has to do, then, is to rid herself of her illusions about the world and get a firm grasp of reality. Once this conviction is securely established in her, the way is open for her to enter on the contemplation of the things of God. We may also take particular note of the parallelism between the three ways and the three sapiential books. Basing himself on Philo, Origen also links the three ways with the three patriarchs, Abraham, Isaac and Jacob. Abraham represents obedience to the commandments, Isaac is natural philosophy, and Jacob, because of his name Israel,[40] stands for contemplation. In Philo, Jacob had represented the soul on the way to perfection and Isaac was the soul that had already reached perfection. The three classes are symbolized in Numbers by the Israelites, the levites and the priests (this again comes from Philo) and in the Song of Songs by the concubines, the bridesmaids and the Bride. They correspond to beginners, those busy acquiring perfection, and the perfect.[41]

The Song of Songs corresponds to the third way. The subject of the poem is spiritual love. Origen reminds his readers in passing that Plato too speaks of spiritual love in the *Symposium*.[42] There are two kinds of love. "There is a kind of love that is physical; the poets also call it desire. There is a spiritual kind of love as well, engendered in spirit by the inner man when he loves. To put it more plainly, anyone who still has the image of the earthly in the outer man goes where earthly desire and *eros* lead him. But one who has the image of the heavenly in the inner man will go where the desire and love of the things of heaven take him. The soul is actuated by this love when she sees how beautiful God's Word is and loves his splendour: he shoots an arrow at her and wounds her with his love."[43] "Children cannot know what the passion of love is. If you are a child where the inner life is concerned, you cannot understand these things."[44] The Hebrews showed their wisdom when they refused to allow everyone indiscriminately to read the book.

The subject of the Song of Songs is the soul whose "one desire is to be made one with God's Word: to go to her heavenly Bridegroom's room—to the mysteries, that is, of his wisdom and knowledge—on her wedding-night."[45] If she is to do that, she must receive the light she needs from the Word himself, as her natural resources, her reason and freewill, are not equal to the task. "The Bridegroom's kiss [Cant. i. 1] is the working of God in the mind, the operation by means of which, with a word of affection, he shows the mind the light and makes plain what had been obscure and unknown to it before; provided, at any rate, that the mind deserves to have God working in it. . . . Every time we turn over in our minds some question about dogma and find out the answer without help from a master, the Word, we may conclude, has kissed us."[46] This shows unmistakably how the unitive way differs from the earlier ones. In the earlier ones, God acts on the soul through masters outside her; in this case there is a master inside the soul, teaching her from within.

Thus, the mystical life appears as a kind of experimental knowledge of the things of God. Origen gives expression to this belief in the doctrine of the spiritual senses, a theory of the utmost importance and one that he was the first to propound. It is hinted at in Scripture, e.g., in the "How gracious the Lord is! Taste and prove it" of Psalm xxxiii. 9. The chief texts relating to it are grouped together at the beginning of Ziegler's *Dulcedo Dei.* Where Origen showed his originality was in interpreting these texts in conjunction with one another and evolving a coherent doctrine out of them. His method has been studied by Fr. Rahner.[47] The spiritual senses are aspects of the life of grace which, as it grows, enables the soul to taste, touch and contemplate the things of God. Fr. Stolz[48] regards them as a restoration of the unsullied sense-activity exercised by man in paradise. In my *Platonisme et théologie mystique,* I argue against this thesis and show that nothing more is involved than a set of metaphors denoting spiritual experience.

Origen expounds the doctrine in the **Contra Celsum.** "If you examine the question more closely," he writes, "you will see that there is, as Scripture says, a common sense for perceiving the divine. Only the blessed will be able to discover it: 'You will discover a sense that can perceive the divine,' the Bible says [cf. Prov. ii. 5]." It is a sense that comprises several subordinate species. There is a sense of sight for seeing noncorporeal things, as is obvious in the case of the cherubim and seraphim; a sense of hearing capable of catching voices that make no sound in the air; a sense of taste with which to taste the living bread that came down from heaven to give life to the world [John vi. 51 et seq.]; a delicate sense of smell—which is what led Paul to say that he was the "good odour of Christ" (2 Cor. ii. 15); a sense of touch such as John used when he handled the "Word of life" (1 John i. 1). We have senses of two different kinds in us, as Solomon knew: one set is mortal, corruptible and human, the other immortal, spiritual and divine.[49] The idea is developed in the ***Commentary on the Song of Songs***. The soul is attracted by the fragrance of the Word's perfumes and is drawn along after him. "What will she do when God's Word comes to occupy her hearing, sight, touch and taste as well? . . . If the eye can see his glory, glory such as belongs to the Father's only-begotten Son [John i. 14], it will not want to look at anything else. If the ears can hear the saving, lifegiving Word, they will want nothing but that to listen to. The Word is life. When a man's hands have touched him, he will never again touch anything that can corrupt or perish. And when his taste has tasted the good Word of God [Heb. vi. 5], tasted life, tasted his flesh, the bread that comes down from heaven, he will be unable after that to bear the taste of anything else. In comparison with the satisfaction that that flavour gives him, all else will seem unappetizing. . . . If a man becomes fit to be with Christ, he will taste the Lord and see how pleasant he is." The pleasure he obtains through his sense of taste will not be his only joy; all his senses will delight in the Word who is life. "I urge my readers, therefore, to mortify their bodily senses and instead of giving admittance to the impressions that come from them, to use the 'inward man's' senses [Rom. vii. 22], the senses that perceive the divine, and to try and understand this by means of them. That is what Solomon was referring to when he said [cf. Prov. ii. 5]: 'You will discover a sense that can perceive the divine'."[50]

That gives us all the factors comprised in the doctrine of the spiritual senses. The spiritual senses are put into operation in the soul by the Word. They are the unfolding of the inner life. They correspond to various spiritual experiences, all concerned with the Word present in the soul. They are thus bound up with the perfection of the spiritual life. "Those who reach the summit of perfection and the height of bliss will find their delight in God's Word." They are bound up with the mortifying of the life of the body: as the outward man declines, the inward man grows strong. In the end, they bewitch the soul and tear her away from herself. Those who taste the things of God find that the things of the body lose their appeal.[51]

From the spiritual point of view, the doctrine was one of the most fruitful of any Origen taught. Gregory of Nyssa worked out its implications at length.[52] His special contribution consisted of grading the different senses in accordance with their bearing on the successive stages of the mystic's ascent to God. He lays considerable stress on the incompatibility of the bodily senses with the spiritual. The spiritual life seems uninviting at first, because the bodily senses are frustrated and the spiritual ones are not yet at work. But if the soul consents to cross this desert, the taste for God will gradually grow in her. St. Augustine owes to the doctrine what is perhaps the finest chapter in

his *Confessions*.[53] St. Bernard makes much of it. Fr. Rahner has shown the use St. Bonaventure makes of it. And the part played by the spiritual sense of touch in St. Teresa's writings is a matter of common knowledge.[54]

Notes

[1] The study of Origen's theology of the spiritual life really began with Walter Völker's book, *Das Volkomenheitsideal des Origenes,* Tübingen, 1931, which regards him as a great mystic and describes the stages of the soul's journey to God as it is mapped out in his works. F. Bornemann had previously studied his influence on the beginnings of monasticism in his *In Inuestiganda Monachatus Origene Quibus de Causis Ratio Habenda Sit Origenis,* Göttingen, 1885. Fr. Jules Lebreton had also written on "Les degrés de la connaissance religieuse" in R.S.R., 1922, p. 265. Völker's book was reviewed by H. C. Puech in an important article, "Un livre récent sur la mystique d'Origène", in the *Rev. Hist. Phil. Rel.,* 1933, pp. 508 et seq. Puech questioned what Völker had said about ecstasy in Origen but otherwise was basically in agreement with him. The chief work written in consequence of Völker's book was Fr. Aloysius Lieske's *Die Logosmystik bei Origenes,* which accused Völker of failing to see that Origen's mystical theology was rooted in dogma and the Church. Those were the main attempts to examine the question. In the way of general studies, M. Bardy's article, "La spiritualité d'Origène", *Vie Spir.,* 1932, [80] - [106], and Nicole Duval's "La vie spirituelle d'après Origène", *Cahiers de Neuilly,* 8, pp. 39 et seq., deserve special mention. Fr. Viller, also, studies Origen's theology of the spiritual life in his book, *La spiritualité des premiers siècles chrétiens,* Paris, 1930, pp. 45 et seq. It has been translated into German and issued with additional matter and a bibliography (Viller-Rahner: *Aszese und Mystik in der Väterzeit,* Freiburg im Breisgrau, 1939, pp. 72 et seq.). A certain number of important monographs on particular points should also be noted—K. Rahner, "La doctrine des sens spirituels chez Origène", *Rev. Asc. Myst.,* 1932, pp. 113 et seq.; Karl Rahner, "Coeur de Jésus chez Origène", *Rev. Asc. Myst.,* 1934, pp. 171 et seq.; Hugo Rahner, "Taufe und geistliches Leben bei Origenes", *Z.A.M.,* 1932, pp. 105, et seq.; Hugo Rahner, "Die Gottesgeburt", ibid., 1935, pp. 351 et seq.; H. Lewy, *Sobria Ebrietas,* Giessen, 1929, p. 119; J. Ziegler, *Dulcedo Dei,* Münster, 1937, pp. 185 et seq.; I. Hausherr, "L'origine de la doctrine occidentale des huit péchés capitaux", *Or. Christ. An.,* xxx, 3, p. 164; "Les grands courants de la spiritualité orientale", *Or. Christ. Per.,* 1935, pp. 114 et seq.; "Penthos: La doctrine de la componction dans l'Orient chrétien", *Or. Christ. An.,* 132, pp. 28 et seq.; Seston, "Remarques sur l'influence d'Origéne sur les origines du monachisme", *Rev. Hist. Rel.,* Sept., 1933, pp. 197 et seq.; Dom E. Bettencourt, *Doctrina Ascetica Origenis,* Rome, 1947.

[2] See my *Platonisme et théologie mystique. Essai sur la doctrine spirituelle de saint Grégoire de Nysse,* Paris, 1943.

[3] H. Urs von Balthasar, *Kosmische Liturgie,* Freiburg im Breisgau, 1941.

[4] D. Marsili, *Giovanni Cassiano e Evagrio Pontico,* Rome, 1936.

[5] "Divinisation du chrétien", *Vie Spir.,* 1939, May, pp. 97 et seq.

[6] Willms, *Εἰκών,* Münster, 1935.

[7] *Hom. Gen.,* 1, 13. See also *Hom. Gen.,* 13, 3; *Hom. Lev.,* 4, 3; 4, 7.

[8] *Hom. Gen.,* 1, 15.

[9] *Comm. Cant.,* 2, 8 (P.G., 12, 123b).

[10] *In Cant.* (P.G., 44, 806).

[11] *Hom. Hex.,* 6, 6, 39.

[12] *Epistola ad Fratres de Monte Dei,* 180.

[13] Plotinus, *Enn.,* 1, 6, 5.

[14] *Hom. Num.,* 27, 1.

[15] *Phaed.,* 69c.

[16] *Hom. Num.,* 27, 3.

[17] Ibid.

[18] *Hom. Ex.,* 5, 5.

[19] *Hom. Num.,* 27, 5.

[20] Loc. cit.

[21] Op. cit., 27, 6. See also *Comm. Jo.,* 1, 91; 6, 103; 28, 37; *Hom. Num.,* 22, 1.

[22] *Hom. Num.,* 27, 9.

[23] Op. cit., 27, 11.

[24] Loc. cit.

[25] Loc. cit.

[26] Op. cit., 27, 12.

[27] *Comm. Matt.,* 12, 5.

[28] *De Princ.,* 2, 11, 15.

[29] *Hom. Num.,* 27, 12.

[30] *Volkommenheitsideal,* pp. 68 et seq.

[31] *Hom. Num.,* 27, 12.

[32] *Comm. Jo.,* 1, 30.

[33] pp. 529-33.

[34] *Quis Rerum Divinarum Heres?,* 249-56.

[35] R.A.M., 1932, p. 135.

[36] Op. cit., 1930, p. 255.

[37] *Or. Christ. Per.,* 1936, p. 129.

[38] *Hom. Num.,* 17, 5.

[39] *Comm. Cant.,* 78.

[40] "Israel" is often interpreted by the fathers as meaning "one who sees God". See, e.g., *De Princ.,* 4, 12 (Tr.).

[41] See K. Rahner, R.A.M., 1932, pp. 125 et seq.

[42] Prologue (Baehrens, p. 63).

[43] *Comm. Cant.,* 67.

[44] Op. cit., 62.

[45] Ibid., 91.

[46] Ibid., 92.

[47] "Les débuts d'une doctrine des cinq sens spirituels chez Origéne", R.A.M., 1932, pp. 113 et seq.

[48] *Théologie de la mystique,* p. 231.

[49] *Cels.,* 1, 48.

[50] *Comm. Cant.,* 1 (Baehrens, pp. 103 et seq.).

[51] See also *De Princ.,* 1, 1, 7 and 9; *Cels.,* 1, 48; 7, 34; *Hom. Lev.,* 31, 7; *Hom. Ez.,* 11, 1; *Comm. Cant.,* 2, Baehrens, p. 167).

[52] See *Platonisme et théologie mystique,* pp. 235 et seq.

[53] 10, 27.

[54] Now that we have come to the end of our study of Origen's spiritual teaching, we see that it is related to his theory that all *logikoi* share in the life of the Logos (see above, ch. 4, s. 1, where the idea is expounded in full). Spiritual progress is the soul's recovery of her

likeness to the Word who dwells within her and enables her to become one with him by seeing and loving him. This is very well brought out by Fr. Lieske in his book, *Die Theologie der Logosmystik bei Origenes,* pp. 120 et seq. But it is also true that Origen's mystical teaching is not a merely speculative thing; it is a consequence of deep spiritual experience. Völker was right in stressing that side of the question. Origen's experience has an independent value of its own and gives him considerable importance in the spiritual sphere properly so-called.

Henry Chadwick (essay date 1966)

SOURCE: "The Illiberal Humanist," in *Early Christian Thought and the Classical Tradition: Studies in Justin, Clement, and Origen,* Oxford at the Clarendon Press, 1966, pp. 66-94.

[*In this essay, Chadwick reviews Origen's life and teachings, showing in what ways Origen is different from Clement, his predecessor. Throughout are discussions of Origen's thinking on revelation, gnosticism, Christian philosophy, human sexuality, and the Incarnation.*]

Origen is not a figure it is easy to see in accurate perspective. This difficulty is not caused merely by the massive dimensions of his work, nor because he is especially obscure, nor even because we do not possess the full original text of his most controversial treatise. The primary reason is perhaps that some of his most characteristic themes, warmly debated during his lifetime and a stone of stumbling to many in the three hundred years following his death, have remained to this day permanently troubling questions in the history of Christian thought. It is notoriously difficult to handle him with that critical spirit which requires sympathy and impartiality from the historian.

Clement was a convert from paganism. Origen's parents were, or at least became, Christians. We have two rival and contradictory accounts of Origen's family, one from Eusebius of Caesarea and one from the inveterate enemy of Christianity, Porphyry.[1] According to Porphyry Origen was born and educated as a pagan. Eusebius says his parents were Christians and that his father, Leonides, was martyred in the persecution of 202 at Alexandria. As Eusebius is able to quote a sentence from a letter from Origen to his father exhorting him to stand firm in his hour of trial,[2] it may reasonably be assumed that Eusebius was at least correct in thinking they became Christians, though it is possible that they were not so at the time of Origen's birth. A large portion of what we know of Origen's life comes from the sixth book of Eusebius's *Ecclesiastical History.* This is not only a high climax of Eusebius's work, but also dependent on a 'Defence of Origen' complied by Eusebius and his teacher, the martyr Pamphilus. (One of the six books of this work survives in a Latin translation by Rufinus.) For Eusebius Origen is a supreme saint and hero, the realization of his highest intellectual and spiritual ideals. The life of Origen is written in a hagiographical tone, and freely uses oral tradition and gossip. But Eusebius had gone to the trouble of assembling over 100 of Origen's letters,[3] several of which he quotes. Whenever Eusebius is using documents contemporary with the events he is describing, his authority is first-class. Whenever he depends on no more than hearsay and oral tradition, his authority is not higher than that of any reasonably conscientious gossip-writer. As he is careful to say when he has documentary authority, it is not hard to distinguish which parts of his life of Origen are authoritative and which should be treated with caution and reserve. For example, the notorious story that Origen castrated himself so as to be able to work more freely in instructing female catechumens[4] may perhaps be true, since such occasional acts of extreme enthusiasm are attested in this period of the early Church.[5] But the story is not among those for which Eusebius quotes contemporary documents. He depends on an unwritten tradition. Near the end of his life Origen wrote a commentary on St. Matthew, in which he deplores the fanaticism of exegetes who have interpreted Matthew xix. 12 literally.[6] Epiphanius in the fourth century records the existence of a rival tradition that Origen's amazing chastity was achieved by drugs rather than by a knife.[7] Possibly both stories were generated by no more than malicious gossip. It is certain, at least, that the extreme self-denial of Origen's life as a young teacher provoked much notice and envious comment, sharpened by the stringency of his own outspoken criticisms of the worldly compromises of clergy and laity. He lived on the minimum of sleep and food. Taking seriously the gospel counsel of poverty, he sold his books of literature and philosophy.

According to Porphyry Origen attended the lectures of Ammonius Saccas,[8] an esoteric eclectic Platonist, with whom some eleven years later Plotinus was to study. Ammonius is a figure largely lost in the mist. The prime source of information about him is Porphyry, who says that Ammonius was the child of Christian parents but abandoned Christianity for the old religion. Ammonius's esoteric teaching moved Plotinus to desire Persian and Indian wisdom (which may suggest some sort of Neopythagoreanism, in spirit akin to that of Numenius of Apamea a generation before him). In his *Life of Plotinus* Porphyry mentions an Origen as one of Plotinus's fellow-students under Ammonius. It is so difficult to reconcile Porphyry's statements about this Origen with what is known of the Christian Origen that almost all scholars recognize the existence of two Origens. The Origen of the *Life of Plotinus* is treated by Porphyry as wholly one of the Neoplatonic circle. It is this Origen who is quoted by later pagan writers such as Eunapius, Hierocles, and especially Proclus, none of whom betrays the least awareness that these quotations might have come from a Christian writer.[9] What the Christian Origen learnt from Ammonius is beyond identification. It is at least certain that his writings display a masterly knowledge of the debates of the Greek philosophical schools and first-hand acquaintance with the works of Plato and Chrysippus.

As a teacher Origen began by giving instruction in grammar (by which he earned enough to keep his bereaved family) and in catechetical teaching. Eusebius says that he began work as a catechist, during the persecution when the normal official instruction (under the bishop) had ceased, at the request of individual converts who desired to be prepared for baptism. Whether this was the beginning of tension with Demetrius, the bishop of Alexandria, can only be a matter for conjecture. Demetrius gave Origen his authorization when the storms of persecution died down. But in Origen's act there may have been some implicit criticism of the fact that the bishop's official teaching was not being given for a time. To a stern ascetic, episcopal 'discretion' might well appear to be moral compromise. The story of his subsequent relations with Demetrius is one of mounting tension and distrust.

Origen divided his pupils into two categories, of which he took the more advanced, while the more elementary teaching was entrusted to Heraclas, a Christian whom he had first met at the lectures of Ammonius Saccas and who was later to become bishop of Alexandria. During this period (from about 212) he learnt Hebrew from a Christian Jew and compiled his Hexapla, a vast synopsis of the various versions of the Old Testament: first the Hebrew, and a transliteration of the Hebrew into Greek characters, the purpose of which is not perfectly clear (the most likely explanation is that some churches had preserved the old synagogue practice of having the Old Testament read in Hebrew even if they did not understand it); then the standard Septuagint version, generally used by the Greek churches and regarded as authoritative, with the rival translations of Aquila, Symmachus, and Theodotion, while, for the Psalms, two additional translations were added, one of which Origen had discovered himself in a jar in the Jordan valley, presumably in some collection of manuscripts very like that found at Qumran. Any words in the Septuagint differing from the Hebrew he marked with an obelus, indicating doubt about their authority, while supplements to the Septuagintal text, marked with asterisks, were added from the version of Theodotion. The Hexapla was designed for use. Origen had learnt from disputations with Rabbis that it was of no value to appeal to books or to a text of which they did not recognize the authority. During the third century the different churches were becoming much more aware

than they had been earlier of divergent customs among themselves in accepting certain books in their lectionary. The majority view regarded the Septuagint as authoritative and inspired, but because of the lack of complete unanimity among churches and because of the continual debate with the synagogue only the Hebrew canon could be regarded as possessing wholly certain authority. The silent implication of Origen's view is that it is not safe to appeal only to the Septuagint to establish a point of fundamental doctrine. It is a consequence of the explicit deduction drawn from this view by Jerome that in English Bibles the overplus of the Septuagint canon over the Hebrew is separately printed, under the thoroughly misleading title 'Apocrypha'.

The text and exposition of the Bible stand at the very centre of Origen's work. The main bulk of his writings consists of sermons preached to congregations (mainly at Caesarea in Palestine whither he migrated in 230-1 after his relations with Bishop Demetrius had reached breaking-point), commentaries giving a full-scale exposition of immense detail, and 'scholia' or brief notes on particular points in certain books (though, as none of the scholia has been preserved directly by the manuscript tradition, their precise character is none too clear and one can argue only from analogy). One of his early works was entitled **Stromateis,** but only a few fragments survive. Among other topics Origen sought in this work to translate into Platonic language some basic New Testament ideas like 'eternal life' and to show the harmony of Jesus and Plato.[10] The endeavour suggests that Origen's **Stromateis** had at least something in common with Clement's, and perhaps he thought of himself as continuing where Clement's work had been left unfinished. On several occasions Clement announced his intention of discussing 'first principles' (*archai*) and the creation of the world,[11] but his intention was never realized. Origen may have wished to fill the gap when he wrote his own fateful treatise 'On First Principles', consisting in the main of an elaborate refutation of gnostic dualism and determinism directed against Marcion, Valentine, and Basilides, and a pioneer attempt to lay down rules for the right interpretation of the Bible.[12] The undertaking necessitated a general statement on the fundamentals of Christian doctrine such as Clement had never produced, but it is wrong to think of Origen's 'First Principles' as a systematic *Summa Theologica*. It is systematic in the sense that Origen opposes to the gnostic theology a coherent and self-consistent view of Christian doctrine, but its essential character is exploratory rather than dogmatic. 'Soundings' might have been an appropriate title for it. On several occasions he reviews various possible opinions and leaves to the reader a decision about the correct view. And although the first four words are a reminiscence of Plato's *Gorgias*, the work is not intended to be a synthesis of Christianity and Platonism. Its primary intention is anti-gnostic polemic; and as in the fourth gospel or the epistle to the Colossians this attack partly takes the form of silent concession, endeavouring to take over any of the positive values of the system of thought Origen is opposing and incorporating them within an orthodox scheme.

A similar need to oppose Valentinian Gnosticism gave Origen the initial impetus to write his commentary on St. John, which became a vast work of thirty-two tomes, of which the medieval scribes only had the courage and energy to transcribe the greater part of nine. This was dedicated to his patron Ambrose, whom he had converted from Valentinianism, and who regretted that, while there existed learned heretical commentaries like that of Heracleon, nothing comparable existed from the orthodox side. The commentary is remarkable for some speculative flights, no doubt designed to show Ambrose that orthodoxy is not duller than heresy. Clement of Alexandria had spoken of St. John as a 'spiritual gospel' in contrast to the three Synoptists who recorded the outward facts.[13] Origen likewise sees that the fourth evangelist's divergences from the synoptic tradition are bound up with theological rather than historical considerations: it was the purpose of the evangelists to give the truth, where possible, at once spiritually and corporeally (or outwardly), but where this was impossible, to prefer the spirit to the body, 'the true spiritual meaning being often preserved, as one might say, in the corporeal falsehood'.[14] None can understand the profundity of the gospel unless he has first, with the author, leant on Jesus's breast.[15] Accordingly, Origen's exposition is in search of a spiritual meaning which is not heretical and yet goes deeper than the surface meaning apparent to ordinary Church readers.

Because much of his work consists of an exposition of scripture Origen's writings bear a closer kinship than Clement's to the great allegorical commentary of Philo on the Pentateuch. 'Philo's commentaries on the Mosaic Law' (he once remarks) 'are read by judicious and intelligent men'.[16] Allegorical principles were securely guaranteed by the authority of St. Paul treating as allegory the story of Hagar and Sarah (Galatians iv) or by his declaration in 2 Corinthians iii that the spirit gives life, while the letter kills. Philo had found in the Pentateuch a mass of Greek philosophy, psychology, ethics, and natural science. Origen takes the method but modifies the results, fusing Philonic allegory with the typological methods of Justin and Irenaeus, by which the Old Testament contained not moralizing generalities expressed in the obscure form of history, geography, or law, but specific foreshadowings of the concrete redemptive acts of God in Christ. Origen takes as axiomatic Philo's principle that nothing unworthy of God can be intended by the inspired writers, and that passages in the Old Testament speaking of God as changing his mind or as angry and threatening prove only that in mercy God accommodates himself to the

level of mean capacities which can only think in such picture language. There is in fact a scale of apprehension, and higher minds perceive truths in the Bible that are obscure to inferior understanding. Most texts in scripture have a literal and historical meaning, but that this is not the only or primary meaning is shown by certain passages which are literally impossible, placed there by providence as evidence to guide the reader to the spiritual truth. The allegorical meaning may not be simple; and two, three, or even four concurrent levels of meaning may be found in some passages. The Song of Songs, for example, has two spiritual interpretations, one concerning Christ and the Church, another concerning the union of the Logos with the individual soul. Origen sometimes justifies this doctrine of concurrent meanings by taking the human analogy of body and soul which Philo and Clement had used before him, only modifying it in accordance with the Pauline division of man into three parts—body, soul, and spirit.[17]

Because revelation is an accommodation to differing levels and capacities, Christian doctrine is capable of varying statements. The higher flights are not only not understood by inferior minds but are actually suspected of being heretical, and therefore have to be treated as esoteric and mysterious. A full account it is hardly safe to commit to writing. But Origen's constant endeavour is to bring the existence of higher insights to the attention of inferior capacities and to provoke them to advance in the spiritual and moral life, so that in time they too may come to understand matters now beyond their range. Literalist exegesis of the Bible produces bizarre crudities, and simple readers of the Old Testament believe things of God that would not be credible of the most savage and unjust men.[18] The diversity of mental capacity in the Church is so great as to impose intense difficulties upon a Christian teacher. He must speak without upsetting the simple, yet without starving the more intelligent.[19] Origen suggests that many Christian teachers are failing in their duty to the sharper minds in their congregations. Probably, he thinks, private instruction is best suited for them—just as the Lord himself spoke in pictures and parables to 'those without', while within the house he explained everything privately to the disciples.[20] Likewise there is the example of St. Paul, who had indeed a higher wisdom expounded to the perfect, but was prepared to accommodate himself to the carnal Corinthians, capable only of milk, not of solid meat. To them the apostle determined to know nothing but the crucified Christ of humiliation; they were not yet worthy of the *theologia gloriae*.[21]

In his commentary on St. John Origen collects from scripture the titles of Christ.[22] It is a consequence of the redeeming grace of Christ that he is all things to all, to each according to his need, and is therefore variously apprehended by believers. We begin by knowing Jesus as redeemer and physician, curing us of sin and passion, but we are to advance to know him under other forms and titles, as life, light, truth, and wisdom. The Logos as the mediator of God's revelation is like the steps leading up to the holy of holies in the Temple,[23] and we are gradually to ascend until we know him, not as he wills to be initially for our sakes, but as he truly is in himself. This is for Origen the principle of the Incarnation, and he finds it powerfully reinforced by the symbolic narrative of the transfiguration: to the inner circle of disciples on the mount Christ's true glory is disclosed, but to those on the plain his appearance may betray nothing of the mystery of his being. So John the Baptist was able to tell the Pharisees that 'there stands one among you whom you do not recognize' (John i. 27). Although Origen emphatically rejects the Docetic doctrine that Christ's body was not real but an optical illusion, nevertheless he found matter very congenial to his conception of the varying levels of apprehension of Christ in the strange doctrine of the apocryphal Acts of John that the physical appearance of Jesus differed in accordance with the spiritual insight of the beholder.[24]

The doctrine of differing degrees of knowledge may be best illustrated by Origen's treatment of the primitive eschatology. The hope of the second coming of Christ is taken in a literal and material sense by simple believers. Origen does not attack their belief; it is better that they should believe the right thing in the wrong way than not believe it at all, and it is the best of which they are capable. But the Christian preacher has a responsibility to educated minds who, so Origen observes, are often distressed by this article of the creed. The spiritual, symbolic meaning of the doctrine of the second coming may be either the universal expansion of the Church throughout the world, bringing all men to the obedience of Christ, or the inward coming of Christ to the soul, when he comes not in humiliation but in glory, uniting the believer to himself in a union so intense that the believer leaves behind the limitations of this mortal state and is raised to be one spirit with the Lord.[25] Similarly, Biblical language about punishment for sinners by everlasting fire is understood literally by very simple believers. They do not perceive that the 'fire' of God's judgement is a purifying process which has a remedial end in view; and this is a truth that ought in general to be concealed from them since many can only be deterred from a sinful life by fear. All such Biblical language is an accommodation to them. In truth the fire of judgement has no measurable temperature. Hell is an inner disintegration of the soul, 'a lack of cohesion'.[26] In the **Contra Celsum** Origen meets the accusation of Celsus that Christian evangelists stampede people into the Church by frightening them with bogywords about God as a torturer. He concedes that simple Christians may understand scriptural language about hell in a superstitious and unworthy way. But their error is only to

misunderstand the purpose of God. As to the fact they are right: 'we teach about God both what is true and what the multitude can understand, though intelligent Christians understand it in a different sense'. In one sense threats of hell are 'more false than true'. But Plato himself thinks it justifiable to tell a lie to a homicidal lunatic.[27]

Again, the resurrection of the flesh is an article of the creed that some unreflecting Christians understand to mean the resuscitation of this physical body, with all its organs.[28] This belief goes with the literal expectation of the reign of Christ for a thousand years at a renewed Jerusalem.[29] Origen regarded as credible neither the millenarian hope of Christ's return to this earth nor the expectation of a literal resuscitation of this body. He discussed the problem in an early work 'On the Resurrection', of which only sparse fragments have been preserved, so that it is difficult to describe Origen's doctrine without being forced to rely on the onslaughts of his critics, especially Methodius and Jerome, who were certainly less than fair to him. Origen entirely agreed with the numerous pagan critics of the Christian hope as literally interpreted, for example, by Justin or Irenaeus, that no appeal might be made to divine omnipotence to justify affirmations unworthy of God. When St. Paul speaks of powers in heaven as 'bowing the knee' to the Father, we are not to suppose that angels have knees.[30] The risen glory of the redeemed transcends this life. The 'body' will be of a kind appropriate to a heavenly environment.

Perhaps Origen's most important statement about the nature of Christian doctrine as he understands it is contained in his preface to his work 'On First Principles'. He begins by laying down those points of doctrine which are plain and unmistakable because they are given in the rule of faith handed down faithfully in the Church from the apostles. The apostles taught certain doctrines as *credenda,* to be believed without discussion, for they had to provide authoritative affirmations intelligible even to the simplest and most uneducated people. But they often did not state the rational grounds underlying their authoritative affirmations; and there are several questions of some importance for theology on which they gave no clear opinion or guidance. So that there is room for investigation and inquiry on two counts. Authority is not arbitrary, and its justification is the ability to give reasons if required and if the recipient possesses the capacity to comprehend them. On the other hand, where authority has prescribed no particular view, the theologian is free to discuss the issues open to him without having to conform to a fixed rule of thought. The doctrines laid down by the rule of faith as given are the following: (*a*) There is one God who created the world out of nothing, the God of both Old and New Testaments, himself both just and good. (*b*) Jesus Christ is God's pre-existent Son, begotten before all worlds, who, without ceasing to be God, became man, born of a virgin and the Holy Spirit; he truly suffered and died, rose again, and ascended to heaven. (*c*) The Holy Spirit is of like rank, but it is not clearly stated in scripture whether he is uncreated or whether he belongs to the created order. What is certain is that the Holy Spirit inspired the Biblical writers. (*d*) The soul will be rewarded for its actions with heaven or hell, and there will be a resurrection of the dead. It is certain that free will must be affirmed. But nothing in scripture makes it clear how the soul comes to be united to the body—whether it is transmitted from the parents together with the seed that grows into the body, or whether it comes into the body from outside, or whether it is created by God or uncreated and immortal. (*e*) It is certain that the devil and evil angels exist. How they came to be and who they are is obscure, though most Christians (of whom Origen is one) think the devil an apostate angel. (*f*) It is certain that this material world was made at a definite time, and will suffer dissolution one day. But it is not clear what existed before it or what will be after it. (*g*) It is certain that scripture is inspired by God and has a meaning deeper than the literal sense; but the elucidation of the true inner meaning is a problem left to the expositor. (*h*) It is not clear beyond discussion whether God and indeed all souls are immaterial beings or whether they have some shape like that of physical bodies. And cognate questions are raised by Church teaching about guardian angels and by the question whether the sun, moon, and stars are ensouled (as the Platonists say) or not.

The presuppositions of this preliminary statement are evidently very different from those governing Irenaeus's theology. For Irenaeus heresy comes of following the itch to speculate where scripture has given no clear guidance; we must be content not to know if the word of God is not explicit, and should maintain as reverent an agnosticism in matters of high theology as we are bound to hold about the causes of bird migration or the sources of the Nile or other matters of natural philosophy which lie beyond the reach of human inquiry.[31] Reason is confronted by a definite frontier, and is precluded from crossing that frontier by the limitations of human knowledge unless it is given in the Bible manifest authority to think about those questions that transcend creaturely capacities. It is the error of the Gnostics that they claim to know what we are not meant to know. Origen is as conscious as Irenaeus of the limitations of human intellectual powers for inquiring into the transcendental world, but thinks it possible for the human mind, with the aid of grace given in answer to prayer and purity of heart, to speculate with becoming diffidence even about questions that are not explicitly set out in the apostolic rule of faith.

Origen begins by eliminating the anthropomorphic notion that God is literally light or fire or spirit in a Stoic sense of a tenuous thinking gas. God is the immaterial ground of being, the cause of all that is. To be is to participate in him who is. He is alone underived, the Monad, transcending all multiplicity, self-sufficient, and beyond the power of the human mind unaided by special grace. In one passage[32] Celsus commends to the Christians a study of Plato if they want to find a reliable theologian: the Platonic school distinguishes three ways in which the knowledge of God is attainable by man, namely, the *via eminentiae* affirming that the highest we know is the least that may be predicated of God, the *via negativa* defining him in terms of what he is not, and the way of analogy, as when we say that God is to the intelligible world what the sun is to the visible and sensible world, making it possible for the eye to see the phenomenal world and indeed itself as well. Origen replies that more than rational dialectic is required for the knowledge of God: 'Human nature is not sufficient to find God unless it is helped by God who is the object of the search; and he is found by those who, after doing all that they can, admit that they need him. He shows himself to those to whom he judges it right to appear, so far as it is possible for God to be known to man and for the human soul which is still in the body to know God.' God is known by a free act of grace on his part, and he reveals himself to those who are pure in heart (so that holiness is an essential requirement, not merely dialectics) through the incarnate Logos. With this large qualification Origen would happily approve of Celsus's statement. The discussion with Celsus illustrates well the double-sided character of Origen's doctrine of God. On the one side he takes for granted the transcendentalist theology of Platonism, that God is the ground of being and even 'beyond being', in need of nothing, though the cosmos has come into being by an overflow of the divine nature which is goodness. On the other side Origen is trying to make room within this scheme for the idea of freedom in God and also in the creatures, and for the notion of a gulf between the infinite Creator and the finite creatures which, by virtue of being created, are strictly dependent and transitory except in so far as they are kept in being by the will of their Maker.

Creation is the consequence of an overflow of divine goodness, its initial object being the order of rational beings, pure spirits unencumbered with material bodies like ours. Since there can never have been a time when divine goodness and power were inactive, there is a sense in which this spiritual cosmos is eternal. If it is not eternally necessary to the being of God, it is certainly an eternal consequence of his nature. Nevertheless Origen also asserts that these rational, spiritual beings are creatures, not uncreated but dependent on the divine will for their existence. Origen is well aware that he is confronting an insoluble problem in trying to reconcile the affirmation that creation is an outflow of the divine nature with the affirmation that it is dependent on a free decision of the divine will. But the affirmation that the discarnate rational beings eternally exist as a correlate of the eternity of the Creator's goodness seems to Origen to be a necessary assertion if the immutability of God is to be upheld. It is on this same ground that he affirms that the generation of the Son is not a temporal act or a moment in a succession of events, but an eternal generation. The Father is eternally Father; there was never a time when the Son was not. Unless this assertion is made, the unchangeableness of God is prejudiced.

The Logos is the image of the Father's power—not an image of the Father so identical with the archetype that he can be said to be as much Father as the Father himself.[33] All rational beings participate in the rationality of the divine Reason who is the archetypal source of their nature, and the mediator between the Father and the creatures. The Logos is therefore God in relation to the lower order; he is God immanent.

The rational beings so created were not self-sufficient, but were turned towards God in adoration. But they came to neglect their love for God. Following an idea suggested by Philo[34] Origen says that they became 'sated' and so fell. By falling from the divine love they cooled and so perhaps became 'souls'[35]—for *psyche* was commonly derived from *psychesthai* by an etymology as old as Plato and Aristotle and exploited by the Stoics who thought that as a newborn baby emerged to the cold air it gasped for its first breath and that at this point the soul first entered its body. To Origen the Pauline trichotomy of body, soul, and spirit suggested that the soul was midway between matter and spirit; it might descend to materialism, but it was called to unite with the highest element, the *pneuma,* and thereby to cease to be *psyche*.[36] (To Origen's later critics this entire notion of spirits falling to become souls seemed very damaging, but the point is not really of central importance for Origen's own thought.)

Origen's next speculation is an adventurous step. He proposes to regard the diversity of spiritual entities, stretching downwards from the archangels through inferior angelic powers and saints to men and yet lower still to demonic powers, as constituting a hierarchy of consubstantial rational beings, which is brought about not, as many of the contemporary Platonists said, by an evolutionary process of necessary emanations from above but by free will being exercised in different ways.[37] The material world is created by God through the Logos by whose power the immense diversity of the hierarchy of being is controlled and so prevented from disintegration. The sensible world is created by God out of nothing, by which Origen means absolute, not merely relative, non-being. 'I cannot understand how so many eminent men have imagined matter to be uncreated.'[38] Origen is strongly critical of the Platonic doctrine of the eternity of the visible world. The words of *Timaeus* 41 that, although the cosmos is created and so in principle destructible, yet in practice by God's

will it will never be destroyed, hold good according to Origen not of this phenomenal world but only of that higher world of discarnate spiritual beings, the realm of saints and angels. Origen likewise rejects the teaching of the *Timaeus* that while the transcendent God is the source and maker of gods derived from himself it is these inferior powers who are responsible for the material world.[39] This doctrine of the *Timaeus* had been freely accepted by Philo, and used by him as an explanation of the problem of evil.[40] But for Origen this view was hopelessly gnostic in its implications, and he would have none of it. In arguing against Celsus he decisively rejects the view that evil inheres in matter, and underlines the point when he says that the Christian doctrine of God as creating matter does not in any way make him responsible for evil.[41]

Nevertheless, Origen never reaches a perfectly clear and decisive opinion on the exact status of matter in the divine purpose, even though the solution of this problem is of the highest importance both for his conception of the nature of man and for his doctrine of the destiny of the redeemed. He reviews three possibilities, but the discussion does not arrive at a decision.[42] First, there is the view that matter is eternal and that it will suffer an eschatological transformation, in which case the resurrection body will be in form like our earthly body but glorified and radiant. Secondly, it is possible that discarnate spirits can exist without any bodies of any kind whatever, though they may need bodies for a time at a certain stage of their education on the way back to God. If so, the material order will be brought into existence as required, which may be from time to time since progress upward may not be constant and there may be occasional set-backs and manifestations of recalcitrance to the divine will. Thirdly, there is the possibility that the visible and corruptible part of the world will be entirely destroyed, but the glorious spirits in the upper spheres of the cosmos may come to have yet more glorious forms than they already possess. Origen simply submits these three views to the reader's judgement. His own sympathy lies more perhaps with either the second or third than the first.[43] There are places in his commentaries where he implies the third view with its implication that all created spirits are in some degree involved in corporeality; in the case of angels (he remarks) the matter of their body will not be heavy and weighed down like ours on this earth, but will be ethereal, like the astral body of which the Neoplatonists speculated; and in principle, it is implied, only the Trinity is intrinsically incorporeal, so that if we speak of angels as 'incorporeal' we mean that they are relatively incorporeal in comparison with us.[44]

This way of thinking of the nature of matter is of course quite remote from our modern notions. But Origen is only giving expression to ideas which were widely assumed by a large number of his Platonizing contemporaries. The whole conception was made easier for him by the current dogma that in itself matter is without form or qualities, a common substratum, upon which various qualities may be imposed in accordance with the archetypal ideas. So the universal, which is the form or species, is imposed on qualityless matter to make each individual thing or animal what it is. To Platonists who objected to the doctrine of the resurrection of the body Origen had an unanswerable argument based precisely on his opponents' presuppositions: why should not the Creator impose a fresh form on the same common matter, so preserving continuity with the personality in this life, while making its new form appropriate to its environment?[45]

Nevertheless, Origen's attitude towards matter is much less positive than Clement's. He is inclined to think that the sun, moon, and stars are ensouled by spiritual beings who, having fallen a certain distance from God, have been incarcerated in these physical bodies, to us very splendid, but a degradation so far as they are concerned, and commanded to indicate to human beings on earth the passing of time.[46] Origen will not accept the gnostic use of astrology, but St. Paul's words about the creation being subjected to futility in hope of deliverance from the bondage of corruption seemed to him to reinforce his view that all spiritual beings, now imprisoned in material bodies, yearn to ascend higher and pray for a release which they cannot be granted before the proper time. Like the apostle in prison they long to depart, but realize that to abide in the flesh is more needful to assist inferior beings.

Certainly this material world is beautiful and noble and shows evidence of its design by a beneficent Creator. But it is not comfortable and is not intended to be. Man is put here as in 'a place of affliction' to educate him to return to his Maker.[47] It would not be good for him to live in a world from which all accidents and all pain are excluded. Natural catastrophes like earthquakes, famines, and plagues may shorten life, but such disasters do not count against the goodness of God, however purposeless they may seem at the time to the sufferers. Many virtues come out of adversity.[48] Evil inheres not in the natural order, but in the resistant will of the creatures.

Clement had regarded sex and marriage as a major crux in the conflict between the Church and Gnosticism, and had emphatically asserted the goodness of the natural order as the gift of God. Origen's tone is markedly different. It is true that he rejects the strict Encratite notion that marriage is incompatible with the profession of the Christian faith, and tolerates second marriages for weaker brethren. But his ascetic mind does not think kindly of the married state. Marriage is inferior to celibacy—on the two grounds, long familiar in pagan thought and by implication (even if it is not stated in so many words) almost given canonical au-

thority within Christianity by St. Paul in 1 Corinthians vii, that sexual intercourse is a defilement interfering with the elevation of the soul above this material world to the realm of spirit, and that one who has dedicated himself to the love of God must forgo the love of mortals. Origen protests that the sexual impulse is indeed natural and instinctive, not (as some Christians think) of diabolical prompting; but it is instinctive in the sense that anger is: sin is inextricably bound up with it.[49] So the priest who offers the Church's sacrifice must be pure.[50] In Origen's time there is no general demand for clerical celibacy as yet, and his demand is addressed to married clergy as much as to unmarried. Conjugal relations in marriage are for the purpose of procreation, and otherwise are disallowed as mere self-indulgence.[51] Because there is a defilement attaching to the reproductive process, the Church baptizes infants.[52] When in Romans v. 14 St. Paul speaks of 'sin in the likeness of Adam's transgression', the simple exegesis is that the universal sinfulness of society is due not to heredity but to environment and education. But deeper inquirers will understand the text to mean that somehow all men existed in Adam's loins and suffered expulsion from paradise with him.[53] All are born impure. In the Bible the only two who celebrate their birthday are Pharaoh and Herod.[54] The purity and sinlessness of Jesus, however, was ensured by the Virgin Birth.[55] Perhaps under the influence of Clement's denial of the notion, Origen reaches no decision about the Philonic and gnostic interpretation of the 'coats of skins' with which Adam and Eve were clothed after their fall: they may be bodies, but this is not certain.[56] But the entire tendency of Origen's ethic is to build on the antithesis of spirit and matter and to think of the way of moral and spiritual advance as a progressive suppression of the mind's responsiveness to the pull of the flesh. Just as in the soul's advance in the spiritual life it comes to understand the mysteries of theology in a deeper way than it did at earlier stages, so also it comes to have a deeper grasp of the nature of sin, so that actions which at the beginning were not regarded as sinful come to be seen in their true light.[57]

The model for the Christian's spiritual progress is not merely the strenuous self-discipline of the prophets but supremely the incarnate Lord. Among all the rational beings originally made by God there was one which inflexibly adhered to the divine love without wavering.[58] This soul was taken to be united to the Logos in a union as inseparable as that of iron in a white-hot fire. (The illustration, it should be said, is a commonplace analogy of Stoic philosophy to describe the union of soul and body as one of complete interpenetration). Even the body which the Logos took of Mary was caught up into the union so that the divine and human united to become one Christ.[59] By this union the properties of the humanity of Christ may be ascribed to the divine Logos and vice versa.[60] The full humanity of

Christ is essential for our salvation, and any part of our threefold nature of body, soul, and spirit not assumed by the Logos is not saved.[61] He possessed a soul of the same substance as all other souls,[62] and is our example as man,[63] but this does not mean that he is a mere man or that he is elevated to divine rank by adoption.[64] He is the pre-existent eternal Logos through whom we pray to the Father,[65] one whom we may even, with appropriate qualifications and explanations, describe as a 'second God' beside the Father.[66] For the Father and the Son are one in power and in will, but differ in their *hypostasis*[67]—and even, as Origen also says, in their *ousia,* though the context makes it clear that this word is being used as virtually synonymous with *hypostasis* on this occasion.[68] Origen is vehemently opposed to the modalist Monarchianism which regarded Father, Son, and Spirit as adjectival names to describe the one divine substance and formally denied that God is in himself three.

The incarnate Lord is the pattern and model for the salvation of humanity. 'With Jesus human and divine nature began to be woven together, so that by sharing with divine life human nature might become divine, not only in Jesus but also in all believers.'[69] So salvation is deification. This means the annihilation not of individuality but of the gulf between finite and infinite. Nor does it mean that the believer, following Christ as example, can find his mystical way to God independently of Christ. 'Even at the very highest climax of contemplation we do not for a moment forget the incarnation.'[70] While the Incarnation is a veritable revelation of God, it is the ladder by which we are to ascend from the flesh to the spirit, from the Son of Man to the Son of God. The incarnate Lord, like the written revelation in inspired scripture, is a veil that must be penetrated.[71] It is an accommodation to our present capacities in this life. The Church's present gospel will one day be superseded by that which the Seer of the Apocalypse calls the everlasting gospel, a heavenly comprehension of truth that will surpass our present understanding by at least as much as the new covenant surpasses the old.[72] But throughout the period of this mortal life we are dependent on the sacramental, external forms of Bible and Church; secondary as they may be, they are an indispensable vehicle.[73]

The Church is a school, making many concessions to weaker brethren, but always seeking to elevate them to higher things and a more intelligent degree of theological literacy. The Christian preacher's task is to rebuke and to encourage, above all to move to penitence.[74] Advance comes as we confess our sins to spiritual advisers, who in Origen's view are to be clergy;

but spiritual power is not always conjoined with ecclesiastical authority, though it ought to be, and the power of the keys is only truly possessed by them if their formal authority is coupled with personal holiness.[75]

Justinian I with his Court.

This process of education is not confined to this life. None is so pure that at death he is fit for the presence of God.[76] Therefore there will be purification hereafter, in which God will purge away the wood, hay, and stubble erected on the foundation laid by Christ.[77] The atonement is a long-continuing process[78] in which Christ is conquering the powers of evil assaulting the soul. Moreover, the very powers of evil themselves are not outside the reach of his care. The beings who are now devils were not created so. They were created good by nature, like all other spiritual beings, and have become evil only in will.[79] It is a gnostic doctrine that any creature of God can become so totally depraved as to become incapable of any goodness at all. 'A totally depraved being could not be censured, but only pitied as a poor unfortunate.'[80] Even the prince of darkness himself retains some vestige of a capacity to recognize truth, some remnants of freedom and some rationality. No creature of God ever passes wholly beyond the bounds of his love and judgement. Origen is emphatic that redemption is not a naturalistic process moving onward of its own motion by an inevitable density. Rebels from God remain for ever free to refuse. But the atoning work of Christ is incomplete until all are redeemed, and 'love never fails'.[81] The process of redemption may take more than one 'age', but the ultimate triumph will surely be God's.[82] Even so, freedom is inalienable from the rational being; if the spiritual creatures once suffered satiety and fell, there can be in principle no ground for denying the possibility that they may fall again. If so, there may be a series of worlds in which providence has to redeem a fallen creation and bring it back to its Maker.[83] Or may we affirm that at the final restoration love will be indefectible, and that those who have seen the glory of the kingdom will never taste of death?[84]

Notes

[1] Quoted by Eusebius, *H.E.* vi. 19. 7.

[2] Ibid. vi. 2. 6. For a recent discussion of Eusebius's life of Origen see M. Hornschuh in *Zeitschrift F. Kirchengeschichte* 71 (1960), 1-25, who makes some valuable observations; but his radical scepticism of Eusebius suffers from the absence of any objective or rational criterion or principle.

[3] Eus. *H.E.* vi. 36. 3.

[4] Ibid. vi. 8.

[5] I have collected some of the evidence in *The Sentences of Sextus* (Cambridge, 1959), pp. 110 f. Cf. also the article 'Castration' in *Dict. d'arch. chr. et de liturgie.*

[6] *Comm. in Matt.* xv. 1 ff.

[7] *Panarion haer.* 64. 3. 11-12. Epiphanius has not, of course, a hundredth part of the authority of Eusebius as an historian; it is precisely the uncritical way in which he sets down incompatible stories that imparts value to what he says, since it argues that at least he had not the intelligence to invent the drug story, which was evidently a current slander against Origen like Epiphanius's other piece of malice that Origen's migration to Caesarea was due to shame that in the persecution at Alexandria, when offered the choice between offering incense and being abused by a homosexual Ethiopian, he had instinctively preferred the former and so became apostate and excommunicate.

Eusebius's story of the castration is sceptically regarded by K. F. Schnitzer, *Origenes über die Grundlehren der Glaubenswissenschaft* (Stuttgart, 1835), pp. xxxiii-xl (a very clear-headed discussion), and briefly by F. Böhringer, *Die Kirche Christi und ihre Zeugen* (Zürich, 1842), pp. 111 f.

[8] Eus. *H.E.* vi. 19. 6. For a recent discussion see H. Dörrie, 'Ammonios der Lehrer Plotins', in *Hermes* 83 (1955), 439-77. For a very different and (I think) highly implausible view see H. Langerbeck's paper in the *Journal of Hellenic Studies* 77 (1957), 67-74, who thinks Ammonius Saccas some sort of Christian heretic. This is at least more likely than the wild theory that Ammonius is Dionysius the Areopagite. The most sober and cautious review of the evidence is given by E. R. Dodds in *Entretiens Hardt* 5 (1960), 24 ff.

[9] For a collection of the fragments of the pagan Origen (at times adventurously interpreted) see K. O. Weber, *Origenes der Neuplatoniker* (Munich, 1962).

[10] *Comm. in Joh.* xiii. 45. 298; Jerome, *Ep.* 8. 4. 3; *Apol. adv. Rufin.* i. 18.

[11] *Quis dives* 26; *Str.* iii. 13. 1; 21. 2; iv. 2. 1; v. 140. 3; vi. 4. 2.

[12] The *de Principiis* survives as a whole only in the paraphrastic Latin translation of Rufinus, which avowedly mitigates passages likely to offend the orthodox ears of Rufinus's contemporaries, especially in books iii-iv which Rufinus treats more cautiously than i-ii. Except for substantial excerpts on the interpretation of the Bible preserved in the Greek of the *Philocalia* of Basil and Gregory Nazianzen, fragments of the original text are few, and are mainly preserved by enemies of Origen like Justinian. A selection of the most damaging passages is translated by Jerome, *Ep.* 124. So much in Rufinus's work can be paralleled, however, in the commentaries and homilies that it is possible to have reasonable confidence about the original sense except in certain instances. The standard text of Koetschau (Leipzig, 1913) is well translated into English by G. W. Butterworth (London, 1936); but the reader should be warned (*a*) that Koetschau, sceptical of Rufinus's reliability, is at times uncritically credulous towards Origen's enemies, and (*b*) that the division of books and chapters is not Origen's. See M. Harl in *Studia Patristica* (ed. F. L. Cross), iii = *T.U.* 78 (1961), pp. 57-67.

[13] Eus. *H.E.* vi. 14. 7.

[14] *Comm. in Joh.* x. 5. 20.

[15] Ibid. i. 4. 23.

[16] *Comm. in Matt.* xv. 3.

[17] *de Princ.* iv. 2. 4; *Hom. in Lev.* v. 1 and 5; *Hom. in Num.* ix. 7. Cf. Philo, *V. Cont.* 78; Clement, *Str.* vi. 132. 3. On Origen's principles of Biblical exegesis the best study is that of H. de Lubac, *Histoire et Esprit* (Paris, 1950); his *Exégèse médiévale* 1. i (Paris, 1959), pp. 198 ff., gives a masterly account of Origen's influence on later commentaries. On typology see especially J. Daniélou, *Sacramentum Futuri* (Paris, 1949); R. P. C. Hanson, *Allegory and Event* (London, 1959); R. M. Grant, *The Letter and the Spirit* (London, 1957).

[18] *de Princ.* iv. 2. 1.

[19] *in Matt. Ser.* 61.

[20] See the exposition of Matt. xiii. 36 in *Comm. in Matt.* x. 1, *c. Cels.* iii. 21, and *Dial. c. Heracl.,* 1st ed.

p. 152 Scherer (the pagination of the first edition is given in the margin of the second).

[21] *c. Cels.* ii. 66; *Comm. in Joh.* i. 7. 43, etc.

[22] *Comm. in Joh.* i. 9 ff. The embryo of Origen's idea is found in Justin's contrast (*Ap.* ii. 6) between the nameless Father and the many names of Christ (cf. *Dial.* 34. 2). That conceptions of God vary according to the believer's capacity is in Philo, *Mut.* 19 ff.

[23] *Comm. in Joh.* xix. 6. 38; cf. Philo, *Leg. Alleg.* iii. 125 f.

[24] *c. Cels.* ii. 64; iv. 16; vi. 68, etc.

[25] *in Matt. Ser.* 50, 56, esp. 70; *Comm. in Matt.* xii. 30, 32. There is a direct attack on materialistic notions of heaven in *de Princ.* ii. 11. 2.

[26] *de Princ.* ii. 10. 5. Philo interprets Hades as tortures of conscience (*Congr.* 57).

[27] *c. Cels.* iii. 78-79; iv. 10, 19; vi. 26, 72.

[28] Ibid. v. 15ff. (Note esp. 22, 'Let no one think I am one of those who deny the Church's doctrine of resurrection; I preserve both the doctrine of the Church and the greatness of God's promise.') Especially important for Origen's position is the fragment on Psalm i preserved by Methodius, *de Resurr.* i. 20 ff. and by Epiphanius, *Panarion hear.* 64. 12; the other main texts are *de Princ.* ii. 10-11; iii. 6. 5-9; *Comm. in Matt.* xvii. 29-33. No text of Origen in either Greek original or translation contains the doctrine ascribed to him in the sixth century that resurrection bodies are spherical (the sphere being the perfect shape according to *Timaeus* 33 B, cf. 44 D, and also the shape of the cosmic god of the Stoics; cf. Seneca, *Apocolocyntosis* 8 of Claudius's rotundity resembling a Stoic god, and Ovid, *Fasti* vi. 271-2). But he believed that the stars have souls (since capable of sin, Job xxv. 5, cf. *Comm. in Joh.* i. 35. 257; *Comm. in Rom.* iii. 6) and spherical bodies (*de Orat.* 31. 3). Plotinus says that souls in heaven, despite their astral spherical bodies, recognize one another by inner character (iv. 4(28). 5. 18; cf. iii. 4(15). 6. 18 ff.). The Platonic and the Christian are fused in Dante's *Paradiso* xiv where the holy souls awaiting resurrection are starry spheres.

For discussion see my remarks in *Harv. Theol. Rev.* 41 (1948), pp. 83-102; A.-J. Festugière in *Revue des sciences philos. et théol.* 43 (1959), 81-86.

[29] Origen's attacks on chiliasm, though rare, are decisive: *Comm. in Matt.* xvii. 35; *de Orat.* xxvii. 13; *Comm. in Cant. Cantic.* prol., (p. 66 Baehrens); frag. in Methodius, *de creatis* 12 (p. 499 Bonwetsch); Origen,

Hom. in Ps. XXXVI, 3.10 (XII. 196f. Lommatzsch).

[30] *de Orat.* 31. 3; *Comm. in Rom.* ix. 41.

[31] Irenaeus, *adv. Haer.* ii. 28. 2-3.

[32] *c. Cels.* vii. 42 ff., well interpreted by Festugière, *La Révélation d'Hermès Trismégiste* iv. 119-123.

[33] *Comm. in Joh.* xiii. 25. Note ii. 23. 149 f.: Because both Father and Son are light, some mistakenly think the *ousia* of the Son not distinct from the Father's (i.e. the argument Justin tries to meet in *Dial.* 128).

[34] Philo, *Heres* 240; *Gig.* 12; *Som.* i. 138 f.; *Opif.* 168; *Post. C.* 145; *Qu. Gen.* iv. 87; *Qu. Ex.* ii. 40.

[35] *de Princ.* ii. 8. 3. Cf. Philo, *Som.* i. 31. See Waszink's commentary on Tert. *de Anima* 25. 2.

[36] e.g. *Comm. in Joh.* xxxii. 18. 218; *Hom. in Luc.* 36. Cf. ch. 4, n. 74. Again the idea is Philonic, e.g. *Leg. Alleg.* iii. 84.

[37] *de Princ.* ii. 1. 1 f. The Platonist Albinus (in Stobaeus i. 49. 37) anticipates Origen's view, saying that souls descend by a mistaken choice, not by a natural destiny resulting from emanations. There is a polemic against this view in Hierocles, *Comm. in Carmen Aureum* i. 1, xi. 17-20 (Mullach, pp. 420 a, 443 a).

[38] *de Princ.* ii. 1. 4. See also *Comm. in Gen.* ap. Eus. *P.E.* vii. 20.

[39] *c. Cels.* iv. 54 ff.

[40] *Opif.* 75; *Conf.* 179; *Abr.* 143; *Fuga* 68 ff.

[41] *c. Cels.* iv. 66; vi. 53.

[42] *de Princ.* ii. 2-3; iii. 6. Both Rufinus and Jerome tendentiously confuse the text. See Karl Müller in *Sitzungsber. Berl. Akad.* 1919, pp. 622 ff.

[43] Cf., however, *de Orat.* 26. 6, where the first view appears.

[44] Cf. *Frag. in Joh.* 13 (p. 495 Preuschen).

[45] *c. Cels.* iii. 41; iv. 57; vi. 77.

[46] *de Princ.* i. 7. 5; iii. 5. 4; *Comm. in Rom.* vii. 4; *Hom. in Num.* xxviii. 2.

[47] *c. Cels.* vii. 50.

[48] The argument is a commonplace of the Stoic theodicy, of which Origen made full use.

[49] *de Princ.* iii. 2. 1-2; *Hom. in Gen.* ii. 6.

[50] *Hom. in Lev.* iv. 6. For a striking anticipation see Philo, *V. Mos.* ii. 68 (Moses practised continence so as to be ready at any time to be the medium of inspired prophecy). Likewise *de Spec. Leg.* i. 150.

[51] *Hom. in Gen.* iii. 6; *Comm. in Matt.* xiv. 1-2.

[52] *Hom. in Lev.* viii. 3; cf. *c. Cels.* vii. 50; *Comm. in Rom.* v. 9; *Hom. in Luc.* 14.

[53] *Comm. in Rom.* v. 1 and 4.

[54] *Hom. in Lev.* viii. 3. Origen takes the idea from Philo, *Ebr.* 208.

[55] *Comm. in Matt.* x. 12; xii. 4.

[56] See *c. Cels.* iv. 40; *Sel. in Gen.* (VIII. 58 Lommatzsch). Clement had rejected this interpretation (*Str.* iii. 95). Ambrose (*ep.* 49. 4) accepts it. It appears also in Porphyry (*de Abst.* i. 31).

[57] *Comm. in Joh.* xxxii. 2; *Comm. in Matt.* x. 24; *Hom. in Luc.* 35. The truth that petty dishonesties and drunkennesses are sins before God no less than pride and other vices is providentially not understood by ignorant believers who, not having the capacity to understand that divine punishment for sin is remedial, would lose heart if they knew: *Hom. in Lev.* xiv. 3; *Hom. in Jerem.* xx. 3; *Dial. c. Heracl.* 1st ed., p. 142 Scherer.

[58] *de Princ.* ii. 6. 6.

[59] *c. Cels.* iii. 41.

[60] *Comm. in Rom.* i. 6; *de Princ.* ii. 6. 2.

[61] *Dial. c. Heracl.*, 1st ed., p. 136; *Comm. in Joh.* xx. 11. 86; xxxii. 18. 218 ff. Origen's argument entirely anticipates the standard Cappadocian objection to Apollinarianism as formulated especially by Gregory Nazianzen; cf. Athanasius, *Tomus ad Antiochenos* 7. Origen attacks those who think the Logos assumed a body, not a human soul, in *de Princ.* iv. 4. 4.

[62] *de Princ.* ii. 8. 5; *Hom. in Lev.* xii. 5.

[63] *Comm. in Cant. Cantic.* ii (p. 153 Baehrens).

[64] *c. Cels.* iii. 14; iv. 32; *Hom. in Iesu Nave* vii. 7.

[65] *de Orat.* xv-xvi; *c. Cels.* v. 4-5; viii. 26.

[66] *c. Cels.* v. 39; vi. 61; vii. 57. Cf. *de Orat.* xv. 1; *Comm. in Joh.* ii. 2; x. 37.

[67] *c. Cels.* viii. 12; *Comm. in Matt.* xvii. 14; *Comm. in Joh.* ii. 10; x. 37.

[68] *de Orat.* xv. 1. See also note 33 above.

[69] *c. Cels.* iii. 28.

[70] *Comm. in Joh.* ii. 8.

[71] For the analogy of the Bible and the Incarnation see *in Matt. Ser.* 27; *Hom. in Exod.* xii. 4; *Hom. in Lev.* i. 1. Cf. ch. 4, n. 13.

[72] *Comm. in Rom.* i. 4; *de Princ.* ii. 8. 7; iii. 6. 8; iv. 2. 4, etc. Jerome (*Ep.* 124. 12), takes exception to Origen's opinion which is paralleled in Irenaeus (*adv. Haer.* iv. 9. 2) and Methodius (*Symp.* ix. 2).

[73] *de Orat.* 5; cf. *Frag. in 1 Cor.* iii. 21 f., ed. Jenkins in *JTS* ix. 353.

[74] *Comm. in Rom.* ix. 1.

[75] *de Orat.* xxviii. 9 f. Origen's doctrine of penitence is extremely complex (and controversial); it is bound up with his ambivalent attitude to the clergy in general, on the one hand profoundly respectful of the office, on the other hand sternly critical of clerical conduct in practice. In Origen's thought about the Church a high sacramentalism crosses with an anti-clerical pietistic strain, and the resulting inconsistencies have led to very diverse interpretations of his words. The most dispassionate account is that of H. von Campenhausen, *Kirchliches Amt und Geistliche Vollmacht* pp. 287 ff.

[76] *Hom. in Num.* xxv. 6.

[77] Origen is the first to read into 1 Cor. iii. 10-15 the doctrine of an ultimate purification for all. For a good examination of the history of this exegesis see J. Gnilka, *Ist I Kor. 3, 10-15 ein Schriftzeugnis für das Fegfeuer?* (Düsseldorf, 1955).

[78] *Comm. in Joh.* vi. 58. 297; *Hom. in Lev.* viii. 5.

[79] *c. Cels.* iv. 65; *Comm. in Joh.* ii. 13. 97.

[80] *Comm. in Joh.* xx. 28. 254.

[81] *Hom. in Num.* xx. 3; *Hom. in Lev.* vii. 2; *Comm. in Joh.* xix. 14 and 21, etc.

[82] *de Orat.* xxvii. 15 and many passages.

[83] *de Princ.* i. 3. 8; *Comm. in Joh.* x. 42.

[84] *Comm. in Matt.* xii. 34; *Comm. in Cant. Cantic.* i. (p. 103 Baehrens): once the soul attains to union with the very *ousia* of the Logos, it is bound by the chains of love and can never again remove, being one spirit with him. *Comm. in Rom.*, Tura papyrus frag. (p. 208

Scherer) distinguishes the indefectibility of faith, which is certain, from that of righteousness which can be lost. (Cf. *JTS* N.S. x (1959), 36).

Rev. H. Chadwick (essay date 1967)

SOURCE: "Origen," in *The Cambridge History of Later Greek and Early Medieval Philosophy,* Cambridge at the University Press, 1967, pp. 182-92.

[*In this essay, Chadwick generally discusses the ways in which Origen's theological and philosophical thinking as well as his principles of allegorical exposition of the Scriptures are distinct from those of his Jewish and pagan contemporaries and predecessors and how they were deeply influenced by them, showing that Origen's thought is a complex patchwork that has been controversial since the sixth century.*]

Origen was born about 184-5 at Alexandria, probably of Christian parents (Porphyry and Eusebius contradict one another on this point). When he was nearly seventeen his father was martyred in the persecution of Severus in 202/3, and the event left a deep mark on Origen's mind. He always writes with an impassioned sense of belonging to a church called to fearless martyrdom and resistance to all compromise with the world which ever threatens it at least as much by the infiltration of merely nominal belief as by external attack and persecution. With this attitude there goes a strongly world-denying strain of personal detachment and ascetic self-discipline, symbolized in the story, told by Eusebius from hearsay and possibly true, that in the zeal of youth Origen took literally Matt. xix. 12 and castrated himself.[1] He lived on the minimum of food and sleep, and took seriously the gospel counsel of poverty.[2]

For a time he studied Greek philosophy in the lecture room of Ammonius Saccas, with whom Plotinus was later to study for eleven years. Ammonius is a mysterious figure.[3] All we know of him probably comes directly or indirectly from Porphyry who describes in his life of Plotinus how Ammonius' esoteric teaching fired Plotinus with a (typically Neopythagorean) desire to investigate the antique wisdom of Persian and Indian sages. But it is a forlorn and foolish undertaking to attempt a reconstruction of Ammonius' metaphysical doctrines by looking for synoptic elements common to Origen and Plotinus. It is impossible to determine what, if anything, Origen really drew from Ammonius. What is certain is that Origen possessed an exhaustive comprehension of the debates of the Greek schools and that to his contemporaries he stood out as an intellectual prodigy. Until 231 Origen worked at Alexandria, though often travelling about on visits elsewhere. But his relations with his bishop were strained and eventually came to breaking point, so that

he had to migrate to Palestinian Caesarea. He died at Tyre about 254.

Origen's work resembles Philo more closely than Clement's, mainly because, except for the two great works *De principiis* and *Contra Celsum,* its form is almost entirely a series of massive commentaries and expository sermons on the Bible. He bases himself on the principles of allegorical interpretation by which Philo had been able to discover in the Pentateuch the doctrines of Greek ethics or natural science. But Origen's evident debt to Philo must not be used to put Origen into a Philonic strait-jacket with the effect of obliterating the important differences between them. The ethical, psychological and scientific exegesis of Philo is now being combined with the typological exegesis of Justin and Irenaeus, seeking in the Old Testament for specific foreshadowings of Christian doctrine in a way that is a natural and easy extension of the argument from prophecy common in the canonical gospels and going back to the earliest Christian generation.[4] Besides the literal and historical meaning (sometimes, but not usually, Origen denies that there is one) and the moral interpretation akin to Philo's, Origen seeks a spiritual meaning that refers to Christ's redemption and a 'mystical' sense that concerns the ascent of the individual soul to union with God and to perfection. In some places Origen tries to schematize his exegesis by boldly arguing from an analogy with St Paul's trichotomy of man's body, soul, and spirit;[5] but in practice he may at times give four or even only two concurrent interpretations.[6] What is impossible is that the text should only have a literal meaning. Much in the Old Testament when interpreted literally and not spiritually is unworthy of God, and this is in itself a sufficient refutation of Judaism.[7] It is blasphemy to ascribe to God human weaknesses like wrath or changes of mind.[8]

Two differences between Origen and Philo are noteworthy in the matter of Scripture. First, controversy with rabbis and differences of opinion within the Church have made Origen hesitant about the authority and inspiration of the Septuagint. Unlike Philo and Justin he never alludes to the propagandist legends about the inspired unanimity of the translators, and, though he feels committed to maintaining the majority view of the Greek churches about the accepted status of the Septuagint, he implies that the Hebrew original is of more certain authority. He accordingly took the trouble to learn Hebrew. Secondly, he provides some positive argument for regarding the Bible as the work of the Holy Spirit, notably in *De principiis* IV, where his crowning point is the power of the Scriptures, as demonstrated by the mission of the Church throughout the world, to set souls on fire with faith and to transform moral life.

In Origen's attitude to philosophy there is not much,

when it comes to detail, that we have not already found in Philo, Justin or Clement. Against the Gnostic exponents of total depravity Origen retorts that 'a totally depraved being could not be censured, only pitied as a poor unfortunate', and insists that in all men some elements of the divine image remain. The Logos lights every man coming into the world; all beings that are rational partake of the true light.[9] The Gospel brings to actuality what in unbelievers is present potentially.[10] The preacher need not hesitate to claim for a Christian possession all that seems sound and good in Hellenic culture. Origen is unmoved by the pagan accusation that he is borrowing Greek tools to rationalize a barbarian superstition.[11]

Philosophy is a valuable preparatory discipline for revealed theology. 'Human wisdom is a means of education for the soul, divine wisdom being the ultimate end.' Philosophy is not indispensable for receiving the truth of God's revelation.[12] If it were, Christ would not have chosen fishermen.[13] To the two (hardly compatible) pagan charges that the Christians are quite uneducated and that Christian teaching is no different from that of Plato and the Stoics, Origen answers that the proportions of educated and uneducated in the Church represent a fair cross-section of society as a whole, and that, while the study of philosophy is confined to an educated élite, the Christians have brought an acceptance of moral truth to classes of society where philosophy has never penetrated.[14] If philosophy is not indispensable, yet it is a valuable tool for understanding the meaning and underlying principles of revelation.[15] In the propositions of the baptismal creed the apostles laid down authoritatively and in language adapted to simple folk what is necessary in Christian belief. The grounds for their statements they left for others to investigate.[16] The Bible does not discourage the pursuit of philosophy.[17] Logic is of great utility in defending Christianity, though the greatest arguments establishing the truth of the Gospel are not natural but the supernatural guarantees of miracle, fulfilled prophecy and the miraculous expansion of the Church in face of powerful prejudice and governmental opposition.[18] To his pupil Gregory (later to become the apostle of Pontus) Origen writes that the Christian may use philosophy as the Hebrews spoiled the Egyptians of their jewels at the Exodus.[19]

In much of this we are frequently reminded of Justin or Clement. But the accent and tone are different. Origen is so much more detached. The reader of Clement is sometimes inclined to suspect him of being so over-anxious to rebut the scornful charge that Christians are uneducated that he indulges in name-dropping. The *Contra Celsum* is wholly without trace of any inferiority complex and is an attack as much as it is a defence. Origen is not one of those apologists who derived encouragement from similarities to Christian ideas in Plato or Chrysippus.[20] He is completely free of

the notion that there is a mystique of authority attaching to the great classical philosophers, and is without the least desire to claim the protection of their name for any statement. Nothing for Origen is true because Plato said it, though he thinks that Plato, being a clever man, said many things that are true. What Origen claims is not an affinity with this or that philosophy, but the right to think and reason from a Christian standpoint.[21]

In the *Contra Celsum* and elsewhere he is occasionally prickly to the point of rudeness towards the classical tradition. This is partly to be explained by the inward psychological effort that a man wholly trained within a metaphysical tradition must make in order to achieve detachment, and partly by the fact that pagan Platonists like Celsus were denying the right of Christians to think at all. The Platonism of Celsus, Porphyry, and, for that matter, Plotinus is in its feeling and temper a scholasticism bound by authority and regarding innovation and originality as synonymous with error. They would not have understood an attitude such as that expressed by Origen when he writes that 'philosophy and the Word of God are not always at loggerheads, neither are they always in harmony. For philosophy is neither in all things contrary to God's law nor is it in all respects consonant.' Origen proceeds in this passage to list some of the points of agreement and disagreement. 'Many philosophers say there is one God who created the world; some have added that God both made and rules all things by his Logos. Again, in ethics and in their account of the natural world they almost all agree with us. But they disagree when they assert that matter is co-eternal with God, when they deny that providence extends below the moon, when they imagine that the power of the stars determines our lives or that the world will never come to an end.'[22]

Like Justin and Clement, Origen attacks the Stoics for their materialism, pantheism and deterministic doctrine of world-cycles.[23] He distinguishes the Christian doctrine of God's providential care from the Stoic idea of God as a material immanent force.[24] The Stoic doctrine of natural law and of 'universal notions' of God and conscience he accepts without the least demur.[25] Every man has an innate awareness of right and wrong.[26] The Sermon on the Mount accords with what natural consent acknowledges to be the ideal pattern in human relations.[27] The Mosaic law spiritually interpreted is the natural law, as Philo said, and both are identified with Christian morality.[28] For Origen there is no distinctively Christian ethic, but rather moral attitudes that are characteristically Christian, above all the recognition that the divine love and righteousness are the ground of this morality. The dormant soul is awakened to this realization by the Gospel.[29] Everyone acknowledges that a truly spiritual religion involves a rejection of polytheistic idolatry, even if he does not act upon that knowledge.[30] The soul of man has an intuitive longing for God; and Origen will not believe that this yearning can have been implanted in man's heart unless it is capable of being satisfied. Just as each faculty of our senses is related to a specific category of objects, so our *nous* is the correlate of God.[31]

Nevertheless, natural religion and natural morality are not enough. There is salvation only in Christ, and good works done before justification are of no avail.[32] The soul of man is so weakened and distracted that it cannot be redeemed apart from the power and grace of God in Christ.[33] The severity of Origen's judgement on 'the good pagan' is, of course, much qualified by his denial that this life is the only chance a man has.

Origen is aware that the Christian estimate of man is in one aspect less exalted than the more aristocratic view of the Stoics with their doctrine of the wise man unmoved by disaster without or passion within, presupposing an innate strength and nobility of soul that is distinguishable from the Christian judgement that, though intended for high things, the soul is frail, bound by the fetters not so much of the body as of sin, and in need of help. Origen occasionally mentions the Stoic moral paradoxes, but with characteristic coolness does not say that he wholeheartedly approves, only that at some more suitable time he might discuss the extent to which these pagan principles accord with Christianity.[34] On the other hand, he makes generous use of the Stoic theodicy. The problem of evil greatly exercised the ingenuity of the Stoic philosophers in their conflict with Sceptics and Academics, and Chrysippus had created an arsenal of argument which Origen exploits. In Christianity the problem of evil was a no less serious question than it was for the Stoics in the time of Carneades. The Gnostics had thrown it into the forefront of the discussion, and had answered the problem by teaching, on the basis of some Platonic support, that evil inhered in matter. This solution was not open to Clement and Origen.[35] Neither, on the other hand, could the Christians happily use the Neoplatonist theodicy that evil is a privation of good. Biblical language about the devil,[36] if not personal experience, ensured that Christian theology must recognize evil to be a positive force, a *depravatio* rather than only a *deprivatio*. Moreover, the Christian belief in a historical revelation having the incarnation at its climax inevitably seemed to link the Christian interest with the Stoic defence of providential care not merely of the cosmos in general but of man in particular. A large part of the second and third books of Origen's *De principiis* is dominated by these questions in the form in which the Gnostics put them, and in the *Contra Celsum* Origen significantly turns for Stoic help in replying to Celsus' Platonizing argument that providence cares for the cosmos as a whole rather than for particularities and has no more concern for mankind than for dolphins.[37] Likewise Origen makes common cause with the Stoa in accepting the argument from

design.[38] He sees difficulties in Scripture as analogous to those encountered in nature—of which he wisely observes that only a fool would try to find an explanation of every single detail.[39]

Origen's attitude towards Platonism is more complicated. He sets an immediate distance between himself and Plato by sharp accusations that Plato was a pagan who, despite the high insights of dialogues such as the *Republic* and the *Phaedo,* failed to break with polytheism.[40] It is significant that the complaint is directed not against Plato's metaphysics but against his behaviour. Origen simply assumes as axiomatic the Platonic conception of the intelligible world with the sensible world as a reflection of it. For Origen the idea is fundamental to his view of revelation. Both the Bible and the Incarnation exemplify the principle that God uses earthly symbols to help us to rise to the spiritual reality that they veil.[41] Furthermore, Origen's doctrine of God unreservedly accepts the traditional Platonic definitions that God is immutable, impassible, beyond time and space, without shape or colour, not needing the world, though creating it by his goodness.[42] He assumes the truth of the late Platonic axiom that, in the hierarchy of being, what is produced must be inferior to that which produces it, an assumption which involved him in difficulties in expounding the doctrine of the Trinity,[43] though his Trinitarian and Christological statements are in fact vastly more 'orthodox' than his later reputation would suggest. Platonic language about the eternity of the cosmos provided him with terminology to express the eternal generation of the Son-Logos from the Father.[44] He echoes Philo's declaration that the Logos stands midway, as high priest and mediator, between the Creator and the created natures.[45] The Logos is the 'idea of ideas'.[46] And so on.

Nevertheless, there are certain points where Origen has substantial disagreements. He rejects the doctrine of the *Timaeus* that the Creator God made souls but delegated the making of bodies to inferior powers.[47] He will not admit that the cosmos is divine or that the stars are gods (though he believes the stars probably have souls).[48] He unambiguously teaches creation *ex nihilo:* creation is not out of relative but out of absolute non-being. 'I cannot understand how so many eminent men have imagined matter to be uncreated.'[49] Origen also rejects the view that this material world will never come to an end. Plato's doctrine that, although the cosmos is created and so in principle corruptible, yet by God's will it will never in fact be destroyed, holds good in Origen's view not of the sensible world, but of the higher world, the heavenly realm of discarnate spirits, saints and angels, which should not be called the realm of ideas lest anyone suppose that it exists only in our minds as a metaphysical hypothesis.[50] All this marks a considerable modification of the Platonic scheme. Nevertheless, Origen was convinced that much of Platonism is true.

In one of his earliest works, the **Stromateis** (extant only in sparse fragments), he even attempted to express the fundamental ideas of Christianity wholly in Platonic language. Neither the theory of Ideas nor the doctrine of Anamnesis plays much part in the structure of Origen's thought, though there are places where he assumes these conceptions. The main problem lay in the nature and origin of the soul.

Origen teaches that souls are not unbegotten and eternal,[51] but created by God, who from overflowing goodness created rational, incorporeal beings. But they neglected to love God, being overcome by 'satiety', and fell, some only a short distance, becoming angels, some a very long way, becoming devils, and some of a middle class, becoming human beings. The material world was not, as the Gnostics declared, an accidental consequence of the Fall, but was made by the goodness of God—not, however, with the intention that anyone should be too comfortable in it, but with the intention of educating humanity by the insecurity and transitoriness of existence to return to God. So in the divine plan some souls are sent down into bodies because of their failures, while others may ascend into bodies because they are showing improvement.

Origen's mythological picture of the hierarchy of being as a diversity resulting from free choices (a conception with which the Neoplatonists could not come to terms) is explicable against the Gnostic background. Origen's anxiety is to defend God from the charge of injustice and arbitrariness. In the doctrine of the soul he was faced by a choice between three possible doctrines: (*a*) the Creationist view that God creates each soul for each individual as conceived and born; (*b*) the Traducianist view that the soul is derived, like the body, from the parents; (*c*) the Platonic Pre-existence theory, according to which immortal and pre-existent souls temporarily reside in the body. Creationism seemed to involve God in endless fuss; Traducianism seemed to endanger the transcendence of the soul in relation to the body by making it something corporeal. Pre-existence had the merit of making a theodicy possible which answered the Gnostics' complaint against the justice and goodness of the Creator. But the final result was a mythological theory of the creation which bore at least a superficial resemblance to the theory it was intended to refute; and orthodox churchmen were disturbed by a doctrine apparently more Platonic than biblical and strongly suggesting the corollary of transmigration. On several occasions Origen disclaims the myth of transmigration as false.[52] Yet his own system presupposes a picture of the soul's course which is strikingly similar. Probably the right solution of this problem is to be found in Origen's insistence on freedom rather than destiny as the key to the universe. In other words, he objected to the fatalistic principles underlying the doctrine of transmigration; he did not object to the idea if its foundations rested on the goodness and justice of God assigning souls to bodies in strict accordance with their merits on the basis of free choices. Because God is good, the process of redemption, which is not confined to this life on earth and does not only include the human race but angels also, will go on and on until God has won back all souls to himself, including even the devil himself who retains freedom and rationality and must therefore have still the power to respond to the wonder of divine mercy. Because freedom is essential to the very constitution of rational beings, universal restoration cannot be asserted to be a predictable end in the sense that the cosmos is moving towards it by an irresistible evolution. But only a belief in total depravity so drastic as to make redemption an act of omnipotent power rather than gracious love can justify the denial of universalist hope. God never abandons anyone. The fire of his judgement is purifying and his punishment is always remedial, even if it may be extremely severe. And because freedom is eternal, even at the summit of the process when all have been restored, it is possible (Origen speculates) that there may be another Fall, so that a series of unending cycles stretches out before the mind.

Origen is not an easy figure to assess. Other, later theologians soon came to look with misgiving upon his devaluation of history as the sphere of divine revelation. Yet his principles of allegorical exposition lived on to become an accepted tradition in medieval commentaries on Scripture. Though his doctrine of the pre-existence of souls (necessary to his theodicy) had occasional later advocates, it seemed too dangerously reminiscent of transmigration to be widely acceptable to the orthodox tradition. His universalism seemed to make redemption almost a natural cosmic process and to eliminate the element of freedom from divine grace and from human responsibility. Despite all his critics and the stormy controversy of the sixth century, culminating in Justinian's condemnation of some of the more extravagant speculations attributed to him by the Origenist monks of Palestine, much in his essential theological position became permanently at home within the Greek orthodox tradition in the revised and restated form given to it by the Cappadocian fathers, especially by Gregory of Nyssa. Widely divergent estimates of him were passed in his lifetime and throughout the patristic and medieval periods. These divergences will no doubt continue so long as there remains debate on the tenability of Christian Platonism.

Notes

[1] Eus. *HE* VI 8; Porphyry's account in VI 19.

[2] Eus. *HE* VI 3. 8 ff.; cf. Origen, *Hom. in Gen.* XVI 5.

[3] For a fuller discussion of Ammonius see Part III, ch. 12, pp. 196-200.

[4] See C. H. Dodd, *According to the Scriptures* (1952), a masterly study; cf. the interesting but speculative book of B. Lindars, *New Testament Apologetic* (1961).

[5] *Princ.* IV 2. 4; *Hom. in Lev.* V 1 and 5; *Hom. in Num.* IX 7.

[6] See H. de Lubac, *Histoire et Esprit* (1950), *Exégèse Médiévale* I i (1959), pp. 198 ff.; J. Daniélou, *Sacramentum Futuri* (1949).

[7] E.g. *Comm. in Rom.* VI 12; *Hom. in Gen.* VI 3; *Hom. in Lev.* X 1.

[8] Cf. *Contra Celsum* IV 72; *Hom. in Jerem.* XVIII 6.

[9] *Comm. in Joh.* XX 28; *Hom. in Jerem.* XIV 10.

[10] *Comm. in Rom.* VIII 2.

[11] *Hom. in Gen.* XIII 3.

[12] *Contra Celsum* III 58; VI 13-14.

[13] *Contra Celsum* I 62.

[14] *Contra Celsum* I 9 f.; III 44 ff.; VI 1 ff.

[15] *Contra Celsum* VI 14.

[16] *Princ.* 1, praef. 3.

[17] *Contra Celsum* VI 7 quotes texts from the Wisdom literature; note the discussion of I Cor. i in I 13 and III 47 f.

[18] *Contra Celsum* I 2. See Gregory Thaumaturgus' account of Origen's educational method in *Paneg.* VII 100 ff.

[19] *Philocalia* 13. Cf. *Hom. in Gen.* XIII 3 (Issac's servants may dig wells on Philistine land).

[20] For the plagiarism thesis cf. *Contra Celsum* IV 39 (the garden of Zeus of *Symp.* 203 from Genesis ii-iii): did Plato hit on it by chance? or did he meet exegetes of Genesis when in Egypt?

[21] *Contra Celsum* VII 46; 49 (disowning captious criticism); *Hom. in Ex.* XI 6. Justin (*Dial.* 6. 1) and Clement (*Str.* VI 66) state the principle.

[22] *Hom. in Gen.* XVI 3; cf. *Princ.* I 3. 1; *Contra Celsum* VI 8; 47 (Plato teaches that the Creator is Son of God).

[23] *Contra Celsum* IV 67-8; V 20; *Princ.* II 3. 4.

[24] *Contra Celsum* VI 71.

[25] E.g. *Comm. in Joh.* I 37; XIII 41; *Contra Celsum* III 40; VIII 52.

[26] *Hom. in Luc.* 35 (p. 196 Rauer).

[27] *Comm. in Rom.* III 7; cf. *Contra Celsum* I 4 f.

[28] *Comm. in Rom.* VI 8; cf. Philo, *Opif.* 3.

[29] *Comm. in Rom.* VIII 2.

[30] *Contra Celsum* III 40.

[31] *Exh. Mart.* 47; *Princ.* II 11. 4; *Sel. in Ps.* (XI, 424 Lommatzsch); cf. *Comm. in Cant. Cantic.* I (p. 91 Baehrens).

[32] *Comm. in Rom.* III 9 (Tura papyrus, p. 166 Scherer); *Hom. in Num.* I 2; XI 7.

[33] *Contra Celsum* IV 19; *Hom. in Ps. 36*, IV 1; *Hom. in Ps. 37*, I 4 (XII, 205; 253 Lommatzsch).

[34] E.g. *Comm. in Joh.* II 16.

[35] *Contra Celsum* IV 66 (decisively rejecting the view that evil inheres in matter); cf. VI 53 (we do not make God responsible for evil by saying he made matter).

[36] To Celsus' remark that 'it is not easy for one who has not studied philosophy to know the origin of evils' Origen replies that it is only possible to begin if one knows (from the Bible) about the devil (IV 65). Celsus finds the idea of Satan impossible (VI 42).

[37] *Contra Celsum* IV 74 ff.

[38] *Contra Celsum* VIII 52; *Princ.* IV 1. 7; *Exh. Mart.* 4.

[39] *Princ.* IV 1. 7; II 9. 4.

[40] *Contra Celsum* III 47; VI 3-4; VII 42; 44.

[41] *Contra Celsum* VI 68.

[42] Immutable: *Contra Celsum* VI 62; *Orat.* XXIV 2; *Comm. in Joh.* II 17; VI 38. Impassible: *Contra Celsum* IV 72 (of wrath); *Hom. in Num.* XVI 3; XXIII 2; *Princ.* II 4. 4; etc. *Hom. in Ezech.* VI 6 accepts passibility in the sense of love and mercy. Transcendent: *Contra Celsum* VI 64 f. (*via negativa* qualified by *via eminentiae*); cf. VII 42 f. Needing nothing: *Hom. in Gen.* VIII 10, etc. Creative goodness: *Princ.* I 4. 3; *Comm. in Joh.* VI 38; cf. *Princ.* I 5. 3 (only the Trinity is good essentially; all else has goodness but can lose it).

43 See, for example, *Comm. in Joh.* XIII 25. (For contacts at this point between the thought of Origen and that of Plotinus see Part III, ch. 12, p. 199.)

44 *Princ.* IV 4. 1 ff.

45 *Princ.* II 6. 1; *Contra Celsum* III 34.

46 *Contra Celsum* VI 64.

47 *Contra Celsum* IV 54. (*Princ.* I 8. 2 attacks a Gnostic variant of this.)

48 *Contra Celsum* V 6-13, disowning not only Plato but Anaxagoras' notion that the stars are masses of hot metal. Origen thinks the stars spiritual beings who have fallen but a little way, are imprisoned in the stars and compelled to regulate earthly weather. He justifies prayer for fine weather on the hypothesis that the sun has free will. (It is fair to add that he regarded all this as speculative.)

49 *Princ.* II 1. 4; *Comm. in Gen. ap.* Eus. *P.E.* VII 20; etc.

50 *Princ.* II 3. 6.

51 *Princ.* I 3. 3. The following résumé is mainly based on the *De principiis*.

52 *Contra Celsum* V 29; *Comm. in Matt.* XIII I (the fullest discussion); etc. Nothing can be based on Koetschau's hypothetical reconstruction of *Princ.* I 8. 4.

Robert W. Smith (essay date 1974)

SOURCE: "Spokesman for Truth (Continued): Christian Preachers," in *The Art of Rhetoric in Alexandria: Its Theory and Practice in the Ancient World.* Martinus Nijhoff, 1974, pp. 73-107.

[*In this excerpt, Smith examines Origen's use of the homily and how in his hands it became an occasion for explaining the meaning of the Scriptures. Discussed as well is Origen's theory and method of preaching. The editors have included only the footnotes that pertain to the part of the chapter devoted to Origen.*]

The homily . . . as a speech form came into its own in the third to fifth centuries in the Byzantine church, but the idea originated centuries earlier. Aeschylus spoke of it (*Thebes, 599*) in the sense of intercourse with or company of people, and Jews had used it in a didactic and explanatory sense of understanding Scriptures. It remained for later and Christian writers and speakers, Clement and Origen among them, to extend its meaning to express what takes place in a meeting between a preacher and his congregation when they are studying Holy Writ.[1] It became an important vehicle not only in Clement's "Hypotyposis", and in the Alexandrian Catechetical School, but in the religious discourse of Origen himself.

In his hands it became an important means of explaining the meaning of biblical passages. Distinguished from the logos . . . or *sermo* which was more in the classical Greek sense of public discourse, the homily was conversational in tone, often lacked a central thesis, and provided a kind of running commentary—verse by verse—of a chapter. It compared one idea with another in the Bible and used allegory and other figures freely—at times too freely, by modern standards.[2]

The homily continued into medieval times and even into the twentieth century, but it reached its zenith in popularity and utility in the third to fifth centuries. P. Oxy 1601 and 1602, dating from this period, are but two of several examples. In each of them the speaker explains the text, then exhorts believers to be chary of Satan ("your adversary the Devil walketh about seeking to devour [you] . . ." 1601) and to follow Christ ("Remain [steadfast] . . . , receive . . . Christ Jesus . . . , accept the word . . . 1602).

When the modern Western reader peruses the homilies of the ancient world he is struck with two vastly different rhetorical products. On the one hand when he reads those of St. John Chrysostom of Antioch or Origen of Alexandria he is struck with solid and mature thought, with preachers whose reflective processes moved ahead of most of their contemporaries, whether secular or sacred. He finds exegesis which, while occasionally a little contrived and fanciful by modern standards, nonetheless has well stood the test of time, and can yet edify the serious reader. One would expect in an age when theological thought was much less crystallized than in the twentieth century that listeners would have greatly profited by such lectures and sermons which, like Demosthenic speeches, smelled of the lamp of diligent work.

On the other hand, the invertebrate products of preachers, like some of those of Athanasius, lacked real substance on occasion and appear today as sweet and insipid. They merit reading only as curious museum pieces. That Alexandrians could and would listen to them testifies to their superficial character and low taste.

As suggested earlier Origen (c. 184-c. 254) was the most important Alexandrian preacher utilizing the homily. This third century teacher/preacher not only commanded the highest respect of any pulpiteer, and headed the famous catechetical school (before he was 20 years old), but also constituted the transition from the traditional sermon to the homily. Modern critics have denied him a place among the ranks of great preachers,[3] but near-contemporary evidence suggests the contrary. While he cannot be placed qualitively in the same rhetorical class as the Attic Ten, he had a large and celebrated following. Eusebius tells us that many and distinguished philosophers came to hear him, and Jerome opines that he was a man of incomparable eloquence and knowledge so that when he opened his mouth he dumbfounded others.[4] A careful scholar, he cared little for Greek rhetoric as taught in the West or practiced in the sophistic schools of Alexandria and Antioch; it was too self-centered and contrived, magnifying men and manner at the expense of mind and matter. If later generations could in retrospect discern profitable features in the rhetorical training of the day, Origen's proximity to the phenomena and his religious zeal hindered his perception of such positive values. Yet, his simplicity of exposition did not prevent occasional loftiness in style nor his seeing allegorical interpretations in it, for whether by grammatico-historical, moral, or spiritual (allegorical) analysis, Scripture had much to teach one who would listen and ponder.[5]

Origen's homilies—some preserved in Greek, others in Latin translation by Rufinus and Jerome—cover both the Old and New Testaments. Of the 206 Migne published in his *Patrologia Graeca* we have texts of them from the Pentateuch (*Genesis, Exodus, Leviticus,* and *Numbers*), the historical books (*Joshua, Judges, I* and *II Samuel*), the Prophets (*Isaiah, Jeremiah,* and *Ezekiel*), as well as the poetic book of the *Canticles*. In the New Testament he wrote on *Matthew, Luke, John,* and some of Paul's *Epistles*. We do not have the original or intermediate source of many of the extant texts which have come to us from the desks of Rufinus and Jerome, but the present ones likely represent at least the substance and probably much of the style of the original homilies. Early in his preaching career he wrote out his homilies, but later in life his extemporaneous delivery called upon the wide and intensive reading of earlier years. Shorthand reporters . . . listening to him recorded his speeches, providing the basis for the later translations into Latin which have survived. The tautology which we sometimes find may stem from scribal errors or (more probably) from the speaker's emphasis of selected portions,[6] as he would have learned from earlier Athenian speeches. But repetition in the texts does occur from time to time.

In his thirteen homilies on *Exodus* he typically begins with a proposition or statement, proceeds through verse by verse exposition and exegesis—a vague resemblance of classical narration (. . . *narratio*)—then ends with the benediction from *I Peter* iv.11, and a final "Amen."[7] In III (*Exodus* iv) on the excuse of Moses that he was not eloquent before Pharoah, Origen replies that all men on occasion lack eloquence and stand mute. God it is who must open their mouths for good causes, while Satan prompts them to buffoonery, obscenities, and useless talk. In VIII (*Exodus* xx) on the First Com-

mandment of the Decalogue we predictably find him acknowledging in a polytheistic society that there are many gods to seduce the faithful from the worship of Jehovah. "To thee also who through Jesus Christ art come out of Egypt and hast been led forth from the house of bondage, it is said, 'Thou shalt have none other gods before me.'" Deliverance was not only for the ancient House of Israel, but for all men: Egypt was not only Israel's prison, but allegorically was contemporary man's as well. Jerusalem and Judea represented the houses of liberty for those leaving their former life and looking for true freedom.

Between A.D. 244 and 249 at an undetermined place Origen preached his 28 homilies on the book of *Numbers* in which he depicted the journey of the ancient Jews as a type of the spiritual odyssey of the Christian.[8] In XX (*Numbers,* xxv), a comparatively long homily taking perhaps a half-hour in delivery, he begins with a prefatory statement recounting the historical seduction of Israel by Moab, then shows the moral sense that luxury can lead to sin. Yet if one arms himself (following Paul in *Ephesians* vi. 14-17) he will withstand the moral battle and finally be united with God. Should he choose otherwise his destiny lies with Satan; there is no middle ground. This speech, like many that he gave, shows the typical three interpretations he normally found in Scripture: grammatico-historical, moral, and spiritual. In XII (*Numbers* xxi. 16) the three are not quite so clear, but we see at least two when he holds that while the Israelites had a literal well Christians have a spiritual one, the Word of God, which brings refreshment from Father, Son, and Holy Spirit.

But sometimes he carried his allegories too far, as in XXVII of the *Numbers* collection. In speaking of the Israelites camping at Thara (Terah; *Numbers* xxxii. 26-27) he understood Thara to mean a mental stupor (*contemplatio stuporis*) into which one might fall because of some great thing (*alicuius magnae rei*) happening to him. But reading the biblical text itself does not support this interpretation. The city was simply one of several places where the Israelites camped. Either he had access to data not mentioned in the original account or he read into the verse what he wished to find. At any rate, the allegory strains the narrative.

The twenty-six *Joshua* homilies came near the end of Origen's preaching career (A.D. 249-50) and while they probably were preached not in Alexandria, but in Caesarea, they merit passing mention because of the speaker himself.[9] He sees many adumbrations for the contemporary Christian: at the Jordan River the Kingdom for the Christian begins and a new conqueror rules; Jericho is the city of evil which falls under the onslaught of the Word of God and the Apostle's doctrines; Rahab prefigures the Gentiles who hear the Good News and believe; and the Canaanites are the demonic powers which war against the soul. Homily II (*Joshua* i. 2) shows not simply the death of Moses and the rising of Joshua, but for contemporary men, the death of the Mosaic Law and the new regime of the Gentiles. Jesus (Joshua; the Hebrew language does not distinguish the two) has supplanted Moses.[10] When one sees, the preacher went on in era of persecution, that Jesus Christ has been crucified, the church grows 30-60-100-fold. When he sees the gathering together of the saints, and the people of God observing the Sabbath, not by abstaining from ordinary affairs (*con versatione communi*), but from acts of sin—when this and more comes about—then know that Jesus, Son of God, holds the leadership.

Luke appears to have been a favorite book of Origen, if we can judge by the thirty-nine homilies devoted to it.[11] They date from A.D. 233-34, but as with most of the other rhetorical works, we find few hints of the occasion. Some of them, III, IX, XV, and XXIV could not have consumed more than 3-5 minutes, if our texts approach completeness. And those numbered XIV, XXI, XXII, and XXIV were probably directed to his catechumens, for he treats explicitly baptism as a necessary preparation for receiving the sacrament of the Lord's Table, while XVIII (*Luke* ii. 40-49) depicts Jesus' parents searching for him at the age of twelve and finding him "not simply in the temple, but sitting in the midst of the doctors." Origen probably had his young students in mind when he said, "Y[ou], therefore, seek Him in the temple of God; seek Him in the Church; seek Him among the teachers who are in the temple, and who depart not from it. If you so seek Him, you will find Him." And in XXXIII in veiled language he invites his listeners to follow the example of Naaman the leper to be cleansed by washing in the Jordan (baptism) and become clean.

Origen's method of preaching was basically a verse by verse exegesis and exposition of Scripture, and probably every verse of every chapter of a selected book. However, in the Lukan homilies which Jerome has preserved for us the first 33 cover for the most part the initial five chapters of the book (chiefly i.1 - iv. 27), but the final six treat only five of the remaining 20 chapters. In view of his normally thorough and systematic approach to his topic, he very likely examined the other chapters as well, but those works have not survived. Because of these qualities his expository homilies far outnumber those of a hortatory nature, and thus they have been copied and recopied until today they constitute an important part of the Origean corpus.

At the close of all 39 he prefaces the last statement in each with some phrase referring to Jesus and then concludes with the brief benediction from *I Peter* iv.11, "to whom belong the glory and dominion for ever and ever. Amen." (*cui est gloria et imperium in saecula*

saeculorum. Amen). The same conclusion occurs in those of *Exodus* and *Numbers* as well, suggesting both a (now) conventionalized liturgical form as well as a basic desire to glorify his Lord. In the Lukan homilies, unlike in his others, there is little introduction, and never any attempt to capture effectively the attention of the audience. He seldom includes a final summary or call to action; this he seems to accomplish in the benediction. While one can theorize that the expositions were intended for a small coterie of disciples and hence no such effort was needed, the supposition remains that they were seemingly composed for the community at large. Probably he was simply following (or entrenching) the custom of making no initial adaptation to either audience or occasion.

Yet Origen concerned himself with his immediate audience, this is abundantly clear. In the first place, he spoke in Greek, not in the native Egyptian tongue of the chora and found in parts of the city. He did so because, as a Hellenistic scholar, he was not only raised in a Greek-speaking family, but was Greek in virtually everything but religion. He therefore spoke to those he most wished to reach. This means that few Egyptians would have found their way into either his classroom or his congregation. It is possible, of course, that he employed interpreters, much as Scythopolis used Procopius in Palestine to interpret into Aramaic,[12] and as the Alexandrian courts came to do for native Egyptians, but not only have we no evidence to support such a theory for his speaking but it is highly unlikely.

Then too we note his overriding concern with the here and now much in keeping with the general disposition of the Alexandrians.[13] While this strikes one as odd in view of his own disciplined study and mastery of earlier works, it shows that he simply accommodated himself to the realities of the speaking situation. One finds little in his preaching to urge his listeners to search out the truth by study and reflection. He often spoke briefly though sometimes his analysis would extend to a half-hour (as in his treatment of *I Samuel* i & ii). The homilies rather play on the restlessness of his listeners and their preoccupation with the present. He was, in a word, relevant.

Since one purpose of the Origean homilies was to teach biblical content and explain Scripture, the speaker drew heavily—almost exclusively—from other parts of the Bible. In his second homily on *Canticles* (i. 12b-ii. 14) he cites the Scriptures 77 times: 35 from the Old Testament (eight from the *Psalms*) and 42 from the New (*Matthew,* 16 times). And in his lengthy exposition of *I Samuel* i and ii he alludes to the Old Testament 83 times (of which 43 come from the books of *Kings*) and 70 times to the New (of which Paul's *Epistles* to the Corinthians are cited 25 times). In XIV (*Luke*) he quotes or refers to Paul's writings nine times from a total of 16 references to the New Testament. This high regard for Paul probably stems from the latter's perception of many allegories and types in the Old Testament, an insight which particularly pleased Origen who also felt that the Scriptures had more to offer than mere history. So Origen's keen memory, thorough grasp of sacred writing, love of allegory (especially found in Paul), and intellectual acumen served him and his audiences well.

Origen's theory of preaching was basically simple. As previously suggested, to him Scripture had three meanings: the grammatico-historical (which established the context), the moral (which applied the verse to the present day) and the spiritual or allegorical (which lifted one to higher heights). He believed that the preacher must know both the Scriptures and the hearts of men, and that he must become as a child to other children, much as God became a child in Jesus, in order to win them for the Kingdom. Thus Origen sought to preach plainly, directly, and often briefly,[14] to allow maximum understanding. One finds in him a "subdued fire that reveals the tale of mental suffering and exhausting toil. Hence that austere solemnity, that absolute sincerity, that breadth and dignity of mind, which grasp and detain the reader with the same spell that was cast upon Gregory."[15] But in arresting his audience he did so not by reference to his own personal experiences or even to those of others around him but by the internal and inherent power of the ideas he developed. If Gregory of Nyssa saw the allegorical interpretation as merely one of several techniques useful to the preacher, Origen conceived of it as the very basis for his preaching.[16] Listeners were intellectually challenged, morally exhorted, and spiritually uplifted with this type of preaching, though twentieth century congregations, accustomed to the Greek *sermo,* would find much of it inadequate.

While Origen made no initial efforts to adapt to his audience, various clues in his sermons suggest that he either tried to recapture waning attention of his listeners, once he had begun, or his amanuenses took more than normal care in their shorthand accounts. In Homily VI (*Luke*) he says that God has given to this our gathering and assembly (*huic coetui nostro atque conventui*) a share of His power, while in VIII (*Exodus*) he declares that Scripture itself, "if you will listen with attention and patience [*si intente et patiente auditis*], will be able to instruct us."[17] Elsewhere on the *Canticles* he exhorts, "you members of the church, speak to the daughters of Jerusalem" [*Et tu, ecclesiastice, ad filias Hieruslem converte sermonem*].[18] One might construe such statements as general exhortations to anyone reading Scripture or worshipping, nonetheless they may have obliquely called back the audience's ebbing attention to the issues at hand. In any event, one must look closely for such adaptation; it is not nearly so obvious as in the more classically oriented sermons summarized in the *Acts of the Apostles.*

We see another side of Origen's rhetorical ability. In the minutes of a recently discovered work, *A Conversation of Origen with Heracleides,* which highlights the trial of Bishop Heracleides probably between A.D. 244 and 249 and perhaps in the bishop's own Alexandrian church,[19] the defendant's orthodoxy had been called into question. Origen, experienced in theological issues and the one under whose preaching Heracleides was converted, was asked to take an active role in the examination of the prelate. The dialogue centered around the beliefs of Heracleides with specific questions like, if Jesus Christ was God, did He really die on the cross? Or, what is the nature of the soul? The account of the trial—some of it is verbatim, as shown by the quotations following the frequent use of "———(name) said . . . —shows Origen in command of the situation at every point. He questions, makes short speeches on theological points such as the essence of the soul, and, as in the homilies, copiously supports his statements with Scriptural references. His sifting and challenging forces the bishop, not his match, to admit two gods in the Christian faith. But Origen's monotheism would not let him rest with that. Quickly drawing the analogy of Adam and Eve becoming one flesh, though not one spirit or soul, and of the righteous man as wedded with Christ, yet distinct from Him, he sought to draw the parallel in the Trinity. But his analogies broke down, and each side was left with two gods, however objectionable it seemed to Christian doctrine.

The audience at the Heracleides trial seems to have drawn both clergy and laymen—perhaps even some non-Christian laymen, for Origen feared he was casting his pearls before swine (xii. 22ff and xv. 7ff). Additional evidence for this stems from the fact that after he was queried on the nature of the soul he hesitated to answer because he feared he might confuse the uninstructed laymen present. The altercation, though confusing to the untutored, must have been charged with excitement and feeling as this highly gifted theologian sought to frame the acceptability of, or their opposites to, specific doctrines.

We do not know the outcome of the trial, whether or not the bishop was acquitted of heresy, but we do see Origen as an advocate thoroughly schooled in his subject, gentle, but with questions which lead to problematic answers. In the courtroom or the classroom he was considerate, kind, and erudite.

Origen's heart and mind moved too rapidly for the church in Alexandria. Demetrius, the local bishop, not only banished him for certain irregular beliefs regarding the Trinity and for his unorthodox ordination in Jerusalem (when Origen was in exile), but even had him excommunicated on grounds curious by some twentieth century theological standards. As Neale points out, in an age when doctrine was not clearly settled,

Origen mixed what today would be called heresy with orthodoxy concerning the Father, Son, and Holy Spirit. When he and others were hammering out beliefs on the anvil of experience and reflection it was difficult to keep paradoxical matters in nice balance.[20]

Notes

[1] Dargan, *History of Preaching*, I, 49. Clement also preached, but his public sermons have not come down to us—unlike the literary product of his namesake of Rome with whom the former is often confused. We shall return to Clement of Alexandria in the next chapter when discussing education.

[2] William F. Arndt and F. Wilbur Gingrich, *Greek-English Lexicon of the New Testament and other Early Christian Literature* (University of Chicago, 1957), v. . . . ; G.W.H. Lampe, *Patristic Greek Lexicon* (Oxford, 1961), v. . . . ; (no editor), *New Catholic Encyclopedia* (New York, 1967), VII, v. "homily;" and James Hastings (ed.), *Encyclopedia of Religion and Ethics*, X (New York, 1955), v. "Preaching."

[3] John Ker, *Lectures on the History of Preaching*, 2nd ed. (London, 1888), p. 63, Edwin C. Dargan, *History of Preaching*, I, 54, and Matter, *Histoire de L'École d'Alexandrie*, III, 85.

[4] . . . H.E., VI. xviii. 1 ff. Conceivably this statement could refer to Origen's teaching in the School. Jerome, *Epistles*, xxxiii. 4: *sed quia gloriam eloquentiae ejus, et scientiae ferre non poterant, et illo dicente, omnes multi putabantur.*

[5] Dargan, *History of Preaching*, I, 51. Origen was not, of course, the first preacher to treat Scripture allegorically. Not only had Philo two centuries before done so, but even the pagan Egyptian priests in the *Book of the Dead* in the second millenium B.C. so treated it. Broadus, *Lectures on the History of Preaching*, p. 54, and R[ichard] B. Tollington, *Selections from the Commentaries and Homilies of Origen* (London, 1929), p. xxxv.

[6] Origen disclaimed any flourishes of style, or perhaps simply lacked the ability. His homilies are at once clear, simple, plain in style, and sometimes dull. His father, Leonides, was probably a rhetorician, though one does not find in the son's works the attention to style he would expect in the era of the Second Sophistic. Philip Schaff, "Ante-Nicene Christianity," *History of the Christian Church* (New York, 1901), II, 786-88, and Paniel, *Pragmatische Geschichte der Christlichen Beredsamkeit*, pp. 175-79.

[7] In considering the *Exodus* homilies I have used chiefly P. Fortier and H. de Lubac, "Origène: Homélies sur L'Exode," *Sources Chrétiennes*, 16 (Paris, 1947).

[8] For the discussion of the *Numbers* homilies I have used André Méhat, "Origène: Homélies sur les Nombres," *Sources Chrétiennes*, 29 (Paris, 1951).

[9] I have used Annie Jaubert, "Origène: Homélies sur Josué," *Sources Chrétiennes*, 71 (Paris, 1960), for the discussion of the *Joshua* homilies.

[10] *Iesus post Moysen suscepit et obtinuit principatum.* Rufinus translation.

[11] In discussing the Lukan homilies I have used Max Rauer, "Homilien zu Luka" in *Origenes Werke*, IX (Berlin, 1959), M.F. Toal, trans., *Sunday Sermons of the Great Fathers* (Chicago, 1957), I, and Henri Crouzel, François Fournier, and Pierre Perichon, "Origène: Homélies sur S. Luc," *Sources Chrétiennes*, 87 (Paris, 1962).

[12] Fergus Millar, "Paul of Samosata, Zenobia and Aurelian: The Church, Local Culture and Political Allegiance in Third-Century Syria," *Journal of Roman Studies*, LXI (1971), 7.

[13] "L'exégèse d'Origène est donc orientée par les préoccupations fondamentales du moment." Jaubert, "Origène," p. 13.

[14] Eusebius, *H.E.*, VI, xxxvi, Bingham, *Antiquities of the Christian Church*, II, 717, Paniel, *Pragmatische Geschichte der Christlichen Beredsamkeit*, pp. 175-83, and Dargan, *History of Preaching*, I, 52.

[15] Bigg, *Church's Task under the Roman Empire*, p. 168.

[16] C.W. Macleod, "Allegory and Mysticism in Origen and Gregory of Nyssa," *Journal of Theological Studies*, N.S. XXII (1972), 371.

[17] Conceivably this could refer to their reading and heeding habits.

[18] So Jerome.

[19] The largely complete Greek text (based on P Cairo Inv 88745) with French translation was first published by Jean Scherer (1949) and may be found in his "Entretien d'Origène avec Héraclide" (Paris, 1960), *Sources Chrétiennes* 77. An English translation is available in John E.L. Oulton and Henry Chadwick, "Alexandrian Christianity," *Library of Christian Classics* (Philadelphia, 1954), II, 430 ff.

[20] Neale, "Patriarchate of Alexandria," pp. 28-35.

P. M. O'Cleirigh (essay date 1980)

SOURCE: "The Meaning of Dogma in Origen," in *Jewish and Christian Self-Definition, Vol. 1.* Fortress Press, 1980, pp. 201-16.

[*In this essay, O'Cleirigh examines the teaching of Origen over against the teachings of Christian orthodoxy with a view to answering the question much in debate among scholars: Did Origen write from a comprehensive view of Christian theology or did he merely apply his philosophical mind to mystical ends?*]

The distinct shape of Origen's achievement is a ground of debate among scholars. It is generally agreed, however, that his work established a model of Christian theology which was to predominate in later centuries.[1] He accomplished this by applying to the scriptures the methods of analysis and demonstration and, some would say, the systematic consistency which he learned from Greek philosophy. In conformity with general philosophical usage he calls each of his conclusions dogma. The nature of this dogma is a question which is appropriate to this seminar, for it lies at the heart of the definition of Christianity as wisdom which Origen wholeheartedly promoted.[2]

A major achievement of Origen scholarship in the past fifty years is the recognition that elements in his works which derive from different traditions are not merely juxtaposed but are transposed into a new context.[3] This is a Christian context, however philosophically conceived. The question is no longer 'Is Origen really a Platonist or a Christian?' but 'What is the philosophy of Origen the Christian?' The main point of debate here is whether Origen writes from the vantage point of a comprehensive system or rather uses his philosophical skill for mystical ends. This cardinal question in determining the nature of Origen's conception of Christian wisdom will be treated in a summary presentation of the arguments by either side. Then the concept of dogma in its twofold reference to the doctrine of common Christianity and the teaching of Origen will be examined with this wider question in view.

Origen as systematician

It will be in place here, before analysing the concept of dogma, to outline the leading points of the argument for and against the view that Origen is a systematic thinker. This is the more appropriate as my paper is a form of postscript to the study by F. H. Kettler of the dogmatics of Origen.[4] His book is the most vigorous assertion of the systematic nature of Origen's thought since that of Hans Jonas,[5] the most convincing since that of Hal Koch.[6] His argument is even more persuasive than Koch's in that he takes due account of Origen's Christianity.

For Kettler, Origen is an independent Christian thinker: he is not a Middle Platonist, a Gnostic, a representative of the church's teaching nor an amalgam of all these (with an emphasis on the third view).[7] In this way he differentiates his view of Origen from that of

Koch, who emphasizes the Middle Platonic roots of Origen's doctrine and concludes that his philosophical system is essentially independent of his Christianity.[8] He distances himself from Jonas, who holds that the structure of Origen's system is Gnostic even if its contents are Christian.[9] For H. Crouzel Origen, as a committed Christian, has no use for merely human systems[10] while for J. Daniélou he has indeed systematic intentions but finds it impossible to contain the Christian truth within a system.[11] The contradictions in his writings come from this tension. In contradistinction to these scholars, Kettler finds that Origen as a Christian thinker succeeds in transposing the traditions he inherited into a consistent system.

The primary reason for finding a philosophical system in Origen is the programme he states at the end of his preface to **On First Principles.** He has set out the doctrines which the apostles preached as necessary for all, observing that they left the grounds of their statements, the how and the why, for investigation by future lovers of wisdom.[12] These doctrines must be taken as elementary and foundation principles in constructing a connected body of doctrine.

> Thus by clear and cogent arguments he will discover the truth about each particular point and so will produce, as we have said, a single body of doctrine with the aid of such illustrations and declarations as he shall find in the holy scriptures and of such conclusions as he shall ascertain to follow logically from them when rightly understood.[13]

The main reason for disputing the existence of such a system in Origen's writings is that the vast bulk of his work is scriptural commentary and is not strikingly systematic in presentation. More particularly, he does not always give the same account of a similar difficulty in exegesis and at times his accounts are positively antithetical. The status of **On First Principles** is disputable and even within this book there are many discussions left inconclusive. The programme of its preface by no means settles the question.[14]

Kettler grants that if Origen intends the discussions to which he suggests two or more answers to remain open questions he cannot be considered a systematic thinker.[15] He sets out to show that Origen means his intelligent readers to draw the proper conclusions from among the alternatives which he suggests. They are enabled to do this by the logic of his system.[16] The reason for Origen's tentative method of presentation has its basis in the tradition of concealing esoteric truth from the uninitiated, but Origen uses this tradition with a double purpose. One part of his purpose is pedagogic—his students must think the question through to the end for themselves. The other part is to reassure the traditionalist Christian who might be shocked to learn the speculative version of his faith.[17]

To this latter end Origen insists many times on the connection between his speculation and the propositions of the *kerygma,* especially when this connection is looser than usual.[18] He also makes frequent use of the distinction between dogma and research, characterizing his inconclusive discussions as research which has not led to a definite conclusion.[19] Kettler studies five passages where this distinction is made—all of which concern his esoteric teaching—and shows how they can be resolved by the logic of the system.[20]

Despite Kettler's close argumentation here, the nature of the evidence—Origen's double intention—precludes a definitive resolution on the grounds of these passages alone. So he proceeds to the relation of research to dogma in the surviving Greek works. Here dogma in most cases means the result of research and is only used in a secondary sense of the propositions of the *kerygma.*[21] This certainly strengthens his thesis on the inconclusive discussions in **On First Principles:** in this work dogma is used with studied ambiguity.[22]

The propositions of the church's proclamation have an ambiguous status. As the elements of Christian teaching they are of fundamental importance, but the notion of fundament is likewise ambiguous. We stand on it but rise above it. Kettler makes a telling point when he notes that Origen never falls back on the *kerygma* when reason fails him.[23] The distinction between common and esoteric dogma of course corresponds to the pervasive distinction in the Alexandrians between mere faith and higher knowledge.

While on earth knowledge is fragmentary. It is a prior grasp on the higher existence. But on the other hand the spiritual man is more than human. On these considerations, Origen, with full acknowledgment of the grace of knowledge, builds his system. He does not know everything and he knows some things more certainly than others, but, according to Kettler, he is absolutely sure of the main lines of his system and their important cross-connections.[24] His problem was not that he did not know the answer to certain questions but that he did not dare to state openly all that was clear to him.

The most resolute opponent of a systematic Origen is Henri Crouzel. No one has shown him that there lies at the centre of Origen's speculation a rational system which could be easily expressed in a series of propositions which derive one from the other.[25] Such a system cannot be found even in **On First Principles** without relying on a large amount of external inimical evidence. The treatise simply does not carry out the programme of the preface. In fact it is not one treatise but three, each of which covers the same material in different degrees of expansion.[26] These are probably three versions of a course given by Origen at Alexandria. They are more concerned with teaching the stu-

dents how to think than with the communication of fixed doctrine. In this way Crouzel accounts for the inconclusive discussions in the work.

Crouzel's attack on the search for a system is made in the context of the proper methodology to be used in studying Origen. He emphasizes the limitations which the assumption of a system has exercised on scholarly work. It is only this assumption which enables the evidence of Jerome and Justinian to be regarded more highly than that of Rufinus.[27] Crouzel's preferred methodology is inductive—all the passages on a given topic must be considered collectively before any conclusion is reached as to Origen's view, and the findings should not be vitiated by alignment with an undemonstrated master system.[28]

He lays stress on the antithetical nature of Origen's expressions. In one passage Origen will insist on the freedom of Judas's action, in another he will write as if Judas, spurred on by the devil, is only a pawn in a combat of spiritual forces.[29] But even though we often find complementary antitheses like this we find them in different writings. Origen is not concerned immediately to restore an equilibrium by stating the complementary consideration. The synthesis of antithetical elements in Origen does not exist on the rational level but on the spiritual level of the *mysterion.*[30]

The *animus* directed against the idea of a system in Origen is aimed ultimately against rationalism. Crouzel does not deny that speculative elements are important in Origen, only that they are the dominant elements. He grants a cosmological perspective, especially in **On First Principles**. He even advocates the dominance of the Platonic perspective of a universe on two levels in its Christian transposition.[31] Indeed he has shown with precision how Origen transposes the Platonic theory of knowledge in terms of Christ as word and wisdom.[32] It is plain that he rejects a system in Origen only if it is the exclusive product of the reasoning and discursive reason with comprehensive ontological claims. Nevertheless he is not persuaded by Kettler's study.[33] Although Kettler is far from treating *nous* in a segregated rational sense, he does extend its reach to the *logos* himself.

Dogma in Origen: background

After this pointing of the debate as to whether Origen is a systematic thinker I now turn to an analysis of the concept of dogma in his writings. For the purposes of his argument Kettler is content to define dogma simply as 'doctrine'.[34] M. Elze, however, in his study of the concept of dogma in the early church, has remarked on the systematic tendency inherent in the Stoic usage of the concept.[35] I follow this suggestion of his in examining the philosophical usage of dogma in Origen and his antecedents. This examination will permit us to make some useful distinctions about the systematic thought of Origen.

First of all we must consider the usage of the concept of dogma in the philosophical tradition before Origen. Already in classical Greek two senses of the word are to be distinguished: on the one hand 'thought', 'opinion', and on the other 'decision', 'decree'. Although these are separate spheres of meaning they derive respectively from the transitive and intransitive meaning of the verb *dokein* (tr. 'to think'; intr. 'to seem good'), and so the range of meaning of dogma is rightly described by Fascher as 'in all cases the outcome of the forming of human ideas which, by common agreement or by a directive from a person in authority, can be made binding either on a philosophical school or on a political community'.[36] It will not be maintained that the doctrine of a philosophical school lacks a certain authority, and it is likewise evident that disagreeable ordinances, at least, inspire reflections on the ruler's capacity for judgment. Nevertheless the separate spheres of meaning which develop whereby dogma in the sense of 'thought' is appropriated by the philosophical schools to mean specifically 'doctrine' and dogma in the sense of 'decree' enters juridical terminology as 'a publicly proclaimed and binding ordinance' are valid distinctions of usage.[37]

It is with the Stoa that dogma first becomes a technical philosophical term and it is on Stoic thinkers that I shall concentrate in this section. Chrysippus, according to Diogenes Laertius (VII. 179), was fond of saying that he needed only to learn the *dogmata* since he was able to work out on his own the arguments by which to demonstrate them. *Dogmata* here must mean the central theses of the school. Although they are reasonable since they can be demonstrated, Chrysippus is emphasizing the priority of these *dogmata* to their demonstration.[38]

The comprehensiveness of Stoic *dogmata* is stressed in Seneca: 'Decreta sunt quae totam vitam totamque rerum naturam simul contineant' (*Ep.* 95.12)—those teachings are *dogmata* which embrace at the same time the whole of (man's) life and the whole of nature.[39] The general concepts of value which form the grounds of worth of individual pursuits are *dogmata*. They are effective at the source of our actions, telling us that money is neither good nor bad, death only happens once, excessive suffering does not last, happiness does not come from pleasure but from the natural life. These *dogmata* expel wrong opinions about good and evil and enable us to judge between them.[40]

Epictetus makes a further distinction in the concept within the area of ethics. Dogma continues to designate the general concepts of value whereby we lay worth on particular things. He frequently writes 'it is not the things themselves that move us and determine our action but the dogma whereby we on our part

value the things'.[41] So dogma makes us tremble before the tyrant while a child does not tremble. But in an even more general sense dogma signifies the *prohairesis,* our ultimate decision about the worth of things.[42]

The undividedness of the ethical and the theoretical as well as the general and comprehensive nature of *dogmata* is seen in a passage from Marcus Aurelius:

> The works of the gods are full of Providence. The works of chance are not divorced from Nature or from the spinning and weaving together of those things which are governed by Providence. Thence everything flows. There is also Necessity and what is beneficient to the whole ordered universe of which you are a part.... That should be enough for you, these should ever be your *dogmata.* Cast out your thirst for books . . .

> (*Medit.* II.3).[43]

Dogmata are here short statements of fundamental principles of the organization of the cosmos and man's place in it. As for Chrysippus such *dogmata* have a priority over demonstration, so for Marcus they are effective guiding principles without further study.

In Sextus Empiricus, the Dogmatists are those who believe they have discovered the truth: 'Aristotle, for example, and Epicurus and the Stoics and certain others.'[44] The dogma which ends the search for truth is not simply a matter of giving it one's approval but can be clearly defined as 'an assent (*synkatathesis*) to one of the non-evident objects (*adēlōn*) of scientific inquiry'.[45] Sextus himself is still seeking for the truth, having neither arrived nor despaired. He has no dogma and *a fortiori* belongs to no *hairesis,* a group with a distinctive common doctrine. Dogmatists have such groups, in which the members give 'adherence to a number of dogmas (assent to a non-evident proposition) which are dependent (*akolouthia*) both on one another and on appearances'.[46] Here, as Elze remarks, the connection of dogma with a distinct tendency to systematic philosophy is clearly expressed.[47]

From this study of philosophical usage we see that dogma, when it becomes a technical term, can designate the statement of a truth not accessible to immediate knowledge but ascertained by scientific inquiry and maintaining a relation to appearances (Sextus). This truth is a general principle: either of explanation of the physical world or of moral action (Seneca). It is effective without (further) demonstration (Marcus, Chrysippus). It has a tendency to join with other *dogmata* in order to form a total explanation of man and the world (Seneca, Sextus).

It was comparatively late when dogma became an accepted term in Hellenistic Judaism, even in the juridical sense. Since dogma specifies etymologically the outcome of human thinking, it seems, as Fascher says, an inappropriate translation for God's 'statutes' and 'judgments' (Deut. 4.1). These are divine directives to be accepted rather than discussed by the people. The wisdom and understanding which they confer come not from a human but a divine source.[48]

Josephus, however, refers to the Mosaic tradition as *dogmata theou* while denying that its directives are subject to amendment (*C. Apion* 1.42). Dogma and law are used equivalently (*Ant.* 15.136). But the use of the philosophical sense of dogma is first found abundantly in Philo. His problem is to combine the use of this serious philosophical term without abandoning the uniqueness of his doctrine as deriving from God.

Philo therefore uses the word in contexts where divine illumination is prominent. Thus the virgins conceive 'those immortal children which only the soul that is dear to God can bring to the birth unaided because the Father has sown in her spiritual rays enabling her to behold the *dogmata* of wisdom' (*Cont.* 68, tr. Colson). 'Others luxuriate and delight in the banquet of *dogmata* which wisdom richly and lavishly supplies' (ibid. 35). Colson translates *dogmata* here as 'verities', 'truths'.

On the other hand, when there is an emphasis on the human source of knowledge Colson translates *dogmata* as 'principles'. God ' . . . lays down a *dogma* which they who belong to the company of the philosophers must not fail to know. The *dogma* is this. God alone in the true sense keeps festival' (*Cher.* 85). Thus in explaining how the mind, as opposed to the eye, needs no medium of light in order to grasp its object, Philo writes, 'The mind applies its eye which never closes or sleeps to the *dogmata* and conclusions set before it and sees them by no borrowed but a genuine light which shines forth from itself' (*Mut.* 5). The latter passage presents a general theory of knowledge in which dogma has its full philosophical sense but the former passage contains two aspects: dogma as a general truth to be known by philosophers, but primarily a principle established by God.[49]

In the New Testament, dogma is used twice of the commandments of the Law (Eph. 2.15; Col. 2.14). The decisions of the Council of Jerusalem are called *dogmata* (Acts 16.4). In these cases the juridical sense of dogma is to the fore.[50] It is not until the Apologists that the philosophic sense of dogma predominates in Christianity. The Apostolic Fathers use it mostly in the juridical meaning. In the Apologists, however, the word is used often of the distinctive doctrine which characterizes a particular 'school' of philosophy. The parallel of Christianity and Greek philosophy which Justin sets up implies that Christianity too has her *dogmata*. But Justin does not often explicitly use the word of Christian teaching.[51]

The Apologists wanted to resist the implication that they were just one 'school' among others. The coincidence of doctrine of the scriptures and the philosophers came to be explained by their common source in the eternal *logos*. The doctrine which philosophers share with Christians are true but Christians live in accord with the entire *logos* and so have the superior philosophy.[52] On this ground Tatian and Athenagoras speak boldly of Christian *dogmata*.

Clement of Alexandria uses *dogmata* of Christian doctrines but it is noteworthy that he does this only in the final completed book of the *Stromateis*.[53] His Gnostic preserves 'the apostolic and ecclesiastical correctness of the *dogmata*'.[54] For the rest he uses the concept only in connection with Greek philosophy and heretical sects. The *dogmata* of the 'Schools' are true in part.[55] The heretics despise the logical consistency (*akolouthia*) of their *dogmata*.[56] The truth is courted by bringing *dogmata* together (*synaphē*) in a comparative way (*antiparathesis*).[57]

Of more specific interest to our inquiry is the presence in book eight of the *Stromateis* of definitions of dogma and *hairesis* which are parallel to those given by Sextus Empiricus.[58] Furthermore, Clement attacks the sceptical 'suspension of judgment' which Sextus advocates. Dogma is a rational *katalepsis* ('cognitive impression'), while *katalepsis* is a state and assent of the mind. A *hairesis* is 'a tendency to a number of *dogmata* which are consistent (*akolouthia*) with one another and with phenomena, tending to a right life'.

The occurrence of these Stoic definitions in both Clement and Sextus is a testimony to their influence at the start of the third century. While in Sextus's dogma assent is given to a 'non-evident proposition', in Clement the assent is a 'cognitive impression'—the mental act is followed by a certainty as immediate as sense perception. Whereas the consistency of *dogmata* issues in moral activity in Clement, Sextus saves this corollary for his definition of the Sceptical position. Finally, after giving these definitions, Clement continues: 'not merely sceptics, but everyone who dogmatizes is accustomed in certain things to suspend his judgment, either through want of strength of mind, or want of clearness in the things, or equal force in the reasons'.[59]

This survey of the usage of dogma in Hellenistic Judaism and Christianity before Origen has shown that in its philosophical sense the concept won only gradual acceptance. As was to be expected it is used of their religious doctrines mostly by men who are also philosophers. In their case too, however, the distinction between human and divine doctrine is consistently upheld. Nevertheless a larger common ground is admitted between philosophical and religious doctrines. The mind is recognized as God's peculiar creation.

Differences over dogma are part of the different interpretations of *logos*.

The ability of the mind to grasp *dogmata* without a medium is acknowledged by Philo. He also writes of God establishing for philosophers a general proposition about his own nature. Justin has a parallel conception of God and the dogma of human freedom. In Clement we get a fuller connection with the systematic tendency noticed above in the Stoic usage of dogma. He criticizes the lack of consistency among the heretics' *dogmata*, defines a *hairesis* in terms of a system of *dogmata* and calls Christianity the best *hairesis*.[60]

Dogma in Origen

Christianity has a mandate to cultivate wisdom. Origen establishes this by quotations 'from the ancient Jewish scriptures, which we also use, and equally from those written after the time of Jesus, which are believed in the churches to be divine'.[61] This wisdom is a revelation of the hidden secrets of God but also includes the learning of the nations. Daniel surpassed the wise men of Babylon (Dan. 1.20) and Moses the Egyptian wise men (Acts 7.22).

Origen in the third book against Celsus rebuts the accusation that Christianity is a religion for the ignorant. 'To have been educated, and to have studied the best doctrines, and to be intelligent does not hinder us from knowing God, but helps us.'[62] 'We do all in our power to call students of philosophical doctrines to our worship of God and to show them its extraordinary purity.'[63] Origen, despite the Christian need for students of philosophy, is also well aware that philosophy could be a dangerous ally of the Christian *sophos*. 'And as for me', he wrote to Gregory, 'I have learned by experience that those men are rare who take what is useful in the land of Egypt and after their departure make what is fitting for the worship of God.'[64] Many use their Greek learning to propound heretical theories. He urges Gregory to use his rational ability not in the philosophical schools but for Christianity. As a general education is propaedeutic to philosophy so philosophy itself should only be propaedeutic to Christianity.[65]

The foregoing quotations outline clearly Origen's independent attitude to the Greek philosophical tradition. Use is to be made of it when it has given good expression to the truth. The truth is not the preserve of any tradition. His general view is that truth is enshrined in the divine scriptures, when rightly interpreted. In this interpretation the heritage of philosophy can be of great assistance in distinguishing meanings and forming demonstrations. In this spirit he is readier than any of his predecessors to call the church's tenets *dogmata*. This greater readiness reflects his conception of Chris-

tianity as the school of the divine educator. But it may also reflect an increased episcopal recognition of the importance of the Christian school to the movement.[66] At any rate Origen allows dogma as an equivalent for the *kerygma*, the gospel which is preached to all.

He starts a discussion 'secundum dogma nostrum, id est, ecclesiasticam fidem'.[67] The *ekklēsiastikon dogma* includes the teaching on Father, Son and Holy Spirit, the economy of the incarnation, resurrection, and the judgment.[68] The followers of heresy have fallen away from God's *dogmata*, the church's teachings, and true reason.[69] Jesus Christ has introduced the saving *dogmata*.[70] Holy are the *dogmata* of the church.[71] The church as bride has an uprightness of *dogmata* and morals.[72]

Against Celsus Origen presents 'the nobility (*to megalophyes*) of the dogma' of the resurrection;[73] against the Gnostics he upholds 'the sublimity (*to hypsos*) of the evangelical proclamation'.[74] In the former case the nobility of the dogma is the reasoned account of Origen as opposed to the version of uneducated people. The sublimity of the gospel proclamation too is not the possession of ill-informed and unreasoning faith but a setting out of the harmony of *dogmata* in Old and New Testament. 'It is in harmony with scripture to say that it is far better to accept *dogmata* with reason and wisdom than with mere faith.'[75] In view of the sharpness with which Origen frequently makes this distinction between mere faith and knowledge, it has to be remembered that the same *kerygma* and the same dogma form the object both of knowledge and of faith. 'We say of God both what is true and what seems to the multitude to be clear, although it is not clear to them in the way that it is to the few who endeavour to understand Christian *dogmata* philosophically.'[76] The difference lies in the mode of clarity of understanding. The simple Christians have more of the truth than the non-Christian philosopher.[77]

This superiority is explained as the consistency of their moral actions with the doctrine they accept. Moral action derives its value from the worth of the *dogmata* out of which it issues.[78] This sense of dogma as constitutive of value we have encountered in Epictetus and Seneca. Here in Origen the *dogmata* function as general principles of action which are accepted without full comprehension. That *dogmata* are accepted before demonstration even by students of philosophy is certainly a common topic in Origen.[79]

For Origen as for the main philosophical tradition any separation of practice from theory is nonsense. That a man should do what follows from what he sees to be true goes without saying. Origen is in fact much more engrossed by questions of *theoria* than of *praxis*, but even the highest contemplation has its moral aspect.

The Christian walks humbly under the great *dogmata* as under the powerful hand of God.[80]

The acceptance of true *dogmata* even without understanding them is good, but Origen is engaged with the clear comprehension of the Christian *dogmata*. This kind of dogma is esoteric in that it requires research, since it is not obvious to common conceptions (*koinai ennoiai*) nor with the clarity (*enargeia*) of visible objects.[81] In this it corresponds substantially with Sextus's definition of dogma.

His method of research, however, has a Christian difference. He states this method frequently and practises it consistently. To common conceptions and clear observation he adds the statements of scripture. These statements are interpreted in the context of the whole Bible in that similar statements are drawn in to clarify the implications of the original statements, consequences are drawn from this and scrutinized to see where they in turn lead.[82]

These *dogmata* in fact are in the scriptures, but have to be read out of them. The truth is grasped in a threefold way: by prayer for the discovery, by the straining of the mind in researching the matter, and by an 'inner perception' of the lack of clarity in the hidden scriptures.[83] This 'inner perception' is compared to violence towards the lack of clearness. In this programme Origen maintains his constant position as to a distinction between divine and human knowledge.[84] Prayer is needed since truth is in the last analysis revealed. But diligent research and passionate commitment are an indispensible condition of this revelation. The role of God and the role of the researcher in the establishment of dogma are here integrated.

Several passages indicate that these *dogmata* of Origen are closely interconnected; one passage leaves no doubt that the connections are systematic. A passage already mentioned comes for first consideration.[85] The sublimity of the evangelical proclamation is full of 'the harmony (*symphōnia*) of the *dogmata* common to the Testament called Old with the Testament named New'. The expression may be slightly pleonastic for 'the harmony of the doctrines of the Old with the doctrines of the New Testament'. This meaning suits the anti-Gnostic context. But the meaning may be fuller, for the *dogmata* are shared (*koinon*) by the Old Testament, presumably with the New Testament. In this case, besides the polemical statement, there would be an intention of harmonizing *dogmata* as well as the scriptures.

A passage from the second volume of the **Commentary on Matthew** compares the scriptures to a single musical instrument of which the seemingly different parts all contribute to one saving song.[86] Here the harmony is between the Old and the New, or the law and the prophets, or gospel and gospel, or evangelists and apostles, or apostles and other apostles. A harmonizing of all scripture is envisaged here in a nonpolemical context. *Dogmata* are not mentioned but if we ask what is harmonized it is undoubtedly the thoughts.

In another passage the divine character of the scriptures is compared to Providence.[87] Human ignorance cannot understand particular instances as part of the providential plan, but this plan is not thereby abolished. 'So neither is the divine character of scripture, which extends through all of it, abolished because our weakness cannot discern in every sentence the hidden splendour of its *dogmata* concealed under a poor and humble style.' To perceive the *dogmata* would be to recognize the pervasive presence of the divine in them. The *dogmata* are thus connected by being equally revelatory of their divine source.

The passage which states a systematic connection between *dogmata* comes from the Greek remains of the **Commentary on the Song of Songs.**[88] The bride is said to conceal the object of contemplation in the depth as if it was seeds of the pomegranate embodied in their proper order (*idioi tagmati sesōmatopoiēmenon*) in the mind; the seeds of the pomegranate under its rind refer to the *dogmata* which are not spoken about (*siōpōmena*).[89]

On the basis of Origen's usage of the concept of dogma, then, one may say that his esoteric *dogmata* do share in the Stoic tendency to systematic connection. His conception of the *logos* as an organized gathering of the ideas suggests this conclusion too.[90] Crouzel's attack on the proponents of a systematic Origen, despite the value of his principles of methodology, is too polemical. It is worth remembering that Walther Völker, the originator of the mystical interpretation of Origen in this century, writes readily of Origen's system, while subordinating it to a mystical purpose.[91]

Without minimizing the seriousness of Origen's rational inquiry and without prejudice to the systematic implications of his usage of dogma, the fact that the Father is beyond the *logos* makes the system which is centred on the *logos* a necessary means rather than an end. To the *dogmata* of Stoic derivation, physical, ethical and logical, Origen adds mystical *dogmata*.[92] This side of Origen's thought cannot be examined here. And although it has an important role in the later history of mysticism,[93] it did not seem to Origen himself to vitiate his rational systematic procedure.

Crouzel emphasizes the antithetical nature of Origen's writing. One can counter by citing passages which are a model of synthesis. A mediating inclusive kind of reasoning is illustrated in the following passage. Two statements of St Paul appear to oppose our power of doing good works (II Tim. 2.21) to God's domination of our actions (Rom. 9.21). Origen comments that 'these statements are not contradictory but must be taken together and one perfect explanation drawn from them both'. This is what he does.[94]

Further, while Origen's pedagogy is characterized by Gregory as Socratic, it is so in its caution in introducing the most necessary study of all, the knowledge of the cause of all things (*Paneg.* 13.7). In this search for the universal cause one must see at least the intention to be systematic. Origen is for Gregory the exemplar of a wise man[95] and wisdom as Origen repeatedly defines it is 'the knowledge of things divine and human and of their causes'.[96] This concern with the reason for things survives in the disembodied soul who will comprehend the reasons which escaped him while in the body (*Peri Archōn* II.11.2). 'It is clear then, that to those who have now in this life a kind of outline of truth and knowledge there shall be added in the future the beauty of the perfect image' (ibid. 4.).[97]

This analysis of Origen's usage of the concept of dogma supports the thesis of Kettler that Origen is a systematic thinker. His system should be seen as a transposition from Stoicism[98]—a harmony of *dogmata* containing an adequate explanation of the world and man. This rational system is integrated with the biblical emphasis on the divine revelation of truth.[99] The height of vision is described in philosophical terms but the eyes are enlightened by command of the Lord.[100]

The systematic connection of *dogmata* in Origen and his development of Christian *gnosis* does not, however, make him a Gnostic, even in the qualified sense which Hans Jonas alleges.[101] One can agree that Origen's is a 'universal-system attempting to comprehend Being in its unconditioned entirety and to present it as a thoroughly connected entity in clear global outlines in which every last element of multiplicity is organically related to its source'.[102] But it does not follow that the form of system distorts Origen's Christian thought. He may with more likelihood be using the form of system as an adequate expression of his Christian thought. It is on the basis of reason that he condemns the Valentinian 'fictions' (*anaplasmata*).[103]

A central point of debate here is Origen's subordination of the Son to the Father. It is often said that here we can put our finger on the distorting effect of philosophy on Origen's Christianity.[104] But in fact Origen may have adopted the philosophical principle that the effect is less than its cause because it correlated with what he found in the New Testament. If it were otherwise it is reasonable to suppose that so central a contradiction would not have escaped his critical eye, devoted as he was to resolving the contradictions men saw in the scriptures.[105]

It is also said that his search for esoteric dogma separated him from the simplicity of the Christian faith.[106]

But his constant aim is to comprehend the unity of the *logos* Christ.[107] It is true that he says the wise man must go beyond the *canon*[108] but he must also go beyond the esoteric meaning of the scriptures.[109] Besides, the ideals which he preached in his homilies at Caesarea, although naturally in more popular forms, are the same as he strove for in his intellectual activity.[110] His *dogmata* are comprehensive postulates for giving an account of the world and man in the light of the revelation of the *logos* in scripture and the human mind.

By presenting Christianity as wisdom in terms of contemporary philosophical culture, Origen to a greater degree than his predecessors broadened one of the bases of Christian self-definition. He extended the universal mission to include the world of understanding and preserved the Christian message in this universal form.

Notes

[1] See, for instance, Henri Crouzel, *Origène et la Philosophie*, Paris 1962, p. 172; R. P. C. Hanson, *Origen's Doctrine of Tradition*, London 1954, pp. 186ff.; F. H. Kettler, *Dogmatik*, p. 47; J. Daniélou, *Origène*, p. 304.

[2] See below, p. 209. In the early third century wisdom and the love of wisdom have very broad connotations. *Philosophia* can mean quite in general the religious and ethical praxis which a particular writer approves either on the grounds that it assumes and applies the fixed results of his reasoning reason (e.g. monotheism, piety, justice, continence) or because it gives a firm purpose to human existence in the defect of reason. In the ranks of the Christians, Tertullian and Tatian recommend Christianity as philosophy for the latter reason while Clement of Alexandria and Origen do so for the former reason. But both Clement and Origen make a further demand on Christians: *theoria*, the contemplation and understanding of the assumptions of their religious praxis. Origen in particular searches for clarity of understanding (see below, p. 212) and this insistence of his places him in the mainstream of Western philosophy proper. Whether and in what way this demand for clarity imposes a comprehension of the whole of reality—since part can only be dubiously clear until the whole is clear—are questions with an important bearing on the present investigation.

[3] W. Völker, *Das Vollkommenheitsideal des Origenes*, Tübingen 1930, p. 146. See also E. Molland, *The Conception of the Gospel in the Alexandrian Theology*, Oslo 1938, pp. 152ff.; H. Crouzel, *Origène et la 'connaissance mystique'*, Bruges/Paris 1961, pp. 7-11, 213-15.

[4] Kettler, *Dogmatik*. My analysis of the concept of dogma

differs from his but the results of this analysis are certainly subsidiary to his more comprehensive argument.

[5] H. Jonas, *Gnosis und spätantiker Geist* II.1, Göttingen 1954, pp. 171-223.

[6] Hal Koch, *Pronoia und Paideusis,* Berlin/Leipzig 1932.

[7] 'Origenes', in *RGG* 4, 1960, col. 1700.

[8] *Pronoia,* pp. 172ff., 202ff. and passim.

[9] *Gnosis,* p. 207.

[10] 'Origène est-il un systématique?' in *Origène et la Philosophie,* p. 190.

[11] *Origène,* p. 306.

[12] *Peri Archōn* 3; *O.W.* 5.9.1ff. In referring to Origen's works I give first the reference to book chapter and paragraph (where applicable), followed by a reference to the volume, page and line of the edition of *Origenes Werke* in the GCS (where available). The second system of reference is preceded by the abbreviation *O.W.*

[13] Ibid., 10; *O.W.* 5.16.9.ff. Translations from *On First Principles* are given in the version of G. W. Butterworth, London 1936.

[14] See below, pp. 204f. The fidelity of Rufinus in translating this passage is not at issue in the dispute. Kettler, *Dogmatik,* p. 1, n. 1, gives a partial retroversion of the passage by adducing parallel expressions from elsewhere in Origen's works. The only unparalleled clause is 'de singulis quibusque quid sit in vero rimetur', and this clause is relevant to Origen's esotericism rather than to his systematic intention. Still, although the elements of this programme can be paralleled, there is no parallel for the programme as a whole in Origen's other surviving works. Therefore it is an external testimony of some weight to Rufinus's fidelity here that Jerome asserts the close interconnection of all elements in *On First Principles.* See Jerome, *Apol.* 3.5 (PL 23.460): 'in this work every element is so woven together and one element derives from another in such a way that should you want to omit or add anything the immediate effect would be like that of putting a patch on a garment.'

[15] *Dogmatik,* p. 24, n. 109.

[16] Ibid., pp. 12, 14.

[17] Ibid., p. 47.

[18] Ibid., p. 32 and the references in n. 127.

[19] Ibid., pp. 12f.

[20] Ibid., pp. 15-39. The passages studied are *Peri Archōn* I.8.4: 'Is there a reincarnation into the bodies of animals?'; II.8.4: 'Is the soul a fallen *nous*?'; I.7.1: an epilogue on the section dealing with rational natures; and I.6.1: a preface to eschatology.

[21] *Dogmatik,* pp. 40-45.

[22] Ibid., p. 45.

[23] Ibid., p. 47.

[24] Ibid., pp. 46f.

[25] *Philosophie,* pp. 180, 184.

[26] Ibid., p. 201, where he adopts the views of B. Steidle, 'Neue Untersuchungen zu Origines *Peri Archon*', *ZNW* 40, 1941, pp. 236-43.

[27] *Philosophie,* p. 182: 'Si la bienveillance de Rufin lui (*sc.* Jonas) est un motif de suspicion, l'animosité qui inspire Jérôme et Justinien constitue pour lui une cause de confiance.'

[28] Ibid., pp. 196ff.

[29] Ibid., pp. 189f. citing S. Laeuchli, 'Origen's interpretation of Judas Iscariot', *CH* 22, 1953, p. 264.

[30] *Philosophie,* p. 190. See below, p. 214, for a 'synthetic' passage.

[31] Ibid., p. 215. A Platonic perspective of a universe on two levels does not preclude a systematic procedure especially in the case of the Middle and Neoplatonists, who adapted so many elements of Aristotelianism and Stoicism to their view. Whatever be said of the aporetic nature of Plato's own writings or the ultimate lack of cohesion in Aristotle's doctrine of substance (see J. Owens, *The Doctrine of Being in Aristotle's 'Metaphysics',* second edition, Toronto 1963), Stoicism is essentially systematic and it is from this source that Origen's usage of dogma finally derives (see below pp. 212, 214).

[32] *Connaissance,* pp. 213ff.

[33] H. Crouzel, *Bibliographie critique d'Origène,* The Hague 1971, pp. 555f.: 'Nouveau plaidoyer pour les conceptions de Harnack, de Faye, Hal Koch et autres, avec les mêmes exclusions et prises de position arbitraires, nécessaires pour trouver un système. A la racine une conception rationaliste de la théologie. Pas de vrai dialogue avec la littérature récente sur Origène'.

[34] *Dogmatik,* p. 17, n. 78.

[35] M. Elze, 'Der Begriff des Dogmas in der alten Kirche', *ZTK* 61, 1964, pp. 421-38, here p. 425.

[36] E. Fascher, 'Dogma II (Sachlich)', *RAC* 4, cols. 1-24, here col. 1.

[37] I disagree with Elze's fundamental distinction of these spheres. Although the concept of dogma did not arise in Greek religion, it is used of correct 'belief' about the gods in Plato (*Laws* 887Eff.). At *Republic* 538C, Plato writes of 'certain *dogmata* about right and honourable conduct, which we have been brought up from childhood to regard with the same sort of reverent obedience that is shown to parents' (tr. Cornford). In this context *dogmata* should be translated 'principles, maxims'. In both cases the meaning of 'thought' is laden with authority. See further n. 40 below.

[38] The Stoic system, writes Goldschmidt, is less concerned with the order of reasons and the logical connection of principles with what follows from them than with the solidarity of the *dogmata*. He continues: 'La qualité systématique est moins dans la conséquence que dans la cohésion, moins dans la succession ordonnée de dogmes que dans leur consonance. Autrement dit, le système est harmonie, bien plus que continuité'. V. Goldschmidt, *Le système stoïcien et l'idée de temps,* second edition, Paris 1969, p. 64. It is especially the logically ordered system which Crouzel cannot find in Origen.

[39] The context is a debate on the connection between physical and ethical doctrine, between *theoria* and *praxis*. Dogma is placed on the theoretical side but so defined as to disallow any disjunction from *praxis:* A. Méhat, *Etude,* p. 84. Within the area of ethical doctrine a similar distinction is debated between *decretum* and *praeceptum:* Seneca, *Ep.* 94 and 95, discussed by Méhat, *Etude,* pp. 81ff. Precepts tell us what should be done in particular cases. Dogmas give us more generally applicable reasons for right living.

[40] Seneca uses the Greek loan-word *dogma* once (*Ep.* 65.10), but prefers to use *decretum,* the translation for it which Cicero introduced into the Latin philosophical vocabulary. Elze notes this and concludes that the juridical sense is to the fore ('Der Begriff des Dogmas', p. 426). This is a testimony that both Cicero and Seneca felt the authoritativeness of philosophical dogma, that the distinction between philosophical and juridical spheres of meaning in the usage of dogma is not absolute but oscillates between more and less.

[41] *Discourses* III.9.2; II.16.24; IV.7.1ff., IV.5.29.

[42] *Discourses* I.17.26. M. Pohlenz, *Die Stoa,* third edition, Göttingen 1964, pp. 444f.

[43] ET Grube. See also *Medit.* IV.51.

[44] *Pyrrhon. Hypotyp.* I.1.3.

[45] Ibid. I.7.3.

[46] Ibid. 16.

[47] See note 35 above. Elze associates this tendency in particular with Stoicism, whose definitions Sextus is using in this passage; but Sextus attributes this tendency to all the Dogmatists—Aristotle, Epicurus, etc. It is worth noticing that Platonism is still for Sextus the Sceptical Academy. He does not seem to think significant the new Platonic dogmatism which we bracket as Middle Platonism.

[48] I am indebted to the references given by Fascher for the usage of dogma in Hellenistic Judaism and to much of his interpretation.

[49] Here we must summarize the complexity of Philo's use of dogma in the conclusion reached by Fascher: the whole range of the concept is clear in Philo—from Chaldean knowledge of celestial phenomena through the doctrines of the Greek philosophers to the interpretation of the Mosaic Law by means of allegory and mystical speculation. It can be said indeed that in his hellenizing of the Old Testament and Judaism, Philo has laid a groundwork that enabled the second and third generations of Christians to hellenize the teaching of Christ as dogma ('Dogma II', col. 6).

[50] Whether the word had lost its radical suggestion so that it could now be applied to the divine law or whether the longer period of political domination by Greek-speakers had brought the sense of authority in the word to the fore is not clear. There is some agreement that the use of *dogmata* in Acts is a purposeful parallel to the dogma of Augustus (Luke 2.1), thereby presenting the Council's decisions as comparable in binding force to imperial edicts.

[51] In this paragraph I am particularly indebted to the article of M. Elze. Two uses of dogma in Justin must be noted. He speaks of man's freedom to act or not to act as being a dogma with God (*Apol.* I.44.11). On the one hand it evokes God as Ruler but on the other states a general proposition about man in the world. In the Acts of his martyrdom Justin confesses that he follows the Christian teachings *meta dogmatos (orthou)* and the Prefect asks what the dogma is (*Acta Martyr.* 2.3). Here, Elze remarks, dogma means the doctrine of the 'school' in a strict sense and expresses at the same time the assent it evokes ('Der Begriff des Dogmas', p. 427).

[52] Justin, *Apol.* II.10.1.

[53] See Stählin's GCS index under dogma.

[54] *Str.* VII.16; GCS 3.73.17.

[55] *Str.* VI.10; GCS 2.56.4.

[56] *Str.* VII.16; GCS 3.68.36.

[57] *Str.* I.2; GCS 2.14.4.

[58] The definitions occur in chapter 5, *Against the Pyrrhonians.*

[59] *Str.* VIII.5.

[60] *Str.* VII.15; GCS 3.65.21.

[61] *CC* III.45-66; *O.W.* 1.240.15ff. Translations from *CC* are given in the version of H. Chadwick, 1953.

[62] *CC* III.49; *O.W.* 1.245.9ff.

[63] *CC* III.57; *O.W.* 1.252.1ff.

[64] *Ep. ad Greg.* 3.65ff. (SC).

[65] Ibid., 4.80ff.

[66] Origen's teaching was welcomed by the bishops in Caesarea, Jerusalem and Arabia. We do not know in what measure doctrinal as distinct from disciplinary differences widened the rift with Demetrius, bishop of Alexandria, but it is certain that Demetrius was not opposed to the very idea of the catechetical school since he appointed Heraclas to replace Origen as its head. Within a few years Heraclas succeeded Demetrius as bishop.

[67] *Peri Archōn* I.7.1; *O.W.* 5.85.28.

[68] *Frag. Comm. I. Cor., JTS* 9, 1908, p. 134 section 4. It will be seen that I make more use of fragments from the *Catenae* than does Kettler. He is rightly suspicious of what doctrines are called dogma in this source. Since, however, I am researching the usage of the concept itself with its philosophical connotations in mind, I am justified in using this source, with due caution.

[69] *Comm. Matt.* 12.23; *O.W.* 10.122.7ff.

[70] *Peri Archōn* IV.1.1; *O.W.* 5.293.7.

[71] *Seln. Psalms* 21 to v. 15.

[72] *Comm. John Frag.* 45; *O.W.* 4.520.15ff.

[73] *CC* 7.32; *O.W.* 2.182.23.

[74] *Comm. John* 5.8; *O.W.* 4.105.14.

[75] *CC* I.13; *O.W.* 1.66.8ff.

[76] *CC* III.79; *O.W.* 1.270.13ff.

[77] *Peri Archōn* IV.1.1; *O.W.* 5.293.9ff.; *Comm. John* 2.3; *O.W.* 2.212.28ff.

[78] *CC* VII.63; *O.W.* 2.212.28ff. The virtue of not building temples comes from the reason why one does not do so.

[79] E.g. *CC* II.5.2; 2.2; *O.W.* 1.103.5ff.; 128.8ff.; *Paneg.* 14 (SC).

[80] *CC* VI.15; *O.W.* 2.85.22ff.; *O.W.* 5.292.18ff.

[81] *Peri Archōn* IV.1.1; *O.W.* 5.292.18ff. 'Now in our discussion of these important subjects we do not rest satisfied with common opinions and the evidence of things that are seen, but we use in addition, for the manifest proof of our statements, testimonies drawn from the scriptures . . .

[82] *Comm. Matt.* 17.30; *O.W.* 10.671.34ff. 'The man in search of dogma shall (lit. let him) behold it when he has taken into his view the whole scripture, the consistency (*akolouthia*) of the various subjects and the corollaries (*ti hepetai*) of adopting such a position.'

[83] *Comm. Matt. Frag.* 138.1; *O.W.* 12.69.1ff. The 'inner feeling' (*synaisthesis*) is the Stoic term for one's appropriation of the sensation of an external object. It is the first step in the active movement of the soul towards that object in order to make it one's own. See Pohlenz, *Die Stoa* I, pp. 57 and 114.

[84] E.g. *CC* VII.44-49; *O.W.* 2.194.25ff. *Peri Archōn* III.3.2; *O.W.* 5.257.16ff.

[85] *Comm. John* 5.8; *O.W.* 4.105.10ff.

[86] Preserved in *Philocalia* 6.2. Part 1 of this chapter speaks of a third kind of peacemaker, he who shows that what to the eyes of others seems like disagreement in the scriptures is not really so, and who proves that harmony and concord exist.

[87] *Peri Archōn* IV.1.7; *O.W.* 5.303.12ff.

[88] This considerable fragment is preserved in the Vatican *Catena* made by Procopius (PG 17.266A). The quotation comes from chapter four to v. 3 (PG 17.272A).

[89] It is unfortunate for the conclusiveness of this passage that it comes from a *Catena,* the text of which the Migne translator admits that he renders 'divinando magis quam interpretando'. Nevertheless the Greek of the present passage is tolerably coherent and the ubiquity of *dogmata* in Rufinus's translation from Origen's *Commentary on the Song of Songs* vouches for the authenticity at least of the terms of the allegory here.

[90] As Kettler argues, *Dogmatik,* p. 2, n. 2.

[91] See e.g. the passage cited in note 3, above. But contrast his statement on p. 83, n. 3 of the same work.

[92] *Frag. Jerem. Lament.* 14; *O.W.* 3.241.2ff. 'Of the observing and contemplative faculty, called Sion, there are many roads of the various *dogmata*—mystical, physical and ethical and perhaps also logical—which bring us to the understanding and vision of the present subjects.'

[93] Gregory of Nyssa is the first chief heir to this side of Origen's thought. See especially his *Life of Moses.*

[94] *Peri Archōn* III.1.24; *O.W.* 5.243.8ff.

[95] *Paneg.* 11.15 (SC).

[96] E.g. *CC* III.72; *O.W.* 1.263.25ff. *Comm. Matt.* 17.2; *O.W.* 10.578.25ff. This is the standard Stoic definition.

[97] The comprehensive rational aspiration of Origen is best conveyed by his description of the repeated double vision of the ascending saint, *Peri Archōn* II.11.6-7.

[98] For an account of the Stoic elements in Origen's conception of the cosmos see E. Corsini, *Commento al Vangelo di Giovanni di Origene,* Torino 1968, pp. 141f., n. 24.

[99] Origen used the Platonic doctrine of illumination as a mediator here.

[100] *Martyr.* 47; *O.W.* 2.43.11ff. 'For then we may enjoy with Christ Jesus the rest which accompanies blessedness, and contemplate him in his wholeness, the living word. Fed by him and comprehending the manifold wisdom in him, and being stamped with the very truth, we may have our minds enlightened by the true and unfailing light of knowledge and have the vision of those things which by that light can be seen by eyes illuminated by the command of the Lord.' The translation is that of H. Chadwick in *Alexandrian Christianity,* London/Philadelphia 1954.

[101] The development of dogma from the New Testament to Origen is parallel to the development of the wider concept of *gnōsis.* The image of *gnōsis* in the New Testament ranges from 'obedient recognition of God's will', a sense derived from Hebrew idiom, to 'theological knowledge, with more emphasis on the theoretical side' (R. Bultmann, *Gnosis,* ET J. R. Coates, London 1952, pp. 36, 40). These meanings of *gnōsis* persist through the second century. All the Christian writers continue the double emphasis that such gnosis is a grace and that it contains a revelation of the last things. (L. Bouyer, 'Gnosis: Le sens orthodoxe de l'expression jusqu'aux pères alexandrins', *JTS* 4, 1953, p. 202.) But this understanding of Christ and his mysteries is neither speculation nor intellectual mysticism (loc. cit.). It becomes both in Origen without losing the emphasis on the charismatic nature of truth or on eschatology. (The grace of truth has been emphasized on p. 213. On eschatology see especially E. Molland, *Gospel,* pp. 144ff.)

[102] *Gnosis,* p. 173 (my translation is a paraphrase).

[103] *Comm. John* 5.8; *O.W.* 4.105.16ff. Ambrose, Origen's patron, had in his love for Jesus sought a rational account of his faith among the heretical doctrines but abandoned them when he used his *synesis:* intelligence. Particular similarities of exegesis and doctrine in Origen and the Gnostic writers have to be interpreted with care. On exegesis see Daniélou, *Origène,* pp. 190ff.; on a similar point of doctrine see especially Jacques-E. Ménard, 'Transfiguration et Polymorphie chez Origène', *Epektasis,* Beauchesne 1972, pp. 367-72.

[104] So Jonas, *Gnosis,* p. 205. Also Endre V. Ivánka, *Plato Christianus,* Einsiedeln 1964, p. 113.

[105] See notes 87 and 94 above.

[106] So St Jerome, *Ep. ad Avitum* 6: 'In talking like this is he not most plainly following the errors of the nations and foisting the ravings of philosophers on the simplicity of the Christian faith?' (ET, Butterworth).

[107] *Comm. John* 5.1-8; *O.W.* 4.240.11ff.; *Comm. John* 13.46; *O.W.* 4.272.29ff.

[108] *Comm. John* 13.16; *O.W.* 2.240.11ff.

[109] *Comm. John* 13.5; *O.W.* 4.229.32ff.

[110] See Kettler, 'Origenes', col. 1694.

Joseph W. Trigg (essay date 1981)

SOURCE: "The Charismatic Intellectual: Origen's Understanding of Religious Leadership," in *Church History,* Vol. 50, No. 1, March, 1981, pp. 5-19.

[*In this essay, Trigg contends that Origen had succeeded in reconciling his two roles as intellectual or philosopher and as a faithful churchman by making churchmanship a function of intellectual achievement.*]

Origen's vocabulary is quite definitely that of an intellectual; it owes little to daily life or to the vernacular of the time. . . . He seems . . . to manufacture his own language, often hermetic, abstract, or difficult to understand, the language of a man concerned above all with ideas, somewhat cut off from the real world, and constitutionally separated from concrete realities. Are we wrong in attaching a particular significance to the fact, so characteristic of his passionate idealism as well as of his intro-version, that he made himself a eunuch?[1]

Thus Marguerite Harl, over twenty years ago, introduced *Origène professeur* to scholars more familiar with *Origène: homme de l'église*, More recently, Pierre Nautin, in *Origène: sa vie et son oeuvre*,[2] has made it starkly apparent how much trouble Origen had in being both an intellectual and a churchman. I contend that Origen's reconciliation of these roles was a coherent theory of religious leadership that merits our attention, a theory in which churchmanship becomes a function of intellectual achievement.

If we were to trust Eusebius's account of Origen's life in the *Ecclesiastical History,* we should think that only the personal jealousy of Bishop Demetrius of Alexandria disturbed Origen's career as a churchman. Nautin shows how the evidence points to Origen's persistent inability to get along with his official ecclesiastical superiors. Reverence for his father, not respect for the church as an institution, accounts for his continued loyalty to the church.[3] The influences that formed his thought were, as far as we know, outside of or on the fringes of the church. He had a pagan literary education, fraternized with gnostics, sought out rabbis and studied under the philosopher Ammonius Saccas. He received his Bible training from his father, and Clement of Alexandria, a free spirit if ever there was one, taught him theology.

Nautin concurs with other scholars that Origen did not consider himself an official catechist, even if Bishop Demetrius may have given his teaching a belated cachet.[4] In fact, he wished to keep his teaching secret and strenuously objected when his treatise **On First Principles,** a fruit of that teaching, was made public.[5] A rich lay patron, Ambrosius, facilitated his independence, as did Origen's eminence beyond the Christian community. His early writings, particularly **On First Principles** and the **Commentary on Genesis,** bespeak such independence by often contradicting received ecclesiastical tradition. Nautin argues that Origen undertook a number of journeys, including one to Rome, due to conflict with bishops.[6] He interprets the "war" that obliged Origen to settle in Palestine for some years before returning to Alexandria as a stage in the conflict with Demetrius that eventuated in his permanent departure from that city. Scholars, with little justification, have conventionally interpreted this "war" as a massacre that occurred during the reign of Caracalla.[7] Nautin thinks that a gift from the Empress Julia Mammaea may have enabled Origen to leave Alexandria for good and that he probably intended to settle in Athens.[8] Once he had left and had been ordained as a presbyter, Demetrius secured from the church in Egypt Origen's condemnation as a heretic. Nautin argues that only Demetrius's timely death prevented him from engineering the condemnation of Origen and his sup-

porters in Palestine. Origen responded to these proceedings, he thinks, with an autobiographical letter that was Eusebius's principal source for his account of Origen's life.[9]

For a time after he settled in Caesarea, where he spent most of his life after about 234, Origen got along well with his bishop. During that period he was able to examine bishops himself as a theological adviser and to preach regularly. But Nautin documents evidence that Origen's homilies met resistance and concludes that he failed to preach on the entire Bible because Theoctistus of Caesarea relieved him of his duties.[10] Nautin also presents evidence that Bishop Heraclas of Alexandria resumed his predecessor's attacks on Origen's orthododoxy.[11] These trials, in Nautin's opinion, account for the unrelieved bitterness against ecclesiastical officials in Origen's last surviving work, the **Commentary on Matthew.**

Nautin does not explain Origen's persistent difficulties with bishops. He seems to consider Origen a third-century Newman, a courageous and loyal thinker on the outs with an obtuse hierarchy.[12] But this is an inadequate parallel. In the church Newman joined there was no question where authority legitimately lay. Newman meekly submitted until his hour arrived, but Origen did not need to be so passive. Demetrius of Alexandria was himself an innovator as Bishop of Alexandria, and the scope of his authority was not clearly defined. Adolf Harnack and Walter Bauer have shown that Demetrius was the first bishop (in the monarchical sense) to direct the Alexandrian church. Before 189, when he took charge, it seems likely that a board of presbyters, one of whom may have been called bishop, governed the church at Alexandria, a church where loose standards of orthodoxy did not exclude gnosticizing tendencies.[13] Demetrius achieved his triumph by associating himself with an interlocking network of bishops who increasingly claimed broad ex officio powers, including the right to excommunicate persons who offended in doctrine or conduct and to readmit them, when penitent, to the church. As the community's official leader, the bishop developed an ideology of religious authority that buttressed his leadership, presenting himself as a successor of the Old Testament priest in his role as an indispensible ritual mediator and as a successor of the New Testament apostles when representing supreme doctrinal authority. Origen, on the other hand, sought to retain his position and dignity as an independent scholar. In doing so he developed a radically "charismatic" ideology of religious authority with which to confront the "official" ideology of the bishops.

I should clarify my understanding of charisma. The term comes, ultimately, from the Apostle Paul, for whom it meant "gift of grace." Rudolf Sohm, in his work on ecclesiastical law, adopted the term from Paul and bequeathed it to modern sociology via Max Weber.[14] Sohm's use of the term is more precise than it is in later writers. I have isolated five leading characteristics, which I illustrate from the epistles of Paul. (1) God confers charismatic authority, not through human mediation (as by ordination) but directly. Paul claimed that he was "an apostle—not from man nor through man, but from Jesus Christ and God the Father."[15] (2) Since God has conferred this authority, it is men's duty to defer to it. Thus charisma demands and elicits free obedience. Paul says to Philemon: "though I am bold enough in Christ to command of you what is required, yet for love's sake I appeal to you."[16] (3) This means that individuals, by recognizing it, verify charismatic authority. Thus Paul says: "If to others I am not an apostle, at least I am to you; for you are the seal of my apostleship in the Lord."[17] (4) Charisma mediates God's word. Thus Paul claimed to speak by the same spirit that inspired the prophets and assigned to his opinions an importance comparable to that of traditional "words of the Lord."[18] (5) Charismatic authority, by its very nature, can belong only to individuals. Thus the point of Paul's simile of the body is to show that God has bestowed his gifts differently on different individuals.[19]

Rudolph Sohm did not apply his concept of charisma to Origen because, in Sohm's view, charisma, which alone had legitimated leadership in the primitive church, had been replaced by legal authority after the apostolic age. But his contemporary, Karl Holl, believed that charismatic authority played a more enduring role in the history of the church. Charisma and legal authority, he argued, had existed side by side even in the primitive church and continued to down to the present. He argued that in Eastern Christianity, charismatic authority had always maintained its legitimacy in the monastic tradition, and he placed Origen in a tradition of charismatic authority that stretched from Paul, through the itinerant apostles of the Didache, down to the *startsy* of contemporary Russia.[20] Holl, though he did no more than sketch out the broad outlines of Origen's understanding of religious authority, thus provided, along with Sohm, a solid foundation for understanding Origen.

Origen's one explicit discussion of the Pauline concept of charisma is his commentary on Ephesians 4:11-12, where he cautiously criticizes the official ecclesiastical leadership and suggests and alternative to it:

> Christ is above all and through all and in all, but grace is given to each of the saints according to the measure of the gift of Christ, so that some are apostles but some are prophets, and others evangelists, and after them pastors and, above all, teachers. If a gift of grace [*charisma*] is given to a teacher according to the measure of the gift of Christ, it is clear that the pastor, exercising his duties with skill, must have the gift of grace to be a pastor. And how, indeed, could anyone be an evangelist, unless the feet—so to speak—of his soul are beautiful? For them to become so, God must supply them with beauty. The prophet as well, testing unbelievers and judging them (for such is the prophet of the new covenant), must be considered as one appointed in the church by God. It is possible for these to exist continually in the church; perhaps apostles also, to whom it is given to work the signs of an apostle, may be found even now.[21]

Notice the insistence that charismata must be empirically verified. The charisma, thus verified, makes someone a teacher, a pastor, an evangelist and so on; ordination alone cannot supply the needed qualifications. Notice also that Origen treats the teacher as the culmination of the list. This illustrates that charisma is, for Origen, predominantly intellectual. Lastly, notice how Origen hints that persons fulfilling the functions of an apostle may still exist in the church. Here he implies that the apostolic function cannot be identified with any specific ecclesiastical office; otherwise there would be no question of its continuing existence. We shall soon see what Origen considered the continuing apostolic function and the works of an apostle to be.

Origen's commentaries on the Pauline epistles survive only in fragments, and he did not write a treatise specifically on religious authority, but we can trace a coherent position in incidental references to the issue throughout his works. I find it convenient to discuss the issue under four heads: (1) the priest, (2) the apostle, (3) criticisms of the established ecclesiastical leadership and (4) penitential discipline. "Priest" was the principal term in the Old Testament that for Origen connoted religious leadership, as was "apostle" in the New Testament. Given Origen's digressive style, therefore, discussions of religious leadership tend to cluster about these terms. Likewise, passages in the Bible critical of religious leaders often led Origen to draw a moral for his own time, and references to forgiveness led him into discussing penitential discipline, a key issue in his time for defining the limits of ecclesiastical authority.

The Old Testament priesthood was appealing to Origen, in the first place, because priests were a tribe apart, entirely consecrated to God's service. On his return to Alexandria after his first sojourn in Caesarea, Origen wrote about this at the beginning of his **Commentary on John**. Priests, he explains, are persons consecrated to the study of the word of God, and high priests are those who excel at such study.[22] There can be no question that these grades correspond to ecclesiastical offices. Priests, and the high priest in particular, also have privileged access to God. Thus Origen follows Clement of Alexandria in interpreting the priest as a spiritual man.[23] But if the priest has a privileged access to divine secrets, this is only so that, as a teacher, he might mediate God's word to others. Origen transforms the Jewish ritual legislation into an exposition of the priest's vocation as a teacher. For example, removing the skin of the sacrificial victim symbolizes removing the veil of the letter from God's word, and taking fine incense in the hand symbolizes making fine distinctions in the interpretation of difficult passages.[24] He also interprets sacrifice as the progressive liberation of the soul from the body that makes possible the apprehension of higher truths.[25] Thus the Levitical priesthood comes to symbolize a moral and intellectual elite of inspired teachers of scripture. This transformation culminates in Origen's interpretation of the high priest's vestments, each item of which symbolizes a spiritual qualification.[26]

The apostle was even more appealing to Origen as a symbol of religious authority. He tacitly claims for himself an apostolic function and dignity in the preface of *On First Principles.* The apostles who wrote the New Testament, he claims, must have had a full, spiritual perception of what they were writing, since it was not God's way to employ automatons. Nonetheless, rather than expounding the deep, spiritual matters that they learned from Jesus, they instead set forth in their writings simple, basic doctrines which they expected to be taken on authority. The disciples did not intend for all Christians to accept these bald statements as the sum and substance of the truth, but they recognized that the more profound doctrines were inappropriate for the majority of believers. They therefore reserved the knowledge of these profound doctrines for future believers worthy to receive them. These are persons who have diligently prepared themselves to receive knowledge and as a result, have received from God the same spiritual gifts that enabled the apostles themselves to write the scriptures.[27] Now *On First Principles* is precisely an investigation of the deeper doctrines that the apostles kept silence about. By undertaking it, therefore, Origen was claiming for himself a God-given comprehension of doctrine comparable to that of the apostles.

He identifies the apostles themselves as inspired exegetes when he interprets the "fields white with the harvest" which the apostles are commissioned to reap in John 4:36 as the legal and prophetic books of the Old Testament.[28] It is clear, moreover, that the deeper, spiritual interpretation that the apostolic man receives is a genuine gift of God, even if it comes only to those who diligently prepare themselves. Origen makes this clear in his interpretation of Matthew 14:22-26. The disciples attempt to cross the lake—that is, to pass from the literal to the spiritual sense of scripture—but they cannot do this without Jesus assisting them after they have come part of the way on their own initiative.[29] But what right do the apostles' successors have to publish doctrines which the apostles themselves saw fit to keep silent about? Here Origen appeals to apostolic discretion, itself a gift from God: if God grants

the spiritual insight into scripture, he grants along with it the discretion to judge how fully and in what circumstances it is to be revealed. An example is the parable of the unmerciful steward in Matthew.[30] Paul is the great example of apostolic discretion. When among the perfect, he was bold to impart a "secret and hidden wisdom of God," but among more simple believers he saw fit to "know nothing . . . save Jesus Christ and him crucified."[31]

If the apostle is an inspired exegete, he is also, like the priest, a teacher by vocation, responsible for mediating God's word to persons at all levels of spiritual progress. Jesus made this clear when he ordered the disciples to allow little children to come to him, thus signifying that more advanced Christians should condescend to the simple.[32] The "works of an apostle" are, in fact, works of teaching. When Jesus commissioned his disciples and gave them power to give sight to the blind and to raise the dead, he had in mind restoring to sight persons "blinded" by false doctrines and raising to life persons "dead" in their sins.[33] Being an apostle is not an official position but a function verified in the doing. In arguing to this effect Origen cites 1 Corinthians 9:2: "If to others I am not an apostle, at least I am to you, for you are the seal of my apostleship in the Lord."[34]

It is readily apparent that Origen's priest and apostle are charismatic figures in Sohm's terms. (1) God confers on them without mediation their spiritual gifts. He alone appoints prophets, makes beautiful the feet of evangelists and provides insight into the deeper doctrines hidden in the mystical interpretation of scripture. (2) The demand for free obedience is not so far explicit, but we shall come to it in Origen's discussion of more practical matters. (3) The requirement that charisma be verified empirically is implicit in Origen's demand that the supposed bearer of charismatic authority prove himself by his deeds. (4) The bearer of charisma mediates God's word in the fullest sense. He has privileged access to divine secrets and responsibility to teach them with discretion. (5) This charisma belongs to individual teachers, not to a collective group.

Origen's choice of these two symbols of religious authority is highly significant. His choice of the priest may appear anomalous, since modern sociologists of religion see the priest as the archetypal representative of a noncharismatic traditional or legal authority.[35] It would seem as if the prophet would be a more congenial symbol of charismatic authority; but, though Origen takes Jeremiah as a model, he rarely treats prophetic authority in this way.[36] One reason Origen found both the priest and the apostle attractive symbols is that they had a privileged access to divine secrets, the priest through ritual and the apostle through personal conversation with Jesus. But there is, I believe, a more significant reason why Origen picked just these two symbols of authority from the Bible. They gave him a way to oppose the pretensions of official authority, which was rapidly appropriating these very symbols to legitimate episcopal authority. "Priest," in Origen's time, was just beginning to become the customary term to describe presbyters and bishops, and bishops were increasingly depicting themselves as successors to the apostles.[37] Origen, by stressing the necessity of personal gifts for these functions, was implicitly criticizing this development. Origen's rejection of Clement's appeal to an "apostolic succession" of esoteric teachers, in which he could have claimed a place, underscores this insistence that charisma is a gift of God alone, unmediatedly accessible through spiritual exegesis.[38]

Opposition to the claims of ecclesiastical authorities is still more apparent in his demand that ecclesiastical offices themselves should be characterized by charismatic authority. The bishop, that is, should belong to the spiritual elite which priests and apostles symbolize. The bishop as an ideal is absolutely essential to Origen's conception of the church; his office symbolizes the continuing possibility of charismatic leadership.[39] Thus the ideal bishop unites in his person a philosophical understanding of scripture, capacity to teach and sanctity of life. In **Contra Celsum** and elsewhere Origen elaborates on the qualifications for the episcopate as set forth in the Pastoral Epistles. The ability to "refute the adversaries" (Titus 1:9) sets forth the intellectual qualifications, since it implies that the bishop has studied dialectic and sought out the hidden doctrines of the Bible.[40] Similarly, the requirement that the bishop be the husband of one wife (1 Timothy 3:2 and Titus 1:6) sets forth allegorically the ethical standards. Taken literally, being the husband of one wife is scarcely an adequate standard of morality, but the marriage in question is not a physical but a spiritual marriage. That is, a person of great holiness is spiritually married to an angel of high rank. Nevertheless, if he sinned, the angel could present him with a bill of divorcement, forcing him to marry an angel of lower rank and thus be "twice married."[41] A person "twice married" in this sense does not, properly speaking, belong to the church, and he could not possibly be a bishop.[42]

Bishops have a special place in the divine economy, since they share responsibility for their congregations with angelic bishops, with whom they cooperate.[43] As a result of these unique responsibilities, bishops have more powers granted to them than are granted to ordinary Christians, though, conversely, more is required of them.[44] Because it is a position that entails such awesome responsibilities, the episcopate must go to just the man whom God has chosen for it, and no human machinations should be involved in the bishop's selection. Moses' selection of Joshua as his successor is thus the pattern for the selection of a bishop:

> Here is no popular acclamation, no thought given to consanguinity or kinship; . . . the government of the

people is handed over to him whom God has chosen, to a man who . . . has in him the Spirit of God and keeps the precepts of God in his sight. Moses knew from personal experience that he was preeminent in the law and in knowledge, so that the children of Israel should obey him. Since all these things are replete with mysteries, we cannot omit what is more precious, although these things commanded literally seem necessary and useful.[45]

Few bishops, however, meet these high standards. Far from exemplifying the proper intellectual standards, they fail to search the scriptures and have contempt for those who do.[46] Worse, many are tainted by heresy. Such bishops are fortunate God no longer deals with heretics as he dealt with Korah, Dathan and Abiram, whom the earth swallowed up alive.[47] In their greed and lust for power many bishops also make a mockery of the ethical standards of their office. The corrupt priests of Pharaoh in the Old Testament provide a more adequate image for most of them than does the Levitical priesthood.[48] In the New Testament the appropriate image is the scribes and Pharisees whom Jesus excoriated rather than the apostles.[49] The bishops utterly fail to exemplify the standard of Christian leadership set forth in Matthew 20:26: "Whoever would be great among you must be your servant." That is, they attempt to rule by force and intimidation rather than by eliciting the free obedience of those set under them.[50] In fact, some bishops, "particularly in the largest cities," make themselves as inaccessible as tyrants in order to overawe their congregations.[51] We might say they do not exercise the style of authority that characterizes a true charismatic leader. But, then, how could they? Their ignorance of the scriptures disqualifies them at the outset as genuine mediators of God's word. Hence, rather than trusting that their ministry will validate itself, they must appeal to the prestige of their office. Origen, as a presbyter at Caesarea, made a point of rejecting any such validation. He urged his congregation to judge for themselves the worth of what he had to say.[52] Confident that he belonged to the spiritual elite which formed the church's true leadership, he welcomed such verification. But he was sadly aware that this elite did not correspond to the church's official leadership. How is it that the church is in such a sorry state? Has God failed to provide the church with worthy leaders? By no means. But the church often fails to give such persons their proper place of honor and responsibility.

> For it frequently happens that he who deals in an humble and abject interpretation and knows earthly things has the preeminent rank of a priest or sits in the chair of a teacher, while he who is spiritual and so free from earthly things that he "judges all things and is judged by no one" either holds a lower rank of ministry or is relegated to the common multitude.[53]

But this anomaly is only external, for on a deeper level the members of the spiritual elite whom Origen describes as priests and apostles are the true leaders of the church:

> Whoever has in himself those things that Paul enumerates about a bishop, even if he is not a bishop before men, is a bishop before God, since he did not come to his position by the ordination of men.[54]

The clear implication is that the bishop at the front of the church may well be bogus while the real bishop is lost in his congregation.

By later standards, such an understanding of Christian ministry is heresy, of course; hence many Origen scholars have attempted to explain away such statements. Chief among these scholars is Hans Urs von Balthasar, whose article "Le Mysterion d'Origène" was seminal for the *nouvelle théologie* school which revived Roman Catholic interest in Origen. Balthasar admitted the existence in Origen's writings of a charismatic hierarchy of spiritual men alongside of the official hierarchy of the church.[55] But this distinction, he argued, is purely formal: the charismatic hierarchy is the invisible institution whose existence assures the validity of the external institution, the official hierarchy, that symbolizes it.[56] Demetrius, in other words, had nothing to worry about. But Balthasar's interpretation will not do. In the first place, it rests on an unproven—and in my view gravely mistaken—assumption about the structure of Origen's thought, the assumption that the symbol necessarily partakes of the reality of the thing it symbolizes. In the second place, it founders on Origen's interpretation of penitential discipline, where Balthasar himself candidly admitted difficulties.[57] Here is one case, the forgiveness of sins, where the bishop clearly posesses no ex officio authority and the spiritual man possesses full authority.

Origen makes the limitation of ex officio powers most explicit in his commentary on Matthew 16:13-20, the passage (obviously a crucial one for any understanding of religious authority) where Peter confesses at Caesarea Philippi that Jesus is the Christ and then receives the power to bind and loose. Origen makes it clear that Peter, as an apostle, symbolizes the member of his spiritual elite. Peter is one who "knows the Son by the revelation of the Father"; that is, he has inward knowledge as opposed to mere faith.[58] To make sure that we do not miss the point, Origen states that if any of us can recognize Jesus as the Christ as Peter did, not by the revelation of flesh and blood but by the light from the Father enlightening us in our hearts, then we are what Peter was.[59] Moreover, if we are what Peter was, the words Jesus spoke to Peter apply to us too: "You are Peter, and upon this rock I will build my church."[60] If so, then it is the spiritual man who holds the keys to the kingdom of heaven, the power to bind and loose.

We cannot mistake the ecclesiological bearing of Origen's argument when he goes on to refute unnamed persons who claim that the church is founded on "one Peter" only, presumably the local bishop. Peter is rather a representative of all the apostles and hence of all who are like them. These men are the "rocks" upon whom Christ founded the church.[61] But a criterion does exist for determining if someone is one of these "rocks." Christ went on to say: "and the gates of Hades will not prevail against it." A "rock," therefore, is one against whom the gates of Hades have not prevailed. And what are the "gates of Hades" but sins, since each sin a person commits is an entranceway to hell? It therefore follows that the "rocks" must be pure and blameless souls, persons against whom sins have not prevailed.[62] This, Origen argues, makes good sense out of Jesus' promise of the keys to the kingdom of heaven; these keys enable the possessor to open for himself the corresponding gates of Zion, the virtues.[63] Thus we have two criteria for the true successor to Peter and the rightful possessor of his power to forgive sins—spiritual insight and holiness of life. Official position has nothing whatsoever to do with it.

Origen goes on to contrast this genuine doctrine of the power of the keys with the spurious claims of ecclesiastical officials. He warns those who use this passage to vindicate the place of the episcopate that the bishop has the power of the keys only in so far as he is a "Peter," a spiritual man.[64] If the bishop attempts to loose others while bound by sin himself, his attempt is vain. Likewise, if he attempts to use his powers of excommunication against a virtuous man, his excommunication is invalid; God himself, much less a Peter, could not bind a virtuous man.[65] Those who claim such authority without possessing the requisite qualifications do not understand the scriptures and have fallen under condemnation for the devil's own sin of pride.[66]

A second passage, not so forthright on ecclesiology, explains why it is that an ex officio power to forgive sins is impossible. In it Origen discusses the power of binding and loosing in the context of so-called unforgivable sins. He clearly rejects the notion, steadily gaining ground during his lifetime, that no sins place the sinner, if repentant, permanently outside the pale of the church. He upholds, that is, a "rigorist," penitential position. This rigorism, by itself, is unimportant, and Origen was later to reject it;[67] what is interesting for my purposes is that he utilizes a strongly charismatic understanding of religious leadership in order to argue against it. The person who has the power to forgive sins has this power because he is directly inspired by God:

> But he who is inspired by God, as the apostles were, and can be known by the fruits, as one who has received the Holy Spirit and has become spiritual by being led by the Spirit as a Son of God to do

everything in accordance with reason—such a one forgives whatever God forgives and retains such sins as are incurable; and even as the prophets serve God in speaking not the things of their own but of the divine will, so he serves him alone who has power to forgive, even God.

Notice that here the apostle is the image of the spiritual man and that, beside being inspired by God (a point Origen belabors by using words with the "pne" root four times in one sentence), he mediates God's word and must be verified by his works. Origen goes on in this passage to explain just how it is that the spiritual man forgives—it is by spiritual insight:

> the apostles, being priests [*nota bene*] of the great high priest, having received knowledge of the healing that comes from God, know, being taught by the Holy Spirit, concerning what sins they ought to offer sacrifices, and when, and in what manner, and they understand concerning what sins they ought not to do this.

This, presumably, is the same sort of insight which the spiritual man has into the mystical meaning of scripture. Thus even the truly apostolic and priestly man who has the power to forgive sins does not have this power as a sort of privilege accruing to his advanced spiritual status. Rather, the power to forgive sins is simply a function of his holiness and spiritual insight. Those who arrogate for themselves powers beyond the priestly office—powers, that is, to pardon incurable sins—do so because they "have no accurate grasp of the knowledge a priest should possess."[68] Origen, like Clement before him, understood the forgiveness of sins as a pastoral process that involves voluntary obedience to a spiritual man. (Here, at last, is the other leading characteristic of charismatic authority.) Origen urged his congregation at Caesarea to choose a physician of their souls carefully on the basis of his personal gifts and then to submit their lives implicitly to him if they truly desired the forgiveness of their sins.[69]

Penitential matters are thus a practical area where Origen's rejection of official claims to authority has concrete implications for ecclesiastical order. This was one area where he found it tactically possible to oppose episcopal pretensions, because the limits of episcopal authority on penitential matters were still uncertain. Since bishops took a laxist position in claiming authority to readmit penitents into the church, Origen adopted for a while the rigorist position on incurable sins which strikes us as anomalous in the larger context of his thought. On other matters, such as teaching authority, he had no such room for maneuver; there we find him allowing bishops to determine the church's public teaching while preserving an esoteric sphere where he had supreme authority. His theological in-

quisition of Bishop Heracleides must have been a thoroughly savored pleasure.

Thus we have an explanation for the consistent tension between Origen and his ecclesiastical superiors that, as Nautin shows, characterized Origen's life. Make no mistake: Origen himself, as one who "searches the deep things of God," was preeminently qualified as a priest, apostle and bishop. Obviously Origen and Demetrius, men with powerful personalities and diametrically opposed positions on authority, could not remain together in the same church. Origen's understanding of religious authority certainly justified his own position, but it would be unjust to imply that it was simply a function of his not being a bishop. The belief that allegorical interpretation of the Bible provides an unparalleled access to divine mysteries, which lies at the basis of his claim to authority, is integral to Origen's thought. So is his notion that the charismatic leader should evoke free obedience. After all, God's providential design to restore all rational creatures to free obedience is the mainspring of his cosmology, and the leader who mediates the divine should scarcely indulge in a compulsion which God himself so rigorously eschews. On the other hand, we cannot imagine that Origen would have maintained this understanding of religious authority had he been a bishop. It is a doctrine which is radically subversive of institutional stability. We can thus understand why Origen should eventually have alienated even a warm admirer like Theoctistus, who had to confront the intractable reality of governing a church. It was inevitable that as the church developed institutionally, charismatic authority of Origen's type should have become increasingly marginal.

How, then, does Origen's understanding of religious leadership fit into the pattern of Christian history? In one respect we might consider Origen as a conservative figure, one who attempted to preserve the charismatic understanding of leadership we find in Paul and the Didache. But Origen's esotericism was an innovation. He is willing to tolerate the outward authority of bishops whom he considers no true bishops before God and speaks complacently of those who "seem, in preeminence, to be bishops and presbyters."[70] He can do so because the authority of the spiritual bishop is unchallenged among the spiritual elite who constitute the true church. However, in Paul or the Didache there is no inner church and the legitimate authorities are openly acknowledged by all. Structurally, Origen's understanding of authority is identical to that which Klaus Koschorke has reconstructed for the Valentinian gnostics.[71] One might suggest, therefore, that Origen mediates to more normative Christianity a gnostic conception of authority in a two-tiered church.

I have already mentioned that Karl Holl assigned Origen's concept of authority considerable influence in the monastic tradition, where the *abba* exercises charismatic authority. Peter Brown also considered

Gregory of Nazianzus.

Origen an illuminating figure in the transformation of perceived reality which made the holy man a key figure of authority in the Late Antique era.[72] In one sense, though, Origen's understanding of authority is distinctive in the Christian tradition: he validates charisma in terms of intellectual gifts acquired through open-minded and disciplined study. Thus, whatever his relationship to the larger tradition, Origen stands out as the theoretician of the charismatic intellectual.

Notes

[1] Marguerite Harl, *Origène et la fonction révélatrice du Verbe incarné* (Paris, 1958), p. 366. All translations are my own unless otherwise noted.

[2] Pierre Nautin, *Origène: sa vie et son oeuvre* (Paris, 1977). See also his *Lettres et écrivains chrétiens des IIe et IIIe siècles* (Paris, 1961).

[3] Nautin, *Origène,* p. 414.

[4] Ibid., p. 48 on Eusebius, *Ecclesiastical History* 6.3.3-8. Hal Koch, "Origenes," in *Paulys Realencyclopädie der classische Altertumswissenschaft,* q. v., 1939), Manfred Hornschuh, "Das Leben des Origenes und die Entstehung der alexandrinischen Schule," *Zeitschrift für Kirchengeschichte* 71 (1960):1-25, 193-214, and F. H. Kettler, "Origenes," in *Religion in Geschichte und Gegenwart,* 3rd. ed., 1960, deny more forthrightly than Nautin that Origen was a catechist.

[5] See Jerome, *Epistle* 84.10.

[6] Nautin, *Origène,* p. 418.

[7] Ibid., p. 316. I can see no plausibility in Hornschuh's contention ("Das Leben des Origenes," pp. 1-2) that Caracalla's measures endangered Origen in his capacity as a philosopher.

[8] Ibid., p. 428.

[9] Ibid., p. 22, and Nautin, *Lettres,* pp. 133-134.

[10] Nautin, *Origène,* pp. 401-405.

[11] Ibid., pp. 437-438.

[12] Ibid., p. 439.

[13] See Adolf Harnack, *The Mission and Expansion of Christianity,* trans. James Moffatt, 2 vols. (New York, 1908), 1:463 and Walter Bauer, *Orthodoxy and Heresy in Earliest Christianity,* trans. Robert Kraft et al. (Philadelphia, 1971), pp. 53-54. Colin H. Roberts's *Manuscript, Society and Belief in Early Christian Egypt* (London, 1977), p. 71, confirms the picture I have presented: "We may surmise that for much of the second century it [the church in Egypt] was a church with no strong central authority and little organization; one of the directions in which it developed was certainly Gnosticism, but a Gnosticism not initially separated from the rest of the Church."

[14] Rudolph Sohm, *Kirchenrecht,* vol. 1 (Leipzig, 1892). See Max Weber, *On Charisma and Institution Building,* ed. S. N. Eisenstadt (Chicago, 1968), p. 46, and Ulrich Brockhaus, *Charisma und Amt* (Wuppertal, 1972).

[15] Sohm, *Kirchenrecht,* pp. 29-35 and 58-59, and Galatians 1:1.

[16] Sohm, *Kirchenrecht,* pp. 27-28 and 56, and Philemon 8.

[17] Sohm, *Kirchenrecht,* pp. 51-52 and 1 Corinthians 9:2 (also 2 Corinthians 3:2, Philippians 4:1, and 1 Thessalonians 2:19).

[18] Sohm, *Kirchenrecht,* p. 29; 2 Corinthians 4:13; and 1 Corinthians 7:30.

[19] Sohm, *Kirchenrecht,* pp. 116-118. See Ernst Käsemann, *Perspectives on Paul* (Philadelphia, 1971) and J. H. Schutz, *Paul and the Anatomy of Apostolic Authority* (London, 1975) for a detailed discussion of charisma in Paul.

[20] See Karl Holl, *Enthusiasmus und Bussgewalt beim griechischen Mönchtum: eine Studie zu Simeon dem Neuen Theologen* (Leipzig, 1898) and *Gesammelte Aufsätze zur Kirchengeschichte II, der Osten* (Tübingen, 1928), pp. 44-67. Walter Volker amplifies Holl's views in *Das Vollkommenheitsideal des Origenes: eine Untersuchung zur Geschichte der Frömmigkeit und zu den Anfängen christlicher Mystik* (Tubingen, 1930) pp. 168-192.

[21] In J.A.F. Gregg, "Origen's Commentary on Ephesians," *Journal of Theological Studies* 3 (1902): 413-414.

[22] Origen, *Commentary on John* 1.2 (4.5.16-6.6). In citing Clement and Origen, I give conventional book and chapter numbers followed, in parentheses, by the volume, page and line in the *Griechische christlische Schriftsteller* edition. See also Homilies on Joshua 9.5 (7.350.27-351.5), where Origen states that the real priest is not just a person who has an outward eminence in the church but one who acts in a priestly manner. These "priests" are presumably those who "abandon themselves to the study of rational argument" so as not to have to accept their faith on authority; Origen, *Contra Celsum* 1.11 (1.62.25-26).

[23] See Clement, *Stromateis* 4.25.157.3-159.3 (2.318.7-319.4), 5.6.32.1-40.1 (2.346.27-354.4) and 7.7.36.2 (3.28.8) and *Excerpts from Theodotus* 27 (3.115.22-116.17). In *Clément d'Alexandrie: Extraits de Théodote* (Paris, 1970), 2nd. ed., pp. 220-223), Francois Sagnard demonstrates Clement's dependence on Philo, *Life of Moses* 2.95-135 for this theme.

[24] Origen, *Homilies on Leviticus* 1.4 (6.285.22-25) and 9.8 (6.433.10-18).

[25] Ibid., 5.4 (6.341-342).

[26] Ibid., 6.5 (6.367).

[27] Origen, *On First Principles* Preface.3 (5.9). See also fragment 47 in Claude Jenkins, "Origen on 1 Corinthians," *The Journal of Theological Studies* 9 (1907-1908): 240.

[28] Origen, *Commentary on John* 13.47.307-308 (4.273.12-22).

[29] Origen, *Commentary on Matthew* 11.5 (10.41.2-42.32).

[30] Ibid., 13.11-12 (10.302.17-305.32).

[31] See, for example, fragment 18 in Jenkins (*JTS* 9:354), where Origen so interprets 1 Corinthians 4:1-4 as to distinguish the functions of the apostle in his exoteric role as a "minister of Christ" from his functions in his esoteric role as a "steward of the mysteries of God." Origen, *Commentary on John* 13.18.109-111 (4.242.10-11) and *Homilies on Leviticus* 4.6 (6.273.12-22) are also informative; in the latter Origen depicts Paul, in his esoteric role, as high priest.

[32] Origen, *Commentary on Matthew* 15.7 (10.365-370).

[33] Origen, *Homilies on Isaiah* 6.4 (8.8.15-9.10).

[34] Origen, *Commentary on John* 32.17 (4.453.6-454.11).

[35] See, for example, Joachim Wach, *Sociology of Religion* (Chicago, 1956), pp. 46-47.

[36] Origen, *Homilies on Jeremiah* 14.15 (3.122.11-21).

[37] See *Syriac Didascalia* 9, trans. Hugh Conolly (Oxford, 1929), p. 86 for the earliest attestation of this usage in the East and the works of Cyprian for its attestation (with regard to bishops) in the West. Origen seems to refer to this practice, though disparagingly, in *Homilies on Jeremiah* 12.3 (3.89.15.27) and *Homilies on Numbers* 2.1 (7.9.22-27).

[38] For Clement's "apostolic succession" see *Stromateis* 1.11.2 (2.8.20-9.3), 1.12.55.1 (2.35.15-17), 5.4.26.5 (2.352.18-19), and 5.10.63.2 (2.368.14-15).

[39] Thus Adolf Harnack argued that the bishop is essential to Origen's understanding of the church (*Der kirchengeschichtliche Ertrag der exegetischen Arbeiten des Origenes,* 2 vols. [Leipzig, 1924], 2:129-130).

[40] Origen, *Contra Celsum* 6.7 (2.106). See also 3.48 (1.244.17-245.2).

[41] Origen, *Commentary on Matthew* 14.21-22 (10.344-349). For angelic marriages see also Hermas, *Shepherd,* Similitude 8.3.3, and the accounts of Ptolemaeus in Irenaeus, *Against Heresies* 1.1.7.1 and Clement, *Excerpts from Theodotus* 64.1 (3.128).

[42] See Origen, *Commentary on John* 6.59 (4.167) and *Homilies on Luke* 17.1 (92.110) as well as the commentary on I Corinthians 1:2, fragment 1 in Jenkins's collection (*JTS* 9:232). Compare Origen, *On Prayer* 6.4 (2.314.15-25).

[43] Origen, *On First Principles* 1.8.1 (5.95) and *Homilies on Luke* 12.3 (92.146).

[44] Origen, *Homilies on Jeremiah* 11.3 (3.80-81) and fragment 50 (3.223).

[45] Origen, *Homilies on Numbers* 22.4 (7.209.3-14).

[46] See *Contra Celsum* 6.7 (2.106) and *Series Commentary on Matthew* 20 (11.35).

[47] Origen, *Homilies on Numbers* 9.1 (7.54.9-10).

[48] Origen, *Homilies on Genesis* 16.5 (6.142.6-11).

[49] Origen, *Commentary on Matthew* 16.22 (10.549-550).

[50] Ibid., 16.8 (10.492.24-31).

[51] Ibid., 16.8 (10.494.3-4).

[52] Origen, *Homilies on Ezechiel* 2.2 (8.342.23-343.3). Compare his *Commentary on John* 19.7 (4.306.32-307.7).

[53] Origen, *Homilies on Numbers* 2.1 (7.9.22-27).

[54] Origen, *Series Commentary on Matthew* 12 (11.23.2-5). Compare Clement, *Stromateis* 6.13.106.2 (2.485.10-17).

[55] Hans Urs von Balthasar, "Le Mysterion d'Origène," *Recherches de science religieuse* 26 (1936): 513-562 and 27 (1937): 38-64, p. 45.

[56] Ibid., pp. 49-50.

[57] Ibid., p. 50.

[58] Origen, *Commentary on Matthew* 12.5 (10.103.29-31 and 10.105.2-5).

[59] Ibid., 12.10 (10.84.24-33).

[60] Ibid., 12.10 (10.85.25-86.2).

[61] Ibid., 12.11 (10.86.15-88.12).

[62] Ibid., 12.12 (10.90.1-11). Such a person is, in fact, the only true Christian; any one disturbed that many ostensible Christians do not meet these standards should remember that "many are called but few are chosen" (Ibid., 12.12 [90.11-91.14] and 17.24 [10.650.1-652.25]).

[63] Ibid., 12.14 (10.96.6-32).

[64] Ibid., 12.14 (10.98.28-99.10). See also *Contra Celsum* 6.77 (2.147.16-22).

[65] Ibid., 12.14 (10.99.27-32). See also his *Homilies on Leviticus* 14.2-4 (6.479-487, especially 479.18-26) and *Homilies on Judges* 2.5 (7.479.1-23).

[66] Ibid., 12.14 (10.100.17-26).

[67] Origen, fragment 24 on 1 Corinthians (Jenkins, *JTS* 9:364), *Commentary on Romans,* Preface (Carl Heinrich Eduard Lommatzsch, ed., *Origenes Opera omnia*, 25 vols. [Berlin, 1831-1848], 6:3-4), *Homilies on Exodus* 6.9 (6.201.12-19), *Contra Celsum* 3.51 (1.247.20-248.5), and *Series Commentary on Matthew* 117 (11.247.9-22), all written later than *On Prayer,* seem to indicate that Origen abandoned the rigorist position.

[68] Origen, *On Prayer* 28.8-10 (2.380-381), trans. J. E. L. Oulton in Henry Chadwick and J.E.L. Oulton, eds., *Alexandrian Christianity* (Philadelphia, 1954), pp. 309-310.

[69] Origen, *Homily on Psalm 37* 2.6 (Lommatzsch ed., 12.267-268).

[70] Origen, *Commentary on John* 32.12 (14.444.31-32).

[71] Klaus Koschorke, *Die Polemik der Gnostiker gegen das kirchliche Christentum* (Leiden, 1978), especially pp. 220-232.

[72] Peter Brown, *The Making of Late Antiquity* (Cambridge, Mass., 1978), pp. 70-73.

Andrew Louth (essay date 1981)

SOURCE: "Origen," in *The Origins of the Christian Mystical Tradition: From Plato to Denys.* Oxford at the Clarendon Press, 1981, pp. 52-74.

[*In this essay, Louth examines the degree to which Platonism permeates Origen's theology, showing how Origen helped found the tradition of intellectual mysticism received by the Eastern Church and, more broadly, the whole of the Christian mystical tradition, having provided a framework within which mystical theology could develop.*]

With Origen we begin to discuss specifically *Christian* mystical theology. So far we have discussed the Platonic background to such theology, and in doing that we may seem to have prejudged the issue as to whether Christian mystical theology has, in fact, a Platonic background at all. However, the idea that Christian mystical theology is nothing but Platonism is a charge often made, and we shall not advance our understanding of this problem by ignoring it. Even without discussing the Fathers, we have seen that this 'Platonic background' is complicated. It is not pure Plato. What we have found in Philo and Plotinus has other philosophical debts than those to Plato. Middle Platonism, of which Philo, as we have seen, can be regarded as an example, and neo-Platonism are indebted to Aristotle and the Stoics for some of their emphases. But it is not by chance that they are called 'Platonist': Plato is their acknowledged master.

The influence of *Middle* Platonism on the Fathers is perhaps more considerable than might at first sight appear likely. Plato and Plotinus are essentially interesting for their own sakes: both were great philosophers. Philo was not, nor were the rest of the so-called Middle Platonists. Rather we find with them a kind of 'accepted wisdom', a way of looking at things which was customary in the early Patristic period and, just for that reason, was influential in the Fathers. How this influence operated, we shall see in what follows.

But even before we come to the Fathers, we have seen something more than the wisdom of pagan philosophy: with Philo we find the influence of the God of the Old Testament, of a God who created man and cares for him and chose Israel to be His people and revealed Himself in His dealings with them. Philo's concern is to show that pagan philosophy could discover nothing not already, for the Jew, a matter of revelation—and the revelation of *God,* moreover, not simply of the divine. This strand assumes even greater importance in the Christian Fathers. Whatever the influence of Platonism, they were concerned with God and not with the divine. Philo's idea of a God who speaks, who declares Himself, is given a sharper edge and more immediacy when, with the Fathers, he becomes the God who speaks and declares Himself in the life, death, and resurrection of Jesus of Nazareth. To know God is to accept that revelation, to participate in God's self-communication thus made known. So for most of the Fathers (with only rare exceptions) the 'mystical life' is the ultimate flowering of the life of baptism, the life we receive when we share in Christ's death and risen life by being baptized in water and the Holy Spirit.

When we begin to examine Origen's understanding of the soul's ascent to God this is the first point to emerge: the ascent begins, or is made possible, by what God has done for us in Christ and made effective in us by baptism. The mystical life is the working-out, the realizing, of Christ's union with the soul effected in baptism, and is a communion, a dialogue between Christ and the soul. Though this is often expressed in language drawn from Plato, when such language is used (as it is in Origen), what these Platonic-sounding concepts mean is very different from what Plato or Plotinus intended. Origen is talking about the life of the baptized Christian within the Church; Plato and Plotinus about the search for ultimate truth by an intellectual élite, either in the company of other like-minded souls, or as 'the alone to the Alone'.

Origen was deeply indebted to Platonism. As we shall see, his theology is permeated through and through by Platonic ways of thought. But his attitude to philosophy is not at all simple.[1] He studied under the philosopher, Ammonius Saccas, who was also Plotinus' master, but he studied *as a Christian.* He was not a convert from philosophy like Justin Martyr or Clement of

Alexandria, and he had none of their welcoming attitude towards philosophy which, for him, was simply a useful study for the Christian theologian as a training in dialectic, and something he justifies by the example of the Israelites' 'spoiling of the Egyptians' at the Exodus.[2] According to a pupil of Origen, Gregory Thaumaturgus, this was Origen's great gift; his capacity to press wisdom into the service of the one Lord wherever it might be found:

> This greatest gift has our friend accepted from God, this goodly portion from heaven, to be the interpreter of God's words to men, to understand the things of God as God's utterances, and to set them forth to men as men hear. Therefore there was nothing unutterable to us, for there was nothing inaccessible. We were privileged to learn every word, Barbarian or Hellenic, mystic or published, divine or human, traversing them all with the fullest freedom, and exploring them, bearing off from all and enjoying the riches of the soul . . . In a word, this was indeed our Paradise, imitating that great Paradise of God, wherein we needed not to till the earth below, not to minister to the body and grow gross, but only to increase the acquisitions of our souls, like some fair plants engrafting themselves, or rather engrafted in us by the Cause of all.[3].

But Origen's real concern was with the interpretation of Scripture. This was the repository of all wisdom and all truth and, as we shall see, the interpretation of Scripture lies at the very heart of his mystical theology. It was certainly the heart of his life's work: most of his writings consist of exposition of Scripture.

It was, then, as an interpreter of the Bible that Origen exercised his greatest influence on later theologians; here was a wealth of reflection on Scripture that could not be ignored and, as the ground of his mystical theology, was to be deeply pervasive in its influence. For him the Song of Songs was *the* book on the summit of the mystical life, the union of the soul with God. This judgement Origen bequeathed to later theology, along with many of the themes he draws out in his interpretation of the Song, in particular, the idea of the three stages of the mystical life—the three ways later called purificatory, illuminative, and unitive—and the notion of the soul's spiritual senses.

Let us begin by looking at his use of the Song of Songs. Origen's **Commentary** and **Homilies** on the Song[4] are not the earliest examples of the genre; there is a commentary, extant only in translation, by Hippolytus, and there is no doubt that Origen made use of this earlier work. However, in Hippolytus' commentary we find an ecclesiological interpretation dominant; that is, the relationship between the Bridegroom and the Bride is interpreted as referring to the relationship between Christ and the Church. The background to that is probably rabbinic interpretation, which saw the Song as expressing the relationship between God and Israel. The interpretation in terms of Christ and the individual soul occurs only occasionally in Hippolytus. With Origen the relationship of the soul to Christ (not that this is isolated from the theme of the relationship of the Church to Christ) becomes more prominent: there is a mystical, as well as an ecclesiological interpretation.

How does Origen justify this use of the Song of Songs? In the Old Testament, there are, he says at the beginning of the first *Homily* on the Song, seven songs, and the Song of Songs is the seventh and the most sublime. Before we can sing this song we must have progressed through the singing of the other six. Origen speaks of the progression through the six songs to the Song of Songs itself thus:

> You must come out of Egypt and, when the land of Egypt lies behind you, you must cross the Red Sea if you are to sing the first song, saying: Let us sing unto the Lord, for He is gloriously magnified [Song of Moses: Exod. 15]. But though you have uttered this first song, you are still a long way from the Song of Songs. Pursue your spiritual journey through the wilderness until you come to the well which the kings dug so that there you may sing the second song [Numbers 21:17-20]. After that, come to the threshold of the holy land that, standing on the bank of Jordan, you may sing another song of Moses, saying: Hear, O heaven, and I will speak, and let the earth give ear to the words of my mouth [Deut. 32]. Again, you must fight under Joshua and possess the holy land as your inheritance; and a bee must prophesy for you and judge you—Deborah, you understand, means 'bee'—in order that you may take that song also on your lips, which is found in the Book of Judges [Judges 5: the Song of Deborah]. Mount up hence to the Book of Kings, and come to the song of David, when he fled out of the hand of all his enemies and out of the hand of Saul, and said: The Lord is my stay and my strength and my refuge and my saviour. [2 Sam. 22:2-end: the Song of David]. You must go on next to Isaiah, so that with him you may say: I will sing to the Beloved the song of my vineyard [Isa. 5]. And when you have been through all the songs, then set your course for greater heights, so that as a fair soul with her spouse you may sing this Song of Songs too.

(*Hom.* I. 1: *GCS,* 27 f)

It is not necessary here to draw out Origen's meaning in any detail[5], it will be sufficient for us to note three points: first, the ascent of the soul to God begins with her 'coming out of Egypt and crossing the Red Sea', that is, with her conversion and baptism. For, as we have already mentioned, the mystical ascent for Origen begins in baptism and is a deepening and bringing to fruition of baptismal grace. Secondly, the way of the soul lies through deserts, and battles, while the soul finds sustenance in wells. And in all this the soul dis-

covers that God is powerful and brings her to victory through His grace. Aridity, moral struggle, consolations: all these are sufficiently familiar in the spiritual life, as also victory through God's grace—though not apart from human effort. Such is the way Origen sees. In the absence, however, of any specific commentary by Origen, I think it would be hazardous to develop a detailed account of the soul's ascent to God from this passage. (In the prologue to the *Commentary* Origen suggests a similar approach with a slightly different list of songs.) And, thirdly, note the songs themselves. At every stage of the Christian life the soul sings: it is full of joy. This is characteristic of Origen's spirituality, which knows nothing of the cloud, the dark night, found in the mysticism of others. His is a mysticism of light. It is optimistic—although balanced by a profound recognition of the necessity of grace. The Song of Songs is the song, then, the joyful song, of the summit of the spiritual life. As Origen puts it in his *Commentary:*

> The soul is not made one with the Word of God and joined with Him until such time as all the winter of her personal disorders and the storm of her vices has passed so that she no longer vacillates and is carried about with every kind of doctrine. When, therefore, all these things have gone out of the soul, and the tempest of desires has fled from her, then the flowers of the virtues can begin to burgeon in her . . . Then also will she hear 'the voice of the turtle-dove', which surely denotes that wisdom which the steward of the Word speaks among the perfect, the deep wisdom of God which is hidden in mystery.

(*Comm. on the Song* III (IV). 14: *GCS* 224)

That is one way in which Origen arrives at his understanding of the Song of Songs as being about the soul's intimate converse with God at the summit of the spiritual life. As far as I know, such a justification is peculiar to Origen. However, also in the *Commentary,* he suggests another way of arriving at this understanding of the Song which is more important, both as laying down a way of mapping out the ascent of the soul to God for later mystics, and also as giving commentaries on the Song of Songs a more specific context.

In the Prologue to the *Commentary* Origen remarks on the fact that philosophers divide their subject into three categories: ethics, physics, and enoptics[6] (enoptics means, roughly, metaphysics). The origin of some such division is Stoic, though Origen is actually referring to the sort of division found among Middle Platonists. He explains:

> That study is called moral (*ethike*) which inculcates a seemly manner of life and gives a grounding in habits that incline to virtue. The study called natural (*physike*) is that in which the nature of each single thing is considered; so that nothing in life may be

done which is contrary to nature, but everything is assigned to the uses for which the Creator brought it into being. The study called inspective (*enoptike*) is that by which we go beyond things seen and contemplate somewhat of things divine and heavenly, beholding them with the mind alone, for they are beyond the range of bodily sight.

(*GCS*, 75)

Origen then goes on to apply this distinction to the three protocanonical books of Wisdom ascribed to Solomon: Proverbs, Ecclesiastes, and the Song of Songs.

Wishing therefore to distinguish one from another these three branches of learning, which we called general just now, that is, the moral, the natural, and the inspective, and to differentiate between then, Solomon issued them in three books, arranged in their proper order. First, in Proverbs, he taught the moral science, putting rules for living into the form of short and pithy maxims, as was fitting. Secondly, he covered the science known as natural in Ecclesiastes. In this, by discussing at length the things of nature, and by distinguishing the useless and vain from the profitable and essential, he counsels us to forsake vanity, and cultivate things useful and upright. The inspective science likewise he has propounded in this little book that we have now in hand, that is, the Song of Songs. In this he instils into the soul the love of things divine and heavenly, using for this purpose the figure of the Bride and Bridegroom, and teaches us that communion with God must be attained by the paths of charity and love.

(*GCS*, 76)

So we have ethics assigned to Proverbs, physics assigned to Ecclesiastes, and enoptics assigned to the Song. There are three stages that the soul must pass through progressively: first, learning virtue (*ethike*), next, adopting a right attitude to natural things (*physike*), then ascending to contemplation of God (*enoptike*). That Origen means a progression is clear when he says, for instance:

If then a man has completed his course in the first subject, as taught in Proverbs, by amending his behaviour and keeping the commandments, and thereafter, having seen how empty is the world and realized the brittleness of transitory things, has come to renounce the world and all that is therein, he will follow on from that point to contemplate and to desire 'the things that are not seen', and 'that are eternal'. To attain to these, however, we need God's mercy; so that, having beheld the beauty of the Word of God, we may be kindled with a saving love for Him, and He Himself may deign to love the soul, whose longings for Himself He has perceived.

(*GCS*, 79)

The idea of the *successiveness* of the stages is often emphasized. For instance, speaking of Jesus as going before us through these stages, he says: 'We should speak of Him first as a beginner in Proverbs; then as advancing in Ecclesiastes; and lastly as more perfect in the Song of Songs.' We clearly have here the beginning of the idea of the three ways of the mystical life, and very nearly the later, familiar language of the way of purification (Origen's *ethike*), the way of illumination (*physike*) and the way of union (*enoptike*).

We have then a threefold division of the soul's ascent. The first, ethics, is concerned with the formation of the virtues. On this there is not much to comment, partly because Origen is here very Platonist and does not say anything we have not already come across, but partly too, because Origen himself does not dwell much on it. As Marguerite Harl remarks, 'Origen is an optimist for whom the struggle against the passions is a preliminary stage in one's interior development, to be passed through quickly.'[7]

Of natural contemplation we need to say a little more. It is clear from the passages already noted that for Origen this means basically not contemplation of the wonder of God in creation but a perception of the transience of the world and a desire to pass beyond it. However, we do sometimes find a more positive understanding of *physike:*

Since, then, it is impossible for a man living in the flesh to know anything of matters hidden and invisible unless he has apprehended some image and likeness thereto among things visible, I think that He who made all things in wisdom so created all the species of visible things upon earth that He placed in them some teaching and knowledge of things invisible and heavenly whereby the human mind might mount to spiritual understanding and seek the grounds of things in heaven; so that, taught by God's wisdom, it might say: The things that are hid and that are manifest have I learned.

(***Comm. on the Song*** III. 12: *GCS*, 209 f.)

This positive understanding of natural contemplation is more developed in the ***Commentary on John,*** where Origen discusses the idea that there are *logoi*, principles, implanted in the created order that can lead man to a conception of God's eternal wisdom:

if anyone is capable of conceiving by thought an incorporeal existence, formed by all sorts of ideas, which embraces the principles of the universe, an existence living and, as it were, animated, he will know the Wisdom of God who is above every creature and who truly says of himself: God created me as the beginning of his ways for his works.

(***Comm. on John*** I. xxxiv: *GCS*, 43)

So much for the first two ways. Origen's understanding of ethics and natural contemplation is deeply Platonic: the aim of these two ways is to subdue the body to the soul and then to free the soul from the body. Only when freed from the body can the soul enter on the way of *enoptike,* contemplation of God Himself, and on this way the soul passes beyond what it can achieve by its own efforts: it can only pass to this way, characterized by love, by reliance on God's mercy.[8] This is stated explicitly in the **Commentary on the Song of Songs** when, discussing the reference to 'midday' in the Song, Origen remarks:

> With regard to the time of vision, then, he 'sits at midday' who puts himself at leisure in order to see God. That is why Abraham is said to sit, not inside the tent but outside, at the door of the tent. For a man's mind also is out of doors and outside of the body, if it be far removed from carnal thoughts and desires; and therefore God visits him who is placed outside all these.

> (II. 4: *GCS* 140)

This also suggests that *enoptike* is properly something the soul can look forward to after death. Released from the body by death, the soul becomes mind, and is free to contemplate invisible reality: the realm of the Platonic Forms. Sometimes Origen gives expression to this in a very explicit way, for instance in **De Principiis:**

> And so the rational being, growing at each successive stage, not as it grew when in this life in the flesh or body and in the soul, but increasing in mind and intelligence, advances as a mind already perfect to perfect knowledge, no longer hindered by its former carnal senses, but developing in intellectual power, ever approaching the pure and gazing 'face to face', if I may so speak, on the causes of things.

> (II. xi. 7: *GCS* 191 f.)

Behind this Platonic distinction between mind and soul, *nous* and *psyche,* lies Origen's whole understanding of the world of spiritual beings and their destiny. Originally all spiritual beings, *logikoi,* were minds, equal to one another, all contemplating the Father through the Word. Most of these minds (all except the future mind of Christ) grew tired of this state of bliss and fell. In falling their ardour cooled and they became souls (*psyche,* supposedly derived from *psychesthai,* to cool). As souls, they dwell in bodies which, as it were, arrest their fall and provide them with the opportunity to ascend again to contemplation of God by working themselves free from their bodies and becoming minds, *noes,* again. As *nous,* the spiritual being can contemplate the Ideas and realize its kinship with this realm.[9] It is clear that this whole pattern is basically Platonist. In particular, for Origen the 'real' world is the realm of spiritual,

non-material beings: the drama of Fall and Redemption belongs essentially to this spiritual realm. Such a presupposition consorts ill with faith in the Incarnate Word, the Word incarnate in a physical, material world. We shall soon see that this is a source of trouble for Origen.

But though this is Platonist, we must qualify. The notion of the world of the Forms has undergone a change since Plato. In some Middle Platonists, Albinus for example, the Forms or Ideas are the *thoughts* of God, that is, they are the objects of God's thought; we come, as it were, within the divine mind when we contemplate them. They are not ultimate in themselves, as in Plato, but the eternal thoughts of the eternal and ultimate God. With Origen this takes the precise form of absorbing the world of the Ideas into the Logos. So Hans Urs von Balthasar can say: 'The world of the Ideas is absorbed in the unity of Christ. Their multiplicity is transformed into the richness of the aspects of the concrete Unity [which is Christ].'[10] The effect of this ought to make Origen's doctrine of contemplation more Christocentric or, at least, Word-centred, than would a merely Platonist theory. We must examine to what extent this is true.

That Origen's doctrine of contemplation is centred on the *Word* is easily seen. In the passage quoted earlier from the **Commentary on the Song of Songs** about *enoptike* it is said that the soul 'having beheld the beauty of the Word of God may be kindled with a saving love for him': such language is characteristic of Origen. But is it *Word*-centred or *Christ*-centred? Is this Word simply the eternal Word, or is it the *Word made flesh?* How much does the distinctively Christian doctrine of the Incarnation affect Origen's Platonist doctrine of contemplation?

In his writings on the Song of Songs we find plenty of evidence that the Incarnation is important for Origen. Take this passage from the second **Homily on the Song of Songs:**

> After this the Bridegroom says: I am the flower of the field and the lily of the valleys. For my sake, who was in the valley, he came down to the valley; and coming to the valley, he became the lily of the valleys in place of the tree of life that was planted in the paradise of God, and was made the flower of the whole field, that is, of the whole world and the entire earth. For what else can so truly be the flower of the world as is the name of Christ?

> (II. G: *GCS,* 49 f.)

Or, in another passage from the same homily, commenting on the passage where the Bridegroom is said to be 'behind our wall, looking out through the windows, becoming visible through the nets', we read:

> The Bridegroom then appears through the nets: Jesus has made a way for you, he has come down to earth

and subjected himself to the nets of the world. Seeing a great throng of mankind entangled in the nets, seeing that nobody except himself could sunder them, he came to the nets when he assumed a human body that was held in the snares of the hostile powers. He broke those nets asunder for you, and you say: 'Behold, he is at the back, behind our wall, looking out through the windows, become visible through the nets.'

(II. 12: *GCS,* 58)

In the **Commentary,** in addition to this interpretation, the nets are made to refer to temptations that Jesus suffered 'before he could enter into union and alliance with his Church' (III. 13: *GCS,* 222). Another passage which yields an interpretation that involves the Incarnation is that where the Bride asks the Bridegroom: 'In the shelter of the rock by the outwork shew me thy face, and let me hear thy voice.' The rock is readily taken to refer to Christ (see I Cor. 10:4), and Origen says: 'Having therefore availed herself of the covering of this rock, the soul comes safely to the place on the outwork, that is, to the contemplation of things incorporeal and eternal.' Origen goes on:

Like to these is the saying of God to Moses: Lo, I have set thee in a cleft of the rock, and thou shalt see my back parts. That rock which is Christ is therefore not completely closed, but has clefts. But the cleft in the rock is he who reveals God to men and makes Him known to them; for no-one knoweth the Father save the Son. So no-one sees the back parts of God, that is to say, the things that are come to pass in the latter times, unless he be placed in the cleft of the rock, that is to say, when he is taught them by Christ's own revealing.

(**Comm. on the Song** IV. 15: *GCS,* 231)

All these passages, in different ways, see the coming of Christ in the Incarnation as that to which the soul responds in its ascent to God. So, *per Christum* is strongly affirmed. Before we ask, how strongly? let us simply ask, how? How is the soul in its ascent to God coming to God through Christ? A full answer to that would have several strands. For instance, the idea that man is created after the image of God obviously has a part to play here, since, for Origen, the image of God is the Word himself, man being made after the fashion of the Word which became flesh. But what seems to be the dominant strand is hinted at in that last quotation about Christ as the rock in the cleft of which we can see God's back parts. God's back parts are here taken to mean (very unusually) prophecies about the last times. These can only be understood through Christ's revealing, which suggests that Christ is being seen as the key to the understanding of Scripture, where these prophecies are contained. If we think back to Philo we shall not, perhaps, be surprised to see this idea emerging here. As with Philo, the understanding

of Scripture is the medium of union with the Word. Commenting on the passage: 'Behold, here he cometh leaping upon the mountains, skipping over the hills,' Origen says:

Now if at any time a soul who is constrained by love for the Word of God is in the thick of an argument about some passage—and everyone knows from his own experience how when one gets into a tight corner like this one gets shut up in the straits of propositions and enquiries—if at such a time some riddles or obscure sayings of the Law or the Prophets hang in the soul, and if then she should chance to perceive him to be present, and from afar should catch the sound of his voice, forthwith she is uplifted. And when he has begun more and more to draw near to her senses and to illuminate the things that are obscure, then she sees him 'leaping upon the mountains and the hills'; that is to say, he then suggests to her interpretations of a high and lofty sort, so that this soul can rightly say: 'Behold, he cometh leaping upon the mountains, skipping over the hills.'

(**Comm. on the Song** III. 11: *GCS* 202)

Understanding Scripture is not for Origen simply an academic exercise but a religious experience. The meaning found in Scripture is received from the Word, and the experience of *discovering* the meaning of Scripture is often expressed in 'mystical' language; he speaks of a 'sudden awakening', of inspiration, and of illumination. It seems to me that a large part of the content of *enoptike* is the discovery of 'spiritual', 'theological' meanings in Scripture through allegory. In this engagement with Scripture, Origen enters more and more deeply into communion with God—and leads others into this communion (something we learn from Gregory Thaumaturgus' *Address to Origen*).[11]

It is quite clear, then, that Origen's mysticism is centred on the Word, and that the Word is apprehended in Scripture. And insofar as Scripture contains the record of the Incarnation, and also prophetic witness to, and apostolic commentary on it, to that extent Origen clearly holds that contemplation of God is possible (in practice, not simply theoretically) only *per Christum.*

But how strongly, how ultimately, does Origen hold to this *per Christum*? Let us start again with a passage from the **Commentary on the Song.** Discussing what is meant by the 'shadow of the apple tree' (*Cant.* 2:3), Origen says:

We must now come to the shadow of the apple tree, and, although one may avail oneself of another shadow, it seems that every soul, as long as she is in this present life, must needs have a shadow, by reason, I think, of that heat of the sun which, when it has arisen, immediately withers and destroys the seed that is not deeply rooted. The shadow of the Law indeed afforded but slight protection from this heat; but the shadow of Christ, under which we now live among the Gentiles, that is to say, the faith of his Incarnation, affords complete protection from it and extinguishes it. For he who used to burn up those who walked in the shadow of the Law was seen to fall as lightning from heaven at the time of the Passion of Christ. Yet the period of this shadow too is to be fulfilled at the end of the age; because, as we have said, after the consummation of the age we shall behold no longer through a glass and in a riddle, but face to face.

(***Comm. on the Song*** III. 5: *GCS,* 183)

The period of the shadow, namely, of faith in the Incarnation is temporary; it will pass away and then we shall see face to face. This idea is often found in Origen. In the ***Homily on Exodus*** he speaks of those 'who do not need to receive the Word of God according to the "it is made flesh", but according to the "Wisdom hidden in a mystery"' (XII. 4: *GCS,* 267) That way of putting it is characteristic: one of the passages quoted earlier about the summit of the soul's ascent spoke of 'that wisdom which the Word dispenses among the perfect, the deep wisdom of God which is hidden in mystery (*Comm.* IV. 14). So the soul, it seems, passes beyond faith in the Incarnation in its ascent to God. The Incarnation is only a stage. It would seem that Origen's Platonist presuppositions here are proof against the impact of the Christian doctrine of the Incarnation: the Incarnation is not really central, but simply a preliminary stage. That is evident in the ***Commentary on John,*** where Origen says: 'Christ said, I am the door. What then must we say of Wisdom, which God created as the beginning of his ways, for his works, in which her Father rejoices, delighting in her manifold intelligible beauty which is seen only by the eyes of the mind, and which arouses a heavenly love which perceives the divine beauty?' (I. ix: *GCS,* 14). At one place, however, in the ***Commentary on John*** this insistence that the Incarnation will be surpassed is tempered, though still substantially affirmed. Commenting on the mantle covered with blood that the Word wears in the Apocalypse, Origen says:

> But he is not naked, the Word that John sees on the horse: he is wearing a robe covered with blood, since the Word made flesh, dying because he was made flesh, because of his blood which was poured on the ground when the soldier pierced his side, bears the marks of his passion. For, if we one day attain to a more elevated and more sublime contemplation of the Word and the Truth, without doubt we shall not entirely forget that we have been led there by his coming in our body.

(II. viii: *GCS,* 62)

We might conclude by saying that Origen's mysticism centred on Christ is ultimately transcended by a mysticism centred on the eternal Word.[12]

We have now seen something of the way in which Origen's Platonist presuppositions qualify and determine his understanding of *enoptike.* But what of the nature of *enoptike* itself? As we have seen, it is by means of love and reliance on God's mercy that the soul enters on this third and highest stage of her mystical ascent. Both these ideas—love, and the soul's reliance on something other than herself—are found in Plato, so there is a fundamental harmony between Plato and Origen here. But we shall see that Origen goes far beyond Plato in his development of these ideas.

Taking up Plato's distinction made in *Symposium* 180 E between common love and heavenly love (*eros pandemos* and *ouranios*), Origen develops from it a similar distinction, in the Prologue to the ***Commentary on the Song,*** between the inner, spiritual man, formed in the image and likeness of God, and the outer, material man, formed of the slime of the earth:

> It follows that, just as there is one love, known as carnal and also known as Cupid [i.e. Eros] by the poets, according to which the lover sows in the flesh; so also there is another, a spiritual love, by which the inner man who loves sows in the spirit . . . And the soul is moved by heavenly love and longing when, having clearly beheld the beauty and fairness of the Word of God, it falls deeply in love with his loveliness and receives from the Word himself a certain dart and wound of love . . . If then a man can so extend his thinking so to ponder and consider the beauty and grace of all the things that have been created in the Word, the very charm of them will so smite him, the grandeur of their brightness will so pierce him as with a chosen dart—as says the Prophet (Isaiah 49:2)—that he will suffer from the dart himself a saving wound and will be kindled with the blessed fire of his love.

(***Comm. on the Song***, Prologue: *GCS,* 66 f.)

Origen goes on to discuss the words for love, *agape* and *eros,* and argues that there is no real difference between them, except that *eros* can be misunderstood (in a carnal way), and so Scripture, as a rule, uses *agape* as being safer. The love that Origen is interested in as far as *enoptike* is concerned is a pure, spiritual longing for that which is invisible; and the two previous stages, ethics and natural contemplation, can be seen as purifying this love. Origen speaks eloquently of the soul's passionate longing for the Word of God, as when explaining the wound of love:

> If there is anyone anywhere who has at some time burned with this faithful love of the Word of God; if there is anyone who has received the sweet wounds of him who is the chosen dart, as the prophet says; if there is anyone who has been pierced with the loveworthy spear of his knowledge, so that he yearns and longs for him by day and by night, can speak of nought but him, would hear of nought but him, can think of nothing else, and is disposed to

no desire nor longing nor yet hope, except for him alone—if such there be, that soul then says in truth: 'I have been wounded by love.'

(**Comm. on the Song**, III. 8: *GCS*, 194)

This is the spiritual love of the inner man as opposed to the carnal love of the outer man, and Origen develops the contrast between them in his teaching that, as the outer man has five senses, so has the inner man five spiritual senses. This doctrine of the five spiritual senses has, it seems, its source in Origen and has great influence thereafter on later mysticism. In an article,[13] Karl Rahner discusses its beginnings in Origen and gives a list of the important passages concerning it.[14] Briefly, this is Rahner's conclusion: Origen sees the biblical foundation for the five spiritual senses in Proverbs 2:5, where his text reads: 'And you will find a divine sense'; and in Hebrews 5:14 in the reference to the 'perfect who by reason of use have their senses exercised to discern good and evil', which, Origen goes on to point out, the bodily senses cannot do. Not all men have these spiritual senses. Some have none, and some have only one or two. It is vice that hinders the operation of these spiritual senses, and two things are necessary if one is to regain them: grace and practice. The Word is the cause of the right use of these senses, for he gives light to the eyes of the soul. The spiritual senses are awakened by grace, and by grace the Word is poured out into our senses. It is also the case that the spiritual senses become effective to the extent that the bodily senses are deadened. The spiritual senses belong properly to the *nous* rather than the soul (which, as we have seen, is fallen for Origen), although his language is by no means consistent on this point. It can be argued that the spiritual senses are not spiritual counterparts of the bodily senses, but are, rather, different figurative expressions for *nous*. In **De Principiis**, for example, Origen speaks of the 'powers of the soul' (I.i.9), which would support such an interpretation. (It must be pointed out, though, that not all references to spiritual senses in Origen's works suggest such a developed theory. Often they appear to be no more than an exegetical device, a way of interpreting such passages as that from the psalm: 'O *taste* and *see* how gracious the Lord is.' Obviously it is not bodily taste and sight that is in question, so there must be *spiritual* taste and sight.)

But what does it mean to talk of such spiritual senses? From Rahner we can see that it is a way of expounding the soul's experience of *enoptike,* contemplation of God. It is, as he puts it, 'the psychology of the doctrine of *theologia* conceived as the highest degree of the spiritual life' (though *theologia* is Evagrius' term, not Origen's). And there seem to be two elements in Origen's doctrine of the spiritual senses. As Rahner points out, and as can be verified by many of Origen's references to spiritual senses, they enable one to discern between good and evil, and are an expression of a kind of deli-

cate spiritual sensitivity the soul learns under the influence of grace in *enoptike,* so that the soul no longer simply avoids breaking God's commandments, but has a feel for God's will, a kind of 'sixth sense' or insight (which is what 'enoptike' would seem to mean: in-sight). 'For that soul only is perfect who has her sense of smell so pure and purged that it can catch the fragrance of the spikenard and myrrh and cypress that proceed from the Word of God, and can inhale the grace of the divine odour' (**Comm. on the Song** II.11: *GCS*, 172). The spiritual senses are a faculty which, as Balthasar puts it, 'can be developed and improved to an infinite delicacy and precision, so as to report to the soul more and more unerringly what is the will of God in every situation'.[15] The other element in the doctrine of the spiritual senses is that it seems to be a way of representing the richness and variety of the soul's experience of God in contemplation: to speak in terms simply of vision or knowledge would be to give too 'flat' an impression of this experience. Both these elements are brought out in the following passage:

And perhaps, as the Apostle says, for those who have their senses exercised to the discerning of good and evil, Christ becomes each of these things in turn, to suit the several senses of the soul. He is called the true sight, therefore, that the soul's eyes may have something to lighten them. He is the Word, so that her ears may have something to hear. Again, he is the Bread of Life so that the soul's palate may have something to taste. And in the same way he is called spikenard or ointment, that the soul's sense of smell may apprehend the fragrance of the Word. For the same reason he is also said to be able to be felt and handled, and is called the Word made flesh so that the hand of the interior soul may touch concerning Word of Life. But all these things are the One, Same Word of God, who adapts himself to the sundry tempers of prayer according to these several guises, and so leaves none of the soul's faculties empty of his grace.

(**Comm. on the Song** II. 9: *GCS*, 167 f.)

The other strand in Origen's understanding of the soul's experience of this highest stage of her ascent is his emphasis on God's mercy. This, we have noted, links up with Plato's idea that at the summit of the mystic ascent the soul passes beyond what it can achieve by its own efforts. The final vision appears suddenly, *exaiphnes,* and this implies, as we saw in our first chapter,[16] both that the soul can do nothing to elicit this final *theoria*, and also that in this final vision the soul is immediately present to the Supreme Beauty. With Origen these two strands are developed in accordance with the modification of his Platonism that we have already noticed. The realm of the Ideas has become the divine *Logos* in all the diversity of its manifestations. So, kinship with the Ideas becomes union with Christ the *Logos*. We have in Origen something that is more like personal encounter than what we find

261

in Plato. And even though, as we have seen, Origen remains too much of a Platonist to allow any final significance to the Incarnation of the Word—it is only a stage—yet the fact that the Word is thought of as meeting men as the Incarnate One (despite the qualifications with which Origen hedges this idea[17]) transforms his understanding of the Word. From being a principle mediating between the One and the many, the Word becomes a person mediating between God and the realm of spiritual beings. Even if the Word that Origen meets in his engagement with Scripture is, in some way, beyond the Incarnate Lord, his encounter with the Word is none the less a personal encounter.

Plato's idea that the soul attains the final vision *exaiphnes* is placed by Origen in a different, and much more fruitful, context, and thus transformed. We have seen something of what this means in the way Origen speaks of the sudden disclosures of the Word as he wrestles with Scripture. More generally, we can say that Plato's bare assertion about the suddenness and immediacy of the vision appears in Origen as the idea of the soul's dereliction and sense of abandonment by God, an abandonment which is suddenly relieved by the coming of the Word. One passage in the first ***Homily on the Song*** is particularly interesting, as it bears witness to Origen's own experience of dereliction:

> The Bride then beholds the Bridegroom; and he, as soon as she has seen him, goes away. He does this frequently throughout the Song; and that is something nobody can understand who has not suffered it himself. God is my witness that I have often perceived the Bridegroom drawing near me and being most intensely present with me; then suddenly he has withdrawn and I could not find him, though I sought to do so. I long therefore for him to come again, and sometimes he does so. Then when he has appeared and I lay hold of him, he slips away once more. And when he has so slipped away my search for him begins anew. So does he act with me repeatedly, until in truth I hold him and go up, 'leaning on my Nephew's arm'.
>
> (I. 7: *GCS*, 39)

Whether this is a 'mystical' experience of dereliction is not quite clear. Passages very similar to this occur elsewhere which quite clearly refer to Origen's experience as an exegete when sometimes he cannot see what a text means and is, in that sense, in difficulty; or when, on the contrary, the meaning 'just comes to him' (cf. *Comm*. III. 11, quoted above . . .). I am unhappy about regarding these passages as directly mystical, as it seems to me quite likely that Origen is clothing in 'mystical' language an experience that is not directly an experience of God at all: namely, the experience one has when the meaning of something suddenly 'comes to one' (as we say, without any mystical metaphor). Even so, if we are to take Origen seriously, this is more than a figure of speech, for he sees his engage-

ment with Scripture as an engagement with God. I suspect that these passages have a spectrum of meaning that ranges from the sort of thing I have mentioned to something which is a genuinely mystical experience of God. Certainly he can speak of these experiences in a way which makes it difficult not to regard the experience as mystical, and as Origen's own. For instance, in the ***Comm. on the Song***, III. 13: '[The Word] does not always stay with her, however, for that for human nature is not possible: He may visit her from time to time, indeed, and yet from time to time she may be forsaken too by Him, that she may long for Him the more' (*GCS*, 218).

Origen understands this experience as the union of the mind with the *Logos,* and only indirectly as contemplation of God. In its union with the *Logos* through contemplation, the soul shares in the Word's contemplation of God. From this flow a number of consequences that are characteristic of Origen's doctrine of contemplation. The soul's contemplation of the *Logos* is natural; in contemplation of the *Logos* the soul regains its proper state. Origen speaks neither of ecstasy, nor of any ultimate unknowability of God or darkness in God. It is possible that Origen dislikes the idea of ecstasy because of the misuse of this idea among the Montanists.[18] Whatever the reason, he develops a doctrine of contemplation where the soul does not pass beyond itself. According to his understanding, the soul does not have to do with a God who is ultimately unknowable. Darkness is only a phase we pass through: it is not ultimate as in Philo, Gregory of Nyssa, or Denys the Areopagite. Partly he sees this darkness as due to our lack of effort. If we strive to know God, the darkness will vanish. But he sometimes speaks of a more ultimate darkness which is the mystery in which God is enveloped. Of this he says in the ***Commentary on John***:

> If one reflects that the richness of what there is in God to contemplate and know is incomprehensible to human nature and perhaps to all beings which are born, apart from Christ and the Spirit, one will understand how God is enveloped in darkness, for no one can formulate any conception rich enough to do Him justice. It is then in darkness that He has made His hiding-place; He has made it thus because no one can know all concerning Him who is infinite.
>
> (II. xxviii: *GCS*, 85)

But he says a few lines later:

> In a manner more paradoxical, I would say also of the darkness taken in a good sense that it hastens towards light, seizing it and becoming light because, not being known, darkness changes its value for him who now does not see, in such a

way that, after instruction, he declares that the darkness which was in him has become light once it has become known.

Origen seems reluctant to entertain the notion of the ultimate unknowability of God. And unlike Philo and Gregory of Nyssa, for instance, for whom God *is* unknowable, Origen quite readily talks about 'knowing God' or 'seeing God'. Only rarely does he raise the question of the implications of God's infinity, while in **De Principiis** (II. iv, 1; IV. iv. 8) he definitely seems unhappy with such an idea.

What does Origen mean by 'knowing God', by contemplation of God? It is clear from the **Commentary on John** (XIX. iv) that Origen is aware that the biblical usage of 'know' means more than intellectual recognition. And he makes use of this in his explanation of what is meant by 'knowing God'. Knowing God is being known by God, and that means that God is united to those who know him, and gives them a share in his divinity. So, knowing God means divinization, *theopoiesis*. Knowing God is having the image of God, which we are, reformed after the likeness: the image is perfected so that we are like God. And contemplation is the means of this, for contemplation is, for Origen, a *transforming* vision. Speaking of the transfiguration of Moses' face when he went into the tabernacle, he says:

According to the literal meaning, something more divine than the manifestation that happened in the tabernacle and the temple was brought into effect in the face of Moses, who consorted with the divine nature. According to the spiritual meaning, those things which are known clearly about God and which are beheld by a mind made worthy by exceeding purity, are said to be the glory of God which is seen. So the mind, purified and passing beyond everything material, so that it perfects its contemplation of God, is made divine in what it contemplates.

(**Comm. on John** XXXII. xxvii: *GCS,* 472)

However, this idea of transforming contemplation is also applied to the Word himself, who, Origen says, would not remain divine (*theos*—without an article) unless he 'remained in unbroken contemplation of the Fatherly depths' (**Comm. on John** II. ii: *GCS,* 55). So we have a view of the world which is in some respects reminiscent of that of Plotinus. There is the ultimate God, *ho theos,* the One, the Father. There is the Word, who derives his divinity from contemplation of the Father (both the contemplation and the divinity that results from this being, in this case, indefectible). And then there is the realm of spiritual beings, the *logikoi,* who, through contemplation of the Word (and through him of God), are divinized.

We can see Origen as a founder of the tradition of intellectualist mysticism that was developed and bequeathed to the Eastern Church by Evagrius. In this tradition, contemplative union is the union of the *nous,* the highest point of the soul, with God through a transforming vision. And in such union the *nous* finds its true nature; it does not pass out of itself into the other; there is no ecstasy. Also the God with whom the soul is united is not unknowable. Consequently darkness is a stage which is left behind in the soul's ascent: there is no ultimate darkness in God. We have a mysticism of light. Origen, however, is not simply the precursor of one tradition, but of the whole of the Christian mystical tradition. Even if, as we shall see, later mystical theology developed emphases which are quite different from those we find in Origen, nevertheless they develop within the framework provided by him.

Notes

[1] See the sharply contrasting accounts in H. Koch, *Pronoia and Paideusis: Studien über Origenes und sein Verhältnis zum Platonismus* (Berlin and Leipzig, 1932) and H. Crouzel, *Origène et la philosophie* (Paris, 1962).

[2] See Origen's letter to Gregory Thaumaturgus (*PG* XI. 88-92) and his *Homilies on Joshua.* (*GCS,* VII. 286-463).

[3] *Address on Origen,* XV (*PG* X. 1096 AB). Metcalfe's trans. (London, 1920), 82 f.

[4] Origen has left us both a commentary (on *Cant.* 1:1-2:15) and two homilies (on *Cant.* 1:1-12a and 1:12b-2:14). The latter are more popular in tone and in them the ecclesiological interpretation is more prominent. All quotations are from R. P. Lawson's translation, published in *Ancient Christian Writers* XXVI (London, 1957) with very valuable annotations. There is also an edition, with translation, of the homilies only, by O. Rousseau (*Sources Chrétiennes* XXXVII, 2nd edn. Paris, 1966). Neither the homilies nor the commentary survive in the original Greek: the homilies are preserved in Jerome's Latin, and the commentary in Rufinus' Latin. I have given the page references to the edition in *Griechischen Christlichen Schriftsteller.*

[5] Such a drawing-out can be found in the introduction to the *Sources Chrétiennes* edition of the homilies.

[6] These terms are derived from the Greek words given with their Latin equivalents (*philosophia moralis, naturalis, inspectiva*) in the Latin version of the *Commentary(GCS,* 75, ll. 7-9). There is not absolute certainty, about them: see H. Crouzel, *Origène et la <<connaissance mystique>>* (Paris, 1961), 50 f., esp. 51 nn. 1 and 2, and Baehrens in *GCS,* ad loc.

[7] *Origène et la fonction révélatrice du Verbe incarné* (Paris, 1958), 321.

[8] See the passage from the Prologue to the *Commentary on the Song,* quoted above, p. 58 f.

[9] For all this see *De Principiis,* esp. I.v and II.viii; and also J. Daniélou, *Origène* (Paris, 1948), 207-18.

[10] *Parole et Mystère chez Origène* (Paris, 1957), 122, n. 26.

[11] On Origen's understanding of Scripture, see H. de Lubac, *Histoire et esprit: l'intelligence de l'écriture d'après Origène* (Paris, 1950), and also C. W. Macleod, 'Allegory and Mysticism', *Journal of Theological Studies* XXII (1971), 362-79.

[12] For further discussion of the importance of the Incarnation in Origen's theology, see Harl, 191-218, and Koch, 62-78.

[13] *'Le Début d'une doctrine des cinq sens spirituals chez Origène', Revue d'ascétique et de mystique* XIII (April 1932), 113-45: now available in an English translation in *Theological Investigations* XVI (London, 1979), 81-103.

[14] To which must be added *Conversation with Heraclides* 16 ff., discovered since Rahner wrote the article.

[15] *Origenes: Geist und Feuer* (2nd edn. Salzburg, 1950), 307, quoted by Lawson in the notes to his translation of the *Commentary* and *Homilies,* 340, note 221. The whole note is of great interest.

[16] See above, 14.

[17] See above, n. 12.

[18] *So Daniélou, Origène,* 296.

Peter Brown (essay date 1988)

SOURCE: "'I Beseech You: Be Transformed': Origen," in *The Body and Society: Men, Women and Sexual Renunciation in Early Christianity,* Columbia University Press, 1988, pp. 160-77.

[*In this excerpt, Peter Brown discusses how Origen in his exposition of Christian theology and his biblical interpretation understood and used the Platonism that permeated the Christian East of his day and how his understanding, profoundly Christian, was fundamentally different from that of his contemporary pagan Platonists.*]

Between May 200 and the middle of 203, Laetus, the Augustal Prefect of Egypt, rounded up a group of Christians from Alexandria and from Egypt proper. The father of Origen had been among them. Origen was sixteen or seventeen at the time, the eldest son of a family of seven. His mother hid his clothes, lest he should rush out to join his father by presenting himself to the authorities. "It was," wrote Eusebius of Caesarea a century later, "an ambition extraordinary in one so young."[1] Origen entered adulthood steeled by closeness to death. For him, the charged antithesis of "true" and "false" paternity, the contrast between continuities created by spiritual guidance and mere physical reproduction, which had been so current in Christian teaching circles in the second century, had become a bitter fact of life. The young man's loyalty to a father who had expected so much from him had been wrenched out of its normal course by the brutal blow of execution. All the continuity, all the loyalty that Origen now wished for lay in the finer, more enduring links of soul to soul, created between a teacher and his disciples within the Christian church.

Settled in Alexandria, Origen became a spiritual guide at a precociously early age. A nucleus of committed young Christians and of recent converts gravitated around the brilliant young teacher and "son of a martyr." When persecution flared up again, between 206 and 210, the group around Origen showed surprising resilience. The Alexandrian clergy discreetly vanished, leaving Origen to maintain the morale of his spiritual charges.[2] Daring the hostile crowd—no small act of courage in a city notorious for its lynch law—the young teacher would step forward to bestow on his spiritual "children" the solemn kiss that declared they had become worthy of their martyr's death.[3]

We know surprisingly little, from Origen's own works, of the texture of the remaining forty years of his life in Alexandria and elsewhere. His career as a teacher in Alexandria ended in 234 with virtual exile and the transfer of his school to Caesarea, on the seacoast of Palestine.[4] He taught there and preached regularly as a priest, expounding the Scriptures in church, until his death some time around 253-254, as a result of the tortures inflicted on him in the previous year in the prison-house of Caesarea.[5]

With Clement, we had been encouraged to look around us, at every detail of the life of a Christian in a great city; with Origen that busy world has vanished: we already breathe the changeless air of the desert.[6] Time stands still in a spiritual Sinai where, for forty years, Origen, the exegete, had gathered from the Scriptures the sweet bread of the angels.[7] Origen thought of himself, above all, as an exegete. Facing the unchanging Word of God, he strove to achieve an icon-like tranquillity, *to make* his *countenance firm before the people.*[8] A man whose heart burned with the hidden fire of the Scriptures,[9] Origen's unhurried, timeless scholarship brought a breath of changelessness into the Christian communities of Alexandria and Caesarea, at the very moment when these communities had begun to hurry headlong into a new age of prosperity, fraught with occasions for compromise with the world and marked by intellectual recrimination and the flagrant quest for power among the clergy.[10] What earned him the admiration of Christian intellectuals in all later centuries was not so much what Origen had taught, exciting and frequently disturbing though that might be; it was the manner in which, as an exegete and spiritual guide, Origen had presented the life of a Christian teacher as suspended above time and space. It was this that made him a role model, a "saint" of Christian culture, a man who could be hailed over a century later as "the whetstone of us all."[11]

From the start, Origen's message had been stark and confident: "I beseech you, therefore, be transformed. Resolve to know that in you there is a capacity to be transformed."[12] (In this phrase we can actually hear Origen speaking: it is taken from a shorthand record of a discussion between Origen and a group of somewhat puzzled bishops, which has survived on a papyrus discovered in Tura, south of Cairo, in 1941.)[13]

By the year 229/230, Origen felt free to commit himself to his most remarkable book, the ***Peri Archôn, On First Principles***. He was then in his late forties, an age when a serious philosopher could be thought to be sufficiently anchored in decades of meditation and direct experience of oral spiritual guidance (and had stirred up enough criticism among his colleagues) to make it worth his time to commit his thoughts to writing. In this book, he took the opportunity to lay bare the assumptions about the position of human beings in the universe that had underlain his personal alchemy as an exegete and guide of souls.

The problem that Origen posed was simple: "In what way has there come to be so great and various a diversity among created beings?"[14]

It was the old Platonic problem—how did the diversity observed in the material world emerge out of the original unity of the world of the Ideas? His answer to the question, however, was magnificently idiosyncratic. In his opinion, each created being had freely chosen to be different from its fellows; and each difference reflected a precise degree of decline from or progress toward an original, common perfection. Originally created equal, as "angelic" spirits, intended by God to stand forever in rapt contemplation of His wisdom, each spirit had "fallen" by choosing of its own free will to neglect, if ever so slightly—and even, in the case of the demons, to reject—the life-giving warmth of the presence of God.[15]

What we now call the "soul," the subjective self, was merely the result of a subtle cooling off of the original ardor of the primal, deepest self: the "spirit." As Origen pointed out, the word *psyché,* for "soul," derived from *psychros,* "cold." Compared with the fiery spirit that flickered upward, always straining to sink back into

the primal fire of God, the conscious self was a dull thing, numbed by the cold absence of love.[16] The baffling diversity of the present universe, divided as it was between ranks of invisible angels and demons, and marked on earth by an apparently infinite variety of human destinies, was the end product of countless particular choices, by which each spirit had freely chosen to be what it now was.

The most obvious feature of such a view was an unrelieved feeling of "divine discontent" with the present limitations of the human person. A vast impatience ran through the universe. Each being—angelic, human, or demonic—had in some way fallen away from God, through the insidious, fatal sin of self-satisfaction. Each mighty spirit had made, and could still make, a dire choice to remain content with its present condition, and to neglect the opportunity to expose itself to the consuming fire of God's love.[17] For Origen, Christ had been the only being whose original deepest self had remained "uncooled" by inertia. Christ's mighty spirit alone had remained inseparably joined to God, much as the white heat of an iron merged with the blaze of the furnace in which it rested.[18] All other beings must experience an unremitting sense of sadness and frustration: the primal, truest, most expansive definition of their self inevitably reached beyond the cramped circumstances of their present mode of existence. A shadow of regret always fell on the body. Whether this "body" was the ethereal frame of an angel or the heavy flesh of a human being, the body was always a limit and a source of frustration. But it was also a challenge; it was a frontier that demanded to be crossed. "Tents," Origen pointed out, were invariably spoken of with favor in the Old Testament. They stood for the limitless horizons of each created spirit, always ready to be struck and to be pitched ever further on. "Houses," by contrast, stood as symbols of dread satiety, "rooted, settled, defined by fixed limits."[19] Even the most resplendent beings were touched by this sadness: Origen believed that the huge soul of the Sun pressed ceaselessly against its radiant disc, and that its spirit sighed, as Saint Paul had sighed: *I could desire to be dissolved and to be with Christ: for it is far better.*[20]

If the tension to transcend the present limits of the self was the most vivid aspect of Origen's view of the human person, it was the least original. What concerned him most was how to reconcile a drive for transformation, shared by many Platonists and Christian Gnostics of the school of Valentinus, with whom he remained in constant dialogue,[21] with a sense of the unfathomable subtlety of God's justice in placing the "fallen" spirit within the temporary limits of a particular material body. The material universe as a whole, in his opinion, had been *subjected to frustration, not of its will;* but it had been *subjected in hope.*[22] For Origen, the fall of each individual spirit into a particular body had not been in any way a cataclysm; to be placed in a body was to experience a positive act of divine mercy. He distanced himself from many of his contemporaries by insisting that the body was necessary for the slow healing of the soul.[23] It was only by pressing against the limitations imposed by a specific material environment that the spirit would learn to recover its earliest yearning to stretch beyond itself, to open itself "ever more fully and more warmly" to the love of God.[24] The body posed a challenge that counteracted the numb sin of self-satisfaction. For this reason, "The world before our eyes became a material world for the sake of those spirits who are in need of a life lived in physical matter."[25] If anything, Origen thought, it was the demons who were to be pitied: turned by their immense self-satisfaction away from the love of God, their bodies had been left perfectly within the control of their proud wills; their eerie flesh was as supple as a chill north wind.[26] "They are regarded as unworthy of this instruction and training whereby, through the flesh, the human race . . . aided by the heavenly powers, is being instructed and trained."[27]

Hence, Origen's profound ambivalence about the human body. Looking at the body at close quarters, as a source of temptation and frustration, Origen offered little comfort to his readers:

> You have coals of fire, you will sit upon them, and they will be of help to you.[28]

Yet, in the eyes of God, each particular human spirit had been allotted a particular physical constitution as its appropriate sparring partner. Each person's *flesh and blood* was particular to that person, and had been exquisitely calibrated by God, "who alone is the searcher of hearts," to challenge the potentially mighty spirit of each to stretch beyond itself.[29] Thus, far from regarding the body as a prison of the soul, Origen arrived at an unexpected familiarity with the body. It always seemed to him that each person's spirit must be as vividly distinctive as were the features of his or her face. The gentle precision of God's mercy ensured that each body was adjusted to the peculiar needs of its soul down to the finest details, much as the lines of each person's handwriting remained unmistakably their own. Each person's relations with the body, therefore, had its own, unfathomably particular story: to the eye of God, the "chastity" of a Peter was as different from the "chastity" of a Paul as was each Apostle's signature.[30] Confronted with their own, irreducibly particular *flesh and blood,* all believers struggled to maintain, in themselves, the huge momentum of their spirit's longing for God.

Origen's view of the spiritual struggle entered the bloodstream of all future traditions of ascetic guidance in the Greek and Near Eastern worlds. It involved the human person in a solemn and continuous dialogue with the intangible powers that brushed against the mind. For "if we are possessed of free will, some spiritual beings may be very likely to be able to urge us on to sin and others to assist us to salvation."[31]

Angels and demons were as close to the Christian of the third century as were adjacent rooms. The free soul expanded in love or slipped back into numbed satiety in as far as it chose to "seek counsellors" in the mighty, unseen spirits that stood so close to every person.[32] At the moment of intense prayer, for instance, the believer could sense, in the undisturbed serenity of the mind, a touch of the stilled silence of the angelic spirits who stood beside all Christians, lovingly concerned that humans should join with them in their own untrammeled worship of God.[33]

Surrounded on every side by invisible helpers and invisible seducers, the thought flow of the Christian could rarely be treated as neutral. Piety and firm resolves rose into consciousness through the soul's willingness to cooperate with its angelic guides. These protecting presences drew the healthful properties of the person to the fore, as mysteriously and as intimately as the contact of healing poultices mobilized the energies of humors that lay far beneath the skin.[34] The themes of a Christian's meditations rose within the "heart" with a power that frequently betrayed resources deeper than those of the isolated, conscious mind:

> *Blessed is the man whose acceptance is in Thee, O Lord: Thy ascents are in his heart.*[35]

It was the same with temptation. Consent to evil thoughts, many of which were occasioned, in the first instance, by the dull creakings of the body—by its need for food and its organic, sexual drives[36]—implied a decision to collaborate with other invisible spirits, the demons, whose pervasive presence, close to the human person, was registered in the "heart" in the form of inappropriate images, fantasies, and obsessions. For these demonic promptings also had a dynamism that could not be explained by the normal stream of conscious thought. Hence, for Origen, as for all later ascetic writers, the "heart" was a place where momentous, faceless options were mercifully condensed in the form of conscious trains of thought—*logismoi*. Little wonder, then, that the wise Solomon had said: *Keep thy heart with all diligence.*[37] For to consent to such *logismoi* was to "consecrate oneself" to demonic partners.[38] It was to give oneself over, on many more levels of the self than the conscious person, to an alternative identity: it was to lose oneself to the powers of numbness that still lurked in the hidden reaches of the universe, and to take on the character of chill demonic spirits who had been content to exist without the ardent search for God.

Origen bequeathed to his successors a view of the human person that continued to inspire, to fascinate, and to dismay all later generations. He conveyed, above all, a profound sense of the fluidity of the body. Basic aspects of human beings, such as sexuality, sexual differences, and other seemingly indestructible attributes of the person associated with the physical body, struck Origen as no more than provisional. The present human body reflected the needs of a single, somewhat cramped moment in the spirit's progress back to a former, limitless identity.

A body, in the sense of a limiting frame for the spirit, would remain with all created beings throughout their long period of healing. But Origen was careful to point out that this body was not necessarily continuous with the present physical organism. It also would become transformed, along with the spirit, "throughout diverse and immeasurable ages," of which the present life was one short interlude.[39] The transformation of the body in the future ages of its existence involved a long, mysterious process, as splendid in its final outcome as was the the pure, "healed" matter that emerged from the alchemist's crucible as gold.[40] The body itself would become less "thick," less "coagulated," less "hardened," as the numbing inertia of the spirit thawed in the growing heat of its yearning for the Wisdom of God. As under the delicious working of fresh wine, the barriers that cramped the person would be dissolved.[41] The "vessel of clay" of the present self would be shattered, to be remolded, ever again, into containers of ever wider capacity, in stages of life that stretched far beyond the grave.[42]

This was a view of the bodies of actual men and women taken from a disturbingly distant vantage point. It meant that Origen was prepared to look at sexuality in the human person as if it were a mere passing phase. It was a dispensable adjunct of the personality that played no role in defining the essence of the human spirit. Men and women could do without it even in this present existence. Human life, lived in a body endowed with sexual characteristics, was but the last dark hour of a long night that would vanish with the dawn. The body was poised on the edge of a transformation so enormous as to make all present notions of identity tied to sexual differences, and all social roles based upon marriage, procreation, and childbirth, seem as fragile as dust dancing in a sunbeam.

Origen was widely believed to have practiced what he preached. It was always said of him that, as a young man of about twenty, around 206, he had discreetly gone to a doctor to have himself castrated.[43] At the time, castration was a routine operation.[44] Origen's supporters were prepared to believe that he had undergone the operation so as to avoid slanderous rumors about the intimacy that he enjoyed with women who were his spiritual charges.[45] Two generations previously, a young Alexandrian had been prepared to undergo the same operation, for the same reason.[46]

When, as a priest at Caesarea, Origen preached against those who took too literally the words of Christ, when He had blessed those who had *made themselves eunuchs for the sake of the kingdom of heaven,* he treated the matter in a manner so unruffled as to reveal a chasm between a third-century audience and ourselves.[47] Given the vivid fantasies that surrounded the adult eunuch, it was far from certain that everyone would have believed that Origen had gained immunity from sexual temptation by such an operation. Postpubertal castration merely made the man infertile; it was, in itself, no guarantee of chastity.[48] What Origen may have sought, at that time, was something more deeply unsettling. The eunuch was notorious (and repulsive to many) because he had dared to shift the massive boundary between the sexes. He had opted out of being male. By losing the sexual "heat" that was held to cause his facial hair to grow, the eunuch was no longer recognizable as a man.[49] He was a human being "exiled from either gender."[50] Deprived of the standard professional credential of a philosopher in late antique circles—a flowing beard—Origen would have appeared in public with a smooth face, like a woman or like a boy frozen into a state of prepubertal innocence. He was a walking lesson in the basic indeterminacy of the body.

This body did not have to be defined by its sexual components, still less by the social roles that were conventionally derived from those components. Rather, the body should act as a blazon of the freedom of the spirit. John the Baptist's soul had been so huge as to have caused his tiny body to leap in his mother's womb. The body of so great a spirit must necessarily have remained a virgin.[51] To reject marriage and sexual activity of any kind was to make plain the fiery spirit's "manifest destiny." Virginity preserved an identity already formed in a former, more splendid existence and destined for yet further glory.

At a stroke, continence ceased to be what it had largely been in the Early Church—a postmarital matter for the middle-aged. Origen, indeed, had been unusual in his early commitment as a Christian, and in the fascination that he had exercised on young persons in Alexandria in the first years of his career. His first years in Alexandria give us a rare glimpse of something like the radicalism of a "youth culture" at work in a church more usually dominated by sober greybeards.[52]

In middle age, Origen tended to present virginity as a state that declared the joining of an "immaculate" spirit with its well-tempered, material frame. As a result of this shift in perspective, virginity could no longer be regarded simply as a perilous state of suspended sexuality, imposed upon the frisky young by their elders in the relatively short period between puberty and marriage. Nor was it an anomaly, made plain by the suspension of a natural destiny to marriage, undergone, in the pagan world, by a few prophetesses and priestesses. Virginity stood for the original state in which every body and soul had joined. It was a physical concretization, through the untouched body, of the preexisting purity of the soul. In the words of an author appreciated by Origen, the continent body was a waxen seal that bore the exact "imprint" of the untarnished soul.[53] Identified in this intimate manner with the pristine soul, the intact flesh of a virgin of either sex stood out also as a fragile oasis of human freedom. Refusal to marry mirrored the right of a human being, the possessor of a preexistent, utterly free soul, not to surrender its liberty to the pressures placed upon the person by society.

Origen was quite prepared to draw this consequence. Social and physical mingled inextricably in his thought. Behind the definition imposed upon the spirit by the body, there lay the definition imposed upon the person, through the body, by society. Origen always thought of a body as more than the physical body, seen in isolation. The body was a "microclimate." It was a vehicle through which the spirit adjusted to its present material environment as a whole.[54] Innumerable subtle filaments led the spirit through the body, into involvement with others, and so into involvement with society. When he spoke of sexually active married persons, Origen took Paul's words on *the present necessity* (or *constraint*) not to refer to the pressure exercised on the soul by the sexual drives of the body. He understood *constraint* in a far wider sense. He thought that Paul had referred to the social bonds that tied the believer to marriage, and, through marriage, to the *frame of this world*—to the great, extended body of society, into which the Christian became inextricably grafted through marriage.[55] To reject sexuality, therefore, did not mean, for Origen, simply to suppress the sexual drives. It meant the assertion of a basic freedom so intense, a sense of identity so deeply rooted, as to cause to evaporate the normal social and physical constraints that tied the Christian to his or her gender. Society might see the Christian virgin, the continent boy, or the young Christian widow as persons defined by their sexual physical nature, and so as potential householders and bearers of children. Origen was less certain: the human spirit did not necessarily need to acquiesce to so self-limiting a definition.

Not to belong to married society was to belong more intensely to others. The invisible world was magnificently sociable. It was a "great city" crowded with angelic spirits. The sense of an invisible, alternative society, of a great communion of human and angelic beings, was central to Origen's notion of the virgin state. Bonds based on physical paternity, on physical love, and on social roles derived from the physical person seemed peculiarly evanescent when compared with the resonant unity of a universe that strained toward the embrace of Christ. In the light of such future intimacy, the humble, physical bonds of human marriage, based as they were on a momentary adjustment of the spirit to the heavy climate of earth, appeared peculiarly insubstantial.[56] A time would come when all relations based upon physical kinship would vanish. His huge identity no longer definable within such narrow limits, even Abraham—so Origen, the son of Leonides the martyr, "dared" to suggest—would no longer be called "father of Isaac," but by some other, deeper name:

> Remember ye not the former things, neither consider the things of old. Behold I will do a new thing.[57]

In thinking in this way, Origen had appropriated, in a characteristically idiosyncratic manner, a distinctive feature of the Platonism of his age, which he may have first encountered through the disciples of Valentinus.[58] The Platonic doctrine of the Ideas was an essential ingredient of Origen's view of the person. The notion that all beauty and order in the visible world was a distant echo of a yet more majestic, unseen harmony haunted contemporaries. For Origen, everything perceived with senses could be thought of as existing in undimmed intensity in God, the source of all being. The spiritual realm was alive with joys whose sensuous delight was veiled from the pious only by the present numbness of their spirits. Those who could thaw their frozen hearts would once again experience the sharp, precise impression of a wealth of spiritual sensations. The prophets and Evangelists had "felt" the original joy of God's Wisdom. In a manner that escaped normal experience, they had actually "tasted," "smelled," and "drunk" it, savoring the sweet taste of the Wisdom of God with a sensibility undulled by long negligence.[59]

It had been Origen's life's labor, as an exegete and guide of souls, to make the "spiritual senses" of his charges come alive again in their original intensity. By withdrawing from the dull anaesthesia of common, physical sensation, the soul of the "spiritual" person might recapture the sharp delights of another, more intensely joyful world. The believer's spirit would stand totally exposed before the Bridegroom, stripped of all sensual joys, to receive on a "naked" sensibility the exquisite touch of His darts.[60]

Origen wrote ***Homilies on the Song of Songs***, around 240, as a peculiarly consequential exponent of what has been aptly called the "wild" Platonism of his generation.[61] In such a Platonism, sensuality could not simply be abandoned or repressed. Rather, the sharpness of sensual experience was brought back to its primordial intensity: it was reawakened, in the mystic's heart, at its true level—the level of the spirit. By contrast, physical pleasure was a stale and bland displacement of true feeling, a deflection of the spirit's huge capacity for delight into the dulled sensations of the body. The spirit must learn to "burn" in its deepest self, to yearn for the indefinable precision of the scent of God, to hope for the delicious particularity of the taste of Christ deep in the mouth, and to prepare itself for the final embrace of the Bridegroom. This meant, in effect—for Origen and for his successors—a discipline of the senses that was all the more searching because what was at stake was no longer simply continence, but the hesitant, fragile growth of a spiritual sense of preternatural sharpness. Physical indulgence, undue eating, undue enjoyment of sight and sound, the physical joys of sexual bonding in marriage: these became subjects of vigilance. Sensual experiences nurtured a counter sensibility. They led to a dulling of the spirit's true capacity for joy. They were a "cushion," which deadened the impact of those deeper, more vivid pleasures that might fall like kisses on the bared spirit.[62]

Origen's attitude to marriage was so much sharper than that of Clement mainly because of the streak of "wild" Platonism that ran through his thought. A refined suspicion came to rest on the joys and duties of the married state for which Clement had still been prepared to praise the providence of God. The pleasures of the marriage bed, the intimacy and loyalty of married life, were slurred echoes of the more clear delights reserved for spirits unnumbed and uncushioned by sensual experience. The refined soul was well advised to shun them: they might bring about a degradation of the spiritual sense that was all the more subtle and anxiety-producing because it could not be pinned down with any great precision. Origen, and many like him in later centuries, felt, with the intangible certainty of a refined, almost an aesthetic, spiritual sensibility, that married intercourse actually coarsened the spirit. The spirit was destined for a moment of startling, unimaginably precise "knowledge" of Christ, of which the subtle "knowledge" of a partner gained through physical love was but a blurred and—so Origen was convinced—a distracting and inapposite echo.[63] The kisses of the Bridegroom would come only in the empty studyroom:

> We find there a certain sensation of an embrace by the Spirit . . . and, oh, that I could be the one who yet might say: *His left hand is beneath my head, and his right arm reaches around me.*[64]

Such a view cast a chill shadow over the marriage bed. As a social institution, the partnership of the married couple—their intimacy, their loyalty to each other, the ordered and benevolent hierarchy of husband and wife (topics on which the author of the pseudo-Pauline Letter to the Ephesians had written with such warmth)—struck Origen as valid symbols of the invisible concord of a redeemed creation. But even they were transient sym-

bols.[65] As for the facts of the marriage-bed, there was something pointedly "inapposite" about them.[66] No amount of decorum in the sexual act could smooth away the incongruities associated with it. Origen did not share Clement's optimism on that score. Rather, seen with high Platonic eyes, married intercourse could be evoked only in terms of what it lacked. It made painfully clear the extent of the hiatus between itself and "true" spiritual joining. In this, Origen's thought resembled that of the Valentinian Gnostics. Married intercourse took place in a "chamber," that is, "in darkness." An undispelled suspicion of "wantonness" lingered over it. Knowledge of married love could not be a stepping stone, by which the soul might rise, through physical experience, to a higher, more spiritual sense of partnership with God. Rather, the experience of sexuality, even in marriage, was delineated with bleak precision, as a darkened antithesis to the blazing, light-filled embrace of Christ in the spirit.[67]

Yet, with Origen, the same "wild" Platonism that would lead him to cast a dark shadow on the physical concomitants of marriage led him to fasten with complete satisfaction on the isolated virgin body. Here, at last, was a physical symbol that reflected without distortion the purity of the spiritual world. Solemnly set apart from married society, the bodies of the continent—men and women alike—stood out as privileged material objects: they were "temples of God:"

> Do not think that just as *the belly* is made *for food and food for the belly,* that in the same way the body is made for intercourse. If you wish to understand the Apostle's train of reasoning, for what reason the body was made, then listen: it was made that it should be a *temple to the Lord;* that the soul, being holy and blessed, should act in it as if it were a priest serving before the Holy Spirit that dwells in you. In this manner, Adam had a body in Paradise; but in Paradise he did not "know" Eve.[68]

Such statements had practical implications. By 248, it was plain that a general persecution was imminent. The onset of persecution had been associated, in many cities, with a positive revival of a sense of the sacred in pagan communities: mobs had rioted at the instigation of pagan priests, angered by insults to the temples; and the Emperor Decius had come to believe that neglect of the visible gestures of sacrifice had jeopardized the safety of the Empire.[69] It was a time when a Christian teacher, such as Origen, had to make clear to pagan critics where exactly the "holy" might be found on earth. In order to reassure his devoted patron and disciple, Ambrosius, Origen began to rebut in great detail an attack on Christianity made by Celsus, a pagan Platonist, written some eighty years previously.

The long work contained quite remarkable statements on the "declaratory" role of the Christian virgin in the

Roman world of the mid-third century. A sense of history comes to run through Origen's presentation of virginity. Virginity was presented as a privileged link between heaven and earth. For it was only through the "holy" body of a virgin woman that God had been able to join Himself to humanity, thus enabling the human race to speak, at last, of Immanuel, "God among us."[70] Christ's Incarnation, through His descent into a virgin body, marked the beginning of a historic mutation: "human and divine began to be woven together, so that by prolonged fellowship with divinity, human nature might become divine."[71]

And the "human nature" that was on its slow way to the divine was a nature most clearly revealed in bodies untouched by sexual experience. In Origen's view, perpetual continence, now upheld, for a wide variety of reasons, by little groups of Christian men and women all over the Mediterranean, made of such persons clearly privileged representatives of God's deepest purposes for the transformation of the human race.

What was at stake, between Celsus, the pagan, and Origen, the Christian, both of them Platonists, was where to find the holy in the visible world, and consequently from what source to derive the authority that the holy might come to exercise among men. A good Platonist, Celsus had looked to the material universe as a whole. Here was a refulgent "body," palpably worthy of the mighty Creator-soul that embraced it.[72] The blazing Sun, the heavy clusters of the Milky Way: these were "bodies" set on fire by the touch of the Ideas. The quiet radiance of the One God, delegated to "angelic" ministers, better known to men in their traditional guise as the ancient gods, filtered down yet further beneath the Moon, to touch the dull earth, bathing with an untroubled light the immemorial holy places of pagan worship. Statues, temples, ancestral rites—these were the symbols that echoed most appositely on earth the blazing holiness of the heavens. Compared with these, the individual human body was too frail a thing to carry so much majesty: it was no more than a needy beggar that had sidled up to the soul, demanding with disagreeable insistence a small share of its attention.[73] Celsus was deeply angry because Jews, and now Christians, were claiming that they stood above all temples—even above the stars themselves. They claimed that they enjoyed direct communion with the One God of the universe. Celsus, and later Plotinus, Origen's younger contemporary (both of them Platonic philosophers steeped in the same culture as Origen), showed deep religious anger that such an overvaluation of their persons should have led Christians to overturn the established hierarchy of the universe. Mere human beings were to know their place, far below the stars; they must not claim that they could brush aside the gods who ministered to them from the distant heavens. Christians, Celsus had said, were like

frogs holding counsel round a marsh, or worms assembling in some filthy corner, saying "God has even deserted the whole world and the motions of the heavens and disregarded the vast earth to give attention to us alone." They are like worms that say, "There is God first, and we are next after Him in rank . . . and all things exist for our benefit."[74]

Faced by such withering indignation, Origen, the Christian Platonist, made the *gran rifiuto* that separated him forever from the "Ancient Wisdom" of his pagan colleagues. Christians, he replied, "have already learned . . . that the body of a rational being that is devoted to the God of the Universe is a temple of the God they worship."[75]

The human body could be "offered up"; it could be "made holy" for God. The humble "ass" of the body could become the "resplendent" vehicle of the soul.[76] Each Christian man or woman could build their body into a "holy tabernacle of the Lord."[77]

> Look now at how you have progressed from being a tiny little human creature on the face of this earth. You have progressed to become a *temple of God,* and you who were mere flesh and blood have reached so far that you are a *limb of Christ's body.*[78]

Let us now follow the fortunes of these "temples of God" in the Christian churches in the Mediterranean and the Near East through the decisive half century that stretched from the death of Origen, through further pagan reaction in the Great Persecution, to the conversion of Constantine and the first public appearance of Saint Anthony.

Notes

[1] Eusebius, *Ecclesiastical History* 6.2.6. On the life of Origen, Pierre Nautin, *Origène: sa vie et son oeuvre* is essential, Henry Chadwick, *Early Christian Thought and the Classical Tradition,* pp. 66-94 is judicious. For Eusebius' presentation of the youth of Origen, see Patricia Cox, *Biography in Late Antiquity: A Quest for the Holy Man,* pp. 69-101. Like all modern scholars, I am particularly indebted to the patient work of F. Crouzel, most especially his *Origène et la "connaissance mystique"* and *Virginité et mariage chez Origène,* and to W. Völker, *Das Vollkommenheitsideal des Origenes.* See also J. W. Trigg, *Origen: the Bible and Philosophy in the Third-Century Church.*

[2] Eusebius, *Ecclesiastical History* 6.3.13-4.3.

[3] Ibid. 6.3.4. and 41.1-23.

[4] See Nautin, *Origène,* pp. 69-101 and 421-432 and Trigg, *Origen,* pp. 130-146.

[5] See Nautin, *Origène,* pp. 433-441 and Trigg, *Origen,* pp. 241-243. G. W. Clarke, *The Letters of Saint Cyprian of Carthage,* Ancient Christian Writers 43, pp. 22-39,

esp. pp. 35-36, gives a masterly account of the pressure put on leading Christians to sacrifice and the consequent discreet release of those who proved too difficult to frighten into conformity.

6 This aspect of Origen is beautifully evoked by Marguerite Harl, *Origène et la fonction révélatrice du Verbe incarné,* pp. 360-363.

7 *In Num.* 17.4, *Griechische christliche Schriftsteller: Origenes Werke* 7, p. 163.

8 *In Ezech.* 3.1, *Origenes Werke* 8, p. 349.

9 *In Joh.* 10.18.105, ed. Cécile Blanc, *Origène: Commentaire sur Saint Jean,* Sources chrétiennes 157, p. 444 and *Hom. in Cant. Cant.* 2.8, in O. Rousseau, ed., *Origène: Homélies sur le Cantique des Cantiques,* p. 95. See esp. Marguerite Harl, "Le langage de l'expérience religieuse chez les pères grecs."

10 Origen's view of contemporary bishops was distinctly unflattering: in *Matt.* 16.6, *Origenes Werke* 10, pp. 493-497.

11 Gregory Nazianzen cited in Suidas, *Lexicon,* A. Adler, ed., 3:619.

12 *Dialogue with Heraclides* 150, in H. E. Chadwick, trans., *Alexandrian Christianity,* p. 446.

13 Chadwick, *Alexandrian Christianity,* pp. 430-436, provides a quite exceptionally good introduction to the incident.

14 *De Principiis.* 2.9.7.245, in F. Crouzel and M. Simonetti, eds., *Origène: Traité des Principes,* Sources chrétiennes 252, p. 368.

15 Ibid. 1.3.8.323, p. 164.

16 Ibid. 2.8.3.120, p. 344.

17 See esp. Marguerite Harl, "Recherches sur l'origénisme d'Origène: la 'satiété' (kóros) de la contemplation comme motif de la chute des âmes."

18 *De Princip.* 2.6.5-6.159-192, pp. 318-320.

19 *In Num.* 17.4, p. 160.

20 *De Princip.* 1.7.5.180, pp. 218-220.

21 See esp. Elaine Pagels, *The Johannine Gospel in Gnostic Exegesis.*

22 Ibid. 1.7.5.156, p. 216, citing Romans 8:19.

23 This has been made plain in general by Hal Koch, *Pronoia und Paideusis. Studien über Origenes und sein Verhältnis zum Platonismus,* esp. pp. 28-30; see now Trigg, *Origen,* pp. 103-120 and Margaret R. Miles, *Fullness of Life,* pp. 49-61.

24 *De Princip.* 1.3.8.319-320, p. 164.

25 *In Joh.* 19.20.132, Sources chrétiennes 292, p. 126.

26 *De Princip.* 1.8.165, p. 86 and 2.8.3.150, p. 346.

27 Ibid. 1.6.3.111, p. 111; in G. W. Butterworth, trans., *Origen: On First Principles,* p. 56.

28 *In Ezech.* 1.3, *Origenes Werke* 8, 324-325.

29 *De Princip.* 3.2.3.157, Sources chrétiennes 268, p. 164.

30 *In Num.* 2.2, p. 11.

31 *De Princip.* Praef. 5.111, p. 84.

32 *In Num.* 20.3, p. 195.

33 Ibid. 11.9, p. 93.

34 *In Jerem.* (Latin version) 2.12, *Origenes Werke* 8:301.

35 *De Princip.* 3.2.4.250, Sources chrétiennes 268: p. 168.

36 Ibid. 3.2.2.89 and 96, p. 158.

37 Ibid. 3.2.4.292, Sources chrétiennes 268: p. 172, citing *Proverbs* 4:23.

38 *In Num.* 20.3, p. 193.

39 *De Princip.* 3.1.23.1025 [Latin of Rufinus], Sources chrétiennes 268, p. 146; Butterworth trans., p. 209.

40 Ibid. 1.6.4.104, p. 204: On gold as "healed" matter, see esp. S. Averincev, "L'or dans le système des symboles de la culture protobyzantine," esp. p. 63.

41 *In Joh.* 1.30.205-206, pp. 160-162.

42 *In Num.* 9.6-7, pp. 62-64.

43 Eusebius, *Eccles. Hist.* 6.8.2-3: see Pierre Nautin, *Lettres et écrivains des iième et iiième siècles,* pp. 121-126. The reader should know that Chadwick, *Early Christian Thought,* p. 67 is unconvinced that such an incident ever happened. I think that the sources for it are sufficiently reliable, that there was nothing impossible about such an action in the third century, and, hence, that—at the very least—Origen could certainly have been viewed as someone who had had himself castrated.

[44] Aline Rousselle, *Porneia: de la maîtrise du corps à la privation sensorielle*, pp. 158-164 takes us into a world little dreamed of by most commentators.

[45] Eusebius, *Eccles. Hist.* 6.8.2.

[46] Justin, *I Apology* 29.2; Henry Chadwick, *The Sentences of Sextus*, p. 111 provides full evidence on the prevalence of castration in third- and fourth-century Christian circles.

[47] *In Matt.* 15.1, pp. 347-353.

[48] See Basil of Ancyra, *de virginitate tuenda* 61, *Patrologia Graeca* 30: 769C for the misdeeds of eunuchs in Christian circles.

[49] *In Matt.* 15.3, p. 356.

[50] Claudius Mamertinus, *Panegyrici latini* 11.19.4.

[51] *In Joh.* 1.31.183 and 187, pp. 330 and 334.

[52] Eusebius, *Eccles. Hist.* 6.3.13-4.3 and *in Jud.* 9.1. *Origenes Werke* 7, p. 518.

[53] *Sentences of Sextus* 346, Chadwick ed., p. 5; see pp. 114-115 on Origen and "Sextus."

[54] Thus fish have a scaly body suited to their watery environment and angels shimmering bodies suited to their life in etherial fire: Origen apud Methodius, *de Resurrectione* 1.22.4-5: see H. Chadwick, "Origen, Celsus and the Resurrection of the Body."

[55] *Fragments on I Corinthians,* 42 C. Jenkins, ed., p. 512.

[56] *In Matt.* 14.22, p. 338.

[57] Ibid., 17.33, pp. 690-691.

[58] On this topic, see the excellent introduction of O. Rousseau, *Origène: Homélies sur le Cantique des Cantiques,* pp. 21-25. I am indebted to John Dillon, "Aesthésis Noété: a doctrine of spiritual senses in Origen and in Plotinus," who makes plain that the final formulation of the notion takes place only in Origen's later years. Patricia Cox, "Origen and the Bestial Soul," and now "Pleasure of the Text, Text of Pleasure: Eros and Language in Origen's *Commentary on the Song of Songs*" are suggestive treatments.

[59] *Contra Celsum* 1.48: see the translation and notes of Henry Chadwick, *Origen: Contra Celsum,* p. 44; cf. *in Num.* 21.1, p. 200—the Levites are those of "undulled" sensibility.

[60] *Hom. in Cant. Cant.* 2.8, p. 132.

[61] The phrase is that of A. H. Armstrong, "Neoplatonic Valuations of Nature, Body and Intellect," at p. 41.

[62] *Hom. in Cant. Cant.* 2.9, p. 134. By the same token, the pains of Hell will be more excruciating for the spirit, just as blows fall more sharply on a naked than on a clothed body: see the citation in Pamphilus, *Apologia for Origen* 8: *Patrologia Graeca* 8: 602D- 603B; trans. Nautin, *Origène,* p. 274.

[63] *In Joh.* 19.4.1, Sources chrétiennes 290, pp. 22-25.

[64] *Hom. in Cant. Cant.* 1.2, p. 65. By contrast, the bedroom is not regarded as a proper place for prayer: *de orat.* 31.4; see esp. Giulia Sfameni Gasparro, *Origene: studi di antropologia,* pp. 234-242.

[65] *Fragments on Ephesians,* 29, J. A. Gregg, ed. p. 566.

[66] *Hom. in Cant. Cant.* 2.1, p. 80.

[67] *Fragments on I Corinthians,* 39, p. 510, citing Romans 13:13.

[68] *Fragments on I Corinthians,* 29, p. 370.

[69] Eusebius, *Eccles. Hist.* 6.41.1: mobs stirred up in Alexandria by pagan priests; on Decius, see Clarke, *Letters of Saint Cyprian,* pp. 21-25, and now Robin Lane Fox, *Pagans and Christians,* pp. 451-454.

[70] *Contra Celsum* 1.35, Chadwick, trans., p. 34.

[71] Ibid. 3.28, p. 146.

[72] This has been particularly well stated, in the case of Plotinus, by A. H. Armstrong, *Saint Augustine and Christian Platonism.* Now in R. A. Markus, *Augustine: A Collection of Critical Essays,* p. 13.

[73] Plotinus, *Enneads* 1.8.14.

[74] *C. Cels.* 4.23, pp. 199-200; compare Plotinus, *Enneads* 2.9: *Against the Gnostics.*

[75] Ibid. 4.26, pp. 201-202.

[76] *in Jud.* 6.5, *Origenes Werke* 7:503.

[77] *In Exod.* 13.5, pp. 277-278.

[78] *in Jes. Nave* 5.5, *Origenes Werke* 7:319.

FURTHER READING

Berchman, Robert M. *From Philo to Origen: Middle Platonism in Translation.* Chico, California: Scholars Press, 1984, 359p.

An historical inquiry into the emergence of the Jewish

and Christian Platonic philosophies in the formative period of Judaism and Christianity in Alexandria.

Butterworth, G.W., ed., trans. *Origen: On First Principles.* Gloucester, MA: Peter Smith, 1973, 342 p.

Contains two good general introductions to Origen's work, one by Henri De Lubac, author of *Histoire et Esprit: L'intelligence de l'Écriture d'après Origene (1950),* and one by Butterworth.

Chadwick, Henry, introduction to *Origen: Contra Celsum,* ed., trans. Chadwick. Cambridge: Cambridge University Press, 1953, pp. ix-xxxii.

Discusses the philosophical background of Origen's dispute with Celsus, as well as the identity, date, and theology of Celsus.

Clark, Elizabeth A. *The Origenist Controversy: The Cultural Construction of an Early Christian Debate.* Princeton: Princeton University Press, 1992, 287p.

An extended discussion of the Origenist controversy of the late fourth and early fifth centuries, showing that it stands at a juncture of several important theological debates over Christian orthodoxy in that general period.

Cox, Patricia. *Biography in Late Antiquity: A Quest for the Holy Man.* Berkeley: University of California Press, 1983, 168p.

Contains an examination of Eusebius' "Life of Origen" according to that work's dual purpose: to defend Origen and to promote unity among the persecuted by using Origen as a rallying figure and as an example of the perfect union of pagan and Christian virtues.

Crouzel, Henri, ed. *Bibliographie Critique D'Origène.* Martinus Nijhoff, Hagae Comitis, 1971, 684p.

A comprehensive bibliography of writings about Origen from the second century to 1969. (Available only in French.)

————. "Current Theology: The Literature on Origen 1970-1988." *Theological Studies* 49, No. 3 (September 1988), 499-516.

A bibliographical review of the new editions, translations, and critical studies of Origen's works throughout Europe and America.

De Lange, N. R. M. *Origen and the Jews: Studies in the Jewish-Christian Relations in Third-Century Palestine.* Cambridge: Cambridge University Press, 1976, 240p.

A study of Origen's position as a biblical scholar in the history of the relations between Jews and Christians, which gave him extraordinary insight into the Jews of his time and their relations with their non-Jewish neighbors.

Drewery, Benjamin. *Origen and the Doctrine of Grace.* London: The Epworth Press, 1960, 214p.

A study of Origen's doctrine of Grace that reveals some of the tensions and latent stresses in his thought that foreshadows Augustine's great contest with Pelagius on the doctrine.

Hanson, R.P.C. *Allegory and Event: A Study of the Sources and Significance of Origen's Interpretation of Scripture.* London: SCM Press, 1959, 400p.

A study of Origen's allegorical method of exegesis, beginning with a survey of the Jewish, pagan, and New Testament sources of Christian allegory and the development of the tradition of biblical allegory.

————. *Origen's Doctrine of Tradition.* London: S. P. C. K., 1954, 213p.

A study of Origen's teaching on tradition, revealing that Origen's thought exhibits an increased definiteness over that of Clement's and is indicative of the general sharpening of the mind of the Church in matters of the Canon, the priesthood, theological doctrine, etc. in the third century.

Heine, Ronald E., ed., trans. *Origen: Homilies on Genesis and Exodus.* The Fathers of the Church, vol. 71. Washington, D. C.: 1981.

Contains an extensive critical introduction that treats of the life and works of Origen as well as the manuscript tradition of his writings.

Jackson, B. Darrell. "Sources of Origen's Doctrine of Freedom." *Church History* XXXV, No. 1 (March 1966), 13-23.

Attempts to show how Origen treats of the doctrine of the rational freedom of the soul in accordance with Scripture and reason.

MacLeod, C. W. "Allegory and the Mysticism in Origen and Gregory of Nyssa." *The Journal of Theological Studies,* N.S. XXII, Part 2 (October 1971), 362-79.

Attempts to show in considering Origen's and Gregory of Nyssa's writings how allegory is related to mysticism and the definite ways in which that relation shapes our understanding of them.

Miller, Patricia Cox. "Poetic Words, Abysmal Words: Reflections on Origen's Hermeneutics." In *Origen of Alexandria: His World and His Legacy.* Edited by Charles Kannengiesser and William L. Petersen. University of Notre Dame Press, 1986, pp. 165-78.

Applies structuralist principles to understand Origen's method of interpreting the Scriptures.

Robertson, J. Armitage. *The Philocalia of Origen.* Cambridge: Cambridge University Press, 1893, 278p.

This text in the original Greek is accompanied by a thorough critical introduction, which, though now a century old, is still very useful. The introduction identifies the sources of the work and provides a history of the text and of its critical acceptance in antiquity.

Rowe, J. Nigel. *Origen's Doctrine of Subordination: A Study in Origen's Christology*. European University Studies, Series XXIII, Theology; vol. 272. Berne: Peter Lang, 1973, 315p.

> Examines and evaluates the Christology of Origen which, it is argued, is drawn less from Scripture than from Origen's own philosophical preconceptions that he brought to his exegesis.

Smith, John Clark. *The Ancient Wisdom of Origen*. Lewisburg: Bucknell University Press and London/ Toronto: Associated University Presses, 1992, 370p.

> A thorough study of Origen's moral theology, beginning with its background of the Greek, Roman, and Jewish religions, pagan philosophy, Gnosticism, Scripture, and a variety of other Christian sources. Also contains an expansive bibliography of primary and secondary sources.

Tzamalikos, Panayiotis. "Origen and the Stoic View of Time." *Journal of the History of Ideas* 52, No. 4 (October/ December 1991), 535-61.

> Argues that Origen began his theology of time with the Stoic concept of time as extension bringing it in line with his general theological framework, which made his view distinctive and original.

Vaspary, Gerard E. *Politics and Exegesis: Origen and the Two Swords*. Berkeley: University of California Press, 1979, 215p.

> Attempts to demonstrate that Origen's theology of politics and his theological principles are the foundation of the medieval political allegory of the two swords.

Widdicombe, Peter. *The Fatherhood of God from Origen to Athanasius*. Oxford: Clarendon Press, 1994, 290p.

> Surveys the Alexandrian background of the early Christian conception of the fatherhood of God, showing how Origen was the most important of Athanasius' Alexandrian predecessors and to whom much of the book is devoted.

Wiles, Maurice. *The Journal of Theological Studies*, N. S. XII, (1961), 284-91.

> Argues that the idea of eternal generation played a very important role in Origen's thought and a very different one than it would ultimately play in the final form of Christian orthodoxy.

Pearl

ca. 1390

Middle English poem.

INTRODUCTION

Pearl is widely regarded as a nearly perfect example of medieval religious poetry. Its depth of thought and emotion and its profound religious message is conveyed through an ornate formal complexity that heightens the readers' experience. Composed by an unknown Northwest Midlands writer, *Pearl* stands first in its manuscript in a group of four works, all probably composed by the same author in the last third of the fourteenth century. The four poems illustrate the religious and courtly interests of the poet and his audience; in each he presents human characters in conflict with spiritual beings. *Pearl* is a dream vision, two of the other poems are verse homilies on Christian virtues, and the fourth is an Arthurian romance. All of the *Pearl*-poet's work enlarges our understanding of the native British tradition of alliterative poetry, but *Pearl* is his most mature religious work. Consisting of 101 twelve-line stanzas of rhyming and alliterative octosyllabic verse, the poem embodies medieval ideas of numeric symbolism and visual symmetry in the beauty of its complex circular form. In *Pearl* readers encounter the medieval interest in the ability of human language to express the divine, ideas about personal redemption and transformation, and the virtues of patience, humility, purity, perfection, and submission to the divine will.

Plot and Major Characters

In this symmetrical dream vision, the despairing narrator wanders through a garden containing the grave of his infant daughter. He has a vision of Paradise lying beyond a river and recognizes the adult woman seated there as his daughter. As she scolds him for his extended grief, she describes her present situation. Married to the Lord of Heaven, she has a status equal to that of other blessed souls (many of whom led long and exemplary Christian lives), which she explains by relating the Parable of the Workers in the Vineyard; the heavenly souls' endless bliss she equates to the pearl of great price of another biblical parable. In answer to his questions, the narrator is allowed to see the New Jerusalem, through which the Lamb of God leads a procession that includes the dreamer's daughter. He tries to join her by crossing the river but awakens to find himself back in his garden, con-

soled by his vision and resolved to accept his lot in life.

Textual History

Pearl is the first of four poems in the British Museum manuscript Cotton Nero A.x, dated by its handwritten script to about 1400; the other poems (the titles of all the poems have been given by modern editors) are *Cleanness*, *Patience* (both verse homilies based on biblical narratives), and *Sir Gawain and the Green Knight* (an Arthurian romance). All four poems are in alliterative verse written by an unknown author in the Northwest Midlands dialect of Middle English, and they form part of a continuous native literary tradition in the North and West of England (a tradition also known as the "alliterative revival"). Internal evidence from all poems shows them to have been composed between approximately 1360 and 1395, with the date of *Pearl* falling near the end of that period. The manuscript was practically unknown until 1753, when the collection of Robert Cotton was given to the British Museum. *Sir Gawain and the Green Knight* was first published in 1839, and the remaining three poems first appeared in Morris's Early English Test Society edition of 1864 (the first in the now extensive EETS series). Israel Gollancz published an edition in 1891 and revised it in 1897; a second edition in 1921 was accompanied by a work of Boccaccio's said to be one of *Pearl*'s sources. A facsimile edition was published in 1923 with an introduction by Gollancz. The 1953 E.V. Gordon edition was considered the the scholarly standard until the publication of Andrew and Waldron's York Medieval Text series edition of 1979.

Major Themes

Demonstrating the interests of the poet and his medieval audience, all four poems by the *Pearl*-poet center around a situation in which a human interacts with an other-worldly being. In *Pearl* the conflict is between the mind of a grieving father and the spirit of his daughter. Thus it is not surprising that the poem's major themes deal with such issues as the adequacy of language to convey spiritual truth and Christian theological concepts of redemption, salvation, and consolation. Other themes emphasize the medieval interest in cardinal virtues and vices. The tension established by the interaction between a human and a spiritual being naturally leads to discussions on the patience, humility, and purity of the *Pearl* maiden in contrast with the impatience, pride, and worldliness of the narrator. The courtly interests of the poet and his audience also allow the modern reader to identify such chivalric ideals as courtesy, chastity, and perfection. Many critics discuss evidence in *Pearl* of Christian theological issues: some find a theme outlining the nature of salvation, others see an emphasis on the redemption of the narrator, noting his progress through the poem and the stages of redemption; still others emphasize that the poem is a Christian *consolatio* about coming to terms with one's mortality. The theme of obedience and submission to God's will has been discussed, and critics who focus on Christian theological concepts see the narrator's growth and transformation as the main issue of the poem. Some commentators emphasize the theme of the inadequacy of language to ever embody the perfect, divine, and ineffable nature of spiritual truth, while others discuss language as incarnational art and emphasize the ornate beauty of the poem's circular form.

Critical Reception

Critical response to *Pearl* in this century has been varied. Early commentators noticed the seemingly autobiographical nature of the poem and speculated about the identity of the poet and possible real-life counterparts of the *Pearl* maiden. Some argued whether the poem was an elegy or an allegory; this debate informed much of the criticism in the first half of this century. Others emphasized symbolism in an attempt to understand the poem's meaning (i.e., pearl as "soul," or "Eucharist," or "the nature of blessedness"). More recently, critics have discussed the intricacy of the poem's interlinked and circular arrangement and discussed the ability of the poem to convey symbolic meaning through its shape. Some have linked these formal issues with the idea of an incarnational art and emphasized numeric symbolism and Gothic visual representations of the sacred. Critics who focus on the narrator connect his progress toward understanding to the stages of redemption or growth in self-knowledge. Some have commented on the poem's ability to convey his intense inner experience; others have examined the relationship between the narrator and the reader. Some scholars who focus on the nature of language and its potential to convey notions of the divine are aided by discussions of the nature of the dream vision. For example, the distance between dreamer and vision is related to the inability of human language to adequately describe divine subjects. The contrast between the experience of the narrator and that of the *Pearl* maiden informs discussions of theological issues, leading most critics who focus on religious matters to emphasize the nature of redemption and the transformation of the narrator as the key issues of the poem.

PRINCIPAL WORKS

Pearl (verse dream vision) late fourteenth century
Cleanness (verse homily) late fourteenth century
Patience (verse homily) late fourteenth century
Sir Gawain and the Green Knight (verse Arthurian romance) late fourteenth century

PRINCIPAL EDITIONS

Early English Alliterative Poems in the West Midlands Dialect of the Fourteenth Century (edited by Richard Morris) 1869
Pearl: An English Poem of the Fourteenth Century, together with Boccaccio's "Olympia" (translated by Israel Gollancz) 1921
Pearl (edited by E. V. Gordon) 1953
The Complete Works of the Gawain-Poet (translated by John Gardner) 1965
The Pearl-Poet: His Complete Works (translated by Margaret A. Williams) 1967
Sir Gawain and the Green Knight, Pearl, and Sir Orfeo (translated by J. R. R. Tolkien) 1975

Pearl, Cleanness, Patience, Sir Gawain and the Green Knight (translated by A. C. Cawley and J. J. Anderson) 1976
Pearl: A New Verse Translation (translated by Marie Borroff) 1977
The Poems of the Pearl Manuscript: Pearl, Cleanness, Patience, Sir Gawain and the Green Knight (edited by Malcolm Andrew and Ronald Waldron) 1979

CRITICISM

Richard Morris (essay date 1869)

SOURCE: A preface to *Early English Alliterative Poems*. Oxford University Press, 1965, pp. ix-xx.

[*In the following excerpt, Morris considers* Pearl *to be a valuable resource for understanding early English and the art and tradition of the poet.*]

[In **"The Pearl"**], the author evidently gives expression to his own sorrow for the loss of his infant child, a girl of two years old, whom he describes as a

> Perle pleasaunte to prynces paye
> *Pearl pleasant to princes' pleasure,*
> To clanly clos in golde so clere
> *Most neatly set in gold so clear.*

Of her death he says:

> Allas! I leste hyr in on erbere
> *Alas! I lost her in an arbour,*
> Þurȝ gresse to grounde hit fro me yot
> *Through grass to ground it from me got.—*
>
> (p. 1.)

The writer then represents himself as visiting his child's grave (or arbour) in the "high season of August," and giving way to his grief (p. 2). He falls asleep, and in a dream is carried toward a forest, where he saw rich rocks gleaming gloriously, hill sides decked with crystal cliffs, and trees the leaves of which were as burnished silver. The gravel under his feet was "precious pearls of orient," and birds "of flaming hues" flew about in company, whose notes were far sweeter than those of the cytole or gittern (guitar) (p. 3). The dreamer arrives at the bank of a stream, which flows over stones (shining like stars in the welkin on a winter's night) and pebbles of emeralds, sapphires, or other precious gems, so

> Þat all the loȝe lemed of lyȝt
> *That all the deep gleamed of light,*
> So dere watȝ hit adubbement
> *So dear was its adornment.—*
>
> (p. 4.)

Following the course of the stream, he perceives on the opposite side a crystal cliff, from which was reflected many a "royal ray" (p. 5).

> At þe fote þer-of þer sete a faunt
> *At the foot thereof there sat a child,*
> A mayden of menske, ful debonere
> *A maiden of honour, full debonnair;*
> Blysnande whyt watȝ hyr bleaunt
> *Glistening white was her robe,*
> (I knew hyr wel, I hade sen hyr ere)
> *(I knew her well, I had seen her before)*
> At glysnande golde þat man con schore
> *As shining gold that man did purify,*
> So schon þat schene an-vnder schore
> *So shone that sheen (bright one) on the opposite shore;*
> On lenghe I loked to hyr þere
> *Long I looked to her there,*
> Þe lenger I knew hyr more & more
> *The longer I knew her, more and more.—*
>
> (pp. 6, 7.)

The maiden rises, and, proceeding along the bank of the stream, approaches him. He tells her that he has done nothing but mourn for the loss of his Pearl, and has been indeed a "joyless jeweller" (p. 8). However, now that he has found his Pearl, he declares that he is no longer sorrowful, but would be a "joyful jeweller" were he allowed to cross the stream (p. 8). The maiden blames her father for his rash speech, tells him that his Pearl is not lost, and that he cannot pass the stream till after death (p. 10). The dreamer is in great grief; he does not, he says, care what may happen if he is again to lose his Pearl. The maiden advises him to bear his loss patiently, and to abide God's doom (p. 11). She describes to him her blissful state in heaven, where she reigns as a queen (p. 12). She explains to him that Mary is the Empress of Heaven, and all others kings and queens (p. 13). The parable of the labourers in the vineyard [Matthew, chapter xx] (pp. 15-18) is then rehearsed at length, to prove that "innocents" are admitted to the same privileges as are enjoyed by those who have lived longer upon the earth (p. 18). The maiden then speaks to her father of Christ and his one hundred and forty thousand brides (p. 24), and describes their blissful state (p. 26), She points out to him the heavenly Jerusalem, which was "all of bright burnished gold, gleaming like glass" (p. 29). Then the dreamer beholds a procession of virgins going to salute the Lamb, among whom he perceives his "little queen" (p. 33). On attempting to cross the stream to follow her, he is aroused from his dream (p. 35), laments his rash curiosity in seeking to know so much of God's mysteries, and declares that man ever desires more happiness than he has any right to expect (p. 35).

. . . . .

This brief outline . . . together with the short extracts from [it], will, it is hoped, give the reader stomach to digest the whole. It is true that [it contains] many "uncouth" terms; but this will be [its] highest merit with the student of language, as is shown, by Dr. Guest's testimony, that [it is] "for several reasons curious, and especially so to the philologist" [History of English Rhythms, vol. i. p. 159]. To those readers who do not appreciate the importance of such a very large addition to the vocabulary of our Early Language as is made by these treatises, let Sir Frederic Madden's opinion of their literary merit suffice. That distinguished editor says, of the author's "poetical talent, the pieces contained in the MS. afford unquestionable proofs; and the description of the change of the seasons, the bitter aspect of winter, the tempest which preceded the destruction of Sodom and Gomorrah, and the sea storm occasioned by the wickedness of Jonas, *are equal to any similar passages* in Douglas or Spenser." Moreover, as to the hardness of the language—inasmuch as the subject matter of the poem will be familiar to all who may take up the present volume, the difficulty on the word-point will not be such as to deter the reader from understanding and appreciating the production of an old English poet, who—though his very name, unfortunately, has yet to be discovered—may claim to stand in the foremost rank of England's early bards.

Carleton F. Brown (essay date 1904)

SOURCE: "The Author of *The Pearl*, Considered in the Light of His Theological Opinions," in *PMLA*, Vol. XIX, No. 1, 1904, pp. 115-45.

[*In the following essay, Brown describes the* Pearl *author as an ecclesiastic who, two hundred years prior to the Protestant Reformation, created a three-hundred-line argument equating the grace received in heaven by a baptized infant with that received by a lifelong active Christian.*]

Among the English poets of the fourteenth century the one who deserves the seat next to Chaucer is the anonymous author of the four poems: *Sir Gawayne and the Green Knight,* **The Pearl,** *Cleanness,* and *Patience.* The singular beauty of these poems has long stimulated scholars to the most diligent efforts to discover their author.

The first attempt to identify the unknown poet was made in 1838 by Dr. Edwin Guest [*History of English Rhythms,* 1882] who confidently assigned these poems to Huchown, the mysterious Scotch poet mentioned by the chronicler Wyntoun. At one time or another, almost every piece of fourteenth century verse which

shows a northerly dialect has been ascribed to Huchown; this identification of our author was therefore natural, if not inevitable. In the following year Sir Frederic Madden, in his edition of *Sir Gawayne* [1839] accepted Dr. Guest's opinion that Huchown was its author. At the same time he recognized the fact that the poem in its present form is not in the Scotch dialect, and suggested as an explanation that it had been rewritten "by a scribe of the Midland counties." With this recognition that *Sir Gawayne* as we have it is in the Midland rather than the Scottish dialect, there was manifestly slender reason for continuing to suppose that Huchown was the author. At length, in 1864, Dr. Richard Morris dealt a decisive blow to the Huchown hypothesis by showing that "the uniformity and consistency of the grammatical forms is so entire that there is indeed no internal evidence of subsequent transcription into any other dialect than that in which they were originally written" [*Early English Alliterative Poems*]. Dr. Morris's conclusion that the language of these poems can be relied on as fixing the author's home in the West Midland district, has been accepted by later philologists. Nevertheless, in the face of the unanimous decision of the philologists that these poems are not the work of a Scottish poet, certain Scotch writers continue to ascribe them to Huchown. Their arguments, however, have not succeeded in carrying conviction.

A fresh attempt to find a name for the author of the Gawayne poetry was made in 1891 by Mr. I. Gollancz. In his edition of **The Pearl,** Mr. Gollancz brought forward the theory that these poems were written by Ralph Strode, but, with a candor which is rare in the advocates of a new theory, he admits that his identification is conjectural. "Though it be possible," he concludes, "to make a plausible surmise, one must acknowledge that the question still remains unanswered."

Here the matter rests at the present time. Nearly seventy years after the attention of scholars was first drawn to these poems, the question as to who wrote them is still an enigma. Some lucky chance may yet reveal the secret, but the probability is that, like the larger part of the literature of that age, they will continue to be unsigned documents. After all, the bare name of the author, if we had it, would not tell us much. It is his personality which we wish most to discover—his outlook on life, his attitude toward the social and religious institutions of his time. Though we lack the author's name, it is still possible through a study of the poems themselves to learn something of his character.

In the present paper, inquiry will be directed to one side of our author's character hitherto almost wholly overlooked: namely, his keen interest in matters of theology.

To begin with, one finds evidence of theological training in the intimate acquaintance with the Bible which the author of **The Pearl** everywhere displays, as well as in the frankly homiletical tone of his lesser poems, *Cleanness* and *Patience*.

In **The Pearl**, besides a paraphrase of the parable of the Laborers in the Vineyard (vv. 500-71), there is a lengthy description of the New Jerusalem (vv. 834-1143), which even in its details closely follows the vision in the Apocalypse. Moreover, in addition to these blocks of Biblical material, there are scattered throughout the poem many quotations of texts and phrases of Scripture, which, perhaps best of all, testify to the fact that the author's mind was saturated with Biblical knowledge.

In the other poems, *Cleanness* and *Patience,* the use of Scriptural material is even greater. In fact these poems are made up for the most part of paraphrases of Biblical stories, which serve the writer's homiletic purpose. Thus *Patience* teaches a lesson of God's long-suffering and readiness to forgive by the story of the Book of Jonah. The poem is introduced by an exposition of the Beatitudes, definitely cited as occurring in the Gospel of Matthew. *Cleanness* affords still better evidence of the wide range of the author's acquaintance with Biblical material. The whole poem consists of a series of Biblical *exempla,* held together, like so many beads on a string, by the thread of the author's purpose, which is to illustrate God's hatred of impurity, and the disasters which have followed uncleanness and sensuality. After relating the parables of the Marriage Feast and the Man without the Wedding Garment, the author turns to the Old Testament for examples of God's punishment of those who lived in impurity. The rest of the poem is taken up with the stories of the Fall of the Angels, the Flood, the Overthrow of Sodom, the Destruction of Jerusalem by Nebuchadnezzar, the Degradation of Nebuchadnezzar, Belshazzar's Feast, and the Capture of Babylon by Darius.

To be sure it is common enough to find compilations of Scriptural stories in the metrical homilies of the fourteenth century. But in several respects these poems are strikingly different from the metrical versions of the ordinary type.

In the first place, one notes the author's intelligent selection and combination of his Biblical material. An excellent example of this occurs in his treatment of the parable of the Marriage Feast [in *Cleanness*]. Here there is a skilful weaving together of the versions of the parable found in Matthew and in Luke. For the most part, the account in *Cleanness* follows Matthew, but the statement of the various excuses offered by the guests is taken from Luke. Clearly, the author was familiar with both versions. Again the story of the Destruction of Jerusalem, though depending in general on Jeremiah (52: 1-26), contains details derived from other portions of the Scriptures.

Furthermore, it should be noticed that our author handles his scriptural material with an accuracy of detail which is not to be met with in any of the other metrical versions. Two or three illustrations will suffice.

Compare, for instance, his version of God's announcement to Noah with the original text:

> Þe ende of alle-kyneʒ flesch þat on vrthe
>   meueʒ,
> Is fallen forþ wyth my face & forþer hit I
>   þenk,
> With her vn-worþelych werk me wlateʒ with-
>   inne,
> Þe gore þer-of me hatʒ greued & þe glette
>   nwyed;
> I schal strenkle my distresse & strye al
>   togeder,
> Boþe ledeʒ & londe & alle þat lyf habbeʒ.

"The end of all flesh is come before me; for the earth is filled with violence through them; and, behold, I will destroy them with the earth."

(Gen. 6:13)

In *Genesis and Exodus,* God's speech to Noah is omitted altogether, while in *Cursor Mundi* (vv. 1633-1660) the rendering is so free that it does not correspond at all to the Biblical phraseology. Again, in *Cleanness* (vv. 314-340) the directions for building the ark follow carefully the text of Genesis (6:14-21). In *Genesis and Exodus,* on the other hand, there is only a brief statement in five lines of the dimensions of the ark. The author of *Cursor Mundi* (vv. 1664-1686), curiously enough, appears to have regarded the dimensions of the ark as given in the Bible as extravagant, and accordingly he cuts down the length, breadth and height by an even half.

To take still another instance, compare the passage in *Cleanness* in which the Lord determines to tell Abraham his intention of destroying Sodom, with the Biblical text:

> How myʒt I hyde myn herte fro Habraham þe
>   trwe,
> Þat I ne dyscouered to his corse my counsayle
>   so dere.
> Syþen he is chosen to be chef chyldryn fader,
> Þat so folk shal falle fro, to flete alle þe
>   worlde,
> & vche blod in þat burne blessed shal worþe.

"And the Lord said, Shall I hide from Abraham that which I do; seeing that Abraham shall surely become a great and mighty nation, and all the nations of the earth shall be blessed in him?"

(Gen. 18:17-18)

There is nothing corresponding to this either in *Genesis and Exodus* or *Cursor Mundi*. One might easily cite a score of other passages in which our author follows the Scriptural narrative more closely than other paraphrasts. Taken together, they assure us that he was dealing with the Biblical text at first hand.

Finally, in *Cleanness* and *Patience* there is an almost complete absence of the legendary and apocryphal material which is so common in other homiletic literature of the time. The following are the only traces of such material which I have been able to discover:

1. The description of the Fall of the Angels. It is a question whether this legend should be classed as apocryphal, inasmuch as it established itself in the church at an early date and was a direct outgrowth of certain passages in the Scriptures themselves. Indeed, in the present case, the author seems to have derived his account of Lucifer's pride and its punishment from *Isaiah* 14:12 ff. This theme has been frequently treated by homilists, theologians and poets, in Latin, French and Anglo-Saxon. None of the mediæval versions which I have consulted, however, appears to be a direct source of the passage in *Cleanness*.

2. The injunction of Lot to his wife to use no salt in preparing the meal for the angel guests. Her disobedience of this command is one of the reasons why she was later turned into a pillar of salt. I have been unable to find the source of this detail of the story. It does not occur in Peter Comestor, *Cursor Mundi,* or *Genesis and Exodus*.

3. The account of the wonderful properties of the Dead Sea, and of the apples of Sodom. These marvels are mentioned in the numerous itineraries of the Holy Land current in the Middle Ages, and were widely copied into the homilies and cyclopedias. It is interesting to note that our author's description depends directly upon the pseudonymous *Book of Sir John Mandeville*.

4. In describing the birth of Jesus, it is stated in *Cleanness* that angels comforted the Madonna with music of organs and pipes, and that the ox and ass worshipped the child. Such details as these were, of course, universal in the stories of Holy Night, and through their very familiarity had ceased to be thought of as legendary.

5. There seems to be a reflection of some apocryphal account in the statement that Christ in cutting bread did not need to make use of a knife but broke it with his hands so that it was cut smoother than it could have been carved by all the "tools of Toulouse."

That one finds no more legendary material in these poems is certainly surprising. In the *Cursor Mundi,* or almost any of the metrical homilies of the mediæval period, the Biblical stories are freely interspersed with material drawn from the apocryphal books or from saints' lives. The contrast in this respect only serves to emphasize again the author's unusual fidelity in dealing with his Biblical material.

From this survey of the Biblical material in **The Pearl,** *Cleanness* and *Patience,* it seems moderately clear that the writer was an ecclesiastic. The extensive and unusually accurate knowledge of the Bible displayed in these poems points strongly in this direction. Moreover, two of them, *Cleanness* and *Patience,* are undisguisedly homiletic, both in purpose and method. It is difficult, therefore, to understand on what ground Mr. Gollancz denies the author's ecclesiastical character. He admits "the intensely religious spirit of these poems" and "the knowledge they everywhere display of Holy Writ," explaining this, however, by supposing that the poet "was at first destined for the service of the church," but that after receiving the first tonsure he went no further in holy orders. "The author of **Pearl,**" he declares, "was certainly no priest." No reason for this assumption is given, however; and I cannot help suspecting that in coming to this conclusion Mr. Gollancz had his eye on his conjectural Ralph Strode rather than on the poems themselves. The only one of the four poems which does not at first suggest the clerical character of its author is *Sir Gawayne*. Yet even in *Sir Gawayne* a careful reading discloses the author's moral and religious nature. The delicacy with which Gawayne's temptations at the castle of Bernlak are related reveals the same love of purity which one finds again in the homily on Cleanness. Nor has the poet been able, even in his romance, to banish wholly his Scriptural allusions. On being informed of the net which had been spread for him, Gawayne is ready with a list of Old Testament worthies who had been beguiled by women.

The opinion that the author of the **Pearl** was an ecclesiastic is confirmed by the fact that he shows a keen interest in the discussion of the theological questions of his day. For evidence of this interest in theology we must depend chiefly on **The Pearl.** *Cleanness* and *Patience,* being wholly homiletical in purpose, raise no questions of doctrine. In **The Pearl,** however, one finds a passage of some three hundred lines (vv. 421-719) which is nothing more or less than a sustained theological argument. This passage is noteworthy in many respects, and affords a basis for judging of the attitude taken by the author in the controversies in which the theologians of his time were engaged.

Before entering upon a consideration of this passage in **The Pearl,** however, it will be necessary to understand in a general way what were the controversies which agitated the theological world of that time. During the first half of the fourteenth century the interest of the theologians centred in two questions: (1) the dispute over predestination and free will, (2) the relative importance of grace and merit in the scheme of salvation. As to the question of predestination, one recalls Chaucer's testimony to the zeal with which it was debated in his time:—

> Witnesse on him that any perfit clerk is,
> That in scole is gret altercacioun
> In this matere, and greet disputisoun,
> And hath ben of an hundred thousand men.

These two questions were not entirely distinct, but were after all merely two phases of the controversy between the Augustinian party and those who inclined toward Pelagianism. Under the schoolmen of the twelfth and thirteenth centuries there had been a steady tendency toward Pelagian opinions. Emphasis was laid more and more upon man's free-will and consequently upon the positive merit obtainable by right conduct, while the doctrine of Augustine, that salvation was entirely a matter of predestination and divine grace, was pushed into the background.

In the first half of the fourteenth century there was a reaction against the Semi-Pelagianism of the schoolmen. The first English theologian who undertook to stem this tide of Pelagian tendency was Thomas Bradwardine—the same whom Chaucer mentions as able to "bulte to the bren" the question of predestination. When Bradwardine sat down to write his learned treatise, *De Causa Dei contra Pelagium,* he compared himself to the prophet Elijah who opposed single-handed the eight hundred and fifty prophets of Baal: "Ita et hodie in hac causa; quot, Domine, hodie cum Pelagio, pro Libero Arbitrio, contra gratuitam gratiam tuam, pugnant, et contra Paulum pugilem gratiae spiritualem? . . . Totus etenim paene mundus post Pelagium abiit in errorem." In another passage he refers to the almost universal prevalence of Pelagian opinions at Oxford when he was a student of theology there. The fundamental doctrine in Bradwardine's theology is that salvation is bestowed through the free grace of God, instead of being achieved by any merits. No less than eight chapters of his treatise are devoted to the defence of this doctrine. It is clear, then, that this doctrine of grace must have been a warmly debated question in fourteenth-century theology, and not merely a doctrinal commonplace.

Turning now to the passage in *The Pearl,* we find that the author takes the side of Bradwardine in exalting the grace of God as the sole ground of salvation. There are no finer or more fervent lines in the poem than the five stanzas that close with the refrain,—

> For þe grace of god is gret inoghe.

Indeed, as I shall attempt to show, the author of *The Pearl* goes beyond Bradwardine in the boldness with which he pushes the doctrine of free grace to its logical conclusion.

Let us first summarize briefly the argument of these three hundred lines of *The Pearl*:—

The "father," beholding in the dream his lost Pearl, and being told by her that she is a crowned queen in the heavenly kingdom, is filled with perplexity. "Is not Mary the queen of heaven?" he asks. In reply the maiden assures him that Mary indeed holds her empire over all that are in heaven, but that the court of the living God has this special property, that each one who arrives there is king or queen of all the realm. Each of the saints is pleased with the honor enjoyed by the others, so that jealousy and strife are unknown among them.

But the father is still unpersuaded that his Pearl can be a queen in the heavenly kingdom. When she died she was a child scarcely two years of age; she had done nothing in her brief life to please God—she did not even know pater noster or creed. With what justice, then, could God advance her to such honor? She might perhaps be a countess or some lady of lower degree, but a queen—that was too high a reward.

The maiden then replies to her father's objections by expounding the parable of the Laborers in the Vineyard. Some of those who were hired by the lord of the vineyard toiled through the heat and burden of the day; others came into the vineyard at the eleventh hour. But all were rewarded equally. She applies this parable to herself: it was eventide when she came to the vineyard, but she received the same reward with those who had toiled for years in the service of the Lord. Even by this parable the father is unconvinced. He tells his Pearl that her tale is unreasonable. God's justice is surely more discriminating than this, or Holy Writ is but a fable. Is it not written in the Psalter: "Thou rewardest every one according to his deserts?" Therefore, those who labor longer ought to receive greater reward.

To this the maiden replies by an exposition of the plan of salvation which extends from verse 600 to verse 743. These lines are the real climax of the poem. It is here that the emotion of the writer reaches its greatest intensity. In the kingdom of God, the maiden declares, there is no question of less and greater. All are paid equally, for upon all is poured the overflowing grace of God. As for the babes who died in infancy, they have been cleansed, at the moment of their birth, by baptism. Why should not the lord of the vineyard allow them their full reward? Paradise was lost through Adam's sin, but Christ paid the penalty and through baptism mankind is restored. There are, indeed, two kinds of persons whom God saves, one is the righteous man, the other is the innocent. But it is better to be saved by innocence than by righteousness. When Jesus walked upon earth he took the children in his arms and blessed them, saying "Of such is the kingdom of heaven."

It is evident, I think, that in this passage the author of **The Pearl** is consciously carrying on a theological discussion. His very earnestness shows that he is engaging in real debate and not merely repeating commonplaces. Furthermore, the objections which he puts into the mouth of the maiden's father appear to represent the arguments of real opponents.

Let us see now what is the main point in this theological argument. The author is laboring to prove that, since salvation is not at all a matter of merit but of grace, even a baptized child dying in infancy will receive in the heavenly kingdom a reward equal to that of the Christian who has lived a life of righteousness and holy works. For all the blessed shall be rewarded equally.

> Þe court of þe kyndom of god alyue,
> Hatȝ a property in hyt self beyng;
> Alle þat may ther-inne aryue
> Of alle þe reme is quene oþer kyng,
> & neuer oþer ȝet schal depryue,
> Bot vchon fayn of oþereȝ hafyng,
> & wolde her corouneȝ wern worþe þo fyue,
> If possyble were her mendyng.
> Bot my lady of quom Iesu con spryng,
> Ho haldeȝ þe empyre ouer vus ful hyȝe,
> & þat dyspleseȝ none of oure gyng,
> For ho is quene of cortaysye.

. . . . .

> "Of more & lasse in godeȝ ryche,"
> Þat gentyl sayde "lys no Ioparde,
> For þer is vch mon payed in-liche,
> Wheþer lyttel oþer much be hys rewarde,
> For þe gentyl cheuentayn is no chyche,
> Queþer-so-euer he dele nesch oþer harde,
> He laueȝ hys gysteȝ as water of dyche,
> Oþer goteȝ of golf þat neuer charde;
> Hys fraunchyse is large; þat euer dard,
> To hym þat matȝ in synne rescoghe
> No blysse betȝ fro hem reparde,
> For þe grace of god is gret Inoghe;

. . . . .

> Bot innoghe of grace hatȝ innocent,
> As sone as þay arn borne bylyne
> In þe water of baptem þay dyssente,
> Þen arne þay boroȝt in-to þe vyne,
> Anon þe day with derk endente,
> Þe myȝt of deth dotȝ to enclyne
> Þat wroȝt neuer wrang er þenne þay wente;
> Þe gentyle lord þenne payeȝ hys hyne,

> Þay dyden hys heste, þay wern þere-ine,
> Why schulde he not her labour alow,
> ȝyrd & pay hym at þe fyrst fyne
> For þe grace of god is grete innoghe?"

This is not the first time that the case of the baptized child dying in infancy has been made the subject of theological speculation. Augustine himself had used it most effectively in his controversies with Pelagius. And from Augustine to the fourteenth century the "baptized infant" played an important rôle in the treatises of the theologians. The author of **The Pearl,** then, is dealing with a familiar case.

It is all the more surprising, therefore, to find that his assertion that the baptized infant will receive equal reward with the adult is directly opposed to the established conclusion of the theologians. Turn, for example, to Bradwardine's treatise. As we have already seen, Bradwardine laid new stress upon the doctrine of grace; yet he never ventured to carry it to the extent of affirming the equality of the heavenly rewards. On the other hand, Bradwardine repeatedly uses this very notion of an infant receiving a reward equal to that of an adult as a convincing *reductio ad absurdam.* Thus, in one passage, he supposes for the sake of argument the case of two sons equal in grace and in all other respects except that one of them has committed some sin which makes him liable to a certain amount of temporal punishment. Now, let both sons, he continues, perform equal works of grace until the one who has sinned is wholly absolved from punishment. The other, then, in addition to absolution from punishment, either will or will not merit a certain reward in the future life:—

> "Non nihil omnino, quia tune posset contingere quod adultus baptizatus, diligens actualiter Deum summe, et in Sanctis operibus actualiter se exercens magno tempore vitae suae, etiam martyrium sustinens pro Christo, et lege ipsius, aequaliter praemiaretur in vita futura cum uno parvulo baptizato, qui nunquam aliquid boni fecit. Hoc enim consequitur evidenter, si haec omnia jungantur in poenitentiam congruam peccatori, aut si haec omnia aeque sufficiant pro satisfactione peccati seu peccatorum suroum; ubi est ergo quod utrumque testamentum creberrime repromittit, quod Deus unicuique secundum opera sua reddet?"

Or take another passage in which the same *reductio ad absurdam* is used to clinch the argument. What quantity of grace, Bradwardine asks, does the sinner immediately merit through his contrition? If you say that it will be large or small in proportion to the degree of his contrition, it would be possible, then, for one through a certain contrition, which we may call A, immediately to merit grace of the grade B, which must be either less than, equal to, or greater than baptismal grace, C:—

"Non minor, quia tune adultus qui per seipsum actualiter meruit, in casu decederet cum minore gratia, et transiret ad minorem gloriam quam parvulus tantummodo baptizatus. Quomodo ergo Deus unicuique secundum opera sua reddet, sicut utrumque Testamentum saepe testatur? . . . Si autem dicatur quod B est aequalis C, consequens est quod in casu, adultus qui per seipsum actualiter meruit, aequaliter praemietur cum parvulo tantummodo baptizato, qui numquam aliquid meruit: Quomodo ergo Deus unum quemque secundum opera sua et merita praemiabit?"

Still other passages of the same tenor are to be found in Bradwardine's treatise.

Now let us place beside these passages from Bradwardine the arguments which the author of **The Pearl** has put into the mouth of the objecting father in his debate with the maiden:

"Þy self in heuen ouer hyȝ þou heue,
To make þe quen þat watȝ so ȝonge,
What more-hond moȝte he a-cheue
Þat hade endured in worlde stronge,
& lyued in penance hys lynez longe,
With bodyly bale hym blysse to byye?
What more worschyp moȝt ho fonge,
Þen coround be kyng by cortayse?

Þat cortayse is to fre of dede,
ȝyf hyt be soth þat þou coneȝ saye,
Þou lyfed not two ȝer in oure þede,
Þou cowþeȝ neuer god nauþer plese ne pray,
Ne neuer nauþer pater ne crede,
& quen mad on þe fyrst day.
I may not traw, so god me spede,
Þat god wolde wryþe so wrange away."

. . . . .

Then more I meled & sayde apert,
"Me thynk þy tale vnresounable,
Goddeȝ ryȝt is redy & euer more ert,
Oþer holy wryt is bot a fable;
In sauter is sayd a verce ouerte
Þat spekeȝ a poynt determynable,
'Þou quyte vchon as hys desserte,
Þou hyȝe kyng ay pretermynable,'
Now he þat stod þe long day stable,
& þou to payment com hym byfore,
Þenne þe lasse in werke to take more able,
& euer þe lenger þe lasse þe more."

It will be observed that the objections raised by the father to the notion that a baptized child will receive equal reward with an adult entirely coincide with the views of Bradwardine—in both, even the very same verse of Scripture is appealed to. It is evident, then, that the author of **The Pearl** is representing real theo-

logical opponents in the statements which he puts into the mouth of the father.

But it is not to Bradwardine alone that the author stands opposed in his assertion that the rewards of the heavenly kingdom are equal. From the beginning of the fifth century, the existence of distinct grades of blessedness in the heavenly kingdom has been the established doctrine of the church. One of the chief grounds on which Jerome († 420 A.D.) attacked the heretic Jovinian, was that he affirmed an equality of rewards among the saints. In the writings of Augustine and Gregory the doctrine of grades of reward in heaven is repeatedly affirmed; and in the hands of the schoolmen it was expanded with rabbinical detail. Nor was this doctrine confined to the Latin treatises on theology; it found its way also into the more popular statements of doctrine which were written in the vernacular. Thus, we read in the *Poema Morale:*—

Ne mai non vuel ne non wane beon inne
  godes riche
Ðeh þer beð wunienges fele elc oþer vn-liche.
Sume þer habbet lasse murhðe and sume
  habbed more
After þan þe hi dude her, after þan þe hi
  swonke sore.

On the other hand, I have been unable to find a single orthodox theologian or poet, from the time of Jerome until the appearance of **The Pearl,** who asserts the equality of the heavenly rewards.

Now, can we suppose that the author of **The Pearl,** in his argument for the equality of the rewards of the blessed, was unaware that he was opposing the traditional doctrine of the theologians? On the face of it, such a supposition is difficult. For, as I have already pointed out, the whole tone of the passage in **The Pearl** suggests that the author was consciously arguing against persons who held an opposite opinion. The possibility that the author's variation from traditional theology was accidental is still further weakened, if not altogether destroyed, when we examine the theological history of the parable of the Laborers in the Vineyard, upon which he relies to establish his position.

It must not be imagined that the author of **The Pearl** was the first to perceive the bearing of this parable on the question of the rewards of the heavenly kingdom. It was this very parable to which the heretical Jovinian had appealed in support of his opinion that the heavenly rewards were equal. And, from Jerome to Duns Scotus, every theologian who discussed the question felt obliged to explain away the apparent inconsistency of this parable with the accepted doctrine of grades of blessedness.

In Augustine, for example, one finds the following:—

"Objectio de denario omnibus reddendo, contra diversitatem praemiorum.

Quid sibi ergo vult, inquiunt, ille denarius, qui opere vineae terminato aequaliter omnibus redditur; sive iis qui ex prima hora, sive iis qui una hora operati sunt? Quid utique, nisi aliquid significat, quod omnes communiter habebunt, sicuti est ipsa vita aeterna, ipsum regnum coelorum, ubi erunt omnes quos Deus praedestinavit, vocavit, justificavit, glorificavit? *Oportet enim corruptibile hoe induere incorruptionem, et mortale hoe induere immortalitatem:* hic est ille denarius, merces omnium.

Stella tamen *ab stella differt in gloria: sic et resurrectio mortuorum:* haec sunt merita diversa sanctorum. . . .

Ita quia ipsa vita aeterna pariter erit omnibus sanctis, aequalis denarius omnibus attributus est; quia vero in ipsa vita aeterna distincte fulgebunt lumina meritorum, multae mansiones sunt apud Patrem: ac per hoc in denario quidem non impari, non vivit alius alio prolixius; in multis autem mansionibus honoratur alius alio clarius."

In this way Augustine explains away the obvious meaning of the parable by making the penny paid to all alike represent the equal duration of the heavenly reward, but denying that it means an equal share in the blessedness of the heavenly kingdom.

The celebrated "Master of the Sentences," Peter Lombard († 1164 A.D.), gave a slightly different interpretation to the parable, but arrived at the same conclusion:—

"Nomine denarii aliquid omnibus electis commune intelligitur, scillicet, vita aeternae, Deus ipse, quo omnes fruentur, sed impariter. Nam sicut erit differens clarificatio corporum, ita differens gloria erit animarum. . . . Dos ergo est una, id est, denarius est unus; sed diversitas est ibi mansionum, id est, differentia claritatis," etc.

In the thirteenth century, Bonaventura discusses at length the question whether all the elect will enjoy equal blessedness:—

"Et quaeritur, utrum omnes habeant aequalem beatitudinem; et quod sic, videtur ex textu ubi dicitur quod omnes acceperunt singulos denarios, et quod Dominus tantum dedit novissimo quantum primo. Et Glossa dicit super illud; *Stella differt a Stella.* Eundem denarium paterfamilias dedit omnibus, qui operati sunt in vinea, quo utique non aliud significatur, quam id quod omnes communiter habebunt, sed illud non est nisi beatitudo: ergo, etc."

Bonaventura, however, is far from assenting to this interpretation of the parable:—

"Contra: *In domo patris mei mansiones multae sunt.* Augustinus; Multae mansiones in una vita erunt, quia variae praemiorum dignitates.

Item Apostolus: *Stella differt a stella in claritate.* Sic ergo claritas cognitionis generat gaudium, et delectationem, et gaudium.

Item ratione videtur, quia praemium respondet merito: sed constat aliquos esse majoris meriti: ergo et praemii."

He concludes, therefore, that although all will have the same blessedness, considered objectively, yet there will be a difference in the "quantity of joy."

Finally, in the treatises of Thomas Aquinas and of Duns Scotus one finds the parable of the Laborers discussed repeatedly, but in every case the obvious meaning of the parable is distorted to fit the theological doctrine of grades of reward among the blessed.

Clearly, then, the parable of the Laborers in the Vineyard was a stock passage in theological literature. Our author could scarcely have found a single discussion of the question of the heavenly rewards in which it was not quoted—and explained away. What is left for us but to conclude that the author of **The Pearl,** in introducing this parable into his argument, deliberately chose to give it an interpretation which he knew to be fundamentally opposed to that of the theologians? In support of his opinions he cites no patristic authority—it is doubtful if he could have found any—but appeals directly to the Scriptures; and, relying on his own interpretation of the biblical text, he ventures to reject the casuistries of scholastic theology.

Let no one suppose, however, that I am seeking to stamp the author of **The Pearl** as a schismatic. Nothing was further from his intention or desire than to separate himself from the great historic Church. Not only was he unswerving in his loyalty to the cardinal doctrines of Christianity, but he also gave his endorsement to some doctrines which to-day are peculiar to the Roman Church. It will be remembered that, according to his view, Mary was still the high empress of the heavenly kingdom. Also, in *Cleanness,* he insists upon the benefits of confession and shrift.

Yet, on the whole, it is evident that our author's attitude toward religious matters was evangelical rather than ecclesiastical.

(1) Holy Church is not once mentioned, nor the benefits to be gained from the prayers and merits of the saints— a favorite topic with religious writers in the Middle Ages.

(2) Again, even in the picture of the New Jerusalem, hierarchichal dignitaries have no place, but, instead, a truly democratic equality among the elect is represented.

(3) Still more significant is our author's disregard of patristic authority and tradition. We miss the familiar "as seynt Austen saith," or "thus writes the holy Gregory," which is so common in writers of the time. Instead, the author of **The Pearl** appeals directly to the authority of the Scriptures.

(4) Finally, one feels, in all four of the poems which he has left us, a deep ethical fervor. At the foundation of his theological system is his strong love of righteousness. His intuitive sense of justice leads him to make short work of doctrinal subtleties:

> Hit is a dom þat neuer god gaue,
> Þat euer þe gyltleȝ schulde be schente.

Cleanness is from first to last a sermon against unrighteousness and impurity. Nor does the author hesitate to administer a stinging rebuke to the unworthy conduct of the dissolute clergy who were the scandal of the religious orders:

> For wonder wroth is þe wyȝ þat wroȝt alle
>   þinge,
> Wyth þe freke þat in fylþe folȝes hym after,
> As renkeȝ of relygioun þat reden & singen,
> & aprochen to hys presens & prestes arn
>   called;
> They teen vnto his temmple & temen to hym
>   seluen,
> Reken with reuerence þay rechen his auter,
> Þay hondel þer his anne body & usen hit
>   boþe.

In this protest against the vices of the religious orders, he is, of course, in entire accord with the author of *Piers Plowman,* with John Wyclif, and with many other of his contemporaries, who were heartily tired of the abuses and scandals connected with the monastic and mendicant orders.

Indeed, these tendencies which I have designated by the term "evangelical," probably represented not alone an individual development on the part of our author, but also the slowly gathering sentiment among the most intelligent and truly religious people of his time. As early as the first half of the fourteenth century had begun the reaction against scholasticism. Even the theologians found the accumulating burden of "authorities" irksome, and appealed to commonsense. Thus Robert Holcot († 1349), in discussing the question whether the saints would rejoice over the sufferings of the damned, decided that they would not, because such jubilation over the misery of others would be in the highest degree despicable even on the part of persons in an imperfect state of grace, and much more so in the saints. Now, Holcot was far from being a heretic, yet in this opinion he turns his back upon Augustine and all the subsequent authorities.

This new emancipation of the religious spirit from the bondage of scholastic theology found one form of expression in the mystical fervors of a man like Richard Rolle of Hampole. At first sight, we might imagine that there was some spiritual kinship between Richard Rolle and the author of **The Pearl**. Both were men of devout spirit and deep religious enthusiasm. Rolle, as well as our author, lays special stress upon Divine grace, very probably having come under the personal influence of Bradwardine while a student at Oxford. There is indeed one sentence in Rolle's *De Gracia Dei* which is worth noting as an interesting parallel to our author's phrases. Rolle says: "God es no chynche of his grace, for he hase therof ynoghe." Compare with this **The Pearl,** vv. 604, 611:

> For þe gentyl cheuantayn is no chyche,
>
>   . . . . .
>
> For þe grace of god is gret Inoghe.

Nevertheless, I do not find evidence of any direct influence of Rolle upon our author. Moreover, there is between the two men a wide difference in temperament. Running through Rolle's writings there is a vein of morbidness; he shows a fondness for disagreeable, even disgusting, pictures of mortality and for excruciating scenes of hell torment, which the finer taste and more wholesome emotion of our author never allow.

Again, Rolle was strongly affected by the symbolism of the mystical school, while the author of **The Pearl** is singularly free from symbolistic interpretations. Surely if a writer cherished any fondness for symbolism he would have had ample opportunity to gratify it in the course of a description of the New Jerusalem, such as one finds in **The Pearl**. Yet our author refrains from introducing any symbolistic interpretation whatever, but contents himself with reproducing the pictures of the Apocalypse. To realize the difference between his method of treatment and that of the mystics, one needs only to turn, for example, to the description of Jerusalem in the writings of Bernard of Clairvaux.

Finally, it remains to inquire in what relation the author of **The Pearl** stood to the Wycliffite movement. On this point Mr. Gollancz is confident; he declares that "his allegiance to the authority of the church, to Papal supremacy, and to the doctrine of Rome, would have brought him most surely into active hostility with Wyclif and his partisans." Mr. Gollancz fails, however, to bring forward any specific passages in which our author declares himself in regard to these questions; and it is difficult to see how his views as to papal supremacy, for example, can be inferred from anything in the poems before us. For my part, I must believe that the assumption of a necessary antagonism between our author and Wyclif is unwarranted.

First of all, it should be remembered that the Wycliffite movement, though it afterwards ripened into a heresy, did not begin as one. In its earlier stages the agitation was concerned with manifest abuses in the church rather than with matters of doctrine. Indeed, in his earlier writings Wyclif showed no dissent from the doctrines of the Church. Take, for example, the question of prayers to Mary. Wyclif actually expressed his doubt whether anyone could be saved without the intercession of the Virgin. Again, one finds him closing one of his sermons with the words: "Truste we unto wordis of þe gospel and worschipe we Jesus and Marie wiþ alle our miȝt." Furthermore, in his system of theology Wyclif followed in the footsteps of Bradwardine, whom he frequently quotes in his treatises. Wyclif, like the author of *The Pearl*, laid emphasis upon the grace of God, rather than on merit, as the ground of salvation. It was not until 1381 that the reformer placed himself definitely in antagonism with the doctrine of the Church by his denial of transubstantiation. If the date ordinarily assigned to *The Pearl*—1370—is to be relied on, this poem would fall in the period of theological ferment, before Wyclif's opinions had thoroughly developed and been denounced as heretical. Whichever way the author's sympathies might have led him in the subsequent division of parties, I can find nothing in his temperament or religious attitude which would have brought him into antagonism with the earlier stages of the Wycliffite movement.

As I have already indicated, the progressive movement which profoundly affected the English church in the fourteenth century, though it afterwards came to be associated with Wyclif's name, was not in its beginning due to any single reformer. It was rather a widespread reaction against an arid and oppressive scholasticism. Such a poem as *The Pearl* well illustrates the new spirit that was stirring the age—the same spirit which later came to expression in Protestantism.

I have noted an interesting passage by Antonius Hiquaeus, the commentator on Duns Scotus, in which the doctrine of the equality of the heavenly rewards,—which, as we have seen, is explicitly taught in *The Pearl*,—is referred to as a distinctively Protestant heresy. Commenting on the passage in Duns Scotus cited above, Hiquaeus says:—

> "Hic se objicit haeresis Joviniani, qui dicebat beatitudinem fore aequalem in patria, ut patet ex Hieronymo contra eundem, ex hoc errore fortasse deducebat nullum esse meritum virginitatis: quem errorem docuit Lutherus, et alii Protestantes, qui

> posuerunt justitiam nostram non esse intrinsecam, sed esse justitiam Christi, et damnant justitiam operum. . . . Eandem veritatem docent omnes Patres et interpretes Scripturae. Patet Joannis 14: *In domo Patris mei mansiones multae sunt*, etc., quem locum de hac veritate inaequalitatis mansionum coelestium quoad gloriam inaequalem exponunt Patres."

Then follows a long list of Fathers and theologians who taught that the rewards of the heavenly kingdon are unequal. Finally, returning to Jovinian, Hiquaeus shows that his heresy had been based upon the parable of the Laborers in the Vineyard, and gives a detailed exposition of the parable in accordance with orthodox teaching.

Thus the theological argument in *The Pearl*, which we have been considering, is seen to be, at least in one respect, a most interesting and remarkable anticipation of sixteenth-century Protestantism.

Israel Gollancz (essay date 1921)

SOURCE: An introduction to *Pearl: An English Poem of the XIVth Century*, Cooper Square Publishers, Inc., 1966, pp. xi-lii.

[*In the following essay, Gollancz discusses the* Pearl *manuscript, its contents and date, the poem's place in English literature; the plan of the poem, its genre, and its relationship to its main sources; its imagery, meter, diction, and style; and the possible identity of its author.*]

'Pearl' *in the Lineage of English Poetry.*—While Chaucer was still learning from Guillaume de Machault and his followers the cult of the Marguerite, flower of flowers, as symbol of womanhood, a contemporary English poet had already found inspiration in the more spiritual associations of the Marguerite as the Pearl of Price.

It is indeed rather with the Prologue of 'The Legend of Good Women' than with Chaucer's earlier effort of 'The Book of the Duchess' that the poem of '**Pearl**' may best be contrasted, though Chaucer's Lament for Blanche the Duchess, as an elegy, invites comparison with '**Pearl**' as elegy. From this point of view, Chaucer's Lament seems somewhat unreal and conventional; our poem exercises its spell, not merely by its artistic beauty, but even more by its simple and direct appeal to what is eternal and elemental in human nature.

Again, its artistic form indicates the peculiar position that this early 'In Memoriam' holds in the progress of English poetry. It represents the compromise between the two schools of poetry that co-existed during the latter half of the fourteenth century, the period with which Chaucer is especially identified as its greatest and noblest product. On the one hand, there were the poets of the East Midland district, with the Court as its literary centre, who sought their first inspiration in the literature of France. Chaucer and his devotees were the representatives of this group, for whom earlier English poetry meant nothing, and whose debt to it was indeed small. These poets preluded 'the spacious times of great Elizabeth'; they were the forward link in our literary history. But there were also poets suggesting the backward link, whose literary ancestors may be found before the Conquest, poets belonging to districts of England where the old English spirit lived on from early times and was predominant, notwithstanding other influences. This school had its home in the West—along the line of the Welsh Marches, in Lancashire, Westmorland and Cumberland, well-nigh to the Tweed; and it is clear that in these regions not only did the old English spirit survive after the days of the Conquest, but also the old English alliterative measure was at no time wholly forgotten, until at last Langland and a band of other poets, whose names have not come down to us, revived this verse as an instrument of literary expression. In these West Midland poets, kinship in feeling with the older English tradition predominated, even as the Norman in the East Midland poets. It was not merely a matter of vocabulary and versification, though indeed Chaucer could not have appreciated Langland's poetry at its proper worth 'right for strangness of his dark langage,' to use the actual words of an East Midland poet concerning another, whose 'manner of speech and style' pronounced him 'of the West country.'[1] Langland, on the other hand, with his intensely didactic purpose, would have had but scant sympathy with the light-hearted and genial spirit of his greater contemporary.

But it would seem that there arose a third class of poets during this period, whose endeavour was to harmonise these diverse elements of Old and New, to blend the archaic Teutonic rhythm with the measures of Romance song. We see this already in the extant remains of lyrical poetry, especially in a number of those preserved in MS. Harl. 2253, dating from some years before the middle of the fourteenth century. The later political ballads of Minot and other fourteenth-century poems point also in this direction. But I can name no sustained piece of literature at all comparable with 'Pearl' as an instance of success in reconciling elements seemingly so irreconcilable. The poet of 'Pearl' holds, as it were, one hand towards Langland and one towards Chaucer; as poet of 'Sir Gawain and the Green Knight,' he was the direct precursor of the poet of the 'Faerie Queene,' and helps us to understand the true significance of Spenser as the Elizabethan poet *par excellence*. 'Pearl' stands on the very threshold of modern English poetry.

The Manuscript.—A kindly fate has preserved this poem from oblivion; a fate that has saved for us so much from the wreckage of time. Indeed, the Old English Muse must have borne a charmed life, surviving the many ills that ancient books were heirs to. Our knowledge of early English literature seems almost miraculous, when we note that so many extant works are preserved to us in unique MSS. 'Cotton Nero A. x.,' in the British Museum, is one of these priceless treasures. Bound up with a dull 'panegyrical oration' on a certain John Chedworth, Archdeacon of Lincoln in the fifteenth century, four English poems are contained in this small quarto volume, each of high intrinsic worth, and of special interest to the student of our early literature. The handwriting of the poems, 'small, sharp, and irregular,' belongs on the best authority to the latter years of the fourteenth century or the early fifteenth. There are neither titles nor rubrics in the MS., but the chief divisions are marked by large initial letters of blue, flourished with red, and several illuminations, coarsely executed, serve by way of illustration, all but one occupying a full page. The difficulty of the language of these poems and the strangeness of the script are no doubt answerable for the treatment they received at the hands of the old cataloguers of the Cottonian collection; probably few modern scholars before Warton, Conybeare, and Madden knew more of the poems than the first page of the MS., and from this they hastily inferred that the whole was a continuous poem 'in Old English, on religious and moral subjects,' or, 'Vetus poema Anglicanum, in quo sub insomnii figmento multa ad religionem et mores spectantia explicantur.' An old librarian, who attempted a transcription of the first four lines, produced the following result:

> Perle pleasaunte to prynces paye
> To claulx clos in gode soeter,
> Oute se wyent I hardely saye
> Ne proved I never her precios pere.

We now know that the MS. came to Sir Robert Cotton from the library of Henry Savile, of Banke in Yorkshire (1568-1617), a great collector, who secured rich spoils from the Northern monasteries and abbeys. To Madden belongs, it would seem, the credit of having shown for the first time that these earlier describers of the MS. had confused four distinct poems, and since his days the poems have received increased, though by no means adequate, attention from all students of our literature.

The Vision and the Allegory.—The first of the four poems, 'Pearl,' tells of a father's grief for a lost child, and how he was comforted, and learnt the lesson of resignation.

This briefly is the theme of the poem of 'Pearl.' A fourteenth-century poet, casting about for the form best suited for such a theme, had two sources of inspiration. On the one hand, there was that great storehouse of 'dream pictures,' 'The Romaunt of the Rose'; on the other, the symbolic pages of Scripture. A poet of the Chaucer school would have chosen the former, and the lost 'Marguerite' would have suggested an allegory of the 'flour that bereth our alder pris in figurynge,' and in his vision the 'Marguerite' would have been transfigured as the type of truest womanhood, a maiden in the train of Love's Queen, Alcestis. But the cult of the 'daisy' seems to have been altogether unknown to our poet, or at least to have had no attraction for him; his lost 'Marguerite,' a beloved child, was for him a lost jewel, a pearl, and 'he bethought him on the man that sought the precious Margarites, and when he had founden one to his liking, he solde all his good to buy that jewell.' The basis of the 'Vision' is this verse of the Gospel, together with the closing chapters of the Apocalypse. Mary, the Queen of Heaven, not Alcestis, Queen of Love, reigns in the visionary Paradise that the poet pictures forth.

The Pearl of the Gospel was a favourite allegorical theme with medieval theologians, but rarely with the poets.[2] I know of but one piece of English literature other than this poem in which it figures strikingly; it is poetical in thought though written in prose, and belongs to a later date than our poem. I allude to the 'Testament of Love,' a rather crude composition, the history of which we know now in relation to the life of its author, Thomas Usk, who was a contemporary and clearly a disciple of Chaucer. It is an obvious imitation of the 'Consolation of Philosophy' of Boethius; but in allegorising the Grace of God by 'a precious Margaret'—'Margarete of virtue,' for whose love he pines—the author may perhaps have been influenced by the poem of **'Pearl.'** Under any circumstances, the poem gives the prose work some interest; the 'Testament' shows how our poet has avoided the danger of being over mystical in the treatment of his subject. Where the poem is simple and direct, the prose is everywhere abstruse and vague, and Usk is forced to close his book with a necessary explanation of his allegory:—

> Right so a jewel betokeneth a gemme, and that is a stoon vertuous or els a perle, Margarite, a woman, betokeneth grace, lerning, or wisdom of God, or els Holy Church. If breed, thorow vertue, is mad holy flesshe, what is that our God sayth? It is the spirit that yeveth lyf; the flesshe, of nothing it profiteth. Flesshe is flesshly understandinge; flessh without grace and love naught is worth. The letter sleeth; the spirit yeveth lyfelich understanding. Charite is love, and love is charite.

God graunt us al therin to be frended!
And thus *The Testament of Love* is ended.

It is not my purpose to deal with the history of the pearl as treated allegorically from far-off times.[3] To do so would lead me into studies of Oriental mysticism; but there can be no doubt that in Hebrew symbolism the soul was likened to a pearl, the 'muddy vesture of decay' being regarded as the mere shell, or as the precious metal in which the jewel was set. 'It is meet,' said the Cabbalistic Rabbi, 'a man should have compassionate regard for his soul, the pure pearl which God has given to him, for it is not proper that he should defile it, but, as is said in the Talmud, should give it back to God pure as he received it.'[4] The Pearl of the Gospel links itself to this fine thought; and our poem emphasises this same aspect of the pearl as the undefiled spirit, the soul of the child, reclaimed by the Prince—the Pearl that He has set in the radiant gold of heaven, transcending its earthly setting in all the grace and charm of child-beauty. The Pearl has now been sundered from the shell. 'The sowle is the precious marguarite vnto God,' the good Knight of La Tour-Landry taught his daughters in his book, which, as I have attempted to show elsewhere, seems to have been well known to our poet.[5]

The Plan of the Poem.—Distraught with grief at the loss of his little daughter, the poet, prone on the child's grave, beholds her in a vision, gloriously transfigured.[6] He sees her radiant, clad in white, her surcoat and kirtle broidered with pearls, and on her head a pinnacled crown, her hair loose upon her shoulders, while 'a wonder pearl' is set upon her breast. The little child, as the very embodiment of Reason, or rather of Divine Sapience, disputes with the father on the error of impious grief, and explains that the whiteness of her robe and the crown on her head betoken her bridal as Queen of Heaven, and that though she has worked but little in the vineyard of earth, her innocence has given her the like reward with those who by righteousness have won the crown. All who enter the realm are kings and queens. The pearl she wears is the token of the bride's betrothal—a token, too, of Truce with God. And the father is begged by his child to purchase his peace, even as the merchant of the Gospel, having found one pearl of price, sold his all to buy it. By her exposition of the Parable of the Vineyard, Pearl explains that, little child as she was, she reached at once the great goal of queenship in the court of heaven, where Mary reigns as Empress. For the father it would have sufficed had she attained the state of countess, or even of a lady of less degree. But, he urges, surely she and her peers dwell in some great manor or within castle-walls. Could he not behold their dwelling-place? In the vision the father is on one side of the stream, his transfigured child on the other, and she tells him that by Divine grace he is to be granted a sight of their glorious home. She bids him follow on his side, while she shows the way on hers, until he reaches a hill. Then, as the seer of Patmos, from a hill he beholds the New Jerusalem descending as a bride from heaven, and the

City of God, as pictured by the Apostle, is revealed to him in all its glory and rich radiance.[7] Amid the golden splendour, dazzling as the light of the sun, suddenly there appears within the citadel a procession of maidens, as moons of glory, all crowned and clad in self-same fashion, gentle 'as modest maids at Mass.' And lo, among them he beholds his 'little queen,' who he thought had stood by him in the glade. The sight of his lost Pearl is too much for his lovelonging, and not-withstanding the earlier warning that no one living could pass the stream, the dreamer dashes forward to plunge, determined to cross. The movement wakes him, and he declares that the lesson of resignation has now been learnt.

The Poem in Relation to its Main Sources.—As I read the poem, it seems to me that its scheme is elaborated from the one thought of the transfiguration of the child, and that the poet successively explains the significance of the spotless whiteness of her attire, of the regal crown she wears, of the pearl of price; and then, by a natural culmination, proceeds to portray the heavenly dwelling—the New Jerusalem.

For the last, he naturally paraphrased Revelation xxi. and other passages from the Apocalypse of St. John, which book indeed inspired his whole conception of the mystical bridal,—'And to her was granted that she should be arrayed in fine linen, clean and white,' Rev. xix. 8. Truly, white is almost the burden of the poet's description of the maiden's robe, her kirtle and all her vesture, her crown, and the pearls that bedeck her. It is of interest to contrast this emphasis on 'white' with the more direct but less effective reference,

> And gode faire *Whyte* she hete,
> That was my lady name right,[8]

and the lines which follow, in which Chaucer appraises Blanche, Duchess of Lancaster. To Chaucer the possibilities of the name with reference to its spiritual significance were hardly present; in our poet's mind the text is uppermost concerning those 'which have not defiled their garments; and they shall walk with me in white, for they are worthy,' Rev. iii. 4.

With obvious delight in pictorial description, the poet depicts the white surcoat,[9] with its hanging lappets, after the fashion of those of highest degree, and leads up to the crown, with its whiteness of pearl and its ornamentation of flowers, the aureole of maidenhood. In the Apocalypse it is the Elders that have on their heads the crowns of gold, but the coronation of the Virgin as empress of heaven, and of the brides as queens, forms a very integral part of medieval homiletic literature as of medieval art.[10] The allegorical interpretation of the Song of Songs in relation to the bridal of the Apocalypse seems to have influenced this idea of the crowning: 'Go forth, O ye daughters of Sion, and behold King

Solomon with the crown wherewith his mother crowned him in the day of his espousals' (Song of Solomon iii. II). A like crown was bestowed upon the bride.[11] 'Come with me from Lebanon, my spouse, with me from Lebanon' (iv. 8), became the burden of the mystical Epithalamium. Thus our poet applies the words in Stanza lxiv, 11. 763-4. So, too, in 'Olympia' we have '*De Libano nunc sponsa veni* sacrosque hymenaeos' as the heavenly songs they sing; and in the 'Song of Great Sweetness,' belonging to the early fifteenth century, there is the same application,—'Veni de Libano . . . veni coronaberis.'[12] The main portion of our poem is drawn from the Parable of the Vineyard and the Apocalypse, and is the amplification of the Gospel text concerning the Pearl of Price in its twofold application, as typifying on the one hand ideal maidenhood, that is, the jewel 'above rubies,'[13] and on the other the Kingdom of Heaven, the Peace of God.

In the earlier part of the poem, both in the description of the spice-garden, where Pearl is at rest, and in the visionary scenes through which the poet passes till he comes to the sundering stream beyond which he sees the 'maiden of mensk,' he is haunted by the dream-pictures of the 'Romaunt of the Rose,' and even Divine Love seems to the bereft father to be 'Luf-Daungere,' that is, Love the Severer, as in the Romaunt, 'Daunger' is the power that keeps the lover from the object of his love. And Pearl, as portrayed and in her utterance, recalls the figure of Reason drawn by William de Lorris (*cp.* Chaucerian version, ll. 3189-216). The wells joined by conduits, in the garden of Sir Mirth, are very directly referred to by our poet in his description of the country of his dream. Thereafter, the Romaunt, save for a few slight echoes, gives place to the Scriptures. The stream is not the artificial conduit of the Garden of the Rose, but, whatever its Biblical source, its beauty has been suggested by the river in the Romaunt described before the Lover reached the garden.

> Et pavé
> *Le fons* de l'iaue de gravele,

which in the Chaucerian rendering is as follows,—

> paved everydel
> With gravel, ful of stones shene
>   (ll. 126-7)

becomes richly transformed in '**Pearl**'; but the words 'in þe founce' betray the direct source of the lines,—

> In þe founce þer stonden stoneȝ stepe,
> As glente þurȝ glas þat glowed & glyȝt,' etc.
>   (ll. 113 ff.).

Metre, Diction, and Style.—The stanzaic form of '**Pearl**,' twelve lines with four accents, rhymed according to the scheme *a b a b a b a b b c b c,* and combining rhyme with alliteration, may have been used by previous poets, but it is diffcult to say whether any of the extant poems in this metre, which seems to have been popular, belong to a date earlier than '**Pearl.**'[14] But not one of them is comparable to our poem in rhythm, beauty of well-defined cæsura, and dignity of movement. There are in '**Pearl**' 101 such stanzas. These divide again into twenty sections, each consisting of five stanzas, having the same refrain; section fifteen is exceptional, with six stanzas. Throughout the poem the last or main word of the refrain is caught up in the first line of the next stanza. Finally, the last line of the poem re-echoes the first, and rounds the whole.

While alliteration is used effectively by the poet, he does not attempt to employ it rigidly, or sacrifice thereto either thought or feeling.

I can point to no direct source to which the poet of '**Pearl**' was indebted for his measure; that it belongs to French or Provencal poetry, I have little doubt. These twelve-line stanzas seem to me to resemble, in effect, the earliest form of the sonnet more than anything else I have as yet discovered. Perhaps students may find 'a billow of tidal music one and whole' in the 'octave,' and in the closing quatrain of the verse the 'ebbing' of the sonnet's 'sestet.' It is noteworthy that the earliest extant sonnet, that of Pier delle Vigne, for a knowledge of which we are indebted to J. A. Symonds, has the same arrangement of rhymes in its octave as the stanzas of '**Pearl**,' viz., *abababab.* Be this as it may, all will, I hope, recognise that there is a distinct gain in giving to the 101 stanzas of the poem the appearance of a sonnet sequence, marking clearly the break between the initial octave and the closing quatrain. In the MS. there is no such indication. When '**Pearl**' was written, the sonnet was still foreign to English literature; the poet, if he knew of this form, wisely chose as its counterpart a measure less 'monumental,' and more suited for lyrical emotion. The refrain, the repetition of the catch-word of each verse, the trammels of alliteration, all seemed to have offered no difficulty; and as far as power over technical trammels contributes to poetic greatness, the author of '**Pearl**' must take high rank among English poets.

To judge by the result, our poet seems to have discovered the artistic form best suited for his subject. With a rich vocabulary at his command, consisting, on the one hand, of alliterative phrases, 'native mother-words,' derived from his local dialect, in which English, French, and Scandinavian elements were strikingly blended, and on the other hand, of words and allusions due to knowledge of Latin and French literature, he succeeded in producing a series of stanzas so simple in syntax, so varied in rhythmical effect, now lyrical, now epical, never undignified, as to leave the impression that no form of metre could have been more suitably chosen for this elegiac theme.

It has been alleged that the diction of the poem is faulty in too great copiousness. On the contrary, the richness of its vocabulary seems to me one of its special charms, and this might be well illustrated by comparing such a section of the poem as the Parable of the Vineyard with the earlier poetical version of the same parable in MS. Harl. 2253, or with the Wycliffite prose version.

Imagery.—The wealth and brilliancy of the poet's descriptions have been the subject of criticism. But surely this richness is what one would expect in a poem, the inspiration of which is mainly derived from the visionary scenes of the Apocalypse, with its pictorial phantasies, and the 'Roman de la Rose,' with its personifications and allegory. The poet's fancy revels in the richness of the heavenly and the earthly paradise, but it is subordinated to his earnestness and intensity. The heightened style of '**Pearl**' responds, moreover, to the poet's own genius for touching vividly his dream-pictures with rich imagery and bright colour. The wealth and brilliancy pervading '**Pearl**' may still delight those theorists who seek in our literature that 'fairy dew of natural magic,' which is supposed to be the peculiar gift of the Celtic genius, and which can be discovered as 'the sheer inimitable Celtic note' in English poetry. It would, I think, be fair to say that the Apocalypse has had a special fascination for the poet because of its almost Romantic fancy, and that he has touched certain scenes of the book with a brilliancy of colour and richness of description altogether foreign to the Germanic strain of our literature. '**Pearl**' finds its truest counterpart in the delicate miniatures of medieval missals, steeped in richest colours and bright with gold, and it is just those scenes of the Apocalypse which the old miniaturists loved to portray, one might better say lived to portray, that seemed to have been uppermost in our poet's mind,—such favourite themes as, 'I looked, and behold, a door was opened in heaven,' which gave special scope to medieval artists. On the title-page of this book will be found an imprint from one of these old miniatures; it is part of an illustration to the verse just quoted, and may well apply to our poet,

> Falling with his weight of cares
> Upon the world's great altar-stairs.

The Poet's Sources: (1) The Bible; (2) The Roman de la Rose.—The poet's main sources of inspiration were, as already indicated, the Bible and the 'Roman de la Rose,' that secular Bible of medieval poets. The latter pervades his fancy, and influences thought, diction, and imagery, while, when once he has chosen as his theme the Pearl of the Gospel and the problem of the Parable of the Vineyard, the former dominates his whole conception. Whatever theological questions may be enunciated in the course of the poem, '**Pearl**' is to my mind, without a doubt, an elegiac poem expressive of personal grief, a poet's lament for the loss of his child, and in its treatment transcends the scholastic and theological discussions of the time.

The Question of Boccaccio's 'Olympia,' and Dante.—An attempt has been made to demonstrate that **'Pearl'** is merely allegorical and theological, but this view ignores or fails to recognise the personal touches whereby the poem soars above all theological questions, and makes its simple and direct appeal to the human heart. It is of great interest that, soon after 1358, some years before **'Pearl,'** Boccaccio wrote an elegy on his young daughter Violante—the Latin Eclogue 'Olympia.' There is no clear evidence that this most charming of Boccaccio's shorter poems was known to our poet, or was one of his sources of inspiration. 'Olympia,' however, may well be considered as a companion poem, of the highest interest and fascination both intrinsically and for the purposes of comparative study. Accordingly, the Latin text, with a translation, is included in the present volume, together with a brief introductory study of its history and the question of its relation to **'Pearl.'**

I can trace no direct influence of Dante on our poet, though parallels may be found, both in the 'Divina Commedia' and the 'Vita Nuova,' as regards conception, imagery, and description. However striking the similarities may appear, these parallels are due, in my opinion, to similar thought, and to the common methods of medieval mysticism. It cannot be proved that our poet was acquainted with the writings of the greatest mind of the medieval age. Yet again, it is not without profit for the student of **'Pearl'** to re-read the Divine Comedy and the New Life, and to recognise Pearl's spiritual kinship to Dante's Beatrice.

The Poet and English Writers.—The author was no doubt acquainted with English poets, his contemporaries and predecessors. He would have been attracted to the writings of Hampole and other mystics, and also to the English homilies on Holy Maidenhood,[15] the English legends of Saints, especially those dealing with St. Margaret. He was a disciple of the alliterative poets. As regards Chaucer, I can discover no trace of influence. The 'Book of the Duchess,' which is adduced as a source of inspiration, is but another elegiac poem belonging to the same *genre* as **'Pearl.'** That Chaucer should refer to Blanche as the Phœnix of Araby, and that the poet of **'Pearl'** applies the same term to the Virgin Mary, cannot be taken seriously as evidence of direct influence; and so, too, with other medieval conventional phrases or ideas common to the two elegies.

We know from his other poems that he was acquainted with French contemporary literature, the romances of chivalry, and mandeville's Travels. In **'Pearl'** so far we have not succeeded in finding any traces of the influence of this secular literature, though perhaps in such a charming touch as we find in ll. 489-92,

> As countess, damosel, *par ma fay*,
> 'Twere fair in heaven to hold estate,
> Or as a lady of lower degree,
> But Queen,—it is too high a goal,

we have a note suggestive of a writer who would have been specially interested in the higher social life depicted in romances of courtesy and chivalry.

The MS. Illustrations of the Poems.—The pictorial character of his poem could not have escaped the poet. The unique MS. of **'Pearl'** contains four crude illustrations depicting its chief episodes. In the first, the author is represented slumbering in a meadow, by the side of a beflowered mound (not a stream, as has been said), clad in a long red gown with falling sleeves, turned up with white, and a blue hood attached round the neck. Madden and others who have described the illustrations have not noticed that there are wings—'wings of fancy'—attached to the shoulders of the dreamer, and a cord reaching up into the foliage above, evidently intended to indicate that the spirit has 'sped forth into space.' In the second, the same figure appears, drawn on a larger scale, and standing by a river. In the third, he is again represented in a similar position, with his hands raised, and on the opposite side. is Pearl, dressed in white, in the costume of the time of Richard the Second and Henry the Fourth; her dress is buttoned tight up to the neck, and on her head is a crown. In the fourth, the author is kneeling by the water, and beyond the stream is depicted a castle or palace, on the embattled walls of which Pearl again appears, with her arm extended towards him. I had the good fortune to induce my ever-revered friend, the late W. Holman Hunt, to give Pearl a place in the history of English art, and by way of contrast to the illustrations of the MS., now reproduced, the portrayal of the poet's theme as conceived by the greatest of modern Pre-Raphaelites is given as frontispiece to the present volume.

Two illustrations follow after the pages of **'Pearl'**; they are evidently intended to represent respectively Noah and his family in the Ark, and the prophet Daniel expounding the writing on the wall to the affrighted Belshazzar and his queen. It is clear that these have nothing to do with the subject of **'Pearl'**; they belong to a second poem, written in a distinctly different metre, the short lines of **'Pearl'** giving place to longer lines, alliterative and rhymeless. The subject of the poem is its first word, 'Cleanness,' and it relates in epic style the lessons of the Flood, the fall of Sodom and Gomorrah, Belshazzar's fate, in order to exemplify the Divine resentment that visits the impenitent who are guilty of faults of 'Uncleanness.' A prelude on the parable of the Marriage Feast precedes, and by way of illustrating Divine moderation, the Fall of the Angels and the Fall of Man are briefly handled.

In the MS. two new pictures precede what is obviously a third poem. The medieval artist is evidently representing episodes in the life of Jonah. The poem is a metrical rendering of the story of Jonah, and is in the same metre as 'Cleanness'; the subject, too, is indicated by its first word, 'Patience.'

It is noteworthy that both these alliterative poems, though rhymeless, are intentionally written in quatrains, and the recognition of this devide is necessary for their right understanding and appreciation.

Links with 'Cleanness' and 'Patience.'—These two poems, 'Cleanness' and 'Patience,' may actually be, or may well be regarded as pendants to **'Pearl,'** dwelling more definitely on its two main themes—purity and submission to the Divine will. The link that binds 'Cleanness' to **'Pearl'** is unmistakable. The significance of the pearl is dwelt on as symbol of the purified spirit:—

> How can'st thou approach His court save thou
>   be clean? . . .
> Through shrift thou may'st shine, though thou
>   hast served shame;
> Thou may'st become pure through penance,
>   till thou art a pearl.
>
> The pearl is praised wherever gems are seen,
> Though it be not the dearest by way of
>   merchandise.
> Why is the pearl so prized, save for its purity,
> That wins praise for it above all white stones?
> It shineth so bright, it is so round of shape,
> Without fault or stain, if it be truly a pearl.
> It becometh never the worse for wear,
> Be it ne'er so old, if it remain but whole.
>
> If by chance 'tis uncared for and becometh
>   dim,
> Left neglected in some lady's bower,
> Wash it worthily in wine, as its nature
>   requireth:
> It becometh e'en clearer than ever before.
>
> So if a mortal be defiled ignobly,
> Yea, polluted in soul, let him seek shrift;
> He may purify him by priest and by penance,
> And grow brighter than beryl or clustering
>   pearls.
>
> One speck of a spot may deprive us even
> Of the Sovereign's sight who sitteth on high. . . .
>
> As the bright burnished beryl ye must be
>   clean,
> That is wholly sound and hath no flaw;

> By ye stainless and spotless as a margery
>   pearl.
> ('Cleanness,' ll. 1110, 1115-32, 551-2, 554-6.)

Similarly, it would be an easy matter to point out links that bind together the poems of 'Cleanness' and 'Patience.' We find in each of them the same didactic purpose, the same strength of descriptive power, the same delight in nature, more especially when agitated by storm and tempest, the same rich gift of expression, and the same diction and rhythm. But if there were any question of the identity of authorship, the descriptions of the Deluge from 'Cleanness' and of the sea-storm which overtook Jonah from 'Patience' would, I think, be almost adequate proof; the writer of the one was most certainly the writer of the other.

'Pearl' and 'Sir Gawain.'—A fourth poem follows 'Cleanness' and 'Patience' in the MS. As one turns the leaves, it becomes clear at a glance that the metre of the poem is a combination of the epic alliterative measure and the rhyming verse of romances of the 'Sir Thopas' type; for a lyrical burden, introduced by a short line of one accent, and rhyming according to the scheme *ababa,* breaks the sequence of the unrhymed alliterative lines at irregular intervals, producing the effect of stanzas averaging some twenty lines.

The poem is illustrated much in the same way as those that precede it, the scriptural pictures yielding to scenes of medieval romance. In the first a headless knight on horse-back carries his head by its hair in his right had, looking benignly at an odd-eyed bill-man before him; while from a raised structure above him a king armed with a knife, his queen, an attendant with a sabre, and another bill-man look on. Three other illustrations, dealing with various episodes of the poem, are added at the end. One of them represents a stolen interview between a lady and a knight. Above the picture is written the following couplet:

> Mi mind is mukel on on, that will me noght
>   amende,
> Sum time was trewe as ston, and fro schame
>   couthe her defende.

The couplet has proved a crux. 'It does not appear,' wrote Sir Frederick Madden, 'how these lines apply to the painting'; Dr. Morris quoted the remark without comment. We shall see the possible value of the cryptic lines later on But first concerning the subject of the poem. It is the well-known romance of Sir Gawain and the Green Knight,—the weird adventure that befell Sir Gawain, the son of Loth and nephew of King Arthur, the favourite hero of medieval romance, popular more especially in the west and northern parts of England, where in all probability traditions of the knight lived on from early times. The English Gawain literature of the fourteenth century, though for the most part derived from

French originals, betrays on all sides the writers' eagerness to satisfy popular enthusiasm for the hero's ideal character. Sir Gawain was indeed the Sir Calydore of Spenser's fourteenth-century precursor,—

> beloved over all,
> In whom it seems that gentlenesse of spright
> And manners mylde were planted naturall,
> To which he adding comely guise withall
> And gracious speech did steal men's hearts
> away.
> Nathless thereto he was full stout and tall,
> And well approved in batteilous affray,
> That did him much renowne, and far his fame
> display.

The fourteenth-century poets of the West and North of England regarded Gawain, 'the falcon of the month of May,' as the traditional embodiment of all that was chivalrous and knightly. The depreciation of the hero in later English literature was doubtless due to the direct influence of one particular class of French romances, and it is from these very romances that modern Englishmen ultimately derive their view of Gawain's character. 'Light was Gawain in life, and light in death,' is the thought that rises now in every English mind at mention of the hero's name. I know but one passage in the whole of early English poetry where the knight is similarly characterised; it is significantly by an East Midland poet, probably the last of English men of letters to write in Anglo-French. In one of his Anglo-French ballades the 'moral' Gower, singing in praise of truest constancy, declares:

> Cil qui tout ditz change sa fortune,
> Et ne voet estre en un soul lieu certein
> Om le poet bien resembler a Gawein,
> _Courtois d'amour, mais il fuist trop volage._

During the second half of the fourteenth century there was special activity in the western districts of England in the making of Gawain romances, the poets vying with each other in their glorification of the hero.

The Arthurian literature of the reign of Edward III. may well be considered in relation to that monarch's attempt to revive at Windsor some of the glories of Camelot, and the present poem may be in some way suggested by the Order of the Garter, or connected with the bestowal of the Order upon some noble, in honour of whom Gawain was depicted with such obvious enthusiasm on the part of the poet. It is noteworthy that at the end of the MS. of the romance a somewhat later hand has written the famous legend of the Order:

> Hony soit qui mal penc.

There is, moreover, stronger confirmation of this aspect of the poem. A later poet, to whom we are indebted for a ballad of 'The Green Knight,'—a _rifacimento_ of this romance, or of some intermediate form of it,—has used the same story to account for the origin of another Order. Evidently aware of its original application, but wishing to make his ballad topical, he ends it with the following reference to the Knighthood of the Bath, then newly instituted:

> All the Court was full faine
> Alive when they saw Sir Gawain,
> They thanked God abone;
> That is the matter and the case,
> Why Knights of the Bath wear the lace,
> Until they have wonnen their shoon.

> Or else a ladye of high estate
> From about his necke shall it take
> For the doughtye deeds that hee hath done;
> It was confirmed by Arthur the King,
> Thorow Sir Gawain's desiringe,
> The King granted him his boone.

This theory gives us, at all events, a _terminus a quo_ for the date of the romance of Gawain; it must belong to some year later than 1345, the probable date of the foundation of the Order of the Garter. Language, diction, thought, rhythm, power of description, moral teaching, vividness of fancy, artistic consciousness, and love of nature, all link this most remarkable Spenserian romance to '**Pearl**,' 'Cleanness,' and 'Patience'; and for a right understanding of the poet and his work the four poems must be treated together. The relation that they bear to one another, as regards time of composition, cannot be definitely determined.

Probable Date.—There is no definite evidence for the date of '**Pearl**.' General considerations of language point to the second half of the fourteenth century. In view, however, of evidence adduced by me enabling us to fix 1373 as the earliest date for 'Cleanness,' it may be safe to accept about 1370 as the date of composition of '**Pearl**,' if we are right in assuming that the elegy preceded the homily. 'Patience' and 'Cleanness' must certainly belong to about the same time. The workmanship and skill of 'Gawain,' to say nothing of its tone and pervading spirit, are so transcendent as to make it difficult for one to assign the poem to a date at all near that of 'Cleanness' and 'Patience,' unless we have here an instance of an early achievement of a poet's genius which, for some cause or other affecting its buoyancy, joy in life, and enthusiasm for romance, failed to maintain its power. On the whole, I am at present inclined to the view that a long period intervened between the homiletic poems and the matured excellence of 'Gawain.' Yet again in this poem we have a striking reference to the pearl:

> As perle bi þe quite pese is of prys more,
> So is Gawayn, in god fayth, bi oþer gay
> knyȝteȝ,—

'as the pearl is of greater price than white pease, so is Gawain, in good faith, than other gay knights.'

Huchown and the Alliterative Poems.—And who was the poet to whom we are indebted for these remarkable poems? The question must still remain unanswered. Unfortunately no tradition concerning their authorship has come down to us, and no definite link has as yet been discovered connecting the poems with any name. Some fifty years back, Dr. Guest, the historian of English Rhythms, set up a claim for a Scotch poet, Huchown by name, but this claim cannot stand the test of philological analysis, in spite of any circumstantial evidence in its favour. The story of Huchown's supposed connection with the poems is an interesting piece of literary history. Andrew of Wyntown, in his 'Orygynale Cronykil' of Scotland, written at the end of the fourteenth century, mentions a poet, Huchown of the 'Awle Ryale,' who, in his 'Gest Hystoriale,'

> Called Lucius Hiberius Emperoure,
> When King of Britain was Arthoure.

The chronicler excuses the poet, for the mistake was not originally his, and adds enthusiastically:

> men off gud dyscretyowne
> Suld excuse and love Huchowne,
> That cunnand was in literature.
> He made the gret Geste of Arthure
> And the Awntyre of Gawane,
> The Pystyll als off Swete Susane.
> He wes curyws in his style,
> Fayre off fecund, and subtylle,
> And ay to plesans and delyte
> Made in metyre mete his dyte,
> Lytil or nocht nevyrtheles
> Waverand fra the suthfastnes.

Huchown was therefore the author of an 'Adventure of Gawain.' Is the poem referred to identical with the 'Gawain' poem described above, the romance written by the author of **'Pearl'**? Most certainly not. The 'Pystyll of Susan' mentioned by Wyntown is extant; all are agreed in regarding it as Huchown's work: it is a rhyming poem, and therefore of special worth as a criterion of dialect. The result of a comparative study of this poem and of **'Pearl'** proves conclusively that they are in different dialects, the one belonging to a district north of the Tweed, the other to a more southern district. **'Pearl'** cannot, therefore, be the work of the poet of the 'Pystyll'; and if this is true of **'Pearl,'** it is equally true of 'Gawain.' It is, moreover, very probable that Huchown's 'gret geste of Arthure' is preserved to us, though in a changed dialect and with some slight intentional modifications, in the alliterative 'Morte Arthur,' and that the 'Awntyre of Gawane' may be identified with the 'Awntyrs off Arthure at the Terne Wathelyne,' which, as far as diction is concerned, is closely connected with the 'Pystyll of Susan.'

Dr. Guest rested his claims for Huchown not merely on this passage from Wyntoun's Chronicle. In the blank space at the head of 'Gawain and the Green Knight,' a hand of the fifteenth century has written 'Hugo de _____,' and this piece of evidence seemed to him to confirm his view of the authorship of the poem. In the first place, it is not certain that the inscription is intended for the name of the author, but even had we clear proof that 'Hugo de aula regali' was to be read, the conclusion, from internal evidence, would be forced upon us, that the writer had made a mistake by no means uncommon in the fifteenth and sixteenth centuries. The great masters of literature have always been made the official fathers of unclaimed productions. It would be easy enough to illustrate this from the pseudo-Chaucerian poems, but an interesting parallel may be adduced from the literary history of Huchown's great contemporary, Barbour. In the Cambridge University Library there is a MS. of Lydgate's 'Troy Book.' Some portion of Lydgate's work has been lost and is replaced by extracts from a version by a northern poet. The scribe definitely assigned these inserted passages to Barbour merely on the evidence of a general likeness in style, but minute investigation places it beyond doubt that the fragments are not from the pen of the author of the 'Bruce.'

The works of five individual poets have, at different times, been fathered on Huchown;[16] of these poems some are undoubtedly West Midland, others genuinely Scottish, but all of them belong to the great period of alliterative poetry, the second half of the fourteenth century or the early years of the fifteenth, and show the influence of that school of English poets that strove on the one hand to revive the old English measure, and on the other to combine this archaic rhythm with the most complex of Romance metres. In the fifteenth century the tradition of this West Midland influence still lived on north of the Tweed, but the greatest of Scottish bards turned to the East Midland poets for their forms, and, following the example of their poet-king, were fascinated by the irresistible spell of Chaucer's genius. This influence of the great English poet on the chief poets of Scotland has received abundant recognition; not so the earlier influence of the West Midland poets, whose best representative is the nameless author of **'Pearl.'**

From among all these poems only one can be singled out as being possibly by the author of **'Pearl.'** On the strength of diction, metre, and other characteristics, the anonymous alliterative poem of 'Erkenwald,' though it lacks the peculiar intensity of 'Cleanness' and 'Patience,' may be an early or very late work, unless we have here an imitation by an enthusiastic disciple. The theme, however, seems to point to London as its place of origin, with about 1386 as its probable date. Anyhow, the poem is a noteworthy product of the school, and must be linked with 'Cleanness' and 'Patience,' even in the matter of the quatrain arrangement.

Imaginary Biography.—But though he be nameless, the poet's personality is so vividly impressed on his work that one may be forgiven the somewhat hazardous task of attempting to evolve an account of his earlier life from mere conjecture and inference. Such an attempt, though fanciful, at all events serves to link together certain facts and impressions, and with this reservation cannot but prove helpful. If documentary evidence is ever discovered, hypothetical conjecture will no doubt be put to a very severe test.

The poet was born about the same time as Chaucer, 1340. His birthplace was somewhere in Lancashire, or perhaps a little to the north, but under no circumstances in any district beyond the Tweed. The evidence of dialect proves this abundantly. The wild solitudes of the Cumbrian coast, near his native home, seem to have had special attraction for him. Like a later and greater poet, he must already as a youth have felt the subtle spell of Nature's varying aspects in those West Midland parts; he too loved to contemplate, even in his childhood,

> . . . Presences of Nature in the sky
> And on the earth! . . . Visions of the hills
> And souls of lonely places!

Wordsworth's country may perhaps justly claim our poet as one of its sons.

Concerning the condition of life to which the boy belonged, we have no definite clue; but I am inclined to infer that his father was closely connected, in some official capacity, with a family of high rank, and that it was amid the gay scenes that brightened life in some great castle that the poet's earliest years were passed. In later life he loved to picture this home, with its battlements and towers, its stately hall and spacious parks. There too, perhaps, the minstrel's tales of chivalry first revealed to him the rich world of medieval Romance, and made him yearn to gain for himself a worthy place among a noble band of contemporary English poets, whose memory is now, for the most part, lost to us for ever.

The English poets were certainly his masters in poetic art, and although he had read the 'Roman de la Rose,' and the chief products of early and contemporary French literature, their influence was comparatively slight as far as the general tone of his poetry is concerned. It is a significant fact that the peot's only direct reference to the 'Roman' speaks of 'Clopyngel's *clene* Rose.' Indeed, the intensely religious spirit of the poems, together with the knowledge they undoubt-

edly display of Holy Writ, makes it probable that the youth may have been destined for the service of the Church. He must have studied sacred and profane literature at some monastic school, or at one of the universities. It is evident that theology and scholasticism had formed an important part of his education. But the author of '**Pearl**' was certainly no priest.

The four poems preserved in the Cottonian collection seem to have belonged to eventful periods of the poet's life. 'Gawain,' written probably for some special occasion, and in honour of some nobleman, perhaps the generous patron to whose household the poet was attached, is remarkable for the evidence it contdains of the writer's minute knowledge of the 'gentle science of woodcraft,' and of all that pertained to the higher social life of that time. He has introduced into his romance elaborate descriptions of the arming of a knight, and of the hunting of the deer, the boar, and the fox. From his evident enthusiasm it is clear that he wrote from personal experience of the pleasures of the chase, and that he was accustomed to the courtly life described by him.

The poet had married; his wedded life was unhappy; the object of his love had disappointed him, and had perhaps proved unfaithful. He had passed through some such experience before 'Gawain' was written. The poet was, I think, speaking for himself when he made his knight exclaim: 'It is no marvel for a man to come to sorrow through woman's wiles; so was Adam beguiled, and Solomon and Samson and David, and many more. It were indeed great bliss for a man to love them well and believe them not-if one but could.'

'Gawain' is the story of a noble knight, bearing the shield of Mary, triumphing over sore temptations that beset his vows of chastity. How often, while drawing his ideal picture of the Knight of Courtesy, did the poet's thoughts recur to the reality of his own life! Perhaps in a musing mood he wrote in the blank space at the head of one of the illustrations in his MS. the suggestive couplet:

> My mind is much on one, who will not make
> amend;
> Sometime she was true as stone, and from
> shame could her defend.

His wedded life had brought him happiness-an only child, his 'little queen.' He perhaps named the child 'Margery' or 'Marguerite'; she was his 'pearl,'—emblem of holiness and innocence. But his happiness was short-lived; before two years had passed the poet's home was desolate.[17] His grief found expression in verse: a heavenly vision of his lost jewel brought him comfort and taught him resignation. On the child's grave he placed a garland of song, blooming yet, after the lapse of five hundred years.

With the loss of his dearest possession a blight seems to have fallen on his life, and even poetry may have lost its charm for him. The lyrist became the stern moralist of 'Cleanness' and 'Patience.' Other troubles, too, seem to have befallen him. 'Patience' seems to us to be almost as autobiographical as **'Pearl.'** The poet is evidently preaching to himself the lesson of fortitude and hope amid misery, pain, and poverty. Something had evidently happened to deprive him of the means of subsistence. 'Poverty and Patience,' he exclaims, 'are needs playfellows':

> Be bold and be patient, in pain and in joy,
> For he that rends his clothes too rashly
> Must sit anon in worse to sew them together.
> Wherefore when poverty presses me and pains
>   enow,
> Calmly in sufferance it behoves me to be
>   patient;
> Despite penance and pain, to prove to men's
>   sight
> That patience is a noble point, though it oft
>   displease.

'Cleanness' and 'Patience' were probably written not long after **'Pearl.'** But the vivid descriptions of the sea in these two poems perhaps justify the inference that the poet may have sought distraction in travel, and may have weathered the fierce tempests he describes.

Perchance new joy came into his life, and into whatever occupation he may have thrown himself, he may still have found in poetry life's chief delight. In this period the attraction of Romance and Chivalry may well have reasserted itself. Was 'Gawain' the outcome of this happier condition, or did it, in spite of many considerations gainsaying the view, belong to the period of his early happiness?

If, late in life, he wrote the poem on 'Erkenwald,' the great Bishop of London, whose magnificent shrine was the glory of St. Paul's Cathedral, and whose festival Bishop Braybroke re-established in the year 1386, it would seem that the poet may have found occupation in the City of London, in some secular office, allowing him leisure for poetry or theology or philosophy, or other intellectual exercise. It is pleasant to think of the possibility of the poet of **'Pearl'** and Chaucer being brought together as London officials. Certainly it was a West Midlander who wrote 'Erkenwald,' but the poem is a London poem, without any doubt, and may, I think, have been associated with Bishop Braybroke's efforts to establish the due observance of St. Erkenwald's Day.

If the poet took any part in the Church controversies then troubling men's minds, his attitude would have been in the main conservative. Full of intense hatred towards all forms of vice, especially immorality, he would have spoken out boldly against ignoble priests and friars, and all such servants of the Church, who, preaching righteousness, lived unrighteously. But whatever his views on theological questions, his allegiance to the authority of the Church, to Papal supremacy, and to the doctrine of Rome, and his attitude towards the amenities of social life and wealth, would have kept him allof from Wycliffe and his partisans. Professor Carleton Brown has well said that his religious outlook was 'evangelical' rather than ecclesiastical.[18]

The 'Philosophical Strode.'—It is indeed remarkable that no tradition has been handed down to us concerning one of the most distinctive of fourteenth-century writers. It can only be accounted for by the fact that, in the first place, his instrument of expression was regarded as uncouth by the generality of cultured Englishmen, and, in the second place, that the bulk of his poetry was small as compared with the writings of his better known contemporaries. Langland was indeed the only West Midland poet who gained anything approaching national recognition and escaped the oblivion of mere local fame. Nevertheless, one must not despair of finding some evidence that may settle, once for all, the problem of the poet's personality. Indeed, of one fourteenth-century writer, whose name and Latin writings are preserved, it is recorded that during his youth and early manhood he was an ardent wooer of the Muses, and that his fame rested on a poem described as an 'Elegy' and possibly as a 'Vision.' Our knowledge of this writer is mainly due to the happy chance that Chaucer seems to have been his friend and admirer, and dedicated to him no less important a poem than his 'Troilus and Creseide':

> O moral Gower this book I direct
> To thee and to the *Philosophical Strode,*
> To vouchsafe there need is for to correct,
> To your benignities and zelis good.

The antiquary Leland was the first to inquire concerning the second of the two names held in such esteem by Chaucer. In an old catalogue of worthies of Merton College, drawn up in the early years of the fifteenth century, and still preserved in the College muniment room, he discovered the following most valuable reference:

> Radulphus Strode, nobilis poeta fuit et versificavit librum elegiacum vocatum Phantasma Radulphi.

This Ralph Strode, poet, is clearly to be identified with the famous philosopher of that name whose philosophical works hold an important place in the history of medieval logic. He was also famous in his time as a controversialist with Wycliffe, and from statements by Wycliffe it is possible to gain some insight into Strode's religious views. But neither his theology nor his philosophy help us to identify him with the writer of the poems in the Cottonian collection.[19]

The evidence, such as it is, tending to connect Strode and the writer of **'Pearl,'** is derived from the following considerations. The Merton description (*if phantasma* may be taken as a somewhat crude Latin rendering of 'dream' or some such word) does not apply to any known poem so well as to **'Pearl.'** Again, the peculiar force of Chaucer's dedication should be considered. Chaucer felt that his 'Troilus and Creseide' was open to the charge of being somewhat too free; wherefore, in a spirit of banter, he evidently offered it to the correction of two fellow-poets whose writings aimed primarily at enforcing moral virtue. Now, if asked to name the very antithesis of 'Tronus,' a student of fourteenth-century literature could choose no better instance than the romance of 'Gawain.' Further, there is a tradition that Strode, leaving his native land, journeyed through France, Germany, and Italy, and visited Syria and the Holy Land. 'An Itinerary to the Holy Land,' by this writer, seems to have been known to Nicholas Brigham, the enthusiastic devotee of Chaucer, to whom we owe his monument in Westminster Abbey. According to Antony Wood, Strode's name as a fellow of Merton occurs for the last time about 1361.

The statement, still repeated in text-books on Chaucer, to the effect that Strode was a Scotch monk in Jedburgh Abbey, was due to the mendacious Dempster, who in his desire to claim the logician for Scotland described Strode as a Scotch monk, who had received his early education at Dryburgh Abbey.

It is noteworthy that a 'Ralph Strode' was Common Serjeant of the City of London. There is every reason for identifying him with Chaucer's 'philosophical Strode.' They were evidently neighbours, for Chaucer lived over the gate at Aldgate, while Strode was living over the gate at Aldersgate. Ralph Strode, the Common Serjeant of the City, died in 1387, and his will was proved in the Archdeaconry Court of London; but, though duly indexed in the archives of the Archdeaconry now at Somerset House, the document itself is missing. He was involved in the municipal politics that distracted London, in the struggles between the partisans of the two great Londoners, Brember and Northampton, the latter the staunch supporter of Wycliffe. The fortunes of Northampton were linked with the fate of Thomas of Usk, the author of the 'Testament of Love.' Usk was executed early in 1388; in the same year Strode's friend and supporter, the former Lord Mayor Brember, paid the same penalty. Strode had died the previous year. But so far as the identity of Strode with the author of **'Pearl'** is concerned, all is mere conjecture; no definite piece of evidence tending to confirm it is adducible. The question still remains unanswered,

> Who and what he was—
> The transitory Being that beheld

This Vision; when and where and how he lived. . . .

Notes

[1] The poet in question was Capgrave; see Prologue to the 'Life of St. Katherine,' printed in Capgrave's 'Chronicle,' edited by Sir E. Maunde Thompson, Rolls Series. . . .

[2] In the really fine poem called 'A Luue Run,' by Thomas de Hales (O. E. Miscellany, E.E.T.S., 1882), the precious gem-stone, maidenhood, more precious than any earthly gem, is dealt with most suggestively. It is set 'in Heaven's gold,' and shines bright in Heaven's bower, but is not specified as the pearl (*cp.* Note on l. 2).

[3] Perhaps the most striking mystical poem on the Pearl is the beautiful gnostic 'Hymn of the Soul,' attributed to the Syrian gnostic Bardaisan, *circa* A.D. 150. Here the Pearl 'lies in the sea, hard by the loud-breathing Serpent.' It has to be brought by the King's son to the House of his Father's Kingdom. I take the Pearl in the Hymn to be symbol of purity amid the defilements of the world. Mr. G. R. S. Mead, in 'The Hymn of the Robe of Glory' (London and Benares, 1908), gives the poem, together with Bibliography, Comments, and Notes. Mr. Mead, in a fascinating article in 'The Quest,' January 1913, discussed a new-found Manichean Treatise, from China, translated and annotated by MM. Ed. Chavannes and P. Pelliot ('Journal Asiatique,' November-December 1911). It would appear probable that certain gnostic elements link this work with the Hymn attributed to Bardaisan. Here we have seven pearls 'hidden in the labyrinth of the impure city of the Démon of Lust.' Also, it is of special interest that the precious pearl called 'moon-light,' with which pity and compassion are compared, is 'the first among all jewels.'

Dr. R. M. Garrett ('University of Washington Publications, IV, 1918) quotes the charming letter of St. Hilary of Poictiers to his twelve-year-old daughter Abra (A.D. 358), concerning a certain Prince who possesses a pearl and a robe of priceless value. He tells her how humbly he begged the gift for the little daughter he so tenderly loved. With the letter he sends a hymn; she is to ask her mother to explain both letter and hymn.

On the Pearl in Mystical Literature, *cp.* also Kunz and Stevenson's 'The Book of the Pearl' (London, 1908).

[4] From the late Cabbalistic work *Reshith Chochmah,* III. i., by Elias de Vidas, who notes that the idea of the soul as a pearl is in the *Zohar,* a medieval Jewish gnostic work containing much ancient lore. I owe this reference to the Rev. Morris Joseph, in whose *Judaism in Creed and Life* the passage is alluded to.

[5] See Preface to 'Cleanness' (Select Early English Poems).

[6] Nothing that has been written attempting to prove that the poem is merely an allegory, and is not inspired by a personal grief, has impressed me in the least degree. The chief exponent of this view was the late Professor Schofield; see Appendix. As further illustration of the personal aspect of the poem, *cp.* De Quincey, on the death of little Kate Wordsworth, who died aged 'not above three' (De Quincey's Works, ed. Masson, 1896, Vol. II. 440-445).

[7] *Cp.* Faerie Queene,' Book I. x.

[8] 'Book of the Duchess,' 948-9.

[9] The surcoat above the robe had probably some special mystical significance. So, too, in the 'Hymn of the Soul' there is the Purple Mantle over the Robe of Glory (*cp.* Mead, p. 46).

[10] Cp. Didron, 'Christian Iconography,' London, 1886.

[11] Cp. Ezek. xvi. 12.

[12] Early English Text Society, Original Series, 24, ed. Furnivall.

[13] The marginal reference in Matt. xiv. 45-6 to Proverbs iii. 14-15 indicates this application. . . .

[14] The metre is fairly common; see poems in Trans. Phil. Soc., 1858, ed. Furnivall; 'Political, Religious and Love Poems,' ed. Furnivall, E.E.T.S. 15; 'Hymns to the Virgin and Christ,' ed. Furnivall, E.E.T.S. 24; 'Twenty-six Political and Other Poems,' ed. Kail, E.E.T.S. 124. Ten Brink was of opinion that 'Pearl' was modelled on the 'Song of Mercy' (Trans. Phil. Soc., 1858, p. 118), but there is no evidence in favour of this, nor can the date be fixed. The only poem in this metre that seems to give evidence of being influenced by 'Pearl' is 'God's Complaint.' 'Thou art an vnkynde omagere' sounds much like an echo of Pearl's 'Þou art no kynde jueler.' Concerning this poem and its author, Glassinbery, and the similar poem, 'This World is Very Vanity,' see my article in 'Athenæum,' March 29, 1902.

The earlier alliterative rhyming poems in Harl. MS. 2253, though not in the same form as 'Pearl,' indicate certain points in common, and have similar characteristics as regards linking and alliteration.

On the metrical structure of the poem, see article by Professor Clark S. Northup, 'Study of the Metrical Structure of *The Pearl,*' Publications of the Modern Language Association of America, XII. pp. 326-40. . . .

[15] Compare especially the thirteenth-century alliterative homily, 'Hali Meidenhad,' ed. Cockayne, E.E.T.S., 1866, which on p. 22 strikingly illustrates certain passages of the poem. . . .

[16] Dr. George Neilson, in his 'Huchown of the Awle Ryale,' 1902, attempted to assign to Huchown the great bulk of anonymous alliterative poetry, including 'Pearl.' Among other criticisms of Dr. Neilson's work, Dr. MacCracken's 'Concerning Huchown' (Publications of the Modern Language Association of America, 1910) should be noted. . . .

[17] It is noteworthy that throughout the poem there is no single refrence, such as one might expect, to the mother of the child. The poet's first words when he beholds his transfigured 'Pearl' are significant:

> "O Pearl," quoth I . . .
> "Art thou my Pearl that I have playned,
> Regretted by me, so lone?"
>
>   [II. 241-3.]

This is consistent with my theory concerning the poet's married life.

[18] Professor Carleton Brown in his article on 'The Author of *The Pearl* considered in the Light of his Theological Opinions' (Publications of the Modern Language Association of America, Vol. XIX., 1904) has some interesting and valuable observations on the relation of the poem to the theology of the time. He holds, against my view, that the assumption of a necessary antagonism between our author and Wycliffe is unwarranted. He deals also with the attitude of the poet, with special reference to the paraphrase of the Parable of the Vineyard, towards the views held by some of his contemporary theologians, notably Bradwardine.

As an indication that the author had in mind the discussions of the theologians, Professor Carleton Brown refers to some of the terms which he employs. He takes as his example the word 'pretermynable,' 1. 596, suggesting a definite acquaintance with the 'predetermination' of the Schoolmen. But see my Note on what I think is the correct interpretation of the word. I am convinced that the poem is not primarily associated with questions of contemporary theology, though, as Professor Brown points out, 'from Augustine to the fourteenth century the "baptized infant" played an important rôle in the treatises of the theologians.'

More recently Dr. R. M. Garrett in 'The Pearl: an Interpretation' (University of Washington Publications, IV., No. 1, 1918), argues that 'Pearl' 'has in its central idea the fundamental teaching of the Eucharist.' The article, though unconvincing, is of special interest for its quotations from the 'Epistola Sancti Hilarii ad Abram

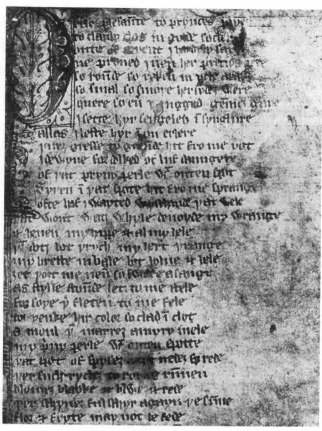

Lines 1-29 from the Cotton MS., Nero A.x. of Pearl.

Filiam Suam' (to which I have already referred); and for calling attention to this charming piece of literature Professor Garrett deserves the best thanks of students of the subject.

[19] In my article on Strode, in the *Dictionary of National Biography,* will be found the first attempt to dispose of the legend of Strode's description as a monk of Jedburgh Abbey, and to write an authentic biography of the famous Schoolman. As regards the possible identification of Chaucer's 'philosophical Strode' with the author of 'Pearl,' the theory, whatever may be its worth, was mine, in spite of a wrongful claim made by Dr. Horstmann.

Professor Carleton Brown, in his article to which I have referred, indicates many points that tell against Strode's authorship, though I do not agree with his attempt to differentiate the poet, the philosopher, and the lawyer.

René Wellek (essay date 1933)

SOURCE: "The Pearl: An Interpretation of the Middle English Poem," in *Sir Gawain and Pearl: Critical Essays,* Indiana University Press, 1966, pp. 3-36.

[*In the following essay, Wellek asserts that* Pearl *is a dream vision that uses allegory to present Pearl as the object of divine grace.*]

A lucky chance has preserved to us two English poems of the fourteenth century which rank not far below the best we have from Chaucer's master hand. MS Cotton Nero A. X. (now A. X. 4) in the British Museum contains the only known text of both *Sir Gawain and the Green Knight* and the ***Pearl***. Since Richard Morris's first edition in 1864 the ***Pearl*** has found an ever increasing number of editors, translators, interpreters and admirers. The aesthetic qualities of the poem—its finished grace, the unearthly loveliness of its descriptions, the heavy brocade of its strange diction, the depth of feeling expressed—have become universally recognized. The linguistic and textual problems it offers have attracted an unusual number of Middle English scholars, and the wide perspectives it opens for speculations in biography, interpretation, comparative literature and history of thought have made this short poem a focus of combat and polemics, in which few Middle English scholars have failed to join. It may be time to look back at what has been achieved: to survey the state of research and to sift the chaff from the wheat and then to give a new interpretation, which would use the reasonable results of the labors done by others in a spirit of gratitude and add a few new points of view and hitherto unnoticed illustrations, which throw a little more light on this sparkling jewel.

The preparatory work, which scholarship has to perform, has been done well and fairly completely in the case of the ***Pearl***. As we have only one MS to go upon, editing does not give us puzzles similar to the amazing MS labyrinths of *Troilus and Criseyde,* so sagaciously solved by Professor Root, or of *Piers the Plowman,* still waiting for a final edition. Nevertheless just because only one MS has been preserved, another type of textual problem is more numerous and free scope is given to emendation of the scribal errors and corruptions and the interpretation of difficult words and passages.

Sir Frederick Madden was the first to give a detailed description of the Cotton MS in his "Syr Gawayne: A Collection of Ancient Romance Poems"[1]—he was at least the first who distinguished between the four poems contained in the MS (***Pearl***, *Purity, Patience* and *Gawain*). *Richard Morris,* in 1864, published the first edition of the ***Pearl*** for the Early English Text Society.[2] To Morris we owe a fair text, which has actually been improved only in details since. *Sir Israel Gollancz* was the next editor in 1891,[3] but his edition, though it meant in some respects a real advance beyond Morris, was vitiated by unnecessary and fanciful emendations. A number of minor contributions in periodicals (by Kölbing, Morris, Holthausen[4]) followed in the next years up to the publication of *C. G. Osgood*'s new edition, which came out in 1906[5] and which meant again a distinct advance in the interpretation and illustration of the text, even if some of his conjectures do not commend themselves to a closer scrutiny. In 1921 *Sir Israel Gollancz* reissued his edition in an entirely recast form,[6] which did away with most of the deficiencies of his earlier work. He uses also Osgood's improvements, though he unjustly denies to him any merit in the advance of textual interpretation.[7] Gollancz's edition, in spite of new and ingenious emendations which mean the solution of many puzzles, still leaves some points of dispute open and is not always consistent and logical in its handling of some textual problems.[8] Larger parts of the poem were edited by *A. Brandl* and *O. Zippel*[9] and by *K. Sisam*[10] and a number of important contributions to textual problems were published by *A. S. Cook,*[11] *O. F. Emerson,*[12] and *E. Tuttle.*[13] Still, there is room for a new and final edition which would incorporate these new results, pay more attention to the evidence of the meter and avoid the arbitrary conjectures of Gollancz. To Gollancz finally we owe a Facsimile reproduction of the MS for the Early English Text Society, though unfortunately the reproduction is technically not quite as perfect as we would wish it to be.[14] Recently *J. P. Oakden*[15] has made an attempt to show that the single scribe of the MS has based his transcription on a MS in which it is still possible to recognize three individual scribal hands, but, it seems, his elaborate theory is unnecessary to account for the phenomena he lists. Translations which can also be called contributions to textual interpretation include prose-versions in modern English, free adaptations and attempts to reproduce the exact rhyme and stanza scheme of the original and even a German and an Italian verse-translation.[16]

The establishment of the text naturally involves the question of the author's dialect and language and the place of provenance of the MS. The MS is undoubtedly written by a hand dating from the late fourteenth or early fifteenth centuries. The evidence found by *J. G. Gilson*[17] points to the fact that it came from the monasteries of the North. The early dialectical research of *R. Morris, F. Knigge, W. Fick,* and *Schwahn*[18] pointed to the conclusion that the poem comes from the extreme North West Midlands, probably from Lancashire. This conclusion has been contested by *J. R. Hulbert,*[19] who judges "that the poems may be from the West Midland, but no significant evidence has yet been given to prove that location." He is altogether sceptical as to whether it is possible to assign a definite locality to the poems considering the state of our knowledge of Middle English dialects. "There is no good evidence to connect alliterative romances with the West; their language should not be called West Midland; and until new facts are found the only safe statement of the location of these poems is that they were probably written in some place which possessed a mixed Northern and Midland dialect."[20] As a solu-

tion Hulbert suggests a sort of κοινή, a conventional language "which had for its basis perhaps some particular dialect (possibly traditionally associated with alliterative verse)" which the writers altered "in the direction of their own native dialect."[21]

But *Karl Luick* in his monumental "Grammatik" has analyzed Middle English dialects much more thoroughly and assigns the poems of the Cotton MS to the type of dialect found in the Ireland MS, written at Hale Hall in Southern Lancashire,[22] and also quotes *Gawain* frequently as having definite West Midland characteristics.[23] Using Luick's results, *R. J. Menner* assembled the evidence for the Northwest. Although he admits the justice of Hulbert's criticism of the older arguments for West Midland, he proves that we actually "possess certain phonological and inflectional characteristics which we have a right to consider West Midland rather than East Midland."[24] But he is careful to state that it would be dangerous to assign these poems to any particular county.

Recently *J. P. Oakden*[25] attempted to narrow down the area even further. On the basis of a complicated map of dialectical boundaries constructed by him, he assigns the **Pearl** to South Lancashire and North West Derbyshire with no preference for either. Because of the strong Scandinavian element in the vocabulary preference is given to South East Lancashire, extreme North West Derbyshire and possibly extreme South West Yorkshire. To make this location even more definite, Oakden makes an elaborate attempt to identify the castle of the Green Knight with the castle Clitheroe near the Ribble, which belonged to John of Gaunt from 1360 to 1398. But the alleged similarity of position is extremely vague and the accuracy of the map of dialect boundaries is also open to grave doubts.[26] Miss *M. S. Serjeantson*[27] recently made another very elaborate attempt to define the region of the **Pearl** more closely. She comes to the conclusion that the **Pearl** may have "originated in an area rather to the east of that in which Sir Gawayne was written." "On the whole, Derbyshire seems the least improbable area to which the Nero MS may be assigned, whatever the original dialects of the poems may have been." But the question does not seem to be settled and, perhaps, it is not possible to settle it with the means at our disposal. In the meantime, we have to rest content with the more cautious conclusions of Menner, especially as the importance of the dialectical evidence is extremely overrated. Though North West Midland must be regarded as the region of provenance, the existence of a special literary language which obscures more definite local traces should not be denied.[28]

The question of the authorship of our poem has naturally attracted many minds. It would be a wonderful find if we should be able to hit on the name of the author of such a large and important body of poetry as the *Pearl, Gawain, Purity,* and *Patience.* The evidence of common authorship of these poems is very strong indeed and should be absolutely beyond any doubt as regards the *Pearl, Purity,* and *Patience.* The evidence as to the common authorship of these poems and *Gawain* seems to me a little less convincing, though the metrical similarities and other links make also this identification highly probable, and the difference in tone and atmosphere can be explained by the French source of *Gawain.*[29] Probably *St. Erkenwald,* that curious legend of London, is also the work of the *Gawain* poet, a view which was forwarded as early as 1881 by *C. Horstmann* and has recently been very ably defended by *H. L. Savage* in his edition of the legend.[30]

But the attempts to connect a name with these poems have hitherto failed completely. There is not a shred of evidence for either *Huchown* or *Strode,* who have been suggested by eminent scholars. On the contrary, enough evidence can be brought against these theories to rule them out of any serious consideration. Huchown of the Awle Ryale can lay claim to nothing except the "Pistel of the Swete Susane," and both the *Pearl* and *Gawain* cannot be by the author of the "Pistel" if only on the ground of the striking dialectical and stylistic differences.[31] Equally flimsy is the case for Ralph Strode, whose authorship has been defended by C. Horstmann and Sir Israel Gollancz. There was, it is true, a poet Ralph Strode who wrote a "Fantasma Radulphi" before 1360, but there is not the slightest evidence that this Fellow of Merton College, Oxford, was a Northerner or that he even wrote in English or that "Ralph's Spectre" is in any way identical with the *Pearl.* Moreover, it has been shown that this Strode was probably not identical with the logician Strode, who played some part in the history of scholastics.[32]

Finally *Oscar Cargill* and *Margaret Schlauch* made a new attempt to identify the poet of the *Pearl.*[33] Though they have no positive evidence to go upon, they identify the child mourned in the poem with Margaret, daughter of John Hastings, Earl of Pembroke, and his wife Margaret, a daughter of Edward III. But they cannot even prove that the child died at the age of two; they have to quote a document dating from 1371, when the girl, born in 1367, was four years old and is unmistakably spoken of as a living person. Another document dated 1369, which makes provisions *in case* her father should die without issue, is certainly no proof— as the authors curiously take it to be—of the child's being actually dead by that time. Also the attempt to press the word "countess" in stanza 41 of the *Pearl* into a literal and earthly significance and to read some importance into the fact that the King has actually given pearls to the supposed mother of the girl are completely unsuccessful. On top of this airy structure Cargill and Schlauch erect a theory about the authorship of the poem. Of five servants of the household of John Hastings, who later came to the Court, they pick two,

John Donne and John Prat, as the likely authors without deciding between them. John Donne was apparently chosen because of his name and not for any other reason, since he is mentioned in a document as "valet of the king's kitchen," and John Prat's case is not much stronger, as we have absolutely nothing to connect him with any definite piece of poetry. It is true that he is called the "King's minstrel" in 1370, but "minstrel" is a term for any fiddler and rope-dancer.

These airy theories disposed of, it will be best to turn to the text of the poem and to ascertain its actual meaning and purpose, as the external evidence has failed to render anything really significant. The history of the *Pearl* research shows that this is not an easy task, as opinions vary with almost every writer on the question. We shall give a brief but critical review of the main interpretations offered and then discuss the poem independently.

All the early editors and interpreters agree in regarding the *Pearl* as an elegy for the death of the poet's daughter. *Bernhard Ten Brink* and *Sir Israel Gollancz* have elaborated this theory in the greatest detail, and hence it has been taken over by almost all handbooks and literary histories.[34] Ten Brink was, I think, the first to construct an imaginary biography of the poet on the base of this interpretation: "Der Dichter," he fancies, "hatte sich verheiratet. Ein Kind, ein holdes, im Reiz der Unschuld strahlendes Mädchen beglückte diese Verbindung. Auf dieses Kind konzentrierte sich die ganze Zärtlichkeit des Vaters mit einer Ausschliesslichkeit, welche uns vermuten lässt, dass die Mutter die Geburt desselben nicht lange überlebt hatte. Da raffte sie im zartesten Alter die Hand des Geschicks unbarmherzig hinweg. Wie dem Vater da zu Mute war, sagt uns seine Dichtung; zugleich aber auch, wie er zur Fassung gelangte."[35] Ten Brink bases his fancy about the mother's death in childbirth on the mere fact that she is never mentioned in the poem, but even he seems nearer to asserted facts, if we compare him with Gollancz, who elaborated Ten Brink's idea in the introduction to his edition in 1891 and repeated his opinions, unshaken by any arguments directed against them, even in the chaper on the *Pearl* in the Cambridge History of English Literature (1901) and in his edition of 1921. Gollancz knows that the author of the *Pearl* was certainly no priest, he knows that his "wedded life was unhappy; the object of his life had disappointed him, and had perhaps proved unfaithful."[36] Nevertheless "his wedded life had brought him happiness-an only child, his 'little queen.' He perhaps named the child Margery or Marguerite. But his happiness was short-lived; before two years had passed the poet's home was desolate. With the loss of his dearest possession a blight seems to have fallen on his life, and even poetry may have lost its charm for him. The lyrist became the stern moralist of the 'Cleanness' and 'Patience'."[37] "'Cleanness' and 'Patience' were probably written not long after the '**Pearl**.' But the vivid descriptions of the sea in these two poems perhaps justify the inference that the poet may have sought distraction in travel. It would seem that late in his life the poet may have found occupation in the City of London, in some secular office" and so on in the most fanciful strain. The text of the poems is utterly silent on the mother, on the name of the child, and flatly contradicts the idea that *Patience* and *Cleanness* could have been written later, as the metrical and artistic advance goes surely the other way round from the earlier homiletic poems to the much more finished *Pearl*.

In 1904 Professor *Carleton Brown* wrote his epoch-making article "The Author of the Pearl Considered in the Light of his Theological Opinions,"[38] where for the first time the actual contents of the poem are taken seriously enough to allow an investigation of its very center, the theological discussion, no longer regarded a mere digression. Professor Brown tries to prove that the poet was an ecclesiastic, as he seems particularly well acquainted with the Bible and the theological controversies of his time. He shows in detail that the poet of the *Pearl* agrees with his contemporary, Thomas Bradwardine, in his fundamental doctrine, directed against the Pelagianism then current, that "salvation is bestowed through the free grace of God, instead of being achieved by any merits." But even further, the author of the *Pearl* "goes beyond Bradwardine in the boldness with which he pushes the doctrine of free grace to its logical conclusion." The assertion that the baptized infant will receive equal reward with the adult is directly opposed to the established opinions of the theologians. The author of the *Pearl* defends the complete equality of the heavenly rewards, a heresy descended from the fourth-century heretic Jovinian. Like Jovinian the poet uses in support of his doctrine the parable of the Vineyard, which he explains literally, implicitly rejecting the scholastic interpretations which tried to smooth over the difficulty. "On the whole, it is evident that our author's attitude towards religious matters was evangelical rather than ecclesiastical." His silence on Holy Church, the absence of any references to apocryphal and legendary matter, his disregard of patristic and scholastic authority, his deep ethical fervor and his assertion of a true equality of the elect are quoted in support of this striking thesis. Professor Brown goes even so far to see, at least in this last respect, a "most interesting and remarkable anticipation of sixteenth century Protestantism."[39]

In the same periodical and in the same year Professor *W. H. Schofield* published an article on "The Nature and Fabric of the Pearl,"[40] which makes a frontal attack on the older interpretation of the *Pearl* as an elegy and tries, besides, to give an allegorical interpretation of the whole poem. He first shows how flimsy is the evidence for the elegiac interpretation and examines further Brown's theory that our author was an ecclesiastic. "An English ecclesiastic in the fourteenth century could not possibly have had any but an illegitimate child and it stands to reason that a priest would not deliberately go out of his way to call people's attention to his child of shame, and then without apology proceed to exalt above all else purity of life." But the poem does not necessitate such a hypothesis, as it is nothing more than an "artistic arrangement of a situation by which certain theological and religious opinions could be effectively presented." The child in the poem is not the daughter of the poet: no kinship is asserted to exist between the two. "One cannot even affirm that it is an imaginary vision of a father without going beyond the information in the text." The Pearl is, in truth, merely an allegorical figure, a being purely and simply of the poet's imagination. The child never had any physical shape on earth. It was the form of a maiden unknown to him, except in his dream, that the poet bodied forth to our view. His poem is no elegy, no lament, no dirge, no *In Memoriam*. What is then the meaning of the allegory? Schofield answers that the vision of the *Pearl* is intended above all to exalt the purity of the maiden, clean virginity. She is merely a symbol of pure maidenhood, a representative bride of the Lamb. However, Schofield's belief in such a one-to-one relation between allegory and its meaning is a little wavering and he quotes the Chaucerian "Testament of Love"[41] to show that the Pearl was a symbol of various connotations. His conclusion is that the Pearl is a purely allegorical figure, similar to those damsels representing Philosophy or Nature or Reason in medieval visions. The poem merely combines the traditional vision of the other world with an equally traditional debate. He asks also, how is it possible that the girl in the vision does not demean herself as a babe of two years and how we can explain "her absolute lack of tenderness in her treatment of her father, her coldly stern rebukes, her never-changing austerity."[42] "Plainly, viewed as an elegy, the poem is ineffective. Unlike the Lady in *Comus*, unlike the Beatrice of Dante, his Pearl, so far as human knowledge can attest, has no stimulating suggestion from a real presence."[43]

In the appendix of his paper, Professor Schofield communicates the interesting discovery of a close parallel to the *Pearl* in Boccaccio's earlier eclogue *Olympia*. Schofield recognizes Boccaccio's eclogue as the starting-point of our author's conception, but, though he does not express any doubt about the elegiac character of Boccaccio's poem written for his daughter Violante, he oddly enough considers this rather a confirmation of his theory. "The Eclogue not only explains the presence of the would-be elegiac atmosphere of the *Pearl*, but accounts also for its unreality." "If as some might possibly argue, the author of the *Pearl* had suffered a loss like Boccaccio's and was led to imitate his poem on that account, he would surely have substituted some of his own for Boccaccio's personal touches. As a matter of fact, however, there is no single remark in the *Pearl,* that by any chance could be autobiographical which is not explicable as an echo of Boccaccio's plainly stated experience."

C. Brown's and Schofield's revolutionary opinions were, however, not accepted by most other scholars, though they forced them to consider the allegorical and theological contents of the poem, which had been hitherto neglected. Professor *Ch. G. Osgood's* edition of 1906 gives a most thorough consideration to these problems, quoting a great deal of new illustrative material, while still holding firmly to the elegiac interpretation. "The poem," he decides, "is first of all an elegy."[44] Professor Osgood is not convinced that the poet is an ecclesiastic, as he may well have been a lay-poet with strong religious interests. The dilemma concerning the illegitimate child is not a real one, as he might very well have been married before taking orders. Several references in the poem exclude a purely allegorical interpretation, nor is the identification of the Pearl with maidenhood very convincing, as the Pearl had dozens of meanings; and, besides, the interpretation given by Schofield is nowhere given or even suggested by the poet.[45] "Considering the poet's work as a whole, it is clear that he is not only no allegorist, but he rather tends to avoid symbolism, even when it lies in his way." Professor Osgood grants, that, though the *Pearl* is not primarily an allegory, it contains certain allegorical elements. But, on the whole, the poet had no preference for allegory and only now and then imparts a certain allegorical cast to his work. The symbolism is merely latent and any such emblematic result was perhaps reached unconsciously, or at any rate did not constitute an important part of the poet's original design.[46] In addition to the allegorical elements Osgood recognizes also the popular medieval theme of the vision of an other world in the *Pearl.* As to the theology propounded, Professor Osgood accepts Brown's conclusion, though he stresses the point that the Jovinian doctrine is only one detail of heresy in a man who, in all other known aspects, was enthusiastically and loyally orthodox. The belief in the equality of heavenly rewards is certainly at variance with the poet's social ideas.[47] It seems, furthermore, to have been of acquisition more recent than the composition of *Purity,* for the orthodox view is there clearly implied.[48] Now this is rather a further indication of the elegiac character of the poem. An isolated point of heresy seems naturally not to have been achieved by reason, but is the reflex of violent emotional experience, the consequence of the poet's affliction by the loss of his daughter. The parallel with *Olympia* Professor Osgood regards rather as based in the general method of treating an elegiac theme, and perhaps in the actual choice of theme, than in the appropriation of poetic details from the eclogue.

Even more thorough is the rejection of Professor Schofield's hypothesis in other papers published in the following years. *C. G. Coulton,* the author of a tasteful

translation of the *Pearl,* wrote in its defense.[49] Coulton shows that the supposition that an ecclesiastic could have had only an illegitimate child is not even well founded because he might have married before taking orders and also because lower orders did not prevent matrimony at that time. Coulton also combats with many telling sarcastic questions Schofield's interpretation of the symbolism of the *Pearl* as denoting maidenhood and notes judiciously that the comparison with Boccaccio's *Olympia* speaks rather against Schofield's thesis than for it.

Similar views are upheld by Professor *Clark S. Northrup,*[50] who points the way out of the unreal dilemma between elegy and allegory. "That the framework of the poem is that of a vision and that the debate effectively expounds and defends the equality of heavenly rewards, no one will doubt; but that this excludes the possibility that the poem is based on a personal experience is still, we think, an open question." The use of the conventional vision is no more strange than "Boccaccio's use of the eclogue in writing of his five-year-old daughter Violante, or Milton's use of conventional pastoral figure in writing of Edward King. Both Boccaccio and Milton managed to express genuine feeling; so, to our thinking, did the author of the *Pearl.*" Also *Gollancz* repeated his earlier opinions, embellishing them with even more fantastic speculations such as the curious suggestion that the Pearl was "perhaps a love-child, hence his *Privy* pearl."[51] More judiciously he states against the allegorical interpretation: "The attempt to read the poem as a theological pamphlet, and as a mere symbolical allegory, ignores its transcendent reality as a poet's lament. The personal side of the poem is clearly marked, though the author nowhere directly refers to his fatherhood . . . the jeweler indicates clearly enough the reality of his loss."[52]

No wonder that Professor *Schofield* wanted to reassert and to explain his theory, when he saw its ill success. The Paper "Symbolism, Allegory and Autobiography in the Pearl"[53] is a labored, almost line-by-line interpretation of the poem in the light of Professor Schofield's theory. He shows well enough that the opening stanza has been hitherto thoroughly misinterpreted, that it contains no mention whatsoever of the maiden and that its style rather resembles that of contemporary lapidaries. But later on his effort to deny all personal references becomes very strained, although he avoids the simplified interpretation of his earlier paper and states now rather surprisingly that the final and chief teaching of the work lies in the line saying that those who dwell with Christ in heavenly joy are pearls, spotless in his sight.[54] Professor Schofield seems right in asserting against Osgood that the allegorical cast of the poem does not appear now and then, but pervasively, wherever it could appear, from the beginning to the end of the work. The emblematic result is an absolutely fundamental part of the poet's design and not an accidental superaddition as Osgood would have us believe. "Take this away and the structure of the poem falls to pieces. On the other hand, take away the would-be 'personal references' and their absence is hardly noticeable."[55]

While Schofield's handling of the symbolism is a little embarrassed and undecided, and, in the second paper at least, fairly non-committal, the allegory of the *Pearl* found bolder interpreters later, who build on Schofield while they reject his detailed application. Professor *R. M. Garrett* is the author of a little pamphlet: "The Pearl: an Interpretation,"[56] where he claims to have found the sesame. The Pearl, according to Garrett, means nothing but the Eucharist. "I have an idea that the whole poem arose from gazing at the Elevated Host in the hands of the Priest." "I believe the poet conceived the poem as taking place within the church, where the Pearl might be buried, quite regardless of the convention of the arbor and the grass." He suggests that the reference to the smell of flowers on the grave-mound is only a quasi-pastoral device, which really hints at the incense in the church. He recapitulates: "Within the frame of the great Pearl the poet see his lost pearl in the presence of the Lamb of God, a very member incorporate in the mystical body of Christ: and she teaches him that through the grace of God as granted in the Eucharist it is given to him to become a member of this body, thus to be forever united with his Pearl as parts of the great Pearl, the mystical body of Christ."[57] However, the only instance of a parallelism between the Pearl and the Eucharist, which Professor Garrett was able to find in the writings of the Western church, is from an obscure hymn by Venantius Fortunatus. The verses in which the poet refers to the Eucharist[58] do not have the meaning which Professor Garrett's curious mistranslation suggests.[59] The whole is merely a string of more or less interesting quotations; the main thesis, however, must be pronounced as unproven.

Professor *Jefferson B. Fletcher*'s comparatively short paper "The Allegory of the Pearl"[60] strikes us as the sanest and most convincing solution of the main questions, and it is a pity that his suggestions have not become the common property of scholarship. First, Professor Fletcher shows that Carleton Brown's interpretation of the theology of the poem is wrong in the essential points: the *Pearl* poet does not actually assert "a flat democracy, or rather oriental despotism of an absolute royal family ruling a dead level of subjects," but he recognizes rank in heaven when he mentions the "aldermen right before God's chair."[61] "The presumption is against a devout fourteenth century Catholic acting the heretic; and if he were to do so, he would certainly try to bolster up his position as strongly as possible." Professor Fletcher shows also that according to the teachings of the Church it is entirely possible to reconcile the equality of the heavenly rewards

expressed by the denarius with the subjective variety of the enjoyment of this beatitude. Also the dilemma between *Pearl* as an elegy or an allegory is justly exposed as a false one. It is possible to grant all the allegorical interpretations which the critics have proposed, and still "believe in the historical existence of the child, just as, for instance, Albertus Magnus in his praise of the Virgin Mary described all the symbolic properties, delights, scents, meteorolog, flora and fauna of Mary quâ Garden without ever doubting her historical reality." Also the symbolism of the *Pearl* cannot be interpreted mechanically by one correspondent abstract as maidenhood. "Though each fact may reflect but one object, the symbol as a whole may at the time reflect many objects."

Sister *M. Madeleva* has devoted a whole book to a new allegorical interpretation. The subtitle of her book *Pearl: A Study in Spiritual Dryness*[62] indicates the surprising conclusion that the poem is a "purely subjective study in spiritual dryness, interior desolation, a lament for the loss of the sensible sweetness of God."[63] The poem "opens with a real case of spiritual 'blues,' followed by a consideration of God's grace, brought to a perfectly consistent climax, the contemplation of heaven."[64] "As to wife, and child, and bereavement, I say that there was no wife, there was no two-year-old daughter and consequently no bereavement."[65] The spot where the poet mourned his pearl is expressedly not a graveyard, but a typical monastery garden.[66] The child could have never been taken into the procession following the Lamb, a child could never have talked in the way the visionary figure is speaking. The Pearl child rather represents "the poet's own soul, as it might be in a state of perfection at this particular time of life."[67] "The Pearl is a token, a symbol of peace; the poet is not seeking a child but a state, a condition of peace, symbolized by a pearl."[68] All this is illustrated or rather darkened by plentiful quotations from medieval literature on mysticism, on spiritual dryness in general, etc., but the actual argument is quite amateurish and frequently enough flies directly into the face of all evidence of the text.

Another revival of the purely allegorical interpretation is represented by *Walter Kirkland Greene's* article: "The Pearl—A New Interpretation."[69] Like Schofield he asserts that the poem is not autobiographical, but parabolical. It does not refer to the actual loss of a child, but the discussion between the dreamer and the maiden is a literary device for imparting a spiritual teaching. The dreamer's function consists solely in introducing the maiden and allowing her to utter her revelations in regard to divine grace and the heavenly rewards. Greene draws a close parallel to Boccaccio's *Olympia* and makes an unconvincing attempt to establish a parallel with Dante's *Purgatorio*.[70] Greene seems to be still convinced of the justness of Professor Brown's description of the poet's heretical theological opinions, but objects to Schofield's interpretation of the Pearl as a symbol of maidenhood as this would not explain the poet's real or apparent grief and subsequent joy. But the way out found by Greene, that the figure of the child is used merely as a literary device to impart the spiritual lesson of divine grace, is surely a blind alley, even though the article has its merit in insisting on the problem of divine grace as the central theological question of the poem.

Finally, an important parallel was first quoted by Miss *Elizabeth Hart* in her article "The heaven of Virgins."[71] She disproves Sister M. Madeleva's argument that a two-year-old child could not be among the procession of the hundred and forty thousand by pointing to a passage in Chaucer's *Prioress's Tale*[72] and drawing attention to the liturgical use of the passage describing the procession in the Apocalypse in the Mass read on the Feast of the Holy Innocents. Curiously enough, Miss Hart has no quarrel with Sister madeleva's main thesis.

It remains for us to reintegrate these interpretations which have passed before our mental eye in a chronological order into one consistent picture which will use the results gained by the study of the literature and will add a few new points of view and illustrations of our own.

The study of the literature showed that several questions about the **Pearl** are still undecided. First of all, we have the dilemma between the elegiacal interpretation and the allegorical interpretation; secondly, there is the moot question about the theological contents of the Pearl's instruction; and thirdly, there is the question about the actual meaning of the symbolism of the Pearl.

The debate which is pervading all literature on the **Pearl,** a debate between elegy and allegory, is very poorly formulated at the outset. There cannot be any doubt that the poem is not an elegy in any sense of the word. The mourning of a beloved object which might conceivably be termed elegiac is merely the starting-point of the poem, which obviously is mainly a vision bringing consolation to the mourner. The point of issue should be rather expressed by a dilemma between a personal interpretation and a purely allegorical one. Professor Fletcher has shown very convincingly that even this dilemma is a false one. We can very well grant the reality of the loss of the child and its historical existence, while we are under no necessity whatever to deny the allegorical intent of the whole. However, it is clear that Ten Brink's, Gollancz's and Osgood's interpretations of the personal background go a good deal beyond the real evidence. We do not know anything about the child mourned, except the fact that it died at two years of age. We do not even know that she was the poet's daughter, though this

interpretation is plausible enough. The only definition of the relationship—and its particular form might have been necessitated by the exigencies of rhyme—can be found in line 233 and asserts merely:

Ho watȝ me nerre þen aunte or nece,

so that the possibility of a young sister is left open. We know nothing whatsoever about the child's name—there is no need to see an allusion to Margarete or Margery in the pervading symbolism of the Pearl. Nor do we know anything at all about the mother, who is never mentioned by the poet. Death in childbirth, unfaithfulness, or the illegitimacy of the relation cannot be deduced from the single passage which says:

Art þou my perle þat I haf playned
Regretted by myn one, on nyȝte,[73]

which means nothing else than that the poet has mourned her in the loneliness of the night. Gollancz derives from these lines even the notion that the child was an only child and interprets the adjective "privy" applied to the "pearl withouten spot" as an allusion to the supposed illegitimacy of the child.[74]

But however sharply we may reject the fanciful speculations of some interpreters, we should not be blind, as others have been, to the essential truth of the personal interpretation. There cannot be any doubt that the poet is mourning the actual loss of a little child, who was not yet two years old when she died, so young and tender of age that she could not please God by good works nor pray to him, as she knew neither Pater nor Creed.[75] All purely allegorical interpretations break down completely at these passages. Nor can there be any doubt that the poet has fallen asleep on her grave, clearly pictured in the illustration to lines 57-64 and not in a monastery garden (Madeleva) or in a church (Garrett). The frequently repeated arguments of all allegorists that the child's behavior to the father is unchildlike is perfectly invalid as the whole supposition on which the poem proceeds is precisely a transformation of the two-year-old child into a wise, majestic inhabitant of the heavens, free from all earthly ignorance and affections. She, who was once so young and simple,[76] is now keen of wit and thoroughly knowing. This is entirely in accordance with the teaching of the church, for which the conferment of heavenly grace always meant a complete regeneration, a becoming similar to God, a state which implies heavenly beauty, heavenly wisdom and joyous freedom from earthly passions like envy, etc.[77] Besides, this transfiguration is nothing unusual in medieval literature: the Olympia of Boccaccio's Eclogue is similarly remote from Boccaccio's six-year-old daughter Violante, and the Beatrice of Dante's Paradise talks very differently from the earthly daughter of Folco Portinari.

Also the argument of those allegorists who grant these personal allusions, but explain them merely as a literary device for imparting a spiritual teaching is not convincing. It is, of course, true that the elegiacal purpose, the mourning of the child, is not the real purpose of the poem, as this is rather contained in the lesson which the beatified child is giving to the poet. The purely elegiac interpretation makes the poem an unartistic conglomerate, as it degrades the very center, the debate between the poet and the visionary girl, to a mere digression detrimental to its artistic unity. Nevertheless it is untrue to say that the personal loss clearly expressed in the poem is a mere device, a mere vehicle destined to convey the revelations in regard to divine grace and the heavenly rewards. All these lessons would, after all, scarcely interest the poet unless they would administer *personal* consolation and reassurement. The point of the poem is the conviction, which the poet carries away at the end of the poem, that the child is saved and that she even sees the face of God. In order to be convinced, the poet must entertain certain theological opinions which cannot therefore be considered in irrelevant digression. That these opinions are expanded by the figure of the girl should not blind us to the fact that they are the real opinions of the author, while the opinions put into the mouth of the dreaming poet are the opinions he is discarding—which he has overcome by the certainty of hope. The logical sequence of events is this: the death of the child, a period of doubt and despair, conviction arrived at by theological study or even confirmed by an actual dream that the child is saved, and lastly the composition of the poem, which embodies this spiritual progress. The essential contrast is that between the wretched will of the fretting mourner, his "del and gret daunger," the "strot" of his rebellious heart[78] and the joyful resignation of the verse towards the end of the poem:

Now al be to þat Prynceȝ paye.[79]

We may therefore very well call the dream and the vision a literary device—there is scarcely anybody who would imagine that it could have happened in this form—but we cannot call the existence of the child and the actuality of its loss a device, as without the reality of the loss the whole vision would manifestly lose any personal appeal to the poet and one could justly be astonished that the poet was at all interested in hearing that a two-year-old child can be saved and even incorporated among the followers of the Lamb. It is irrelevant whether the poet ever really dreamt such a dream: we shall never know it and if we knew that he did, we should still have to say that the poem is necessarily an elaboration, a concretization of a dream-reality and therefore more real and lasting than any dream could ever have been. Vision and theological lesson are closely intertwined: as a matter of fact the argument of the girl is nothing but a justification of the vision. The theological instruction is a ratiocination, which tries to defend the justness, possibility and likelihood of the vision, and on the other hand, the vision is also a device to give authority and weight to the theological opinions revealed by the girl. If we consider the question of the type or "genre" of the poem as at all important, we have to answer that the poem is a vision of the other world, in which the poet is administering consolation to himself for a personal loss. Inside of this vision we have a debate between the dreaming poet and the girl. In addition, the whole is permeated by the allegory of the Pearl.

The vision asserts that it is possible for a baptized child, who died before it was two years old and therefore had no opportunity to perform good works or to exercise Christian faith, to be saved and even to be received among the host which follows the Lamb of God. The debate merely reinforces the vision by arguments. Professor Brown has doubted the orthodoxy of this view advanced by the poet and has even made him out a sort of precursor of the Reformation. He quotes Bradwardine's testimony[80] to the fact that Pelagianism was widely accepted in fourteenth-century England. On grounds of Pelagianism, which, however, scarcely was ever held in this extreme form, there would be no possibility for a small child to acquire heavenly grace, as grace is entirely dependent on good works. But our author's rejection of this view is by no means heterodox. On the contrary, it is in perfect accordance with the views of the church, even though at the time of our poet doubt was still possible.

Let us examine the opinions of the church fathers on this point. The most important authority is, of course, St. Augustine, as he especially fought Pelagius in numerous writings and is very explicit on our question, as the grace of baptized children was a chief argument against Pelagius' exclusive stress on good works. The fundamental assumption is that God could not condemn an innocent, baptized child, as "all the ways of the Lord are mercy and truth."[81] The question is, rather, by what right a child, though devoid of any merits which it could not possibly earn, can nevertheless be granted eternal beatitude. The possibility is opened by a distinction between two titles to salvation: one the hereditary title which we have as God's children, the other the title by reward as God's laborers. The children have therefore a title to salvation merely as "filii Dei," which is a "titulus haereditatis," while grown-up persons either lose their title to grace, conferred by baptism, by committing sins or add to their title by good works (titulus mercedis). This means actually that there are two kinds of grace, which modern theology has come to distinguish as "gratia prima" and "gratia secunda." "Gratia prima" is completely free grace, "gratis data, donata, non reddita,"[82] while the second grace is additional and proportional to our merits. This first grace is given by God as the remittance of original sin in baptism. All the church fathers insist that the innocent children also have inherited the sin of Adam and that they would be condemned to eternal damnation if the death of Christ did not save them in baptism.[83] In baptism, says Augustine, "parvulis infundi occultissimam gratiam per quam ad Deum convertuntur."[84] The efficacy of baptism is so great that it gives them also a consciousness of the grace received[85] and a belief in the Son of Man. "Inter credentes igitur baptizatos parvulos numerabis, nec juidicare nullo modo aliter audebis, si non vis esse apertus hereticus. Ergo ideo habent vitam aeternam, quia qui credit in filium, habet vitam aeternam."[86] Exactly the same opinion is also held by St. Chrysostomus and other fathers of the church,[87] but apparently in the course of the Middle Ages the salvation of baptized children does not seem to have been received quite without question, though the prevalent view held to the kindly theory of the fathers. This development can be illustrated by the difference between two Popes. Pope Innocent III (1198 till 1216) simply thought that there are two opinions about the question, but does not decide in favor of either: "Aliis asserentibus pervirtutem baptismi parvulis quidem culpam remitti, sed gratiam non conferri; nonnullis vero dicentibus ed elimitti peccatum et virtutes infundi habentibus illas quoad habitum non quoad usum,"[88] that is, the child is not getting any assistance for his actions, but a form of being, a state of existence. But already Pope Clement V (1305-1314) considers the majority of opinions as inclining toward the second view favorable to the salvation of children. He declared at the council held at Vienne in 1311: "Quantum ad effectum baptismi in parvulis reperiuntur doctores quidam theologi opiniones contrarias habuisse, quibusdam ex ipsis dicentibus, per virtutem baptismi parvulis quidem culpam remitti, sed gratiam non conferri: aliis e contra asserentibus quod et culpa eisdem in baptismo remittitur et virtutes ac informans gratia infunduntur quoad habitum, etsi non pro illotempore quoad usum. Nos attendentes generalem efficaciam mortis Christi, quae per baptisma applicatur pariter omnibus baptizatis, opinionem secundam tamquam probaliorem et dictis sanctorum et modernorum theologorum magis consonam et conformem sacro approbante Concilio duximus eligendam."[89] Also St. Bernhard of Clairvaux defends the salvation of children and considers envy to be the cause of the doubts expressed against this view.[90] In the sixteenth century the Council of Trent codified this doctrine in so many words,[91] and also the founders of Jesuit neo-scholasticism of that time all accept the view expressed by Pope Clement V, e.g., Canisius, Vasquez and Suarez.[92] The quotations and references may be sufficient to show that our poet was completely in the line of orthodox teaching and that he lived at a time when doubt seemed still to be possible about this question. But a famous Pope decided in agreement with our poet and the ultimate decision of the Catholic Church lay with him. It is essentially a Christian doctrine to put such efficacy

into the act of baptism. It not only remits original sin, but also infuses sanctifying grace. The point of view expressed in the *Pearl* is therefore precisely un-Protestant, as in the theory of sixteenth-century Protestantism, the justification of children by baptism remained unexplained. This is the reason why radical Protestant sects like the Anabaptists and the Menonites denied the possibility of efficient infant baptism. In this point certainly our poet is not a forerunner of Protestantism. He is absolutely at one with the opinions we have here expounded: he considers grace completely free, merely depending on God's liberality, it is the "heritage"[93] with which the bride is decorated. Baptism washes away the guilt of Adam:

> Þat wascheȝ away þe gylteȝ felle
> Þat Adam wyth in deth vus drounde.
> Now is þer noȝt in þe worlde rounde
> By-twene vus & blysse . . . [94]

The fact that the child did not know Pater or Creed is irrelevant, for the "grace of God is gret in-nogh."[95]

A question apart from the assertion of the possibility of salvation for the child is raised by her status in heaven. That she can be saved we have shown to be clearly orthodox, but there has been expressed doubt whether it is possible that she could be received among the followers of the Lamb. Professor Brown even suspected the poet of teaching a complete equality of heavenly rewards, in anticipation of Luther's famous sermon "De nativitate Mariae," where he says: "omnes Christiani aeque magni sumus, sicut mater Dei, et aeque sancti sicut ipsa." Our poet has been connected by Professor Brown with the Jovinian heresy asserting the same. It is not surprising that Professor Brown "had been unable to find a single orthodox theologian or poet, from the time of Jerome until the appearance of the Pearl, who asserts the equality of heavenly rewards."[96] We actually have in the poem passages which seem to assert that the poet is holding this view in order to promote the child, most clearly e.g. in the verses:

> "Of more & lasse in Godeȝ ryche,"
> Þat gentyl sayde, "lys no joparde,
> For þer is vch mon payed inlyche,
> Wheþer lyttel oþer much be hys rewarde."[97]

But with such an interpretation many other passages are in conflict, which implicitly recognize the established teaching of the church. The very idea that the girl is in the procession following the Lamb implies a distinction in heaven, and, even though the heavenly hierarchy is nowhere enumerated, the fact of its existence is clearly in the mind of our poet throughout the vision. He speaks not only of the hundred and forty-four thousand virgins of the procession, but also of the four beasts and especially of the "aldermen so sadde of chere" "ryȝt byfore Godeȝ chayere."[98] The aldermen occur once more coupled with "legyounes of aungeleȝ"[99] who cannot be imagined to be identical with the virgins in whose procession the girl is walking.

It is also not true that the poet would deny the importance of good works altogether. He says the opposite twice:

Þe ryȝt-wys man schal se hys face

and

Þe ryȝt-wys man also sertayn
Aproche he schal þat proper pyle.[100]

Though the poet is no doubt not very definite about the hierarchy in heaven and though he makes no attempt to reconcile the assumption of the traditional distinctions with his assertion of the equality of the heavenly rewards, we must assume that he did not feel this contradiction and that he felt no qualms about the orthodoxy of his opinion. Actually his ideas are absolutely orthodox, only that the church felt more clearly the necessity of reconciling the parable of the vineyard and the denarius given to every laborer with the generally accepted ideas about a heavenly hierarchy. In our poet we have the parable stated and the traditional picture of heaven accepted side by side without a sense of contradiction. The church is merely conscious of the difficulty and solves it in a way satisfactory to religious thought. All the church fathers assert the inequality of the heavenly rewards, while dwelling on the perfect harmony and lack of envy in heaven. According to St. Augustine there is the same difference between the just as between the sinners.[101] As biblical support the passage about the many mansions in the house of the father[102] and the passage in the Corinthians which asserts that one star differs from the other in brightness[103] are constantly quoted. The Parable of the Vineyard is interpreted in such a way that the contradiction is solved rather ingeniously. John Chrysostomus, archbishop of Constantinople,[104] solves the question by suggesting that those who have come earlier in the parable of the vineyard were after all subject to the low passion of envy and jealousy in claiming a higher payment. The actual purpose of the parable is merely to give courage to those who became converted only in later years and to convince them that they are not worse off than others. St. Irenaeus, bishop of Lyons, does not seem to see the contradiction between the parable and the teaching about the inequality of heavenly rewards. Once[105] he elaborates the differences between those who are going to dwell in the heavens, those who will enjoy the joys of Paradise, and others who will own the splendid city. When he is explaining the parable of the vineyard,[106] he simply says that it means the same master of the house: some he has called immediately at the creation of the world, others in the middle of time and still others when the time had progressed and others again, when it was at an end, for

there are many laborers, each one at his time, but only one father of the house, who calls them to work. There is only one vineyard, there is only one major domus, the Spirit of God, who arranges everything, and similarly only one reward, since all received the denarius with the picture and the inscription of the king, the knowledge of the Son of God, which is immortality. Only St. Augustine saw the difficulty and solved it thus: "Objectio de denario omnibus reddendo, contra diversitatem praemiorum. Quid sibi ergo vult, inquiunt, ille denarius, qui opera vineae terminato aequaliter omnibus redditur; sive iis qui ex prima hora, sive iis qui una hora operati sunt? Quid utique (Matth. XX, 9) nisi aliquid significat, quod omnes communiter habebunt, sicuti est ipsa vita aeterna, ipsum regnum coelorum, ubi erunt omnes quos Deus praedestinavit, vocavit, justificavit, glorificavit? Oportet enim corruptibile hoc induere incorruptionem, et mortale hoc induere immortalitatem: hic est ille denarius, merces omnium." Nevertheless it is true: "Stella tamen ab stella differt in gloria: sic et resurrectio mortuorum: haec sunt merita diversa sanctorum. Ita quia ipsa vita aeterna pariter erit omnibus sanctis, aequalis denarius omnibus attributus est; quia vero in ipsa vita aeterna distincte fulgebant lumina meritorum, multae mansiones sunt apud Patrem (Joan. XIV, 2): ac per hoc in denario quidem non impari, non vivit alius alio prolixius; in multis autem mansionibus honoratur alius alio clarius."[107] This theory was restated and simplified by the great codifier of dogma, Gregory the Great: "Ipse propter electos in Evangelio dicit: In domo patris mei mansiones multae sunt. Si enim dispar retributio in illa aeterna beatitudine non esset una potius mansio quam multae essent. Multae ergo mansiones sunt, in quibus et distincti bonorum ordines, et propter meritorum consortia communiter laetantur; et tamen unum denarium omnes laborantes accipiunt. Qui multis mansionibus distinguuntur: quia et una est beatitudo quam illic percipiunt, dispar retributionis qualitas, quam per opera diversa consequuntur."[108] Bonaventura[109] teaches a similar way out, asserting that though all will have the same blessedness, considered objectively, yet there will be a difference in the quantity of joy. The same point of view is succinctly phrased by St. Thomas: "Unitas denarii significat unitatem beatitudinis ex parte objecti; sed diversitas mansionum significat diversitatem beatitudinis secundum diversum gradum fruitionis."[110] Similar opinions can be found in Petrus Lombardus, Duns Scotus and Prosper.[111] The author of the ***Pearl*** might have been unacquainted with these solutions of the difficulty, since he stresses much more the obvious sense of the Parable without, however, drawing radical consequences which led Jovinian and Luther to quite different solutions. He is content to show that this parable justifies his belief that his child could be beatified, and not only beatified, but, thanks to God's unbounded grace, be received among the very followers of the Lamb.

That this particular elevation is quite possible was shown conclusively by Miss Hart, who drew attention to a passage in Chaucer's *Prioress's Tale,* where a seven-year-old child is definitely associated with the hundred and forty-four thousand.[112] "Chaucer calls the little boy's mother 'his newe Rachel (B 1817), alluding to Matthew 2, 18. This verse is the conclusion of the Gospel read in the Mass on the Feast of the Holy Innocents (Dec. 28); and the Epistle of that Feast is the very passage in which John describes the procession of the virgins. This is the only liturgical use of this particular passage from the Apocalypse and the association of the Holy Innocents with the procession must have been familiar enough in the Middle Ages. The fact that the liturgy describes such small children, 'a bimatu et infra' (Matthew 2, 16), as forming part of the procession of the centum quadraginta quatuor milia—this fact would seem amply to explain the poet's assigning a place therein to a little girl" of two years' age.[113] We may add in support of Miss Hart's thesis that in the All Saints' Day litany, in the third liturgical order the classes of saints are enumerated in the following order: "Maria—Angeli—Patriarchae et Prophetae—Apostoli et Evangelistae—Discipuli Domini—*Innocentes*—Martyres—Pontifices et Confessores—Doctores—Sacerdotes et Levitae—Monachi et Eremitae—*Virgines* et Viduae."[114] Occam finally gives a theological justification of this special position of the children by drawing a distinction between two kinds of predestination, one which he calls absolute and one which he calls hypothetic. To the hypothetic kind belong all ordinary people, as God has here to decide "post praevisa merita." To the privileged of the first class belong the Virgin Mary, the prophets and apostles, certain saints and all children dying in the grace of baptism.[115] The theology of the poem reveals itself then as entirely orthodox, consistent with the best teachings of the church and well informed on almost all points, though, of course, one cannot deny that it is used for purposes of special pleading. The conclusion drawn from this that the poet must have been an ecclesiastic is not entirely convincing, as we can well imagine an educated layman, interested in these things and well read in his Latin, to have acquired sufficient knowledge in these matters, which touched so intimately the fate of a beloved child or sister.

The third question raised by any study of the **Pearl** is the question of the meaning of its allegory. Here again one must grant to the defenders of the personal interpretation that it would be quite possible to imagine the poem, i.e., the vision and the teaching conveyed by the child without the allegory of the Pearl. It is undoubtedly true that the poem has no allegorical key to it: neither maidenhood (Schofield) nor the Eucharist (Garrett) nor the own soul of the poet (Madeleva) will do. There is no such solution of the allegory. On the other hand, it is true that the allegory of the Pearl is the chief decoration of the poem, one of the main devices of the poet to give it artistic charm and unity. The title **Pearl,** which modern scholarship has given to the poem, is therefore perfectly justified, as the whole poem from the beginning to the end is playing variations on the theme of the Pearl, even though the actual contents are a vision and a theological debate.

The Pearl represents several different things in the poem: first of all the earthly child that went through the grass to the ground-a use of the word, to which the visionary girl herself objects, as she on earth could be rather compared to a flowering and fading rose.[116] Then it means the visionary child in heaven, which at the same time is richly decorated with pearls, especially with one "wonder perle, wythouten wemme" in the midst of her breast, a Pearl which is also worn by all the other virgins in the host following the Lamb.[117] This Pearl in the midst of her breast is identical with the Pearl which the merchant in the Parable bought with all his treasures and this is like the realm of heaven's sphere,[118] i.e., it is nothing but eternal beatitude. The poet is then counseled by the maiden to forsake the mad world and to purchase this spotless Pearl.[119] When he will have purchased this Pearl, he will himself have become a Pearl, a precious pearl unto His pleasure, which is also the final aim and wish of all men on earth.[120]

The symbolism then is not simple and cannot be solved by a one-to-one identification with some abstract virtue, as maidenhood, cleanliness, or by identifying it with the Eucharist or the soul of the poet, but it is complex or rather double. First the Pearl is the girl before she is lost-here obviously Pearl is merely an ordinary symbol for the preciousness, uniqueness, beauty, purity, etc. of the dead girl. When she is found again in heaven, the Pearl is a symbol of an immaculate, pure blessed person in the hands of God. The poet and all men are aspiring to become such a one. Parallel with this symbolism which identifies Pearl with a person, runs the second symbolism, that of the Pearl which the girl is wearing on her breast and which the poet is counseled to purchase for himself. This is obviously the realm of heaven or the grace of God. The symbolism of the Pearl—while not exactly Protean—is shifting subtly, from the conventional and mere earthly meaning of preciousness to the heavenly symbol of grace and the realm of grace. This is really very simple and completely in agreement with traditional symbolism.

All allegorical use of the Pearl descends from the Parable, cited also by our poet, about the merchant who sold all his goods in order to win one precious pearl.[121] This Pearl is most frequently identified with Christ, e.g., as early as in Bishop Melito's Clavis de Metallibus, which is supposed to date back to the second century.[122] But very frequently indeed it means the blessed, the saints themselves, a symbolism which agrees with what we have considered the first meaning of the Pearl in our poem. We find this interpreatation in Rupert of Deutz, in Hrabanus Maurus, the famous archbishop of Mayence, and in St. Bonaventura. The last says e.g.: "Bonae margaritae sunt omnes sancit; una vero pretiosa est Christus."[123] Even more frequent is the identification of the Pearl with the heavenly kingdom and heavenly grace or similar concepts as the word of God, the faith of the church. To Gregory the Great "margarita vero mystice significat evangelicam doctrinam sue dulcetudinem coelestis vitae,"[124] to Petrus Chrysologus it is identical with "vita aeterna,"[125] to Petrus Capuanus, a Parisian theologian at the end of the twelfth century, who gives a very elaborate symbolism of the Pearl, it means "Fides ecclesiae," "verbum dei" and the Apostles.[126] More confused is the symbolism of the Pearl in the "Testament of Love," a prose piece, which was first printed in Thynne's edition of Chaucer in 1532, but was probably written by one Thomas Usk about 1387. The allegory of the Pearl there returns again and again, but always in some connection with grace or mercy. At the end the writer says with extraordinary bluntness: "Margarite, a woman, betokeneth grace, lerning, or wisdom of god, or els holy church."[127] That this interpretation was a current one can be also shown from a fifteenth-century source, i.e., from Beati Alani (Redivivi Rupensis) Tractatus Mirabilis De Ortu atque Progressu Psalterii Christi et Mariae.[128] This curious book gives a whole synopsis of fifteen gems explaining or rather running parallel to the "Ave Maria, gratia plena." Gratia in the text of the Annunciation is identified with margarita, a symbol of Grace, while e.g. Ave is identified with Adamas, a symbol of Innocence, etc. The text gives a long and involved explanation, fortified by many authorities, why Mary can be represented by a Pearl, and why and how she is full of grace. Somebody who would make a closer search into allegorical literature might probably discover many more similar passages, which, however shifting the symbolism may seem, are perfectly consistent in the main point. We see the Pearl is even here perfectly well set into the tradition of its time. The difficulties of the poem appear then largely as illusory, as many of them were stirred up by scholarship which lost contact with the actual text and indulged in mysterious interpretations or fanciful speculations.

All these debates, we feel, about dialect, authorship, elegy versus allegory, theology, symbolism, etc., though they have been almost the only occupation of scholarship, say very little about the *Pearl* as a work of art. We may grant that a right conception of the contents of the poem has cleared the way for an artistic appreciation, but the actual study of the artistic value of the poem is still in its beginnings. Even the obvious approach through questions of meter and structure has not been much utilized hitherto. Professor *Northup*'s paper, "A Study of the Metrical Structure of the Middle English Poem the Pearl"[129] is rather a contribution to the history of final unstressed -*e* in the West Midland than a metrical investigation proper. Also Oakden's

treatment of the meter is rather a statistical survey of the alliteration and its use[130] than an attempt at artistic interpretation. In these questions much is still to be done by a judicious use of modern methods, which, on the whole, could come to many new results in Middle English scholarship.[131]

Notes

[1] London 1839, for the Ballantyne Club, pp. XLVII-L.

[2] In "Early English Alliterative Poems in the West-Midland Dialect of the Fourteenth Century." Ed. by R. Morris. London 1864. There are revised editions dating from 1869, 1885, 1896 and 1901.

[3] Pearl. An English Poem of the Fourteenth Century. Ed. with a Modern Rendering by I. Gollancz. London 1891.

[4] E. Kölbing, Englische Studien XVI. 268-273, a review of Gollancz's edition. The debate R. Morris-Gollancz in the Academy (No. 999, 1001, 1003 and 1005, 39, 602; 40, 36, 76, 116). F. Holthausen, Zur Textkritik me. Dichtungen, in Herrigs Archiv, Vol. XC, p. 144-8.

[5] The Pearl. A Middle English Poem. Ed. with Introduction, Notes, and Glossary by Charles Grosvenor Osgood. In the Belles Lettres Series. Boston 1906.

[6] Pearl. An English Poem of the Fourteenth Century. Edited with Modern Rendering, together with Boccaccio's Olympia, by Sir Israel Gollancz. London 1921, in the Medieval Library. Gollancz's edition of the Pearl in "Select Early English Poems" (Milford, Oxford University Press) is only a large paper edition of the same.

[7] Cp. Gollancz's introduction p. L. But dozens of Gollancz's changes compared to the 1891 edition follow simply Osgood.

[8] Cp. e. g. J. R. Hulbert's review in Modern Philology. Vol. XXV. (1927), p. 118-9.

[9] Mittelenglische Sprach- und Literaturproben. Berlin 1917, pp. 114-4, an edition of ll. 1-360.

[10] In Fourteenth Century Verse and Prose (Oxford 1925, p. 59), a well annotated edition of lines 361-612 (p. 59 seq.).

[11] In Modern Philology VI (1908), 197 seq. on ll. 215/6.

[12] Some Notes on the Pearl, PMLA March 1922. Vol. XXXVII, pp. 52-93, and More Notes on Pearl. PMLA. Dec. 1927. Vol. XLII, pp. 807-31.

[13] Notes on the Pearl. MLR (1920). Vol. XV, pp. 298-300.

[14] Early English Text Society. Vol. 162, 176 plates, compare the review by W. W. Greg in the MLR. Vol. 19, p. 223.

[15] Alliterative Poetry in Middle English. The Dialectical and Metrical Survey. Manchester University Press. 1930, p. 262 seq.

[16] Gollancz in his editions in rhymeless verses. A. R. Brown in Poet Lore V, 434-6, rendering of ll. 158-172. F. T. Palgrave, Landscape in Poetry. London 1897, pp. 115-7, rendering of st. 4 in metre. S. Weir Mitchell, Pearl, rendered into Modern English Verse, New York 1906. 46 stanzas mostly from the first half, also Portland, Maine, 1908, in the "Bibelot." C. G. Coulton, Pearl rendered into Modern English, London 1906 in the metre of the original (also 1921). Charles G. Osgood, The Pearl rendered in Prose. Princeton 1907. Two poor translations by Sophie Jewett (New York 1908) and Marian Mead (Portland, Maine 1908). Jessie Weston in "Romance, Vision and Satire" (London 1912). W. A. Neilson and K. G. T. Webster in Chief British Poets of the Fourteenth and Fifteenth Centuries, London 1916, a prose-translation by Professor Webster. The German translation by Otto Decker, Schwerin 1916, the Italian by Frederico Olivero (Milano e Turino 1927), with a good introduction.

[17] J. P. Gilson: The Library of the Henry Savile of Banke. A paper read before the Bibliographical Society Nov. 18, 1907, London 1909, proves that the MS comes from this library (1568-1617, Banke in Yorkshire).

[18] Morris, introduction to his edition, F. Knigge, Die Sprache des Dichters von Sir Gawain and the Green Knight, der sogenannten Early English Alliterative Poems and De Erkenwalde. Marburg 1885. W. Fick, Zum mittelenglischen Gedicht von der Perle. Eine Lautuntersuchung. Kiel 1885. Schwahn, Die Conjugation in Sir Gawayn and the Green Knight und den sogenannten Early English Alliterative Poems. Strassburg 1884.

[19] "The 'West Midland' of the Romances" in Modern Philology XIX. 1921-2, p. 9 and p. 11.

[20] Ibidem p. 16.

[21] Ib. p. 12.

[22] Historische Grammatik der Englischen Sprache. Leipzig 1921. Vol. I. I, 47.

[23] Ib. § 33, § 357, Anm. 1; § 397, Anm. I; § 399, Anm. 1; § 408, Anm. 3; § 460, Anm. 1.

[24] "Sir Gawain and the Green Knight and the West Midland" in PMLA, Vol. XXXVII (1922), p. 503, especially p. 505 and 519.

[25] Loc. cit. p. 85-6.

[26] Ib. p. 257 seq. compare A. Brandl's unfavorable review in Herrigs Archiv. Vol. 86 (158) 1931, p. 293. "Die grosse Dialektkarte ist nicht ernsthaft zu nehmen" etc.

[27] In "The Dialects of the West Midlands" in "Review of English Studies." Vol. 3 (1927), p. 327 seq.

[28] Cp. on this R. Huchon's "Histoire de la langue anglaise," Vol. II, 235 who studies the vocabulary and comes to the conclusion: "Il tend à se constituer ainsi une langue littéraire spéciale, qui se superpose à l'idiome courant, le dépasse et diffère de lui par la tonalité et par l'orgine des matériaux employés." Also H. L. Savage's opinion (ed. of St. Erkenwald, p. XXXIII).

[29] The best summary for the evidence of common authorship of these poems in Prof. Menner's edition of *Purity* (Yale University Press. 1920). Additional points in Oakden loc. cit. p. 251 seq. On the sources of *Gawain* cp. G. L. Kittredge: A. Study of Gawain and the Green Knight. Cambridge, Mass. 1916. The idea of a French source for *Sir Gawain* has been contested by E. v. Schaubert, Der englische Ursprung von Sir Gawain in "Englische Studien," Vol. 57, pp. 330-446. If her thesis should be accepted, the common authorship of *Gawain* and *Pearl* would become rather doubtful.

[30] *St. Erkenwald,* Yale Press, 1926, p. XLVIII seq. cp. C. Horstmann, "Altenglische Legenden" (Neue Folge), Heilbronn 1881, p. 266.

[31] The Huchown theory was advocated mainly by George Neilson e. g. in "Huchown of the Awle Ryale, the Alliterative Poet" (Glasgow 1902), or "Cross-links between Pearl and the Adventures of Arthur" in "Scottish Antiquary" 16, p. 67-78. Already M. Trautmann destroyed the theory in "Der Dichter Huchown und seine Werke," Anglia I, 190-49. Best discussion by H. N. McCracken "Concerning Huchown" PMLA. Vol. XXV (1910, p. 507 seq.).

[32] The Strode theory advanced by Gollancz in his editions (p. XLVI of the 1921 ed.), in the DNB under Strode and the CHEL I (1901) p. 320 seq. Carleton Brown (The Author of the Pearl Considered in the Light of his Theological Opinions in PMLA. Vol. XXIX, pp. 146-8) destroys the theory completely.

[33] PMLA. Vol. XLIII (March 1928), p. 177-9.

[34] E. g. Jusserand, Legouis, Wülker, H. Hecht, Snell, Saintsbury, V. Mathesius etc.

[35] Quoted according to "Geschichte der englischen Literatur." 2nd ed. Strassburg 1899, p. 406-7.

[36] 1921 ed., p. XLIII.

[37] Ib. p. XLIV.

[38] PMLA. Vol. XIX (1904), pp. 115-153.

[39] Ib. p. 145.

[40] PMLA. Vol. XIX (1904), pp. 154-215.

[41] Cp. below p. 27.

[42] Loc. cit. p. 201.

[43] Ib. p. 202.

[44] Osgood's ed. p. XXVIII.

[45] Ib. p. XXXIV.

[46] Ib. p. XXXVI.

[47] Osgood points to ll. 35-50 of "Purity."

[48] "Purity," ll. 13-124.

[49] "In Defence of the Pearl," in "Modern Language Review." Vol. II (1907), p. 39.

[50] "Recent Studies of the Pearl" in "Modern Language Notes." Vol. XXII (1907), p. 21.

[51] Cambridge History of English Literature I, 331.

[52] Ib. p. 320.

[53] PMLA. Vol. XXIV (1909), pp. 585-675.

[54] Ib. p. 618.

[55] Ib. p. 631.

[56] University of Washington Publications in English. Vol. IV, No. 1. April 1918. Seattle, Washington, 45 pp.

[57] Ib. p. 36.

[58] Ll. 1205-6 of the Pearl.

[59] Cp. the severe, but just review by Professor C. Brown in the "Modern Language Notes." Vol. XXXIV, p. 42-3.

[60] In "Journal of English and Germanic Philology." Jan. 1921. Vol. XX, 1-21.

[61] Ll. 885-7 of the Pearl. cp. below p. 23.

[62] D. Appleton, New York 1925, pp. 226.

[63] Ib. p. 22.

[64] Ib. p. 89.

[65] Ib. p. 90.

[66] Ib. p. 208.

[67] Ib. p. 191.

[68] Ib. p. 175.

[69] PMLA, Dec. 1925. Vol. XL, pp. 814-27.

[70] Canto XXVIII.

[71] In "Modern Language Notes." Vol. XLII. 2. (1927), pp. 113-6.

[72] B text of the Canterbury Tales 11. 1769-75. Skeat's Chaucer. Vol. IV, p. 185.

[73] Ll. 243-4 of the Pearl.

[74] Ed. of the Pearl 1921, p. XLII and CHEL I, 331. "Privy" in l. 12.

[75] Ll. 483-5 of the Pearl.

[76] Ll. 473, 483-5.

[77] Any text-book of dogmatics shows this e. g. J. Pohle, Lehrbuch der Dogmatik II, 566, II, 665 etc. From Corinthians I, 13, 9 it can be concluded that the blessed inhabitants of heaven shall see everything clearly in God, what on earth is only an object of theological faith. The absence of envy and competition is inforced in our poem by a comparison with the relation between members of the same body. (ll. 457 seq.), a comparison which descends also from 1 Corinthians (6, 15 and Ch. 12) and which is e. g. elaborated by St. Augustine in "De Civitate Dei" (XXII, 30).

[78] "My wreched wylle" in l. 56, "del and gret daunger" in l. 250, "strot" in l. 353.

[79] L. 1176.

[80] In "De Causa Dei contra Pelagium" ed. 1618. Preface, quoted in Brown loc. cit.

[81] Psalm 24. 10, quoted by Augustine in the letter to Paulinus written in 417, No. 186.

[82] Augustinus, Tractatus 3 in Jovinianum n. 9.

[83] Cp. the letter of Augustine quoted above, besides "De Civitate Dei" XXI, 16. In Evangelium Joannis Tractatus 41, 5, also Chrysostomus, homilia de Adam et Eva; Cyprianus epistola 59, and Fidum etc.

[84] De Peccatorum Meritis et Remissione, Liber I. Caput 9. Migne, Patrologia Latina, Vol. 44, p. 114.

[85] Augustine, Letter to Mercator No. 193, dating from 418, also to Bishop Bonifacius, No. 98, written in 408, and De Peccatorum Meritis etc. Lib. 1, cap. 19 and lib. 3, c. 2.

[86] Sermo 14 de verbis Apostoli.

[87] Cp. the list of authorities quoted in Suarez, De gratia VI, 1, 7, Moguntiae 1621, p. 2, and Canisius, Opus catechisticum, Parisiis 1585, p. 413.

[88] In Cap. Maiores. Decret 1, 3 tit. 42 de baptismo, quoted by Pohle, Lehrbuch der Dogmatik II, 554.

[89] Clement, de summa Trinit. et fide cath. quoted ib.

[90] Sermo 66 super Cantica and Epistola ducentesima quadragesima ad Hildefonsum comitem, de Henrico haeretico, printed e. g. in S. Bernardi selectarum epistolarum Liber unicus, Parisiis 1614, p. 351. Bernardus uses the passage "Sinite parvulos venire a me," which the Pearl poet also uses in ll. 718 seq.

[91] Sess. 5, canon. 5 de Baptismo and sess. 7 can. 13 de Baptismo. Suarez summarizes the decisions thus: Concilium definit infantes baptizatos vere computari inter fideles, intelligit autem inter fideles justos. Et constant, quia sunt digni regno coelorum. De Gratia, VII, 8, 6, p. 88.

[92] Canisius, Opus catechisticum, Parisiis 1585, p. 413 Suarez, De gratia VI, 3, 6 (p. 8), and Gabriele Vasquez, Commentarium ac Disputationum in primam secundae S. Thomae tomus secundus. Antverpiae. MDCXX, disp. CCII. Cap. VI, p. 610-11.

[93] L. 417 of the Pearl.

[94] Ll. 655-8.

[95] L. 660.

[96] Brown loc. cit. p. 137.

[97] Ll. 447-9, 601-4, 863-4 etc. ll. 601-4 quoted.

[98] L. 885.

[99] L. 1121.

[100] Ll. 675 and 685/6.

[101] Epistola No. 167. n. 3. "Induti sunt sancti justitia (Job 29, 14) alius magis, alius minus."

[102] John 14, 2.

[103] 1 Cor. 15, 41.

[104] Commentary to Matthew. Homilium 64. ad Ch. XX, 1-16.

[105] Contra haereticos, Lib V, 36, 1-2.

[106] Ib. IV, 36, 7.

[107] Augustinus, De Sancta Virginitate cap. 26. Migne, Patrologia Vol. XL, col. 410. The same interpretation in "In Joannis Evangelium" Trac. LXVII, cap. 14. Migne, Patrologia Vol. XXX, col. 1812. Canisius loc. cit. p. 1115.

[108] Libro Quarto dialogorum, capite tregesimoquinto, quoted by Canisius, loc. cit.

[109] Libri IV Sententiarum Dist. XLIX. Paris 1. Q VI. Ed. 1668. Vol. II, p. 533.

[110] Summa Theologica I-II. V, 2.

[111] Petrus Lombardus, Dist. XLIX Pars I. Migne, Patrologia. Vol. CXCII, col. 957, Duns Scotus, In Lib. IV Sententiarum Dist. L. Qu. V. (ed. 1639, tom. X, pp. 641 and 651). Prosper, De vita contemplativa lib. I, cap. IV, quoted by Canisius, loc. cit. p. 1670.

[112] Cp. note 73.

[113] "Modern Language Notes" XLII, 2 (1927), pp. 113-6.

[114] Quoted in R. Stroppel, Liturgie u. geistliche Dichtung 1050-1300. Frankfurt 1927.

[115] In L. dist. 41 Qu. 1, quoted according to Pohle, loc. cit. II, 479.

[116] L. 269.

[117] L. 221 and cp. l. 1103-4.

[118] L. 735.

[119] L. 743-4.

[120] The last verse of the poem l. 1212.

[121] Matthew XII, 46.

[122] Episcopus Sardensium, cp. about him A. Harnack, Geschichte der altchristlichen Literatur I (1893), p. 246-

55, the passage from Clavis LXVI quoted in J. B. Pitra, Spicilegium Solesmense. Tom. II, 341. Parisiis 1855. Pitra quotes a passage, where the Pearl is also among the ninety-two names of Christ, from a Parisian cod. 36 f. 164, 165 III, 447, and passages from Phoebadius Barcinonensis, Eucherius, a bishop of Lyon, etc. Osgood (his ed. p. 82) quotes Augustine, Chrysostomus, Ephren the Syrian for this interpretation.

[123] Bonaventura (1221-1257) in serm. 3 dom. 17 p. Pent. in Opera Omnia. Tom. 7 Lugduni 1668, t. 3, p. 199 A and sermo 6 in Rogat. Rupert of Deutz quoted by Osgood p. 82 from Patr. Lat. Vol. 169, col. 1202. Hrabanus Maurus (died in 856) quoted by Pitra loc. cit.

[124] Homilia in Evangelia 11, 2 quoted by Osgood p. 82-3.

[125] Patrologia Lat. Vol. 184, col. 1069, quoted by Osgood loc. cit.

[126] Ad. litt. XII, art. 46, quoted by Pitra loc. cit.

[127] Chaucerian and other pieces. Ed. by W. W. Skeat. Oxford 1897, p. 145.

[128] Venetiis 1565. Apud Paulum Baleonium. Pars Quarta, Caput XXIV, Sermo I, preached in 1471, p. 232.

[129] PMLA. Vol. XII (1897), p. 326-40.

[130] Oakden loc. cit. p. 235, 241.

[131] I am thinking especially of the new study of poetical language and meter based on functional linguistics initiated in Russia and happily continued by members of the Prague Linguistic Circle.

Charles Moorman (essay date 1955)

SOURCE: "The Role of the Narrator in Pearl," in *The Middle English Pearl: Critical Essays,* University of Notre Dame Press, 1970, pp. 103-21.

[*In the following essay, Moorman defines the poem's real subject as the narrator's mind: the stages of his conversation with the Pearl maiden represent stages leading to his personal redemption and acceptance of his situation.*]

It is decidedly *not* the intention of this paper to introduce a radically new interpretation of the Middle English *Pearl,* a poem which has already been done almost to death by its interpreters. The criticism already devoted to the poem contains judgments as to its meaning and purpose so varied and, at times, so downright contradictory that *Pearl* is in danger of becoming a scholarly free-for-all, another "Who was Homer?" or "Why did Hamlet delay?" The disputed question in *Pearl* is, of course, "What is the pearl-maiden?" So far it has been suggested that she is the poet's daughter,[1] clean maidenhood,[2] the Eucharist,[3] innocence,[4] the lost sweetness of God,[5] the Blessed Virgin,[6] heaven itself,[7] and a literary fiction functioning only as an introduction to theological debate.[8] Such interest in the figure of the girl and in the peripheral aspects of source and imagery is understandable. A poem containing possible allusions to the *Roman de la rose,* Boccaccio, Chaucer, Dante, and the Vulgate and utilizing possibly heretical theology, the medieval dream-vision, the elegy, and the *débat* is a critic's land of heart's desire. However, such interpretive scholarship, while undeniably of great interest and value in opening up new avenues of critical insight, is nevertheless fragmentary, in that it is all too seldom directed, except in the most parenthetical manner, toward exploring the total meaning of the poem. We become easily lost in exploring the technicalities of the theology, the possible levels of symbolism in the maiden, and the details of the vision of the New Jerusalem and so are content to leave the center of the poem untouched or to murmur that its theme is obvious and pass on.

I would suggest that the quickest way to come to the heart of the poem would be to waive entirely all questions of allegory and symbolism and to concentrate not upon the figure of the girl but upon that of the narrator. For whatever else the poem may be—dream-vision, elegy, allegory, debate—it is, first of all, a fiction presented from a clearly defined and wholly consistent point of view; we accompany the "I" of the poem through his vision, and it is through his eyes that we see the magical landscapes and the girl. In the terms of Henry James, the narrator-poet is the "central intelligence" of the poem; in those of Brooks and Warren, the poem is the "narrator's story," in that we are never allowed to see and judge the experience presented by the poem objectively and for ourselves but are, instead, forced, by the point of view which the poet adopts, to accept the experience of the vision only in terms of its relationship to him. The mind of the narrator in *Pearl,* like the mind of Strether in *The Ambassadors* or, to come closer home, the mind of Dante the voyager, is the real subject under consideration. It is with the figure of the narrator alone in an "erbere" [arbor] that the poem begins and ends; it is he who controls the argument with the pearl-maiden by introducing the subjects for debate and by directing the path of the discussion with his questions; it is for his benefit that the maiden relates the parable of the vineyard and allows him to view the New Jerusalem.

The girl—to most critics the center of attraction simply because of her enigmatic and apparently shifting nature—is not introduced until line 161 and does not become actively engaged in the poem until line 241, when she is addressed by the narrator. She then disappears at line 976, to appear only once thereafter in a single reference within the vision of the New Jerusalem. In a poem of 1,212 lines, the girl herself is present on the scene for only 815 lines and can be said to participate in the action for only 735 lines, a little over half the length of the poem. Moreover, the pearl-maiden cannot be said to function, except peripherally, in the narrative movement of the poem. During that middle section of the poem which she seems to dominate by her presence, the poet never allows us to lose our sense of the narrator's presence. We know that he is there and listening carefully, interjecting questions and remarks from time to time. We are constantly aware of the fact that it is for his benefit that the girl talks and that it is his consciousness which is directly affected by her remarks. In short, the poet has so constructed the poem that it becomes obligatory that the reader judge the figure of the pearl-maiden not in isolation but entirely in terms of her relation to the narrator, the "I," the central intelligence of the poem.

The effect of this fact upon interpretation would seem to be twofold. First, it forces the reader to regard the action of the poem within the implied dramatic framework which the poet provides, and, second, it requires the reader to fit into that framework all the details, however seemingly unrelated, which the poet introduces—most significantly, the parable of the vineyard, the debate over grace and merit and the ensuing description of the place of the innocent in the heavenly hierarchy, the girl's description of her life in the New Jerusalem, and the vision of the New Jerusalem which is given to the poet.

The poem begins with a direct statement by the poet-narrator that he has lost "in on erbere"[9] [in an arbor] a certain pearl of great value, one which is to him without peer in all the world. He is so terribly grieved by the loss of the pearl that he cannot forget his former delight in possessing the gem; he laments his loss, "wyschande þat wele, / Þat wont watȝ whyle deuoyde [his] wrange / And heuen [his] happe and al [his] hele" [wishing that happiness / That once (him) freed from care / And restored (his) hap and all (his) joy] (14-16). But his grief takes another form also: it brings into his mind a series of paradoxes concerning the relationship of beauty and death or, more specifically, of growth and death. He knows that he sang "neuer so swete a sange" [never so sweet a song] (19) as that which he sings now in his hour of deepest grief; he reflects that the pearl's presence in the earth of the arbor will cause "blomeȝ blayke and blwe and rede" [golden and blue and red blossoms] (27) to prosper over her grave; he knows that "vch gresse mot grow of grayneȝ dede" [each blade must grow from dead seed] (31). In short, the narrator's grief-stricken statements reflect more than

personal sorrow over the loss of the pearl. In his grief he begins to consider the paradoxical nature of the universe in which he lives, a universe in which the decay of the body contributes directly to the beauty of nature, where "Flor and fryte may not be fede / Þer hit doun drof in moldeȝ dunne" [flowers and fruit may not fail where this pearl dropped down into dark earth] (29-30). Like Shelley in "Adonais," he wonders how

> The leprous corpse, touched by this spirit
>   tender,
> Exhales itself in flowers of gentle breath;
> Like incarnations of the stars, when splendour
> Is changed to fragrance, they illumine death
> And mock the merry worm that wakes
>   beneath.

Having established the narrator's grief and, more importantly, this questioning of the nature and justice of the universe which his grief inspires, the poet goes on to begin the dramatic movement of the poem. The narrator states that he has come to "þat spot" (49) where he lost the pearl; he has come there, moreover, in the very midst of August, when all growing things have blossomed, when the corn must be cut and the flowers—gillyflowers, ginger, gromwells, and peonies—are "schyre and schene" [bright and shining] (42). Here, in the midst of joy, his sorrow becomes even more acute, and in spite both of "resoun," which offers only the most temporary relief to his "deuely dele" [dreadful care] (51), and of the "kynde of Kryst," his "wreched wylle in wo ay wraȝte" [nature of Christ], [wretched will in woe was caught] (56). It is in this mood that the vision begins.

Thus in the first section of the poem we are introduced, even before we know that the poem is to take the form of a vision, to two facts about the situation of the narrator. First, we learn that he is overcome with inconsolable grief, and from the allusion to the "huyle" [mound] (41) we judge that the poet is grieving the death of a loved one. Second, we learn that his grief has taken the form of an awareness, almost of an indictment, of the mixed nature of the world. Standing amid the joyful flowers of August, he can think only of death and of the fact that the rotting body of his beloved child, "so clad in clot" [clothed in clay] (22), has produced this profusion of color. The two are so connected in the mind of the narrator, moreover, that his last thoughts upon going to sleep are of his own "wreched wylle" and, paradoxically, of the fragrance which springs into his senses as he falls asleep. In short, the poet's immediate grief has developed at the very beginning of the poem into a pondering of universal problems of life and death.

This questioning of the nature of things introduced at the outset is to occupy the poet throughout the poem. In order to assuage his grief, the poet must thus accomplish a reconciliation of the apparently dual nature of heavenly justice. And it is precisely this struggle for understanding which gives the poem its permanence and its enduring appeal. We are seldom, if ever, satisfied with the purely occasional poem, and the elegy which records only a particular grief never becomes in any way meaningful to us. In the elegy, moreover, the poet's grief is made universal and thus meaningful by exactly the process we see at work here in *Pearl*. The reader's attention is directed by the elegiac poet not toward the figure of the deceased, but toward the poet's own struggle to accept his loss and, more importantly, toward his struggle to understand in universal terms the final meaning of death and the conditions under which death may be meaningful to him. In "Lycidas," we remember, we are not allowed to become interested in the figure of Edward King. Our attention instead is focused from the beginning upon the struggle of the young Milton, first, to accept the possibility of his own premature death and, second, to understand, in both personal and universal terms, the significance of King's death. Likewise, in "In Memoriam" the figure of Arthur Hallam moves out of our consciousness as Tennyson explores the terms upon which he can accept a traditional faith in a skeptical age. "Adonais" and "Thyrsis" are more concerned with the struggles of the living Shelley and the living Arnold than with the praises of the dead Keats and the dead Clough.

And so it is with *Pearl*. The first section of the poem introduces the poet's struggle to reconcile the apparent contradiction expressed for him in the contrast of the flowers and the corpse; stanzas 2-5 introduce the means whereby he can approach a resolution of that contradiction. From the side of the grave his "spyryt þer sprang in space" [spirit leapt through space] (61), and his body "on balke þer bod in sweuen" [remained in a dream on the mound] (62). He finds himself in a strange world, far removed from the familiar earthly garden where he fell asleep; he "ne wyste in þis worlde quere þat hit wace" [new not in this world where it was] (65). He sees about him the items of the natural world— cliffs, forests, trees; but here these familiar sights are transformed into strange shapes and materials: crystal cliffs, forests filled with "rych rokkeȝ" (68), silver leaves, and pearls scattered about as gravel. This is the Earthly Paradise, where the ordinary natural objects of earth are displayed within and altered by a supernatural context. As Wendell Stacy Johnson points out, the images of the garden here reflect a brightness and light coming from outside themselves.[10]

Yet even this vision is not the ultimate perfection. Across the stream by which he walks lies the Heavenly Paradise, the complete antithesis of earth. The images pass here from "the vision of nature arrayed in (reflecting) light to one of a land and a person [the pearl-maiden] set in gems and adorned by an 'inner' lightness."[11] Both gardens, however, have a recupera-

tive effect upon the narrator; the first "Bylde in [him] blys, abated [his] baleȝ, / Fordidden [his] stresse, dystryed [his] payneȝ" [increased (his) joy, relieved (his) sorrow, / Allayed (his) distress, destroyed (his) pain] (123-124). But the second paradise, that which lies across the stream, seems even more wonderful to him; there, he feels, lies the answer to his dilemma:

> Forþy I þoȝt þat Paradyse
> Watȝ þer ouer gayn þo bonkeȝ brade.
> I hoped þe water were a deuyse
> Bytwene myrþeȝ by mereȝ made;
> Byȝonde þe broke, by slente oþer slade,
> I hoped þat mote merked wore.
>
>   (137-142)

> [Indeed I thought that Paradise
> Beyond broad banks lay there displayed.
> I thought the stream to be a ruse,
> Between two joys a boundary made;
> Beyond the stream, on slope, in dell,
> I thought to see the City laid.]

But the water is deep, and, in spite of his longing, the narrator cannot cross.

The narrator has now reached a position midway between earth, with its unsolvable riddles of life and death, and heaven, where all contradictories are united. In mythical terms, the narrator has arrived at a testing point; he is midway in the hero's mythical initiation cycle from earth to the strange land of adventure to earth again. Having accomplished the necessary journey to a strange land, having accepted the "call to adventure,"[12] he finds his mind "radically cut away from the attitudes, attachments, and life patterns of the stage left behind [his normal earthly life]."[13] In the more familiar terms of Arnold Toynbee, the narrator has accomplished a "withdrawal" from society which "makes it possible for the personality to realize powers within himself which might have remained dormant if he had not been released for the time being from his social toils and trammels."[14] Within the context of the poem, the narrator is at a point midway between problem (the apparently paradoxical nature of death) and solution (the resolving of that paradox). His world has become neither earth nor heaven but a middle ground, where earth and heaven can, under certain conditions as in the dream-vision, meet. In the midst of his wonderment, just as he is about to attempt a crossing, he sees before him, on the other side of the stream, the lost pearl, and at this point the debate begins.

What I have just called the "debate," which is to say simply the conversation between the narrator and the pearl-maiden, falls conveniently, as I have implied, into four parts: (1) the parable of the vineyard, (2) the girl's discussion of the relative grounds of grace and merit as means of salvation and her ensuing explanation of the place of the innocent in the heavenly hierarchy, (3) her description of Our Lord's suffering in the Old Jerusalem and of her life with him in the New Jerusalem, and (4) the vision of the New Jerusalem. I would claim that these episodes in the discussion are not digressions used either for their own sakes or for purposes of general instruction but that they are well-defined and climactically arranged stages in the process by which the narrator is made to understand the meaning of the girl's death and so is freed from the burden of his grief. It is my general thesis here that the long debate between the narrator and the girl is the only means by which the narrator can resolve the paradox of beauty and decay, of growth and death, which has troubled him and, by that resolution, come to accept the death of his daughter. For it becomes quite clear in the course of the conversation between the living narrator-poet and the dead maiden that their differences are profound. He is a man, she an angel, and the nature of the stream that divides them and the function of the vision itself become clear within the context of those differences. Earth cannot receive her; he is not ready for heaven. The debate in which they engage thus becomes a contest between two points of view, the earthly and the heavenly, between a point of view which sees natural death only as an irreducible paradox of decay and growth and a point of view which can reconcile that paradox in terms of a higher unity. Thus the terms of the central episode of the debate—grace and merit—are of no great consequence in themselves but have meaning within the dramatic framework of the poem only as they relate to the attitudes which they serve to reveal in the course of the talk.

Wendell Stacy Johnson has already shown, by means of a careful study of the imagery of the poem, that *Pearl* involves "an emphasis upon a ubiquitous sense of contrast between the nature of heaven and the nature of earth, the revelation of which seems, for our [Johnson's] present reading, to be the poem's main purpose."[15] I would agree with Johnson's demonstration of the contrast between earthly values and heavenly values, but this contrast seems to me to constitute only the means used by the poet to attain a yet higher end. The poet's earthbound nature, which we, as readers, share and which causes him to balk and quibble at each of her explanations, is in reality the source of his discontent. The girl's purpose in the debate is thus not primarily to prove to him the theological validity of the saving doctrine of grace but to demonstrate to him a point of view which will allow him to accept the differences in their attitudes and, through this acceptance, to come to a realization of the meaning and purpose of her death. To show the successful resolution of the two points of view exhibited in the poem and, through this resolution, the concomitant acceptance by the narrator of the fact of death thus becomes the main purpose and theme of the poem.

It remains to chart briefly the progress of the argument. The narrator—who, we remember, is the central intelligence and thus, in a sense, the reader—begins with the most natural of questions, a question which stems from his own interrogation of the justness of God and from his earthbound point of view:

> "O perle," quod I, "in perleȝ pyȝt,
> Art þou my perle þat I haf playned,
> Regretted by myn one on nyȝte?
> Much longenyg haf I for þe layned,
> Syþen into gresse þou me aglyȝte.
> Pensyf, payred, I am forpayned,
> And þou in a lyf of lykyng lyȝte,
> In Paradys erde, of stryf vnstrayned.
> What wyrde hatȝ hyder my iuel vayned,
> And don me in þys del and gret daunger?"
> (241-250)

> ["O Pearl," I said, "in pearls bedight,
> Are you the pearl that I have mourned
> And grieved for by myself at night?
> By grief for you have I been torn
> Since into grass you slipped away.
> Pensive and careworn, I have grieved,
> While you enjoy a life of play
> In Paradise from strife relieved.
> What fate has there my jewel placed
> And left to me this pain and care?"]

If both the tone and substance of his question reveal his earthly point of view, both the tone and substance of the pearlmaiden's answer reveal the gulf between them:

> "Sir, ȝe haf your tale mysetente,
> To say your perle is al awaye,
> Þat is in cofer so comly clente
> As in þis gardyn gracios gaye,
> Hereinne to lenge for euer and play,
> Þer mys nee mornyng com neuer nere.
> Her were a forser for þe, in faye,
> If þou were a gentyl jueler."
> (257-264)

> [Sir, you have your tale mistold,
> To say your pearl was snatched away,
> Since now she lies in royal state
> In this fair garden sweet and gay,
> Herein to dwell in constant joy
> With loss and mourning never near.
> Here might you see a treasured tomb
> If you were a gentle jeweler.]

As E. V. Gordon has said, "In the manner of the maiden is portrayed the effect upon a clear intelligence of the persistent earthliness of the father's mind: all is revealed to him, and he has eyes, yet he cannot see."[16]

The narrator, as quick to be comforted here by the girl's answer as he was by his first glimpse of the earthly paradise, suggests that he join her by crossing the stream. She replies, as of course she must, that he is "madde" (290). The narrator, at this point, though professing to understand the blessed state of the girl, quite obviously can interpret their relationship only in the familiar terms of earth, a sort of relationship which to her can no longer exist. He is human, he has our sympathy, but he is still completely dominated by earthly standards. The pearl-maiden must thus rebuke him, reminding him of his status as a living man:

> "Deme now þyself if þou con dayly
> As man to God wordeʒ schulde heue.
> Þou saytʒ þou schal won in þis bayly;
> Me þynk þe burde fyrst aske leue,
> And ʒet of graunt þou myʒteʒ fayle."
>
> (313-317)

> [Judge now yourself if you have said
> Those words to God you daily ought.
> You think this land to be your own;
> I think permission should be sought
> Even though that gift might be denied.]

The first section of the argument, a sort of prelude to the debate proper, thus establishes the nature of the differences between the narrator and the maiden. He asks pity; she demands full understanding. Neither can grant the other's request or acknowledge the other's point of view.

Then the narrator, in the course of blaming the girl for her happiness at his expense ("In blysse I se þe blyþely blent, / And I a man al mornyf mate; / ʒe take þeron ful lyttel tente, / Þaʒ I hente ofte harmeʒ hate" [In joy I see you blithely blent, / And I a man by mourning dazed; / You take thereof full little heed / That I am oft by sorrow razed] [385-388]), questions her right to the high place which she holds in the heavenly hierarchy; if she is

> . . . quen þat watʒ so ʒonge.
> What more honour moʒte he acheue
> Þat hade endured in worlde stronge,
> And lyued in penaunce hys lyueʒ longe
> Wyth bodyly bale hym blysse to byye?
>
> (474-478)

> [. . . queen while yet so young,
> What greater honor might he achieve
> Who had endured this world's distress,
> And lived in penance all his life
> To buy by pain true happiness?]

She lived, he says, for only two years; she never learned how to pray, knew neither "Pater ne Crede" [the Our Father nor the Creed]. Her position is thus to the nar-

rator "to dere a date" [too great a reward] (492). It is at this point in her explanation that the girl replies to the narrator's objections with the parable of the vineyard, in which first and last are paid alike, and she ends her telling of the story with an assertion which serves, significantly at this point, to emphasize the differences between the points of view which separate father and daughter:

> More haf I of ioye and blysse hereinne,
> Of ladyschyp gret and lyueʒ blom,
> Þen alle þe wyʒeʒ in þe worlde myʒt wynne
> By þe way of ryʒt to aske dome.
>
> (577-580)

> [More have I of joy and bliss herein,
> Of ladyship true and honor's height
> Than all men in the world might win
> Who sought reward by way of right.]

But, at this stage of the poem, the narrator, relying wholly upon his earthly standard of value, cannot begin to accept such a departure from what he considers true justice, and he, matching her appeal to biblical authority with his own, tells her that her tale is "vnresounable" (590). Thus her first attempt at conversion fails, since the narrator refuses to acknowledge, or even to recognize, her point of view and instead continues to advance earthly standards in opposition to her.

The maiden, however, pursues her case by the only means left open to her, by explaining carefully and in detail the relationship between grace and merit and the place of the innocent, "saf by ryʒt" [safe by right] (684), in heaven in order to assert that the grace of God is "gret inoghe" (612) to overcome earthly difficulties and standards of justice based entirely upon merit and "gret inoghe" to allot to each a full share of heavenly grace. Moreover, toward the end of her description of the place of the innocent in heaven, which concludes the second main episode of the debate, the maiden sharply underlines her point in continuing the debate thus far. She says:

> Harmleʒ, trwe, and vndefylde,
> Wythouten mote oþer mascle of sulpande
>   synne,
> Quen such þer cnoken on þe bylde,
> Tyt schal hem men þe ʒate vnpynne.
> Þer is þe blys þat con not blynne
> Þat þe jueler soʒte burʒ perré pres,
> And solde alle hys goud, boþe wolen and
>   lynne,
> To bye hym a perle watʒ mascelleʒ.
>
> (725-732)

> [The innocent, true, and undefiled
> By spot or stain of filthy sin,

When these come knocking at the door
The warders quick the gate unpin.
Within is the joy that never fails,
Which the jeweler thought in gems to catch
And sold his goods, linens and wool,
To buy him a pearl without a match.]

And she ends her speech by admonishing her father to forsake his earthly standards:

I rede þe forsake þe worlde wode
And porchace þy perle maskelles.

(743-744)

[I bid you forsake this madding world
And purchase this pearl without a match.]

The point of her remark, occurring as it does at the end of her attempt to explain to him heavenly standards of justice, is that the difference in standards between heaven and earth is such that the achieving of the pearl (here plainly symbolizing beatitude) demands a complete renunciation of wealth and hence earthly standards of wealth. That the narrator is beginning to see the point of the girl's remarks is evident in that, for the first time in the poem, he himself seems to perceive the nature and width of the river which separates them:

O maskeleʒ perle in perlez pure,

.   .   .   .   .

Quo formed þe þy fayre fygure?

.   .   .   .   .

Þy beauté com neuer of nature;
Pymalyon paynted neuer þy vys,
Ne Arystotel nawþer by his lettrure
Of carped þe kynde þese propertéʒ.
Þy colour passeʒ þe flour-de-lys;
Þyn angel-hauyng so clene corteʒ.

(745-754)

[O matchless Pearl arrayed in pearls

.   .   .   .   .

Who framed for you your figure's grace?

.   .   .   .   .

Your grace springs not from natural source
Nor did Pygmalion paint your matchless face.
Aristotle did not in all his works
Include your gentle properties,
Your color surpassing fleur-de-lis,
Your heaven-sent pure courtesy.]

Gordon, in his edition of the poem, notes of these lines that they are reminiscent of a passage in the *Roman de la rose* "where it is argued that neither the 'philosopher' . . . nor the artist, not even Pygmalion, can imitate successfully the works of Nature."[17] But this is plainly not the function of the comparison in this context. The narrator here would seem to realize for the first time the fact that the maiden before him is no longer the girl he knew on earth as his daughter. Her beauty is a new, an unnatural, beauty; her face and color derive from supernatural sources and from a realm of experience which even Aristotle, who catalogued all the forms of natural things, left untouched. Thus the parable of the vineyard and the discussion of grace and merit and of the place of the innocent in heaven are by no means digressive in character; they are integral to the movement and purpose of the poem as the first steps in the process whereby the poet-narrator comes to understand, or if not to understand, at least to accept, the heavenly point of view which the pearl-maiden represents.

But in spite of this sudden revelation of the central meaning of the maiden's speech, the narrator cannot as yet apply to his own situation the lesson he has apparently learned. For at the maiden's statement that Christ has "pyʒt [her] in perleʒ maskelleʒ" [robed (her) in matchless pearls] (768), he reiterates his argument that she is unworthy to surpass those women who "For Kryst han lyued in much stryf" [lived for Christ in sore distress] (776) and so, in effect, reopens the discussion.

The maiden's third attempt to assauge the poet's grief by explaining to him the differences in attitude which separate them takes the form of a description of Christ's sufferings in the Old Jerusalem and of her life in the New Jerusalem. Again, her point is the same, that heavenly standards are not earthly standards, but this time she deals directly with the paradox which lies at the root of the narrator's difficulty:

Alþaʒ oure corses in clotteʒ clynge,
And ʒe remen for rauþe wythouten reste,
We þourʒoutly hauen cnawyng;
Of on dethe ful oure hope is drest.
Þe Lombe vus gladeʒ, oure care is kest. . . .
(857-861)

[Although our corpses lie in graves
And you in grief remain alive,
We still have knowledge sure enough
That from one death our hopes derive.
The Lamb us gladdens, our cares are gone. . . .]

Upon hearing this statement, the narrator comes closer than before to a true and lasting understanding of their differences:

319

I am bot mokke and mul among,
And þou so ryche a reken rose,
And bydeȝ here by þys blysful bonc
Þer lyueȝ lyste may neuer lose.

(905-908)

[I am but muck and mold indeed
And you a rich and noble rose,
Who on this blissful shore reside
And never may life's savor lose.]

He realizes, in short, that his world of "mokke and mul" is forever separate from the world "by þys blysful bonc." Yet, for one last time, he cannot resist asking a favor; he would see the New Jerusalem himself. The reasons for his asking such a question again stem from his earthly point of view. He has looked about on the other side of the stream and has seen no hint of "castel-walle, / Ne maner þer [the girl] may mete and won" [a castle wall, / Nor manor where (the girl) might dwell] (917-918). He has seen only "þyse holteȝ" [these groves] (921), and he knows with all the dogmatic surety of earth that Jerusalem is *really* "in Judee" (922). It is the most natural of questions for him. He has come, by now, largely to accept the girl's point; he realizes that out of "mokke and mul" may come a "reken rose" and that even though the mysteries of heaven are forever incomprehensible to man, yet death, even his daughter's death, has a place in the divine plan, however unknowable it may be. As yet, he is still a man, and seeing is, after all, believing. And so the vision follows.

The vision, the final step in the process by which the poet comes to understand the meaning of death, involves, as did the parable of the vineyard, the debate on grace and merit, and the description of life in heaven, the distinction between earthly and heavenly standards of value. Here, in the New Jerusalem, the separation is complete; there is no need of earthly light or even of earthly religious forms:

Sunne ne mone schon neuer so swete
As þat foysoun flode out of þat flet;
Swyþe hit swange þurȝ vch a strete
Wythouten fylþe oþer galle oþer glet.
Kyrk þerinne watȝ non ȝete,
Chapel ne temple þat euer watȝ set;
Þe Almyȝty watȝ her mynster mete,
Þe Lombe þe sakerfyse þer to refet.

(1057-1064)

[Sun nor moon shone never so sweet
As that fair flood flowed from the throne;
Swiftly it poured through every street,
Unchecked by filth or scum or stone.
No church was ever built therein,
No crypt, no temple ever set;
Almighty God was church enough,
The Lamb their sacrifice complete.]

The climax of the vision, and of the poem, comes when the poet perceives, with his own eyes, his "lyttel quene" (1147) sitting among her peers, happy and again "wyth lyf" (1146), though a different kind of life from that he had first wished for her. And at this vision of an existence forever separate from earth, all his doubts disappear. In an ecstasy, he wishes to cross over to her but is awakened from his dream and finds himself again in the garden, his head upon the grave.

It is significant that the narrator's first words upon awakening show his single-hearted devotion to Christ. "Now al be to þat Prynceȝ paye" [Now all be to that Prince's joy] (1176), he says, and we are to understand, I think, that all doubts, all challenges, all questionings, have been removed from him. He realizes his own unworthiness to enter as yet into the heavenly life, his own incapacity to know finally the mysteries of the universe. But through a *rite de passage,* he has journeyed to the strange land and has returned, having been initiated into a new and more meaningful life. He will thus accept the standards of God, for the most part without understanding but also without questioning. It is enough for him; "wel is me," he says, "in þys doel-doungoun / Þat þou art to þat Prynseȝ paye" [well for me . . . in this dungeon of sorrow / since you are that Prince's joy.] (1187-1188). The poem thus ends with the narrator's lamenting, not, as before, the death of his daughter and the corruption of her body, but the corruptness of his own soul which has kept him from her and with his prayer that he may himself eventually be counted among the lowly servants and "precious perleȝ" of God.

The theme and the poetic method of *Pearl* are thus the theme and the poetic method of most elegies, the acceptance, through suffering and revelation, of death as a part of the universal plan. In *Pearl,* the parts of the dream-vision become the stages of redemption. The narrator here comes to learn, through a series of trials, to accept his place among the living. Like Milton's Adam, he can be said to say:

Greatly instructed I shall hence depart,
Greatly in peace of thought, and have my fill
Of knowledge, what this vessel can contain;
Beyond which was my folly to aspire.
Henceforth I learn that to obey is best,
And love with fear the only God.

Notes

[1] See the commentaries in the editions of the poem by R. Morris (London, 1864); I. Gollancz (London, 1891); and C. G. Osgood (Boston, 1906); and especially G. G. Coulton's defense of the autobiographical basis of the poem in *MLR,* II (1906), 39-43.

Illustration for Cotton MS.lines 57-64.

[2] W. H. Schofield, "The Nature and Fabric of *The Pearl*," *PMLA*, XIX (1904), 154-215, and "Symbolism, Allegory, and Autobiography in *The Pearl*," *ibid.*, XXIV (1909), 585-675.

[3] R. M. Garrett, *"The Pearl": An Interpretation* ("University of Washington Publications in English," Vol. IV, No. 1 [Seattle, 1918]).

[4] See Jefferson B. Fletcher, "The Allegory of the *Pearl*," *JEGP*, XX (1921), 1-21; and D. W. Robertson, "The 'Heresy' of *The Pearl*" and "The Pearl as Symbol," *MLN*, LXV (1950), 152-161.

[5] Sister Mary Madeleva, *"Pearl": A Study in Spiritual Dryness* (New York, 1925).

[6] Fletcher.

[7] Sister Mary Hillman, "Some Debatable Words in *Pearl* and Its Theme," *MLN*, LX (1945), 241-248.

[8] W. K. Greene, "*The Pearl*: A New Interpretation," *PMLA*, XL (1925), 814-827.

[9] *Pearl*, ed. E. V. Gordon (Oxford, 1953), l. 9. All line references in the text are to this edition.

[10] "The Imagery and Diction of *The Pearl:* Toward an Interpretation," *ELH*, XX (1953), 169. . . .

[11] *Ibid.*

[12] Joseph Campbell, *The Hero with a Thousand Faces* (New York, 1949), pp. 49-59.

[13] *Ibid.*, p. 10.

[14] Arnold Toynbee, *A Study of History*, abridged by D. C. Somervell (Oxford, 1947), p. 217.

[15] P. 163 . . .

[16] *Pearl*, p. xviii.

[17] *Ibid.*, p. 72.

Dorothy Everett (essay date 1955)

SOURCE: "The Alliterative Revival," in *Essays on Middle English*, Oxford at the Clarendon Press, 1955, pp. 46-96.

[*In this excerpt, Everett argues that the so-called alliterative revival was actually part of a continuous tradition and that* Pearl *can be compared to Milton's* Lycidas *and Dante's* Divine Comedy.]

The Alliterative *Morte Arthure* and other poems

Nothing that has survived from the early Middle English period prepares us for that later outpouring of alliterative poetry which has conveniently, though probably inaccurately, been termed the 'alliterative revival'. Suddenly (so it appears to us), in the middle of the fourteenth century, a number of poets began to use alliterative verse in the kinds of poetry then most popular—romances, chronicles, political satire, religious and moral allegory—and, continuing throughout this century and the next, they produced, among a good deal that is second-rate or worse, some of the most spirited of Middle English poems, and a few that can stand comparison with good poems of any age. The fact that so much in this poetry is obviously traditional suggests that the suddenness of its beginning must be illusory; for, if it be supposed that the traditional features were the result of a deliberate revival, this demands answers to the questions—what were the models, and, how were they known? Laȝamon's *Brut* does not provide a satisfactory answer, if only because its uncertain rhythms could not have inspired the far more confident rhythms of the later poems. To answer that other earlier works, now lost, might have been preserved in written or oral form till the second half of the fourteenth century is tantamount to admitting a continuous interest in alliterative verse; and such an interest is at least as likely to have resulted in new compositions as in the constant repetition of old. Moreover, as will appear, the nature of one of the earliest poems of the group seems to indicate that it was not the first of its kind. It is likely then, that alliterative poetry continued to be composed on a considerable scale from generation to generation without a break, and that the features in fourteenth-century verse that appear to be new to the alliterative tradition were adopted gradually, to meet the demands of new subjects and new tastes.

These new features are of various kinds. The traditional vocabulary is often enlarged by a wealth of technical terms, usually French, to do with hunting, architecture, armour, and so forth. The influence of stanzaic verse is seen in the occasional grouping of the alliterative long lines, sometimes in quatrains, sometimes in stanzas using rhyme. Fashionable formal devices such as the dream or the debate are employed, and alliterative poets become as addicted as any others to describing spring mornings, hunting scenes, and elaborate feasts. Yet their poetry remains distinctive in manner and feeling, as well as in metre. Some of the most striking differences between Middle English alliterative poetry and poetry written in other metres are in manner, a liking for specific detail resulting in solid, realistic description; in feeling, a seriousness of outlook which gives unusual strength and purpose, at least to the best of the poems.

There are many and puzzling resemblances in phraseology, style, and theme between the various alliterative poems. Some of these can undoubtedly be explained as the result of deliberate imitation, though ignorance of the exact date of most of the poems often makes it impossible to decide which way the borrowing went. Common authorship has been held to account for some others; but the game of hunting for similar phrases and assigning all works that contain them to a single author was carried much too far by some early critics. It has been shown that many of the poems which were at one time attributed on this evidence to the poet Huchoun, whose name we chance to know from Andrew Wyntoun's *Orygynale Cronykil,* differ in dialect and in important points of style and metrical technique. Nowadays theories of common authorship are viewed with caution, and scholars prefer to leave the authors of most of the alliterative poems unnamed.

Something is known, however, about where the authors lived. From the remark of Chaucer's Parson:

> But trusteth wel, I am a Southern man,
> I kan nat geeste 'rum, ram, ruf,' by lettre,
> Ne, God woot, rym holde I but litel bettre
>   *(Canterbury Tales,* 1. 42-44)

we may judge, not, as is often suggested, that Chaucer despised alliterative verse (there are good reasons for not believing this), but that he did not think such verse was composed in his own southern district. The investigations of modern scholars show him, on the whole, to have been right. The original dialects of the alliterative poems, so far as they can be ascertained, have, with very few exceptions, been localized in the western counties from Gloucestershire to Cumberland; the majority of them in the northern half of this district.

If, as we may also infer, Chaucer thought these poems 'provincial', he was right in this too; for most of them came from districts which, as the southerner Trevisa tells us, 'þe kynges of Englelond woneþ fer fram'—districts, that is, far removed from the recognized centres of culture. Yet the odd thing is that some of these poems are not at all what we should expect a provincial poem to be. They have a self-assured air, as if their writers, who were evidently familiar with polite literature, knew what they wanted to achieve and how to set about it. In the no doubt extreme case of *Sir Gawain and the Green Knight,* there is a knowledge of aristocratic society as complete as in Chaucer's poetry. Such a poem must have been written for a cultured society of some kind, and it is possible that some great families of the west who were in opposition to the king—the Mortimers, Bohuns, and Beauchamps, for instance—may deliberately have fostered verse of native origin as a rival to that poetry, more closely dependent on French, which was written for the court by Chaucer and others. We know that one alliterative poem at least, *William of Palerne,* was written at the request of Humphrey de Bohun, Earl of Hereford.

Not all alliterative poetry can have been intended for aristocratic society, however. The greatness of *Piers Plowman* does not obscure its comparative lack of art, and, however successful modern critics may have been in showing that it is not the shapeless mass that it once seemed to be, it still remains evident that its writer (or writers) felt no compulsion to polish his work. This does not prove that *Piers Plowman* was written for the common people, though John Ball's letter to the peasants of Essex (1381) shows that they knew of it; but it does suggest that it was intended for a public less literary and less critical than that for which *Sir Gawain* was written. We must not draw too sharp distinctions between the poems, dividing them into 'aristocratic' and 'popular', for some of the interconnexions that have been mentioned cut across any groupings that might be made. But we may suppose that, in the later fourteenth century, in the districts where it flourished, alliterative poetry was popular in more than one stratum of society. Perhaps there had been, in the preceding period, separate streams of tradition, kept alive in different classes of society, which for some reason or other, and to some extent, intermingled in the fourteenth century.

. . . . .

Pearl

Pearl stands much father apart from other Middle English writings than *Sir Gawain*. Though its form is influenced by the familiar dream convention, and though it is thoroughly medieval in spirit and workmanship, yet as a whole it is unlike any other Middle English poem. In some respects it is nearer to *Lycidas* than to anything else in English, for—without prejudice to the controversial question of whether or not *Pearl* is an elegy—it begins, like *Lycidas,* by lamenting a loss; from this the poet is led on to consider certain spiritual and moral problems, and he finally reaches understanding and acceptance of God's will. Like *Lycidas, Pearl* is cast in a conventional literary form, is built with scrupulous artistry and expressed in highly charged language—language, that is, selected and ordered for particular ends. Though the differences between the two poems are, of course, many and important, they are essentially of the same order.

So far as *Pearl* is concerned, there is much in this statement that needs justification, and it would be well to begin by outlining the poem as impartially as possible. It opens with praise of the pearl which the poet has lost in an 'erbere' ['herb garden'] and he tells how, on going back to the spot, he finds it covered with so many sweet flowering plants that he is overpowered by their fragrance and falls asleep. He passes in spirit into a marvellous country and, on the other side of a river, he perceives a maiden clad in gleaming white garments set with pearls. He recognizes her: 'I knew hyr wel, I hade sen hyr ere',[1] 'Ho watȝ me nerre þen aunte or nece';[2] and he begins to question her: 'What fate has carried away my jewel and plunged me in such grief?' (249-50). The maiden rebukes him, saying that he has no cause for grief, for, though she was but young when she departed, her Lord the Lamb took her in marriage and crowned her queen.

The dreamer cannot believe this, for surely Mary is the Queen of Heaven. But the maiden explains that in heaven no one dispossesses any other, and all are kings and queens; and then, as he protests that she is too young to be a queen, she relates the parable of the workers in the vineyard to show that the first shall be last, and the last first. The dreamer still protests, for this means that he who works less receives more. The maiden replies that there is no question of more or less in God's kingdom; His grace is enough for all. The sinner who repents finds grace, why not the innocent who never sinned? 'When such knock there upon the dwelling, quickly shall the gate be unlatched for them' (727-8). In the kingdom of heaven is endless bliss, the pearl of great price, which the merchant sold all that he had to purchase. In answer to the dreamer's further questions, he is permitted to see the New Jerusalem

and, in the streets of it, a procession headed by the Lamb. In the throng that follows Him he sees his 'lyttel quene'.

Longing to be with her, he is about to start into the stream, but he suddenly awakes, to find himself back in the 'erbere'. Though full of grief at his banishment from the fair country of his vision, he cries:

> If hit be ueray and soth sermoun,
> Þat þou so strykeȝ in garlande gay,
> So wel is me in þys doel-doungoun,
> Þat þou art to þat Prynseȝ paye.[3]

He reflects that, had he been more submissive to God's will, he might have come to know more of His mysteries, and he ends by offering up his vision to God, praying that God may 'grant us to be the servants of His household and precious pearls for His pleasure'.

This summary is perhaps sufficient to suggest the nature of the appeal made by *Pearl,* but it cannot convey the qualities which make it an outstanding example of poetic art.

In this poem, as in all great poems, form and content are not separable; and both are evident alike in the smallest detail and in the conception and shaping of the whole.

As in *Sir Gawain and the Green Knight,* the matter of *Pearl* is ordered so as to form a pattern. Naturally the means by which this is done here differ from those employed in the narrative poem, and the pattern is all-embracing, as it is not in *Sir Gawain.* Of the twenty equal sections of the poem[4] the first four are mainly devoted to presenting the dreamer's state of mind and to description of the dream-country and of Pearl herself; argument and exposition occupy the central twelve sections, and the last four again contain description, this time of the New Jerusalem, and end with the poet's reflections. This pattern is emphasized by the echoing of the first line of the poem, 'Perle, plesaunte to pryncez paye',[5] in the last, 'Ande precious perleȝ vnto his pay'. The metrical scheme, which subdivides the poem into smaller sections and at the same time links all its parts into a continuous sequences, forms a second pattern, subsidiary to the main one but concurrent with it. There are 101 stanzas of twelve four-stressed lines, rhyming a b a b a b a b b c b c. Two or more of the stresses are usually marked by alliteration. The stanzas fall into groups of five, the same refrain being used in the last line of each of the five, and it is thus that the poem is divided into the twenty equal sections, though section XV, exceptionally, contains six stanzas. A keyword or phrase in the refrain is always echoed in the first line of the following stanza; this means that the sections are linked to one another, since a significant word is repeated, in the first line of each new section, from the refrain of the preceding one. The echo between the first and last lines of the poem gives the effect of a completed circle, intended perhaps to suggest the idea of the pearl, which in 1. 738 is called 'endeleʒ rounde'.[6]

The same stanza form, and the linking, are found elsewhere in Middle English, in some lyrics in the Vernon MS. for instance; but nowhere else is there anything like this complex scheme, nor is the stanza handled with such mastery. This poet makes good use of the natural break after the eighth line, and, within the line, he allows himself freedom in the use of alliteration and varies the rhythm and the number of syllables. Thus, within the rigid metrical scheme of the whole, the line, its smallest unit, is flexible. The following stanzas, one descriptive, one argumentative, illustrate some of these characteristics. They also illustrate what appears to be a general practice, the greater use of alliteration in description:

The dubbemente of þo derworth depe
Wern bonkeʒ bene of beryl bryʒt;
Swangeande swete þe water con swepe,
Wyth a rownande rourde raykande aryʒt;
In þe founce þer stonden stoneʒ stepe,
As glente þurʒ glas þat glowed and glyʒt;
As stremande sterneʒ, quen stroþe men slepe,
Staren in welkyn in wynter nyʒt;
For vche a pobbel in pole þer pyʒt
Watz emerad, saffer, oþer gemme gente,
Þat alle þe loʒe lemed of lyʒt,
So dere watʒ hit adubbement.[7]

Grace innogh þe mon may haue
Þat synneʒ þenne new, ʒif him repente,
Bot wyth sorʒ and syt he mot hit craue,
And byde þe payne þerto is bent.
Bot resoun of ryʒt þat con not raue
Saueʒ euermore þe innossent;
Hit is a dom þat neuer God gaue,
Þat euer þe gylteʒ schulde be schente.
Þe gyltyf may contryssyoun hente,
And be þurʒ mercy to grace þryʒt;
Bot he to gyle þat neuer glente,
As innocente is saf by ryʒte.[8]

The refrains are the most difficult part of this scheme to manage, but on the whole the poet is amazingly successful with them. Often they appear to fit naturally into his train of thought, but when necessary he will vary them slightly. The emphasis which certain words receive from so much repetition is rarely misplaced; indeed, most of the reiterated words and pharses are so essential to the poem as a whole that, taken in order, they almost form a key to its contents. There are some sections, certainly, in which the repetition seems mechanical, and others in which the meaning of the repeated word or phrase has to be ingeniously stretched to fit every context in which it is used. Yet the poet

can make a poetic virtue even of this kind of ingenuity, or of something very closely akin to it. In Section VIII the refrain word 'cortasye', is used to mean, not only 'courtesy', 'courtliness', but 'generosity', 'benevolence', and, as critics have pointed out, it is sometimes almost a synonym for 'grace' (divine favour or condescension). No one of these meanings fits every context in this section, but the poet uses now one, now another, while keeping all the time some reflection of the basic meanings 'courtliness', 'courtesy', and its implications. This is achieved by the use of many words such as 'queen', 'king', 'emperor', 'empress', 'court' which are naturally associated with 'courtliness' and 'courtesy'. So the lesson of Section VII—that though Mary is Queen of Heaven, she is also Queen of Courtesy, and none who comes there is, or feels himself to be, dispossessed, but each is 'king and queen by courtesy'—is doubly conveyed by clear statement which can be intellectually apprehended and by all the associations of the word 'courtesy'.

Such exploitation of the association of words is a marked feature of the whole poem and takes many forms, from mere word-play, dependent on similarity of sound, as in the line 'So is hys mote wythouten moote',[9] to the vividly metaphorical language of the following lines:

I loked among his meyny schene
How þay wyth lyf wern laste and lade[10]

or of these:

For þoʒ þou daunce as any do,
Braundysch and bray þy braþe breme,
When þou no fyrre may, to ne fro,
Þou moste abyde þat he schal deme.[11]

Some words already have poetic or literary associations which are of value to the context in which they are used. So, 'douth', having dignified associations from its use in old heroic poetry, but having lost the precise significance of the Old English 'duguþ',[12] is at once impressive and mysterious enough to be used of the hosts of hell, earth, and heaven that gaze upon the Lamb (839-10). In writing of his longing for the Pearl the poet evokes, by the word 'luf-daungere',[13] memories of the separation of lovers, and of the love-longing so often described by poets of the *Roman de la Rose* tradition. Especially in descriptive passages, his phrasing is full of echoes; and it is here that they have most value, for in all his descriptions the poet is attempting to present something transcending ordinary human experience. In the description of the maiden, he calls to his aid conceptions of feminine beauty by using terms from the romances, and throughout the opening descriptions there are reminiscences, verbal and otherwise, of the Garden of Love in the *Roman de la Rose*. The flowers on the spot where Pearl was lost are, like those in the Garden of Love, fragrant spices known for their healing properties; and the trees, the birds, the river of the country of the poet's vision could not fail to remind his readers of that beautiful garden. Yet the details—the 'flaumbande hweȝ'[14] of the birds, the tree-trunks 'blwe as ble of ynde',[15] the emeralds, sapphires, and other gems that lie at the bottom of the stream—are peculiar to this description and less realistic than those in the *Roman*; for this land is more remote from normal experience than the Garden of Love and surpasses it in beauty. At one point the poet compares the banks of the river to 'fyldor fyn',[16] normally associated with jewellery or, in simile, with golden hair, and the effect of this fantastic comparison is to convey the splendour of the banks and at the same time their unreality. To the modern mind, however, the associations with nature evoked by some of the poet's similes are probably more effective—the comparison, for instance, of the precious stones glinting through the water to stars that shine on a winter night,[17] or of the sudden appearance of the procession of Virgins to the rising of the moon:

> Ryȝt as þe maynful mone con rys
> Er þenne þe day-glem dryue al doun,
> So sodanly on a wonder wyse
> I watȝ war of a prosessyoun.[18]

More than any secular book it is the Bible that fills the poet's mind and imagination. When he describes his distress, 'My herte watȝ al wyth mysse remorde, As wallande water gotȝ out of welle',[19] he is recalling the Psalmist's 'Sicut aqua effusus sum'; at the words of the Lamb, 'Cum hyder to me, my lemman swete, For mote ne spot is non in þe' (763-4), the maiden is invested with the associations of the Song of Songs ('et macula non est in te. Veni de Libano sponsa mea . . . '). In the central portion of the poem the poet makes constant appeal to the authority of the Bible, buttressing his argument by passages drawn from it. The ease with which he passes from one part of it to another is an indication both of his familiarity with it and of the alert independence of his mind. In Section XIV and the beginning of XV, where the maiden is replying to the dreamer's question 'Quat kyn þyng may be þat Lambe?',[20] her answer is a tissue of reminiscences of Isaiah liii, of the Gospels, of the Book of Revelation and of other passages, all co-ordinated into a coherent and moving statement.

However closely dependent on the Bible the poet may be, he always follows his own line of thought. The parable of the workers in the vineyard, which is a close paraphrase of Matthew xx. 1-16, is interpreted in a way that is relevant to the argument and, so far as is known, unique; and, in the description of the New Jerusalem, the poet makes his own choice of details from the Book of Revelation and presents them in his own order.

With the parable of the pearl of great price (Matthew xiii. 45-46), from which the symbolism of the poem largely derives, it is not the Bible alone that the poet has in mind, but, in addition, various interpretations of it. The parable is alluded to and partly paraphrased in ll. 729-32, just after the reference to Jesus calling the little children to Him, and the implication would seem to be that the precious pearl (the 'spotless pearl' in the words of the poem) means innocence. But at the same time it means the kingdom of heaven, the reward of innocence, for ll. 729 ff. state explicitly that the pearl which the merchant sought is 'the joy that cannot cease' which is found in the kingdom of heaven, and in the next stanza (lxii) the maiden shows in what respects the pearl resembles that kingdom. She finally identifies it with the pearl she wears upon her breast which, she says, her Lord the Lamb placed there in token of peace. Of the many interpretations of the pearl of great price which might have been familiar to the poet, Gregory's statement that 'margarita vero mystic significat . . . dulcitudinem coelestis vitae', or that of Petrus Chrysologus that the pearl is 'vita aeterna', may lie behind his thought here; and there may even be a hint at the interpretation, used in Usk's *Testament of Love*, that the pearl of great price means grace. The poet shifts to yet another interpretation in the first line of stanza lxiii, when the maiden herself is addressed as the 'spotless pearl'. Here he is probably thinking of St. Bonaventura's 'Bonae margaritae sunt omnes sancti'. It is evident that in this passage the poet is playing upon various ideas connected with the pearl of great price in much the same way as he plays upon the meanings of the word 'cortasye', and he sums up the complex symbolism of the passage in the lines which the dreamer addresses to the maiden:

> 'O maskeleȝ Perle in perleȝ pure,
> Þat bereȝ', quod I, 'þe perle of prys . . . '[21]

It is likely that, to a medieval lover of poetry, many of the passages that have been quoted in the preceding pages would have conveyed a rather different impression from that which they make on a modern critic. While not less alive to their effects, he would at the same time have recognized them as examples of the rhetorical 'figures' and colours which Chaucer's Host begs the Clerk to keep till he composes in the 'high style'; and he would have noticed many others, for rhetorical devices of all kinds abound in the poem. In *Pearl*, as in *Sir Gawain and the Green Knight*, the whole method of composition, including the planning of the poem, is determined by the precepts of the rhetoricians. But, again as in *Sir Gawain*, it is not rhetorical doctrine but the poet's artistic sense that is the ultimate court of appeal. In some of his descriptive passages, where he needs to create an impression of gorgeous beauty, he writes in the 'high style' enriching his expression by every means he knows; but when he wishes, he can write simply, with few devices, comparatively little alliteration, and few words that were not in common use. The paraphrase of the parable of the workers in the vineyard is for the most part in this simple style, and a comparison of this passage with the description of the dream-country makes it possible to answer the criticism that the poet's vocabulary is 'faulty in too great copiousness'. It is obvious that there is 'copiousness' where it is in place, but not everywhere.

Another objection might perhaps more legitimately be brought against *Pearl*. It might be argued that a work so meticulously wrought must be lacking in vital force, that such close attention to form and expression cannot be compatible with the creation of poetry that is 'the breath and finer spirit of all knowledge'. To this the only answer is a personal one. To many readers, the present writer among them, the human emotion manifested in the poem appears to be its driving force and its motive. Whether the poet is describing his grief, or wrestling in argument, or realizing the joy of those who follow the Lamb, there is an urgency and a passionate sincerity in his writing which forbids one to regard it as a mere exercise in the poetic art. This has been widely felt, even though there has been no general agreement about the nature of the poet's loss or the meaning of his poem.

These are problems still in dispute, and possibly incapable of final solution, since it will not do to argue that, because the poet makes us feel a sense of loss, Pearl must represent a real child and cannot be the allegorical representation of some virtue or, as has even been suggested, of the poet's own soul in a state of perfection. For men have grieved for such losses as much as for the loss of a child. Yet, on the whole, it seems most satisfactory to assume that the poem was inspired by the death of a loved child, not necessarily a daughter or a sister, for the line 'Ho^{22} wat$_3$ me nerre^{23} þen aunte or nece' need not imply blood-relationship. The poet's grief is intensified by his uncertainty about her fate, for she died too young to please God by works or even to pray (484). In the vision that is granted him, he is convinced, both by argument and by the sight of his 'lyttel quene' in the New Jerusalem, that she is saved and that she is among those who follow the Lamb; and with this reassurance he is able to resign himself to God's will.

R. Wellek has shown that the child's fate could have presented a real problem at the time when *Pearl* was written.^{24} Though belief in the salvation of the baptized child through free grace was widely held from the time of Augustine, yet the matter was still under discussion in the fourteenth century. The reaffirmation by Thomas Bradwardine (d. 1340), in *De Causa Dei contra Pelagium,* of the doctrine of salvation by grace, against those who held the Pelagian heresy of salvation by merit, points to an interest in fourteenth-century England in matters fundamentally connected with

this. Hence the poet's anxiety to know what had happened to the child, and his concern with the nature of grace, are understandable. Clearly the maiden's answer, that the innocent who have been baptized (626-7) are saved, 'For þe grace of God is gret innoghe',^{25} is not, as one critic has suggested, unorthodox; and it would appear that R. Wellek was right in maintaining that there is nothing unorthodox, either, in the high position in heaven which is assigned to the child. The intellectual and spiritual struggle presented in the poem is not waged against orthodox beliefs; rather, it is a struggle to accept the teaching of the Church by one who wishes to do so, but is beset by doubts.

The battle must, of course, have been won before the poem was written, since it is the poet who, in the person of Pearl, provides the answers to his own difficulties. But it is not the least of his powers as a poet that he conveys the agony of the struggle as if it were still to win. There is a close parallel to the *Divina Commedia* here. Small as the scale of *Pearl* is compared with Dante's poem, the method is essentially the same. In both, the process of enlightenment is presented by means of a dialogue between a mortal seeking it and a celestial being, once a loved mortal, who now possesses knowledge, by virtue of her position in heaven. In both, the poet has, as it were, split himself into two, so that he can present at once his ignorance and uncertainty and his knowledge and confidence; and, since his serene confidence, and even his power to understand, was not achieved unaided, but was the result of divine revelation both direct and through the teaching of the Church, the person of the instructor is rightly represented as insusceptible of human emotion, remote and incomprehensible, while the person of the instructed remains human and prone to emotion, and for that reason able to arouse emotion. Though the dialogue form is often used in medieval literature to convey instruction, the similarity here is unusually close; and it is between something so fundamental to each poem that it affords far better grounds for thinking that the poet of *Pearl* knew the *Divina Commedia* than some of the lesser parallels that have been cited.

If this be the right way of looking at the poem, there is little point in the old argument as to whether *Pearl* is an elegy or an allegory. Though it has, of course, elegiac and allegorical elements in it, it is not to be comprehended by either term, and it could with as much justice be called a homily, a debate (*disputatio*), or a vision of the other world. None of these labels, by itself, is any more illuminating than the bare terms 'elegy' or 'pastoral' would be, if applied to *Lycidas*.

This brings us back to the starting-point and by now it should have become clearer in what respects *Lycidas* and *Pearl* are alike and in what they differ. Perhaps the most surprising thing is the marked similarity of their conclusions. The vision of the Catholic poet of *Pearl* ends where the Protestant Milton's does:

> For Lycidas your sorrow is not dead,
> . . . but mounted high
> Through the dear might of him that walked
>   the waves. . . .
> And hears the unexpressive nuptial Song,
> In the blest Kingdoms meek of joy and love,
> There entertain him all the Saints above,
> In solemn troops and sweet Societies.

Notes

[1] 'I knew her well, I had seen her before' (164).

[2] 'She was nearer to me than aunt or niece' (233).

[3] 'If it is indeed sober truth that thou movest thus in a gay garland, then I am content, in this prison of grief, that thou art to the Prince's pleasure' (1158-8).

[4] Indicated by initial capitals in the manuscript.

[5] 'Pearl, a precious thing for the Prince's pleasure'.

[6] 'endlessly round'.

[7] 'The beauties of those precious deeps [i.e. deep waters] were pleasant banks of bright beryl; swinging softly, the water swept with a whispering voice, flowing straight on. In the depth there lay bright stones that glowed and glittered like lights through glass; shimmering like stars, which, while men on earth are sleeping, gleam in the heavens on a winter night. For every pebble set there in the pool was an emerald, sapphire or precious gem, so that all the water shimmered with light, so splendid was its adornment' (109-20).

[8] 'Grace enough may that man have who sins afresh, if he will repent; but with sorrow and lamentation he must crave it and endure the pain that is bound with it. But Reason, Who cannot swerve from justice, evermore saves the innocent. It is a judgment that God never gave that ever the innocent should be discomfited. The guilty man may cling to contrition and by mercy be drawn back to grace—but he who never turned aside to sin, being innocent is saved by right' (661-72, emending MS. *at* to *as,* and MS. & to *by* in the last line.)

[9] 'So is His dwelling without spot' (948).

[10] 'I gazed among His radiant following [and saw] how they were loaded and weighed down with life' (1145-6).

[11] 'For, though you skip about like any doe, rush to and fro, and bray out your fierce wrath, when you can

go no further, forwards or backwards, you must put up with what He decrees' (345-8).

[12] 'a band of noble retainers'.

[13] 'separation in love' (11). 'Danger', in the *Roman de la Rose,* comes between the lover and the beloved.

[14] 'flaming colours'.

[15] 'blue as indigo'.

[16] 'fine gold thread'.

[17] See p. 88.

[18] 'Even as the mighty moon rises before the gleam of day has quite descended thence, so suddenly, in a miraculous way, I was aware of a procession' (1093-6).

[19] 'My heart was all stricken with grief [so that I was] like rushing water pouring from a stream' (364-5).

[20] 'What kind of thing may that Lamb be?

[21] ' "Oh spotless Pearl, in pure pearls, that wears", said I, "the pearl of price" ' (745-6).

[22] 'She'.

[23] 'nearer'.

[24] '*The Pearl*: an interpretation of the Middle English Poem', *Studies in English by Members of the English Seminar at the Charles University,* iv (Prague, 1933).

[25] 'enough'.

John Gardner (essay date 1965)

SOURCE: "Conventions and Traditions in the Poems," in *The Complete Works of the Gawain-Poet,* The University of Chicago Press, 1965, pp. 13-36.

[*In the following essay, Gardner places* Pearl *in the tradition of alliterative courtly verse and comments on the poet's skillful use of the elaborate ornamentation created with patterns of rhyme, alliteration, numeric symbolism, and the important symbolism emanating from the four-level system of biblical exegesis.*]

In their selection of poetic forms, Chaucer and the *Gawain*-poet differ. Chaucer's parson disparages the ancient English "rum, ram, ruf" school of poetry, and whether or not Chaucer agrees with his parson, his poems are not alliterative. The *Gawain*-poet, on the other hand, announces at once in *Sir Gawain and the Green Knight* that he intends to tell his story

> Rightly, as it is written,
> A story swift and strong
> With letters locked and linking,
> As scōps have always sung.
>
> [part 1, st. 2, ll. 33-36]

And whereas Chaucer explores numerous poetic genres and more often than not completely transforms them, the *Gawain*-poet for the most part holds to the old conventions, within them writing homilies, a courtly dream-vision, a saint's legend, and, surprisingly, a most unconventional Arthurian romance. In both his choice of form and his choice of subject, the *Gawain*-poet is mainly, though not entirely, a conscious traditionalist.

To call a poet a traditionalist is not to call him unoriginal. The questions to be asked concerning such a poet are: Where was the tradition when he found it? How did he reinterpret or extend the tradition? For the most part we can only speculate, drawing inferences from the poems and from the practice of other poets of the day. The chief hindrance is our lack of information concerning the courts where the provincial poets wrote. It must be understood that, generally speaking, a poet of the fourteenth century wrote for an audience, not primarily for himself or posterity. To allude to books or build symbols from philosophical systems his immediate audience could not possibly know might suggest overweening pride. In practice poets frequently put together extremely familiar materials in new ways to achieve new effects, at best a new vision of reality. Thus in the *Troilus,* for instance, Chaucer combines Dante, Boethius, a story from Boccaccio, and possibly the story of the Fall of Man, among other things, to create something strikingly new.

All the surviving west and northwest Midlands alliterative poetry shows a similar manipulation of conventional materials. A stock May morning passage—shining leaves, birds singing like angels, fields full of flowers—enters the *Morte Arthure* as an ironic contrast to Arthur's warlike deeds; in *The Parliament of the Three Ages* the same materials comment on the narrator's poaching of a deer; in *Winner and Waster* the stock passage, slightly modified, establishes the parallel between winning and wasting in Nature, on one hand, and winning and wasting in human society, on the other; in *Piers Plowman* the same convention, treated more realistically and localized at Malvern Hills, becomes the foundation for a series of allegorical dreams. Many of these alliterative poems present arming scenes like those in *Sir Gawain,* and *The Parliament of the Three Ages* presents a hunt which seems designed to contrast with legal and noble hunts like those in *Sir Gawain.* The description of Youth in the *Parliament* may or may not be conventional but certainly calls to mind the *Gawain*-poet's description of the Green Knight. The *Parliament*-poet says of Youth (ll. 109-23):

> The first was a fierce man, fairer than the others,
> A bold knight on a steed and dressed to ride,
> A knight on a noble horse, a hawk on his wrist.
> He was big in the chest and broad in the shoulders,
> And his arms, likewise, were large and long,
> And his waist was handsomely shaped as a maiden's;
> His legs were long and sturdy, handsome to see.
> He straightened up in his stirrups and stood aloft,
> And he had neither hood nor hat to hide his hair,
> But a garland on his head, a glorious one
> Arrayed with bright red roses, richest of flowers,
> With trefoils and true-love knots and delicate pearls,
> And there in the center a splendid carbuncle.
> He was outfitted in green interwoven with gold,
> Adorned with golden coins and beautiful beryl. . . .

Other parts of the description of Youth recall the **Pearl**. Like the child in the **Pearl**, Youth's garments are sewn all around with gems, but the gems are, instead of pearls, the chalcedonies, sapphires, emeralds, amethysts, and so forth which are associated in the **Pearl** with the New Jerusalem. Two of the alliterative poems, *Morte Arthure* and "Summer Sunday," present elaborate descriptions of Lady Fortune spinning her wheel. And a host of poems in Middle English, from *The Owl and the Nightingale* to *Winner and Waster,* make use of the formal debate. In short, the new use of old materials is a central feature of the medieval poet's practice.

But though some literary sources of the provincial poetry have been identified, we still know relatively little about what books poets had at hand in the provincial centers or what the audiences there were like. This much is certain: the works which emanated from them demonstrate a high culture. All of the great poems from the provincial centers reveal a common interest in the gentleman's pursuits—hunting, hawking, music, chess, law, the old code of chivalry, theoretical discussion of heaven and earth. It is now generally agreed that the poems also reveal something more: the technical mastery of Old English meter in the many alliterative poems from the various sections of rural England in the thirteenth and fourteenth centuries argues not so much an "alliterative revival" as a fourteenth-century renaissance within a continuous poetic tradition from Anglo-Saxon to late medieval times.

Continuous or not, it is clear that the tradition did not come down to the *Gawain*-poet in its tenth-century form. Between the Anglo-Saxon era of "wide gabled halls" and the High Middle Ages with its "chalk-white chimneys," life in England changed drastically. Simple adornment of jewels and gold plate evolved to splendid ornamental shields, carved fretwork, gold-trammeled tapestry work from Toulouse and Tars; the plated boar's head helmet gave way to riveted steel and the Near Eastern helmet cover intricately wrought of crochet work, rubies, diamonds, and plumes; the simple scheme of protector and retainers became the elaborate feudal system emanating from God. Poetic theory reflected this efoliation. (One can see the change coming, perhaps, in the Old English poetry of Cynewulf, when he fashions a picture of the cross in the scheme of human relationships in *Elene*, when he weaves a runic signature into his verse, or when he shifts, in his comments on art, into rhyme.) By the late fourteenth century, especially in the northwest and in Scotland, elaborate prosodic devices are the fashion. *Gawain* is only one of many poems which play classic Old English alliterative long lines against French rhyme in a bob and wheel. The **Pearl** is only one of many poems in which stanzas are interlinked by verbal repetition. Consider the extreme ingenuity of "Summer Sunday," a poem the *Gawain*-poet may have known:

SUMMER SUNDAY

[? *A Lament for Edward II, 1327*]
—Anonymous

On a summer Sunday I saw the sun
  Rising up early on the rim of the east:
Day dawned on the dunes, dark lay the town;
  I caught up my clothes, I would go to the
  groves in haste;
With the keenest of kennel-dogs, crafty and
  quick to sing,
  And with huntsmen, worthies, I went at
  once to the woods.
So rife on the ridge the deer and dogs would
  run
  That I liked to loll under limbs in the cool
  glades
    And lie down.
    The kennel-dogs quested the kill
    With barking bright as a bell;
    Disheartened the deer in the dell
    And made the ridge resound.

Ridge and rill resounded with the rush of the
  roes in terror
  And the boisterous barking the brilliant
  bugle bade.

I stood, stretched up, saw dogs and deer
  together
  Where they slipped under shrubs or scattered
  away in the shade.
There lords and ladies with lead-leashes
  loitered
  With fleet-footed greyhounds that frolicked
  about and played.
And I came to the ground where grooms
  began to cry orders,
  And walked by wild water and saw on the
  other side
    Deep grass.
  I sauntered by the stream, on the strand,
  And there by the flood found
  A boat lying on the land;
    And so I left the place.

So I left the place, more pleased with my own
  way,
  And wandered away in the woods to find
  who I'd find.
I lounged a long while and listened—on a
  slope I lay—
  Where I heard not a hound or a hunter or
  hart or hind.
So far I'd walked I'd grown weary of the
  way;
  Then I left my little game and leaned on a
  limb
And standing there I saw then, clear as day,
  A woman with a wonderful wheel wound by
  the wind.
    I waited then.
    Around that wheel were gathered
    Merry men and maids together;
    Most willingly I went there
    To try my fortune.

Fortune, friend and foe, fairest of the dear,
  Was fearful, false, and little of faith, I found.
She spins the wheel to weal and from weal to
  woe
  In the running ring like a roebuck running
  round.
At a look from that lovely lady there,
  I gladly got into the game, cast my goods to
  the ground.
Ah, could I recount, count up, cunning and clear,
  The virtues of that beauty who in bitterness
  bound
    Me tight!
  Still, some little I'll stay
  To tell before turning away—
  All my reasons in array
    I'll readily write.

Readily I'll write dark runes to read:
  No lady alive is more lovely in all this land;

I'd go anywhere with that woman and think
   myself glad,
     So strangely fair her face; at her waist, I
     found,
The gold of her kirtle like embers gleamed
   and glowed.
     But in bitter despair that gentle beauty soon
     bound
Me close, when her laughing heart I had given
   heed.
     Wildly that wonderful wheel that woman
     wound
        With a will.
     A woman of so much might,
     So wicked a wheel-wright,
     Had never struck my sight,
        Truth to tell.
Truth to tell, sitting on the turf I saw then
   A gentleman looking on, in a gaming mood,
   gay,
Bright as the blossoms, his brows bent
   To the wheel the woman whirred on its way.
It was clear that with him all was well as the
   wheel went,
   For the laughed, leaned back, and seemed at
   ease as he lay.
A friendly look toward me that lord sent,
   And I could imagine no man more merry
   than he
     In his mind.
     I gave the knight greeting.
     He said, "You see, my sweeting,
     The crown of that handsome king?
        I claim it as mine!

     "As mine to me it will come:
     As King I claim the kingdom,
     The kingdom is mine.
     To me the wheel will wind.
     Wind well, worthy dame;
     Come fortune, friendly game;
     Be game now, and set
     Myself on that selfsame seat!"

I saw him seated then at splendid height,
   Right over against the rim of the running
   ring;
He cast knee over knee as a great king might,
   Handsomely clothed in a cloak and crowned
   as a king.
Then high of heart he grew in his gambling
   heat;
   Laid one leg on the other leg and sat
   lounging;
Unlikely it looked that his lordship would fall
   in the bet;
   All the world, it seemed, was at his
   wielding
        By right.

     On my knees I kissed that king.
     He said, "You see, my sweeting,
     How I reign by the ring,
        Most high in might?

     "Most high in might, queen and knight
     Come at my call.
     Foremost in might,
     Fair lords at my foot fall.
     Lordly the life I lead,
     No lord my like is living,
     No duke living need I dread,
     For I reign by right as King."
Of kings it seems most sad to speak and set
   down
   How they sit on that seemly seat awhile,
   then in wastes are in sorrow
   sought.
I beheld a man with hair like the leaves of the
   horehound,
   All black were his veins, his brow to
   bitterness brought;
His diadem with diamonds dripped down
   But his robes hung wild, though beautifully
   wrought;
Torn away was his treasure—tent, tower,
   town—
   Needful and needing, naked; and nought
     His name.
     Kindly I kissed that prince.
     He spoke words, wept tears;
     Now he, pulled down from his place,
     A captive had become.

     "Become a captive outcast,
     Once mighty kings would call
     Me king. From friends I fall,
     Long time from all love, now little, lo! at
   the last.
     Fickle is fortune, now far from me;
     Now weal, now woe,
     Now knight, now king, now captive."
A captive he had become, his life a care;
   Many joys he had lost and all his mastery.
Then I saw him sorrier still and hurt still
   more:
   A bare body in a bed, on a bier they bore
   him past me,
A duke driven down into death, hidden in the
   dark.

The ornamental devices in "Summer Sunday" are un-usually intricate. Lines both alliterate and rhyme, and in certain sections the last word of a line is the same as the first word of the next line in the same stanza; stanzas are linked by verbal repetition; separate epi-sodes are linked by the image of the circle; and the shape of the stanzas in the poem comes to be reversed, reflecting the thematic reversal of Fortune. But though this poem is, like the work of the *Gawain*-poet, intricate, many of the same devices are to be found, in isolation or together, in even the most slipshod popular poetry of the day. And since they appear frequently, rhyme linking, combined alliteration and rhyme, and other entirely ornamental devices can doubtless be considered conventional. Thus, to the extent that it is merely ornamental, we probably ought to consider conventional even the *Gawain*-poet's "signature," his characteristic use of a particular phrase or stylistic device at the beginning and end of each of his poems. (The same device appears in some Scottish poetry.)

The real significance of the *Gawain*-poet's devices is not simply that he uses them, but rather that his use of them is meticulous—his alliterative rules are unusually rigorous—and that his devices normally embody a direct fusion of form and content. Take, for example, the *Pearl.* Gollancz pointed out that the twelve-line stanzas of the *Pearl* are perhaps best viewed as primitive sonnets. (His view has for some reason not been widely accepted, but he is right that sonnets of roughly the same type appear in Italy before Dante.) If we accept Gollancz' suggestion, or at any rate if we are able to see each stanza as, at least much of the time, more or less a unit in itself, developing a single dramatic tension, image, or philosophical idea, then the linked ring of one hundred (or, surely by accident, one hundred and one)[1] stanzas in the *Pearl* has symbolic relationship to the transmutation within the poem of flower imagery into jewel imagery (Nature into Art), reflecting the contrast between mortal life and eternal life. Thus the circular poem becomes the artistic reflection of the "garland" of the blessed (a circle of artificial flowers) about the throne of God.[2]

If we believe that the poet had some reason for linking stanzas and organizing other material as he did, we are, I think, forced to conclude that number symbolism of an ingenious sort is also used in the poem. *Three* is the mystical number of the Trinity, complement of the tripartite soul in man, and it may also suggest unity and completion, the Pythagorean "beginning, middle, and end." This Pythagorean (and Christian) use of three appears as an element in the five-part structure of the poem. The first and last five-stanza sections frame a dream that comes in three parts which, as we shall see later, may be interpreted as presenting together the whole of Christian illumination. *Five,* the number of linked stanzas in each section, has various associations as we learn in the *Gawain,* but most commonly suggests the five joys of Mary and the five wounds of Christ, both of which associations are appropriate in the *Pearl,* where the Virgin is both emblem and road of man's salvation and where the blood of Christ functions throughout as a controlling symbol. In the first of the three sections of the dream the central image is a stream, a detail borrowed from courtly French and Italian poetry but explicitly identified here as the river in

Paradise, which for the patristic exegetes is a "sign" or foreshadowing of the "well-spring," Christ (cf. John 7:38). The second section of the dream focuses first on the parable of the vineyard, hence, symbolically—and this too is made explicit in the poem—the "wine" or blood by which man is redeemed, and then (starting at stanza 51) on grace, which comes to be identified with "Water and blood of the wide wound." The third section of the dream identifies blood, grace, light, and music. *Ten* is in a different way a number of completion. (Ten times ten is the number of stanzas probably intended.) St. Augustine writes:

> Again, the number ten signifies a knowledge of the Creator and the creature; for the trinity is the Creator and the septenary indicates the creature by reason of his life and body. For with reference to life there are three, whence we should love God with all our hearts, with all our souls, and with all our minds; and with reference to the body there are very obviously four elements of which it is made.[3]

Four, or the square, is traditionally associated with world-wide extension (four winds, four evangelists), and for Augustine it is also emblematic of time (four seasons, four parts of the day). Thus at the end of time, on the day of the Last Judgment, Christ reads from a book with square pages. (This image is not found in the Apocalypse but is introduced by the poet.) *Twelve*—a number repeatedly mentioned in the final section of the *Pearl*—is the number of the Mystical Body, the Church Universal, and is thus also the number of salvation. In addition to the relevance of specific symbolic numbers to the theme of the *Pearl,* number symbolism has a general relevance in that mathematical relationships, unlike human beings or roses, are immutable. Boethius writes that mathematics deals with the *intelligible* and finds that

> it itself includes the first or *intellectible* part in virtue of its own thought and understanding, directed as these are to the celestial works of supernal divinity and to whatever sublunary beings enjoy more blessed mind and purer substance, and, finally, to human souls. All of these things, though they once consisted of that primary intellectible substance, have since, by contact with bodies, degenerated from the level of intellectibles to that of intelligibles; as a result, they are less objects of understanding than active agents of it, and they find greater happiness by the purity of their understanding whenever they apply themselves to the study of things intellectible.[4]

And Hugh of St. Victor, commenting on this passage, writes:

> For the nature of spirits and souls, because it is incorporeal and simple, participates in intellectible substance; but because through the sense organs spirit or soul descends in different ways to the

apprehension of physical objects and draws into itself a likeness of them through its imagination, it deserts its simplicity somehow by admitting a type of composition.[5]

Thus by the use of mystical numbers the poet reinforces the central contrast in the poem between the soul in Nature and the soul liberated from Nature.

The "signature" in the ***Pearl*** is equally functional. The contrast between the first and last lines of the poem focuses the conflict between unselfishness and selfishness, or in exegetical language, between a proper and reasonable view of earthly treasure, on one hand, and on the other, "concupiscence" in the theological sense, an undue regard for the things of this world.

Ornamental devices are less conspicuous in the *Gawain,* mainly because the symbolic extension of the surface action is more deeply embedded in the poem. The alliterative long lines are appropriate, though only in the most general way, reflecting the ancient English poetic mode in a poem purporting to deal with ancient native tradition. (The *Gawain*-stanza, sometimes modified in one way or another, is common in courtly provincial verse and may itself have been regarded as traditional.) The bob and wheel device found in this poem is sometimes merely decorative, but it does often have an important thematic or dramatic function. For instance, in the opening lines the poet writes:

> Felix Brutus
> On the slopes of many broad hills established
> Britain
>   with joy,
> Where war and wrack and wonder
> Have sometimes since held sway,
> And now bliss, now blunder,
> Turned like dark and day.
>   [Part I, st. I, ll. 13-19]

Here all that follows the pivotal phrase "with joy" (the "bob") contrasts with the force of that phrase, setting up an irony which extends to the whole of the poem. (The four lines which follow the "bob" comprise the "wheel.") The "signature" in the *Gawain,* the opening and closing concern with the fall of Troy, is relevant to the central conflict in the poem between the vulnerability of mortal kingdoms and the permanence of the Kingdom of God.

In some respects the most interesting of the *Gawain*-poet's signature—if we may rightly call it a full-blown signature—is that in *St. Erkenwald.* The signature here involves not verbal repetition but the repetition of a stylistic device. The poem opens:

> At London in England no long while since—
> Since when Christ suffered on the cross and

Christendom was built—
There was a bishop . . .

The last two stanzas of the poem read:

> For as soon as that soul was established in
>   bliss,
> That other creation that covered the bones
>   corrupted;
> For the everlasting life, the life without end,
> Voids all that vanity that avails man nothing.

> Then was there praising of the Lord and the
>   lifting of hymns:
> Mourning and joy in that moment came
>   together.
> They passed forth in procession, and all the
>   people followed,
> And all the bells of the city sang out at once.

The poet's repetition is stylistic: "since, since" in the opening lines has its echo in "all the people . . . all the bells" which appears in the closing lines. The echo calls attention to the relationship between the two passages. Both contrast London (a particular point in space) and the spatial concept of universal Christendom, earth and heaven; and both passages also contrast historical time and time as it exists in the mind of God. The opening lines set up a concept of time stretching backward out of sight. In terms of such a concept, St. Erkenwald lived not long ago and Christ not a very long while before that. The end of the poem, on the other hand, focuses on "the everlasting life, the life without end," introducing a concept of time stretching forward out of sight. The contrast of finite and infinite time and space is central to the organization of the poem, accounting not only for the historical material and the bishop's prayer for more than mortal wisdom, but also for specific images throughout—the runes on the coffin, undecipherable to mortal reason; the crowd which gathers like "all the world . . . in an instant"; the chess image in which, when the human mind is checkmated, God moves one pawn and recasts the whole game. At last this contrast between the finite and the infinite becomes the poet's artistic justification of the miracle. And so what might have been merely ornamental in the work of another medieval poet becomes in the hands of the *Gawain*-poet both the thing said and the way of saying it.

For the *Gawain*-poet, plots, images, and certain rhetorical devices were also largely a matter of convention. It has often been pointed out that the two most elaborately developed symbols in *Sir Gawain and the Green Knight,* the shield and the girdle, are standard devices for characterization in medieval poetry. In the alliterative *Morte Arthure* (almost certainly earlier than the *Gawain*) shields are the usual means of identifying a knight's particular virtues; and in *The Parliament of the Three Ages,* as in Chaucer and elsewhere, the girdle or waistband (on which one hangs one's moneybags) is the usual detail singled out to suggest a man's concern with possessions. But the *Gawain*-poet's use of the standard devices is ingenious. The emblem on Arthur's shield in the *Morte Arthure,* a picture of the Virgin, is transferred to the *inside* of Gawain's shield to show, as the poet explicitly tells us, the source of Gawain's inner strength; and for the usual gryphon on the outside of Gawain's shield the poet substitutes a pentangle indicative of his strength—that is, his virtues—as seen from outside. With the shield, as Donald R. Howard has pointed out, Gawain serves the world but stands aloof from it; with the girdle he serves himself.[6] No such ingenious use of the two images, and no such juxtaposition of the two, can be found outside *Sir Gawain and the Green Knight.*

Borrowing plots, descriptions, even especially elegant lines from the work of other poets was standard practice in the Middle Ages—as it has been among good poets of almost every age, for that matter. At its best this borrowing becomes imperatorial confiscation. Thus Chaucer seized Boccaccio's elegant and slight *Il Filostrato* and transformed it into the greatest tragic poem in English; and thus Shakespeare transformed the curious tragedies of earlier poets into the world's most powerful modern drama.

The artistry in poetic borrowing can also lie in adapting borrowed material to its new context without obscuring its meaning in the original context, for here the poet's object is not to confiscate but rather to enrich meaning by playing one context against another. Only if the reader remembers that the revels of Arthur's court are usually licentious can he see the humor in the poet's pious celebration of the Christmas revels which open the *Gawain.*[7] It is as though the revels were being seen through the eyes of the innocent Sir Gawain himself. It is impossible, however, to know the extent to which the *Gawain*-poet's work is meant to operate in this way. Knowing virtually nothing of his audience, we cannot know how much knowledge the poet was able to assume; and knowing almost as little of his immediate sources, we cannot be perfectly sure how much of the given poem is the poet's own. Scholarship on the *Gawain*-poet has veered between two extremes: the tendency to attribute nearly everything to the poet himself and the tendency to trace all virtues to a hypothetical source.

Undoubtedly our best clue to the poet's method is provided, as Professor Mabel Day has sensibly suggested, by the homiletic *Purity,* for here we do know most, if not all, of the poet's sources. We find in *Purity* the clear influence of the *Roman de la Rose,* Mandeville's *Travels* (in the French version), *Cursor Mundi, The Knight of La Tour-Landry* (probably in French), and the Vulgate Bible. In a complicated plot

made up of three linked biblical episodes the poet brings these materials together, associating each episode with the other two by means of puns and verbal repetitions, and at the end of the poem he tells us that he has preached "in three ways" the same moral lesson. Since puns and verbal repetitions of the same sort appear in the other poems, we may safely suppose that he combined other materials with equal freedom and ingenuity in *Gawain, Patience,* the **Pearl,** and *St. Erkenwald.*

If we make this supposition, we can make guesses concerning the extent to which the poet extended or modified tradition in such poems as the *Gawain,* even though the exact sources are unknown. In the *Gawain* two old motifs appear, the Beheading Game (parts 1 and 4) and the Temptation (part 3).[8] Both the general outline of the Green Knight's challenge and the general outline of the Temptation are common, the first deriving from a Cuchulain legend of about the ninth century, the second perhaps deriving from the thirteenth-century French *Yder.* The parallels are slight between the *Gawain* and known versions of the two motifs, especially with regard to the Temptation, and many details in the *Gawain*-poet's treatment of the two motifs come from sources which have nothing to do with either. Given the poet's combination of diverse materials in *Purity* and given the obvious coherence of the *Gawain,* we have every reason to suppose that the combination of diverse materials here is the poet's own work and not, as Kittredge suggested in 1916, work done in a lost French original. Certain details are unquestionably of English origin (the legendary founding of Britain and the arming of Gawain); and a few details are clearly peculiar to our poet (for instance, the stanzas on the turning of the seasons at the beginning of part 2). And to the extent that all elements in the poem are interrelated to form a coherent and balanced whole—both literal and symbolic—from which no part can be removed without serious damage to the poem on both levels, we can be absolutely certain that the interrelationship, together with the resulting aesthetic effect, is to be credited to the *Gawain*-poet himself. Once the structure of the poem has been understood, once it has been recognized that we are dealing here not with borrowing but with total transformation of old material, the search outside the poem for the poem's meaning becomes pure pedantry. But internal analysis does have a limitation, nevertheless. What it cannot show, and what must therefore be left to the scholarship of the future, is the straight or ironic play of text against source. Reading the *Gawain* may be roughly equivalent to reading "The Waste Land" without knowledge of Eliot's sources.

Perhaps the single most important set of poetic conventions open to the medieval poet came from the poetry of courtly love. The central metaphor in the *Divine Comedy,* the identification of Beatrice as the Neoplatonic Christian image of the ideal—Truth,

Beauty, Goodness—derives from this poetry. Chaucer's dream-visions, *Troilus,* and much of the *Canterbury Tales* all draw from the same well. A good deal of the *Gawain*-poet's meaning will escape us if we are not familiar with the common devices used in the poetry of courtly love. Take, for example, the conventional love bower or garden. In the *Book of the Duchess,* the dreamer comes upon a "floury grene" which is

> Ful thikke of gras, ful softe and swete,
> With floures fele, faire under fete,
> And litel used, hyt semed thus;
> For both Flora and Zephirus,
> They two that make floures growe,
> Had mad her dwellynge ther, I trowe;
> For hit was, on to beholde
> As thogh the erthe envye wolde
> To be gayer than the heven,
> To have moo floures, swiche seven
> As in the welken sterres bee.
> Hyt had forgete the povertee
> That wynter, thorgh hys colde morwes,
> Had mad hyt suffre, and his sorwes,
> All was forgeten, and that was sene.
> For al the woode was waxen grene. . . .
>   [*Book of the Duchess,* ll. 399-414]

The same sort of garden is to be found in the *Roman de la Rose,* in Dante, and in a hundred other places. It is a garden from which mutability has been banished—or rather, one is usually given to understand, a garden from which mutability *appears* to have been banished. The garden looks back to the unfallen Paradise, a poetic subject at least as old as the *Ave Phoenice,* source of the Old English *Phoenix.*[9] It represents Nature at her best, and so it contrasts both with Nature as we usually see her and with the immutable idea of which Nature is a corporeal embodiment. If we are familiar with this conventional garden, there is a beautiful irony for us in that passage in *Patience* where Jonah, sheltered from the burning sun by a lovely green bower of woodbine which God has erected around him, thinks of his arbor as a lover's bower. God is indeed Jonah's lover—a point poor Jonah misses—and this bower, like every lover's paradise, is a mutable thing which can be thrown to the ground in an instant. Looking at the bower in worldly terms, Jonah puts his hopes on false felicity. In the *Pearl* the idea of the earthly paradise is explored in quite different terms. The poem opens in a garden which is the conventional love garden in all respects but one: it is a real arbor, where mutability has *not* been banished. The tension between the actuality of the garden and the idealism of the convention suggested by its description is moving in itself, and it also prepares for the narrator's vision of the true Paradise in his dream. But the poet's most complex treatment of the conventional garden comes in *Sir Gawain and the Green Knight.* The white castle Gawain comes upon, surprisingly, in the center of a grim, dark forest, is a

paradise of ambiguous meaning as are most such paradises, but ambiguous in unusually ominous ways. It is at once an unfallen Paradise, a factitious heaven, a garden of Venus, the land of Faery, Asgaard, and the haunt of Druids.

The garden is only one of many conventional devices from courtly-love poetry used in old or new ways in the work of the *Gawain*-poet. Another is the formal paradox familiar to every reader through Renaissance Petrarchan poetry or through Chaucer. Chaucer's Black Knight says:

> My song ys turned to pleynynge,
> And al my laughtre to wepynge,
> My glade thoghtes to hevynesse;
> In travayle ys myn ydelnesse
> And eke my reste; my wele is woo,
> My good ys harm, and evermoo
> In wrathe ys turned my pleynge
> And my delyt into sorwynge. . . .
>   [*Book of the Duchess,* ll. 599-606]

This formal balance of opposing concepts is used by the *Gawain*-poet when Sir Abraham bargains with God to save Sodom; it is transformed into a vehicle for strong emotion in the dreamer's plea for the compassion of his pearl; and it becomes rich comedy in Sir Gawain's sophistical attempts to fend off the amorous lady of the castle. Still another conventional element is, of course, the device of the dream-vision itself. The device is obviously central in the **Pearl,** and combining with traditions of fairy magic it becomes the basis of the mystery and uncertainty which pervade the *Gawain.* When the Green Knight enters King Arthur's court all sounds die out as if everyone in the hall had suddenly slipped off into sleep, and the green man seems a magical phantom or an illusion. By means of a pun, Middle English *prayere,* the *Gawain*-poet leaves a trace of doubt whether the castle in the forest is "pitched on a prairie" or pitched "on a prayer." That trace of doubt is perhaps strengthened by our recollection that dream paradises so often come after pathless wandering in great, dark forests; and for the poet's immediate audience that hint may have been further reinforced by the recognition that whereas the general area of Gawain's search and the Green Chapel to which he comes in the end were real and recognizable places, there had never in the memory of man been a castle or any sign of one in the area.[10] On the other hand, the castle does not go up in smoke as Morgan's phantom castles ordinarily do. Nothing is certain. That is an important part of the meaning of the poem.

As all we have said thus far should suggest, another very important aspect of medieval poetic convention is what we may call the idea of symbolic equation. The idea is rooted in the medieval view of the cosmos. Scholastic thinkers speak of two "books" by which man may learn his road to salvation. One is Nature; the other, Scripture. Before the Fall, man could pe ceive God's revelation of Himself directly, by looking at His created works. But, as Bonaventura puts it, "turning himself away from the true light to mutable goods, he was bent over by his own sin, and the whole human race by original sin, which doubly infected human nature, ignorance infecting man's mind and concupiscence his flesh."[11] Now Nature carries, for man, only "vestiges" or "traces" of the divine hand, and to be saved he needs a clearer text, one which, incidentally, helps him to understand that first text, Nature, which has become hopelessly obscured. The clearer text is Scripture, God's new revelation not only of Himself but also of what he wished man to see, in allegorical and moral terms, when he looked at the oak tree, the serpent, the rose. As elements of God's self-revelation, all superficially similar things in Nature may be seen as types of one another and of something higher; thus (as the earlier exegetes had it) all Nature is a vast array of emblems.

The literary importance of patristic exegesis may easily be exaggerated or misunderstood, but exegetical symbolism can by no means be dismissed as a possibility within any given poem by anyone seriously concerned with the meaning of medieval poetry to its immediate audience. Indeed, the basic technique has come down to us practically unchanged in the work of, for instance, Melville and Faulkner. Petrarch, Boccaccio, and Dante—poets of enormous influence in their day—all subscribed to a theory of criticism developed roughly in terms of the three-fold system of the exegetes. They would all differ profoundly, however, with the New Exegetes. Boccaccio, for instance, denies that any good poet would ever intentionally introduce obscurities for the purpose of withholding his meaning from any reader,[12] and neither in his criticism (in the *Genealogy of the Gods*) nor in his own poetry does he apply this system or any other system rigidly. But the early Italian poets were unanimous in their opinion that good poetry was inspired and that the method of poetry was the method of the Holy Ghost. Indeed, the theory that poetry comes from God was still vital enough in Sidney's day to provide the first argument in his *Defence,* though Sideny was not much interested in what was earlier supposed to be the exact method of divine inspiration.

It is a commonplace that the Middle Ages saw the world as ordered, but in a practical way we might as easily characterize the medieval world as one of celestial disturbances, terrestrial plagues, witch-hunts, slums, devastating fires, crop failures, earthquakes, physical and mental sickness, bloodletting, peasant revolts, corruption in church and state, wolves and boars a mile outside London, and, above all, endless, apparently hopeless, thoroughly wasteful war. Men have always known that what *is* is not necessarily what ought to be, and

disorder seen on every hand heightens man's need for a conceptual scheme of order. On the basis of divine revelation and the essential, though not always evident, order in Nature—the regular succession of generation, corruption, and regeneration—the Middle Ages worked out its schemes. The best minds of the period went into the work, drawing hints wherever they might be found—from Aristotle, from fragmentary third-hand accounts of Plato's thought, from Vergil, Ovid, Statius, old mythologies, and, above all, of course, from the Bible.

That the Bible was directly inspired by God went without saying; and since the Bible, the work of perfect wisdom, had obvious obscurities and seeming contradictions, it was clear that when speaking to man, God chose to speak in dark conceits. The whole truth, embracing infinite time and space, would doubtless be too much for mortal minds. Moreover, a man had to prove himself worthy of truth; it must not come to him easily but must follow from diligence.[13] Man's work, then, was to decipher as well as possible the dark conceits of God and thus to discover as much as he could of the total system. What medieval exegetes found, playing one scriptural text against another in accordance with the accepted principles of classical Greek literary criticism, was that, like ancient Greek poetry, the Bible worked on several levels—sometimes on one level at a time, sometimes on all levels at once. The levels were these:[14]

1. *The Literal or Historical Sense.* On the first and most obvious level, the intent of Scripture is that which the words signify in their natural and proper acceptation, as in John 10:30, "I and the Father are one," in which passage the deity of Christ and His equality with God the Father are distinctly asserted. The literal sense has also been called the grammatical sense, the term *grammatical* having the same reference to the Greek language as the term *literal* to the Latin, both referring to the elements of a word. When words are taken metaphorically or figuratively, diverted to a meaning they do not naturally carry but which they nevertheless intend, as when the properties of one person or thing are attributed to another, they operate not on the literal level but on some other. Thus the adjective "hardness" applies literally to stone, figuratively to the heart. On the literal level, those narratives which purport to be true accounts of historical events are to be read as certain history; but this is not to say that they may not operate on other levels as well. When the Jews are said to "possess" or "inherit the land"—phrases of frequent occurrence in the Old Testament—the literal meaning is that the Jews are to hold secure and undisturbed possession of their promised land; but the phrases have figurative meaning as well, having reference to the Christian's possession of the life everlasting.

2. *The Allegorical Sense* (sometimes treated as merely a mode of the anagogical and tropological senses). On

a second level, Scripture signifies, besides or instead of the literal meaning, things having to do with faith or spiritual doctrine. It is this level that is most likely to embarrass the modern reader, for it frequently does violence to obvious surface meaning. And it is their insistence upon reading medieval poetry as though it worked in this way and in no other that is most troublesome in the interpretations of the New Exegetes, Robertson and Huppé, for instance.[15] Bonaventura's comments upon Christ's cry on the cross, "I thirst," will serve to illustrate. Bonaventura writes:

> Earlier, as the hour of His passion was approaching, the most sweet Jesus *fell prostrate and prayed, saying: "Father, if it is possible, let this cup pass away from Me."* He said this not once but a second and a third time; and by the cup He was to drink He meant the passion He was to suffer. Now, having emptied this same cup of the passion, He says: "*I thirst.*" What does He mean?

> Before tasting the cup, O good Jesus, You prayed that it might be taken away from You; but now, after emptying it, You thirst. How wonderful this appears! Was Your cup perhaps filled with the wine of delight, instead of humiliation and the worst bitterness? Emphatically not! It was filled with the most withering shame. This should not produce thirst, but rather aversion to drink.

> When, before You suffered, You prayed that the cup be removed from You, we must believe it was not a refusal of the passion itself. You had come for this very suffering, without which mankind would not have been saved. But it might have been said that, true man though You are, since You are also one with God, the bitterness of the passion did not really affect You. That is why You prayed once, twice, and even three times that the cup be removed from You: to prove to the doubters how supremely bitter was Your suffering. . . . By praying before You suffered that this cup might be taken away from You, and by saying, after it was emptied: "I thirst," You showed us how immeasurable is Your love. For this seemed to mean: Although My passion was so dreadful that, because of My human sensibility, I prayed to be saved from it, My love for you, O man, triumphed even over the torments of the cross, making Me thirst for more and greater tortures, if need be. . . .[16]

It is important to resist the temptation to dismiss commentary of this sort as lunacy, childishness, or pernicious sophistry. The practice of contemporary writers of prose fiction leads us closer, perhaps, than some generations have been to the symbolic mode of thought common in the Middle Ages, but we are nevertheless sufficiently committed to the literal or realistic to be made uncomfortable by such insistent allegorical reading. If we were in the habit of finding "signs" or "fig-

ures" all around us as some medieval people clearly were, or if, like James Joyce, we were accustomed to seeing profound philosophical significance, not mere linguistic accident, in puns, we would probably find interpretation like Bonaventura's somewhat less farfetched than we do. If he can avoid pursuing the principle intemperately, the student of medieval literature will do well to bear in mind Augustine's warning that

> when that which is said figuratively is taken as though it were literal, it is understood carnally. Nor can anything more appropriately be called the death of the soul than that condition in which the thing which distinguishes us from beasts, which is the understanding, is subjected to the flesh in the pursuit of the letter. He who follows the letter takes figurative expressions as though they were literal and does not refer the things signified to anything else.[17]

The corollary to this is, "Every analysis *begins* from things which are finite, or defined, and *proceeds* in the direction of things which are infinite, or undefined."[18] (The italics are mine.) One must watch for signs, particularly where no other explanation will account for details within the poem, but one should not abandon the literal level until forced to do so by the text.

3. *The Anagogical or "Typical" Sense.* On a third level, objects, actions, or prophetic visions secretly represent things present or future; more particularly, events recorded in the Old Testament presignify or adumbrate events related in the New Testament. The exegetes declare that, rightly understood, Moses' story is parallel to the stories of Adam, Noah, Joseph, Christ. The water which gushes from the rock Moses strikes is a "type" or presignification of the blood and water which gush from Christ's side; it is obversely analogous to the flood of Noah's time and symbolically analogous to the flood of sin in which man was drowned with the fall of Adam (the fiery lake in *St. Erkenwald*); and it is analogous to the flood of grace from the throne of God (first seen in the visions of Ezekiel), introduced on earth by the Holy Ghost (cf. light and water imagery in the *Pearl*). The job of patristic exegesis was to determine the exact nature of the relationships, and the result of exegesis was an elaborate symbology (or "typology") in which, for instance, grapes, wine, blood, wheat, bread, the lamb, the lily, the rose, the pearl, the lion, the falcon, the temple, the number *eight,* and so forth, become emblematic of Christ or attributes of Christ. Appearing in paintings, church windows, fretwork, sermons, and popular songs, this system of relationships comes to be—at least potentially—the shared tradition of all medieval men and thus material for poetry. Within the framework of typology the poet has two alternatives. He may retell biblical stories, introducing new typic images or situations which further elaborate or extend an orthodox typic interpreta-

tion; or he may introduce into a non-biblical story images or situations which establish a biblical parallel or group of parallels and which thus encourage an allegorical reading of the otherwise realistic or literal story.

4. *The Moral or Tropological Sense.* On the final level, Scripture tells us of the progress of the soul: the nature of man before and after the Fall, the conditions of his salvation, and the terms and impediments of redemption. The parable of the talents, for example, shows on the tropological level (according to one account) that the duties which men are called to perform are suited to their situations and the talents which they have received, that whatever a good man possesses he has received from God, together with the ability to improve that good, and that the grace and temporal mercies of God are suited to the power a man has of improving his talents.

But there is more to medieval symbolism than the system of the exegetes. Classical philosophy and feudalism introduce complications. Aristotle's basically Platonic notion of order extending from a Prime Mover through various natures or, to use the English word, kinds, became in the Middle Ages "plenitude," the scheme founded on the view that everything that could be created had been created, completing the whole range of the possible from best (the angels) to worst (the basest form of earth). The whole scheme of plenitude can be divided into discrete categories, the links of the so-called great chain of being, and within each category of Nature can be found another hierarchy from best to worst: the angels, carefully ranked from the Virtues of Heaven down, are higher than men, who are also carefully ranked from king to serf; eagles are higher than ducks; lions are higher than cows; roses are higher than brambles; gold is higher than lead. Given such hierarchies, it becomes possible to identify a station in one hierarchy in terms of the corresponding station of some other. A king might be emblematically represented by an eagle or by gold; God, or some attribute of God, might be represented by a crown or, as in Dante and Chaucer, an eagle.

Luckily for poets, the idea of equation was not altogether rigid. Certain emblems—particularly those having Scripture as their basis—tended to be of fixed significance; but whereas Chaucer's eagles in the *Parliament of Fowls* had to be eagles, to his goose and turtledove, for instance, he could assign meanings of his own, based on his private intuition of what geese and turtledoves would be if they were people.

Medieval symbolism is further complicated by heraldry with all its monsters, lions, deer, boars, birds, fish, reptiles, insects, plants, flowers, rocks, each with its specific meaning, and complicated also by the "language and sentiment of flowers," whereby the soldier or lover might send quite complicated messages in a simple bouquet. Still another complication comes through courtly love, a system developed by analogy to feudalism and Scholastic Neoplatonism. If the mistress is identified, in jest or in earnest, with God or the Supreme Good, and if Love is treated as a feudal lord, all symbols applicable to Christianity or feudalism may be transferred to the scheme of love.

The modern reader may well inquire how he is to make sense of poetry written for an audience which took all this symbolism for granted. For the most part he probably cannot without the help of scholars. But great poetry operates on the literal as well as on symbolic levels. One need not know heraldry to understand the importance and even, in a general way, the nature of the lady's temptation of Sir Gawain, and one need not know about jewel symbolism to sense the power of the vision which concludes the *Pearl*. The discovery of symbolic reinforcement and enrichment of the poet's literal narrative is not a starting point but a time for refining interpretation.

Finally, though, one does want to know what the *Gawain*-poet's symbols mean and the extent to which his handling of symbols is merely conventional. Where scholars can offer no sure explanations, the meanings of symbols—indeed, the extent to which the poems are symbolic—must be a matter of personal conjecture. As for the poet's contribution to tradition, we know at least this: most of the identifiable symbolism to be found in the *Pearl, Purity, Patience,* and *St. Erkenwald* can be found outside the work of the *Gawain*-poet; but the transitions from one symbolic identification to another and the personal emotion which charges the symbolic identifications are certainly the poet's own contributions. The symbolism in the *Gawain* gives more trouble. Structure points to possible symbolic identifications, but just what the identifications may mean no one has so far shown convincingly. The armor and appearance of the Green Knight are described in detail in part 1; in part 2, the arming of Gawain is developed in a parallel way; in part 3, Gawain is dressed up for Christmas festivities; and in part 4, the arming of Gawain is described once again. So far we have little idea what, if anything, the ritualistic armings mean. Critics have had just as much trouble with the Green Knight himself. How close was the poet to his ultimate mythical source (Gawain as sungod)?[19] Did he intend a direct identification of the Green Knight as the "green man"? What is the meaning of the poet's consistent characterization of the Green Knight as a sophisticated adult with a keen sense of humor, a man thoroughly unlike those overly earnest "beardless babes," King Arthur and his court? Is there any significance in the fact that the huge knight's colors are green, gold, and red? And what is the significance of his hunting trips? It is possible to work out by internal analysis convincing answers to many of these questions, but the answers remain conjectural.

Illustration for Cotton MS. lines 101-08.

Notes

[1] Most scholars agree that one of the six stanzas in the fifteenth group of linked stanzas was meant to be canceled or revised out.

[2] It has recently been argued that the "garland" in stanza 99 is not, as Gordon thought, "a metaphorical description of the heavenly procession," and not, in fact, a garland at all, but a crown, symbol, like Dante's *ghirlande,* of the New Jerusalem. It is surely both and thus the earliest example of this later conventional image in English poetry. The New Jerusalem and the blessed or the elevated Church are interchangeable terms in exegetical writing, and the shifting symbolic identifications of the pearl image in this poem would support a view of other symbols in the poem as having double or triple meaning. The argument that the procession is not circular carries no weight (there is no evidence either way—except, perhaps, for the moon image, which supports the view that the procession is circular). We are told that the whole celestial city is filled. More important, the shifting imagery throughout, from the mutable to the immutable, the natural to the supernatural (see my interpretation of the poem), justifies the guess that individual pearls (liberated, pure souls), for-

merly mutable flowers, become, together, a garland of perfected flowers (flowers "figured" out of pearls) and become, finally, the heavenly city itself. Concerned as he seems to be with the Platonic image of unity and completion, the sphere, the poet would be unlikely to miss a chance of introducing one more circle.

[3] Augustine, *On Christian Doctrine,* trans. D. W. Robertson, Jr. (New York: Liberal Arts Press, 1958), p. 52.

[4] Quoted by Hugh of St. Victor, *The Didascalicon of Hugh of St. Victor,* trans. Jerome Taylor (New York: Columbia University Press, 1961), p. 63.

[5] *Ibid.*

[6] Donald R. Howard, "Structure and Symmetry in *Sir Gawain,*" *Speculum,* XXXIX (July, 1964), 425-33.

[7] If we think of the poems in the *Pearl* manuscript as a unified group, then the parallel description of the revels at Belshazzar's court in *Purity* would also tend to cast ironic light over the revels at Camelot. The Belshazzar passage may be sufficient in itself to account for the irony, without recourse to a theory that allusion is involved. But if the concluding section of *Purity* was written after *Sir Gawain and the Green Knight,* a possibility very attractive in certain respects, and at any rate one we cannot rule out, we are back where we began.

For a brilliant, partly conjectural treatment of ironic allusion and parody in *Sir Gawain and the Green Knight,* see Marie Borroff, *Sir Gawain and the Green Knight: A Stylistic and Metrical Study* (New Haven: Yale University Press, 1962), pp. 52-129.

[8] For a discussion of the origins of the story, see the introduction by Mabel Day and Mary S. Serjeantson to Gollancz' edition of *Sir Gawain and the Green Knight,* pp. xx ff.

[9] See J. A. W. Bennett, *The Parlement of Foules: An Interpretation* (Oxford: Clarendon Press, 1957), pp. 62 ff.

[10] See Professor Day's discussion of the Green Chapel in Gollancz' *Sir Gawain and the Green Knight,* pp. xix-xx. The evidence for this identification of the mound is strong but not conclusive.

[11] Bonaventura, *The Mind's Road to God,* trans. George Boas (New York: The Liberal Arts Press, 1953), p. 9.

[12] See *Boccaccio on Poetry,* ed. C. G. Osgood (New York: The Liberal Arts Press, 1930), p. 60.

[13] See, for example, Augustine, *On Christian Doctrine,* p. 37.

[14] There are two main traditions. For Gregory the Great, Jerome, and Hugh of St. Victor, among others, Scripture works on three levels—the literal, the allegorical, and the tropological (in this formulation, the allegorical is a mode of the anagogical); for Bede, Augustine, and others, Scripture works on the four levels I have outlined in the Introduction. The difference is merely clerical, since identical interpretations might be catalogued in either way. It might be mentioned that poets seem to favor the three-level system; at any rate that is the system expounded by Boccaccio, Petrarch, and Dante.

[15] See Professor E. Talbot Donaldson's opposition to the method of patristic exegesis in his "Patristic Exegesis: The Opposition," *Critical Approaches to Medieval Literature,* ed. Dorothy Bethurum (New York: Columbia University Press, 1960), pp. 1-26.

[16] *The Works of Bonaventure,* trans. Jose de Vinck (Paterson, N.J.: St. Anthony Guild Press, 1963), I, 79-80.

[17] Augustine, *On Christian Doctrine,* p. 84.

[18] Hugh of St. Victor, *The Didascalicon,* p. 92.

[19] For an argument that the poet was very close indeed to his mythic source, see John Speirs' interpretation of the poem in *Medieval English Poetry: The Non-Chaucerian Tradition* (London: Faber and Faber, 1957), pp. 215 ff.

Ian Bishop (essay date 1968)

SOURCE: An introduction "The Maiden as an Innocent" and "The Priviledges of the Newly Baptized," in *Pearl in Its Setting: A Critical Study of the Structure and Meaning of the Middle English Poem,* Basil Blackwell, 1968, pp. 101-03, 104-112, 113-21.

[*In the following essay, Bishop finds that the liturgy in use during the twelfth and thirteenth centuries provides important information for understanding the poet's characterization of the Pearl maiden..*]

Introductory

In order to represent the apparition of the child's beatified soul, the author has to supply her with a visionary body of appropriate stature and appearance; with suitable clothing; and with arguments that will justify her status in the Kingdom of Heaven and that will console her earthly father.

Scholars have provided explanations of several details of the poet's presentation of her. There is, for example,

the fact that, although she died before she was two years old, she appears to the dreamer as a maiden of adult stature. Osgood has observed that this is in accordance with St. Augustine's teaching about the body which those who die in infancy will assume after the General Resurrection.[1] It is true that Osgood seems to have forgotten that the maiden's body has not yet risen from the dead: at 1. 857 she says, referring to herself and the other brides of the Lamb: 'Alþaȝ oure courseȝ in clotteȝ clynge'. But, as it is necessary for her to assume a 'visionary body' in order to manifest herself to the dreamer, it is appropriate that this body should have the appearance of the one which, according to the highest patristic authority, she will assume after the General Resurrection. Together with her adult stature goes the ability to communicate with the dreamer in adult language and concepts. Another observation made by Osgood is that her costume is cut according to the fashions of the later fourteenth century[2]; she is also appropriately adorned with pearls, and her robes are white because she is included in the procession of the hundred and forty-four thousand virgin brides of the Lamb. She wears the white 'coroun', or aureole, of virginity. There has been disagreement among scholars about the status that the poet accords her in the heavenly kingdom. René Wellek, however, was able to show that the author's opinion on this matter was not heterodox.[3] In order to demonstrate this he cites Papal decrees and more or less contemporary theological controversies.

The fundamental reason for the poet's presenting the maiden in the way that he does is that she had died while in a state of post-baptismal innocence. This simple fact, I believe, affords the true explanation of the way in which she is dressed as well as the essential reason for the status that she possesses in heaven. I shall suggest later that the best commentary on the author's intentions is to be found, not in theological disputations, Papal decrees or Biblical commentaries, but in liturgical contexts—both in the text of the liturgy itself and in the principal commentaries on it that were compiled during the twelfth and thirteenth centuries. Besides providing sources for the details I have just mentioned, these texts and commentaries supply practically all the arguments that the maiden uses in the course of her *apologia*. It is a reasonable assumption that, if the poet could have encountered these supposedly controversial doctrines in such an uncontroversial source as the text of the liturgy and the standard commentaries upon it, he would probably have taken them for granted. So there is no need to assume that he was familiar with the niceties of contemporary theological controversies on the subject of the salvation of those who die in infancy.

These elements in the characterization of the maiden, which the author could have derived from liturgical sources, are blended with others that belong to the poetic traditions of the later Middle Ages; mainly literary procedures and formulas of imagery and diction, some of which are set forth in the twelfth-century *Artes Poeticae,* but all of which are commonplace in the Latin and vernacular poetry of the succeeding centuries. He also derives details of characterization from the realm of *courtoisie* and other secular sources. His blending of the various elements is sometimes quite subtle, but its very success has perhaps been partly responsible for disguising from the modern reader the poem's true *sentence.*

Throughout the following chapters all references to the text of the liturgy (i.e. to the *Missal, Breviary, Processional,* etc.) follow the use of Sarum, unless otherwise stated.[4] Although other medieval English rites existed, the Use of Sarum was the English rite *par excellence* in the fourteenth century; it was, for example, the one used at Oxford. The liturgical commentary to which I most often refer is the *Rationale Divinorum Officiorum* by Durandus of Mende.[5] This work is to liturgical writings what the *Summa Theologiae* of St. Thomas Aquinas is to theological compilations. It makes use of all previous writings on this subject that are of any importance, and marks the culminating point in the history of this species of commentary. After the composition of the *Rationale* towards the end of the thirteenth century, no work of comparable importance appeared.[6] There are, however, two earlier sources (both of the twelfth century) that will be mentioned in this argument, although they were both used by Durandus. The first of these consists of the writings of Honorius (usually known as 'Honorius of Autun'), in particular his *Gemma Animae, Sacramentarium,* and sermons in the collection *Speculum Ecclesiae.*[7] There is a certain amount of material among these writings which is of particular interest for the present argument, but which is not included by Durandus in his *Rationale.* The other source is the work of Johannes Belethus, rector of the University of Paris, which has the same title as that of Durandus.[8] Although this work has little of relevance that is not also mentioned by Durandus, occasional references to it are given below, because there is some definite evidence of its being known in England: it was used by Bartholomaeus Anglicus (Bartholomaeus de Glanvilla) in the portion of his encyclopaedia, *De Proprietatibus Rerum,* that is entitled 'Of Times' (Book 9) in Trevisa's translation. He acknowledges his indebtedness to Belethus in Book IX, chapter 28: 'All this is take & drawe of the sentence of John Beleth, whose auctorite is solemne in holy chirch namely in ordening of office & service of holi chirch.'[9]

· · · · ·

The Maiden as an Innocent

(i) THE LITURGY FOR CHILDERMAS

Miss Elizabeth Hart has shown how a knowledge of the liturgy for Holy Innocents' Day will elucidate a

certain difficulty in *Pearl.*[10] She observes that the poet's inclusion of an infant in the procession of the hundred and forty-four thousand virgins of *Revelation* xiv may be explained by the fact that this passage occurs in the Missal as the Epistle for Innocents' Day. She also notices how Chaucer, in the *Prioress's Tale,* included his child martyr in this procession[11] and a few stanzas later called his mother 'This newe Rachel',[12] alluding to the closing words of the Gospel for the same day: 'Vox in Rama audita est, ploratus et ululatus multus: Rachel plorans filios suos, et noluit consolari, quia non sunt' (*Matt.* ii). In *Pearl* there is, of course, no question of martyrdom, but Miss Hart does not fail to notice that the Gospel for the day mentions the age of the Innocents at the time of their death as 'a bimatu et infra' (*Matt.* ii, 16), and that the dreamer remarks to the child: 'Þou lyfed not two ȝer in oure þede'. Miss Hart remarks that 'the association of the Innocents with this procession must have been common throughout the Middle Ages, being brought home to the laity by means of homilies and sermons'.

The present chapter is concerned to support this view by suggesting that the association would have been brought home by even more striking means than homilies and sermons alone, and by attempting to show that the homilies, sermons, and other liturgical pieces prescribed for this particular Feast, will account for other interesting and important details in *Pearl.*

(ii) THE PROCESSION OF THE INNOCENTS; THE BOY BISHOP; THE LITURGICAL DRAMA

One way in which the association of the Innocents with the faultless company who follow the Lamb would have been brought home in the fourteenth century is through the offices of the Breviary, in which various portions of the Epistle for the Mass appear as Antiphons and Responses. At Vespers on St. John's Day (the Vigil of the Feast in question) a *responsorium* beginning with the words 'Centum quadraginta . . . ' is chanted; this versicle and other portions of the Epistle recur in every office for the day itself and upon its octave. There is no need to suppose that the poet would have to be a religious in order to become familiar with the Breviary, or that he was less acquainted with his 'Antiphoner' than the schoolchildren in *The Prioress's Tale.*[13] Thus, a detail in the Epistle that left only a slight impression would be confirmed by the antiphons, if only for the reason that when a few words are sung or chanted they are—*pace* Wyclif—apt to call more attention to themselves than when they occur in the middle of a long passage that is read or intoned at a comparatively faster speed. His familiarity with the Breviary could also account for our author's remembering, and expecting his audience to remember, the mere detail in the Gospel narrative about the precise age of the Innocents, since the antiphon between the first and second psalms for Lauds on Innocents' Day consists of the words: 'A bimatu et infra occidit multos pueros Herodes propter Dominum.'[14] It also occurs as the first antiphon for Terce.

The effect made by the text of the Breviary would, in the fourteenth century, have been enhanced by certain ceremonies and customs which were observed on that occasion, particularly by those associated with the institution of the Boy Bishop.[15] In the Middle Ages the feast of the Holy Innocents was recognized as the special property of children, just as St. Stephen's Day was claimed by the deacons as their own.[16] Children played a prominent part in the offices for the Feast, beginning with Vespers on St. John's Day, where the Sarum Breviary gives the following rubric:

> *Tunc eat processio puerorum ad altare Innocentium, vel Sanctae Trinitatis, cum capis sericis et cereis illuminatis in manibus suis, cantando, R. Centum Quadraginta . . . etc.*[17]

Anyone who witnessed this procession could not fail to perceive the association of the Innocents and the company described in *Revelation* xiv. But what is still more important for my present purpose is the fact that anyone who witnessed this procession (and similar processions on the following day) would be inclined to associate the antiphon 'Centum Quadraginta' and the company of which it sings with children in general.

The celebration of the figure of the child, and of the state of Innocence which it represents, culminated in the practice of electing the Boy Bishop, who normally took office at Vespers on St. John's Day when, during the singing of the *Magnificat,* the precentro surrendered his staff of office at the reference to the deposition of the mighty from their seat. A child was invested with the authority (within prescribed limits) of a bishop, and even went so far as to preach a sermon. Unfortunately, no text of any such sermon preached before the late fifteenth century is extant, but a reference to the practice is to be found in a will of 1328.[18] Of the three late examples that have been preserved, one (preached in Gloucester Cathedral) takes for its text—as might be expected—*Matthew* xviii, 3; it dwells upon the Christian new birth and urges the audience themselves to become as little children.[19] Vestments of considerable expense were provided for the boy: an inventory of St. Paul's, London, of 1295 mentions a white mitre embroidered with flowers; another refers to a new white mitre with orphreys, used on these occasions.[20] One of the symbolic functions of the Boy Bishop is indicated in another Sarum rubric concerned with the singing of the *responsorium* 'Centum Quadraginta' at Vespers on St. John's Day:

> *Solus Episcopus Innocencium si assit, Christum puerum, uerum et aeternum Pontificem designans incipiat, R. Centum quadraginta . . . etc.*[21]

From this account it can be seen that the feast of the Holy Innocents was made the occasion for the exaltation of the ideas of humility and innocence embodied in the figure of the child, who is, for the occasion, set in authority over his elders to admonish them and to be imitated by them. So, if he was acquainted with these practices, our author would have a clear precedent for putting a discourse on humility, innocence and spiritual renewal into the mouth of the dreamer's former child as well as for placing her in the company which is described in *Revelation* xiv. Further, it is reasonable to suppose that the impression made by a child, dressed in a bishop's robes with a white mitre set with flowers or gems, would not be forgotten by him or his audience. So it is possible that some part of the characterization of the transfigured child in ***Pearl,*** as she appears in 'a pyȝt coroune . . . Hiȝe pynakled of cler quyt perle . . . Wyth flurted flowreȝ perfet vpon',[22] to admonish him, with 'semblaunt sade for doc oþer erle',[23] may have been suggested by these ceremonies.[24]

There remains to be considered one other development from the liturgy for Innocents' Day that associates the victims of Herod with the hundred and forty-four thousand; namely, the liturgical drama of the slaughter of the Innocents. Unfortunately, texts of the liturgical dramas performed in England have not survived, but E. K. Chambers believes that there is evidence that they continued to be performed side by side with the vernacular Mysteries in the fourteenth century.[25] Karl Young has shown that the texts of the dramas that have survived all belong to a French development.[26] In a version in a service book from Laon Cathedral the choir boys enter in procession, supporting a lamb and singing: 'Ecce Agnus Dei, ecce qui tollit peccata mundi.'[27] More interesting is the example in the Fleury play-book (from a thirteenth-century MS. at Orleans).[28] It begins with the following rubric:

> *Ad interfectionem puerorum, inducantur* Innocentes *stolis albis, et gaudentes* [gradientes?] *per monasterium, orent Dominum dicentes* "Quam gloriosum etc.". *Tunc Agnus ex improviso veniens, portans crucem, antecedat eos huc et illuc, et illi sequentes cantent:* "Quam gloriosum est regnum./ Emitte Agnum, Domine."
>
> (*Isa.* xvi, 1)

Another direction reads:

> *Interea* Innocentes *adhuc gradientes post Agnum decantent:*
> Agno sacrato pro nobis mortificato,
> Splendorem patris, splendorem virginitatis,
> Offerimus Christo sub signo numinis [*MS.* luminis] isto . . .

—the (somewhat corrupt) text continues with a reference to Herod. Thus, the Epistle is dramatized as well as the incident that is narrated in the Gospel.

Anyone who believes that **Pearl** is more a *consolatio* than an elegy will be particularly interested by another episode in the drama. The reference at the conclusion of the Gospel to Rachel's lamentation and her refusal to be consoled is represented. She appears with two 'consolatrices', who ask her why she weeps for those who possess the Kingdom of Heaven; but she persists in her grief. Eventually an angel appears above the prostrate forms of the slaughtered children, saying: 'Sinite paruulos et nolite eos prohibere ad me venire; talium est enim regnum caelorum' (*Matthew* xix, 14). At these words, the children rise and enter the choir. The various aspects of the liturgy for the day are amalgamated into this piece, which brings out the association of the children with the Lamb and with the Apocalyptic procession. It is impossible to say whether any representation of this kind was known in England in the fourteenth century, but the example is instructive, in any case, because it illustrates the way in which the liturgy for the day was interpreted, and indicates the kind of ideas and associations that the feast evoked in the Middle Ages.[29]

In the light of what has been considered in the foregoing paragraphs, it is reasonable to suggest that a fourteenth-century poet, who was concerned with the death of an infant and her fortunes after death, would quite naturally recall the liturgy and customs of this feast when composing his *consolatio*. This hypothesis is investigated more closely in the following section.

(iii) *Lectiones* AND HOMILIES

I have mentioned that Miss Hart is aware of a possible objection to her thesis about the child in **Pearl**[30]: unlike the Innocents and the boy in *The Prioress's Tale,* this child did not suffer a martyr's death. Such an objection is, however, easily answered. The most important reason for the maiden's right to salvation is that she died soon after baptism. Similarly, the Holy Innocents died immediately after their baptism—or rather, simultaneously with it, because their martyrdom constituted their baptism, according to contemporary doctrine.[31] Thus, in establishing a relationship between the Innocents and the child in **Pearl,** the proximity of their baptism to their death is of considerable importance; the difference between the two instances is simply that, whereas the former suffered 'fullyng in blode-schedynge', the latter received 'fullyng of fonte', so that the former received martyrs' crowns in Heaven, whereas Pearl does not. The resemblances between the two instances certainly outweigh the single difference, whose significance is still further reduced when another fact is recognized: the child's baptism 'in fonte' is made efficacious only by means of a 'blodeschedynge'— although a vicarious one. Our author shows, in the course of his central argument about salvation by 'innocence' or 'ryȝt' (which, as will appear below, has other affinities with the liturgy for this day), that he is

fully aware of this. In ll. 649 ff. he refers to the wound, that Christ received from the spear, as a well or font; and of the water that flowed from it he says:

> "Þe water is baptem, þe soþe to telle,
> Þat folȝed þe glayue so grymly grounde . . ."
> (ll. 653-54)

These lines are spoken by the maiden herself as she explains the origin of her own innocence through baptism. The part that the Crucifixion plays in this process is emphasized in the middle stanza of the three that carry this explanation.[32]

With the single exception of this detail, the Innocents are represented in the liturgy as dying in the same state as Pearl. The fact that the Innocents were within two years of age at the time of their death is also emphasized in a homily in Mirk's *Festial*. He sees in this fact a special significance:

> Þis Innocentes þat holy chyrche syngeþ of, lyueden her wyþout schame, for þay wer all wiþin two ȝer of age . . . þes chyldyr lyued not so long forto know þe good from þe euell, but wern jslayne wiþin degre of jnnocentes. Wherfor þay lyuedon here wyþout schame.[33]

The homily proceeds to explain the merits of Innocence. In this quotation the Innocents' early death is considered to have been a positive advantage to them, and this corresponds to what the author of **Pearl** maintains. A whole series of homilies that pursue this development of thought is afforded by the *lectiones* for Matins in the Sarum Breviary.[34] The second *lectio* is taken from Severianus, and it argues that Christ did not desert these children in permitting their early death, but was, on the contrary, bestowing a particular privilege upon them:

> Christus non despexit suos milites sed provexit; quibus ante dedit triumphare quam vivere; quos fecit capere sine concertatione victoriam; quos donavit coronis antequam membris; quos voluit virtutibus vitia praeterire; ante caelum possidere quam terram. Praemisit ergo Christus suos milites non anisit.[35]

The implications of the word 'milites' in this quotation, as well as all references to martyrdom in those that follow, must be discounted for the purpose of the present argument. The point is that these passages are all concerned with children who suffer death before they are two years old.

The third *lectio* broaches the subject of salvation by Grace or merit and comes to the conclusion that is presupposed by our author; namely, that infants, who have not the power to earn their glory through meritorious deeds, are saved through Grace, since, for adult and infant alike, eternal life is a divine gift and is not due to human deserts. This homily, like the previous one, is concerned with martyrdom, but allowance can easily be made for that.

> Hoc loco attendat auditor, et intelligat martyrium non constare per meritum, sed venire per gratiam. In parvulis, quae voluntas, quod arbitrium, ubi captiva fuit et ipsa natura? De martyrio ergo demus totum Deo, nichil nobis. Vincere dyabolum, corpus tradere, contemnere viscera, tormenta expendere, lassare tortorem, capere de injuriis gloriam, de morte vitam, non virtutis humanae, sed muneris est divini.[36]

The second series of *lectiones* ('In Secundo Nocturno') are taken from St. John Chrysostom. Before we examine the homilies themselves, it is worth considering the liturgical text with which the first one is associated. The office ('In Secundo Nocturno') begins with the antiphon: 'Norunt infantes laudare Deum, qui loqui non noverant: fiunt periti laude qui fuerant imperiti sermone.' This antiphon is followed by Psalm xiv (Vulgate),[37] 'Domine, quis habitabit?', after which comes another antiphon on the same Psalm: 'Exigitur itaque infantium aetas in laudem, quae delictorum non noverat crimen.' This Psalm is used in *Pearl* at ll. 678 ff., in conjunction with the similar vv. 3 and 4 of Psalm xxiv (*A.V.*; xxiii in Vulgate), during the argument in which the maiden weighs her own claims (as an infant) against those of the workers in the vineyard who 'stod þe long day stable', and who rely upon the length of their service for their reward. Speaking of one of these, she says:

> "Where wysteʒ þou euer any bourne abate
> Euer so holy in hys *prayere*
> Þat he ne forfeted by sumkyn gate
> Þe mede sumtyme of heueneʒ clere?
> And ay þe ofter þe alder þay were,
> Þay laften ryʒt and wroʒten woghe."
> (ll. 617-22—my italics)

She is referring to the dreamer's earlier argument in which he upheld the claims of the man

> "Þat hade endured in worlde stronge,
> And lyued in penaunce hys lyueʒ longe
> Wyþ bodyly bale hym blysse to byye . . ."
> (ll. 476-79)

He had argued that it seemed unfair that she should have been rewarded before such a man, and he proceeded to make a comparison of these qualifications with her own—a comparison which was not to her advantage:

> "Þou lyfed not two ʒer in oure þede;
> Þou cowþeʒ neuer God nauþer plese ne pray,
> Ne neuer nawþer Pater ne Crede."
> (ll. 483-85)

The occurrence of the word 'pray' in l. 484 and that of the word 'prayere' in l. 618 are significant. The point of the maiden's answer to the dreamer's objection is that, although she was ignorant of the very rudiments ('Pater' and 'Crede') of religious instruction, she could nevertheless 'plese' God, even if she could not 'pray' to Him. The reason for this is—she asserts—that she is undefiled by any fleck of sin, because she has never known any. In fact, she answers to the description, of the man fit to stand in God's holy place, that is delineated in Psalm xxiv, 4 (*A.V.*). This is precisely the point which the antiphons 'In Secundo Nocturno' make about the Innocents who died before they were two years old. In the *lectio* (iv) that follows, St. John Chrysostom elaborates this doctrine;

> Fiunt interea pueri sine magistro diserti, docti sine doctore, periti sine eruditore. Agnoscunt infantes Christum, praedicant Dominum, non quem persuasio humana docuerat, sed quem divinitas innocentibus inspirabat. Cessant enim humana cum divina tractantur: quia humana ipsa prodesse non poterunt, nisi divinorum solatio subleventur. Necesse est enim terrena succumbere, cum caelestia praedicantur; naturalia silere, cum virtutes loquuntur. Exigitur itaque infantium aetas in laudem, quae delictorum non noverat crimen.[38]

The liturgy for Childermas goes some way towards accounting for the presence of certain details in the poet's characterization of the maiden, as well as providing a possible source for some of the doctrines about the salvation of those who die in infancy, which are asserted in the *debate* between the maiden and the dreamer.[39] There remain some important details and arguments of which it gives no account. But there are other liturgical writings that supply what is here missing and confirm much of what has already been conjectured.

. . . . .

The Privileges of the Newly Baptized

(i) THE DESCRIPTION OF THE MAIDEN

The maiden is the subject of something like a formal *effictio* that occurs between ll. 161 and 240. Several of the details of her appearance that are stated there and elsewhere in the poem conform to the paradigm of ideal feminine beauty that is often associated with formal descriptions of ladies in medieval literature: for example, she has golden hair and 'yʒen graye', and her complexion is compared to the 'flour-de-lys'. The whiteness of her complexion is emphasized by two other stereotyped similes: 'Hyr vysage whyt as playn yuore' and 'Her ble more blaʒt þan whalleʒ bon'. But one detail of the regular paradigm is absent: it was customary to mention the blend of white and red in the lady's cheeks and to express this idea by means of a simile about lilies mingling with red roses. In the account of the maiden's 'colour' there is no mention of red roses. The reason for this departure from the usual pattern is, of course, that the poet wishes the maiden to look as much as possible like a pearl. This fact is clearly brought out in ll. 215-16, where her 'depe colour' is compared to that of the pearls that are set in the embroidery of her dress. In fact, the poet is here observing a precept laid down by one of those very rhetoricians whose *Artes Poeticae* raised the description to the place of honour among methods of *amplificatio* and helped to establish the almost invariable features of the paragon of female beauty. Matthew of Vendôme stipulates: 'Debet autem qualibet persona ab illo intitulari epitheto quod in ea prae coeteris dominatur.'[40] 'White' is the epithet that predominates in the initial description of the maiden, and the final impression of her appearance that we carry away from the poem is of her whiteness: the very last visual impression of the heavenly country that the dreamer receives before his expulsion is of 'my lyttel quene . . . þat watȝ so *quyt*' (ll. 1147-50).

Just as the description of the maiden's personal appearance is affected by the poet's desire to make her look like a pearl, so the way in which she is dressed is determined by considerations of symbolic propriety. If we discount the fashionable cut of her raiment and disregard its other ornamental details, we find that her attire consists basically of two things: her white robes and her crown or mitre, 'Hiȝe pynakled of cler quyt perle'. She wears the white robes because she belongs to the company that follows the Lamb. But we saw in the last chapter that it is necessary to ask why she is entitled to join that company. The crown has been identified by editors as the 'aureolc' that a virgin is entitled to wear in Heaven. Indeed, the maiden herself says that the Lamb 'coronde [me] clene in vergynté' (l. 767). But much earlier in the poem she had stated that He 'Corounde me *quene* in blysse to brede' (l. 415). That is surely the primary significance of her crown: the debate about her status as queen occupies a far more important place in the scheme of the poem than does the later exchange about her status as a virgin bride of the Lamb. In the next section I shall show that the basis of the maiden's apparel consists of nothing other than the ceremonial dress of the newly baptized. These vestments carried certain symbolic significations that are of considerable relevance to the meaning of *Pearl*.

(ii) THE SIGNIFICANCE OF THE MAIDEN'S 'LIVERY'

Honorius 'of Autun', in the course of a commentary on the baptismal rites celebrated on Holy Saturday, remarks that when the neophyte emerges from the font:

> Deinde mitra capiti ejus imponitur, veste alba induitur, quia in regnum et in sacerdotium assumitur.

Per mitram corona regni, per albam sacerdotalis dignitas exprimitur, quia videlicet Christi regis et sacerdotis membrum efficitur. Per albam quoque vestem innocentia designatur, quia hanc nunc per Christum in baptismo recipit, quam in primo parente amisit.

> (*Gemma Animae*, III, cxi)[41]

The final chapter of the first book of the same work (cap. cxliii) is entitled 'Baptizati albas portant vestes', and reads as follows:

> Baptizati autem ideo vestes albas portant, quae amissam innocentiam se recepisse insinuant. Illorum *mitra* regni coronam, *alba* vero sacerdotii praefert stolam. Jam enim facti sunt reges et sacerdotes et Christi regis et sacerdotis cohaeredes.[42]

Honorius is speaking of the baptism of adult catechumens in the days when baptism by immersion was practised. This is because he is not so much concerned to explain the sacrament of baptism itself, or the contemporary baptismal rite, as to consider the liturgical ceremonies of Holy Saturday, for an understanding of which a knowledge of the baptismal practices of the primitive Church is necessary.[43] Thus, although the ceremonies that he describes had become generally outmoded by the time at which he was writing, and had been replaced by something much nearer to the modern Roman baptismal rite,[44] the memory of them was nevertheless kept alive by the liturgy for Holy Saturday and Easter Week. What I would emphasize here is the fact that since the author of *Pearl* represents the child in Heaven as having acquired full adult stature in body and in intellect, it is fitting that the basis of her 'livery' should be the dress of the adult catechumen rather than the simplified adaptation of it that was placed upon infants at their baptism during the Middle Ages.

The question of the relationship between the dress of the catechumen and that of baptized infants must now be considered. In the baptism of infants, the counterpart to the white robes of the catechumens was certainly the cloth of white linen known as the *chrisom*, and, since it was placed on the infant's head, it would do duty for the *corona* or *mitra* as well. The way in which this adaptation of the catechumen's dress was brought about can be seen from the following remark by Johannes Belethus, which occurs in his commentary on the liturgy for Holy Saturday:

> Inuncto chrismate baptizato, imponitur capite ejus chrismale, rotunda quaedam mitra quae coronam vitae significat, vel candida induitur vestis, quae ad similitudinem cuculli ex albissimo panno conficitur filo rubro supertexto. Candida illa vestis innocentiae stolam designat, quae nobis redditur in baptismo . . .[45]

The detail of the red thread seems to have been only a local addition and need not concern us.[46] This passage should make it clear how the *chrisom* is related to both the *corona* and the *alba*. The observations of Durandus on the significance of the dress of the newly baptized are still more explicit. He remarks that in certain places the white robe is given to the neophyte in token of priesthood, and 'quaedam rotunda mitra, signum coronae regni vitae, quia ipse est membrum Christi, qui est rex et sacerdos'.[47] He shows that there is Scriptural authority for this doctrine in I *Peter* ii, 9:

> Omnes enim veri christiani reges, et sacerdotes dicuntur, unde Petrus Apostolus ait: "Vos autem genus electum, regale sacerdotium". Reges, quia seipsos et alios regunt . . . etc.[48]

The second verse of this chapter of St. Peter's epistle shows that the apostle was himself thinking of those who have been reborn into the Christian community.[49] So these liturgical commentators all agree that baptism carries with it the privilege of kingship in Christ's kingdom. If, therefore, a child were to die soon after baptism, so that it was still within what Mirk calls 'degre of jnnocentes' at the time of its death, it would acquire the status of king (or queen) upon entering the Kingdom of Heaven.

This very point is the central subject of the first part of the *debate* in **Pearl;** it has also been the subject of controversy among students of the poem. This controversy has ranged in two directions. First, it has been suggested that in the fourteenth century it would have been heretical to believe that a baptized infant could be saved; and, second, that it was heretical of the poet to argue that in Heaven everyone is 'payed inlyche / wheþer lyttel oþer much be hys rewarde'.[50] Professor Wellek disposed of both these charges by referring to theological controversies of the time, and it is not intended to renew this dispute here.[51] What is here suggested is that there is no need to suppose that the poet had an expert knowledge of the theological controversies of the time; the essence of his argument can be found in these twelfth- and thirteenth-century commentaries on the liturgy.

Doctrines that closely resemble those formulated by the commentators in the course of their discussion of the dress of the newly baptized are present in the poem. The 'rotunda mitra' is, according to our commentators, a symbol of the *corona* of the Kingdom of Heaven. The maiden in **Pearl** is, of course, not represented as wearing a baptismal head-dress, but this heavenly crown which it symbolizes. She declares that the Lamb 'Corounde me quene in blysse to brede . . .', although she was of a tender age when she died. The dreamer, aware of the fact that in any given kingdom there can be only one king and one queen, asks her whether she is the Queen of Heaven. The maiden explains that the

Kingdom of Heaven has a mysterious 'property' (l. 446), whereby everyone who becomes an inhabitant also becomes a king or queen. The dreamer objects that he could understand her being a countess or 'lady of lasse aray' because she died before she was two years of age without knowing 'Pater or Creed', whereas the positions of greater honour should be reserved for those who have had to endure more on Earth. But these objections are shown to be irrelevant, since 'Of more and lasse in Godez ryche . . . lys no joparde' (ll. 601 ff.). At this point the maiden clinches her argument by referring to the privileged status of the newly baptized (ll. 613-72), who are in a stronger position by virtue of their innocence than those who have lived longer and had time to lose it (and so to forfeit the privileges acquired at baptism)—even if it is still possible for them to regain it. It is true that in the poem it is never explicitly stated that the neophyte becomes a king by virtue of his baptism, but this idea is clearly presupposed throughout this argument. Since the neophyte is a co-heir with Christ of God's kingdom,[52] it follows that if a child dies while still in its baptismal innocence, it will, when it goes to Heaven, be 'Sesed in alle hys herytage' (l. 417).

At ll. 457-68 the maiden refers to the doctrine of the mystical body of Christ, in order to illustrate her statement in the previous stanza about the mysterious 'property' of the Kingdom of Heaven. The fact that the poet chooses to put this doctrine into her mouth at this point in her argument provides another link with the status of the newly baptized. It will be recalled that Honorius declares that the *mitra* and the *alba* are given to the newly baptized, 'quia . . . Christi regis et sacerdotis *membrum* efficitur'—he becomes a king (our author is not concerned in the poem with the priestly status) by becoming 'a longande lym to þe Mayster of myste'.[53] The point I would emphasize is that the poet does not simply derive the doctrinal material for this stanza from I *Corinthians* xii (where, incidentally, there is a direct allusion to baptism at *v*. 13), but uses this text to illustrate and support his argument that the inhabitants of the heavenly kingdom can all be kings without depriving one another of their kingship. This is precisely what the liturgical commentators say, when they discuss the status of the newly baptized.

Having considered the liturgical elements in the poem that are centred upon the signification of the 'coroune', we may now examine those that are associated with the other basic part of the maiden's dress; namely, her white robes. In quotations that have already been made from the three principal liturgical writers who are mentioned in this study, it was stated that the white vestments of the newly baptized signify the innocence which was lost through Adam and restored through the sacrament of baptism. The poet makes no explicit statement about what is signified by the white robes, but the argument of the poem shows that the innocence which the maiden received at baptism is an important element in her characterization. It is the subject of the central portion of the debate about innocence and 'riȝt'. As soon as the subject of innocence is introduced at ll. 625 ff., it is associated with baptism, and the two succeeding stanzas discuss the institution of this sacrament through the Crucifixion as a means of restoring what was withdrawn from mankind through Adam's sin. Certainly, innocence is the maiden's principal virtue, comprehending within itself subsidiary virtues such as chastity, virginity and purity.

The maiden's white robes are mentioned for the first time at l. 197: 'Al blysnande whyt watȝ hir beau biys'. In defence of the emendation of MS. *uiys*, Gordon shows that the line is a rendering of *Revelation* xix, 8, which states that it was allowed to the bride of the Lamb to clothe herself in shining white bysse.[54] As that verse from *Revelation* is unquestionably the source of this line, it may seem an act of supererogation to inquire any further into the significance of the word *biys*. Nevertheless, it is interesting to see that Durandus associates it with baptism and with the new, supernatural life that is bestowed by the sacrament. Like Honorius and Belethus, he remarks that the alb, or white robe, is the appropriate one for those who are reborn through baptism.[55] In III, iii, 1, he says that the Alb is made of bysse, or linen, because it is written: 'for the fine linen is the righteousness of saints' (*Revelation* xix, 8). In the next paragraph he remarks that *byssus* is an Egyptian linen, whose whiteness is produced by beating—and he goes on to give an allegorical meaning for this. It is not the allegorical signification given here that is of interest to us, however, but the one which is given in 5 of the same chapter, where he observes that the alb, because it is made of linen, is completely unlike the garments made from the skins of dead animals which Adam put on after the Fall, and, therefore, it symbolizes the new supernatural life that is given in baptism, and exemplified in Christ. For the same reason, the white vestments are a fitting dress for Christ, the head of His mystical body, as well as for those who have become members (limbs) through baptism:

> Porro, secundum quod capiti, scilicet Christo, convenit alba, quae est lineum vestimentum, longissime distans a tunicis pelliceis, quae ex mortuis animalibus fiunt, quibus Adam vestitus est post peccatum, novitatem vitae significat, quam Christus et habuit, et docuit, et tribuit in baptismo, de qua dicit Apostolus: "[Expellentes] veterem hominem cum actibus suis . . . et induite novum, qui secundum Deum creatus est" (*Eph.* iv). Nam in transfiguratione "resplenduit facies ejus sicut sol, et vestimenta ejus facta sunt alba, sicut nix" (*Matt.* xvii). Semper enim vestimenta munda fuerunt, et candida, quia "peccatum non facit, nec inventus est dolus in ore ejus."
>
> (I *Peter* ii).[56]

So, when the neophyte puts on the white robe, he assumes, not only the virtue of innocence, but the new, supernatural life as well. Moreover, he also puts on the robes that are worn by the inhabitants of the Heavenly Kingdom and the garments that are, above all, those most fitting for Christ. In fact, he puts on Christ's own livery.

The white garments of the maiden in *Pearl* have much the same pattern of interrelated functions and meanings. It would be possible to tabulate the various significations of the white robes, both in *Pearl* and in liturgical practice, according to the fourfold allegorical system of the theologians and Biblical commentators—at least, in a fairly loose, analogical manner. Their 'tropological' meaning would be 'innocence'; 'allegorically' they would symbolize rebirth in Christ, whose own livery they are; 'anagogically' they would represent the fact that baptism entitles the neophyte to become after death one of the white-robed company of the New Jerusalem. The liturgical commentators did, indeed, regularly make use of this fourfold method of interpretation.[57] A particular instance of their doing this will serve to introduce a final observation. The example is not directly concerned with white robes, but it does establish the association between the newly baptized and the hundred and forty-four thousand faultless virgins. Honorius 'of Autun', in the course of his commentary on the liturgy for Holy Saturday, considers the reason for the singing of the canticle, 'Sicut cervus desiderat', during the procession to the font, which was undertaken on that day and was repeated daily throughout the following Easter Week. He sees an anagogical significance in this practice:

> Anagoge, id est sensus ad superiores ducens, locutio est, quae de praeteritis, futuris, et ea quae in coelis est vita futura, sive mysticis sive apertis sermonibus disputat; unde catechumenis dicitur in Cantico: "Sicut cervus desiderat ad fontes aquarum". Canticum ideo cantatur, quia ipsi sunt futuri in baptismo de centum quadraginta quatuor milium coetu, qui cantant canticum novum, quod nemo potuerat dicere nisi illi.[58]

Similarly, Durandus observes:

> Ideo autem Cantica cantantur, quia catechumeni, quorum est hujus diei officium, futuri sunt in proximo de coetu centum quadraginta quatuor millium cantantium canticum novum (*Rev.* xiv). Cantatur etiam propter futuram renovationem in veram innocentiam, quasi jam factum sit quod cito futurum sit . . .[59]

The liturgy for Holy Saturday was instituted at a time when baptism of adult catechumens by immersion was generally practised, and when that sacrament was celebrated only twice a year: on Holy Saturday and at

Pentecost—of which the former was, liturgically, the more important occasion. In the fourteenth century, when the candidates for baptism were infants rather than adults, and the sacrament was celebrated independently of these dates, the conditions that originally determined the structure of the liturgy for this season no longer obtained. There could, for example, be no procession of neophytes to the font throughout Easter Week. So certain adaptations were made. Thus, the procession was undertaken by the clergy and choir dressed in albs.[60] Again, although there may sometimes have been nobody to baptize on Holy Saturday,[61] the idea of baptism retained its pre-eminence in the liturgy on account of the ceremony of the blessing of the font. The liturgy would, normally, no longer be performed for the benefit of the neophyte, but for the edification of adults who had been baptized as infants. So these portions of the liturgy would acquire an allegorical rather than a literal significance. The baptismal ceremonies would provide an annual opportunity for an act of spiritual renewal; the figure of the neophyte would become a symbol, inciting the faithful to return to the state of innocence which they possessed after their baptism.

Similarly, the Epistle in the Mass for the Saturday in Easter Week, originally intended for the exhortation of the neophytes, would serve to impress upon Christians who had been baptized many years earlier a *sentence* similar to the one that is implied in **Pearl**. It was taken from I *Peter* ii and urged its hearers to lay aside guile and envy, and 'like new-born babes, desire the rational milk without guile, that thereby you may grow unto salvation'. The faithful were again urged to imitate the virtues of the infant in the Introit for the following day (Low Sunday): 'Quasi modo geniti infantes, alleluia: rationabile, sine dolo lac concupiscite, alleluia, alleluia, alleluia'.[62] The day came to be known as 'Quasimodo Sunday'.

Notes

[1] *Ed. cit.,* p. xxv, n. 3; cf. *De Civitate Dei,* xxii, 14 and 15. Dante's assumption (*Paradiso,* xxxii, 46-47) that children retain their childish faces and voices in Heaven is contrary to the normal medieval opinion.

[2] *Ed. cit.,* 63-64; n. on l. 197.

[3] 'The Pearl: An Interpretation of the Middle English Poem', *Studies in English,* iv (Charles University, Prague, 1933)—esp. pp. 20-24. Reprinted in Blanch, *op. cit.* (see Bibliographical Note, above, p. 128); esp. pp. 24 ff.

[4] All references to the Sarum Missal and Breviary are to the following edd.: *The Sarum Missal,* ed. J. Wickham Legg (Oxford, 1916); F. Proctor and C. Wordsworth, *Breviarium ad Usum Insignis Ecclesiae Sarum* (Cambridge, 1879-86), 3 vols.

[5] I give references to book, chapter and paragraph. The edition from which I quote is that published at Naples in 1859. Many helpful annotations will be found in the French translation of this work: *Rational ou Manuel des Divins Offices de Guillaume Durand,* ed. Charles Barthélemy (Paris, 1854), 5 vols. An English trans. of Book I appears in J. M. Neale and B. Webb, *The Symbolism of Churches and Church Ornaments* (Leeds, 1843), and of Book III in T. H. Passmore, *The Sacred Vestments* (London, 1899).

[6] Durandus acknowledges the fact that his work is a compilation from other sources (VIII, xiv). For a list of some of the authors whom he consulted, see Barthélemy, *ed. cit.,* I, xxv. In V, 467-79, he gives a list of the principal liturgical commentators arranged chronologically.

[7] Honorius's works are edited in *PL,* clxxii.

[8] It is printed in the edition of Durandus's *Rationale* (Naples, 1859) mentioned above. A text of Belethus's *Rationale* will also be found in *PL,* ccii.

[9] Text from the following edition: 'Bartholomaeus de proprietatibus rerum . . translated from latin into our vulgaire langage by John of Trevisa. Londoni in aedibus Thomae Bertheleti [1535]'.

[10] *MLN,* xlii, 113-16.

[11] *CT,* B.1769-75.

[12] *Ibid.,* B.1817.

[13] Cf. *CT,* B. 1709.

[14] *Sarum Breviary, ed. cit.,* I, ccxlii. For Wyclif's opinion that muscial settings—among other features of the Salisbury ritual—distract attention from the *sentence,* see his treatise 'Of Feigned Contemplative Life' in *The English Works of Wyclif,* ed. F. D. Matthew (*EETS,* O.S., 74), pp. 187-96.

[15] On the Boy Bishop see (apart from primary sources mentioned in subsequent notes): E. K. Chambers, *The Medieval Stage* (Oxford, 1903), i, 336-71; Daniel Rock, *The Church of Our Fathers,* new edn. by G. W. Hart and W. H. Frere (London, 1904), iv, 250-56; J. M. J. Fletcher, *The Boy Bishop at Salisbury and Elsewhere* (Salisbury, 1921); W. C. Meller, *The Boy Bishop* (London, 1923). Meller does little more than follow Fletcher.

[16] See Durandus of Mende, *Rationale,* VII, xlii, 15, as well as secondary sources mentioned in preceding note.

[17] *Sarum Breviary, ed. cit.,* I, ccxxix.

[18] See Meller, *op. cit.,* p. 13.

[19] Text is given in *Camden Miscellany,* VII (Publications of the Camden Society, N.S., No. xiv, 1875), pp. 14 ff.; see Fletcher, *op. cit.,* p. 18; Meller, *op. cit.,* p. 14.

[20] Meller, *op. cit.,* pp. 12-13.

[21] C. Wordsworth, *Ceremonies and Processions of the Cathedral Church of Salisbury* (Cambridge, 1901), p. 52.

[22] Lines 205-7.

[23] Line 211.

[24] The available evidence suggests that these ceremonies were widespread throughout England during the fourteenth century: see Fletcher, *op. cit.,* pp. 9-10; Meller, *op. cit.,* pp. 10-11.

[25] *Medieval Stage,* ii, 148; *English Literature at the Close of the Middle Ages* (Oxford, 1945), pp. 7-9.

[26] *The Drama of the Medieval Church* (Oxford, 1933), ii, 102-24.

[27] *Ibid.,* p. 105.

[28] *Ibid.,* pp. 110-13. Text also given in T. Wright, *Early Mysteries and Other Latin Poems of the Twelfth and Thirteenth Centuries* (London, 1838), pp. 29-31; E. du Méril, *Origines Latines Du Théâtre Moderne* (Paris, 1849), pp. 175-79.

[29] The Innocents are also associated with the procession of *Revelation* xiv in hymns, such as that by Bede (*Anal. Hymnica,* L, p. 102 and see XLII, p. 225); see also the carol by John Audelay, mentioned by Gordon, *ed. cit.,* p. xxv, n. 2. Gordon also refers to the Towneley play of Herod.

[30] See above, p. 104.

[31] On baptism by martyrdom, cf. *Piers Plowman,* B. xii, 282-83:

> 'For there is fullyng of fonte . and fullyng in
>   blode-shedynge,
> And through fuire is fullyng . and that is
>   ferme bileue.'

(W. W. Skeat, *The Vision of William Concerning Piers the Plowman. In Three Parallel Texts*—London, 1886 —i, 382.)

[32] Lines 645-48.

[33] *Mirk's Festial,* ed. T. Erbe, I (*EETS,* E.S., 96), p. 35.

[34] They do not appear in the modern Roman Breviary; neither are they included in the medieval York Breviary: see *Breviarium ad Usum Insignis Ecclesiae Eboracensis,* i (Surtees Society, lxxi (1880; 1879 on spine), coll. 112-20). The three final *lectiones* (which do not, in fact, concern us here) are, like the corresponding ones in *Sarum,* taken from Bede—but they are not identical with them.

[35] *Sarum Breviary, ed. cit.,* I, ccxxxiv. The *lectio* is concerned with the antiphon: 'quare non defendis . . .'

[36] *Ibid.* col. ccxxxv (by Severianus).

[37] Psalm xv in *A.V.*

[38] *Sarum Breviary, ed. cit.,* I ccxxxvi.

[39] Moreover, it may also provide a possible source for an important aspect of the poem's didactic *sentence.* In addition to evidence already mentioned, we may observe an annotation by Barthélemy (see above, p. 143, n. 5) on a passage in which Durandus discusses the liturgy for Holy Innocents' Day. He calls attention to a homily for the Feast by Pope St. Leo the Great [i.e. Leo I] (Barthélemy, *ed. cit.,* v, 342-45). The homily exhorts its audience to become as children and is concerned with the spiritual renewal of life; it urges a return to infancy, not in ignorance, but in harmlessness.

[40] Text from Edmond Faral, *Les Arts Poétiques du XIIe et du XIIIe Siècle* (Paris, 1924), p. 120. This is Matthew's adaptation, for purposes of the *descriptio,* of Horace's precept about consistency of characterization (De Arte Poetica, II, 120 ff.).

[41] *PL,* clxxii, 673.

[42] *Ibid.,* col. 616.

[43] See P. Guéranger, *The Liturgical Year:* the vol. entitled 'Passiontide and Holy Week' in the trans. by L. Shepherd (Dublin, 1870), pp. 614-19.

[44] For the form of baptism observed in medieval England, see W. Maskell, *Monumenta Ritualia Ecclesiae Anglicanae* (London, 1846), i, 22-36. Maskell reproduces the text of the Sarum rite, but in footnotes he observes discrepancies between it and the other medieval English rites.

[45] *Rationale,* cap. cx (*PL,* ccii, 114).

[46] See Durandus, *op. cit.,* VI, lxxxiii, 17.

[47] *Ibid.,* 15.

[48] *Ibid.*

[49] See above, p. 121.

[50] Lines 603-4.

[51] See above. . . .

[52] See Honorius as quoted above. . . .

[53] . . . So also Durandus: ' . . . quia ipse est *membrum* Christi, qui est rex et sacerdos'. . . .

[54] *Ed. cit.,* p. 54.

[55] *Op. cit.,* VI, lxxxiii, 16, where he is discussing the significance of the chrisom. See also *ibid.,* III, xviii, 2. This [section] is concerned with the various uses of the four liturgical colours.

[56] *Ibid.,* III, iii, 5. The opening of the quotation from *Ephesians* is a corruption of *Ephesians* iv, 22: 'Deponere vos secundum pristinam conversationem veterem hominem . . . ' Cf. *Colossians* iii, 9 and 10.

[57] The application of the four allegorical 'senses' to the liturgical text as well as to the vestments and ecclesiastical ornaments is a common feature of the liturgical commentaries. See Durandus, *op. cit.,* I, *Proemium,* 6-12.

[58] *PL,* clxxii, 749.

[59] *Op. cit.,* VI, lxxxi, 13.

[60] *Sarum Breviary, ed. cit.,* I, dcccxviii-dcccxxii.

[61] But usually, no doubt, there were infants to be baptized on that day. The Sarum Missal makes provision for baptism in the course of the Holy Saturday ceremonies, giving instructions for the putting on of the chrisom (*ed. cit.,* p. 131).

[62] *Sarum Missal, ed. cit.,* p. 144.

A. C. Spearing (essay date 1970)

SOURCE: "Pearl," in *The Gawain-Poet: A Critical Study,* Cambridge at the University Press, 1970, pp. 96-170.

[*In the following excerpt, Spearing describes* Pearl *as an extended dramatic narrative in which the literal-minded dreamer interacts with the celestial maiden in a way that reveals the difference between earthly human relationships and spiritual relationships.*]

. . . In the fourteenth century the pearl could symbolize any of a very wide range of things; if a coherence is established within this variety, it is established by the poem itself, not by its sources and analogues.[1] In some ways it may be that we can better take **Pearl** as a guide to medieval symbolism than medieval symbolism as a guide to **Pearl**.

My purpose in what follows, then, is to read the poem with care: by no means an original aim, but more novel than it ought to be. It will be found, I believe, that Schofield was right in saying that 'The author's plan is to let the symbolism of his poem disclose itself slowly'.[2] The pearl image is not static but dynamic. It will be recalled that we found the same to be true of the central concept of *clannesse* in the poem *Purity*. We saw how, in the course of his poem, the *Gawain*-poet redefined that concept so completely as in effect to re-create it, and how he did so by setting it in a variety of contexts taken from real situations, so that the idea developed in meaning as the poem extended itself in time. In **Pearl** the poet treats his central image, and perhaps other images such as that of the jeweller, in the same way, but now the development in meaning is co-ordinated with and expressed through a single developing human drama—the encounter between the Dreamer and the Pearl Maiden. The result is a poem more economical and more powerfully moving than *Purity*. The whole force and poignancy of **Pearl** derives from its basic structure as an encounter involving human relationship; and it is through the synthesis of symbol with this human drama that the poet conveys his meaning, and not, I believe, through any concealed layers of allegory.

Symbol and drama

The pearl symbol is first mentioned as the first word of the poem's first line—'Perle, plesaunte to prynces paye'—and the similarity between this line and the closing lines of the poem has not escaped notice. At the end, the reference is to the Prince of heaven, to whom the pearl now belongs; the narrator wishes that we too may be 'precious perlez unto his pay'. I have suggested that the poem has a circular effect, its head biting its own tail; but this does not mean that its tail is the same as its head. None the less, even so moderate an interpreter of the poem as Gordon has followed the earlier commentators cited by Schofield and has claimed that the prince of the first line means 'literally a prince of this world and symbolically Christ'.[3] It is true of course that the parallel between the opening and closing lines is deliberate, and that on a second and subsequent readings of the poem the first line may recall the last, so that we shall have from the very beginning a sense of the nature of the development in meaning which is to take place. But this is not to say that the first line will mean the last, even symbolically. To agree that it does mean the last is surely to deny the nature of the poem as an object which, for its reader, is extended in time, and is therefore capable of discursive or dramatic development. And in this case we may miss the point of the first section of the poem. It begins with an exclamation in praise of 'the pearl' (i.e. pearls in general), and already a development in meaning begins as 'the pearl' slides unobtrusively across into another sense (i.e. one particular pearl):

> Perle, plesaunte to prynces paye
> To clanly clos in golde so clere!
> Oute of oryent, I hardyly saye,
> Ne proved I never her precios pere.
>
> (1-4)

Those lines, taken by themselves, might belong to a verse lapidary, and refer to the pearl as a literal precious stone, valued by literal earthly princes. This sense remains throughout the opening section: we can always understand that the narrator is referring to a jewel, and to the loss of a jewel. But there are also suggestions in this opening section that he is using the language of a lapidary in order to refer to something else: a girl or woman. They begin with the reference to the pearl as *her*. This indication that the pearl is feminine might be simply a matter of grammatical gender, *perle* deriving from a word which is feminine in French.[4] But the next two lines intensify the suggestion of femininity in such a way as to hint at sex rather than gender:

> So rounde, so reken in uche araye,
> So smal, so smothe, her sydez were.
>
> (5-6)

Here *araye* could mean either the setting of a stone or the dress of a person, and *sydez* could mean either the surface of a pearl or the flanks of a woman. Other suggestions that the pearl is an image used of a person come from what the narrator goes on to tell us of his feelings about its loss, particularly when the loss is first mentioned:

> Allas! I leste hyr in on erbere;
> Thurgh gresse to grounde hit fro me yot.
> I dewyne, fordolked of luf-daungere,
> Of that pryvy perle wythouten spot.
>
> (9-12)

In later stanzas in the opening section he speaks of the grievous affliction of his heart, the burning and swelling of his breast, of clasping his hands in misery, of the fierce obstinacy of his grief. These are feelings that would be highly extravagant, Shylock-like indeed, if directed towards a jewel, but which are normal as part of the conventional language of love-suffering in medieval poetry. We noted earlier that *luf-daungere* suggests *fine amour*. It remains a case of suggestion, however: the implications of the phrasing are not pinned down by any explicit statement. We are faced with suggestiveness of a kind that belongs to poetry rather than to theology, and what it suggests is that the rela-

tionship between the narrator and the lost pearl is in some sense a human love-relationship, and that the loss involved is the death of a beloved girl or woman. She is 'clad in clot' (22) rather than in 'golde so clere', the earth is accused of marring her beauty, and she is now rotting. Yet at the same time as these hints of a human relationship broken by death are given, the original indications that the pearl is simply a pearl are by no means dropped. The refrain line throughout this section is some variant of 'that precios perle wythouten spotte', and the pearl is also referred to as a 'myry juele' (23) which 'trendeled doun' on to a 'huyle' (41), and as 'such rychez' (26).

Now we may, if we choose, refer to this deliberate intermingling of human suggestions and jewel suggestions as 'allegory', though the word is usually employed to indicate some more precise system of equivalences. But if we do call it allegory we need to recognize that it is the narrator who is being an allegorist, not necessarily the poet. This narrator is imposing on waking reality some vague equivalent to the kind of allegorical structure that the Lover in the *Roman de la Rose* finds ready-made in the world of his dream. The narrator, we gather, has lost by her death someone dear to him, and he thinks it appropriate to speak of the death of a person in terms of the loss of a precious stone: that is to say, that he sees it as the total and irrevocable loss of a valuable object, towards which the proper response is one of passionate and hopeless mourning. His attitude in this opening section is somewhat reminiscent of that of the man in black in *The Book of the Duchess*, a poem from which all hint of an otherworldly consolation is carefully excluded, even to the extent of omitting the consolatory metamorphosis from the story of Ceyx and Alcyone. In *Pearl*, even more than in Chaucer's dream-poem, this dramatic grief is made attractive, framed as it is in a scene which delights the senses with strange music and with the brightness and fragrance of flowers and herbs. But our response to the narrator's grief should not be one simply of surrender. The garden in which it is set forms a traditional pleasance or *locus amoenus*,[5] but the season in which the narrator enters it is not the traditional one of spring or Maytime but August, harvest-time, 'Quen corne is corven wyth crokez kene' (40). This unusual season may have had symbolic associations of one sort or another, as indeed may the flowers and herbs,[6] but it also has a compelling poetic effect. This effect is in harmony with the landscape's noticeable lack of one constant feature of the traditional *locus amoenus*, namely the stream or river. The landscape provides, we may say, an 'objective correlative' to the emotions of the narrator. About both there is a hint of the over-ripe, the unrefreshed, the drowsy, and perhaps of the merely passive: the corn awaiting the sickle, the narrator surrendering to his overpowering emotion. He does not see things with May-morning clarity; though he feels deeply the value of the lost pearl, by relying merely on feeling he underestimates its preciousness, seeing it not, as at the end of the poem, as precious to the Prince of heaven, but as precious only to earthly princes. As the opening lines hint, and as is made explicit later in the poem, the narrator is defined as a 'jeweller', aware only of material values.

That we are intended to adopt a critical attitude towards the narrator, even while feeling fully the pathos of his situation, is suggested by the way in which he refers to the flowers growing on the spot where his pearl was lost (that is, in human terms, the grave of the beloved):

> Blomez blayke and blwe and rede
> Ther schynez ful schyr agayn the sunne.
> Flor and fryte may not be fede
> Ther hit doun drof in moldez dunne;
> For uch gresse mot grow of graynez dede;
> No whete were ellez to wonez wonne.
>
> (27-32)

The last two lines embody an allusion to a familiar Scriptural text, John xii. 24-5:

> Amen, amen dico vobis, nisi granum frumenti
>   cadens in terram mortuum fuerit,
>   Ipsum solum manet; si autem mortuum
>   fuerit, multum fructum affert.
> (Amen, amen, I say to you, unless the grain
>   of wheat falling into the ground die,
>   Itself remaineth alone. But if it die, it
>   bringeth forth much fruit.)

But it is clear that the narrator has misunderstood this text: he has taken the fruit which grows from the dead grain to be material, like the flowers on the grave. If he recalled the next words in John, he would have understood that it was the spiritual fruit of eternal life:

> Qui amat animam suam, perdet eam; et qui odit animam suam in hoc mundo, in vitam aeternam custodit eam.
>
> (John xii. 25)

> (He that loveth his life shall lose it; and he that hateth his life in this world keepeth it unto life eternal.)

The narrator, then, has been mistaken to talk about the dead person as something which can be lost as completely as a jewel. Once a pearl is lost in the earth, it is lost for ever, but a person is an immortal soul as well as a corruptible body, and, by physical death, can gain eternal life. The narrator's grief, however touching and understandable, is mistaken, because it leaves out of account the immortality of the dead person's soul. His pearl may be lost to him for the time being, but it is not absolutely lost. His mistakenness comes

close to being explicitly acknowledged in the final stanza of the opening section, where the earliest openly Christian reference occurs:

> A devely dele in my hert denned,
> Thagh resoun sette myselven saght.
> I playned my perle that ther watz spenned
> Wyth fyrce skyllez that faste faght;
> Thagh kynde of Kryst me comfort kenned,
> My wreched wylle in wo ay wraghte.
>
> (51-6)

It is not clear to what extent this perception represents the narrator's awareness at the time, or the awareness he achieved later as a result of the experience recorded in the poem. It does not need to be clear (we have noted that such ambiguity is part of the poem's technique), for its work has been done once it points towards a conflict between the narrator's violent and persuasive emotions and some as yet undefined rational and Christian attitude. The conflict is not immediately developed, for at this point the narrator is overcome by sleep, and becomes the Dreamer.

His body remains *in hoc mundo*, in the garden, but his spirit is transported to the new landscape of 'life eternal'. It is, as we have seen, another 'gardyn gracios gaye' (260), another version of the traditional *locus amoenus*, but this time a different version, shining with brilliant light and hard with metal and precious stones. This other world is conceived with the *Gawain*-poet's usual concreteness, but the concreteness is not used in quite the same way as when he recreates Old Testament scenes in *Purity* or *Patience*. There the purpose of the concreteness is to naturalize and familiarize: it is a matter of introducing table-cloths and oaktrees into the deserts of Palestine. Coming from *Purity*, we might expect in **Pearl** to find the other world full of angels having picnics under the oaktrees, but in fact what the poet does is to evoke an exotic and genuinely otherworldly landscape, but still to re-create it in full solidity, with no hint of any vagueness or uncertainty. The more homely aspects of the Old Testament poems here become part of the Dreamer's naïveté, not part of the reality he naïvely regards. In this other world, the crystal cliffs, the blue-trunked trees with silver leaves, the gravel made of pearls, make up a kind of science-fiction landscape: it is planetary or lunar in its strangeness, and has a technicolour harshness in its brilliance. We have seen how the poet uses metallic similes to sharpen the sensory effect. He also employs one or two ingeniously precise similes of the 'as mote in at a munster dore' type for the same purpose. For example:

> In the founce ther stonden stonez stepe,
> As glente thurgh glas that glowed and glyght,
> As stremande sternez, quen strothe-men slepe,
> Staren in welkyn in wynter nyght.
>
> (113-16)

In the first of these similes describing the stones at the bottom of the rivers, the suggestion is perhaps of stained glass with the sun shining through it. The second simile, while seeming to be developed into an independent scene almost for its own sake, in fact heightens the original sensory effect with its strongly evocative details of the winter night and of men sleeping while the stars burn. Sound and rhythm, as always, have their part to play in calling up the scene, as in the two lines preceding those just quoted, where s's and r's create a whispering effect, while repeated present participles suggest the irregular, halting progress of the swirling water as it turns back on itself:

> Swangeande swete the water con swepe,
> With a rownande rourde raykande aryght.
>
> (111-12)

Or one might mention the pebbly feel of

> The gravayl that on grounde con grynde
> Wern precious perlez of oryente.
>
> (81-2)

That last line contains the first mention of pearls in the poem's second section, and the context of the landscape of which it forms part draws out two further aspects of the meaning latent in the pearl symbol: its brilliance and its hard permanence. Light, the effusion of God, is the favourite medieval image of beauty, and here the more human beauty which the pearl had at first in the narrator's memory—'So smal, so smothe her sydez were'—has begun, through emphasis on new aspects of the same symbol, to merge into a heavenly beauty. The pearl is now part of a landscape dazzling, overpowering in its brightness:

> For urthely herte myght not suffyse
> To the tenthe dole of tho gladnez glade.
>
> (135-6)

And the preciousness which was susceptible of death has in the same way begun to turn into a more permanent but harder preciousness. Thus, although the pearl symbol has for the moment reverted to its original sense of a precious stone, it has done so only to develop in new directions. We shall find that none of its separate senses is abandoned in the course of the poem, but any of them may momentarily come to the surface for the sake of a further development of associations.

This is the only mention of pearls in the second or third sections of the poem, but in the third section the Maiden appears for the first time. She is not at once identified with the lost pearl; by making use of the slow perception of his Dreamer, the poet is able to unfold his symbol gradually. At first what the Dreamer sees in her is the hard brilliance of the pearl, and an almost unbearable purity of whiteness. She is sitting on the other side of the river that cuts through the dream landscape, at the foot of a glittering crystal cliff, a courteous and gracious lady, dressed in a gleaming white mantle, who shines 'As glysnande golde that man con schere' (165): another characteristically precise simile—not just like gold, but like freshly cut gold. Not even in the feverish jargon of washing-powder advertisements does modern English have enough words meaning shining, glittering, radiant, and so on, to translate all the poet's different ways of expressing the effusion of light. Within all this overpowering glitter, the Dreamer comes only slowly to recognize the Maiden; and he says so with a naïve simplicity that will be characteristic of his attitude towards her in this encounter. He remarks only, 'I knew hyr wel, I hade sen hyr ere' (164), and again:

> On lenghe I loked to hyr there;
> The lenger, I knew hyr more and more.
>
> (167-8)

At last, this figure, at first still as a statue, begins to move. First she raises her head, so that the Dreamer can see 'Hyr vysayge whyt as playn yvore' (178), then she rises to her feet, and walks down to the river bank. This slow process of encounter and recognition is one of great emotional turmoil for the Dreamer. His heart is stunned (*blunt,* 176) and full of astonished confusion (*ful stray atount,* 179), and he is afraid that having seen her he may lose her again. It is through this moving and convincing crisis of human feeling that the meaning of the symbol is developed for us, rather than through the existence from the beginning of parallel allegorical layers.

At this point it is still not perfectly clear who it is that the Dreamer recognizes when he recognizes the Maiden, but it becomes clear in the course of the next section of the poem, section IV, in which her appearance and dress are described in great detail. Here pearls are mentioned again and again, as part of a 'fashion plate' description of her dress. The normal medieval descriptive method, of accumulation rather than selection, is used, but more effectively here than in the description of the temple vessels in *Purity,* because it is directed to a single end, the intensification of pearl qualities. (It has often been pointed out that there was a special enthusiasm for pearls in fourteenth-century courtly society, so that at the same time the Maiden is shown to be a great and fashionable lady.)[7] She is wearing a white linen mantle, open at the sides, and trimmed with pearls, with hanging sleeves also decorated with pearls. Her kirtle is to match, and again is covered with pearls. She wears a crown of pearls, and her complexion is as pearl-like as the pearls with which she is adorned:

> Her depe colour yet wonted non
> Of precios perle in porfyl pyghte.
>
> (215-16)

The culmination of this description is reached with a single flawless pearl at her breast:

> Bot a wonder perle wythouten wemme
> Inmyddez hyr breste watz sette so sure;
> A mannez dome moght dryghly demme
> Er mynde moght malte in hit mesure.
> I hope no tong moght endure
> No saverly saghe say of that syght,
> So watz hit clene and cler and pure,
> That precios perle ther hit watz pyght.
>
> (221-8)

To attempt to distinguish the symbolic significance of this one pearl from that of the Pearl Maiden herself would be to misunderstand, indeed to resist, the poet's methods. Certainly this pearl seems to have special associations with purity or virginity, in such phrases as *wythouten wemme,* but these only recall and develop an idea which had been present from the first section of the poem, with its use of *wythouten spot* as the refrain phrase. The *order* in which the poem's symbolism is unfolded is significant, but it is a single symbol, with a single though complex meaning, which is being evolved, and any attempt at minute allegorical distinctions will only obscure the poem's central achievement. Even more mistaken is Sister Hillmann's attempt to distinguish the Pearl Maiden from the lost pearl. It is true that the Maiden 'does not identify herself with the material pearl'[8] explicitly, but the continuity of the symbol is beyond question. When the Dreamer first sees the Maiden move there are striking verbal reminiscences of the lost pearl of the poem's opening stanza:

> That gracios gay wythouten galle,
> So smothe, so smal, so seme slyght,
> Rysez up in hir araye ryalle,
> A precios pyece in perlez pyght.
>
> (189-92)

'So smothe, so smal' recalls 'So smal, so smothe her sydez were' (6), while 'hir araye ryalle' is in keeping with the royal associations of 'Perle, plesaunte to prynces paye' (1). The Maiden curtsies to the Dreamer, takes off her crown to him, and greets him; and his first words to her, though their form is interrogative, work through their repetitions to complete the identification of the Maiden with the lost jewel:

> 'O perle,' quod I, 'in perlez pyght,
> Art thou my perle that I haf playned,
> Regretted by myn one on nyghte?'
>
> (241-3)

There can surely be no doubt, if only we respond to the poem, that this Pearl Maiden *is* (though no doubt in some complex sense of the word 'is') his lost pearl. I have already argued that the lost pearl is to be seen as a person, and that, if we wish to reconstruct a specific human situation, she is most plausibly seen as the Dreamer's daughter dead in infancy. This is a convenient point to pause and ask why the poet did not make it easier for us to reconstruct this situation. Why did he mystify us with talk about aunts and nieces, and why did he allow the Dreamer to use the language of *fine amour* as well as that of fatherly love in referring to the pearl? We have been seeing how the poem works not by making clear-cut identifications and distinctions of the kind that belong to theology, but by vague mergings and emergings of an essentially poetic kind. We may now be prepared to see that the same could be true of the (fictional) situation 'behind' the poem. If the poet left the relationship between the Dreamer and the Maiden vague, perhaps he did so because he wanted it to be vague. It is true, of course, that he gained certain advantages by the hints of a father-daughter relationship. It has been pointed out, for example, that 'there seems to be a special significance in the situation where the doctrinal lesson given by the celestial maiden comes from one of no earthly wisdom to her proper teacher and instructor in the natural order'.[9] Because the Dreamer at once recognizes the Maiden as one who in her earthly existence was 'So smothe, so smal, so seme slyght' (190), he is unable for a long time to grasp that the statement

> A mannez dom moght dryghly demme
> Er mynde moght malte in hit mesure
>
> (223-4)

is true of her doctrine as well as of the pearl at her breast. But the poet could gain further advantages by leaving the father-daughter relationship as a matter of hints only, and adding to it hints of other relationships, such as that of lover and beloved. One such advantage would be that of widening the poem's appeal for a courtly audience, who would be used to poems about *fine amour,* but less ready to respond to a poem about fatherly love. A more important advantage was that it enabled the poet to write a poem not about one particular relationship, but about human relationship in general: about earthly relationship, and its meaning in the context of death and of the other world beyond death. It was for this reason, no doubt, that he reserved the clinching phrase 'In Krystez dere blessyng and myn' (1208) for the final stanza: he did not wish to pin the poem down to a single specific relationship until the last possible moment. My argument has been that the *Gawain*-poet's central subject is the impact of the more than human upon the human, and the reassessment of human values that must follow from this. This is, I believe, the central subject of *Pearl* too, and before returning to the text of the poem I shall examine this idea further.

The situation in which the Dreamer finds himself in the heavenly world of *Pearl* reminds me of an incident in the life of Jesus recorded by St Matthew. The Sadducees, 'who say there is no resurrection' (Matthew xxii. 23), put to Jesus a problem about a woman who was married seven times in succession, to seven men who were all brothers—an imaginary situation, no doubt, intended to trap Jesus, rather than a difficulty that was always cropping up in real life. She outlived them all, and then eventually died herself, and the Sadducees wanted to know whose wife she would be in the resurrection. Jesus answered, 'in the resurrection they shall neither marry nor be married, but shall be as the angels of God in heaven' (xxii. 30). One meaning of this answer is to indicate that in the heavenly world the terminology of earthly relationship simply ceases to apply. One way of seeing *Pearl* is as an imaginative extension of this statement and of other New Testament statements like it (for example, in some of the parables of the kingdom) about the nature of the heavenly world. In our world, people exist above all through human relationships. Man is a social animal, and his very personality is largely formed by a succession of relationships: a series of marriages, as it were, including that with his parents and that with his children, and centring usually in marriage itself. Take away this network of human relationships, and the individual withers. Nevertheless, in the kingdom of heaven as postulated by the Christian revelation, this familiar network is dissolved away, and yet the individual soul survives. In *Pearl,* this is the state of which the Dreamer has a visionary foretaste: human relationship itself is dissolved away, and in the case of the Maiden, who, through having died, truly belongs to this other world, it has been replaced by relationship of a different and utterly strange kind. We shall be examining that in detail shortly, but for the moment let us consider simply how the Maiden explains to the Dreamer that in the heavenly world she is a bride of the Lamb and Queen of Heaven. He protests that this position can belong to the Blessed Virgin alone, but she explains further that *all* the 144,000 virgins in the heavenly city are also brides of the Lamb and Queens of Heaven. Now in human terms this is meaningless nonsense: we are obviously not to imagine something like the Wife of Bath's 'octogamye' multiplied many times over. But it is evidently only by inventing such nonsense that human language can be used to hint at the transcendent system of relationships, centring in God, that exists in the heavenly world. All that is clear to the Dreamer is that he is excluded from this new order: he has lost his pearl on earth, through her death, and even by visiting the other world in a vision he cannot regain her, because he has no part in this new system of relationships, and cannot even understand it except in terms of the old. Hence the pain his vision causes him; and he seems to feel an even sharper anguish at being confronted with the Maiden inexplicably at home in an incomprehensible other world than he did at the simple fact of her death in this world. It is in this sense, then, that *Pearl* can be said to be about relationship itself. To say 'Ho watz me nerre then aunte or nece', without specifying further, implies *all* close human relationships, in such a way as to enable

the individual reader or listener to fill out the vagueness with his own experiences of human relationship. At the same time, to talk of aunts and nieces when confronted with a transfigured heavenly being betrays an inability to see reality in any other terms than those of the family relationships with which we are most familiar. The effect of this inability on the Dreamer's part is one of mingled pathos and comedy.

In the heavenly world of his dream, the Dreamer is certainly a figure at once pathetic and comic. At first, on seeing the Maiden, he is simply stunned:

> Wyth yyen open and mouth ful clos,
> I stod as hende as hawk in halle.
>
> (183-4)

Then he discloses expectations that not only contradict his earlier attitude in the garden but are quite out of keeping with the heavenly order of things. In the garden, he had mourned his pearl as though she were irrevocably lost. In the dream, recognizing that she still exists, he expresses new assumptions, though still of a kind familiar to us. We find them innocently and pathetically expressed nowadays in the obituary and memorial columns of newpapers. In the heavenly world, we shall achieve a reunion with the dear departed 'on the other shore'; the threads of earthly relationship will be picked up just where they were dropped, nothing essential will be altered, but all the difficulties and tensions involved in earthly relationships will miraculously be dissolved away. These are the dreams with which modern Christians often console themselves, despite all that the Gospels have to say about the essential strangeness and incomprehensibility of the heavenly order. And they are the Dreamer's expectations too. His first words to the Maiden (to return to the text where we left it) express his surprise at finding her alive after all, when previously, for all his theoretical Christianity, he had assumed that she was dead. He is almost reproachful towards her. He has been suffering the agonies of a rejected lover, yet now he finds her very pleasantly accommodated after all:

> 'O perle', quod I, 'in perlez pyght,
> Art thou my perle that I haf playned,
> Regretted by myn one on nyghte?
> Much longeyng haf I for the layned,
> Sythen into gresse thou me aglyghte.
> Pensyf, payred, I am forpayned,
> And thou in a lyf of lykyng lyghte,
> In Paradys erde, of stryf unstrayned.
> What wyrde hatz hyder my juel vayned,
> And don me in thys del and gret daunger?'
>
> (241-50)

Along with the genuineness of this suffering, which arouses our compassion, the last question, coming from a Christian, is almost ridiculously inept. What else could he have expected to find? The Maiden answers him without giving the reassurance he is groping for. She is grave, exact, and severe: 'Sir, ye haf your tale mysetente' (257). She goes on to explain, in a passage we have already examined, that all that he lost was in fact a rose, subject to the natural process of decay; but the rose has now proved to be 'a perle of prys' (272). The Dreamer begs her pardon for his misunderstanding, only to flounder confidently into the further error of the 'on the other shore' theory:

> 'Iwyse,' quod I, 'my blysfol beste,
> My grete dystresse thou al todrawez.
> To be excused I make requeste;
> I trawed my perle don out of dawez.
> Now haf I fonde hyt, I schal ma feste,
> And wony wyth hyt in schyr wod-schawez,
> And love my Lorde and al his lawez
> That hatz me broght thys blys ner.
> Now were I at yow byyonde thise wawez,
> I were a joyful jueler.'
>
> (279-88)

This facile hope of a happy-ever-after reunion is met with an even more stinging rebuke from the Maiden, and a devastatingly complete analysis of his error, divided into three parts. She begins with a question and an exclamation which decisively withdraw her from the realm of humanity—you human beings!—'Wy borde ye men? So madde ye be!' (290). In the cruelty of this one might sense the callousness of a small child, not seeing how much words can hurt; yet at the same time it can be seen as deliberate and necessary harshness, for the Dreamer has no hope of gaining further understanding unless he can be shocked out of his fool's paradise. She continues:

> Thre wordez hatz thou spoken at ene:
> Unavysed, for sothe, wern alle thre.
> Thou ne woste in worlde quat on dotz mene;
> Thy worde byfore thy wytte con fle.
> Thou says thou trawez me in this dene,
> Bycawse thou may wyth yyen me se;
> Another thou says, in thys countré
> Thyself schal won wyth me ryght here;
> The thrydde, to passe thys water fre—
> That may no joyfol jueler.
>
> (291-300)

She then corrects each of his false statements separately. In the case of the first, it is important not to misunderstand her correction. She is not saying that he is mistaken in trusting the evidence of his eyes that she is 'in this dene' of paradise, but that he is mistaken in believing her to be there *only* because he can see her with his eyes.[10] She really is there (there is no hint of her being in the dream landscape only potentially), but he should have known that she would be without seeing her, because, as a Christian, he knew of God's

promise of immortality for the soul. Her answer helps to define the failing that the Dreamer has in common with most Christians: the failure to take with full seriousness, to realize to himself, religious truths that he knows perfectly well in theory:

> I halde that jueler lyttel to prayse
> That levez wel that he segh wyth yye,
> And much to blame and uncortayse
> That levez oure Lorde wolde make a lyye,
> That lelly hyghte your lyf to rayse,
> Thagh fortune dyd your flesch to dyye.
> Ye setten hys wordez ful westernays
> That levez nothynk bot ye hit syye.
>
> And that is a poynt o sorquydryye,
> That uche god mon may evel byseme,
> To leve no tale be true to tryye
> Bot that hys one skyl may deme.
>
> (301-12)

The Dreamer's second error, in supposing that he can now dwell with the maiden 'in this bayly' (315), she corrects by pointing out that he must first ask permission, and that this may not be granted. His third error, in proposing to cross the river-barrier which separates them, she corrects by reminding him that Adam's sin makes it necessay that he should die before he can do so.

Discourse and drama

At this point, a complete change has begun to come over the course of the poem. Previously, the burden of meaning had been carried by the pearl symbol itself; but, by his evident failure to understand the Maiden's complex and highly poetic image of the transformation of the rose into the pearl, the Dreamer has shown that he is unable to make any further progress through the development of symbolism. He is hopelessly literal-minded, as dreamers in fourteenth-century poems tend to be. We may recall, for example, how in *The Book of the Duchess* the man in black tries to explain the nature of his loss to the Dreamer by using chess imagery: he was playing at chess with Fortune and lost his queen. The Chaucerian Dreamer is utterly bewildered by this:

> ther is no man alyve her
> Wolde for a fers make this woo!
>
> (740-1)

And so the man in black has to turn to more literal language, and tell his life-story. In *The Book of the Duchess*, however, chess imagery is only peripheral; in **Pearl** pearl imagery is absolutely central, and it is therefore all the more striking that from this point on it is simply dropped. For more than four hundred lines the pearl symbol undergoes no further development, and simpler, more explicit forms of exposition take its place. The Maiden's division of the Dreamer's error into three parts occurs at the end of section v. In section VI the word *perle* occurs only twice, as a name:

> My precios perle dotz me gret pyne;
>
> (330)

> When I am partlez of perle myne.
>
> (335)

In section VII it again occurs only twice, in the form of references to what has already occurred when the poem begins:

> Fro thou watz wroken fro uch a wothe,
> I wyste never quere my perle watz gon;
>
> (375-6)

> Thow wost wel when thy perle con schede,
> I watz ful yong and tender of age.
>
> (411-12)

In sections VIII, IX, X, XI and XII the word *perle* does not occur at all. Throughout this large central part of the poem the human drama of the encounter between Dreamer and Maiden continues to unfold itself, but it is accompanied not by any symbolic development but by the development of argument and explicit doctrine.

This has begun with the Maiden's threefold analysis of the Dreamer's error. In answer to her correction, the Dreamer persists in seeing the situation in terms of his own misery; for him (and this is eminently natural) the crucial fact about her careful statement is not that it is true but that it hurts him. It throws him into a despair like that in which Jonah wishes that God would slay him, though in the Dreamer's case the misery is more genuine and less histrionic:

> Now rech I never for to declyne,
> Ne how fer of folde that man me fleme.
> When I am partlez of perle myne,
> Bot durande doel what may men deme?
>
> (333-6)

Once more the Maiden rebukes him with what seems like cruelty—a cruelty that may again suggest a child in its apparent inability even to understand his suffering. The rebuke is now more clearly directed not at his opinions and expectations, but at the attitude of mind that underlies them:

> 'Thow demez noght bot doel-dystresse,'
> Thenne sayde that wyght. 'Why dotz thou so?
> For dyne of doel of lurez lesse,
> Ofte mony mon forgos the mo.
> The oghte better thyselven blesse,

> And love ay God, in wele and wo,
> For anger gaynez the not a cresse.
> Who nedez schal thole, be not so thro.
> For thogh thou daunce as any do,
> Braundysch and bray thy brathez breme,
> When thou no fyrre may, to ne fro,
> Thou moste abyde that he schal deme.'
>
> (337-48)

The picture the Maiden paints of him here is a cruel caricature, using an undignified animal image like the image of the hawk he had earlier applied to himself, and suggesting a thwarted child stamping and shouting in anger. It relates him very clearly to the anti-hero of *Patience,* the impatient man who foolishly resists the power of God, refusing to acknowledge that he lives in a world over which God has absolute control, and in which ultimately man has no choice but to do God's will. The conclusion 'Thou moste abyde that he schal deme' is hard but just, and a full response to the poem will take account of both its hardness and its justice. Our own thoughts and feelings should be engaged on both sides of the encounter; we shall recognize the absurdity of the Dreamer's position, and yet—because it is based on a completely natural human response, and because the Dreamer is 'I', not 'he'—we shall also share in his suffering.

The Dreamer now begins to undergo a development that was beyond the scope of Jonah, and still more of any of the examples of *fylthe* in *Purity.* He learns from the Maiden's insistence on the need to recognize facts, and especially the fact of God's omnipotence. He apologizes to God—'Ne worthe no wraththe unto my Lorde' (362)—and shows a new humility towards the Maiden:

> Rebuke me never wyth wordez felle,
> Thagh I forloyne, my dere endorde.
>
> (367-8)

He begins to recognize that there is a distance between them, but he persists in seeing that distance in earthly terms. Sometimes this produces an acute pathos, as when he begs her:

> God forbede we be now wrothe,
> We meten so selden by stok other ston.
>
> (379-80)

Here the tag 'by stok other ston' has an effect similar to that of the other tag 'aunte or nece': by its very nature as a cliché belonging to earthly meetings and separations it makes us feel the Dreamer's loneliness in the strange world of his dream. Such tags seem to be used for this purpose almost systematically. In the next stanza the Dreamer begs the Maiden to tell him 'What lyf ye lede erly and late' (392), and there again 'erly and late' touches one by its reminder of the familiar earthly world in the midst of the timeless heavenly world to which it is so strikingly inapplicable. Having grasped that there is now an unbridgeable distance between himself and the Maiden, the Dreamer can only see that distance as it might be in this world: as a social distance. She has somehow gone up in the world, and joined an aristocracy before the courtly grandeur of which he feels as abashed as the Chaucerian dreamer faced with the man in black or the God of Love. The distance between them is one of manners:

> Thagh cortaysly ye carp con,
> I am bot mol and manerez mysse.
>
> (381-2)

Yet he can at least take vicarious pleasure in her advancement:

> For I am ful fayn that your astate
> Is worthen to worschyp and wele, iwysse.
>
> (393-4)

And he is naturally curious about her new way of life.

At this point a digression may be necessary if I am to make my view of the poem clear. The *Gawain*-poet really is presenting the transcendent heavenly order in terms of material royalty, luxury and grandeur; it really is the case that for him an earthly kingdom is a valid 'image . . . of the Kingdom (significant word) of Heaven'.[11] And in this he is following a powerful tradition in medieval religious writing, found in English from the time of such twelfth-century texts as the *Ancrene Riwle,* where God is figured as a powerful and knightly king, full of *deboneirté,* who woos a lady besieged in her castle; or as *The Wooing of Our Lord,* where Christ is represented as wooing the human soul, and possessing in himself all the qualities that would be most desirable in an aristocratic husband—wealth, *largesce,* power, beauty. (The images of wooing and marriage, deriving from the Song of Songs, also reappear in ***Pearl****.*) And of course in the medieval visual arts God is regularly represented as a king, and heaven as an earthly court. If the heavenly order is to be represented in earthly images at all (and earthly images are all we know), what images could an aristocratic society better choose than those of earthly royalty? But intelligent people in the fourteenth century knew as well as we do that these images were only images, not realities; and so we find the author of *The Cloud of Unknowing* referring scathingly to those naïvely devout men who 'wil make a God as hem lyst, and clothen Hym ful richely in clothes, and set Hym in a trone, fer more curiously than ever was He depeynted in this erthe. Thees men wil maken aungelles in bodely licnes, and set hem aboute ich one with diverse minstralsie, fer more corious than ever was any seen or herde in this liif.'[12] What the *Gawain*-poet has done in ***Pearl*** is to find a way of simultaneously using such material images for the divine and making us aware of

their inadequacy. He does this by means of his naïve Dreamer, who can see the grandeur into which his pearl entered on the other side of death only in grossly material terms, as a higher social status. It would not be a great exaggeration to think of him as something of a snob; he has at least a keen sense of social status, a tendency to see reality in terms of social differences (one of his first thoughts on seeing the Maiden in her new state was that her face was 'sade *for doc other erle'* [211]), and a powerful curiosity about how the great live in their heavenly world. This must not be taken to imply that the *Gawain*-poet is as scornful as the *Cloud*-author of the use of royal and courtly images for heaven, or that he totally dissociates himself from the Dreamer's view of them. On the contrary, they are an essential part of his poem, and he clearly takes a real and unashamed delight in describing the grandeur and glitter of the heavenly world and the heavenly city. For him, as not perhaps for us, such images remained natural and viable. But it is significant that he represents God himself not as a great king or lord, but (following the Apocalypse) as the Lamb, a far more mysterious and unearthly image, in which magnificence is strangely mingled with suffering.

To return to the text: the Maiden expresses her approval of the Dreamer's new humility:

> 'Now blysse, burne, mot the bytyde,'
> Then sayde that lufsoum of lyth and lere,
> 'And welcum here to walk and byde,
> For now thy speche is to me dere.
> Maysterful mod and hyghe pryde,
> I hete the, arn heterly hated here.'
>
> (397-402)

His emotional readjustment makes possible further intellectual progress, and she at once explains, simply and openly, the terms of her new life. She is married to the Lamb of God, he has crowned her as his queen forever, and as such she is 'sesed in alle hys herytage' (417). Inevitably, the Dreamer takes this explanation with complete literalness, and understands it in earthly terms. Taken in this way, it is indeed startling, and his first reaction is a shocked remark, halfway between question and exclamation: ' "Blysful," quod I, "may thys be trwe?"' (421). He quickly pulls himself up, afraid of having offended her, only to repeat the question:

> Dysplesez not if I speke errour.
> Art thou the quene of hevenez blwe,
> That al thys world schal do honour?
>
> (422-4)

He imagines that she must be claiming to have supplanted the Blessed Virgin herself, for the kingdom of heaven, like earthly kingdoms, can surely have only one queen at a time. She carefully explains that this is not so:

The court of the kyndom of God alyve
Hatz a property in hytself beyng:
Alle that may therinne aryve
Of alle the reme is quen other kyng,
And never other yet schal depryve,
But uchon fayn of otherez hafyng.

(445-50)

This straightforward explanation makes as clear as possible the difficulty of using the language of everyday affairs, rather than that of poetic symbolism, about the divine. The Maiden's words are as exact as possible, *depryve* belonging (like *herytage* earlier) to the technical language of law, and *property* either to the same technical language or to that of scholastic philosophy,[13] yet taken together they make up a statement which in earthly terms is nonsensical. The Dreamer makes the best effort he can to accommodate himself to what he says:

'Cortaysé,' quod I, 'I leve,
And charyté grete, be yow among.'

(469-70)

But he still cannot swallow it entirely, and, with indignation breaking through his caution, he continues:

Bot—my speche that yow ne greve—
Thyself in heven over hygh thou heve,
To make the quen that watz so yonge!

(471-4)[14]

It is her youth that sticks in his throat. If only she were a little older, she might somehow deserve this extraordinary promotion; as it is, he cannot bring himself either to believe or to approve anything so out of keeping with his ideas of justice:

That cortaysé is to fre of dede,
Yyf hyt be soth that thou conez saye.
Thou lyfed not two yer in oure thede;
Thou cowthez never God nauther plese ne
    pray,
Ne never nawther Pater ne Crede;
And quen mad on the fyrst day!
I may not traw, so God me spede,
That God wolde wrythe so wrange away.
Of countes, damysel, par ma fay,
Wer fayr in heven to hald asstate,
Other ellez a lady of lasse aray;
Bot a quene! Hit is to dere a date.

(481-92)

It is delightful that he should think of the court of heaven in such thoroughly earthly terms as to feel that it would be tolerable for her to be a countess in it, but not a queen; and this is perfectly in keeping with the sense of social distinctions he showed on first seeing her, when he thought her face 'sade for doc other erle'

(211). A countess is the wife of an earl. And the speech is amusing not only in its naïve assumptions, but in the vigorous colloquialism of their expression. His indignation reaches its height when he has to mention the offensive word 'queen': we notice the almost angrily emphatic monosyllables of 'And quen mad on the fyrst day!' and the outraged squeak in the last line of the stanza: 'Bot a quene! Hit is to dere a date.' He would rather accuse God of extravagance than accept *that*. As everywhere in his work, the *Gawain*-poet shows a brilliant gift for mimicking tones of voice; to do this within the intricate metrical form of **Pearl** demands a virtuosity unusual even for him.

It is in answer to this indignant incredulity of the Dreamer's that the Maiden repeats and expounds the parable of the vineyard, which we examined earlier. That part of the poem (lines 493-588) is purely discursive, not even dramatic, and I need say no more about it here. Not till after the Maiden has finished re-telling the parable does the Dreamer once more intervene, with his insistence on judging things for himself—an insistence for which we may feel grateful, even while recognizing its unwisdom, since he voices doubts we may share. He has made some progress; though his tone of voice has its usual resolute earthliness, he is now measuring the Maiden's statements not merely against common sense but against Biblical authority:

Then more I meled and sayde apert,
'Me thynk thy tale unresounable.
Goddez ryght is redy and evermore rert,
Other Holy Wryt is bot a fable.
In Sauter is sayde a verce overte.'

(589-93)

Perhaps his characteristic 'Me thynk' may remind us of the repeated 'uus thynk' (552-3) of the disgruntled workmen in the parable; he has much in common with them. The Maiden recognizes his mood of scholastic disputatiousness—'Bot now thou motez, me for to mate' (613)—and once more answers in purely discursive terms, with an exposition of the roles of grace and justice in determining the fate of human souls, in which she first reverts to the parable to expound it allegorically, and then produces appropriate Scriptural texts to confirm her argument. We examined her treatment of these at an earlier stage. She concludes by referring to the Crucifixion as a deed more powerful than any abstract argument:

Forthy to corte quen thou schal com
Ther alle oure causez schal be tryed,
Alegge the ryght, thou may be innome,
By thys ilke spech I have asspyed;
Bot he on rode that blody dyed,
Delfully thurgh hondez thryght,
Gyve the to passe, when thou arte tryed,
By innocens and not by ryghte.

(701-8)

After so much discourse, this plain reference to the Crucifixion as an irreducible human event has an extraordinary emotive power. It leads the Maiden back to speak of the Ministry of Christ, again in simple and human terms: her place in heaven is to be justified ultimately not by bandying texts and arguments but by Christ's saying,

> Do way, let chylder unto me tyght,
> To suche is hevenryche arayed.
>
> (718-19)

Symbolism resumed

On the question of the salvation of the innocent there is no more to be said; but now that this question has been settled, the poem can at last revert to its former course and former method of developing symbolism. Christ's words about 'the kingdom of heaven' lead naturally into another parable of the kingdom, this time one of the shortest, that of the pearl of great price:

> Iterum simile est regnum caelorum homini negotiatori quaerenti bonas margaritas;
>
> Inventa autem una pretiosa margarita, abiit, et vendidit omnia quae habuit, et emit eam.
>
> (Matthew xiii. 45-6)
>
> (Again the kingdom of heaven is like to a merchant seeking good pearls.
>
> Who, when he had found one pearl of great price, went his way and sold all that he had and bought it.)

The mention of pearls makes possible the resumption of pearl symbolism, after the long discursive central section:

> Ther is the blys that con not blynne
> That the jueler soghte thurgh perré pres,
> And solde alle hys goud, bothe wolen and
>   lynne,
> To bye hym a perle watz mascellez.
>
> (729-32)

The fact that we have here a planned resumption of the symbolism, rather than one dependent on chance associations, is demonstrated by the way in which the symbol is taken up again in section XIII at precisely the point at which it was abandoned in section V. The point at which the Dreamer's understanding failed was the image of the transformation of the rose into the pearl, and at that point, for the first time, the pearl was called a 'perle of prys' (272). Now, over 450 lines later, comes the parable of the pearl of great price. Moreover, in the refrain-lines of section V, the Dreamer

was being referred to as a jeweller, with implications perhaps of materialism. The Maiden, for example, seemed to be using the language of trade, of profit and loss, for his benefit in a very pointed way:

> And thou hatz called thy wyrde a thef,
> That oght of noght hatz mad the cler.
>
> (273-4)[15]

Now the image of the jeweller is redeemed by that of the merchant of the parable. Both the pearl and the jeweller remain viable as symbols, because they can include heavenly as well as earthly meanings. Recognition of this should perhaps modify the light in which one sees the human drama of the encounter between Dreamer and Maiden. I have been emphasizing mainly the gap between the two, with its consequences of the Dreamer's misunderstanding and the Maiden's apparent cruelty towards him. But symbols provide the means of bridging the gap between earthly and heavenly understanding, as the Scriptural parables of the kingdom bear witness. There is difference between the heavenly and earthly worlds, but there is also continuity, a continuity figured, for example, in the fact that the 'gardyn gracios gaye' of the dream is only another version of the 'erber grene' in which the narrator fell asleep. The earthly rose does not disappear, to be replaced by the heavenly pearl; it is 'put in pref' to (proves to be) a pearl. This complex relationship between the earthly and the heavenly is easily misunderstood. It is misunderstood by the Dreamer, who persistently sees only continuity between them; it is misunderstood by those modern scholars who see only difference.[16] But the poem itself, with the delicacy and subtlety of poetic symbolism, opens the way to a truer understanding.

The Maiden proceeds immediately with a stanza in exposition of the parable of the pearl which seems designed to sum up the pearl symbolism as so far developed, and to take it further through the association with the kingdom of heaven:

> This makellez perle, that boght is dere,
> The joueler gef fore alle hys god,
> Is lyke the reme of hevenesse clere:
> So sayde the Fader of folde and flode;
> For hit is wemlez, clene, and clere,
> And endelez rounde, and blythe of mode,
> And commune to alle that ryghtwys were.
> Lo, even inmyddez my breste hit stode.
> My Lorde the Lombe, that schede hys blode,
> He pyght hit there in token of pes.
> I rede the forsake the worlde wode
> And porchace thy perle maskelles.
>
> (733-44)

Here some of the associations previously accumulated by the symbol are gathered together. 'Wemlez, clene, and clere' reminds one of previous phrases such as 'wythouten wemme' and 'wythouten spot', and attention is now focused on the single pearl at the Maiden's breast, as it were the symbol of the symbol. This is available to the Dreamer as well as to the Maiden; but there would surely be no point in trying to distinguish separate layers of meaning in the pearl, and to differentiate between the pearl as the Maiden and the pearl as the kingdom of heaven, which is not her private possession but is 'commune to alle that ryghtwys were'. These figurative senses are inextricably entangled, and any attempt to schematize them is only too likely to result in an impoverished perception of the richness of the symbolic whole. The poetry works not by distinction but by fusion. The mingling of the various senses is recognized by the Dreamer in the very phrasing of his answer, in which 'he sums up the complex symbolism of the passage'[17] we have been discussing:

> 'O maskelez perle in perlez pure,
> That berez,' quod I, 'the perle of prys.'
>
>   (745-6)

The Dreamer goes on to ask who created her beauty, but before she can answer that question he asks another, which betrays once more his preoccupation with status: 'quat kyn offys' (755) does she hold in heaven? She answers that she is the bride of the Lamb of God, and repeats the invitation of the Song of Songs which he addressed to her:

> Cum hyder to me, my lemman swete,
> For mote ne spot is non in the.
>
>   (763-4)

The Dreamer then asks who this Lamb of God is; and in doing so he shows in its most materialistic form his preoccupation with social advancement. He imagines her progress as one of ruthless social climbing, elbowing aside all possible rivals, and culminating in an unparalleled triumph over them:

> Quat kyn thyng may be that Lambe
> That the wolde wedde unto hys vyf?
> Over alle other so hygh thou clambe
> To lede wyth hym so ladyly lyf.
> So mony a comly on-uunder cambe
> For Kryst han lyved in much stryf;
> And thou con alle tho dere out dryf
> And fro that maryag al other depres,
> Al only thyself so stout and styf,
> A makelez may and maskellez.
>
>   (771-80)

The Dreamer is now prepared to accept that the Maiden really has achieved the highest rank, but he has clearly not understood her earlier explanation of the universal kingship and queenship of the blessed. The tone of his remarks is roughly that of a bourgeois father's aston-

ished admiration at his daughter's unexpected marriage with the royal family's most eligible bachelor. And this tone is supported by the strikingly secular implications of some of the terms he applies to her. 'Comly on-uunder cambe' is a formula belonging to a formulaic system regularly applied to ladies in romances and love-poems; two other examples are 'lufsum under lyne', applied to the lady in *Sir Gawain and the Green Knight* (1814), and 'geynest under gore' from the Harley lyric *Alysoun*.[18] 'Stout and styf' is another alliterative formula, belonging to medieval romance, but implying the heroic resolution of the warrior rather than the modesty appropriate to a lady.[19] We can reasonably deduce that such phrases would have seemed glaringly inappropriate to the Maiden's true nature, and it is possible that for a courtly fourteenth-century audience they would have called up the vulgar world of popular romance (such as Chaucer parodies in *Sir Thopas*). Certainly they reveal the Dreamer's absurd failure to grasp the truth about the Maiden's position.

Patiently, she explains once more that she is *maskelles* but not *makeles;* indeed, she is only one of the Lamb's 144,000 brides. She goes on to attempt an answer to the question 'Quat kyn thyng may be that Lambe?' She does so by quoting the main Scriptural sources for the doctrine of the Lamb of God. The first of these is in Isaiah liii, the passage concerning the 'man of sorrows' on whom the sins of the world were laid, and who 'shall be led as a sheep to the slaughter and shall be dumb as a lamb before his shearer, and he shall not open his mouth' (Isaiah liii. 7). She relates this in turn to the second source, John the Baptist's welcoming of Christ as the fulfilment of the prophecy in Isaiah: 'The next day, John saw Jesus coming to him; and he saith: Behold the Lamb of God. Behold him who taketh away the sin of the world' (John i. 29). Finally she links these two texts to the Apocalypse, in which the other St John saw the Lamb standing in the midst of the throne of God (Apocalypse v. 6). Thus the poet brings together the three chief Scriptural occurrences of the Lamb: the foreshadowing in Isaiah, the historical event in St John's Gospel, and the heavenly fulfilment in the Apocalypse. The typological pattern is complete, explicitly completed by the poet, rather than left hidden as an allegory.

The Maiden repeats her earlier explanation that, by being married to the Lamb, she is not keeping out anyone else: every day, she says, the Lamb brings in a new supply of brides, and yet they never quarrel with each other. On the contrary, their attitude is 'the more the merrier'; this is the very phrase she uses: 'The mo the myryer, so God me blesse' (850). The down-to-earth colloquialism is no doubt intentionally comic, and it throws a comic light back upon the Dreamer, whose materialism makes it necessary. The Maiden proceeds to quote the Apocalypse to him at some length, to prove that what she says is true, but we need not examine the passage here. Now at last it seems that the Dreamer has grasped that she is only one among many royal brides, but this leads him to think of another question, in which his materialism shows itself once more. He prefaces it with an elaborate complimentary address, very different from his blunt contradictions earlier in the poem. He has understood and accepted the distance between them, and has found a *cortays* rhetoric appropriate to her grandeur and his lowliness:

> 'Never the les let be my thonc,'
> Quod I, 'My perle, thagh I appose;
> I schulde not tempte thy wyt so wlonc,
> To Krystez chambre that art ichose.
> I am bot mokke and mul among,
> And thou so ryche a reken rose,
> And bydez here by thys blysful bonc
> Ther lyvez lyste may never lose.
> Now, hynde, that sympelnesse conez enclose,
> I wolde the aske a thynge expresse,
> And thagh I be bustwys as a blose,
> Let my bone vayl nevethelese.
>
> 'Nevethelese cler I you bycalle,
> If ye con se hyt be to done;
> As thou art gloryous wythouten galle,
> Wythnay thou never my ruful bone.'
>
> (901-16)

In this open acknowledgement of his own inferiority the Dreamer achieves a real dignity, but at last he brings out his naïve question. If she is only one of a great company of brides, wherever do they live?

> Haf ye no wonez in castel-walle,
> Ne maner ther ye may mete and won?
>
> (917-18)

In giving the Dreamer these thoughts of a castle or mansion as possible dwelling-places, the poet is of course following the technique explained earlier: he is making use of the traditional images for heavenly things used in his time, but at the same time, by letting the Dreamer employ them with exaggerated and comic naïveté, he is indicating that they cannot really be taken literally. The Maiden has spoken of Jerusalem, but the Dreamer knows that that is in Judaea, so the brides cannot dwell there, yet their sheer numbers must demand a great city for them to live in:

> Thys motelez meyny thou conez of mele,
> Of thousandez thryght so gret a route,
> A gret ceté, for ye arn fele,
> Yow byhod have, wythouten doute.
> So cumly a pakke of joly juele,
> Wer evel don schulde lyy theroute!
>
> (925-30)

One would not be wrong, I think, to detect in those last two lines a delightfully breezy colloquialism, which at the same time conveys the Dreamer's innocently kindly masculine concern at the thought of a crowd of helpless girls sleeping rough.

The Maiden reassures him with her explanation of the existence of two Jerusalems, one earthly and the other heavenly. In answer to his request to see the heavenly city where she dwells, she tells him that 'thurgh gret favor' (968) of the Lamb he may see it from outside, though not from within. There follows the detailed description, closely based on the Apocalypse. This again is a passage we have considered already, with its jewel imagery and brilliant light, and the Dreamer's assurance that his experience would not have been possible 'in the body'. Just as during the earlier long passage based on Scripture (the parable of the vineyard, lines 497 ff.), symbol and drama are here in abeyance. There they gave way to narrative and exposition; here to description. Miss Kean is right, I think, in judging that there is a certain lack of pressure in the poetry of this part of *Pearl:* 'Necessary as an effective set piece is to the plan of the poem, it does not, in fact, seem to engage the poet's concentrated attention; and he seems to depend on his reader's reaction to the general effect, and to recognition of a familiar context, rather than on his usual technical skill'.[20] We found a similar failing (so it appears to a modern reader) in the description of the temple vessels in *Purity*: a mere collection of details, in which poetry attempts to do the work of painting, and necessarily fails to embody the required significance. Such failures are so common in medieval literature that we can perhaps do no better than to record that we have encountered something that appealed to medieval taste but does not appeal to ours. For medieval poets and their audiences, exhaustive descriptions and lists seem to have had an attraction so great that they often demanded nothing more. A parallel example from a fourteenth-century dream-poem is the list of fourteen varieties of trees in *The Parlement of Foules;* one from elsewhere in the *Gawain*-poet's work is the lengthy explanation in *Sir Gawain and the Green Knight* of the various symbolic significances of the pentangle. In none of these cases would we be prepared to call the passage poetry; it is rather an inset into the poem of a different kind of material, highly relevant to its significance but not continuous with it in literary substance. This descriptive passage, however, becomes once more enlivened with drama from the point at which the Dreamer reminds us of his own presence as a witness, so overcome as to be certain that he could not have been 'in the body', and amusingly undignified in his stunned state: 'I stod as stylle as dased quayle' (1085). What follows certainly is poetry. Heralded by the haunting simile of moonrise in daylight comes the procession of virgin-brides, in which the development of the pearl symbolism is taken a stage further, for they are all arrayed like his own pearl:

> Depaynt in perlez and wedez qwyte;
> In uchonez breste watz bounden boun
> The blysful perle wyth gret delyt.
>
> (1102-4)

The Dreamer can now see for himself that they are not jostling for position, as an earthly procession might, and he innocently notes this surprising fact: 'Thagh thay wern fele, no pres in plyt' (1114). At their head is the Lamb himself. In describing the Lamb, the poet does not, as we might expect, allow the Dreamer's naïve vision to make him familiar or homely. On the contrary, he brings out the full exoticism of the Apocalypse, the almost nightmare quality of St John's apprehension of the nature of God. The Lamb, 'Wyth hornez seven of red golde cler' (1111) and pearly-white coat, surrounded by prostrate elders and incense-scattering angels, suggests for the moment the god of a totemistic cult stranger and crueller than Christianity as we usually think of it. Only for the moment, however. This is no cruel beast-god, but one with 'lokez symple, hymself so gent' (1134), and he has in his side the bleeding wound of the crucified Christ. The wound is described with the simplest of alliterative formulas, 'wyde and weete' (1135)[21]—it is an ordinary wound, gaping and messy—and it arouses in the Dreamer a touchingly simple compassion and incredulity that anyone could have been so cruel as to cause it. It is as if he were feeling the reality of Christ's sufferings for the first time:

> Bot a wounde ful wyde and weete con wyse
> Anende hys herte, thurgh hyde torente.
> Of hys quyte syde his blod outsprent.
> Alas, thoght I, who did that spyt?
> Ani breste for bale aght haf forbrent
> Er he therto hade had delyt.
>
> (1135-40)[22]

The mixture of feelings aroused by this description of the Lamb and his procession has, I find, an extraordinarily disturbing power: squalor in majesty, pain in triumph. Already disturbed by this, the Dreamer is still more agitated by the sight of his 'lyttel quene' (1147) among the virgin-brides. All that he has learned about the necessary distance between them is overwhelmed by 'luf-longyng' (1152), and he makes his ill-fated attempt to cross the stream.

This attempt, as the Dreamer ought to have recognized before making it, is displeasing to God—'Hit watz not at my Pryncez paye' (1164)—and in consequence 'That braththe out of my drem me brayde' (1170). He is suddenly returned to the waking world, to the garden and pearl of the poem's opening:

> Then wakned I in that erber wlonk;
> My hede upon that hylle watz layde
> Ther as my perle to grounde strayd.
>
> (1171-3)

He has shown the sin of Jonah, impatience, and he ruefully reflects that if he had submitted to the will of God he might have seen more of his secrets:

> To that Pryncez paye hade I ay bente,
> And yerned no more then watz me gyven,
> And halden me ther in trwe entent,
> As the perle me prayed that watz so thryven,
> As helde, drawn to Goddez present,
> To mo of his mysterys I hade ben dryven.
>
> (1189-94)

The moral he draws is entirely in keeping with *Patience*:

> Lorde, mad hit arn that agayn the stryven,
> Other proferen the oght agayn thy paye.
>
> (1199-1200)

But the situation is more complex than at the end of *Patience*. The 'hero' of *Patience* is 'he', and there is no sign that Jonah has learned anything from his experience: the moral is for us. But the 'hero' of *Pearl* is 'I', and the Dreamer has learned something himself, as well as providing an *exemplum* for us. The dream-experience has not been wasted on him, for the moral he draws from it also applies to the rebellious feelings he had been displaying at the beginning of the poem towards the loss of his pearl. Now, assured by his vision that she is not really lost, but is one of the circle of the blessed, he is able to win through to acceptance of her death and even, through seeing how happy her state now is, to rejoicing at it:

> If hit be veray and soth sermoun
> That thou so stykez in garlande gay,
> So wel is me in thys doel-doungoun
> That thou art to that Prynsez paye.
>
> (1185-8)

The Dreamer has been changed by his dream, yet we feel the change to be precarious—as precarious, say, as the change brought about at the end of *The Tempest*. It will always be possible to return from the end of the poem to its beginning, and to start the wheel revolving once more. But for the moment a genuine change of attitude has occurred, and it is not implausibly extreme. The Dreamer still finds the world a 'doel-doungoun', but he can now recognize his own impatience, and is ready to commit his pearl voluntarily into the hands of God:

> And sythen to God I hit bytaghte,
> In Krystez dere blessyng and myn.
>
> (1207-8)

One question remains to be considered: does the poem tell us anything about the nature of the further *mysterys* that the Dreamer might have seen if he had not been impatient and tried to cross the river? It is of the essence of **Pearl** that, through the Dreamer's imperfection, the visionary experience should remain incomplete, and indeed, if the poem is to remain a poem, it has to break off short of any closer approach to the ineffable. But the necessary sense of incompleteness, by which the Dreamer is made miserable at the end—

Me payed ful ille to be outfleme
So sodenly of that fayre regioun,
Fro alle tho syghtez so quyke and queme.
A longeyng hevy me strok in swone . . .

(1177-80)

—could be conveyed to us all the more fully if we had some hint of what further illumination he had lost. I believe that the poem does offer such a hint, and that the clue to it is found once more in the development of the pearl symbolism. A final and incomplete stage in this development has been taking place during the long passage based on the Apocalypse. The qualities of the pearl have been gradually extended, as we have seen, to include the other world of the dream, the kingdom of heaven and the new Jerusalem, which had

uch yate of a margyrye,
A parfyt perle that never fatez.

(1037-8)

But in particular there are suggestions that the Lamb of God too can be seen as an aspect of the poem's central symbol (or rather that the pearl can be seen as a reflection of the Lamb). In answering the Dreamer's question 'Quat kyn thyng may be that Lambe?' (771), the Maiden has referred to Christ as 'My Lombe, my Lorde, my dere juelle' (795). *Juelle* is a term which has previously been applied to the Maiden herself—

That juel thenne in gemmez gente

(253)

A juel to me then watz thys geste,
And juelez wern hyr gentyl sawez

(277-8)

—and it is later applied once more to the Lamb, whose followers 'Al songe to love that gay juelle' (1124). Other key qualities of the pearl are also found in him. He is white and spotless:

Thys Jerusalem Lombe hade never pechche
Of other huee bot quyt jolyf

That mot ne masklle moght on streche,
For wolle quyte so ronk and ryf;

(841-4)

The Lompe ther wythouten spottez blake.

(945)

Finally, when the Dreamer actually sees the Lamb for the first time he sees this whiteness as explicitly pearl-like; 'As praysed perlez his wedez wasse' (1112). We seem to have here the briefest glimpse of a potential culmination of the visionary experience, by which the Lamb and the pearl would be identified, and the Dreamer would see in the precious stone the ground of its own preciousness; or, to put it differently, would recognize in the human soul the image of God. Such a perception would belong to mystical experience, however, and, as I have argued earlier, though the *Gawain*-poet probably knew the devotional writings of his time, he neither was nor supposed himself to be a mystic. Still less is his Dreamer a mystic; but I think it likely that, in the potential identification of Lamb and pearl (similar to, but higher than, the achieved identification of pearl and rose), the poet hinted at a culmination from which the Dreamer was excluded.

Notes

[1] This point is forcefully made by A. R. Heiserman, 'The Plot of *Pearl*', *PMLA,* LXXX (1965), 164-71.

[2] 'Symbolism, Allegory, and Autobiography in *The Pearl*', p. 588.

[3] Schofield, *ibid.* pp. 589 ff.; Gordon, ed. *Pearl,* note on lines 1-4, p. 45.

[4] Cf. M. W. Bloomfield, 'A Grammatical Approach to Personification Allegory', *MP,* LX (1962-3), 161-71: 'One might say that languages with grammatical gender, unlike [modern] English, have automatically built-in personification of some sort' (p. 162).

[5] For this literary convention, see E. R. Curtius, *European Literature and the Latin Middle Ages,* trans. W. R. Trask (New York, 1953), pp. 183-202.

[6] C. A. Luttrell, '*Pearl:* Symbolism in a Garden Setting', *Neophilologus,* XLIX (1965), 160-76, points out that the 'harvest-time and August opening' is by no means unique: there is an example in Nicole de Margival's *Panthere d'Amors.* It remains unusual, however. For suggestions as to the possible symbolic associations of the season, see Gollancz, ed. *Pearl,* pp. 118-19 (Lammas); C. G. Osgood, ed. *Pearl* (Boston, Mass., 1906), p. xvi (Assumption of the Virgin); Schofield, 'Symbolism, Allegory, and Autobiography in *The Pearl*', p. 616, n. 2 (St. John's Great Reaper); Kean, pp. 48-52 (cycle of seasons connected with Passion and Resurrection, and with sin and regenera-

Illusttration for Cotton MS. lines 193-228.

tion). Miss Kean also considers the possible symbolism of flowers at some length (p. 59-70). As is usual with scholarly discussions of medieval symbolism, the scholars disagree so thoroughly among themselves that they can scarcely be said to clarify the poem for us, or even to convince us that there was any generally accepted system of symbols in the poet's own time, on which he was drawing. August could perhaps 'mean' almost as as many different things in the fourteenth century as it can today; and we are left with the poem.

[7] See Gordon, ed. *Pearl*, p. xxxiv and note on line 228.

[8] Hillmann, ed. *The Pearl*, p. xx.

[9] Gordon, ed. *Pearl*, p. xiii.

[10] Miss Kean appears to take it that 'in this dene' means 'on earth', and that the Dreamer 'had believed that she was on earth' (Kean, p. 128). But if this were so, why should the Maiden not explain that she is not on earth, rather than (as she does) that she is where she is not because he can see her, but because that was God's promise? Miss Kean asserts that 'As the Maiden points out, she is not, in fact, in the country in which he thinks she is' (p. 129), but without giving any line-

reference. There is no equivalent in *Pearl* to the statement of Beatrice in the *Paradiso* which Miss Kean quotes as a parallel: "Tu non se' in terra, sì come tu credi."

[11] D.S. Brewer, 'Courtesy and the *Gawain*-Poet', p. 59.

[12] Ed. Phyllis Hodgson, p. 105.

[13] On legal terminology in *Pearl*, see Kean, pp. 185 ff.

[14] There is a discrepancy in the line-numbering here, because Gordon and other editors assume that a line has accidentally been omitted from the manuscript between *greve* and *Thyself.*

[15] I think this a more plausible interpretation of the lines than A. L. Kellogg's suggestion (*Traditio*, XII [1956], 406-7) that they allude to the doctrine of *creatio ex nihilo*, for this would not explain *thef* or *cler* (cf. 'a clear profit').

[16] For example, Sister Hillmann, ed. *The Pearl*; W. S. Johnson, 'The Imagery and Diction of *The Pearl*', *ELH*, XX (1953), 161-80: 'The result is an emphasis upon a ubiquitous sense of contrast between the nature of heaven and the nature of earth, the revelation of which seems, for our present reading, to be the poem's main purpose' (p. 163); and S. de Voren Hoffman, 'The *Pearl*: Notes for an Interpretation', *MP*, LVIII (1960-1), 73-80: 'in the poem we find together several meanings of the pearl figure and . . . they are kept distinct' (p. 76).

[17] Dorothy Everett, *Essays on Middle English Literature*, p. 93.

[18] *English Lyrics of the Thirteenth Century*, ed. Carleton Brown (Oxford, 1932), p. 140.

[19] See the detailed discussion of *styf* in Borroff, pp. 79-81.

[20] Kean, p. 215.

[21] Cf. *The Destruction of Troy*, ed. Panton and Donaldson, 'wyde woundes and wete' (1329); *York Mystery Plays*, ed. Lucy Toulmin Smith, 'woundes wete' (p. 406, line 200 and p. 411, line 283) (these are Christ's wounds).

[22] Miss Kean (p. 210) notes the 'prosaic terms' in which the wound is described, and compares the Dreamer's reaction, which she sees as 'lack of comprehension', with that of the Chaucerian Dreamer in *The Book of the Duchess* to the news that the man in black's lady is dead. She remarks; 'What is appropriate to a courtly poem addressed to a patron, seems oddly at variance with a moment which, we feel,

would normally call for a much higher emotional tension.' It is true that 'the glimpse of the New Jerusalem and its triumphant host cannot be a personal triumph for the Dreamer' (p. 211), but I think Miss Kean underrates the emotional charge that can be carried by simple language. To see and feel for the first time the reality of Christ's suffering, and to see that suffering as borne at the very heart of triumph, is to achieve illumination (admittedly not of an advanced kind), not misunderstanding.

Anne Howland Schotter (essay date 1984)

SOURCE: "Vernacular Style and the Word of God: The Incarnational Art of Pearl," in *Ineffability: Naming the Unnamable from Dante to Beckett.* AMS Press, 1984, pp. 23-34.

[*In the following essay, Schotter considers the theme of* Pearl *to be the inadequacy of both images and human language to convey the idea of the Divine.*]

Any Christian visionary writer must confront the problem of how to convey the Divine in human terms. Throughout history theologians have spoken of two ways, the positive, which proposes analogies for God, and the negative, which denies that any analogies are valid. The two ways tend to work in a dialectical manner, the latter continually warning against the idolatry that the former might encourage.[1] The author of the fourteenth-century English **Pearl** confronts this traditional problem when he tries to convey the kingdom of heaven to his readers. His solution is to suggest it by various analogical devices, while at the same time using a naive dreamer as a warning against taking them literally. Among the devices that he chooses are parables (those of the vineyard and the pearl of great price), images (the paradisal garden, the Lamb, and the New Jerusalem), and an enigma (the Pearl maiden herself). It has often been pointed out that by using the maiden to criticize the dreamer's earthbound perception of these analogies, the poet makes the inadequacy of images in conveying the Divine an explicit theme of the poem.[2] I would like to argue that he makes the inadequacy of *language* in conveying the Divine an implicit theme as well. He uses the limitations of his specific poetic medium—the West Midland dialect of Middle English on which alliterative poetry was based—to explore the general problems of language in its attempt to express the ineffable. For at the same time that he exploits the most splendid resources of his medium, he includes some of its pedestrian characteristics as a warning against excessive trust in language. His rhetorical concerns thus take on a theological dimension as he uses human words to try to convey God's Word, while paradoxically insisting that it is impossible for them to do so.[3]

In this respect the poet follows Augustinian sign theory, which, although it is profoundly distrustful of signs of any kind, justifies the use of both words and visual images for Christian purposes. Saint Augustine frequently pointed out that words are inadequate to convey an ineffable Godhead, saying, for instance, in *De Doctrina Christiana,*

God should not be said to be ineffable, for when this is said, something is said. And a contradiction in terms is created, since if that is ineffable which cannot be spoken, that is not ineffable which can be called ineffable. This contradiction is to be passed over in silence rather than resolved verbally.[4]

And yet, Augustine argued, if man could not use language to *express* God he could nevertheless use it to *praise* Him, and the Christian preacher, moreover, was obligated to spread God's Word with human words as best he could.[5] Since language was a mediation made necessary by fallen understanding, rhetoric was a weapon with which God's friends should be armed, despite the danger that their hearers might enjoy beautiful language for its own sake. Such idolatry could be prevented if language would warn against its own inadequacy—if the signs would warn against being taken for the thing they signified.[6] The justification for using human language was to be found in an analogy with the Incarnation, for if language had fallen with Adam, it had been redeemed by Christ's condescending to take on human flesh—and, therefore, human speech.[7]

Augustine held, furthermore, that a similar incarnational model justified using a low style to express the Word of God: the gap between literary styles was insignificant compared to that between human language and Divine. In reformulating Ciceronian rhetoric, he abandoned the distinction between three levels of style which was based on subject matter, arguing that no aspect of the Christian story could be considered "low." Hence, as Erich Auerbach has shown, he urged the Christian rhetorician to adopt a *sermo humilis*—a low style for a lofty theme.[8] In this way Augustine was able to defend the style of the Old Latin version of the Bible to the cultivated Romans who thought it barbarous, even while he continued to use elaborate figures of speech in his own writing.

The **Pearl**-poet does not put forth his linguistic principles at all, let alone do so with the explicitness of Augustine. But Augustinian sign theory persisted in Europe through the fourteenth century, as can be seen in Dante's dependence on it to justify the use of the Italian vernacular for elevated literary subjects.[9] It is likely, therefore, that our poet's thoughts on language were informed by Augustine's. I would like to argue that he perceived the gap between the high and low elements in his own alliterative poetic tradition in the same way that Augustine perceived that which stood between the styles of Ciceronian and biblical Latin. And furthermore, although in trying to convey the heavenly vision he employed the high elements, he also used the low elements of his tradition to warn against them. In this way he sought a *sermo humilis* in which to achieve a poetic incarnation of the Word of God.

The certain elements of alliterative poetry can be considered low is a reflection of the complex sociolinguistic situation of Middle English in the fourteenth century: after three hundred years of domination by French, the language was being used increasingly for imaginative literature, but because of the great dialectal differences, those who used it had little sense of shared literary values. Rather than one standard literary dialect, as South East Midland was to become in the fifteenth century, there were several dialects, of which West Midland, with its traditional alliterative poetry, was just one.[10] All Middle English poetry was prone to infelicities of style, because of its dependence on conventional devices left over from an earlier, simpler age when performance, if not composition, was oral.[11]

Such devices, which might be called "low" elements, include both general topoi and more specific verbal formulas. While the topos I shall discuss in *Pearl*—that of "inexpressibility"—is part of the general European tradition which Middle English inherited, the formula, *se wyth syʒt*, is specific to alliterative poetry. Formulas developed largely out of the requirement that the poetry alliterate three words per line, a situation which led poets to choose stereotyped groups of words, such as *on erthe* or *sothly to say,* on purely phonetic grounds.[12] The resulting style, wordy and highly conventional, has not been well regarded by modern critics, one of whom objects that alliterative poets show an excessive tolerance to "pleonasm, and sometimes to sheer vacuity of expression."[13]

But while the style of alliterative poetry as a whole has been little esteemed, that of the *Pearl* itself has been consistently praised, often for qualities which are just as characteristic of its tradition as the empty formulas: writers speak of a "high style" in which poets use words "as if they were jewels" and resort to "elaborate and colourful rhetoric for sheer pride of craftsmanship."[14] One characteristic of this style is the use of certain archaic adjectives, many of them "elevated" because they appear only in poetic contexts, to describe courtly and heroic subjects—adjectives such as *bryʒt, clere, mery, ryche,* and *schene*.[15] In employing not only these words, but also such examples of the medieval rhetorician's "difficult ornament" as word-play, stanza-linking, and complex rhyme scheme, *Pearl* is acknowledged to be the most exquisite example of the alliterative high style that we have.

The poem has received praise not only for using the high elements, but also for transcending the low ones. But such a view overlooks the poet's intentional use of low formulas for a rhetorical purpose. For although he exploits all the resources of the alliterative high style at the supreme visionary moments—when the dreamer catches sight of the paradisal garden, the maiden, and the New Jerusalem—he also introduces at those moments certain low elements which work with the high in a dialectical fashion to warn against the distractions offered by beautiful language. By undercutting his own linguistic virtuosity, he demonstrates that language, for all its power, is inadequate to convey the Word of God. He thus uses the limitations of his own vernacular literary language to point out the limitations of human language in general.

In this process of undercutting, the *Pearl*-poet uses what J. A. Burrow considers the most common device with which Middle English poets dissociated themselves from their inherited literary medium: the naive narrator.[16] While the *Pearl* dreamer is apparently unaware of the conventional nature of his stylistic devices, the poet is extremely aware, and uses these elements to dramatize the limitations of human language. His strategy becomes especially clear in the debate section of the poem, where the poet has the maiden, as his spokesman, correct the dreamer's misconceptions.

The alliterative formula which the dreamer uses to describe his vision of heaven, *se wyth syʒt* (or *se wyth yʒe*), is one which points to the inadequacy of both words and images. Of all the formulas that have been criticized as being mere fillers to facilitate composition, this has been singled out as one of the most meaningless, something to be fitted in whenever a poet needed a second half-line alliterating on "S."[17] Marie Borroff, however, has justified its use in certain contexts where emphasis on vision is significant, notably in the work of the *Pearl*-poet himself. For she argues that when in *Sir Gawain* the members of King Arthur's court think that nothing so extraordinary as the Green Knight has ever been "sene in þat sale wyth syʒt er þat tyme, / wyth yʒe" (seen in that hall with sight before that time, with eye), the double pleonasm in the formula underscores the court's stupefaction, and slows down the action in a way appropriate to a mood of wonder.[18]

I believe that the poet uses *se wyth syʒt* self-consciously, fully aware of its limitations, both theological and rhetorical. The former lie in the faith which it implies in the ability of visual images to accurately convey the Divine. The dreamer in using the formula to describe his vision thereby expresses this faith; the poet, however, wants us to recognize that we see God through such images "through a glass darkly," rather than, as in heaven, "face to face" (I Cor. XIII.12). The theological limitations of the formula are further underscored by the fact that it is often used by the narrators of secular alliterative dream visions to express their astonishment at the splendor of earthly marvels. By putting the formula in the *Pearl* dreamer's mouth, the poet classes him with such dreamers as the narrator of *Wynnere and Wastoure,* to whom the king is one of the handsomest lords that anyone ever "sawe with his eghne," or that of "Summer Sunday," to whom Lady Fortune is such a woman as he never "sey . . . wiþ syȝth."[19]

The rhetorical limitation of *se wyth syȝt,* on the other hand, is simply that it is hackneyed. It is useful for pointing up the inadequacy of words for expressing the Divine, for it allows the poet to undercut the effect of the language of the alliterative high style. Thus, in the midst of describing the maiden's dress with such elevated phrases as "beau biys" (fair linen), "al blysnande whyt" (all shining white), and "Wyth precios perleȝ al vmbepyȝte" (with precious pearls adorned all about), the poet inserts a "low" formula when he has the dreamer call her pearls the loveliest "þat euer I seȝ ȝet with myn ene" (that ever I saw yet with my eyes).[20]

That the poet is using *se wyth syȝt* pointedly in this case is suggested by the fact that the maiden soon repeats the formula when reproaching him for depending on the evidence of his eyes. She scolds him for believing that she is still alive, simply because he can "wyth yȝen [her] se" (l. 296), and goes on to say

> I halde þat iueler lyttel to prayse
> Þat leueȝ wel þat he seȝ wyth yȝe,
> And much to blame and vncortayse
> Þat leueȝ oure Lorde wolde make a lyȝe,
> Þat lelly hyȝte your lyf to rayse,
> Þaȝ fortune dyd your flesch to dyȝe.
> ȝe setten hys wordeȝ ful westernays
> Þat leueȝ noþynk bot ȝe hit syȝe.
>
>   (*ll.* 301-308)

> I hold that jeweler hardly worthy of praise
> Who believes fully what he sees with eye,
> And worthy of blame and lacking courtesy
> Who believes our Lord would tell a lie,
> He who faithfully promised to raise your life,
> Though Fortune caused your flesh to die.
> You take his words entirely amiss
> You who believe nothing unless you see it.

The dreamer doubts the resurrection, she says, because he believes nothing unless "[he] hit syȝe," and believes everything that he can "seȝ wyth yȝe." By using a formula which the dreamer himself has used—one which has been tainted by having been used to describe too many secular marvels—the maiden points out at once the inadequacy of images and the inadequacy of words for conveying the Divine.

Later in the poem, when the dreamer has made some spiritual progress and is granted a vision of the Heavenly City, the same formula is used to emphasize his dependence on the book of Apocalypse, the source of his vision, and on St. John, its mediator. "As John þe apostel hit syȝ wyth syȝt, / I syȝe þat cyty" (As John the apostle saw it with sight, I saw that city, ll. 985-986), says the dreamer, and his continued allusion to John's seeing the New Jerusalem (emphasized in the refrain of this stanza group) becomes almost iconographic, like the image of St. John peering through a door into heaven in the popular illuminated Apocalypse books.[21] But although the dreamer is using the formula to authenticate his vision, the poet is using it to point out the dreamer's too earthly perception. This is further suggested by the fact that in contemporary mystical writings St. John's vision is classified in Augustinian terms as a "spiritual" one, which, because reliant on figures and images, is inferior to an "intellectual" vision—presumably the Beatific Vision—involving the sight of God face to face.[22] The Beatific Vision is a major concern of the poet's in his biblical narrative *Purity,* where it is generally expressed by the formula *se wyth syȝt* or *se wyth yȝe.*[23] *Pearl,* however, must be characterized as a failed Beatific Vision to the extent that the dreamer never sees God's face. It is likely therefore that the poet, in having the dreamer use *se wyth syȝt* to describe what he *does* see, is pointing up the limited, mediated quality of the vision, as well as of the language with which he recounts it.

The second kind of conventional language which the poet uses to call attention to the inadequacy of words is a rhetorical commonplace—the "inexpressibility topos."[24] This topos is not by any means limited to alliterative poetry, but is part of a larger literary inheritance. As a strategic device of self-deprecation for the purpose of winning the audience's approval, it was, indeed, traditional. But as Burrow has shown, this strategy became greatly intensified among fourteenth-century English poets who were trying to accommodate themselves to their awkward medium.[25] In the *Pearl* the inexpressibility topos is used to suggest that the poet recognizes the limitations of the alliterative style—that he is deliberately using conventional apologies for the conventionality of his language. For while the dreamer uses these apologies conventionally, the poet expects us to recognize them as justified—expressions of the inadequacy of language not only on a rhetorical, but also on a theological level.

Here as elsewhere the poet uses the dreamer to exploit the ambiguity of the religious and secular connotations of words. In a Christian context, the inexpressibility topos was an important device of the negative way, part of the "rhetoric of ineffability" by which mystical poets sought to express the Divine.[26] Words which admitted their own inadequacy were held to be less likely to lead to idolatry than those which took themselves for granted, as Augustine, following Plato and Plotinus, bad pointed out.[27] Dante of course makes the most notable use of the topos in such a context in the *Paradiso,* where he continually complains that language falls short of describing the Beatific Vision. It is possible, as one critic has argued, that the **Pearl**-poet knew the *Divine Comedy,* and it is even more likely that he knew the anonymous Middle English mystical work *The Cloud of Unknowing,* which refers to mysteries "whiche man may not, ne kan not, speke."[28] Certainly he would have been aware of the mystical Latin hymns which assert, in paradoxical terms, God's ineffability.[29] The poet could thus measure the dreamer against writers whose linguistic doubts were profound and theological. But despite the frequent use of the topos in Christian contexts, it was originally classical, and it occurred throughout the Middle Ages in secular descriptions of any marvelous subject to which "words could not do justice."[30] It even had a form specific to alliterative poetry in the formula *it is to tor* [too difficult] *to telle,* which the **Pearl**-poet himself uses in *Sir Gawain* to describe indescribable luxury.[31]

Although this alliterative form of the topos is not used in **Pearl,** other forms are. The dreamer's mistake is to apply them in the conventional secular sense, without a true recognition of the inadequacy of human language. Thus, he paints a dazzling picture of the paradisal garden which foreshadows the New Jerusalem, drawing heavily on the language of the alliterative tradition:

> Dubbed wern alle þo downeʒ sydeʒ
> Wyth crystal klyffeʒ so cler of kynde.
> Holtewodeʒ bryʒt aboute hem bydeʒ
> Of bolleʒ as blwe as ble of Ynde;
>
> As bornyst syluer þe lef on slydeʒ,
> Þat þike con trylle on vch a tynde.
> Quen glem of glodeʒ agayneʒ hem glydeʒ,
> Wyth schymeryng schene ful schrylle þay
>   schynde.
>
>   (*ll.* 73-80)

> Adorned were all the slopes of the hills
> With crystal cliffs of so clear a sort.
> Woodlands bright were set about them
> Whose trunks were blue as the color indigo;
> As burnished silver the leaves swayed,
> That trembled closely on each branch.
> When a gleam of the sky fell against them,
> They shone very brilliantly with a bright
>   shimmering.

The dreamer devotes fifty-five lines to the garden, making it appear like a *locus amoenus* in a secular alliterative dream vision.[32] His understanding, if not his sincerity, is thus open to question when, in the midst of this description, he asserts that

> þe derþe þerof for to deuyse
> Nis no wyʒ worþé þat tonge bereʒ.
>
>   (*ll.* 99-100)

> To describe the splendor thereof
> There is no one worthy who bears a tongue.

The poet puts this conventional disclaimer in the dreamer's mouth to warn against the beauty of the rest of the description, for he knows that the unworthiness of human speech is far greater than the dreamer realizes.

A similar strategy is used when the maiden appears to the dreamer in the garden. He takes her earthly guise for reality, describing her in the intensifying language of alliterative poetry, which is more appropriate to a romance heroine than to the beatified spirit of a child who died in infancy. As far as he is concerned, it is in keeping with this language that he claims inexpressibility when portraying the allegorical pearl on her breast:

> A manneʒ dom moʒt dryʒly demme,
> Er mynde moʒt malte in hit mesure.
> I hope no tong moʒt endure
> No sauerly saghe say of þat syʒt.
>
>   (*ll.* 223-226)

> A man's judgment would be utterly baffled
> Before his mind could comprehend its value.
> I believe no tongue could endure
> Nor say an adequate word of that sight.

But despite his assertion that human judgment and speech are inadequate, and despite his earlier claim to having been struck dumb when first seeing the maiden ("I stod ful stylle and dorste not calle; / Wyth yʒen open and mouth ful clos," ll. 182-183), the dreamer goes on to describe her with all the resources at an alliterative poet's disposal. He thus lacks the humility of the pilgrim Dante, who, when Beatrice appears to him in a similar situation near the end of the *Paradiso,* resolves to remain silent, his poetic abilities having been so overcome that he cannot describe her beauty.[33] The **Pearl**-poet, then, exploits the simultaneous secular and religious connotations of the inexpressibility topos in order to emphasize the split between the dreamer's and the reader's perception. And because this topos *is* a commonplace, a piece of "used" language, it paradoxically embodies in itself the very inadequacy of language to which it refers.

The likelihood that the poet is using these two types of conventional language—the formula and the topos— self-consciously in the visionary sections is strengthened by his discursive treatment of the limits of language in the debate section of the poem. The maiden, speaking for the poet, makes it clear that language is a much more fundamental issue than the dreamer, with his stock confessions of inexpressibility, perceives, as she touches, implicitly, on the Christian concept of the problematical relation between human words and the Divine Word discussed by Augustine. First, she points out that human language is a medium which encourages error; the dreamer does in fact "speke errour," as he puts it in a conventional apology to her (l. 422). While warning him against depending on the evidence of his eyes, the maiden says,

Þre wordeʒ hatʒ þou spoken at ene:
Vnavysed, for soþe, wern alle þre.
Þou ne woste in worlde quat on dotʒ mene;
Þy worde byfore þy wytte con fle.

(ll. 291-294)

Three words have you spoken at once:
All ill-advised, indeed, were all three.
You don't know what in the world one of
   them means;
Your word has fled before your wit.

She characterizes the dreamer's three misconceptions (that she is in the paradise that he sees, that he can join her there, that he can cross the water) as three ill-advised "wordeʒ." And she points out that his "worde" fled before his "wytte"—that is, that he failed to achieve the embodiment of thought in language which Augustine considered a metaphor for the Incarnation.[34]

But despite the fact that the dreamer's language has failed, the maiden implies that human language *may* be used to bridge the gap between God and man. The early part of the debate deals with this problem, as can be seen from the prominence given to *deme,* the link-word in stanza-group 6 (ll. 301-360). In its ten occurrences in the stanza's refrain, the word ranges in meaning from "to judge" to "to speak," and it is applied in turn to God, the dreamer, and the maiden in a way that explicitly contrasts Divine and human speech as well as judgment. The maiden makes it clear, as Augustine had, that whatever the limitations of human language, man is entitled to use it to try to communicate with God ("þy prayer may hys pyté byte" [your prayer may move his pity], l. 355), and is in fact obligated to do so ("man to God wordeʒ schulde heue" [man should lift words to God], l. 314). She is recognizing here the Christian paradox that although God is ineffable, He has nevertheless, in Augustine's words, "accepted the tribute of the human voice, and wished us to take joy in prasing Him with our words."[35] Human language, furthermore, is valid as a means of communication from God to man, as in His revelation in Scripture, but scriptural words are often misconstrued by fallen human beings. Thus the maiden, in a passage quoted earlier, scolds the dreamer for thinking that Christ would "make a lyʒe" about the resurrection (l. 304), and for taking Christ's words amiss ("ʒe setten hys wordeʒ ful

westernays," l. 306). The dreamer continues his misunderstanding till near the end of the debate, when he complains that it would contradict Scripture if the maiden had indeed been made a queen in heaven—then "Holy Wryt" would be "bot a fable" (l. 592).

The maiden, then, implies that although man is obligated to try to communicate with God through language, his attempt will be doomed to failure—words are insufficient. More devastating in its consequences for the dreamer, however, is the suggestion that the ability to use language is *unnecessary* for salvation, since the maiden, who died while an inarticulate child, was saved. The dreamer's main objection to her high position in heaven is that she died too young to have earned that status. The linguistic implications of this point are brought forward when he argues that a child of two would have been unable to pray—to praise God with language:

Þou lyfed not two ʒer in oure þede;
Þou cowþeʒ neuer God nauþer plese ne pray,
Ne neuer nawþer Pater ne Crede.

(ll. 483-485)

You lived not two years in our land;
You never knew how to please God, nor pray
   to him,
Nor knew either Paternoster or Creed.

The maiden answers him with the parable of the vineyard, whose moral is that earthly status is reversed in heaven ("þe laste schal be þe fyrst . . . /And þe fyrst þe laste," ll. 507-571). She sharpens the moral with the standard medieval gloss that the "laste"—those who entered the vineyard late in the day—are the innocents, those who died in infancy (ll. 625-636). She further blosters her argument by citing Christ's insistence that the Kingdom of Heaven is open to children ("let chylder vnto me tyʒt./To suche is heuenryche arayed," ll. 718-719) and that one can enter it *only* if he becomes like a child ("hys ryche no wyʒ myʒt wynne/Bot he com þyder ryʒt as a chylde," ll. 722-723). In using these allusions to support her own position in heaven, the maiden is implicitly drawing on the Christian concept that the humility of the child is specifically linguistic. Augustine in particular was intrigued by the idea of the speechless (*infans*) or barely articulate child. In justifying the *sermo humilis* of the Bible, he frequently mentions its accessibility to children, saying for instance that Scripture, while it "suits itself to babes," nevertheless lets our understanding rise to the sublime.[36] Again in the *Confessions* he tells of his initial contempt for scriptural Latin because its style was unworthy of Cicero: "as the child grows these books grow with him. But I was too proud to call myself a child. I was inflated with self-esteem, which made me think myself a great man."[37] The *Pearl*-dreamer, as he insists on the efficacy of language, is very like the young Augustine in rhetorical arrogance. The maiden's claim that she was elevated to the rank of queen in heaven is thus especially humiliating: she has shown that adult linguistic facility is insignificant from a Divine perspective.

Language, then, is a far more important theme of the **Pearl** than has generally been recognized. This theme has both rhetorical and theological implications, since the poet's sense of the inadequacy of his Middle English poetic style is sharpened by his recognition of the inadequacy of man's words *vis à vis* God's Word. The former he dramatizes by placing conventional and sometimes hackneyed language in the dreamer's mouth; the latter he treats discursively through the maiden's criticisms of the dreamer. By using language which warns against itself, the poet is able to achieve a poetic incarnation on the Augustinian model—to suggest the Divine Word through the limited medium of his own words.

Notes

[1] For a succinct discussion, see John MacQuarrie, *God-Talk: An Examination of the Language and Logic of Religion* (New York: Harper and Row, 1967), pp. 25, 28-29.

[2] E.g., A. C. Spearing, *The Gawain-Poet: A Critical Study* (Cambridge, Eng.: Cambridge Univ. Press, 1970), pp. 155-56, 165, and Pamela Gradon, *Form and Style in Early English Literature* (London: Methuen, 1971), pp. 207-211.

[3] Two articles deal with the theme of language in *Pearl* in ways that differ from mine. James Milroy's "*Pearl*: The Verbal Texture and the Linguistic Theme" (*Neophilologus*, 55 [1971], 195-208) discusses the dreamer's earthbound understanding of words, but in a context which is only implicitly theological; John M. Hill's "Middle English Poets and the Word: Notes toward an Appraisal of Linguistic Consciousness" (*Criticism*, 16 [1974], 153-169) is much closer to my work in treating the inadequacy of language in Augustinian terms, but, like Milroy's article, does not relate this inadequacy to the limitations of Middle English verse.

[4] Trans. D. W. Robertson, Jr., *On Christian Doctrine* (Indianapolis: Bobbs-Merrill, 1958), I.vi.6; *PL* XXXIV, 21.

[5] See, e.g., *Confessions* I.iv.4; *PL* XXXII, 622-623.

[6] Augustine's statements about language are part of his larger concern that anything intended to move men toward blessedness not be enjoyed for its own sake. For Augustinian sign theory, see Stanley E. Fish, *Self-Consuming Artifacts: The Experience of Seventeenth-Century Literature* (1972; rpt. Berkeley: Univ. of California Press, 1974), pp. 21-43, and Joseph Anthony Mazzeo, "St. Augustine's Rhetoric of Silence: Truth vs. Eloquence and Things vs. Signs," *Renaissance and Seventeenth-Century Studies* (New York: Columbia Univ. Press, 1964), pp. 1-28.

[7] See Marcia L. Colish, *The Mirror of Language: A Study in the Medieval Theory of Knowledge* (New Haven: Yale Univ. Press, 1968), pp. 22, 33-35, and more generally, the chapter "St. Augustine: the Experience of the Word," pp. 8-81.

[8] "Sermo humilis," in *Literary Language and its Public in Late Latin Antiquity and in the Middle Ages*, trans. Ralph Manheim (Princeton: Princeton Univ. Press, 1965), pp. 27-52.

[9] Especially in *De Vulgari Eloquentia;* on this point and on the general continuity of the theory, see Colish, pp. 264-265, 315-316. The case for the influence of Augustinian sign theory on two Middle English poems contemporary with *Pearl* is made by Mary Carruthers (*The Search for St. Truth: A Study of Meaning in Piers Plowman* [Evanston: Northwestern Univ. Press, 1973], esp. pp. 10-19), and Eugene Vance ("*Mervelous Signals*: Poetics, Sign Theory, and Politics in Chaucer's *Troilus*," *NLH*, 10 [1979], 296). Robert O. Payne points out that the Augustinian concern that rhetoric would encourage idolatry continued through the fourteenth century ("Chaucer's Realization of Himself as Rhetor," in *Medieval Eloquence: Studies in the Theory and Practice of Medieval Rhetoric*, ed. James J. Murphy [Berkeley: Univ. of California Press, 1978], pp. 280-282).

[10] See Albert C. Baugh, *A History of the English Language*, 2nd ed. (New York: Appleton-Century-Crofts, 1957), pp. 150-187, 227-237, and Basil Cottle, *The Triumph of English, 1350-1400* (New York: Barnes and Noble, 1969), pp. 15-50.

[11] On the debasement of Middle English style, see J. A. Burrow, *Ricardian Poetry: Chaucer, Gower, Langland, and the Gawain-Poet* (New Haven: Yale Univ. Press, 1971), pp. 25-28. On oral performance in medieval literature, see Robert Kellogg, "Oral Literature," *NLH*, 5 (1973), 55-66.

[12] For a brief account of the nature of the alliterative line, see Thorlac Turville-Petre, *The Alliterative Revival* (Totowa, N.J.: Rowman and Littlefield, 1977), pp. 51-56.

[13] Burrow, p. 26. See also J. P. Oakden, *Alliterative Poetry in Middle English: A Survey of the Traditions*, II (Manchester: Manchester Univ. Press, 1935), 381-401.

[14] Elizabeth Salter, *Piers Plowman: An Introduction* (Cambridge, Mass.: Harvard Univ. Press, 1961), p. 17.

She refers to the "high rhetoric" and "formality" of many of the poets (pp. 15-17).

[15] See especially Marie Borroff, *Sir Gawain and the Green Knight: A Stylistic and Metrical Study* (New Haven: Yale Univ. Press, 1962), pp. 52-90, and Larry D. Benson, *Art and Tradition in Sir Gawain and the Green Knight* (New Brunswick: Rutgers Univ. Press, 1965), pp. 126-143.

[16] Burrow, pp. 39-40.

[17] Burrow, p. 27.

[18] Borroff, pp. 71-72; *Sir Gawain and the Green Knight,* ed. J. R. R. Tolkien and E. V. Gordon, 2nd ed. rev. Norman Davis (Oxford: Oxford Univ. Press, 1968), ll. 197-98. My translation.

[19] *Wynnere and Wastoure,* ed. Sir Israel Gollancz (London: Oxford Univ. Press, 1930), l. 89, and "Summer Sunday," in *Historical Poems of the Fourteenth and Fifteenth Centuries,* ed. Rossell Hope Robbins (New York: Columbia Univ. Press, 1959), p. 100, l. 64. Similarly, the dreamer in "The Crowned King" tells of the marvelous crowd of people which he "sawe in [his] sight" (in Robbins, p. 228, l. 33).

[20] *Pearl,* ed. E. V. Gordon (1953; rpt. Oxford: Clarendon Press, 1966), ll. 197, 204, 200. This and subsequent translations of the poem are my own.

[21] See George Henderson, *Gothic* (1967; rpt. Baltimore: Penguin, 1972), p. 149.

[22] Edward Wilson, "'Gostly Drem' in 'Pearl'," *NM,* 69 (1968), 90-101.

[23] See C. G. Osgood, ed. *Pearl* (Boston: D. C. Heath, 1906), n. to l. 675, and Robert J. Menner, ed. *Purity* (New Haven: Yale Univ. Press, 1920), n. to l. 25.

[24] So named by Ernst Robert Curtius, in *European Literature and the Latin Middle Ages,* trans. Willard R. Trask (1953; rpt. New York: Harper and Row, 1963), p. 159.

[25] Burrow. pp. 39-42.

[26] See Lowry Nelson, "The Rhetoric of Ineffability: Toward a Definition of Mystical Poetry," *CL,* 8 (1956), 323-336, Luigi Tonelli, *Dante e la poesia dell'ineffabile* (Florence: G. Barbèra, 1934), pp. 45-77, and Robin Kirkpatrick, *Dante's Paradiso and the Limitations of Modern Criticism* (Cambridge: Cambridge Univ. Press, 1978), pp. 36-50.

[27] Peter S. Hawkins, "Saint Augustine and the Language of Ineffability," unpub. ms., pp. 8-11.

[28] For the former point, see P. M. Kean, *Pearl: An Interpretation* (New York: Barnes and Noble, 1967), pp. 120-132; for the latter, *The Cloud of Unknowing and the Book of Privy Counselling,* ed. Phyllis Hodgson (London: EETS, 1944), p. 62.

[29] See Nelson, p. 327, and Tonelli, pp. 70-75.

[30] Curtius' examples are limited to secular ones (pp. 159-162). In Dante the secular topos coalesces with the Christian, and Tonelli has shown that the poet drew on its use by Provencal love poets as well as by the mystics (pp. 80, ff.).

[31] He says that it is "to tor for to telle" of all the ornamental figures embroidered on the Green Knight's clothing (l. 165). See *OED,* Tor, a., for further examples in alliterative poetry. My interpretation of the formula as a use of the inexpressibility topos depends on a translation of *tor* as "difficult"; the more common translation, "tiresome, tedious," would make it an instance of *occupattio*—the announcement that the poet will curtail his description (see Benson, p. 172).

[32] E.g., the landscapes in *Wynnere and Wastoure* (ll. 33-44) and the *Parlement of the Thre Ages* (ed. M.Y. Offord [London: EETS, 1959], ll. 1-20). On the conventionality of such landscapes, see Ralph W. V. Elliott, "Landscape and Rhetoric in Middle English Alliterative Poetry," *Melbourne Critical Review,* 4 (1961), 65-76.

[33] *La Commedia seconda antica vulgata,* ed. Giorgio Petrocchi, IV (Rome: Arnoldo Mondadori, 1967), XXX. 16-33.

[34] *De Trinitate* XV.x. 19; *PL* XLII, 1071, and *De Doctrina Christiana* I. xiii; *PL* XXXIV, 24.

[35] *On Christian Doctrine* I. vi. 6; *PL* XXXIV, 21.

[36] *De Trinitate* 1.2 (trans. Arthur West Haddan in *A Select Library of the Nicene and Post-Nicene Fathers of the Christian Church,* ed. Philip Schaff [Grand Rapids, Mich.: Wm. B. Eerdmans, 1956], III, 18; *PL* XLII, 820).

[37] *Confessions* III.v (trans. R. S. Pine-Coffin [Harmondsworth: Penguin, 1961], p. 60); *PL* XXXII, 686.

Lynn Staley (essay date 1991)

SOURCE: "The Pearl Dreamer and the Eleventh Hour," in *Text and Matter: New Critical Perspectives of the Pearl-Poet,* The Whitston Publishing Company, 1991, pp. 3-15.

[*In the following essay, Staley argues that because the poet placed the dreamer's experience in the month of harvest, the dreamer recognizes the importance of time as a catalyst for his spiritual transformation.*]

In this essay I would like to examine the poet's handling of time in *Pearl*. His awareness, not only of various ways of considering time, but of the potential artistic uses of a temporal cycle or cycles, is apparent throughout his works. In *Sir Gawain,* he juxtaposes Camelot with Cyclic, Degenerative, and Regenerative schemes of time, in each case to the concept of motion.[1] His use of time in that poem points up Camelot's genuine instability; the city is not capable of withstanding motion but only of tracing its own cycle of declension. In addition, the poet's handling of the seasonal cycle at the beginning of the second section of *Sir Gawain* testifies to his awareness of the implications of judgment and warning inherent in medieval treatments of the period of time from spring to harvest. In *Patience* and *Purity* he dramatizes significant events of biblical history in such a way as to highlight those cycles of time that define and circumscribe human action and human choice. His handling of time in *Pearl* is equally purposeful, for, even as he specifies August as the month of the narrator's experience, he provides for this experience a setting that locates the dreamer within an entirely different temporal framework.

That much-discussed reference to August comes early in the poem, in section 1, lines 37-40:

> To þat spot þat I in speche expoun
> I entred in þat erber grene,
> In Auguste in a hyȝ seysoun,
> Quen corne is coruen wyth crokeȝ kene.[2]

There have been numerous suggestions about the exact date the poet intends us to associate with this "hyȝ seysoun." We can interpret the phrase as referring to Lammas (Gollancz, Gordon, and Andrew and Waldron), to the Feast of the Transfiguration (Madeleva, Knightley), or to the Feast of the Assumption (Hamilton, Osgood, Schofield). Or we can take Charles Moorman's ingenious suggestion that "hyȝ" is an unlisted alternative spelling of "hiȝ" or "heȝ" (hay), the phrase then referring simply to the "hay season."[3] Despite the fact that I incline toward the Feast of the Assumption, especially since *Pearl* seems to reflect many of the lessons, themes, and figures identified with this day, I would like to explore the poet's possible reasons for linking the dreamer's experience to a date in late summer, for that experience seems rather to belong to a genre of visionary narrative traditionally connected to late spring or early summer. By shifting the seasonal context of the dream, the poet offers an implied commentary upon the dreamer, the nature of his problem, and the Parable of the Vineyard, through

which the maiden examines the proper use of time, a medium the dreamer seems initially to squander without regard for its limits. Ultimately, the reference to August early in the poem prepares us to apply the Parable of the Vineyard to the sorrowing dreamer as well as to the maiden, who describes herself as having begun vineyard labor at the eleventh hour.

The lines themselves describe two conventional but distinct scenes, whose separate elements the poet joins in a single sentence and a single pictorial frame. First, as several critics have pointed out, the description of August as the time when grain is scythed reflects the traditional occupation for August in both literary descriptions and pictorial sequences of the Labors of the Months.[4] As Trevisa describes the month in his translation of Bartholomaeus Anglicus' *De Proprietatibus Rerum,* "in þis moneþ corn is igadred into bernes and þerfore he is ypeynt wiþ a fleile þrossching corn . . ."[5] That the relatively uniform iconographic treatments of the month of August have their origin in the actual agricultural cycle is no doubt the case as Emile Mâle observed; when translated into art, however, man's labors also acquired meanings rooted in the medieval understanding of time. Put simply, time was conceived of as a medium for change or growth. Again I quote Trevisa:

> Tyme is mesure of chaungeable þingis, as Aristotel seiþ *de quinque substanciis* . . . Oþir as Rabanus seiþ, tyme is dymensioun of chaungeabil þingis, touchinge meovinge and abidinge, and duriþ in meovable þingis. As Austyn seiþ, noþing is more precious þan tyme . . . Tyme is schort, chaungeable, & vncurable . . .[6]

In each case, the attempt to define time depends upon a recognition of finitude, for—Aristotle, Rabanus Maurus, and St. Augustine agree—time is a medium for change, which can be measured just as a line that begins at one point and ends at another can be measured. However, medieval discussions of time are less abstract considerations of the nature of time than they are urgent preambles to exhortations regarding the use of time, since man can do little about time itself but can do much within his own time. As Rosemond Tuve noted, the urgency that informed references to the seasonal cycle and to the sequence of the Labors of the Months is characteristic of English verse, making "English seasons-descriptions from before Lydgate until after Spenser a contribution to that apology for poetry which sees in it the teaching of an active virtue."[7]

The reference to August notwithstanding, the first 180 lines of *Pearl,* up to the dreamer's first sight of the maiden, suggest the outlines of another convention, that of the love vision, linked not to late summer but to spring or early summer, the more timely season for dreams pertaining to or arising from frustrated desire.[8]

The opening sections of *Pearl* could, in fact, be described as an especially focused and intelligent transformation of the traditions of the French love vision as handed on to later writers by Guillaume de Lorris. Moreover, the author of *Pearl* seems to be conscious of the ties between the *Romance of the Rose* and the biblical imagery of desire, since he adapts certain key elements of Amant's experience in ways that highlight the *Pearl* dreamer's state of mind. Guillaume de Lorris' account of the Garden of Deduit seems to provide the *Pearl*-Poet with the subtext for his description of the garden in which the dreamer goes to mourn the loss of his pearl:[9]

> On huyle þer perle hit trendeled doun
> Schadowed þis worteʒ ful schyre and schene,
> Gilofre, gyngure and gromylyoun,
> And pyonys powdered ay bytwene.
>
> (41-44)

These lines, together with the first two lines of the preceding quatrain ("To þat spot þat I in speche expoun / I entred in þat erber grene") distill an entire tradition, thereby suggesting a series of *topoi* linked to the literature of love, search, vision.

With only a few brushstrokes, the poet conjures up a garden inextricably joined to the visionary experiences of late spring or early summer. Like the innermost sanctum of the Garden of Deduit, the spot of the pearl's loss is doubly enclosed, first, in a garden, implied by the phrase "I entred in," and, second, by the plants that shade the spot, making of it a kind of bower.[10] The plants themselves evoke earlier spice gardens of desire. For example, the more elaborate garden Guillaume de Lorris describes, which boasts its own complicated literary and biblical pedigree, contains many exotic spices—cloves, licorice, fresh grains of paradise (or cardamom), zedoary (a ginger-like spice), anise, and cinnamon—a number of trees and animals, and an abundance of unnamed flowers—red, yellow, and white—in addition to violets and periwinkles. The Middle English translator of these lines, whom I will call Chaucer, is faithful to his original; following both the spirit and the letter of the French text, he ends his description of the garden's lushness by saying of the ground that it is "poudred, as men had it peynt."[11] Both verbs imply art rather than nature, design rather than accident, thereby conveying the garden's concealed artifice. The *Pearl*-Poet's description of the dreamer's garden focuses our attention upon those few details that establish the spot of loss as the setting for a certain type of experience. Like Chaucer, he translates Guillaume de Lorris' cloves as gillyflowers or clove pinks; he includes ginger but adds "gromylyoun," or gromwell, a commonly grown medicinal herb, which fits nicely into the line's alliterative pattern. On the other hand, as Gollancz also noticed, the word might reflect the poet's assumption that the gromwell's white

seed and the "greyn de parys" mentioned in the Middle English *Romance of the Rose* were identical. Although I would not want to dismiss this possibility, I do not care to make too much of it. The poet may also have expected his audience to remember that the gromwell's white, pearl-like seeds are the source of the herb's medicinal benefits, perhaps hinting at an elaborate metaphoric pun whereby the lost pearl had indeed been transformed through the natural process of seasonal decay and growth and had borne fruit, the curative potential of which the self-absorbed dreamer is oblivious.[12] Finally, the *Pearl*-Poet uproots the violet and the periwinkle from the garden, replacing them with peonies, which, like the gromwell, were grown for medicinal purposes. He, too, indicates the garden's artfulness by describing the peonies as "powdered" between the other plants.

These comments may seem to represent undue attention to an ostensibly random group of plants, but the tightly woven description functions as a trope, placing us, not in a real garden where pinks, peonies, ginger, and gromwell are all blooming simultaneously, but in a garden setting where both culinary and curative herbs form a bower for a lover's dream. The first of the manuscript illustrations to the poem suggests a similar contemporary awareness of the almost mannerist character of the poet's description of this spot. Its depiction of a male figure sleeping in a highly stylized pastoral setting could serve to introduce any number of works that recount moments of revelation or vision. For example, on the stalls of Carlyle Cathedral is placed a sequence of paintings depicting scenes from a life of St. Augustine. The panels portraying Augustine's experience of conversion in the garden are particularly striking, especially when we compare them to the manuscript illustrations for *Pearl;* both sequences are indebted to the iconographic conventions of the literature of love or vision, or, as Courcelle puts it, of conversion. Thus, the panel tracing that central moment in Augustine's spiritual life shows him reclining near an open book in a garden whose mounds are powdered with flowers while an angel leans toward him and carries a banner on which is inscribed *Tolle, lege.* If we erased the angel's wings and removed the banner, the picture, which looks remarkably like a reverse image of the first of the illustrations for *Pearl,* could be used in an edition of *The Legend of Good Women, The Romance of the Rose,* or *Pearl.*[13]

The poet's description of this garden would be less significant, or more conventional, did not the poem itself take place in August. By joining in one sentence in lines 37-40 a reference to an August field and to an enclosed garden, the poet seems to insist that we see the dreamer and his garden within a larger frame. In effect, he sketches for us a scene whose fundamental disunity underlines the spiritual conflict in the dreamer between himself and time. Thus the poet seems to mix metaphors on rather a large scale, dislocating the conventional protagonist of the literary dream vision and placing him and his garden of desire in the midst of a larger and equally significant frame—a calendar, open to August.[14] There are at least two other instances in the poem where the poet hints at an association between a calendrical sequence and the dreamer's experience, the first in the dreamer's initial reaction to the landscape of his vision and the second in the maiden's account of the Parable of the Vineyard.

When the dreamer first "awakens" in his vision, he finds himself in a realm whose characteristics identify it as a *locus amoenus,* an edenic landscape whose heightened clarity and sensual appeal serve as an *accessus* to the debate between the dreamer and his beloved guide. Here, the poet's awareness of the connections between literary convention and biblical imagery is particularly apparent, for he recasts materials that Guillaume de Lorris and others had drawn from the Song of Songs and the Book of Apocalypse in their attempts to describe other efforts to regain paradise. For example, in Apocalypse 22:2, St. John describes the River of Life as flowing from the throne of God. That river was thought to flow here on earth in baptismal water, thereby creating at once a rite of passage and a passageway for the man seeking entry to paradise. Guillaume de Lorris employs this detail in his depiction of Amant's gradual apprehension of another sort of paradise, for, when Amant first "awakens" in his dream landscape, he hears the sound of water. Drawn to the sound, he discovers a river whose cold water gushes from a nearby hill. While washing his face in the water—a social rite that ironically evokes the more fundamental cleansing of the baptismal fount—he notices the gravel that covers the streambed, a detail that adds to the richness and mystery of the landscape he inhabits. The ***Pearl***-Poet restores this river to the landscape of the New Jerusalem; its force and majesty and the splendor of the stones along its bottom impel the dreamer towards revelation, not towards the outer reaches of fantasy. By drawing upon the details of such conventions, the poet not only indicates a relationship between his dreamer and other literary lovers and dreamers, but establishes his experience in a season appropriate for desire, when the year's fruit is yet nascent in the flowers dotting these landscapes.

But if the outlines of the narrator's visionary experience characterize him as a lover whose plaint is set in the beginnings of the annual cycle, the maiden insists that he recognize actual, not imaginary, time. She does so by recounting the Parable of the Vineyard (Matthew 20:1-16), a parable in which human activity is circumscribed by the period of time from sunrise to sunset. Labor in the vineyard begins with first light and continues until the sun goes down, "þe date of day of euensonge, / On oure byfore þe sonne go doun"

(529-30). Those who commence work at the "eleventh hour" begin, not at one hour before midnight, but in late afternoon, probably around four o'clock.[15]

In addition to recounting a parable whose message is bound up with the sun's daily motion, the poet describes a scriptural labor associated with the sun's annual movement through the zodiac, for the harvest of the grapes was linked to the month of September, or to the sign of Libra. As Trevisa describes September, "And þis moneþ is ende of somyr and biginny[n]g of haruest. In þis monthe grapis beþ ripe and þerfore he is ipeint in a vineȝerd as a gardeynere gadringe grapis in a basket."[16] Trevisa here evokes both the pictorial and the philosophical traditions, describing, first, September as a particular labor, and, second, the symbol for that labor. The description could be turned around so that we perceive, as the maiden seems to expect the dreamer to understand, that the gardener gathering grapes in a basket is a sign of the end of summer, a sign of harvest. When Virgo gives way to Libra, the season changes from one of growth to one of reckoning. It is Libra, or the Scales, that hangs low in the horizon over Chaucer's pilgrims as the Parson begins his tale of penance, a tale fittingly introduced by Harry Bailly with "Beeth fructuous, and that in little space." Here, as so often in *The Canterbury Tales,* Harry Bailly speaks more wisely than he may know, for the subject of fruitfulness was inevitably raised in considerations of Libra. If we extend Chaucer's allusion to Libra, with Libra in the sky, the Parson has but little space— or little daylight—left to urge spiritual fruitfulness upon the pilgrims, whose diverse loves the *Tales* recount, and who, in turn, have little time to repent.

The fact that September was frequently described as signifying the day of judgment makes the maiden's use of the Parable of the Vineyard even more pointed. As the first month of autumn, September is the month of the equinox, signalling days of shorter length and thus of diminished opportunity for human activity.[17] The maiden's handling of this parable captures the urgency associated with September and the sign of Libra, thus calling attention to the brevity of time available for human labor. Not only does she stress the passing of each hour, but she uses "date," connoting a specific period of time, as a link word in section IX, the section in which she describes the labor in the vineyard. Moreover, she uses "date" here in reference both to an annual and a diurnal measurement of time. First, she applies "date" to that time of year when the grapes are ready for harvest (lines 500-08); if we examine both the traditional associations between September and the gathering of grapes and the relationship between the parable and the theme of judgment, it seems likely that "date" in this case refers to September. However, she also uses the word to denote a time of day, as in "date of daye" (517), "welneȝwyl day watȝ passed date" (528); and "At þe date of day of euensonge" (529). Her use of the word underscores the relationship between the two ways of telling time in the poem, implying that sundown and September are, in fact, the same date, particularly since she refers to evensong as one hour before sundown or as the eleventh hour, when she herself entered the vineyard. Indeed, the theme of judgment that informs her narration of the parable is most evident in her description of sundown,

> ȝe sunne watȝ doun and hit wex late.
> To take her hyre he made sumoun;
> ȝe day watȝ al apassed date.
>
> (538-40)

The end words for each line—"late," "sumoun," and "date" suggest that sundown, like that date when the sun moves into Libra, can be understood as the time of balance when the results of spring's planting and summer's growth are put to the scales. It is the note of finality struck by those words "late," "sumoun," and "date," that ought to alert the dreamer to the time of year in which he exists—August, one hour before sundown.

The maiden's account of the Parable of the Vineyard and the dreamer's account of the landscape of vision, are cast in strikingly visual language that evokes not only the language of the dream vision and of the Bible, but pictures of Spring or early summer, and of August and September. Such pictures can only be understood as individual elements of a larger sequence, the sequence of the year, the scheme by which man measures time. If we consider these pictures in relation to the early portrayal of the dreamer in his garden in the midst of August, we can detect the outlines of a calendrical sequence within *Pearl,* a sequence that underlies both the poem's patterns of language and imagery and its broader thematic concerns.

First, and most obviously, the references to time adumbrate a movement from spring to harvest that is directly relevant to the dreamer's efforts to come to terms with the fact or effect of mutability. Ultimately, the vision of the New Jerusalem, the Tree of Life with its twelve fruits for the twelve months at its heart, provides the dreamer, as it provides the poem's reader, with a visual token of permanence, offsetting the sense of time and transience that seems to dominate the poem. In the stanza describing the Tree of Life (1069-80), the narrator emphasizes the permanence and the clarity of the landscape of paradise. Those bodies by which we tell time here on earth, the moon, the planets, and the sun, are not only unnecessary in a realm without time, but pale in relationship to the refulgence of heaven. The splendor of that transcendent sphere is mirrored in the River of Life, which also reflects the trees growing by its bank:

> Aboute þat water arn tres ful schym,
> þat twelue fryteȝ of lyf con bere ful sone;
> Twelue syþeȝ on ȝer þay beren ful frym,
> And renowleȝ nwe in vche a mone.
>
> (1077-80)

Whereas in the sun's movement through the sky and in the rotation of the months we on earth find our symbols for earth's impermanence, those twelve endlessly renewing fruits are visual symbols for eternity. The moon, our most persistent referent for change, not only has no power in heaven's sky ("The mone may þerof aproche no myȝte" [1069]), but is subsumed into a greater motion, the cycle of endless renewal played out by the banks of the River of Life.

Second, the implied movement from August to September adds one more strand to the poem's rich weave of allusions to cultivation and harvest. On the most basic level, "corn" is a generic term, referring to any grain. The dreamer's use of it echoes his allusion to John 12:24 only a few lines previously, "For vch gresse mot grow of grayneȝ dede; / No whete were elleȝ to woneȝ wonne" (31-32). From this early and rather arid reference to the natural cycle to his final description of the citizens of heaven as harvested pearls, his language sketches his growing recognition of a more fundamental process of cultivation and harvest. Thus his initial hopelessly literal reference to wheat is transformed—by a process as mysterious as transubstantiation itself—into the truly nourishing bread of the Mass mentioned in the poem's closing lines, grain that has not only been cut but ground, bolted, and baked. From the rotting body of the lost pearl to the risen body of Christ, the poem traces a pattern of resurrection and transformation, of spiritual harvest. If we interpret the dreamer's reference to corn in a more metaphoric sense, we should note that the word also was used to denote the end result of something, the desired product, associations that reverberate in the poem's many allusions to spiritual fruitfulness and cultivation. If the dreamer's early expressions of grief can be described as the barren harvest of his sorrow, then the poem that begins "Perle, plesaunte to prynces paye" surely can suggest true fruit, the bountiful harvest of love and labor.

Finally, and most importantly, the poet's emphasis upon time implies that the dreamer himself is in his eleventh hour. If we take the "hyȝ seysoun" as referring to the Feast of the Assumption, celebrated on August 15, the sun has indeed just entered the eleventh sign, Virgo, symbolized by a woman bearing sheaves of grain.[18] It is not improbable that the poet intends an annual cycle organized around the period from spring to harvest or around the sun's movement through the zodiac of human labor. First, medievel writers had many ways of organizing time, depending, in each case, upon the message they sought to illustrate. In his introductory remarks to *The Golden Legend,* Jacobus de Voragine

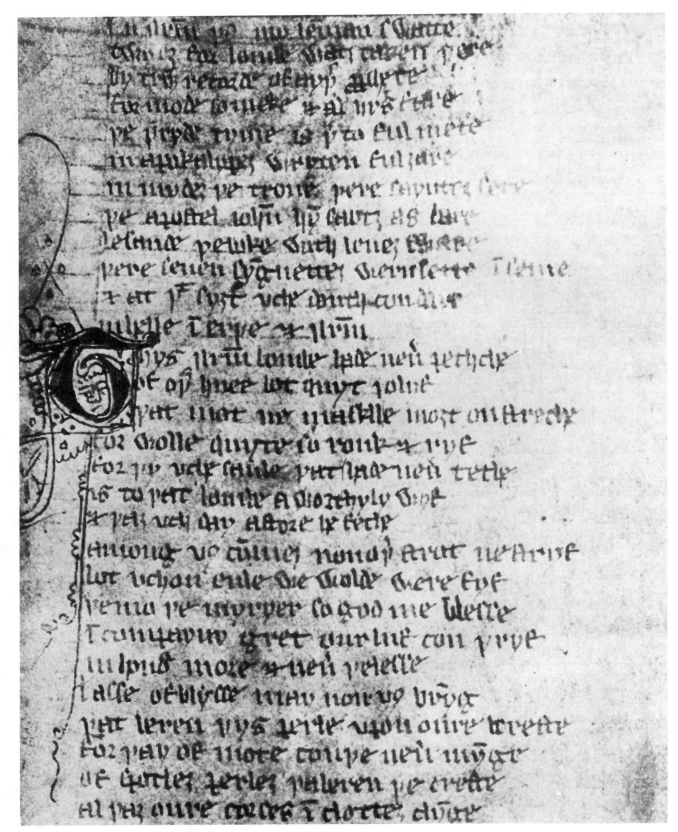

Lines 829-57 from the Cotton MS. Nero A.x. of Pearl.

uses a cycle that begins in winter with Advent and ends in fall; the poet's description of autumn in *Sir Gawain* directly contrasts seasonal change and the idea of harvest with natural fruitfulness, or implicitly, with human activity. Moreover, the Parable of the Vineyard at the center of **Pearl** focuses upon the sun's movement from dawn to evening or from first light to last. The poet's choice of August as the month for the dreamer's experience is particularly significant in relation to the picture outlined by the maiden's parable; a man gathering grapes is a sign for September, for Libra, when the equinox occurs, thus signalling days of shorter duration. If September corresponds to sundown, then August, like evensong, occurs in the last hour of light.

The August date of the poem marks the dreamer as sorely in need of an eleventh-hour work permit.[19] Whereas he is initially content to sleep (and, ironically enough, to inhabit a garden we associate with an earlier season of the year and other occupations) while all around him the fields are white with harvest, the maiden urges upon him timely labor, August's spiritual work that must precede the balance scales of September. The maiden's appearance is, however, timely in more ways than one, for, while the dreamer exists in a state of disharmony with the natural cycle, she verifies the essential orderliness of the natural cycle even as she bears witness to a realm whose cycles transcend our own. The dreamer's description of himself as a laborer in the closing lines of the poem, therefore, highlights his own awareness of time, a recognition of its use. By stepping away from the artificial spring he at first inhabits and by leaving the love-garden of his self-involved grief, he steps into his true place, a field whose ripe grain awaits the worker. Furthermore, if the dreamer's perception of the movement from August to September or his genuine comprehension of time serves as a catalyst for his spiritual transformation, the poem functions as such a reminder for its audience. Just as the maiden offers the dreamer the clemency figured in Virgo, the poem, like a true calendar, fulfills its end, rooting us in and reminding us of time and the uses of time, only to impel us beyound time to timeless harvests.

Notes

[1] See my study, *The Voice of the* Gawain-*Poet* (Madison: The University of Wisconsin Press, 1984), pp. 40-69.

[2] *Pearl,* ed. E. V. Gordon (Oxford: Clarendon Press, 1953, rpt., 1970). All quotations from *Pearl* refer to this edition and are cited by line number within the text.

[3] For a brief discussion of these suggestions, see William Vantuono's comments on lines 39-40 in *The Pearl Poems: An Omnibus Edition, Vol.1*: Pearl *and* Clean-ness, ed. W. Vantuono, The Renaissance Imagination, No. 5 (New York: Garland Publishing, 1984), p. 220. For Moorman's more etymological remarks, see his comment on the line in *Pearl* in *The Works of the Gawain-Poet,* ed. Charles Moorman (Jackson: University of Mississippi Press, 1977).

[4] See particularly Ian Bishop, Pearl *in Its Setting* (Oxford: Basil Blackwell, 1968), p. 86; Theodore Bogdanos, Pearl: *Image of the Ineffable* (University Park: The Pennsylvania State University Press, 1983), p. 27.

[5] *On the Properties of Things, John Trevisa's translation of Bartholomaeus Anglicus' De Proprietatibus Rerum,* (Oxford: Clarendon Press, 1975), I, 532, hereafter cited as Trevisa. For discussions of the iconography of the Labors of the Months, see Emile Mâle, *The Gothic Image: Religious Art in France of the Thirteenth Century* trans. from 3rd ed. by Dora Nussey (1913; rpt. New York: Harper and Row, 1958), pp. 72-93; Rosemond Tuve, *Seasons and Months: Studies in a Tradition of Middle English Poetry* (Totowa, New Jersey: Rowman and Littlefield, 1976).

[6] Trevisa, I, 517-518.

[7] Tuve, *Seasons and Months,* p. 122.

[8] For this tradition, see the collection recently edited and translated by B. A. Windeatt, *Chaucer's Dream Poetry: Sources and Analogues* (Totowa, New Jersey: Rowman and Littlefield, 1982). Here I except Nicole de Margival's *Le Dit de la Panthere d'Amours,* c. 1300, which Windeatt also includes in this collection; this poem, like *Pearl,* is set at harvest time on the eve of the Feast of the Assumption. For discussions of the spring setting for poems recounting visions, love visions in particular, see Tuve's remarks in *Seasons and Months,* pp. 110-11; in addition, see A. B. Giamatti, *The Earthly Paradise and the Renaissance Epic* (Princeton: Princeton University Press, 1966, rpt. 1969), Chapter 1; Marc M. Pelen, "Form and Meaning of the Old French Love Vision: the *Fableau dou Dieu d'Amours* and Chaucer's *Parliament of Fowls,*" *The Journal of Medieval and Renaissance Studies* 9 (1979): 277-305; J. I. Wimsatt, "Chaucer and French Poetry," in *Geoffrey Chaucer: Writers and Their Background,* ed. Derek Brewer (Athens: Ohio University Press, 1975).

[9] On literary influence, see Thomas M. Greene, *The Light in Troy* (New Haven: Yale University Press, 1982), particularly the remarks on pp. 48-53. For a differently directed study from my own concerning the relationship between elements of the *Romance of the Rose* and *Parl,* see Herbert Pilch, "The Middle English *Pearl:* Its Relation to the *Roman de la Rose,*" in *The Middle English Pearl: Critical Essays,* ed. John Conley

(Notre Dame: University of Notre Dame Press, 1970), pp. 163-84.

[10] On the characteristic details of medieval literary gardens, see D. W. Robertson, Jr., "The Doctrine of Charity in Mediaeval Literary Gardens: A Topical Approach through Symbolism and Allegory," *Speculum* 26 (1951): 24-49. On the garden in *The Romance of the Rose,* see John V. Fleming, *The Roman de la Rose: A Study in Allegory and Iconography* (Princeton: Princeton University Press, 1969), Chapter 2: *"The Hortus Deliciarum."* See also Charles Dahlberg's remarks in his edition, *The Romance of the Rose* (Princeton: Princeton University Press, 1971), Notes to Chapter 1, pp. 357-65.

[11] *The Romaunt of the Rose* in *The Riverside Chaucer,* ed. Larry D. Benson (Boston: Houghton Mifflin Co., 1987), 1436. The description of the garden is found in lines 1349-1438.

[12] For an understanding of the ways in which these plants appear in medieval writing, see the entries for each of them in the *Middle English Dictionary,* ed. Sherman M. Kuhn (Ann Arbor: The University of Michigan Press). Sir Israel Gollancz in his edition of *Pearl* (1891; rpt. New York: Cooper Square Publishers, 1966), p. 120, also makes this point about the gromwell. For a study of the details of this site, see C. A. Luttrell, "Pearl: Symbolism in a Garden Setting," in *The Middle English Pearl,* pp. 297-324. Luttrell (p. 311) also notes the harvest time opening in *Le Dit de la Panthere.* See also, Bogdanos, *Ineffable,* pp. 23-26.

[13] See Pierre Courcelle, *Les Confessions de Saint Augustin dans la tradition litteraire* (Paris, 1963). As Courcelle notes, the same cathedral has a life of Saint Cuthbert, for which (see B. Colgrave, "The Saint Cuthbert Paintings on the Carlisle Cathedral Stalls," *Burlington Magazine* 73 [1938]: 17) the artist copied the miniatures of a "Life" from the late twelfth century. It is, as Courcelle remarks, probable that the same is the case for the life of St. Augustine; the conception of scenes, iconography, and form seem to evoke the illustrations of the "epoque romane." For any analysis of *Pearl,* especially the link between that poem and the motif of the *Noli me tangere* that I have suggested in *The Voice of the* Gawain *Poet* (pp. 148-78), the inscriptions for two of the scenes in this "Life" are particularly tantalizing. The inscription for a scene depicting Augustine and Alypius in the garden includes the following details: "Her sore wepying for hys gret syn / He went to morne a garth wythin." For the "Tolle, lege," the inscription is noted: "Her wepyng and walyng as he lay / Sodenly a voice thus herd he say: Tolle, lege, tolle lege." Both inscriptions emphasize the sorrow that precedes recognition and conversion, for Augustine is cast, like Mary Magdalene or the *Pearl* dreamer, as a mourner in a garden.

[14] Just how purposeful are these lines is even more apparent if we compare them, not only to the opening stanzas of French love visions, but to the opening of Boccaccio's "Olympia," a poem whose similarity to *Pearl* suggests *Pearl's* elegiac form and purpose.

[15] For a discussion of the poet's use of the "eleventh hour" to describe the maiden's status in the vineyard, see D. W. Robertson, Jr., "The 'Heresy' of *The Pearl,*" in *The Middle English Pearl,* pp. 291-96. As Roberson notes, the maiden seems to follow Bruno Astensis' lead in associating the "eleventh hour" with those individuals baptized only shortly before death rather than with those who become Christians in old age. I concur with Robertson's reading of the passage, but would like to suggest that we apply the parable to the dreamer whose life, like any life, can be divided into twelve hours. For the "eleventh hour" as a time of day, see Chauncey Wood, *Chaucer and the Country of the Stars* (Princeton: Princeton University Press, 1970), p. 294; see also C. R. Cheney, *Handbook of Dates for Students of English History* (London: Office of the Royal Historical Society, 1945, rpt. 1970), p. 9.

[16] Trevisa, I, 533. In *The Pearl: An Interpretation* (New York: Barnes and Noble, 1967) p. 52, P. M. Kean associates the labor of the parable with March or early Spring, especially since the maiden describes the workers as cutting and tying up the vines: "Wryþen and worchen and don gret pyne, / Keruen and caggen and man hit clos" (*Pearl,* 511-12). There are, however, several reasons for linking the labor of the parable to fall, despite the fact that pruning was assigned to March in the schema of the Labors of the Months. (On March, see Trevisa, I, 530; Mâle, *The Gothic Image,* p. 71; Tuve, *Seasons and Months,* pp. 161-62.) First, the pruning ascribed to March could involve trees or vines whereas the more specific image of the vineyard was linked to September. Second, though it is unlikely the poet had any direct experience of viticulture, Virgil in the *Georgics* (Book II, 397ff.) recommends dressing the vines three or four times a year, contending that the soil should be broken up and the grove lightened of its foliage. He then notes that the vines should be cut and pruned into shape in the fall. On vinedressing and pruning in the fall, see also William Robert Prince, *Treatise on the Vine* (New York, 1830), pp. 276-281. Furthermore, as Fernande Braudel points out in *The Structure of Everyday life* (vol. 1 of *Civilization and Capitalism,* trans. and revised by Sian Reynolds [New York: Harper and Row, 1979], p. 487), fall was the season in which landowners most frequently hired day laborers, the season, in fact, when the scene described in the parable was likely to have been a common one in the agricultural districts of Europe. However tempting it is to speculate about the reality that may underlie the poet's fiction, I think his account of the labors of the vineyard has more to do with commentaries on the Parable of the Vineyard than with medieval agricul-

tural practices. Most obviously, his description of the labor is general enough to suggest how little he knew about such matters, particularly if we juxtapose this section of *Pearl* with certain passages of *Sir Gawain,* wherein he demonstrates a more intimate knowledge of the customs of late fourteenth-century aristocratic life. More importantly, if we turn to the commentaries on the Parable of the Vineyard, we find the labor in the vineyard depicted in general terms, emphasizing its strenuousness and focusing on the broader issues of cultivation and fruitfulness. By interpreting the vineyard as a figure for the Church or for the Kingdom of Heaven, the commentators stress the theme of harvest, directing our attention to our duties in the time left before the twelfth and final hour. Thus, the laborers' complaint in the parable that those who have borne the day's heat should receive the same wage as those who began work at the eleventh hour, together with the parable's inherent urgency, evokes a scene near the end of the yearly agricultural cycle. For comentaries on the parable, see St. Augustine, Sermo LXXXVII in *Sermones de Scripturis, PL* 38, cols, 530-39; Bede, *In Matthaei Evangelium Expositio, PL* 92, cols. 87-88; St. Gregory, Hom. XIX in *XL Homiliarum in Evangelia, PL* 76, cols. 1153-59; Rabanus Maurus, *Comment. in Matthaeum, PL* 107, cols. 1025-30. Finally, the poet may have taken a hint from St. Gregory in linking the parable to a particular month; near the end of his sermon, Gregory, in exhorting his hearers to penance, specifically relates his audience. He says: "Mense autem Julio nuper elapso, hujus quam nostis pestilentiae clade percussus est, qui, ad extremum veniens, urgeri coepit ut animam redderet" (col. 1158).

[17] See Wood, *Chaucer and the Country of the Stars,* pp. 272-97, for a discussion of Libra. In his massive encyclopedia, the *Reductorium Morale* (Colona, 1730), Petrus Berchorius says of September, "Iste mensis significat diem judicii" V, p. 128). In discussing Libra (p. 108), Berchorius says: "Quando Sol est in libra, tunc facit noctes & dies aequos, & ideo dicitur libra, quia monstrat ponderum aequitatem. Sic vere quando Judex est in libra justitiae, tunc necessario facit aequinoctium, i.e. aequale judicium inter virum & proximum suum, alias non. Vel dic, quod quando Sol, i.e. Christus ascendet signum librae, i.e. thronum judicii, ubi facta omnium librabit & ponderabit."

[18] See Trevisa's remarks about the appropriate signs for both August and September (I, 1, 532-33). For remarks linking the Feast of the Assumption to this same issue of fruitfulness, see Bruno Astensis, "De Humilitate," in *Sententiae,* Lib. II, v, *PL* 165, col. 198.

[19] The dreamer's idleness in the midst of an August harvest may also have been charged with more immediate ironies for the poem's first audience; as Georges Duby in *Rural Economy and Country Life in the Medieval West* (trans. Cynthia Postan, Columbia, South

Carolina: University of South Carolina Press, Book IV, "Change and Upheaval in the XVth Century") points out, harvest time was a period of real activity throughout rural England, a time when each potential laborer was pressed into service.

Sarah Stanbury (essay date 1991)

SOURCE: "Gazing Toward Jerusalem: Space and Perception in *Pearl*," in *Seeing the Gawain-Poet: Description and the Act of Perception,* University of Pennsylvania Press, 1991, pp. 12-41.

[*In the following essay, Stanbury describes the poem as an allegorical fiction and compares it to the pilgrimage-narrative genre of travel literature and to the tradition of medieval illustrated Apocalypses.*]

Pearl is a story of a journey to Jerusalem. Like popular narrative accounts of actual pilgrimages—526 accounts of journeys to Jerusalem have survived from the period 1100 to 1500—*Pearl*'s itinerary culminates in a sacred city and also takes its pilgrim to that holy city through an exotic land of marvels. The diaries and narratives in which pilgrims logged their impressions are filled with details of exotic experiences; and as Donald Howard has shown in his discussion of pilgrimage narratives, they record graphic visual details of distant places.[1] William von Boldensele, a German Dominican whose record of his 1332-33 pilgrimage to the Holy Land was a major source for John Mandeville's mid fourteenth-century *Travels,* dwells at length on elephants, on the Dead Sea, and on the wonders of bananas.[2] Of the pilgrimage accounts surviving from 1100 to 1300, many to be sure are little more than itineraries of places visited. Yet in the fourteenth century, which Howard labels the great age of pilgrimage narrative, accounts of travels to the Holy Land came to describe the sights, delights, and curiosities of travel as they struck the imagination of the pilgrim. Pilgrimage narratives became personal records, recounted as direct experience—"I saw," "I heard"—and describing new places in the language of wonder.

In *Pearl,* of course, the narrator's journey to the heavenly city is an allegorical fiction cast in the conventional modes of a dream vision and a journey to the Otherworld. Nevertheless, the dream is recorded in the rhetoric of discovery.[3] Like the pilgrims' diaries, *Pearl* offers a visual record of experience, centering the perception and interpretation of what is seen on a single fictional witness, the narrator/jeweler recording his dream. Recounting his vision, the narrator repeatedly describes his encounters with the strange and the marvelous in sensory terms and consistently organizes descriptions according to his own eyes, senses, and emotions. When he first describes the transformed valley, he describes the paradox of being "lost" in a place that nevertheless offers vivid sensory cues: "I ne wyste [knew] in þis worlde quere þat hit wace, / Bot I knew me keste þer klyfeȝ cleuen [rose aloft]" (65-66). Being "lost" allows for a new kind of knowledge, one marked by the certain grasp of sensory phenomena. All the dreamer can know of his location is his placement in relation to a set of spatial properties—in this case, the cliffs that rise above him.

If we understand *Pearl* to be not just a dream vision but also a work of travel literature—in fact a pilgrimage narrative—it can help us account not only for the treatment of specific images, in particular the image of the New Jerusalem, but also for the extraordinary control the narrator's senses exert over the poem's presentation of spatial relationships. Much as the poet's contemporaries were delighting in actual discoveries of the wonders of the East, *Pearl*'s narrator also becomes a pilgrim, one self-consciously engaged in the discovery of new worlds. The descriptions of the paradisal landscape and the New Jerusalem are not simply visions but precise visualizations, recording a process of apprehension through the fiction of an imaginary extraterrestrial world. The methodology of that process is as significant for understanding the poem as are the artifacts described.[4] The dream in *Pearl* is a visual drama in which the details of the landscape are optically coherent, focused according to the visual resolution of a fictional viewer. Terms for sight, such as "I saugh," "I loked," appear every few lines in the description of the New Jerusalem, which is described as a visual apotheosis that imitates a vision: "As John þe apostel hit syȝ wyth syȝt, / I syȝe þat cyty of gret renoun" (985-986).[5] Even the dreamer's final act, and the one that awakens him from his vision, is described as a response to sensory and especially visual stimuli, for he tries to ford the stream when "[d]elyt me drof in yȝe and ere" (1153). Throughout the poem, references to the narrator's faculties of sight and hearing reiterate that *Pearl* is a record of a private experience, one known subjectively on the level of sensation. Through descriptions of things that are seen and through references to sight itself, the poet centers the *Pearl* narrator in a visual and sensory scenario, tying descriptive detail to the narrator's fictional acts of perception.

In this chapter, I examine the poet's sensory map of his pilgrimage by looking at the relationships between description and eyewitness in several of the poem's lavish descriptive passages. In its presentation of a series of focused or focalized descriptive scenes, I will argue, the text of *Pearl* reveals and communicates acts of perception. *Pearl* is a poem in part about sight; yet sight in this poem is enacted throughout by its twin valences, sight as sensory faculty and as spiritual metaphor, vision and visionary, and perception itself is realized as a complex and multivalent experience.

Through the subjective voice of the dreamer, *Pearl* dramatizes the aporia between visual experience and other ways of knowing, such as the instruction by doctrine the Maiden provides. In contrast with other texts that have been suggested as models for *Pearl*'s genre, *Pearl* is singular in its use of visual perception to structure the narrative.[6] Indeed, *Pearl* resists easy categorization by genre, for although it has been called a dream vision,[7] a vision of the Otherworld,[8] and also a "carefully structured poetic account of a spiritual itinerary culminating in an ecstasy of mystical contemplation,"[9] it remains strikingly original, especially in its sensory reification of the New Jerusalem and in the termination of its vision through, paradoxically, the stimuli of sensation, marked by the dreamer's account of sensory excess, "[d]elyt me drof in yȝe and ere." The narrator's physical presence in the text is not only intrusive but also volatile, finally subverting, as he wills to cross the stream, the very visionary system that controls what he sees.

A brief look at the debate about *Pearl*'s visionary system can help to outline some of the mystical and contemplative patterns that the descriptive itinerary of the poem both replicates and resists. Readers have attempted to identify the poem's spiritual mode, relating the narrator's transitional experience to contemplative methodologies that would have been widely known in the poet's time. Augustine, Aquinas, Hugh of Saint Victor, and Bonaventure, who all offer contemplative programs that demonstrate the ways sensory perceptions can aid in the process of spiritual ascent, divide the experience of spiritual realignment into stages, normally three. Augustine divides the spirit hierarchically into memory, understanding, and will, stages that arguably conform to the states of the dreamer in *Pearl* as he moves in spirit from the *erber* to the paradisal landscape to the New Jerusalem.[10] The dreamer's spiritual progress also corresponds in suggestive ways to the stages of the history of the world as they were widely understood in the Middle Ages, the *lex naturalis* or law of nature (the garden), the *lex scripta* or law of scripture (the debate), and the *tempus gratiae* or time of grace (the New Jerusalem).[11] The dreamer moves from a world of nature through scriptural indoctrination into a revelation of the Heavenly City, a gift of grace at the end of history.

The mystical itineraries of Hugh of Saint Victor and of Saint Bonaventure also map stages of understanding, but are particularly interesting for understanding *Pearl* in the way they address the apparent contradictions inherent in using sensory experience to understand something that is incorporeal. Hugh of Saint Victor describes three levels of cognition: cogitation, meditation, and contemplation.[12] In the stage of contemplation, the mind "comprehends all with clear vision" [manifesta visione comprehendit], attaining perfected sight that can be compared to the dreamer's clear and scripturally authorized vision of the Heavenly City.[13] In his *Itinerarium mentis in deum,* Bonaventure details in a carefully schematized narrative the steps one can take from apprehension of natural form, realized as God's *Vestigia* or traces in the corporeal and especially natural world, to a spiritual vision of God. Like Hugh, Bonaventure also describes the ascent as a threefold process, or a movement through corporeal, spiritual, and divine realms. As Louis Blenkner points out in his study of the application of these contemplative strategies to *Pearl,* Bonaventure also says that in mystical ascent we move from without to within to above, a progression that applies aptly to the Middle English poem.[14] The dreamer's progress can be mapped as a movement from without the *erber* to the vision above, the New Jerusalem that descends from the sky. Indeed, of the mystical treatises available to the poet of *Pearl,* Bonaventure's *Itinerarium* may be its closest analogue. In addition to offering an account of spiritual ascent that proceeds by gradations and transitions, the *Itinerarium* also offers one of the best known and most concise manuals on the use of sensible form in spiritual ascent. Bonaventure maintains that the contemplative must first learn to see and delight in God's creation before he can proceed upward to the next stage of the hierarchy: "Therefore, from visible things the soul rises to the consideration of the power, wisdom, and goodness of God" (*Itin.* 1.13, 46-47).[15] The process of contemplation begins with the "first way of seeing," the consideration of things in themselves, which reveal information about weight, number, and measure (*Itin.* 1.11, 44-45).

Yet the *Itinerarium* does not, like *Pearl,* culminate in a clear and ecstatic vision of God or the Heavenly City. Rather, Bonaventure says that the contemplative progresses from sight of corporeal things to a sight of inner verities, effectively transcending reliance on sensory faculties. The condition of our lives is one of being a *viator* or wayfarer (*Itin.* 7.2, 96-97), and when we have reached "peace" we have arrived "as in an inner Jerusalem" ("tanquam in interiori Hierosolyma" [*Itin.* 7.1, 96-97]) apprehended only metaphorically through the darkness of "supreme illumination": "Thus our mind, accustomed as it is to the opaqueness in beings and the phantasms of visible things, appears to be seeing nothing when it gazes upon the light of the highest being. It does not understand that this very darkness is the supreme illumination of our mind, just as when the eye sees pure light, it seems to be seeing nothing" (*Itin.* 5.4, 82-83).[16] Instead of constructing a vision of Jerusalem or of suggesting that we can see the city, Bonaventure uses Jerusalem as a metaphor, "as in an inner Jerusalem," for a spiritual state. In the final state of mystical transport we abandon the senses and "ascend to the superessential gleam of the divine darkness by an incommensurable and absolute transport of a pure mind" (*Itin.* 7.5, 100-101).[17]

Pearl's use of a visionary who continues throughout the poem to visualize and respond to sensory forms dramatizes the conflicts of human perception even more poignantly than it illustrates mystical transport and consolation. This fact may account for the poem's originality and resistance to easy classification by genre. The dreamer's serial perceptions of focused scenes describe not only objective correlatives of his spiritual progress but also his infatuation with physical forms, a condition for which the Maiden faults him early in her discourse. She scolds the dreamer for believing what he sees, or more specifically for believing that she is a corporeal being to whose side of the stream he can cross:

> I halde þat iueler lyttel to prayse
> Þat leueʒ wel þat he seʒ wyth yʒe.
>
> (301-302)[18]

Refining her critique of the dreamer, she goes on to explain that reliance on sight or one's "one skyl" is a point of pride:

> ʒe setten hys wordeʒ ful westernays
> Þat leueʒ noþynk bot ʒe hit syʒe.
> And þat is a poynt o sorquydryʒe,
> Þat vche god mon may euel byseme,
> To leue no tale be true to tryʒe
> Bot þat hys one skyl may dem.
>
> (307-312)[19]

This argument is an exhortation to what we might call ocular skepticism. Her terms, that he should not entirely trust what he sees and also that he should have faith in things even if he cannot see them, echo the Chaucerian commonplace most precisely articulated in the Prologue to *The Legend of Good Women*: "But God forbede but men shulde leve / Wel more thing then men han seen with ye" (*Legend of Good Women* F, 10-12).[20] Her complaint also sets forth the dreamer's central epistemological dilemma in terms that would have been very familiar to a fourteenth- or fifteenth-century reader. In the Maiden's analysis, the dreamer's perceptual problem is one of relying on experience rather than authority. Authority here is not, of course, the validation given by books, but the authority of Scripture, the one book, or the validation of faith. Nevertheless, by centering perception on the dreamer, together with the primary interpretation of what is seen or heard, the poet exploits a technique of narrative engagement that subverts the Maiden's text on ocular skepticism without offering an alternative epistemological model, dramatizing rather a crisis of interpretation. The method of the dreamer's visionary process is vision itself, a faculty that is finally selfconsuming when sense impressions seduce him to attempt to ford the stream, and he awakens.

Seeing in the Garden

In spite of the Pearl Maiden's suggestion that the dreamer discredit visual perception in favor of knowledge of God to be gained through faith and Scripture, the vision in its entirety progresses as a dynamic between sensory perception, interpretation, and reaction— principally a joyful yearning that leads the dreamer both physically and metaphorically upward. In **Pearl,** in fact, the dreamer's spiritual progress mirrors his sensory, and chiefly visual, itinerary. The narrator's record of focused descriptive scenes, his attention to sensory detail, and his suspended recognition of his location are specular acts, serving to center reception and interpretation of the visionary landscape self-reflexively on the viewer.[21] But the process of perception is itself dynamic and transitional, even though the dreamer's submission to sense perception at first precludes an active search for consolation. Through the mechanics of visual sensation and an altering perception of the dimensions of his fictive physical space, the dreamer reveals his spiritual condition even as his acts of sensory perception themselves prompt a system of change.

The use of focused description to reveal and define the spatial relationships between the dreamer and his locations appears not only in the paradisal landscape, but also in the *erber,* as the narrator immediately establishes that the garden is a circumscribed space in which he is the central figure. This enclosed space serves both as the locus of the jeweler's spiritual change and as a metaphor for his spiritual stasis. The narrator at the first encloses his own troubled spirit within an enclosed garden, mourning the loss of a tiny pearl that paradoxically seems to enclose or subsume both the emotional and physical space of the poem. When the jeweler/dreamer enters the *erber,* he crosses into what was for the Middle Ages one of the most familiar images of enclosed space, that of the *hortus conclusus,* the enclosed Eden of the Fall (*Deduit*), a garden of earthly delight. But this garden, structured around mementos of mourning, is the place of the jeweler's spiritual transition; and in fact, as the imagery of decay and regeneration in the description suggests (lines 29-36), the garden, though structured as a fixed space, belongs to the realm of mutability. The experience the narrator relates, however, is one of physical stasis, where his acts of sensory perception in the *erber* oppose either physical or spiritual change. In contrast to the ensuing description of the paradisal landscape, the description of the *erber* includes few focused visual impressions, and instead is descriptively characterized by lists, such as the short catalogue of flowers, "Gilofre, gyngure and gromylyoun, / And pyonys powdered ay bytwene" (43-44) [gilly-flower, ginger and gromwell, and peonies scattered everywhere between], and by diffuse sense impressions, such as the vague "odour" (58) that finally precipitates his swoon. The few spe-

cific visual details that the *erber* section provides serve to frame and define this space less in relation to the narrator's senses than in relation to cosmic or temporal dimensions.[22] Flowers of the *erber,* for instance, shine against the sun. It is August, a temporal location the poet reinforces by an allusion to pastoral activity, the reaping of grain, outside the garden in the realm of mutability. Within the garden, sense impressions are dominated by emotions, the dreamer's psychic torment. Grain is cut (40), the pearl trundles down the hill (41), flowers cast shadows (42), he collapses (57); the vertical motion is downward.[23]

When the narrator embarks on his journey through a visionary realm, the split between his physical stasis, asleep on a grave in an enclosed garden, and visionary motion repeats the very structural incongruities of the *erber* itself. Presented entirely as an eyewitness account and with minute attention to visual detail as recorded through natural perspective, the spatial construction of the dreamer's account of the earthly paradise as he becomes a pilgrim to Jerusalem undergoes a subtle but important shift. By detailing juxtapositions in the dreamer's visual focus, imaginary motion, and physical stasis, the description of the paradisal garden communicates, as does description in the *erber,* that the dreamer's understanding of spiritual verities parallels his perception of space: what he believes permanent is in fact transitional. No longer the fixed and central figure in a walled garden, the dreamer looks up as well as down and moves linearly, "as fortune fares," across a changing terrain. Whereas the descriptive frame of the *erber,* an enclosed garden that evokes the "imprisoned" pearl [*spenned,* 53], seems metonymic for the narator's own spirit, home of warring emotions, the "fyrce skylleʒ þat faste faʒt" (54), the spatial system of his dream expands dramatically. In his dream he gives himself over to fortune and the grace of God:

> Fro spot my spyryt þer sprang in space;
> My body on balke þer bod in sweuen.
> My goste is gon in Godeʒ grace
> In auenture þer meruayleʒ meuen.
>
> (61-64)[24]

The dreamer now moves in a horizontal direction, never knowing quite what he will find around the next cliff or bend in the river. In contrast to the vertical and circular axes that shape the *erber,* this horizontal plane in the paradisal garden dramatizes the dreamer's enhanced sensory responsiveness as well as his release from the earlier emotional self-absorption and physical stasis.

Just as the addition of a horizontal plane reflects the dreamer's motion, an altered construction of vertical dimensions also indicates the developing perceptual acuity of his eye. In the *erber* the spatial axes repeatedly reveal vertical and especially descending motion, yet in the earthly paradise the dreamer's gaze and his very steps move both up and down in response to his wondering appraisal of sensory forms. Governing the composition of the text's spatial relationships, his gaze reveals a methodology of perception that mirrors his mind. For example, his initial awareness of his spirit's location in a place "þer klyfeʒ cleuen" indicates an altered perception of himself in relation to the space he inhabits. Suddenly he is a small figure surrounded by cliffs that rise above him. No longer focusing exclusively or even myopically on mementos of his personal loss, he perceives the relationships and agencies of light, as his eye seems to follow patterns of illumination. He first notices the cliffs rising above him gleaming luminously. When he takes a closer look, he perceives how the trees and leaves that adorn the cliff sides take their beauty from the movement and reflection of light:

> Quen glem of glodeʒ agaynʒ hem glydeʒ,
> Wyth schymeryng schene ful schrylle þay
>   schynde.
> Þe grauayl þat on grounde con grynde
> Wern precious perleʒ of oryente:
> Þe sunnebemeʒ bot blo and blynde
> In respecte of þat adubbement.
>
> (79-84)[25]

The careful visual focusing in this magnificent descriptive passage not only locates the fictional observer—the dreamer—but it also comments on his processes of enhanced perception, suggesting that perception of the world (Bonaventure's *vestigia*) is metonymic for the psychic or moral life.[26] The dreamer's gaze is led by motion and reflection, for his account of the gravel of pearls has a visual analogue in the leaves moving against the illuminated background of the sky. In contrast to the references to light in the *erber,* which describe illumination only through shadows and reflection ("Þer schyneʒ ful schyr agayn þe sunne" [28]; "Schadowed þis worteʒ [plants]" [42]), The dreamer's gaze moves in all directions, perceiving the varying illuminations of leaves and pebbles against a backdrop of still greater brilliance.

The pattern of upward and downward glances that characterizes the dreamer's gaze in lines 79 to 84 is repeated and amplified in stanza 10 when he looks at the gemstones lining the riverbed and compares them to stars:

> In þe founce þer stonden stoneʒ stepe,
> As glente þurʒ glas þat glowed and glyʒt,
> As stremande sterneʒ, quen stroþe-men slepe,
> Staren in welkyn in wynter nyʒt.
>
> (113-116)[27]

In an even clearer reference to the analogues between the objects of this world and celestial bodies, this pas-

sage repeats the pattern of the dreamer's gaze—although the vividly realized image of "stremande strneʒ" is only a long simile—with emphasis on the gaze of the fictional viewer. *Stroþe* is translated as swampy and overgrown land, and according to Gordon's note, "would probably carry with it also, pictorially, a suggestion of the dark, low earth onto which the high stars look down."[28] The sense of great distances between heaven and earth is also enhanced by the verb *slepe,* for the stars *stremande,* or streaming with light, and *staren,* or staring, assert power and motion independent of human concerns. Paradoxically, however, the fact that the stars "stare" while people sleep also emphasizes the act of sensory perception; because the viewers are asleep, we are even more aware of an imaginative eye that looks simultaneously up at the celestial motion, horizontally at the sleepers, and literally down at the pebbles in the pool.

The topography of the dreamer's paradisal landscape is thus vastly more complex than that of the *erber* in which his body literally lies, for it contains a vertical axis of trees and cliffs, and (in a simile) stars, as well as a horizontal plane that transforms as the dreamer moves through the valley. Spatially complex as it is, however, the description of the valley is as systematically tied to the senses and perceptual system of a single consciousness as is the description of the *erber*. The description of the landscape thus suggests that the dreamer who sees should also interpret; yet his interpretive skills or inclinations seem suspended, a silencing that itself offers a partial reading of his stance as an interpreter of sensory forms. His role as visionary in a sensory drama seems in part to comment on the processes of sensory awakening, on the psychic drama of the soul's progressive discovery of divinity through the tuning of the outer senses to the world. Like Bonaventure's Wayfarer in the *Itinerarium,* he embarks on a spiritual pilgrimage, the first steps of which involve rediscovery of sensory harmony; and if the dreamer simply records those perceptions with little interpretive commentary, that record itself glosses a process, that of learning how to see.

The Vision of the New Jerusalem

In the final four stanza groups of **Pearl,** the dreamer returns to direct sensory apprehension after the twelve groups spent in verbal debate with the Maiden. His record of the New Jerusalem, of the Lamb within, and of the procession of the virgins thus recalls, by a simple structural parallel, the descriptions of the garden and landscape at the beginning. The dreamer's emotional and visual frameworks immediately appear to be radically altered. As he describes the City, not only are his physical senses suspended, at least at first, but he is also bodily at a remove from the object of vision. The perspective of the dreamer's gaze contrasts sharply with his angle of sight in the *erber,* where he is the central presence in the garden. His vision of the New Jerusalem, where the Lamb, the City, and his Pearl are all removed from himself, on one level testifies to his enhanced intellectual understanding of death and redemption. With the stream the boundary between the world of creatures and the rule of eternity is clearly set, and God's kingdom, the Heavenly City, awaits the just man.

Yet the process by which the vision of the Heavenly City is recorded also dramatizes a crisis, the dreamer's separation from the perfect proportions and harmony he perceives. During his vision of the New Jerusalem, the dreamer records two very different responses to his vision. After he has surveyed the building rising in elevation, brilliant with its own light, and has visually penetrated to the throne at the center, he stands astonished, as still "as a dazed quail." He is enraptured; he feels no bodily sensations, "nawþer reste ne trauayle." Later, however, after he watches the procession of virgins, his emotions change. He sees not simply the edifice of the city but also the mystery that yokes eternity with human pity. He is stricken with delight. He first grieves at the bleeding Lamb—"alas, þoʒt I, who did þat spyt?" (1138), then rejoices at the hundred thousand virgins. Finally, when he spots his "lyttel quene" among the company, delight driving in through his "eye and ear" gives way to frenzy, and he rushes into the stream.

Nowhere in *Pearl* is the reader more aware than in these two scenes of the dreamer's bodily relationship to space. Led by the Pearl Maiden, he stands on a hill across a stream as he watches the New Jerusalem descending from the sky, just as John watches in the Book of Revelation. Because the poet makes repeated references to the dreamer's emotional responses to what he sees during these three stanza groups that comprise the vision of the New Jerusalem, the reader is regularly reminded that the vision is being recorded by an eyewitness, a human eye-of-the-beholder who sees, but does not enter. When the Maiden promises him a vision, she expressly states, in fact, that it is a purely optical experience. He may not inhabit the space he will see:

> Þou may not enter wythinne hys tor,
> Bot of þe Lombe I have þe aquylde
> For a syʒt þerof þurʒ gret fauor.
>
> (966-968)[29]

When the dreamer spies the City, he also reiterates the visual nature of his experience, even emphasizing visionary authority. He sees as John saw:

> As John þe apostel hit syʒ wyth syʒt,
> I syʒe þat cyty of gret renoun.
>
> (985-986)[30]

> As John deuysed [described] ʒet saʒ I þare.
>
> (1021)[31]

> As John hym wryteʒ ʒet more I syʒe.
>
> (1033)[32]

In the next group the dreamer describes how his sight passes through the wall of the city, thus again reminding us of his position on the other side of the stream:

> Þurʒ woʒe and won my lokyng ʒede,
> For sotyle cler noʒt lette no lyʒt.
>
> (1049-1050)[33]

These references to sight thus create an emphatic sense that describing is a focalized, self-referential activity; even though the description is first offered as a visual artifact, with little account of his response to what he sees, the dreamer never permits his reader to forget his presence. He stands on one side of the stream, describing what exists fictively in another place.

Although he continues to refer to his own senses as organizers of his vision, "I watʒ war of a prosessyoun" (1096), "I loked among his meyny schene [fair company]" (1145), "þen saʒ I þer my lyttel quene" (1147), as the vision progresses, the dreamer increasingly describes his emotional responses:

> An-vnder mone so great merwayle
> No fleschly hert ne myʒt endeure,
> As quen I blusched vpon þat bayle,
> So ferly þerof watʒ þe fasure.
> I stod as stylle as dased quayle
> For ferly of þat frelich fygure,
> Þat felde I nawþer reste ne trauayle,
> So watʒ I rauyste wyth glymme pure.
>
> (1081-1088)[34]

References to sensation remind us that the dreamer's body is fixed in space, thus rendering this transformation of his emotions all the more poignant. This is initially a spiritual apotheosis, and the dreamer, "rauyste wyth glymme pure," recalls Dante at the summit of Paradise: "for my sight, becoming pure, was entering more and more through the beam of the lofty light which in itself is true" (*Par.* 33.52-54).[35] Yet when the dreamer witnesses the bleeding Lamb, his spiritual eye penetrating to the center of the Christian mystery, his gaze turns to his "lyttel quene" and he is overwhelmed by the "luf-longing" that tempts him to ford the water. He yearns to join not the Lamb, not Christ, but his Pearl.

A look at medieval illustrated Apocalypses, which pictorialize a dream vision narrative that culminates, as does *Pearl*, in a vision of the New Jerusalem, can add to our appreciation of the poet's descriptive achievement in this section of the narrative. The dreamer's desire to join his "lyttel quene," the desire that fractures the boundary between time *in aevo,*[36] the visionary moment, and time in the world of creatures describes a crisis, dramatized through the technique of focalized description, that is centered in the experiences of allegiances torn between sensory truth and spiritual abstraction. A similar crisis is depicted as well in the illustrated Apocalypses. As several scholars have convincingly argued, the *Pearl*-poet may well have known the illustrated cycles.[37] He was even more likely to have been familiar with commentaries on the Apocalypse. Illustrated Apocalypses were extremely popular in England in the thirteenth and early fourteenth centuries, many of them evolving into fashionable picture books for wealthy patrons.[38] Features of some Apocalypse manuscripts that also appear in *Pearl* include a bleeding Lamb, a City that is twelve furlongs (not the 12,000 furlongs of Revelation 21.16), a river that separates John from the New Jerusalem, and an angel-guide who leads and directs the visionary throughout.[39]

Pictorially, perhaps the most important feature the Apocalypse books share with *Pearl* is the treatment of the New Jerusalem, for both texts record the city graphically, either visually or verbally. This similarity is a persuasive argument that an Apocalypse manuscript or manuscripts may have afforded a source for *Pearl,* an argument that is further bolstered by the fact that *Pearl*'s description of the New Jerusalem has no analogues in Middle English narrative. Critics have often condemned the description of the City, especially the first part with the catalogue of gems, for its simple recapitulation of the biblical text,[40] yet they have not sufficiently recognized the originality of this section, detailing as it does a city that is most often cited as a spiritual abstraction.[41] Even in the few English texts where the Heavenly City is apprehended and described, the accounts are briefer and more allusive, such as the descriptions in *The Vision of Tundale* and in Walter Hilton's *Scale of Perfection,* which is actually taken from Ezekiel's vision, and not from Revelation at all.[42] The portracted description in *Pearl,* which details both the exterior construction of the City and its interior—including river, trees, virgins, and Lamb—visualizes a place and an event that were most often understood in medieval scriptural exegesis to reflect a spiritual ideal. Even though the description is clearly indebted to a pictorial tradition, in breaking with poetic conventions in its reification of the City, the description invites us in particular to examine the processes of perception that generate its images.

Perhaps the most important similarity between *Pearl* and the illustrated Apocalypses, and the one that is most suggestive for understanding *Pearl*'s attention to eyewitness experience and visual epistemology, is the treatment of the visionary himself. In the illustrated cycles, Saint John becomes an important character, more involved with the images of his vision than is the passive observer in the biblical text of Revelation. He is, as Barbara Nolan has shown, an emotionally responsive witness to the End, engaged passionally in the experience of observing and recording what he sees.[43] Not only John's emotional responses but also his spatial relationship to his vision, as conveyed by his placement graphically on the page, contribute to his role as a commentator on visionary experience in many of the Apocalypse manuscripts. In the Cloisters Apocalypse, an early fourteenth-century Continental manuscript that was based on a thirteenth-century English source and shares many features with several other manuscripts, John dominates spatially, even when he is placed to one side of the panel. In size he is usually greater than or equal to his angel-guide and is often larger than the figures he observes. This spatial dominance augments a commentary on visionary experience, for John in the illustrations, like the *Pearl* dreamer, lends individual scenes spatial coherence and ties the construction of spatial relationships to an act of fictional perception. In many manuscripts, John's placement on the page suggests that he mediates at an intersection of multiple levels of time. In the early pages of the Cloisters Apocalypse, John is often shown outside the scene entirely, standing in the margin and looking in through a door at the Court of Heaven. . . .[44] The text of Revelation describes a door open in Heaven; yet the use of the device predominantly in the early folios of the manuscript initially sets the Evangelist at a remove from his vision. The distance is further magnified by the graphic design of the page, which, though traditional, evokes three separate but simultaneous operations of time. The elders worship in rectangles; Christ in majesty sits in a mandorla, a sign of eternity; and John stands without in the realm of mutability.[45]

Similar graphics in other Apocalypse manuscripts also place John within a design that depicts the simultaneous operations of multiple levels of time, even as the design illustrates the evangelist's separation or even exclusion from the events he sees. In a page depicting the Court of Heaven in the Trinity Apocalypse, a thirteenth-century English manuscript that was seminal in the development of the English Apocalypse cycles, John stands without, separated in his own rectangle from the Court of Heaven, which itself is made of units of rectangles and circles[46]. His enclosure resembles a church, which announces John's role as a prophet of God.

The illustrated cycles, portraying as they do both the human witness and the sacred realm that he knows through sound and sight, share with *Pearl* an interest in the sensory processes of visionary experience. Their similar spatial use of an eyewitness in an encounter with images from the Apocalypse continues as John, like the *Pearl* dreamer, moves to change his dimensional relationship with what he sees, becoming spatially engaged. Led to the New Jerusalem by his angel-guide, John becomes not only a prophet but also a pilgrim on a spiritual quest. In the Cloisters and the Trinity manuscripts, the pilgrim's visionary achievement is illustrated in the final folios. First he is led by the angel up the hill, where he sees the City descending from the sky. Then he looks down in reverence, his sight penetrating to the center of the mystery as he sees Christ and the Lamb in a mandorla, the worshipers, and the river and trees of life. Trinity also illustrates the optical miracle of the City, for the New Jerusalem is depicted in both elevation and projection. The lavishly gilded illustration of the City in projection pictures John's comprehensive and penetrating vision as he witnesses the foursquare City while his sight encompasses the Lamb, the river of life, and the angel with the measuring rod.

These scenes from the Cloisters and Trinity Apocalypses depict the New Jerusalem as a spatially coherent and complex structure; and like *Pearl,* both attempt to portray that structure according to the view of a textual witness as they depict the reaction of the viewer as well as his optical process that sees through the walls to a simultaneous perception of the Lamb and the river of life. Also like *Pearl,* however, the final folios of many Apocalypse cycles frequently depict a scene of crisis, John's turn after his vision of the City to worship the angel, and the angel's redirection of John's affections to God. In the Trinity Apocalypse the angel's command, "Worship God!" touchingly illustrates the conflict between human and divine love. As John bends to the angel, the angel tenderly raises his chin to God. Human gesture is then supplanted by a gesture of worship, for at the right John kneels and folds his hands in prayer while the object of his devotion sits separated by a rectangle and mandorla in a pose of benediction.

This conflict between human and divine love is illustrated even more strikingly in a scene from a thirteenth-century French Apocalypse where John worships the angel after he has seen the wedding of the Lamb . . . .[47] This scene illustrates the second of two similar scenes in Revelation, where John falls down to worship at the feet of the angel who has shown him his vision. The first time comes after the angel tells John, "Blessed are those who are invited to the marriage supper of the Lamb" (19.9); the second follows John's vision of the New Jerusalem (22.8). Both times the angel commands John, "Worship God!" This episode was understood by some medieval commentators on the Apocalypse to illustrate the conflict between faith and the seductions of the senses, a conflict powerfully dramatized in the concluding scenes of *Pearl.* The Berengaudus commentary, a gloss of Revelation that was often used in the illustrated Apocalypses,[48] explains that John worships the angel only after those times that he has seen the union of Christ with his Church:

But when he comes to the place, where he says that the angel showed him how the bride was joined to Christ, where he says: because the marriage feast of the Lamb came, he wanted to adore the angel. And when he showed him how Holy Church, after the resurrection, will be joined to Christ, and will reign with him eternally, he wanted to adore the angel. . . . Wherefore St. John wanted to adore the angel twice, because the two unions of Holy Church with Christ were shown to him.[49]

The image of union, this commentary suggests, the yoking of man with God in the marriage of Church and Christ, inspires a human desire that repeatedly needs to be redirected to God. The dreamer's turning to his Pearl Maiden, who has been his angel-guide, may find its source in the image from Revelation and in the available commentaries, for it follows a pattern similar to John's and indicates a like frailty before a symbol of union. The symbol of spiritual marriage is made even more powerful in *Pearl* by the poet's dressing of his Pearl Maiden in white as for a wedding[50] and by the conflation of two separate scenes from Revelation—the New Jerusalem and the vision of the 144,000 virgins.

The dreamer's vision is thus one of fusion, but finally of a spiritual wedding to which he has not yet been invited. Although the aim of visionary experience, as medieval mystical handbooks describe with varying methodologies, is fusion with God and loss of self, *Pearl* finally pictures separation. The dreamer's mortality, his inhabitation of the human world, permits him to transcend the suspension of his bodily senses— "as still as a dazed quail"—and to be inflamed by love; yet his very capacity for human love causes his exclusion from the Heavenly City.

The conflict between human and divine love, described through the *Pearl* dreamer's sudden shift from the image of the Lamb to the image of the Maiden, is also illustrated in the Apocalypse illustrations of John's turn to the angel. These representations are strikingly suggestive, in fact, of the dreamer's turn to the Maiden at the end of *Pearl,* for they use an image from erotic iconography to denote the sensuous bond between John and his angel-guide. Chucking John under the chin, the angel uses a gesture that conventionally signifies human love, and more often even an erotic interchange. A commonplace in illustrations of lovers in medieval ivories, the gesture even appears in one of the Cotton Nero illustrations to *Sir Gawain and the Green Knight,* where the Lady, standing by Gawain's bedside, chucks him lightly on his beard. . . .

How the visual language of erotic love can be appropriated by sacred images is a complex semiotic problem, and one that has been addressed in relation to this gesture by art historian. Leo Steinberg in his study of the sexuality of Christ. In his excursus on the chin-chucking gesture in Madonna and Child paintings, where the hand of the infant cups the chin of the mother, Steinberg argues that the use of the motif derives from Canticles 2.6, "his left hand is under my head and his right hand shall embrace me," words that medieval commentators took to signify the spiritual marriage or coitus between Christ and his Church.[51] The appearance of the chin-chuck in Madonna and Child paintings emphasizes Christ's humanity through Christ's use of a gesture from the iconography of eros: Steinberg writes, "No Christian artist, medieval or Renaissance, would have taken this long-fixed convention for anything but a sign of erotic communion, either carnal or spiritual."[52] When it appears in the French Apocalypse . . . and in other illustrations of Saint John and the angel, the gesture of the touched chin would certainly evoke this rich system of conventions. Similar to the dreamer in *Pearl,* yearning to join his Maiden/daughter as soon as he sees the Lamb, John turns from the static perfection of his heavenly vision to a human likeness close at hand. That this temptation is inherent in the process of mystical rapture is suggested by the French Apocalypse master's use of the chin-chuck. The angel receives John's worship with a gesture of eroticized tenderness, but then directs the Evangelist's gaze to the Majesty above.

The illustrated Apocalypses as they evolved in the thirteenth and fourteenth centuries thus share with *Pearl* an interest in human, sensory processes and desire through their picturing of locations as they are seen and experienced serially by an eyewitness. The complex relationship between the seer and visionary truth is further illustrated in the Apocalypse cycles through the *vitae* of John that often accompany the visionary sequences.[53] In these lives of John so often appended to the illustrated Apocalypses—appearing before and after the visionary sequence—John is portrayed as active, engaged in life, whereas in the scenes describing his vision he becomes principally an observer, standing to one side of the page or beyond its border. Yet it is in this life that John is prepared for a vision of another level of union. The Book of Revelation is about union, the Berengaudus commentary repeatedly suggests: union as revealed by the concordances of the Old Testament with the New, union as shown by the revelation at the eschaton of the whole history of the world, and union as signified by the marriage of Christ with His Church. St. John in the *vita,* like the dreamer in *Pearl,* prepares for a vision of union at the coming End by confronting death. He is condemned, boiled alive, and cast out on Patmos from the human community. It is there, in isolation, that he has a vision about anagogical death and eternal life, and he returns to the world.

By appending a *vita* to the text of Revelation, compilers of such illustrated Apocalypses as Trinity thus ef-

fectively place visionary and transcendent experience within the framework of temporality. In *Pearl,* this conflict between the world of vision, *in aevo,* and the world of quotidian reality is expressly illustrated as the dreamer awakens, but it is also the principal subject of his meditations in the poem's final section. These passages describe the dreamer's brusque awakening; his disappointment on finding himself cast out from the place of joy; his grudging concession that even if he has to be an outcast from paradise, at least his Pearl should reside within it; his rankling sense that if he had just been content with the vision he could have seen even greater mysteries. Finally, in the last stanza, he remarks—astonishingly—how easy it is to be a good Christian. Even as the narrator tells of his reconciliation with his lot, he describes again the experience of loss, although here it is a vision that is lost rather than his daughter.

Most critics of *Pearl* have understood the poem to be finally a Christian comedy, reading in the ending consolation and reconciliation, the altar of the sacramental eucharist replacing the grave of human loss.[54] In the final stanzas, however, the narrator repeatedly refers to the bitterness of his loss rather than the joy of consolation. In the penultimate stanza he even tells himself that his expulsion from paradise was his own doing, forgetting that residence in paradise is not possible for the living, and certainly not part of the Maiden's intent when she led him to the vision:

> To þat Prynceȝ paye hade I ay bente,
> And ȝerned no more þen watȝ me gyuen,
> And halden me þer in trwe entent,
> As þe perle me prayed þat watȝ so þryuen,
> As helde, drawen to Goddeȝ present,
> To mo of his mysterys I hade ben dryuen;
> Bot ay wolde man of happe more hente
> Þen moȝte by ryȝt vpon hem clyuen.
> Þerfore my ioye watȝ sone toriuen,
> And I kaste of kytheȝ þat lasteȝ aye.
> (1189-1198)[55]

This system of causalities is technically accurate; that is, the dreamer correctly blames his own desire for excessive joy for his expulsion from his paradisal dream. The causal system that casts the dreamer from his visionary state is larger than the question of will or cupidity that the dreamer here cites, however, for it is the system or condition of humanity itself, the Fall that the dreamer's expulsion from a visionary paradise recapitulates.[56] Human grief may be, of course, a consequence of cupidity; yet it does not follow that the dreamer's greed directly causes his fall from Paradise. Even at the end, the narrator still seems to believe that he could have stayed in the visionary realm; he still is unwilling to accept that the condition of living in the world is a condition of exile.

The final stanza of *Pearl,* though it expresses reconciliation with bereavement and a comfort with the consolations provided by Christian ritual, "þe forme of bred and wyn" (1209), thus fails to be fully convincing, for up to the last stanza the poem's brilliantly focalized descriptions have embodied desire and loss, even as the poem has posed mystical union as an eschatological ideal for the human pilgrimage. In *Pearl* the approach to visionary union as well as separation from that union are both realized spatially through the medium of the eyewitness, the dreamer, who is set in a complex perceptual relationship to the series of events he records. The value of looking at the illustrated Apocalypses for understanding the dreamer's development in *Pearl* lies in a tension between sensory ontology and the promises of Scripture, linear temporality juxtaposed to the eschaton where time ends. As Theodore Bogdanos points out, *Pearl* differs markedly from the text of Revelation in giving the New Jerusalem a "concrete topography,"[57] noting that the dreamer's spatialized city contrasts to John's sequential and spatially incoherent perception of objects and events, described in Revelation with the reiterated "I saw." For his description of a city with a complex topography, the poet seems to be drawing instead on the pictorial traditions of Apocalypse illustrations that depict a city in both projection and elevation, and even more important, that describe the city's concrete dimensions as they are perceived by an eyewitness who is himself led by an angel-guide. Furthermore, in addition to sharing with *Pearl* an interest in visionary apprehension as a process, the illustrated Apocalypses also dramatize the visionary moment, *in aevo,* against a backdrop of human works, the scenes from John's vita that are often depicted before and after the visionary sequence. Within the visions themselves, the illustrated cycles and *Pearl* also record a similar paradox, the impulse to human love that in the cycles inspires John to worship the angel and that in *Pearl* tempts the dreamer both before and after his doctrinal instruction to try to join the Maiden.

The Reader and the Interpretive Gaze

The crisis of fusion and separation that is created in *Pearl* by the vision of the New Jerusalem involves not only the dreamer but also the reader in a complex visual hermeneutic. By creating a visual system that includes a spatially complex city and an eyewitness recording that scene, the poet establishes vision as an act of interpretation; the dreamer is both respondent and interpreter, his very reactions to his vision prompting the engagement of a second interpreter, the reader, who knows all that he knows, and more. This interactive interpretive process can be illustrated, for instance, when the dreamer spies the Lamb with His wound and grieves, "Alas, þoȝt I, who did þat spyt?" (1138). By phrasing the question, the dreamer locates himself, in this case, as both a physical and an emotional witness,

experiencing the direct impact of the Christian tragedy. Yet the question also illustrates his own subjective placement in this vision, suspended from history, Scripture, and an iconographic tradition that tell the Christian again and again "who did þat spyt," and indeed, make knowledge of the answer critical to an anagogical understanding of the image at all. The reader, of course, supplies the answer, or at least recognizes how the dreamer, in his very *lack* of knowledge, has a suspended historical consciousness. The rhetoric of questioning itself invites the engagement of the reader; this question in particular illustrates the experience of contemplative union as well as the dramas of crisis and separation, for the voice of the dreamer locates his physical presence, separate from the scene he witnesses, identifies the gap between his emotional union and intellectual understanding, and by asking a question that *we* answer, invites us as readers to formulate his position and our own.

And what is the role of the reader who approaches the New Jerusalem through the eyes of the dreamer? A reader in the fourteenth century would certainly be familiar with *Pearl*'s depiction of the New Jerusalem from the description of the city in Revelation; and a fourteenth-century reader might well be acquainted both with commentaries on Revelation that frequently accompany the illuminations in picture books and with an exegetical tradition in which the images of Revelation are read as historical and prophetic signs. A method of reading a pictorial Apocalypse cycle is described in a late medieval Prologue to an Apocalypse in Magdalene College, Cambridge. According to this poem, our encounter, seriatim, with the pictures and words of the manuscript will lead us through a process of interpretation, a process that has our own salvation as its end:

> Who redes þis boke of ymagerie
> Hit will hom counfort & make redie,
> And vndirstonde hor witte to clere,
> By þes beestis purtreyed here;
> And ful knowyng of mykel treuth
> Þat now is hidde, hit is grete reuth;
> What þei by-meenen in hor kynde,
> Waytnas þo gloose & ȝe shal fynde
> Hit is as keye þat wil vnloken
> Þo dore þat is ful faste stoken;
> Þis keye were gode men to fynde,
> To make hom se þat now ben blynde;
> God gif vs grace þat sight to haue,
> To reule vs riȝt we may be saue.[58]

In this text, seeing and reading are conflated, even transposed, as equivalent processes, such that one "reads" the book of imagery and "witnesses" the gloss. The pictures, "þes beestis purtreyed here," make us desire to unlock their meaning, which the gloss provides, as if, in an image appropriate to the text of the

Book of Revelation ("I looked, and lo, in heaven an open door!" [Rev. 4.1]), the gloss were a key to a door. Understanding the full meaning, we see who were formerly blind; and with that sight or knowledge we have the means to hasten our salvation.

The description of the New Jerusalem in **Pearl** does not afford such a precisely articulated hermeneutics, however. Whereas the Magdalene Apocalypse Prologue describes how an encounter with both image and text in an Apocalypse cycle can lead to an incremental growth in understanding, **Pearl** uses material from the Apocalypse cycles and the text of Revelation to depict, in verbal form, a visual encounter in which visual images function not as "hidden" signs that a verbal key can unlock but as concrete and sensuous perceptions. There is no gloss; or more precisely, there is only the extratextual gloss that the reader may provide, educated perhaps in a tradition of reading the events of John's vision as signs of the history of the Church and of the world to come. The dreamer's principal activity, however, is one of reaction to scenes as they are recorded on a strictly sensuous and perceptual level.

This is not to suggest that we as readers stand in critical scorn of the dreamer for his repeated failures in understanding, though some critics seem to have found themselves in this position.[59] The brilliant topography of the dreamer's visual pilgrimage should keep us from such easy dismissals or cancellations, since the textual space we inhabit as we read the poem is principally constructed of the dreamer's visual universe. The dreamer's pilgrimage to the heavenly Jerusalem is actualized as a journey to a city, and his spiritual education occurs in counterpoint to his encounter with visual and fictively physical form. The dreamer's vision of the city is a powerful dramatization of the experience of not knowing or of seeing that which cannot be fully grasped. If **Pearl** is intended to describe a contemplative methodology in which the dreamer uses the physical beauties of the world to lead him to anagogical truths, then that process must be said to be a failure. The dreamer never attains the kind of blind vision Bonaventure and the English mystics celebrate as the goal of contemplative experience, nor does he understand intellectually the spiritual content of his dream. The vision the dreamer does attain, including his preparatory sensory pilgrimage through the Earthly Paradise, describes instead an epistemological system, sensory processes in linear time, that frames its perceptions through the body.

Notes

[1] Donald R. Howard, *Writers and Pilgrims: Medieval Pilgrimage Narratives and Their Posterity* (Berkeley: University of California Press, 1980), 17-52.

Illustration from Cotton MS. lines 961-72.

[2] Account edited by C. L. Grotefend in *Die Edelherren von Boldensele oder Boldensen* (Hanover, 1855); see Howard, *Writers and Pilgrims,* 29-31.

[3] On the basis of descriptions of the Dead Sea given in *Purity,* it is clear that the Cotton Nero poet was familiar with Mandeville's travels. The poet's use of Jerusalem, here the New Jerusalem of the spiritual journey, and his detailed record of the pilgrim's visual and sensory experiences on that journey also suggest that he may have known not only Mandeville's account, but also others of the many pilgrimage narratives describing a journey to a sacred city. For a fuller discussion of *Pearl*'s uses of Jerusalem and of motifs from travel literature, see my essay, "*Pearl* and the Idea of Jerusalem," *Medievalia et Humanistica* 16 (1988): 117-131. For a discussion of the influence of Mandeville on Chaucer and on the *Gawain*-poet, see Josephine Waters Bennett, *The Rediscovery of Sir John Mandeville* (1954; rpt. New York: Kraus Reprint Co., 1971), 221-227.

[4] Although many studies have focused on the plight of the narrator, few have looked at the mechanics of his perceptual process. For studies of the narrator, see in

particular Charles Moorman, "The Role of the Narrator in *Pearl,*" *Modern Philology* 53 (1955): 73-81; Elton Higgs, "The Progress of the Dreamer in *Pearl,*" *Studies in Medieval Culture* 4 (1974): 388-400; Larry Sklute, "Expectation and Fulfillment in *Pearl,*" *Philological Quarterly* 52 (1973): 663-679; A. C. Spearing, *Medieval Dream Poetry* (Cambridge: Cambridge University Press, 1976), 111-129; and S. L. Clark and Julian N. Wasserman, "The Spatial Argument of *Pearl:* Perspectives on a Venerable Bead," *Interpretations* 11 (1979): 1-12. Among studies that explore the processes of the narrator's perception of his vision, my argument owes a particular debt to John Finlayson, who maps the visionary realm as an objective correlative to the dreamer's spiritual growth ("*Pearl:* Landscape and Vision," *Studies in Philology,* 71 (1974): 314-343). Theodore Bogdanos also discusses the narrator's perceptual methodology, but with particular attention to the multivalent symbolism of images (*Pearl: Image of the Ineffable* [University Park, PA: Pennsylvania State University Press, 1983]); see, for example, 27, 33-34, 42-43, 103.

[5] See lines 979, 1021, 1032, 1033, 1035, 1049, 1083, 1143, 1145, 1147, 1151. Citations from *Pearl* are from the edition by E. V. Gordon (Oxford: Oxford University Press, 1953).

[6] In early scholarship on *Pearl,* debate centered around its affiliations with elegy, allegory, or Christian *consolatio,* with the question of genre for many years being the principal topic of inquiry. More recent studies have tended to look at *Pearl*'s debt to popular devotional or iconographic traditions in the poet's time, such as the cult of the Magdalene or the interest in apocalyptic themes and images. See, for example, the *Pearl* chapter in Lynn Staley Johnson, *The Voice of the Gawain-Poet* (Madison: University of Wisconsin Press, 1984), esp. 148-161; the *Pearl* chapter in Barbara Nolan, *The Gothic Visionary Perspective,* (Princeton, NJ: Princeton University Press, 1977), 156-204; and Muriel Whitaker, "*Pearl* and Some Illustrated Apocalypse Manuscripts," *Viator* 12 (1981): 183-196.

[7] See, for instance, Constance Hieatt, "*Pearl* and the Dream-Vision Tradition," *Studia Neophilologica* 37 (1965): 139-145.

[8] As a vision of the Otherworld, *Pearl* is part of a long tradition that includes the apocryphal *Apocalypse of Peter,* the sixth-century Latin *Visio sancti Pauli,* the enormously popular twelfth-century *Vision of Tundale,* which was translated in the late Middle Ages into German, French, Italian, Icelandic, and English, and that naturally includes Dante's *Divine Comedy. Pearl*'s relationship to these traditions is discussed by Thomas C. Niemann, "*Pearl* and the Christian Other World," *Genre* 7 (1974): 213-232.

[9] For a discussion of *Pearl*'s theology, see Louis Blenkner, "The Theological Structure of *Pearl,*" *Traditio* 24 (1968): 43-75; rpt. in *The Middle English Pearl: Critical Essays,* ed. John Conley (Notre Dame, IN: University of Notre Dame Press, 1970), 221. See also A. P. Baldwin, "The Tripartite Reformation of the Soul in *The Scale of Perfection, Pearl,* and *Piers Plowman,*" in *The Medieval Mystical Tradition in England,* ed. Marion Glasscoe (Cambridge: D. S. Brewer, 1984), 136-149.

[10] See the discussions in Blenkner, 228, 251; and in Finlayson, "Landscape and Vision," 336.

[11] See the discussion in Chapter 3 of the ages of the world in *Purity*'s historiography. Hugh of Saint Victor, one of the most important medieval historiographers, describes the stages of the world in *De Sacramentis,* in J.-P. Migne, *Patrologiae cursus completus, series latina* (Paris 1844-1864) (*PL*), 176-346; see *Hugh of Saint Victor on the Sacraments of the Christian Faith (De Sacramentis),* trans. Roy J. Deferrari (Cambridge: Mediaeval Academy, 1954), 185-186. See also Blenkner, 235.

[12] *PL,* 175.116-117. Hugh recognizes the power and importance of sensory images, and delights in the paradox that profound spiritual truths can be revealed in minute natural organisms. See the discussion in Bogdanos, 7; see also Blenkner, 227; and John Gatta, "Transformation Symbolism and the Liturgy of the Mass in *Pearl,*" *Modern Philology* 71 (1974): 248, discussing *Pearl*'s sacramental view of reality and debt to Scholastic valorization of the senses as a mode of spiritual perception.

[13] *PL,* 175.177; cited in Blenkner, 228.

[14] "Secundum hunc triplicem progressum mens nostra tres habet aspectus principales. Unus est ad corporalia exteriora, secundum quem vocatur *animalitas* seu sensualitas; alius intra se et in se, secundum quem dicitur *spiritus;* tertius supra se, secundum quem dicitur *mens*" [In keeping with this threefold progression, our mind has three principal ways of perceiving. In the first way it looks at the corporeal things outside itself, and so acting, it is called animality or sensitivity. In the second, it looks within itself, and is then called spirit. In the third, it looks above itself, and is then called mind] (*Itinerarium Mentis in Deum,* 1.4, 40-41, ed. and tr. Philotheus Boehner [St. bonaventure, NY: Franciscan Institute, 1956], 41). All subsequent translations and citations from the *Itinerarium* are taken from Boehner's edition. See also Blenkner, 228-229; and see the discussion of Bonaventure in Chapter 6.

[15] "Ex his ergo visibilibus consurgit ad considerandum Dei potentiam, sapientiam et bonitatem. . . .''

[16] "Quia assuefactus ad tenebras entium et phantasmata sensibilium, cum ipsam lucem summi *esse* intuetur, videtur sibi nihil videre; non intelligens, quod ipsa caligo summa est mentis nostrae illumination, sicut, quando videt oculus puram lucem, videtur sibi nihil videre."

[17] "[A]d superessentialem divinarum tenebrarum radium, omnia deserens et ab omnibus absolutus, ascendes."

[18] "I hold that jeweler little to praise who fully believes what he sees with his eyes."

[19] "In believing nothing but what you see, you misinterpret his words. And that is a point of pride, which ill becomes each good man, to believe no tale can be trusted but that which his own reason can judge."

[20] *The Riverside Chaucer,* 3rd ed., ed. Larry Benson (Boston: Houghton Mifflin, 1987), 588. I discuss the visual imagery of the *Prologue* in my article, "Cupid's Sight in the Prologue to the *Legend of Good Women,*" *Centerpoint* 15 (1981) 95-102.

[21] Finlayson discusses the relationship of the dreamer to his locations, but sees this relationship as strictly progressive; in the *erber* his "inability to see the divine truths made concrete in the physical phenomena around him indicates his earthbound state of spiritual blindness" ("*Pearl:* Landscape and Vision," 320), whereas in his vision of the New Jerusalem "there is emotional involvement in what is observed, to the point of an attempt being made to join the throng in the Heavenly City" (336). Finlayson draws parallels between *Pearl* and Walter Hilton's *Scale of Perfection,* arguing that "the purpose and meaning of *Pearl* lie . . . in the dramatic, imaginative *creation* of the mystical experience" (336).

[22] On the paucity of sensory images in the *erber,* see, for instance, Patricia M. Kean's argument that the *erber* is a "frame into which a series of closely interwoven images and scriptural references are fitted, all of which work together to establish and elaborate the theme of mortality and regeneration" (*The* Pearl: *An Interpretation* [London: Routledge & Kegan Paul, 1967], 34). Only a few readers have discussed the description as a construct of the narrator's perceptual processes; see Finlayson, who points out that the dreamer "observes the natural phenomena which surround him, but sees them only as objects; he is in a natural landscape bursting with reminders of the cyclical process of death, rebirth and due season, but cannot, because of his grief, see it as Nature" (319); and Johnson, who notes that the description of the *erber* is important in the sequence of the narrator's visionary transitions (180-205).

[23] On the use of the *erber* in a commentary on decay and regeneration and on the relationship of this terrestrial image with the Maiden's argument, see especially Kean, 31-85; Edward Vasta, "Immortal Flowers and the Pearl's Decay," *JEGP* 66 (1967): 519-531, rpt. in Conley, 185-202; and C. A. Luttrell, "*Pearl:* Symbolism in a Garden Setting," *Neophilologus* 49 (1965): 160-176, rpt. in *Sir Gawain and Pearl: Critical Essays,* ed. Robert J. Blanch (Bloomington: Indiana University Press, 1966), 60-85.

[24] "From that spot my spirit sprang there in space; my body rested in sleep on the bank. My spirit was gone in the grace of God in adventures where marvels exist."

[25] "When patches of sky glide against them, they shone with a shimmering sheen. The gravel that crunched on the ground was made of precious Oriental pearls. The sunbeams were dusky and dim by comparison with that adornment."

[26] See the discussion of this passage in Chapter 1.

[27] "In the bottom there stood bright stones that glinted and gleamed like fire through glass, like streaming stars, when earth [marshland]-men sleep, stare in the heavens on winter nights."

[28] Gordon, 52.

[29] "You may not enter within his castle, but from the lamb I have obtained a sight of it for you through great grace."

[30] "As the apostle John saw it with sight, I saw that city of great renoun."

[31] "As John described, I also saw there."

[32] "As John himself writes I saw even more."

[33] "Through the wall and the dwelling my gaze passed, for the clear transparency could not hinder any light."

[34] "Human hearts might not survive such a great marvel under the moon, as when I gazed upon that wall, the form was so marvelous. I stood as still as a dazed quail, in amazement of that noble figure; I was so ravished with the pure gleam that I felt neither rest nor toil."

[35] "[C]hè la mia vista, venendo sincera, / e più e più intrava per lo raggio / dell'altra luce che da sè è vera." Citations and translations are from the edition by John D. Sinclair, *The Divine Comedy of Dante Alighieri: III. Paradiso* (rpt. 1972; New York: Oxford University Press, 1939).

[36] The term *aevum* came in the twelfth and thirteenth centuries to denote the time the spirit exists in the

visionary moment. For a discussion of the term, see Nolan, *Gothic Visionary Perspective,* 38-40.

[37] Rosalind Field, "The Heavenly Jerusalem in *Pearl,*" *Modern Language Review* 81 (1986): 7-17; and Whitaker, 183-196.

[38] For a general study of the development of the English Apocalypse, see George Henderson, "Studies in English Manuscript Illumination," *Journal of the Warburg and Courtauld Institutes* 30 (1967): 17-137 and 31 (1968): 103-147. See also Peter Brieger, *English Art: 1216-1307,* Oxford History of English Art 4 (Oxford: Oxford University Press, 1957), 159-170; and Nolan, 54-83.

[39] The reduction in the size of the New Jerusalem is the most persuasive argument offered to demonstrate that the poet was familiar with commentaries on the Apocalypse. The use of twelve furlongs appears, for instance, in both Bede's *Explanatio Apocalypsis* (*PL,* 113.196) and in the Berengaudus commentary. For a discussion of illustrated Apocalypses that depict a wounded lamb, see Field, 11-13.

[40] See, for instance, Ian Bishop, *Pearl in its Setting: A Critical Study of the Structure and Meaning of the Middle English Poem* (Oxford: Blackwell, 1968), 37; Finlayson, 333; and Kean, 210. Both Finlayson and Kean justify the poet's use of a "mere catalogue" by arguing that the description reveals the inadequacy of the dreamer's spiritual state.

[41] For Bonaventure, the New Jerusalem is a contemplative goal: "Quibus adeptis, efficitur spiritus noster *hierarchicus* ad conscendendum sursum secundum conformitatem ad illam Ierusalem supernam, in quam nemo intrat, nisi prius per gratiam ipsa in cor descendat, sicut vidit Ioannes in Apocalypsi sua" [These things attained, our spirit, in as much as it is in conformity with the heavenly Jerusalem, is made hierarchic in order to mount upward. For into this heavenly Jerusalem no one enters unless it first comes down into his heart by grace, as St. John beheld in the Apocalypse] (*Itin.* 4.4, 74-75). See also *Itin.* 7.1, 96-97. In the New Testament, the New Jerusalem is a complex image, both an eschatological event and symbol of Christian residence, the city where all Christians are fellow citizens: see Phil 4.3, Luke 10.206, and esp. Rev. 21.27. For a discussion of the City in Scripture, see James Calvin De Young, *Jerusalem in the New Testament: The Significance of the City in the History of Redemption and in Eschatology* (Kampen: J. H. Kok, 1960), 117-127. For a discussion of the two cities, heavenly and earthly, see my essay, "*Pearl* and the Idea of Jerusalem" *Medievalia et Humianistica* 16 1988: 117-131; see also Stephen G. Nichols, Jr., *Romanesque Signs: Early Medieval Narrative and Iconography* (New Haven, CT: Yale University Press, 1983), 24-25; and Spearing, *The*

Gawain *Poet: A Critical Study* (Cambridge: Cambridge University Press, 1970), 114.

[42] Tundale first sees the Earthly Paradise and then, from the top of a second wall, the greatest joy, God's face and all the saints and bishops. See *Das Mittelenglische Gedicht über die Vision des Tundalus,* ed. Albrecht Wagner (Halle: Niemeyer, 1893), 120, lines 2082-2234. Walter Hilton, *The Scale of Perfection,* trans. Dom Gerard Sitwell, O.S.B. (London: Burns Oates, 1953), vol. 2, sec. 25, follows the Augustinian tradition of using Jerusalem metaphorically as the city of peace, though he does briefly describe the soul's encounter with the city in graphic terms taken from Ezekiel 40: " . . . you have come very near to Jerusalem. You have not yet reached it, but by the gleams of light that escape from it you will be able to see it in the distance before you come to it" (210). Through the New Jerusalem, Hilton explores the perceptual shifts effected through inner "sight": "This city signifies the perfect love of God, and it is set on the hill of contemplation. To the soul that has had no experience of it but that strives for it with desire it seems only small, six cubits and a palm in length. . . . He sees that there is something which surpasses the attainment of all human effort, as the palm goes beyond the six cubits, but he does not see what this is. But if he is able to get inside the city of contemplation, he sees much more than he saw at first" (*Scale,* vol. 2, sec. 25, 211).

[43] Nolan, 64-66.

[44] See the discussion in *The Cloisters Apocalypse,* vol. 2, ed. Florens Deuchler, Jeffrey M. Hoffeld, and Helmut Nickel (New York: Metropolitan Museum of Art, 1971), 10, and volume 1 for facsimile illustrations.

[45] Discussing the central west portal at Chartres, Nichols argues that the tympanum with its similar fusive composition of elders, Majesty, and parishioner creates a "biaxial narrative structure" in which linear time coalesces with the eschaton (*Romanesque Signs,* 42).

[46] Trinity, produced in England in the second quarter of the thirteenth century, is a lavishly illustrated book which served as a prototype for later versions. It was unique in its use of a French text and commentary, in its insistence on the concordance of Old and New Testaments, and on its optimistic view of the triumph of the Church. See Peter A. Brieger's commentary in *The Trinity College Apocalypse* (London: Eugrammia Press, 1967), 5.

[47] Johnson argues that *Pearl* is based on the *noli me tangere* episode, the encounter of Mary Magdelene with Christ, with Mary's desire to touch Christ a direct parallel with the dreamer's desire to join the Maiden (*The Voice of the* Gawain-*Poet,* 148-161). The episode from the Apocalypse offers a more direct parallel with *Pearl;* certainly the popularity in the thirteenth and

fourteenth centuries of both the *noli me tangere* and of the worship of the angel from Revelation attest to a fascination with the corporeal processes of spiritual perception.

[48] The date of the commentary (*PL,* 17.763-970) is uncertain. It has been placed variously in the ninth and the twelfth centuries, with most recent scholarship supporting the later date. For a discussion of the commentary, see Brieger, ed., *Trinity College Apocalypse,* 5-6; R. Freyhan, "Joachism and the English Apocalypse," *Journal of the Warburg and Courtauld Institutes* 18 (1955): 211-244; and Nolan, 67-71.

[49] Trans. Brieger, *Trinity College Apocalypse,* 52 (fol. 27v). Trinity contains a French condensation of the Berengaudus commentary.

[50] Gordon's note on *biys,* line 197, points out that the Bride of the Lamb also arrays herself in "bysse" in Rev. 19.8.

[51] Leo Steinberg, *The Sexuality of Christ in Renaissance Art and Modern Oblivion* (New York: Pantheon, 1983), 3-5, 110-116.

[52] Steinberg, 113.

[53] An innovation of the Trinity Apocalypse, the *vitae* of John also occurred in most of the later English cycles; see the discussion in Brieger, *Trinity Apocalypse,* 6.
[54] See Johnson, *Voice of the* Gawain-*Poet,* 162, 177. See also Bishop, 92-93; John Conley, "*Pearl* and a Lost Tradition," *JEGP: Journal of English and Germanic Philology,* 54 (1955): 232-247, rpt. in Conley, ed., *Middle English Pearl,* 50-72; Blenkner, "Theological Structure of *Pearl*"; and A. C. Spearing, "The *Gawain*-Poet's Sense of an Ending," in *Readings in Medieval Poetry* (New York: Cambridge University Press, 1987), 213-215, who says the final two stanzas of *Pearl* provide a "subtle and consoling closure." Theodore Bogdanos has provided an important dissenting voice, arguing instead that the dreamer experiences a "process, of symbolic alienation" that reflects "the poet's radical sense of man's spiritual alienation and the inaccessibility of divine reality to him" (*Pearl: Image of the Ineffable,* 145).

[55] "Had I always bent myself to that Prince's pay and yearned for no more than was given to me, and held myself there in true intent as the lovely pearl asked me—quite probably, drawing to God's presence, I would have been led to more of his mysteries; but men would always take more happiness than might be theirs by right. Therefore my joy was soon torn from me and I was cast out from the eternal regions."

[56] See Bogdanos, 144.

[57] Bogdanos, 115.

[58] Magdalene College, Cambridge, MS. 5, in *Secular Lyrics of the XIVth and XVth Centuries,* ed. Rossell Hope Robbins (Oxford: Clarendon Press, 1952), 93-94.

[59] See, for example, Spearing, *The* Gawain *Poet,* 167-170; and Kean, *The Pearl,* 213, 227-242; and the discussion in Bogdanos, 143-144.

Jim Rhodes (essay date 1994)

SOURCE: "The Dreamer Redeemed: Exile and the Kingdom in the Middle English Pearl," in *Studies in the Age of Chaucer,* Vol. 16, 1994, pp. 119-42.

[*In the following essay, Rhodes argues that instead of regarding the dreamer as a mere foil to the Maiden, the dreamer should be viewed as her equal and the poem should be seen as accurately reflecting the theological debate taking place in the fourteenth century.*]

> One might maintain, not too paradoxically, that every medieval poetic form (on whatever level one may define it) *tends* toward double meaning: and I don't mean the doubling deciphered by an allegoristic reading but, superimposing or complexifying its effects, a perpetual *sic et non,* yes and no, obverse/reverse. Every meaning, in the last analysis, would present itself as enigmatic, the enigma being resolved into simultaneous and contradictory propositions, one of which always more or less parodies the other.[1]

With the possible exception of *Sir Gawain and the Green Knight,* all of the works of the **Pearl** poet have been regarded as didactic or imitative of the form and content of a medieval sermon. Of these poems **Pearl** has been portrayed as the most controlled and sustained example of his homiletic art. Thus for one reader **Pearl** is about the drama of faith or the "tension of belief" which lies at the core of medieval spirituality; for another it is about the fallen soul and its salvation; for most others it is about the education of the Dreamer, his progress under the guidance of the Maiden toward learning to shift his focus from earthly to heavenly love, from the Maiden to the love of Christ.[2] What these readings share is a confidence in the authority of the **Pearl** Maiden's discourse, particularly her interpretation of the Vineyard parable as prologue to her formal instruction of the Dreamer in the traditional theology of salvation and penance. At the same time, these readings treat the Dreamer as a sympathetic but somewhat naïve figure who does not understand the full meaning of Christian doctrine.

Recently readers have begun to position the Dreamer more centrally in the narrative and to award him a more active role in the experience of his spiritual education. David Aers, for example, after acknowledging the psychological complexity and theological sophistication of the Dreamer, detects a degree of Lollard individualism and interpretiveness in his response to the vineyard parable.[3] Aers argues that the Dreamer's self-absorption has prevented him from gaining self-transcendence and from renewing his bonds with the human community, but that the dream and the encounter with the Maiden give the Dreamer the "time, space, and provocation to *change*, to redirect his being from identification with the dead person, to redirect his love."[4] In the symbolic structure of the poem the Dreamer moves from the solitary "I" at the beginning of the poem to the communal "we" at the close.

This approach goes a long way toward redeeming the Dreamer, but it still makes him too dependent on the Maiden for his personal renewal, and it allows the Maiden's theological argument or position to stand uncontested. The aim of this article is to show that the Dreamer's voice counts as much as the Maiden's in the theological and social discourse of the poem and that he shares the theological and moral center of the poem with her. Accordingly, this article proposes that we read *Pearl* in terms of Bakhtinian dialogic instead of as Boethian dialogue, the traditional approach to the poem. In Boethian dialogue the interlocutor holds unquestioned superiority over the correspondent, whereas in Bakhtinian dialogic no such superiority is apportioned. For Bakhtin, both sides have equal authority, even when the dialogue takes place within only one party, usually as a struggle or interplay between two categories: the authoritative word (religious, political, or moral discourse, the word of the fathers or teachers) and internally persuasive discourse (translating external discourse into one's own words or vocabulary, with one's own accents, gestures, modifications) which, Bakhtin says, is denied all privilege, backed by no authority, and goes unrecognized by scholarly norms or opinions.[5] Applied to *Pearl,* this means that the Dreamer is no mere foil who feeds the Maiden easy questions that permit her to expatiate on doctrine to a passive listener. His questions, whether they are practical, personal, or economic, enlarge the scope of the debate and press the discourse of the Maiden to satisfy the very real problems that concern him. His voice gives expression to views on justification and salvation that were current in the fourteenth century and in opposition to her view. Once elevated to the level of the Maiden, the Dreamer brings the poem into line with the tenor and terms of the theological debate that did arise outside the poem.

The dialogical structure also allows the reader to assume a more active role in the reception of the narrative. Inasmuch as the theological issues under examination in the poem—salvation and justification, the claims of this world against those of the other world—are topics that directly concern the reader, the dialogical structure invites the audience to discriminate among the various positions advanced without having to commit itself to any one of them. This will be especially true of the poet's presentation of the vineyard parable. In themselves parables appeal to the interpretive skills of every reader, and the *Pearl* poet accommodates the interests of his readers in the way that he sustains the tension between the Dreamer and the Maiden through their separate readings and responses to the vineyard parable. The Maiden treats the parable primarily as a metaphor for the kingdom of heaven, or as a lesson in the eternal values, in God's love for the innocent and in the consolation gained by those who resign their will to the supreme will of God. Her vision encompasses the whole scheme of salvation, and her theology centers on the reward of heaven as the free gift of God's grace. The Dreamer responds to the parable more existentially and pragmatically: the vineyard is like the human order in its ordinariness and its workaday familiarity. It represents an area of human activity that is self-contained and autonomous; it pertains to events or conditions in this world, to matters of justice or merit or proper reward for work rendered. His vision settles first on the sense world of immediate experience and does not separate what is theological from what is social, political, or economic.

Normally in a narrative such as this one, as Marie McLean explains it, a narrator gains and holds authority as teller by controlling or co-opting the power of the narratee, or the text of the narrator shapes the audience into its ideal narratee.[6] In the vineyard parable, however, the Maiden-narrator fails to achieve her desired control over the Dreamer-narratee because he continues to rely on his reason and sense impressions throughout, despite her several attempts to wean him from them, and because his practical intellect persistently interrogates the absolute authority of the explanations and conclusions. By interposing himself between the Maiden and the audience through his seemingly naïve questions, the Dreamer mediates the authority of her discourse so that the reader is neither "recruited" nor "seduced" by the Maiden (to borrow Ross Chambers's vocabulary of narrative persuasion) and thus remains free to be an active reader who can search the text for alternative meanings beneath the stipulated one.[7]

I intend to discuss the dynamic relationship between the Maiden and the Dreamer in more pointed detail below, but first I want to say something about the place of the vineyard parable in the theological debates about salvation, justification, and human freedom in the fourteenth century. In this way we can approach the poem with a clearer understanding of how *Pearl* unfolds as a debate within the narrator, wherein the earthbound voice of the Dreamer counters the idealizing voice of the Maiden, and a theology of immanence balances against a theology of transcendence.

The vineyard parable apparently has always been an enigmatic one, no less so in the fourteenth century, primarily because a literal reading leaves the impression that both sides in the dispute, workers and householder, have a just and reasonable claim. Judging from the commentary it attracted, the parable enjoyed widespread popularity in late-medieval discussions of justification, yielding what Paul Zumthor calls a multiplicity of "simultaneous and contradictory propositions." The traditional or orthodox understanding of the parable, articulated by Augustine against the Pelagians, interprets it as a defense of the necessity of God's prevenient grace in the work of salvation. In Augustine's analysis, the workers have no claim to the money in terms of the work done, but they do have a claim on the basis of the promise made to them by the owner of the vineyard. Analogously, human beings have no claim on the grace of God on the basis of their works, only on the basis of the obligation of God to live up to his promise.[8]

Augustine's view remained prominent throughout the late Middle Ages, but its authority was seriously challenged by the nominalist anthropology of the *via moderna* (those theologians who assign a positive role to human beings in the work of their own salvation)[9] in the fourteenth century and refined in the fifteenth century by Gabriel Biel.[10] Extrapolating from William of Ockham's and Pierre D'Auriole's "semi-pelagian" treatment of justification, Biel offers an interpretation of the vineyard parable that epitomizes the theological precepts of the *via moderna* with its characteristic emphasis on human dignity and reward for meritorious deeds. Biel accepts that both God and human beings are teleologically oriented but contends that God's *telos* and humankind's *telos* may not coincide. Whereas the employee works for his wages, the employer, Biel says, is motivated not by the wages of the employee but rather by the work performed. Biel's analogy, in Heiko Oberman's view, emphasizes the intrinsic importance of the life of the *viator* on earth, "the value of which was now less exclusively defined in terms of the *eternal Jerusalem* (italics added), the final destination of the *viator,* and more in terms of the journey itself."[11]

The notion of the *viator* relates directly to our discussion because it conforms with the Dreamer's disposition to pursue a happiness attainable in this life and to grant greater recognition to work or activity carried out in this world. Without diminishing the importance of salvation theology, the thinkers supporting the notion of the *viator* stressed hermeneutical over soteriological values, and moral problems over dogmatic theology, priorities of the Dreamer, as we shall see. The notion of the *viator* also radically changed

theological geography by projecting human beings into history horizontally as well as vertically, equipped with their own set of existential objectives and moral determinants. As Oberman observes, the concept of the *viator* apportioned a realm for human beings established by the *potentia ordinata* within which they could come into their own, free to realize their own innate endowment of dignity.[12] Finally, the idea of the *viator* enabled the *moderni* first to confront then to offset the legacy of "negative progress" inherited from an older Augustinianism (but revived by Thomas Bradwardine in the fourteenth century), whereby the human will has been so weakened by sin that it cannot effect its own regeneration, and human nature itself, without grace, can do little more than contribute to the sum of evil in the world.[13]

To reorient people toward this world, the *moderni* devised what is called covenantal theology, a partnership or legal *pactum* with God that broadened the basis of *iustitia Dei* and brought it into harmony with a theology of merit. Before covenantal theology, Alistair McGrath argues, there was no definitive concept of justification in the late Middle Ages. The twelfth century and scholasticism in general, McGrath says, determined that justification involved an ontological change in human beings, thus requiring an ontological intermediary or intermediate, which was identified with the created habit of grace or charity.[14] Hence *ex natura rei* such a habit was implicated in the process of human justification. In the fourteenth century, however, both the *via moderna* and the *schola Augustiniana moderna* began to conceive of justification in personal or relational terms. In place of the ontological intermediary the *via moderna* substituted the *pactum,* wherein God, in his unlimited freedom (*de potentia Dei absoluta*), wills to limit himself within the chosen order (*de potentia Dei ordinata*).[15] The *pactum* or covenant, McGrath says, constitutes the turning point in the doctrine of justification associated with the *via moderna,* because in it God imposes upon himself the obligation to reward the individual who does *quod in se est* with the gift of justifying grace.[16]

Although formal debate of these issues remained the special domain of the schoolmen, the issues of justification, human and divine agency, freedom and responsibility were made available to the whole of English society. According to Janet Coleman, "Not only were the issues of the schools discussed by those who were not schoolmen, but the language, the jargon of the schools filtered down to a very great extent into literature that was meant for the edification of the nonclerical literate."[17] Similarly, William Courtenay tells us that the themes we can expect to find in Middle English literature are those that were of concern to scholars and poets alike: "These common interests were biblical themes and imagery, and the penitential themes of vices and virtues, grace and justification, moral choice, sin and repentance, predenstination and human liberty, and the conflicts and ambiguities that life presents to the average Christian."[18] In the second half of the fourteenth century, then, in the period when the *Pearl* poet was composing his biblically oriented poems, vernacular writings of all kinds had begun to reproduce scenes and stories from the Bible, providing greater access to the word of God and personal knowledge of the law of Christ, what Wyclif had declared was the fundamental right of every Christian. Wider distribution and broader understanding of basic doctrine and of biblical materials evidently increased the public appetite for themes and works applicable to everyday life. As Walter Ullmann accurately describes it, a new spiritual ethos took root in art and literature that complemented the anthropological and Christological advances evolving in theology:

> The development in the arts might be said to be "From the future life to the present," or "From deity to humanity." Or, as has rightly been said, men now tried to bring God down to earth and to see and touch him. . . . The type began to give way to the portrayal of real and natural people. . . . This direct approach—evidenced also by the contemporaneous Bible translations—powerfully stimulated the pictorial representation of gospel stories, with the result that they came to be set in natural surroundings which actually meant the environs with which the artist himself was familiar; their setting was contemporaneous. . . . As might be expected, every artist perceived a gospel story in a different light, and in this way his product represented the subjective impact which biblical events and situations had made upon him.[19]

Instead of a "waning" or "dissolution" of order, then, the second half of the fourteenth century was a period of robust theological activity, when the lay activism encouraged by the Fourth Lateran Council came to fruition, and when the disintegration of some traditional structures signaled not moral decay but a not-to-be-missed opportunity to effect reform of both the church and society.[20]

By this account the *Pearl* poet is writing in the midst of a theological and literary renaissance in which a new image of human nature and human society is being forged. Metaphysical problems now are being analyzed from our or the human side of the issue, and the question of greatest importance has become what is expected of human beings, or, as Chaucer's eschatologically disillusioned Monk puts it, "How shal the world be served?" (*GP* 187).[21]

The *Pearl* poet is as well equipped as anyone else to answer that question for the fourteenth century. Despite suffering from the reputation that he is too "accepting and unquestioning of the orthodox forms of Christianity and feudalism," the *Pearl* poet proves,

through his artful appropriation of biblical parables, that he is engaged with the social and political issues that beset his church and society.[22] Biblical hermeneutics is simply the way he chooses to inscribe crisis into his poetry. While maintaining a readily identifiable link to the order, sequence, and language of the original parable, he enriches his own version with the kinds of contemporary details, nuance, and shifts of emphasis that induce the text to speak afresh to an audience that seeks to comprehend its kerygma in the context of their own experience and historical moment. In all of his poems, however, he does not press upon his audience the sociohistorical or moral concerns built into each of them; instead he leads his audience, through the gradual self-realization of his narrators, to discover for themselves the connection between the moral lesson and contemporary social or theological problems. Rather than mounting a pointed counterargument, he lets style become a manner of seeing things. The realism or language of particularity characteristic of his poems and parables attests to his desire to fix human beings more securely in this world and in a way that allows them to be "reborn as historical beings in their manifest unity of body and spirit."[23] This, I emphasize, is the task that he sets for himself in his depiction of the Dreamer in *Pearl*.

The Prologue or opening movement of *Pearl* takes place in the erber, a curious mixture of cloister garden and romantic bower, where the Dreamer repairs to commune with his absent pearl. More than a place of contemplation and retreat from this world, the erber stands in for this world as the natural physical environment in which the Dreamer is situated. It is the site where the poet problematizes the figure of the Dreamer before we meet the Maiden and where the Dreamer reveals himself to us as a complex and introspective representative of the human condition. The conversation the Dreamer holds with himself in the erber shows us that he is aware of his loss emotionally and intellectually and that he feels it physically. The appeal of the Dreamer himself, who strikes us as an ordinary layman or bereaved father, draws us into the world of the poem and makes the theological debate that swirls in his mind all the more personal and substantive to our own way of confronting the world.

From the outset it is apparent that the Dreamer refuses to act as a predictable player in a conventional dream vision. In the opening stanza when he tells us that he suffers "fordolked of luf-daungere,"[24] we are led to expect one kind of poem only to discover that it is going to be entirely of another sort. The poet's manipulation of a term familiar to love poetry has a calculated effect nevertheless; it acts as a verbal prod that disorients us and sticks in our mind because of its incongruity, both complicating the narrative and individuating the Dreamer. It puts the audience on notice that it has to adjust to his way of articulating and internalizing things. The erotic potentiality in the term "luf-daungere" is not misplaced either if we see it as an expression of the limitations of spiritual consolation and as an admission of the need human love has for the physical or bodily presence of the beloved.

At this point it is helpful if we draw upon the language of modern psychology, especially that of Lacan, if we are to unpack what the poet has wound so tightly in his phrase "luf-daungere." As Lacan describes it, personal grief exists in the frame of a discourse. We the living give the dead over to the symbolic order. That is, we bury them according to the rituals of our society, and we resituate them in a discourse. Only the reference to discourse prevents the grief from becoming chronic.[25] Stuart Schneiderman explains this transaction in the Freudian vocabulary of the ego:

> When the experience of love is made out to be primary, the dominion of the ego is extended and death is reduced to a loss of love. The ego denies death by *idealizing* love and life; the dead remain alive in the strong ego, still loving and beloved. Thus the ego may recover from its loss by believing that, through death, love has been made eternal. . . . It is through the symbolic order and through the rituals it prescribes that the object is truly given up, truly buried. [Italics added.][26]

Schneiderman goes on to say that if the deceased is not buried metaphorically, which means forgotten, the subject will have no sense of loss or lack and will be alienated from a desire that can only be seen as a threat to the perfect harmony of the truest love.

In layman's terms, what the Dreamer needs to learn is that burying his daughter does not mean obliterating her from his mind altogether. Burying her, in fact, may lead to the release of an even greater capacity to love, one that could expand the human community to embrace the dead as well as the living. Consolation then will come not only from his vision of the New Jerusalem with the Maiden in it but also from the regeneration of his "luf-longyng" in his encounter in the other world. If his vision teaches him that his pearl is lost forever to this world—living in this world entails the loss of precious things—it also may teach him that such loss need not result in his surrender of the whole earthly enterprise.

The Dreamer's reluctance to let go of his daughter is revealed in the ambivalence he shows toward the erber itself. He is drawn to the spot, even though it fills him with sorrowful reminders, because it also secretly arouses him and energizes him (lines 13-20):

> Syþen in þat spote hit fro me sprange,
> Ofte haf I wayted, wyschande þat wele
> Þat wont watz whyle deuoyde my wrange

> And heuen my happe and al my hele—
> Þat dotz bot þrych my hert þrange,
> My breste in bale bot bolne and bele.
> ȝet þoȝt me neuer so swete a sange
> As stylle stounde let to me stele.

The paradoxical state of the Dreamer's mental frame—his sensations oscillate between near-violence and extreme sensitivity—reveals to us the depth of his attachment to earthly things. In contrast to the Maiden's comprehensive vision, the Dreamer is more inductive in his outlook. His mind does not advert immediately to the symbolic signification hidden beneath the concrete reality. Whatever meaning readers may assign to the flowers, the spices, and the pearl itself, the Dreamer sees them first as natural objects of beauty in their own right and not as shadowy reminders of some higher, invisible reality. His attention to the sights, sounds, and odors of the garden indicate his attachment to the physical world and point to his sensitivity to human finitude, change, and the problem of death.[27]

Memories of the death of his daughter, and his inability to expel the demons of loss that torment him, provoke the Dreamer to speculate about the resurrection of the body and the prospect of an afterlife. His rational faculties and animal soul seem to understand and accept death and regeneration as an integral part of the cycle of nature (lines 29-32):

> Flor and fryte may not be fede
> Þer hit doun drof in moldez dunne,
> For vch gresse mot grow of graynez dede;
> No whete were ellez to wonez wonne.[28]

However much his "special spyce" may enrich the seed, he wonders whether some more perdurable quality is due her, and he cannot fully reconcile himself to the thought that she has dissolved into mere mud or clay. Yet the comfort he might derive from the Resurrection eludes him: "Þaȝ kynde of Kryst me comfort kenned, / My wreched wylle in wo ay wraȝte" (lines 55-56); it does not master his will and emotions, which incline toward the consolations of the erber. The erber in its colors, odors, and natural beauty thus imposes on our consciousness an acute awareness of the Dreamer's presence in his body and in a familiar human setting that remains embedded in our mind even after we take flight with him to traverse the landscape of the other world.

These two currents converge in the Dreamer's mind when he identifies the occasion as both a religious holiday and the height of the harvest season. Aers has shown that the holiday and the suggestion of human activity unfolding outside or beyond the erber bring out the poignancy of the Dreamer's isolation and distance from the community.[29] The Dreamer's words "In Auguste in a hyȝ seysoun, / Quen corne is coruen wyth crokez kene" (lines 39-40) pit the imagery of the coming of winter and impending death against the celebration of life in its plenitude. The particularity of the Dreamer's language allows us to visualize this particular August, this field of corn, these workers with their sharp sickles. His consciousness of the organic growth from seed to flower and of the interpenetration of nature and human beings offsets the earlier images of disintegration and decay and serves as a buffer for his loss. The continuity and self-renewal of nature in its annual cycles thus vies in his mind with the linear plane of eschatological time or salvation history.[30]

Suffused with the scent of the flowers that surround him, he drifts into sleep. He dreams of a vineyard, not only because the parable centers on a harvest but also because it contains all the conflicting tensions he has been turning over in his mind. For when he departs from the erber, he explicitly leaves his body behind: "My body on balke þer bod. In sweuen" (line 62). The separation of the soul from the body as prerequisite for entry into the other world illuminates the source of much of his anguish. His eventual return to his body could imply a plea for the resurrection of the body, an appeal to heal the body-spirit schism and thus restore human nature to its original dignity. The Dreamer's return to the erber also posits a theology open to the world, and thus a counter to the *contemptus mundi* motif inherent in the Maiden's discourse.

The lines of the dialectic are sharply drawn once the Dreamer meets the Maiden in his dream. What disrupts the joy of their reconciliation is his dismay over her disclosure that she has been made a queen of heaven, when Christians here on earth accept only Mary as queen. The Maiden patiently explains to the Dreamer that many strive for heaven and many achieve it but that there are no "supplanters" within the place and all who arrive are made kings or queens. Then, drawing on Paul's analogy to the body in 1 Cor. 12:12-31, the Maiden explains to him that the heavenly order differs from the earthly norm. In heaven, she says, everyone cares for and belongs to the other (lines 457-68):

> Of courtaysye, as saytz Saynt Poule,
> Al arn we membrez of Jesu Kryst:
> As heued and arme and legg and naule
> Temen to hys body ful trwe and tryste,
> Ryȝt so is vch a Krysten sawle
> A longande lym to þe Mayster of myste.
> Þenne loke: what hate oþer any gawle
> Is tached oþer tyȝed þy lymmez bytwyste?
> Þy heued hatz nauþer greme ne gryste
> On arme oþer fynger þaȝ þou ber byȝe.
> So fare we alle wyth luf and lyste
> To kyng and quene by cortaysye.

Although the Maiden's aim is to attend to the invisible or heavenly application of the analogy, her language exceeds her announced intention. Christ's body in its physical dimensions obtrudes and takes on a significance of its own. As David Jeffrey has shown in respect to medieval painting, when the natural world is made fully natural, it may no longer signify the spiritual. That is, when the vividness or realism of the visible, physical object that refers is more pronounced than the spiritual or invisible thing to which it refers, the signs cease to function with the same directness.[31] Accordingly, in this passage, we are more likely to register an impression of the physical or material body of Christ, than the mystical concept—more so if we have been an audience that had become increasingly exposed to what Ullmann identified as the growing pervasiveness of incarnational images.

Christ's navel, the most unusual and arresting item in the catalogue of Christ's physical properties, does the most work to capture our attention and prevents us from responding passively to an otherwise metaphoric commonplace. Making *navel* a rhyme word with *sawle* and with *Poule* draws added attention to it and suggests the inseparable link of the body with the soul. More suggestively, the navel is what connects the audience to and reminds it of their common origins in Adam and redemption in Christ, whose birth from a human mother and acceptance of a complete human nature characterized incarnational devotion at that time.

The incarnational strain in fourteenth-century theology, in concert with the *via moderna* and Franciscan spirituality in general, called attention to Christ's body as a further indication that human nature was created in the image and likeness of Christ. Here again the aim was to stress the positive aspect of human nature, its inherent nobility and its capacity to act ethically. This theology was also secular in its outlook, insofar as it sought the political as well as moral improvement of human society. Graeco-Roman body-politic ideology had been revived for the later Middle Ages by John of Salisbury, and, Peter Travis tells us, Paul's exaltation of Christ's body stimulated the imagination of the poets and artists, as well as the theologians, to use it as a metaphor for social unity and social harmony:

> Recognizing the tendency of social bodies to break up into misaligned fragments, yet appreciating the special importance of the *most lowly organs* [Christ's navel?], Paul's version of Christ's body and the unifying and disunifying function of its discrete parts is a version that ramifies throughout the Middle Ages. Not only was this living metaphor sacralized in peculiarly complicated ways in the idea of the king's two bodies, but it blended with various late medieval ways of conceiving the polis, the city on earth perceived as a sacred human organism of interdependent economic, social, political, and geographic units. [Italics added.][32]

One effect of the incarnational emphasis, then, was to transpose to the human plane, as a this-worldly possibility and as a specifically human goal, the social harmony and spirit of mutuality that the Maiden presents as an (exclusively) other-worldly ideal.

What the Dreamer does not yet grasp, and will not until after he has his vision and beholds the Eucharist in the Mass, is an incarnational understanding of the world. Nor does he as yet see the body of Christ as the sign of a continuity between this world and the other world, life and death, human and divine, that eluded him in the erber.[33] But his receptivity of the incarnational is implicit in his language, even if it is not articulated in a theological vocabulary, first in his impression of a redeemed nature in the erber and here in the confidence he shows toward the moral responsibility of the human community. Those who have endured the trials of this world and have lived their penance in it, he proclaims, are the ones most deserving to wear the crown and be at one with Christ's body (lines 475-80):

> What more honour moȝte he acheue
> Þat hade endured in worlde stronge,
> And lyued in penaunce hys lyuez longe
> With bodyly bale hym blysse to byye?
> What more worschyp moȝt he fonge
> Þen corounde be kyng by cortaysé?

His reluctance to celebrate the Maiden's heavenly status is not intended to deny her a place in heaven, only that it seems to him that human beings purchase their salvation with "bodyly bale." Indirectly the Dreamer's argument summarizes the view of the *moderni* on justification. His emphasis on work in the world assumes the essential goodness of human nature and accepts the obligation to work in the vineyard as the human side of the *pactum*.[34]

In response to the Dreamer's contention that God's "courtesy" is too generous if it allows someone to be queen who has scarcely lived two years in the world and who, he says, "cowþez neuer God nauþer plese ne pray, / Ne neuer nawþer Pater ne Crede" (lines 484-85),[35] the Maiden recites the vineyard parable as an object lesson (it is she who is didactic, not the poet) that will teach him that there is no "date" or limit to God's mercy and goodness (lines 495-500):

> For al is trawþe þat He con dresse,
> And He may do noþynk bot ryȝt.
> As Mathew melez in your messe
> In sothfol Gospel of God almyȝt:
> In sample He can ful grayþely gesse
> And lyknez hit to heuen lyȝte.

Her interpretation of the parable conforms to the Augustinian theme of salvation in the other world, but her homely, familiar recitation of the parable itself pulls against the soteriological meaning she tries to extract from it. As with her allusion to Christ's body, the physical object that refers is more pronounced than the invisible thing to which it refers, and we see more than just the heavenly application when we become absorbed in the vivid details of a contemporary harvest scene Brueghelian in its realism.[36]

First the householder is given a ring of authenticity by the skill he displays in knowing the most propitious time to secure the vines: "Of tyme of ȝere þe terme watz tyȝt, / To labor vyne watz dere þe date. / Þat date of ȝere wel knawe þys hyne" (lines 503-505). Chaucer employs similar language to characterize the acumen of his Reeve: "Wel wiste he by the droghte and by the reyn / The yeldynge of his seed and of his greyn" (*GP* 595-96) (the *Pearl* poet's "reve" also controls the purse strings of his master; lines 541-48). The emphasis in both of these passages falls on experience and the knowledge that accrues to human beings who are in harmony with nature and nature's time.

The *Pearl* poet's feel for human beings in rhythm with their surroundings and in tune with their work, such as the sailors in *Patience* and the armorers in *Sir Gawain and the Green Knight* (or the masons in *Saint Erkenwald* with their "eggit toles"—a scene worthy if not imitative of the *Pearl* poet), not only heightens the realism of his poems but also helps reorient his audience toward the purposefulness of the ordinary in this world. Most of these scenes and the workers themselves are evidently peripheral to the main focus of the poem, yet it is precisely through them that the poet is able to articulate an important theme of his poem: humble, routine labor and those in the margins of society are vitally connected to the concerns of the community. And, since the work activity occurs in poems that revolve around a moral or theological crisis, he appears to be imputing a sacramental purpose to work no matter how remote it may stand from official spiritual activity.

In the parable the poet synchronizes the labor of the vine workers with the rise and fall of the sun and with the canonical hours. Time is measured by the change in the color of the sky and by the pleasure or pain the workers feel as they "Wryþen and worchen and don gret pyne, / Keruen and caggen and man hit clos" (lines 511-12). The Maiden's narrative respects, perhaps privileges, the generosity of the householder, but the heat of the day, its length, and its exhausting toll on the workers, suretched out by the effective use of polysyndeton in the lines just cited, generates sympathy for the disgruntled day laborers, who feel unfairly compensated for their efforts (lines 549-56):

> And þenne þe fyrst bygonne to pleny
> And sayden þat þay hade trauayled sore:

"Þese bot on oure hem con streny;
Vus þynk vus oȝe to take more.
More haf we serued, vus þynk so,
Þat suffred han þe dayez hete,
Þenn þyse þat wroȝt not hourez two,
And þou dotz hem vus to counterfete."

The workers evidently believe in a merit system wherein reward is proportionate to performance. To them the householder's generosity appears arbitrary and unjust. The real day laborers in the fourteenth century often worked exceedingly long hours for deplorably low wages and were systematically exploited by householders or the seigneurial class lends credence to the protests uttered by the vineyard workers.[37] In the poet's version of Matthew's parable, moreover, the workers are granted a greater recognition scene than they get in the biblical passage, rooting the poem, and the parable, more firmly in the social and economic milieu of the fourteenth century and making the question of justice in this world a more pointed one.

The householder defends his actions on the grounds of the covenant, the agreement he struck with the individual groups of workers before they entered the vineyard—although no mention is made of wages in the employment of the one-hour workers (lines 558-68):

Frende, no waning I wyl þe ȝete;
Take þat is þyn owne, and go.
And I hyred þe for a peny agrete,
Quy bygynneȝ þou now to þrete?
Watz not a pené þy couenaunt þore?
Fyrre þen couenaunde is noȝt to plete;
Wy schalte þou þenne ask more?
More, weþer louyly is me my gyfte—
To do wyth myn quatso me lykez?
Oþer ellez þyn yȝe to lyþer is lyfte
For I am goude and non byswykez?

The householder speaks placatingly to the day laborers here (he calls their leader "frende"), but he stands firm in his conviction that he has the right to reward as he pleases, as long as he does not violate his promise to the first in his generosity to the last. Legally or technically, the householder is correct in his stance, but the strength of any covenant lies in its mutuality, and any sense of injustice or unfairness could result in discontent or loss of respect, as expressed by the day laborers.

The concept of the covenant itself (no equivalent of which is in Matthew's version), however, does leave room for some reconciliation of grievances to be negotiated, which the poet underscores by its repetition in lines 562 and 563. For, in addition to its theological signification as the bond or working arrangement between God and humankind outlined by the *moderni,* the concept of the convenant had a rich heritage in English law, dating to the feudal period during which the lord and his vassals were united by reciprocal rights and duties.[38] Feudal law had or presupposed the cooperation of both lord and vassal toward a common goal, a cooperation that emanated from a concept of mutual fidelity.[39]

In the vineyard parable the vineyard itself, this earth, is the mutual ground that unites the workers and householder together, and on its growth and development depends the economic salvation of both laborers and landowner. Throughout the parable the householder's repeated injunctions against idleness and his several forays into the marketplace to recruit eager workers whose "hyre watz nawhere boun," that is, not fixed by covenant, and who are asked to do whatever they can (lines 531-36), open the vineyard to the entire community, giving the parable a Dantean turn. It is Dante who contends that only through the effort of all human beings working collectively toward peace and justice will humanity and human history actuate the totality of its *humanitas.*[40] For this enterprise all are called and all are chosen.

The *Pearl* poet does not seek to resolve the conflict between the laborers and the householder openly. He neither privileges the view of the householder nor discredits the complaints of the workers. Rather, he prefers to sustain the paradox built into the parable and its several levels of meaning so that the impasse between the parties serves as a provocation that both frustrates closure and allows questions of social justice and divine justice to arise naturally from the situation he depicts. Similarly, the narration of the parable itself does not settle the differences between the Dreamer and the Maiden, each of whom seems strengthened in his or her position by its recitation. At the close of the parable the Maiden likens the householder to Christ, who sheds his mercy graciously on the innocent "Þaȝ þay com late and lyttel wore, / And þaȝ her sweng wyth lyttel atslykez" (lines 574-75). She supports her argument by drawing on the moral force contained in the double epigram that concludes the parable: "Þe laste schal be þe fyrst þat strykez" (line 570), and "For mony ben called, þaȝ fewe be rnykez" (line 572). In her gloss the Maiden alludes to paradigms of universal and timeless significance, preeminently to the ideal of innocence and to the figure of the child as the highest beatitude. Because Christ beckons us to come to him as little children, she says, the innocent receive a greater portion of glory and bliss than all the people of the world might claim by seeking judgment on the grounds of their righteousness. The tag lines that echo throughout sections 11 and 12 respectively carry the burden of her argument: "Þe grace of God is gret innoȝe" and "Þe innosent is ay saf by ryȝt."

The Dreamer reacts boldly to her gloss ("Then more I meled and sayde apert"; line 589), telling her that her explication of hte text is unreasonable. Confidently expressing his own understanding of Scripture, he cites David's psalm as a more accurate reflection of the meaning of the parable (lines 595-600):

> "Þou quytez vchon as hys desserte,
> Þou hyȝe Kyng ay pertermynable."
> Now he þat stod þe long day stable,
> And þou to payment com hym byfore,
> Þenne þe lasse in werke to take more able,
> And euer þe lenger þe lasse þe more.

It is apparent that the Dreamer identifies with the point of view of the workers; he refuses to regard them abstractly, and his enthusiasm for those who "stand the long day stable," the many who are called, matches her zeal for the few who are chosen. In his persistence the Dreamer should not be dismissed as recalcitrant or simpleminded, as some have concluded, when his words show that he is as committed to his own theological convictions and moral values as the Maiden is to hers. What the Maiden attributes to the transcendent, the Dreamer continues to show is also part of the immanent, the personal, and the human.

The Maiden goes on to expound on the power of God's grace and the redemption of the innocent, at the end of which the Dreamer still expresses his wonderment— and doubt—that she should be exalted above those who have suffered for Christ "onvunder cambe" (line 775). The Dreamer's hesitancy sets the Maiden off on another lengthy disquisition, this time on salvation history. In her lesson the Maiden schools the Dreamer in the sinfulness of human life, Christ's suffering in the world at the hands of "boyez bolde" (line 806), his transformation into the Lamb, and the evolution of the New Jerusalem out of the earthly one. More and less, she tells him, are not relevant in God's kingdom; what does count is the salvation of one's soul. For her, recovery of the pearl in the other world is compensation enough for loss or death in this world. Hence she urges him (lines 743-44) to forsake this world if he wants to purchase his spotless pearl. She warns him that no one is righteous enough to warrant heaven (lines 697-700) on his or her own merits: "Forþy to corte quen þou schal com / Þer alle oure causez schal be cryed, / Alegge þe ryȝt, þou may be innome" (lines 701-703). She completes her lesson and brings the poem to its climax with an allusion to death and salvation that goes to the heart of the distress suffered by the Dreamer in the erber—his fear of death and bodily decay set against the promise of permanence and the release from all tension in the New Jerusalem. She assures him (lines 857-61):

> Alþaȝ oure corses in clottez clynge,
> And ȝe remen for rauþe wythouten reste,
> We þurȝoutly hauen cnawyng;
> Of on dethe ful oure hope is drest.
> Þe Lombe vus gladez, oure care is kest.

The Maiden's appeal situates intimacy—the lost intimacy the Dreamer had mourned for in the erber—in the New Jerusalem and in the Lamb who relieves all cares. Aware that she is a "reken rose" and he "bot mokke and mul among" (lines 905-906), he asks to be taken to that "blysful bor" (line 964) where peace reigns "withouten reles" (line 956).

Some readers have been disappointed with the Dreamer's description of the New Jerusalem; they find it flat and insipid, or a lapse of attention on the poet's part. More likely it is another instance of style creating meaning. Throughout the sequence the Dreamer defers his own responses to those he has read in John's Apocalypse. John's description, like the Maiden's lengthy speech, appeals to him intellectually but also shows the limitations of theological formulations to personal crises. The repetition in every stanza of some phrase that acknowledges John's description, "as Johan deuysed" or "as Johan hym wrytez," points up the Dreamer's role as reader and interpreter, but also his independence as a seer. He is no mere conduit for John's vision, and his own vision does not result in the renunciation of this world that the Maiden had urged on him. As impressed as he is with the vision, the Dreamer, like Dante, shows that one's ascent to the pinnacle of the other world need not obliterate the mutable world. Rather, the vision encourages the viewer, including John, another poet, to return to this world to work or to write in order to make this world approximate the heavenly ideal they had the privilege of seeing. So it is with the Dreamer.

His personal response does enter the moment he sees Christ's body, the wound in his side still spurting blood (lines 1135-37). Redemption of a personal kind is made real to him when he spies his daughter in the procession frolicking joyfully with her companions. What moves him is his irrepressible desire to join his daughter, to be part of the Body of Christ. Equally strong is the attraction of the "meyny schene," and how "þay wyth lyf wern laste and lade" (lines 1145-46). His sudden impulse to cross the river, "For luf-longyng in gret delyt" (line 1152), *is* his act of self-transcendence, his determination to be reunited to society, to be part of the human community again. His "luf-longyng" recalls the "luf-daungere" he felt in the opening passage of the poem, which no longer seems mysterious but identifies itself as that love of the earth which calls him back to his "erber grene" and to the fundamental human desire for the life of the body: back to the harvest, and back to the work that remains in the fields and in the vineyard.[41]

His self-assertion wakes him up, the vision dissipated, and we are constrained to ask, Is this the fall of man?[42] Does the Dreamer awaken in a "doel-doungoun" (line 1187) or in an "erber wlonk" (line 1187)? Viewed from one perspective, with one eye on his "lyttel quene" (line 1147) set in a "garlande gay" (line 1186) in the New Jerusalem, and the other eye on the Dreamer prostrate on her grave mound, this world (the "old muck ball," Beckett calls it) may seem indeed a place of exile. Yet the heavenly view need not invalidate the earthly one. At the end the narrator, who is at once the Dreamer and the one who has had the dream, can accept the vision of the eternal world, God's world, and its fulfillment. But he also accepts the fact that there is, contrary to Augustine, a real world here and a need to enjoy its pleasures and pains, to understand his purpose in the present life, and to comprehend still further his work here. To love the things of this world, the Dreamer has learned, is not to be attached overly to the material world or to be resistant to God's love and will. It is to understand and love better by seeing how such love brings about the full realization of one's humanness. The immanent world is not a rejection of the transcendent world; the Dreamer has buried his daughter. Rather, the presence of the transcendent—the knowledge of her continuity—compensates for the awareness at the root of Western consciousness of a profound sadness, or inescapable lack, to human existence.

Reawakened to the world around him, the Dreamer finds that he is not alone in the world. He discovers in the Eucharist, in the Body of Christ, "a frende ful fyin" (line 1204). Calling the Eucharist a "frende" echoes the householder's conciliatory gesture toward the day laborers in the vineyard parable (line 558), making the Eucharist a sign of the covenant or bond of mutual fidelity that joins the human with the divine. As Caroline Bynum remarks about eucharistic devotion in the late Middle Ages: "it stood for Christ's humanness and therefore for ours. Eating it and, in that eating, fusing with Christ's hideous physical suffering, the Christian not so much *escaped* as *became* the human."[43] The Eucharist thus becomes for the Dreamer a daily reminder of the dream, of the vineyard, of the vision of his daughter, and, finally, of a fully human redemption.

Like Dante, then, the Dreamer sees to see better. It is his vision, after all, not the Maiden's, and the writing or retelling of it affords him the retrospective view that yields meaning. He has lost one vision only to discern by his human sight a vision right in front of him. It is the Dreamer himself who draws the link between seed, penny, pearl, and Eucharist, the harvests of grain and grape, bread and wine. He knows he cannot lose himself in the seasons or the cycles of nature, nor can he withdraw to the heavenly Jerusalem. But he now knows who he is and to what kingdom he belongs. That he returns to the erber and reinhabits his body without any sense that he has fallen back into a sinful world assures us that he is not in exile here. Like Jonah in his woodbine, the Dreamer is at home in his "erber wlonk."

Notes

[1] Paul Zumthor, *Speaking of the Middle Ages,* trans. Sarah White (Lincoln: University of Nebraska Press, 1986), p. 63.

[2] See Theodore Bogdanos, *Pearl: Image of the Ineffable: A Study in Medieval Poetic Symbolism* (University Park: Pennsylvania State University Press, 1970); Ian Bishop, pearl *in Its Setting: A Critical Study of the Structure and Meaning of the Middle English Poem* (Oxford: Blackwell, 1968); Lynn Staley Johnson, *The Voice of the* Gawain-*Poet* (Madison: University of Wisconsin Press, 1984). Other texts that influenced my reacing of the poem are W. A. Davenport, *The Art of the* Gawain-*Poet* (London: Athlone, 1978); and, most recently, the excellent study by Sarah Stanbury, *Seeing the* Gawain *Poet: Description and the Act of Perception* (Philadelphia: University of Pennsylvania Press, 1992).

[3] See David Aers, "The Self Mourning: Reflections on *Pearl,*" *Speculum* 68 (1993): 54-73, esp. pp. 65-66.

[4] Ibid., p. 59.

[5] See M. M. Bakhtin, *The Dialogical Imagination,* ed. Michael Holquist, trans. Caryl Emerson and Michael Holquist (Austin: University of Texas Press, 1981), pp. 342-46.

[6] See Marie McLean, *Narrative as Performance: The Baudelairean Experiment* (London: Routledge, 1988), p. 20.

[7] Cited in ibid., pp. 20-21.

[8] For a detailed discussion of Augustine's argument and its influence in the later Middle Ages, see Alistair McGrath, *Iustitia Dei: A History of the Christian Doctrine of Justification,* vol. 1, *The Beginnings to the Reformation* (Cambridge: Cambridge University Press, 1986), pp. 53-70.

[9] For a clear statement of the nominalist anthropology of the *via moderna,* see Heiko Oberman, "Some Notes on the Theology of Nominalism," *HTR* 53 (1960): 47-76.

[10] I do not wish to give the impression that Biel was an opponent of Augustinianism, and I follow Francis Oakley in this regard (*The Western Church in the Later Middle Ages* [Ithaca, N.Y.: Cornell University Press, 1979], esp. pp. 131-74). Oakely shows that, while Augustinian terms did govern the theological discourse of the later Middle Ages, there were as many Augustinians in the thirteenth and fourteenth centuries as there were Platonists in the twelfth. Much of the intensification of the Augustinian language in the era,

he says, was as a response to the rise of a humanist sensibility in distinction to it (p. 136), and by the fourteenth century Augustine's views on justification were not the dominant ones.

[11] See Heiko Oberman, *The Harvest of Medieval Theology: Gabriel Biel and Late Medieval Nominalism* (Grand Rapids, Mich.: William E. Eerdmans, 1967), p. 214.

[12] Ibid., pp. 214-15.

[13] For a discussion of this point, see Gordon Leff, *Bradwardine and the Pelagians: A Study of His* De Causa Dei *and Its Opponents* (Cambridge: Cambridge University Press, 1957), pp. 140-59. See also Oberman, "Some Notes," p. 53.

[14] McGrath provides a detailed and extensive analysis of this entire subject in *Iustitia Dei,* pp. 109-55, 166-80. He also provides a more abbreviated discussion, which I rely on here, that superbly conveys the gist of the matter as it applies to the social and political issues involved. See Alistair McGrath, *The Intellectual Origins of the European Reformation* (Oxford: Blackwell, 1993), pp. 69-93.

[15] See McGrath, *Intellectual Origins,* pp. 80-82. In general, covenantalism characterizes the theology of Ockham and Duns Scotus, particularly in the areas of merit, the two powers of God, and the contingency of the world. In Oberman's words, covenantal theology sought to replace the hierarchy with a partnership or legal *pactum,* by designating human beings as "the appointed representatives of God, responsible for their own life, society, and world, within the limits of the covenant stipulated by God"; Heiko Oberman, "The Shape of Late Medieval Thought: The Birth Pangs of the Modern Era," in Heiko Oberman and Charles Trinkaus, eds., *The Pursuit of Holiness in the Later Middle Ages* (Leiden: Bril, 1974), p. 15. For additional discussion, see William Courtenay, *Covenant and Causality in Medieval Thought.* (London: Variorum Reprints, 1984), esp. pp. 94-115; and William Courtenay, *Schools and Scholars in Fourteenth Century England* (Princeton, N.J.: Princeton University Press, 1987), pp. 250-307. See also Steven Ozment, *The Age of Reform, 1250-1550: An Intellectual and Religious History of Late Medieval Europe* (New Haven, Conn.: Yale University Press, 1980), pp. 15-72.

[16] McGrath, *Intellectual Origins,* p. 81. For Ockham's view on God's freedom and the *pactum,* see William of Ockham, *Oxoniensis, 4 Sent.* q. 3 Q: "God freely institutes the conditions of beatitude and creates every creature from His will. He can, therefore, will anything with respect to creatures. If someone should love God and perform all the works approved by God, still God could annihilate him without offence, or he could

'reward' him with eternal punishment, for God is debtor to no one." See also ibid., 1 *Sent.* d, 17 q. 2 C: "God of his own free will can accept as meritorious an act arising *ex puris naturalibus* without the *habitus of caritas*"; cited in Janet Coleman, Piers Plowman *and the* Moderni (Rome: Edizioni Di Storia E Letteratura, 1981), pp. 201-202 n. 30.

[17] See Coleman, Piers Plowman *and the* Moderni, p. 15. See also Margaret Aston's comment: "Interest in scholastic theology radiated beyond the schools. In the 1330's William of Ockham remarked that the topic of free will attracted lay disputants, so that 'laymen and old women' were ready to take on 'even learned men and those skilled in theology'"; *Lollards and Reformers: Images and Literacy in Late Medieval Religion* (London: Hambledon, 1984), p. 130.

[18] Courtenay, *Schools and Scholars,* p. 380.

[19] Walter Ullmann, *The Medieval Foundations of Renaissance Humanism* (Ichaca, N.Y.: Cornell University Press, 1977), p. 84. See also Maurice Keen's observation that the widespread use of vernacular manuals with their emphasis on the humanity of Christ and attention to contemporary moral issues, "a strand in late medieval English religion very different from its preoccupation with the fate of the soul after death," may have had an influence on what he sees as a pronounced growth in charitable and socially directed activity in the fourteenth century; Maurice Keen, *English Society in the Later Middle Ages, 1348-1500* (London: Penguin, 1990), p. 284.

[20] See Heiko Oberman, *The Dawn of the Reformation* (Edinburgh: T&T Clark, 1986), pp. 15-16; Oberman, "The Shape of Late Medieval Thought," pp. 10-15.

[21] All citations of Chaucer's works are taken from Robert A. Pratt, ed., *The Tales of Canterbury, Complete, by Geoffrey Chaucer* (Boston: Houghton Mifflin, 1966).

[22] See Charles Muscatine, *Poetry and Crisis in the Age of Chaucer* (South Bend, Ind.: University of Notre Dame Press, 1972), p. 37.

[23] Erich Auerbach, *Dante: Poet of the Secular World,* trans. Ralph Manheim (Chicago: University of Chicago Press, 1961), p. 178.

[24] All citations of *Pearl* are taken from Malcolm Andrew and Ronald Waldron, eds., *The Poems of the* Pearl *Manuscript* (Berkeley and Los Angeles: University of California Press, 1978).

[25] For a general and informative introduction to Lacan's ideas as they relate to this discussion, see Stuart Schneiderman, *Jacques Lacan: The Death of an In-*

tellectual Hero (Cambridge, Mass.: Harvard University Press, 1983), pp. 150-55; see also Malcolm Bowie, *Freud, Proust, and Lacan: Theory as Fiction* (Cambridge: Cambridge University Press, 1988), pp. 99-135.

[26]Schneiderman, *Jacques Lacan,* pp. 151-52.

[27]Stanbury, *Seeing the* Gawain *Poet,* pp. 16-17, makes a perceptive comment on the poet's strategy: "In the Maiden's analysis, the dreamer's perceptual problem is one of relying on experience rather than authority. Authority here is not, of course, the validation given by books, but the authority of Scripture, the one book, or the validation of faith. Nevertheless, by centering perception on the dreamer, together with the primary interpretation of what is seen or heard, the poet exploits a technique of narrative engagement that subverts the Maiden's text on ocular skepticism without offering an alternative epistemological model, dramatizing rather a crisis of interpretation."

[28]For a discussion of flower and fruit imagery, or vegetation imagery in general, and its relation to personal renewal, see Gerhart B. Ladner, "Vegetation Symbolism and the Concept of Renaissance," in Millard Meiss, ed., *Essays in Honor of Erwin Panofsky, De Artibus Opuscula XL* (New York: New York University Press, 1961), pp. 303-22.

[29]Aers, "Self Mourning," pp. 57-58.

[30]For further discussion of this point see Aron Gurevich, *Medieval Popular Culture: Problems of Belief and Perception,* trans. Janos M. Bak and Paul A. Hollingsworth (Cambridge: Cambridge University Press, 1988), pp. 99-103.

[31]David Jeffrey, "Postscript," in David Jeffrey, ed., *By Things Seen: Reference and Recognition in Medieval Thought* (Ottawa: University of Ottawa Press, 1979), p. 251. See also Jeffrey's suggestion, p. 240, that with the appearance of Aristotelean thought the current from Being to becoming reverses and it is the rich experience of the created order which leads men to an apprehension of its eternal model. Immanence itself, he says, does not prevail until vertical organization—the principle of reference—gives way to horizontal order.

[32]Peter W. Travis, "The Semiotics of Christ's Body in the English Cycles," in Richard Emmerson, ed., *Approaches to Teaching Medieval English Drama* (New York: MLA Publications, 1990), pp. 72-73. See also Peter W. Travis, "The Social Body of the Dramatic Christ in Medieval England," *Acta* 13 (1985): 17-36.

[33]For a general discussion of the poet's reliance on incarnational images and its theology in *Pearl,* see Bogdanos, *Pearl,* pp. 10-12.

[34] See Anonymous, "Our Daily Work: A Mirror of Discipline," in David Jeffrey, *The Law of Love: English Spirituality in the Age of Wyclif* (Grand Rapids, Mich.: Eerdmans, 1988), pp. 236-64. The anonymous author emphasizes the importance of work to salvation and likens Christians to servants in God's vineyard who are called upon to work. He goes on to say that "that person prays without ceasing who is always doing good"; p. 246.

[35] The Dreamer's references to the "Pater" and the "Creed" indicate how seriously he took the responsibility to learn the minimum that was required of the laity in one's understanding of the faith. In addition to the Creed and Paternoster, the laity were expected to know the Ave Maria, the sacraments, the seven deadly sins, works of charity, the acts of mercy, and the seven virtues, all of which attested to a concerted desire to have a more active as well as more informed laity. See also R. N. Swanson, *Church and Society in Late Medieval England* (London: Blackwell, 1993), pp. 275-99.

[36] Those critics who have linked the vineyard parable to the harvest or have recognized its special appeal to the agricultural society of the fourteenth century are Paul Piehler, *The Visionary Landscape: A Study of Medieval Allegory* (Montreal: McGill-Queens University Press, 1971), pp. 150-52; Spearing, *The* Gawain *Poet,* p. 101; and Bogdanos, *Pearl,* p. 91.

[37] In fourteenth-century France the vineyard day laborers had a widespread reputation for standing up for wage and work reform against strong opposition from their noble and ecclesiastical employers. See Jacques LeGoff, *Time, Work, and Culture in the Middle Ages,* trans. Arthur Goldhammer (Chicago: University of Chicago Press, 1980), p. 47 and n. 25. For a discussion of labor conditions, clocks, and the social effects of both the Ordinance of Labourers and the Statute of Labourers, see Christopher Dyer, *Standards of Living in the Later Middle Ages: Social Change in England, c. 1200-1520* (Cambridge: Cambridge University Press, 1989), pp. 27-86, 219-32; see also Keen, *English Society,* pp. 27-47.

[38] In this regard see the arrangement between the Reeve and his master in Chaucer's *General Prologue:* "His swyn, his hors, his stoor, and his pultrye / Was hoolly in this Reves governynge, / And by his covenant yaf the rekenynge" (lines 598-600).

[39] Ullmann, *Medieval Foundations.*

[40] For Dante's view of history and human development, see Gerald Groveland Walsh, "Dante's Philosophy of History," *Catholic Historical Review* 20 (1934): 117-34; Ullmann, *Medieval Foundations,* pp. 128-38. For the connection between Dante and the *Pearl* poet,

see R. A. Shoaf, "*Purgatorio* and *Pearl:* Transgression and Transcendence," *TSLL* 32 (1990): 152-68.

[41] Lee Patterson's comment about Chaucer's poetry seems equally suitable to apply to the Dreamer and the *Pearl* poet himself: "the characteristic location of Chaucerian poetry is precisely the middle ground, the space between an atemporal beginning and a transcendent end. . . . Man is a creature of the middle, a historical being who dreams of a moment before and after history that he can never finally attain"; Lee Patterson, "'What man artow?': Authorial Self-Definition in *The Tale of Sir Thopas* and *The Tale of Melibee,*" *SAC* 11 (1989): 174.

[42] Bogdanos, *Pearl,* p. 114, among others, answers this question affirmatively.

[43] Caroline Bynum, *Fragmentation and Redemption: Essays on Gender and the Human Body in Medieval Religion* (New York: Zone Books, 1991), p. 44. See also Miri Rubin's masterful study of the Eucharist in the late Middle Ages, *Corpus Christi: The Eucharist in Late Medieval Culture* (Cambridge: Cambridge University Press, 1991). Rubin says that the Eucharist as symbol bound together the essential narratives of the Incarnation, the Crucifixion, and the Redemption: "It was this-worldly in emphasizing that channels of regeneration and salvation were available and attainable, renewable and never exhaustible. It possessed little of the eschatological pull which informed the cultural worlds of late antiquty, or of the early modern era, but was geared toward the present, was fulfilled here and now, offering powerful and tangible rewards to the living in the present, as well as to their relatives the dead"; p. 348.

FURTHER READING

Aers, David. "The Self Mourning: Reflections on *Pearl.*" *Speculum* 68, No. 1 (1993): 59-73.

> Finds that the institution of the church is strangely absent in a poem that deals with the self and Christian teaching.

Andrew, Malcolm and Ronald Waldron, editors. *The Poems of the Pearl Manuscript: Pearl, Cleanness, Patience, Sir Gawain and the Green Knight.* York Medieval Texts, 2nd series. Berkeley: University of California Press, 1979, 15-17, 29-36.

> Places *Pearl* in the dream-vision tradition and emphasizes spiritual transformation of the dreamer. Also has a select bibliography.

Blenkner, Louis. "The Pattern of Traditional Images in *Pearl.*" *Studies in Philology* 68, No. 1 (1971): 26-49.

> Shows how traditional patterns found in medieval theories of imagery are used in the poem to demonstrate the proper signification of the pearl symbol.

————. "The Theological Structure of *Pearl*" (1968). In *The Middle English Pearl: Critical Essays,* edited by John Conley, 220-65. Notre Dame, Indiana: University of Notre Dame Press, 1970.

> Makes an analogy between the poem's tripartite structure and the traditional three-part ascent of the soul to God.

Bloomfield, Morton W. "Some Notes on *Pearl* (lines 1-12, 61, 775-76, 968)" (1964). In *Studies in Language, Literature, and Culture of the Middle Ages and Later,* edited by E. Bagby Atwood and Archibald A. Hill, 300-02. Austin: University of Texas Press, 1969.

> Offers corrections to previous translations of four passages.

Bogdanos, Theodore. *Pearl, Image of the Ineffable: A Study in Medieval Poetic Symbolism.* University Park: Pennsylvania State University Press, 1983. 168 p.

> Interprets *Pearl* through a study of medieval poetic symbolism.

Borroff, Marie, translator. *Pearl: A New Verse Translation.* New York: Norton, 1977, vii-xxi.

> Discusses thematic links with the other poems in the manuscript as well as symbolism, literary background, and design.

Brewer, D. S. "Courtesy and the *Gawain*-Poet." In *Patterns of Love and Courtesy: Essays in Memory of C. S. Lewis,* edited by John Lawlor, 54-85. London: Edward Arnold, 1966.

> Describes the poet's use of fourteenth-century terms to convey the abstraction of 'courtesy' (the good), which he identifies with Christian love.

Conley, John. "*Pearl* and a Lost Tradition" (1955). In *The Middle English Pearl: Critical Essays,* edited by John Conley, 50-72. Notre Dame, Indiana: University of Notre Dame Press, 1970.

> Insists that *Pearl* is a Christian consolatio.

Davenport, W. A. *The Art of the Gawain-Poet.* London: Athlone Press, 1978, 7-18, 51-4.

> Argues that the poem is a fiction in which the narrator reveals his change from depression to a more balanced state of mind.

Eckhardt, Caroline D. "Woman as Mediator in the Middle English Romances." *Journal of Popular Culture* 14, No. 1 (1980): 94-107.

> Discusses the role of woman as intercessor revealed in the narratives of Middle English romances and the response of audiences to them.

Finlayson, John. "*Pearl*: Landscape and Vision." *Studies in Philology* 71, No. 3 (1974): 314-43.
Explains the relationship of the dreamer to his three locations and shows what this progression reveals about his experience.

Garrett, Robert Max. *The Pearl: An Interpretation.* Seattle: University of Washington Press, 1918. 45 p.
Sees the pearl as a symbol for the Holy Eucharist.

Gordon, E. V., editor. Introduction to *Pearl.* Oxford: Clarendon Press, 1953, ix-lii.
Covers manuscript, form, theme, symbolism, sources, language and author, as well as major points of critical controversy.

Greene, Walter Kirkland. "The Pearl—A New Interpretation." *PMLA* 40, No. 4 (1925): 814-27.
Emphasizes the theme of the fallen soul and its redemption.

Hieatt, Constance. "*Pearl* and the Dream-Vision Tradition." *Studia Neophilologica* 37 (1965): 139-45.
Argues that the poet uses the dream both as a unifying device for his poem and as a valid way of presenting ambiguous or difficult material.

Hoffman, Stanton de Voren. "The *Pearl*: Notes for an Interpretation." *Modern Philology* 58, No. 2 (1960): 73-80.
Basing his interpretation on the pearl symbol and motifs of innocence, death, and renewal, argues that the poem is an elegy with the theme of spiritual adventure, a quest of the soul towards truth.

Horgan, A. D. "Justice in *The Pearl*." *Review of English Studies* 32 (1981): 173-80.
Shows how the debate about the child's salvation contrasts traditional Western ideas of justice with the spiritual concept of justice revealed in God's unlimited grace and mercy.

Johnson, Lynn Staley. *The Voice of the Gawain-Poet.* Madison: University of Wisconsin Press, 1984, xvi-xix, 144-210.
Shows how the complex imagery of *Pearl* can be understood by revealing parallels between the narrator's spiritual growth and elements of the medieval Mary Magdalene tradition.

Johnson, Wendell Stacy. "The Imagery and Diction of the *Pearl*: Toward an Interpretation." *ELH* 20, No. 3 (1953): 161-80.
Argues that the poem embodies the contrasting meaning revealed by two groups of images, those depicting this world and those depicting the next.

McGalliard, John C. "Links, Language, and Style in the *Pearl*" (1963). In *Studies in Language, Literature, and Culture of the Middle Ages and Later*, edited by E. Bagby Atwood and Archibald A. Hill, 279-299. Austin: University of Texas Press, 1969.
Describes concatenating links among stanzas and their groups; mentions difficulties in meter, dialect, and syntax; and discusses the intensity of connotation produced by "symbolic forms" where sound is especially suited to meaning in some word groups.

Madeleva, Sister Mary. *Pearl: A Study in Spiritual Dryness.* New York: Appleton, 1925, 89-193.
Regards the pearl as a symbol for the poet's soul, and sees the poem as an exposition on interior desolation.

Moorman, Charles. *The Pearl-Poet.* Twayne English Author Series. New York: Twayne, 1968, 1-63.
Suggests elegiac theme of acceptance through suffering and the revelation of death as part of the universal plan.

Nichols, Jonathan. "Expectations of Courtesy Confounded: The Dreamer and the Maiden in *Pearl*." In *The Matter of Courtesy: Medieval Courtesy Books and the Gawain-Poet.* Suffolk, Great Britain: D. S. Brewer, 1985, 103-111.
Argues that the poet overturns dreamer's and readers' dual expectations regarding authority in family and medieval social order to illustrate differences between heavenly and earthly kingdoms.

Nolan, Barbara. *The Gothic Visionary Perspective.* Princeton: Princeton University Press, 1977, xiii-xvii, 156-204.
Shows how the poet combines symbolism of form and number with dream-vision genre to demonstrate the spiritual transformation of the narrator.

Petroff, Elizabeth. "Landscape in Pearl: Transformation of Nature." *Chaucer Review* 16, No. 2 (1981): 181-93.
Landscape imagery of the poem is related both to the liturgy for the Assumption of the Virgin and to the blessing of medicinal herbs and agricultural harvests.

Richardson, F. E. "The Pearl: A Poem and Its Audience." *Neophilologus* 46 (1962): 308-15.
Discusses the action by which the four great themes of *Pearl* are developed.

Robertson, D. W., Jr. "The 'Heresy' of *The Pearl*" (1955). In *The Middle English Pearl: Critical Essays*, edited by John Conley, 291-96. Notre Dame, Indiana: University of Notre Dame Press, 1970.
Answers the charge of heresy in the poem by demonstrating the orthodoxy of the poet's use of the parable of the Workers in the Vineyard.

————. "The Pearl as Symbol." *Modern Language Notes* 65, No. 3 (1950): 155-61.
Discusses the pearl symbol in terms of the four levels of scriptural exegesis in use during the Middle Ages.

Russell, J. Stephen. *The English Dream Vision: Anatomy of a Form.* Columbus: Ohio State University Press, 1988, 139-42, 159-74.

Discusses the dream-vision form followed by deconstructionist criticism of *Pearl* and Chaucer's *Book of the Duchess* and *House of Fame.*

Sklute, Larry M. "Expectation and Fulfillment in *Pearl.*" *Philological Quarterly* 52, No. 4 (1973): 663-79.

Focuses on readers, whose expectations about consolation are fulfilled because they, like the narrator, have struggled to understand by faith truths about the divine.

Spearing, A. C. "Symbolic and Dramatic Development in *Pearl*" (1962). In *The Middle English Pearl: Critical Essays*, edited by John Conley, 122-48. Notre Dame, Indiana: University of Notre Dame Press, 1970.

Discusses how the poem embodies a dramatic process of both symbolic and human development.

Stern, Milton R. "An Approach to the *Pearl*" (1955). In *The Middle English Pearl: Critical Essays*, edited by John Conley, 73-85. Notre Dame, Indiana: University of Notre Dame Press, 1970.

Discusses the poem in terms of gemology and the four levels of scriptural exegesis in use during the Middle Ages.

Tolkien, J. R. R., trans. Introduction to *Sir Gawain and the Green Knight, Pearl, and Sir Orfeo.* London: Allen and Unwin, 1975, 13-24.

Discusses dramatization as well as formal relationships among debate, elegy, allegory, symbolism, and dream-vision.

Turville-Petre, Thorlac. *The Alliterative Revival.* Cambridge: D. S. Brewer, 1977, 66-8.

Describes the poem's circular form in terms of its rhyming alliterative stanzas, their numerical symbolism, patterns of stanza linking and refrains, and the grouping of stanzas and group themes.

Williams, Margaret A., translator. Introduction to *The Pearl-Poet: His Complete Works.* New York: Random House, 1967, 3-18, 62-83.

Discusses manuscript, language and author, and the alliterative movement, and places *Pearl* in its literary tradition.

Wilson, Edward. "Pearl." In *The Gawain-Poet.* Medieval and Renaissance Authors Series. Leiden: E. J. Brill, 1976, 1-45.

Emphasizes *Pearl*'s rhetorical arrangement and recognizes many of its medieval analogues, especially the Middle English Abraham and Isaac dramas.

CLASSICAL AND MEDIEVAL LITERATURE CRITICISM

INDEXES

Literary Criticism Series
Cumulative Author Index

Literary Criticism Series
Cumulative Topic Index

CMLC Cumulative Nationality Index

CMLC Cumulative Title Index

CMLC Cumulative Critic Index

How to Use This Index

The main references

Calvino, Italo
1923-1985.....CLC 5, 8, 11, 22, 33, 39,
73; SSC 3

list all author entries in the following Gale Literary Criticism series:

BLC = *Black Literature Criticism*
CLC = *Contemporary Literary Criticism*
CLR = *Children's Literature Review*
CMLC = *Classical and Medieval Literature Criticism*
DA = *DISCovering Authors*
DAB = *DISCovering Authors: British*
DAC = *DISCovering Authors: Canadian*
DAM = *DISCovering Authors Modules*
   DRAM: Dramatists module
   MST: Most-studied authors module
   MULT: Multicultural authors module
   NOV: Novelists module
   POET: Poets module
   POP: Popular/genre writers module

DC = *Drama Criticism*
HLC = *Hispanic Literature Criticism*
LC = *Literature Criticism from 1400 to 1800*
NCLC = *Nineteenth-Century Literature Criticism*
PC = *Poetry Criticism*
SSC = *Short Story Criticism*
TCLC = *Twentieth-Century Literary Criticism*
WLC = *World Literature Criticism, 1500 to the Present*

The cross-references

See also CANR 23; CA 85-88;
obituary CA 116

list all author entries in the following Gale biographical and literary sources:

AAYA = *Authors & Artists for Young Adults*
AITN = *Authors in the News*
BEST = *Bestsellers*
BW = *Black Writers*
CA = *Contemporary Authors*
CAAS = *Contemporary Authors Autobiography Series*
CABS = *Contemporary Authors Bibliographical Series*
CANR = *Contemporary Authors New Revision Series*
CAP = *Contemporary Authors Permanent Series*
CDALB = *Concise Dictionary of American Literary Biography*
CDBLB = *Concise Dictionary of British Literary Biography*

DLB = *Dictionary of Literary Biography*
DLBD = *Dictionary of Literary Biography Documentary Series*
DLBY = *Dictionary of Literary Biography Yearbook*
HW = *Hispanic Writers*
JRDA = *Junior DISCovering Authors*
MAICYA = *Major Authors and Illustrators for Children and Young Adults*
MTCW = *Major 20th-Century Writers*
NNAL = *Native North American Literature*
SAAS = *Something about the Author Autobiography Series*
SATA = *Something about the Author*
YABC = *Yesterday's Authors of Books for Children*

Literary Criticism Series
Cumulative Author Index

A. E. . . . . TCLC 3, 10
See also Russell, George William

Abasiyanik, Sait Faik 1906-1954
See Sait Faik
See also CA 123

Abbey, Edward 1927-1989 . . . . . . CLC 36, 59
See also CA 45-48; 128; CANR 2, 41

Abbott, Lee K(ittredge) 1947- . . . . . . CLC 48
See also CA 124; CANR 51; DLB 130

Abe, Kobo
1924-1993 . . . . CLC 8, 22, 53, 81;
DAM NOV
See also CA 65-68; 140; CANR 24; MTCW

Abelard, Peter c. 1079-c. 1142 . . . CMLC 11
See also DLB 115

Abell, Kjeld 1901-1961 . . . . CLC 15
See also CA 111

Abish, Walter 1931- . . . . CLC 22
See also CA 101; CANR 37; DLB 130

Abrahams, Peter (Henry) 1919- . . . . . CLC 4
See also BW 1; CA 57-60; CANR 26;
DLB 117; MTCW

Abrams, M(eyer) H(oward) 1912- . . . CLC 24
See also CA 57-60; CANR 13, 33; DLB 67

Abse, Dannie
1923- . . . CLC 7, 29; DAB; DAM POET
See also CA 53-56; CAAS 1; CANR 4, 46;
DLB 27

Achebe, (Albert) Chinua(lumogu)
1930- . . . . . CLC 1, 3, 5, 7, 11, 26, 51, 75;
BLC; DA; DAB; DAC; DAM MST,
MULT, NOV; WLC
See also AAYA 15; BW 2; CA 1-4R;
CANR 6, 26, 47; CLR 20; DLB 117;
MAICYA; MTCW; SATA 40;
SATA-Brief 38

Acker, Kathy 1948- . . . . CLC 45
See also CA 117; 122

Ackroyd, Peter 1949- . . . . CLC 34, 52
See also CA 123; 127; CANR 51; DLB 155;
INT 127

Acorn, Milton 1923- . . . . CLC 15; DAC
See also CA 103; DLB 53; INT 103

Adamov, Arthur
1908-1970 . . . . CLC 4, 25; DAM DRAM
See also CA 17-18; 25-28R; CAP 2; MTCW

Adams, Alice (Boyd) 1926- . . . CLC 6, 13, 46
See also CA 81-84; CANR 26, 53;
DLBY 86; INT CANR-26; MTCW

Adams, Andy 1859-1935 . . . . TCLC 56
See also YABC 1

Adams, Douglas (Noel)
1952- . . . . CLC 27, 60; DAM POP
See also AAYA 4; BEST 89:3; CA 106;
CANR 34; DLBY 83; JRDA

Adams, Francis 1862-1893 . . . . NCLC 33

Adams, Henry (Brooks)
1838-1918 . . . . . . TCLC 4, 52; DA; DAB;
DAC; DAM MST
See also CA 104; 133; DLB 12, 47

Adams, Richard (George)
1920- . . . . CLC 4, 5, 18; DAM NOV
See also AAYA 16; AITN 1, 2; CA 49-52;
CANR 3, 35; CLR 20; JRDA; MAICYA;
MTCW; SATA 7, 69

Adamson, Joy(-Friederike Victoria)
1910-1980 . . . . CLC 17
See also CA 69-72; 93-96; CANR 22;
MTCW; SATA 11; SATA-Obit 22

Adcock, Fleur 1934- . . . . CLC 41
See also CA 25-28R; CAAS 23; CANR 11,
34; DLB 40

Addams, Charles (Samuel)
1912-1988 . . . . CLC 30
See also CA 61-64; 126; CANR 12

Addison, Joseph 1672-1719 . . . . LC 18
See also CDBLB 1660-1789; DLB 101

Adler, Alfred (F.) 1870-1937 . . . . . . TCLC 61
See also CA 119

Adler, C(arole) S(chwerdtfeger)
1932- . . . . CLC 35
See also AAYA 4; CA 89-92; CANR 19,
40; JRDA; MAICYA; SAAS 15;
SATA 26, 63

Adler, Renata 1938- . . . . CLC 8, 31
See also CA 49-52; CANR 5, 22, 52;
MTCW

Ady, Endre 1877-1919 . . . . TCLC 11
See also CA 107

Aeschylus
525B.C.-456B.C. . . . . CMLC 11; DA;
DAB; DAC; DAM DRAM, MST

Afton, Effie
See Harper, Frances Ellen Watkins

Agapida, Fray Antonio
See Irving, Washington

Agee, James (Rufus)
1909-1955 . . . . TCLC 1, 19; DAM NOV
See also AITN 1; CA 108; 148;
CDALB 1941-1968; DLB 2, 26, 152

Aghill, Gordon
See Silverberg, Robert

Agnon, S(hmuel) Y(osef Halevi)
1888-1970 . . . . CLC 4, 8, 14
See also CA 17-18; 25-28R; CAP 2; MTCW

Agrippa von Nettesheim, Henry Cornelius
1486-1535 . . . . LC 27

Aherne, Owen
See Cassill, R(onald) V(erlin)

Ai 1947- . . . . CLC 4, 14, 69
See also CA 85-88; CAAS 13; DLB 120

Aickman, Robert (Fordyce)
1914-1981 . . . . CLC 57
See also CA 5-8R; CANR 3

Aiken, Conrad (Potter)
1889-1973 . . . . CLC 1, 3, 5, 10, 52;
DAM NOV, POET; SSC 9
See also CA 5-8R; 45-48; CANR 4;
CDALB 1929-1941; DLB 9, 45, 102;
MTCW; SATA 3, 30

Aiken, Joan (Delano) 1924- . . . . CLC 35
See also AAYA 1; CA 9-12R; CANR 4, 23,
34; CLR 1, 19; DLB 161; JRDA;
MAICYA; MTCW; SAAS 1; SATA 2,
30, 73

Ainsworth, William Harrison
1805-1882 . . . . NCLC 13
See also DLB 21; SATA 24

Aitmatov, Chingiz (Torekulovich)
1928- . . . . CLC 71
See also CA 103; CANR 38; MTCW;
SATA 56

Akers, Floyd
See Baum, L(yman) Frank

Akhmadulina, Bella Akhatovna
1937- . . . . CLC 53; DAM POET
See also CA 65-68

Akhmatova, Anna
1888-1966 . . . . CLC 11, 25, 64;
DAM POET; PC 2
See also CA 19-20; 25-28R; CANR 35;
CAP 1; MTCW

Aksakov, Sergei Timofeyvich
1791-1859 . . . . NCLC 2

Aksenov, Vassily
See Aksyonov, Vassily (Pavlovich)

Aksyonov, Vassily (Pavlovich)
1932- . . . . CLC 22, 37
See also CA 53-56; CANR 12, 48

Akutagawa Ryunosuke
1892-1927 . . . . TCLC 16
See also CA 117

Alain 1868-1951 . . . . TCLC 41

Alain-Fournier . . . . TCLC 6
See also Fournier, Henri Alban
See also DLB 65

Alarcon, Pedro Antonio de
1833-1891 . . . . NCLC 1

Alas (y Urena), Leopoldo (Enrique Garcia)
1852-1901 . . . . TCLC 29
See also CA 113; 131; HW

Albee, Edward (Franklin III)
1928- . . . . . . CLC 1, 2, 3, 5, 9, 11, 13, 25,
53, 86; DA; DAB; DAC; DAM DRAM,
MST; WLC
See also AITN 1; CA 5-8R; CABS 3;
CANR 8; CDALB 1941-1968; DLB 7;
INT CANR-8; MTCW

Alberti, Rafael 1902- . . . . CLC 7
See also CA 85-88; DLB 108

Albert the Great 1200(?)-1280 . . . . CMLC 16
See also DLB 115

411

Alcala-Galiano, Juan Valera y
See Valera y Alcala-Galiano, Juan

Alcott, Amos Bronson 1799-1888 .. **NCLC 1**
See also DLB 1

Alcott, Louisa May
1832-1888 .... **NCLC 6; DA; DAB;**
DAC; DAM MST, NOV; WLC
See also CDALB 1865-1917; CLR 1, 38;
DLB 1, 42, 79; DLBD 14; JRDA;
MAICYA; YABC 1

Aldanov, M. A.
See Aldanov, Mark (Alexandrovich)

Aldanov, Mark (Alexandrovich)
1886(?)-1957 .... **TCLC 23**
See also CA 118

Aldington, Richard 1892-1962...... **CLC 49**
See also CA 85-88; CANR 45; DLB 20, 36,
100, 149

Aldiss, Brian W(ilson)
1925- .... **CLC 5, 14, 40; DAM NOV**
See also CA 5-8R; CAAS 2; CANR 5, 28;
DLB 14; MTCW; SATA 34

Alegria, Claribel
1924- .... **CLC 75; DAM MULT**
See also CA 131; CAAS 15; DLB 145; HW

Alegria, Fernando 1918-........... **CLC 57**
See also CA 9-12R; CANR 5, 32; HW

Aleichem, Sholom .... **TCLC 1, 35**
See also Rabinovitch, Sholem

Aleixandre, Vicente
1898-1984 .... **CLC 9, 36; DAM POET;**
PC 15
See also CA 85-88; 114; CANR 26;
DLB 108; HW; MTCW

Alepoudelis, Odysseus
See Elytis, Odysseus

Aleshkovsky, Joseph 1929-
See Aleshkovsky, Yuz
See also CA 121; 128

Aleshkovsky, Yuz .... **CLC 44**
See also Aleshkovsky, Joseph

Alexander, Lloyd (Chudley) 1924- .. **CLC 35**
See also AAYA 1; CA 1-4R; CANR 1, 24,
38; CLR 1, 5; DLB 52; JRDA; MAICYA;
MTCW; SAAS 19; SATA 3, 49, 81

Alexie, Sherman (Joseph, Jr.)
1966- .... **CLC 96; DAM MULT**
See also CA 138; NNAL

Alfau, Felipe 1902-............... **CLC 66**
See also CA 137

Alger, Horatio, Jr. 1832-1899 ..... **NCLC 8**
See also DLB 42; SATA 16

Algren, Nelson 1909-1981 .... **CLC 4, 10, 33**
See also CA 13-16R; 103; CANR 20;
CDALB 1941-1968; DLB 9; DLBY 81,
82; MTCW

Ali, Ahmed 1910- .... **CLC 69**
See also CA 25-28R; CANR 15, 34

Alighieri, Dante 1265-1321 .... **CMLC 3, 18**

Allan, John B.
See Westlake, Donald E(dwin)

Allen, Edward 1948-.............. **CLC 59**

Allen, Paula Gunn
1939- .... **CLC 84; DAM MULT**
See also CA 112; 143; NNAL

Allen, Roland
See Ayckbourn, Alan

Allen, Sarah A.
See Hopkins, Pauline Elizabeth

Allen, Woody
1935- .... **CLC 16, 52; DAM POP**
See also AAYA 10; CA 33-36R; CANR 27,
38; DLB 44; MTCW

Allende, Isabel
1942- .... **CLC 39, 57; DAM MULT,**
NOV; HLC
See also AAYA 18; CA 125; 130;
CANR 51; DLB 145; HW; INT 130;
MTCW

Alleyn, Ellen
See Rossetti, Christina (Georgina)

Allingham, Margery (Louise)
1904-1966 .... **CLC 19**
See also CA 5-8R; 25-28R; CANR 4;
DLB 77; MTCW

Allingham, William 1824-1889 ... **NCLC 25**
See also DLB 35

Allison, Dorothy E. 1949- .... **CLC 78**
See also CA 140

Allston, Washington 1779-1843.... **NCLC 2**
See also DLB 1

Almedingen, E. M. .... **CLC 12**
See also Almedingen, Martha Edith von
See also SATA 3

Almedingen, Martha Edith von 1898-1971
See Almedingen, E. M.
See also CA 1-4R; CANR 1

Almqvist, Carl Jonas Love
1793-1866 .... **NCLC 42**

Alonso, Damaso 1898-1990 .... **CLC 14**
See also CA 110; 131; 130; DLB 108; HW

Alov
See Gogol, Nikolai (Vasilyevich)

Alta 1942-...................... **CLC 19**
See also CA 57-60

Alter, Robert B(ernard) 1935-...... **CLC 34**
See also CA 49-52; CANR 1, 47

Alther, Lisa 1944-.............. **CLC 7, 41**
See also CA 65-68; CANR 12, 30, 51;
MTCW

Altman, Robert 1925-............. **CLC 16**
See also CA 73-76; CANR 43

Alvarez, A(lfred) 1929-.......... **CLC 5, 13**
See also CA 1-4R; CANR 3, 33; DLB 14,
40

Alvarez, Alejandro Rodriguez 1903-1965
See Casona, Alejandro
See also CA 131; 93-96; HW

Alvarez, Julia 1950-.............. **CLC 93**
See also CA 147

Alvaro, Corrado 1896-1956 .... **TCLC 60**

Amado, Jorge
1912- .... **CLC 13, 40; DAM MULT,**
NOV; HLC
See also CA 77-80; CANR 35; DLB 113;
MTCW

Ambler, Eric 1909-............ **CLC 4, 6, 9**
See also CA 9-12R; CANR 7, 38; DLB 77;
MTCW

Amichai, Yehuda 1924- ...... **CLC 9, 22, 57**
See also CA 85-88; CANR 46; MTCW

Amiel, Henri Frederic 1821-1881 .. **NCLC 4**

Amis, Kingsley (William)
1922-1995 ..... **CLC 1, 2, 3, 5, 8, 13, 40,**
44; DA; DAB; DAC; DAM MST, NOV
See also AITN 2; CA 9-12R; 150; CANR 8,
28; CDBLB 1945-1960; DLB 15, 27, 100,
139; INT CANR-8; MTCW

Amis, Martin (Louis)
1949- .... **CLC 4, 9, 38, 62**
See also BEST 90:3; CA 65-68; CANR 8,
27; DLB 14; INT CANR-27

Ammons, A(rchie) R(andolph)
1926- .... **CLC 2, 3, 5, 8, 9, 25, 57;**
DAM POET; PC 16
See also AITN 1; CA 9-12R; CANR 6, 36,
51; DLB 5, 165; MTCW

Amo, Tauraatua i
See Adams, Henry (Brooks)

Anand, Mulk Raj
1905- .... **CLC 23, 93; DAM NOV**
See also CA 65-68; CANR 32; MTCW

Anatol
See Schnitzler, Arthur

Anaya, Rudolfo A(lfonso)
1937- .... **CLC 23; DAM MULT, NOV;**
HLC
See also CA 45-48; CAAS 4; CANR 1, 32,
51; DLB 82; HW 1; MTCW

Andersen, Hans Christian
1805-1875 .... **NCLC 7; DA; DAB;**
DAC; DAM MST, POP; SSC 6; WLC
See also CLR 6; MAICYA; YABC 1

Anderson, C. Farley
See Mencken, H(enry) L(ouis); Nathan,
George Jean

Anderson, Jessica (Margaret) Queale
.... **CLC 37**
See also CA 9-12R; CANR 4

Anderson, Jon (Victor)
1940- .... **CLC 9; DAM POET**
See also CA 25-28R; CANR 20

Anderson, Lindsay (Gordon)
1923-1994 .... **CLC 20**
See also CA 125; 128; 146

Anderson, Maxwell
1888-1959 ...... **TCLC 2; DAM DRAM**
See also CA 105; 152; DLB 7

Anderson, Poul (William) 1926- .... **CLC 15**
See also AAYA 5; CA 1-4R; CAAS 2;
CANR 2, 15, 34; DLB 8; INT CANR-15;
MTCW; SATA-Brief 39

Anderson, Robert (Woodruff)
1917- .... **CLC 23; DAM DRAM**
See also AITN 1; CA 21-24R; CANR 32;
DLB 7

Anderson, Sherwood
1876-1941 .... **TCLC 1, 10, 24; DA;**
DAB; DAC; DAM MST, NOV; SSC 1;
WLC
See also CA 104; 121; CDALB 1917-1929;
DLB 4, 9, 86; DLBD 1; MTCW

Andier, Pierre
See Desnos, Robert

Andouard
See Giraudoux, (Hippolyte) Jean

Andrade, Carlos Drummond de ...... **CLC 18**
See also Drummond de Andrade, Carlos

Andrade, Mario de 1893-1945..... **TCLC 43**

Andreae, Johann V(alentin)
1586-1654 .... **LC 32**
See also DLB 164

Andreas-Salome, Lou 1861-1937... **TCLC 56**
See also DLB 66

Andrewes, Lancelot 1555-1626 .... **LC 5**
See also DLB 151

Andrews, Cicily Fairfield
See West, Rebecca

Andrews, Elton V.
See Pohl, Frederik

Andreyev, Leonid (Nikolaevich)
1871-1919 .... **TCLC 3**
See also CA 104

Andric, Ivo 1892-1975 .... **CLC 8**
See also CA 81-84; 57-60; CANR 43;
DLB 147; MTCW

Angelique, Pierre
See Bataille, Georges

Angell, Roger 1920- .... **CLC 26**
See also CA 57-60; CANR 13, 44

Angelou, Maya
1928- .... **CLC 12, 35, 64, 77; BLC; DA;**
DAB; DAC; DAM MST, MULT, POET,
POP
See also AAYA 7; BW 2; CA 65-68;
CANR 19, 42; DLB 38; MTCW;
SATA 49

Annensky, Innokenty Fyodorovich
1856-1909 .... **TCLC 14**
See also CA 110

Anon, Charles Robert
See Pessoa, Fernando (Antonio Nogueira)

Anouilh, Jean (Marie Lucien Pierre)
1910-1987 ...... **CLC 1, 3, 8, 13, 40, 50;**
DAM DRAM
See also CA 17-20R; 123; CANR 32;
MTCW

Anthony, Florence
See Ai

Anthony, John
See Ciardi, John (Anthony)

Anthony, Peter
See Shaffer, Anthony (Joshua); Shaffer,
Peter (Levin)

Anthony, Piers 1934- .. **CLC 35; DAM POP**
See also AAYA 11; CA 21-24R; CANR 28;
DLB 8; MTCW; SAAS 22; SATA 84

Antoine, Marc
See Proust, (Valentin-Louis-George-Eugene-)
Marcel

Antoninus, Brother
See Everson, William (Oliver)

Antonioni, Michelangelo 1912- ..... **CLC 20**
See also CA 73-76; CANR 45

Antschel, Paul 1920-1970
See Celan, Paul
See also CA 85-88; CANR 33; MTCW

Anwar, Chairil 1922-1949 .... **TCLC 22**
See also CA 121

Apollinaire, Guillaume
1880-1918 .... **TCLC 3, 8, 51;**
DAM POET; PC 7
See also Kostrowitzki, Wilhelm Apollinaris
de
See also CA 152

Appelfeld, Aharon 1932- .... **CLC 23, 47**
See also CA 112; 133

Apple, Max (Isaac) 1941- .... **CLC 9, 33**
See also CA 81-84; CANR 19; DLB 130

Appleman, Philip (Dean) 1926- ..... **CLC 51**
See also CA 13-16R; CAAS 18; CANR 6,
29

Appleton, Lawrence
See Lovecraft, H(oward) P(hillips)

Apteryx
See Eliot, T(homas) S(tearns)

Apuleius, (Lucius Madaurensis)
125(?)-175(?) .... **CMLC 1**

Aquin, Hubert 1929-1977......... **CLC 15**
See also CA 105; DLB 53

Aragon, Louis
1897-1982 ..... **CLC 3, 22; DAM NOV,**
POET
See also CA 69-72; 108; CANR 28;
DLB 72; MTCW

Arany, Janos 1817-1882........ **NCLC 34**

Arbuthnot, John 1667-1735 .... **LC 1**
See also DLB 101

Archer, Herbert Winslow
See Mencken, H(enry) L(ouis)

Archer, Jeffrey (Howard)
1940- .... **CLC 28; DAM POP**
See also AAYA 16; BEST 89:3; CA 77-80;
CANR 22, 52; INT CANR-22

Archer, Jules 1915- .... **CLC 12**
See also CA 9-12R; CANR 6; SAAS 5;
SATA 4, 85

Archer, Lee
See Ellison, Harlan (Jay)

Arden, John
1930- ..... **CLC 6, 13, 15; DAM DRAM**
See also CA 13-16R; CAAS 4; CANR 31;
DLB 13; MTCW

Arenas, Reinaldo
1943-1990 ...... **CLC 41; DAM MULT;**
HLC
See also CA 124; 128; 133; DLB 145; HW

Arendt, Hannah 1906-1975 .... **CLC 66**
See also CA 17-20R; 61-64; CANR 26;
MTCW

Aretino, Pietro 1492-1556 .... **LC 12**

Arghezi, Tudor................... **CLC 80**
See also Theodorescu, Ion N.

Arguedas, Jose Maria
1911-1969 .... **CLC 10, 18**
See also CA 89-92; DLB 113; HW

Argueta, Manlio 1936- .... **CLC 31**
See also CA 131; DLB 145; HW

Ariosto, Ludovico 1474-1533 .... **LC 6**

Aristides
See Epstein, Joseph

Aristophanes
450B.C.-385B.C......... **CMLC 4; DA;**
DAB; DAC; DAM DRAM, MST; DC 2

Arlt, Roberto (Godofredo Christophersen)
1900-1942 ..... **TCLC 29; DAM MULT;**
HLC
See also CA 123; 131; HW

Armah, Ayi Kwei
1939- .... **CLC 5, 33; BLC;**
DAM MULT, POET
See also BW 1; CA 61-64; CANR 21;
DLB 117; MTCW

Armatrading, Joan 1950- .... **CLC 17**
See also CA 114

Arnette, Robert
See Silverberg, Robert

Arnim, Achim von (Ludwig Joachim von
Arnim) 1781-1831 .... **NCLC 5**
See also DLB 90

Arnim, Bettina von 1785-1859.... **NCLC 38**
See also DLB 90

Arnold, Matthew
1822-1888 ..... **NCLC 6, 29; DA; DAB;**
DAC; DAM MST, POET; PC 5; WLC
See also CDBLB 1832-1890; DLB 32, 57

Arnold, Thomas 1795-1842 ...... **NCLC 18**
See also DLB 55

Arnow, Harriette (Louisa) Simpson
1908-1986 .... **CLC 2, 7, 18**
See also CA 9-12R; 118; CANR 14; DLB 6;
MTCW; SATA 42; SATA-Obit 47

Arp, Hans
See Arp, Jean

Arp, Jean 1887-1966............... **CLC 5**
See also CA 81-84; 25-28R; CANR 42

Arrabal
See Arrabal, Fernando

Arrabal, Fernando 1932- ... **CLC 2, 9, 18, 58**
See also CA 9-12R; CANR 15

Arrick, Fran.................... **CLC 30**
See also Gaberman, Judie Angell

Artaud, Antonin (Marie Joseph)
1896-1948 ... **TCLC 3, 36; DAM DRAM**
See also CA 104; 149

Arthur, Ruth M(abel) 1905-1979.... **CLC 12**
See also CA 9-12R; 85-88; CANR 4;
SATA 7, 26

Artsybashev, Mikhail (Petrovich)
1878-1927 .... **TCLC 31**

Arundel, Honor (Morfydd)
1919-1973 .... **CLC 17**
See also CA 21-22; 41-44R; CAP 2;
CLR 35; SATA 4; SATA-Obit 24

Asch, Sholem 1880-1957 .... **TCLC 3**
See also CA 105

Ash, Shalom
See Asch, Sholem

Ashbery, John (Lawrence)
1927- ...... **CLC 2, 3, 4, 6, 9, 13, 15, 25,**
41, 77; DAM POET
See also CA 5-8R; CANR 9, 37; DLB 5,
165; DLBY 81; INT CANR-9; MTCW

Ashdown, Clifford
See Freeman, R(ichard) Austin

Ashe, Gordon
See Creasey, John

Ashton-Warner, Sylvia (Constance)
1908-1984 . . . . **CLC 19**
See also CA 69-72; 112; CANR 29; MTCW

Asimov, Isaac
1920-1992 . . . . . . **CLC 1, 3, 9, 19, 26, 76,
92; DAM POP**
See also AAYA 13; BEST 90:2; CA 1-4R;
137; CANR 2, 19, 36; CLR 12; DLB 8;
DLBY 92; INT CANR-19; JRDA;
MAICYA; MTCW; SATA 1, 26, 74

Astley, Thea (Beatrice May)
1925- . . . . **CLC 41**
See also CA 65-68; CANR 11, 43

Aston, James
See White, T(erence) H(anbury)

Asturias, Miguel Angel
1899-1974 . . . . **CLC 3, 8, 13;
DAM MULT, NOV; HLC**
See also CA 25-28; 49-52; CANR 32;
CAP 2; DLB 113; HW; MTCW

Atares, Carlos Saura
See Saura (Atares), Carlos

Atheling, William
See Pound, Ezra (Weston Loomis)

Atheling, William, Jr.
See Blish, James (Benjamin)

Atherton, Gertrude (Franklin Horn)
1857-1948 . . . . **TCLC 2**
See also CA 104; DLB 9, 78

Atherton, Lucius
See Masters, Edgar Lee

Atkins, Jack
See Harris, Mark

Attaway, William (Alexander)
1911-1986 . . . . **CLC 92; BLC;
DAM MULT**
See also BW 2; CA 143; DLB 76

Atticus
See Fleming, Ian (Lancaster)

Atwood, Margaret (Eleanor)
1939- . . . . . **CLC 2, 3, 4, 8, 13, 15, 25, 44,
84; DA; DAB; DAC; DAM MST, NOV,
POET; PC 8; SSC 2; WLC**
See also AAYA 12; BEST 89:2; CA 49-52;
CANR 3, 24, 33; DLB 53;
INT CANR-24; MTCW; SATA 50

Aubigny, Pierre d'
See Mencken, H(enry) L(ouis)

Aubin, Penelope 1685-1731(?) . . . . **LC 9**
See also DLB 39

Auchincloss, Louis (Stanton)
1917- . . . . **CLC 4, 6, 9, 18, 45;
DAM NOV; SSC 22**
See also CA 1-4R; CANR 6, 29; DLB 2;
DLBY 80; INT CANR-29; MTCW

Auden, W(ystan) H(ugh)
1907-1973 . . . . . . **CLC 1, 2, 3, 4, 6, 9, 11,
14, 43; DA; DAB; DAC; DAM DRAM,
MST, POET; PC 1; WLC**
See also AAYA 18; CA 9-12R; 45-48;
CANR 5; CDBLB 1914-1945; DLB 10,
20; MTCW

Audiberti, Jacques
1900-1965 . . . . . . **CLC 38; DAM DRAM**
See also CA 25-28R

Audubon, John James
1785-1851 . . . . **NCLC 47**

Auel, Jean M(arie)
1936- . . . . **CLC 31; DAM POP**
See also AAYA 7; BEST 90:4; CA 103;
CANR 21; INT CANR-21

Auerbach, Erich 1892-1957 . . . . . . **TCLC 43**
See also CA 118

Augier, Emile 1820-1889 . . . . **NCLC 31**

August, John
See De Voto, Bernard (Augustine)

Augustine, St. 354-430 . . . . . **CMLC 6; DAB**

Aurelius
See Bourne, Randolph S(illiman)

Aurobindo, Sri 1872-1950 . . . . **TCLC 63**

Austen, Jane
1775-1817 . . . . . **NCLC 1, 13, 19, 33, 51;
DA; DAB; DAC; DAM MST, NOV;
WLC**
See also CDBLB 1789-1832; DLB 116

Auster, Paul 1947- . . . . **CLC 47**
See also CA 69-72; CANR 23, 52

Austin, Frank
See Faust, Frederick (Schiller)

Austin, Mary (Hunter)
1868-1934 . . . . **TCLC 25**
See also CA 109; DLB 9, 78

Autran Dourado, Waldomiro
See Dourado, (Waldomiro Freitas) Autran

Averroes 1126-1198 . . . . **CMLC 7**
See also DLB 115

Avicenna 980-1037 . . . . **CMLC 16**
See also DLB 115

Avison, Margaret
1918- . . . . **CLC 2, 4; DAC; DAM POET**
See also CA 17-20R; DLB 53; MTCW

Axton, David
See Koontz, Dean R(ay)

Ayckbourn, Alan
1939- . . . . . . **CLC 5, 8, 18, 33, 74; DAB;
DAM DRAM**
See also CA 21-24R; CANR 31; DLB 13;
MTCW

Aydy, Catherine
See Tennant, Emma (Christina)

Ayme, Marcel (Andre) 1902-1967 . . . **CLC 11**
See also CA 89-92; CLR 25; DLB 72

Ayrton, Michael 1921-1975 . . . . **CLC 7**
See also CA 5-8R; 61-64; CANR 9, 21

Azorin . . . . **CLC 11**
See also Martinez Ruiz, Jose

Azuela, Mariano
1873-1952 . . . . . **TCLC 3; DAM MULT;
HLC**
See also CA 104; 131; HW; MTCW

Baastad, Babbis Friis
See Friis-Baastad, Babbis Ellinor

Bab
See Gilbert, W(illiam) S(chwenck)

Babbis, Eleanor
See Friis-Baastad, Babbis Ellinor

Babel, Isaak (Emmanuilovich)
1894-1941(?) . . . . . . **TCLC 2, 13; SSC 16**
See also CA 104

Babits, Mihaly 1883-1941 . . . . **TCLC 14**
See also CA 114

Babur 1483-1530 . . . . **LC 18**

Bacchelli, Riccardo 1891-1985 . . . . . **CLC 19**
See also CA 29-32R; 117

Bach, Richard (David)
1936- . . . . . . **CLC 14; DAM NOV, POP**
See also AITN 1; BEST 89:2; CA 9-12R;
CANR 18; MTCW; SATA 13

Bachman, Richard
See King, Stephen (Edwin)

Bachmann, Ingeborg 1926-1973 . . . . . **CLC 69**
See also CA 93-96; 45-48; DLB 85

Bacon, Francis 1561-1626 . . . . **LC 18, 32**
See also CDBLB Before 1660; DLB 151

Bacon, Roger 1214(?)-1292 . . . . . . **CMLC 14**
See also DLB 115

Bacovia, George . . . . **TCLC 24**
See also Vasiliu, Gheorghe

Badanes, Jerome 1937- . . . . **CLC 59**

Bagehot, Walter 1826-1877 . . . . . . **NCLC 10**
See also DLB 55

Bagnold, Enid
1889-1981 . . . . . . **CLC 25; DAM DRAM**
See also CA 5-8R; 103; CANR 5, 40;
DLB 13, 160; MAICYA; SATA 1, 25

Bagritsky, Eduard 1895-1934 . . . . . **TCLC 60**

Bagrjana, Elisaveta
See Belcheva, Elisaveta

Bagryana, Elisaveta . . . . **CLC 10**
See also Belcheva, Elisaveta
See also DLB 147

Bailey, Paul 1937- . . . . **CLC 45**
See also CA 21-24R; CANR 16; DLB 14

Baillie, Joanna 1762-1851 . . . . **NCLC 2**
See also DLB 93

Bainbridge, Beryl (Margaret)
1933- . . . . **CLC 4, 5, 8, 10, 14, 18, 22, 62;
DAM NOV**
See also CA 21-24R; CANR 24; DLB 14;
MTCW

Baker, Elliott 1922- . . . . **CLC 8**
See also CA 45-48; CANR 2

Baker, Nicholson
1957- . . . . **CLC 61; DAM POP**
See also CA 135

Baker, Ray Stannard 1870-1946 . . . **TCLC 47**
See also CA 118

Baker, Russell (Wayne) 1925- . . . . . . **CLC 31**
See also BEST 89:4; CA 57-60; CANR 11,
41; MTCW

Bakhtin, M.
See Bakhtin, Mikhail Mikhailovich

Bakhtin, M. M.
See Bakhtin, Mikhail Mikhailovich

Bakhtin, Mikhail
See Bakhtin, Mikhail Mikhailovich

Bakhtin, Mikhail Mikhailovich
1895-1975 . . . . **CLC 83**
See also CA 128; 113

Bauchart
See Camus, Albert

Baudelaire, Charles
1821-1867 . . . . NCLC 6, 29, 55; DA;
DAB; DAC; DAM MST, POET; PC 1;
SSC 18; WLC

Baudrillard, Jean 1929- . . . . CLC 60

Baum, L(yman) Frank 1856-1919 . . . TCLC 7
See also CA 108; 133; CLR 15; DLB 22;
JRDA; MAICYA; MTCW; SATA 18

Baum, Louis F.
See Baum, L(yman) Frank

Baumbach, Jonathan 1933- . . . . . . CLC 6, 23
See also CA 13-16R; CAAS 5; CANR 12;
DLBY 80; INT CANR-12; MTCW

Bausch, Richard (Carl) 1945- . . . . . . CLC 51
See also CA 101; CAAS 14; CANR 43;
DLB 130

Baxter, Charles
1947- . . . . CLC 45, 78; DAM POP
See also CA 57-60; CANR 40; DLB 130

Baxter, George Owen
See Faust, Frederick (Schiller)

Baxter, James K(eir) 1926-1972 . . . . CLC 14
See also CA 77-80

Baxter, John
See Hunt, E(verette) Howard, (Jr.)

Bayer, Sylvia
See Glassco, John

Baynton, Barbara 1857-1929 . . . . . TCLC 57

Beagle, Peter S(oyer) 1939- . . . . CLC 7
See also CA 9-12R; CANR 4, 51;
DLBY 80; INT CANR-4; SATA 60

Bean, Normal
See Burroughs, Edgar Rice

Beard, Charles A(ustin)
1874-1948 . . . . TCLC 15
See also CA 115; DLB 17; SATA 18

Beardsley, Aubrey 1872-1898 . . . . . NCLC 6

Beattie, Ann
1947- . . . . CLC 8, 13, 18, 40, 63;
DAM NOV, POP; SSC 11
See also BEST 90:2; CA 81-84; CANR 53;
DLBY 82; MTCW

Beattie, James 1735-1803 . . . . NCLC 25
See also DLB 109

Beauchamp, Kathleen Mansfield 1888-1923
See Mansfield, Katherine
See also CA 104; 134; DA; DAC;
DAM MST

Beaumarchais, Pierre-Augustin Caron de
1732-1799 . . . . DC 4
See also DAM DRAM

Beaumont, Francis
1584(?)-1616 . . . . LC 33; DC 6
See also CDBLB Before 1660; DLB 58, 121

Beauvoir, Simone (Lucie Ernestine Marie
Bertrand) de
1908-1986 . . . . CLC 1, 2, 4, 8, 14, 31, 44,
50, 71; DA; DAB; DAC; DAM MST,
NOV; WLC
See also CA 9-12R; 118; CANR 28;
DLB 72; DLBY 86; MTCW

Becker, Carl 1873-1945 . . . . TCLC 63:
See also DLB 17

Becker, Jurek 1937- . . . . CLC 7, 19
See also CA 85-88; DLB 75

Becker, Walter 1950- . . . . CLC 26

Beckett, Samuel (Barclay)
1906-1989 . . . . . CLC 1, 2, 3, 4, 6, 9, 10,
11, 14, 18, 29, 57, 59, 83; DA; DAB;
DAC; DAM DRAM, MST, NOV;
SSC 16; WLC
See also CA 5-8R; 130; CANR 33;
CDBLB 1945-1960; DLB 13, 15;
DLBY 90; MTCW

Beckford, William 1760-1844 . . . . NCLC 16
See also DLB 39

Beckman, Gunnel 1910- . . . . CLC 26
See also CA 33-36R; CANR 15; CLR 25;
MAICYA; SAAS 9; SATA 6

Becque, Henri 1837-1899 . . . . NCLC 3

Beddoes, Thomas Lovell
1803-1849 . . . . NCLC 3
See also DLB 96

Bedford, Donald F.
See Fearing, Kenneth (Flexner)

Beecher, Catharine Esther
1800-1878 . . . . NCLC 30
See also DLB 1

Beecher, John 1904-1980 . . . . CLC 6
See also AITN 1; CA 5-8R; 105; CANR 8

Beer, Johann 1655-1700 . . . . LC 5
See also DLB 168

Beer, Patricia 1924- . . . . CLC 58
See also CA 61-64; CANR 13, 46; DLB 40

Beerbohm, Henry Maximilian
1872-1956 . . . . TCLC 1, 24
See also CA 104; DLB 34, 100

Beerbohm, Max
See Beerbohm, Henry Maximilian

Beer-Hofmann, Richard
1866-1945 . . . . TCLC 60
See also DLB 81

Begiebing, Robert J(ohn) 1946- . . . . CLC 70
See also CA 122; CANR 40

Behan, Brendan
1923-1964 . . . . CLC 1, 8, 11, 15, 79;
DAM DRAM
See also CA 73-76; CANR 33;
CDBLB 1945-1960; DLB 13; MTCW

Behn, Aphra
1640(?)-1689 . . . . . . LC 1, 30; DA; DAB;
DAC; DAM DRAM, MST, NOV,
POET; DC 4; PC 13; WLC
See also DLB 39, 80, 131

Behrman, S(amuel) N(athaniel)
1893-1973 . . . . CLC 40
See also CA 13-16; 45-48; CAP 1; DLB 7,
44

Belasco, David 1853-1931 . . . . TCLC 3
See also CA 104; DLB 7

Belcheva, Elisaveta 1893- . . . . CLC 10
See also Bagryana, Elisaveta

Beldone, Phil "Cheech"
See Ellison, Harlan (Jay)

Beleno
See Azuela, Mariano

Belinski, Vissarion Grigoryevich
1811-1848 . . . . NCLC 5

Belitt, Ben 1911- . . . . CLC 22
See also CA 13-16R; CAAS 4; CANR 7;
DLB 5

Bell, James Madison
1826-1902 . . . . TCLC 43; BLC;
DAM MULT
See also BW 1; CA 122; 124; DLB 50

Bell, Madison (Smartt) 1957- . . . . . . CLC 41
See also CA 111; CANR 28

Bell, Marvin (Hartley)
1937- . . . . CLC 8, 31; DAM POET
See also CA 21-24R; CAAS 14; DLB 5;
MTCW

Bell, W. L. D.
See Mencken, H(enry) L(ouis)

Bellamy, Atwood C.
See Mencken, H(enry) L(ouis)

Bellamy, Edward 1850-1898 . . . . . . NCLC 4
See also DLB 12

Bellin, Edward J.
See Kuttner, Henry

Belloc, (Joseph) Hilaire (Pierre)
1870-1953 . . . TCLC 7, 18; DAM POET
See also CA 106; 152; DLB 19, 100, 141;
YABC 1

Belloc, Joseph Peter Rene Hilaire
See Belloc, (Joseph) Hilaire (Pierre)

Belloc, Joseph Pierre Hilaire
See Belloc, (Joseph) Hilaire (Pierre)

Belloc, M. A.
See Lowndes, Marie Adelaide (Belloc)

Bellow, Saul
1915- . . . . . . CLC 1, 2, 3, 6, 8, 10, 13, 15,
25, 33, 34, 63, 79; DA; DAB; DAC;
DAM MST, NOV, POP; SSC 14; WLC
See also AITN 2; BEST 89:3; CA 5-8R;
CABS 1; CANR 29, 53;
CDALB 1941-1968; DLB 2, 28; DLBD 3;
DLBY 82; MTCW

Belser, Reimond Karel Maria de 1929-
See Ruyslinck, Ward
See also CA 152

Bely, Andrey . . . . TCLC 7; PC 11
See also Bugayev, Boris Nikolayevich

Benary, Margot
See Benary-Isbert, Margot

Benary-Isbert, Margot 1889-1979 . . . CLC 12
See also CA 5-8R; 89-92; CANR 4;
CLR 12; MAICYA; SATA 2;
SATA-Obit 21

Benavente (y Martinez), Jacinto
1866-1954 . . . . . TCLC 3; DAM DRAM,
MULT
See also CA 106; 131; HW; MTCW

Benchley, Peter (Bradford)
1940- . . . . CLC 4, 8; DAM NOV, POP
See also AAYA 14; AITN 2; CA 17-20R;
CANR 12, 35; MTCW; SATA 3, 89

Benchley, Robert (Charles)
1889-1945 . . . . TCLC 1, 55
See also CA 105; DLB 11

Benda, Julien 1867-1956 . . . . TCLC 60
See also CA 120

Benedict, Ruth 1887-1948 . . . . TCLC 60

Benedikt, Michael 1935- . . . . CLC 4, 14
See also CA 13-16R; CANR 7; DLB 5

Benet, Juan 1927- . . . . CLC 28
See also CA 143

Benet, Stephen Vincent
1898-1943 . . . . . . TCLC 7; DAM POET;
SSC 10
See also CA 104; 152; DLB 4, 48, 102;
YABC 1

Benet, William Rose
1886-1950 . . . . . . TCLC 28; DAM POET
See also CA 118; 152; DLB 45

Benford, Gregory (Albert) 1941- . . . . CLC 52
See also CA 69-72; CANR 12, 24, 49;
DLBY 82

Bengtsson, Frans (Gunnar)
1894-1954 . . . . TCLC 48

Benjamin, David
See Slavitt, David R(ytman)

Benjamin, Lois
See Gould, Lois

Benjamin, Walter 1892-1940 . . . . . TCLC 39

Benn, Gottfried 1886-1956. . . . . TCLC 3
See also CA 106; DLB 56

Bennett, Alan
1934- . . . CLC 45, 77; DAB; DAM MST
See also CA 103; CANR 35; MTCW

Bennett, (Enoch) Arnold
1867-1931 . . . . TCLC 5, 20
See also CA 106; CDBLB 1890-1914;
DLB 10, 34, 98, 135

Bennett, Elizabeth
See Mitchell, Margaret (Munnerlyn)

Bennett, George Harold 1930-
See Bennett, Hal
See also BW 1; CA 97-100

Bennett, Hal . . . . CLC 5
See also Bennett, George Harold
See also DLB 33

Bennett, Jay 1912- . . . . CLC 35
See also AAYA 10; CA 69-72; CANR 11,
42; JRDA; SAAS 4; SATA 41, 87;
SATA-Brief 27

Bennett, Louise (Simone)
1919- . . . . . CLC 28; BLC; DAM MULT
See also BW 2; CA 151; DLB 117

Benson, E(dward) F(rederic)
1867-1940 . . . . TCLC 27
See also CA 114; DLB 135, 153

Benson, Jackson J. 1930- . . . . CLC 34
See also CA 25-28R; DLB 111

Benson, Sally 1900-1972 . . . . CLC 17
See also CA 19-20; 37-40R; CAP 1;
SATA 1, 35; SATA-Obit 27

Benson, Stella 1892-1933. . . . . TCLC 17
See also CA 117; DLB 36, 162

Bentham, Jeremy 1748-1832 . . . . . NCLC 38
See also DLB 107, 158

Bentley, E(dmund) C(lerihew)
1875-1956 . . . . TCLC 12
See also CA 108; DLB 70

Bentley, Eric (Russell) 1916- . . . . CLC 24
See also CA 5-8R; CANR 6; INT CANR-6

Beranger, Pierre Jean de
1780-1857 . . . . NCLC 34

Berendt, John (Lawrence) 1939- . . . . CLC 86
See also CA 146

Berger, Colonel
See Malraux, (Georges-)Andre

Berger, John (Peter) 1926- . . . . . . CLC 2, 19
See also CA 81-84; CANR 51; DLB 14

Berger, Melvin H. 1927- . . . . CLC 12
See also CA 5-8R; CANR 4; CLR 32;
SAAS 2; SATA 5, 88

Berger, Thomas (Louis)
1924- . . . . CLC 3, 5, 8, 11, 18, 38;
DAM NOV
See also CA 1-4R; CANR 5, 28, 51; DLB 2;
DLBY 80; INT CANR-28; MTCW

Bergman, (Ernst) Ingmar
1918- . . . . CLC 16, 72
See also CA 81-84; CANR 33

Bergson, Henri 1859-1941 . . . . TCLC 32

Bergstein, Eleanor 1938- . . . . CLC 4
See also CA 53-56; CANR 5

Berkoff, Steven 1937- . . . . CLC 56
See also CA 104

Bermant, Chaim (Icyk) 1929- . . . . . . CLC 40
See also CA 57-60; CANR 6, 31

Bern, Victoria
See Fisher, M(ary) F(rances) K(ennedy)

Bernanos, (Paul Louis) Georges
1888-1948 . . . . TCLC 3
See also CA 104; 130; DLB 72

Bernard, April 1956- . . . . CLC 59
See also CA 131

Berne, Victoria
See Fisher, M(ary) F(rances) K(ennedy)

Bernhard, Thomas
1931-1989 . . . . CLC 3, 32, 61
See also CA 85-88; 127; CANR 32;
DLB 85, 124; MTCW

Berriault, Gina 1926- . . . . CLC 54
See also CA 116; 129; DLB 130

Berrigan, Daniel 1921- . . . . CLC 4
See also CA 33-36R; CAAS 1; CANR 11,
43; DLB 5

Berrigan, Edmund Joseph Michael, Jr.
1934-1983
See Berrigan, Ted
See also CA 61-64; 110; CANR 14

Berrigan, Ted . . . . CLC 37
See also Berrigan, Edmund Joseph Michael,
Jr.
See also DLB 5, 169

Berry, Charles Edward Anderson 1931-
See Berry, Chuck
See also CA 115

Berry, Chuck . . . . CLC 17
See also Berry, Charles Edward Anderson

Berry, Jonas
See Ashbery, John (Lawrence)

Berry, Wendell (Erdman)
1934- . . . . CLC 4, 6, 8, 27, 46;
DAM POET
See also AITN 1; CA 73-76; CANR 50;
DLB 5, 6

Berryman, John
1914-1972 . . . . . . CLC 1, 2, 3, 4, 6, 8, 10,
13, 25, 62; DAM POET
See also CA 13-16; 33-36R; CABS 2;
CANR 35; CAP 1; CDALB 1941-1968;
DLB 48; MTCW

Bertolucci, Bernardo 1940- . . . . CLC 16
See also CA 106

Bertrand, Aloysius 1807-1841 . . . . NCLC 31

Bertran de Born c. 1140-1215 . . . . . CMLC 5

Besant, Annie (Wood) 1847-1933 . . . TCLC 9
See also CA 105

Bessie, Alvah 1904-1985. . . . . CLC 23
See also CA 5-8R; 116; CANR 2; DLB 26

Bethlen, T. D.
See Silverberg, Robert

Beti, Mongo. . . . CLC 27; BLC; DAM MULT
See also Biyidi, Alexandre

Betjeman, John
1906-1984 . . . . CLC 2, 6, 10, 34, 43;
DAB; DAM MST, POET
See also CA 9-12R; 112; CANR 33;
CDBLB 1945-1960; DLB 20; DLBY 84;
MTCW

Bettelheim, Bruno 1903-1990 . . . . . . CLC 79
See also CA 81-84; 131; CANR 23; MTCW

Betti, Ugo 1892-1953 . . . . TCLC 5
See also CA 104

Betts, Doris (Waugh) 1932- . . . . CLC 3, 6, 28
See also CA 13-16R; CANR 9; DLBY 82;
INT CANR-9

Bevan, Alistair
See Roberts, Keith (John Kingston)

Bialik, Chaim Nachman
1873-1934 . . . . TCLC 25

Bickerstaff, Isaac
See Swift, Jonathan

Bidart, Frank 1939- . . . . CLC 33
See also CA 140

Bienek, Horst 1930- . . . . CLC 7, 11
See also CA 73-76; DLB 75

Bierce, Ambrose (Gwinett)
1842-1914(?) . . . . TCLC 1, 7, 44; DA;
DAC; DAM MST; SSC 9; WLC
See also CA 104; 139; CDALB 1865-1917;
DLB 11, 12, 23, 71, 74

Biggers, Earl Derr 1884-1933 . . . . . TCLC 65
See also CA 108

Billings, Josh
See Shaw, Henry Wheeler

Billington, (Lady) Rachel (Mary)
1942- . . . . CLC 43
See also AITN 2; CA 33-36R; CANR 44

Binyon, T(imothy) J(ohn) 1936- . . . . CLC 34
See also CA 111; CANR 28

Bioy Casares, Adolfo
1914- . . . . CLC 4, 8, 13, 88;
DAM MULT; HLC; SSC 17
See also CA 29-32R; CANR 19, 43;
DLB 113; HW; MTCW

Bird, Cordwainer
See Ellison, Harlan (Jay)

Bird, Robert Montgomery
1806-1854 . . . . NCLC 1

Birney, (Alfred) Earle
1904- . . . . CLC 1, 4, 6, 11; DAC;
DAM MST, POET
See also CA 1-4R; CANR 5, 20; DLB 88;
MTCW

Bishop, Elizabeth
1911-1979 . . . . . CLC 1, 4, 9, 13, 15, 32;
DA; DAC; DAM MST, POET; PC 3
See also CA 5-8R; 89-92; CABS 2;
CANR 26; CDALB 1968-1988; DLB 5,
169; MTCW; SATA-Obit 24

Bishop, John 1935- . . . . CLC 10
See also CA 105

Bissett, Bill 1939- . . . . CLC 18; PC 14
See also CA 69-72; CAAS 19; CANR 15;
DLB 53; MTCW

Bitov, Andrei (Georgievich) 1937- . . . CLC 57
See also CA 142

Biyidi, Alexandre 1932-
See Beti, Mongo
See also BW 1; CA 114; 124; MTCW

Bjarme, Brynjolf
See Ibsen, Henrik (Johan)

Bjornson, Bjornstjerne (Martinius)
1832-1910 . . . . TCLC 7, 37
See also CA 104

Black, Robert
See Holdstock, Robert P.

Blackburn, Paul 1926-1971 . . . . . . CLC 9, 43
See also CA 81-84; 33-36R; CANR 34;
DLB 16; DLBY 81

Black Elk
1863-1950 . . . . . TCLC 33; DAM MULT
See also CA 144; NNAL

Black Hobart
See Sanders, (James) Ed(ward)

Blacklin, Malcolm
See Chambers, Aidan

Blackmore, R(ichard) D(oddridge)
1825-1900 . . . . TCLC 27
See also CA 120; DLB 18

Blackmur, R(ichard) P(almer)
1904-1965 . . . . CLC 2, 24
See also CA 11-12; 25-28R; CAP 1; DLB 63

Black Tarantula, The
See Acker, Kathy

Blackwood, Algernon (Henry)
1869-1951 . . . . TCLC 5
See also CA 105; 150; DLB 153, 156

Blackwood, Caroline 1931-1996 . . . CLC 6, 9
See also CA 85-88; 151; CANR 32;
DLB 14; MTCW

Blade, Alexander
See Hamilton, Edmond; Silverberg, Robert

Blaga, Lucian 1895-1961 . . . . CLC 75

Blair, Eric (Arthur) 1903-1950
See Orwell, George
See also CA 104; 132; DA; DAB; DAC;
DAM MST, NOV; MTCW; SATA 29

Blais, Marie-Claire
1939- . . . . CLC 2, 4, 6, 13, 22; DAC;
DAM MST
See also CA 21-24R; CAAS 4; CANR 38;
DLB 53; MTCW

Blaise, Clark 1940- . . . . CLC 29
See also AITN 2; CA 53-56; CAAS 3;
CANR 5; DLB 53

Blake, Nicholas
See Day Lewis, C(ecil)
See also DLB 77

Blake, William
1757-1827 . . . . NCLC 13, 37, 57; DA;
DAB; DAC; DAM MST, POET; PC 12;
WLC
See also CDBLB 1789-1832; DLB 93, 163;
MAICYA; SATA 30

Blake, William J(ames) 1894-1969 . . . PC 12
See also CA 5-8R; 25-28R

Blasco Ibanez, Vicente
1867-1928 . . . . . . TCLC 12; DAM NOV
See also CA 110; 131; HW; MTCW

Blatty, William Peter
1928- . . . . CLC 2; DAM POP
See also CA 5-8R; CANR 9

Bleeck, Oliver
See Thomas, Ross (Elmore)

Blessing, Lee 1949- . . . . CLC 54

Blish, James (Benjamin)
1921-1975 . . . . CLC 14
See also CA 1-4R; 57-60; CANR 3; DLB 8;
MTCW; SATA 66

Bliss, Reginald
See Wells, H(erbert) G(eorge)

Blixen, Karen (Christentze Dinesen)
1885-1962
See Dinesen, Isak
See also CA 25-28; CANR 22, 50; CAP 2;
MTCW; SATA 44

Bloch, Robert (Albert) 1917-1994 . . . CLC 33
See also CA 5-8R; 146; CAAS 20; CANR 5;
DLB 44; INT CANR-5; SATA 12;
SATA-Obit 82

Blok, Alexander (Alexandrovich)
1880-1921 . . . . TCLC 5
See also CA 104

Blom, Jan
See Breytenbach, Breyten

Bloom, Harold 1930- . . . . CLC 24
See also CA 13-16R; CANR 39; DLB 67

Bloomfield, Aurelius
See Bourne, Randolph S(illiman)

Blount, Roy (Alton), Jr. 1941- . . . . . CLC 38
See also CA 53-56; CANR 10, 28;
INT CANR-28; MTCW

Bloy, Leon 1846-1917 . . . . TCLC 22
See also CA 121; DLB 123

Blume, Judy (Sussman)
1938- . . . CLC 12, 30; DAM NOV, POP
See also AAYA 3; CA 29-32R; CANR 13,
37; CLR 2, 15; DLB 52; JRDA;
MAICYA; MTCW; SATA 2, 31, 79

Blunden, Edmund (Charles)
1896-1974 . . . . CLC 2, 56
See also CA 17-18; 45-48; CAP 2; DLB 20,
100, 155; MTCW

Bly, Robert (Elwood)
1926- . . . . CLC 1, 2, 5, 10, 15, 38;
DAM POET
See also CA 5-8R; CANR 41; DLB 5;
MTCW

Boas, Franz 1858-1942 . . . . TCLC 56
See also CA 115

Bobette
See Simenon, Georges (Jacques Christian)

Boccaccio, Giovanni
1313-1375 . . . . CMLC 13; SSC 10

Bochco, Steven 1943- . . . . CLC 35
See also AAYA 11; CA 124; 138

Bodenheim, Maxwell 1892-1954 . . . TCLC 44
See also CA 110; DLB 9, 45

Bodker, Cecil 1927- . . . . CLC 21
See also CA 73-76; CANR 13, 44; CLR 23;
MAICYA; SATA 14

Boell, Heinrich (Theodor)
1917-1985 . . . . CLC 2, 3, 6, 9, 11, 15, 27,
32, 72; DA; DAB; DAC; DAM MST,
NOV; SSC 23; WLC
See also CA 21-24R; 116; CANR 24;
DLB 69; DLBY 85; MTCW

Boerne, Alfred
See Doeblin, Alfred

Boethius 480(?)-524(?) . . . . CMLC 15
See also DLB 115

Bogan, Louise
1897-1970 . . . . CLC 4, 39, 46, 93;
DAM POET; PC 12
See also CA 73-76; 25-28R; CANR 33;
DLB 45, 169; MTCW

Bogarde, Dirk . . . . CLC 19
See also Van Den Bogarde, Derek Jules
Gaspard Ulric Niven
See also DLB 14

Bogosian, Eric 1953- . . . . CLC 45
See also CA 138

Bograd, Larry 1953- . . . . CLC 35
See also CA 93-96; SAAS 21; SATA 33, 89

Boiardo, Matteo Maria 1441-1494 . . . . LC 6

Boileau-Despreaux, Nicolas
1636-1711 . . . . LC 3

Bojer, Johan 1872-1959 . . . . TCLC 64

Boland, Eavan (Aisling)
1944- . . . . CLC 40, 67; DAM POET
See also CA 143; DLB 40

Bolt, Lee
See Faust, Frederick (Schiller)

Bolt, Robert (Oxton)
1924-1995 . . . . . . CLC 14; DAM DRAM
See also CA 17-20R; 147; CANR 35;
DLB 13; MTCW

Bombet, Louis-Alexandre-Cesar
See Stendhal

Bomkauf
See Kaufman, Bob (Garnell)

Bonaventura . . . . NCLC 35
See also DLB 90

Bond, Edward
1934- . . . CLC 4, 6, 13, 23; DAM DRAM
See also CA 25-28R; CANR 38; DLB 13;
MTCW

Bonham, Frank 1914-1989 . . . . CLC 12
See also AAYA 1; CA 9-12R; CANR 4, 36;
JRDA; MAICYA; SAAS 3; SATA 1, 49;
SATA-Obit 62

Bonnefoy, Yves
1923- ...... **CLC 9, 15, 58; DAM MST,
POET**
See also CA 85-88; CANR 33; MTCW

Bontemps, Arna(ud Wendell)
1902-1973 .... **CLC 1, 18; BLC;
DAM MULT, NOV, POET**
See also BW 1; CA 1-4R; 41-44R; CANR 4,
35; CLR 6; DLB 48, 51; JRDA;
MAICYA; MTCW; SATA 2, 44;
SATA-Obit 24

Booth, Martin 1944-.............. **CLC 13**
See also CA 93-96; CAAS 2

Booth, Philip 1925-.............. **CLC 23**
See also CA 5-8R; CANR 5; DLBY 82

Booth, Wayne C(layson) 1921- ..... **CLC 24**
See also CA 1-4R; CAAS 5; CANR 3, 43;
DLB 67

Borchert, Wolfgang 1921-1947 ..... **TCLC 5**
See also CA 104; DLB 69, 124

Borel, Petrus 1809-1859........ **NCLC 41**

Borges, Jorge Luis
1899-1986 ... **CLC 1, 2, 3, 4, 6, 8, 9, 10,
13, 19, 44, 48, 83; DA; DAB; DAC;
DAM MST, MULT; HLC; SSC 4; WLC**
See also CA 21-24R; CANR 19, 33;
DLB 113; DLBY 86; HW; MTCW

Borowski, Tadeusz 1922-1951...... **TCLC 9**
See also CA 106

Borrow, George (Henry)
1803-1881 .... **NCLC 9**
See also DLB 21, 55, 166

Bosman, Herman Charles
1905-1951 .... **TCLC 49**

Bosschere, Jean de 1878(?)-1953... **TCLC 19**
See also CA 115

Boswell, James
1740-1795 ...... **LC 4; DA; DAB; DAC;
DAM MST; WLC**
See also CDBLB 1660-1789; DLB 104, 142

Bottoms, David 1949-.............. **CLC 53**
See also CA 105; CANR 22; DLB 120;
DLBY 83

Boucicault, Dion 1820-1890...... **NCLC 41**

Boucolon, Maryse 1937(?)-
See Conde, Maryse
See also CA 110; CANR 30, 53

Bourget, Paul (Charles Joseph)
1852-1935 .... **TCLC 12**
See also CA 107; DLB 123

Bourjaily, Vance (Nye) 1922- .... **CLC 8, 62**
See also CA 1-4R; CAAS 1; CANR 2;
DLB 2, 143

Bourne, Randolph S(illiman)
1886-1918 .... **TCLC 16**
See also CA 117; DLB 63

Bova, Ben(jamin William) 1932-.... **CLC 45**
See also AAYA 16; CA 5-8R; CAAS 18;
CANR 11; CLR 3; DLBY 81;
INT CANR-11; MAICYA; MTCW;
SATA 6, 68

Bowen, Elizabeth (Dorothea Cole)
1899-1973 ..... **CLC 1, 3, 6, 11, 15, 22;
DAM NOV; SSC 3**
See also CA 17-18; 41-44R; CANR 35;
CAP 2; CDBLB 1945-1960; DLB 15, 162;
MTCW

Bowering, George 1935-........ **CLC 15, 47**
See also CA 21-24R; CAAS 16; CANR 10;
DLB 53

Bowering, Marilyn R(uthe) 1949-... **CLC 32**
See also CA 101; CANR 49

Bowers, Edgar 1924- .... **CLC 9**
See also CA 5-8R; CANR 24; DLB 5

Bowie, David .... **CLC 17**
See also Jones, David Robert

Bowles, Jane (Sydney)
1917-1973 .... **CLC 3, 68**
See also CA 19-20; 41-44R; CAP 2

Bowles, Paul (Frederick)
1910- .... **CLC 1, 2, 19, 53; SSC 3**
See also CA 1-4R; CAAS 1; CANR 1, 19,
50; DLB 5, 6; MTCW

Box, Edgar
See Vidal, Gore

Boyd, Nancy
See Millay, Edna St. Vincent

Boyd, William 1952-........ **CLC 28, 53, 70**
See also CA 114; 120; CANR 51

Boyle, Kay
1902-1992 ..... **CLC 1, 5, 19, 58; SSC 5**
See also CA 13-16R; 140; CAAS 1;
CANR 29; DLB 4, 9, 48, 86; DLBY 93;
MTCW

Boyle, Mark
See Kienzle, William X(avier)

Boyle, Patrick 1905-1982......... **CLC 19**
See also CA 127

Boyle, T. C. 1948-
See Boyle, T(homas) Coraghessan

Boyle, T(homas) Coraghessan
1948- ..... **CLC 36, 55, 90; DAM POP;
SSC 16**
See also BEST 90:4; CA 120; CANR 44;
DLBY 86

Boz
See Dickens, Charles (John Huffam)

Brackenridge, Hugh Henry
1748-1816 .... **NCLC 7**
See also DLB 11, 37

Bradbury, Edward P.
See Moorcock, Michael (John)

Bradbury, Malcolm (Stanley)
1932- .... **CLC 32, 61; DAM NOV**
See also CA 1-4R; CANR 1, 33; DLB 14;
MTCW

Bradbury, Ray (Douglas)
1920- .... **CLC 1, 3, 10, 15, 42; DA;
DAB; DAC; DAM MST, NOV, POP;
WLC**
See also AAYA 15; AITN 1, 2; CA 1-4R;
CANR 2, 30; CDALB 1968-1988; DLB 2,
8; INT CANR-30; MTCW; SATA 11, 64

Bradford, Gamaliel 1863-1932..... **TCLC 36**
See also DLB 17

Bradley, David (Henry, Jr.)
1950- ..... **CLC 23; BLC; DAM MULT**
See also BW 1; CA 104; CANR 26; DLB 33

Bradley, John Ed(mund, Jr.)
1958- .... **CLC 55**
See also CA 139

Bradley, Marion Zimmer
1930- .... **CLC 30; DAM POP**
See also AAYA 9; CA 57-60; CAAS 10;
CANR 7, 31, 51; DLB 8; MTCW

Bradstreet, Anne
1612(?)-1672 ...... **LC 4, 30; DA; DAC;
DAM MST, POET; PC 10**
See also CDALB 1640-1865; DLB 24

Brady, Joan 1939- .... **CLC 86**
See also CA 141

Bragg, Melvyn 1939- .... **CLC 10**
See also BEST 89:3; CA 57-60; CANR 10,
48; DLB 14

Braine, John (Gerard)
1922-1986 .... **CLC 1, 3, 41**
See also CA 1-4R; 120; CANR 1, 33;
CDBLB 1945-1960; DLB 15; DLBY 86;
MTCW

Brammer, William 1930(?)-1978 .... **CLC 31**
See also CA 77-80

Brancati, Vitaliano 1907-1954..... **TCLC 12**
See also CA 109

Brancato, Robin F(idler) 1936-..... **CLC 35**
See also AAYA 9; CA 69-72; CANR 11,
45; CLR 32; JRDA; SAAS 9; SATA 23

Brand, Max
See Faust, Frederick (Schiller)

Brand, Millen 1906-1980.......... **CLC 7**
See also CA 21-24R; 97-100

Branden, Barbara .... **CLC 44**
See also CA 148

Brandes, Georg (Morris Cohen)
1842-1927 .... **TCLC 10**
See also CA 105

Brandys, Kazimierz 1916-......... **CLC 62**

Branley, Franklyn M(ansfield)
1915- .... **CLC 21**
See also CA 33-36R; CANR 14, 39;
CLR 13; MAICYA; SAAS 16; SATA 4,
68

Brathwaite, Edward Kamau
1930- .... **CLC 11; DAM POET**
See also BW 2; CA 25-28R; CANR 11, 26,
47; DLB 125

Brautigan, Richard (Gary)
1935-1984 .... **CLC 1, 3, 5, 9, 12, 34, 42;
DAM NOV**
See also CA 53-56; 113; CANR 34; DLB 2,
5; DLBY 80, 84; MTCW; SATA 56

Brave Bird, Mary 1953-
See Crow Dog, Mary
See also NNAL

Braverman, Kate 1950- .... **CLC 67**
See also CA 89-92

Brecht, Bertolt
1898-1956 ...... **TCLC 1, 6, 13, 35; DA;
DAB; DAC; DAM DRAM, MST; DC 3;
WLC**
See also CA 104; 133; DLB 56, 124; MTCW

Brecht, Eugen Berthold Friedrich
See Brecht, Bertolt

Bremer, Fredrika 1801-1865 . . . . . **NCLC 11**

Brennan, Christopher John
1870-1932 . . . . **TCLC 17**
See also CA 117

Brennan, Maeve 1917- . . . . **CLC 5**
See also CA 81-84

Brentano, Clemens (Maria)
1778-1842 . . . . **NCLC 1**
See also DLB 90

Brent of Bin Bin
See Franklin, (Stella Maraia Sarah) Miles

Brenton, Howard 1942- . . . . **CLC 31**
See also CA 69-72; CANR 33; DLB 13;
MTCW

Breslin, James 1930-
See Breslin, Jimmy
See also CA 73-76; CANR 31; DAM NOV;
MTCW

Breslin, Jimmy . . . . **CLC 4, 43**
See also Breslin, James
See also AITN 1

Bresson, Robert 1901- . . . . **CLC 16**
See also CA 110; CANR 49

Breton, Andre
1896-1966 . . . . . **CLC 2, 9, 15, 54; PC 15**
See also CA 19-20; 25-28R; CANR 40;
CAP 2; DLB 65; MTCW

Breytenbach, Breyten
1939(?)- . . . . . . **CLC 23, 37; DAM POET**
See also CA 113; 129

Bridgers, Sue Ellen 1942- . . . . **CLC 26**
See also AAYA 8; CA 65-68; CANR 11,
36; CLR 18; DLB 52; JRDA; MAICYA;
SAAS 1; SATA 22

Bridges, Robert (Seymour)
1844-1930 . . . . . . **TCLC 1; DAM POET**
See also CA 104; 152; CDBLB 1890-1914;
DLB 19, 98

Bridie, James . . . . **TCLC 3**
See also Mavor, Osborne Henry
See also DLB 10

Brin, David 1950- . . . . **CLC 34**
See also CA 102; CANR 24;
INT CANR-24; SATA 65

Brink, Andre (Philippus)
1935- . . . . **CLC 18, 36**
See also CA 104; CANR 39; INT 103;
MTCW

Brinsmead, H(esba) F(ay) 1922- . . . . **CLC 21**
See also CA 21-24R; CANR 10; MAICYA;
SAAS 5; SATA 18, 78

Brittain, Vera (Mary)
1893(?)-1970 . . . . **CLC 23**
See also CA 13-16; 25-28R; CAP 1; MTCW

Broch, Hermann 1886-1951 . . . . **TCLC 20**
See also CA 117; DLB 85, 124

Brock, Rose
See Hansen, Joseph

Brodkey, Harold (Roy) 1930-1996 . . **CLC 56**
See also CA 111; 151; DLB 130

Brodsky, Iosif Alexandrovich 1940-1996
See Brodsky, Joseph
See also AITN 1; CA 41-44R; 151;
CANR 37; DAM POET; MTCW

Brodsky, Joseph . . **CLC 4, 6, 13, 36, 50; PC 9**
See also Brodsky, Iosif Alexandrovich

Brodsky, Michael Mark 1948- . . . . . **CLC 19**
See also CA 102; CANR 18, 41

Bromell, Henry 1947- . . . . **CLC 5**
See also CA 53-56; CANR 9

Bromfield, Louis (Brucker)
1896-1956 . . . . **TCLC 11**
See also CA 107; DLB 4, 9, 86

Broner, E(sther) M(asserman)
1930- . . . . **CLC 19**
See also CA 17-20R; CANR 8, 25; DLB 28

Bronk, William 1918- . . . . **CLC 10**
See also CA 89-92; CANR 23; DLB 165

Bronstein, Lev Davidovich
See Trotsky, Leon

Bronte, Anne 1820-1849 . . . . **NCLC 4**
See also DLB 21

Bronte, Charlotte
1816-1855 . . . . **NCLC 3, 8, 33; DA;
DAB; DAC; DAM MST, NOV; WLC**
See also AAYA 17; CDBLB 1832-1890;
DLB 21, 159

Bronte, Emily (Jane)
1818-1848 . . . . **NCLC 16, 35; DA; DAB;
DAC; DAM MST, NOV, POET; PC 8;
WLC**
See also AAYA 17; CDBLB 1832-1890;
DLB 21, 32

Brooke, Frances 1724-1789 . . . . **LC 6**
See also DLB 39, 99

Brooke, Henry 1703(?)-1783 . . . . **LC 1**
See also DLB 39

Brooke, Rupert (Chawner)
1887-1915 . . . . . . **TCLC 2, 7; DA; DAB;
DAC; DAM MST, POET; WLC**
See also CA 104; 132; CDBLB 1914-1945;
DLB 19; MTCW

Brooke-Haven, P.
See Wodehouse, P(elham) G(renville)

Brooke-Rose, Christine 1926- . . . . . . **CLC 40**
See also CA 13-16R; DLB 14

Brookner, Anita
1928- . . . . **CLC 32, 34, 51; DAB;
DAM POP**
See also CA 114; 120; CANR 37; DLBY 87;
MTCW

Brooks, Cleanth 1906-1994 . . . . . **CLC 24, 86**
See also CA 17-20R; 145; CANR 33, 35;
DLB 63; DLBY 94; INT CANR-35;
MTCW

Brooks, George
See Baum, L(yman) Frank

Brooks, Gwendolyn
1917- . . . . . . **CLC 1, 2, 4, 5, 15, 49; BLC;
DA; DAC; DAM MST, MULT, POET;
PC 7; WLC**
See also AITN 1; BW 2; CA 1-4R;
CANR 1, 27, 52; CDALB 1941-1968;
CLR 27; DLB 5, 76, 165; MTCW;
SATA 6

Brooks, Mel . . . . **CLC 12**
See also Kaminsky, Melvin
See also AAYA 13; DLB 26

Brooks, Peter 1938- . . . . **CLC 34**
See also CA 45-48; CANR 1

Brooks, Van Wyck 1886-1963 . . . . . . **CLC 29**
See also CA 1-4R; CANR 6; DLB 45, 63,
103

Brophy, Brigid (Antonia)
1929-1995 . . . . **CLC 6, 11, 29**
See also CA 5-8R; 149; CAAS 4; CANR 25,
53; DLB 14; MTCW

Brosman, Catharine Savage 1934- . . . . **CLC 9**
See also CA 61-64; CANR 21, 46

Brother Antoninus
See Everson, William (Oliver)

Broughton, T(homas) Alan 1936- . . . **CLC 19**
See also CA 45-48; CANR 2, 23, 48

Broumas, Olga 1949- . . . . **CLC 10, 73**
See also CA 85-88; CANR 20

Brown, Charles Brockden
1771-1810 . . . . **NCLC 22**
See also CDALB 1640-1865; DLB 37, 59,
73

Brown, Christy 1932-1981 . . . . **CLC 63**
See also CA 105; 104; DLB 14

Brown, Claude
1937- . . . . . **CLC 30; BLC; DAM MULT**
See also AAYA 7; BW 1; CA 73-76

Brown, Dee (Alexander)
1908- . . . . **CLC 18, 47; DAM POP**
See also CA 13-16R; CAAS 6; CANR 11,
45; DLBY 80; MTCW; SATA 5

Brown, George
See Wertmueller, Lina

Brown, George Douglas
1869-1902 . . . . **TCLC 28**

Brown, George Mackay
1921-1996 . . . . **CLC 5, 48**
See also CA 21-24R; 151; CAAS 6;
CANR 12, 37; DLB 14, 27, 139; MTCW;
SATA 35

Brown, (William) Larry 1951- . . . . . . **CLC 73**
See also CA 130; 134; INT 133

Brown, Moses
See Barrett, William (Christopher)

Brown, Rita Mae
1944- . . . . . **CLC 18, 43, 79; DAM NOV,
POP**
See also CA 45-48; CANR 2, 11, 35;
INT CANR-11; MTCW

Brown, Roderick (Langmere) Haig-
See Haig-Brown, Roderick (Langmere)

Brown, Rosellen 1939- . . . . **CLC 32**
See also CA 77-80; CAAS 10; CANR 14, 44

Brown, Sterling Allen
1901-1989 . . . . **CLC 1, 23, 59; BLC;
DAM MULT, POET**
See also BW 1; CA 85-88; 127; CANR 26;
DLB 48, 51, 63; MTCW

Brown, Will
See Ainsworth, William Harrison

Brown, William Wells
1813-1884 . . . . NCLC 2; BLC;
DAM MULT; DC 1
See also DLB 3, 50

Browne, (Clyde) Jackson 1948(?)-. . . CLC 21
See also CA 120

Browning, Elizabeth Barrett
1806-1861 . . . . . NCLC 1, 16; DA; DAB;
DAC; DAM MST, POET; PC 6; WLC
See also CDBLB 1832-1890; DLB 32

Browning, Robert
1812-1889 . . . . NCLC 19; DA; DAB;
DAC; DAM MST, POET; PC 2
See also CDBLB 1832-1890; DLB 32, 163;
YABC 1

Browning, Tod 1882-1962 . . . . CLC 16
See also CA 141; 117

Brownson, Orestes (Augustus)
1803-1876 . . . . NCLC 50

Bruccoli, Matthew J(oseph) 1931- . . CLC 34
See also CA 9-12R; CANR 7; DLB 103

Bruce, Lenny . . . . CLC 21
See also Schneider, Leonard Alfred

Bruin, John
See Brutus, Dennis

Brulard, Henri
See Stendhal

Brulls, Christian
See Simenon, Georges (Jacques Christian)

Brunner, John (Kilian Houston)
1934-1995 . . . . . . CLC 8, 10; DAM POP
See also CA 1-4R; 149; CAAS 8; CANR 2,
37; MTCW

Bruno, Giordano 1548-1600. . . . . LC 27

Brutus, Dennis
1924- . . . . . CLC 43; BLC; DAM MULT,
POET
See also BW 2; CA 49-52; CAAS 14;
CANR 2, 27, 42; DLB 117

Bryan, C(ourtlandt) D(ixon) B(arnes)
1936- . . . . CLC 29
See also CA 73-76; CANR 13;
INT CANR-13

Bryan, Michael
See Moore, Brian

Bryant, William Cullen
1794-1878 . . . . . NCLC 6, 46; DA; DAB;
DAC; DAM MST, POET
See also CDALB 1640-1865; DLB 3, 43, 59

Bryusov, Valery Yakovlevich
1873-1924 . . . . TCLC 10
See also CA 107

Buchan, John
1875-1940 . . . . TCLC 41; DAB;
DAM POP
See also CA 108; 145; DLB 34, 70, 156;
YABC 2

Buchanan, George 1506-1582 . . . . LC 4

Buchheim, Lothar-Guenther 1918- . . . CLC 6
See also CA 85-88

Buchner, (Karl) Georg
1813-1837 . . . . NCLC 26

Buchwald, Art(hur) 1925-. . . . . CLC 33
See also AITN 1; CA 5-8R; CANR 21;
MTCW; SATA 10

Buck, Pearl S(ydenstricker)
1892-1973 . . . . CLC 7, 11, 18; DA; DAB;
DAC; DAM MST, NOV
See also AITN 1; CA 1-4R; 41-44R;
CANR 1, 34; DLB 9, 102; MTCW;
SATA 1, 25

Buckler, Ernest
1908-1984 . . CLC 13; DAC; DAM MST
See also CA 11-12; 114; CAP 1; DLB 68;
SATA 47

Buckley, Vincent (Thomas)
1925-1988 . . . . CLC 57
See also CA 101

Buckley, William F(rank), Jr.
1925- . . . . CLC 7, 18, 37; DAM POP
See also AITN 1; CA 1-4R; CANR 1, 24,
53; DLB 137; DLBY 80; INT CANR-24;
MTCW

Buechner, (Carl) Frederick
1926- . . . . . . CLC 2, 4, 6, 9; DAM NOV
See also CA 13-16R; CANR 11, 39;
DLBY 80; INT CANR-11; MTCW

Buell, John (Edward) 1927-. . . . . CLC 10
See also CA 1-4R; DLB 53

Buero Vallejo, Antonio 1916- . . . CLC 15, 46
See also CA 106; CANR 24, 49; HW;
MTCW

Bufalino, Gesualdo 1920(?)-. . . . . CLC 74

Bugayev, Boris Nikolayevich 1880-1934
See Bely, Andrey
See also CA 104

Bukowski, Charles
1920-1994 . . . . CLC 2, 5, 9, 41, 82;
DAM NOV, POET
See also CA 17-20R; 144; CANR 40;
DLB 5, 130, 169; MTCW

Bulgakov, Mikhail (Afanas'evich)
1891-1940 . . . . TCLC 2, 16;
DAM DRAM, NOV; SSC 18
See also CA 105; 152

Bulgya, Alexander Alexandrovich
1901-1956 . . . . TCLC 53
See also Fadeyev, Alexander
See also CA 117

Bullins, Ed
1935- . . . . CLC 1, 5, 7; BLC;
DAM DRAM, MULT; DC 6
See also BW 2; CA 49-52; CAAS 16;
CANR 24, 46; DLB 7, 38; MTCW

Bulwer-Lytton, Edward (George Earle Lytton)
1803-1873 . . . . NCLC 1, 45
See also DLB 21

Bunin, Ivan Alexeyevich
1870-1953 . . . . TCLC 6; SSC 5
See also CA 104

Bunting, Basil
1900-1985 . . . . CLC 10, 39, 47;
DAM POET
See also CA 53-56; 115; CANR 7; DLB 20

Bunuel, Luis
1900-1983 . . . . CLC 16, 80;
DAM MULT; HLC
See also CA 101; 110; CANR 32; HW

Bunyan, John
1628-1688 . . . . . . LC 4; DA; DAB; DAC;
DAM MST; WLC
See also CDBLB 1660-1789; DLB 39

Burckhardt, Jacob (Christoph)
1818-1897 . . . . NCLC 49

Burford, Eleanor
See Hibbert, Eleanor Alice Burford

Burgess, Anthony
. CLC 1, 2, 4, 5, 8, 10, 13, 15, 22, 40, 62,
81, 94; DAB
See also Wilson, John (Anthony) Burgess
See also AITN 1; CDBLB 1960 to Present;
DLB 14

Burke, Edmund
1729(?)-1797 . . . . LC 7; DA; DAB; DAC;
DAM MST; WLC
See also DLB 104

Burke, Kenneth (Duva)
1897-1993 . . . . CLC 2, 24
See also CA 5-8R; 143; CANR 39; DLB 45,
63; MTCW

Burke, Leda
See Garnett, David

Burke, Ralph
See Silverberg, Robert

Burke, Thomas 1886-1945 . . . . TCLC 63
See also CA 113

Burney, Fanny 1752-1840 . . . . NCLC 12, 54
See also DLB 39

Burns, Robert 1759-1796. . . . . PC 6
See also CDBLB 1789-1832; DA; DAB;
DAC; DAM MST, POET; DLB 109;
WLC

Burns, Tex
See L'Amour, Louis (Dearborn)

Burnshaw, Stanley 1906-. . . . . CLC 3, 13, 44
See also CA 9-12R; DLB 48

Burr, Anne 1937-. . . . . CLC 6
See also CA 25-28R

Burroughs, Edgar Rice
1875-1950 . . . . TCLC 2, 32; DAM NOV
See also AAYA 11; CA 104; 132; DLB 8;
MTCW; SATA 41

Burroughs, William S(eward)
1914- . . . . CLC 1, 2, 5, 15, 22, 42, 75;
DA; DAB; DAC; DAM MST, NOV,
POP; WLC
See also AITN 2; CA 9-12R; CANR 20, 52;
DLB 2, 8, 16, 152; DLBY 81; MTCW

Burton, Richard F. 1821-1890. . . . NCLC 42
See also DLB 55

Busch, Frederick 1941- . . . CLC 7, 10, 18, 47
See also CA 33-36R; CAAS 1; CANR 45;
DLB 6

Bush, Ronald 1946- . . . . CLC 34
See also CA 136

Bustos, F(rancisco)
See Borges, Jorge Luis

Bustos Domecq, H(onorio)
See Bioy Casares, Adolfo; Borges, Jorge
Luis

Butler, Octavia E(stelle)
1947- . . . . . CLC 38; DAM MULT, POP
See also AAYA 18; BW 2; CA 73-76;
CANR 12, 24, 38; DLB 33; MTCW;
SATA 84

Butler, Robert Olen (Jr.)
1945- . . . . **CLC 81; DAM POP**
See also CA 112; INT 112

Butler, Samuel 1612-1680 . . . . **LC 16**
See also DLB 101, 126

Butler, Samuel
1835-1902 . . . . . . **TCLC 1, 33; DA; DAB;**
DAC; DAM MST, NOV; WLC
See also CA 143; CDBLB 1890-1914;
DLB 18, 57

Butler, Walter C.
See Faust, Frederick (Schiller)

Butor, Michel (Marie Francois)
1926- . . . . **CLC 1, 3, 8, 11, 15**
See also CA 9-12R; CANR 33; DLB 83;
MTCW

Buzo, Alexander (John) 1944- . . . . . . **CLC 61**
See also CA 97-100; CANR 17, 39

Buzzati, Dino 1906-1972 . . . . **CLC 36**
See also CA 33-36R

Byars, Betsy (Cromer) 1928- . . . . **CLC 35**
See also CA 33-36R; CANR 18, 36; CLR 1,
16; DLB 52; INT CANR-18; JRDA;
MAICYA; MTCW; SAAS 1; SATA 4,
46, 80

Byatt, A(ntonia) S(usan Drabble)
1936- . . . **CLC 19, 65; DAM NOV, POP**
See also CA 13-16R; CANR 13, 33, 50;
DLB 14; MTCW

Byrne, David 1952- . . . . **CLC 26**
See also CA 127

Byrne, John Keyes 1926-
See Leonard, Hugh
See also CA 102; INT 102

Byron, George Gordon (Noel)
1788-1824 . . . . . **NCLC 2, 12; DA; DAB;**
DAC; DAM MST, POET; PC 16; WLC
See also CDBLB 1789-1832; DLB 96, 110

C. 3. 3.
See Wilde, Oscar (Fingal O'Flahertie Wills)

Caballero, Fernan 1796-1877 . . . . . **NCLC 10**

Cabell, Branch
See Cabell, James Branch

Cabell, James Branch 1879-1958 . . . **TCLC 6**
See also CA 105; 152; DLB 9, 78

Cable, George Washington
1844-1925 . . . . **TCLC 4; SSC 4**
See also CA 104; DLB 12, 74; DLBD 13

Cabral de Melo Neto, Joao
1920- . . . . **CLC 76; DAM MULT**
See also CA 151

Cabrera Infante, G(uillermo)
1929- . . . . . **CLC 5, 25, 45; DAM MULT;**
HLC
See also CA 85-88; CANR 29; DLB 113;
HW; MTCW

Cade, Toni
See Bambara, Toni Cade

Cadmus and Harmonia
See Buchan, John

Caedmon fl. 658-680 . . . . **CMLC 7**
See also DLB 146

Caeiro, Alberto
See Pessoa, Fernando (Antonio Nogueira)

Cage, John (Milton, Jr.) 1912- . . . . . **CLC 41**
See also CA 13-16R; CANR 9;
INT CANR-9

Cain, G.
See Cabrera Infante, G(uillermo)

Cain, Guillermo
See Cabrera Infante, G(uillermo)

Cain, James M(allahan)
1892-1977 . . . . **CLC 3, 11, 28**
See also AITN 1; CA 17-20R; 73-76;
CANR 8, 34; MTCW

Caine, Mark
See Raphael, Frederic (Michael)

Calasso, Roberto 1941- . . . . **CLC 81**
See also CA 143

Calderon de la Barca, Pedro
1600-1681 . . . . **LC 23; DC 3**

Caldwell, Erskine (Preston)
1903-1987 . . . . **CLC 1, 8, 14, 50, 60;**
DAM NOV; SSC 19
See also AITN 1; CA 1-4R; 121; CAAS 1;
CANR 2, 33; DLB 9, 86; MTCW

Caldwell, (Janet Miriam) Taylor (Holland)
1900-1985 . . . . **CLC 2, 28, 39;**
DAM NOV, POP
See also CA 5-8R; 116; CANR 5

Calhoun, John Caldwell
1782-1850 . . . . **NCLC 15**
See also DLB 3

Calisher, Hortense
1911- . . . . . **CLC 2, 4, 8, 38; DAM NOV;**
SSC 15
See also CA 1-4R; CANR 1, 22; DLB 2;
INT CANR-22; MTCW

Callaghan, Morley Edward
1903-1990 . . . . **CLC 3, 14, 41, 65; DAC;**
DAM MST
See also CA 9-12R; 132; CANR 33;
DLB 68; MTCW

Callimachus
c. 305B.C.-c. 240B.C. . . . . **CMLC 18**

Calvino, Italo
1923-1985 . . . . . **CLC 5, 8, 11, 22, 33, 39,**
73; DAM NOV; SSC 3
See also CA 85-88; 116; CANR 23; MTCW

Cameron, Carey 1952- . . . . **CLC 59**
See also CA 135

Cameron, Peter 1959- . . . . **CLC 44**
See also CA 125; CANR 50

Campana, Dino 1885-1932 . . . . **TCLC 20**
See also CA 117; DLB 114

Campanella, Tommaso 1568-1639 . . . . **LC 32**

Campbell, John W(ood, Jr.)
1910-1971 . . . . **CLC 32**
See also CA 21-22; 29-32R; CANR 34;
CAP 2; DLB 8; MTCW

Campbell, Joseph 1904-1987 . . . . **CLC 69**
See also AAYA 3; BEST 89:2; CA 1-4R;
124; CANR 3, 28; MTCW

Campbell, Maria 1940- . . . . **CLC 85; DAC**
See also CA 102; NNAL

Campbell, (John) Ramsey
1946- . . . . **CLC 42; SSC 19**
See also CA 57-60; CANR 7; INT CANR-7

Campbell, (Ignatius) Roy (Dunnachie)
1901-1957 . . . . **TCLC 5**
See also CA 104; DLB 20

Campbell, Thomas 1777-1844 . . . . **NCLC 19**
See also DLB 93; 144

Campbell, Wilfred . . . . **TCLC 9**
See also Campbell, William

Campbell, William 1858(?)-1918
See Campbell, Wilfred
See also CA 106; DLB 92

Campion, Jane . . . . **CLC 95**
See also CA 138

Campos, Alvaro de
See Pessoa, Fernando (Antonio Nogueira)

Camus, Albert
1913-1960 . . . . **CLC 1, 2, 4, 9, 11, 14, 32,**
63, 69; DA; DAB; DAC; DAM DRAM,
MST, NOV; DC 2; SSC 9; WLC
See also CA 89-92; DLB 72; MTCW

Canby, Vincent 1924- . . . . **CLC 13**
See also CA 81-84

Cancale
See Desnos, Robert

Canetti, Elias
1905-1994 . . . . **CLC 3, 14, 25, 75, 86**
See also CA 21-24R; 146; CANR 23;
DLB 85, 124; MTCW

Canin, Ethan 1960- . . . . **CLC 55**
See also CA 131; 135

Cannon, Curt
See Hunter, Evan

Cape, Judith
See Page, P(atricia) K(athleen)

Capek, Karel
1890-1938 . . . . . . **TCLC 6, 37; DA; DAB;**
DAC; DAM DRAM, MST, NOV; DC 1;
WLC
See also CA 104; 140

Capote, Truman
1924-1984 . . . . . . **CLC 1, 3, 8, 13, 19, 34,**
38, 58; DA; DAB; DAC; DAM MST,
NOV, POP; SSC 2; WLC
See also CA 5-8R; 113; CANR 18;
CDALB 1941-1968; DLB 2; DLBY 80,
84; MTCW

Capra, Frank 1897-1991 . . . . **CLC 16**
See also CA 61-64; 135

Caputo, Philip 1941- . . . . **CLC 32**
See also CA 73-76; CANR 40

Card, Orson Scott
1951- . . . . . . **CLC 44, 47, 50; DAM POP**
See also AAYA 11; CA 102; CANR 27, 47;
INT CANR-27; MTCW; SATA 83

Cardenal, Ernesto
1925- . . . . **CLC 31; DAM MULT,**
POET; HLC
See also CA 49-52; CANR 2, 32; HW;
MTCW

Cardozo, Benjamin N(athan)
1870-1938 . . . . **TCLC 65**
See also CA 117

Carducci, Giosue 1835-1907 . . . . **TCLC 32**

Carew, Thomas 1595(?)-1640 . . . . **LC 13**
See also DLB 126

Carey, Ernestine Gilbreth 1908- .... CLC 17
See also CA 5-8R; SATA 2

Carey, Peter 1943- .... CLC 40, 55, 96
See also CA 123; 127; CANR 53; INT 127;
MTCW

Carleton, William 1794-1869 ...... NCLC 3
See also DLB 159

Carlisle, Henry (Coffin) 1926- .... CLC 33
See also CA 13-16R; CANR 15

Carlsen, Chris
See Holdstock, Robert P.

Carlson, Ron(ald F.) 1947- .... CLC 54
See also CA 105; CANR 27

Carlyle, Thomas
1795-1881 .... NCLC 22; DA; DAB;
DAC; DAM MST
See also CDBLB 1789-1832; DLB 55; 144

Carman, (William) Bliss
1861-1929 .... TCLC 7; DAC
See also CA 104; 152; DLB 92

Carnegie, Dale 1888-1955 .... TCLC 53

Carossa, Hans 1878-1956......... TCLC 48
See also DLB 66

Carpenter, Don(ald Richard)
1931-1995 .... CLC 41
See also CA 45-48; 149; CANR 1

Carpentier (y Valmont), Alejo
1904-1980 .... CLC 8, 11, 38;
DAM MULT; HLC
See also CA 65-68; 97-100; CANR 11;
DLB 113; HW

Carr, Caleb 1955(?)- .... CLC 86
See also CA 147

Carr, Emily 1871-1945.......... TCLC 32
See also DLB 68

Carr, John Dickson 1906-1977 ...... CLC 3
See also CA 49-52; 69-72; CANR 3, 33;
MTCW

Carr, Philippa
See Hibbert, Eleanor Alice Burford

Carr, Virginia Spencer 1929-....... CLC 34
See also CA 61-64; DLB 111

Carrere, Emmanuel 1957- .... CLC 89

Carrier, Roch
1937- ... CLC 13, 78; DAC; DAM MST
See also CA 130; DLB 53

Carroll, James P. 1943(?)- .... CLC 38
See also CA 81-84

Carroll, Jim 1951- .... CLC 35
See also AAYA 17; CA 45-48; CANR 42

Carroll, Lewis .... NCLC 2, 53; WLC
See also Dodgson, Charles Lutwidge
See also CDBLB 1832-1890; CLR 2, 18;
DLB 18, 163; JRDA

Carroll, Paul Vincent 1900-1968.... CLC 10
See also CA 9-12R; 25-28R; DLB 10

Carruth, Hayden
1921- ...... CLC 4, 7, 10, 18, 84; PC 10
See also CA 9-12R; CANR 4, 38; DLB 5,
165; INT CANR-4; MTCW; SATA 47

Carson, Rachel Louise
1907-1964 .... CLC 71; DAM POP
See also CA 77-80; CANR 35; MTCW;
SATA 23

Carter, Angela (Olive)
1940-1992 ...... CLC 5, 41, 76; SSC 13
See also CA 53-56; 136; CANR 12, 36;
DLB 14; MTCW; SATA 66;
SATA-Obit 70

Carter, Nick
See Smith, Martin Cruz

Carver, Raymond
1938-1988 .... CLC 22, 36, 53, 55;
DAM NOV; SSC 8
See also CA 33-36R; 126; CANR 17, 34;
DLB 130; DLBY 84, 88; MTCW

Cary, Elizabeth, Lady Falkland
1585-1639 .... LC 30

Cary, (Arthur) Joyce (Lunel)
1888-1957 .... TCLC 1, 29
See also CA 104; CDBLB 1914-1945;
DLB 15, 100

Casanova de Seingalt, Giovanni Jacopo
1725-1798 .... LC 13

Casares, Adolfo Bioy
See Bioy Casares, Adolfo

Casely-Hayford, J(oseph) E(phraim)
1866-1930 .... TCLC 24; BLC;
DAM MULT
See also BW 2; CA 123; 152

Casey, John (Dudley) 1939-........ CLC 59
See also BEST 90:2; CA 69-72; CANR 23

Casey, Michael 1947-.............. CLC 2
See also CA 65-68; DLB 5

Casey, Patrick
See Thurman, Wallace (Henry)

Casey, Warren (Peter) 1935-1988 ... CLC 12
See also CA 101; 127; INT 101

Casona, Alejandro................. CLC 49
See also Alvarez, Alejandro Rodriguez

Cassavetes, John 1929-1989........ CLC 20
See also CA 85-88; 127

Cassill, R(onald) V(erlin) 1919-... CLC 4, 23
See also CA 9-12R; CAAS 1; CANR 7, 45;
DLB 6

Cassirer, Ernst 1874-1945 .... TCLC 61

Cassity, (Allen) Turner 1929- .... CLC 6, 42
See also CA 17-20R; CAAS 8; CANR 11;
DLB 105

Castaneda, Carlos 1931(?)-........ CLC 12
See also CA 25-28R; CANR 32; HW;
MTCW

Castedo, Elena 1937- .... CLC 65
See also CA 132

Castedo-Ellerman, Elena
See Castedo, Elena

Castellanos, Rosario
1925-1974 ...... CLC 66; DAM MULT;
HLC
See also CA 131; 53-56; DLB 113; HW

Castelvetro, Lodovico 1505-1571..... LC 12

Castiglione, Baldassare 1478-1529 ... LC 12

Castle, Robert
See Hamilton, Edmond

Castro, Guillen de 1569-1631....... LC 19

Castro, Rosalia de
1837-1885 ...... NCLC 3; DAM MULT

Cather, Willa
See Cather, Willa Sibert

Cather, Willa Sibert
1873-1947 .... TCLC 1, 11, 31; DA;
DAB; DAC; DAM MST, NOV; SSC 2;
WLC
See also CA 104; 128; CDALB 1865-1917;
DLB 9, 54, 78; DLBD 1; MTCW;
SATA 30

Catton, (Charles) Bruce
1899-1978 .... CLC 35
See also AITN 1; CA 5-8R; 81-84;
CANR 7; DLB 17; SATA 2;
SATA-Obit 24

Catullus c. 84B.C.-c. 54B.C. ..... CMLC 18

Cauldwell, Frank
See King, Francis (Henry)

Caunitz, William J. 1933-1996 ..... CLC 34
See also BEST 89:3; CA 125; 130; 152;
INT 130

Causley, Charles (Stanley) 1917-..... CLC 7
See also CA 9-12R; CANR 5, 35; CLR 30;
DLB 27; MTCW; SATA 3, 66

Caute, David 1936-.... CLC 29; DAM NOV
See also CA 1-4R; CAAS 4; CANR 1, 33;
DLB 14

Cavafy, C(onstantine) P(eter)
1863-1933 .... TCLC 2, 7; DAM POET
See also Kavafis, Konstantinos Petrou
See also CA 148

Cavallo, Evelyn
See Spark, Muriel (Sarah)

Cavanna, Betty .... CLC 12
See also Harrison, Elizabeth Cavanna
See also JRDA; MAICYA; SAAS 4;
SATA 1, 30

Cavendish, Margaret Lucas
1623-1673 .... LC 30
See also DLB 131

Caxton, William 1421(?)-1491(?)..... LC 17

Cayrol, Jean 1911-................ CLC 11
See also CA 89-92; DLB 83

Cela, Camilo Jose
1916- ..... CLC 4, 13, 59; DAM MULT;
HLC
See also BEST 90:2; CA 21-24R; CAAS 10;
CANR 21, 32; DLBY 89; HW; MTCW

Celan, Paul ...... CLC 10, 19, 53, 82; PC 10
See also Antschel, Paul
See also DLB 69

Celine, Louis-Ferdinand
.... CLC 1, 3, 4, 7, 9, 15, 47
See also Destouches, Louis-Ferdinand
See also DLB 72

Cellini, Benvenuto 1500-1571 .... LC 7

Cendrars, Blaise .... CLC 18
See also Sauser-Hall, Frederic

Cernuda (y Bidon), Luis
1902-1963 .... CLC 54; DAM POET
See also CA 131; 89-92; DLB 134; HW

Cervantes (Saavedra), Miguel de
1547-1616 .... LC 6, 23; DA; DAB;
DAC; DAM MST, NOV; SSC 12; WLC

Cesaire, Aime (Fernand)
1913- .... **CLC 19, 32; BLC;**
DAM MULT, POET
See also BW 2; CA 65-68; CANR 24, 43;
MTCW

Chabon, Michael 1965(?)- .... **CLC 55**
See also CA 139

Chabrol, Claude 1930- .... **CLC 16**
See also CA 110

Challans, Mary 1905-1983
See Renault, Mary
See also CA 81-84; 111; SATA 23;
SATA-Obit 36

Challis, George
See Faust, Frederick (Schiller)

Chambers, Aidan 1934- .... **CLC 35**
See also CA 25-28R; CANR 12, 31; JRDA;
MAICYA; SAAS 12; SATA 1, 69

Chambers, James 1948-
See Cliff, Jimmy
See also CA 124

Chambers, Jessie
See Lawrence, D(avid) H(erbert Richards)

Chambers, Robert W. 1865-1933... **TCLC 41**

Chandler, Raymond (Thornton)
1888-1959 .... **TCLC 1, 7; SSC 23**
See also CA 104; 129; CDALB 1929-1941;
DLBD 6; MTCW

Chang, Jung 1952- .... **CLC 71**
See also CA 142

Channing, William Ellery
1780-1842 .... **NCLC 17**
See also DLB 1, 59

Chaplin, Charles Spencer
1889-1977 .... **CLC 16**
See Chaplin, Charlie
See also CA 81-84; 73-76

Chaplin, Charlie
See Chaplin, Charles Spencer
See also DLB 44

Chapman, George
1559(?)-1634 ..... **LC 22; DAM DRAM**
See also DLB 62, 121

Chapman, Graham 1941-1989 ...... **CLC 21**
See also Monty Python
See also CA 116; 129; CANR 35

Chapman, John Jay 1862-1933 ..... **TCLC 7**
See also CA 104

Chapman, Lee
See Bradley, Marion Zimmer

Chapman, Walker
See Silverberg, Robert

Chappell, Fred (Davis) 1936-.... **CLC 40, 78**
See also CA 5-8R; CAAS 4; CANR 8, 33;
DLB 6, 105

Char, Rene(-Emile)
1907-1988 .... **CLC 9, 11, 14, 55;**
DAM POET
See also CA 13-16R; 124; CANR 32;
MTCW

Charby, Jay
See Ellison, Harlan (Jay)

Chardin, Pierre Teilhard de
See Teilhard de Chardin, (Marie Joseph)
Pierre

Charles I 1600-1649 .... **LC 13**

Charyn, Jerome 1937- .... **CLC 5, 8, 18**
See also CA 5-8R; CAAS 1; CANR 7;
DLBY 83; MTCW

Chase, Mary (Coyle) 1907-1981 ...... **DC 1**
See also CA 77-80; 105; SATA 17;
SATA-Obit 29

Chase, Mary Ellen 1887-1973 .... **CLC 2**
See also CA 13-16; 41-44R; CAP 1;
SATA 10

Chase, Nicholas
See Hyde, Anthony

Chateaubriand, Francois Rene de
1768-1848 .... **NCLC 3**
See also DLB 119

Chatterje, Sarat Chandra 1876-1936(?)
See Chatterji, Saratchandra
See also CA 109

Chatterji, Bankim Chandra
1838-1894 .... **NCLC 19**

Chatterji, Saratchandra .... **TCLC 13**
See also Chatterje, Sarat Chandra

Chatterton, Thomas
1752-1770 .... **LC 3; DAM POET**
See also DLB 109

Chatwin, (Charles) Bruce
1940-1989 .. **CLC 28, 57, 59; DAM POP**
See also AAYA 4; BEST 90:1; CA 85-88;
127

Chaucer, Daniel
See Ford, Ford Madox

Chaucer, Geoffrey
1340(?)-1400 .... **LC 17; DA; DAB;**
DAC; DAM MST, POET
See also CDBLB Before 1660; DLB 146

Chaviaras, Strates 1935-
See Haviaras, Stratis
See also CA 105

Chayefsky, Paddy .... **CLC 23**
See also Chayefsky, Sidney
See also DLB 7, 44; DLBY 81

Chayefsky, Sidney 1923-1981
See Chayefsky, Paddy
See also CA 9-12R; 104; CANR 18;
DAM DRAM

Chedid, Andree 1920- .... **CLC 47**
See also CA 145

Cheever, John
1912-1982 ...... **CLC 3, 7, 8, 11, 15, 25,**
64; DA; DAB; DAC; DAM MST, NOV,
POP; SSC 1; WLC
See also CA 5-8R; 106; CABS 1; CANR 5,
27; CDALB 1941-1968; DLB 2, 102;
DLBY 80, 82; INT CANR-5; MTCW

Cheever, Susan 1943-.......... **CLC 18, 48**
See also CA 103; CANR 27, 51; DLBY 82;
INT CANR-27

Chekhonte, Antosha
See Chekhov, Anton (Pavlovich)

Chekhov, Anton (Pavlovich)
1860-1904 ..... **TCLC 3, 10, 31, 55; DA;**
DAB; DAC; DAM DRAM, MST; SSC 2;
WLC
See also CA 104; 124

Chernyshevsky, Nikolay Gavrilovich
1828-1889 .... **NCLC 1**

Cherry, Carolyn Janice 1942-
See Cherryh, C. J.
See also CA 65-68; CANR 10

Cherryh, C. J. .... **CLC 35**
See Cherry, Carolyn Janice
See also DLBY 80

Chesnutt, Charles W(addell)
1858-1932 .... **TCLC 5, 39; BLC;**
DAM MULT; SSC 7
See also BW 1; CA 106; 125; DLB 12, 50,
78; MTCW

Chester, Alfred 1929(?)-1971....... **CLC 49**
See also CA 33-36R; DLB 130

Chesterton, G(ilbert) K(eith)
1874-1936 .... **TCLC 1, 6, 64;**
DAM NOV, POET; SSC 1
See also CA 104; 132; CDBLB 1914-1945;
DLB 10, 19, 34, 70, 98, 149; MTCW;
SATA 27

Chiang Pin-chin 1904-1986
See Ding Ling
See also CA 118

Ch'ien Chung-shu 1910-........... **CLC 22**
See also CA 130; MTCW

Child, L. Maria
See Child, Lydia Maria

Child, Lydia Maria 1802-1880 .... **NCLC 6**
See also DLB 1, 74; SATA 67

Child, Mrs.
See Child, Lydia Maria

Child, Philip 1898-1978 .... **CLC 19, 68**
See also CA 13-14; CAP 1; SATA 47

Childers, (Robert) Erskine
1870-1922 .... **TCLC 65**
See also CA 113; DLB 70

Childress, Alice
1920-1994 .... **CLC 12, 15, 86, 96; BLC;**
DAM DRAM, MULT, NOV; DC 4
See also AAYA 8; BW 2; CA 45-48; 146;
CANR 3, 27, 50; CLR 14; DLB 7, 38;
JRDA; MAICYA; MTCW; SATA 7, 48,
81

Chislett, (Margaret) Anne 1943-.... **CLC 34**
See also CA 151

Chitty, Thomas Willes 1926-....... **CLC 11**
See also Hinde, Thomas
See also CA 5-8R

Chivers, Thomas Holley
1809-1858 .... **NCLC 49**
See also DLB 3

Chomette, Rene Lucien 1898-1981
See Clair, Rene
See also CA 103

Chopin, Kate
.... **TCLC 5, 14; DA; DAB; SSC 8**
See also Chopin, Katherine
See also CDALB 1865-1917; DLB 12, 78

Chopin, Katherine 1851-1904
See Chopin, Kate
See also CA 104; 122; DAC; DAM MST,
NOV

Chretien de Troyes
c. 12th cent. - .... **CMLC 10**

Christie
See Ichikawa, Kon

Christie, Agatha (Mary Clarissa)
1890-1976 ...... **CLC 1, 6, 8, 12, 39, 48; DAB; DAC; DAM NOV**
See also AAYA 9; AITN 1, 2; CA 17-20R; 61-64; CANR 10, 37; CDBLB 1914-1945; DLB 13, 77; MTCW; SATA 36

Christie, (Ann) Philippa
See Pearce, Philippa
See also CA 5-8R; CANR 4

Christine de Pizan 1365(?)-1431(?) .... **LC 9**

Chubb, Elmer
See Masters, Edgar Lee

Chulkov, Mikhail Dmitrievich
1743-1792 .... **LC 2**
See also DLB 150

Churchill, Caryl 1938- ... **CLC 31, 55; DC 5**
See also CA 102; CANR 22, 46; DLB 13; MTCW

Churchill, Charles 1731-1764 .... **LC 3**
See also DLB 109

Chute, Carolyn 1947- .... **CLC 39**
See also CA 123

Ciardi, John (Anthony)
1916-1986 .... **CLC 10, 40, 44; DAM POET**
See also CA 5-8R; 118; CAAS 2; CANR 5, 33; CLR 19; DLB 5; DLBY 86; INT CANR-5; MAICYA; MTCW; SATA 1, 65; SATA-Obit 46

Cicero, Marcus Tullius
106B.C.-43B.C. .... **CMLC 3**

Cimino, Michael 1943- .... **CLC 16**
See also CA 105

Cioran, E(mil) M. 1911-1995 .... **CLC 64**
See also CA 25-28R; 149

Cisneros, Sandra
1954- ..... **CLC 69; DAM MULT; HLC**
See also AAYA 9; CA 131; DLB 122, 152; HW

Cixous, Helene 1937- .... **CLC 92**
See also CA 126; DLB 83; MTCW

Clair, Rene .... **CLC 20**
See also Chomette, Rene Lucien

Clampitt, Amy 1920-1994 .... **CLC 32**
See also CA 110; 146; CANR 29; DLB 105

Clancy, Thomas L., Jr. 1947-
See Clancy, Tom
See also CA 125; 131; INT 131; MTCW

Clancy, Tom .... **CLC 45; DAM NOV, POP**
See also Clancy, Thomas L., Jr.
See also AAYA 9; BEST 89:1, 90:1

Clare, John
1793-1864 .... **NCLC 9; DAB; DAM POET**
See also DLB 55, 96

Clarin
See Alas (y Urena), Leopoldo (Enrique Garcia)

Clark, Al C.
See Goines, Donald

Clark, (Robert) Brian 1932- .... **CLC 29**
See also CA 41-44R

Clark, Curt
See Westlake, Donald E(dwin)

Clark, Eleanor 1913-1996 .... **CLC 5, 19**
See also CA 9-12R; 151; CANR 41; DLB 6

Clark, J. P.
See Clark, John Pepper
See also DLB 117

Clark, John Pepper
1935- .... **CLC 38; BLC; DAM DRAM, MULT; DC 5**
See also Clark, J. P.
See also BW 1; CA 65-68; CANR 16

Clark, M. R.
See Clark, Mavis Thorpe

Clark, Mavis Thorpe 1909- .... **CLC 12**
See also CA 57-60; CANR 8, 37; CLR 30; MAICYA; SAAS 5; SATA 8, 74

Clark, Walter Van Tilburg
1909-1971 .... **CLC 28**
See also CA 9-12R; 33-36R; DLB 9; SATA 8

Clarke, Arthur C(harles)
1917- .... **CLC 1, 4, 13, 18, 35; DAM POP; SSC 3**
See also AAYA 4; CA 1-4R; CANR 2, 28; JRDA; MAICYA; MTCW; SATA 13, 70

Clarke, Austin
1896-1974 ...... **CLC 6, 9; DAM POET**
See also CA 29-32; 49-52; CAP 2; DLB 10, 20

Clarke, Austin C(hesterfield)
1934- .... **CLC 8, 53; BLC; DAC; DAM MULT**
See also BW 1; CA 25-28R; CAAS 16; CANR 14, 32; DLB 53, 125

Clarke, Gillian 1937- .... **CLC 61**
See also CA 106; DLB 40

Clarke, Marcus (Andrew Hislop)
1846-1881 .... **NCLC 19**

Clarke, Shirley 1925- .... **CLC 16**

Clash, The
See Headon, (Nicky) Topper; Jones, Mick; Simonon, Paul; Strummer, Joe

Claudel, Paul (Louis Charles Marie)
1868-1955 .... **TCLC 2, 10**
See also CA 104

Clavell, James (duMaresq)
1925-1994 .... **CLC 6, 25, 87; DAM NOV, POP**
See also CA 25-28R; 146; CANR 26, 48; MTCW

Cleaver, (Leroy) Eldridge
1935- ..... **CLC 30; BLC; DAM MULT**
See also BW 1; CA 21-24R; CANR 16

Cleese, John (Marwood) 1939- ..... **CLC 21**
See also Monty Python
See also CA 112; 116; CANR 35; MTCW

Cleishbotham, Jebediah
See Scott, Walter

Cleland, John 1710-1789 .... **LC 2**
See also DLB 39

Clemens, Samuel Langhorne 1835-1910
See Twain, Mark
See also CA 104; 135; CDALB 1865-1917; DA; DAB; DAC; DAM MST, NOV; DLB 11, 12, 23, 64, 74; JRDA; MAICYA; YABC 2

Cleophil
See Congreve, William

Clerihew, E.
See Bentley, E(dmund) C(lerihew)

Clerk, N. W.
See Lewis, C(live) S(taples)

Cliff, Jimmy .... **CLC 21**
See also Chambers, James

Clifton, (Thelma) Lucille
1936- .... **CLC 19, 66; BLC; DAM MULT, POET**
See also BW 2; CA 49-52; CANR 2, 24, 42; CLR 5; DLB 5, 41; MAICYA; MTCW; SATA 20, 69

Clinton, Dirk
See Silverberg, Robert

Clough, Arthur Hugh 1819-1861 .. **NCLC 27**
See also DLB 32

Clutha, Janet Paterson Frame 1924-
See Frame, Janet
See also CA 1-4R; CANR 2, 36; MTCW

Clyne, Terence
See Blatty, William Peter

Cobalt, Martin
See Mayne, William (James Carter)

Cobbett, William 1763-1835 ..... **NCLC 49**
See also DLB 43, 107, 158

Coburn, D(onald) L(ee) 1938- ...... **CLC 10**
See also CA 89-92

Cocteau, Jean (Maurice Eugene Clement)
1889-1963 .... **CLC 1, 8, 15, 16, 43; DA; DAB; DAC; DAM DRAM, MST, NOV; WLC**
See also CA 25-28; CANR 40; CAP 2; DLB 65; MTCW

Codrescu, Andrei
1946- .... **CLC 46; DAM POET**
See also CA 33-36R; CAAS 19; CANR 13, 34, 53

Coe, Max
See Bourne, Randolph S(illiman)

Coe, Tucker
See Westlake, Donald E(dwin)

Coetzee, J(ohn) M(ichael)
1940- ...... **CLC 23, 33, 66; DAM NOV**
See also CA 77-80; CANR 41; MTCW

Coffey, Brian
See Koontz, Dean R(ay)

Cohan, George M. 1878-1942 ..... **TCLC 60**

Cohen, Arthur A(llen)
1928-1986 .... **CLC 7, 31**
See also CA 1-4R; 120; CANR 1, 17, 42; DLB 28

Cohen, Leonard (Norman)
1934- .... **CLC 3, 38; DAC; DAM MST**
See also CA 21-24R; CANR 14; DLB 53; MTCW

Cohen, Matt 1942- . . . . **CLC 19; DAC**
See also CA 61-64; CAAS 18; CANR 40;
DLB 53

Cohen-Solal, Annie 19(?)- . . . . **CLC 50**

Colegate, Isabel 1931- . . . . **CLC 36**
See also CA 17-20R; CANR 8, 22; DLB 14;
INT CANR-22; MTCW

Coleman, Emmett
See Reed, Ishmael

Coleridge, Samuel Taylor
1772-1834 . . . . . **NCLC 9, 54; DA; DAB;**
DAC; DAM MST, POET; PC 11; WLC
See also CDBLB 1789-1832; DLB 93, 107

Coleridge, Sara 1802-1852 . . . . **NCLC 31**

Coles, Don 1928- . . . . **CLC 46**
See also CA 115; CANR 38

Colette, (Sidonie-Gabrielle)
1873-1954 . . . . **TCLC 1, 5, 16;**
DAM NOV; SSC 10
See also CA 104; 131; DLB 65; MTCW

Collett, (Jacobine) Camilla (Wergeland)
1813-1895 . . . . **NCLC 22**

Collier, Christopher 1930- . . . . **CLC 30**
See also AAYA 13; CA 33-36R; CANR 13,
33; JRDA; MAICYA; SATA 16, 70

Collier, James L(incoln)
1928- . . . . **CLC 30; DAM POP**
See also AAYA 13; CA 9-12R; CANR 4,
33; CLR 3; JRDA; MAICYA; SAAS 21;
SATA 8, 70

Collier, Jeremy 1650-1726 . . . . **LC 6**

Collier, John 1901-1980 . . . . **SSC 19**
See also CA 65-68; 97-100; CANR 10;
DLB 77

Collins, Hunt
See Hunter, Evan

Collins, Linda 1931- . . . . **CLC 44**
See also CA 125

Collins, (William) Wilkie
1824-1889 . . . . **NCLC 1, 18**
See also CDBLB 1832-1890; DLB 18, 70,
159

Collins, William
1721-1759 . . . . **LC 4; DAM POET**
See also DLB 109

Collodi, Carlo 1826-1890 . . . . **NCLC 54**
See also Lorenzini, Carlo
See also CLR 5

Colman, George
See Glassco, John

Colt, Winchester Remington
See Hubbard, L(afayette) Ron(ald)

Colter, Cyrus 1910- . . . . **CLC 58**
See also BW 1; CA 65-68; CANR 10;
DLB 33

Colton, James
See Hansen, Joseph

Colum, Padraic 1881-1972 . . . . **CLC 28**
See also CA 73-76; 33-36R; CANR 35;
CLR 36; MAICYA; MTCW; SATA 15

Colvin, James
See Moorcock, Michael (John)

Colwin, Laurie (E.)
1944-1992 . . . . **CLC 5, 13, 23, 84**
See also CA 89-92; 139; CANR 20, 46;
DLBY 80; MTCW

Comfort, Alex(ander)
1920- . . . . **CLC 7; DAM POP**
See also CA 1-4R; CANR 1, 45

Comfort, Montgomery
See Campbell, (John) Ramsey

Compton-Burnett, I(vy)
1884(?)-1969 . . . . . . **CLC 1, 3, 10, 15, 34;**
DAM NOV
See also CA 1-4R; 25-28R; CANR 4;
DLB 36; MTCW

Comstock, Anthony 1844-1915 . . . . **TCLC 13**
See also CA 110

Comte, Auguste 1798-1857 . . . . . . **NCLC 54**

Conan Doyle, Arthur
See Doyle, Arthur Conan

Conde, Maryse
1937- . . . . **CLC 52, 92; DAM MULT**
See also Boucolon, Maryse
See also BW 2

Condillac, Etienne Bonnot de
1714-1780 . . . . **LC 26**

Condon, Richard (Thomas)
1915-1996 . . . . **CLC 4, 6, 8, 10, 45;**
DAM NOV
See also BEST 90:3; CA 1-4R; 151;
CAAS 1; CANR 2, 23; INT CANR-23;
MTCW

Confucius
551B.C.-479B.C. . . . . **CMLC 19; DA;**
DAB; DAC; DAM MST

Congreve, William
1670-1729 . . . . **LC 5, 21; DA; DAB;**
DAC; DAM DRAM, MST, POET;
DC 2; WLC
See also CDBLB 1660-1789; DLB 39, 84

Connell, Evan S(helby), Jr.
1924- . . . . **CLC 4, 6, 45; DAM NOV**
See also AAYA 7; CA 1-4R; CAAS 2;
CANR 2, 39; DLB 2; DLBY 81; MTCW

Connelly, Marc(us Cook)
1890-1980 . . . . **CLC 7**
See also CA 85-88; 102; CANR 30; DLB 7;
DLBY 80; SATA-Obit 25

Connor, Ralph . . . . **TCLC 31**
See also Gordon, Charles William
See also DLB 92

Conrad, Joseph
1857-1924 . . . . **TCLC 1, 6, 13, 25, 43, 57;**
DA; DAB; DAC; DAM MST, NOV;
SSC 9; WLC
See also CA 104; 131; CDBLB 1890-1914;
DLB 10, 34, 98, 156; MTCW; SATA 27

Conrad, Robert Arnold
See Hart, Moss

Conroy, Pat
1945- . . . **CLC 30, 74; DAM NOV, POP**
See also AAYA 8; AITN 1; CA 85-88;
CANR 24; DLB 6; MTCW

Constant (de Rebecque), (Henri) Benjamin
1767-1830 . . . . **NCLC 6**
See also DLB 119

Conybeare, Charles Augustus
See Eliot, T(homas) S(tearns)

Cook, Michael 1933- . . . . **CLC 58**
See also CA 93-96; DLB 53

Cook, Robin 1940- . . . . **CLC 14; DAM POP**
See also BEST 90:2; CA 108; 111;
CANR 41; INT 111

Cook, Roy
See Silverberg, Robert

Cooke, Elizabeth 1948- . . . . **CLC 55**
See also CA 129

Cooke, John Esten 1830-1886 . . . . . **NCLC 5**
See also DLB 3

Cooke, John Estes
See Baum, L(yman) Frank

Cooke, M. E.
See Creasey, John

Cooke, Margaret
See Creasey, John

Cook-Lynn, Elizabeth
1930- . . . . **CLC 93; DAM MULT**
See also CA 133; NNAL

Cooney, Ray . . . . **CLC 62**

Cooper, Douglas 1960- . . . . **CLC 86**

Cooper, Henry St. John
See Creasey, John

Cooper, J. California
. . . . **CLC 56; DAM MULT**
See also AAYA 12; BW 1; CA 125

Cooper, James Fenimore
1789-1851 . . . . **NCLC 1, 27, 54**
See also CDALB 1640-1865; DLB 3;
SATA 19

Coover, Robert (Lowell)
1932- . . . . **CLC 3, 7, 15, 32, 46, 87;**
DAM NOV; SSC 15
See also CA 45-48; CANR 3, 37; DLB 2;
DLBY 81; MTCW

Copeland, Stewart (Armstrong)
1952- . . . . **CLC 26**

Coppard, A(lfred) E(dgar)
1878-1957 . . . . **TCLC 5; SSC 21**
See also CA 114; DLB 162; YABC 1

Coppee, Francois 1842-1908 . . . . . . **TCLC 25**

Coppola, Francis Ford 1939- . . . . **CLC 16**
See also CA 77-80; CANR 40; DLB 44

Corbiere, Tristan 1845-1875 . . . . . **NCLC 43**

Corcoran, Barbara 1911- . . . . **CLC 17**
See also AAYA 14; CA 21-24R; CAAS 2;
CANR 11, 28, 48; DLB 52; JRDA;
SAAS 20; SATA 3, 77

Cordelier, Maurice
See Giraudoux, (Hippolyte) Jean

Corelli, Marie 1855-1924 . . . . **TCLC 51**
See also Mackay, Mary
See also DLB 34, 156

Corman, Cid . . . . **CLC 9**
See also Corman, Sidney
See also CAAS 2; DLB 5

Corman, Sidney 1924-
See Corman, Cid
See also CA 85-88; CANR 44; DAM POET

Cormier, Robert (Edmund)
1925- .... **CLC 12, 30; DA; DAB; DAC; DAM MST, NOV**
See also AAYA 3; CA 1-4R; CANR 5, 23; CDALB 1968-1988; CLR 12; DLB 52; INT CANR-23; JRDA; MAICYA; MTCW; SATA 10, 45, 83

Corn, Alfred (DeWitt III) 1943- ... **CLC 33**
See also CA 104; CANR 44; DLB 120; DLBY 80

Corneille, Pierre
1606-1684 .... **LC 28; DAB; DAM MST**

Cornwell, David (John Moore)
1931- .... **CLC 9, 15; DAM POP**
See also le Carre, John
See also CA 5-8R; CANR 13, 33; MTCW

Corso, (Nunzio) Gregory 1930- ... **CLC 1, 11**
See also CA 5-8R; CANR 41; DLB 5, 16; MTCW

Cortazar, Julio
1914-1984 ...... **CLC 2, 3, 5, 10, 13, 15, 33, 34, 92; DAM MULT, NOV; HLC; SSC 7**
See also CA 21-24R; CANR 12, 32; DLB 113; HW; MTCW

CORTES, HERNAN 1484-1547..... **LC 31**

Corwin, Cecil
See Kornbluth, C(yril) M.

Cosic, Dobrica 1921- .... **CLC 14**
See also CA 122; 138

Costain, Thomas B(ertram)
1885-1965 .... **CLC 30**
See also CA 5-8R; 25-28R; DLB 9

Costantini, Humberto
1924(?)-1987 .... **CLC 49**
See also CA 131; 122; HW

Costello, Elvis 1955-.............. **CLC 21**

Cotter, Joseph Seamon Sr.
1861-1949 .... **TCLC 28; BLC; DAM MULT**
See also BW 1; CA 124; DLB 50

Couch, Arthur Thomas Quiller
See Quiller-Couch, Arthur Thomas

Coulton, James
See Hansen, Joseph

Couperus, Louis (Marie Anne)
1863-1923 .... **TCLC 15**
See also CA 115

Coupland, Douglas
1961- .... **CLC 85; DAC; DAM POP**
See also CA 142

Court, Wesli
See Turco, Lewis (Putnam)

Courtenay, Bryce 1933-........... **CLC 59**
See also CA 138

Courtney, Robert
See Ellison, Harlan (Jay)

Cousteau, Jacques-Yves 1910-...... **CLC 30**
See also CA 65-68; CANR 15; MTCW; SATA 38

Coward, Noel (Peirce)
1899-1973 .... **CLC 1, 9, 29, 51; DAM DRAM**
See also AITN 1; CA 17-18; 41-44R; CANR 35; CAP 2; CDBLB 1914-1945; DLB 10; MTCW

Cowley, Malcolm 1898-1989 .... **CLC 39**
See also CA 5-8R; 128; CANR 3; DLB 4, 48; DLBY 81, 89; MTCW

Cowper, William
1731-1800 ...... **NCLC 8; DAM POET**
See also DLB 104, 109

Cox, William Trevor
1928- .... **CLC 9, 14, 71; DAM NOV**
See also Trevor, William
See also CA 9-12R; CANR 4, 37; DLB 14; INT CANR-37; MTCW

Coyne, P. J.
See Masters, Hilary

Cozzens, James Gould
1903-1978 .... **CLC 1, 4, 11, 92**
See also CA 9-12R; 81-84; CANR 19; CDALB 1941-1968; DLB 9; DLBD 2; DLBY 84; MTCW

Crabbe, George 1754-1832....... **NCLC 26**
See also DLB 93

Craddock, Charles Egbert
See Murfree, Mary Noailles

Craig, A. A.
See Anderson, Poul (William)

Craik, Dinah Maria (Mulock)
1826-1887 .... **NCLC 38**
See also DLB 35, 163; MAICYA; SATA 34

Cram, Ralph Adams 1863-1942.... **TCLC 45**

Crane, (Harold) Hart
1899-1932 .... **TCLC 2, 5; DA; DAB; DAC; DAM MST, POET; PC 3; WLC**
See also CA 104; 127; CDALB 1917-1929; DLB 4, 48; MTCW

Crane, R(onald) S(almon)
1886-1967 .... **CLC 27**
See also CA 85-88; DLB 63

Crane, Stephen (Townley)
1871-1900 .... **TCLC 11, 17, 32; DA; DAB; DAC; DAM MST, NOV, POET; SSC 7; WLC**
See also CA 109; 140; CDALB 1865-1917; DLB 12, 54, 78; YABC 2

Crase, Douglas 1944-............. **CLC 58**
See also CA 106

Crashaw, Richard 1612(?)-1649...... **LC 24**
See also DLB 126

Craven, Margaret
1901-1980 .... **CLC 17; DAC**
See also CA 103

Crawford, F(rancis) Marion
1854-1909 .... **TCLC 10**
See also CA 107; DLB 71

Crawford, Isabella Valancy
1850-1887 .... **NCLC 12**
See also DLB 92

Crayon, Geoffrey
See Irving, Washington

Creasey, John 1908-1973 .... **CLC 11**
See also CA 5-8R; 41-44R; CANR 8; DLB 77; MTCW

Crebillon, Claude Prosper Jolyot de (fils)
1707-1777 .... **LC 28**

Credo
See Creasey, John

Creeley, Robert (White)
1926- ..... **CLC 1, 2, 4, 8, 11, 15, 36, 78; DAM POET**
See also CA 1-4R; CAAS 10; CANR 23, 43; DLB 5, 16, 169; MTCW

Crews, Harry (Eugene)
1935- .... **CLC 6, 23, 49**
See also AITN 1; CA 25-28R; CANR 20; DLB 6, 143; MTCW

Crichton, (John) Michael
1942- .... **CLC 2, 6, 54, 90; DAM NOV, POP**
See also AAYA 10; AITN 2; CA 25-28R; CANR 13, 40; DLBY 81; INT CANR-13; JRDA; MTCW; SATA 9, 88

Crispin, Edmund .... **CLC 22**
See also Montgomery, (Robert) Bruce
See also DLB 87

Cristofer, Michael
1945(?)- .... **CLC 28; DAM DRAM**
See also CA 110; 152; DLB 7

Croce, Benedetto 1866-1952 ...... **TCLC 37**
See also CA 120

Crockett, David 1786-1836 .... **NCLC 8**
See also DLB 3, 11

Crockett, Davy
See Crockett, David

Crofts, Freeman Wills
1879-1957 .... **TCLC 55**
See also CA 115; DLB 77

Croker, John Wilson 1780-1857 .. **NCLC 10**
See also DLB 110

Crommelynck, Fernand 1885-1970 .. **CLC 75**
See also CA 89-92

Cronin, A(rchibald) J(oseph)
1896-1981 .... **CLC 32**
See also CA 1-4R; 102; CANR 5; SATA 47; SATA-Obit 25

Cross, Amanda
See Heilbrun, Carolyn G(old)

Crothers, Rachel 1878(?)-1958..... **TCLC 19**
See also CA 113; DLB 7

Croves, Hal
See Traven, B.

Crow Dog, Mary .... **CLC 93**
See also Brave Bird, Mary

Crowfield, Christopher
See Stowe, Harriet (Elizabeth) Beecher

Crowley, Aleister .... **TCLC 7**
See also Crowley, Edward Alexander

Crowley, Edward Alexander 1875-1947
See Crowley, Aleister
See also CA 104

Crowley, John 1942-.............. **CLC 57**
See also CA 61-64; CANR 43; DLBY 82; SATA 65

Crud
See Crumb, R(obert)

Crumarums
See Crumb, R(obert)

Davis, Richard Harding
1864-1916 . . . . **TCLC 24**
See also CA 114; DLB 12, 23, 78, 79;
DLBD 13

Davison, Frank Dalby 1893-1970 . . . **CLC 15**
See also CA 116

Davison, Lawrence H.
See Lawrence, D(avid) H(erbert Richards)

Davison, Peter (Hubert) 1928- . . . . . **CLC 28**
See also CA 9-12R; CAAS 4; CANR 3, 43;
DLB 5

Davys, Mary 1674-1732 . . . . **LC 1**
See also DLB 39

Dawson, Fielding 1930- . . . . **CLC 6**
See also CA 85-88; DLB 130

Dawson, Peter
See Faust, Frederick (Schiller)

Day, Clarence (Shepard, Jr.)
1874-1935 . . . . **TCLC 25**
See also CA 108; DLB 11

Day, Thomas 1748-1789 . . . . **LC 1**
See also DLB 39; YABC 1

Day Lewis, C(ecil)
1904-1972 . . . . **CLC 1, 6, 10;**
DAM POET; PC 11
See also Blake, Nicholas
See also CA 13-16; 33-36R; CANR 34;
CAP 1; DLB 15, 20; MTCW

Dazai, Osamu . . . . **TCLC 11**
See also Tsushima, Shuji

de Andrade, Carlos Drummond
See Drummond de Andrade, Carlos

Deane, Norman
See Creasey, John

**de Beauvoir, Simone (Lucie Ernestine Marie
Bertrand)**
See Beauvoir, Simone (Lucie Ernestine
Marie Bertrand) de

de Brissac, Malcolm
See Dickinson, Peter (Malcolm)

de Chardin, Pierre Teilhard
See Teilhard de Chardin, (Marie Joseph)
Pierre

Dee, John 1527-1608 . . . . **LC 20**

Deer, Sandra 1940- . . . . **CLC 45**

De Ferrari, Gabriella 1941- . . . . **CLC 65**
See also CA 146

Defoe, Daniel
1660(?)-1731 . . . . **LC 1; DA; DAB; DAC;**
DAM MST, NOV; WLC
See also CDBLB 1660-1789; DLB 39, 95,
101; JRDA; MAICYA; SATA 22

de Gourmont, Remy(-Marie-Charles)
See Gourmont, Remy (-Marie-Charles) de

de Hartog, Jan 1914- . . . . **CLC 19**
See also CA 1-4R; CANR 1

de Hostos, E. M.
See Hostos (y Bonilla), Eugenio Maria de

de Hostos, Eugenio M.
See Hostos (y Bonilla), Eugenio Maria de

Deighton, Len . . . . **CLC 4, 7, 22, 46**
See also Deighton, Leonard Cyril
See also AAYA 6; BEST 89:2;
CDBLB 1960 to Present; DLB 87

Deighton, Leonard Cyril 1929-
See Deighton, Len
See also CA 9-12R; CANR 19, 33;
DAM NOV, POP; MTCW

Dekker, Thomas
1572(?)-1632 . . . . . **LC 22; DAM DRAM**
See also CDBLB Before 1660; DLB 62

Delafield, E. M. 1890-1943 . . . . **TCLC 61**
See also Dashwood, Edmee Elizabeth
Monica de la Pasture
See also DLB 34

de la Mare, Walter (John)
1873-1956 . . . . **TCLC 4, 53; DAB; DAC;**
DAM MST, POET; SSC 14; WLC
See also CDBLB 1914-1945; CLR 23;
DLB 162; SATA 16

Delaney, Franey
See O'Hara, John (Henry)

Delaney, Shelagh
1939- . . . . **CLC 29; DAM DRAM**
See also CA 17-20R; CANR 30;
CDBLB 1960 to Present; DLB 13;
MTCW

Delany, Mary (Granville Pendarves)
1700-1788 . . . . **LC 12**

Delany, Samuel R(ay, Jr.)
1942- . . . . **CLC 8, 14, 38; BLC;**
DAM MULT
See also BW 2; CA 81-84; CANR 27, 43;
DLB 8, 33; MTCW

De La Ramee, (Marie) Louise 1839-1908
See Ouida
See also SATA 20

de la Roche, Mazo 1879-1961 . . . . . . **CLC 14**
See also CA 85-88; CANR 30; DLB 68;
SATA 64

Delbanco, Nicholas (Franklin)
1942- . . . . **CLC 6, 13**
See also CA 17-20R; CAAS 2; CANR 29;
DLB 6

del Castillo, Michel 1933- . . . . **CLC 38**
See also CA 109

Deledda, Grazia (Cosima)
1875(?)-1936 . . . . **TCLC 23**
See also CA 123

Delibes, Miguel . . . . **CLC 8, 18**
See also Delibes Setien, Miguel

Delibes Setien, Miguel 1920-
See Delibes, Miguel
See also CA 45-48; CANR 1, 32; HW;
MTCW

DeLillo, Don
1936- . . . . . **CLC 8, 10, 13, 27, 39, 54, 76;**
DAM NOV, POP
See also BEST 89:1; CA 81-84; CANR 21;
DLB 6; MTCW

de Lisser, H. G.
See De Lisser, Herbert George
See also DLB 117

De Lisser, Herbert George
1878-1944 . . . . **TCLC 12**
See also de Lisser, H. G.
See also BW 2; CA 109; 152

Deloria, Vine (Victor), Jr.
1933- . . . . **CLC 21; DAM MULT**
See also CA 53-56; CANR 5, 20, 48;
MTCW; NNAL; SATA 21

Del Vecchio, John M(ichael)
1947- . . . . **CLC 29**
See also CA 110; DLBD 9

de Man, Paul (Adolph Michel)
1919-1983 . . . . **CLC 55**
See also CA 128; 111; DLB 67; MTCW

De Marinis, Rick 1934- . . . . **CLC 54**
See also CA 57-60; CAAS 24; CANR 9, 25,
50

Dembry, R. Emmet
See Murfree, Mary Noailles

Demby, William
1922- . . . . . **CLC 53; BLC; DAM MULT**
See also BW 1; CA 81-84; DLB 33

Demijohn, Thom
See Disch, Thomas M(ichael)

de Montherlant, Henry (Milon)
See Montherlant, Henry (Milon) de

Demosthenes 384B.C.-322B.C. . . . **CMLC 13**

de Natale, Francine
See Malzberg, Barry N(athaniel)

Denby, Edwin (Orr) 1903-1983 . . . . . **CLC 48**
See also CA 138; 110

Denis, Julio
See Cortazar, Julio

Denmark, Harrison
See Zelazny, Roger (Joseph)

Dennis, John 1658-1734 . . . . **LC 11**
See also DLB 101

Dennis, Nigel (Forbes) 1912-1989 . . . . **CLC 8**
See also CA 25-28R; 129; DLB 13, 15;
MTCW

De Palma, Brian (Russell) 1940- . . . . **CLC 20**
See also CA 109

De Quincey, Thomas 1785-1859 . . . **NCLC 4**
See also CDBLB 1789-1832; DLB 110; 144

Deren, Eleanora 1908(?)-1961
See Deren, Maya
See also CA 111

Deren, Maya . . . . **CLC 16**
See also Deren, Eleanora

Derleth, August (William)
1909-1971 . . . . **CLC 31**
See also CA 1-4R; 29-32R; CANR 4;
DLB 9; SATA 5

Der Nister 1884-1950 . . . . **TCLC 56**

de Routisie, Albert
See Aragon, Louis

Derrida, Jacques 1930- . . . . **CLC 24, 87**
See also CA 124; 127

Derry Down Derry
See Lear, Edward

Dersonnes, Jacques
See Simenon, Georges (Jacques Christian)

Desai, Anita
1937- . . . **CLC 19, 37; DAB; DAM NOV**
See also CA 81-84; CANR 33, 53; MTCW;
SATA 63

de Saint-Luc, Jean
See Glassco, John

de Saint Roman, Arnaud
See Aragon, Louis

Descartes, Rene 1596-1650 ...... **LC 20, 35**

De Sica, Vittorio 1901(?)-1974 ..... **CLC 20**
See also CA 117

Desnos, Robert 1900-1945....... **TCLC 22**
See also CA 121; 151

Destouches, Louis-Ferdinand
1894-1961 .... **CLC 9, 15**
See also Celine, Louis-Ferdinand
See also CA 85-88; CANR 28; MTCW

Deutsch, Babette 1895-1982 .... **CLC 18**
See also CA 1-4R; 108; CANR 4; DLB 45;
SATA 1; SATA-Obit 33

Devenant, William 1606-1649 .... **LC 13**

Devkota, Laxmiprasad
1909-1959 .... **TCLC 23**
See also CA 123

De Voto, Bernard (Augustine)
1897-1955 .... **TCLC 29**
See also CA 113; DLB 9

De Vries, Peter
1910-1993 .... **CLC 1, 2, 3, 7, 10, 28, 46;**
DAM NOV
See also CA 17-20R; 142; CANR 41;
DLB 6; DLBY 82; MTCW

Dexter, John
See Bradley, Marion Zimmer

Dexter, Martin
See Faust, Frederick (Schiller)

Dexter, Pete
1943- .... **CLC 34, 55; DAM POP**
See also BEST 89:2; CA 127; 131; INT 131;
MTCW

Diamano, Silmang
See Senghor, Leopold Sedar

Diamond, Neil 1941- .... **CLC 30**
See also CA 108

Diaz del Castillo, Bernal 1496-1584 .. **LC 31**

di Bassetto, Corno
See Shaw, George Bernard

Dick, Philip K(indred)
1928-1982 .... **CLC 10, 30, 72;**
DAM NOV, POP
See also CA 49-52; 106; CANR 2, 16;
DLB 8; MTCW

Dickens, Charles (John Huffam)
1812-1870 ...... **NCLC 3, 8, 18, 26, 37,**
50; DA; DAB; DAC; DAM MST, NOV;
SSC 17; WLC
See also CDBLB 1832-1890; DLB 21, 55,
70, 159, 166; JRDA; MAICYA; SATA 15

Dickey, James (Lafayette)
1923- .... **CLC 1, 2, 4, 7, 10, 15, 47;**
DAM NOV, POET, POP
See also AITN 1, 2; CA 9-12R; CABS 2;
CANR 10, 48; CDALB 1968-1988;
DLB 5; DLBD 7; DLBY 82, 93;
INT CANR-10; MTCW

Dickey, William 1928-1994 ...... **CLC 3, 28**
See also CA 9-12R; 145; CANR 24; DLB 5

Dickinson, Charles 1951- .... **CLC 49**
See also CA 128

Dickinson, Emily (Elizabeth)
1830-1886 .... **NCLC 21; DA; DAB;**
DAC; DAM MST, POET; PC 1; WLC
See also CDALB 1865-1917; DLB 1;
SATA 29

Dickinson, Peter (Malcolm)
1927- .... **CLC 12, 35**
See also AAYA 9; CA 41-44R; CANR 31;
CLR 29; DLB 87, 161; JRDA; MAICYA;
SATA 5, 62

Dickson, Carr
See Carr, John Dickson

Dickson, Carter
See Carr, John Dickson

Diderot, Denis 1713-1784 .... **LC 26**

Didion, Joan
1934- .. **CLC 1, 3, 8, 14, 32; DAM NOV**
See also AITN 1; CA 5-8R; CANR 14, 52;
CDALB 1968-1988; DLB 2; DLBY 81,
86; MTCW

Dietrich, Robert
See Hunt, E(verette) Howard, (Jr.)

Dillard, Annie
1945- .... **CLC 9, 60; DAM NOV**
See also AAYA 6; CA 49-52; CANR 3, 43;
DLBY 80; MTCW; SATA 10

Dillard, R(ichard) H(enry) W(ilde)
1937- .... **CLC 5**
See also CA 21-24R; CAAS 7; CANR 10;
DLB 5

Dillon, Eilis 1920-1994........... **CLC 17**
See also CA 9-12R; 147; CAAS 3; CANR 4,
38; CLR 26; MAICYA; SATA 2, 74;
SATA-Obit 83

Dimont, Penelope
See Mortimer, Penelope (Ruth)

Dinesen, Isak .... **CLC 10, 29, 95; SSC 7**
See also Blixen, Karen (Christentze
Dinesen)

Ding Ling .... **CLC 68**
See also Chiang Pin-chin

Disch, Thomas M(ichael) 1940-... **CLC 7, 36**
See also AAYA 17; CA 21-24R; CAAS 4;
CANR 17, 36; CLR 18; DLB 8;
MAICYA; MTCW; SAAS 15; SATA 54

Disch, Tom
See Disch, Thomas M(ichael)

d'Isly, Georges
See Simenon, Georges (Jacques Christian)

Disraeli, Benjamin 1804-1881 .. **NCLC 2, 39**
See also DLB 21, 55

Ditcum, Steve
See Crumb, R(obert)

Dixon, Paige
See Corcoran, Barbara

Dixon, Stephen 1936-..... **CLC 52; SSC 16**
See also CA 89-92; CANR 17, 40; DLB 130

Dobell, Sydney Thompson
1824-1874 .... **NCLC 43**
See also DLB 32

Doblin, Alfred .... **TCLC 13**
See also Doeblin, Alfred

Dobrolyubov, Nikolai Alexandrovich
1836-1861 .... **NCLC 5**

Dobyns, Stephen 1941-............ **CLC 37**
See also CA 45-48; CANR 2, 18

Doctorow, E(dgar) L(aurence)
1931- ..... **CLC 6, 11, 15, 18, 37, 44, 65;**
DAM NOV, POP
See also AITN 2; BEST 89:3; CA 45-48;
CANR 2, 33, 51; CDALB 1968-1988;
DLB 2, 28; DLBY 80; MTCW

Dodgson, Charles Lutwidge 1832-1898
See Carroll, Lewis
See also CLR 2; DA; DAB; DAC;
DAM MST, NOV, POET; MAICYA;
YABC 2

Dodson, Owen (Vincent)
1914-1983 .... **CLC 79; BLC;**
DAM MULT
See also BW 1; CA 65-68; 110; CANR 24;
DLB 76

Doeblin, Alfred 1878-1957....... **TCLC 13**
See also Doblin, Alfred
See also CA 110; 141; DLB 66

Doerr, Harriet 1910- .... **CLC 34**
See also CA 117; 122; CANR 47; INT 122

Domecq, H(onorio) Bustos
See Bioy Casares, Adolfo; Borges, Jorge
Luis

Domini, Rey
See Lorde, Audre (Geraldine)

Dominique
See Proust, (Valentin-Louis-George-Eugene-)
Marcel

Don, A
See Stephen, Leslie

Donaldson, Stephen R.
1947- .... **CLC 46; DAM POP**
See also CA 89-92; CANR 13;
INT CANR-13

Donleavy, J(ames) P(atrick)
1926- .... **CLC 1, 4, 6, 10, 45**
See also AITN 2; CA 9-12R; CANR 24, 49;
DLB 6; INT CANR-24; MTCW

Donne, John
1572-1631 .... **LC 10, 24; DA; DAB;**
DAC; DAM MST, POET; PC 1
See also CDBLB Before 1660; DLB 121,
151

Donnell, David 1939(?)-........... **CLC 34**

Donoghue, P. S.
See Hunt, E(verette) Howard, (Jr.)

Donoso (Yanez), Jose
1924- .... **CLC 4, 8, 11, 32;**
DAM MULT; HLC
See also CA 81-84; CANR 32; DLB 113;
HW; MTCW

Donovan, John 1928-1992 .... **CLC 35**
See also CA 97-100; 137; CLR 3;
MAICYA; SATA 72; SATA-Brief 29

Don Roberto
See Cunninghame Graham, R(obert)
B(ontine)

Doolittle, Hilda
1886-1961 ..... **CLC 3, 8, 14, 31, 34, 73; DA; DAC; DAM MST, POET; PC 5; WLC**
See also H. D.
See also CA 97-100; CANR 35; DLB 4, 45; MTCW

Dorfman, Ariel
1942- .... **CLC 48, 77; DAM MULT; HLC**
See also CA 124; 130; HW; INT 130

Dorn, Edward (Merton) 1929-... **CLC 10, 18**
See also CA 93-96; CANR 42; DLB 5; INT 93-96

Dorsan, Luc
See Simenon, Georges (Jacques Christian)

Dorsange, Jean
See Simenon, Georges (Jacques Christian)

Dos Passos, John (Roderigo)
1896-1970 ...... **CLC 1, 4, 8, 11, 15, 25, 34, 82; DA; DAB; DAC; DAM MST, NOV; WLC**
See also CA 1-4R; 29-32R; CANR 3; CDALB 1929-1941; DLB 4, 9; DLBD 1; MTCW

Dossage, Jean
See Simenon, Georges (Jacques Christian)

Dostoevsky, Fedor Mikhailovich
1821-1881 ...... **NCLC 2, 7, 21, 33, 43; DA; DAB; DAC; DAM MST, NOV; SSC 2; WLC**

Doughty, Charles M(ontagu)
1843-1926 .... **TCLC 27**
See also CA 115; DLB 19, 57

Douglas, Ellen .... **CLC 73**
See also Haxton, Josephine Ayres; Williamson, Ellen Douglas

Douglas, Gavin 1475(?)-1522 .... **LC 20**

Douglas, Keith 1920-1944 .... **TCLC 40**
See also DLB 27

Douglas, Leonard
See Bradbury, Ray (Douglas)

Douglas, Michael
See Crichton, (John) Michael

Douglass, Frederick
1817(?)-1895 .... **NCLC 7, 55; BLC; DA; DAC; DAM MST, MULT; WLC**
See also CDALB 1640-1865; DLB 1, 43, 50, 79; SATA 29

Dourado, (Waldomiro Freitas) Autran
1926- .... **CLC 23, 60**
See also CA 25-28R; CANR 34

Dourado, Waldomiro Autran
See Dourado, (Waldomiro Freitas) Autran

Dove, Rita (Frances)
1952- .... **CLC 50, 81; DAM MULT, POET; PC 6**
See also BW 2; CA 109; CAAS 19; CANR 27, 42; DLB 120

Dowell, Coleman 1925-1985 .... **CLC 60**
See also CA 25-28R; 117; CANR 10; DLB 130

Dowson, Ernest (Christopher)
1867-1900 .... **TCLC 4**
See also CA 105; 150; DLB 19, 135

Doyle, A. Conan
See Doyle, Arthur Conan

Doyle, Arthur Conan
1859-1930 .... **TCLC 7; DA; DAB; DAC; DAM MST, NOV; SSC 12; WLC**
See also AAYA 14; CA 104; 122; CDBLB 1890-1914; DLB 18, 70, 156; MTCW; SATA 24

Doyle, Conan
See Doyle, Arthur Conan

Doyle, John
See Graves, Robert (von Ranke)

Doyle, Roddy 1958(?)- .... **CLC 81**
See also AAYA 14; CA 143

Doyle, Sir A. Conan
See Doyle, Arthur Conan

Doyle, Sir Arthur Conan
See Doyle, Arthur Conan

Dr. A
See Asimov, Isaac; Silverstein, Alvin

Drabble, Margaret
1939- .... **CLC 2, 3, 5, 8, 10, 22, 53; DAB; DAC; DAM MST, NOV, POP**
See also CA 13-16R; CANR 18, 35; CDBLB 1960 to Present; DLB 14, 155; MTCW; SATA 48

Drapier, M. B.
See Swift, Jonathan

Drayham, James
See Mencken, H(enry) L(ouis)

Drayton, Michael 1563-1631 .... **LC 8**

Dreadstone, Carl
See Campbell, (John) Ramsey

Dreiser, Theodore (Herman Albert)
1871-1945 .... **TCLC 10, 18, 35; DA; DAC; DAM MST, NOV; WLC**
See also CA 106; 132; CDALB 1865-1917; DLB 9, 12, 102, 137; DLBD 1; MTCW

Drexler, Rosalyn 1926- .... **CLC 2, 6**
See also CA 81-84

Dreyer, Carl Theodor 1889-1968 .... **CLC 16**
See also CA 116

Drieu la Rochelle, Pierre(-Eugene)
1893-1945 .... **TCLC 21**
See also CA 117; DLB 72

Drinkwater, John 1882-1937 ..... **TCLC 57**
See also CA 109; 149; DLB 10, 19, 149

Drop Shot
See Cable, George Washington

Droste-Hulshoff, Annette Freiin von
1797-1848 .... **NCLC 3**
See also DLB 133

Drummond, Walter
See Silverberg, Robert

Drummond, William Henry
1854-1907 .... **TCLC 25**
See also DLB 92

Drummond de Andrade, Carlos
1902-1987 .... **CLC 18**
See also Andrade, Carlos Drummond de
See also CA 132; 123

Drury, Allen (Stuart) 1918- .... **CLC 37**
See also CA 57-60; CANR 18, 52; INT CANR-18

Dryden, John
1631-1700 .... **LC 3, 21; DA; DAB; DAC; DAM DRAM, MST, POET; DC 3; WLC**
See also CDBLB 1660-1789; DLB 80, 101, 131

Duberman, Martin 1930- .... **CLC 8**
See also CA 1-4R; CANR 2

Dubie, Norman (Evans) 1945- ...... **CLC 36**
See also CA 69-72; CANR 12; DLB 120

Du Bois, W(illiam) E(dward) B(urghardt)
1868-1963 .... **CLC 1, 2, 13, 64, 96; BLC; DA; DAC; DAM MST, MULT, NOV; WLC**
See also BW 1; CA 85-88; CANR 34; CDALB 1865-1917; DLB 47, 50, 91; MTCW; SATA 42

Dubus, Andre 1936-... **CLC 13, 36; SSC 15**
See also CA 21-24R; CANR 17; DLB 130; INT CANR-17

Duca Minimo
See D'Annunzio, Gabriele

Ducharme, Rejean 1941- .... **CLC 74**
See also DLB 60

Duclos, Charles Pinot 1704-1772 ..... **LC 1**

Dudek, Louis 1918- .... **CLC 11, 19**
See also CA 45-48; CAAS 14; CANR 1; DLB 88

Duerrenmatt, Friedrich
1921-1990 ...... **CLC 1, 4, 8, 11, 15, 43; DAM DRAM**
See also CA 17-20R; CANR 33; DLB 69, 124; MTCW

Duffy, Bruce (?)- .... **CLC 50**

Duffy, Maureen 1933- .... **CLC 37**
See also CA 25-28R; CANR 33; DLB 14; MTCW

Dugan, Alan 1923- .... **CLC 2, 6**
See also CA 81-84; DLB 5

du Gard, Roger Martin
See Martin du Gard, Roger

Duhamel, Georges 1884-1966 .... **CLC 8**
See also CA 81-84; 25-28R; CANR 35; DLB 65; MTCW

Dujardin, Edouard (Emile Louis)
1861-1949 .... **TCLC 13**
See also CA 109; DLB 123

Dumas, Alexandre (Davy de la Pailleterie)
1802-1870 .... **NCLC 11; DA; DAB; DAC; DAM MST, NOV; WLC**
See also DLB 119; SATA 18

Dumas, Alexandre
1824-1895 .... **NCLC 9; DC 1**

Dumas, Claudine
See Malzberg, Barry N(athaniel)

Dumas, Henry L. 1934-1968 ..... **CLC 6, 62**
See also BW 1; CA 85-88; DLB 41

du Maurier, Daphne
1907-1989 .... **CLC 6, 11, 59; DAB; DAC; DAM MST, POP; SSC 18**
See also CA 5-8R; 128; CANR 6; MTCW; SATA 27; SATA-Obit 60

Dunbar, Paul Laurence
1872-1906 ..... **TCLC 2, 12; BLC; DA; DAC; DAM MST, MULT, POET; PC 5; SSC 8; WLC**
See also BW 1; CA 104; 124; CDALB 1865-1917; DLB 50, 54, 78; SATA 34

Dunbar, William 1460(?)-1530(?) .... **LC 20**
See also DLB 132, 146

Duncan, Lois 1934-............... **CLC 26**
See also AAYA 4; CA 1-4R; CANR 2, 23, 36; CLR 29; JRDA; MAICYA; SAAS 2; SATA 1, 36, 75

Duncan, Robert (Edward)
1919-1988 .... **CLC 1, 2, 4, 7, 15, 41, 55; DAM POET; PC 2**
See also CA 9-12R; 124; CANR 28; DLB 5, 16; MTCW

Duncan, Sara Jeannette
1861-1922 .... **TCLC 60**
See also DLB 92

Dunlap, William 1766-1839....... **NCLC 2**
See also DLB 30, 37, 59

Dunn, Douglas (Eaglesham)
1942-.................... **CLC 6, 40**
See also CA 45-48; CANR 2, 33; DLB 40; MTCW

Dunn, Katherine (Karen) 1945-..... **CLC 71**
See also CA 33-36R

Dunn, Stephen 1939- .... **CLC 36**
See also CA 33-36R; CANR 12, 48, 53; DLB 105

Dunne, Finley Peter 1867-1936.... **TCLC 28**
See also CA 108; DLB 11, 23

Dunne, John Gregory 1932-........ **CLC 28**
See also CA 25-28R; CANR 14, 50; DLBY 80

Dunsany, Edward John Moreton Drax
Plunkett 1878-1957
See Dunsany, Lord
See also CA 104; 148; DLB 10

Dunsany, Lord................ **TCLC 2, 59**
See also Dunsany, Edward John Moreton Drax Plunkett
See also DLB 77, 153, 156

du Perry, Jean
See Simenon, Georges (Jacques Christian)

Durang, Christopher (Ferdinand)
1949-.................... **CLC 27, 38**
See also CA 105; CANR 50

Duras, Marguerite
1914-1996 .. **CLC 3, 6, 11, 20, 34, 40, 68**
See also CA 25-28R; 151; CANR 50; DLB 83; MTCW

Durban, (Rosa) Pam 1947-........ **CLC 39**
See also CA 123

Durcan, Paul
1944- .... **CLC 43, 70; DAM POET**
See also CA 134

Durkheim, Emile 1858-1917 ...... **TCLC 55**

Durrell, Lawrence (George)
1912-1990 .... **CLC 1, 4, 6, 8, 13, 27, 41; DAM NOV**
See also CA 9-12R; 132; CANR 40; CDBLB 1945-1960; DLB 15, 27; DLBY 90; MTCW

Durrenmatt, Friedrich
See Duerrenmatt, Friedrich

Dutt, Toru 1856-1877........... **NCLC 29**

Dwight, Timothy 1752-1817...... **NCLC 13**
See also DLB 37

Dworkin, Andrea 1946-........... **CLC 43**
See also CA 77-80; CAAS 21; CANR 16, 39; INT CANR-16; MTCW

Dwyer, Deanna
See Koontz, Dean R(ay)

Dwyer, K. R.
See Koontz, Dean R(ay)

Dylan, Bob 1941-...... **CLC 3, 4, 6, 12, 77**
See also CA 41-44R; DLB 16

Eagleton, Terence (Francis) 1943-
See Eagleton, Terry
See also CA 57-60; CANR 7, 23; MTCW

Eagleton, Terry.................... **CLC 63**
See also Eagleton, Terence (Francis)

Early, Jack
See Scoppettone, Sandra

East, Michael
See West, Morris L(anglo)

Eastaway, Edward
See Thomas, (Philip) Edward

Eastlake, William (Derry) 1917-..... **CLC 8**
See also CA 5-8R; CAAS 1; CANR 5; DLB 6; INT CANR-5

Eastman, Charles A(lexander)
1858-1939 ..... **TCLC 55; DAM MULT**
See also NNAL; YABC 1

Eberhart, Richard (Ghormley)
1904- .. **CLC 3, 11, 19, 56; DAM POET**
See also CA 1-4R; CANR 2; CDALB 1941-1968; DLB 48; MTCW

Eberstadt, Fernanda 1960-........ **CLC 39**
See also CA 136

Echegaray (y Eizaguirre), Jose (Maria Waldo)
1832-1916 .... **TCLC 4**
See also CA 104; CANR 32; HW; MTCW

Echeverria, (Jose) Esteban (Antonino)
1805-1851 .... **NCLC 18**

Echo
See Proust, (Valentin-Louis-George-Eugene-) Marcel

Eckert, Allan W. 1931-........... **CLC 17**
See also AAYA 18; CA 13-16R; CANR 14, 45; INT CANR-14; SAAS 21; SATA 29; SATA-Brief 27

Eckhart, Meister 1260(?)-1328(?) .. **CMLC 9**
See also DLB 115

Eckmar, F. R.
See de Hartog, Jan

Eco, Umberto
1932-... **CLC 28, 60; DAM NOV, POP**
See also BEST 90:1; CA 77-80; CANR 12, 33; MTCW

Eddison, E(ric) R(ucker)
1882-1945 .... **TCLC 15**
See also CA 109

Edel, (Joseph) Leon 1907-...... **CLC 29, 34**
See also CA 1-4R; CANR 1, 22; DLB 103; INT CANR-22

Eden, Emily 1797-1869 .... **NCLC 10**

Edgar, David
1948-......... **CLC 42; DAM DRAM**
See also CA 57-60; CANR 12; DLB 13; MTCW

Edgerton, Clyde (Carlyle) 1944-.... **CLC 39**
See also AAYA 17; CA 118; 134; INT 134

Edgeworth, Maria 1768-1849... **NCLC 1, 51**
See also DLB 116, 159, 163; SATA 21

Edmonds, Paul
See Kuttner, Henry

Edmonds, Walter D(umaux) 1903-.. **CLC 35**
See also CA 5-8R; CANR 2; DLB 9; MAICYA; SAAS 4; SATA 1, 27

Edmondson, Wallace
See Ellison, Harlan (Jay)

Edson, Russell.................... **CLC 13**
See also CA 33-36R

Edwards, Bronwen Elizabeth
See Rose, Wendy

Edwards, G(erald) B(asil)
1899-1976 .... **CLC 25**
See also CA 110

Edwards, Gus 1939-.............. **CLC 43**
See also CA 108; INT 108

Edwards, Jonathan
1703-1758 .... **LC 7; DA; DAC; DAM MST**
See also DLB 24

Efron, Marina Ivanovna Tsvetaeva
See Tsvetaeva (Efron), Marina (Ivanovna)

Ehle, John (Marsden, Jr.) 1925-.... **CLC 27**
See also CA 9-12R

Ehrenbourg, Ilya (Grigoryevich)
See Ehrenburg, Ilya (Grigoryevich)

Ehrenburg, Ilya (Grigoryevich)
1891-1967 .... **CLC 18, 34, 62**
See also CA 102; 25-28R

Ehrenburg, Ilyo (Grigoryevich)
See Ehrenburg, Ilya (Grigoryevich)

Eich, Guenter 1907-1972 .... **CLC 15**
See also CA 111; 93-96; DLB 69, 124

Eichendorff, Joseph Freiherr von
1788-1857 .... **NCLC 8**
See also DLB 90

Eigner, Larry.................... **CLC 9**
See also Eigner, Laurence (Joel)
See also CAAS 23; DLB 5

Eigner, Laurence (Joel) 1927-1996
See Eigner, Larry
See also CA 9-12R; 151; CANR 6

Einstein, Albert 1879-1955 .... **TCLC 65**
See also CA 121; 133; MTCW

Eiseley, Loren Corey 1907-1977..... **CLC 7**
See also AAYA 5; CA 1-4R; 73-76; CANR 6

Eisenstadt, Jill 1963-............. **CLC 50**
See also CA 140

Eisenstein, Sergei (Mikhailovich)
1898-1948 .... **TCLC 57**
See also CA 114; 149

Eisner, Simon
See Kornbluth, C(yril) M.

Esterbrook, Tom
See Hubbard, L(afayette) Ron(ald)

Estleman, Loren D.
1952- . . . . . . CLC 48; DAM NOV, POP
See also CA 85-88; CANR 27;
INT CANR-27; MTCW

Eugenides, Jeffrey 1960(?)- . . . . CLC 81
See also CA 144

Euripides c. 485B.C.-406B.C. . . . . DC 4
See also DA; DAB; DAC; DAM DRAM,
MST

Evan, Evin
See Faust, Frederick (Schiller)

Evans, Evan
See Faust, Frederick (Schiller)

Evans, Marian
See Eliot, George

Evans, Mary Ann
See Eliot, George

Evarts, Esther
See Benson, Sally

Everett, Percival L. 1956- . . . . CLC 57
See also BW 2; CA 129

Everson, R(onald) G(ilmour)
1903- . . . . CLC 27
See also CA 17-20R; DLB 88

Everson, William (Oliver)
1912-1994 . . . . CLC 1, 5, 14
See also CA 9-12R; 145; CANR 20; DLB 5,
16; MTCW

Evtushenko, Evgenii Aleksandrovich
See Yevtushenko, Yevgeny (Alexandrovich)

Ewart, Gavin (Buchanan)
1916-1995 . . . . CLC 13, 46
See also CA 89-92; 150; CANR 17, 46;
DLB 40; MTCW

Ewers, Hanns Heinz 1871-1943 . . . TCLC 12
See also CA 109; 149

Ewing, Frederick R.
See Sturgeon, Theodore (Hamilton)

Exley, Frederick (Earl)
1929-1992 . . . . CLC 6, 11
See also AITN 2; CA 81-84; 138; DLB 143;
DLBY 81

Eynhardt, Guillermo
See Quiroga, Horacio (Sylvestre)

Ezekiel, Nissim 1924- . . . . CLC 61
See also CA 61-64

Ezekiel, Tish O'Dowd 1943- . . . . CLC 34
See also CA 129

Fadeyev, A.
See Bulgya, Alexander Alexandrovich

Fadeyev, Alexander . . . . TCLC 53
See also Bulgya, Alexander Alexandrovich

Fagen, Donald 1948- . . . . CLC 26

Fainzilberg, Ilya Arnoldovich 1897-1937
See Ilf, Ilya
See also CA 120

Fair, Ronald L. 1932- . . . . CLC 18
See also BW 1; CA 69-72; CANR 25;
DLB 33

Fairbairns, Zoe (Ann) 1948- . . . . CLC 32
See also CA 103; CANR 21

Falco, Gian
See Papini, Giovanni

Falconer, James
See Kirkup, James

Falconer, Kenneth
See Kornbluth, C(yril) M.

Falkland, Samuel
See Heijermans, Herman

Fallaci, Oriana 1930- . . . . CLC 11
See also CA 77-80; CANR 15; MTCW

Faludy, George 1913- . . . . CLC 42
See also CA 21-24R

Faludy, Gyoergy
See Faludy, George

Fanon, Frantz
1925-1961 . . . . CLC 74; BLC;
DAM MULT
See also BW 1; CA 116; 89-92

Fanshawe, Ann 1625-1680 . . . . LC 11

Fante, John (Thomas) 1911-1983 . . . CLC 60
See also CA 69-72; 109; CANR 23;
DLB 130; DLBY 83

Farah, Nuruddin
1945- . . . . . . CLC 53; BLC; DAM MULT
See also BW 2; CA 106; DLB 125

Fargue, Leon-Paul 1876(?)-1947 . . . TCLC 11
See also CA 109

Farigoule, Louis
See Romains, Jules

Farina, Richard 1936(?)-1966 . . . . CLC 9
See also CA 81-84; 25-28R

Farley, Walter (Lorimer)
1915-1989 . . . . CLC 17
See also CA 17-20R; CANR 8, 29; DLB 22;
JRDA; MAICYA; SATA 2, 43

Farmer, Philip Jose 1918- . . . . CLC 1, 19
See also CA 1-4R; CANR 4, 35; DLB 8;
MTCW

Farquhar, George
1677-1707 . . . . LC 21; DAM DRAM
See also DLB 84

Farrell, J(ames) G(ordon)
1935-1979 . . . . CLC 6
See also CA 73-76; 89-92; CANR 36;
DLB 14; MTCW

Farrell, James T(homas)
1904-1979 . . . . CLC 1, 4, 8, 11, 66
See also CA 5-8R; 89-92; CANR 9; DLB 4,
9, 86; DLBD 2; MTCW

Farren, Richard J.
See Betjeman, John

Farren, Richard M.
See Betjeman, John

Fassbinder, Rainer Werner
1946-1982 . . . . CLC 20
See also CA 93-96; 106; CANR 31

Fast, Howard (Melvin)
1914- . . . . CLC 23; DAM NOV
See also AAYA 16; CA 1-4R; CAAS 18;
CANR 1, 33; DLB 9; INT CANR-33;
SATA 7

Faulcon, Robert
See Holdstock, Robert P.

Faulkner, William (Cuthbert)
1897-1962 . . . . . CLC 1, 3, 6, 8, 9, 11, 14,
18, 28, 52, 68; DA; DAB; DAC;
DAM MST, NOV; SSC 1; WLC
See also AAYA 7; CA 81-84; CANR 33;
CDALB 1929-1941; DLB 9, 11, 44, 102;
DLBD 2; DLBY 86; MTCW

Fauset, Jessie Redmon
1884(?)-1961 . . . . CLC 19, 54; BLC;
DAM MULT
See also BW 1; CA 109; DLB 51

Faust, Frederick (Schiller)
1892-1944(?) . . . . . TCLC 49; DAM POP
See also CA 108; 152

Faust, Irvin 1924- . . . . CLC 8
See also CA 33-36R; CANR 28; DLB 2, 28;
DLBY 80

Fawkes, Guy
See Benchley, Robert (Charles)

Fearing, Kenneth (Flexner)
1902-1961 . . . . CLC 51
See also CA 93-96; DLB 9

Fecamps, Elise
See Creasey, John

Federman, Raymond 1928- . . . . . . CLC 6, 47
See also CA 17-20R; CAAS 8; CANR 10,
43; DLBY 80

Federspiel, J(uerg) F. 1931- . . . . CLC 42
See also CA 146

Feiffer, Jules (Ralph)
1929- . . . . . . CLC 2, 8, 64; DAM DRAM
See also AAYA 3; CA 17-20R; CANR 30;
DLB 7, 44; INT CANR-30; MTCW;
SATA 8, 61

Feige, Hermann Albert Otto Maximilian
See Traven, B.

Feinberg, David B. 1956-1994 . . . . . . CLC 59
See also CA 135; 147

Feinstein, Elaine 1930- . . . . CLC 36
See also CA 69-72; CAAS 1; CANR 31;
DLB 14, 40; MTCW

Feldman, Irving (Mordecai) 1928- . . . . CLC 7
See also CA 1-4R; CANR 1; DLB 169

Fellini, Federico 1920-1993 . . . . . CLC 16, 85
See also CA 65-68; 143; CANR 33

Felsen, Henry Gregor 1916- . . . . CLC 17
See also CA 1-4R; CANR 1; SAAS 2;
SATA 1

Fenton, James Martin 1949- . . . . CLC 32
See also CA 102; DLB 40

Ferber, Edna 1887-1968 . . . . CLC 18, 93
See also AITN 1; CA 5-8R; 25-28R; DLB 9,
28, 86; MTCW; SATA 7

Ferguson, Helen
See Kavan, Anna

Ferguson, Samuel 1810-1886 . . . . . NCLC 33
See also DLB 32

Fergusson, Robert 1750-1774 . . . . LC 29
See also DLB 109

Ferling, Lawrence
See Ferlinghetti, Lawrence (Monsanto)

Fornes, Maria Irene 1930-...... CLC 39, 61
See also CA 25-28R; CANR 28; DLB 7;
HW; INT CANR-28; MTCW

Forrest, Leon 1937-.............. CLC 4
See also BW 2; CA 89-92; CAAS 7;
CANR 25, 52; DLB 33

Forster, E(dward) M(organ)
1879-1970 ..... CLC 1, 2, 3, 4, 9, 10, 13,
15, 22, 45, 77; DA; DAB; DAC;
DAM MST, NOV; WLC
See also AAYA 2; CA 13-14; 25-28R;
CANR 45; CAP 1; CDBLB 1914-1945;
DLB 34, 98, 162; DLBD 10; MTCW;
SATA 57

Forster, John 1812-1876 .... NCLC 11
See also DLB 144

Forsyth, Frederick
1938-.. CLC 2, 5, 36; DAM NOV, POP
See also BEST 89:4; CA 85-88; CANR 38;
DLB 87; MTCW

Forten, Charlotte L. .... TCLC 16; BLC
See also Grimke, Charlotte L(ottie) Forten
See also DLB 50

Foscolo, Ugo 1778-1827.......... NCLC 8

Fosse, Bob .... CLC 20
See also Fosse, Robert Louis

Fosse, Robert Louis 1927-1987
See Fosse, Bob
See also CA 110; 123

Foster, Stephen Collins
1826-1864 .... NCLC 26

Foucault, Michel
1926-1984 .... CLC 31, 34, 69
See also CA 105; 113; CANR 34; MTCW

Fouque, Friedrich (Heinrich Karl) de la Motte
1777-1843 .... NCLC 2
See also DLB 90

Fourier, Charles 1772-1837 ...... NCLC 51

Fournier, Henri Alban 1886-1914
See Alain-Fournier
See also CA 104

Fournier, Pierre 1916-............ CLC 11
See also Gascar, Pierre
See also CA 89-92; CANR 16, 40

Fowles, John
1926-...... CLC 1, 2, 3, 4, 6, 9, 10, 15,
33, 87; DAB; DAC; DAM MST
See also CA 5-8R; CANR 25; CDBLB 1960
to Present; DLB 14, 139; MTCW;
SATA 22

Fox, Paula 1923-................ CLC 2, 8
See also AAYA 3; CA 73-76; CANR 20,
36; CLR 1; DLB 52; JRDA; MAICYA;
MTCW; SATA 17, 60

Fox, William Price (Jr.) 1926-..... CLC 22
See also CA 17-20R; CAAS 19; CANR 11;
DLB 2; DLBY 81

Foxe, John 1516(?)-1587 .... LC 14

Frame, Janet
1924-......... CLC 2, 3, 6, 22, 66, 96
See also Clutha, Janet Paterson Frame

France, Anatole.................. TCLC 9
See also Thibault, Jacques Anatole Francois
See also DLB 123

Francis, Claude 19(?)-........... CLC 50

Francis, Dick
1920-....... CLC 2, 22, 42; DAM POP
See also AAYA 5; BEST 89:3; CA 5-8R;
CANR 9, 42; CDBLB 1960 to Present;
DLB 87; INT CANR-9; MTCW

Francis, Robert (Churchill)
1901-1987 .... CLC 15
See also CA 1-4R; 123; CANR 1

Frank, Anne(lies Marie)
1929-1945 .... TCLC 17; DA; DAB;
DAC; DAM MST; WLC
See also AAYA 12; CA 113; 133; MTCW;
SATA 87; SATA-Brief 42

Frank, Elizabeth 1945-........... CLC 39
See also CA 121; 126; INT 126

Frankl, Viktor E(mil) 1905-........ CLC 93
See also CA 65-68

Franklin, Benjamin
See Hasek, Jaroslav (Matej Frantisek)

Franklin, Benjamin
1706-1790 ..... LC 25; DA; DAB; DAC;
DAM MST
See also CDALB 1640-1865; DLB 24, 43,
73

Franklin, (Stella Maraia Sarah) Miles
1879-1954 .... TCLC 7
See also CA 104

Fraser, (Lady) Antonia (Pakenham)
1932-...................... CLC 32
See also CA 85-88; CANR 44; MTCW;
SATA-Brief 32

Fraser, George MacDonald 1925-.... CLC 7
See also CA 45-48; CANR 2, 48

Fraser, Sylvia 1935-.............. CLC 64
See also CA 45-48; CANR 1, 16

Frayn, Michael
1933-.............. CLC 3, 7, 31, 47;
DAM DRAM, NOV
See also CA 5-8R; CANR 30; DLB 13, 14;
MTCW

Fraze, Candida (Merrill) 1945-..... CLC 50
See also CA 126

Frazer, J(ames) G(eorge)
1854-1941 .... TCLC 32
See also CA 118

Frazer, Robert Caine
See Creasey, John

Frazer, Sir James George
See Frazer, J(ames) G(eorge)

Frazier, Ian 1951-................ CLC 46
See also CA 130

Frederic, Harold 1856-1898...... NCLC 10
See also DLB 12, 23; DLBD 13

Frederick, John
See Faust, Frederick (Schiller)

Frederick the Great 1712-1786 ...... LC 14

Fredro, Aleksander 1793-1876..... NCLC 8

Freeling, Nicolas 1927-........... CLC 38
See also CA 49-52; CAAS 12; CANR 1, 17,
50; DLB 87

Freeman, Douglas Southall
1886-1953 .... TCLC 11
See also CA 109; DLB 17

Freeman, Judith 1946-............ CLC 55
See also CA 148

Freeman, Mary Eleanor Wilkins
1852-1930 .... TCLC 9; SSC 1
See also CA 106; DLB 12, 78

Freeman, R(ichard) Austin
1862-1943 .... TCLC 21
See also CA 113; DLB 70

French, Albert 1943-............. CLC 86

French, Marilyn
1929-................. CLC 10, 18, 60;
DAM DRAM, NOV, POP
See also CA 69-72; CANR 3, 31;
INT CANR-31; MTCW

French, Paul
See Asimov, Isaac

Freneau, Philip Morin 1752-1832.. NCLC 1
See also DLB 37, 43

Freud, Sigmund 1856-1939 .... TCLC 52
See also CA 115; 133; MTCW

Friedan, Betty (Naomi) 1921-...... CLC 74
See also CA 65-68; CANR 18, 45; MTCW

Friedlander, Saul 1932-........... CLC 90
See also CA 117; 130

Friedman, B(ernard) H(arper)
1926-...................... CLC 7
See also CA 1-4R; CANR 3, 48

Friedman, Bruce Jay 1930-..... CLC 3, 5, 56
See also CA 9-12R; CANR 25, 52; DLB 2,
28; INT CANR-25

Friel, Brian 1929-........... CLC 5, 42, 59
See also CA 21-24R; CANR 33; DLB 13;
MTCW

Friis-Baastad, Babbis Ellinor
1921-1970 .... CLC 12
See also CA 17-20R; 134; SATA 7

Frisch, Max (Rudolf)
1911-1991 ..... CLC 3, 9, 14, 18, 32, 44;
DAM DRAM, NOV
See also CA 85-88; 134; CANR 32;
DLB 69, 124; MTCW

Fromentin, Eugene (Samuel Auguste)
1820-1876 .... NCLC 10
See also DLB 123

Frost, Frederick
See Faust, Frederick (Schiller)

Frost, Robert (Lee)
1874-1963 .... CLC 1, 3, 4, 9, 10, 13, 15,
26, 34, 44; DA; DAB; DAC; DAM MST,
POET; PC 1; WLC
See also CA 89-92; CANR 33;
CDALB 1917-1929; DLB 54; DLBD 7;
MTCW; SATA 14

Froude, James Anthony
1818-1894 .... NCLC 43
See also DLB 18, 57, 144

Froy, Herald
See Waterhouse, Keith (Spencer)

Fry, Christopher
1907-..... CLC 2, 10, 14; DAM DRAM
See also CA 17-20R; CAAS 23; CANR 9,
30; DLB 13; MTCW; SATA 66

Frye, (Herman) Northrop
1912-1991 .... CLC 24, 70
See also CA 5-8R; 133; CANR 8, 37;
DLB 67, 68; MTCW

Fuchs, Daniel 1909-1993 .... **CLC 8, 22**
See also CA 81-84; 142; CAAS 5;
CANR 40; DLB 9, 26, 28; DLBY 93

Fuchs, Daniel 1934- .... **CLC 34**
See also CA 37-40R; CANR 14, 48

Fuentes, Carlos
1928- ...... **CLC 3, 8, 10, 13, 22, 41, 60;**
DA; DAB; DAC; DAM MST, MULT,
NOV; HLC; WLC
See also AAYA 4; AITN 2; CA 69-72;
CANR 10, 32; DLB 113; HW; MTCW

Fuentes, Gregorio Lopez y
See Lopez y Fuentes, Gregorio

Fugard, (Harold) Athol
1932- .... **CLC 5, 9, 14, 25, 40, 80;**
DAM DRAM; DC 3
See also AAYA 17; CA 85-88; CANR 32;
MTCW

Fugard, Sheila 1932- .... **CLC 48**
See also CA 125

Fuller, Charles (H., Jr.)
1939- .... **CLC 25; BLC; DAM DRAM,**
MULT; DC 1
See also BW 2; CA 108; 112; DLB 38;
INT 112; MTCW

Fuller, John (Leopold) 1937- .... **CLC 62**
See also CA 21-24R; CANR 9, 44; DLB 40

Fuller, Margaret .... **NCLC 5, 50**
See also Ossoli, Sarah Margaret (Fuller
marchesa d')

Fuller, Roy (Broadbent)
1912-1991 .... **CLC 4, 28**
See also CA 5-8R; 135; CAAS 10;
CANR 53; DLB 15, 20; SATA 87

Fulton, Alice 1952- .... **CLC 52**
See also CA 116

Furphy, Joseph 1843-1912 .... **TCLC 25**

Fussell, Paul 1924- .... **CLC 74**
See also BEST 90:1; CA 17-20R; CANR 8,
21, 35; INT CANR-21; MTCW

Futabatei, Shimei 1864-1909 ..... **TCLC 44**

Futrelle, Jacques 1875-1912 ...... **TCLC 19**
See also CA 113

Gaboriau, Emile 1835-1873 ...... **NCLC 14**

Gadda, Carlo Emilio 1893-1973 .... **CLC 11**
See also CA 89-92

Gaddis, William
1922- ..... **CLC 1, 3, 6, 8, 10, 19, 43, 86**
See also CA 17-20R; CANR 21, 48; DLB 2;
MTCW

Gaines, Ernest J(ames)
1933- .... **CLC 3, 11, 18, 86; BLC;**
DAM MULT
See also AAYA 18; AITN 1; BW 2;
CA 9-12R; CANR 6, 24, 42;
CDALB 1968-1988; DLB 2, 33, 152;
DLBY 80; MTCW; SATA 86

Gaitskill, Mary 1954- .... **CLC 69**
See also CA 128

Galdos, Benito Perez
See Perez Galdos, Benito

Gale, Zona
1874-1938 ...... **TCLC 7; DAM DRAM**
See also CA 105; DLB 9, 78

Galeano, Eduardo (Hughes) 1940-... **CLC 72**
See also CA 29-32R; CANR 13, 32; HW

Galiano, Juan Valera y Alcala
See Valera y Alcala-Galiano, Juan

Gallagher, Tess
1943- .. **CLC 18, 63; DAM POET; PC 9**
See also CA 106; DLB 120

Gallant, Mavis
1922- .... **CLC 7, 18, 38; DAC;**
DAM MST; SSC 5
See also CA 69-72; CANR 29; DLB 53;
MTCW

Gallant, Roy A(rthur) 1924- .... **CLC 17**
See also CA 5-8R; CANR 4, 29; CLR 30;
MAICYA; SATA 4, 68

Gallico, Paul (William) 1897-1976 ... **CLC 2**
See also AITN 1; CA 5-8R; 69-72;
CANR 23; DLB 9; MAICYA; SATA 13

Gallo, Max Louis 1932- .... **CLC 95**
See also CA 85-88

Gallois, Lucien
See Desnos, Robert

Gallup, Ralph
See Whitemore, Hugh (John)

Galsworthy, John
1867-1933 ...... **TCLC 1, 45; DA; DAB;**
DAC; DAM DRAM, MST, NOV;
SSC 22; WLC 2
See also CA 104; 141; CDBLB 1890-1914;
DLB 10, 34, 98, 162

Galt, John 1779-1839 .... **NCLC 1**
See also DLB 99, 116, 159

Galvin, James 1951- .... **CLC 38**
See also CA 108; CANR 26

Gamboa, Federico 1864-1939 ..... **TCLC 36**

Gandhi, M. K.
See Gandhi, Mohandas Karamchand

Gandhi, Mahatma
See Gandhi, Mohandas Karamchand

Gandhi, Mohandas Karamchand
1869-1948 ..... **TCLC 59; DAM MULT**
See also CA 121; 132; MTCW

Gann, Ernest Kellogg 1910-1991.... **CLC 23**
See also AITN 1; CA 1-4R; 136; CANR 1

Garcia, Cristina 1958- .... **CLC 76**
See also CA 141

Garcia Lorca, Federico
1898-1936 ... **TCLC 1, 7, 49; DA; DAB;**
DAC; DAM DRAM, MST, MULT,
POET; DC 2; HLC; PC 3; WLC
See also CA 104; 131; DLB 108; HW;
MTCW

Garcia Marquez, Gabriel (Jose)
1928- .... **CLC 2, 3, 8, 10, 15, 27, 47, 55,**
68; DA; DAB; DAC; DAM MST,
MULT, NOV, POP; HLC; SSC 8; WLC
See also AAYA 3; BEST 89:1, 90:4;
CA 33-36R; CANR 10, 28, 50; DLB 113;
HW; MTCW

Gard, Janice
See Latham, Jean Lee

Gard, Roger Martin du
See Martin du Gard, Roger

Gardam, Jane 1928- .... **CLC 43**
See also CA 49-52; CANR 2, 18, 33;
CLR 12; DLB 14, 161; MAICYA;
MTCW; SAAS 9; SATA 39, 76;
SATA-Brief 28

Gardner, Herb(ert) 1934- .... **CLC 44**
See also CA 149

Gardner, John (Champlin), Jr.
1933-1982 ..... **CLC 2, 3, 5, 7, 8, 10, 18,**
28, 34; DAM NOV, POP; SSC 7
See also AITN 1; CA 65-68; 107;
CANR 33; DLB 2; DLBY 82; MTCW;
SATA 40; SATA-Obit 31

Gardner, John (Edmund)
1926- .... **CLC 30; DAM POP**
See also CA 103; CANR 15; MTCW

Gardner, Miriam
See Bradley, Marion Zimmer

Gardner, Noel
See Kuttner, Henry

Gardons, S. S.
See Snodgrass, W(illiam) D(e Witt)

Garfield, Leon 1921-1996.......... **CLC 12**
See also AAYA 8; CA 17-20R; 152;
CANR 38, 41; CLR 21; DLB 161; JRDA;
MAICYA; SATA 1, 32, 76

Garland, (Hannibal) Hamlin
1860-1940 .... **TCLC 3; SSC 18**
See also CA 104; DLB 12, 71, 78

Garneau, (Hector de) Saint-Denys
1912-1943 .... **TCLC 13**
See also CA 111; DLB 88

Garner, Alan
1934- .... **CLC 17; DAB; DAM POP**
See also AAYA 18; CA 73-76; CANR 15;
CLR 20; DLB 161; MAICYA; MTCW;
SATA 18, 69

Garner, Hugh 1913-1979 .... **CLC 13**
See also CA 69-72; CANR 31; DLB 68

Garnett, David 1892-1981 .... **CLC 3**
See also CA 5-8R; 103; CANR 17; DLB 34

Garos, Stephanie
See Katz, Steve

Garrett, George (Palmer)
1929- .... **CLC 3, 11, 51**
See also CA 1-4R; CAAS 5; CANR 1, 42;
DLB 2, 5, 130, 152; DLBY 83

Garrick, David
1717-1779 .... **LC 15; DAM DRAM**
See also DLB 84

Garrigue, Jean 1914-1972 .... **CLC 2, 8**
See also CA 5-8R; 37-40R; CANR 20

Garrison, Frederick
See Sinclair, Upton (Beall)

Garth, Will
See Hamilton, Edmond; Kuttner, Henry

Garvey, Marcus (Moziah, Jr.)
1887-1940 .... **TCLC 41; BLC;**
DAM MULT
See also BW 1; CA 120; 124

Gary, Romain .... **CLC 25**
See also Kacew, Romain
See also DLB 83

Gascar, Pierre .... **CLC 11**
See also Fournier, Pierre

Gascoyne, David (Emery) 1916- .... **CLC 45**
See also CA 65-68; CANR 10, 28; DLB 20;
MTCW

Gaskell, Elizabeth Cleghorn
1810-1865 .. **NCLC 5; DAB; DAM MST**
See also CDBLB 1832-1890; DLB 21, 144,
159

Gass, William H(oward)
1924- ... **CLC 1, 2, 8, 11, 15, 39; SSC 12**
See also CA 17-20R; CANR 30; DLB 2;
MTCW

Gasset, Jose Ortega y
See Ortega y Gasset, Jose

Gates, Henry Louis, Jr.
1950- .... **CLC 65; DAM MULT**
See also BW 2; CA 109; CANR 25, 53;
DLB 67

Gautier, Theophile
1811-1872 ...... **NCLC 1; DAM POET;**
SSC 20
See also DLB 119

Gawsworth, John
See Bates, H(erbert) E(rnest)

Gay, Oliver
See Gogarty, Oliver St. John

Gaye, Marvin (Penze) 1939-1984 ... **CLC 26**
See also CA 112

Gebler, Carlo (Ernest) 1954-....... **CLC 39**
See also CA 119; 133

Gee, Maggie (Mary) 1948-......... **CLC 57**
See also CA 130

Gee, Maurice (Gough) 1931-....... **CLC 29**
See also CA 97-100; SATA 46

Gelbart, Larry (Simon) 1923- ... **CLC 21, 61**
See also CA 73-76; CANR 45

Gelber, Jack 1932-........**CLC 1, 6, 14, 79**
See also CA 1-4R; CANR 2; DLB 7

Gellhorn, Martha (Ellis) 1908- .. **CLC 14, 60**
See also CA 77-80; CANR 44; DLBY 82

Genet, Jean
1910-1986 ...... **CLC 1, 2, 5, 10, 14, 44,**
46; DAM DRAM
See also CA 13-16R; CANR 18; DLB 72;
DLBY 86; MTCW

Gent, Peter 1942-................ **CLC 29**
See also AITN 1; CA 89-92; DLBY 82

Gentlewoman in New England, A
See Bradstreet, Anne

Gentlewoman in Those Parts, A
See Bradstreet, Anne

George, Jean Craighead 1919-...... **CLC 35**
See also AAYA 8; CA 5-8R; CANR 25;
CLR 1; DLB 52; JRDA; MAICYA;
SATA 2, 68

George, Stefan (Anton)
1868-1933 .... **TCLC 2, 14**
See also CA 104

Georges, Georges Martin
See Simenon, Georges (Jacques Christian)

Gerhardi, William Alexander
See Gerhardie, William Alexander

Gerhardie, William Alexander
1895-1977 .... **CLC 5**
See also CA 25-28R; 73-76; CANR 18;
DLB 36

Gerstler, Amy 1956-............. **CLC 70**
See also CA 146

Gertler, T. .... **CLC 34**
See also CA 116; 121; INT 121

gfgg....................... **CLC XvXzc**

Ghalib........................ **NCLC 39**
See also Ghalib, Hsadullah Khan

Ghalib, Hsadullah Khan 1797-1869
See Ghalib
See also DAM POET

Ghelderode, Michel de
1898-1962 .... **CLC 6, 11; DAM DRAM**
See also CA 85-88; CANR 40

Ghiselin, Brewster 1903-.......... **CLC 23**
See also CA 13-16R; CAAS 10; CANR 13

Ghose, Zulfikar 1935-............. **CLC 42**
See also CA 65-68

Ghosh, Amitav 1956-............. **CLC 44**
See also CA 147

Giacosa, Giuseppe 1847-1906 ...... **TCLC 7**
See also CA 104

Gibb, Lee
See Waterhouse, Keith (Spencer)

Gibbon, Lewis Grassic .... **TCLC 4**
See also Mitchell, James Leslie

Gibbons, Kaye
1960- .... **CLC 50, 88; DAM POP**
See also CA 151

Gibran, Kahlil
1883-1931 .... **TCLC 1, 9; DAM POET,**
POP; PC 9
See also CA 104; 150

Gibran, Khalil
See Gibran, Kahlil

Gibson, William
1914- .... **CLC 23; DA; DAB; DAC;**
DAM DRAM, MST
See also CA 9-12R; CANR 9, 42; DLB 7;
SATA 66

Gibson, William (Ford)
1948- .... **CLC 39, 63; DAM POP**
See also AAYA 12; CA 126; 133; CANR 52

Gide, Andre (Paul Guillaume)
1869-1951 .... **TCLC 5, 12, 36; DA;**
DAB; DAC; DAM MST, NOV; SSC 13;
WLC
See also CA 104; 124; DLB 65; MTCW

Gifford, Barry (Colby) 1946-....... **CLC 34**
See also CA 65-68; CANR 9, 30, 40

Gilbert, W(illiam) S(chwenck)
1836-1911 ..... **TCLC 3; DAM DRAM,**
POET
See also CA 104; SATA 36

Gilbreth, Frank B., Jr. 1911-....... **CLC 17**
See also CA 9-12R; SATA 2

Gilchrist, Ellen
1935- .... **CLC 34, 48; DAM POP;**
SSC 14
See also CA 113; 116; CANR 41; DLB 130;
MTCW

Giles, Molly 1942-............... **CLC 39**
See also CA 126

Gill, Patrick
See Creasey, John

Gilliam, Terry (Vance) 1940-....... **CLC 21**
See also Monty Python
See also CA 108; 113; CANR 35; INT 113

Gillian, Jerry
See Gilliam, Terry (Vance)

Gilliatt, Penelope (Ann Douglass)
1932-1993 .... **CLC 2, 10, 13, 53**
See also AITN 2; CA 13-16R; 141;
CANR 49; DLB 14

Gilman, Charlotte (Anna) Perkins (Stetson)
1860-1935 .... **TCLC 9, 37; SSC 13**
See also CA 106; 150

Gilmour, David 1949-............. **CLC 35**
See also CA 138, 147

Gilpin, William 1724-1804....... **NCLC 30**

Gilray, J. D.
See Mencken, H(enry) L(ouis)

Gilroy, Frank D(aniel) 1925-........ **CLC 2**
See also CA 81-84; CANR 32; DLB 7

Ginsberg, Allen
1926- ......**CLC 1, 2, 3, 4, 6, 13, 36, 69;**
DA; DAB; DAC; DAM MST, POET;
PC 4; WLC 3
See also AITN 1; CA 1-4R; CANR 2, 41;
CDALB 1941-1968; DLB 5, 16, 169;
MTCW

Ginzburg, Natalia
1916-1991 .... **CLC 5, 11, 54, 70**
See also CA 85-88; 135; CANR 33; MTCW

Giono, Jean 1895-1970.......... **CLC 4, 11**
See also CA 45-48; 29-32R; CANR 2, 35;
DLB 72; MTCW

Giovanni, Nikki
1943- ...... **CLC 2, 4, 19, 64; BLC; DA;**
DAB; DAC; DAM MST, MULT, POET
See also AITN 1; BW 2; CA 29-32R;
CAAS 6; CANR 18, 41; CLR 6; DLB 5,
41; INT CANR-18; MAICYA; MTCW;
SATA 24

Giovene, Andrea 1904-............. **CLC 7**
See also CA 85-88

Gippius, Zinaida (Nikolayevna) 1869-1945
See Hippius, Zinaida
See also CA 106

Giraudoux, (Hippolyte) Jean
1882-1944 .... **TCLC 2, 7; DAM DRAM**
See also CA 104; DLB 65

Gironella, Jose Maria 1917-....... **CLC 11**
See also CA 101

Gissing, George (Robert)
1857-1903 .... **TCLC 3, 24, 47**
See also CA 105; DLB 18, 135

Giurlani, Aldo
See Palazzeschi, Aldo

Gladkov, Fyodor (Vasilyevich)
1883-1958 .... **TCLC 27**

Glanville, Brian (Lester) 1931-...... **CLC 6**
See also CA 5-8R; CAAS 9; CANR 3;
DLB 15, 139; SATA 42

Glasgow, Ellen (Anderson Gholson)
1873(?)-1945 .... **TCLC 2, 7**
See also CA 104; DLB 9, 12

Glaspell, Susan (Keating)
1882(?)-1948 .... **TCLC 55**
See also CA 110; DLB 7, 9, 78; YABC 2

Glassco, John 1909-1981 . . . . CLC 9
See also CA 13-16R; 102; CANR 15;
DLB 68

Glasscock, Amnesia
See Steinbeck, John (Ernst)

Glasser, Ronald J. 1940(?)- . . . . CLC 37

Glassman, Joyce
See Johnson, Joyce

Glendinning, Victoria 1937-. . . . . CLC 50
See also CA 120; 127; DLB 155

Glissant, Edouard
1928- . . . . CLC 10, 68; DAM MULT

Gloag, Julian 1930- . . . . CLC 40
See also AITN 1; CA 65-68; CANR 10

Glowacki, Aleksander
See Prus, Boleslaw

Gluck, Louise (Elisabeth)
1943- . . . . CLC 7, 22, 44, 81;
DAM POET; PC 16
See also CA 33-36R; CANR 40; DLB 5

Gobineau, Joseph Arthur (Comte) de
1816-1882 . . . . NCLC 17
See also DLB 123

Godard, Jean-Luc 1930-. . . . . CLC 20
See also CA 93-96

Godden, (Margaret) Rumer 1907-. . . CLC 53
See also AAYA 6; CA 5-8R; CANR 4, 27,
36; CLR 20; DLB 161; MAICYA;
SAAS 12; SATA 3, 36

Godoy Alcayaga, Lucila 1889-1957
See Mistral, Gabriela
See also BW 2; CA 104; 131; DAM MULT;
HW; MTCW

Godwin, Gail (Kathleen)
1937- . . . . CLC 5, 8, 22, 31, 69;
DAM POP
See also CA 29-32R; CANR 15, 43; DLB 6;
INT CANR-15; MTCW

Godwin, William 1756-1836. . . . . . NCLC 14
See also CDBLB 1789-1832; DLB 39, 104,
142, 158, 163

Goethe, Johann Wolfgang von
1749-1832 . . . . NCLC 4, 22, 34; DA;
DAB; DAC; DAM DRAM, MST,
POET; PC 5; WLC 3
See also DLB 94

Gogarty, Oliver St. John
1878-1957 . . . . TCLC 15
See also CA 109; 150; DLB 15, 19

Gogol, Nikolai (Vasilyevich)
1809-1852 . . . . NCLC 5, 15, 31; DA;
DAB; DAC; DAM DRAM, MST; DC 1;
SSC 4; WLC

Goines, Donald
1937(?)-1974 . . . . CLC 80; BLC;
DAM MULT, POP
See also AITN 1; BW 1; CA 124; 114;
DLB 33

Gold, Herbert 1924-. . . . . . . CLC 4, 7, 14, 42
See also CA 9-12R; CANR 17, 45; DLB 2;
DLBY 81

Goldbarth, Albert 1948-. . . . . CLC 5, 38
See also CA 53-56; CANR 6, 40; DLB 120

Goldberg, Anatol 1910-1982 . . . . . . CLC 34
See also CA 131; 117

Goldemberg, Isaac 1945- . . . . CLC 52
See also CA 69-72; CAAS 12; CANR 11,
32; HW

Golding, William (Gerald)
1911-1993 . . . . CLC 1, 2, 3, 8, 10, 17, 27,
58, 81; DA; DAB; DAC; DAM MST,
NOV; WLC
See also AAYA 5; CA 5-8R; 141;
CANR 13, 33; CDBLB 1945-1960;
DLB 15, 100; MTCW

Goldman, Emma 1869-1940. . . . . . TCLC 13
See also CA 110; 150

Goldman, Francisco 1955-. . . . . CLC 76

Goldman, William (W.) 1931-. . . . CLC 1, 48
See also CA 9-12R; CANR 29; DLB 44

Goldmann, Lucien 1913-1970 . . . . . CLC 24
See also CA 25-28; CAP 2

Goldoni, Carlo
1707-1793 . . . . LC 4; DAM DRAM

Goldsberry, Steven 1949-. . . . . CLC 34
See also CA 131

Goldsmith, Oliver
1728-1774 . . . . . . LC 2; DA; DAB; DAC;
DAM DRAM, MST, NOV, POET;
WLC
See also CDBLB 1660-1789; DLB 39, 89,
104, 109, 142; SATA 26

Goldsmith, Peter
See Priestley, J(ohn) B(oynton)

Gombrowicz, Witold
1904-1969 . . . . CLC 4, 7, 11, 49;
DAM DRAM
See also CA 19-20; 25-28R; CAP 2

Gomez de la Serna, Ramon
1888-1963 . . . . CLC 9
See also CA 116; HW

Goncharov, Ivan Alexandrovich
1812-1891 . . . . NCLC 1

Goncourt, Edmond (Louis Antoine Huot) de
1822-1896 . . . . NCLC 7
See also DLB 123

Goncourt, Jules (Alfred Huot) de
1830-1870 . . . . NCLC 7
See also DLB 123

Gontier, Fernande 19(?)- . . . . CLC 50

Goodman, Paul 1911-1972. . . . CLC 1, 2, 4, 7
See also CA 19-20; 37-40R; CANR 34;
CAP 2; DLB 130; MTCW

Gordimer, Nadine
1923- . . . . CLC 3, 5, 7, 10, 18, 33, 51, 70;
DA; DAB; DAC; DAM MST, NOV;
SSC 17
See also CA 5-8R; CANR 3, 28;
INT CANR-28; MTCW

Gordon, Adam Lindsay
1833-1870 . . . . NCLC 21

Gordon, Caroline
1895-1981 . . . CLC 6, 13, 29, 83; SSC 15
See also CA 11-12; 103; CANR 36; CAP 1;
DLB 4, 9, 102; DLBY 81; MTCW

Gordon, Charles William 1860-1937
See Connor, Ralph
See also CA 109

Gordon, Mary (Catherine)
1949- . . . . CLC 13, 22
See also CA 102; CANR 44; DLB 6;
DLBY 81; INT 102; MTCW

Gordon, Sol 1923-. . . . . CLC 26
See also CA 53-56; CANR 4; SATA 11

Gordone, Charles
1925-1995 . . . . . CLC 1, 4; DAM DRAM
See also BW 1; CA 93-96; 150; DLB 7;
INT 93-96; MTCW

Gorenko, Anna Andreevna
See Akhmatova, Anna

Gorky, Maxim. . . . . TCLC 8; DAB; WLC
See also Peshkov, Alexei Maximovich

Goryan, Sirak
See Saroyan, William

Gosse, Edmund (William)
1849-1928 . . . . TCLC 28
See also CA 117; DLB 57, 144

Gotlieb, Phyllis Fay (Bloom)
1926-. . . . . CLC 18
See also CA 13-16R; CANR 7; DLB 88

Gottesman, S. D.
See Kornbluth, C(yril) M.; Pohl, Frederik

Gottfried von Strassburg
fl. c. 1210-. . . . . CMLC 10
See also DLB 138

Gould, Lois . . . . CLC 4, 10
See also CA 77-80; CANR 29; MTCW

Gourmont, Remy (-Marie-Charles) de
1858-1915 . . . . TCLC 17
See also CA 109; 150

Govier, Katherine 1948-. . . . . CLC 51
See also CA 101; CANR 18, 40

Goyen, (Charles) William
1915-1983 . . . . CLC 5, 8, 14, 40
See also AITN 2; CA 5-8R; 110; CANR 6;
DLB 2; DLBY 83; INT CANR-6

Goytisolo, Juan
1931- . . . . . CLC 5, 10, 23; DAM MULT;
HLC
See also CA 85-88; CANR 32; HW; MTCW

Gozzano, Guido 1883-1916 . . . . PC 10
See also DLB 114

Gozzi, (Conte) Carlo 1720-1806 . . NCLC 23

Grabbe, Christian Dietrich
1801-1836 . . . . NCLC 2
See also DLB 133

Grace, Patricia 1937-. . . . . CLC 56

Gracian y Morales, Baltasar
1601-1658 . . . . LC 15

Gracq, Julien. . . . . CLC 11, 48
See also Poirier, Louis
See also DLB 83

Grade, Chaim 1910-1982 . . . . CLC 10
See also CA 93-96; 107

Graduate of Oxford, A
See Ruskin, John

Graham, John
See Phillips, David Graham

Graham, Jorie 1951-. . . . . CLC 48
See also CA 111; DLB 120

Graham, R(obert) B(ontine) Cunninghame
See Cunninghame Graham, R(obert)
B(ontine)
See also DLB 98, 135

Graham, Robert
See Haldeman, Joe (William)

Graham, Tom
See Lewis, (Harry) Sinclair

Graham, W(illiam) S(ydney)
1918-1986 .... CLC 29
See also CA 73-76; 118; DLB 20

Graham, Winston (Mawdsley)
1910- .... CLC 23
See also CA 49-52; CANR 2, 22, 45;
DLB 77

Grahame, Kenneth
1859-1932 .... TCLC 64; DAB
See also CA 108; 136; CLR 5; DLB 34, 141;
MAICYA; YABC 1

Grant, Skeeter
See Spiegelman, Art

Granville-Barker, Harley
1877-1946 ..... TCLC 2; DAM DRAM
See also Barker, Harley Granville
See also CA 104

Grass, Guenter (Wilhelm)
1927- ..... CLC 1, 2, 4, 6, 11, 15, 22, 32,
49, 88; DA; DAB; DAC; DAM MST,
NOV; WLC
See also CA 13-16R; CANR 20; DLB 75,
124; MTCW

Gratton, Thomas
See Hulme, T(homas) E(rnest)

Grau, Shirley Ann
1929- .... CLC 4, 9; SSC 15
See also CA 89-92; CANR 22; DLB 2;
INT CANR-22; MTCW

Gravel, Fern
See Hall, James Norman

Graver, Elizabeth 1964-.......... CLC 70
See also CA 135

Graves, Richard Perceval 1945- .... CLC 44
See also CA 65-68; CANR 9, 26, 51

Graves, Robert (von Ranke)
1895-1985 ...... CLC 1, 2, 6, 11, 39, 44,
45; DAB; DAC; DAM MST, POET;
PC 6
See also CA 5-8R; 117; CANR 5, 36;
CDBLB 1914-1945; DLB 20, 100;
DLBY 85; MTCW; SATA 45

Graves, Valerie
See Bradley, Marion Zimmer

Gray, Alasdair (James) 1934- ...... CLC 41
See also CA 126; CANR 47; INT 126;
MTCW

Gray, Amlin 1946- .... CLC 29
See also CA 138

Gray, Francine du Plessix
1930- .... CLC 22; DAM NOV
See also BEST 90:3; CA 61-64; CAAS 2;
CANR 11, 33; INT CANR-11; MTCW

Gray, John (Henry) 1866-1934 .... TCLC 19
See also CA 119

Gray, Simon (James Holliday)
1936- .... CLC 9, 14, 36
See also AITN 1; CA 21-24R; CAAS 3;
CANR 32; DLB 13; MTCW

Gray, Spalding 1941-.. CLC 49; DAM POP
See also CA 128

Gray, Thomas
1716-1771 ...... LC 4; DA; DAB; DAC;
DAM MST; PC 2; WLC
See also CDBLB 1660-1789; DLB 109

Grayson, David
See Baker, Ray Stannard

Grayson, Richard (A.) 1951-....... CLC 38
See also CA 85-88; CANR 14, 31

Greeley, Andrew M(oran)
1928- .... CLC 28; DAM POP
See also CA 5-8R; CAAS 7; CANR 7, 43;
MTCW

Green, Anna Katharine
1846-1935 .... TCLC 63
See also CA 112

Green, Brian
See Card, Orson Scott

Green, Hannah
See Greenberg, Joanne (Goldenberg)

Green, Hannah .... CLC 3
See also CA 73-76

Green, Henry.................. CLC 2, 13
See also Yorke, Henry Vincent
See also DLB 15

Green, Julian (Hartridge) 1900-
See Green, Julien
See also CA 21-24R; CANR 33; DLB 4, 72;
MTCW

Green, Julien................ CLC 3, 11, 77
See also Green, Julian (Hartridge)

Green, Paul (Eliot)
1894-1981 ...... CLC 25; DAM DRAM
See also AITN 1; CA 5-8R; 103; CANR 3;
DLB 7, 9; DLBY 81

Greenberg, Ivan 1908-1973
See Rahv, Philip
See also CA 85-88

Greenberg, Joanne (Goldenberg)
1932- .... CLC 7, 30
See also AAYA 12; CA 5-8R; CANR 14,
32; SATA 25

Greenberg, Richard 1959(?)-....... CLC 57
See also CA 138

Greene, Bette 1934- .... CLC 30
See also AAYA 7; CA 53-56; CANR 4;
CLR 2; JRDA; MAICYA; SAAS 16;
SATA 8

Greene, Gael .... CLC 8
See also CA 13-16R; CANR 10

Greene, Graham
1904-1991 .... CLC 1, 3, 6, 9, 14, 18, 27,
37, 70, 72; DA; DAB; DAC; DAM MST,
NOV; WLC
See also AITN 2; CA 13-16R; 133;
CANR 35; CDBLB 1945-1960; DLB 13,
15, 77, 100, 162; DLBY 91; MTCW;
SATA 20

Greer, Richard
See Silverberg, Robert

Gregor, Arthur 1923-.............. CLC 9
See also CA 25-28R; CAAS 10; CANR 11;
SATA 36

Gregor, Lee
See Pohl, Frederik

Gregory, Isabella Augusta (Persse)
1852-1932 .... TCLC 1
See also CA 104; DLB 10

Gregory, J. Dennis
See Williams, John A(lfred)

Grendon, Stephen
See Derleth, August (William)

Grenville, Kate 1950-.............. CLC 61
See also CA 118; CANR 53

Grenville, Pelham
See Wodehouse, P(elham) G(renville)

Greve, Felix Paul (Berthold Friedrich)
1879-1948
See Grove, Frederick Philip
See also CA 104; 141; DAC; DAM MST

Grey, Zane
1872-1939 .... TCLC 6; DAM POP
See also CA 104; 132; DLB 9; MTCW

Grieg, (Johan) Nordahl (Brun)
1902-1943 .... TCLC 10
See also CA 107

Grieve, C(hristopher) M(urray)
1892-1978 ..... CLC 11, 19; DAM POET
See also MacDiarmid, Hugh; Pteleon
See also CA 5-8R; 85-88; CANR 33;
MTCW

Griffin, Gerald 1803-1840 .... NCLC 7
See also DLB 159

Griffin, John Howard 1920-1980.... CLC 68
See also AITN 1; CA 1-4R; 101; CANR 2

Griffin, Peter 1942- .... CLC 39
See also CA 136

Griffiths, Trevor 1935-......... CLC 13, 52
See also CA 97-100; CANR 45; DLB 13

Grigson, Geoffrey (Edward Harvey)
1905-1985 .... CLC 7, 39
See also CA 25-28R; 118; CANR 20, 33;
DLB 27; MTCW

Grillparzer, Franz 1791-1872...... NCLC 1
See also DLB 133

Grimble, Reverend Charles James
See Eliot, T(homas) S(tearns)

Grimke, Charlotte L(ottie) Forten
1837(?)-1914
See Forten, Charlotte L.
See also BW 1; CA 117; 124; DAM MULT,
POET

Grimm, Jacob Ludwig Karl
1785-1863 .... NCLC 3
See also DLB 90; MAICYA; SATA 22

Grimm, Wilhelm Karl 1786-1859 .. NCLC 3
See also DLB 90; MAICYA; SATA 22

Grimmelshausen, Johann Jakob Christoffel
von 1621-1676 .... LC 6
See also DLB 168

Grindel, Eugene 1895-1952
See Eluard, Paul
See also CA 104

Grisham, John 1955-.. CLC 84; DAM POP
See also AAYA 14; CA 138; CANR 47

Grossman, David 1954- . . . . CLC 67
See also CA 138

Grossman, Vasily (Semenovich)
1905-1964 . . . . CLC 41
See also CA 124; 130; MTCW

Grove, Frederick Philip . . . . TCLC 4
See also Greve, Felix Paul (Berthold
Friedrich)
See also DLB 92

Grubb
See Crumb, R(obert)

Grumbach, Doris (Isaac)
1918- . . . . CLC 13, 22, 64
See also CA 5-8R; CAAS 2; CANR 9, 42;
INT CANR-9

Grundtvig, Nicolai Frederik Severin
1783-1872 . . . . NCLC 1

Grunge
See Crumb, R(obert)

Grunwald, Lisa 1959- . . . . CLC 44
See also CA 120

Guare, John
1938- . . . . CLC 8, 14, 29, 67;
DAM DRAM
See also CA 73-76; CANR 21; DLB 7;
MTCW

Gudjonsson, Halldor Kiljan 1902-
See Laxness, Halldor
See also CA 103

Guenter, Erich
See Eich, Guenter

Guest, Barbara 1920- . . . . CLC 34
See also CA 25-28R; CANR 11, 44; DLB 5

Guest, Judith (Ann)
1936- . . . . CLC 8, 30; DAM NOV, POP
See also AAYA 7; CA 77-80; CANR 15;
INT CANR-15; MTCW

Guevara, Che . . . . CLC 87; HLC
See also Guevara (Serna), Ernesto

Guevara (Serna), Ernesto 1928-1967
See Guevara, Che
See also CA 127; 111; DAM MULT; HW

Guild, Nicholas M. 1944- . . . . CLC 33
See also CA 93-96

Guillemin, Jacques
See Sartre, Jean-Paul

Guillen, Jorge
1893-1984 . . . . . . CLC 11; DAM MULT,
POET
See also CA 89-92; 112; DLB 108; HW

Guillen, Nicolas (Cristobal)
1902-1989 . . . . CLC 48, 79; BLC;
DAM MST, MULT, POET; HLC
See also BW 2; CA 116; 125; 129; HW

Guillevic, (Eugene) 1907- . . . . CLC 33
See also CA 93-96

Guillois
See Desnos, Robert

Guillois, Valentin
See Desnos, Robert

Guiney, Louise Imogen
1861-1920 . . . . TCLC 41
See also DLB 54

Guiraldes, Ricardo (Guillermo)
1886-1927 . . . . TCLC 39
See also CA 131; HW; MTCW

Gumilev, Nikolai Stephanovich
1886-1921 . . . . TCLC 60

Gunesekera, Romesh . . . . CLC 91

Gunn, Bill . . . . CLC 5
See also Gunn, William Harrison
See also DLB 38

Gunn, Thom(son William)
1929- . . . . CLC 3, 6, 18, 32, 81;
DAM POET
See also CA 17-20R; CANR 9, 33;
CDBLB 1960 to Present; DLB 27;
INT CANR-33; MTCW

Gunn, William Harrison 1934(?)-1989
See Gunn, Bill
See also AITN 1; BW 1; CA 13-16R; 128;
CANR 12, 25

Gunnars, Kristjana 1948- . . . . CLC 69
See also CA 113; DLB 60

Gurganus, Allan
1947- . . . . CLC 70; DAM POP
See also BEST 90:1; CA 135

Gurney, A(lbert) R(amsdell), Jr.
1930- . . . . CLC 32, 50, 54; DAM DRAM
See also CA 77-80; CANR 32

Gurney, Ivor (Bertie) 1890-1937 . . . TCLC 33

Gurney, Peter
See Gurney, A(lbert) R(amsdell), Jr.

Guro, Elena 1877-1913 . . . . TCLC 56

Gustafson, Ralph (Barker) 1909- . . . . CLC 36
See also CA 21-24R; CANR 8, 45; DLB 88

Gut, Gom
See Simenon, Georges (Jacques Christian)

Guterson, David 1956- . . . . CLC 91
See also CA 132

Guthrie, A(lfred) B(ertram), Jr.
1901-1991 . . . . CLC 23
See also CA 57-60; 134; CANR 24; DLB 6;
SATA 62; SATA-Obit 67

Guthrie, Isobel
See Grieve, C(hristopher) M(urray)

Guthrie, Woodrow Wilson 1912-1967
See Guthrie, Woody
See also CA 113; 93-96

Guthrie, Woody . . . . CLC 35
See also Guthrie, Woodrow Wilson

Guy, Rosa (Cuthbert) 1928- . . . . CLC 26
See also AAYA 4; BW 2; CA 17-20R;
CANR 14, 34; CLR 13; DLB 33; JRDA;
MAICYA; SATA 14, 62

Gwendolyn
See Bennett, (Enoch) Arnold

H. D. . . . . CLC 3, 8, 14, 31, 34, 73; PC 5
See also Doolittle, Hilda

H. de V.
See Buchan, John

Haavikko, Paavo Juhani
1931- . . . . CLC 18, 34
See also CA 106

Habbema, Koos
See Heijermans, Herman

Hacker, Marilyn
1942- . . . . CLC 5, 9, 23, 72, 91;
DAM POET
See also CA 77-80; DLB 120

Haggard, H(enry) Rider
1856-1925 . . . . TCLC 11
See also CA 108; 148; DLB 70, 156;
SATA 16

Hagiosy, L.
See Larbaud, Valery (Nicolas)

Hagiwara Sakutaro 1886-1942 . . . . TCLC 60

Haig, Fenil
See Ford, Ford Madox

Haig-Brown, Roderick (Langmere)
1908-1976 . . . . CLC 21
See also CA 5-8R; 69-72; CANR 4, 38;
CLR 31; DLB 88; MAICYA; SATA 12

Hailey, Arthur
1920- . . . . CLC 5; DAM NOV, POP
See also AITN 2; BEST 90:3; CA 1-4R;
CANR 2, 36; DLB 88; DLBY 82; MTCW

Hailey, Elizabeth Forsythe 1938- . . . CLC 40
See also CA 93-96; CAAS 1; CANR 15, 48;
INT CANR-15

Haines, John (Meade) 1924- . . . . CLC 58
See also CA 17-20R; CANR 13, 34; DLB 5

Hakluyt, Richard 1552-1616 . . . . LC 31

Haldeman, Joe (William) 1943- . . . . . CLC 61
See also CA 53-56; CANR 6; DLB 8;
INT CANR-6

Haley, Alex(ander Murray Palmer)
1921-1992 . . . . CLC 8, 12, 76; BLC; DA;
DAB; DAC; DAM MST, MULT, POP
See also BW 2; CA 77-80; 136; DLB 38;
MTCW

Haliburton, Thomas Chandler
1796-1865 . . . . NCLC 15
See also DLB 11, 99

Hall, Donald (Andrew, Jr.)
1928- . . CLC 1, 13, 37, 59; DAM POET
See also CA 5-8R; CAAS 7; CANR 2, 44;
DLB 5; SATA 23

Hall, Frederic Sauser
See Sauser-Hall, Frederic

Hall, James
See Kuttner, Henry

Hall, James Norman 1887-1951 . . . TCLC 23
See also CA 123; SATA 21

Hall, (Marguerite) Radclyffe
1886-1943 . . . . TCLC 12
See also CA 110; 150

Hall, Rodney 1935- . . . . CLC 51
See also CA 109

Halleck, Fitz-Greene 1790-1867 . . NCLC 47
See also DLB 3

Halliday, Michael
See Creasey, John

Halpern, Daniel 1945- . . . . CLC 14
See also CA 33-36R

Hamburger, Michael (Peter Leopold)
1924- . . . . CLC 5, 14
See also CA 5-8R; CAAS 4; CANR 2, 47;
DLB 27

Hamill, Pete 1935- . . . . CLC 10
See also CA 25-28R; CANR 18

Hamilton, Alexander
1755(?)-1804 . . . . **NCLC 49**
See also DLB 37

Hamilton, Clive
See Lewis, C(live) S(taples)

Hamilton, Edmond 1904-1977 . . . . . . **CLC 1**
See also CA 1-4R; CANR 3; DLB 8

Hamilton, Eugene (Jacob) Lee
See Lee-Hamilton, Eugene (Jacob)

Hamilton, Franklin
See Silverberg, Robert

Hamilton, Gail
See Corcoran, Barbara

Hamilton, Mollie
See Kaye, M(ary) M(argaret)

Hamilton, (Anthony Walter) Patrick
1904-1962 . . . . **CLC 51**
See also CA 113; DLB 10

Hamilton, Virginia
1936- . . . . **CLC 26; DAM MULT**
See also AAYA 2; BW 2; CA 25-28R;
CANR 20, 37; CLR 1, 11, 40; DLB 33,
52; INT CANR-20; JRDA; MAICYA;
MTCW; SATA 4, 56, 79

Hammett, (Samuel) Dashiell
1894-1961 . . . . **CLC 3, 5, 10, 19, 47;**
SSC 17
See also AITN 1; CA 81-84; CANR 42;
CDALB 1929-1941; DLBD 6; MTCW

Hammon, Jupiter
1711(?)-1800(?) . . . . **NCLC 5; BLC;**
DAM MULT, POET; PC 16
See also DLB 31, 50

Hammond, Keith
See Kuttner, Henry

Hamner, Earl (Henry), Jr. 1923- . . . **CLC 12**
See also AITN 2; CA 73-76; DLB 6

Hampton, Christopher (James)
1946- . . . . **CLC 4**
See also CA 25-28R; DLB 13; MTCW

Hamsun, Knut . . . . **TCLC 2, 14, 49**
See also Pedersen, Knut

Handke, Peter
1942- . . . . **CLC 5, 8, 10, 15, 38;**
DAM DRAM, NOV
See also CA 77-80; CANR 33; DLB 85,
124; MTCW

Hanley, James 1901-1985 . . . **CLC 3, 5, 8, 13**
See also CA 73-76; 117; CANR 36; MTCW

Hannah, Barry 1942- . . . . **CLC 23, 38, 90**
See also CA 108; 110; CANR 43; DLB 6;
INT 110; MTCW

Hannon, Ezra
See Hunter, Evan

Hansberry, Lorraine (Vivian)
1930-1965 . . . . . . **CLC 17, 62; BLC; DA;**
DAB; DAC; DAM DRAM, MST,
MULT; DC 2
See also BW 1; CA 109; 25-28R; CABS 3;
CDALB 1941-1968; DLB 7, 38; MTCW

Hansen, Joseph 1923- . . . . **CLC 38**
See also CA 29-32R; CAAS 17; CANR 16,
44; INT CANR-16

Hansen, Martin A. 1909-1955 . . . . . **TCLC 32**

Hanson, Kenneth O(stlin) 1922- . . . . **CLC 13**
See also CA 53-56; CANR 7

Hardwick, Elizabeth
1916- . . . . **CLC 13; DAM NOV**
See also CA 5-8R; CANR 3, 32; DLB 6;
MTCW

Hardy, Thomas
1840-1928 . . . . . . **TCLC 4, 10, 18, 32, 48,**
53; DA; DAB; DAC; DAM MST, NOV,
POET; PC 8; SSC 2; WLC
See also CA 104; 123; CDBLB 1890-1914;
DLB 18, 19, 135; MTCW

Hare, David 1947- . . . . **CLC 29, 58**
See also CA 97-100; CANR 39; DLB 13;
MTCW

Harford, Henry
See Hudson, W(illiam) H(enry)

Hargrave, Leonie
See Disch, Thomas M(ichael)

Harjo, Joy 1951- . . . **CLC 83; DAM MULT**
See also CA 114; CANR 35; DLB 120;
NNAL

Harlan, Louis R(udolph) 1922- . . . . . **CLC 34**
See also CA 21-24R; CANR 25

Harling, Robert 1951(?)- . . . . **CLC 53**
See also CA 147

Harmon, William (Ruth) 1938- . . . . . **CLC 38**
See also CA 33-36R; CANR 14, 32, 35;
SATA 65

Harper, F. E. W.
See Harper, Frances Ellen Watkins

Harper, Frances E. W.
See Harper, Frances Ellen Watkins

Harper, Frances E. Watkins
See Harper, Frances Ellen Watkins

Harper, Frances Ellen
See Harper, Frances Ellen Watkins

Harper, Frances Ellen Watkins
1825-1911 . . . . **TCLC 14; BLC;**
DAM MULT, POET
See also BW 1; CA 111; 125; DLB 50

Harper, Michael S(teven) 1938- . . **CLC 7, 22**
See also BW 1; CA 33-36R; CANR 24;
DLB 41

Harper, Mrs. F. E. W.
See Harper, Frances Ellen Watkins

Harris, Christie (Lucy) Irwin
1907- . . . . **CLC 12**
See also CA 5-8R; CANR 6; DLB 88;
JRDA; MAICYA; SAAS 10; SATA 6, 74

Harris, Frank 1856-1931 . . . . **TCLC 24**
See also CA 109; 150; DLB 156

Harris, George Washington
1814-1869 . . . . **NCLC 23**
See also DLB 3, 11

Harris, Joel Chandler
1848-1908 . . . . **TCLC 2; SSC 19**
See also CA 104; 137; DLB 11, 23, 42, 78,
91; MAICYA; YABC 1

Harris, John (Wyndham Parkes Lucas)
Beynon 1903-1969
See Wyndham, John
See also CA 102; 89-92

Harris, MacDonald . . . . **CLC 9**
See also Heiney, Donald (William)

Harris, Mark 1922- . . . . **CLC 19**
See also CA 5-8R; CAAS 3; CANR 2;
DLB 2; DLBY 80

Harris, (Theodore) Wilson 1921- . . . . **CLC 25**
See also BW 2; CA 65-68; CAAS 16;
CANR 11, 27; DLB 117; MTCW

Harrison, Elizabeth Cavanna 1909-
See Cavanna, Betty
See also CA 9-12R; CANR 6, 27

Harrison, Harry (Max) 1925- . . . . . . **CLC 42**
See also CA 1-4R; CANR 5, 21; DLB 8;
SATA 4

Harrison, James (Thomas)
1937- . . . . **CLC 6, 14, 33, 66; SSC 19**
See also CA 13-16R; CANR 8, 51;
DLBY 82; INT CANR-8

Harrison, Jim
See Harrison, James (Thomas)

Harrison, Kathryn 1961- . . . . **CLC 70**
See also CA 144

Harrison, Tony 1937- . . . . **CLC 43**
See also CA 65-68; CANR 44; DLB 40;
MTCW

Harriss, Will(ard Irvin) 1922- . . . . . . **CLC 34**
See also CA 111

Harson, Sley
See Ellison, Harlan (Jay)

Hart, Ellis
See Ellison, Harlan (Jay)

Hart, Josephine
1942(?)- . . . . **CLC 70; DAM POP**
See also CA 138

Hart, Moss
1904-1961 . . . . . . **CLC 66; DAM DRAM**
See also CA 109; 89-92; DLB 7

Harte, (Francis) Bret(t)
1836(?)-1902 . . . . **TCLC 1, 25; DA; DAC;**
DAM MST; SSC 8; WLC
See also CA 104; 140; CDALB 1865-1917;
DLB 12, 64, 74, 79; SATA 26

Hartley, L(eslie) P(oles)
1895-1972 . . . . **CLC 2, 22**
See also CA 45-48; 37-40R; CANR 33;
DLB 15, 139; MTCW

Hartman, Geoffrey H. 1929- . . . . **CLC 27**
See also CA 117; 125; DLB 67

Hartmann von Aue
c. 1160-c. 1205 . . . . **CMLC 15**
See also DLB 138

Hartmann von Aue 1170-1210 . . . . **CMLC 15**

Haruf, Kent 1943- . . . . **CLC 34**
See also CA 149

Harwood, Ronald
1934- . . . . **CLC 32; DAM DRAM, MST**
See also CA 1-4R; CANR 4; DLB 13

Hasek, Jaroslav (Matej Frantisek)
1883-1923 . . . . **TCLC 4**
See also CA 104; 129; MTCW

Hass, Robert 1941- . . . . . **CLC 18, 39; PC 16**
See also CA 111; CANR 30, 50; DLB 105

Hastings, Hudson
See Kuttner, Henry

Hastings, Selina. . . . . **CLC 44**

Hatteras, Amelia
 See Mencken, H(enry) L(ouis)

Hatteras, Owen .... **TCLC 18**
 See also Mencken, H(enry) L(ouis); Nathan,
  George Jean

Hauptmann, Gerhart (Johann Robert)
 1862-1946 ...... **TCLC 4; DAM DRAM**
 See also CA 104; DLB 66, 118

Havel, Vaclav
 1936- .... **CLC 25, 58, 65;**
  DAM DRAM; DC 6
 See also CA 104; CANR 36; MTCW

Haviaras, Stratis .... **CLC 33**
 See also Chaviaras, Strates

Hawes, Stephen 1475(?)-1523(?) ..... **LC 17**

Hawkes, John (Clendennin Burne, Jr.)
 1925- ...... **CLC 1, 2, 3, 4, 7, 9, 14, 15,**
  27, 49
 See also CA 1-4R; CANR 2, 47; DLB 2, 7;
  DLBY 80; MTCW

Hawking, S. W.
 See Hawking, Stephen W(illiam)

Hawking, Stephen W(illiam)
 1942- .... **CLC 63**
 See also AAYA 13; BEST 89:1; CA 126;
  129; CANR 48

Hawthorne, Julian 1846-1934 ..... **TCLC 25**

Hawthorne, Nathaniel
 1804-1864 .... **NCLC 39; DA; DAB;**
  DAC; DAM MST, NOV; SSC 3; WLC
 See also AAYA 18; CDALB 1640-1865;
  DLB 1, 74; YABC 2

Haxton, Josephine Ayres 1921-
 See Douglas, Ellen
 See also CA 115; CANR 41

Hayaseca y Eizaguirre, Jorge
 See Echegaray (y Eizaguirre), Jose (Maria
  Waldo)

Hayashi Fumiko 1904-1951 ...... **TCLC 27**

Haycraft, Anna
 See Ellis, Alice Thomas
 See also CA 122

Hayden, Robert E(arl)
 1913-1980 ...... **CLC 5, 9, 14, 37; BLC;**
  DA; DAC; DAM MST, MULT, POET;
  PC 6
 See also BW 1; CA 69-72; 97-100; CABS 2;
  CANR 24; CDALB 1941-1968; DLB 5,
  76; MTCW; SATA 19; SATA-Obit 26

Hayford, J(oseph) E(phraim) Casely
 See Casely-Hayford, J(oseph) E(phraim)

Hayman, Ronald 1932- .... **CLC 44**
 See also CA 25-28R; CANR 18, 50;
  DLB 155

Haywood, Eliza (Fowler)
 1693(?)-1756 .... **LC 1**

Hazlitt, William 1778-1830 ...... **NCLC 29**
 See also DLB 110, 158

Hazzard, Shirley 1931- .... **CLC 18**
 See also CA 9-12R; CANR 4; DLBY 82;
  MTCW

Head, Bessie
 1937-1986 .... **CLC 25, 67; BLC;**
  DAM MULT
 See also BW 2; CA 29-32R; 119; CANR 25;
  DLB 117; MTCW

Headon, (Nicky) Topper 1956(?)- ... **CLC 30**

Heaney, Seamus (Justin)
 1939- ...... **CLC 5, 7, 14, 25, 37, 74, 91;**
  DAB; DAM POET
 See also CA 85-88; CANR 25, 48;
  CDBLB 1960 to Present; DLB 40;
  DLBY 95; MTCW

Hearn, (Patricio) Lafcadio (Tessima Carlos)
 1850-1904 .... **TCLC 9**
 See also CA 105; DLB 12, 78

Hearne, Vicki 1946- .... **CLC 56**
 See also CA 139

Hearon, Shelby 1931- .... **CLC 63**
 See also AITN 2; CA 25-28R; CANR 18,
  48

Heat-Moon, William Least .... **CLC 29**
 See also Trogdon, William (Lewis)
 See also AAYA 9

Hebbel, Friedrich
 1813-1863 .... **NCLC 43; DAM DRAM**
 See also DLB 129

Hebert, Anne
 1916- .... **CLC 4, 13, 29; DAC;**
  DAM MST, POET
 See also CA 85-88; DLB 68; MTCW

Hecht, Anthony (Evan)
 1923- ...... **CLC 8, 13, 19; DAM POET**
 See also CA 9-12R; CANR 6; DLB 5, 169

Hecht, Ben 1894-1964 .... **CLC 8**
 See also CA 85-88; DLB 7, 9, 25, 26, 28, 86

Hedayat, Sadeq 1903-1951 .... **TCLC 21**
 See also CA 120

Hegel, Georg Wilhelm Friedrich
 1770-1831 .... **NCLC 46**
 See also DLB 90

Heidegger, Martin 1889-1976 ...... **CLC 24**
 See also CA 81-84; 65-68; CANR 34;
  MTCW

Heidenstam, (Carl Gustaf) Verner von
 1859-1940 .... **TCLC 5**
 See also CA 104

Heifner, Jack 1946- .... **CLC 11**
 See also CA 105; CANR 47

Heijermans, Herman 1864-1924 ... **TCLC 24**
 See also CA 123

Heilbrun, Carolyn G(old) 1926- ..... **CLC 25**
 See also CA 45-48; CANR 1, 28

Heine, Heinrich 1797-1856 .... **NCLC 4, 54**
 See also DLB 90

Heinemann, Larry (Curtiss) 1944- .. **CLC 50**
 See also CA 110; CAAS 21; CANR 31;
  DLBD 9; INT CANR-31

Heiney, Donald (William) 1921-1993
 See Harris, MacDonald
 See also CA 1-4R; 142; CANR 3

Heinlein, Robert A(nson)
 1907-1988 ...... **CLC 1, 3, 8, 14, 26, 55;**
  DAM POP
 See also AAYA 17; CA 1-4R; 125;
  CANR 1, 20, 53; DLB 8; JRDA;
  MAICYA; MTCW; SATA 9, 69;
  SATA-Obit 56

Helforth, John
 See Doolittle, Hilda

Hellenhofferu, Vojtech Kapristian z
 See Hasek, Jaroslav (Matej Frantisek)

Heller, Joseph
 1923- .... **CLC 1, 3, 5, 8, 11, 36, 63; DA;**
  DAB; DAC; DAM MST, NOV, POP;
  WLC
 See also AITN 1; CA 5-8R; CABS 1;
  CANR 8, 42; DLB 2, 28; DLBY 80;
  INT CANR-8; MTCW

Hellman, Lillian (Florence)
 1906-1984 ...... **CLC 2, 4, 8, 14, 18, 34,**
  44, 52; DAM DRAM; DC 1
 See also AITN 1, 2; CA 13-16R; 112;
  CANR 33; DLB 7; DLBY 84; MTCW

Helprin, Mark
 1947- .... **CLC 7, 10, 22, 32;**
  DAM NOV, POP
 See also CA 81-84; CANR 47; DLBY 85;
  MTCW

Helvetius, Claude-Adrien
 1715-1771 .... **LC 26**

Helyar, Jane Penelope Josephine 1933-
 See Poole, Josephine
 See also CA 21-24R; CANR 10, 26;
  SATA 82

Hemans, Felicia 1793-1835 ...... **NCLC 29**
 See also DLB 96

Hemingway, Ernest (Miller)
 1899-1961 .... **CLC 1, 3, 6, 8, 10, 13, 19,**
  30, 34, 39, 41, 44, 50, 61, 80; DA; DAB;
  DAC; DAM MST, NOV; SSC 1; WLC
 See also CA 77-80; CANR 34;
  CDALB 1917-1929; DLB 4, 9, 102;
  DLBD 1; DLBY 81, 87; MTCW

Hempel, Amy 1951- .... **CLC 39**
 See also CA 118; 137

Henderson, F. C.
 See Mencken, H(enry) L(ouis)

Henderson, Sylvia
 See Ashton-Warner, Sylvia (Constance)

Henley, Beth .... **CLC 23; DC 6**
 See also Henley, Elizabeth Becker
 See also CABS 3; DLBY 86

Henley, Elizabeth Becker 1952-
 See Henley, Beth
 See also CA 107; CANR 32; DAM DRAM,
  MST; MTCW

Henley, William Ernest
 1849-1903 .... **TCLC 8**
 See also CA 105; DLB 19

Hennissart, Martha
 See Lathen, Emma
 See also CA 85-88

Henry, O. .... **TCLC 1, 19; SSC 5; WLC**
 See also Porter, William Sydney

Henry, Patrick 1736-1799 .... **LC 25**

443

Henryson, Robert 1430(?)-1506(?).... **LC 20**
See also DLB 146

Henry VIII 1491-1547............. **LC 10**

Henschke, Alfred
See Klabund

Hentoff, Nat(han Irving) 1925-..... **CLC 26**
See also AAYA 4; CA 1-4R; CAAS 6;
CANR 5, 25; CLR 1; INT CANR-25;
JRDA; MAICYA; SATA 42, 69;
SATA-Brief 27

Heppenstall, (John) Rayner
1911-1981 .... **CLC 10**
See also CA 1-4R; 103; CANR 29

Herbert, Frank (Patrick)
1920-1986 ...... **CLC 12, 23, 35, 44, 85;**
DAM POP
See also CA 53-56; 118; CANR 5, 43;
DLB 8; INT CANR-5; MTCW; SATA 9,
37; SATA-Obit 47

Herbert, George
1593-1633 .... **LC 24; DAB;**
DAM POET; PC 4
See also CDBLB Before 1660; DLB 126

Herbert, Zbigniew
1924-......... **CLC 9, 43; DAM POET**
See also CA 89-92; CANR 36; MTCW

Herbst, Josephine (Frey)
1897-1969 .... **CLC 34**
See also CA 5-8R; 25-28R; DLB 9

Hergesheimer, Joseph
1880-1954 .... **TCLC 11**
See also CA 109; DLB 102, 9

Herlihy, James Leo 1927-1993 ...... **CLC 6**
See also CA 1-4R; 143; CANR 2

Hermogenes fl. c. 175-........... **CMLC 6**

Hernandez, Jose 1834-1886...... **NCLC 17**

Herodotus c. 484B.C.-429B.C..... **CMLC 17**

Herrick, Robert
1591-1674 ..... **LC 13; DA; DAB; DAC;**
DAM MST, POP; PC 9
See also DLB 126

Herring, Guilles
See Somerville, Edith

Herriot, James
1916-1995 .... **CLC 12; DAM POP**
See also Wight, James Alfred
See also AAYA 1; CA 148; CANR 40;
SATA 86

Herrmann, Dorothy 1941-......... **CLC 44**
See also CA 107

Herrmann, Taffy
See Herrmann, Dorothy

Hersey, John (Richard)
1914-1993 .... **CLC 1, 2, 7, 9, 40, 81;**
DAM POP
See also CA 17-20R; 140; CANR 33;
DLB 6; MTCW; SATA 25;
SATA-Obit 76

Herzen, Aleksandr Ivanovich
1812-1870 .... **NCLC 10**

Herzl, Theodor 1860-1904........ **TCLC 36**

Herzog, Werner 1942-............. **CLC 16**
See also CA 89-92

Hesiod c. 8th cent. B.C.-......... **CMLC 5**

Hesse, Hermann
1877-1962 .... **CLC 1, 2, 3, 6, 11, 17, 25,**
69; DA; DAB; DAC; DAM MST, NOV;
SSC 9; WLC
See also CA 17-18; CAP 2; DLB 66;
MTCW; SATA 50

Hewes, Cady
See De Voto, Bernard (Augustine)

Heyen, William 1940- .... **CLC 13, 18**
See also CA 33-36R; CAAS 9; DLB 5

Heyerdahl, Thor 1914-............ **CLC 26**
See also CA 5-8R; CANR 5, 22; MTCW;
SATA 2, 52

Heym, Georg (Theodor Franz Arthur)
1887-1912 .... **TCLC 9**
See also CA 106

Heym, Stefan 1913-.............. **CLC 41**
See also CA 9-12R; CANR 4; DLB 69

Heyse, Paul (Johann Ludwig von)
1830-1914 .... **TCLC 8**
See also CA 104; DLB 129

Heyward, (Edwin) DuBose
1885-1940 .... **TCLC 59**
See also CA 108; DLB 7, 9, 45; SATA 21

Hibbert, Eleanor Alice Burford
1906-1993 .... **CLC 7; DAM POP**
See also BEST 90:4; CA 17-20R; 140;
CANR 9, 28; SATA 2; SATA-Obit 74

Hichens, Robert S. 1864-1950..... **TCLC 64**
See also DLB 153

Higgins, George V(incent)
1939-................ **CLC 4, 7, 10, 18**
See also CA 77-80; CAAS 5; CANR 17, 51;
DLB 2; DLBY 81; INT CANR-17;
MTCW

Higginson, Thomas Wentworth
1823-1911 .... **TCLC 36**
See also DLB 1, 64

Highet, Helen
See MacInnes, Helen (Clark)

Highsmith, (Mary) Patricia
1921-1995 .... **CLC 2, 4, 14, 42;**
DAM NOV, POP
See also CA 1-4R; 147; CANR 1, 20, 48;
MTCW

Highwater, Jamake (Mamake)
1942(?)-..................... **CLC 12**
See also AAYA 7; CA 65-68; CAAS 7;
CANR 10, 34; CLR 17; DLB 52;
DLBY 85; JRDA; MAICYA; SATA 32,
69; SATA-Brief 30

Highway, Tomson
1951-..... **CLC 92; DAC; DAM MULT**
See also CA 151; NNAL

Higuchi, Ichiyo 1872-1896....... **NCLC 49**

Hijuelos, Oscar
1951-.... **CLC 65; DAM MULT, POP;**
HLC
See also BEST 90:1; CA 123; CANR 50;
DLB 145; HW

Hikmet, Nazim 1902(?)-1963....... **CLC 40**
See also CA 141; 93-96

Hildesheimer, Wolfgang
1916-1991 .... **CLC 49**
See also CA 101; 135; DLB 69, 124

Hill, Geoffrey (William)
1932-... **CLC 5, 8, 18, 45; DAM POET**
See also CA 81-84; CANR 21;
CDBLB 1960 to Present; DLB 40;
MTCW

Hill, George Roy 1921-........... **CLC 26**
See also CA 110; 122

Hill, John
See Koontz, Dean R(ay)

Hill, Susan (Elizabeth)
1942-.. **CLC 4; DAB; DAM MST, NOV**
See also CA 33-36R; CANR 29; DLB 14,
139; MTCW

Hillerman, Tony
1925-............ **CLC 62; DAM POP**
See also AAYA 6; BEST 89:1; CA 29-32R;
CANR 21, 42; SATA 6

Hillesum, Etty 1914-1943 .... **TCLC 49**
See also CA 137

Hilliard, Noel (Harvey) 1929-...... **CLC 15**
See also CA 9-12R; CANR 7

Hillis, Rick 1956-................ **CLC 66**
See also CA 134

Hilton, James 1900-1954......... **TCLC 21**
See also CA 108; DLB 34, 77; SATA 34

Himes, Chester (Bomar)
1909-1984 .... **CLC 2, 4, 7, 18, 58; BLC;**
DAM MULT
See also BW 2; CA 25-28R; 114; CANR 22;
DLB 2, 76, 143; MTCW

Hinde, Thomas .... **CLC 6, 11**
See also Chitty, Thomas Willes

Hindin, Nathan
See Bloch, Robert (Albert)

Hine, (William) Daryl 1936-....... **CLC 15**
See also CA 1-4R; CAAS 15; CANR 1, 20;
DLB 60

Hinkson, Katharine Tynan
See Tynan, Katharine

Hinton, S(usan) E(loise)
1950- .... **CLC 30; DA; DAB; DAC;**
DAM MST, NOV
See also AAYA 2; CA 81-84; CANR 32;
CLR 3, 23; JRDA; MAICYA; MTCW;
SATA 19, 58

Hippius, Zinaida .... **TCLC 9**
See also Gippius, Zinaida (Nikolayevna)

Hiraoka, Kimitake 1925-1970
See Mishima, Yukio
See also CA 97-100; 29-32R; DAM DRAM;
MTCW

Hirsch, E(ric) D(onald), Jr. 1928-... **CLC 79**
See also CA 25-28R; CANR 27, 51;
DLB 67; INT CANR-27; MTCW

Hirsch, Edward 1950- .... **CLC 31, 50**
See also CA 104; CANR 20, 42; DLB 120

Hitchcock, Alfred (Joseph)
1899-1980 .... **CLC 16**
See also CA 97-100; SATA 27;
SATA-Obit 24

Hitler, Adolf 1889-1945.......... **TCLC 53**
See also CA 117; 147

Hoagland, Edward 1932-.......... **CLC 28**
See also CA 1-4R; CANR 2, 31; DLB 6;
SATA 51

Hoban, Russell (Conwell)
1925- . . . . CLC 7, 25; DAM NOV
See also CA 5-8R; CANR 23, 37; CLR 3;
DLB 52; MAICYA; MTCW; SATA 1,
40, 78

Hobbs, Perry
See Blackmur, R(ichard) P(almer)

Hobson, Laura Z(ametkin)
1900-1986 . . . . CLC 7, 25
See also CA 17-20R; 118; DLB 28;
SATA 52

Hochhuth, Rolf
1931- . . . . . CLC 4, 11, 18; DAM DRAM
See also CA 5-8R; CANR 33; DLB 124;
MTCW

Hochman, Sandra 1936- . . . . CLC 3, 8
See also CA 5-8R; DLB 5

Hochwaelder, Fritz
1911-1986 . . . . . . CLC 36; DAM DRAM
See also CA 29-32R; 120; CANR 42;
MTCW

Hochwalder, Fritz
See Hochwaelder, Fritz

Hocking, Mary (Eunice) 1921- . . . . . CLC 13
See also CA 101; CANR 18, 40

Hodgins, Jack 1938- . . . . CLC 23
See also CA 93-96; DLB 60

Hodgson, William Hope
1877(?)-1918 . . . . TCLC 13
See also CA 111; DLB 70, 153, 156

Hoeg, Peter 1957- . . . . CLC 95
See also CA 151

Hoffman, Alice
1952- . . . . CLC 51; DAM NOV
See also CA 77-80; CANR 34; MTCW

Hoffman, Daniel (Gerard)
1923- . . . . CLC 6, 13, 23
See also CA 1-4R; CANR 4; DLB 5

Hoffman, Stanley 1944- . . . . CLC 5
See also CA 77-80

Hoffman, William M(oses) 1939- . . . CLC 40
See also CA 57-60; CANR 11

Hoffmann, E(rnst) T(heodor) A(madeus)
1776-1822 . . . . NCLC 2; SSC 13
See also DLB 90; SATA 27

Hofmann, Gert 1931- . . . . CLC 54
See also CA 128

Hofmannsthal, Hugo von
1874-1929 . . . . TCLC 11; DAM DRAM;
DC 4
See also CA 106; DLB 81, 118

Hogan, Linda
1947- . . . . CLC 73; DAM MULT
See also CA 120; CANR 45; NNAL

Hogarth, Charles
See Creasey, John

Hogarth, Emmett
See Polonsky, Abraham (Lincoln)

Hogg, James 1770-1835 . . . . NCLC 4
See also DLB 93, 116, 159

Holbach, Paul Henri Thiry Baron
1723-1789 . . . . LC 14

Holberg, Ludvig 1684-1754 . . . . LC 6

Holden, Ursula 1921- . . . . CLC 18
See also CA 101; CAAS 8; CANR 22

Holderlin, (Johann Christian) Friedrich
1770-1843 . . . . NCLC 16; PC 4

Holdstock, Robert
See Holdstock, Robert P.

Holdstock, Robert P. 1948- . . . . CLC 39
See also CA 131

Holland, Isabelle 1920- . . . . CLC 21
See also AAYA 11; CA 21-24R; CANR 10,
25, 47; JRDA; MAICYA; SATA 8, 70

Holland, Marcus
See Caldwell, (Janet Miriam) Taylor
(Holland)

Hollander, John 1929- . . . . . . CLC 2, 5, 8, 14
See also CA 1-4R; CANR 1, 52; DLB 5;
SATA 13

Hollander, Paul
See Silverberg, Robert

Holleran, Andrew 1943(?)- . . . . CLC 38
See also CA 144

Hollinghurst, Alan 1954- . . . . CLC 55, 91
See also CA 114

Hollis, Jim
See Summers, Hollis (Spurgeon, Jr.)

Holly, Buddy 1936-1959 . . . . TCLC 65

Holmes, John
See Souster, (Holmes) Raymond

Holmes, John Clellon 1926-1988. . . . CLC 56
See also CA 9-12R; 125; CANR 4; DLB 16

Holmes, Oliver Wendell
1809-1894 . . . . NCLC 14
See also CDALB 1640-1865; DLB 1;
SATA 34

Holmes, Raymond
See Souster, (Holmes) Raymond

Holt, Victoria
See Hibbert, Eleanor Alice Burford

Holub, Miroslav 1923- . . . . CLC 4
See also CA 21-24R; CANR 10

Homer
c. 8th cent. B.C.- . . . . . CMLC 1, 16; DA;
DAB; DAC; DAM MST, POET

Honig, Edwin 1919- . . . . CLC 33
See also CA 5-8R; CAAS 8; CANR 4, 45;
DLB 5

Hood, Hugh (John Blagdon)
1928- . . . . CLC 15, 28
See also CA 49-52; CAAS 17; CANR 1, 33;
DLB 53

Hood, Thomas 1799-1845. . . . . NCLC 16
See also DLB 96

Hooker, (Peter) Jeremy 1941- . . . . . . CLC 43
See also CA 77-80; CANR 22; DLB 40

hooks, bell . . . . CLC 94
See also Watkins, Gloria

Hope, A(lec) D(erwent) 1907- . . . . CLC 3, 51
See also CA 21-24R; CANR 33; MTCW

Hope, Brian
See Creasey, John

Hope, Christopher (David Tully)
1944- . . . . CLC 52
See also CA 106; CANR 47; SATA 62

Hopkins, Gerard Manley
1844-1889 . . . . NCLC 17; DA; DAB;
DAC; DAM MST, POET; PC 15; WLC
See also CDBLB 1890-1914; DLB 35, 57

Hopkins, John (Richard) 1931- . . . . . . CLC 4
See also CA 85-88

Hopkins, Pauline Elizabeth
1859-1930 . . . . TCLC 28; BLC;
DAM MULT
See also BW 2; CA 141; DLB 50

Hopkinson, Francis 1737-1791 . . . . . . LC 25
See also DLB 31

Hopley-Woolrich, Cornell George 1903-1968
See Woolrich, Cornell
See also CA 13-14; CAP 1

Horatio
See Proust, (Valentin-Louis-George-Eugene-)
Marcel

Horgan, Paul (George Vincent O'Shaughnessy)
1903-1995 . . . . . . CLC 9, 53; DAM NOV
See also CA 13-16R; 147; CANR 9, 35;
DLB 102; DLBY 85; INT CANR-9;
MTCW; SATA 13; SATA-Obit 84

Horn, Peter
See Kuttner, Henry

Hornem, Horace Esq.
See Byron, George Gordon (Noel)

Hornung, E(rnest) W(illiam)
1866-1921 . . . . TCLC 59
See also CA 108; DLB 70

Horovitz, Israel (Arthur)
1939- . . . . CLC 56; DAM DRAM
See also CA 33-36R; CANR 46; DLB 7

Horvath, Odon von
See Horvath, Oedoen von
See also DLB 85, 124

Horvath, Oedoen von 1901-1938. . . TCLC 45
See also Horvath, Odon von
See also CA 118

Horwitz, Julius 1920-1986. . . . . CLC 14
See also CA 9-12R; 119; CANR 12

Hospital, Janette Turner 1942- . . . . . CLC 42
See also CA 108; CANR 48

Hostos, E. M. de
See Hostos (y Bonilla), Eugenio Maria de

Hostos, Eugenio M. de
See Hostos (y Bonilla), Eugenio Maria de

Hostos, Eugenio Maria
See Hostos (y Bonilla), Eugenio Maria de

Hostos (y Bonilla), Eugenio Maria de
1839-1903 . . . . TCLC 24
See also CA 123; 131; HW

Houdini
See Lovecraft, H(oward) P(hillips)

Hougan, Carolyn 1943- . . . . CLC 34
See also CA 139

Household, Geoffrey (Edward West)
1900-1988 . . . . CLC 11
See also CA 77-80; 126; DLB 87; SATA 14;
SATA-Obit 59

Housman, A(lfred) E(dward)
1859-1936 . . . . . . TCLC 1, 10; DA; DAB;
DAC; DAM MST, POET; PC 2
See also CA 104; 125; DLB 19; MTCW

Housman, Laurence 1865-1959 ..... **TCLC 7**
See also CA 106; DLB 10; SATA 25

Howard, Elizabeth Jane 1923- ... **CLC 7, 29**
See also CA 5-8R; CANR 8

Howard, Maureen 1930- ..... **CLC 5, 14, 46**
See also CA 53-56; CANR 31; DLBY 83;
INT CANR-31; MTCW

Howard, Richard 1929- ...... **CLC 7, 10, 47**
See also AITN 1; CA 85-88; CANR 25;
DLB 5; INT CANR-25

Howard, Robert Ervin 1906-1936 ... **TCLC 8**
See also CA 105

Howard, Warren F.
See Pohl, Frederik

Howe, Fanny 1940- .... **CLC 47**
See also CA 117; SATA-Brief 52

Howe, Irving 1920-1993 .... **CLC 85**
See also CA 9-12R; 141; CANR 21, 50;
DLB 67; MTCW

Howe, Julia Ward 1819-1910 ..... **TCLC 21**
See also CA 117; DLB 1

Howe, Susan 1937- .... **CLC 72**
See also DLB 120

Howe, Tina 1937- .... **CLC 48**
See also CA 109

Howell, James 1594(?)-1666 .... **LC 13**
See also DLB 151

Howells, W. D.
See Howells, William Dean

Howells, William D.
See Howells, William Dean

Howells, William Dean
1837-1920 .... **TCLC 7, 17, 41**
See also CA 104; 134; CDALB 1865-1917;
DLB 12, 64, 74, 79

Howes, Barbara 1914-1996 .... **CLC 15**
See also CA 9-12R; 151; CAAS 3;
CANR 53; SATA 5

Hrabal, Bohumil 1914- .... **CLC 13, 67**
See also CA 106; CAAS 12

Hsun, Lu
See Lu Hsun

Hubbard, L(afayette) Ron(ald)
1911-1986 .... **CLC 43; DAM POP**
See also CA 77-80; 118; CANR 52

Huch, Ricarda (Octavia)
1864-1947 .... **TCLC 13**
See also CA 111; DLB 66

Huddle, David 1942- .... **CLC 49**
See also CA 57-60; CAAS 20; DLB 130

Hudson, Jeffrey
See Crichton, (John) Michael

Hudson, W(illiam) H(enry)
1841-1922 .... **TCLC 29**
See also CA 115; DLB 98, 153; SATA 35

Hueffer, Ford Madox
See Ford, Ford Madox

Hughart, Barry 1934- .... **CLC 39**
See also CA 137

Hughes, Colin
See Creasey, John

Hughes, David (John) 1930- .... **CLC 48**
See also CA 116; 129; DLB 14

Hughes, Edward James
See Hughes, Ted
See also DAM MST, POET

Hughes, (James) Langston
1902-1967 ..... **CLC 1, 5, 10, 15, 35, 44;**
BLC; DA; DAB; DAC; DAM DRAM,
MST, MULT, POET; DC 3; PC 1;
SSC 6; WLC
See also AAYA 12; BW 1; CA 1-4R;
25-28R; CANR 1, 34; CDALB 1929-1941;
CLR 17; DLB 4, 7, 48, 51, 86; JRDA;
MAICYA; MTCW; SATA 4, 33

Hughes, Richard (Arthur Warren)
1900-1976 ...... **CLC 1, 11; DAM NOV**
See also CA 5-8R; 65-68; CANR 4;
DLB 15, 161; MTCW; SATA 8;
SATA-Obit 25

Hughes, Ted
1930- .... **CLC 2, 4, 9, 14, 37; DAB;**
DAC; PC 7
See also Hughes, Edward James
See also CA 1-4R; CANR 1, 33; CLR 3;
DLB 40, 161; MAICYA; MTCW;
SATA 49; SATA-Brief 27

Hugo, Richard F(ranklin)
1923-1982 .... **CLC 6, 18, 32;**
DAM POET
See also CA 49-52; 108; CANR 3; DLB 5

Hugo, Victor (Marie)
1802-1885 .... **NCLC 3, 10, 21; DA;**
DAB; DAC; DAM DRAM, MST, NOV,
POET; WLC
See also DLB 119; SATA 47

Huidobro, Vicente
See Huidobro Fernandez, Vicente Garcia

Huidobro Fernandez, Vicente Garcia
1893-1948 .... **TCLC 31**
See also CA 131; HW

Hulme, Keri 1947- .... **CLC 39**
See also CA 125; INT 125

Hulme, T(homas) E(rnest)
1883-1917 .... **TCLC 21**
See also CA 117; DLB 19

Hume, David 1711-1776 .... **LC 7**
See also DLB 104

Humphrey, William 1924- .... **CLC 45**
See also CA 77-80; DLB 6

Humphreys, Emyr Owen 1919- ..... **CLC 47**
See also CA 5-8R; CANR 3, 24; DLB 15

Humphreys, Josephine 1945- .... **CLC 34, 57**
See also CA 121; 127; INT 127

Huneker, James Gibbons
1857-1921 .... **TCLC 65**
See also DLB 71

Hungerford, Pixie
See Brinsmead, H(esba) F(ay)

Hunt, E(verette) Howard, (Jr.)
1918- .... **CLC 3**
See also AITN 1; CA 45-48; CANR 2, 47

Hunt, Kyle
See Creasey, John

Hunt, (James Henry) Leigh
1784-1859 ...... **NCLC 1; DAM POET**

Hunt, Marsha 1946- .... **CLC 70**
See also BW 2; CA 143

Hunt, Violet 1866-1942 .... **TCLC 53**
See also DLB 162

Hunter, E. Waldo
See Sturgeon, Theodore (Hamilton)

Hunter, Evan
1926- .... **CLC 11, 31; DAM POP**
See also CA 5-8R; CANR 5, 38; DLBY 82;
INT CANR-5; MTCW; SATA 25

Hunter, Kristin (Eggleston) 1931- ... **CLC 35**
See also AITN 1; BW 1; CA 13-16R;
CANR 13; CLR 3; DLB 33;
INT CANR-13; MAICYA; SAAS 10;
SATA 12

Hunter, Mollie 1922- .... **CLC 21**
See also McIlwraith, Maureen Mollie
Hunter
See also AAYA 13; CANR 37; CLR 25;
DLB 161; JRDA; MAICYA; SAAS 7;
SATA 54

Hunter, Robert (?)-1734............. **LC 7**

Hurston, Zora Neale
1903-1960 .... **CLC 7, 30, 61; BLC; DA;**
DAC; DAM MST, MULT, NOV; SSC 4
See also AAYA 15; BW 1; CA 85-88;
DLB 51, 86; MTCW

Huston, John (Marcellus)
1906-1987 .... **CLC 20**
See also CA 73-76; 123; CANR 34; DLB 26

Hustvedt, Siri 1955- .... **CLC 76**
See also CA 137

Hutten, Ulrich von 1488-1523....... **LC 16**

Huxley, Aldous (Leonard)
1894-1963 ..... **CLC 1, 3, 4, 5, 8, 11, 18,**
35, 79; DA; DAB; DAC; DAM MST,
NOV; WLC
See also AAYA 11; CA 85-88; CANR 44;
CDBLB 1914-1945; DLB 36, 100, 162;
MTCW; SATA 63

Huysmans, Charles Marie Georges
1848-1907
See Huysmans, Joris-Karl
See also CA 104

Huysmans, Joris-Karl.............. **TCLC 7**
See also Huysmans, Charles Marie Georges
See also DLB 123

Hwang, David Henry
1957- .... **CLC 55; DAM DRAM; DC 4**
See also CA 127; 132; INT 132

Hyde, Anthony 1946-.............. **CLC 42**
See also CA 136

Hyde, Margaret O(ldroyd) 1917- ... **CLC 21**
See also CA 1-4R; CANR 1, 36; CLR 23;
JRDA; MAICYA; SAAS 8; SATA 1, 42,
76

Hynes, James 1956(?)-............. **CLC 65**

Ian, Janis 1951- .... **CLC 21**
See also CA 105

Ibanez, Vicente Blasco
See Blasco Ibanez, Vicente

Ibarguengoitia, Jorge 1928-1983 .... **CLC 37**
See also CA 124; 113; HW

Ibsen, Henrik (Johan)
1828-1906 .... **TCLC 2, 8, 16, 37, 52;**
DA; DAB; DAC; DAM DRAM, MST;
DC 2; WLC
See also CA 104; 141

Jean Paul   1763-1825 .... NCLC 7

Jefferies, (John) Richard
      1848-1887 .... NCLC 47
   See also DLB 98, 141; SATA 16

Jeffers, (John) Robinson
      1887-1962 .... CLC 2, 3, 11, 15, 54; DA;
                  DAC; DAM MST, POET; WLC
   See also CA 85-88; CANR 35;
      CDALB 1917-1929; DLB 45; MTCW

Jefferson, Janet
   See Mencken, H(enry) L(ouis)

Jefferson, Thomas   1743-1826 .... NCLC 11
   See also CDALB 1640-1865; DLB 31

Jeffrey, Francis   1773-1850........ NCLC 33
   See also DLB 107

Jelakowitch, Ivan
   See Heijermans, Herman

Jellicoe, (Patricia) Ann   1927-...... CLC 27
   See also CA 85-88; DLB 13

Jen, Gish .... CLC 70
   See also Jen, Lillian

Jen, Lillian   1956(?)-
   See Jen, Gish
   See also CA 135

Jenkins, (John) Robin   1912-....... CLC 52
   See also CA 1-4R; CANR 1; DLB 14

Jennings, Elizabeth (Joan)
      1926- .... CLC 5, 14
   See also CA 61-64; CAAS 5; CANR 8, 39;
      DLB 27; MTCW; SATA 66

Jennings, Waylon   1937-........... CLC 21

Jensen, Johannes V.   1873-1950.... TCLC 41

Jensen, Laura (Linnea)   1948-...... CLC 37
   See also CA 103

Jerome, Jerome K(lapka)
      1859-1927 .... TCLC 23
   See also CA 119; DLB 10, 34, 135

Jerrold, Douglas William
      1803-1857 .... NCLC 2
   See also DLB 158, 159

Jewett, (Theodora) Sarah Orne
      1849-1909 .... TCLC 1, 22; SSC 6
   See also CA 108; 127; DLB 12, 74;
      SATA 15

Jewsbury, Geraldine (Endsor)
      1812-1880 .... NCLC 22
   See also DLB 21

Jhabvala, Ruth Prawer
      1927- .... CLC 4, 8, 29, 94; DAB;
                                DAM NOV
   See also CA 1-4R; CANR 2, 29, 51;
      DLB 139; INT CANR-29; MTCW

Jibran, Kahlil
   See Gibran, Kahlil

Jibran, Khalil
   See Gibran, Kahlil

Jiles, Paulette   1943-........... CLC 13, 58
   See also CA 101

Jimenez (Mantecon), Juan Ramon
      1881-1958 ..... TCLC 4; DAM MULT,
                            POET; HLC; PC 7
   See also CA 104; 131; DLB 134; HW;
      MTCW

Jimenez, Ramon
   See Jimenez (Mantecon), Juan Ramon

Jimenez Mantecon, Juan
   See Jimenez (Mantecon), Juan Ramon

Joel, Billy .... CLC 26
   See also Joel, William Martin

Joel, William Martin   1949-
   See Joel, Billy
   See also CA 108

John of the Cross, St.   1542-1591 .... LC 18

Johnson, B(ryan) S(tanley William)
      1933-1973 .... CLC 6, 9
   See also CA 9-12R; 53-56; CANR 9;
      DLB 14, 40

Johnson, Benj. F. of Boo
   See Riley, James Whitcomb

Johnson, Benjamin F. of Boo
   See Riley, James Whitcomb

Johnson, Charles (Richard)
      1948- .... CLC 7, 51, 65; BLC;
                                DAM MULT
   See also BW 2; CA 116; CAAS 18;
      CANR 42; DLB 33

Johnson, Denis   1949-............. CLC 52
   See also CA 117; 121; DLB 120

Johnson, Diane   1934-........ CLC 5, 13, 48
   See also CA 41-44R; CANR 17, 40;
      DLBY 80; INT CANR-17; MTCW

Johnson, Eyvind (Olof Verner)
      1900-1976 .... CLC 14
   See also CA 73-76; 69-72; CANR 34

Johnson, J. R.
   See James, C(yril) L(ionel) R(obert)

Johnson, James Weldon
      1871-1938 .... TCLC 3, 19; BLC;
                            DAM MULT, POET
   See also BW 1; CA 104; 125;
      CDALB 1917-1929; CLR 32; DLB 51;
      MTCW; SATA 31

Johnson, Joyce   1935-............. CLC 58
   See also CA 125; 129

Johnson, Lionel (Pigot)
      1867-1902 .... TCLC 19
   See also CA 117; DLB 19

Johnson, Mel
   See Malzberg, Barry N(athaniel)

Johnson, Pamela Hansford
      1912-1981 .... CLC 1, 7, 27
   See also CA 1-4R; 104; CANR 2, 28;
      DLB 15; MTCW

Johnson, Samuel
      1709-1784 ..... LC 15; DA; DAB; DAC;
                            DAM MST; WLC
   See also CDBLB 1660-1789; DLB 39, 95,
      104, 142

Johnson, Uwe
      1934-1984 .... CLC 5, 10, 15, 40
   See also CA 1-4R; 112; CANR 1, 39;
      DLB 75; MTCW

Johnston, George (Benson)   1913-... CLC 51
   See also CA 1-4R; CANR 5, 20; DLB 88

Johnston, Jennifer   1930-........... CLC 7
   See also CA 85-88; DLB 14

Jolley, (Monica) Elizabeth
      1923- .... CLC 46; SSC 19
   See also CA 127; CAAS 13

Jones, Arthur Llewellyn   1863-1947
   See Machen, Arthur
   See also CA 104

Jones, D(ouglas) G(ordon)   1929-.... CLC 10
   See also CA 29-32R; CANR 13; DLB 53

Jones, David (Michael)
      1895-1974 .... CLC 2, 4, 7, 13, 42
   See also CA 9-12R; 53-56; CANR 28;
      CDBLB 1945-1960; DLB 20, 100; MTCW

Jones, David Robert   1947-
   See Bowie, David
   See also CA 103

Jones, Diana Wynne   1934-........ CLC 26
   See also AAYA 12; CA 49-52; CANR 4,
      26; CLR 23; DLB 161; JRDA; MAICYA;
      SAAS 7; SATA 9, 70

Jones, Edward P.   1950-........... CLC 76
   See also BW 2; CA 142

Jones, Gayl
      1949- .... CLC 6, 9; BLC; DAM MULT
   See also BW 2; CA 77-80; CANR 27;
      DLB 33; MTCW

Jones, James   1921-1977.... CLC 1, 3, 10, 39
   See also AITN 1, 2; CA 1-4R; 69-72;
      CANR 6; DLB 2, 143; MTCW

Jones, John J.
   See Lovecraft, H(oward) P(hillips)

Jones, LeRoi .... CLC 1, 2, 3, 5, 10, 14
   See also Baraka, Amiri

Jones, Louis B. .... CLC 65
   See also CA 141

Jones, Madison (Percy, Jr.)   1925-... CLC 4
   See also CA 13-16R; CAAS 11; CANR 7;
      DLB 152

Jones, Mervyn   1922-.......... CLC 10, 52
   See also CA 45-48; CAAS 5; CANR 1;
      MTCW

Jones, Mick   1956(?)-............. CLC 30

Jones, Nettie (Pearl)   1941-........ CLC 34
   See also BW 2; CA 137; CAAS 20

Jones, Preston   1936-1979 .... CLC 10
   See also CA 73-76; 89-92; DLB 7

Jones, Robert F(rancis)   1934-....... CLC 7
   See also CA 49-52; CANR 2

Jones, Rod   1953-................. CLC 50
   See also CA 128

Jones, Terence Graham Parry
      1942- .... CLC 21
   See also Jones, Terry; Monty Python
   See also CA 112; 116; CANR 35; INT 116

Jones, Terry
   See Jones, Terence Graham Parry
   See also SATA 67; SATA-Brief 51

Jones, Thom   1945(?)-............. CLC 81

Jong, Erica
      1942-............ CLC 4, 6, 8, 18, 83;
                            DAM NOV, POP
   See also AITN 1; BEST 90:2; CA 73-76;
      CANR 26, 52; DLB 2, 5, 28, 152;
      INT CANR-26; MTCW

Jonson, Ben(jamin)
1572(?)-1637 ..... LC 6, 33; DA; DAB;
DAC; DAM DRAM, MST, POET;
DC 4; WLC
See also CDBLB Before 1660; DLB 62, 121

Jordan, June
1936- ..... CLC 5, 11, 23; DAM MULT,
POET
See also AAYA 2; BW 2; CA 33-36R;
CANR 25; CLR 10; DLB 38; MAICYA;
MTCW; SATA 4

Jordan, Pat(rick M.) 1941- .... CLC 37
See also CA 33-36R

Jorgensen, Ivar
See Ellison, Harlan (Jay)

Jorgenson, Ivar
See Silverberg, Robert

Josephus, Flavius c. 37-100 ..... CMLC 13

Josipovici, Gabriel 1940- .... CLC 6, 43
See also CA 37-40R; CAAS 8; CANR 47;
DLB 14

Joubert, Joseph 1754-1824 .... NCLC 9

Jouve, Pierre Jean 1887-1976 ..... CLC 47
See also CA 65-68

Joyce, James (Augustine Aloysius)
1882-1941 .... TCLC 3, 8, 16, 35, 52;
DA; DAB; DAC; DAM MST, NOV,
POET; SSC 3; WLC
See also CA 104; 126; CDBLB 1914-1945;
DLB 10, 19, 36, 162; MTCW

Jozsef, Attila 1905-1937 .... TCLC 22
See also CA 116

Juana Ines de la Cruz 1651(?)-1695 ... LC 5

Judd, Cyril
See Kornbluth, C(yril) M.; Pohl, Frederik

Julian of Norwich 1342(?)-1416(?) .... LC 6
See also DLB 146

Juniper, Alex
See Hospital, Janette Turner

Junius
See Luxemburg, Rosa

Just, Ward (Swift) 1935- .... CLC 4, 27
See also CA 25-28R; CANR 32;
INT CANR-32

Justice, Donald (Rodney)
1925- .... CLC 6, 19; DAM POET
See also CA 5-8R; CANR 26; DLBY 83;
INT CANR-26

Juvenal c. 55-c. 127 .... CMLC 8

Juvenis
See Bourne, Randolph S(illiman)

Kacew, Romain 1914-1980
See Gary, Romain
See also CA 108; 102

Kadare, Ismail 1936- .... CLC 52

Kadohata, Cynthia .... CLC 59
See also CA 140

Kafka, Franz
1883-1924 .... TCLC 2, 6, 13, 29, 47, 53;
DA; DAB; DAC; DAM MST, NOV;
SSC 5; WLC
See also CA 105; 126; DLB 81; MTCW

Kahanovitsch, Pinkhes
See Der Nister

Kahn, Roger 1927- .... CLC 30
See also CA 25-28R; CANR 44; SATA 37

Kain, Saul
See Sassoon, Siegfried (Lorraine)

Kaiser, Georg 1878-1945 .... TCLC 9
See also CA 106; DLB 124

Kaletski, Alexander 1946- .... CLC 39
See also CA 118; 143

Kalidasa fl. c. 400- .... CMLC 9

Kallman, Chester (Simon)
1921-1975 .... CLC 2
See also CA 45-48; 53-56; CANR 3

Kaminsky, Melvin 1926-
See Brooks, Mel
See also CA 65-68; CANR 16

Kaminsky, Stuart M(elvin) 1934- ... CLC 59
See also CA 73-76; CANR 29, 53

Kane, Paul
See Simon, Paul

Kane, Wilson
See Bloch, Robert (Albert)

Kanin, Garson 1912- .... CLC 22
See also AITN 1; CA 5-8R; CANR 7;
DLB 7

Kaniuk, Yoram 1930- .... CLC 19
See also CA 134

Kant, Immanuel 1724-1804 ...... NCLC 27
See also DLB 94

Kantor, MacKinlay 1904-1977 ...... CLC 7
See also CA 61-64; 73-76; DLB 9, 102

Kaplan, David Michael 1946- ...... CLC 50

Kaplan, James 1951- .... CLC 59
See also CA 135

Karageorge, Michael
See Anderson, Poul (William)

Karamzin, Nikolai Mikhailovich
1766-1826 .... NCLC 3
See also DLB 150

Karapanou, Margarita 1946- .... CLC 13
See also CA 101

Karinthy, Frigyes 1887-1938 ...... TCLC 47

Karl, Frederick R(obert) 1927- ..... CLC 34
See also CA 5-8R; CANR 3, 44

Kastel, Warren
See Silverberg, Robert

Kataev, Evgeny Petrovich 1903-1942
See Petrov, Evgeny
See also CA 120

Kataphusin
See Ruskin, John

Katz, Steve 1935- .... CLC 47
See also CA 25-28R; CAAS 14; CANR 12;
DLBY 83

Kauffman, Janet 1945- .... CLC 42
See also CA 117; CANR 43; DLBY 86

Kaufman, Bob (Garnell)
1925-1986 .... CLC 49
See also BW 1; CA 41-44R; 118; CANR 22;
DLB 16, 41

Kaufman, George S.
1889-1961 ...... CLC 38; DAM DRAM
See also CA 108; 93-96; DLB 7; INT 108

Kaufman, Sue .... CLC 3, 8
See also Barondess, Sue K(aufman)

Kavafis, Konstantinos Petrou 1863-1933
See Cavafy, C(onstantine) P(eter)
See also CA 104

Kavan, Anna 1901-1968 ...... CLC 5, 13, 82
See also CA 5-8R; CANR 6; MTCW

Kavanagh, Dan
See Barnes, Julian

Kavanagh, Patrick (Joseph)
1904-1967 .... CLC 22
See also CA 123; 25-28R; DLB 15, 20;
MTCW

Kawabata, Yasunari
1899-1972 .... CLC 2, 5, 9, 18;
DAM MULT; SSC 17
See also CA 93-96; 33-36R

Kaye, M(ary) M(argaret) 1909- ..... CLC 28
See also CA 89-92; CANR 24; MTCW;
SATA 62

Kaye, Mollie
See Kaye, M(ary) M(argaret)

Kaye-Smith, Sheila 1887-1956 ..... TCLC 20
See also CA 118; DLB 36

Kaymor, Patrice Maguilene
See Senghor, Leopold Sedar

Kazan, Elia 1909- .... CLC 6, 16, 63
See also CA 21-24R; CANR 32

Kazantzakis, Nikos
1883(?)-1957 .... TCLC 2, 5, 33
See also CA 105; 132; MTCW

Kazin, Alfred 1915- .... CLC 34, 38
See also CA 1-4R; CAAS 7; CANR 1, 45;
DLB 67

Keane, Mary Nesta (Skrine) 1904-1996
See Keane, Molly
See also CA 108; 114; 151

Keane, Molly .... CLC 31
See also Keane, Mary Nesta (Skrine)
See also INT 114

Keates, Jonathan 19(?)- .... CLC 34

Keaton, Buster 1895-1966 .... CLC 20

Keats, John
1795-1821 .... NCLC 8; DA; DAB;
DAC; DAM MST, POET; PC 1; WLC
See also CDBLB 1789-1832; DLB 96, 110

Keene, Donald 1922- .... CLC 34
See also CA 1-4R; CANR 5

Keillor, Garrison .... CLC 40
See also Keillor, Gary (Edward)
See also AAYA 2; BEST 89:3; DLBY 87;
SATA 58

Keillor, Gary (Edward) 1942-
See Keillor, Garrison
See also CA 111; 117; CANR 36;
DAM POP; MTCW

Keith, Michael
See Hubbard, L(afayette) Ron(ald)

Keller, Gottfried 1819-1890 .... NCLC 2
See also DLB 129

Kellerman, Jonathan
1949- .... CLC 44; DAM POP
See also BEST 90:1; CA 106; CANR 29, 51;
INT CANR-29

Kelley, William Melvin 1937- . . . . . . CLC 22
See also BW 1; CA 77-80; CANR 27;
DLB 33

Kellogg, Marjorie 1922- . . . . CLC 2
See also CA 81-84

Kellow, Kathleen
See Hibbert, Eleanor Alice Burford

Kelly, M(ilton) T(erry) 1947- . . . . CLC 55
See also CA 97-100; CAAS 22; CANR 19,
43

Kelman, James 1946- . . . . CLC 58, 86
See also CA 148

Kemal, Yashar 1923- . . . . CLC 14, 29
See also CA 89-92; CANR 44

Kemble, Fanny 1809-1893 . . . . NCLC 18
See also DLB 32

Kemelman, Harry 1908- . . . . CLC 2
See also AITN 1; CA 9-12R; CANR 6;
DLB 28

Kempe, Margery 1373(?)-1440(?) . . . . . LC 6
See also DLB 146

Kempis, Thomas a 1380-1471 . . . . LC 11

Kendall, Henry 1839-1882 . . . . NCLC 12

Keneally, Thomas (Michael)
1935- . . . . . . CLC 5, 8, 10, 14, 19, 27, 43;
DAM NOV
See also CA 85-88; CANR 10, 50; MTCW

Kennedy, Adrienne (Lita)
1931- . . . . . CLC 66; BLC; DAM MULT;
DC 5
See also BW 2; CA 103; CAAS 20; CABS 3;
CANR 26, 53; DLB 38

Kennedy, John Pendleton
1795-1870 . . . . NCLC 2
See also DLB 3

Kennedy, Joseph Charles 1929-
See Kennedy, X. J.
See also CA 1-4R; CANR 4, 30, 40;
SATA 14, 86

Kennedy, William
1928- . . . CLC 6, 28, 34, 53; DAM NOV
See also AAYA 1; CA 85-88; CANR 14,
31; DLB 143; DLBY 85; INT CANR-31;
MTCW; SATA 57

Kennedy, X. J. . . . . CLC 8, 42
See also Kennedy, Joseph Charles
See also CAAS 9; CLR 27; DLB 5;
SAAS 22

Kenny, Maurice (Francis)
1929- . . . . CLC 87; DAM MULT
See also CA 144; CAAS 22; NNAL

Kent, Kelvin
See Kuttner, Henry

Kenton, Maxwell
See Southern, Terry

Kenyon, Robert O.
See Kuttner, Henry

Kerouac, Jack . . . . . CLC 1, 2, 3, 5, 14, 29, 61
See also Kerouac, Jean-Louis Lebris de
See also CDALB 1941-1968; DLB 2, 16;
DLBD 3; DLBY 95

Kerouac, Jean-Louis Lebris de 1922-1969
See Kerouac, Jack
See also AITN 1; CA 5-8R; 25-28R;
CANR 26; DA; DAB; DAC; DAM MST,
NOV, POET, POP; MTCW; WLC

Kerr, Jean 1923- . . . . CLC 22
See also CA 5-8R; CANR 7; INT CANR-7

Kerr, M. E. . . . . CLC 12, 35
See also Meaker, Marijane (Agnes)
See also AAYA 2; CLR 29; SAAS 1

Kerr, Robert . . . . CLC 55

Kerrigan, (Thomas) Anthony
1918- . . . . CLC 4, 6
See also CA 49-52; CAAS 11; CANR 4

Kerry, Lois
See Duncan, Lois

Kesey, Ken (Elton)
1935- . . . . . . CLC 1, 3, 6, 11, 46, 64; DA;
DAB; DAC; DAM MST, NOV, POP;
WLC
See also CA 1-4R; CANR 22, 38;
CDALB 1968-1988; DLB 2, 16; MTCW;
SATA 66

Kesselring, Joseph (Otto)
1902-1967 . . . . . CLC 45; DAM DRAM,
MST
See also CA 150

Kessler, Jascha (Frederick) 1929- . . . . CLC 4
See also CA 17-20R; CANR 8, 48

Kettelkamp, Larry (Dale) 1933- . . . . CLC 12
See also CA 29-32R; CANR 16; SAAS 3;
SATA 2

Key, Ellen 1849-1926 . . . . TCLC 65

Keyber, Conny
See Fielding, Henry

Keyes, Daniel
1927- . . . . CLC 80; DA; DAC;
DAM MST, NOV
See also CA 17-20R; CANR 10, 26;
SATA 37

Keynes, John Maynard
1883-1946 . . . . TCLC 64
See also CA 114; DLBD 10

Khanshendel, Chiron
See Rose, Wendy

Khayyam, Omar
1048-1131 . . . . CMLC 11; DAM POET;
PC 8

Kherdian, David 1931- . . . . CLC 6, 9
See also CA 21-24R; CAAS 2; CANR 39;
CLR 24; JRDA; MAICYA; SATA 16, 74

Khlebnikov, Velimir . . . . TCLC 20
See also Khlebnikov, Viktor Vladimirovich

Khlebnikov, Viktor Vladimirovich 1885-1922
See Khlebnikov, Velimir
See also CA 117

Khodasevich, Vladislav (Felitsianovich)
1886-1939 . . . . TCLC 15
See also CA 115

Kielland, Alexander Lange
1849-1906 . . . . TCLC 5
See also CA 104

Kiely, Benedict 1919- . . . . CLC 23, 43
See also CA 1-4R; CANR 2; DLB 15

Kienzle, William X(avier)
1928- . . . . CLC 25; DAM POP
See also CA 93-96; CAAS 1; CANR 9, 31;
INT CANR-31; MTCW

Kierkegaard, Soren 1813-1855 . . . . NCLC 34

Killens, John Oliver 1916-1987 . . . . . CLC 10
See also BW 2; CA 77-80; 123; CAAS 2;
CANR 26; DLB 33

Killigrew, Anne 1660-1685 . . . . LC 4
See also DLB 131

Kim
See Simenon, Georges (Jacques Christian)

Kincaid, Jamaica
1949- . . . . CLC 43, 68; BLC;
DAM MULT, NOV
See also AAYA 13; BW 2; CA 125;
CANR 47; DLB 157

King, Francis (Henry)
1923- . . . . CLC 8, 53; DAM NOV
See also CA 1-4R; CANR 1, 33; DLB 15,
139; MTCW

King, Martin Luther, Jr.
1929-1968 . . . . CLC 83; BLC; DA; DAB;
DAC; DAM MST, MULT
See also BW 2; CA 25-28; CANR 27, 44;
CAP 2; MTCW; SATA 14

King, Stephen (Edwin)
1947- . . . . CLC 12, 26, 37, 61;
DAM NOV, POP; SSC 17
See also AAYA 1, 17; BEST 90:1;
CA 61-64; CANR 1, 30, 52; DLB 143;
DLBY 80; JRDA; MTCW; SATA 9, 55

King, Steve
See King, Stephen (Edwin)

King, Thomas
1943- . . . . . CLC 89; DAC; DAM MULT
See also CA 144; NNAL

Kingman, Lee . . . . CLC 17
See also Natti, (Mary) Lee
See also SAAS 3; SATA 1, 67

Kingsley, Charles 1819-1875 . . . . . NCLC 35
See also DLB 21, 32, 163; YABC 2

Kingsley, Sidney 1906-1995 . . . . CLC 44
See also CA 85-88; 147; DLB 7

Kingsolver, Barbara
1955- . . . . CLC 55, 81; DAM POP
See also AAYA 15; CA 129; 134; INT 134

Kingston, Maxine (Ting Ting) Hong
1940- . . . . CLC 12, 19, 58; DAM MULT,
NOV
See also AAYA 8; CA 69-72; CANR 13,
38; DLBY 80; INT CANR-13; MTCW;
SATA 53

Kinnell, Galway
1927- . . . . CLC 1, 2, 3, 5, 13, 29
See also CA 9-12R; CANR 10, 34; DLB 5;
DLBY 87; INT CANR-34; MTCW

Kinsella, Thomas 1928- . . . . CLC 4, 19
See also CA 17-20R; CANR 15; DLB 27;
MTCW

Kinsella, W(illiam) P(atrick)
1935- . . . . CLC 27, 43; DAC;
DAM NOV, POP
See also AAYA 7; CA 97-100; CAAS 7;
CANR 21, 35; INT CANR-21; MTCW

Kipling, (Joseph) Rudyard
1865-1936 . . . . . . **TCLC 8, 17; DA; DAB; DAC; DAM MST, POET; PC 3; SSC 5; WLC**
See also CA 105; 120; CANR 33; CDBLB 1890-1914; CLR 39; DLB 19, 34, 141, 156; MAICYA; MTCW; YABC 2

Kirkup, James 1918- . . . . **CLC 1**
See also CA 1-4R; CAAS 4; CANR 2; DLB 27; SATA 12

Kirkwood, James 1930(?)-1989 . . . . . . **CLC 9**
See also AITN 2; CA 1-4R; 128; CANR 6, 40

Kirshner, Sidney
See Kingsley, Sidney

Kis, Danilo 1935-1989 . . . . **CLC 57**
See also CA 109; 118; 129; MTCW

Kivi, Aleksis 1834-1872 . . . . **NCLC 30**

Kizer, Carolyn (Ashley)
1925- . . . . . **CLC 15, 39, 80; DAM POET**
See also CA 65-68; CAAS 5; CANR 24; DLB 5, 169

Klabund 1890-1928 . . . . **TCLC 44**
See also DLB 66

Klappert, Peter 1942- . . . . **CLC 57**
See also CA 33-36R; DLB 5

Klein, A(braham) M(oses)
1909-1972 . . . . **CLC 19; DAB; DAC; DAM MST**
See also CA 101; 37-40R; DLB 68

Klein, Norma 1938-1989 . . . . **CLC 30**
See also AAYA 2; CA 41-44R; 128; CANR 15, 37; CLR 2, 19; INT CANR-15; JRDA; MAICYA; SAAS 1; SATA 7, 57

Klein, T(heodore) E(ibon) D(onald)
1947- . . . . **CLC 34**
See also CA 119; CANR 44

Kleist, Heinrich von
1777-1811 . . . . **NCLC 2, 37; DAM DRAM; SSC 22**
See also DLB 90

Klima, Ivan 1931- . . . . . **CLC 56; DAM NOV**
See also CA 25-28R; CANR 17, 50

Klimentov, Andrei Platonovich 1899-1951
See Platonov, Andrei
See also CA 108

Klinger, Friedrich Maximilian von
1752-1831 . . . . **NCLC 1**
See also DLB 94

Klopstock, Friedrich Gottlieb
1724-1803 . . . . **NCLC 11**
See also DLB 97

Knebel, Fletcher 1911-1993 . . . . **CLC 14**
See also AITN 1; CA 1-4R; 140; CAAS 3; CANR 1, 36; SATA 36; SATA-Obit 75

Knickerbocker, Diedrich
See Irving, Washington

Knight, Etheridge
1931-1991 . . . . **CLC 40; BLC; DAM POET; PC 14**
See also BW 1; CA 21-24R; 133; CANR 23; DLB 41

Knight, Sarah Kemble 1666-1727 . . . . . **LC 7**
See also DLB 24

Knister, Raymond 1899-1932 . . . . . **TCLC 56**
See also DLB 68

Knowles, John
1926- . . . . . . **CLC 1, 4, 10, 26; DA; DAC; DAM MST, NOV**
See also AAYA 10; CA 17-20R; CANR 40; CDALB 1968-1988; DLB 6; MTCW; SATA 8, 89

Knox, Calvin M.
See Silverberg, Robert

Knye, Cassandra
See Disch, Thomas M(ichael)

Koch, C(hristopher) J(ohn) 1932- . . . **CLC 42**
See also CA 127

Koch, Christopher
See Koch, C(hristopher) J(ohn)

Koch, Kenneth
1925- . . . . **CLC 5, 8, 44; DAM POET**
See also CA 1-4R; CANR 6, 36; DLB 5; INT CANR-36; SATA 65

Kochanowski, Jan 1530-1584 . . . . **LC 10**

Kock, Charles Paul de
1794-1871 . . . . **NCLC 16**

Koda Shigeyuki 1867-1947
See Rohan, Koda
See also CA 121

Koestler, Arthur
1905-1983 . . . . **CLC 1, 3, 6, 8, 15, 33**
See also CA 1-4R; 109; CANR 1, 33; CDBLB 1945-1960; DLBY 83; MTCW

Kogawa, Joy Nozomi
1935- . . . . . . **CLC 78; DAC; DAM MST, MULT**
See also CA 101; CANR 19

Kohout, Pavel 1928- . . . . **CLC 13**
See also CA 45-48; CANR 3

Koizumi, Yakumo
See Hearn, (Patricio) Lafcadio (Tessima Carlos)

Kolmar, Gertrud 1894-1943 . . . . . . **TCLC 40**

Komunyakaa, Yusef 1947- . . . . . . **CLC 86, 94**
See also CA 147; DLB 120

Konrad, George
See Konrad, Gyoergy

Konrad, Gyoergy 1933- . . . . . . **CLC 4, 10, 73**
See also CA 85-88

Konwicki, Tadeusz 1926- . . . . . **CLC 8, 28, 54**
See also CA 101; CAAS 9; CANR 39; MTCW

Koontz, Dean R(ay)
1945- . . . . . . **CLC 78; DAM NOV, POP**
See also AAYA 9; BEST 89:3, 90:2; CA 108; CANR 19, 36, 52; MTCW

Kopit, Arthur (Lee)
1937- . . . . . **CLC 1, 18, 33; DAM DRAM**
See also AITN 1; CA 81-84; CABS 3; DLB 7; MTCW

Kops, Bernard 1926- . . . . **CLC 4**
See also CA 5-8R; DLB 13

Kornbluth, C(yril) M. 1923-1958 . . . . **TCLC 8**
See also CA 105; DLB 8

Korolenko, V. G.
See Korolenko, Vladimir Galaktionovich

Korolenko, Vladimir
See Korolenko, Vladimir Galaktionovich

Korolenko, Vladimir G.
See Korolenko, Vladimir Galaktionovich

Korolenko, Vladimir Galaktionovich
1853-1921 . . . . **TCLC 22**
See also CA 121

Korzybski, Alfred (Habdank Skarbek)
1879-1950 . . . . **TCLC 61**
See also CA 123

Kosinski, Jerzy (Nikodem)
1933-1991 . . . . **CLC 1, 2, 3, 6, 10, 15, 53, 70; DAM NOV**
See also CA 17-20R; 134; CANR 9, 46; DLB 2; DLBY 82; MTCW

Kostelanetz, Richard (Cory) 1940- . . **CLC 28**
See also CA 13-16R; CAAS 8; CANR 38

Kostrowitzki, Wilhelm Apollinaris de
1880-1918
See Apollinaire, Guillaume
See also CA 104

Kotlowitz, Robert 1924- . . . . **CLC 4**
See also CA 33-36R; CANR 36

Kotzebue, August (Friedrich Ferdinand) von
1761-1819 . . . . **NCLC 25**
See also DLB 94

Kotzwinkle, William 1938- . . . **CLC 5, 14, 35**
See also CA 45-48; CANR 3, 44; CLR 6; MAICYA; SATA 24, 70

Kozol, Jonathan 1936- . . . . **CLC 17**
See also CA 61-64; CANR 16, 45

Kozoll, Michael 1940(?)- . . . . **CLC 35**

Kramer, Kathryn 19(?)- . . . . **CLC 34**

Kramer, Larry 1935- . . **CLC 42; DAM POP**
See also CA 124; 126

Krasicki, Ignacy 1735-1801 . . . . **NCLC 8**

Krasinski, Zygmunt 1812-1859 . . . . **NCLC 4**

Kraus, Karl 1874-1936 . . . . **TCLC 5**
See also CA 104; DLB 118

Kreve (Mickevicius), Vincas
1882-1954 . . . . **TCLC 27**

Kristeva, Julia 1941- . . . . **CLC 77**

Kristofferson, Kris 1936- . . . . **CLC 26**
See also CA 104

Krizanc, John 1956- . . . . **CLC 57**

Krleza, Miroslav 1893-1981 . . . . **CLC 8**
See also CA 97-100; 105; CANR 50; DLB 147

Kroetsch, Robert
1927- . . . . **CLC 5, 23, 57; DAC; DAM POET**
See also CA 17-20R; CANR 8, 38; DLB 53; MTCW

Kroetz, Franz
See Kroetz, Franz Xaver

Kroetz, Franz Xaver 1946- . . . . **CLC 41**
See also CA 130

Kroker, Arthur 1945- . . . . **CLC 77**

Kropotkin, Peter (Aleksieevich)
1842-1921 . . . . **TCLC 36**
See also CA 119

Krotkov, Yuri 1917- . . . . **CLC 19**
See also CA 102

Krumb
See Crumb, R(obert)

Krumgold, Joseph (Quincy)
1908-1980 .... **CLC 12**
See also CA 9-12R; 101; CANR 7;
MAICYA; SATA 1, 48; SATA-Obit 23

Krumwitz
See Crumb, R(obert)

Krutch, Joseph Wood 1893-1970.... **CLC 24**
See also CA 1-4R; 25-28R; CANR 4;
DLB 63

Krutzch, Gus
See Eliot, T(homas) S(tearns)

Krylov, Ivan Andreevich
1768(?)-1844 .... **NCLC 1**
See also DLB 150

Kubin, Alfred (Leopold Isidor)
1877-1959 .... **TCLC 23**
See also CA 112; 149; DLB 81

Kubrick, Stanley 1928-............ **CLC 16**
See also CA 81-84; CANR 33; DLB 26

Kumin, Maxine (Winokur)
1925- ..... **CLC 5, 13, 28; DAM POET;**
PC 15
See also AITN 2; CA 1-4R; CAAS 8;
CANR 1, 21; DLB 5; MTCW; SATA 12

Kundera, Milan
1929- .... **CLC 4, 9, 19, 32, 68;**
DAM NOV
See also AAYA 2; CA 85-88; CANR 19,
52; MTCW

Kunene, Mazisi (Raymond) 1930-... **CLC 85**
See also BW 1; CA 125; DLB 117

Kunitz, Stanley (Jasspon)
1905- .... **CLC 6, 11, 14**
See also CA 41-44R; CANR 26; DLB 48;
INT CANR-26; MTCW

Kunze, Reiner 1933-.............. **CLC 10**
See also CA 93-96; DLB 75

Kuprin, Aleksandr Ivanovich
1870-1938 .... **TCLC 5**
See also CA 104

Kureishi, Hanif 1954(?)-.......... **CLC 64**
See also CA 139

Kurosawa, Akira
1910- .... **CLC 16; DAM MULT**
See also AAYA 11; CA 101; CANR 46

Kushner, Tony
1957(?)- .... **CLC 81; DAM DRAM**
See also CA 144

Kuttner, Henry 1915-1958........ **TCLC 10**
See also CA 107; DLB 8

Kuzma, Greg 1944-............... **CLC 7**
See also CA 33-36R

Kuzmin, Mikhail 1872(?)-1936 .... **TCLC 40**

Kyd, Thomas
1558-1594 ...... **LC 22; DAM DRAM;**
DC 3
See also DLB 62

Kyprianos, Iossif
See Samarakis, Antonis

La Bruyere, Jean de 1645-1696...... **LC 17**

Lacan, Jacques (Marie Emile)
1901-1981 .... **CLC 75**
See also CA 121; 104

Laclos, Pierre Ambroise Francois Choderlos
de 1741-1803 .... **NCLC 4**

Lacolere, Francois
See Aragon, Louis

La Colere, Francois
See Aragon, Louis

La Deshabilleuse
See Simenon, Georges (Jacques Christian)

Lady Gregory
See Gregory, Isabella Augusta (Persse)

Lady of Quality, A
See Bagnold, Enid

La Fayette, Marie (Madelaine Pioche de la
Vergne Comtes 1634-1693...... **LC 2**

Lafayette, Rene
See Hubbard, L(afayette) Ron(ald)

Laforgue, Jules
1860-1887 .... **NCLC 5, 53; PC 14;**
SSC 20

Lagerkvist, Paer (Fabian)
1891-1974 .... **CLC 7, 10, 13, 54;**
DAM DRAM, NOV
See also Lagerkvist, Par
See also CA 85-88; 49-52; MTCW

Lagerkvist, Par .... **SSC 12**
See also Lagerkvist, Paer (Fabian)

Lagerloef, Selma (Ottiliana Lovisa)
1858-1940 .... **TCLC 4, 36**
See also Lagerlof, Selma (Ottiliana Lovisa)
See also CA 108; SATA 15

Lagerlof, Selma (Ottiliana Lovisa)
See Lagerloef, Selma (Ottiliana Lovisa)
See also CLR 7; SATA 15

La Guma, (Justin) Alex(ander)
1925-1985 .... **CLC 19; DAM NOV**
See also BW 1; CA 49-52; 118; CANR 25;
DLB 117; MTCW

Laidlaw, A. K.
See Grieve, C(hristopher) M(urray)

Lainez, Manuel Mujica
See Mujica Lainez, Manuel
See also HW

Laing, R(onald) D(avid)
1927-1989 .... **CLC 95**
See also CA 107; 129; CANR 34; MTCW

Lamartine, Alphonse (Marie Louis Prat) de
1790-1869 ..... **NCLC 11; DAM POET;**
PC 16

Lamb, Charles
1775-1834 .... **NCLC 10; DA; DAB;**
DAC; DAM MST; WLC
See also CDBLB 1789-1832; DLB 93, 107,
163; SATA 17

Lamb, Lady Caroline 1785-1828 .. **NCLC 38**
See also DLB 116

Lamming, George (William)
1927- .... **CLC 2, 4, 66; BLC;**
DAM MULT
See also BW 2; CA 85-88; CANR 26;
DLB 125; MTCW

L'Amour, Louis (Dearborn)
1908-1988 .... **CLC 25, 55; DAM NOV,**
POP
See also AAYA 16; AITN 2; BEST 89:2;
CA 1-4R; 125; CANR 3, 25, 40;
DLBY 80; MTCW

Lampedusa, Giuseppe (Tomasi) di ... **TCLC 13**
See also Tomasi di Lampedusa, Giuseppe

Lampman, Archibald 1861-1899 .. **NCLC 25**
See also DLB 92

Lancaster, Bruce 1896-1963........ **CLC 36**
See also CA 9-10; CAP 1; SATA 9

Landau, Mark Alexandrovich
See Aldanov, Mark (Alexandrovich)

Landau-Aldanov, Mark Alexandrovich
See Aldanov, Mark (Alexandrovich)

Landis, John 1950-............... **CLC 26**
See also CA 112; 122

Landolfi, Tommaso 1908-1979... **CLC 11, 49**
See also CA 127; 117

Landon, Letitia Elizabeth
1802-1838 .... **NCLC 15**
See also DLB 96

Landor, Walter Savage
1775-1864 .... **NCLC 14**
See also DLB 93, 107

Landwirth, Heinz 1927-
See Lind, Jakov
See also CA 9-12R; CANR 7

Lane, Patrick
1939- .... **CLC 25; DAM POET**
See also CA 97-100; DLB 53; INT 97-100

Lang, Andrew 1844-1912......... **TCLC 16**
See also CA 114; 137; DLB 98, 141;
MAICYA; SATA 16

Lang, Fritz 1890-1976 .... **CLC 20**
See also CA 77-80; 69-72; CANR 30

Lange, John
See Crichton, (John) Michael

Langer, Elinor 1939- .... **CLC 34**
See also CA 121

Langland, William
1330(?)-1400(?) ...... **LC 19; DA; DAB;**
DAC; DAM MST, POET
See also DLB 146

Langstaff, Launcelot
See Irving, Washington

Lanier, Sidney
1842-1881 ...... **NCLC 6; DAM POET**
See also DLB 64; DLBD 13; MAICYA;
SATA 18

Lanyer, Aemilia 1569-1645 ...... **LC 10, 30**
See also DLB 121

Lao Tzu .... **CMLC 7**

Lapine, James (Elliot) 1949-....... **CLC 39**
See also CA 123; 130; INT 130

Larbaud, Valery (Nicolas)
1881-1957 .... **TCLC 9**
See also CA 106; 152

Lardner, Ring
See Lardner, Ring(gold) W(ilmer)

Lardner, Ring W., Jr.
See Lardner, Ring(gold) W(ilmer)

Lee-Hamilton, Eugene (Jacob)
1845-1907 .... **TCLC 22**
See also CA 117

Leet, Judith 1935- .... **CLC 11**

Le Fanu, Joseph Sheridan
1814-1873 .... **NCLC 9; DAM POP;**
SSC 14
See also DLB 21, 70, 159

Leffland, Ella 1931- .... **CLC 19**
See also CA 29-32R; CANR 35; DLBY 84;
INT CANR-35; SATA 65

Leger, Alexis
See Leger, (Marie-Rene Auguste) Alexis
Saint-Leger

Leger, (Marie-Rene Auguste) Alexis
Saint-Leger
1887-1975 .... **CLC 11; DAM POET**
See also Perse, St.-John
See also CA 13-16R; 61-64; CANR 43;
MTCW

Leger, Saintleger
See Leger, (Marie-Rene Auguste) Alexis
Saint-Leger

Le Guin, Ursula K(roeber)
1929- ...... **CLC 8, 13, 22, 45, 71; DAB;**
DAC; DAM MST, POP; SSC 12
See also AAYA 9; AITN 1; CA 21-24R;
CANR 9, 32, 52; CDALB 1968-1988;
CLR 3, 28; DLB 8, 52; INT CANR-32;
JRDA; MAICYA; MTCW; SATA 4, 52

Lehmann, Rosamond (Nina)
1901-1990 .... **CLC 5**
See also CA 77-80; 131; CANR 8; DLB 15

Leiber, Fritz (Reuter, Jr.)
1910-1992 .... **CLC 25**
See also CA 45-48; 139; CANR 2, 40;
DLB 8; MTCW; SATA 45;
SATA-Obit 73

Leibniz, Gottfried Wilhelm von
1646-1716 .... **LC 35**
See also DLB 168

Leimbach, Martha 1963-
See Leimbach, Marti
See also CA 130

Leimbach, Marti .... **CLC 65**
See also Leimbach, Martha

Leino, Eino .... **TCLC 24**
See also Loennbohm, Armas Eino Leopold

Leiris, Michel (Julien) 1901-1990 ... **CLC 61**
See also CA 119; 128; 132

Leithauser, Brad 1953- .... **CLC 27**
See also CA 107; CANR 27; DLB 120

Lelchuk, Alan 1938- .... **CLC 5**
See also CA 45-48; CAAS 20; CANR 1

Lem, Stanislaw 1921- .... **CLC 8, 15, 40**
See also CA 105; CAAS 1; CANR 32;
MTCW

Lemann, Nancy 1956- .... **CLC 39**
See also CA 118; 136

Lemonnier, (Antoine Louis) Camille
1844-1913 .... **TCLC 22**
See also CA 121

Lenau, Nikolaus 1802-1850 ...... **NCLC 16**

L'Engle, Madeleine (Camp Franklin)
1918- .... **CLC 12; DAM POP**
See also AAYA 1; AITN 2; CA 1-4R;
CANR 3, 21, 39; CLR 1, 14; DLB 52;
JRDA; MAICYA; MTCW; SAAS 15;
SATA 1, 27, 75

Lengyel, Jozsef 1896-1975 .... **CLC 7**
See also CA 85-88; 57-60

Lennon, John (Ono)
1940-1980 .... **CLC 12, 35**
See also CA 102

Lennox, Charlotte Ramsay
1729(?)-1804 .... **NCLC 23**
See also DLB 39

Lentricchia, Frank (Jr.) 1940- ...... **CLC 34**
See also CA 25-28R; CANR 19

Lenz, Siegfried 1926- .... **CLC 27**
See also CA 89-92; DLB 75

Leonard, Elmore (John, Jr.)
1925- ...... **CLC 28, 34, 71; DAM POP**
See also AITN 1; BEST 89:1, 90:4;
CA 81-84; CANR 12, 28, 53;
INT CANR-28; MTCW

Leonard, Hugh .... **CLC 19**
See also Byrne, John Keyes
See also DLB 13

Leonov, Leonid (Maximovich)
1899-1994 .... **CLC 92; DAM NOV**
See also CA 129; MTCW

Leopardi, (Conte) Giacomo
1798-1837 .... **NCLC 22**

Le Reveler
See Artaud, Antonin (Marie Joseph)

Lerman, Eleanor 1952- .... **CLC 9**
See also CA 85-88

Lerman, Rhoda 1936- .... **CLC 56**
See also CA 49-52

Lermontov, Mikhail Yuryevich
1814-1841 .... **NCLC 47**

Leroux, Gaston 1868-1927 .... **TCLC 25**
See also CA 108; 136; SATA 65

Lesage, Alain-Rene 1668-1747 .... **LC 28**

Leskov, Nikolai (Semyonovich)
1831-1895 .... **NCLC 25**

Lessing, Doris (May)
1919- ..... **CLC 1, 2, 3, 6, 10, 15, 22, 40,**
94; DA; DAB; DAC; DAM MST, NOV;
SSC 6
See also CA 9-12R; CAAS 14; CANR 33;
CDBLB 1960 to Present; DLB 15, 139;
DLBY 85; MTCW

Lessing, Gotthold Ephraim
1729-1781 .... **LC 8**
See also DLB 97

Lester, Richard 1932- .... **CLC 20**

Lever, Charles (James)
1806-1872 .... **NCLC 23**
See also DLB 21

Leverson, Ada 1865(?)-1936(?) .... **TCLC 18**
See also Elaine
See also CA 117; DLB 153

Levertov, Denise
1923- ...... **CLC 1, 2, 3, 5, 8, 15, 28, 66;**
DAM POET; PC 11
See also CA 1-4R; CAAS 19; CANR 3, 29,
50; DLB 5, 165; INT CANR-29; MTCW

Levi, Jonathan .... **CLC 76**

Levi, Peter (Chad Tigar) 1931- ..... **CLC 41**
See also CA 5-8R; CANR 34; DLB 40

Levi, Primo
1919-1987 .... **CLC 37, 50; SSC 12**
See also CA 13-16R; 122; CANR 12, 33;
MTCW

Levin, Ira 1929- ..... **CLC 3, 6; DAM POP**
See also CA 21-24R; CANR 17, 44;
MTCW; SATA 66

Levin, Meyer
1905-1981 .... **CLC 7; DAM POP**
See also AITN 1; CA 9-12R; 104;
CANR 15; DLB 9, 28; DLBY 81;
SATA 21; SATA-Obit 27

Levine, Norman 1924- .... **CLC 54**
See also CA 73-76; CAAS 23; CANR 14;
DLB 88

Levine, Philip
1928- .... **CLC 2, 4, 5, 9, 14, 33;**
DAM POET
See also CA 9-12R; CANR 9, 37, 52;
DLB 5

Levinson, Deirdre 1931- .... **CLC 49**
See also CA 73-76

Levi-Strauss, Claude 1908- .... **CLC 38**
See also CA 1-4R; CANR 6, 32; MTCW

Levitin, Sonia (Wolff) 1934- .... **CLC 17**
See also AAYA 13; CA 29-32R; CANR 14,
32; JRDA; MAICYA; SAAS 2; SATA 4,
68

Levon, O. U.
See Kesey, Ken (Elton)

Lewes, George Henry
1817-1878 .... **NCLC 25**
See also DLB 55, 144

Lewis, Alun 1915-1944 .... **TCLC 3**
See also CA 104; DLB 20, 162

Lewis, C. Day
See Day Lewis, C(ecil)

Lewis, C(live) S(taples)
1898-1963 ..... **CLC 1, 3, 6, 14, 27; DA;**
DAB; DAC; DAM MST, NOV, POP;
WLC
See also AAYA 3; CA 81-84; CANR 33;
CDBLB 1945-1960; CLR 3, 27; DLB 15,
100, 160; JRDA; MAICYA; MTCW;
SATA 13

Lewis, Janet 1899- .... **CLC 41**
See also Winters, Janet Lewis
See also CA 9-12R; CANR 29; CAP 1;
DLBY 87

Lewis, Matthew Gregory
1775-1818 .... **NCLC 11**
See also DLB 39, 158

Lewis, (Harry) Sinclair
1885-1951 ..... **TCLC 4, 13, 23, 39; DA;**
DAB; DAC; DAM MST, NOV; WLC
See also CA 104; 133; CDALB 1917-1929;
DLB 9, 102; DLBD 1; MTCW

Lord, Bette Bao 1938- . . . . **CLC 23**
See also BEST 90:3; CA 107; CANR 41;
INT 107; SATA 58

Lord Auch
See Bataille, Georges

Lord Byron
See Byron, George Gordon (Noel)

Lorde, Audre (Geraldine)
1934-1992 . . . . **CLC 18, 71; BLC;
DAM MULT, POET; PC 12**
See also BW 1; CA 25-28R; 142; CANR 16,
26, 46; DLB 41; MTCW

Lord Jeffrey
See Jeffrey, Francis

Lorenzini, Carlo 1826-1890
See Collodi, Carlo
See also MAICYA; SATA 29

Lorenzo, Heberto Padilla
See Padilla (Lorenzo), Heberto

Loris
See Hofmannsthal, Hugo von

Loti, Pierre . . . . **TCLC 11**
See also Viaud, (Louis Marie) Julien
See also DLB 123

Louie, David Wong 1954- . . . . **CLC 70**
See also CA 139

Louis, Father M.
See Merton, Thomas

Lovecraft, H(oward) P(hillips)
1890-1937 . . . . **TCLC 4, 22; DAM POP;
SSC 3**
See also AAYA 14; CA 104; 133; MTCW

Lovelace, Earl 1935- . . . . **CLC 51**
See also BW 2; CA 77-80; CANR 41;
DLB 125; MTCW

Lovelace, Richard 1618-1657 . . . . **LC 24**
See also DLB 131

Lowell, Amy
1874-1925 . . . . **TCLC 1, 8; DAM POET;
PC 13**
See also CA 104; 151; DLB 54, 140

Lowell, James Russell 1819-1891 . . **NCLC 2**
See also CDALB 1640-1865; DLB 1, 11, 64,
79

Lowell, Robert (Traill Spence, Jr.)
1917-1977 . . . **CLC 1, 2, 3, 4, 5, 8, 9, 11,
15, 37; DA; DAB; DAC; DAM MST,
NOV; PC 3; WLC**
See also CA 9-12R; 73-76; CABS 2;
CANR 26; DLB 5, 169; MTCW

Lowndes, Marie Adelaide (Belloc)
1868-1947 . . . . **TCLC 12**
See also CA 107; DLB 70

Lowry, (Clarence) Malcolm
1909-1957 . . . . **TCLC 6, 40**
See also CA 105; 131; CDBLB 1945-1960;
DLB 15; MTCW

Lowry, Mina Gertrude 1882-1966
See Loy, Mina
See also CA 113

Loxsmith, John
See Brunner, John (Kilian Houston)

Loy, Mina . . . . **CLC 28; DAM POET; PC 16**
See also Lowry, Mina Gertrude
See also DLB 4, 54

Loyson-Bridet
See Schwob, (Mayer Andre) Marcel

Lucas, Craig 1951- . . . . **CLC 64**
See also CA 137

Lucas, George 1944- . . . . **CLC 16**
See also AAYA 1; CA 77-80; CANR 30;
SATA 56

Lucas, Hans
See Godard, Jean-Luc

Lucas, Victoria
See Plath, Sylvia

Ludlam, Charles 1943-1987 . . . . . **CLC 46, 50**
See also CA 85-88; 122

Ludlum, Robert
1927- . . . **CLC 22, 43; DAM NOV, POP**
See also AAYA 10; BEST 89:1, 90:3;
CA 33-36R; CANR 25, 41; DLBY 82;
MTCW

Ludwig, Ken . . . . **CLC 60**

Ludwig, Otto 1813-1865 . . . . **NCLC 4**
See also DLB 129

Lugones, Leopoldo 1874-1938 . . . . . **TCLC 15**
See also CA 116; 131; HW

Lu Hsun 1881-1936 . . . . . . **TCLC 3; SSC 20**
See also Shu-Jen, Chou

Lukacs, George . . . . **CLC 24**
See also Lukacs, Gyorgy (Szegeny von)

Lukacs, Gyorgy (Szegeny von) 1885-1971
See Lukacs, George
See also CA 101; 29-32R

Luke, Peter (Ambrose Cyprian)
1919-1995 . . . . **CLC 38**
See also CA 81-84; 147; DLB 13

Lunar, Dennis
See Mungo, Raymond

Lurie, Alison 1926- . . . . **CLC 4, 5, 18, 39**
See also CA 1-4R; CANR 2, 17, 50; DLB 2;
MTCW; SATA 46

Lustig, Arnost 1926- . . . . **CLC 56**
See also AAYA 3; CA 69-72; CANR 47;
SATA 56

Luther, Martin 1483-1546 . . . . **LC 9**

Luxemburg, Rosa 1870(?)-1919 . . . . **TCLC 63**
See also CA 118

Luzi, Mario 1914- . . . . **CLC 13**
See also CA 61-64; CANR 9; DLB 128

L'Ymagier
See Gourmont, Remy (-Marie-Charles) de

Lynch, B. Suarez
See Bioy Casares, Adolfo; Borges, Jorge
Luis

Lynch, David (K.) 1946- . . . . **CLC 66**
See also CA 124; 129

Lynch, James
See Andreyev, Leonid (Nikolaevich)

Lynch Davis, B.
See Bioy Casares, Adolfo; Borges, Jorge
Luis

Lyndsay, Sir David 1490-1555 . . . . . . **LC 20**

Lynn, Kenneth S(chuyler) 1923- . . . . **CLC 50**
See also CA 1-4R; CANR 3, 27

Lynx
See West, Rebecca

Lyons, Marcus
See Blish, James (Benjamin)

Lyre, Pinchbeck
See Sassoon, Siegfried (Lorraine)

Lytle, Andrew (Nelson) 1902-1995 . . **CLC 22**
See also CA 9-12R; 150; DLB 6; DLBY 95

Lyttelton, George 1709-1773 . . . . **LC 10**

Maas, Peter 1929- . . . . **CLC 29**
See also CA 93-96; INT 93-96

Macaulay, Rose 1881-1958 . . . . . **TCLC 7, 44**
See also CA 104; DLB 36

Macaulay, Thomas Babington
1800-1859 . . . . **NCLC 42**
See also CDBLB 1832-1890; DLB 32, 55

MacBeth, George (Mann)
1932-1992 . . . . **CLC 2, 5, 9**
See also CA 25-28R; 136; DLB 40; MTCW;
SATA 4; SATA-Obit 70

MacCaig, Norman (Alexander)
1910- . . . . . **CLC 36; DAB; DAM POET**
See also CA 9-12R; CANR 3, 34; DLB 27

MacCarthy, (Sir Charles Otto) Desmond
1877-1952 . . . . **TCLC 36**

MacDiarmid, Hugh
. . . . **CLC 2, 4, 11, 19, 63; PC 9**
See also Grieve, C(hristopher) M(urray)
See also CDBLB 1945-1960; DLB 20

MacDonald, Anson
See Heinlein, Robert A(nson)

Macdonald, Cynthia 1928- . . . . . . **CLC 13, 19**
See also CA 49-52; CANR 4, 44; DLB 105

MacDonald, George 1824-1905 . . . . . **TCLC 9**
See also CA 106; 137; DLB 18, 163;
MAICYA; SATA 33

Macdonald, John
See Millar, Kenneth

MacDonald, John D(ann)
1916-1986 . . . . **CLC 3, 27, 44;
DAM NOV, POP**
See also CA 1-4R; 121; CANR 1, 19;
DLB 8; DLBY 86; MTCW

Macdonald, John Ross
See Millar, Kenneth

Macdonald, Ross . . . . . **CLC 1, 2, 3, 14, 34, 41**
See also Millar, Kenneth
See also DLBD 6

MacDougal, John
See Blish, James (Benjamin)

MacEwen, Gwendolyn (Margaret)
1941-1987 . . . . **CLC 13, 55**
See also CA 9-12R; 124; CANR 7, 22;
DLB 53; SATA 50; SATA-Obit 55

Macha, Karel Hynek 1810-1846 . . **NCLC 46**

Machado (y Ruiz), Antonio
1875-1939 . . . . **TCLC 3**
See also CA 104; DLB 108

Machado de Assis, Joaquim Maria
1839-1908 . . . . **TCLC 10; BLC**
See also CA 107

Machen, Arthur . . . . **TCLC 4; SSC 20**
See also Jones, Arthur Llewellyn
See also DLB 36, 156

Machiavelli, Niccolo
1469-1527 ...... LC 8; DA; DAB; DAC;
DAM MST

MacInnes, Colin 1914-1976 ...... CLC 4, 23
See also CA 69-72; 65-68; CANR 21;
DLB 14; MTCW

MacInnes, Helen (Clark)
1907-1985 ..... CLC 27, 39; DAM POP
See also CA 1-4R; 117; CANR 1, 28;
DLB 87; MTCW; SATA 22;
SATA-Obit 44

Mackay, Mary 1855-1924
See Corelli, Marie
See also CA 118

Mackenzie, Compton (Edward Montague)
1883-1972 .... CLC 18
See also CA 21-22; 37-40R; CAP 2;
DLB 34, 100

Mackenzie, Henry 1745-1831 .... NCLC 41
See also DLB 39

Mackintosh, Elizabeth 1896(?)-1952
See Tey, Josephine
See also CA 110

MacLaren, James
See Grieve, C(hristopher) M(urray)

Mac Laverty, Bernard 1942- .... CLC 31
See also CA 116; 118; CANR 43; INT 118

MacLean, Alistair (Stuart)
1922-1987 .... CLC 3, 13, 50, 63;
DAM POP
See also CA 57-60; 121; CANR 28; MTCW;
SATA 23; SATA-Obit 50

Maclean, Norman (Fitzroy)
1902-1990 .... CLC 78; DAM POP;
SSC 13
See also CA 102; 132; CANR 49

MacLeish, Archibald
1892-1982 .... CLC 3, 8, 14, 68;
DAM POET
See also CA 9-12R; 106; CANR 33; DLB 4,
7, 45; DLBY 82; MTCW

MacLennan, (John) Hugh
1907-1990 .... CLC 2, 14, 92; DAC;
DAM MST
See also CA 5-8R; 142; CANR 33; DLB 68;
MTCW

MacLeod, Alistair
1936- ...... CLC 56; DAC; DAM MST
See also CA 123; DLB 60

MacNeice, (Frederick) Louis
1907-1963 ...... CLC 1, 4, 10, 53; DAB;
DAM POET
See also CA 85-88; DLB 10, 20; MTCW

MacNeill, Dand
See Fraser, George MacDonald

Macpherson, James 1736-1796 ...... LC 29
See also DLB 109

Macpherson, (Jean) Jay 1931- ...... CLC 14
See also CA 5-8R; DLB 53

MacShane, Frank 1927- .... CLC 39
See also CA 9-12R; CANR 3, 33; DLB 111

Macumber, Mari
See Sandoz, Mari(e Susette)

Madach, Imre 1823-1864 .... NCLC 19

Madden, (Jerry) David 1933- .... CLC 5, 15
See also CA 1-4R; CAAS 3; CANR 4, 45;
DLB 6; MTCW

Maddern, Al(an)
See Ellison, Harlan (Jay)

Madhubuti, Haki R.
1942- .... CLC 6, 73; BLC;
DAM MULT, POET; PC 5
See also Lee, Don L.
See also BW 2; CA 73-76; CANR 24, 51;
DLB 5, 41; DLBD 8

Maepenn, Hugh
See Kuttner, Henry

Maepenn, K. H.
See Kuttner, Henry

Maeterlinck, Maurice
1862-1949 ...... TCLC 3; DAM DRAM
See also CA 104; 136; SATA 66

Maginn, William 1794-1842 ...... NCLC 8
See also DLB 110, 159

Mahapatra, Jayanta
1928- .... CLC 33; DAM MULT
See also CA 73-76; CAAS 9; CANR 15, 33

Mahfouz, Naguib (Abdel Aziz Al-Sabilgi)
1911(?)-
See Mahfuz, Najib
See also BEST 89:2; CA 128; DAM NOV;
MTCW

Mahfuz, Najib .... CLC 52, 55
See also Mahfouz, Naguib (Abdel Aziz
Al-Sabilgi)
See also DLBY 88

Mahon, Derek 1941- .... CLC 27
See also CA 113; 128; DLB 40

Mailer, Norman
1923- ...... CLC 1, 2, 3, 4, 5, 8, 11, 14,
28, 39, 74; DA; DAB; DAC; DAM MST,
NOV, POP
See also AITN 2; CA 9-12R; CABS 1;
CANR 28; CDALB 1968-1988; DLB 2,
16, 28; DLBD 3; DLBY 80, 83; MTCW

Maillet, Antonine 1929- ...... CLC 54; DAC
See also CA 115; 120; CANR 46; DLB 60;
INT 120

Mais, Roger 1905-1955 .... TCLC 8
See also BW 1; CA 105; 124; DLB 125;
MTCW

Maistre, Joseph de 1753-1821 .... NCLC 37

Maitland, Frederic 1850-1906 ..... TCLC 65

Maitland, Sara (Louise) 1950- ...... CLC 49
See also CA 69-72; CANR 13

Major, Clarence
1936- .... CLC 3, 19, 48; BLC;
DAM MULT
See also BW 2; CA 21-24R; CAAS 6;
CANR 13, 25, 53; DLB 33

Major, Kevin (Gerald)
1949- .... CLC 26; DAC
See also AAYA 16; CA 97-100; CANR 21,
38; CLR 11; DLB 60; INT CANR-21;
JRDA; MAICYA; SATA 32, 82

Maki, James
See Ozu, Yasujiro

Malabaila, Damiano
See Levi, Primo

Malamud, Bernard
1914-1986 ...... CLC 1, 2, 3, 5, 8, 9, 11,
18, 27, 44, 78, 85; DA; DAB; DAC;
DAM MST, NOV, POP; SSC 15; WLC
See also AAYA 16; CA 5-8R; 118; CABS 1;
CANR 28; CDALB 1941-1968; DLB 2,
28, 152; DLBY 80, 86; MTCW

Malaparte, Curzio 1898-1957 ..... TCLC 52

Malcolm, Dan
See Silverberg, Robert

Malcolm X .... CLC 82; BLC
See also Little, Malcolm

Malherbe, Francois de 1555-1628 ..... LC 5

Mallarme, Stephane
1842-1898 .... NCLC 4, 41;
DAM POET; PC 4

Mallet-Joris, Francoise 1930- ...... CLC 11
See also CA 65-68; CANR 17; DLB 83

Malley, Ern
See McAuley, James Phillip

Mallowan, Agatha Christie
See Christie, Agatha (Mary Clarissa)

Maloff, Saul 1922- .... CLC 5
See also CA 33-36R

Malone, Louis
See MacNeice, (Frederick) Louis

Malone, Michael (Christopher)
1942- .... CLC 43
See also CA 77-80; CANR 14, 32

Malory, (Sir) Thomas
1410(?)-1471(?) ...... LC 11; DA; DAB;
DAC; DAM MST
See also CDBLB Before 1660; DLB 146;
SATA 59; SATA-Brief 33

Malouf, (George Joseph) David
1934- .... CLC 28, 86
See also CA 124; CANR 50

Malraux, (Georges-)Andre
1901-1976 ...... CLC 1, 4, 9, 13, 15, 57;
DAM NOV
See also CA 21-22; 69-72; CANR 34;
CAP 2; DLB 72; MTCW

Malzberg, Barry N(athaniel) 1939- ... CLC 7
See also CA 61-64; CAAS 4; CANR 16;
DLB 8

Mamet, David (Alan)
1947- .... CLC 9, 15, 34, 46, 91;
DAM DRAM; DC 4
See also AAYA 3; CA 81-84; CABS 3;
CANR 15, 41; DLB 7; MTCW

Mamoulian, Rouben (Zachary)
1897-1987 .... CLC 16
See also CA 25-28R; 124

Mandelstam, Osip (Emilievich)
1891(?)-1938(?) ...... TCLC 2, 6; PC 14
See also CA 104; 150

Mander, (Mary) Jane 1877-1949 ... TCLC 31

Mandeville, John fl. 1350- .... CMLC 19
See also DLB 146

Mandiargues, Andre Pieyre de .... CLC 41
See also Pieyre de Mandiargues, Andre
See also DLB 83

Mandrake, Ethel Belle
See Thurman, Wallace (Henry)

Mason, Lee W.
See Malzberg, Barry N(athaniel)

Mason, Nick 1945- .... CLC 35

Mason, Tally
See Derleth, August (William)

Mass, William
See Gibson, William

Masters, Edgar Lee
1868-1950 ..... TCLC 2, 25; DA; DAC;
DAM MST, POET; PC 1
See also CA 104; 133; CDALB 1865-1917;
DLB 54; MTCW

Masters, Hilary 1928- .... CLC 48
See also CA 25-28R; CANR 13, 47

Mastrosimone, William 19(?)- ...... CLC 36

Mathe, Albert
See Camus, Albert

Matheson, Richard Burton 1926- ... CLC 37
See also CA 97-100; DLB 8, 44; INT 97-100

Mathews, Harry 1930- .... CLC 6, 52
See also CA 21-24R; CAAS 6; CANR 18,
40

Mathews, John Joseph
1894-1979 ...... CLC 84; DAM MULT
See also CA 19-20; 142; CANR 45; CAP 2;
NNAL

Mathias, Roland (Glyn) 1915- ...... CLC 45
See also CA 97-100; CANR 19, 41; DLB 27

Matsuo Basho 1644-1694 .... PC 3
See also DAM POET

Mattheson, Rodney
See Creasey, John

Matthews, Greg 1949- .... CLC 45
See also CA 135

Matthews, William 1942- .... CLC 40
See also CA 29-32R; CAAS 18; CANR 12;
DLB 5

Matthias, John (Edward) 1941- ...... CLC 9
See also CA 33-36R

Matthiessen, Peter
1927- .... CLC 5, 7, 11, 32, 64;
DAM NOV
See also AAYA 6; BEST 90:4; CA 9-12R;
CANR 21, 50; DLB 6; MTCW; SATA 27

Maturin, Charles Robert
1780(?)-1824 .... NCLC 6

Matute (Ausejo), Ana Maria
1925- .... CLC 11
See also CA 89-92; MTCW

Maugham, W. S.
See Maugham, W(illiam) Somerset

Maugham, W(illiam) Somerset
1874-1965 ...... CLC 1, 11, 15, 67, 93;
DA; DAB; DAC; DAM DRAM, MST,
NOV; SSC 8; WLC
See also CA 5-8R; 25-28R; CANR 40;
CDBLB 1914-1945; DLB 10, 36, 77, 100,
162; MTCW; SATA 54

Maugham, William Somerset
See Maugham, W(illiam) Somerset

Maupassant, (Henri Rene Albert) Guy de
1850-1893 ..... NCLC 1, 42; DA; DAB;
DAC; DAM MST; SSC 1; WLC
See also DLB 123

Maupin, Armistead
1944- .... CLC 95; DAM POP
See also CA 125; 130; INT 130

Maurhut, Richard
See Traven, B.

Mauriac, Claude 1914-1996 .... CLC 9
See also CA 89-92; 152; DLB 83

Mauriac, Francois (Charles)
1885-1970 .... CLC 4, 9, 56
See also CA 25-28; CAP 2; DLB 65;
MTCW

Mavor, Osborne Henry 1888-1951
See Bridie, James
See also CA 104

Maxwell, William (Keepers, Jr.)
1908- .... CLC 19
See also CA 93-96; DLBY 80; INT 93-96

May, Elaine 1932- .... CLC 16
See also CA 124; 142; DLB 44

Mayakovski, Vladimir (Vladimirovich)
1893-1930 .... TCLC 4, 18
See also CA 104

Mayhew, Henry 1812-1887 ...... NCLC 31
See also DLB 18, 55

Mayle, Peter 1939(?)- .... CLC 89
See also CA 139

Maynard, Joyce 1953- .... CLC 23
See also CA 111; 129

Mayne, William (James Carter)
1928- .... CLC 12
See also CA 9-12R; CANR 37; CLR 25;
JRDA; MAICYA; SAAS 11; SATA 6, 68

Mayo, Jim
See L'Amour, Louis (Dearborn)

Maysles, Albert 1926- .... CLC 16
See also CA 29-32R

Maysles, David 1932- .... CLC 16

Mazer, Norma Fox 1931- .... CLC 26
See also AAYA 5; CA 69-72; CANR 12,
32; CLR 23; JRDA; MAICYA; SAAS 1;
SATA 24, 67

Mazzini, Guiseppe 1805-1872 .... NCLC 34

McAuley, James Phillip
1917-1976 .... CLC 45
See also CA 97-100

McBain, Ed
See Hunter, Evan

McBrien, William Augustine
1930- .... CLC 44
See also CA 107

McCaffrey, Anne (Inez)
1926- .... CLC 17; DAM NOV, POP
See also AAYA 6; AITN 2; BEST 89:2;
CA 25-28R; CANR 15, 35; DLB 8;
JRDA; MAICYA; MTCW; SAAS 11;
SATA 8, 70

McCall, Nathan 1955(?)- .... CLC 86
See also CA 146

McCann, Arthur
See Campbell, John W(ood, Jr.)

McCann, Edson
See Pohl, Frederik

McCarthy, Charles, Jr. 1933-
See McCarthy, Cormac
See also CANR 42; DAM POP

McCarthy, Cormac 1933- ..... CLC 4, 57, 59
See also McCarthy, Charles, Jr.
See also DLB 6, 143

McCarthy, Mary (Therese)
1912-1989 ... CLC 1, 3, 5, 14, 24, 39, 59
See also CA 5-8R; 129; CANR 16, 50;
DLB 2; DLBY 81; INT CANR-16;
MTCW

McCartney, (James) Paul
1942- .... CLC 12, 35
See also CA 146

McCauley, Stephen (D.) 1955- ..... CLC 50
See also CA 141

McClure, Michael (Thomas)
1932- .... CLC 6, 10
See also CA 21-24R; CANR 17, 46;
DLB 16

McCorkle, Jill (Collins) 1958- ...... CLC 51
See also CA 121; DLBY 87

McCourt, James 1941- .... CLC 5
See also CA 57-60

McCoy, Horace (Stanley)
1897-1955 .... TCLC 28
See also CA 108; DLB 9

McCrae, John 1872-1918 .... TCLC 12
See also CA 109; DLB 92

McCreigh, James
See Pohl, Frederik

McCullers, (Lula) Carson (Smith)
1917-1967 .... CLC 1, 4, 10, 12, 48; DA;
DAB; DAC; DAM MST, NOV; SSC 9;
WLC
See also CA 5-8R; 25-28R; CABS 1, 3;
CANR 18; CDALB 1941-1968; DLB 2, 7;
MTCW; SATA 27

McCulloch, John Tyler
See Burroughs, Edgar Rice

McCullough, Colleen
1938(?)- .... CLC 27; DAM NOV, POP
See also CA 81-84; CANR 17, 46; MTCW

McDermott, Alice 1953- .... CLC 90
See also CA 109; CANR 40

McElroy, Joseph 1930- .... CLC 5, 47
See also CA 17-20R

McEwan, Ian (Russell)
1948- .... CLC 13, 66; DAM NOV
See also BEST 90:4; CA 61-64; CANR 14,
41; DLB 14; MTCW

McFadden, David 1940- .... CLC 48
See also CA 104; DLB 60; INT 104

McFarland, Dennis 1950- .... CLC 65

McGahern, John
1934- .... CLC 5, 9, 48; SSC 17
See also CA 17-20R; CANR 29; DLB 14;
MTCW

McGinley, Patrick (Anthony)
1937- .... CLC 41
See also CA 120; 127; INT 127

McGinley, Phyllis 1905-1978 ...... CLC 14
See also CA 9-12R; 77-80; CANR 19;
DLB 11, 48; SATA 2, 44; SATA-Obit 24

McGinniss, Joe 1942-............. **CLC 32**
See also AITN 2; BEST 89:2; CA 25-28R;
CANR 26; INT CANR-26

McGivern, Maureen Daly
See Daly, Maureen

McGrath, Patrick 1950-.......... **CLC 55**
See also CA 136

McGrath, Thomas (Matthew)
1916-1990 .... **CLC 28, 59; DAM POET**
See also CA 9-12R; 132; CANR 6, 33;
MTCW; SATA 41; SATA-Obit 66

McGuane, Thomas (Francis III)
1939- .... **CLC 3, 7, 18, 45**
See also AITN 2; CA 49-52; CANR 5, 24,
49; DLB 2; DLBY 80; INT CANR-24;
MTCW

McGuckian, Medbh
1950- .... **CLC 48; DAM POET**
See also CA 143; DLB 40

McHale, Tom 1942(?)-1982....... **CLC 3, 5**
See also AITN 1; CA 77-80; 106

McIlvanney, William 1936-........ **CLC 42**
See also CA 25-28R; DLB 14

McIlwraith, Maureen Mollie Hunter
See Hunter, Mollie
See also SATA 2

McInerney, Jay
1955- .... **CLC 34; DAM POP**
See also AAYA 18; CA 116; 123;
CANR 45; INT 123

McIntyre, Vonda N(eel) 1948- ..... **CLC 18**
See also CA 81-84; CANR 17, 34; MTCW

McKay, Claude
.... **TCLC 7, 41; BLC; DAB; PC 2**
See also McKay, Festus Claudius
See also DLB 4, 45, 51, 117

McKay, Festus Claudius 1889-1948
See McKay, Claude
See also BW 1; CA 104; 124; DA; DAC;
DAM MST, MULT, NOV, POET;
MTCW; WLC

McKuen, Rod 1933-............. **CLC 1, 3**
See also AITN 1; CA 41-44R; CANR 40

McLoughlin, R. B.
See Mencken, H(enry) L(ouis)

McLuhan, (Herbert) Marshall
1911-1980 .... **CLC 37, 83**
See also CA 9-12R; 102; CANR 12, 34;
DLB 88; INT CANR-12; MTCW

McMillan, Terry (L.)
1951- .... **CLC 50, 61; DAM MULT,**
NOV, POP
See also BW 2; CA 140

McMurtry, Larry (Jeff)
1936- .... **CLC 2, 3, 7, 11, 27, 44;**
DAM NOV, POP
See also AAYA 15; AITN 2; BEST 89:2;
CA 5-8R; CANR 19, 43;
CDALB 1968-1988; DLB 2, 143;
DLBY 80, 87; MTCW

McNally, T. M. 1961-............ **CLC 82**

McNally, Terrence
1939- ... **CLC 4, 7, 41, 91; DAM DRAM**
See also CA 45-48; CANR 2; DLB 7

McNamer, Deirdre 1950-.......... **CLC 70**

McNeile, Herman Cyril 1888-1937
See Sapper
See also DLB 77

McNickle, (William) D'Arcy
1904-1977 ...... **CLC 89; DAM MULT**
See also CA 9-12R; 85-88; CANR 5, 45;
NNAL; SATA-Obit 22

McPhee, John (Angus) 1931- ...... **CLC 36**
See also BEST 90:1; CA 65-68; CANR 20,
46; MTCW

McPherson, James Alan
1943- .... **CLC 19, 77**
See also BW 1; CA 25-28R; CAAS 17;
CANR 24; DLB 38; MTCW

McPherson, William (Alexander)
1933- .... **CLC 34**
See also CA 69-72; CANR 28;
INT CANR-28

Mead, Margaret 1901-1978........ **CLC 37**
See also AITN 1; CA 1-4R; 81-84;
CANR 4; MTCW; SATA-Obit 20

Meaker, Marijane (Agnes) 1927-
See Kerr, M. E.
See also CA 107; CANR 37; INT 107;
JRDA; MAICYA; MTCW; SATA 20, 61

Medoff, Mark (Howard)
1940- .... **CLC 6, 23; DAM DRAM**
See also AITN 1; CA 53-56; CANR 5;
DLB 7; INT CANR-5

Medvedev, P. N.
See Bakhtin, Mikhail Mikhailovich

Meged, Aharon
See Megged, Aharon

Meged, Aron
See Megged, Aharon

Megged, Aharon 1920-............ **CLC 9**
See also CA 49-52; CAAS 13; CANR 1

Mehta, Ved (Parkash) 1934-....... **CLC 37**
See also CA 1-4R; CANR 2, 23; MTCW

Melanter
See Blackmore, R(ichard) D(oddridge)

Melikow, Loris
See Hofmannsthal, Hugo von

Melmoth, Sebastian
See Wilde, Oscar (Fingal O'Flahertie Wills)

Meltzer, Milton 1915-............ **CLC 26**
See also AAYA 8; CA 13-16R; CANR 38;
CLR 13; DLB 61; JRDA; MAICYA;
SAAS 1; SATA 1, 50, 80

Melville, Herman
1819-1891 ..... **NCLC 3, 12, 29, 45, 49;**
DA; DAB; DAC; DAM MST, NOV;
SSC 1, 17; WLC
See also CDALB 1640-1865; DLB 3, 74;
SATA 59

Menander
c. 342B.C.-c. 292B.C........ **CMLC 9;**
DAM DRAM; DC 3

Mencken, H(enry) L(ouis)
1880-1956 .... **TCLC 13**
See also CA 105; 125; CDALB 1917-1929;
DLB 11, 29, 63, 137; MTCW

Mercer, David
1928-1980 .... **CLC 5; DAM DRAM**
See also CA 9-12R; 102; CANR 23;
DLB 13; MTCW

Merchant, Paul
See Ellison, Harlan (Jay)

Meredith, George
1828-1909 .. **TCLC 17, 43; DAM POET**
See also CA 117; CDBLB 1832-1890;
DLB 18, 35, 57, 159

Meredith, William (Morris)
1919- .. **CLC 4, 13, 22, 55; DAM POET**
See also CA 9-12R; CAAS 14; CANR 6, 40;
DLB 5

Merezhkovsky, Dmitry Sergeyevich
1865-1941 .... **TCLC 29**

Merimee, Prosper
1803-1870 .... **NCLC 6; SSC 7**
See also DLB 119

Merkin, Daphne 1954-............ **CLC 44**
See also CA 123

Merlin, Arthur
See Blish, James (Benjamin)

Merrill, James (Ingram)
1926-1995 .... **CLC 2, 3, 6, 8, 13, 18, 34,**
91; DAM POET
See also CA 13-16R; 147; CANR 10, 49;
DLB 5, 165; DLBY 85; INT CANR-10;
MTCW

Merriman, Alex
See Silverberg, Robert

Merritt, E. B.
See Waddington, Miriam

Merton, Thomas
1915-1968 .. **CLC 1, 3, 11, 34, 83; PC 10**
See also CA 5-8R; 25-28R; CANR 22, 53;
DLB 48; DLBY 81; MTCW

Merwin, W(illiam) S(tanley)
1927- ...... **CLC 1, 2, 3, 5, 8, 13, 18, 45,**
88; DAM POET
See also CA 13-16R; CANR 15, 51; DLB 5,
169; INT CANR-15; MTCW

Metcalf, John 1938-.............. **CLC 37**
See also CA 113; DLB 60

Metcalf, Suzanne
See Baum, L(yman) Frank

Mew, Charlotte (Mary)
1870-1928 .... **TCLC 8**
See also CA 105; DLB 19, 135

Mewshaw, Michael 1943-.......... **CLC 9**
See also CA 53-56; CANR 7, 47; DLBY 80

Meyer, June
See Jordan, June

Meyer, Lynn
See Slavitt, David R(ytman)

Meyer-Meyrink, Gustav 1868-1932
See Meyrink, Gustav
See also CA 117

Meyers, Jeffrey 1939- .... **CLC 39**
See also CA 73-76; DLB 111

Meynell, Alice (Christina Gertrude Thompson)
1847-1922 .... **TCLC 6**
See also CA 104; DLB 19, 98

Meyrink, Gustav .... **TCLC 21**
See also Meyer-Meyrink, Gustav
See also DLB 81

Nerval, Gerard de
1808-1855 ..... **NCLC 1; PC 13; SSC 18**

Nervo, (Jose) Amado (Ruiz de)
1870-1919 .... **TCLC 11**
See also CA 109; 131; HW

Nessi, Pio Baroja y
See Baroja (y Nessi), Pio

Nestroy, Johann 1801-1862...... **NCLC 42**
See also DLB 133

Neufeld, John (Arthur) 1938- ...... **CLC 17**
See also AAYA 11; CA 25-28R; CANR 11,
37; MAICYA; SAAS 3; SATA 6, 81

Neville, Emily Cheney 1919-...... **CLC 12**
See also CA 5-8R; CANR 3, 37; JRDA;
MAICYA; SAAS 2; SATA 1

Newbound, Bernard Slade 1930-
See Slade, Bernard
See also CA 81-84; CANR 49;
DAM DRAM

Newby, P(ercy) H(oward)
1918- .... **CLC 2, 13; DAM NOV**
See also CA 5-8R; CANR 32; DLB 15;
MTCW

Newlove, Donald 1928- .... **CLC 6**
See also CA 29-32R; CANR 25

Newlove, John (Herbert) 1938-..... **CLC 14**
See also CA 21-24R; CANR 9, 25

Newman, Charles 1938-......... **CLC 2, 8**
See also CA 21-24R

Newman, Edwin (Harold) 1919- .... **CLC 14**
See also AITN 1; CA 69-72; CANR 5

Newman, John Henry
1801-1890 .... **NCLC 38**
See also DLB 18, 32, 55

Newton, Suzanne 1936-.......... **CLC 35**
See also CA 41-44R; CANR 14; JRDA;
SATA 5, 77

Nexo, Martin Andersen
1869-1954 .... **TCLC 43**

Nezval, Vitezslav 1900-1958 ...... **TCLC 44**
See also CA 123

Ng, Fae Myenne 1957(?)-.......... **CLC 81**
See also CA 146

Ngema, Mbongeni 1955- .... **CLC 57**
See also BW 2; CA 143

Ngugi, James T(hiong'o)........ **CLC 3, 7, 13**
See also Ngugi wa Thiong'o

Ngugi wa Thiong'o
1938- ..... **CLC 36; BLC; DAM MULT,
NOV**
See also Ngugi, James T(hiong'o)
See also BW 2; CA 81-84; CANR 27;
DLB 125; MTCW

Nichol, B(arrie) P(hillip)
1944-1988 .... **CLC 18**
See also CA 53-56; DLB 53; SATA 66

Nichols, John (Treadwell) 1940-.... **CLC 38**
See also CA 9-12R; CAAS 2; CANR 6;
DLBY 82

Nichols, Leigh
See Koontz, Dean R(ay)

Nichols, Peter (Richard)
1927-................. **CLC 5, 36, 65**
See also CA 104; CANR 33; DLB 13;
MTCW

Nicolas, F. R. E.
See Freeling, Nicolas

Niedecker, Lorine
1903-1970 .... **CLC 10, 42; DAM POET**
See also CA 25-28; CAP 2; DLB 48

Nietzsche, Friedrich (Wilhelm)
1844-1900 .... **TCLC 10, 18, 55**
See also CA 107; 121; DLB 129

Nievo, Ippolito 1831-1861 .... **NCLC 22**

Nightingale, Anne Redmon 1943-
See Redmon, Anne
See also CA 103

Nik. T. O.
See Annensky, Innokenty Fyodorovich

Nin, Anais
1903-1977 ...... **CLC 1, 4, 8, 11, 14, 60;
DAM NOV, POP; SSC 10**
See also AITN 2; CA 13-16R; 69-72;
CANR 22, 53; DLB 2, 4, 152; MTCW

Nishiwaki, Junzaburo 1894-1982 .... **PC 15**
See also CA 107

Nissenson, Hugh 1933-........... **CLC 4, 9**
See also CA 17-20R; CANR 27; DLB 28

Niven, Larry .... **CLC 8**
See also Niven, Laurence Van Cott
See also DLB 8

Niven, Laurence Van Cott 1938-
See Niven, Larry
See also CA 21-24R; CAAS 12; CANR 14,
44; DAM POP; MTCW

Nixon, Agnes Eckhardt 1927-...... **CLC 21**
See also CA 110

Nizan, Paul 1905-1940........... **TCLC 40**
See also DLB 72

Nkosi, Lewis
1936- ..... **CLC 45; BLC; DAM MULT**
See also BW 1; CA 65-68; CANR 27;
DLB 157

Nodier, (Jean) Charles (Emmanuel)
1780-1844 .... **NCLC 19**
See also DLB 119

Nolan, Christopher 1965-......... **CLC 58**
See also CA 111

Noon, Jeff 1957-................. **CLC 91**
See also CA 148

Norden, Charles
See Durrell, Lawrence (George)

Nordhoff, Charles (Bernard)
1887-1947 .... **TCLC 23**
See also CA 108; DLB 9; SATA 23

Norfolk, Lawrence 1963-......... **CLC 76**
See also CA 144

Norman, Marsha
1947- .... **CLC 28; DAM DRAM**
See also CA 105; CABS 3; CANR 41;
DLBY 84

Norris, Benjamin Franklin, Jr.
1870-1902 .... **TCLC 24**
See also Norris, Frank
See also CA 110

Norris, Frank
See Norris, Benjamin Franklin, Jr.
See also CDALB 1865-1917; DLB 12, 71

Norris, Leslie 1921- .... **CLC 14**
See also CA 11-12; CANR 14; CAP 1;
DLB 27

North, Andrew
See Norton, Andre

North, Anthony
See Koontz, Dean R(ay)

North, Captain George
See Stevenson, Robert Louis (Balfour)

North, Milou
See Erdrich, Louise

Northrup, B. A.
See Hubbard, L(afayette) Ron(ald)

North Staffs
See Hulme, T(homas) E(rnest)

Norton, Alice Mary
See Norton, Andre
See also MAICYA; SATA 1, 43

Norton, Andre 1912- .... **CLC 12**
See also Norton, Alice Mary
See also AAYA 14; CA 1-4R; CANR 2, 31;
DLB 8, 52; JRDA; MTCW

Norton, Caroline 1808-1877...... **NCLC 47**
See also DLB 21, 159

Norway, Nevil Shute 1899-1960
See Shute, Nevil
See also CA 102; 93-96

Norwid, Cyprian Kamil
1821-1883 .... **NCLC 17**

Nosille, Nabrah
See Ellison, Harlan (Jay)

Nossack, Hans Erich 1901-1978..... **CLC 6**
See also CA 93-96; 85-88; DLB 69

Nostradamus 1503-1566............ **LC 27**

Nosu, Chuji
See Ozu, Yasujiro

Notenburg, Eleanora (Genrikhovna) von
See Guro, Elena

Nova, Craig 1945-............... **CLC 7, 31**
See also CA 45-48; CANR 2, 53

Novak, Joseph
See Kosinski, Jerzy (Nikodem)

Novalis 1772-1801 .... **NCLC 13**
See also DLB 90

Nowlan, Alden (Albert)
1933-1983 .. **CLC 15; DAC; DAM MST**
See also CA 9-12R; CANR 5; DLB 53

Noyes, Alfred 1880-1958 .... **TCLC 7**
See also CA 104; DLB 20

Nunn, Kem 19(?)-................ **CLC 34**

Nye, Robert
1939- .... **CLC 13, 42; DAM NOV**
See also CA 33-36R; CANR 29; DLB 14;
MTCW; SATA 6

Nyro, Laura 1947- .... **CLC 17**

Oates, Joyce Carol
1938- ...... **CLC 1, 2, 3, 6, 9, 11, 15, 19,
33, 52; DA; DAB; DAC; DAM MST,
NOV, POP; SSC 6; WLC**
See also AAYA 15; AITN 1; BEST 89:2;
CA 5-8R; CANR 25, 45;
CDALB 1968-1988; DLB 2, 5, 130;
DLBY 81; INT CANR-25; MTCW

Orwell, George
..... TCLC 2, 6, 15, 31, 51; DAB; WLC
See also Blair, Eric (Arthur)
See also CDBLB 1945-1960; DLB 15, 98

Osborne, David
See Silverberg, Robert

Osborne, George
See Silverberg, Robert

Osborne, John (James)
1929-1994 ..... CLC 1, 2, 5, 11, 45; DA;
DAB; DAC; DAM DRAM, MST; WLC
See also CA 13-16R; 147; CANR 21;
CDBLB 1945-1960; DLB 13; MTCW

Osborne, Lawrence 1958- .... CLC 50

Oshima, Nagisa 1932- .... CLC 20
See also CA 116; 121

Oskison, John Milton
1874-1947 ..... TCLC 35; DAM MULT
See also CA 144; NNAL

Ossoli, Sarah Margaret (Fuller marchesa d')
1810-1850
See Fuller, Margaret
See also SATA 25

Ostrovsky, Alexander
1823-1886 .... NCLC 30, 57

Otero, Blas de 1916-1979......... CLC 11
See also CA 89-92; DLB 134

Otto, Whitney 1955-.............. CLC 70
See also CA 140

Ouida .... TCLC 43
See also De La Ramee, (Marie) Louise
See also DLB 18, 156

Ousmane, Sembene 1923- .... CLC 66; BLC
See also BW 1; CA 117; 125; MTCW

Ovid
43B.C.-18(?) ... CMLC 7; DAM POET;
PC 2

Owen, Hugh
See Faust, Frederick (Schiller)

Owen, Wilfred (Edward Salter)
1893-1918 ...... TCLC 5, 27; DA; DAB;
DAC; DAM MST, POET; WLC
See also CA 104; 141; CDBLB 1914-1945;
DLB 20

Owens, Rochelle 1936-............. CLC 8
See also CA 17-20R; CAAS 2; CANR 39

Oz, Amos
1939- .... CLC 5, 8, 11, 27, 33, 54;
DAM NOV
See also CA 53-56; CANR 27, 47; MTCW

Ozick, Cynthia
1928- .... CLC 3, 7, 28, 62; DAM NOV,
POP; SSC 15
See also BEST 90:1; CA 17-20R; CANR 23;
DLB 28, 152; DLBY 82; INT CANR-23;
MTCW

Ozu, Yasujiro 1903-1963 .... CLC 16
See also CA 112

Pacheco, C.
See Pessoa, Fernando (Antonio Nogueira)

Pa Chin .... CLC 18
See also Li Fei-kan

Pack, Robert 1929-.............. CLC 13
See also CA 1-4R; CANR 3, 44; DLB 5

Padgett, Lewis
See Kuttner, Henry

Padilla (Lorenzo), Heberto 1932- ... CLC 38
See also AITN 1; CA 123; 131; HW

Page, Jimmy 1944-................ CLC 12

Page, Louise 1955-.............. CLC 40
See also CA 140

Page, P(atricia) K(athleen)
1916- .... CLC 7, 18; DAC; DAM MST;
PC 12
See also CA 53-56; CANR 4, 22; DLB 68;
MTCW

Page, Thomas Nelson 1853-1922.... SSC 23
See also CA 118; DLB 12, 78; DLBD 13

Paget, Violet 1856-1935
See Lee, Vernon
See also CA 104

Paget-Lowe, Henry
See Lovecraft, H(oward) P(hillips)

Paglia, Camille (Anna) 1947-....... CLC 68
See also CA 140

Paige, Richard
See Koontz, Dean R(ay)

Pakenham, Antonia
See Fraser, (Lady) Antonia (Pakenham)

Palamas, Kostes 1859-1943 .... TCLC 5
See also CA 105

Palazzeschi, Aldo 1885-1974....... CLC 11
See also CA 89-92; 53-56; DLB 114

Paley, Grace
1922- .... CLC 4, 6, 37; DAM POP;
SSC 8
See also CA 25-28R; CANR 13, 46;
DLB 28; INT CANR-13; MTCW

Palin, Michael (Edward) 1943-..... CLC 21
See also Monty Python
See also CA 107; CANR 35; SATA 67

Palliser, Charles 1947-............ CLC 65
See also CA 136

Palma, Ricardo 1833-1919........ TCLC 29

Pancake, Breece Dexter 1952-1979
See Pancake, Breece D'J
See also CA 123; 109

Pancake, Breece D'J............... CLC 29
See also Pancake, Breece Dexter
See also DLB 130

Panko, Rudy
See Gogol, Nikolai (Vasilyevich)

Papadiamantis, Alexandros
1851-1911 .... TCLC 29

Papadiamantopoulos, Johannes 1856-1910
See Moreas, Jean
See also CA 117

Papini, Giovanni 1881-1956....... TCLC 22
See also CA 121

Paracelsus 1493-1541.............. LC 14

Parasol, Peter
See Stevens, Wallace

Parfenie, Maria
See Codrescu, Andrei

Parini, Jay (Lee) 1948- .... CLC 54
See also CA 97-100; CAAS 16; CANR 32

Park, Jordan
See Kornbluth, C(yril) M.; Pohl, Frederik

Parker, Bert
See Ellison, Harlan (Jay)

Parker, Dorothy (Rothschild)
1893-1967 .... CLC 15, 68;
DAM POET; SSC 2
See also CA 19-20; 25-28R; CAP 2;
DLB 11, 45, 86; MTCW

Parker, Robert B(rown)
1932- ...... CLC 27; DAM NOV, POP
See also BEST 89:4; CA 49-52; CANR 1,
26, 52; INT CANR-26; MTCW

Parkin, Frank 1940-.............. CLC 43
See also CA 147

Parkman, Francis, Jr.
1823-1893 .... NCLC 12
See also DLB 1, 30

Parks, Gordon (Alexander Buchanan)
1912- ... CLC 1, 16; BLC; DAM MULT
See also AITN 2; BW 2; CA 41-44R;
CANR 26; DLB 33; SATA 8

Parnell, Thomas 1679-1718 .... LC 3
See also DLB 94

Parra, Nicanor
1914- ...... CLC 2; DAM MULT; HLC
See also CA 85-88; CANR 32; HW; MTCW

Parrish, Mary Frances
See Fisher, M(ary) F(rances) K(ennedy)

Parson
See Coleridge, Samuel Taylor

Parson Lot
See Kingsley, Charles

Partridge, Anthony
See Oppenheim, E(dward) Phillips

Pascal, Blaise 1623-1662 .... LC 35

Pascoli, Giovanni 1855-1912 ...... TCLC 45

Pasolini, Pier Paolo
1922-1975 .... CLC 20, 37
See also CA 93-96; 61-64; DLB 128;
MTCW

Pasquini
See Silone, Ignazio

Pastan, Linda (Olenik)
1932- .... CLC 27; DAM POET
See also CA 61-64; CANR 18, 40; DLB 5

Pasternak, Boris (Leonidovich)
1890-1960 ...... CLC 7, 10, 18, 63; DA;
DAB; DAC; DAM MST, NOV, POET;
PC 6; WLC
See also CA 127; 116; MTCW

Patchen, Kenneth
1911-1972 ... CLC 1, 2, 18; DAM POET
See also CA 1-4R; 33-36R; CANR 3, 35;
DLB 16, 48; MTCW

Pater, Walter (Horatio)
1839-1894 .... NCLC 7
See also CDBLB 1832-1890; DLB 57, 156

Paterson, A(ndrew) B(arton)
1864-1941 .... TCLC 32

Paterson, Katherine (Womeldorf)
1932- .... CLC 12, 30
See also AAYA 1; CA 21-24R; CANR 28;
CLR 7; DLB 52; JRDA; MAICYA;
MTCW; SATA 13, 53

Piers, Robert
See Anthony, Piers

Pieyre de Mandiargues, Andre 1909-1991
See Mandiargues, Andre Pieyre de
See also CA 103; 136; CANR 22

Pilnyak, Boris .... TCLC 23
See also Vogau, Boris Andreyevich

Pincherle, Alberto
1907-1990 ..... CLC 11, 18; DAM NOV
See also Moravia, Alberto
See also CA 25-28R; 132; CANR 33;
MTCW

Pinckney, Darryl 1953- .... CLC 76
See also BW 2; CA 143

Pindar 518B.C.-446B.C. .... CMLC 12

Pineda, Cecile 1942- .... CLC 39
See also CA 118

Pinero, Arthur Wing
1855-1934 ..... TCLC 32; DAM DRAM
See also CA 110; DLB 10

Pinero, Miguel (Antonio Gomez)
1946-1988 .... CLC 4, 55
See also CA 61-64; 125; CANR 29; HW

Pinget, Robert 1919- .... CLC 7, 13, 37
See also CA 85-88; DLB 83

Pink Floyd
See Barrett, (Roger) Syd; Gilmour, David;
Mason, Nick; Waters, Roger; Wright,
Rick

Pinkney, Edward 1802-1828 ..... NCLC 31

Pinkwater, Daniel Manus 1941- .... CLC 35
See also Pinkwater, Manus
See also AAYA 1; CA 29-32R; CANR 12,
38; CLR 4; JRDA; MAICYA; SAAS 3;
SATA 46, 76

Pinkwater, Manus
See Pinkwater, Daniel Manus
See also SATA 8

Pinsky, Robert
1940- .. CLC 9, 19, 38, 94; DAM POET
See also CA 29-32R; CAAS 4; DLBY 82

Pinta, Harold
See Pinter, Harold

Pinter, Harold
1930- ..... CLC 1, 3, 6, 9, 11, 15, 27, 58,
73; DA; DAB; DAC; DAM DRAM,
MST; WLC
See also CA 5-8R; CANR 33; CDBLB 1960
to Present; DLB 13; MTCW

Piozzi, Hester Lynch (Thrale)
1741-1821 .... NCLC 57
See also DLB 104, 142

Pirandello, Luigi
1867-1936 ...... TCLC 4, 29; DA; DAB;
DAC; DAM DRAM, MST; DC 5;
SSC 22; WLC
See also CA 104

Pirsig, Robert M(aynard)
1928- .... CLC 4, 6, 73; DAM POP
See also CA 53-56; CANR 42; MTCW;
SATA 39

Pisarev, Dmitry Ivanovich
1840-1868 .... NCLC 25

Pix, Mary (Griffith) 1666-1709 .... LC 8
See also DLB 80

Pixerecourt, Guilbert de
1773-1844 .... NCLC 39

Plaidy, Jean
See Hibbert, Eleanor Alice Burford

Planche, James Robinson
1796-1880 .... NCLC 42

Plant, Robert 1948- .... CLC 12

Plante, David (Robert)
1940- ...... CLC 7, 23, 38; DAM NOV
See also CA 37-40R; CANR 12, 36;
DLBY 83; INT CANR-12; MTCW

Plath, Sylvia
1932-1963 ..... CLC 1, 2, 3, 5, 9, 11, 14,
17, 50, 51, 62; DA; DAB; DAC;
DAM MST, POET; PC 1; WLC
See also AAYA 13; CA 19-20; CANR 34;
CAP 2; CDALB 1941-1968; DLB 5, 6,
152; MTCW

Plato
428(?)B.C.-348(?)B.C. ..... CMLC 8; DA;
DAB; DAC; DAM MST

Platonov, Andrei .... TCLC 14
See also Klimentov, Andrei Platonovich

Platt, Kin 1911- .... CLC 26
See also AAYA 11; CA 17-20R; CANR 11;
JRDA; SAAS 17; SATA 21, 86

Plautus c. 251B.C.-184B.C. .... DC 6

Plick et Plock
See Simenon, Georges (Jacques Christian)

Plimpton, George (Ames) 1927- ..... CLC 36
See also AITN 1; CA 21-24R; CANR 32;
MTCW; SATA 10

Plomer, William Charles Franklin
1903-1973 .... CLC 4, 8
See also CA 21-22; CANR 34; CAP 2;
DLB 20, 162; MTCW; SATA 24

Plowman, Piers
See Kavanagh, Patrick (Joseph)

Plum, J.
See Wodehouse, P(elham) G(renville)

Plumly, Stanley (Ross) 1939- ...... CLC 33
See also CA 108; 110; DLB 5; INT 110

Plumpe, Friedrich Wilhelm
1888-1931 .... TCLC 53
See also CA 112

Poe, Edgar Allan
1809-1849 .... NCLC 1, 16, 55; DA;
DAB; DAC; DAM MST, POET; PC 1;
SSC 1, 22; WLC
See also AAYA 14; CDALB 1640-1865;
DLB 3, 59, 73, 74; SATA 23

Poet of Titchfield Street, The
See Pound, Ezra (Weston Loomis)

Pohl, Frederik 1919- .... CLC 18
See also CA 61-64; CAAS 1; CANR 11, 37;
DLB 8; INT CANR-11; MTCW;
SATA 24

Poirier, Louis 1910-
See Gracq, Julien
See also CA 122; 126

Poitier, Sidney 1927- .... CLC 26
See also BW 1; CA 117

Polanski, Roman 1933- .... CLC 16
See also CA 77-80

Poliakoff, Stephen 1952- .... CLC 38
See also CA 106; DLB 13

Police, The
See Copeland, Stewart (Armstrong);
Summers, Andrew James; Sumner,
Gordon Matthew

Polidori, John William
1795-1821 .... NCLC 51
See also DLB 116

Pollitt, Katha 1949- .... CLC 28
See also CA 120; 122; MTCW

Pollock, (Mary) Sharon
1936- .... CLC 50; DAC; DAM DRAM,
MST
See also CA 141; DLB 60

Polo, Marco 1254-1324 .... CMLC 15

Polonsky, Abraham (Lincoln)
1910- .... CLC 92
See also CA 104; DLB 26; INT 104

Polybius c. 200B.C.-c. 118B.C. .... CMLC 17

Pomerance, Bernard
1940- .... CLC 13; DAM DRAM
See also CA 101; CANR 49

Ponge, Francis (Jean Gaston Alfred)
1899-1988 ..... CLC 6, 18; DAM POET
See also CA 85-88; 126; CANR 40

Pontoppidan, Henrik 1857-1943 ... TCLC 29

Poole, Josephine .... CLC 17
See also Helyar, Jane Penelope Josephine
See also SAAS 2; SATA 5

Popa, Vasko 1922-1991 .... CLC 19
See also CA 112; 148

Pope, Alexander
1688-1744 ...... LC 3; DA; DAB; DAC;
DAM MST, POET; WLC
See also CDBLB 1660-1789; DLB 95, 101

Porter, Connie (Rose) 1959(?)- ..... CLC 70
See also BW 2; CA 142; SATA 81

Porter, Gene(va Grace) Stratton
1863(?)-1924 .... TCLC 21
See also CA 112

Porter, Katherine Anne
1890-1980 ...... CLC 1, 3, 7, 10, 13, 15,
27; DA; DAB; DAC; DAM MST, NOV;
SSC 4
See also AITN 2; CA 1-4R; 101; CANR 1;
DLB 4, 9, 102; DLBD 12; DLBY 80;
MTCW; SATA 39; SATA-Obit 23

Porter, Peter (Neville Frederick)
1929- .... CLC 5, 13, 33
See also CA 85-88; DLB 40

Porter, William Sydney 1862-1910
See Henry, O.
See also CA 104; 131; CDALB 1865-1917;
DA; DAB; DAC; DAM MST; DLB 12,
78, 79; MTCW; YABC 2

Portillo (y Pacheco), Jose Lopez
See Lopez Portillo (y Pacheco), Jose

Post, Melville Davisson
1869-1930 .... TCLC 39
See also CA 110

Potok, Chaim
1929- .... **CLC 2, 7, 14, 26; DAM NOV**
See also AAYA 15; AITN 1, 2; CA 17-20R;
CANR 19, 35; DLB 28, 152;
INT CANR-19; MTCW; SATA 33

Potter, Beatrice
See Webb, (Martha) Beatrice (Potter)
See also MAICYA

Potter, Dennis (Christopher George)
1935-1994 .... **CLC 58, 86**
See also CA 107; 145; CANR 33; MTCW

Pound, Ezra (Weston Loomis)
1885-1972 ...... **CLC 1, 2, 3, 4, 5, 7, 10,
13, 18, 34, 48, 50; DA; DAB; DAC;
DAM MST, POET; PC 4; WLC**
See also CA 5-8R; 37-40R; CANR 40;
CDALB 1917-1929; DLB 4, 45, 63;
MTCW

Povod, Reinaldo 1959-1994 .... **CLC 44**
See also CA 136; 146

Powell, Adam Clayton, Jr.
1908-1972 .... **CLC 89; BLC;
DAM MULT**
See also BW 1; CA 102; 33-36R

Powell, Anthony (Dymoke)
1905- .... **CLC 1, 3, 7, 9, 10, 31**
See also CA 1-4R; CANR 1, 32;
CDBLB 1945-1960; DLB 15; MTCW

Powell, Dawn 1897-1965 .... **CLC 66**
See also CA 5-8R

Powell, Padgett 1952- .... **CLC 34**
See also CA 126

Power, Susan .... **CLC 91**

Powers, J(ames) F(arl)
1917- .... **CLC 1, 4, 8, 57; SSC 4**
See also CA 1-4R; CANR 2; DLB 130;
MTCW

Powers, John J(ames) 1945-
See Powers, John R.
See also CA 69-72

Powers, John R. .... **CLC 66**
See also Powers, John J(ames)

Powers, Richard (S.) 1957- .... **CLC 93**
See also CA 148

Pownall, David 1938- .... **CLC 10**
See also CA 89-92; CAAS 18; CANR 49;
DLB 14

Powys, John Cowper
1872-1963 .... **CLC 7, 9, 15, 46**
See also CA 85-88; DLB 15; MTCW

Powys, T(heodore) F(rancis)
1875-1953 .... **TCLC 9**
See also CA 106; DLB 36, 162

Prager, Emily 1952- .... **CLC 56**

Pratt, E(dwin) J(ohn)
1883(?)-1964 .... **CLC 19; DAC;
DAM POET**
See also CA 141; 93-96; DLB 92

Premchand .... **TCLC 21**
See also Srivastava, Dhanpat Rai

Preussler, Otfried 1923- .... **CLC 17**
See also CA 77-80; SATA 24

Prevert, Jacques (Henri Marie)
1900-1977 .... **CLC 15**
See also CA 77-80; 69-72; CANR 29;
MTCW; SATA-Obit 30

Prevost, Abbe (Antoine Francois)
1697-1763 .... **LC 1**

Price, (Edward) Reynolds
1933- .... **CLC 3, 6, 13, 43, 50, 63;
DAM NOV; SSC 22**
See also CA 1-4R; CANR 1, 37; DLB 2;
INT CANR-37

Price, Richard 1949- .... **CLC 6, 12**
See also CA 49-52; CANR 3; DLBY 81

Prichard, Katharine Susannah
1883-1969 .... **CLC 46**
See also CA 11-12; CANR 33; CAP 1;
MTCW; SATA 66

Priestley, J(ohn) B(oynton)
1894-1984 .... **CLC 2, 5, 9, 34;
DAM DRAM, NOV**
See also CA 9-12R; 113; CANR 33;
CDBLB 1914-1945; DLB 10, 34, 77, 100,
139; DLBY 84; MTCW

Prince 1958(?)- .... **CLC 35**

Prince, F(rank) T(empleton) 1912- .. **CLC 22**
See also CA 101; CANR 43; DLB 20

Prince Kropotkin
See Kropotkin, Peter (Aleksieevich)

Prior, Matthew 1664-1721 .... **LC 4**
See also DLB 95

Pritchard, William H(arrison)
1932- .... **CLC 34**
See also CA 65-68; CANR 23; DLB 111

Pritchett, V(ictor) S(awdon)
1900- .... **CLC 5, 13, 15, 41;
DAM NOV; SSC 14**
See also CA 61-64; CANR 31; DLB 15,
139; MTCW

Private 19022
See Manning, Frederic

Probst, Mark 1925- .... **CLC 59**
See also CA 130

Prokosch, Frederic 1908-1989 .... **CLC 4, 48**
See also CA 73-76; 128; DLB 48

Prophet, The
See Dreiser, Theodore (Herman Albert)

Prose, Francine 1947- .... **CLC 45**
See also CA 109; 112; CANR 46

Proudhon
See Cunha, Euclides (Rodrigues Pimenta) da

Proulx, E. Annie 1935- .... **CLC 81**

**Proust, (Valentin-Louis-George-Eugene-)
Marcel**
1871-1922 .... **TCLC 7, 13, 33; DA;
DAB; DAC; DAM MST, NOV; WLC**
See also CA 104; 120; DLB 65; MTCW

Prowler, Harley
See Masters, Edgar Lee

Prus, Boleslaw 1845-1912 .... **TCLC 48**

Pryor, Richard (Franklin Lenox Thomas)
1940- .... **CLC 26**
See also CA 122

Przybyszewski, Stanislaw
1868-1927 .... **TCLC 36**
See also DLB 66

Pteleon
See Grieve, C(hristopher) M(urray)
See also DAM POET

Puckett, Lute
See Masters, Edgar Lee

Puig, Manuel
1932-1990 .... **CLC 3, 5, 10, 28, 65;
DAM MULT; HLC**
See also CA 45-48; CANR 2, 32; DLB 113;
HW; MTCW

Purdy, Al(fred Wellington)
1918- .... **CLC 3, 6, 14, 50; DAC;
DAM MST, POET**
See also CA 81-84; CAAS 17; CANR 42;
DLB 88

Purdy, James (Amos)
1923- .... **CLC 2, 4, 10, 28, 52**
See also CA 33-36R; CAAS 1; CANR 19,
51; DLB 2; INT CANR-19; MTCW

Pure, Simon
See Swinnerton, Frank Arthur

Pushkin, Alexander (Sergeyevich)
1799-1837 ..... **NCLC 3, 27; DA; DAB;
DAC; DAM DRAM, MST, POET;
PC 10; WLC**
See also SATA 61

P'u Sung-ling 1640-1715 .... **LC 3**

Putnam, Arthur Lee
See Alger, Horatio, Jr.

Puzo, Mario
1920- ..... **CLC 1, 2, 6, 36; DAM NOV,
POP**
See also CA 65-68; CANR 4, 42; DLB 6;
MTCW

Pym, Barbara (Mary Crampton)
1913-1980 .... **CLC 13, 19, 37**
See also CA 13-14; 97-100; CANR 13, 34;
CAP 1; DLB 14; DLBY 87; MTCW

Pynchon, Thomas (Ruggles, Jr.)
1937- ..... **CLC 2, 3, 6, 9, 11, 18, 33, 62,
72; DA; DAB; DAC; DAM MST, NOV,
POP; SSC 14; WLC**
See also BEST 90:2; CA 17-20R; CANR 22,
46; DLB 2; MTCW

Qian Zhongshu
See Ch'ien Chung-shu

Qroll
See Dagerman, Stig (Halvard)

Quarrington, Paul (Lewis) 1953- .... **CLC 65**
See also CA 129

Quasimodo, Salvatore 1901-1968 ... **CLC 10**
See also CA 13-16; 25-28R; CAP 1;
DLB 114; MTCW

Quay, Stephen 1947- .... **CLC 95**

Quay, The Brothers
See Quay, Stephen; Quay, Timothy

Quay, Timothy 1947- .... **CLC 95**

Queen, Ellery .... **CLC 3, 11**
See also Dannay, Frederic; Davidson,
Avram; Lee, Manfred B(ennington);
Sturgeon, Theodore (Hamilton); Vance,
John Holbrook

Queen, Ellery, Jr.
See Dannay, Frederic; Lee, Manfred
B(ennington)

Queneau, Raymond
1903-1976 . . . . **CLC 2, 5, 10, 42**
See also CA 77-80; 69-72; CANR 32;
DLB 72; MTCW

Quevedo, Francisco de 1580-1645 . . . . **LC 23**

Quiller-Couch, Arthur Thomas
1863-1944 . . . . **TCLC 53**
See also CA 118; DLB 135, 153

Quin, Ann (Marie) 1936-1973 . . . . . . **CLC 6**
See also CA 9-12R; 45-48; DLB 14

Quinn, Martin
See Smith, Martin Cruz

Quinn, Peter 1947- . . . . **CLC 91**

Quinn, Simon
See Smith, Martin Cruz

Quiroga, Horacio (Sylvestre)
1878-1937 . . . . . **TCLC 20; DAM MULT;**
HLC
See also CA 117; 131; HW; MTCW

Quoirez, Francoise 1935- . . . . **CLC 9**
See also Sagan, Francoise
See also CA 49-52; CANR 6, 39; MTCW

Raabe, Wilhelm 1831-1910 . . . . **TCLC 45**
See also DLB 129

Rabe, David (William)
1940- . . . . . . **CLC 4, 8, 33; DAM DRAM**
See also CA 85-88; CABS 3; DLB 7

Rabelais, Francois
1483-1553 . . . . . . **LC 5; DA; DAB; DAC;**
DAM MST; WLC

Rabinovitch, Sholem 1859-1916
See Aleichem, Sholom
See also CA 104

Racine, Jean
1639-1699 . . . . **LC 28; DAB; DAM MST**

Radcliffe, Ann (Ward)
1764-1823 . . . . **NCLC 6, 55**
See also DLB 39

Radiguet, Raymond 1903-1923 . . . . **TCLC 29**
See also DLB 65

Radnoti, Miklos 1909-1944 . . . . **TCLC 16**
See also CA 118

Rado, James 1939- . . . . **CLC 17**
See also CA 105

Radvanyi, Netty 1900-1983
See Seghers, Anna
See also CA 85-88; 110

Rae, Ben
See Griffiths, Trevor

Raeburn, John (Hay) 1941- . . . . **CLC 34**
See also CA 57-60

Ragni, Gerome 1942-1991 . . . . **CLC 17**
See also CA 105; 134

Rahv, Philip 1908-1973 . . . . **CLC 24**
See also Greenberg, Ivan
See also DLB 137

Raine, Craig 1944- . . . . **CLC 32**
See also CA 108; CANR 29, 51; DLB 40

Raine, Kathleen (Jessie) 1908- . . . **CLC 7, 45**
See also CA 85-88; CANR 46; DLB 20;
MTCW

Rainis, Janis 1865-1929 . . . . **TCLC 29**

Rakosi, Carl . . . . **CLC 47**
See also Rawley, Callman
See also CAAS 5

Raleigh, Richard
See Lovecraft, H(oward) P(hillips)

Raleigh, Sir Walter 1554(?)-1618 . . . . **LC 31**
See also CDBLB Before 1660

Rallentando, H. P.
See Sayers, Dorothy L(eigh)

Ramal, Walter
See de la Mare, Walter (John)

Ramon, Juan
See Jimenez (Mantecon), Juan Ramon

Ramos, Graciliano 1892-1953 . . . . . **TCLC 32**

Rampersad, Arnold 1941- . . . . **CLC 44**
See also BW 2; CA 127; 133; DLB 111;
INT 133

Rampling, Anne
See Rice, Anne

Ramsay, Allan 1684(?)-1758 . . . . **LC 29**
See also DLB 95

Ramuz, Charles-Ferdinand
1878-1947 . . . . **TCLC 33**

Rand, Ayn
1905-1982 . . . . . . **CLC 3, 30, 44, 79; DA;**
DAC; DAM MST, NOV, POP; WLC
See also AAYA 10; CA 13-16R; 105;
CANR 27; MTCW

Randall, Dudley (Felker)
1914- . . . . . . **CLC 1; BLC; DAM MULT**
See also BW 1; CA 25-28R; CANR 23;
DLB 41

Randall, Robert
See Silverberg, Robert

Ranger, Ken
See Creasey, John

Ransom, John Crowe
1888-1974 . . . . **CLC 2, 4, 5, 11, 24;**
DAM POET
See also CA 5-8R; 49-52; CANR 6, 34;
DLB 45, 63; MTCW

Rao, Raja 1909- . . . **CLC 25, 56; DAM NOV**
See also CA 73-76; CANR 51; MTCW

Raphael, Frederic (Michael)
1931- . . . . **CLC 2, 14**
See also CA 1-4R; CANR 1; DLB 14

Ratcliffe, James P.
See Mencken, H(enry) L(ouis)

Rathbone, Julian 1935- . . . . **CLC 41**
See also CA 101; CANR 34

Rattigan, Terence (Mervyn)
1911-1977 . . . . **CLC 7; DAM DRAM**
See also CA 85-88; 73-76;
CDBLB 1945-1960; DLB 13; MTCW

Ratushinskaya, Irina 1954- . . . . **CLC 54**
See also CA 129

Raven, Simon (Arthur Noel)
1927- . . . . **CLC 14**
See also CA 81-84

Rawley, Callman 1903-
See Rakosi, Carl
See also CA 21-24R; CANR 12, 32

Rawlings, Marjorie Kinnan
1896-1953 . . . . **TCLC 4**
See also CA 104; 137; DLB 9, 22, 102;
JRDA; MAICYA; YABC 1

Ray, Satyajit
1921-1992 . . . **CLC 16, 76; DAM MULT**
See also CA 114; 137

Read, Herbert Edward 1893-1968 . . . . **CLC 4**
See also CA 85-88; 25-28R; DLB 20, 149

Read, Piers Paul 1941- . . . . . . **CLC 4, 10, 25**
See also CA 21-24R; CANR 38; DLB 14;
SATA 21

Reade, Charles 1814-1884 . . . . **NCLC 2**
See also DLB 21

Reade, Hamish
See Gray, Simon (James Holliday)

Reading, Peter 1946- . . . . **CLC 47**
See also CA 103; CANR 46; DLB 40

Reaney, James
1926- . . . . . . **CLC 13; DAC; DAM MST**
See also CA 41-44R; CAAS 15; CANR 42;
DLB 68; SATA 43

Rebreanu, Liviu 1885-1944 . . . . **TCLC 28**

Rechy, John (Francisco)
1934- . . . . **CLC 1, 7, 14, 18;**
DAM MULT; HLC
See also CA 5-8R; CAAS 4; CANR 6, 32;
DLB 122; DLBY 82; HW; INT CANR-6

Redcam, Tom 1870-1933 . . . . **TCLC 25**

Reddin, Keith . . . . **CLC 67**

Redgrove, Peter (William)
1932- . . . . **CLC 6, 41**
See also CA 1-4R; CANR 3, 39; DLB 40

Redmon, Anne . . . . **CLC 22**
See also Nightingale, Anne Redmon
See also DLBY 86

Reed, Eliot
See Ambler, Eric

Reed, Ishmael
1938- . . . . **CLC 2, 3, 5, 6, 13, 32, 60;**
BLC; DAM MULT
See also BW 2; CA 21-24R; CANR 25, 48;
DLB 2, 5, 33, 169; DLBD 8; MTCW

Reed, John (Silas) 1887-1920 . . . . . . **TCLC 9**
See also CA 106

Reed, Lou . . . . **CLC 21**
See also Firbank, Louis

Reeve, Clara 1729-1807 . . . . **NCLC 19**
See also DLB 39

Reich, Wilhelm 1897-1957 . . . . **TCLC 57**

Reid, Christopher (John) 1949- . . . . . **CLC 33**
See also CA 140; DLB 40

Reid, Desmond
See Moorcock, Michael (John)

Reid Banks, Lynne 1929-
See Banks, Lynne Reid
See also CA 1-4R; CANR 6, 22, 38;
CLR 24; JRDA; MAICYA; SATA 22, 75

Reilly, William K.
See Creasey, John

Reiner, Max
See Caldwell, (Janet Miriam) Taylor
(Holland)

Reis, Ricardo
See Pessoa, Fernando (Antonio Nogueira)

Remarque, Erich Maria
1898-1970 .... **CLC 21; DA; DAB; DAC; DAM MST, NOV**
See also CA 77-80; 29-32R; DLB 56; MTCW

Remizov, A.
See Remizov, Aleksei (Mikhailovich)

Remizov, A. M.
See Remizov, Aleksei (Mikhailovich)

Remizov, Aleksei (Mikhailovich)
1877-1957 .... **TCLC 27**
See also CA 125; 133

Renan, Joseph Ernest
1823-1892 .... **NCLC 26**

Renard, Jules 1864-1910 .... **TCLC 17**
See also CA 117

Renault, Mary .... **CLC 3, 11, 17**
See also Challans, Mary
See also DLBY 83

Rendell, Ruth (Barbara)
1930- .... **CLC 28, 48; DAM POP**
See also Vine, Barbara
See also CA 109; CANR 32, 52; DLB 87; INT CANR-32; MTCW

Renoir, Jean 1894-1979 .... **CLC 20**
See also CA 129; 85-88

Resnais, Alain 1922- .... **CLC 16**

Reverdy, Pierre 1889-1960 .... **CLC 53**
See also CA 97-100; 89-92

Rexroth, Kenneth
1905-1982 ...... **CLC 1, 2, 6, 11, 22, 49; DAM POET**
See also CA 5-8R; 107; CANR 14, 34; CDALB 1941-1968; DLB 16, 48, 165; DLBY 82; INT CANR-14; MTCW

Reyes, Alfonso 1889-1959 .... **TCLC 33**
See also CA 131; HW

Reyes y Basoalto, Ricardo Eliecer Neftali
See Neruda, Pablo

Reymont, Wladyslaw (Stanislaw)
1868(?)-1925 .... **TCLC 5**
See also CA 104

Reynolds, Jonathan 1942- .... **CLC 6, 38**
See also CA 65-68; CANR 28

Reynolds, Joshua 1723-1792 .... **LC 15**
See also DLB 104

Reynolds, Michael Shane 1937- .... **CLC 44**
See also CA 65-68; CANR 9

Reznikoff, Charles 1894-1976 .... **CLC 9**
See also CA 33-36; 61-64; CAP 2; DLB 28, 45

Rezzori (d'Arezzo), Gregor von
1914- .... **CLC 25**
See also CA 122; 136

Rhine, Richard
See Silverstein, Alvin

Rhodes, Eugene Manlove
1869-1934 .... **TCLC 53**

R'hoone
See Balzac, Honore de

Rhys, Jean
1890(?)-1979 .... **CLC 2, 4, 6, 14, 19, 51; DAM NOV; SSC 21**
See also CA 25-28R; 85-88; CANR 35; CDBLB 1945-1960; DLB 36, 117, 162; MTCW

Ribeiro, Darcy 1922- .... **CLC 34**
See also CA 33-36R

Ribeiro, Joao Ubaldo (Osorio Pimentel)
1941- .... **CLC 10, 67**
See also CA 81-84

Ribman, Ronald (Burt) 1932- .... **CLC 7**
See also CA 21-24R; CANR 46

Ricci, Nino 1959- .... **CLC 70**
See also CA 137

Rice, Anne 1941- ..... **CLC 41; DAM POP**
See also AAYA 9; BEST 89:2; CA 65-68; CANR 12, 36, 53

Rice, Elmer (Leopold)
1892-1967 ...... **CLC 7, 49; DAM DRAM**
See also CA 21-22; 25-28R; CAP 2; DLB 4, 7; MTCW

Rice, Tim(othy Miles Bindon)
1944- .... **CLC 21**
See also CA 103; CANR 46

Rich, Adrienne (Cecile)
1929- .... **CLC 3, 6, 7, 11, 18, 36, 73, 76; DAM POET; PC 5**
See also CA 9-12R; CANR 20, 53; DLB 5, 67; MTCW

Rich, Barbara
See Graves, Robert (von Ranke)

Rich, Robert
See Trumbo, Dalton

Richard, Keith .... **CLC 17**
See also Richards, Keith

Richards, David Adams
1950- .... **CLC 59; DAC**
See also CA 93-96; DLB 53

Richards, I(vor) A(rmstrong)
1893-1979 .... **CLC 14, 24**
See also CA 41-44R; 89-92; CANR 34; DLB 27

Richards, Keith 1943-
See Richard, Keith
See also CA 107

Richardson, Anne
See Roiphe, Anne (Richardson)

Richardson, Dorothy Miller
1873-1957 .... **TCLC 3**
See also CA 104; DLB 36

Richardson, Ethel Florence (Lindesay)
1870-1946
See Richardson, Henry Handel
See also CA 105

Richardson, Henry Handel .... **TCLC 4**
See also Richardson, Ethel Florence (Lindesay)

Richardson, John
1796-1852 .... **NCLC 55; DAC**
See also DLB 99

Richardson, Samuel
1689-1761 ...... **LC 1; DA; DAB; DAC; DAM MST, NOV; WLC**
See also CDBLB 1660-1789; DLB 39

Richler, Mordecai
1931- .... **CLC 3, 5, 9, 13, 18, 46, 70; DAC; DAM MST, NOV**
See also AITN 1; CA 65-68; CANR 31; CLR 17; DLB 53; MAICYA; MTCW; SATA 44; SATA-Brief 27

Richter, Conrad (Michael)
1890-1968 .... **CLC 30**
See also CA 5-8R; 25-28R; CANR 23; DLB 9; MTCW; SATA 3

Ricostranza, Tom
See Ellis, Trey

Riddell, J. H. 1832-1906 .... **TCLC 40**

Riding, Laura .... **CLC 3, 7**
See also Jackson, Laura (Riding)

Riefenstahl, Berta Helene Amalia 1902-
See Riefenstahl, Leni
See also CA 108

Riefenstahl, Leni .... **CLC 16**
See also Riefenstahl, Berta Helene Amalia

Riffe, Ernest
See Bergman, (Ernst) Ingmar

Riggs, (Rolla) Lynn
1899-1954 ..... **TCLC 56; DAM MULT**
See also CA 144; NNAL

Riley, James Whitcomb
1849-1916 .... **TCLC 51; DAM POET**
See also CA 118; 137; MAICYA; SATA 17

Riley, Tex
See Creasey, John

Rilke, Rainer Maria
1875-1926 .... **TCLC 1, 6, 19; DAM POET; PC 2**
See also CA 104; 132; DLB 81; MTCW

Rimbaud, (Jean Nicolas) Arthur
1854-1891 ..... **NCLC 4, 35; DA; DAB; DAC; DAM MST, POET; PC 3; WLC**

Rinehart, Mary Roberts
1876-1958 .... **TCLC 52**
See also CA 108

Ringmaster, The
See Mencken, H(enry) L(ouis)

Ringwood, Gwen(dolyn Margaret) Pharis
1910-1984 .... **CLC 48**
See also CA 148; 112; DLB 88

Rio, Michel 19(?)- .... **CLC 43**

Ritsos, Giannes
See Ritsos, Yannis

Ritsos, Yannis 1909-1990 ..... **CLC 6, 13, 31**
See also CA 77-80; 133; CANR 39; MTCW

Ritter, Erika 1948(?)- .... **CLC 52**

Rivera, Jose Eustasio 1889-1928... **TCLC 35**
See also HW

Rivers, Conrad Kent 1933-1968...... **CLC 1**
See also BW 1; CA 85-88; DLB 41

Rivers, Elfrida
See Bradley, Marion Zimmer

Riverside, John
See Heinlein, Robert A(nson)

Rizal, Jose 1861-1896 .... **NCLC 27**

Roa Bastos, Augusto (Antonio)
1917- ..... **CLC 45; DAM MULT; HLC**
See also CA 131; DLB 113; HW

Robbe-Grillet, Alain
1922- ...... **CLC 1, 2, 4, 6, 8, 10, 14, 43**
See also CA 9-12R; CANR 33; DLB 83;
MTCW

Robbins, Harold
1916- .... **CLC 5; DAM NOV**
See also CA 73-76; CANR 26; MTCW

Robbins, Thomas Eugene 1936-
See Robbins, Tom
See also CA 81-84; CANR 29; DAM NOV,
POP; MTCW

Robbins, Tom .... **CLC 9, 32, 64**
See also Robbins, Thomas Eugene
See also BEST 90:3; DLBY 80

Robbins, Trina 1938- .... **CLC 21**
See also CA 128

Roberts, Charles G(eorge) D(ouglas)
1860-1943 .... **TCLC 8**
See also CA 105; CLR 33; DLB 92;
SATA 88; SATA-Brief 29

Roberts, Kate 1891-1985 .... **CLC 15**
See also CA 107; 116

Roberts, Keith (John Kingston)
1935- .... **CLC 14**
See also CA 25-28R; CANR 46

Roberts, Kenneth (Lewis)
1885-1957 .... **TCLC 23**
See also CA 109; DLB 9

Roberts, Michele (B.) 1949-........ **CLC 48**
See also CA 115

Robertson, Ellis
See Ellison, Harlan (Jay); Silverberg, Robert

Robertson, Thomas William
1829-1871 .... **NCLC 35; DAM DRAM**

Robinson, Edwin Arlington
1869-1935 .... **TCLC 5; DA; DAC;**
DAM MST, POET; PC 1
See also CA 104; 133; CDALB 1865-1917;
DLB 54; MTCW

Robinson, Henry Crabb
1775-1867 .... **NCLC 15**
See also DLB 107

Robinson, Jill 1936-.............. **CLC 10**
See also CA 102; INT 102

Robinson, Kim Stanley 1952- ...... **CLC 34**
See also CA 126

Robinson, Lloyd
See Silverberg, Robert

Robinson, Marilynne 1944-........ **CLC 25**
See also CA 116

Robinson, Smokey................. **CLC 21**
See also Robinson, William, Jr.

Robinson, William, Jr. 1940-
See Robinson, Smokey
See also CA 116

Robison, Mary 1949-.............. **CLC 42**
See also CA 113; 116; DLB 130; INT 116

Rod, Edouard 1857-1910 .... **TCLC 52**

Roddenberry, Eugene Wesley 1921-1991
See Roddenberry, Gene
See also CA 110; 135; CANR 37; SATA 45;
SATA-Obit 69

Roddenberry, Gene .... **CLC 17**
See also Roddenberry, Eugene Wesley
See also AAYA 5; SATA-Obit 69

Rodgers, Mary 1931-............. **CLC 12**
See also CA 49-52; CANR 8; CLR 20;
INT CANR-8; JRDA; MAICYA;
SATA 8

Rodgers, W(illiam) R(obert)
1909-1969 .... **CLC 7**
See also CA 85-88; DLB 20

Rodman, Eric
See Silverberg, Robert

Rodman, Howard 1920(?)-1985..... **CLC 65**
See also CA 118

Rodman, Maia
See Wojciechowska, Maia (Teresa)

Rodriguez, Claudio 1934-......... **CLC 10**
See also DLB 134

Roelvaag, O(le) E(dvart)
1876-1931 .... **TCLC 17**
See also CA 117; DLB 9

Roethke, Theodore (Huebner)
1908-1963 ...... **CLC 1, 3, 8, 11, 19, 46;**
DAM POET; PC 15
See also CA 81-84; CABS 2;
CDALB 1941-1968; DLB 5; MTCW

Rogers, Thomas Hunton 1927- ..... **CLC 57**
See also CA 89-92; INT 89-92

Rogers, Will(iam Penn Adair)
1879-1935 ...... **TCLC 8; DAM MULT**
See also CA 105; 144; DLB 11; NNAL

Rogin, Gilbert 1929-.............. **CLC 18**
See also CA 65-68; CANR 15

Rohan, Koda .... **TCLC 22**
See also Koda Shigeyuki

Rohmer, Eric.................... **CLC 16**
See also Scherer, Jean-Marie Maurice

Rohmer, Sax .... **TCLC 28**
See also Ward, Arthur Henry Sarsfield
See also DLB 70

Roiphe, Anne (Richardson)
1935- .... **CLC 3, 9**
See also CA 89-92; CANR 45; DLBY 80;
INT 89-92

Rojas, Fernando de 1465-1541 ...... **LC 23**

Rolfe, Frederick (William Serafino Austin
Lewis Mary) 1860-1913...... **TCLC 12**
See also CA 107; DLB 34, 156

Rolland, Romain 1866-1944....... **TCLC 23**
See also CA 118; DLB 65

Rolvaag, O(le) E(dvart)
See Roelvaag, O(le) E(dvart)

Romain Arnaud, Saint
See Aragon, Louis

Romains, Jules 1885-1972 .... **CLC 7**
See also CA 85-88; CANR 34; DLB 65;
MTCW

Romero, Jose Ruben 1890-1952 ... **TCLC 14**
See also CA 114; 131; HW

Ronsard, Pierre de
1524-1585 .... **LC 6; PC 11**

Rooke, Leon
1934- .... **CLC 25, 34; DAM POP**
See also CA 25-28R; CANR 23, 53

Roper, William 1498-1578 .... **LC 10**

Roquelaure, A. N.
See Rice, Anne

Rosa, Joao Guimaraes 1908-1967 ... **CLC 23**
See also CA 89-92; DLB 113

Rose, Wendy
1948- .... **CLC 85; DAM MULT; PC 13**
See also CA 53-56; CANR 5, 51; NNAL;
SATA 12

Rosen, Richard (Dean) 1949-....... **CLC 39**
See also CA 77-80; INT CANR-30

Rosenberg, Isaac 1890-1918....... **TCLC 12**
See also CA 107; DLB 20

Rosenblatt, Joe .... **CLC 15**
See also Rosenblatt, Joseph

Rosenblatt, Joseph 1933-
See Rosenblatt, Joe
See also CA 89-92; INT 89-92

Rosenfeld, Samuel 1896-1963
See Tzara, Tristan
See also CA 89-92

Rosenthal, M(acha) L(ouis)
1917-1996 .... **CLC 28**
See also CA 1-4R; 152; CAAS 6; CANR 4,
51; DLB 5; SATA 59

Ross, Barnaby
See Dannay, Frederic

Ross, Bernard L.
See Follett, Ken(neth Martin)

Ross, J. H.
See Lawrence, T(homas) E(dward)

Ross, Martin
See Martin, Violet Florence
See also DLB 135

Ross, (James) Sinclair
1908- ...... **CLC 13; DAC; DAM MST**
See also CA 73-76; DLB 88

Rossetti, Christina (Georgina)
1830-1894 ..... **NCLC 2, 50; DA; DAB;**
DAC; DAM MST, POET; PC 7; WLC
See also DLB 35, 163; MAICYA; SATA 20

Rossetti, Dante Gabriel
1828-1882 .... **NCLC 4; DA; DAB;**
DAC; DAM MST, POET; WLC
See also CDBLB 1832-1890; DLB 35

Rossner, Judith (Perelman)
1935- ....**CLC 6, 9, 29**
See also AITN 2; BEST 90:3; CA 17-20R;
CANR 18, 51; DLB 6; INT CANR-18;
MTCW

Rostand, Edmond (Eugene Alexis)
1868-1918 ...... **TCLC 6, 37; DA; DAB;**
DAC; DAM DRAM, MST
See also CA 104; 126; MTCW

Roth, Henry 1906-1995 .... **CLC 2, 6, 11**
See also CA 11-12; 149; CANR 38; CAP 1;
DLB 28; MTCW

Roth, Joseph 1894-1939.......... **TCLC 33**
See also DLB 85

Roth, Philip (Milton)
1933- ...... **CLC 1, 2, 3, 4, 6, 9, 15, 22,**
31, 47, 66, 86; DA; DAB; DAC;
DAM MST, NOV, POP; WLC
See also BEST 90:3; CA 1-4R; CANR 1, 22,
36; CDALB 1968-1988; DLB 2, 28;
DLBY 82; MTCW

Rothenberg, Jerome 1931-........ **CLC 6, 57**
See also CA 45-48; CANR 1; DLB 5

Salisbury, John
See Caute, David

Salter, James 1925- .... **CLC 7, 52, 59**
See also CA 73-76; DLB 130

Saltus, Edgar (Everton)
1855-1921 .... **TCLC 8**
See also CA 105

Saltykov, Mikhail Evgrafovich
1826-1889 .... **NCLC 16**

Samarakis, Antonis 1919- .... **CLC 5**
See also CA 25-28R; CAAS 16; CANR 36

Sanchez, Florencio 1875-1910..... **TCLC 37**
See also HW

Sanchez, Luis Rafael 1936-........ **CLC 23**
See also CA 128; DLB 145; HW

Sanchez, Sonia
1934- ...... **CLC 5; BLC; DAM MULT;**
PC 9
See also BW 2; CA 33-36R; CANR 24, 49;
CLR 18; DLB 41; DLBD 8; MAICYA;
MTCW; SATA 22

Sand, George
1804-1876 .... **NCLC 2, 42, 57; DA;**
DAB; DAC; DAM MST, NOV; WLC
See also DLB 119

Sandburg, Carl (August)
1878-1967 .... **CLC 1, 4, 10, 15, 35; DA;**
DAB; DAC; DAM MST, POET; PC 2;
WLC
See also CA 5-8R; 25-28R; CANR 35;
CDALB 1865-1917; DLB 17, 54;
MAICYA; MTCW; SATA 8

Sandburg, Charles
See Sandburg, Carl (August)

Sandburg, Charles A.
See Sandburg, Carl (August)

Sanders, (James) Ed(ward) 1939- ... **CLC 53**
See also CA 13-16R; CAAS 21; CANR 13,
44; DLB 16

Sanders, Lawrence
1920- .... **CLC 41; DAM POP**
See also BEST 89:4; CA 81-84; CANR 33;
MTCW

Sanders, Noah
See Blount, Roy (Alton), Jr.

Sanders, Winston P.
See Anderson, Poul (William)

Sandoz, Mari(e Susette)
1896-1966 .... **CLC 28**
See also CA 1-4R; 25-28R; CANR 17;
DLB 9; MTCW; SATA 5

Saner, Reg(inald Anthony) 1931- .... **CLC 9**
See also CA 65-68

Sannazaro, Jacopo 1456(?)-1530 ...... **LC 8**

Sansom, William
1912-1976 ...... **CLC 2, 6; DAM NOV;**
SSC 21
See also CA 5-8R; 65-68; CANR 42;
DLB 139; MTCW

Santayana, George 1863-1952 ..... **TCLC 40**
See also CA 115; DLB 54, 71; DLBD 13

Santiago, Danny .... **CLC 33**
See also James, Daniel (Lewis)
See also DLB 122

Santmyer, Helen Hoover
1895-1986 .... **CLC 33**
See also CA 1-4R; 118; CANR 15, 33;
DLBY 84; MTCW

Santos, Bienvenido N(uqui)
1911-1996 ...... **CLC 22; DAM MULT**
See also CA 101; 151; CANR 19, 46

Sapper .... **TCLC 44**
See also McNeile, Herman Cyril

Sappho
fl. 6th cent. B.C.- .... **CMLC 3;**
DAM POET; PC 5

Sarduy, Severo 1937-1993 .... **CLC 6, 96**
See also CA 89-92; 142; DLB 113; HW

Sargeson, Frank 1903-1982 .... **CLC 31**
See also CA 25-28R; 106; CANR 38

Sarmiento, Felix Ruben Garcia
See Dario, Ruben

Saroyan, William
1908-1981 ..... **CLC 1, 8, 10, 29, 34, 56;**
DA; DAB; DAC; DAM DRAM, MST,
NOV; SSC 21; WLC
See also CA 5-8R; 103; CANR 30; DLB 7,
9, 86; DLBY 81; MTCW; SATA 23;
SATA-Obit 24

Sarraute, Nathalie
1900- .... **CLC 1, 2, 4, 8, 10, 31, 80**
See also CA 9-12R; CANR 23; DLB 83;
MTCW

Sarton, (Eleanor) May
1912-1995 .... **CLC 4, 14, 49, 91;**
DAM POET
See also CA 1-4R; 149; CANR 1, 34;
DLB 48; DLBY 81; INT CANR-34;
MTCW; SATA 36; SATA-Obit 86

Sartre, Jean-Paul
1905-1980 .... **CLC 1, 4, 7, 9, 13, 18, 24,**
44, 50, 52; DA; DAB; DAC;
DAM DRAM, MST, NOV; DC 3; WLC
See also CA 9-12R; 97-100; CANR 21;
DLB 72; MTCW

Sassoon, Siegfried (Lorraine)
1886-1967 .... **CLC 36; DAB;**
DAM MST, NOV, POET; PC 12
See also CA 104; 25-28R; CANR 36;
DLB 20; MTCW

Satterfield, Charles
See Pohl, Frederik

Saul, John (W. III)
1942- ...... **CLC 46; DAM NOV, POP**
See also AAYA 10; BEST 90:4; CA 81-84;
CANR 16, 40

Saunders, Caleb
See Heinlein, Robert A(nson)

Saura (Atares), Carlos 1932-....... **CLC 20**
See also CA 114; 131; HW

Sauser-Hall, Frederic 1887-1961.... **CLC 18**
See also Cendrars, Blaise
See also CA 102; 93-96; CANR 36; MTCW

Saussure, Ferdinand de
1857-1913 .... **TCLC 49**

Savage, Catharine
See Brosman, Catharine Savage

Savage, Thomas 1915- .... **CLC 40**
See also CA 126; 132; CAAS 15; INT 132

Savan, Glenn 19(?)- .... **CLC 50**

Sayers, Dorothy L(eigh)
1893-1957 ..... **TCLC 2, 15; DAM POP**
See also CA 104; 119; CDBLB 1914-1945;
DLB 10, 36, 77, 100; MTCW

Sayers, Valerie 1952-............. **CLC 50**
See also CA 134

Sayles, John (Thomas)
1950- .... **CLC 7, 10, 14**
See also CA 57-60; CANR 41; DLB 44

Scammell, Michael .... **CLC 34**

Scannell, Vernon 1922- .... **CLC 49**
See also CA 5-8R; CANR 8, 24; DLB 27;
SATA 59

Scarlett, Susan
See Streatfeild, (Mary) Noel

Schaeffer, Susan Fromberg
1941- .... **CLC 6, 11, 22**
See also CA 49-52; CANR 18; DLB 28;
MTCW; SATA 22

Schary, Jill
See Robinson, Jill

Schell, Jonathan 1943-............ **CLC 35**
See also CA 73-76; CANR 12

Schelling, Friedrich Wilhelm Joseph von
1775-1854 .... **NCLC 30**
See also DLB 90

Schendel, Arthur van 1874-1946 ... **TCLC 56**

Scherer, Jean-Marie Maurice 1920-
See Rohmer, Eric
See also CA 110

Schevill, James (Erwin) 1920-....... **CLC 7**
See also CA 5-8R; CAAS 12

Schiller, Friedrich
1759-1805 .... **NCLC 39; DAM DRAM**
See also DLB 94

Schisgal, Murray (Joseph) 1926-..... **CLC 6**
See also CA 21-24R; CANR 48

Schlee, Ann 1934-................ **CLC 35**
See also CA 101; CANR 29; SATA 44;
SATA-Brief 36

Schlegel, August Wilhelm von
1767-1845 .... **NCLC 15**
See also DLB 94

Schlegel, Friedrich 1772-1829 .... **NCLC 45**
See also DLB 90

Schlegel, Johann Elias (von)
1719(?)-1749 .... **LC 5**

Schlesinger, Arthur M(eier), Jr.
1917- .... **CLC 84**
See also AITN 1; CA 1-4R; CANR 1, 28;
DLB 17; INT CANR-28; MTCW;
SATA 61

Schmidt, Arno (Otto) 1914-1979.... **CLC 56**
See also CA 128; 109; DLB 69

Schmitz, Aron Hector 1861-1928
See Svevo, Italo
See also CA 104; 122; MTCW

Schnackenberg, Gjertrud 1953-..... **CLC 40**
See also CA 116; DLB 120

Schneider, Leonard Alfred 1925-1966
See Bruce, Lenny
See also CA 89-92

Sexton, Anne (Harvey)
1928-1974 .... CLC 2, 4, 6, 8, 10, 15, 53;
DA; DAB; DAC; DAM MST, POET;
PC 2; WLC
See also CA 1-4R; 53-56; CABS 2;
CANR 3, 36; CDALB 1941-1968; DLB 5,
169; MTCW; SATA 10

Shaara, Michael (Joseph, Jr.)
1929-1988 .... CLC 15; DAM POP
See also AITN 1; CA 102; 125; CANR 52;
DLBY 83

Shackleton, C. C.
See Aldiss, Brian W(ilson)

Shacochis, Bob .... CLC 39
See also Shacochis, Robert G.

Shacochis, Robert G. 1951-
See Shacochis, Bob
See also CA 119; 124; INT 124

Shaffer, Anthony (Joshua)
1926- .... CLC 19; DAM DRAM
See also CA 110; 116; DLB 13

Shaffer, Peter (Levin)
1926- ...... CLC 5, 14, 18, 37, 60; DAB;
DAM DRAM, MST
See also CA 25-28R; CANR 25, 47;
CDBLB 1960 to Present; DLB 13;
MTCW

Shakey, Bernard
See Young, Neil

Shalamov, Varlam (Tikhonovich)
1907(?)-1982 .... CLC 18
See also CA 129; 105

Shamlu, Ahmad 1925- .... CLC 10

Shammas, Anton 1951-............ CLC 55

Shange, Ntozake
1948- .... CLC 8, 25, 38, 74; BLC;
DAM DRAM, MULT; DC 3
See also AAYA 9; BW 2; CA 85-88;
CABS 3; CANR 27, 48; DLB 38; MTCW

Shanley, John Patrick 1950-....... CLC 75
See also CA 128; 133

Shapcott, Thomas W(illiam) 1935- .. CLC 38
See also CA 69-72; CANR 49

Shapiro, Jane..................... CLC 76

Shapiro, Karl (Jay) 1913- .. CLC 4, 8, 15, 53
See also CA 1-4R; CAAS 6; CANR 1, 36;
DLB 48; MTCW

Sharp, William 1855-1905 .... TCLC 39
See also DLB 156

Sharpe, Thomas Ridley 1928-
See Sharpe, Tom
See also CA 114; 122; INT 122

Sharpe, Tom...................... CLC 36
See also Sharpe, Thomas Ridley
See also DLB 14

Shaw, Bernard................... TCLC 45
See also Shaw, George Bernard
See also BW 1

Shaw, G. Bernard
See Shaw, George Bernard

Shaw, George Bernard
1856-1950 ... TCLC 3, 9, 21; DA; DAB;
DAC; DAM DRAM, MST; WLC
See also Shaw, Bernard
See also CA 104; 128; CDBLB 1914-1945;
DLB 10, 57; MTCW

Shaw, Henry Wheeler
1818-1885 .... NCLC 15
See also DLB 11

Shaw, Irwin
1913-1984 .... CLC 7, 23, 34;
DAM DRAM, POP
See also AITN 1; CA 13-16R; 112;
CANR 21; CDALB 1941-1968; DLB 6,
102; DLBY 84; MTCW

Shaw, Robert 1927-1978 .... CLC 5
See also AITN 1; CA 1-4R; 81-84;
CANR 4; DLB 13, 14

Shaw, T. E.
See Lawrence, T(homas) E(dward)

Shawn, Wallace 1943- .... CLC 41
See also CA 112

Shea, Lisa 1953-................. CLC 86
See also CA 147

Sheed, Wilfrid (John Joseph)
1930- .... CLC 2, 4, 10, 53
See also CA 65-68; CANR 30; DLB 6;
MTCW

Sheldon, Alice Hastings Bradley
1915(?)-1987
See Tiptree, James, Jr.
See also CA 108; 122; CANR 34; INT 108;
MTCW

Sheldon, John
See Bloch, Robert (Albert)

Shelley, Mary Wollstonecraft (Godwin)
1797-1851 .... NCLC 14; DA; DAB;
DAC; DAM MST, NOV; WLC
See also CDBLB 1789-1832; DLB 110, 116,
159; SATA 29

Shelley, Percy Bysshe
1792-1822 .... NCLC 18; DA; DAB;
DAC; DAM MST, POET; PC 14; WLC
See also CDBLB 1789-1832; DLB 96, 110,
158

Shepard, Jim 1956-................ CLC 36
See also CA 137

Shepard, Lucius 1947- .... CLC 34
See also CA 128; 141

Shepard, Sam
1943- .... CLC 4, 6, 17, 34, 41, 44;
DAM DRAM; DC 5
See also AAYA 1; CA 69-72; CABS 3;
CANR 22; DLB 7; MTCW

Shepherd, Michael
See Ludlum, Robert

Sherburne, Zoa (Morin) 1912-...... CLC 30
See also AAYA 13; CA 1-4R; CANR 3, 37;
MAICYA; SAAS 18; SATA 3

Sheridan, Frances 1724-1766........ LC 7
See also DLB 39, 84

Sheridan, Richard Brinsley
1751-1816 .... NCLC 5; DA; DAB;
DAC; DAM DRAM, MST; DC 1; WLC
See also CDBLB 1660-1789; DLB 89

Sherman, Jonathan Marc........... CLC 55

Sherman, Martin 1941(?)- .... CLC 19
See also CA 116; 123

Sherwin, Judith Johnson 1936-... CLC 7, 15
See also CA 25-28R; CANR 34

Sherwood, Frances 1940-......... CLC 81
See also CA 146

Sherwood, Robert E(mmet)
1896-1955 ...... TCLC 3; DAM DRAM
See also CA 104; DLB 7, 26

Shestov, Lev 1866-1938.......... TCLC 56

Shevchenko, Taras 1814-1861 .... NCLC 54

Shiel, M(atthew) P(hipps)
1865-1947 .... TCLC 8
See also CA 106; DLB 153

Shields, Carol 1935-......... CLC 91; DAC
See also CA 81-84; CANR 51

Shiga, Naoya 1883-1971... CLC 33; SSC 23
See also CA 101; 33-36R

Shilts, Randy 1951-1994 .... CLC 85
See also CA 115; 127; 144; CANR 45;
INT 127

Shimazaki, Haruki 1872-1943
See Shimazaki Toson
See also CA 105; 134

Shimazaki Toson................. TCLC 5
See also Shimazaki, Haruki

Sholokhov, Mikhail (Aleksandrovich)
1905-1984 .... CLC 7, 15
See also CA 101; 112; MTCW;
SATA-Obit 36

Shone, Patric
See Hanley, James

Shreve, Susan Richards 1939-...... CLC 23
See also CA 49-52; CAAS 5; CANR 5, 38;
MAICYA; SATA 46; SATA-Brief 41

Shue, Larry
1946-1985 ...... CLC 52; DAM DRAM
See also CA 145; 117

Shu-Jen, Chou 1881-1936
See Lu Hsun
See also CA 104

Shulman, Alix Kates 1932- ...... CLC 2, 10
See also CA 29-32R; CANR 43; SATA 7

Shuster, Joe 1914- .... CLC 21

Shute, Nevil..................... CLC 30
See also Norway, Nevil Shute

Shuttle, Penelope (Diane) 1947- ..... CLC 7
See also CA 93-96; CANR 39; DLB 14, 40

Sidney, Mary 1561-1621 .... LC 19

Sidney, Sir Philip
1554-1586 ..... LC 19; DA; DAB; DAC;
DAM MST, POET
See also CDBLB Before 1660; DLB 167

Siegel, Jerome 1914-1996 .... CLC 21
See also CA 116; 151

Siegel, Jerry
See Siegel, Jerome

Sienkiewicz, Henryk (Adam Alexander Pius)
1846-1916 .... TCLC 3
See also CA 104; 134

Sierra, Gregorio Martinez
See Martinez Sierra, Gregorio

Sierra, Maria (de la O'LeJarraga) Martinez
See Martinez Sierra, Maria (de la O'LeJarraga)

Sigal, Clancy 1926-. . . . . **CLC 7**
See also CA 1-4R

Sigourney, Lydia Howard (Huntley)
1791-1865 . . . . **NCLC 21**
See also DLB 1, 42, 73

Siguenza y Gongora, Carlos de
1645-1700 . . . . **LC 8**

Sigurjonsson, Johann 1880-1919 . . . **TCLC 27**

Sikelianos, Angelos 1884-1951 . . . . **TCLC 39**

Silkin, Jon 1930- . . . . **CLC 2, 6, 43**
See also CA 5-8R; CAAS 5; DLB 27

Silko, Leslie (Marmon)
1948- . . . . **CLC 23, 74; DA; DAC; DAM MST, MULT, POP**
See also AAYA 14; CA 115; 122; CANR 45; DLB 143; NNAL

Sillanpaa, Frans Eemil 1888-1964. . . **CLC 19**
See also CA 129; 93-96; MTCW

Sillitoe, Alan
1928- . . . . **CLC 1, 3, 6, 10, 19, 57**
See also AITN 1; CA 9-12R; CAAS 2; CANR 8, 26; CDBLB 1960 to Present; DLB 14, 139; MTCW; SATA 61

Silone, Ignazio 1900-1978 . . . . **CLC 4**
See also CA 25-28; 81-84; CANR 34; CAP 2; MTCW

Silver, Joan Micklin 1935- . . . . **CLC 20**
See also CA 114; 121; INT 121

Silver, Nicholas
See Faust, Frederick (Schiller)

Silverberg, Robert
1935- . . . . **CLC 7; DAM POP**
See also CA 1-4R; CAAS 3; CANR 1, 20, 36; DLB 8; INT CANR-20; MAICYA; MTCW; SATA 13

Silverstein, Alvin 1933- . . . . **CLC 17**
See also CA 49-52; CANR 2; CLR 25; JRDA; MAICYA; SATA 8, 69

Silverstein, Virginia B(arbara Opshelor)
1937- . . . . **CLC 17**
See also CA 49-52; CANR 2; CLR 25; JRDA; MAICYA; SATA 8, 69

Sim, Georges
See Simenon, Georges (Jacques Christian)

Simak, Clifford D(onald)
1904-1988 . . . . **CLC 1, 55**
See also CA 1-4R; 125; CANR 1, 35; DLB 8; MTCW; SATA-Obit 56

Simenon, Georges (Jacques Christian)
1903-1989 . . . . **CLC 1, 2, 3, 8, 18, 47; DAM POP**
See also CA 85-88; 129; CANR 35; DLB 72; DLBY 89; MTCW

Simic, Charles
1938- . . . . **CLC 6, 9, 22, 49, 68; DAM POET**
See also CA 29-32R; CAAS 4; CANR 12, 33, 52; DLB 105

Simmel, Georg 1858-1918 . . . . **TCLC 64**

Simmons, Charles (Paul) 1924- . . . . . **CLC 57**
See also CA 89-92; INT 89-92

Simmons, Dan 1948-. . . **CLC 44; DAM POP**
See also AAYA 16; CA 138; CANR 53

Simmons, James (Stewart Alexander)
1933- . . . . **CLC 43**
See also CA 105; CAAS 21; DLB 40

Simms, William Gilmore
1806-1870 . . . . **NCLC 3**
See also DLB 3, 30, 59, 73

Simon, Carly 1945-. . . . . **CLC 26**
See also CA 105

Simon, Claude
1913- . . . . **CLC 4, 9, 15, 39; DAM NOV**
See also CA 89-92; CANR 33; DLB 83; MTCW

Simon, (Marvin) Neil
1927- . . . . **CLC 6, 11, 31, 39, 70; DAM DRAM**
See also AITN 1; CA 21-24R; CANR 26; DLB 7; MTCW

Simon, Paul 1942(?)- . . . . **CLC 17**
See also CA 116

Simonon, Paul 1956(?)- . . . . **CLC 30**

Simpson, Harriette
See Arnow, Harriette (Louisa) Simpson

Simpson, Louis (Aston Marantz)
1923- . . . . **CLC 4, 7, 9, 32; DAM POET**
See also CA 1-4R; CAAS 4; CANR 1; DLB 5; MTCW

Simpson, Mona (Elizabeth) 1957-. . . **CLC 44**
See also CA 122; 135

Simpson, N(orman) F(rederick)
1919- . . . . **CLC 29**
See also CA 13-16R; DLB 13

Sinclair, Andrew (Annandale)
1935- . . . . **CLC 2, 14**
See also CA 9-12R; CAAS 5; CANR 14, 38; DLB 14; MTCW

Sinclair, Emil
See Hesse, Hermann

Sinclair, Iain 1943-. . . . . **CLC 76**
See also CA 132

Sinclair, Iain MacGregor
See Sinclair, Iain

Sinclair, Mary Amelia St. Clair 1865(?)-1946
See Sinclair, May
See also CA 104

Sinclair, May. . . . . **TCLC 3, 11**
See also Sinclair, Mary Amelia St. Clair
See also DLB 36, 135

Sinclair, Upton (Beall)
1878-1968 . . . . . . **CLC 1, 11, 15, 63; DA; DAB; DAC; DAM MST, NOV; WLC**
See also CA 5-8R; 25-28R; CANR 7; CDALB 1929-1941; DLB 9; INT CANR-7; MTCW; SATA 9

Singer, Isaac
See Singer, Isaac Bashevis

Singer, Isaac Bashevis
1904-1991 . . . . **CLC 1, 3, 6, 9, 11, 15, 23, 38, 69; DA; DAB; DAC; DAM MST, NOV; SSC 3; WLC**
See also AITN 1, 2; CA 1-4R; 134; CANR 1, 39; CDALB 1941-1968; CLR 1; DLB 6, 28, 52; DLBY 91; JRDA; MAICYA; MTCW; SATA 3, 27; SATA-Obit 68

Singer, Israel Joshua 1893-1944 . . . **TCLC 33**

Singh, Khushwant 1915-. . . . . **CLC 11**
See also CA 9-12R; CAAS 9; CANR 6

Sinjohn, John
See Galsworthy, John

Sinyavsky, Andrei (Donatevich)
1925- . . . . **CLC 8**
See also CA 85-88

Sirin, V.
See Nabokov, Vladimir (Vladimirovich)

Sissman, L(ouis) E(dward)
1928-1976 . . . . **CLC 9, 18**
See also CA 21-24R; 65-68; CANR 13; DLB 5

Sisson, C(harles) H(ubert) 1914-. . . . . **CLC 8**
See also CA 1-4R; CAAS 3; CANR 3, 48; DLB 27

Sitwell, Dame Edith
1887-1964 . . . . **CLC 2, 9, 67; DAM POET; PC 3**
See also CA 9-12R; CANR 35; CDBLB 1945-1960; DLB 20; MTCW

Sjoewall, Maj 1935-. . . . . **CLC 7**
See also CA 65-68

Sjowall, Maj
See Sjoewall, Maj

Skelton, Robin 1925- . . . . **CLC 13**
See also AITN 2; CA 5-8R; CAAS 5; CANR 28; DLB 27, 53

Skolimowski, Jerzy 1938- . . . . **CLC 20**
See also CA 128

Skram, Amalie (Bertha)
1847-1905 . . . . **TCLC 25**

Skvorecky, Josef (Vaclav)
1924- . . . . **CLC 15, 39, 69; DAC; DAM NOV**
See also CA 61-64; CAAS 1; CANR 10, 34; MTCW

Slade, Bernard. . . . . **CLC 11, 46**
See also Newbound, Bernard Slade
See also CAAS 9; DLB 53

Slaughter, Carolyn 1946-. . . . . **CLC 56**
See also CA 85-88

Slaughter, Frank G(ill) 1908- . . . . . . **CLC 29**
See also AITN 2; CA 5-8R; CANR 5; INT CANR-5

Slavitt, David R(ytman) 1935-. . . . **CLC 5, 14**
See also CA 21-24R; CAAS 3; CANR 41; DLB 5, 6

Slesinger, Tess 1905-1945 . . . . **TCLC 10**
See also CA 107; DLB 102

Slessor, Kenneth 1901-1971. . . . . . . **CLC 14**
See also CA 102; 89-92

Slowacki, Juliusz 1809-1849 . . . . . **NCLC 15**

Smart, Christopher
1722-1771 . . . **LC 3; DAM POET; PC 13**
See also DLB 109

Smart, Elizabeth 1913-1986. . . . . **CLC 54**
See also CA 81-84; 118; DLB 88

Smiley, Jane (Graves)
1949- . . . . **CLC 53, 76; DAM POP**
See also CA 104; CANR 30, 50; INT CANR-30

Smith, A(rthur) J(ames) M(arshall)
1902-1980 . . . . **CLC 15; DAC**
See also CA 1-4R; 102; CANR 4; DLB 88

Smith, Anna Deavere 1950- . . . . **CLC 86**
See also CA 133

Smith, Betty (Wehner) 1896-1972 . . . **CLC 19**
See also CA 5-8R; 33-36R; DLBY 82;
SATA 6

Smith, Charlotte (Turner)
1749-1806 . . . . **NCLC 23**
See also DLB 39, 109

Smith, Clark Ashton 1893-1961 . . . . **CLC 43**
See also CA 143

Smith, Dave . . . . **CLC 22, 42**
See also Smith, David (Jeddie)
See also CAAS 7; DLB 5

Smith, David (Jeddie) 1942-
See Smith, Dave
See also CA 49-52; CANR 1; DAM POET

Smith, Florence Margaret 1902-1971
See Smith, Stevie
See also CA 17-18; 29-32R; CANR 35;
CAP 2; DAM POET; MTCW

Smith, Iain Crichton 1928- . . . . **CLC 64**
See also CA 21-24R; DLB 40, 139

Smith, John 1580(?)-1631 . . . . **LC 9**

Smith, Johnston
See Crane, Stephen (Townley)

Smith, Joseph, Jr. 1805-1844 . . . . **NCLC 53**

Smith, Lee 1944- . . . . **CLC 25, 73**
See also CA 114; 119; CANR 46; DLB 143;
DLBY 83; INT 119

Smith, Martin
See Smith, Martin Cruz

Smith, Martin Cruz
1942- . . . . . **CLC 25; DAM MULT, POP**
See also BEST 89:4; CA 85-88; CANR 6,
23, 43; INT CANR-23; NNAL

Smith, Mary-Ann Tirone 1944- . . . . . **CLC 39**
See also CA 118; 136

Smith, Patti 1946- . . . . **CLC 12**
See also CA 93-96

Smith, Pauline (Urmson)
1882-1959 . . . . **TCLC 25**

Smith, Rosamond
See Oates, Joyce Carol

Smith, Sheila Kaye
See Kaye-Smith, Sheila

Smith, Stevie . . . . **CLC 3, 8, 25, 44; PC 12**
See also Smith, Florence Margaret
See also DLB 20

Smith, Wilbur (Addison) 1933- . . . . . **CLC 33**
See also CA 13-16R; CANR 7, 46; MTCW

Smith, William Jay 1918- . . . . **CLC 6**
See also CA 5-8R; CANR 44; DLB 5;
MAICYA; SAAS 22; SATA 2, 68

Smith, Woodrow Wilson
See Kuttner, Henry

Smolenskin, Peretz 1842-1885 . . . . **NCLC 30**

Smollett, Tobias (George) 1721-1771 . . **LC 2**
See also CDBLB 1660-1789; DLB 39, 104

Snodgrass, W(illiam) D(e Witt)
1926- . . . . **CLC 2, 6, 10, 18, 68;**
DAM POET
See also CA 1-4R; CANR 6, 36; DLB 5;
MTCW

Snow, C(harles) P(ercy)
1905-1980 . . . . **CLC 1, 4, 6, 9, 13, 19;**
DAM NOV
See also CA 5-8R; 101; CANR 28;
CDBLB 1945-1960; DLB 15, 77; MTCW

Snow, Frances Compton
See Adams, Henry (Brooks)

Snyder, Gary (Sherman)
1930- . . **CLC 1, 2, 5, 9, 32; DAM POET**
See also CA 17-20R; CANR 30; DLB 5, 16,
165

Snyder, Zilpha Keatley 1927- . . . . . . **CLC 17**
See also AAYA 15; CA 9-12R; CANR 38;
CLR 31; JRDA; MAICYA; SAAS 2;
SATA 1, 28, 75

Soares, Bernardo
See Pessoa, Fernando (Antonio Nogueira)

Sobh, A.
See Shamlu, Ahmad

Sobol, Joshua . . . . **CLC 60**

Soderberg, Hjalmar 1869-1941 . . . . **TCLC 39**

Sodergran, Edith (Irene)
See Soedergran, Edith (Irene)

Soedergran, Edith (Irene)
1892-1923 . . . . **TCLC 31**

Softly, Edgar
See Lovecraft, H(oward) P(hillips)

Softly, Edward
See Lovecraft, H(oward) P(hillips)

Sokolov, Raymond 1941- . . . . **CLC 7**
See also CA 85-88

Solo, Jay
See Ellison, Harlan (Jay)

Sologub, Fyodor . . . . **TCLC 9**
See also Teternikov, Fyodor Kuzmich

Solomons, Ikey Esquir
See Thackeray, William Makepeace

Solomos, Dionysios 1798-1857 . . . **NCLC 15**

Solwoska, Mara
See French, Marilyn

Solzhenitsyn, Aleksandr I(sayevich)
1918- . . . . . . **CLC 1, 2, 4, 7, 9, 10, 18, 26,**
34, 78; DA; DAB; DAC; DAM MST,
NOV; WLC
See also AITN 1; CA 69-72; CANR 40;
MTCW

Somers, Jane
See Lessing, Doris (May)

Somerville, Edith 1858-1949 . . . . . . **TCLC 51**
See also DLB 135

Somerville & Ross
See Martin, Violet Florence; Somerville,
Edith

Sommer, Scott 1951- . . . . **CLC 25**
See also CA 106

Sondheim, Stephen (Joshua)
1930- . . . . **CLC 30, 39; DAM DRAM**
See also AAYA 11; CA 103; CANR 47

Sontag, Susan
1933- . . . . **CLC 1, 2, 10, 13, 31;**
DAM POP
See also CA 17-20R; CANR 25, 51; DLB 2,
67; MTCW

Sophocles
496(?)B.C.-406(?)B.C. . . . . . **CMLC 2; DA;**
DAB; DAC; DAM DRAM, MST; DC 1

Sordello 1189-1269 . . . . **CMLC 15**

Sorel, Julia
See Drexler, Rosalyn

Sorrentino, Gilbert
1929- . . . . **CLC 3, 7, 14, 22, 40**
See also CA 77-80; CANR 14, 33; DLB 5;
DLBY 80; INT CANR-14

Soto, Gary
1952- . . . . **CLC 32, 80; DAM MULT;**
HLC
See also AAYA 10; CA 119; 125;
CANR 50; CLR 38; DLB 82; HW;
INT 125; JRDA; SATA 80

Soupault, Philippe 1897-1990 . . . . . . **CLC 68**
See also CA 116; 147; 131

Souster, (Holmes) Raymond
1921- . . . **CLC 5, 14; DAC; DAM POET**
See also CA 13-16R; CAAS 14; CANR 13,
29, 53; DLB 88; SATA 63

Southern, Terry 1924(?)-1995 . . . . **CLC 7**
See also CA 1-4R; 150; CANR 1; DLB 2

Southey, Robert 1774-1843 . . . . **NCLC 8**
See also DLB 93, 107, 142; SATA 54

Southworth, Emma Dorothy Eliza Nevitte
1819-1899 . . . . **NCLC 26**

Souza, Ernest
See Scott, Evelyn

Soyinka, Wole
1934- . . . . **CLC 3, 5, 14, 36, 44; BLC;**
DA; DAB; DAC; DAM DRAM, MST,
MULT; DC 2; WLC
See also BW 2; CA 13-16R; CANR 27, 39;
DLB 125; MTCW

Spackman, W(illiam) M(ode)
1905-1990 . . . . **CLC 46**
See also CA 81-84; 132

Spacks, Barry 1931- . . . . **CLC 14**
See also CA 29-32R; CANR 33; DLB 105

Spanidou, Irini 1946- . . . . **CLC 44**

Spark, Muriel (Sarah)
1918- . . . . . **CLC 2, 3, 5, 8, 13, 18, 40, 94;**
DAB; DAC; DAM MST, NOV; SSC 10
See also CA 5-8R; CANR 12, 36;
CDBLB 1945-1960; DLB 15, 139;
INT CANR-12; MTCW

Spaulding, Douglas
See Bradbury, Ray (Douglas)

Spaulding, Leonard
See Bradbury, Ray (Douglas)

Spence, J. A. D.
See Eliot, T(homas) S(tearns)

Spencer, Elizabeth 1921- . . . . **CLC 22**
See also CA 13-16R; CANR 32; DLB 6;
MTCW; SATA 14

Spencer, Leonard G.
See Silverberg, Robert

Stewart, Mary (Florence Elinor)
1916- .... CLC 7, 35; DAB
See also CA 1-4R; CANR 1; SATA 12

Stewart, Mary Rainbow
See Stewart, Mary (Florence Elinor)

Stifle, June
See Campbell, Maria

Stifter, Adalbert 1805-1868 ...... NCLC 41
See also DLB 133

Still, James 1906- .... CLC 49
See also CA 65-68; CAAS 17; CANR 10,
26; DLB 9; SATA 29

Sting
See Sumner, Gordon Matthew

Stirling, Arthur
See Sinclair, Upton (Beall)

Stitt, Milan 1941- .... CLC 29
See also CA 69-72

Stockton, Francis Richard 1834-1902
See Stockton, Frank R.
See also CA 108; 137; MAICYA; SATA 44

Stockton, Frank R. .... TCLC 47
See also Stockton, Francis Richard
See also DLB 42, 74; DLBD 13;
SATA-Brief 32

Stoddard, Charles
See Kuttner, Henry

Stoker, Abraham 1847-1912
See Stoker, Bram
See also CA 105; DA; DAC; DAM MST,
NOV; SATA 29

Stoker, Bram
1847-1912 .... TCLC 8; DAB; WLC
See also Stoker, Abraham
See also CA 150; CDBLB 1890-1914;
DLB 36, 70

Stolz, Mary (Slattery) 1920- .... CLC 12
See also AAYA 8; AITN 1; CA 5-8R;
CANR 13, 41; JRDA; MAICYA;
SAAS 3; SATA 10, 71

Stone, Irving
1903-1989 .... CLC 7; DAM POP
See also AITN 1; CA 1-4R; 129; CAAS 3;
CANR 1, 23; INT CANR-23; MTCW;
SATA 3; SATA-Obit 64

Stone, Oliver 1946- .... CLC 73
See also AAYA 15; CA 110

Stone, Robert (Anthony)
1937- .... CLC 5, 23, 42
See also CA 85-88; CANR 23; DLB 152;
INT CANR-23; MTCW

Stone, Zachary
See Follett, Ken(neth Martin)

Stoppard, Tom
1937- ...... CLC 1, 3, 4, 5, 8, 15, 29, 34,
63, 91; DA; DAB; DAC; DAM DRAM,
MST; DC 6; WLC
See also CA 81-84; CANR 39;
CDBLB 1960 to Present; DLB 13;
DLBY 85; MTCW

Storey, David (Malcolm)
1933- ..... CLC 2, 4, 5, 8; DAM DRAM
See also CA 81-84; CANR 36; DLB 13, 14;
MTCW

Storm, Hyemeyohsts
1935- .... CLC 3; DAM MULT
See also CA 81-84; CANR 45; NNAL

Storm, (Hans) Theodor (Woldsen)
1817-1888 .... NCLC 1

Storni, Alfonsina
1892-1938 ..... TCLC 5; DAM MULT;
HLC
See also CA 104; 131; HW

Stout, Rex (Todhunter) 1886-1975 ... CLC 3
See also AITN 2; CA 61-64

Stow, (Julian) Randolph 1935- .. CLC 23, 48
See also CA 13-16R; CANR 33; MTCW

Stowe, Harriet (Elizabeth) Beecher
1811-1896 ..... NCLC 3, 50; DA; DAB;
DAC; DAM MST, NOV; WLC
See also CDALB 1865-1917; DLB 1, 12, 42,
74; JRDA; MAICYA; YABC 1

Strachey, (Giles) Lytton
1880-1932 .... TCLC 12
See also CA 110; DLB 149; DLBD 10

Strand, Mark
1934- .. CLC 6, 18, 41, 71; DAM POET
See also CA 21-24R; CANR 40; DLB 5;
SATA 41

Straub, Peter (Francis)
1943- .... CLC 28; DAM POP
See also BEST 89:1; CA 85-88; CANR 28;
DLBY 84; MTCW

Strauss, Botho 1944- .... CLC 22
See also DLB 124

Streatfeild, (Mary) Noel
1895(?)-1986 .... CLC 21
See also CA 81-84; 120; CANR 31;
CLR 17; DLB 160; MAICYA; SATA 20;
SATA-Obit 48

Stribling, T(homas) S(igismund)
1881-1965 .... CLC 23
See also CA 107; DLB 9

Strindberg, (Johan) August
1849-1912 ...... TCLC 1, 8, 21, 47; DA;
DAB; DAC; DAM DRAM, MST; WLC
See also CA 104; 135

Stringer, Arthur 1874-1950 ...... TCLC 37
See also DLB 92

Stringer, David
See Roberts, Keith (John Kingston)

Strugatskii, Arkadii (Natanovich)
1925-1991 .... CLC 27
See also CA 106; 135

Strugatskii, Boris (Natanovich)
1933- .... CLC 27
See also CA 106

Strummer, Joe 1953(?)- .... CLC 30

Stuart, Don A.
See Campbell, John W(ood, Jr.)

Stuart, Ian
See MacLean, Alistair (Stuart)

Stuart, Jesse (Hilton)
1906-1984 .... CLC 1, 8, 11, 14, 34
See also CA 5-8R; 112; CANR 31; DLB 9,
48, 102; DLBY 84; SATA 2;
SATA-Obit 36

Sturgeon, Theodore (Hamilton)
1918-1985 .... CLC 22, 39
See also Queen, Ellery
See also CA 81-84; 116; CANR 32; DLB 8;
DLBY 85; MTCW

Sturges, Preston 1898-1959 .... TCLC 48
See also CA 114; 149; DLB 26

Styron, William
1925- .... CLC 1, 3, 5, 11, 15, 60;
DAM NOV, POP
See also BEST 90:4; CA 5-8R; CANR 6, 33;
CDALB 1968-1988; DLB 2, 143;
DLBY 80; INT CANR-6; MTCW

Suarez Lynch, B.
See Bioy Casares, Adolfo; Borges, Jorge
Luis

Su Chien 1884-1918
See Su Man-shu
See also CA 123

Suckow, Ruth 1892-1960 .... SSC 18
See also CA 113; DLB 9, 102

Sudermann, Hermann 1857-1928 .. TCLC 15
See also CA 107; DLB 118

Sue, Eugene 1804-1857 .... NCLC 1
See also DLB 119

Sueskind, Patrick 1949- .... CLC 44
See also Suskind, Patrick

Sukenick, Ronald 1932- ..... CLC 3, 4, 6, 48
See also CA 25-28R; CAAS 8; CANR 32;
DLBY 81

Suknaski, Andrew 1942- .... CLC 19
See also CA 101; DLB 53

Sullivan, Vernon
See Vian, Boris

Sully Prudhomme 1839-1907 ...... TCLC 31

Su Man-shu .... TCLC 24
See also Su Chien

Summerforest, Ivy B.
See Kirkup, James

Summers, Andrew James 1942- ..... CLC 26

Summers, Andy
See Summers, Andrew James

Summers, Hollis (Spurgeon, Jr.)
1916- .... CLC 10
See also CA 5-8R; CANR 3; DLB 6

Summers, (Alphonsus Joseph-Mary Augustus)
Montague 1880-1948 .... TCLC 16
See also CA 118

Sumner, Gordon Matthew 1951- .... CLC 26

Surtees, Robert Smith
1803-1864 .... NCLC 14
See also DLB 21

Susann, Jacqueline 1921-1974 ...... CLC 3
See also AITN 1; CA 65-68; 53-56; MTCW

Su Shih 1036-1101 .... CMLC 15

Suskind, Patrick
See Sueskind, Patrick
See also CA 145

Sutcliff, Rosemary
1920-1992 .... CLC 26; DAB; DAC;
DAM MST, POP
See also AAYA 10; CA 5-8R; 139;
CANR 37; CLR 1, 37; JRDA; MAICYA;
SATA 6, 44, 78; SATA-Obit 73

Sutro, Alfred 1863-1933.......... TCLC 6
See also CA 105; DLB 10

Sutton, Henry
See Slavitt, David R(ytman)

Svevo, Italo .... TCLC 2, 35
See also Schmitz, Aron Hector

Swados, Elizabeth (A.) 1951-....... CLC 12
See also CA 97-100; CANR 49; INT 97-100

Swados, Harvey 1920-1972 .... CLC 5
See also CA 5-8R; 37-40R; CANR 6;
DLB 2

Swan, Gladys 1934- .... CLC 69
See also CA 101; CANR 17, 39

Swarthout, Glendon (Fred)
1918-1992 .... CLC 35
See also CA 1-4R; 139; CANR 1, 47;
SATA 26

Sweet, Sarah C.
See Jewett, (Theodora) Sarah Orne

Swenson, May
1919-1989 .... CLC 4, 14, 61; DA; DAB;
DAC; DAM MST, POET; PC 14
See also CA 5-8R; 130; CANR 36; DLB 5;
MTCW; SATA 15

Swift, Augustus
See Lovecraft, H(oward) P(hillips)

Swift, Graham (Colin) 1949-.... CLC 41, 88
See also CA 117; 122; CANR 46

Swift, Jonathan
1667-1745 ...... LC 1; DA; DAB; DAC;
DAM MST, NOV, POET; PC 9; WLC
See also CDBLB 1660-1789; DLB 39, 95,
101; SATA 19

Swinburne, Algernon Charles
1837-1909 ...... TCLC 8, 36; DA; DAB;
DAC; DAM MST, POET; WLC
See also CA 105; 140; CDBLB 1832-1890;
DLB 35, 57

Swinfen, Ann .... CLC 34

Swinnerton, Frank Arthur
1884-1982 .... CLC 31
See also CA 108; DLB 34

Swithen, John
See King, Stephen (Edwin)

Sylvia
See Ashton-Warner, Sylvia (Constance)

Symmes, Robert Edward
See Duncan, Robert (Edward)

Symonds, John Addington
1840-1893 .... NCLC 34
See also DLB 57, 144

Symons, Arthur 1865-1945 .... TCLC 11
See also CA 107; DLB 19, 57, 149

Symons, Julian (Gustave)
1912-1994 .... CLC 2, 14, 32
See also CA 49-52; 147; CAAS 3; CANR 3,
33; DLB 87, 155; DLBY 92; MTCW

Synge, (Edmund) J(ohn) M(illington)
1871-1909 .... TCLC 6, 37;
DAM DRAM; DC 2
See also CA 104; 141; CDBLB 1890-1914;
DLB 10, 19

Syruc, J.
See Milosz, Czeslaw

Szirtes, George 1948-............. CLC 46
See also CA 109; CANR 27

Tabori, George 1914-............. CLC 19
See also CA 49-52; CANR 4

Tagore, Rabindranath
1861-1941 .... TCLC 3, 53;
DAM DRAM, POET; PC 8
See also CA 104; 120; MTCW

Taine, Hippolyte Adolphe
1828-1893 .... NCLC 15

Talese, Gay 1932-................ CLC 37
See also AITN 1; CA 1-4R; CANR 9;
INT CANR-9; MTCW

Tallent, Elizabeth (Ann) 1954- ..... CLC 45
See also CA 117; DLB 130

Tally, Ted 1952-................ CLC 42
See also CA 120; 124; INT 124

Tamayo y Baus, Manuel
1829-1898 .... NCLC 1

Tammsaare, A(nton) H(ansen)
1878-1940 .... TCLC 27

Tan, Amy
1952- .... CLC 59; DAM MULT, NOV,
POP
See also AAYA 9; BEST 89:3; CA 136;
SATA 75

Tandem, Felix
See Spitteler, Carl (Friedrich Georg)

Tanizaki, Jun'ichiro
1886-1965 .... CLC 8, 14, 28; SSC 21
See also CA 93-96; 25-28R

Tanner, William
See Amis, Kingsley (William)

Tao Lao
See Storni, Alfonsina

Tarassoff, Lev
See Troyat, Henri

Tarbell, Ida M(inerva)
1857-1944 .... TCLC 40
See also CA 122; DLB 47

Tarkington, (Newton) Booth
1869-1946 .... TCLC 9
See also CA 110; 143; DLB 9, 102;
SATA 17

Tarkovsky, Andrei (Arsenyevich)
1932-1986 .... CLC 75
See also CA 127

Tartt, Donna 1964(?)-............. CLC 76
See also CA 142

Tasso, Torquato 1544-1595 .... LC 5

Tate, (John Orley) Allen
1899-1979 .... CLC 2, 4, 6, 9, 11, 14, 24
See also CA 5-8R; 85-88; CANR 32;
DLB 4, 45, 63; MTCW

Tate, Ellalice
See Hibbert, Eleanor Alice Burford

Tate, James (Vincent) 1943- ... CLC 2, 6, 25
See also CA 21-24R; CANR 29; DLB 5,
169

Tavel, Ronald 1940-............... CLC 6
See also CA 21-24R; CANR 33

Taylor, C(ecil) P(hilip) 1929-1981... CLC 27
See also CA 25-28R; 105; CANR 47

Taylor, Edward
1642(?)-1729 .... LC 11; DA; DAB;
DAC; DAM MST, POET
See also DLB 24

Taylor, Eleanor Ross 1920-......... CLC 5
See also CA 81-84

Taylor, Elizabeth 1912-1975 ... CLC 2, 4, 29
See also CA 13-16R; CANR 9; DLB 139;
MTCW; SATA 13

Taylor, Henry (Splawn) 1942-...... CLC 44
See also CA 33-36R; CAAS 7; CANR 31;
DLB 5

Taylor, Kamala (Purnaiya) 1924-
See Markandaya, Kamala
See also CA 77-80

Taylor, Mildred D. .... CLC 21
See also AAYA 10; BW 1; CA 85-88;
CANR 25; CLR 9; DLB 52; JRDA;
MAICYA; SAAS 5; SATA 15, 70

Taylor, Peter (Hillsman)
1917-1994 ..... CLC 1, 4, 18, 37, 44, 50,
71; SSC 10
See also CA 13-16R; 147; CANR 9, 50;
DLBY 81, 94; INT CANR-9; MTCW

Taylor, Robert Lewis 1912-........ CLC 14
See also CA 1-4R; CANR 3; SATA 10

Tchekhov, Anton
See Chekhov, Anton (Pavlovich)

Teasdale, Sara 1884-1933.......... TCLC 4
See also CA 104; DLB 45; SATA 32

Tegner, Esaias 1782-1846......... NCLC 2

Teilhard de Chardin, (Marie Joseph) Pierre
1881-1955 .... TCLC 9
See also CA 105

Temple, Ann
See Mortimer, Penelope (Ruth)

Tennant, Emma (Christina)
1937-.................... CLC 13, 52
See also CA 65-68; CAAS 9; CANR 10, 38;
DLB 14

Tenneshaw, S. M.
See Silverberg, Robert

Tennyson, Alfred
1809-1892 .... NCLC 30; DA; DAB;
DAC; DAM MST, POET; PC 6; WLC
See also CDBLB 1832-1890; DLB 32

Teran, Lisa St. Aubin de .... CLC 36
See also St. Aubin de Teran, Lisa

Terence 195(?)B.C.-159B.C....... CMLC 14

Teresa de Jesus, St. 1515-1582...... LC 18

Terkel, Louis 1912-
See Terkel, Studs
See also CA 57-60; CANR 18, 45; MTCW

Terkel, Studs .... CLC 38
See also Terkel, Louis
See also AITN 1

Terry, C. V.
See Slaughter, Frank G(ill)

Terry, Megan 1932-............... CLC 19
See also CA 77-80; CABS 3; CANR 43;
DLB 7

Tertz, Abram
See Sinyavsky, Andrei (Donatevich)

Tesich, Steve 1943(?)-1996...... **CLC 40, 69**
See also CA 105; 152; DLBY 83

Teternikov, Fyodor Kuzmich 1863-1927
See Sologub, Fyodor
See also CA 104

Tevis, Walter 1928-1984 .... **CLC 42**
See also CA 113

Tey, Josephine.................. **TCLC 14**
See also Mackintosh, Elizabeth
See also DLB 77

Thackeray, William Makepeace
1811-1863 .... **NCLC 5, 14, 22, 43; DA;**
DAB; DAC; DAM MST, NOV; WLC
See also CDBLB 1832-1890; DLB 21, 55,
159, 163; SATA 23

Thakura, Ravindranatha
See Tagore, Rabindranath

Tharoor, Shashi 1956- .... **CLC 70**
See also CA 141

Thelwell, Michael Miles 1939- ..... **CLC 22**
See also BW 2; CA 101

Theobald, Lewis, Jr.
See Lovecraft, H(oward) P(hillips)

Theodorescu, Ion N. 1880-1967
See Arghezi, Tudor
See also CA 116

Theriault, Yves
1915-1983 .. **CLC 79; DAC; DAM MST**
See also CA 102; DLB 88

Theroux, Alexander (Louis)
1939-..................... **CLC 2, 25**
See also CA 85-88; CANR 20

Theroux, Paul (Edward)
1941- .... **CLC 5, 8, 11, 15, 28, 46;**
DAM POP
See also BEST 89:4; CA 33-36R; CANR 20,
45; DLB 2; MTCW; SATA 44

Thesen, Sharon 1946-............. **CLC 56**

Thevenin, Denis
See Duhamel, Georges

Thibault, Jacques Anatole Francois
1844-1924
See France, Anatole
See also CA 106; 127; DAM NOV; MTCW

Thiele, Colin (Milton) 1920- .... **CLC 17**
See also CA 29-32R; CANR 12, 28, 53;
CLR 27; MAICYA; SAAS 2; SATA 14,
72

Thomas, Audrey (Callahan)
1935- .... **CLC 7, 13, 37; SSC 20**
See also AITN 2; CA 21-24R; CAAS 19;
CANR 36; DLB 60; MTCW

Thomas, D(onald) M(ichael)
1935- .... **CLC 13, 22, 31**
See also CA 61-64; CAAS 11; CANR 17,
45; CDBLB 1960 to Present; DLB 40;
INT CANR-17; MTCW

Thomas, Dylan (Marlais)
1914-1953 ... **TCLC 1, 8, 45; DA; DAB;**
DAC; DAM DRAM, MST, POET;
PC 2; SSC 3; WLC
See also CA 104; 120; CDBLB 1945-1960;
DLB 13, 20, 139; MTCW; SATA 60

Thomas, (Philip) Edward
1878-1917 ...... **TCLC 10; DAM POET**
See also CA 106; DLB 19

Thomas, Joyce Carol 1938-........ **CLC 35**
See also AAYA 12; BW 2; CA 113; 116;
CANR 48; CLR 19; DLB 33; INT 116;
JRDA; MAICYA; MTCW; SAAS 7;
SATA 40, 78

Thomas, Lewis 1913-1993 .... **CLC 35**
See also CA 85-88; 143; CANR 38; MTCW

Thomas, Paul
See Mann, (Paul) Thomas

Thomas, Piri 1928-.............. **CLC 17**
See also CA 73-76; HW

Thomas, R(onald) S(tuart)
1913- .... **CLC 6, 13, 48; DAB;**
DAM POET
See also CA 89-92; CAAS 4; CANR 30;
CDBLB 1960 to Present; DLB 27;
MTCW

Thomas, Ross (Elmore) 1926-1995 .. **CLC 39**
See also CA 33-36R; 150; CANR 22

Thompson, Francis Clegg
See Mencken, H(enry) L(ouis)

Thompson, Francis Joseph
1859-1907 .... **TCLC 4**
See also CA 104; CDBLB 1890-1914;
DLB 19

Thompson, Hunter S(tockton)
1939- .... **CLC 9, 17, 40; DAM POP**
See also BEST 89:1; CA 17-20R; CANR 23,
46; MTCW

Thompson, James Myers
See Thompson, Jim (Myers)

Thompson, Jim (Myers)
1906-1977(?) .... **CLC 69**
See also CA 140

Thompson, Judith .... **CLC 39**

Thomson, James
1700-1748 ..... **LC 16, 29; DAM POET**
See also DLB 95

Thomson, James
1834-1882 ..... **NCLC 18; DAM POET**
See also DLB 35

Thoreau, Henry David
1817-1862 ..... **NCLC 7, 21; DA; DAB;**
DAC; DAM MST; WLC
See also CDALB 1640-1865; DLB 1

Thornton, Hall
See Silverberg, Robert

Thucydides c. 455B.C.-399B.C.... **CMLC 17**

Thurber, James (Grover)
1894-1961 .... **CLC 5, 11, 25; DA; DAB;**
DAC; DAM DRAM, MST, NOV; SSC 1
See also CA 73-76; CANR 17, 39;
CDALB 1929-1941; DLB 4, 11, 22, 102;
MAICYA; MTCW; SATA 13

Thurman, Wallace (Henry)
1902-1934 .... **TCLC 6; BLC;**
DAM MULT
See also BW 1; CA 104; 124; DLB 51

Ticheburn, Cheviot
See Ainsworth, William Harrison

Tieck, (Johann) Ludwig
1773-1853 .... **NCLC 5, 46**
See also DLB 90

Tiger, Derry
See Ellison, Harlan (Jay)

Tilghman, Christopher 1948(?)-..... **CLC 65**

Tillinghast, Richard (Williford)
1940-...................... **CLC 29**
See also CA 29-32R; CAAS 23; CANR 26,
51

Timrod, Henry 1828-1867 .... **NCLC 25**
See also DLB 3

Tindall, Gillian 1938-.............. **CLC 7**
See also CA 21-24R; CANR 11

Tiptree, James, Jr. .... **CLC 48, 50**
See also Sheldon, Alice Hastings Bradley
See also DLB 8

Titmarsh, Michael Angelo
See Thackeray, William Makepeace

Tocqueville, Alexis (Charles Henri Maurice
Clerel Comte) 1805-1859..... **NCLC 7**

Tolkien, J(ohn) R(onald) R(euel)
1892-1973 ...... **CLC 1, 2, 3, 8, 12, 38;**
DA; DAB; DAC; DAM MST, NOV,
POP; WLC
See also AAYA 10; AITN 1; CA 17-18;
45-48; CANR 36; CAP 2;
CDBLB 1914-1945; DLB 15, 160; JRDA;
MAICYA; MTCW; SATA 2, 32;
SATA-Obit 24

Toller, Ernst 1893-1939 .... **TCLC 10**
See also CA 107; DLB 124

Tolson, M. B.
See Tolson, Melvin B(eaunorus)

Tolson, Melvin B(eaunorus)
1898(?)-1966 .... **CLC 36; BLC;**
DAM MULT, POET
See also BW 1; CA 124; 89-92; DLB 48, 76

Tolstoi, Aleksei Nikolaevich
See Tolstoy, Alexey Nikolaevich

Tolstoy, Alexey Nikolaevich
1882-1945 .... **TCLC 18**
See also CA 107

Tolstoy, Count Leo
See Tolstoy, Leo (Nikolaevich)

Tolstoy, Leo (Nikolaevich)
1828-1910 ...... **TCLC 4, 11, 17, 28, 44;**
DA; DAB; DAC; DAM MST, NOV;
SSC 9; WLC
See also CA 104; 123; SATA 26

Tomasi di Lampedusa, Giuseppe 1896-1957
See Lampedusa, Giuseppe (Tomasi) di
See also CA 111

Tomlin, Lily..................... **CLC 17**
See also Tomlin, Mary Jean

Tomlin, Mary Jean 1939(?)-
See Tomlin, Lily
See also CA 117

Tomlinson, (Alfred) Charles
1927-.............. **CLC 2, 4, 6, 13, 45;**
DAM POET
See also CA 5-8R; CANR 33; DLB 40

Tonson, Jacob
See Bennett, (Enoch) Arnold

Toole, John Kennedy
1937-1969 .... **CLC 19, 64**
See also CA 104; DLBY 81

Vicker, Angus
See Felsen, Henry Gregor

Vidal, Gore
　1925- ..... **CLC 2, 4, 6, 8, 10, 22, 33, 72;**
　　　　　　DAM NOV, POP
　See also AITN 1; BEST 90:2; CA 5-8R;
　CANR 13, 45; DLB 6, 152;
　INT CANR-13; MTCW

Viereck, Peter (Robert Edwin)
　1916- .... **CLC 4**
　See also CA 1-4R; CANR 1, 47; DLB 5

Vigny, Alfred (Victor) de
　1797-1863 ..... **NCLC 7; DAM POET**
　See also DLB 119

Vilakazi, Benedict Wallet
　1906-1947 .... **TCLC 37**

Villiers de l'Isle Adam, Jean Marie Mathias
　Philippe Auguste Comte
　1838-1889 .... **NCLC 3; SSC 14**
　See also DLB 123

Villon, Francois 1431-1463(?) .... **PC 13**

Vinci, Leonardo da 1452-1519 ...... **LC 12**

Vine, Barbara .... **CLC 50**
　See also Rendell, Ruth (Barbara)
　See also BEST 90:4

Vinge, Joan D(ennison) 1948- ...... **CLC 30**
　See also CA 93-96; SATA 36

Violis, G.
See Simenon, Georges (Jacques Christian)

Visconti, Luchino 1906-1976 .... **CLC 16**
　See also CA 81-84; 65-68; CANR 39

Vittorini, Elio 1908-1966 ...... **CLC 6, 9, 14**
　See also CA 133; 25-28R

Vizinczey, Stephen 1933- .... **CLC 40**
　See also CA 128; INT 128

Vliet, R(ussell) G(ordon)
　1929-1984 .... **CLC 22**
　See also CA 37-40R; 112; CANR 18

Vogau, Boris Andreyevich 1894-1937(?)
　See Pilnyak, Boris
　See also CA 123

Vogel, Paula A(nne) 1951- .... **CLC 76**
　See also CA 108

Voight, Ellen Bryant 1943- .... **CLC 54**
　See also CA 69-72; CANR 11, 29; DLB 120

Voigt, Cynthia 1942- .... **CLC 30**
　See also AAYA 3; CA 106; CANR 18, 37,
　40; CLR 13; INT CANR-18; JRDA;
　MAICYA; SATA 48, 79; SATA-Brief 33

Voinovich, Vladimir (Nikolaevich)
　1932- .... **CLC 10, 49**
　See also CA 81-84; CAAS 12; CANR 33;
　MTCW

Vollmann, William T.
　1959- ...... **CLC 89; DAM NOV, POP**
　See also CA 134

Voloshinov, V. N.
See Bakhtin, Mikhail Mikhailovich

Voltaire
　1694-1778 ..... **LC 14; DA; DAB; DAC;**
　　　DAM DRAM, MST; SSC 12; WLC

von Daeniken, Erich 1935- .... **CLC 30**
　See also AITN 1; CA 37-40R; CANR 17,
　44

von Daniken, Erich
See von Daeniken, Erich

von Heidenstam, (Carl Gustaf) Verner
See Heidenstam, (Carl Gustaf) Verner von

von Heyse, Paul (Johann Ludwig)
See Heyse, Paul (Johann Ludwig von)

von Hofmannsthal, Hugo
See Hofmannsthal, Hugo von

von Horvath, Odon
See Horvath, Oedoen von

von Horvath, Oedoen
See Horvath, Oedoen von

von Liliencron, (Friedrich Adolf Axel) Detlev
See Liliencron, (Friedrich Adolf Axel)
Detlev von

Vonnegut, Kurt, Jr.
　1922- ...... **CLC 1, 2, 3, 4, 5, 8, 12, 22,**
　40, 60; DA; DAB; DAC; DAM MST,
　　　NOV, POP; SSC 8; WLC
　See also AAYA 6; AITN 1; BEST 90:4;
　CA 1-4R; CANR 1, 25, 49;
　CDALB 1968-1988; DLB 2, 8, 152;
　DLBD 3; DLBY 80; MTCW

Von Rachen, Kurt
See Hubbard, L(afayette) Ron(ald)

von Rezzori (d'Arezzo), Gregor
See Rezzori (d'Arezzo), Gregor von

von Sternberg, Josef
See Sternberg, Josef von

Vorster, Gordon 1924- .... **CLC 34**
　See also CA 133

Vosce, Trudie
See Ozick, Cynthia

Voznesensky, Andrei (Andreievich)
　1933- ...... **CLC 1, 15, 57; DAM POET**
　See also CA 89-92; CANR 37; MTCW

Waddington, Miriam 1917- .... **CLC 28**
　See also CA 21-24R; CANR 12, 30;
　DLB 68

Wagman, Fredrica 1937- .... **CLC 7**
　See also CA 97-100; INT 97-100

Wagner, Richard 1813-1883 .... **NCLC 9**
　See also DLB 129

Wagner-Martin, Linda 1936- .... **CLC 50**

Wagoner, David (Russell)
　1926- .... **CLC 3, 5, 15**
　See also CA 1-4R; CAAS 3; CANR 2;
　DLB 5; SATA 14

Wah, Fred(erick James) 1939- ...... **CLC 44**
　See also CA 107; 141; DLB 60

Wahloo, Per 1926-1975 .... **CLC 7**
　See also CA 61-64

Wahloo, Peter
See Wahloo, Per

Wain, John (Barrington)
　1925-1994 .... **CLC 2, 11, 15, 46**
　See also CA 5-8R; 145; CAAS 4; CANR 23;
　CDBLB 1960 to Present; DLB 15, 27,
　139, 155; MTCW

Wajda, Andrzej 1926- .... **CLC 16**
　See also CA 102

Wakefield, Dan 1932- .... **CLC 7**
　See also CA 21-24R; CAAS 7

Wakoski, Diane
　1937- .... **CLC 2, 4, 7, 9, 11, 40;**
　　　　　　DAM POET; PC 15
　See also CA 13-16R; CAAS 1; CANR 9;
　DLB 5; INT CANR-9

Wakoski-Sherbell, Diane
See Wakoski, Diane

Walcott, Derek (Alton)
　1930- .... **CLC 2, 4, 9, 14, 25, 42, 67, 76;**
　BLC; DAB; DAC; DAM MST, MULT,
　　　　　　POET
　See also BW 2; CA 89-92; CANR 26, 47;
　DLB 117; DLBY 81; MTCW

Waldman, Anne 1945- .... **CLC 7**
　See also CA 37-40R; CAAS 17; CANR 34;
　DLB 16

Waldo, E. Hunter
See Sturgeon, Theodore (Hamilton)

Waldo, Edward Hamilton
See Sturgeon, Theodore (Hamilton)

Walker, Alice (Malsenior)
　1944- .... **CLC 5, 6, 9, 19, 27, 46, 58;**
　BLC; DA; DAB; DAC; DAM MST,
　　MULT, NOV, POET, POP; SSC 5
　See also AAYA 3; BEST 89:4; BW 2;
　CA 37-40R; CANR 9, 27, 49;
　CDALB 1968-1988; DLB 6, 33, 143;
　INT CANR-27; MTCW; SATA 31

Walker, David Harry 1911-1992.... **CLC 14**
　See also CA 1-4R; 137; CANR 1; SATA 8;
　SATA-Obit 71

Walker, Edward Joseph 1934-
See Walker, Ted
　See also CA 21-24R; CANR 12, 28, 53

Walker, George F.
　1947- .... **CLC 44, 61; DAB; DAC;**
　　　　　　DAM MST
　See also CA 103; CANR 21, 43; DLB 60

Walker, Joseph A.
　1935- .... **CLC 19; DAM DRAM, MST**
　See also BW 1; CA 89-92; CANR 26;
　DLB 38

Walker, Margaret (Abigail)
　1915- .... **CLC 1, 6; BLC; DAM MULT**
　See also BW 2; CA 73-76; CANR 26;
　DLB 76, 152; MTCW

Walker, Ted..................... **CLC 13**
　See also Walker, Edward Joseph
　See also DLB 40

Wallace, David Foster 1962- .... **CLC 50**
　See also CA 132

Wallace, Dexter
See Masters, Edgar Lee

Wallace, (Richard Horatio) Edgar
　1875-1932 .... **TCLC 57**
　See also CA 115; DLB 70

Wallace, Irving
　1916-1990 ..... **CLC 7, 13; DAM NOV,**
　　　　　　POP
　See also AITN 1; CA 1-4R; 132; CAAS 1;
　CANR 1, 27; INT CANR-27; MTCW

Wallant, Edward Lewis
　1926-1962 .... **CLC 5, 10**
　See also CA 1-4R; CANR 22; DLB 2, 28,
　143; MTCW

Walley, Byron
See Card, Orson Scott

Walpole, Horace 1717-1797. . . . . LC 2
See also DLB 39, 104

Walpole, Hugh (Seymour)
1884-1941 . . . . TCLC 5
See also CA 104; DLB 34

Walser, Martin 1927-. . . . . CLC 27
See also CA 57-60; CANR 8, 46; DLB 75,
124

Walser, Robert
1878-1956 . . . . TCLC 18; SSC 20
See also CA 118; DLB 66

Walsh, Jill Paton. . . . . CLC 35
See also Paton Walsh, Gillian
See also AAYA 11; CLR 2; DLB 161;
SAAS 3

Walter, Villiam Christian
See Andersen, Hans Christian

Wambaugh, Joseph (Aloysius, Jr.)
1937- . . . . CLC 3, 18; DAM NOV, POP
See also AITN 1; BEST 89:3; CA 33-36R;
CANR 42; DLB 6; DLBY 83; MTCW

Ward, Arthur Henry Sarsfield 1883-1959
See Rohmer, Sax
See also CA 108

Ward, Douglas Turner 1930-. . . . . . . CLC 19
See also BW 1; CA 81-84; CANR 27;
DLB 7, 38

Ward, Mary Augusta
See Ward, Mrs. Humphry

Ward, Mrs. Humphry
1851-1920 . . . . TCLC 55
See also DLB 18

Ward, Peter
See Faust, Frederick (Schiller)

Warhol, Andy 1928(?)-1987. . . . . CLC 20
See also AAYA 12; BEST 89:4; CA 89-92;
121; CANR 34

Warner, Francis (Robert le Plastrier)
1937- . . . . CLC 14
See also CA 53-56; CANR 11

Warner, Marina 1946-. . . . . CLC 59
See also CA 65-68; CANR 21

Warner, Rex (Ernest) 1905-1986. . . . CLC 45
See also CA 89-92; 119; DLB 15

Warner, Susan (Bogert)
1819-1885 . . . . NCLC 31
See also DLB 3, 42

Warner, Sylvia (Constance) Ashton
See Ashton-Warner, Sylvia (Constance)

Warner, Sylvia Townsend
1893-1978 . . . . CLC 7, 19; SSC 23
See also CA 61-64; 77-80; CANR 16;
DLB 34, 139; MTCW

Warren, Mercy Otis 1728-1814. . . NCLC 13
See also DLB 31

Warren, Robert Penn
1905-1989 . . . . CLC 1, 4, 6, 8, 10, 13, 18,
39, 53, 59; DA; DAB; DAC; DAM MST,
NOV, POET; SSC 4; WLC
See also AITN 1; CA 13-16R; 129;
CANR 10, 47; CDALB 1968-1988;
DLB 2, 48, 152; DLBY 80, 89;
INT CANR-10; MTCW; SATA 46;
SATA-Obit 63

Warshofsky, Isaac
See Singer, Isaac Bashevis

Warton, Thomas
1728-1790 . . . . LC 15; DAM POET
See also DLB 104, 109

Waruk, Kona
See Harris, (Theodore) Wilson

Warung, Price 1855-1911. . . . . TCLC 45

Warwick, Jarvis
See Garner, Hugh

Washington, Alex
See Harris, Mark

Washington, Booker T(aliaferro)
1856-1915 . . . . TCLC 10; BLC;
DAM MULT
See also BW 1; CA 114; 125; SATA 28

Washington, George 1732-1799. . . . . . LC 25
See also DLB 31

Wassermann, (Karl) Jakob
1873-1934 . . . . TCLC 6
See also CA 104; DLB 66

Wasserstein, Wendy
1950- . . . . CLC 32, 59, 90;
DAM DRAM; DC 4
See also CA 121; 129; CABS 3; CANR 53;
INT 129

Waterhouse, Keith (Spencer)
1929- . . . . CLC 47
See also CA 5-8R; CANR 38; DLB 13, 15;
MTCW

Waters, Frank (Joseph)
1902-1995 . . . . CLC 88
See also CA 5-8R; 149; CAAS 13; CANR 3,
18; DLBY 86

Waters, Roger 1944-. . . . . CLC 35

Watkins, Frances Ellen
See Harper, Frances Ellen Watkins

Watkins, Gerrold
See Malzberg, Barry N(athaniel)

Watkins, Gloria 1955(?)-
See hooks, bell
See also BW 2; CA 143

Watkins, Paul 1964-. . . . . CLC 55
See also CA 132

Watkins, Vernon Phillips
1906-1967 . . . . CLC 43
See also CA 9-10; 25-28R; CAP 1; DLB 20

Watson, Irving S.
See Mencken, H(enry) L(ouis)

Watson, John H.
See Farmer, Philip Jose

Watson, Richard F.
See Silverberg, Robert

Waugh, Auberon (Alexander) 1939- . . CLC 7
See also CA 45-48; CANR 6, 22; DLB 14

Waugh, Evelyn (Arthur St. John)
1903-1966 . . . . . . CLC 1, 3, 8, 13, 19, 27,
44; DA; DAB; DAC; DAM MST, NOV,
POP; WLC
See also CA 85-88; 25-28R; CANR 22;
CDBLB 1914-1945; DLB 15, 162; MTCW

Waugh, Harriet 1944- . . . . CLC 6
See also CA 85-88; CANR 22

Ways, C. R.
See Blount, Roy (Alton), Jr.

Waystaff, Simon
See Swift, Jonathan

Webb, (Martha) Beatrice (Potter)
1858-1943 . . . . TCLC 22
See also Potter, Beatrice
See also CA 117

Webb, Charles (Richard) 1939-. . . . . . CLC 7
See also CA 25-28R

Webb, James H(enry), Jr. 1946-. . . . CLC 22
See also CA 81-84

Webb, Mary (Gladys Meredith)
1881-1927 . . . . TCLC 24
See also CA 123; DLB 34

Webb, Mrs. Sidney
See Webb, (Martha) Beatrice (Potter)

Webb, Phyllis 1927-. . . . . CLC 18
See also CA 104; CANR 23; DLB 53

Webb, Sidney (James)
1859-1947 . . . . TCLC 22
See also CA 117

Webber, Andrew Lloyd. . . . . CLC 21
See also Lloyd Webber, Andrew

Weber, Lenora Mattingly
1895-1971 . . . . CLC 12
See also CA 19-20; 29-32R; CAP 1;
SATA 2; SATA-Obit 26

Webster, John
1579(?)-1634(?) . . . . . . LC 33; DA; DAB;
DAC; DAM DRAM, MST; DC 2; WLC
See also CDBLB Before 1660; DLB 58

Webster, Noah 1758-1843 . . . . NCLC 30

Wedekind, (Benjamin) Frank(lin)
1864-1918 . . . . . . TCLC 7; DAM DRAM
See also CA 104; DLB 118

Weidman, Jerome 1913-. . . . . CLC 7
See also AITN 2; CA 1-4R; CANR 1;
DLB 28

Weil, Simone (Adolphine)
1909-1943 . . . . TCLC 23
See also CA 117

Weinstein, Nathan
See West, Nathanael

Weinstein, Nathan von Wallenstein
See West, Nathanael

Weir, Peter (Lindsay) 1944- . . . . CLC 20
See also CA 113; 123

Weiss, Peter (Ulrich)
1916-1982 . . . . CLC 3, 15, 51;
DAM DRAM
See also CA 45-48; 106; CANR 3; DLB 69,
124

Weiss, Theodore (Russell)
1916- . . . . CLC 3, 8, 14
See also CA 9-12R; CAAS 2; CANR 46;
DLB 5

Whittlebot, Hernia
See Coward, Noel (Peirce)

Wicker, Thomas Grey   1926-
See Wicker, Tom
See also CA 65-68; CANR 21, 46

Wicker, Tom . . . . CLC 7
See also Wicker, Thomas Grey

Wideman, John Edgar
1941- . . . . CLC 5, 34, 36, 67; BLC;
DAM MULT
See also BW 2; CA 85-88; CANR 14, 42;
DLB 33, 143

Wiebe, Rudy (Henry)
1934- . . . . CLC 6, 11, 14; DAC;
DAM MST
See also CA 37-40R; CANR 42; DLB 60

Wieland, Christoph Martin
1733-1813 . . . . NCLC 17
See also DLB 97

Wiene, Robert   1881-1938 . . . . TCLC 56

Wieners, John   1934- . . . . CLC 7
See also CA 13-16R; DLB 16

Wiesel, Elie(zer)
1928- . . . . . . CLC 3, 5, 11, 37; DA; DAB;
DAC; DAM MST, NOV
See also AAYA 7; AITN 1; CA 5-8R;
CAAS 4; CANR 8, 40; DLB 83;
DLBY 87; INT CANR-8; MTCW;
SATA 56

Wiggins, Marianne   1947- . . . . CLC 57
See also BEST 89:3; CA 130

Wight, James Alfred   1916-
See Herriot, James
See also CA 77-80; SATA 55;
SATA-Brief 44

Wilbur, Richard (Purdy)
1921- . . . CLC 3, 6, 9, 14, 53; DA; DAB;
DAC; DAM MST, POET
See also CA 1-4R; CABS 2; CANR 2, 29;
DLB 5, 169; INT CANR-29; MTCW;
SATA 9

Wild, Peter   1940- . . . . CLC 14
See also CA 37-40R; DLB 5

Wilde, Oscar (Fingal O'Flahertie Wills)
1854(?)-1900 . . . . TCLC 1, 8, 23, 41; DA;
DAB; DAC; DAM DRAM, MST, NOV;
SSC 11; WLC
See also CA 104; 119; CDBLB 1890-1914;
DLB 10, 19, 34, 57, 141, 156; SATA 24

Wilder, Billy . . . . CLC 20
See also Wilder, Samuel
See also DLB 26

Wilder, Samuel   1906-
See Wilder, Billy
See also CA 89-92

Wilder, Thornton (Niven)
1897-1975 . . . . . . CLC 1, 5, 6, 10, 15, 35,
82; DA; DAB; DAC; DAM DRAM,
MST, NOV; DC 1; WLC
See also AITN 2; CA 13-16R; 61-64;
CANR 40; DLB 4, 7, 9; MTCW

Wilding, Michael   1942- . . . . CLC 73
See also CA 104; CANR 24, 49

Wiley, Richard   1944- . . . . CLC 44
See also CA 121; 129

Wilhelm, Kate . . . . CLC 7
See also Wilhelm, Katie Gertrude
See also CAAS 5; DLB 8; INT CANR-17

Wilhelm, Katie Gertrude   1928-
See Wilhelm, Kate
See also CA 37-40R; CANR 17, 36; MTCW

Wilkins, Mary
See Freeman, Mary Eleanor Wilkins

Willard, Nancy   1936- . . . . CLC 7, 37
See also CA 89-92; CANR 10, 39; CLR 5;
DLB 5, 52; MAICYA; MTCW;
SATA 37, 71; SATA-Brief 30

Williams, C(harles) K(enneth)
1936- . . . . CLC 33, 56; DAM POET
See also CA 37-40R; DLB 5

Williams, Charles
See Collier, James L(incoln)

Williams, Charles (Walter Stansby)
1886-1945 . . . . TCLC 1, 11
See also CA 104; DLB 100, 153

Williams, (George) Emlyn
1905-1987 . . . . . . CLC 15; DAM DRAM
See also CA 104; 123; CANR 36; DLB 10,
77; MTCW

Williams, Hugo   1942- . . . . CLC 42
See also CA 17-20R; CANR 45; DLB 40

Williams, J. Walker
See Wodehouse, P(elham) G(renville)

Williams, John A(lfred)
1925- . . . CLC 5, 13; BLC; DAM MULT
See also BW 2; CA 53-56; CAAS 3;
CANR 6, 26, 51; DLB 2, 33;
INT CANR-6

Williams, Jonathan (Chamberlain)
1929- . . . . CLC 13
See also CA 9-12R; CAAS 12; CANR 8;
DLB 5

Williams, Joy   1944- . . . . CLC 31
See also CA 41-44R; CANR 22, 48

Williams, Norman   1952- . . . . CLC 39
See also CA 118

Williams, Sherley Anne
1944- . . . . . CLC 89; BLC; DAM MULT,
POET
See also BW 2; CA 73-76; CANR 25;
DLB 41; INT CANR-25; SATA 78

Williams, Shirley
See Williams, Sherley Anne

Williams, Tennessee
1911-1983 . . . . . CLC 1, 2, 5, 7, 8, 11, 15,
19, 30, 39, 45, 71; DA; DAB; DAC;
DAM DRAM, MST; DC 4; WLC
See also AITN 1, 2; CA 5-8R; 108;
CABS 3; CANR 31; CDALB 1941-1968;
DLB 7; DLBD 4; DLBY 83; MTCW

Williams, Thomas (Alonzo)
1926-1990 . . . . CLC 14
See also CA 1-4R; 132; CANR 2

Williams, William C.
See Williams, William Carlos

Williams, William Carlos
1883-1963 . . . . CLC 1, 2, 5, 9, 13, 22, 42,
67; DA; DAB; DAC; DAM MST, POET;
PC 7
See also CA 89-92; CANR 34;
CDALB 1917-1929; DLB 4, 16, 54, 86;
MTCW

Williamson, David (Keith)   1942- . . . . CLC 56
See also CA 103; CANR 41

Williamson, Ellen Douglas   1905-1984
See Douglas, Ellen
See also CA 17-20R; 114; CANR 39

Williamson, Jack . . . . CLC 29
See also Williamson, John Stewart
See also CAAS 8; DLB 8

Williamson, John Stewart   1908-
See Williamson, Jack
See also CA 17-20R; CANR 23

Willie, Frederick
See Lovecraft, H(oward) P(hillips)

Willingham, Calder (Baynard, Jr.)
1922-1995 . . . . CLC 5, 51
See also CA 5-8R; 147; CANR 3; DLB 2,
44; MTCW

Willis, Charles
See Clarke, Arthur C(harles)

Willy
See Colette, (Sidonie-Gabrielle)

Willy, Colette
See Colette, (Sidonie-Gabrielle)

Wilson, A(ndrew) N(orman)   1950- . . CLC 33
See also CA 112; 122; DLB 14, 155

Wilson, Angus (Frank Johnstone)
1913-1991 . . CLC 2, 3, 5, 25, 34; SSC 21
See also CA 5-8R; 134; CANR 21; DLB 15,
139, 155; MTCW

Wilson, August
1945- . . . . . . CLC 39, 50, 63; BLC; DA;
DAB; DAC; DAM DRAM, MST,
MULT; DC 2
See also AAYA 16; BW 2; CA 115; 122;
CANR 42; MTCW

Wilson, Brian   1942- . . . . CLC 12

Wilson, Colin   1931- . . . . CLC 3, 14
See also CA 1-4R; CAAS 5; CANR 1, 22,
33; DLB 14; MTCW

Wilson, Dirk
See Pohl, Frederik

Wilson, Edmund
1895-1972 . . . . CLC 1, 2, 3, 8, 24
See also CA 1-4R; 37-40R; CANR 1, 46;
DLB 63; MTCW

Wilson, Ethel Davis (Bryant)
1888(?)-1980 . . . . CLC 13; DAC;
DAM POET
See also CA 102; DLB 68; MTCW

Wilson, John   1785-1854 . . . . NCLC 5

Wilson, John (Anthony) Burgess   1917-1993
See Burgess, Anthony
See also CA 1-4R; 143; CANR 2, 46; DAC;
DAM NOV; MTCW

Wilson, Lanford
1937- . . . . . CLC 7, 14, 36; DAM DRAM
See also CA 17-20R; CABS 3; CANR 45;
DLB 7

Yakumo Koizumi
See Hearn, (Patricio) Lafcadio (Tessima Carlos)

Yanez, Jose Donoso
See Donoso (Yanez), Jose

Yanovsky, Basile S.
See Yanovsky, V(assily) S(emenovich)

Yanovsky, V(assily) S(emenovich)
1906-1989 .... CLC 2, 18
See also CA 97-100; 129

Yates, Richard 1926-1992 ..... CLC 7, 8, 23
See also CA 5-8R; 139; CANR 10, 43;
DLB 2; DLBY 81, 92; INT CANR-10

Yeats, W. B.
See Yeats, William Butler

Yeats, William Butler
1865-1939 ..... TCLC 1, 11, 18, 31; DA;
DAB; DAC; DAM DRAM, MST,
POET; WLC
See also CA 104; 127; CANR 45;
CDBLB 1890-1914; DLB 10, 19, 98, 156;
MTCW

Yehoshua, A(braham) B.
1936- .... CLC 13, 31
See also CA 33-36R; CANR 43

Yep, Laurence Michael 1948- ...... CLC 35
See also AAYA 5; CA 49-52; CANR 1, 46;
CLR 3, 17; DLB 52; JRDA; MAICYA;
SATA 7, 69

Yerby, Frank G(arvin)
1916-1991 .... CLC 1, 7, 22; BLC;
DAM MULT
See also BW 1; CA 9-12R; 136; CANR 16,
52; DLB 76; INT CANR-16; MTCW

Yesenin, Sergei Alexandrovich
See Esenin, Sergei (Alexandrovich)

Yevtushenko, Yevgeny (Alexandrovich)
1933- .... CLC 1, 3, 13, 26, 51;
DAM POET
See also CA 81-84; CANR 33; MTCW

Yezierska, Anzia 1885(?)-1970 ..... CLC 46
See also CA 126; 89-92; DLB 28; MTCW

Yglesias, Helen 1915- .... CLC 7, 22
See also CA 37-40R; CAAS 20; CANR 15;
INT CANR-15; MTCW

Yokomitsu Riichi 1898-1947 ...... TCLC 47

Yonge, Charlotte (Mary)
1823-1901 .... TCLC 48
See also CA 109; DLB 18, 163; SATA 17

York, Jeremy
See Creasey, John

York, Simon
See Heinlein, Robert A(nson)

Yorke, Henry Vincent 1905-1974 ... CLC 13
See also Green, Henry
See also CA 85-88; 49-52

Yosano Akiko 1878-1942 .. TCLC 59; PC 11

Yoshimoto, Banana .... CLC 84
See also Yoshimoto, Mahoko

Yoshimoto, Mahoko 1964-
See Yoshimoto, Banana
See also CA 144

Young, Al(bert James)
1939- ..... CLC 19; BLC; DAM MULT
See also BW 2; CA 29-32R; CANR 26;
DLB 33

Young, Andrew (John) 1885-1971 .... CLC 5
See also CA 5-8R; CANR 7, 29

Young, Collier
See Bloch, Robert (Albert)

Young, Edward 1683-1765 .... LC 3
See also DLB 95

Young, Marguerite (Vivian)
1909-1995 .... CLC 82
See also CA 13-16; 150; CAP 1

Young, Neil 1945- .... CLC 17
See also CA 110

Young Bear, Ray A.
1950- .... CLC 94; DAM MULT
See also CA 146; NNAL

Yourcenar, Marguerite
1903-1987 .... CLC 19, 38, 50, 87;
DAM NOV
See also CA 69-72; CANR 23; DLB 72;
DLBY 88; MTCW

Yurick, Sol 1925- .... CLC 6
See also CA 13-16R; CANR 25

Zabolotskii, Nikolai Alekseevich
1903-1958 .... TCLC 52
See also CA 116

Zamiatin, Yevgenii
See Zamyatin, Evgeny Ivanovich

Zamora, Bernice (B. Ortiz)
1938- ..... CLC 89; DAM MULT; HLC
See also CA 151; DLB 82; HW

Zamyatin, Evgeny Ivanovich
1884-1937 .... TCLC 8, 37
See also CA 105

Zangwill, Israel 1864-1926 .... TCLC 16
See also CA 109; DLB 10, 135

Zappa, Francis Vincent, Jr. 1940-1993
See Zappa, Frank
See also CA 108; 143

Zappa, Frank .... CLC 17
See also Zappa, Francis Vincent, Jr.

Zaturenska, Marya 1902-1982 .... CLC 6, 11
See also CA 13-16R; 105; CANR 22

Zelazny, Roger (Joseph)
1937-1995 .... CLC 21
See also AAYA 7; CA 21-24R; 148;
CANR 26; DLB 8; MTCW; SATA 57;
SATA-Brief 39

Zhdanov, Andrei A(lexandrovich)
1896-1948 .... TCLC 18
See also CA 117

Zhukovsky, Vasily 1783-1852 .... NCLC 35

Ziegenhagen, Eric .... CLC 55

Zimmer, Jill Schary
See Robinson, Jill

Zimmerman, Robert
See Dylan, Bob

Zindel, Paul
1936- ..... CLC 6, 26; DA; DAB; DAC;
DAM DRAM, MST, NOV; DC 5
See also AAYA 2; CA 73-76; CANR 31;
CLR 3; DLB 7, 52; JRDA; MAICYA;
MTCW; SATA 16, 58

Zinov'Ev, A. A.
See Zinoviev, Alexander (Aleksandrovich)

Zinoviev, Alexander (Aleksandrovich)
1922- .... CLC 19
See also CA 116; 133; CAAS 10

Zoilus
See Lovecraft, H(oward) P(hillips)

Zola, Emile (Edouard Charles Antoine)
1840-1902 ...... TCLC 1, 6, 21, 41; DA;
DAB; DAC; DAM MST, NOV; WLC
See also CA 104; 138; DLB 123

Zoline, Pamela 1941- .... CLC 62

Zorrilla y Moral, Jose 1817-1893 .. NCLC 6

Zoshchenko, Mikhail (Mikhailovich)
1895-1958 .... TCLC 15; SSC 15
See also CA 115

Zuckmayer, Carl 1896-1977 .... CLC 18
See also CA 69-72; DLB 56, 124

Zuk, Georges
See Skelton, Robin

Zukofsky, Louis
1904-1978 .... CLC 1, 2, 4, 7, 11, 18;
DAM POET; PC 11
See also CA 9-12R; 77-80; CANR 39;
DLB 5, 165; MTCW

Zweig, Paul 1935-1984 .... CLC 34, 42
See also CA 85-88; 113

Zweig, Stefan 1881-1942 .... TCLC 17
See also CA 112; DLB 81, 118

Literary Criticism Series
Cumulative Topic Index

This index lists all topic entries in Gale's *Classical and Medieval Literature Criticism, Contemporary Literary Criticism, Literature Criticism from 1400 to 1800, Nineteenth-Century Literature Criticism,* and *Twentieth-Century Literary Criticism.*

Topic Index

Topic Index

CMLC Cumulative Nationality Index

RUSSIAN
　Slovo o polku Igoreve (*The Igor Tale*) **1**

SPANISH
　Poema de mio Cid (*Poem of the Cid*) **4**
　Razón de amor **16**
TURKISH
　Kitab-i-dedem Qorkut (*Book of Dede Korkut*) **8**

WELSH
　Mabinogion **9**

CMLC Cumulative Title Index

Title Index

211-12, 214, 221, 225-26, 232, 244, 249-51, 254, 256-57, 285, 288, 296-98

De rerum generatione ex elementis (Bacon) **14**:62

De Resurrectione (Albert the Great) **16**:118, 125

De Sacrificio Missae (Albert the Great) **16**:42

De scientia experimentali (Bacon) **14**:5, 80

De Scientia Perspectiva (Bacon) **14**:20, 47

De senectute (Cicero) **3**:193, 195, 202, 204, 227, 231, 288

De sensu et sensato (Albert the Great) **16**:61, 106, 110

De sinderesi (Albert the Great) **16**:49

De somno et vigilia (Albert the Great) **16**:7, 61, 110

De Spiritu et Anima (Albert the Great) **16**:128

De spiritu et respiratione (Albert the Great) **16**:61

De statibus (Hermogenes)
　　See *On Stases*

De temporibus meis (Cicero) **3**:198

De termino Paschali (Bacon) **14**:63

De topicis differentiis (Boethius) **15**:7, 27, 29, 88, 129, 131, 136

De tranquillitate animi (Seneca) **6**:344, 382, 393

De Trinitate (Augustine) **6**:21, 27, 62, 68, 70, 77, 85-7, 90-1, 116, 119-21, 138-40

De trinitate (Boethius) **15**:31-2, 43, 56, 59, 79, 86, 95, 125-30, 136, 141

de Unitate et Trinitate Divina (Abelard)
　　See *Theologia 'Summi boni'*

De utilitate grammaticae (Bacon) **14**:46, 64

De utilitate mathematicae (Bacon) **14**:5

De vegetabilibus (Albert the Great) **16**:20, 36-7, 61, 64

De vera religione (Augustine) **6**:68

De vita beata (Seneca) **6**:382, 412

De vulgari eloquentia (Boccaccio) **13**:65

"The Death of Edward the Confessor" **4**:13

"The Death of Enkidu" **3**:336

"The Death of Gilgamesh" **3**:333, 336-37, 349

Decameron (Boccaccio) **13**:3-28, 30-8, 42-3, 45, 47-52, 55-7, 59-65, 67, 71-2, 74-5, 82-4, 86, 88-91, 94, 114-8, 122-31

Decisive Treatise (Averroes)
　　See *Fasl al-maqal*

Dede Korkut
　　See *Kitabi-i Dedem Qorkut*

Dede Korkut nameh
　　See *Kitabi-i Dedem Qorkut*

"The Defence of Walled Towns" (Sordello) **15**:330, 344

Defense (Plato)
　　See *Apologia*

Defense (Xenophon)
　　See *Apology*

Deification of Arsinoe (Callimachus) **18**: 34, 39, 60

Descent of Heracles into the Underworld (Pindar) **12**:321

Descent of the Gods (Hesiod)
　　See *Theogony*

Desconort (Llull) **12**:108, 120, 122

Destructio destructionis philosophorum (Averroes)
　　See *Tahafut al-tahafut*

Destructio Destructionum (Averroes)
　　See *Tahafut al-tahafut*

Destruction of the Destruction (Averroes)
　　See *Tahafut al-tahafut*

"Deus Amanz" (Marie de France)
　　See "Les Dous Amanz"

"The Devout Prince" **2**:40

Dialectica (Abelard) **11**:62, 64, 66

Dialogi (Seneca) **6**:374, 381-82, 410, 413

Dialogue between a Christian and a Jew (Abelard)
　　See *Dialogue between a Philosopher, a Jew and A Christian*

Dialogue between a Philosopher, a Jew and A Christian (Abelard) **11**:4, 11, 21, 24, 51-53, 67

Dialogue of the Philosopher with a Jew and a Christian (Abelard)
　　See *Dialogue between a Philosopher, a Jew and A Christian*

Dialogue of Trismegistus (Apuleius) **1**:17

Dialogues (Seneca)
　　See *Dialogi*

Dialogues on the Supreme Good, the End of All Moral Action (Cicero)
　　See *De finibus*

Diana's Hunt (Boccaccio)
　　See *Caccia di Diana*

Dictyluci (Aeschylus)
　　See *Net-Draggers*

"Dido" (Ovid) **7**:312

"Dirge for Blacatz" (Sordello)
　　See "Planher vuelh en Blacatz"

Dis Exapaton (Menander) **9**:258, 270

"Discourse on Dragon and Tiger (Lead and Mercury)" (Su Shih) **15**:400

"Discourse on Literature" (Su Shih) **15**:420

Disputation (Llull) **12**:119

Dithyrambs (Pindar) **12**:320, 355

Divine Song
　　See *Bhagavad Gita*

Divisions (Boethius) **15**:27, 29-30

The Divisions of Oratory (Cicero)
　　See *Partiones oratoriae*

Doctrina pueril (Llull) **12**:104-05, 107, 121

"The Doe and Her Fawn" (Marie de France) **8**:193-94

"Dompna meillz qu om pot pensar" (Sordello) **15**:361

A Double Deceit (Menander)
　　See *Dis Exapaton*

The Dour Man (Menander)
　　See *Dyskolos*

"Les Dous Amanz" (Marie de France) **8**:116-17, 121, 131, 133-34, 136-39, 147, 153-54, 156, 162-65, 181, 187

"A Draught of Sesamum" (Su Shih) **15**:383, 391

Dream (Cicero)
　　See *Somnium Scipionis*

Dream of Scipio (Cicero)
　　See *Somnium Scipionis*

The Dream of the Rood **14**:215-294

"Dreams of the Sky-land" (Li Po) **2**:134

"Drinking Alone by Moonlight" (Li Po) **2**:132, 143, 163

Drunkenness (Menander) **9**:248

"A Dung-Beetle" (Marie de France)
　　See "A Wolf and a Dung-Beetle"

Duties (Cicero)
　　See *De officiis*

The Dynasty of Raghu (Kalidasa)
　　See *Raghuvamsa*

Dyskolos (Menander) **9**:231-33, 235-41, 243-52, 257, 260-65, 269-70, 272-77, 279-84, 286-87

"The Ebony Horse" **2**:51

Ecclesiazusae (Aristophanes)
　　See *Ekklesiazousai*

The Education of Cyrus (Xenophon)
　　See *Cyropaedia*

Egyptians (Aeschylus) **11**:88, 160, 179

"Eight Sights of Feng-hsiang" (Su Shih) **15**:410

Eighth Isthmian (Pindar)
　　See *Isthmian 8*

Eighth Olympian (Pindar)
　　See *Olympian 8*

"Eighty some paces" (Su Shih) **15**:398

Eirene (Aristophanes) **4**:44-5, 60-2, 78, 87, 93, 108-09, 124-26, 132-33, 138, 142-44, 148-49, 153-54, 160, 162-63. 165-68

Ekklesiazousai (Aristophanes) **4**:44, 60-62, 65, 68, 78, 87, 94, 110, 124-26, 128-29, 147, 149-50, 152, 155-56, 161-62, 166, 168-77, 179-80

Elegia di Constanza (Boccaccio) **13**:62-4, 73

Elegia di madonna Fiammetta (Boccaccio)
　　See *Fiammetta*

Elegies (Ovid)
　　See *Tristia*

Elegies of Gloom (Ovid)
　　See *Tristia*

Elektra (Sophocles) **2**:289, 293, 300, 314-15, 319-22, 324, 326-27, 331, 335, 338-40, 347, 349, 351, 353-54, 357-58, 368, 380, 384-85, 395-96, 417-18, 421

Elementary Exercises (Hermogenes)
　　See *Progymnasmata*

Eleusinians (Aeschylus) **11**:192

Eleventh Nemean (Pindar)
　　See *Nemean 11*

Eleventh Olympian (Pindar)
　　See *Olympian 11*

Eleventh Pythian (Pindar)
　　See *Pythian 11*

"Eliduc" (Marie de France) **8**:114, 118, 121, 129-30, 133, 135, 140, 144-45, 147-49, 152, 158, 160-61, 164-66, 170, 182

Embassy (Demosthenes)
　　See *On the Misconduct of the Embassy*

"An Emperor and his Ape" (Marie de France) **8**:175

"Emril Son of Beyril" **8**:105

Enarration on Psalm 90 (Augustine) **6**:111

Enarration on Psalm 136 (Augustine) **6**:116

Enarrationes in psalmos (Augustine) **6**:83

Enchiridion ad laurentium (Augustine) **6**:9, 21, 68

Encomia (Pindar) **12**:320-21, 357, 363-64

Encomion on Sosibius (Callimachus) **18**: 43

Encomium (Pindar)
　　See *Encomia*

Enid (Chretien de Troyes)
　　See *Erec et Enide*

Ensegnamen d'Onor (Sordello) **15**:331-32, 354, 256, 270, 376-76

Epic of Gilgamesh **3**:301-75

Epicleros (Menander) **9**:203

Epigrams (Callimachus) **18**: 18, 25, 32, 34-8, 48

Epinicia (Pindar) **12**:320-22

Epinomis (Plato) **8**:248, 305-06, 311

"Episode of Nala"
　　See *Nalopakhyana*

Epistle ad P. Lentulum (Cicero)
　　See *Ad P. Lentulum*

Epistle XLVII (Seneca) **6**:384

Epistles (Ovid)
　　See *Heroides*

Epistles (Plato) **8**:305, 311

Epistles (Seneca)

Title Index

See *Epistulae morales*
"Letting the Intellect Go and Experiencing Pure Ignorance" (Eckhart) 9:24
Li (Confucius)
　See *Li Chi*
Li Chi (Confucius) 19:11, 20-21, 26-28, 35-36, 38, 40, 46, 69
Libation Bearers (Aeschylus) 11:85, 87-8, 102, 104-05, 107, 116, 118-19, 131, 138, 140, 151, 153-54, 159, 162-64, 181, 184-85, 191, 193-95, 202, 205-07, 211, 217, 223
Libation-Pourers (Aeschylus)
　See *Libation Bearers*
Libellus de Alchimia (Albert the Great) 16:65
Liber contemplationis (Llull) 12:104
Liber de ascensu et descensu intellectus (Llull) 12:107. 111
Liber de lumine (Llull) 12:110
Liber de retardatione accidentium senectutis (Bacon) 14:64
Liber de sancta virginitate (Augustine) 6:38
Liber Hymnorum (Abelard) 11:45
Liber mineralium (Albert the Great) 16:55, 62-4, 97, 100-02
Liber Positionum (Eckhart) 9:56
Liber praedicationis contra Iudaeos (Llull) 12:117
Liber principiorum medicinae (Llull) 12:107
Liberum arbitrium voluntatis (Augustine)
　See *De libero arbitrio voluntatis*
Libre d'amic e Amat (Llull)
　See *Book of the Lover and the Beloved*
Libre de meravelles (Llull)
　See *Felix*
Libre del orde de cavalleria (Llull) 12:104, 107
Life (Josephus)
　See *Vita*
Life of Dante (Boccaccio)
　See *Vita di Dante*
Liki (Confucius)
　See *Li Chi*
Le Livre de l'Espurgatorie (Marie de France)
　See *L'Espurgatoire Saint Patrice*
Le Livre de Marco Polo (Polo)
　See *The Travels of Marco Polo the Venetian*
Lock of Berenice (Callimachus) 18: 15-17, 30, 35, 43, 59, 61, 63-4
Locri (Menander) 9:203
Logica 'Ingredientibus' (Abelard) 11:63, 64, 66
Logica 'Nostrorum' (Abelard) 11:62, 64, 66
Logical Treatises (Albert the Great) 16:4
"The Lonely Wife" (Li Po) 2:132
Long Commentary on the Metaphysics (Averroes)
　See *Tafsir ma ba'd al-tabi'ah*
Longer Work (Bacon)
　See *Opus Majus*
Lord's Song
　See *Bhagavadgita*
The Lord's Song
　See *Bhagavad Gita*
Love-Poems (Ovid)
　See *Amores*
"The Lovers of the Benou Udreh" 2:40
"A Lu Mountain Song for the Palace Censor Empty-Boat Lu" (Li Po) 2:152, 164
Lun Yu (Confucius) 19:10-11, 17-23, 26, 28-33, 35-36, 38-42, 48-50, 68-69, 72-76, 78-85, 88-89, 95-101
Lykourgeia (Aeschylus) 11:192

Lysis (Plato) 8:254, 264-66, 306, 314
Lysistrata (Aristophanes) 4:44, 60-2, 65, 68, 88, 93-94, 107-10, 113, 123-26, 133, 142, 144-45, 151, 153-56, 160, 163, 166, 169-75
The Mabinogion
　See *Pedeir Keinc y Mabinogi*
Mad Hercules (Seneca)
　See *Hercules furens*
"The Mad Lover" 2:40
"The Magic Horse" 2:49
Mahabharata 5:177-287
The Maid of Andros (Terence)
　See *Andria*
Makura no soshi (Sei Shonagon) 6:291-96, 299-309, 311-26
Makura Zoshi (Sei Shonagon)
　See *Makura no soshi*
Malavika and Agnimitra (Kalidasa)
　See *Malavikagnimitra*
Malavikagnimitra (Kalidasa) 9:82, 85, 90, 96-7, 99-102, 126, 128, 131-33, 137-38
"Maldon"
　See "The Battle of Maldon"
The Man from Sikyon (Menander)
　See *Sikyonios*
"The Man of Yemen and His Six Slave Girls" 2:40
The Man She Hated (Menander)
　See *Misoumenos*
"The Man Who Never Laughed Again" 2:40
The Man Who Punished Himself (Menander)
　See *Heautontimorumenus*
Manahij (Averroes)
　See *Kitab al-kashf 'an manahij al-adilla fi 'aqa'id al-milla, wa ta'rif ma waqa'a fiha bi-hasb at-ta'wil min ash-shibah al-muzigha wal-bida 'al-mudilla*
Mandeville's Travels (Mandeville) 19:107-80
Manilian (Cicero)
　See *Pro Lege Manilia*
Marco Polo (Polo)
　See *The Travels of Marco Polo the Venetian*
Marco Polo's Travels (Polo)
　See *The Travels of Marco Polo the Venetian*
Mariale (Albert the Great) 16:42
Marius (Cicero) 3:198
Marriage of Arsinoe (Callimachus) 18: 34
Masters of the Frying Pan (Aristophanes) 4:167
Medea (Ovid) 7:312 7:286, 297, 336, 346-47, 376, 420, 425, 444-45
Medea (Seneca) 6:336, 344-45, 363, 366, 371, 373, 377-81, 404-10, 413-18, 426-27, 432-33, 436, 441
Medicamina Faciei (Ovid) 7:346
Megalopolis (Demosthenes)
　See *For Megalopolis*
Meghaduta (Kalidasa) 9:89-90, 92, 95, 102, 107, 113, 115, 125-26, 129
Meister Eckhart: The Essential Sermons, Commentaries, Treatises, and Defense (Eckhart) 9:67
Memoirs (Xenophon)
　See *Memorabilia*
Memorabilia (Xenophon) 17:329, 331, 335, 337, 340, 341, 342, 343, 344, 345, 349, 362, 374, 375
"A Memorial of Self-Introduction Written for Assistant Director of the Censorate Sung" (Li Po) 2:173-74
Menexenus (Plato) 8:305-07

Meno (Plato) 8:206, 218, 250, 264, 283-85, 305-07, 311, 320-22, 328, 356-57, 362
Menon (Plato)
　See *Meno*
Metamorphoses (Apuleius) 1:3, 7-8, 12-13, 15, 17-24, 26-27, 29-37, 39-43, 45
Metamorphoses (Ovid) 7:286, 291-92, 298-99, 304-05, 314-16, 322, 324-36, 335-44, 346, 349, 357, 361-63, 365, 368-77, 379, 383-93, 395-96, 398-402, 404, 412-18, 430-32, 434-35, 438, 443-46
Metamorphosis (Ovid)
　See *Metamorphoses*
Metaphysics (Avicenna) 16:159-60, 164
Meteora (Albert the Great)
　See *De meteoris*
Meteororum (Albert the Great)
　See *De meteoris*
Middle Commentary on Porphyry's Isagoge and on Aristotle's Categoriae (Averroes) 7:67
Midiana (Demosthenes)
　See *Against Midias*
"Milun" (Marie de France) 8:121, 128, 131-34, 147-50, 159, 162-66, 170, 175, 182, 187
Mineralia (Albert the Great)
　See *Liber mineralium*
Minos (Plato)
　See *Meno*
Misoumenos (Menander) 9:258, 260, 269-70, 276, 287
"Misty Yangtze" (Su Shih) 15:397
"Modern Music in the Yen Ho Palace" (Su Shih) 15:385
"The Monkey and Her Baby" (Marie de France) 8:191
"The Monkey King" (Marie de France) 8:191
Moral Epistles (Seneca)
　See *Epistulae morales*
Morte Arthure "Alliterative" 10:375-436
The Mother-in-Law (Terence)
　See *Hecyra*
"A Mouse and a Frog" (Marie de France) 8:174
Movement of Animals (Albert the Great) 5:
"Moving to Lin-kao Pavilion" (Su Shih) 15:410
La Mule sans frein (Chretien de Troyes) 10:178-79, 232
Multiplication of Species (Bacon)
　See *Tractatus de Mulitiplicatione Specierum*
Murasaki Shikibu nikki (Murasaki) 1:457
Music (Boethius)
　See *In topica Ciceronis*
Music (Confucius)
　See *Yueh*
"The Muslim Champion and the Christian Damsel" 2:27
"My Trip in a Dream to the Lady of Heaven Mountain" (Li Po) 2:150
Myrmidons (Aeschylus) 11:101, 125, 193
Mystère d'Adam
　See *Ordo Representacionis Ade*
Mystery of Adam
　See *Ordo Representacionis Ade*
Mystical Theology (Albert the Great) 16:29, 119
N. 4 (Pindar)
　See *Nemean 4*
N. 6 (Pindar)
　See *Nemean 6*
N. 7 (Pindar)
　See *Nemean 7*

"On a Picture Screen" (Li Po) **2**:136
"On Anactoria" (Sappho)
  See "Ode to Anactoria"
On Ancient Medicine (Thucydides) **17**:253
On Anger (Seneca)
  De ira
On Animals (Albert the Great)
  See De animalibus
On Armaments (Demosthenes) **13**:158
On Christian Doctrine (Augustine)
  See De doctrina Christiana
On Clemency (Seneca)
  De clementia
On Consolation (Seneca) **6**:344
On Divination (Cicero)
  See De divinatione
On Division (Boethius)
  See *Divisions*
On Duties (Cicero)
  See De officiis
On First Principles (Origen)
  See De Principiis
On Forms (Hermogenes)
  See *On Types of Style*
On Free Will (Augustine)
  See De libero arbitrio voluntatis
On Friendship (Cicero)
  See De amicitia
On Gentleness (Seneca) **6**:423
On Giving and Receiving Favours (Seneca)
  De beneficiis
On Glory (Cicero) **3**:177
On Good Deeds (Seneca) **6**:427
On Grace and Free Will (Augustine)
  See De gratia et libero arbitrio
On Halonnesus (Demosthenes) **13**:165
On His Consulship (Cicero)
  See De consulatu suo
On Household Economy (Xenophon)
  See *Oeconomicus*
On Ideas (Hermogenes)
  See *On Types of Style*
On Invention (Cicero)
  See De inventione
On Invention (Hermogenes) **6**:170-72, 185-86,
  188, 191, 198-202
On Laws (Cicero)
  See De legibus
On Martyrdom (Origen) **19**:187
On Mercy (Seneca)
  De clementia
On Method (Hermogenes)
  See On the Method of Deinotes
On Misconduct of Ambassadors (Demosthenes)
  See *On the Misconduct of the Embassy*
"On Nourishing Life" (Su Shih) **15**:401
On Old Age (Cicero)
  See De senectute
On Order (Augustine)
  See De ordine
On Peace of Mind (Seneca)
  See De tranquillitate animi
On Providence (Seneca)
  De providentia
On Qualities of Style (Hermogenes)
  See On Types of Style
On Sleep and Waking (Albert the Great) **16**:16
On Staseis (Hermogenes)
  See *On Stases*

On Stases (Hermogenes) **6**:158, 170-74, 185-86,
  191, 196, 198-202
"On Taking Leave of Tzu-yu at Ying-chou: Two
  Poems" (Su Shih) **15**:411
On the Affairs in the Chersonese (Demosthenes)
  See *On the Chersonese*
On the Best Kind of Orators (Cicero)
  See De optimo genere oratorum
On the Blessed Life (Cicero)
  See *Tusculan Disputations*
On the Categoric Syllogism (Apuleius) **1**:12-13
On the Categorical Syllogism (Boethius) **15**:27
On the Catholic Faith (Boethius)
  See De fide catholica
*On the Causes and Properties of the Elements and
  of the Planets* (Albert the Great)
  See De causis et proprietatibus elementorum et
    planetarum
On the Chersonese (Demosthenes) **13**:138, 146,
  148-9, 152, 161, 166, 193, 195
On the Chief Good and Evil (Cicero)
  See De finibus
On the Christian Struggle (Augustine) **6**:21
On the City of God (Augustine)
  See De civitate Dei
On the Crown (Demosthenes) **13**:139, 143, 145,
  147-52, 162, 166, 172-5, 179, 183-4, 189, 191-
  5, 197
On the Divine Unity and Trinity (Abelard)
  See *Theologia 'Summi boni'*
On the False Embassy (Demosthenes)
  See *On the Misconduct of the Embassy*
On the Fraudulent Embassy (Demosthenes)
  See *On the Misconduct of the Embassy*
On the Freedom of Rhodes (Demosthenes)
  See *For the Rhodians*
On the God of Socrates (Apuleius) **1**:4, 7, 12-13,
  23, 32
On the Greatest Degree of Good and Evil (Cicero)
  See De finibus
On the Happy Life (Seneca)
  De vita beata
On the Hypothetical Syllogism (Boethius) **15**: 9,
  27,
On the Lacedaemonian Polity (Xenophon)
  See Constitution of Sparta
On the Method of Deinotes (Hermogenes) **6**:158,
  188, 191, 202
On the Method of Force (Hermogenes)
  See *On the Method of Deinotes*
On the Misconduct of the Embassy (Demosthenes)
  13:138, 147-9, 165, 168, 172, 183-4, 189, 194-
  5
On the Nature of Gods (Cicero)
  See De natura deorum
On the Nature of Good (Augustine) **6**:9
On the Orator (Cicero)
  See De oratore
On the Pattern for Rhetorical Effectiveness
  (Hermogenes) **6**:170
On the Peace (Demosthenes) **13**:138, 148-9, 159-
  60, 165
"On the Red Cliff" (Su Shih)
  See "Rhymeprose on the Red Cliff"
On the Reorganization (Demosthenes) **13**:165
"On the Restoration of the Examination System"
  (Su Shih) **15**:385
On the Resurrection (Origen) **19**:186
On the Rhodians (Demosthenes)

  See *For the Rhodians*
On the Science of Moral Habits (Avicenna)
  16:164
On the Shortness of Life (Seneca)
  De brevitate vitae
On the Soul (Avicenna) **16**:164
On the State (Cicero)
  See De republica
On the Symmories (Demosthenes) **13**:145, 148,
  159, 163-4, 171, 197
On the Treaties with Alexander (Demosthenes)
  13:166
On the Trinity (Augustine)
  See De Trinitate
On the Trinity (Boethius)
  See De trinitate
"On the twelfth night" (Su Shih) **15**:398
On the Unity of the Intellect: against Averroes
  (Augustine) **16**:57
On the Universe (Apuleius)
  See De mundo
On the Usefulness of Mathematics (Bacon)
  See De utilitate mathematicae
On the Vices Contracted in the Study of Theology
  (Bacon) **14**:92
On Types of Style (Hermogenes) **6**:158, 170, 185-
  92, 196, 200-02, 204
Optics (Bacon) **14**:20
Opus imperfectum contra Julianum (Augustine)
  6:149
Opus Maius (Bacon)
  See *Opus Majus*
Opus Majus (Bacon) **14**:3-5, 7-8, 15, 18, 20, 22-
  23, 29-31, 34-35, 37, 40, 42, 47, 49-50, 53-54,
  59, 61-65, 68-70, 73, 76-77, 80, 82, 84, 86, 92-
  94, 100, 102, 106-15
Opus Minus (Bacon) **14**:15, 18-20, 29, 40, 48, 52,
  54, 62-63, 66-68, 80, 100, 102-03
Opus Sermonum (Eckhart) **9**:57
Opus Tertium (Bacon) **14**:15, 19-21, 29-30, 40,
  47-48, 52, 54, 58-59, 62-63, 65, 67-68, 80, 83,
  86, 100-05, 108
Opus Tripartitum (Eckhart) **9**:55
The Orator (Cicero)
  See De optimo genere dicendi
Orator ad M. Brutum (Cicero)
  See De optimo genere dicendi
The Orator: To Marcus Brutus (Cicero)
  See De optimo genere dicendi
Ordo Representacionis Ade **4**:182-221
Oresteia (Aeschylus) **11**:77, 100-01, 105-06, 109,
  117-19, 123, 128, 130, 132-34, 136-40, 153-56,
  158-59, 160, 162-63, 167-68, 180, 184, 190-91,
  193-95, 197-99, 206, 209, 211, 217-19, 222-23
Orestes (Aeschylus) **11**:134
Orge (Menander) **9**:244, 248, 250, 284
Ornithes (Aristophanes) **4**:44-6, 58, 62-7, 87, 93-
  6. 100. 110, 114, 124-26. 131-33, 135, 142,
  144, 146-49, 155, 159-61, 165-66, 168
P. 1 (Pindar)
  See *Pythian 1*
P. 2 (Pindar)
  See *Pythian 2*
P. 3 (Pindar)
  See *Pythian 3*
P. 4 (Pindar)
  See *Pythian 4*
P. 5 (Pindar)
  See *Pythian 5*

Title Index

P. 6 (Pindar)
　See *Pythian 6*
P. 8 (Pindar)
　See *Pythian 8*
Paean for Ceos (Pindar) 12:318
Paean for the Abderites (Pindar)
　See *Paean 2*
Paean 1 (Pindar) 12:355
Paean 2 (Pindar) 12:321, 351, 360-61
Paean 4 (Pindar) 12:352, 382
Paean 5 (Pindar) 12:359
Paean 6 (Pindar) 12:271, 300, 358-59
Paean 8 (Pindar) 12:
Paean 9 (Pindar) 12:266, 308-09, 356
Paeans (Pindar) 12:318, 320-21, 352
"The Palace of the Grotto of Mists" (Sordello)
　15:391
Paraphrase (Caedmon)
　See "Genesis"
Paraphrase of Genesis (Caedmon)
　See "Genesis"
A Parasite's Brain to the Rescue (Terence)
　See *Phormio*
Parisian Questions and Prologues (Eckhart) 9:69
Parliament of Women (Aristophanes)
　See *Ekklesiazousai*
Parmenides (Plato) 8:232, 234, 240, 258-60, 264,
　282, 293, 306, 310, 317, 320, 328, 333-34, 338,
　340-41, 361, 364
Partheneia (Pindar) 12:320-21, 351, 356
"The Parting" (Li Po) 2:138
"A Parting Banquet for the Collator Shu-yün at the
　Hsieh T'iao Lodge in Hsüan-chou" (Li Po)
　2:163
Partiones oratoriae (Cicero) 3:201, 218, 259-60,
　263
Partitiones (Cicero)
　See *Partiones oratoriae*
Parzival (Wolfram von Eschenbach) 5:293-94,
　296-302, 304-05, 307-10, 312, 314-17, 320-23,
　325-26, 333-45, 347, 350-54, 357-58, 360, 362,
　366, 369-71, 373, 376, 380-83, 385-86, 390-92,
　395-96, 400-01, 403-04, 409, 411, 416-17, 419-
　23, 425, 429-32
"Passing the Huai" (Su Shih) 15:413
The Pastorals of Daphnis and Chloe (Longus)
　See *Daphnis and Chloe*
Patrologia Graeca (Origen) 19:231
"The Pavilion of Flying Cranes" (Su Shih) 15:382
"The Pavilion to Glad Rain" (Su Shih) 15:382
Peace (Aristophanes)
　See *Eirene*
The Peace (Demosthenes)
　See *On the Peace*
Pearl 19:275-407
"A Peasant and a Dung-Beetle" (Marie de France)
　8:174
"The Peasant Who Saw His Wife with Her Lover"
　(Marie de France) 8:190
Pedeir Keinc y Mabinogi 9:144-98
"*Peleus and Thetis*" (Catullus)
　See "*Poem 64*"
Penelope (Aeschylus) 11:124
Perceval (Chretien de Troyes) 10:133, 137, 139,
　143, 145-46, 150, 157, 159, 161-66, 169, 178-
　79, 183, 189-90, 195-96, 199, 206-09, 216-20,
　223-26, 228-40
Perceval le Gallois (Chretien de Troyes)
　See *Perceval*

Percevax le viel (Chretien de Troyes)
　See *Perceval*
Peri hermeneias (Apuleius) 1:24
Perikeiromene (Menander) 9:207, 210-11, 213,
　215, 217, 221, 223, 225, 228, 230, 232, 238-39,
　246-48, 250-52, 260, 267, 269-71, 276-77, 281,
　288
Perr Archon (Origen)
　See *De Principiis*
Persae (Aeschylus)
　See *Persians*
Persians (Aeschylus) 11:77, 85, 88, 96, 102, 112-
　13, 117-18, 121, 127, 133-35, 139, 151-53,
　156, 158-60, 179, 181-84, 191, 193-95, 198,
　200, 202-03, 205, 211, 215-20
Perspective (Bacon)
　See *De Scientia Perspectiva*
Phaedo (Plato) 8:204-07, 209, 233, 235-36, 239,
　261, 268, 305-07, 312, 320, 322-25, 328, 331,
　340-41, 358, 361-62
Phaedra (Seneca) 6:341, 366, 368-70, 377, 379-
　81, 389, 403-06, 413-16, 418, 424-26, 432, 448
Phaedrus (Plato) 8:205, 210, 220, 230, 232-33,
　241, 244, 254-55, 259, 262, 264-66, 270, 275,
　283, 299, 306-07, 317, 322-25, 331, 334, 355,
　359, 362, 364
Philebus (Plato) 8:248, 260, 264-68, 270, 306,
　310, 333, 341, 361, 363-64
Philippic I (Demosthenes) 13:137, 148-9, 152,
　165, 171, 183, 190-2, 195, 197
Philippic II (Demosthenes) 13:138, 148-9, 151,
　160, 165, 172
Philippic III (Demosthenes) 13:138, 143-5, 148,
　161, 166, 172, 177, 180, 192-3, 195
Philippic IV (Demosthenes) 13:162, 166
Philippics (Cicero) 3:192-93, 196, 198-99, 229-
　30, 253, 268, 271-73
Philippics (Demosthenes) 13:139, 142-3, 149-52,
　158, 161-2, 172, 174, 180, 183, 189
Philoctetes (Aeschylus) 11:125, 140
Philoctetes at Troy (Sophocles) 2:341
Philoktetes (Sophocles) 2:289, 294-95, 302-05,
　314, 316, 318, 320, 325, 338, 341, 346, 352-54,
　357, 367-68, 377, 385-87, 397-408, 415-16,
　419, 426
Philomena (Chretien de Troyes) 10:137
Philosopher (Plato) 8:259
Phineus (Aeschylus) 11:159, 174
The Phoenician Women (Seneca)
　See *Phoenissae*
Phoenissae (Seneca) 6:363, 366, 379-80, 402,
　413, 421, 432, 437
"Phoenix Song" (Li Po) 2:152
Phormio (Terence) 14:303, 306-07, 311, 313-18,
　320, 333, 335, 340, 341, 347-49, 352-53, 356-
　57, 364, 376-80, 383-85, 389-90
Phychostasia (Aeschylus)
　See *Weighing of Souls*
"Phyllis" (Ovid) 7:311
Physica (Albert the Great) 16:4, 36, 61
Physicorum (Albert the Great) 16:
Physics (Albert the Great)
　See *Physica*
The Pillow Book of Sei Shonagon (Sei Shonagon)
　See *Makura no soshi*
Pillow Sketches (Sei Shonagon)
　See *Makura no soshi*
Pinakes (Callimachus) 18: 38, 45-8, 62-4, 68-70
"Pine Wine of the Middle Mountains" (Su Shih)

　15:382
"The Pious Black Slave" 2:40
Planctus (Abelard) 11:55, 68
"Planher vuelh en Blacatz" (Sordello) 15:332, 337,
　343, 365, 375, 377
Plants (Albert the Great)
　See *De vegetabilibus*
Ploutos (Aristophanes) 4:44, 46, 62, 67, 76, 90,
　94, 111, 115, 124-26, 147-48, 153, 161, 165-68,
　174-75, 177-80
"The Plunder of the Home of Salur-Kazan" 8:97,
　103, 109
Plutus (Aristophanes)
　See *Ploutos*
"*Poem 1*" (Catullus) 18: 104, 108, 110-11, 117,
　122-23, 130-32, 150, 167-78, 185-93
"*Poem 2*" (Catullus) 18: 116, 161, 178, 187-93,
　196
"*Poem 3*" (Catullus) 18: 166, 174, 178, 187-88
"*Poem 4*" (Catullus) 18: 108, 117, 167, 180, 187-
　88
"*Poem 5*" (Catullus) 18: 102, 137-38, 141, 159,
　166, 179, 186, 188, 196-97
"*Poem 6*" (Catullus) 18: 99, 106, 122, 125-27,
　129-30, 133, 138, 188, 195-96
"*Poem 7*" (Catullus) 18: 102, 108, 118, 137-38,
　140, 150, 160-61, 166, 181, 186, 188, 196-97
"*Poem 8*" (Catullus) 18: 138, 153, 160-61, 166,
　188, 192
"*Poem 9*" (Catullus) 18: 121, 128, 186, 188
"*Poem 10*" (Catullus) 18: 99, 107, 122-26, 129-
　30, 188
"*Poem 11*" (Catullus) 18: 99, 116, 119, 126, 133,
　162, 166-67, 179, 181-82, 185, 187-88, 192,
　194
"*Poem 12*" (Catullus) 18: 122, 181, 188
"*Poem 13*" (Catullus) 18: 102, 109, 127, 180,
　186
"*Poem 14*" (Catullus) 18: 99-101, 166, 186, 188
"*Poem 14b*" (Catullus) 18: 122, 193
"*Poem 15*" (Catullus) 18: 119, 133-34, 188-90,
　193-95, 197
"*Poem 16*" (Catullus) 18: 119, 132, 134, 137,
　167, 186, 188-90, 193-97
"*Poem 17*" (Catullus) 18: 122, 129-30, 181
"*Poem 18*" (Catullus) 18:127 18:127
"*Poem 18*" (Filderman) 18: 127
"*Poem 21*" (Catullus) 18: 119, 134, 181, 188
"*Poem 22*" (Catullus) 18: 100-01, 145
"*Poem 23*" (Catullus) 18: 99, 119, 133-34, 181,
　188
"*Poem 24*" (Catullus) 18: 99, 132, 134, 188
"*Poem 25*" (Catullus) 18: 132-33, 166
"*Poem 26*" (Catullus) 18: 99, 119, 134, 188
"*Poem 28*" (Catullus) 18: 99, 121, 132, 188
"*Poem 29*" (Catullus) 18: 99, 118, 144, 166, 181,
　187-88
"*Poem 30*" (Catullus) 18: 99, 125, 169, 171
"*Poem 31*" (Catullus) 18: 103, 117, 146, 166-67,
　186-88
"*Poem 32*" (Catullus) 18: 115, 122-23, 130, 133,
　137-38, 146, 181
"*Poem 33*" (Catullus) 18: 122, 132-33, 146
"*Poem 34*" (Catullus) 18: 110-11, 166-67, 176,
　181-82
"*Poem 35*" (Catullus) 18: 93, 99-102, 122, 128,
　130, 147, 167, 186
"*Poem 36*" (Catullus) 18: 100-01, 121, 127, 145,
　167, 186

Aristotelis (Bacon) **14**:49, 66
"Quatre Dols" (Marie de France)
   See "Le Chaitivel"
Queen Arsinoe (Callimachus) **18**: 5-6
Questions on Aristotle (Bacon)
   See *Quaestiones super libros i-vi Physicorum*
      Aristotelis
Questions on Aristotle's Physics (Bacon)
   See *Quaestiones super libros i-vi Physicorum*
      Aristotelis
Raghuvamsa (Kalidasa) **9**:82, 84-5, 89-91, 102,
   115, 118-19, 121, 125-26, 138
"Raising a Cup of Wine to Query the Moon" (Li
   Po) **2**:166
"The Rajah's Diamond" **2**:36
Ransom of Hector (Aeschylus) **11**:125, 193
The Rape of the Locks (Menander)
   See *Perikeiromene*
Razón de amor **16**:336-376
Razón de amor con los denuestos del agua y el
   vino
   See *Razón de amor*
Rbaiyyat (Khayyam)
   See *Rubáiyát*
"Ready for a Drink" (Li Po) **2**:166
Record of Rites (Confucius)
   See *Li Chi*
"The Red Cliff" (Su Shih)
   See "Rhymeprose on the Red Cliff"
Rede der Unterscheidungen (Eckhart) **9**:35, 42
Remedia Amoris (Ovid) **7**:344-46, 353, 377, 379,
   398, 429, 440, 444
Remedia studii (Bacon) **14**:62
Remedies of Love (Ovid)
   See *Remedia Amoris*
The Republic (Cicero)
   See *De republica*
Republic (Plato) **8**:206, 211, 217, 219, 223, 225-
   28, 232-33, 236, 239, 241, 243-44, 246, 248-
   50, 252-53, 255, 259-61, 263-68, 270, 276-83,
   285, 287, 290-92, 294, 299, 305-06, 308-11,
   313, 317, 322, 324-25, 328-29, 331, 339-48,
   352, 357-58, 363-64
Retractiones (Augustine) **6**:9, 32, 116
Reysen und Wenderschafften duch des Gelobte
   Land (Mandeville)
   See *Mandeville's Travels*
"Rhapsody of Remorse" (Li Po) **2**:169
Rhetorica (Cicero)
   See *De inventione*
"Rhymeprose on the Red Cliff" (Su Shih) **15**:382,
   385, 398, 419, 421-24
Risalat al-Adwiyyah (Avicenna) **16**:147
Rituals (Confucius)
   See *Li Chi*
Rivals (Plato) **8**:305, 311
"Rock of Yen-yu" (Su Shih) **15**:387
Roman
   See *Le Roman de la Rose*
The Roman Calendar (Ovid)
   See *Fasti*
Le Roman de la Rose **8**:374-453
The Romance
   See *Le Roman de la Rose*
The Romance of the Rose
   See *Le Roman de la Rose*
Romanz de la Rose
   See *Le Roman de la Rose*
Rood

   See *The Dream of the Rood*
Rosciana (Cicero)
   See *Pro Roscio Amerino*
Rose
   See *Le Roman de la Rose*
"Rose in Bloom" **2**:23
Rtusamhara (Kalidasa) **9**:89-90, 103-05, 107
Ruba'iyat (Khayyam)
   See *Rubáiyát*
Rubáiyát (Khayyam) **11**:228-309
Sacred Treatises (Boethius)
   See *Theological Tractates*
"Saif El-Mulûk" **2**:43
Sakuntala (Kalidasa)
   See *Abhijñana-sakuntala*
Samia (Menander) **9**:205-06, 211, 213, 215, 217,
   220-21, 224, 238, 246, 249, 252-53, 255, 257-
   61, 264, 269-72, 275-78, 281, 287-88
The Samian Woman (Menander)
   See *Samia*
"Satire Agaimst Three Disinherited Lords"
   (Sordello) **15**:276
Satires (Juvenal) **8**:7, 14, 19, 22, 27-8, 59-60, 66,
   68-9, 73-8
"Saying Farewell to the Children at Nanling as I
   Leave for the Capital" (Li Po) **2**:174
"The Scavenger and the Noble Lady" **2**:40
Schionatulander (Wolfram von Eschenbach)
   See *Titurèl*
Scipio's Dream (Cicero)
   See *Somnium Scipionis*
Scite Teipsum (Abelard)
   See *Scito Te Ipsum*
Scito Te Ipsum (Abelard) **11**:5, 10, 12, 16, 20, 24,
   49, 51, 53, 54, 57, 68
Scripta Super Sententias (Albert the Great)
   See *Commentary on the Book of the Sentences*
Scriptum Principale (Bacon) **14**:15
The Seasons (Kalidasa)
   See *Rtusamhara*
Second Alcibiades (Plato)
   See *Alcibiades II*
Second Olympian (Pindar)
   See *Olympian 2*
Second Olynthiac (Demosthenes)
   See *Olynthiac II*
Second Philippic (Cicero)
   See *Philippics*
Second Philippic (Demosthenes)
   See *Philippic II*
Second Pythian (Pindar)
   See *Pythian 2*
"Seeing off Wei Wan, Recluse of Wang-wu
   Mountain, on His Trip Home" (Li Po) **2**:168
"Segrek Son of Ushun Koja" **8**:103
Sei Shonagon ga Makura-no-Soshi (Sei Shonagon)
   See *Makura no soshi*
Sei Shonagon's Pillow Book (Sei Shonagon)
   See *Makura no soshi*
"Seizure" (Sappho)
   See "Ode to Anactoria"
Self-Punishment (Terence)
   See *Heautontimoreumenos*
The Self-Tormentor (Terence)
   See *Heautontimoreumenos*
"Senh' En Sordel mandamen" (Sordello) **15**:362
Sentences (Albert the Great)
   See *Commentary on the Book of the Sentences*
Septem (Aeschylus)

   See *Seven against Thebes*
Sermon on St. John the Baptist (Abelard) **11**:66
Seven against Thebes (Aeschylus) **11**:77, 83-5, 88,
   96, 102-03, 107, 111, 113, 117, 119, 124, 127,
   133-35, 137-39, 142, 151-54, 156, 159, 167,
   173, 179, 181, 184, 194, 200, 205, 207, 217
Seven before Thebes (Aeschylus)
   See *Seven against Thebes*
Seventh Epistle (Plato)
   See *Seventh Letter*
Seventh Isthmian (Pindar)
   See *Isthmian 7*
Seventh Letter (Plato) **8**:222, 305-06, 334, 338-
   41, 349
Seventh Nemean (Pindar)
   See *Nemean 7*
The Sham Eunich (Terence)
   See *Eunuchus*
Shearing of Glycera (Menander)
   See *Perikeiromene*
The Shield (Menander)
   See *Aspis*
Shield of Heracles (Hesiod)
   See *Shield of Herakles*
Shield of Herakles (Hesiod) **5**:74, 82-83, 118, 174
Shih (Confucius)
   See *Shih Ching*
Shih Chi (Confucius) **19**:21, 84
Shih Ching (Confucius) **19**:6, 19, 21, 29, 31, 34-
   35, 38-39, 46, 51
Shorn Lady (Menander)
   See *Perikeiromene*
Short Treatise in Praise of Dante (Boccaccio)
   See *Trattatello in lode di Dante*
The Short-Haired Lass (Menander)
   See *Perikeiromene*
Shoulder Bite (Chretien de Troyes) **10**:232
Shu (Confucius)
   See *Shu Ching*
Shu Ching (Confucius) **19**:6, 9, 19-20, 28, 34-35,
   38, 46, 67
"Si co'l malaus ge no se sap gardar" (Sordello)
   15:363
Sic et Non (Abelard) **11**:4, 7, 9, 10, 14, 16, 21, 24,
   27, 31, 48, 66
The Sikyonian (Menander)
   See *Sikyonios*
Sikyonios (Menander) **9**:260, 269-70, 278, 288
Sir Gawain and The Green Knight **2**:181-287
"Sirmio" (Catullus)
   See "*Poem 31*"
Sisyphus (Aeschylus) **11**:123
Sixth Isthmian (Pindar)
   See *Isthmian 6*
Sixth Nemean (Pindar)
   See *Nemean 6*
Sixth Olympian (Pindar)
   See *Olympian 6*
Sixth Paean (Pindar)
   See *Paean 6*
Sixth Pythian (Pindar)
   See *Pythian 6*
"Sleeper Awakened" **2**:20
Slovo o polku Igoreve **1**:477-530
Soliloquia (Augustine) **6**:53, 62, 68-9, 90, 126
Soliloquies (Augustine)
   See *Soliloquia*
Soliloquy (Abelard) **11**:67
Somnium Scipionis (Cicero) **3**:181, 200, 211, 289,

Title Index

CMLC Cumulative Critic Index

Critic Index

Sophocles 2:312

Niles, John D.
Beowulf 1:150

Nisbet, R. G. M.
Cicero, Marcus Tullius 3:263

Nisetich, Frank J.
Pindar 12:335

Nissen, Christopher
Boccaccio, Giovanni 13:122

Noble, Peter S.
Chrétien de Troyes 10:210

Nohrnberg, James
Inferno 3:139

Nordal, Sigurður
Hrafnkel's Saga 2:91

Norinaga, Motoori
Murasaki, Lady 1:415

Northcott, Kenneth J.
Wolfram von Eschenbach 5:403

Norton, Charles Eliot
Khayyám 11:236
Vita Nuova 18:318

Norwood, Frances
Apuleius 1:26

Norwood, Gilbert
Aeschylus 11:116
Aristophanes 4:92
Menander 9:205
Pindar 12:266
Terence 14:309, 315

Nothnagle, John T.
Chrétien de Troyes 10:157

Nutt, Alfred
Wolfram von Eschenbach 5:299

Nyland, Waino
Kalevala 6:238

Obata, Shigeyoshi
Li Po 2:133

Obuchowski, Mary Dejong
Murasaki, Lady 1:444

O'Cleirigh, P.M.
Origen 19:234

Odenkirchen, Carl V.
Mystery of Adam 4:205

Ogilvy, J. D. A.
Beowulf 1:154

Oinas, Felix J.
Kalevala 6:254

Oldfather, W. A.
Cicero, Marcus Tullius 3:206

Olschki, Leonardo
Polo, Marco 15:293

Oppenheim, A. Leo
Epic of Gilgamesh 3:321

Origen
Song of Songs 18:200

Ormsby, John
Poem of the Cid 4:226

Osgood, Charles G.
Boccaccio, Giovanni 13:37

Osterud, Svein
Hesiod 5:145

Otis, Brooks
Aeneid 9:429
Ovid 7:356

Otto, Rudolph
Meister Eckhart 9:35

Ovid
Ovid 7:281

Owen, D. D. R.
Chrétien de Troyes 10:173
The Song of Roland 1:191, 236

Owen, S. G.
Juvenal 8:25

Owen, Stephen
Li Po 2:156

Paden, William D., Jr.
Bertran de Born 5:51, 61

Page, Denys
Odyssey 16:300
Sappho 3:430

Pagels, Elaine
Augustine, St. 6:140

Palgrave, Francis T.
Ovid 7:299
Sappho 3:386

Pálsson, Hermann
Hrafnkel's Saga 2:108

Palumbo, Donald
Arabian Nights 2:71

Pancoast, Henry S.
Layamon 10:314

Pandiri, Thalia A.
Longus 7:265

Pandit, R. S.
Kalidasa 9:103

Papini, Giovanni
Augustine, St. 6:37

Park, Katharine
Albert the Great 16:112

Parker, Douglass
Terence 14:352

Parry, Adam
Aeneid 9:421

Parshall, Linda B.
Wolfram von Eschenbach 5:378

Patch, Howard R.
Boethius 15:15
The Dream of the Rood 14:218

Pater, Walter
Apuleius 1:14
Plato 8:252

Paterson, John
The Book of Psalms 4:395

Paton, Lucy Allen
Layamon 10:315

Patrick, Mary Mills
Sappho 3:393

Patten, Faith H.
The Dream of the Rood 14:268

Patterson, Annabel M.
Hermogenes 6:178

Patton, John H.
Meister Eckhart 9:60

Paul, Herbert
Cicero, Marcus Tullius 3:194

Payne, John
Arabian Nights 2:12

Pearson, C. H.
Juvenal 8:11

Pearson, Karl
Meister Eckhart 9:9

Pearson, Lionel
Demosthenes 13:182

Pease, Samuel James
Xenophon 17:329

Peck, Russell A.
Morte Arthure 10:406

Peers, E. Allison
Llull, Ramon 12:92, 95

Pei, Mario A.
The Song of Roland 1:178

Pekarik, Andrew
Murasaki, Lady 1:460

Penwill, J. L.
Apuleius 1:42
Penzer, N. M.
Polo, Marco 15:276

Perrier, Joseph Louis
Bertran de Born 5:24

Perry, Ben Edwin
Apuleius 1:34

Perry, Henry Ten Eyck
Menander 9:214
Terence 14:333

Perse, St.-John
Inferno 3:131

Petrarch, Francesco
Augustine, St. 6:7
Boccaccio, Giovanni 13:4
Cicero, Marcus Tullius 3:181, 182

Petronio, Giuseppe
Boccaccio, Giovanni 13:47

Pfeiffer, Rudolf
Callimachus 18:43

Philippides, Marios
Longus 7:260

Philostratus
Hermogenes 6:158

Pickering, Charles J.
Khayyám 11:249
Avicenna 16:156

Pickering, F. P.
Hartmann von Aue 15:218

Pidal, Ramón Menéndez
Poem of the Cid 4:234

Pinkerton, Percy E.
Wolfram von Eschenbach 5:293

Piramus, Denis
Marie de France 8:113

Plato
Aristophanes 4:38
Iliad 1:270
Plato 8:200

Plumptre, E. H.
Bacon, Roger 14:10

Plutarch
Aeschylus 11:84
Aristophanes 4:40
Demosthenes 13:148, 163, 185
Herodotus 17:50
Menander 9:203
Sappho 3:379

Poag, James F.
Wolfram von Eschenbach 5:400

Podlecki, Anthony J.
Pindar 12:351
Sappho 3:491

Poe, Joe Park
Seneca, Lucius Annaeus 6:389

Poggioli, Renato
The Igor Tale 1:507
Inferno 3:123

Critic Index

Critic Index

Critic Index